ISBN 978-0-428-66045-1
PIBN 11300913

1 MONTH OF
FREE
READING

at

www.ForgottenBooks.com

By purchasing this book you are eligible for one month membership to ForgottenBooks.com, giving you unlimited access to our entire collection of over 1,000,000 titles via our web site and mobile apps.

To claim your free month visit:
www.forgottenbooks.com/free1300913

U. S. DEPARTMENT OF AGRICULTURE.

Department Bulletins

Nos. 1126–1150,

WITH CONTENTS
AND INDEX.

Prepared in the Office of Editorial Work.

WASHINGTON:
GOVERNMENT PRINTING OFFICE.
1924.

CONTENTS.

INDEX.

○

UNITED STATES DEPARTMENT OF AGRICULTURE

DEPARTMENT BULLETIN No. 1126

Washington, D. C. ▼ April 23, 1923

THE EFFECT OF BORAX ON THE GROWTH AND YIELD OF CROPS.

By J. J. SKINNER and B. E. BROWN, *Biochemists*, and F. R. REID, *Assistant Biochemist*, *Office of Soil-Fertility Investigations, Bureau of Plant Industry*.

CONTENTS.

INTRODUCTION.

The United States Department of Agriculture issued a report (*12*)[1] early in 1920 on crop injury by borax in fertilizers which was based partly on field experiments conducted in 1919 in cooperation with farmers in the States of Maine, New York, New Jersey, Virginia, North Carolina, South Carolina, and Georgia and partly on investigations of the crop injury by borax in commercial fields of potatoes and cotton in certain Eastern States.

These investigations were made by the department in 1919, as a result of appeals from farmers and fertilizer dealers in many sections of the Eastern States which indicated that important crops to which certain fertilizers had been applied were very seriously affected. As a result of the investigation by the department and by several of the State experiment stations, the trouble was traced to the use of a potash salt containing borax which came from Searles Lake, Calif.

The results of the experiments in the States enumerated above showed that this potash salt containing borax was injurious to potatoes and cotton, but that the degree of injury was dependent upon the type of soil and the climatic conditions. In experiments

---

[1] Serial numbers (italic) in parentheses refer to "Literature cited" at the end of this bulletin.

carried on with potatoes, a decreased yield resulted in some cases where the potash was applied in quantities which would give 7.5 pounds of borax per acre, while in other experiments as much as 18 pounds was required to show injury. In some of the experiments with cotton a reduction in yield resulted where as little as 4 pounds of borax per acre were used, while on other soils no decreased yield resulted with the use of less than 12 pounds.

That the injury caused by the Searles Lake potash was due to the borax it contained has been further demonstrated by experiments made in 1920. In these tests the effect of Searles Lake potash free from borax gave good results and compared very favorably with potash materials from other sources.

Owing to the great interest taken in the subject and its bearing on crop production it was felt essential to conduct further field studies in order to obtain detailed evidence on the effect of borax upon different crops with respect to growth as well as yield.

This bulletin embodies the results of these field studies conducted cooperatively in the States of Maine, New Jersey, Virginia, and Alabama on several important types of soil.

REVIEW OF THE LITERATURE.

The injurious effects of borax in corn fertilizers were noted in Indiana in 1917 by Conner, which seem to be the first recorded field observations on the effect of borax and its occurrence in fertilizer practice. Conner (3) reached the conclusion from his experiments in pots that 100 pounds per acre of a fertilizer containing 2 per cent of borax when applied in the furrow caused injury to the corn plant. Work previous to this by Lipman (8) was confined to pot tests, and the work of Cook (5, 6, 7) was chiefly concerned with the action of borax in manure and is not directly applicable to present-day commercial-fertilizer practice; neither are the experiments of a number of European workers which are reviewed in Cook's paper.

Conner's more recent report (4), giving the results of his work with borax on corn in two field experiments, confirms the data obtained from the pot tests. He found that borax caused the greatest injury when the fertilizer in which it was contained was applied in the row. From 0.5 of a pound up to 4 pounds of anhydrous borax per acre produced injury when drilled in the row, and 16 to 18 pounds were required to produce injury when the fertilizer was sown broadcast and worked into the surface soil. Conner also found that borax injury varies with the method of application, type of soil, seasonal conditions, and the crop grown.

In field experiments reported by Blackwell and Collings (1), designated a progress report, applications of a potash salt containing 17.75 per cent borax ($Na_2B_4O_7$), used in quantities varying from 25 to 1,000 pounds per acre, did not prevent germination of cotton and corn seed under the conditions of the experiment or hinder the normal growth of the young plants. Their experiments were discontinued when the young ants were 18 inches in height. Nor did applications of commercial borax ranging from 54 to 400 pounds per acre prevent germination and normal growth of either cotton or corn. The planting was followed immediately by heavy rains, which it is stated may account in a large measure for the failure of these quantities of borax to show harmful results. The plantings in these experiments were made late in the summer, and the crops did not mature.

A general survey of the injury to the 1919 potato crop in Maine by borax in fertilizers is given by Morse (9), together with a report on pot experiments with borax fertilizer on potatoes, beans, oats, wheat, and buckwheat. Fertilizers applied to soil in pots so as to add 17.6 pounds of anhydrous borax per acre produced severe leaf injury when the fertilizer was mixed in the upper 6 inches of the pot or when placed in the 3 inches of soil below the seed piece. The larger application of borax caused greater root injury and more stunting of the plants, but less tip and marginal injury to the leaves. An application by means of the drill of fertilizer containing anhydrous borax equivalent to 4.4 pounds per acre caused severe injury to beans, while the same fertilizers sown broadcast in quantity equivalent to 8.8 pounds of borax per acre caused no apparent injury to oats, wheat, and buckwheat.

The work of Neller and Morse (10) is also very conclusive in showing that borax is extremely poisonous to plants. A number of pot experiments are reported which were conducted under the joint auspices of eight different institutions, namely, the experiment stations of the States of Maine, New Hampshire, Vermont, Massachusetts, Rhode Island, Connecticut, New York, and New Jersey. The work was planned in order to determine whether injury previously observed both in the field and in the greenhouse was due alone to the borax present in the fertilizer applied and to determine the maximum quantity per acre that can be safely applied to land on which important food crops are to be grown. Potatoes, corn, and beans were grown, and borax was applied with fertilizers in quantities varying from 1 to 20 pounds per acre. While these experiments were made in pots and a direct comparison with field conditions can not be made, the results obtained are very valuable and show conclusively that very small quantities of borax can be injurious to plant life. Corn and beans proved to be more susceptible than potatoes to the injurious effects of borax. Three pounds of borax per acre was the largest quantity that could be applied in drills with safety to beans; the limit for corn was under 5 pounds and for potatoes slightly above 5 pounds per acre. Mixing the fertilizer with the soil decreased the injury and slightly raised the quantity of borax that could be applied per acre with safety. These results were obtained with a typical greenhouse o t n soil which had a water-holding capacity of 37.5 per cent and was kept at an optimum water content of 19.2 per cent. Subsequent experiments with beans showed that greater injury occurred where the soil moisture was kept at 15.2 per cent than where it was kept at 30.4 per cent.

The damage to crops in North Carolina, principally cotton, tobacco, corn, and peaches, by borax in fertilizers, observed in 1919, is given in a report by Plummer and Wolf (11) in which they also include the results of their experimental work. Their experiments, using pots containing a sandy soil to which 5 pounds of borax per acre were applied, showed considerable injury to corn, and when 10 pounds of borax were applied the plants were entirely lacking in green color and soon died. Cotton did not grow where 5 pounds per acre were used. In clay soil both cotton and corn showed marked injury when the quantity of borax exceeded 7 pounds per acre, although in sandy soil as little as 1 pound per acre injured tobacco. The authors state that colloidal absorption is an important factor in enabling plants to tolerate larger quantities of borax when grown on clay soils.

The effect of borax on Sassafras loam (a brown or yellowish brown moderately heavy loam with a reddish yellow subsoil) in New Jersey, as presented by Blair and Brown (2), was to depress the yield of potatoes when as much as 30 pounds per acre was used in the drill and the seed planted immediately, while no appreciable decreased yield resulted with 50 pounds when the planting of seed was delayed. With 100 pounds of borax per acre the yield was cut one half. Where fertilizers were sown broadcast 50 pounds of borax per acre markedly decreased the yields. Applications of 100, 200, and 400 pounds of borax per acre either prevented germination or resulted in delayed germination. With corn, where fertilizers were applied in the drill, there was some depression in yield beginning with the 5-pound application, and with 50 pounds per acre and over the injury was severe. When the fertilizer was sown broadcast at the rate of 50 pounds of borax per acre there was a marked decrease in yield. It is noted that the rainfall at New Brunswick during the summer of 1920 was unusually heavy, there being a precipitation of 2.01 inches in the 10 days following the fertilizer application.

In the experiments on the Caribou loam[2] (a yellowish brown silt loam with yellow subsurface soil and gray subsoil) at Presque Isle, Me., injury occurred when an application as low as 5 pounds of borax per acre when put in the furrow and planting done immediately. As the quantity of borax applied increased, the injury became progressively worse. There was a moderate but not excessive rainfall in the early summer, which very likely accounts in part for the difference in the degree of harmfulness shown in this and the New Brunswick experiments.

The results of the investigation with cotton at Muscle Shoals,[3] Ala., on two soil types showed that harmful effects resulted from the use of a quantity of borax as small as 5 pounds per acre. The use of 10 pounds of borax per acre delayed and seriously affected germination. In some cases the plant outgrew its early shock where the smaller quantities were used. The degree of harmfulness of the borax in the experiments planted at different times correlates with the rainfall to a certain extent. When the rainfall was heavy shortly after the fertilizer application was made, the effect of the borax was less.

Other experiments with cotton on both the Clarksville silt loam (a light-gray silt loam with heavy yellowish subsoil) and Colbert silt loam (a gray-brown silt loam with heavy reddish yellow subsoil) were made at Muscle Shoals, Ala., in cooperation with the Fixed-Nitrogen Research Laboratory.

SCOPE AND PLAN OF THE INVESTIGATIONS IN 1920.

Extensive series of tests were made at the department experimental farm at Arlington, Va., on a silty clay loam soil. Corn, Lima beans, snap beans, potatoes, and cotton were grown. Records were kept as to the influence of borax on germination, on early growth, and on the

---

[2] Brown, B. E. Effect of borax in fertilizer on the growth and yield of potatoes. U. S. Dept. Agr. Bul. 998, 8 p., 1 fig., 4 pl. 1922

[3] Skinner, J. J., and Allison, F. E. The influence of fertilizers containing borax on the growth and fruiting of cotton. Unpublished manuscript.

final yield of each crop matured. The records of these experiments, together with the data obtained in some of the experiments located in the States mentioned, are given in detail in this bulletin. Other tests were made cooperatively with the Maine and New Jersey Agricultural Experiment Stations, potatoes being grown on Caribou loam at Presque Isle, Me., and potatoes and corn on Sassafras loam at New Brunswick, N. J.

The experiments at Arlington, Presque Isle, New Brunswick, and Muscle Shoals were of the same general plan and afforded an opportunity of studying the effects of borax on five soil types and five crops under different climatic conditions. Borax in all of these experiments was mixed with a fertilizer analyzing 4 per cent NH_3, 8 per cent P_2O_5, and 4 per cent K_2O and the fertilizer applied at a standard rate for each crop, namely, 400 pounds per acre to corn, 1,000 pounds to cotton and to beans, 1,500 to 2,000 pounds to potatoes. Fertilizer free from borax was used as a control. Sufficient borax was added and mixed with the fertilizer so that when applied at the rates just named 1 to 400 pounds of anhydrous borax per acre would be added.

In addition to the experiments made on this general plan at these four locations, other experiments were made at Arlington, Va., with corn and cotton and at Muscle Shoals, Ala., with cotton, using a no-borax fertilizer, one which supplied 5 pounds, another 10 pounds, and a third 20 pounds of borax per acre. These experiments were inaugurated at intervals of about 10 days, to study the influence of weather conditions on the action of borax upon these crops growing on the same type of soil.

The experiments in each location involved applying the fertilizer in three ways: (1) In the seed drill and planting after an interval of a week or 10 days, (2) in the seed drill and planting immediately after applying the fertilizer, (3) broadcasting the fertilizer and planting immediately.

Other experiments with potatoes were made in order to compare the effectiveness of commercial Searles Lake potash, designated 1920 grade, which contained no borax with Searles Lake potash containing borax as it occurred in the trade prior to that year. The latter salt is called the 1919 grade. These experiments were made cooperatively with growers in the potato-producing regions of Virginia, New Jersey, and Maine.

EXPERIMENTS WITH BORAX AT ARLINGTON, VA.

The soil on which the experiments at Arlington were conducted is a silty clay loam, well suited to the growing of vegetables and general farm crops. The land in question was filled with river-bottom material from the Potomac River some ten years ago. It has been tile-drained and in wet seasons does not suffer from an excess of water. In dry seasons it has a sufficient water-holding capacity to support good crop growth. The land was cultivated to corn for several years preceding the inauguration of the borax experiment.

The area used for the experiment was 132 by 400 feet. Each row 132 feet long was divided into three equal sections, providing plats one two-hundred-and-seventieth of an acre in extent. In section 1 the fertilizer was put in the drill, covered and mixed with soil to a depth of about 2 inches and the planting of seed delayed for 7 days.

In section 2 the fertilizer was put in the furrow and otherwise treated as in section 1, except that the seed was planted immediately after the fertilizer was applied. In section 3 the fertilizer was sown broadcast over an area approximately 12 inches wide along the seed furrow.

A fertilizer analyzing 4 per cent NH_3, 8 per cent P_2O_5, and 4 per cent K_2O was applied at the rate of 1,000 pounds per acre to beans, 1,800 pounds per acre to potatoes, and 400 pounds per acre to corn. The materials used in preparing the 4–8–4 mixture were acid phosphate, sodium nitrate, ammonium sulphate, cottonseed meal, and potassium chlorid. Sufficient borax was added and well mixed with the fertilizer so as to apply 1, 2, 3, 4, 5, 10, 20, 30, 50, 100, 200, and 400 pounds of anhydrous borax ($Na_2B_4O_7$) per acre. Five plats were used as checks, and to these was added the fertilizer which contained no borax.

Three adjoining rows were used for each treatment; in the first row Lima beans were planted, in the second snap beans, and in the third potatoes. The experiment with corn was made on plats adjoining those in the truck-crop tests. Records of the effect of the borax on germination, on the growth of the plant in its early stage, and on the yield were made in each case. The daily rainfall was recorded, and this factor will be considered in connection with the experiments.

EFFECT OF BORAX ON LIMA BEANS.

Lima beans were planted in sections 2 and 3 on May 26, immediately after the application of the fertilizers. The seeds in section 1 were planted 7 days later. Each section was planted with 90 seeds and on June 25 thinned to a stand of 70 plants. The experiment was discontinued on September 22, when the vines were cut and weighed green. The beans were picked as they matured, and the yield of beans in the hull as well as vine growth was recorded.

In order to determine the effect of the borax on germination and on early growth, a count of the number of plants in each plat was made one month after date of planting and a measurement made of their height. These data together with the yields are given in Table 1.

The influence of borax on germination can be seen by a study of columns 2, 6, and 10 of Table 1. The data for the two outside control rows are not given, as these were influenced by other experiments in adjoining plats.

In section 1, where the fertilizer was put in the drill and planting delayed for 7 days, the three no-borax or check plats germinated 73, 82, and 83 seeds out of a possible 90. The 400-pound borax plat germinated 4 seeds, the 200-pound plat 37 seeds, and the 100-pound plat 48 seeds. The remaining plats receiving 50 pounds or less germinated fewer seeds than the no-borax plats, but the effect was not so marked as in section 2.

In section 2 only a few seeds germinated in the 100, 200, and 400 pound plats. Less than half germinated in the 30 and 50 pound plats, and a marked effect was produced by the smaller quantities of borax, especially the 10 and 20 pound applications. The three checks in section 2 germinated 82, 75, and 73 seeds, respectively, out of a possible 90.

In section 3, where the fertilizer was sown broadcast, there was a marked effect on germination with 20 pounds of borax per acre; smaller quantities than this had only a slight effect. There was no germination on the 400-pound plat, and only 7 seeds germinated where 200 pounds were used.

TABLE 1.—*Effect of various quantities of borax on Lima beans in field plats on silty clay loam at Arlington, Va., in 1920.*

Borax per acre.	Sec. 1.—Fertilizer applied in drill 7 days before planting.				Sec. 2.—Fertilizer applied in drill at time of planting.				Sec. 3.—Fertilizer applied broadcast at time of planting.			
	Plants up June 25.		Yield per plat (pounds).		Plants up June 25.		Yield per plat (pounds).		Plants up June 25.		Yield per plat (pounds).	
	Num- ber.	Height, inches.	Beans.	Vines.	Num- ber.	Height, inches.	Beans.	Vines.	Num- ber.	Height, inches.	Beans.	Vines.
1	2	3	4	5	6	7	8	9	10	11	12	13
1 pound.....	72	8.0	25.0	49	60	7.7	21.0	52	80	7.7	23.0	51
2 pounds....	75	9.2	26.0	57	52	7.7	22.5	46	63	8.6	26.1	47
3 pounds....	62	7.8	26.4	46	60	7.7	23.5	47	58	8.0	25.0	47
None........	73	9.4	24.7	43	82	8.7	20.0	47	78	8.9	22.9	49
4 pounds....	70	7.5	21.7	42	76	8.1	21.8	44	76	6.8	21.0	46
5 pounds....	77	7.0	27.5	45	71	7.4	27.7	46	72	6.8	25.1	43
10 pounds...	85	6.8	21.6	48	42	6.7	16.9	37	63	6.3	23.2	41
None........	82	9.0	18.8	46	75	9.1	22.8	49	70	8.8	23.5	40
20 pounds...	65	6.9	19.7	39	48	6.1	20.8	35	41	5.7	15.9	38
30 pounds...	77	6.2	19.8	31	32	5.2	12.0	31	63	5.6	19.2	45
50 pounds...	74	5.2	19.0	34	19	3.8	9.5	21	39	4.1	11.7	38
None........	83	9.3	19.9	46	73	8.1	16.5	42	83	8.7	17.8	45
100 pounds..	48	2.6	5.2	15	9	....	2.6	15	17	....	3.5	15
200 pounds..	37	....	4.8	16	8	....	2.4	10	7	....	0	0
400 pounds..	4	....	0	0	5	....	0	0	0	....	0	0

Where the fertilizer was applied in the drill, the borax in as small quantities as 1, 2, 3, and 4 pounds per acre had a retarding effect on the early growth of the beans, and 10 pounds of borax markedly stunted the plants. There was not much noticeable depression of growth by borax in quantities under 4 pounds, and when the bean vines reached maturity they had outgrown all injury.

In section 1, 20 pounds of borax decreased the growth of vines, but the production of beans was not influenced by quantities under 100 pounds per acre. In section 2, 10 pounds per acre caused marked depression in the final yield of both vines and beans. In the broadcasted section 20 pounds per acre depressed the production of beans, but vine growth was not influenced by quantities smaller than 50 pounds. There was some stimulation in all sections by the smaller applications.

EFFECT OF BORAX ON SNAP BEANS.

The experiment with snap beans was similar in all details to that of the Lima beans. The seeds were planted on May 26, somewhat thick in the row and thinned to 125 per plat on June 15. They had matured by August 13, on which date the experiment was terminated. The beans were picked weekly, and the record is given in pounds of green beans produced.

The snap beans proved to be very sensitive to borax. During the first month the plants where 1, 2, 3, 4, and 5 pounds of borax were applied in section 2 showed a slightly lighter color of foliage than the no-borax plat, although there was no distinct bleaching. There was a distinct and marked bleaching of leaves with 10 pounds and upward. This effect was distinguished by a curled leaf having yellow and brown tips, and often the entire leaf was affected. This characteristic became severe where 20 pounds were used. These same effects were noticeable in sections 1 and 3, but relatively large quantities were required to produce the symptoms. In section 1 there was no apparent change in color of foliage with quantities under 5 pounds per acre. The complete data are given in Table 2.

TABLE 2.—*Effect of various quantities of borax on snap beans in field plats on silty clay loam at Arlington, Va., in 1920.*

Borax per acre.	Sec. 1.—Fertilizer applied in drill 7 days before planting.				Sec. 2.—Fertilizer applied in drill at time of planting.				Sec. 3.—Fertilizer applied broadcast at time of planting.			
	Plants up June 15.		Yield per plat (pounds).		Plants up June 15.		Yield per plat (pounds).		Plants up June 15.		Yield per plat (pounds).	
	Number.	Height, inches.	Beans	Vines.	Number.	Height, inches.	Beans.	Vines.	Number.	Height, inches.	Beans.	Vines.
None........	210	6.2	27.8	37.0	162	7.6	24.7	34.0	132	7.9	25.5	30.0
1 pound.....	180	6.6	29.6	34.0	154	6.8	26.0	32.0	149	6.5	23.8	29.0
2 pounds....	208	4.8	26.7	34.5	93	6.7	22.6	29.0	129	6.7	20.5	29.0
3 pounds....	213	5.5	26.7	34.5	91	6.4	20.0	27.0	125	7.0	19.1	26.0
None........	203	5.9	24.8	33.0	109	7.0	21.6	31.0	139	7.8	20.8	28.5
4 pounds....	180	5.2	21.0	32.0	113	5.5	20.8	27.0	150	6.6	19.2	24.5
5 pounds....	224	4.2	19.6	25.5	84	6.0	17.5	21.0	42	5.8	21.2	28.0
10 pounds....	208	4.8	19.5	25.5	63	4.6	12.6	16.0	80	4.6	16.7	21.0
None........	190	6.4	24.7	33.0	94	6.0	22.4	25.0	128	7.9	20.0	25.0
20 pounds...	223	4.1	10.8	15.0	62	3.6	9.2	10.5	103	5.5	12.2	15.5
30 pounds...	210	4.1	12.5	17.0	55	4.0	7.3	9.0	83	4.4	8.4	11.5
50 pounds...	142	4.0	10.4	15.0	20	3.7	2.4	2.0	68	3.6	7.5	7.5
None........	231	5.8	24.3	33.5	115	6.5	21.8	27.0	128	7.5	20.6	24.0
100 pounds..	119	3.0	3.6	5.0	27	....	1.1	2.0	28	....	1.1	1.5
200 pounds..	58	....	0	0	15	....	0	.7	8	....	0	0
400 pounds..	7	....	0	0	13	....	0	0	0	....	0	0
None........	203	5.9	23.8	33.5	114	6.5	21.4	25.5	130	7.1	16.8	23.5

Table 2 shows that borax in small quantities materially affected germination, especially in section 2, and that there was considerable retardation in growth in the early life of the plant. The effect on germination and growth is shown in Plate I, Figure 1. The plants shown were dug from the various plats in section 2 on June 15, each being a representative plant from the plat on which it grew. Where 200 and 400 pounds of borax were used, the seeds germinated, but the sprout withered and died without pushing through the soil. The plants from the 50 and 100 pound borax plats were abnormal, weak, and very badly bleached.

The weights of beans and vines tell the story of the final influence of borax on the production of this crop. In sections 1 and 2 its harmful effect is first noticeable with 5 pounds per acre, which increases in degree as the quantity added increases. In the broadcasted section there is not shown much influence from quantities under 10 pounds per acre.

Plates II and III show the Lima and snap beans which were photographed on July 17. In Plate II, Figures 1, 2, and 3 show the Lima and snap beans grown on the no-borax, 5-pound, and 10-pound borax plats, respectively. In Plate III, Figures 1, 2, and 3 show the beans in the 20, 50, and 100 pound borax plats. Figure 3 also shows the plats having 200 and 400 pounds of borax. Here it is seen that these higher borax plats have supported no vegetation whatever. The effect of the varying quantities of borax is apparent and does not call for further comment.

FIG. I.—SNAP BEANS DUG FROM FIELD PLATS TREATED WITH VARIOUS
QUANTITIES OF BORAX.

Seeds planted May 26; plants removed from the soil and photographed June 15.

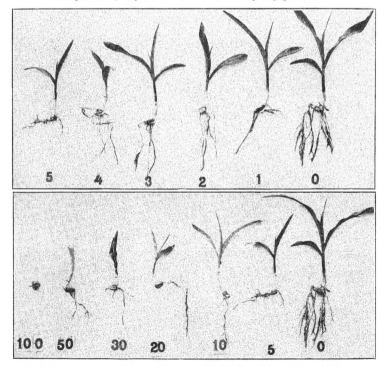

FIGS. 2 AND 3.—CORN PLANTS DUG FROM FIELD PLATS TREATED WITH VARIOUS
QUANTITIES OF BORAX.

Seeds planted May 3; plants dug from the soil and photographed May 28.

EFFECT OF BORAX ON PLANTS IN THEIR EARLY STAGES OF GROWTH.

The figures shown in connection with the plants indicate the number of pounds of borax applied
per acre in the fertilizer used.

FIG. 1.—NO BORAX APPLIED.

FIG. 2.—APPLICATION OF 5 POUNDS OF BORAX PER ACRE.

FIG. 3.—APPLICATION OF 10 POUNDS OF BORAX PER ACRE.

EFFECT OF BORAX ON BEANS AT ARLINGTON, VA.—I.

Seeds planted on silty clay loam May 26, using a 4-8-4 fertilizer with and without borax: Snap
beans at left, Lima beans at right, plants photographed July 17. (Compare with Pl. III)

FIG. I.—APPLICATION OF 20 POUNDS OF BORAX PER ACRE: SNAP BEANS AT
LEFT, LIMA BEANS AT RIGHT.

FIG. 2.—APPLICATION OF 50 POUNDS OF BORAX PER ACRE: SNAP BEANS AT
LEFT, LIMA BEANS AT RIGHT.

FIG. 3.—APPLICATION OF 100 POUNDS OF BORAX PER ACRE ON RIGHT, 200
POUNDS IN CENTER, AND 400 POUNDS ON LEFT.

EFFECT OF BORAX ON BEANS AT ARLINGTON, VA.—II.

Seeds planted May 26 on silty clay loam, using a 4–8–4 fertilizer with and without borax; plants
photographed July 17. (Compare with Pl. II.)

YIELDS OF POTATOES OBTAINED WITH VARIOUS QUANTITIES OF BORAX IN FERTILIZERS AT ARLINGTON, VA.

A, No borax, 5, 10, 20, and 30 pounds of borax per acre, respectively. B, No borax, 50, 100, 200, and 400 pounds of borax per acre, respectively. C, Ten pounds of borax per acre applied by different methods: Sec. 1.—In the drill with delayed planting. Sec. 2.—In the drill at time of planting. Sec. 3.—Sown broadcast at time of planting. All plats, 1/270 acre.

EFFECT OF BORAX ON POTATOES.

The potatoes grown in the experiment were McCormicks and were planted on July 1 and dug on October 26. Each of the three sections was planted with 40 seed pieces. The record of the number of pieces that germinated in each plat is given, and it is seen here that the yield is coordinated to a certain extent with the percentage of germination. The rainfall in the first 7 days of July was approximately 2 inches, which was sufficient to thoroughly wet the surface soil a few inches, and the fertilizers doubtless were well diffused in section 1 before the seeds were planted. During July there were 4.97 inches of rainfall and in August 4.91 inches, fairly well distributed, which made conditions ideal for potato growing during the first two months of this experiment.

The yields and the germination records obtained in the experiment are given in Table 3.

TABLE 3.—*Effect of various quantities of borax on potatoes in field plats on silty clay loam at Arlington, Va., in 1920.*

Borax per acre.	Sec. 1.—Fertilizer applied in drill 7 days before planting. Yield per plat (pounds).			Sec. 2.—Fertilizer applied in drill at time of planting. Yield per plat (pounds).			Plants up July 30.	Sec. 3.—Fertilizer applied broadcast at time of planting. Yield per plat (pounds).			Plants up July 30.
	Primes.	Culls.	Total.	Primes.	Culls.	Total.		Primes.	Culls.	Total.	
None.......	34	1	35	39	2	41	40	43	2	45	42
1 pound....	38	2	40	45	1	46	43	46	2	48	43
2 pounds....	38	1	39	38	2	40	41	50	3	53	44
3 pounds....	40	3	43	40	2	42	44	49	4	53	44
None.......	37	3	40	39	2	41	40	42	3	45	44
4 pounds....	40	4	44	54	1	55	44	42	1	43	42
5 pounds....	39	1	40	33	1	34	39	45	1	46	44
10 pounds...	36	3	39	39	1	40	38	49	1	50	42
None.......	31	5	36	35	1	36	42	51	1	52	44
20 pounds...	32	2	34	30	2	32	35	45	1	46	43
30 pounds...	24	2	26	25	1	26	28	45	1	46	44
50 pounds...	22	3	25	23	1	24	20	35	1	36	40
None.......	30	3	33	33	2	35	39	55	1	56	43
100 pounds..	14	2	16	14	1	15	9	24	0	24	24
200 pounds..	2	2	4	0	0	0	2	0	0	0	4
400 pounds..	0	0	0	0	0	0	2	0	0	0	3
None.......	39	2	41	44	2	46	41	42	2	44	43

In section 1, where the fertilizer was put in the furrow and the planting of potatoes delayed, there was a slight stimulation with the smaller quantities of borax. The yield was depressed by 30 pounds per acre; quantities larger than this proved still more harmful.

In section 2, where the potatoes were planted immediately (Pl. IV, Figs. 1 and 2), the germination was affected, and there was a depression of yield with 20 pounds of borax per acre, while 30 pounds were more harmful. Where 200 and 400 pounds of borax were used there was no germination. In section 3, 50 pounds of borax was the smallest quantity which proved harmful and 100 pounds were decidedly injurious, reducing germination and yield approximately 50 per cent. In Plate IV, Figure 3 shows the effect of 10 pounds of borax per acre in the three sections with different methods of fertilizer application.

The following conclusions can be drawn from the potato experiment: Borax in quantities of 4 pounds per acre and less was stimulating, in harmony with the effect of small quantities of poisons generally; the 5 and 10 pound applications showed no unusual effects; the application of 20 pounds per acre affected germination and reduced the yield when the fertilizer was applied in the drill and the potatoes planted immediately; 30 pounds decreased the growth where the fertilizer was applied in the drill and the planting delayed; and 50 pounds were injurious to germination and depressed the yield where the fertilizer was sown broadcast.

EFFECT OF BORAX ON CORN.

The experiment with corn differed from that with beans and potatoes in that each plat was three rows instead of one, which made the area for each treatment one-ninetieth of an acre instead of one two-hundred-and-seventieth. The fertilizer was applied on May 3, and the seed planted in sections 2 and 3 on that date, while planting in section 1 was delayed until May 12.

The corn was planted thick, using approximately the same number of grains in each plat, afterwards thinning to a stand of 105 plants per section. Before thinning, a record was made of the number of plants which had come up in each plat and the average height of the plants was taken on that date. Notes made 25 days after the seeds were planted (on May 28) showed that in section 2 there was a decided difference in the color of the young plants where 2 and 3 pounds per acre of borax were used. Where 5 pounds were used they were badly discolored and the leaves were slightly curled. In the 10-pound plat the leaves were badly bleached. In section 3, where the fertilizer was sown broadcast, there was no leaf discoloration or bleaching with any quantity under 10 pounds per acre. This characteristic effect was very marked where 20 pounds were used.

A representative plant from each plat in section 2 is shown in Plate I, Figures 2 and 3. Here the characteristic effect of borax is shown. The records showing its effect on germination and on the plant in the early stages of growth, together with the final yields of stover and corn, are given in Table 4.

Borax in quantities as low as 4 pounds per acre slightly depressed the yield of both stover and corn when the fertilizer was applied in the drill. Quantities larger than this decreased the yield considerably more. The use of 20 pounds was very detrimental, and there was an utter failure where 100 pounds were applied.

In the section sown broadcast 20 pounds per acre caused some decrease in yield; the 50-pound application was very harmful; and there was no growth at all where 200 and 400 pounds were used.

Plates V and VI show the corn in section 2 photographed on July 9. The corn in the 3-pound borax plat had not made as much growth as in the no-borax plat, and the corn in the 10-pound plat was a great deal smaller at this stage of its growth than the corn in the no-borax plat. On the 30-pound borax plat shown in Plate VI, Figure 2, the broken stand and uneven growth of the corn is quite striking. An inspection made on July 9 showed that the corn on the no-borax and on the 4-pound borax plats in the broadcasted section of the experiment had made practically the same growth.

FIG. I.—PLAT TO WHICH NO BORAX WAS APPLIED.

FIG. 2.—PLAT RECEIVING 3 POUNDS OF BORAX PER ACRE.

EFFECT OF BORAX ON CORN AT ARLINGTON, VA.—I.

Fertilizers applied in the drill; seed planted May 7 on silty clay loam; photographed July 9
Compare with Pl. VI.)

FIG. I.—PLAT RECEIVING 10 POUNDS OF BORAX PER ACRE.

FIG. 2.—PLAT RECEIVING 30 POUNDS OF BORAX PER ACRE.

EFFECT OF BORAX ON CORN AT ARLINGTON, VA.—II.

Seed planted May 7 on silty clay loam; fertilizers applied in the drill; photographed July 9
(Compare with Pl. V.)

TABLE 4.—*Effect of various quantities of borax on corn in field plats on silty clay loam at Arlington, Va., in 1920.*

Borax per acre.	Sec. 1.—Fertilizer applied in drill 7 days before planting.				Sec. 2.—Fertilizer applied in drill at time of planting.				Sec. 3.—Fertilizer applied broadcast at time of planting.			
	Plants up June 8.		Yield per plat, pounds.		Plants up May 28		Yield per plat, pounds.		Plants up May 28.		Yield per plat, pounds.	
	Number.	Height, inches.	Stover.	Ears.	Number.	Height, inches.	Stover.	Ears.	Number.	Height, inches.	Stover	Ears.
None........	207	8.6	153	106	214	6.5	136	91	237	6.0	120	96
1 pound.....	177	8.1	147	81	221	5.2	118	88	244	5.5	113	91
2 pounds....	167	7.7	136	96	191	4.5	113	89	206	4.8	123	81
3 pounds....	194	8.0	147	93	209	3.7	135	80	208	4.2	92	84
None........	170	8.6	156	94	210	5.5	132	87	202	5.6	122	90
4 pounds....	162	7.9	120	87	179	4.2	128	72	156	4.5	131	84
5 pounds....	145	7.0	131	86	168	4.1	125	75	184	4.6	131	97
10 pounds...	153	5.9	114	89	111	3.2	116	72	180	4.3	131	92
None........	170	8.5	146	94	225	5.5	140	97	229	5.4	148	96
20 pounds...	127	5.7	129	87	76	3.1	107	71	175	4.0	142	85
30 pounds...	74	5.3	90	66	70	3.4	90	60	187	3.9	140	54
50 pounds...	51	4.9	75	44	24	......	82	59	44	......	72	56
None........	177	8.7	157	105	211	5.5	156	109	182	5.6	133	100
100 pounds..	26	3.5	50	33	9	......	17	9	77	......	74	64
200 pounds..	6	3.4	16	13	7	......	18	10	0	......	0	0
400 pounds..	0	0	0	0	9	......	0	0	1	......	0	0
None........	189	8.4	135	96	133	5.2	137	99	82	4.3	115	86

In section 1, as far as concerns the 200 and 400 pound plats, nothing grew. Where borax was sown broadcast over the entire area and mixed with the soil the growth of either grass or weeds was prevented throughout the entire summer. In section 2 these same plats allowed only a few plants to mature, and these were outside the drill rows.

From the data presented in the foregoing pages it is apparent that borax is injurious to plant growth. The degree of harmfulness seems to vary considerably with the crop grown and the method of applying the fertilizer. It is apparent from the data presented in this bulletin and from the work of others previously cited that borax is much less harmful when sown broadcast than when concentrated in the drill. Weather conditions following the time of applying the fertilizer and during the early life of the crop are an important factor which influences the action of the borax, as was pointed out in considering the work already reported.

INFLUENCE OF RAINFALL ON THE EFFECT OF BORAX.

A daily record of the rainfall at Arlington was kept, which affords an opportunity to study its influence on the effect of borax on the various crops. The daily rainfall for May, June, July, August, and September is given in Table 5.

Considering first the weather conditions connected with the planting of beans on May 26, it is seen from a study of the rainfall record that there was no precipitation for 10 days preceding the application of the fertilizer and none for 10 days following the inauguration of the experiment. The first rainfall occurred on June 5, amounting to 1.19 inches. The rainfall for the remainder of the month was well distributed and was sufficient to keep the soil in good moist condition. At the time of planting the beans and for 10 days following the soil was dry. This period was followed by two weeks of optimum soil-moisture conditions. The effect of the borax in retarding the germination of the beans and stunting the growth of the young plants was probably more pronounced than if there had been heavy rainfall for this period.

TABLE 5.—*Record of daily rainfall at Arlington, Va., for the five-month period from May to September, inclusive, in 1920.*

[Data in inches.]

Date.	May.	June.	July.	Aug.	Sept.	Date.	May.	June.	July.	Aug.	Sept.
1........	0.38	0	0	0	0	17.......	0	0.21	0.07	0.18	0
2........	0	0	0	.44	0	18........	0	.21	.08	.16	0
3........	0	0	1.96	0	0	19........	0	0	0	.17	0
4........	0	0	0	0	0	20........	0	0	.89	.80	0
5........	0	1.19	0	0	0	21........	0	1.25	0	1.00	0
6........	0	.83	0	.26	0	22........	0	.15	0	0	0
7........	0	0	0	.01	.22	23........	0	0	.22	.11	0
8........	.41	0	.62	0	0	24........	0	.04	0	0	0
9........	0	0	0	0	0	25........	0	.24	.80	0	.03
10.......	0	0	0	.04	1.09	26........	0	0	0	0	0
11.......	0	0	0	.38	.70	27........	0	0	0	0	0
12.......	0	.25	0	0	0	28........	0	0	0	.18	.07
13.......	.76	0	0	.71	.01	29........	0	0	0	0	.02
14.......	0	.05	0	0	0	30........	0	0	0	.11	1.34
15.......	.05	0	.31	0	0	31........	0	....	0	0	....
16.......	0	.09	.02	.36	0						

The weather conditions at the time of planting the potatoes on July 1 were somewhat different. For 10 days preceding the inauguration of the experiment about 1 inch of rain had fallen, and the soil was sufficiently moist to cause germination and to support normal growth. On July 3, two days after the fertilizer was applied and the seed planted in sections 2 and 3, there was a rainfall of 1.96 inches. While this depth of rainfall would not be likely to cause any considerable quantity of borax to be leached, it probably would be sufficient to dissolve the borax. By the natural movement of the soil moisture the borax would be well diffused in the soil. The borax in section 1, where the delayed planting was made, was probably well distributed before planting was done. Occasional rains during July kept the soil well supplied with moisture except in the last of the month, when a period of about a week without rainfall occurred. The rainfall in August was favorable, so that the potatoes germinated and grew under rather favorable moisture conditions, and only slight borax injury was experienced. It required relatively large quantities to produce a pronounced injury.

The corn which was planted early in May started its growth under somewhat different weather conditions than did the beans and potatoes. When planted on May 3 the soil was in a good moist condition and during the following 12 days there was a well-distributed rainfall of 1.22 inches, which was during the germination stage. The rainfall was sufficient to keep the surface soil in a moist condition, and at no time during the 12-day germinating period did the surface become dry. The following 3 weeks, which was the period when the young plants were beginning their growth, were without rainfall, As was pointed out earlier, there was considerable injury to the young corn by small quantities of borax, except possibly in the 3 plats of section 1 which received 1, 2, and 3 pounds of borax per acre.

It would seem that weather conditions at the time of planting exerted considerable influence on the effect of borax on the crops in the Arlington work. As this was apparent early in the investigation, experiments with corn and cotton were planned and inaugurated early in June to determine especially the effect of rainfall and weather conditions on the action of borax. Experiments with these two crops were begun on June 2 and repeated at intervals of about one week for a number of weeks.

PERIODIC PLANTING OF CORN AND COTTON.

CORN.

The experiments planned especially to study the effect of borax under different weather conditions were similar in design to the former experiments described as far as the method of applying the fertilizer is concerned. Only two quantities of borax were used, however, namely 5 and 10 pounds per acre, and these are compared with a fertilizer containing no borax. Each treatment comprised one row 44 feet long, which is one two-hundred-and-seventieth of an acre. The outline of the experiments with dates on which each was inaugurated is given in Table 6, together with the data obtained.

TABLE 6.—*Influence of weather conditions on the action of borax on corn at Arlington, Va., in 1920.*

| | Yield per plat. | | | | | | | | | | | |
| | Sec. 1.—Fertilizer applied in drill 7 days before planting. | | | Sec. 2.—Fertilizer applied in drill at time of planting. | | | | Sec. 3.—Fertilizer applied broadcast at time of planting. | | | |
Experiment, date started, and borax per acre.	Sto-ver.	In-crease or de-crease.	Ears.	In-crease or de-crease.	Sto-ver.	In-crease or de-crease.	Ears.	In-crease or de-crease.	Sto-ver.	In-crease or de-crease	Ears.	In-crease or de-crease.
	Lbs.	P. ct.	Lbs.	P. ct.	Lbs.	P. ct.	Lbs.	P. ct.	Lbs.	P. ct.	Lbs.	P. ct.
Series A, June 2:												
None...............	30	....	25	....	32	....	24	....	33	....	31	......
5 pounds..........	45	+50	31	+24	44	+37.5	33	+37.5	41	+24.2	36	+16.1
10 pounds.........	33	+10	28	+12	39	+21.9	34	+41.7	34	+ 3	32	+ 3.2
Series B, June 9:												
None...............	33	....	24	....	67	....	39	....	53	....	38	......
5 pounds..........	29	−12.1	20	−16.7	47	−29.8	28	−28.2	46	−13.2	33	−13.1
10 pounds.........	28	−15.1	19	−20.8	50	−25.4	33	−15.4	58	+ 9.4	46	+21
Series C, July 7:												
None...............	132	....			138	....			153	....		......
5 pounds..........	133	+ .75			137	− .7			143	− 6.5		......
10 pounds.........	123	− 6.8			97	−30			126	−17.6		......
Series D, July 15:												
None...............	93	....			122	....			124	....		......
5 pounds..........	89	− 4.3			109	−10.6			117	− 5.6		......
10 pounds.........	64	−31.2			97	−20.5			127	+ 2.4		......
Series E, August 3:												
None...............	81	....			91	....			91	....		......
5 pounds..........	82	+ 1.23			73	−19.8			76	−16.5		......
10 pounds.........	66	−18.5			58	−36.2			71	−22		......

In the first experiments of the series, A, the fertilizers were applied on June 2, and the seeds were planted on that date in sections 2 and 3 and on June 9 in section 1. There was an increased yield of both stover and corn in the 5 and 10 pound borax plats in each section over the no-borax plat. There was a marked stimulation apparently due to borax, which was as much as 50 per cent in stover in one case and 37.5 per cent in ear production in another case. The third day after the fertilizers were applied there was a rainfall of 1.19 inches and the fourth day 0.83 inch. This depth of moisture falling in 2 days undoubtedly diffused the borax in the soil. At any rate the borax in the quantities applied, 5 and 10 pounds per acre, under these weather conditions had no harmful action.

In series B, which was started on June 9, the borax caused some decrease in both stover and corn. This decrease was most severe in section 2, where the yield of stover was decreased nearly 30 per cent and of ears 28.2 per cent by 5 pounds of borax. The yield of stover was decreased 25.4 per cent and that of ears 15.4 per cent by 10 pounds of borax. At the time of applying fertilizers and planting the soil was moist, but there had been no rain for several days. The light showers which fell within the 10 days following the planting were not more than would moisten the surface inch of soil.

Series C was not planted until July 7, and no yield of ear corn was produced by this and the subsequent planting, as the planting was made too late in the season to mature. The yield of stover, however, is given. The effect of the borax in this planting was to cause no decrease with 5 pounds in section 1, and only slight decreases in sections 2 and 3. The decrease with 10 pounds was more marked in sections 1 and 3 and especially in section 2, where it was as much as 30 per cent. The soil was moist at planting time, and there was 0.62 of an inch precipitation the next day, after which there was no precipitation for a week. The second week after planting there were light showers daily which were sufficient to keep the surface moist.

Series D was planted on July 15, and the action of the borax was somewhat more severe than in series C. A slightly decreased yield in each section was caused by 5 pounds of borax. The use of 10 pounds of borax caused a considerable decrease in sections 1 and 2, but a slight increase in section 3. The first 10 days after this experiment was begun the soil was rather moist. There were light showers for the 4 days following the planting, amounting in all to 0.48 of an inch rainfall, and on the sixth day, July 20, there was 0.89 inch precipitation.

The last planting was made on August 3, and series E in Table 6 shows that the borax was harmful to growth in sections 2 and 3 with 5 pounds per acre, and its harmful effects were very marked in each section where 10 pounds were used, amounting to a decrease of 36.2 per cent in growth in section 2. The rainfall in the 10-day period following the planting was moderate, amounting to 0.69 of an inch, which was well distributed. In the second 10-day period, 3.38 inches precipitation occurred, but this, too, was well distributed, and there were no heavy rains during the 20-day period.

In each of these series, excepting A, the borax had a harmful action. However, the degree of harmfulness in the several series varied, and in series C it was very mild. The experiments generally were made under favorable moisture conditions, the depth of rainfall which occurred shortly after the fertilizer was applied in each test did not vary greatly, except in series A, where there was a precipitation of 2.02 inches in the four days following the fertilizer application, and in series C, where the planting was followed on the second day by a rainfall of 0.62 of an inch.

COTTON.

Experiments with the Cleveland Big Boll variety of cotton similar to those with corn just described were also made and some interesting results obtained. Cotton planted as late as June at Arlington could not mature. The effects of borax, however, were noted on germination, growth, and boll formation. In these tests each treatment occupied one row or an area of one two-hundred-and-seventieth of an acre. The 4–8–4 fertilizer was used at the rate of 1,000 pounds per acre. The cotton was planted thick and thinned to 45 hills per plat, with 2 plants to each hill. The complete data are given in Table 7.

TABLE 7.—*Effect of various quantities of borax on the growth and fruiting of cotton on silty clay loam at Arlington, Va., in 1920.*

[The measurements of height of plants were made in experiment series A and B, for sections 2 and 3, on July 27; for section 1, on August 3; those for experiment series C, sections 2 and 3, on August 3, and for section 1, on August 10.]

Experiment, date started, and borax per acre.	Sec. 1.—Fertilizer applied in drill 7 days before planting.					Sec. 2.—Fertilizer applied in drill at time of planting.					Sec. 3.—Fertilizer applied broadcast at time of planting.				
	Height.	Weight, green.	Increase or decrease.	Bolls and squares.	Increase or decrease.	Height.	Weight, green.	Increase or decrease.	Bolls and squares.	Increase or decrease.	Height.	Weight, green.	Increase or decrease.	Bolls and squares.	Increase or decrease.
	Ins.	Lbs.	P.ct.	No.	P.ct.	Ins.	Lbs.	P.ct.	No.	P.ct.	Ins.	Lbs.	P.ct.	No.	P.ct.
Series A, June 2:															
None	16.9	61	.....	1,680	.....	12.5	60	.....	1,777	.....	14.8	73	.....	1,435	.....
5 pounds	12.4	56	− 8.2	1,295	−22.9	11.6	59	− 1.7	1,000	−43.7	14.1	80	+ 9.6	1,252	−12.7
10 pounds	11.2	58	− 5	1,315	−21.7	10.1	61	+ 1.7	967	−45.6	11.0	55	−24.7	901	−37.2
Series B, June 9:															
None	8.8	67	.....	1,478	.....	11.5	72	.....	1,441	.....	13.0	72	.....	1,525	.....
5 pounds	8.1	69	+ 3	1,400	− 5.3	7.3	62	−14	1,305	− 9.4	10.0	79	+ 9.7	1,503	− 1.4
10 pounds	6.9	67	0	1,302	−11.9	6.5	58	−19.5	1,361	− 5.6	8.8	68	− 5.6	1,600	+ 5
Series C, June 18:															
None	9.6	62	.....	1,500	.....	10.2	69	.....	1,697	.....	10.7	68	.....	1,692	.....
5 pounds	7.0	62	0	1,590	+ 6	9.6	70	+ 1.4	1,750	+ 3.1	9.1	71	+ 4.4	1,800	+ 6.4
10 pounds	6.7	57	− 8	1,490	− .7	8.7	72	+ 4.4	1,505	−11.3	7.8	64	− 5.9	1,613	− 4.7
20 pounds	6.5	56	− 9.7	1,380	− 8	6.8	49	−29	1,480	−12.8	7.2	53	−22	1,520	−10.2
Series D, July 7:															
None		40	.....	1,100	.....		45	.....	1,539	.....		54	.....	1,610	.....
5 pounds		37	− 7.5	1,000	− 9.1		49	+ 8.9	1,392	− 9.5		51	− 5.6	1,630	+ 1.2
10 pounds		29	−27.7	760	−30.9		33	−26.7	1,050	−31.7		41	−24.2	1,210	−24.8
20 pounds		21	−47.5	597	−45.7		29	−35.5	930	−39.5		35	−35.2	1,030	−36
Series E, July 15:															
None		26	.....	622	.....		28	.....	823	.....		35	.....	1,146	.....
5 pounds		26	0	680	+ 9		24	−14.3	822	− .1		36	− 2.9	1,137	− 0.8
10 pounds		21	−19.2	585	− 6		23	−18	718	−12.7		33	− 5.8	1,005	−12.3
20 pounds		21	−19.2	560	−10		18	−36	434	−47.2		30	−14.3	1,020	−11
Series F, August 5:															
None		10	.....	0	.....		13	.....	0	.....		17	.....	0	.....
5 pounds		10	0	0	.....		11	−15.4	0	.....		14	−17.6	0	.....
10 pounds		8	−20	0	.....		12	− 7.7	0	.....		14	−17.6	0	.....
20 pounds		9	−10	0	.....		8	−38.4	0	.....		13	−23.5	0	.....

An examination of the data given in Table 7 shows generally that the growth was checked and the fruiting decreased by the borax. A record of the height of the plants, made when the crop was young, shows that the growth was checked in the very beginning by the borax. The degree of injury, however, varies with the different plantings and with the different methods of applying the fertilizers. The germination was rather irregular where 20 pounds of borax were applied, and in spots the young cotton died. The use of 10 pounds of borax had a decided effect on the color of the foliage in each experiment, as the foliage was much lighter where the borax was applied.   The 5-pound application of borax produced the least injury.

In section 3, where 5 pounds of borax per acre were applied, no injury was observed in series A, B, and C, and the reduction noted in the fruiting of the plants in series A and B was not serious.   With 10 pounds of borax there was a further decrease in growth and, in general, in the number of bolls formed.   Where 20 pounds of borax were used there was a decided harmful effect.   In series C, D, E, and F there was a reduction in growth of 22, 35.2, 14.3, and 23.5 per cent respectively; and in series C, D, and E a reduction in boll formation of 10.2, 36, and 11 per cent, respectively.

In section 2, where the fertilizer was applied in the drill and the seed planted immediately, the harmfulness of borax with 10 and 20 pounds per acre was quite marked, especially in series D, E, and F, and the fruiting in series A was adversely affected.   The growth was checked more in this section than where the fertilizer was sown broadcast.   The use of 5 pounds per acre reduced growth to a much less extent than the 10 or 20 pound applications.

In section 1, where the planting was not made until after the fertilizer was applied, the harmfulness of the borax was on the whole less than in sections 2 and 3, except in series D and E, which is probably due to drier soil conditions.

In connection with the rainfall record, it was stated that the moisture condition of the soil was about optimum at the time and after the plantings were made in series A, B, and C.   The rainfall was, however, very light during the weeks of July 4 and July 11 and was again light the weeks of July 25 and August 3.   The effect of the borax in series D and E, which were planted in the period of dry weather, was more severe than in the experiments which were planted when the moisture was more nearly normal.   For example, in section 1, 20 pounds of borax per acre reduced the growth 9.7 per cent in series C, 47.5 per cent in series D, and 19.2 per cent in series E.   In section 2 the growth was reduced 29 per cent in series C, 35.5 per cent in series D, and 36 per cent in series E.   In section 3 growth was reduced 22 per cent in series C, 35.2 per cent in series D, and 14.3 per cent in series E.   The formation of bolls was also reduced more in series D and E than in C.   A few days after the plantings were made in series D, E, and F, a light rain fell, which was followed by a dry period.   While the plants were young in the earlier experiments there were occasional heavy rains, and at no time did the soil become very dry.   It is not probable that a rainfall of 1 to 1.7 inches in one week distributed over a period of several days would wash very much borax out of reach of the roots of the cotton.   However, it would result in the diffusion of the borax through the soil, and this diffusion might easily account for the lesser extent of injury in series A, B, and C.   Under the rainfall conditions of series D and E the borax was concentrated in locations surrounding the roots of the young plants and would naturally cause a more severe injury and a greater retardation of growth.

The data in general show that the action of borax on cotton under the weather conditions prevailing at the time of this test was decidedly harmful when 20 pounds per acre were applied in the drill or sown broadcast.   This quantity showed harmful effects whether the seed was planted immediately after the fertilizers were applied or whether they were planted after the intervening of a light rain. The use of 10 pounds per acre decidedly checked growth when applied in the drill, but was only slightly harmful when sown broadcast.

FIELD EXPERIMENTS USING FERTILIZERS WITH AND WITHOUT BORAX.

A COMPARISON OF TWO GRADES OF SEARLES LAKE POTASH IN THE FIELD.

In connection with certain studies in commercial fields to determine the comparative effectiveness of different potash carriers on the potato, a test of two grades of muriate of potash from Searles Lake was included. The two grades differed in that one, the so-called 1919 grade, contained 6.25 per cent of borax, while the other grade, designated 1920, contained practically none.

The tests were conducted cooperatively in Virginia, New Jersey, and Maine, as follows:

At Cape Charles, Va., in cooperation with the Virginia Truck Experiment Station; on Sassafras sandy loam; fertilizer application, 1,800 pounds per acre; average control, 7–8–0; variety grown, Irish Cobbler; yield, 161.7 bushels per acre.

At Norfolk, Va., in cooperation with the Virginia Truck Experiment Station; on Norfolk sandy loam; fertilizer application, 1,800 pounds per acre; average control, 7–7–0; variety grown, Irish Cobbler; yield, 221.3 bushels per acre.

At Holmdel, N. J., in cooperation with the New Jersey Agricultural Experiment Station; on Sassafras loam; fertilizer application, 1,500 pounds per acre; average control, 4–10–0; variety grown, American Giant; yield, 246 bushels per acre.

At Presque Isle, Me., in cooperation with the Maine Agricultural Experiment Station; on Caribou loam; fertilizer application, 1,800 pounds per acre; average control, 5–10–0; variety grown, Irish Cobbler; yield, 243.7 bushels per acre.

The detailed results are shown in Table 8.

The data in Table 8 disclose the fact that in most of the tests, especially as the quantity of borax was increased, the yields were reduced. At two of the stations the fertilizer mixtures containing the 1919 potash salt (6.25 per cent borax) were applied in two ways: (1) by means of the planter which applies the fertilizer in a furrow made by the planter plow and (2) by means of a fertilizer distributer which gives a somewhat greater spread to the application. It will be noted that the former method, which presumably afforded a greater concentration of the fertilizer-borax mixtures near the potato seed pieces, gave the poorer results. The fertilizer mixtures containing the so-called 1920 grade of potash salt (practically free from borax) gave excellent returns, comparing very favorably with other potash carriers.[4] In the experiment at Holmdel, N. J., it will be observed that the fertilizer-borax mixtures gave better results than the no-borax mixtures when applied with the distributer. The chief explanation for this lies perhaps in the heavy rainfall following planting which undoubtedly was sufficient to reduce the concentration of the borax to a point whereby stimulation, rather than injury, may have resulted to the extent of increasing the yields. When applied with the p an er in the drill row, as is ordinarily done by the potato grower, the degree of injury was considerable, as is shown in the first figure column of Table 8. It is well to state in this connection that the results obtained during the same season at New Brunswick, N. J. (2), tend to support the foregoing explanation. At New Bruns-

---

[4] A report on the effect of various potash salts upon crop yields on prominent soil types is in course of preparation.

wick it was found that a fairly high concentration of borax was required to produce injury, and it is significant, moreover, that the rainfall there, which would be approximately the same as at Holmdel, was quite heavy.

TABLE 8.—*Total yields of potatoes grown on different types of soil treated with fertilizers of stated composition, applied at given rates per acre, and containing varying percentages of borax, tests of 1920.*

Items of comparison.	Application of muriate of potash.			Composition of fertilizer (per cent).		
	With planter in drill row, 1919 grade.	With distributer.		NH₃.	P₂O₅.	K₂O.
		1919 grade.	1920 grade.			
At Cape Charles, Va., on Sassafras sandy loam:						
Potash (K₂O) per acre.............pounds..		54	54			
Borax (Na₂B₄O₇) per acre.............do....		8.85	....	7	8	3
Yield per acre.....................bushels..		178.1	203.6			
Potash (K₂O) per acre.............pounds..		90	90			
Borax (Na₂B₄O₇) per acre.............do....		14.75	....	7	8	5
Yield per acre.....................bushels..		161.9	199.7			
Potash (K₂O) per acre.............pounds..		126	126			
Borax (Na₂B₄O₇) per acre.............do....		20.65	....	7	8	7
Yield per acre.....................bushels..		127.4	228.9			
At Norfolk, Va., on Norfolk sandy loam:						
Potash (K₂O) per acre.............pounds..		54	54			
Borax (Na₂B₄O₇) per acre.............do....		8.85	....	7	7	3
Yield per acre.....................bushels..		221.1	245.9			
Potash (K₂O) per acre.............pounds..		90	90			
Borax (Na₂B₄O₇) per acre.............do....		14.75	....	7	7	5
Yield per acre.....................bushels..		231.8	232.5			
Potash (K₂O) per acre.............pounds..		126	126			
Borax (Na₂B₄O₇) per acre.............do....		20.65	....	7	7	7
Yield per acre.....................bushels..		193.6	229.8			
At Holmdel, N. J., on Sassafras loam:						
Potash (K₂O) per acre.............pounds..	45	45	45			
Borax (Na₂B₄O₇) per acre.............do....	7.5	7.5	7.5	4	10	3
Yield per acre.....................bushels..	262	284	278			
Potash (K₂O) per acre.............pounds..	75	75	75			
Borax (Na₂B₄O₇) per acre.............do....	12.5	12.5	12.5	4	10	5
Yield per acre.....................bushels..	256.0	292.6	285.3			
Potash (K₂O) per acre.............pounds..	105	105	105			
Borax (Na₂B₄O₇) per acre.............do....	17.5	17.5	17.5	4	10	7
Yield per acre.....................bushels..	226.0	203.3	276.0			
At Presque Isle, Me., on Caribou loam:						
Potash (K₂O) per acre.............pounds..	54	54	54			
Borax (Na₂B₄O₇) per acre.............do....	8.85	8.85	....	5	10	3
Yield per acre.....................bushels..	331.4	355.5	340.2			
Potash (K₂O) per acre.............pounds..	90	90	90			
Borax (Na₂B₄O₇) per acre.............do....	14.75	14.75	....	5	10	5
Yield per acre.....................bushels..	301.5	316.0	368.0			
Potash (K₂O) per acre.............pounds..	126	126	126			
Borax (Na₂B₄O₇) per acre.............do....	20.65	20.65	....	5	10	7
Yield per acre.....................bushels..	232.1	311.7	495.9			

At the other stations the fertilizer-borax mixtures were injurious and when applied in the drill caused lower yields than when applied with a fertilizer distributer. The illustrations shown in Plate VII, Figures 1 and 2, and Plate VIII, Figures 1 and 2, will give some idea of the effect of borax in fertilizer upon the yield of potatoes on two soil types.

What is brought out here as well as in other parts of this bulletin is convincing proof that borax caused injury. Even were the rainfall heavy in one section, thereby mitigating the injury, it does not follow that the same weather conditions would prevail elsewhere or in another season, and since it has been definitely brought out herein that borax is quite apt to be harmful, it should be practically eliminated from fertilizer salts. Fortunately, this is already fully recognized. The fact is further brought out from the field tests on several soil types that practically borax-free potash salts give good results.

FURTHER RESULTS WITH POTATOES AND CORN.

Results obtained with potatoes and corn at New Brunswick, N. J. (2), and with potatoes at Presque Isle, Me.,[5] are again referred to here, with certain tabular presentations of yields and rainfall data, in order that the results may be assembled in their entirety, the details having been presented elsewhere.

The plan of the experiments in New Jersey and in Maine was similar to that at Arlington, Va., particularly as applies to the quantity of borax used. In New Jersey, fertilizer at the rate of 1,500 pounds per acre was applied to potatoes and at the rate of 400 pounds to corn; and in Maine, at the rate of 2,000 pounds to potatoes. The results are presented in Tables 9, 10, and 12.

TABLE 9.—*Effect of various quantities of borax on potatoes in plats on Sassafras loam at New Brunswick, N. J., in 1920.*

[Fertilizer application, 1,500 pounds per acre; variety grown, Irish Cobbler.]

Borax per acre.	Yield per plat (pounds).								
	Sec. 1.—Fertilizer applied in drill some time previous to planting.			Sec. 2.—Fertilizer applied in drill at time of planting.			Sec. 3.—Fertilizer applied broadcast at time of planting.		
	Primes.	Seconds.	Total.	Primes.	Seconds.	Total.	Primes.	Seconds.	Total.
None (check 1)	78.25	7.50	85.75	75.50	5.50	81.00	58.25	7.50	65.75
1 pound	64.20	5.75	69.95	56.30	6.85	63.15	41.40	5.00	46.40
2 pounds	75.55	4.65	80.20	72.50	9.00	81.50	58.05	5.80	63.85
3 pounds	75.65	6.65	82.30	65.60	9.10	74.70	60.15	5.75	65.90
None (check 2)	79.75	7.70	87.45	62.95	10.35	73.30	65.70	4.45	70.15
4 pounds	88.35	6.40	94.75	69.55	7.60	77.15	66.35	4.95	71.30
5 pounds	85.20	6.00	91.20	77.15	4.65	81.80	62.20	8.00	70.20
10 pounds	88.60	5.90	94.50	64.55	6.45	71.00	60.80	5.10	65.90
None (check 3)	86.90	5.75	92.65	67.75	8.60	76.35	65.80	4.10	69.90
20 pounds	85.70	3.75	89.45	68.75	6.90	75.65	79.00	3.00	82.00
30 pounds	76.95	3.00	79.95	55.00	3.85	58.85	74.00	3.55	77.55
50 pounds	67.95	3.55	71.50	25.35	1.40	26.75	45.70	2.00	47.70
None (check 4)	65.15	7.65	72.80	60.35	6.00	66.35	66.85	6.55	73.40
100 pounds	43.75	3.00	46.75	2.00	1.00	3.00	1.25	.50	1.75
200 pounds	22.50	1.25	23.75	None.	.125	.125	None.	None.	None.
400 pounds	4.00	.50	4.50	None.	None.	None.	None.	None.	None.

[5] Brown B. E. Effect of borax in fertilizer on the growth and yield of potatoes. U. S. Dept. Agr. Bul. 998, 8 p., 1 fig., 4 pl. 1922.

In section 1 of Table 9 it is shown that the yields of potatoes were not greatly influenced by the borax until large quantities were applied. In this section the fertilizer-borax mixtures were applied some time before planting, and during this period the rainfall was at times quite heavy. In section 1 an application of 100 pounds was required before any marked depression in the yield took place.

In section 2, where the fertilizer-borax mixtures were applied and planting done immediately, the first obvious depression in yield took place with the 30-pound application of borax.

In section 3, where the fertilizer-borax mixtures were sown broadcast as much as practicable, no distinct depression in yield can be attributed to concentrations of borax under 50 pounds.

TABLE 10.—*Effect of various quantities of borax on corn in plats on Sassafras loam at New Brunswick, N. J., in 1920.*

[Yields stated in pounds, air-dry basis; fertilizer application, 400 pounds per acre.]

Borax per acre.	Grain.			Cobs.			Stalks.		
	Sec. 1.[a]	Sec. 2.[b]	Sec. 3.[c]	Sec. 1.[a]	Sec. 2.[b]	Sec. 3.[c]	Sec. 1.[a]	Sec. 2.[b]	Sec. 3.[c]
None (check 1).....	11.30	19.88	19.59	2.43	4.32	4.33	24.25	22.00	21.40
1 pound.............	7.96	16.79	17.39	1.63	3.73	3.44	23.00	26.95	18.90
2 pounds...........	8.87	14.93	20.53	1.81	3.18	4.33	23.00	25.75	23.60
3 pounds...........	14.30	13.36	16.79	3.05	2.69	3.44	21.15	18.20	20.80
None (check 2).....	13.47	13.00	13.91	2.81	2.35	2.82	19.30	18.55	20.20
4 pounds...........	9.82	12.00	11.97	2.07	2.50	2.36	14.60	17.50	17.05
5 pounds...........	8.79	8.60	9.97	2.00	1.65	2.04	14.20	12.55	13.80
10 pounds..........	10.85	9.47	11.73	2.30	1.97	2.61	14.85	15.90	16.70
None (check 3).....	7.95	11.68	15.90	1.83	2.44	3.16	18.70	16.52	19.85
20 pounds..........	8.64	9.24	13.90	1.93	1.78	2.84	18.10	15.13	21.05
30 pounds..........	11.77	7.57	12.63	2.67	1.99	2.88	22.95	16.70	21.70
50 pounds..........	11.08	3.41	6.79	2.62	.92	1.66	18.75	7.30	15.65
None (check 4).....	10.55	19.12	20.90	2.23	4.27	4.90	22.50	24.35	31.50
100 pounds.........	6.44	.62	2.82	1.76	.19	.86	20.90	1.70	9.46
200 pounds.........	1.23	0	0	.32	0	0	2.60	0	0
400 pounds.........	.40	0	0	.15	0	0	2.70	0	0

a Fertilizer applied in drill some time previous to planting.
b Fertilizer applied in drill at time of planting.
c Fertilizer applied broadcast at time of planting.

In the corn experiment (Table 10) the normal fertilizer and fertilizer-borax mixtures were applied at the rate of 400 pounds per acre; the quantity of borax, however, was the same as that applied to the potatoes.

In section 1 very little depression in yield, if any, occurred below the 50-pound application, but with quantities in excess of 50 pounds the injury was quite severe.

In section 2 the yields are somewhat confusing, but there was some indication that, beginning with the 5-pound application, some injury ensued, although it will be noted that with applications of 10 and 20 pounds per acre the yields were approximately the same as with the 5-pound application.

In section 3 some evidence is shown that, under the seasonal conditions prevailing, fairly high concentrations of borax were required to produce serious injury.

It will be noted (Table 11), as previously brought out, that the rainfall at New Brunswick during the growing season of 1920 was unusually heavy, which probably reduced the concentration of borax through solution and diffusion into the soil mass. At other stations

FIG. 1.—COMPARISON OF PLATS 43 AND 46.

FIG. 2.—COMPARISON OF PLATS 45, 46, AND 47.

EFFECT OF BORAX ON POTATOES AT CAPE CHARLES, VA.

Quantities of borax applied per acre: Plat 43, none; plat 45, 8.85 pounds; plat 46, 14.75 pounds plat 47, 20.65 pounds.   Soil, Sassafras sandy loam; area of each plat, one-fortieth acre.

FIG. I.—EFFECT OF BORAX ON POTATOES AT NORFOLK, VA.

Quantities of borax applied per acre: Plat 45 (at left), 8.85 pounds; plat 46 (in center), 14.75 pounds; plat 47 (at right), 20.65 pounds   Soil, Norfolk sandy loam; area of each plat, one-fortieth acre.

FIG. 2.—EFFECT OF BORAX ON POTATOES AT PRESQUE ISLE, ME.

Quantities of borax per acre applied with fertilizer: Plat 44 (at left), none; plat 47 (in center, applied with distributer), 20.65 pounds; plat 50 (at right, applied in the furrow with planter), 20.65 pounds. Soil, Caribou loam; area of each plat, one-fortieth acre.

YIELDS OF POTATOES FROM 1/200 ACRE WITH VARIOUS QUANTITIES OF BORAX IN FERTILIZERS.

On Caribou loam. Fertilizer applied at time of planting; *A*, No borax, 5, 10, 20, and 30 pounds of borax per acre, respectively; *B*, 50, 100, 200, and 400 pounds of borax per acre, respectively.

where the rainfall was not so heavy and.was more uniformly distributed the injurious action of borax was much greater.

TABLE 11.—*Record of rainfall at New Brunswick, N. J., during the growing season, in 1920.*

[Data in inches.]

Items of comparison.	Apr.	May.	June.	July.	Aug.	Sept.
1920	4.28	3.56	9.64	6.00	8.21	2.23
10-year average, 1910 to 1919	3.66	3.85	3.52	4.67	5.07	2.95

Table 12 shows the results obtained with potatoes in Maine.

TABLE 12.—*Effect of various quantities of borax on potatoes in plats on Caribou loam, at Presque Isle, Me., in 1920.*

[Yields in bushels per acre; variety grown, Irish Cobbler; fertilizer application, 2,000 pounds per acre.]

Borax per acre.	Sec. 1.*a*	Sec. 2.*b*	Sec. 3.*c*	Borax per acre.	Sec. 1.*a*	Sec. 2.*b*	Sec. 3.*c*.
None (check 1)	362.7	326.6	337.3	20 pounds	201.3	150.7	200.0
1 pound	370.0	349.3	318.7	30 pounds	118.7	52.0	81.3
2 pounds	381.3	362.7	324.0	50 pounds	88.0	26.7	56.7
3 pounds	390.7	305.3	304.0	None (check 4)	338.7	294.7	321.7
None (check 2)	342.7	376.0	317.3	100 pounds	9.3	5.3	10.7
4 pounds	341.3	330.3	328.0	200 pounds	4.0	1.3	2.7
5 pounds	328.7	302.7	329.3	400 pounds	1.3	.67	1.3
10 pounds	293.3	228.0	264.0	None (check 5)	309.3	316.0	237.3
None (check 3)	348.0	350.7	313.3				

a Fertilizer applied in drill some time previous to planting.
b Fertilizer applied in drill at time of planting.
c Fertilizer applied broadcast at time of planting.

In section 1, where borax was applied in the furrow, injury definitely occurred in the case of the 10-pound application of borax and became progressively worse. It will be noted, however, that the degree of injury was less than in section 2, where the borax was applied in the furrow and planting done immediately. The application of 1, 2, and 3 pounds of borax per acre apparently stimulated plant growth.

In section 2, the borax showed injury with the 5-pound application, and the injury with 10 pounds and larger quantities was great. The yields obtained from the plats receiving the large applications of borax, namely, 50, 100, 200, and 400 pounds per acre, are shown in Plate IX.

In section 3, the general trend of the results is fairly similar to that in sections 1 and 2, the first sign of injury occurring in the case of the 10-pound application of borax. In this section the method of applying the fertilizer-borax mixture in the case of the 400-pound application apparently depressed the yield of the last check.

The record for Presque Isle, Me. (Table 13), indicates that the rain which fell during June, subsequent to planting on June 5, was fairly well distributed. It would seem that there was hardly enough rainfall to cause the borax to be leached to any marked extent; in fact, only sufficient to keep the soil in good condition and the borax concentrated at the seed piece. The relation of the rainfall to the degree of injury sustained by the plants during the period is emphasized at this point, owing to the fact that the first three or four weeks after planting embraces germination and the early life of the plant.

TABLE 13.—*Record of rainfall at Presque Isle, Me., for June, July, and August, 1920.*

[Data in inches.]

Date.	June.	July.	Aug.	Date.	June.	July.	Aug.	Date.	June.	July.	Aug.
1		0.45	0.17	12			0.46	22	0.57		0.23
2	0.13			13		0.04		23	1.02	0.06	1.32
3	.50	.37	.63	14			.01	24	.10	.03	
4		.43		15			.01	25	.12	.02	
5		1.10		16	0.04		.09	26			.01
7	.73	.11		18			.03	27	.03		
8		1.00		19		.20	.42	29	1.09		
10			.43	20			.05	30	1.01	.08	.08
11	.49		.12	21		.06		31			.15

EFFECT OF BORAX ON COTTON AT MUSCLE SHOALS, ALA.[6]

PLANTINGS ON COLBERT SILT LOAM.

An experiment with cotton similar in plan to that at Arlington and at other locations with potatoes and corn was made on Colbert silt loam at Muscle Shoals, Ala. It included the application of fertilizer in the row as well as broadcast and also the immediate and delayed planting of seed after applying fertilizer. The quantity of borax used varied from 1 to 400 pounds per acre, and two rows each 70 feet long were used for each treatment. The fertilizers were applied on May 10. The rainfall for the month prior to starting the experiment and for a like period afterwards was exceedingly heavy. The soil became very compact from the excessive rains, and a very poor stand over the entire area was secured. The experiment was continued, however, in order to observe the effects of the borax, but a harvest was not made, as the broken stand appeared to make it useless.

TABLE 14.—*Effect of various quantities of borax on the growth of cotton on Colbert silt loam, at Muscle Shoals, Ala., in 1920.*

Borax per acre.	Fertilizer applied in the row.		Fertilizer applied broadcast at time of planting.
	At time of planting.	Planted 10 days later.	
None			
1 pound	Normal	Normal	Normal.
2 pounds	do	do	Do.
3 pounds	do	do	Do.
None			
4 pounds	do	do	Do.
5 pounds	Normal	Normal	Do.
10 pounds	do	do	Do.
None			
20 pounds	Slight injury	Slight retarding	Slight retarding.
30 pounds	Plants small; many dying	Somewhat stunted	Slightly retarded.
50 pounds	Germination low; plants dying.	Germination low; plants show yellowing.	Somewhat stunted.
None			
100 pounds	Only an occasional seed germinated: plants dying.	Germination about 50 per cent; plants dying.	Germination decreased and plants dying.
200 pounds	7 seeds germinated; plants about dead.	Only an occasional seed germinated; plants about dead.	Germination decreased about 70 per cent; most plants dead.
400 pounds	No germination	No germination	12 seeds germinated, and plants died.
None			

[6] The immediate supervision of this experiment was under the direction of Dr. F. E. Allison, of the Fixed-Nitrogen Research Laboratory of the United States Department of Agriculture.

Borax caused the greatest injury to cotton in the early stages, either preventing germination or in lesser amounts merely retarding growth and preventing chlorophyll formation. A record of observations three weeks after planting is given in Table 14.

The quantity of borax required to produce a noticeable injury to cotton receiving fertilizer in the row was 20 pounds. Fifty pounds were necessary to appreciably lower germination and cause the death of any very large percentage of the plants. Where the fertilizer was used in the row and planting delayed for 10 days the injury seemed to be decreased about 50 to 75 per cent. Distributing the fertilizer broadcast decreased the injurious effects as much or possibly slightly more than delaying planting. It is shown that any method employed which decreased the concentration of the borax around the plant roots markedly decreased the injury.

During the 10 days preceding planting, May 1 to 10, 2.06 inches of rain fell, and for the 10-day period following planting 3.34 inches of rain fell. The second day after planting 1.6 inches precipitation occurred, which was followed by light showers for several days. The seventh day after planting there was a rainfall of 1.56 inches. The total rainfall for the month was 5.70 inches.

Even with this great depth of rainfall there was unquestionable injury from the borax with 30 pounds per acre. With 50 pounds per acre germination was low, and many of the plants died after germinating when the fertilizer was put in the drill and seed planted immediately. When the borax was sown broadcast the plants were stunted. With 100 pounds of borax per acre and over there was practically no germination.

PLANTINGS ON CLARKSVILLE SILT LOAM.

An experiment at Muscle Shoals, Ala., was also made on Clarksville silt loam located on a gentle slope and well drained. The soil is fairly retentive of moisture and does not become compact. The plan of the experiment differed somewhat from that at Arlington, Va., with cotton in that the fertilizer was applied only in the drill and the seed planted immediately, as in section 2 of the Arlington test (see Table 7). The 4-8-4 fertilizer was used at the same rate of application per acre, namely, 1,000 pounds, and borax applied at 5, 10, and 20 pounds per acre. The test was repeated six times; the first test was started on June 12, and the others followed at intervals of about one week. The separate plats are designated as series A, B, C, D, E, and F. The Cleveland Big-Boll variety was used.

Table 15 shows the results for this set of plats, including the height of the cotton plants at intervals during growth, the number of bolls which formed, and the green and dry weights of the plants, including the roots. Table 16 shows the weekly record of rainfall, so that the relation of the rainfall to the degree of harmfulness of borax in the different series can be compared. The effects of borax on germination, growth, and boll formation are noted. The cotton did not mature, so no yield records were obtained.

TABLE 15.—*Effect of various quantities of borax on the growth of cotton on Clarksville silt loam at Muscle Shoals, Ala., in 1920.*

Experiment, date started, and borax per acre.	Average height of plants (inches).			Bolls Oct. 26.	Green weight of plants.		Dry weight of plants (lbs.).
	July 28.	Aug. 20.	Oct. 16.		Pounds.	Increase or decrease (per cent).	
Series A, June 12:							
None....	12.9	25.3	45.5	667	93.0	....	36.0
5 pounds....	9.6	21.8	44.4	583	86.0	−7.5	33.5
10 pounds....	7.1	17.3	42.1	456	85.0	−8.6	32.0
20 pounds....	4.9	13.2	32.6	242	44.0	−52.7	15.0
Series B, June 19:							
None....	12.0	28.6	50.0	716	104.0	....	40.0
5 pounds....	10.5	25.7	43.3	563	84.0	−19.2	34.5
10 pounds....	8.6	24.1	43.0	576	78.0	−25.	31.5
20 pounds....	6.9	15.6	39.1	383	63.0	−39.4	25.0
Series C, June 26:							
None....	9.4	18.1	45.2	337	86.0	....	34.0
5 pounds....	6.3	15.1	40.5	220	78.0	− 9.3	28.5
10 pounds....	6.9	12.9	39.9	224	75.0	−12.8	26.0
20 pounds....	5.0	9.6	31.5	97	43.0	−50.	15.0
Series D, July 3:							
None....	6.2	16.1	42.2	112	63.0	....	25.5
5 pounds....	5.2	15.1	41.6	94	62.0	− 1.6	24.0
10 pounds....	4.1	12.0	32.9	92	59.0	− 6.3	23.0
20 pounds....	3.2	7.2	29.3	53	39.0	−38.1	13.0
Series E, July 11:							
None....	....	12.3	36.8	45	55.0	....	17.5
5 pounds....	....	11.5	33.7	48	56.5	+ 2.7	20.0
10 pounds....	....	9.9	31.3	46	50.5	− 8.2	20.0
20 pounds....	....	8.4	26.1	14	38.0	−30.9	11.0
Series F, July 20:							
None....	....	10.0	28.2	5	46.5	....	15.0
5 pounds....	....	8.9	29.1	7	47.0	+ 1.1	15.0
10 pounds....	....	8.7	25.7	4	41.0	−11.8	11.0
20 pounds....	....	7.6	22.4	1	35.0	−24.8	8.0

TABLE 16.—*Temperature and rainfall at Florence, Ala. (near Muscle Shoals), in June and July, 1920.*

Week of—	Rainfall (inches).	Temperature (°F.).		Week of—	Rainfall (inches).	Temperature (°F.).	
		Max.	Min.			Max.	Min.
June 6 to 12..........	0	97	53	Aug. 1 to 7............	0	94	60
13 to 19..........	.52	98	63	8 to 14..........	5.10	90	66
20 to 26..........	.58	92	56	15 to 21..........	4.46	91	64
27 to July 3..........	.08	93	61	22 to 28..........	.59	91	56
July 4 to 10..........	.76	94	62	29 to Sept. 4......	.42	96	61
11 to 17..........	.98	93	61	Sept. 5 to 11..........	2.17	93	55
18 to 24..........	1.50	98	63	12 to 18..........	.32	93	55
25 to 31..........	.06	95	57	19 to 25..........	.54	92	55
				26 to Oct. 2......	0	92	37

The relation of rainfall to the degree of harmfulness of borax to cotton is apparent from a study of Tables 15 and 16, and this has been considered in detail in an earlier paper.[7] From the results of the experiment as a whole it will be observed that 5 pounds of borax per acre produced some injury to cotton when applied in the rows, and larger quantities showed even greater toxic effects. The results are in harmony with those obtained at Arlington, Va., showing that

---

[7] Skinner, J. J., and Allison, F. E. The influence of fertilizers containing borax on the growth and fruiting of cotton. Unpublished manuscript.

borax in small amounts is harmful to cotton and that its effect is influenced to a certain degree by weather conditions. Wherever light rains occurred soon after planting, followed by a dry spell, the effect was severest. If heavy rains followed periodically after planting the effect was less severe.

THE RESIDUAL EFFECT OF BORAX.

In order to determine whether there was any residual effect of borax on the succeeding crop, the field which was used for beans, potatoes, and corn in the experiments at Arlington, Va., was planted to wheat in October, 1920, following the harvesting of summer crops. The soil was disked and harrowed and the seed drilled over the entire field.

As the wheat pushed through the soil, the plants in the drill rows immediately over the area where the borax fertilizer had been applied in quantities of 50, 100, 200, and 400 pounds per acre showed a bleached appearance, and the stand on the 200 and 400 pound plats was poor. Plants taken from the fertilizer drill rows are shown in Plate X. These plants weakened as the winter came on, and by early spring the stand was not more than 25 per cent on the plats with the 200 and 400 pound applications. At harvest time in June, 1921, the single drill rows immediately over the original fertilizer-borax drill row were cut separately and the weight of straw and grain is given in Table 17.

TABLE 17.—*Effect of borax on wheat planted after potatoes and corn which had received fertilizer containing borax in various quantities, at Arlington, Va., in 1920.*

Borax per acre.	Yield of wheat per plat (pounds).				Borax per acre.	Yield of wheat per plat (pounds).			
	Potato section.		Corn section.			Potato section.		Corn section.	
	Straw.	Grain.	Straw.	Grain.		Straw.	Grain.	Straw.	Grain.
1 pound..........	21.0	1.75	21	3.0	20 pounds.......	21.0	1.5	18	1.75
2 pounds..........	14.5	2.0	21	2.25	30 pounds.......	20.0	1.5	19	2.0
3 pounds..........	12.0	1.5	19	3.2	50 pounds.......	18.0	1.0	17	1.6
None..............	21.0	1.75	20	2.5	None.............	23.0	2.25	21	3.0
4 pounds..........	16.5	1.5	19	2.7	100 pounds......	10.0	1.0	19	1.25
5 pounds..........	14.5	1.2	18	2.6	200 pounds......	8.0	.75	12	1.0
10 pounds.........	17.0	1.2	17	2.75	400 pounds......	4.0	.6	6	.75
None..............	26.0	2.0	18	2.25	None.............	19.0	1.6	18	2.0

The yield of straw and grain from each drill row in the potato section varies considerably among the checks. While the growth was less in the rows where the smaller quantities of borax were used, it was as great as in the rows which had received 20 and 30 pound applications, so it would be presumed that these decreases may be due to causes other than borax. The yield from the 50-pound plat is slightly under the no-borax plat, and where larger quantities of borax were used the yield is cut more than 50 per cent. A somewhat similar effect is noted in the corn section. It is apparent that the borax, when used in the higher quantities, still remained of sufficient concentration in the soil to exert a harmful residual effect on the succeeding crop. It should be remembered, however, that the soil was disked and not plowed in the preparation for the wheat, so there was very little mixing of the soil. The only plants which were damaged were those in the seed drill row immediately over the old fertilizer-borax drill row.

An interesting case was encountered where cotton in a commercial field was damaged by Searles Lake potash in 1919. This field was again planted to cotton in 1921. The growing crops for both seasons on the same field are shown in Plate XI. In Figure 1 of Plate XI (photographed August 27) is shown the cotton in 1919 which had been fertilized with a mixture analyzing 3 per cent NH_3, 8 per cent P_2O_5, and 3 per cent K_2O at the rate of 800 pounds per acre and in addition had received 100 pounds of Searles Lake potash containing 12 per. cent of borax. This is a 12-acre field. and yielded that year between 3 and 4 bales of cotton. The soil is the Norfolk sandy loam and is well suited for cotton production. In Figure 2 of Plate XI (photographed August 22) the field of cotton is shown as it appeared in 1921 after being fertilized with a similar mixture containing no borax, and it was estimated that the 12 acres would yield about 12 bales of cotton. From this it is apparent that all effects of the borax applied in 1919 had disappeared.

SYMPTOMS OF BORAX-AFFECTED PLANTS.

The descriptions of borax-affected plants as observed by the various investigators are here given in order that the reader may recognize the abnormal characteristics produced by this chemical, especially if compared with the photographs shown in this and the other papers cited. These characteristics are as follows:

Potatoes.—Potato plants affected by borax present rather striking characteristics, as noted in the field experiments reported. The seed piece often fails entirely to germinate, or it may be delayed in germination. When germination has failed, there was an abundance of decay in the seed piece even after the lapse of considerable time. In cases where germination is not seriously affected, the young sprouts are often killed. There is an absence of roots at the seed piece, but root development often occurs above the seed piece in the upper layers of soil. The small plants always have a poor root development. The stalks of affected plants are not as thick as those of normal plants and are very spindling, the leaves are small and narrowed, light in color, and bleached, or at least there is a marginal yellowing of the leaflet. This is prominent on the more severely injured and dwarfed plants. The yellowing is of a bright golden color and not the pale yellowing usually present in plants that are normally or prematurely ripening. In milder cases the abnormal color is restricted to the extreme edges of the leaves, particularly the lower ones. While the lower leaf was badly affected, young shoots formed on its axis would appear entirely healthy only to suffer the same difficulty in their later development. The dead tissues suggest more of an olive color than a green and resemble most closely a potato leaf which had been rapidly killed and quickly dried with little yellowing. The marginal injury appeared to be caused by an accumulation of borax. In severe cases the leaves at the top of the plant are noted as folded upward on the midrib. Commercial fields where borax caused injury presented a broken appearance in stand, with plants of irregular size, often very weak and spindling.

Corn.—The toxic action of borax on corn may result in the prevention or delay of germination and in distorted and bleached plants. In severe cases following germination the seedling has not sufficient vitality to push through the soil, and in such cases it withers and dies. The stalk frequently fails to develop its leaves after having pushed through the soil. With as small a quantity as 5 pounds per acre, borax was observed to produce a slight bleaching when the plant was 2 to 3 weeks old. Badly bleached and distorted plants resulted where larger quantities were present. The injury by borax is always at germination and during early growth, for if the stalks were not killed they finally produced good ears of corn. Young plants injured by borax tend to be lighter in color and in some cases are bleached entirely white. This prevention of chlorophyll formation may be due to an interference with the

United States Department of Agriculture, Depart-

ment Bulletin No. 1126, "The Effect of Borax

on the Growth and Yield of Crops."

The following error crept in during the print-

ing of the above bulletin and should be corrected

in the copy sent you: Page 26, line 29, "abundance"

should be "absence."

assimilation of iron, similar to the action of an excess of calcium, or, as observed, with an excess of manganese compounds. Injurious quantities of borax cause tipburn; in still stronger concentrations wilting ensues, first of the older leaves and then of the entire plant. Borax toxicity is also evidenced in the foliage by a banded bleaching of the chlorophyll of the leaves especially marked at the margins. The extreme tips are often killed, but not the margins. When the injury is less severe the leaves are at first streaked with pale green and may later regain their normal color.

Beans.—Borax is especially injurious to beans and is harmful at germination and retards development in the early stages of growth. The injury first appears on the margins of the first leaves which unfold, especially the tips. Where injury is severe, the entire leaf soon turns yellow, then white, which is followed by a killing of the tissues, working from the margin inward. It has been observed that the taproot of the bean plant was the most injured portion in the poisoned seedling. The root nodules were markedly reduced in size and number. In all cases of borax injury to beans, a dwarfed plant resulted with a final reduction of both vines and fruit.

Cotton.—Cotton plants affected by borax both in pots and under field conditions are weak, slender, and frequently die after having made a growth of an inch or two. At the time when the first pair of true leaves should appear, the seedlings show no apparent growth for several weeks, dead sections appearing along the margins of the seed leaves which eventually become dry, and the plant dies. Where injury is less, the plant shows a stunted growth and early maturity. The foliage shows a yellowed effect, and the leaves become dish shaped. The resultant effect is a broken stand, and plants in the field of the same age vary greatly in size. The yield is greatly reduced.

Tobacco.—Plummer and Wolf (*11*) describe the effects of borax on tobacco as follows: The roots of borax-affected plants are severely stunted, tend to be densely clustered near the end of the main root, and are all short and fibrous. The lower leaves are pale green, thicker, and less broad. The tissues most distant from the principal veins are palest and may become dead and dry. The leaf margins and tips are rolled downward and become rimbound. The root development of plants which made considerable growth is near the surface of the soil and near the tip of the main root, with few or no roots between these two groups. The stand in borax-treated fields is broken, and the plants lack uniformity in size.

It would appear from the symptoms described for the various crops that the main characteristics of borax-affected plants are (1) retarded germination; (2) general dwarfing of the plant including both roots and tops; (3) absence of normal color, which may be characterized by bleached and yellowed foliage, especially leaf tips and margins; and (4) reduced growth and yield.

SUMMARY.

The results presented herein show that borax proved to be harmful to plant growth. The experimental work was designed in order to preclude any other possible harmful factors. For one thing, practically pure borax was employed to mix with the fertilizers. The fertilizer itself was made from practically borax-free nitrogen, phosphoric acid, and potash salts. Varying quantities of borax, ranging from 1 to 400 pounds per acre were mixed with fertilizer and applied to the soil in three different ways. In order to properly compare the effect of the borax, one application of borax-free fertilizer was made in the same way and applied in the same quantity. Finally it was decided essential to carry on the experimental work on a number of soil types and with different crop plants as indicators of borax injury.

The results show that the potato can tolerate a greater quantity of borax than plants like corn or beans, which were injured by comparatively small quantities of borax. The degree of injury, however, was modified considerably according to the rainfall. Apparently the depth and distribution of rainfall is the most prominent factor concerned. Heavy rainfall in one section caused the borax to leach or diffuse into the soil mass, thereby enabling plants to withs and greater applications of it than in other sections where less rainfall had occurred and where only light applications were necessary to produce injury.

The way in which the fertilizer was applied exerted considerable influence, and in practically every case the fertilizer-borax mixtures drilled in the furrow, followed by immediate planting, produced much worse injury and with lower concentrations than by applying the fertilizer-borax mixtures some time before planting or by broadcasting and planting immediately.

The effect of borax on the germination and yield of Lima beans at Arlington, Va., was most noticed where the fertilizer-borax mixtures were applied in the furrow and planting done at once. Less than 50 per cent germinated with an application of 10 pounds of borax per acre, and with even less quantities the effect was marked. The 10-pound application of borax caused marked depression in the final yield of both vines and beans. In the section where the mixtures were sown broadcast, it required 20 pounds to produce injury, while in the section where the fertilizer-borax mixtures were applied in the drill some time before planting, 20 pounds also were required to produce injury.

The effect of borax on snap beans at Arlington, Va., was quite marked, injury being noticeable with small quantities of borax, and the yield was curtailed with an application of 5 pounds of borax per acre, and with quantities below 5 pounds the vines showed a color lighter than the no-borax plats.

The effect of borax on potatoes at Arlington, Va., when used in quantities less than 5 pounds per acre was one of stimulation. Where the borax application immediately preceded planting, 20 pounds of borax produced injury and a depression in yield. With the other methods of applying the borax mixtures the potato withstood greater concentration of borax.

Corn displayed a marked reaction to borax. In the case of immediate planting, where the fertilizer was drilled in the furrow, only 2 or 3 pounds of borax were required to produce lighter colored plants, and with 5 pounds marked discoloration ensued. When the fertilizer was sown broadcast no discoloration took place until 10 pounds or more of borax per acre had been applied.

Four pounds of borax in the drill depressed the yield of both stover and corn. When sown broadcast, 20 pounds were required to depress the yield. Practically no plant growth took place where the application exceeded 50 pounds of borax per acre.

The effect of borax on cotton in experiments conducted at Arlington, Va., and Muscle Shoals, Ala., was to severely injure the plants with 20 pounds of borax per acre and to slightly injure the plants with 10 pounds per acre. With high rainfall the degree of injury was slight, and with low rainfall the injury was more severe.

In experimental work in Virginia, New Jersey, and Maine the effect of borax was more marked on sandy soils than on the heavier soil types, and the effect of the borax was modified by rainfall.

Experimental work conducted at New Brunswick, N. J., with corn and potatoes on Sassafras loam showed strikingly the influence of rainfall, for it required comparatively high initial applications of borax to produce the degree of injury noted elsewhere.

UNITED STATES DEPARTMENT OF AGRICULTURE

In Cooperation with the
Louisiana Agricultural Experiment Station

DEPARTMENT BULLETIN No. 1127

| Washington, D. C. | PROFESSIONAL PAPER | January 12, 1923 |

SOME NEW VARIETIES OF RICE.

By CHARLES E. CHAMBLISS, *Agronomist in Charge of Rice Investigations, Office of Cereal Investigations, Bureau of Plant Industry,* and J. MITCHELL JENKINS, *Superintendent, Rice Experiment Station, Crowley, La.,* and *Assistant Agronomist, Office of Cereal Investigations, Bureau of Plant Industry.*

CONTENTS.

INTRODUCTION.

This bulletin includes a description of the rice plant and a botanical and agronomic description of seven new varieties that have been developed in the course of cooperative experiments at the Rice Experiment Station, Crowley, La., and of four varieties now widely grown in this country. The agronomic performance and adaptation of each variety, including a full description of the conditions under which the experiments were conducted, are discussed in detail. The commercial value of the milled rice of the new varieties from a culinary standpoint is indicated.

CONDITIONS UNDER WHICH THE RICE VARIETIES DESCRIBED WERE GROWN.

The seven new varieties of rice herein described were developed from pure-line selections at the Rice Experiment Station, Crowley, La., and grown under the same conditions as the four long-established varieties which also are described in this bulletin.

The station is operated by the Louisiana Agricultural Experiment Station in cooperation with the Office of Cereal Investigations of the Bureau of Plant Industry. It is located 1 mile west of Crowley and is within a few miles of the eastern border of the

10062°—23——1

prairie region of southwestern Louisiana, where rice is the important money crop.

The soil of the experiment station is the Crowley silt loam. It is the typical rice soil of the prairies in this section of the State and contains approximately 4 per cent of very fine sand, 69 per cent of silt, and 23 per cent of clay. It is of a brown or ash-gray color and rather compact in structure, with a tendency to puddle when plowed in a wet state. The subsoil, which lies at an average depth of 16 inches, is a mottled blue and yellow clay which is so impervious that there is no vertical seepage through it. Levees that contain much of this clay are practically water-tight.

The varietal experiments were made on tenth-acre plats, measuring 2 rods wide and 8 rods long. They were arranged side by side in series, each plat being separated from that on either side by a 5-foot alley. The series were inclosed by levees in which were located gates that could be operated to discharge water into or from the plats whenever it was desired. The irrigation water was obtained from a deep well and conveyed to the series through ditches. These ditches also served for drainage purposes.

The land used in testing these varieties was plowed in late autumn or early winter to the depth of 5 to 7 inches and well drained during the winter. Under these conditions, the necessary field operations for making a good seed bed in spring consisted usually of one double disking and one harrowing before seeding. A float always was used after disking. As a rule, this preparation left the surface soil loose and finely divided to a depth of several inches and made a seed bed which retained moisture so well that irrigation was seldom used to promote germination.

The varieties were grown each year on land that grew soy beans in the previous year. The beans were sown at the rate of 30 pounds per acre in rows 4½ feet apart and were cultivated. The seed was harvested and the stems and leaves plowed under. The vegetable matter thus added to the soil greatly improved its physical condition. The frequent cultivations of the soy beans served to control weeds, especially red rice. By the use of this legume, plant food in the form of nitrogen was stored in the soil. No commercial fertilizers were applied to the plats.

The rice seed was sown with a drill to a depth of 2 inches during the first week of May at the rate of 80 pounds per acre.

The irrigation water was applied to the plats approximately 30 days after the rice plants emerged. At this time the average height of the plants of the different varieties ranged from 8 to 13 inches. Throughout the remainder of the growing season an average depth of 5 inches of water was maintained. Fresh water was admitted to the plats when needed to equal the losses from seepage, evaporation, and transpiration.

The plats were drained when the panicles were well turned down. The grain was harvested with a hand hook and put in large shocks, where it remained for weeks before it was thrashed. The shocks were strongly built to withstand the wind and so capped that the grain was protected from rain as well as sun.

DESCRIPTION OF THE RICE PLANT.

Most of the varieties of rice cultivated in this country belong to the species *Oryza sativa* L. They are annual grasses with fibrous roots extending outward and downward in all directions from the crown, which is located about 1½ inches above the lower end of the culm. The distribution of the roots usually is outward and very near the surface of the soil. Under normal conditions most of the roots do not extend to a greater depth than 3 to 5 inches. When grown without irrigation and before the irrigation water is applied when irrigated, the roots penetrate the soil more deeply than when the soil is submerged. Adventitious roots (Fig. 1, *B*) arise from the first, second, and third nodes. They are more conspicuous in some varieties than in others and often are produced under irrigation when the water level is suddenly lowered or raised.

The culms of the rice plant are erect, cylindrical, and hollow, with solid nodes. They vary in length from approximately 2 to 6 feet, depending largely upon the variety, but to a certain extent upon the soil and probably other factors. The number of culms to a plant varies greatly, usually ranging from 3 to 12. The wall of the culm in the lower internodes is thick. That of the peduncle, below the panicle, is much thinner but still strong. In color the internodes are light green to yellowish green. They are sometimes streaked with brown or purple. The nodes usually are darker green or brown.

The leaves vary in number from five to eight. As a rule, there are six, including two basal leaves, one of which may wither and become detached before the plant matures. The sheath nodes, or swollen bases of the leaf sheaths (Fig. 1, *A*), are conspicuous and usually a light green. The sheaths (Fig. 1, *C*), which are open in part, are much shorter than the blades. They are green and occasionally marked with purple on their inner surface near the base. The auricles are hairy and prominent (Fig. 2, *B*), and may be light yellow or green, cartilaginous or membranous. The ligules (Fig. 2, *A*) are prominent, light yellow or sometimes light green, acute or obtuse, and often split for their entire length. The blades (Fig. 2, *D*) vary in width from a little less than half an inch to 1 inch and in length from 16 to 20 inches. They are erect or ascending, usually the latter, and prominently veined. Their surfaces are glabrous or puberulent, though sometimes rough, particularly toward the apex. The apex is acute or acuminate. Narrow blades are characteristic of the short-grain varieties of rice.

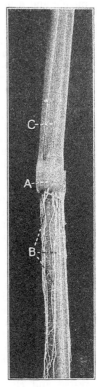

FIG. 1.—A part of the two lower internodes of a culm of rice, showing sheath node (*A*), adventitious roots (*B*), and leaf sheath (*C*). The leaf sheath has been removed to expose the adventitious roots. (Natural size.)

was increased from nursery to plat experiments in 1915. The plat yields are given in Table 2. The variety was distributed in southwestern Louisiana for commercial growing in 1918. Enough seed of Fortuna (C. I. No. 1344) was grown in 1921 to sow approximately 100,000 acres in 1922.

The stout green culms of the Fortuna variety are striped with purple and usually number five to the plant. Their average height, including the panicles, is 51 inches. The nodes are brown, marked on their lower margin with green. The sheath nodes are light green and marked on their upper margin with purple. The outer surface of the leaf sheaths is green, streaked with purple, and their inner surface is purple, especially toward the base. The auricles are membranous and persistent. The ligules average five-eighths of an inch in length. The leaf blades are broad, averaging five-eighths of an inch in width. The panicles have an average length of 11½ inches, and each bears on an average 187 seeds. Before maturity the glumes are dark purplish brown, and the distal end of the spikelets is purple. The stigmas are dark purple.

The seeds (kernel plus hull; Pl. I, D and E) average 10.1 millimeters in length and 3.1 millimeters in thickness. The glumes are light brown and distinctly notched on the margins. The hull (lemma and palea) is pale yellow, medium in thickness, and thinly covered with short white hairs. The apex of the hull terminates in two dark-brown conical teeth, located on the meson, and unequal in length. The conical lateral teeth usually are absent and when present are inconspicuous.

The kernels (Pl. I, F and G) average in length 7.7 millimeters, in width (lateral diameter) 1.8 millimeters, and in thickness (dorsiventral diameter) 2.5 millimeters. Viewed laterally, the dorsal and ventral margins are unequally convex, the ventral being the less so. The distal end is obtuse. The opaque area when present is narrow and located near the center of the kernel.

This variety matures in approximately 142 days and has produced an average yield of 2,530 pounds of paddy and 2,210 pounds of straw per acre. On the lighter soil of southwestern Louisiana it produced 2,199 pounds of paddy per acre. Acre yields of 2,775 pounds of paddy have been obtained from it on old prairie land which had been rested and closely pastured for two years. On new land in the Mississippi River section of Louisiana near Carville this variety has produced 5,366 pounds of excellent grain per acre. It produces good yields on poor soil. When grown on very rich soil it shows a tendency to lodge. Its grain is likely to shatter if harvest is delayed too long after maturity.

ACADIA.

The Acadia variety is a pure-line selection from the Omachi variety, which was imported from Japan in 1910 by a rice farmer of Crowley, La.

This selection was made at the Rice Experiment Station, Crowley, La., by the writers in 1911. The name Acadia is the name of the parish in which the station is located and was applied to this selection in 1917. The selection was increased from nursery to plat experiments in 1916. The plat yields are given in Table 2. The variety

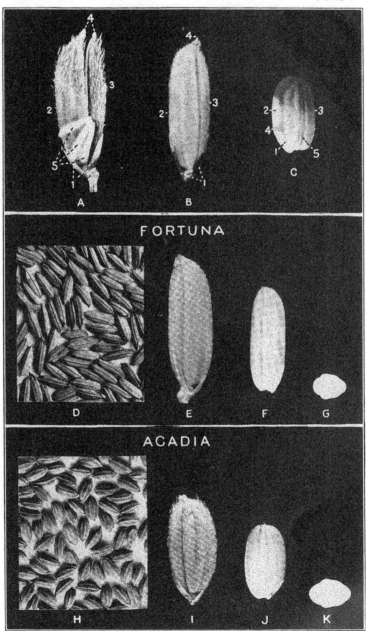

SPIKELET, SEEDS, AND KERNELS OF RICE.

A, Spikelet; B, seed; C, kernel. Fortuna and Acadia varieties: D, E, H, I, Seeds; F, J, kernels;
G, K, transverse sections of kernels. (Figures D and H, natural size; all others, × 4.)

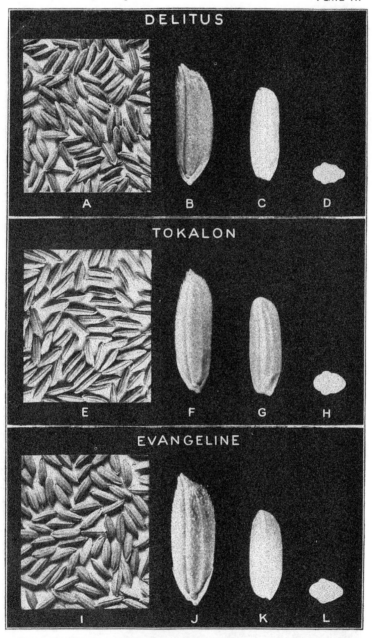

SEEDS AND KERNELS OF RICE OF THE DELITUS, TOKALON, AND EVANGELINE VARIETIES.

A, B, E, F, I, J, Seeds; C, G, K, kernels; D, H, L, transverse sections of kernels.   (Figures A, E, and I, natural size; all others, × 4.)

was distributed in southwestern Louisiana for commercial growing in 1918. Enough seed of Acadia (C. I. No. 1988) was grown in 1921 to sow at least 40,000 acres in 1922.

The slender culms of the Acadia variety are light green and usually number 10 to the plant. The average height, including the panicle, is 50 inches. The culm and sheath nodes are dark green. The auricles are deciduous. The ligules average half an inch in length. The leaf blades are narrow, averaging three-eighths of an inch in width. The panicles have an average length of 9 inches, and each bears on an average 132 seeds.

The seeds (Pl. I, *H* and *I*) average 7.2 millimeters in length and 3.7 millimeters in thickness. The glumes are very pale yellow and have entire margins. The hull loosely incloses the kernel and is of medium thickness and yellow. Its surface has a burlaplike appearance and is thinly covered with white hairs, which are long and conspicuous toward the apex. The apex of the hull terminates in four conical yellow teeth. The two that are prominent are located on the meson and are of equal length. The other two are lateral, very short, and inconspicuous.

The kernels (Pl. I, *J* and *K*) average in length 5.7 millimeters, in width 2.1 millimeters, and in thickness 3.2 millimeters. Viewed laterally, the dorsal and ventral margins are equally convex, and their distal end is broadly obtuse. The opaque area, when present, usually is small and located on the dorsal margin.

This variety matures in approximately 139 days. It produced an average yield of 2,884 pounds of paddy and 2,020 pounds of straw per acre. It has produced 4,702 pounds of paddy per acre on old rice land in the Mississippi River section of Louisiana and as much as 5,155 pounds on new land in the same locality. On the prairies of southwestern Louisiana yields of 3,800 pounds per acre have been obtained.

DELITUS.

The Delitus variety is a pure-line selection from the Bertone variety, which was obtained by the United States Department of Agriculture in 1904 from Vilmorin, Andrieux & Co., Paris, France. The selection was made at the Rice Experiment Station, Crowley, La., by the writers in 1911. The name Delitus is an abbreviation of the Latin word meaning delicate and was chosen also on account of its similarity in sound to the words " delight us." It was applied to this selection in 1917. This selection was increased from nursery to plat experiments in 1914. The plat yields are given in Table 2. The variety was distributed in southwestern Louisiana for commercial growing in 1918. The acreage of Delitus (C. I. No. 1206) is small, as at present it is grown only for home use.

The culms of the Delitus variety are medium in size, brown, slightly flexed at the fourth node, and usually number seven to the plant. Their average height, including the panicles, is 53 inches. The nodes are dark brown and the sheath nodes light green. The inner surface of the lower part of the sheaths and the outer surface of the sheaths near the base are purple. The auricles are not prominent, but are persistent. The ligules average five-eighths of an inch in length. The leaf blades are broad, averaging five-eighths of an inch in width. The panicles have an average length of

9¾ inches, and each bears on an average 122 seeds. Before maturity the glumes and the distal end of the spikelets are purplish brown. The stigmas are tinged with purple.

The seeds (Pl. II, *A* and *B*) average 8.9 millimeters in length and 2.9 millimeters in thickness. The glumes are light brown and plainly notched on the margins. The thin hull, which loosely incloses the kernel, is light brown and sparingly covered with short white hairs, which are more numerous toward the apex. The apex of the hull terminates in two conical dark-brown teeth, located on the meson, which are unequal in length and slightly bent ventrad. The conical lateral teeth usually are absent and when present are very inconspicuous.

The kernels (Pl. II, *C* and *D*) average in length 7.1 millimeters, in width 1.6 millimeters, and in thickness 2.4 millimeters. Viewed laterally, the dorsal and ventral margins are unequally convex, the ventral being the less so. Their distal end is more or less obtuse. The opaque area is seldom present.

This variety matures in approximately 131 days and produces an average yield of 1,862 pounds of paddy and 1,350 pounds of straw per acre. Although its yielding capacity is not large, this rice is worthy of cultivation on account of the distinct flavor of its kernels, resembling that of pop corn. This character is not possessed by any other rice except Salvo grown in the United States.

TOKALON.

The Tokalon variety is a pure-line selection from the Carangiang variety, which was obtained in 1904 by the United States Department of Agriculture from the rice exhibit of the Philippine Islands at the Louisiana Purchase Exposition.

The selection was made at the Rice Experiment Station, Crowley, La., by the writers in 1911. The name Tokalon is derived from the Greek, meaning the beautiful, and was applied to this variety in 1917. The selection was increased from nursery to plat experiments in 1915. The plat yields are given in Table 2. The variety was distributed in southwestern Louisiana for commercial growing in 1918. Enough seed of Tokalon (C. I. No. 51) was grown in 1921 to sow 6,000 acres in 1922.

The thick culms of the Tokalon variety are green and usually number six to the plant. Their average height, including the panicles, is 50 inches. The culm nodes are brown; the sheath nodes green. The inner surface of the leaf sheaths is light purple. The auricles are deciduous. The ligules average five-eighths of an inch in length. The leaf blades are broad, measuring five-eighths of an inch in width. The panicles have an average length of 10¼ inches, and each bears on an average 152 seeds. Before maturity the distal end of the spikelets is reddish brown.

The seeds (Pl. II, *E* and *F*) average 9.3 millimeters in length and 2.9 millimeters in thickness. The glumes are pale yellow and have smooth margins. The hull firmly incloses the kernel. It is light yellow, medium in thickness, and thinly covered with short white hairs. The apex of the hull terminates in four conical brown teeth. The two located on the meson are prominent, unequal in length, and bent ventrad. The other two are lateral and very short.

The kernels (Pl. II, *G* and *H*) average in length 7.5 millimeters, in width 1,8 millimeters, and in thickness 2.4 millimeters. Viewed laterally, the dorsal and ventral margins are equally convex, and their distal end is obtuse. The opaque area when present is narrow and located near the center of the kernel.

This variety matures in approximately 143 days and has produced an average acre yield of 2,443 pounds of paddy and 2,310 pounds of straw. It seems well adapted to southwestern Louisiana, producing larger yields on the clay soils of the prairies than on the alluvial Delta lands. This rice shows a strong tendency to shatter when it matures in late autumn. This loss may be prevented by early seeding. Production on poor soils is greater from this variety than from any of the varieties now grown on the Coastal Plain in the Louisiana-Texas rice belt. On account of the white thin bran of the kernel it might be used to meet the increasing demand for "brown" or "natural" rice.

EVANGELINE.

The Evangeline is a pure-line selection from an unnamed variety which was obtained by the United States Department of Agriculture in 1904 from the rice exhibit of Guatemala at the Louisiana Purchase Exposition. The selection was made at the Rice Experiment Station, Crowley, La., by the writers in 1911. The name Evangeline is taken from Longfellow's poem of the same name and was applied to this selection in 1917. It was increased from nursery to plat experiments in 1914. The plat yields are given in Table 2. The variety was distributed in southwestern Louisiana for commercial growing in 1918. No accurate estimate of the acreage of Evangeline (C. I. No. 1162) can be made at present. It probably will be grown more extensively on the Delta lands than in the prairie sections of Louisiana.

The stout green culms of the Evangeline variety are slightly flexed at the second node and usually number six to the plant. Their average height, including the panicles, is 45 inches. The culm nodes are dark green; sheath nodes light green. The auricles are prominent and persistent. The ligules average three-fourths of an inch in length. The leaf blades are broad, averaging three-fourths of an inch in width. The panicles have an average length of $8\frac{1}{2}$ inches, and each bears on an average 140 seeds.

The seeds (Pl. II, *I* and *J*) average 9 millimeters in length and 3.1 millimeters in thickness. The glumes are pale yellow and have smooth margins. The hull tightly incloses the kernel, is light yellow, medium in thickness, and thinly covered with very short white hairs. The apex of the hull terminates in two conical light-yellow teeth. These are located on the meson, are unequal in length, and distinctly bent ventrad. The conical lateral teeth are usually absent and when present are inconspicuous.

The kernels (Pl. II, *K* and *L*) average in length 7 millimeters, in width 1.8 millimeters, and in thickness 2.6 millimeters. Viewed laterally, the dorsal and ventral margins are equally convex, and their distal end is obtuse. The opaque area often extends from the dorsal margin to the center.

This variety matures in approximately 122 days and has produced an average acre yield of 2,027 pounds of paddy and 1,191 pounds of straw. On the ordinary prairie lands of southwestern Louisiana it produced 1,850 pounds of paddy per acre. It grows on very rich land without showing a tendency to lodge and has produced acre yields under these conditions as high as 3,420 pounds of grain. The production of 2,500 pounds of paddy per acre has been reported from the Delta lands of the Mississippi River section of Louisiana.

VINTULA.

The Vintula variety is a pure-line selection from an unnamed variety from Ceylon which was obtained by the United States Department of Agriculture from the Botanical Gardens, Georgetown, British Guiana, where it had been grown experimentally for several years.

The selection was made at the Rice Experiment Station, Crowley, La., by the writers in 1911. The name Vintula, composed of the first four letters of Vinton, the name of a town in southwestern Louisiana, and the abbreviation of Louisiana, with the letter u inserted for euphony, was applied to this selection in 1917. This selection was increased from nursery to plat experiments in 1914. The plat yields are given in Table 2. The variety was distributed in southwestern Louisiana for commercial growing in 1918. Enough seed of Vintula (C. I. No. 1241) was grown in 1921 to sow approximately 10,000 acres.

The culms of the Vintula variety are medium in size, green, and usually number seven to the plant. Their average height, including the panicles, is 51 inches. The culm and sheath nodes are green. The auricles are conspicuous and deciduous. The ligules average five-eighths of an inch in length. The leaf blades are broad, averaging half an inch in width. The panicles, which are more or less open, have an average length of 10 inches, and each bears on an average 145 seeds.

The seeds (Pl. III, A and B) average 9.6 millimeters in length and 3.1 millimeters in thickness. The glumes are pale yellow and have smooth margins. The hull loosely incloses the kernel, is thin, and sparingly covered with short white hairs. The apex of the hull terminates in two conical light-yellow teeth. These are located on the meson, are unequal in length, and slightly bent ventrad. The conical lateral teeth usually are absent and when present are inconspicuous.

The kernels (Pl. III, C and D) average in length 7.2 millimeters, in width 1.8 millimeters, and in thickness 2.6 millimeters. Viewed laterally, their dorsal and ventral margins are unequally convex, the ventral being the less so. Their distal ends are obtuse, but sharply curved toward the ventral margin. The opaque area is never prominent and when present is narrow and located on or near the dorsal margin.

This variety matures in approximately 123 days and has produced an average acre yield of 2,086 pounds of paddy and 1,149 pounds of straw. It has yielded slightly over 2,000 pounds of grain per acre on the lighter prairie soils of southwestern Louisiana and has averaged about 4,000 pounds per acre on the Delta lands of the Mississippi River section of the State.

SALVO.

The Salvo is a pure-line selection from the Djember variety, which was obtained by the United States Department of Agriculture in 1904 from Charles A. Franc, Soerabaya, Java.

The selection was made at the Rice Experiment Station, Crowley, La., by the writers in 1911. The name Salvo is derived from the Latin, meaning safe, and was applied to this selection in 1917. The selection was increased from nursery to plat experiments in 1914. The plat yields are given in Table 2. The variety was distributed in southwestern Louisiana for commercial growing in 1918. The acreage of Salvo (C. I. No. 1297) is not definitely known, as at present it is grown only for home use.

The stout culms of this variety are green and usually number six to the plant. Their average height, including the panicles, is 51 inches. The culm nodes are green, marked with brown; the sheath nodes are light green. The auricles are conspicuous and persistent. The ligules average three-fourths of an inch in length. The leaf blades are broad, averaging three-fourths of an inch in width. The panicles have an average length of 10½ inches, and each bears on an average 143 seeds.

The seeds (Pl. III, *E* and *F*) average 10.3 millimeters in length and 3.1 millimeter in thickness. The glumes are brown and have smooth margins. The hull, which loosely incloses the kernel, is light yellow and medium in thickness. Its surface is thickly covered with short white hairs, which obscure in part its burlaplike appearance. The apex of the hull terminates in two conical purple teeth, which are located on the meson. These are unequal in length and bent ventrad. The conical lateral teeth are usually absent and when present are very inconspicuous.

The kernels (Pl. III, *G* and *H*) average in length 7.7 millimeters, in width 1.9 millimeters, and in thickness 2.4 millimeters. Viewed laterally, the dorsal and ventral margins are unequally convex, the ventral margin being the less so. The distal end is obtuse and slightly curved toward the ventral margin. The opaque area is narrow and located near the center.

This variety matures in approximately 144 days and has produced an average acre yield of 1,774 pounds of paddy and 1,790 pounds of straw. It seems to be well adapted to the lighter soils of southwestern Louisiana. Salvo, like Delitus, has a pop-cornlike flavor.

HONDURAS.

The name Honduras was applied to a long-grain rice that was imported from Honduras into Louisiana through commercial sources, probably as early as 1890. On account of its productiveness it soon supplanted the Carolina varieties on the Delta lands of the State and later was introduced into southwestern Louisiana, where it was the leading variety as long as new land was available for rice culture. It probably is a strain of the Creole variety, which is extensively grown in Morelos, Mexico.

The very stout green culms of the Honduras variety usually number five to the plant. Their average height, including the panicles, is 54 inches. The culm nodes are dark green; sheath nodes light green. The auricles are deciduous. The ligules are three-fourths of an inch long. The leaf blades are broad, averaging five-eighths of an inch in width. The panicles (Fig. 3) have an average length of 9¾ inches, and each bears on an average 157 seeds.

The seeds (Pl. III, *I* and *J*) average 10 millimeters in length and 3.4 millimeters in thickness. The glumes are pale yellow and have smooth margins. The hull loosely incloses the kernel, is light yellow, and medium in thickness. Its surface has a burlaplike appearance and is thinly and evenly covered with white hairs. The apex of the hull terminates in four conical light-yellow teeth. The two that are prominent are located on the meson, the dorsal one being the longer and sometimes spinelike. This conical tooth may develop into an awn when the variety is grown on very rich soil. The other two are lateral and small.

The kernels (Pl. III, *K* and *L*) average in length 8 millimeters, in width 1.9 millimeters, and in thickness 2.8 millimeters. Viewed laterally, the dorsal and ventral margins are equally convex, and the distal end is obtuse. The opaque area, when present, is usually located on or near the dorsal margin.

This variety matures in approximately 123 days and has produced an average acre yield of 1,834 pounds of paddy and 2,363 pounds of straw. It is the principal long-grain rice grown in Louisiana, Texas, and Arkansas. It has yielded at the rate of 1,914 pounds of paddy per acre on the Delta lands of the Mississippi River in Louisiana and as high as 2,045 pounds of paddy on new prairie lands in Arkansas. When grown on land that has been cropped too heavily to rice, it produces low yields of paddy, often too inferior in quality to make a good milled product. Because of its lack of productiveness on the poorer lands, the acreage of Honduras rice has been greatly reduced in southwestern Louisiana. In the Mississippi and Teche River sections of Louisiana this variety produces its maximum yields and should be grown there on a larger acreage.

The milled product of this rice always has a ready market. Its popularity is due to the fact that the kernels do not form a pastelike mass when boiled. These properties are highly valued by those who eat rice regularly. This class of consumers also uses the broken as well as the whole kernels of this variety, which indicates rather strongly that something more is necessary than a whole kernel (head rice) to make an attractive and palatable dish of rice.

WATARIBUNE.

The Wataribune variety was grown for the first time in this country at Webster, Tex.. in 1908, by S. Sabaira, a Japanese farmer, who imported the seed from Japan. The seed from this crop was sold by J. A. Lambert, Houston, Tex., under the name "Watari." Although a rice of high-yielding capacity and excellent quality, it has never been grown extensively in Louisiana, Texas, and Arkansas. Wataribune and selections from it are the principal varieties cultivated in California.

The rather thick culms of this variety are light green, streaked with dark green, and usually number eight to the plant. Their average height, including the panicles, is 43 inches. The culm nodes

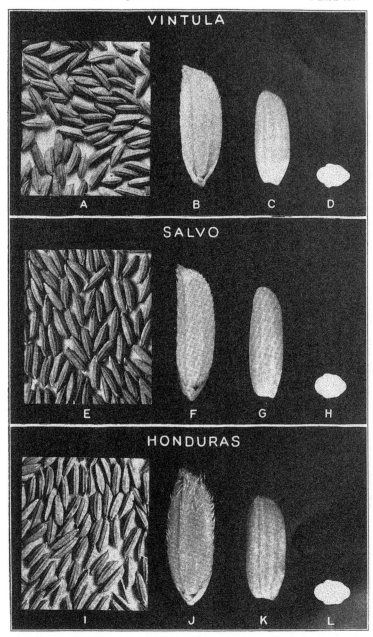

SEEDS AND KERNELS OF RICE OF THE VINTULA, SALVO, AND HONDURAS
VARIETIES.

A, *B*, *E*, *F*, *I*, *J*, Seeds; *C*, *G*, *K*, kernels; *D*, *H*, *L*, transverse sections of kernels.   (Figures *A*, *E*, and *I*, natural size; all others, × 4),

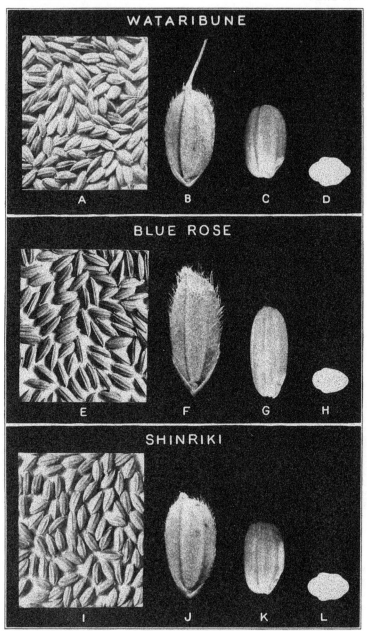

SEEDS AND KERNELS OF RICE OF THE WATARIBUNE, BLUE ROSE, AND
SHINRIKI VARIETIES.

A, B, E, F, I, J, Seeds; *C, G, K,* kernels; *D, H, I,* transverse sections of kernels. (Figures *A,*
E, and *I,* natural size; all others, × 4.)

are dark green streaked with light green, the sheath nodes light green. The auricles are persistent. The ligules are five-eighths of an inch in length. The leaf blades are narrow, averaging three-eighths of an inch in width. The panicles have an average length of 8¾ inches, and each bears on an average 137 seeds.

The seeds (Pl. IV, *A* and *B*) average 7.4 millimeters in length and 3.7 millimeters in thickness. The glumes are pale yellow and have smooth margins. The hull, which loosely incloses the kernel, is light yellow and medium in thickness. Its surface has a burlaplike appearance and is thinly covered with white hairs. These hairs are longer and more conspicuous toward the apex and are usually prominent on the veins. A light-yellow awn with a very short conical yellow tooth at its base on each side is characteristic of the variety. The awn varies in length from 10 to 26 millimeters, is deciduous, and sometimes not present on all spikelets of the panicle. When the awn is absent, the apex of the hull terminates in four conical yellow teeth. The two that are prominent are located on the meson and are unequal in length, the longer one lying dorsally. The other two are lateral and rather short.

The kernels (Pl. IV, *C* and *D*) average in length 5.5 millimeters, in width 2.1 millimeters, and in thickness 3.2 millimeters. Viewed laterally, their dorsal and ventral margins are equally convex, and their distal end is broadly obtuse. The opaque area when present is small and is located on or near the dorsal margin.

This variety matures in approximately 137 days and has produced an average acre yield of 2,727 pounds of paddy and 1,777 pounds of straw. It may be grown on the poorer prairie lands of Louisiana and Texas with more profit than may be obtained from Blue Rose, which has a longer period of growth and requires richer soil for high production. Wataribune rice should not be sown on very rich soil, for under such conditions it shows a tendency to lodge.

BLUE ROSE.

The Blue Rose variety is the result of a selection made by Sol. Wright, of Crowley, La., from an unknown variety which was found by J. F. Shoemaker, also of Crowley, La., in 1907, in a field of Japanese rice that he was growing east of Jennings, La., near the Mermentau River. Many plants of this unknown variety were cut at maturity by Mr. Shoemaker and given by him to Mr. Wright, who isolated a strain which he later offered for sale under the name Blue Rose.

The stout light-green culms of this variety are striped with dark green and usually number seven to the plant. Their average height, including the panicles, is 44 inches. The culm nodes are dark green; sheath nodes light green. The auricles are deciduous. The ligules are half an inch long. The leaf blades are broad, averaging five-eighths of an inch in width. The panicles have an average length of 8½ inches, and each bears, on an average, 144 seeds.

The seeds (Pl. IV, *E* and *F*) average 8.7 millimeters in length and 3.4 millimeters in thickness. The glumes are pale yellow and have smooth margins. The hull loosely incloses the kernel and is yellow and thick. Its surface has a burlaplike appearance and is thinly covered with long white hairs which are longer and more numerous toward the apex. The apex of the bull terminates in four conical pale-yellow teeth. The two prominent ones are located on the meson, are unequal in length, and are slightly bent ventrad. The other two are lateral and very short.

The kernels (Pl. IV, *G* and *H*) average in length 6.6 millimeters, in width 1.9 millimeters, and in thickness 2.8 millimeters. Viewed laterally, the dorsal and ventral margins are equally convex, and the distal end is obtuse. The opaque area when present is small and located on or near the dorsal margin.

This variety matures in approximately 148 days and has produced an average acre yield of 2,086 pounds of paddy and 2,520 pounds of straw. Although it has the longest growing period of any of the varieties cultivated in this country, Blue Rose is preferred in the Southern States to the more productive Japanese varieties because of the general similarity of its kernels to those of the Honduras variety, which is so widely known and valued as a rice of excellent cooking quality. It lacks, however, the culinary properties of Honduras rice, but it produces a larger yield of head rice, upon which, unfortunately, the miller has placed too high a premium. Large mill yields are important, and varieties that can produce them are desirable, but a rice must also possess certain qualities for table use before it can become a highly marketable product for the occasional as well as the daily consumer.

SHINRIKI.

The principal introduction of the Shinriki variety was made from Japan in 1902 by Dr. S. A. Knapp, then an agricultural explorer of the United States Department of Agriculture. Prior to 1910 Shinriki was probably the best known of the Japanese varieties grown in Louisiana and Texas.

The slender wiry culms of this variety are light green and usually number 13 to the plant. Their average height, including the panicles, is 37 inches. The culm and sheath nodes are light green. The auricles are deciduous. The ligules are half an inch long. The leaf blades are very narrow, averaging three-eighths of an inch in width. The panicles have an average length of 8 inches, and each bears on an average 105 seeds.

The seeds (Pl. IV, *I* and *J*) average 7.3 millimeters in length and 3.6 millimeters in thickness. The glumes are pale yellow and have smooth margins. The hull, which loosely incloses the kernel, is light yellow and medium in thickness. Its surface has a burlaplike appearance and is thinly covered with short white hairs, which are longer and more conspicuous toward the apex. The apex of the hull terminates in four conical light-green teeth. The two prominent ones are located on the meson and are unequal in length. The other two are lateral and very short.

The kernels (Pl. IV, *K* and *L*) average in length 5.4 millimeters, in width 2.1 millimeters, and in thickness 3.1 millimeters. Viewed laterally, the dorsal and ventral margins are equally convex, and the distal end is broadly obtuse. The opaque area is seldom conspicuous and when present is located on the dorsal margin.

This variety matures in approximately 143 days and has produced an average acre yield of 2,500 pounds of paddy and 1,734 pounds of straw. It is not grown on a large acreage in the United States, mainly because its culms are too short to be cut with a binder without the loss of some grain, even when the plants produce a normal yield. This loss, of course, does not occur in Japan, where the variety is extensively grown, because the crop is cut with hand hooks. The Shinriki and Wataribune varieties are usually quoted as "Japan rice" in the southern rice markets of the United States.

COMPARISON OF VARIETIES.

The stems and foliage of the varieties described, except Delitus, Evangeline, Vintula, and Honduras, retain their green color after the grain ripens. Usually the entire plant of these four varieties matures rapidly, the leaves turning yellow as the grain ripens.

Uniformity in the size of the seed is strikingly characteristic of the Fortuna, Acadia, Delitus, Tokalon, Wataribune, and Shinriki varieties. The seeds on the lower part of the panicles of Evangeline and Honduras often vary in size. When grown on poor soil, Evangeline, Honduras, and Blue Rose often produce stunted panicles, bearing imperfect seeds. The dimensions of the seeds of all varieties are shown in Table 1.

None of these varieties shows complete resistance to the fungous disease (rotten-neck) caused by *Piricularia oryzae* Br. and Cav. Honduras is very susceptible, and all of them may be seriously affected by this disease if they are left uncut too long after maturity. The conditions which produce the straighthead disease have no effect upon Fortuna and Vintula, as so far observed.

TABLE 1.—*Average dimensions of seeds and kernels of seven new and four long-established varieties of rice grown at the Rice Experiment Station, Crowley, La.*

[Thickness=dorsiventral diameter; width=lateral diameter.]

Class and variety.	C. I. No.	Dimensions (millimeters).					
		Seeds (spikelets).			Kernels.		
		Length.	Thickness.	Width.	Length.	Thickness.	Width.
Long-grain varieties:							
Fortuna	1344	10.1	3.1	2.1	7.7	2.5	1.8
Delitus	1206	8.9	2.9	2.0	7.1	2.4	1.6
Tokalon	51	9.3	2.9	2.1	7.5	2.4	1.8
Evangeline	1162	9.0	3.1	2.1	7.0	2.6	1.8
Vintula	1241	9.6	3.1	2.0	7.2	2.6	1.8
Salvo	1297	10.3	3.1	2.1	7.7	2.4	1.9
Honduras	1643	10.0	3.4	2.3	8.0	2.8	1.9
Medium-grain variety:							
Blue Rose	1962	8.7	3.4	2.1	6.6	2.8	1.9
Short-grain varieties:							
Acadia	1988	7.2	3.7	2.5	5.7	3.2	2.1
Wataribune	1561	7.4	3.7	2.5	5.5	3.2	2.1
Shinriki	1642	7.3	3.6	2.3	5.4	3.1	2.1

Losses from shattering may be greatly lessened by the prompt harvesting of varieties that are known to thrash easily and by the early seeding of varieties which have a long growing period. The long-grain varieties, which are late in maturing, show a greater tendency to shatter their grain than the short-grain rices that ripen at the same time. The early-maturing varieties, which as a rule have long grains, seldom shatter unless left standing too long after the irrigation water has been drained from the field. When maturity occurs in late autumn there always is greater shattering, regardless of the variety of rice. The agronomic characters, including yield, of the 11 varieties here described are given in Table 2.

TABLE 2.—*Average agronomic data and annual and average yields of seven new and four long-established varieties of rice grown on tenth-acre plats at the Rice Experiment Station, Crowley, La., during periods of varying length in the 9-year period from 1913 to 1921, inclusive.*

AVERAGE AGRONOMIC DATA.

Class and variety.	C. I. No.	Date of—					Time to maturity (days) from—		Days of sub-mer-gence.
		Seed-ing.	Emer-gence.	Sub-mer-gence.	First head-ing.	Matur-ity.	Seed-ing.	First head-ing.	
Long-grain varieties:		*May*	*May*	*June*	*Aug.*	*Sept.*			
Fortuna	1344	2	17	17	20	21	142	32	96
Delitus	1206	4	19	15	7	12	131	36	89
Tokalon	51	3	17	17	23	23	143	31	98
Evangeline	1162	3	17	18	3	2	122	30	76
Vintula	1241	2	17	15	3	2	123	30	79
Salvo	1297	3	18	17	21	24	144	34	99
Honduras	1643	3	17	16	3	3	123	31	79
Medium-grain variety:									
Blue Rose	1962	1	19	19	26	26	148	31	99
Short-grain varieties:									
Acadia	1988	3	17	18	16	19	139	34	93
Wataribune	1561	3	18	16	14	17	137	34	93
Shinriki	1642	3	20	17	19	23	143	34	98

Class and variety.	Culms per plant.	Dimensions (inches).			Seeds per pan-icle.	Weight of product (pounds).			
		Height of plant at—		Length of pan-icle.		Acre yield.		Per bushel.	Hulls in 100 pounds of paddy.
		Date of sub-mer-gence.	Matu-rity.[1]			Grain.	Straw.		
Long-grain varieties:									
Fortuna	5	13.4	51	11.50	187	2,530	2,210	43	21.0
Delitus	7	11.9	53	9.70	122	1,862	1,350	43	22.0
Tokalon	6	14.3	50	10.35	152	2,443	2,310	44	18.2
Evangeline	6	13.3	45	8.50	140	2,027	1,191	44	21.6
Vintula	7	12.9	51	10.00	145	2,086	1,149	42	20.6
Salvo	6	11.9	51	10.50	143	1,774	1,790	41	22.0
Honduras	5	15.5	54	9.75	157	1,834	2,363	41	20.6
Medium-grain variety:									
Blue Rose	7	14.5	44	8.50	144	2,086	2,520	44	20.6
Short-grain varieties:									
Acadia	10	12.3	50	8.98	132	2,884	2,020	44	17.2
Wataribune	8	10.6	43	8.65	137	2,727	1,777	44	18.0
Shinriki	13	8.8	37	8.00	105	2,500	1,734	46	19.0

[1] Including panicle.

Annual and Average Yields

Yields per acre, pounds.]

Class and variety.	Annual.								
	1913	1914	1915	1916	1917	1918	1919	1920	1921
Long-grain varieties:									
Fortuna			1,590	2,730	3,420	3,020	2,750	1,900	2,300
Delitus		2,100	1,980	2,010	1,255	1,840	1,710	1,220	2,780
Tokalon			2,555	2,350	2,870	2,550	2,680	2,050	2,050
Evangeline		1,660	2,650	1,890	1,798	2,010	2,530	1,430	2,250
Vintula		2,800	2,240	2,085	1,457	2,070	2,140	1,310	2,590
Salvo		2,610	1,500	2,130	1,760	2,060	1,590	1,150	1,390
Honduras	1,850	1,500	1,900	2,230	1,920	2,000	1,470	1,900	1,740
Medium-grain variety:									
Blue Rose			1,888		3,130	2,770	1,690	1,290	1,750
Short-grain varieties:									
Acadia				3,665	3,610	2,910	2,620	2,170	2,330
Wataribune	2,570	2,180	2,833	3,530	1,894	3,390	3,080	3,240	1,830
Shinriki	2,700	2,180	2,500	2,590	2,362	2,980	1,900	2,960	2,330

Class and variety.	Average for years stated, dates inclusive.					
	5 years, 1917 to 1921.	6 years, 1916 to 1921.	6 years, 1915 and 1917 to 1921.	7 years, 1915 to 1921.	8 years, 1914 to 1921.	9 years, 1913 to 1921.
Long-grain varieties:						
Fortuna	2,678	2,687	2,497	2,530		
Delitus	1,761	1,803	1,798	1,828	1,862	
Tokalon	2,440	2,425	2,459	2,443		
Evangeline	2,004	1,985	2,111	2,080	2,027	
Vintula	1,913	1,942	1,968	1,985	2,086	
Salvo	1,590	1,680	1,575	1,654	1,774	
Honduras	1,806	1,877	1,822	1,880	1,833	1,834
Medium-grain variety:						
Blue Rose	2,126		2,086			
Short-grain varieties:						
Acadia	2,728	2,884				
Wataribune	2,687	2,827	2,711	2,828	2,747	2,727
Shinriki	2,506	2,520	2,505	2,517	2,475	2,500

The grain of the Acadia, Wataribune, Blue Rose, and Shinriki varieties is not easily removed from the straw. Unless the separator is fed very slowly when these varieties are thrashed, there is considerable loss of grain. Similar care must be exercised for another reason in thrashing Honduras and Evangeline. Their straw becomes very brittle after drying in the shock and is not easily separated from the grain when the thrasher is fed too rapidly.

The culinary properties of the new varieties described in this bulletin have a commercial value, and if properly exploited by the trade they should greatly increase the demand for rice as a daily article of food. The rice-eating people of this country, like the orientals, eat this cereal mainly in the boiled state and show a preference for those varieties whose kernels retain their general shape and remain separate when prepared in this way. These varieties possess this characteristic and for this reason should be more marketable than those which form a pastelike mass when boiled.

ORGANIZATION OF THE UNITED STATES DEPARTMENT OF AGRICULTURE.

Secretary of Agriculture_____HENRY C. WALLACE.
Assistant Secretary_____C. W. PUGSLEY.
Director of Scientific Work_____E. D. BALL.
Director of Regulatory Work_____
Weather Bureau_____CHARLES F. MARVIN, Chief.
Bureau of Agricultural Economics_____HENRY C. TAYLOR, Chief.
Bureau of Animal Industry_____JOHN R. MOHLER, Chief.
Bureau of Plant Industry_____WILLIAM A. TAYLOR, Chief.
Forest Service_____W. B. GREELEY, Chief.
Bureau of Chemistry_____WALTER G. CAMPBELL, Acting Chief.
Bureau of Soils_____MILTON WHITNEY, Chief.
Bureau of Entomology_____L. O. HOWARD, Chief.
Bureau of Biological Survey_____E. W. NELSON, Chief.
Bureau of Public Roads_____THOMAS H. MacDONALD, Chief.
Fixed-Nitrogen Research Laboratory_____F. G. COTTRELL, Director.
Division of Accounts and Disbursements___A. ZAPPONE, Chief.
Division of Publications_____JOHN L. COBBS, Jr., Chief.
Library_____CLARIBEL R. BARNETT, Librarian.
States Relations Service_____A. C. TRUE, Director.
Federal Horticultural Board_____C. L. MARLATT, Chairman.
Insecticide and Fungicide Board_____J. K. HAYWOOD, Chairman.
Packers and Stockyards Administration___⎫ CHESTER MORRILL,
Grain Future-Trading Act Administration___⎭   Assistant to the Secretary.
Office of the Solicitor_____R. W. WILLIAMS, Solicitor.

This bulletin is a contribution from—

Bureau of Plant Industry_____WILLIAM A. TAYLOR, Chief;
    Office of Cereal Investigations_____CARLETON R. BALL,
                                                Cerealist in Charge.

18

BULLETIN No. 1128

DECAYS AND DISCOLORATIONS IN AIRPLANE WOODS.

By J. S. BOYCE, *Pathologist, Office of Investigations in Forest Pathology, Bureau of Plant Industry.*

CONTENTS.

INTRODUCTION.

The purpose of this bulletin is to enumerate and describe the more important decays and discolorations to which woods used in aircraft construction are subject and the conditions under which they occur. It is well known that the initial or incipient stages of decay—that is, the first steps in weakening wood—are indicated by discolorations, but wood is subject to many color variations from the normal not caused by wood-destroying fungi.

The value of recognizing the true nature of any given discoloration or other abnormality is immediately apparent, since such knowledge will permit the free use of wood which, though seriously reduced in value from an æsthetic standpoint by a disagreeable discoloration, is not mechanically weakened, while at the same time dangerous color variations can be detected. In the airplane industry, where the very finest quality of high-grade wood is demanded, and in which there is a maximum of unavoidable waste in the remanufacture of the lumber, it is imperative that no suitable material be wasted or diverted to another purpose, while at the same time it is equally important that all weakened material be excluded.

This bulletin first considers certain defects in airplane woods not due to decay, but which must be readily recognized in order to avoid confusion. Next are described the various discolorations in airplane woods caused by mechanical injuries to the living trees, chemical reactions, harmless fungi, and decay-inducing fungi in relation to their actual effect on the strength of wood. In the case of those defects and properties which it is not within the province of this bulletin to discuss in detail, references to available literature are given.

GENERAL CONSIDERATIONS.

There are certain basic principles in the manufacture of high-grade lumber which should be most rigidly adhered to in the case of stock for airplanes. The purchaser should be certain that the manufacturer supplying his requirements is both willing and able to fulfill these conditions, so that defects very difficult to detect are not introduced.

When trees are felled the logs should be removed from the woods with reasonable promptness, because as soon as the timber is down it becomes subject to decay, sap-stain, checking, and the attacks of wood-boring insects. Leaving logs in the woods over winter is particularly poor practice. If the logs must be stored for any considerable length of time they should be kept in the pond, where the defects mentioned will be largely prevented.

After the logs are sawed the lumber should be carefully inspected and those pieces unsuitable for use in airplanes diverted to other uses. Next comes seasoning. Drying with artificial heat in dry kilns is preferable. The kilns should be of proper construction, so that the temperature and relative humidity can be completely controlled and the lumber brought to an average final moisture content of about 8 per cent, within the limits of 5 to 10 per cent (based on oven-dry weight), without checking or other injury. If it is necessary to store the dry lumber at the mill it should be placed in a dry shed, completely protected from the weather. The shed should have a board floor. Concrete, particularly if new, or dirt floors may give off considerable moisture. The stock should be shipped in box cars completely protected from moisture. When it reaches the factory the lumber should be shop seasoned; that is, placed in a room under uniform shop conditions, for about two weeks. During the entire process of manufacture the stock should be carefully protected from the absorption of moisture. Piling lumber or partly fabricated parts on damp floors or under the drip from steam or water pipes are two not uncommon offenses.

In case it is impossible to kiln-dry the stock, air drying must be resorted to. As a rule it is not possible to get the moisture content below 11 per cent by this process, except in arid regions. When the lumber comes from the saw it may be necessary to dip it in a chemical solution to prevent sap-stain in regions where lumber is especially subject to this discoloration; but under any conditions the stock should be carefully open-piled on elevated foundations to assure a circulation of air throughout and only sound, bright, thoroughly seasoned stickers used between courses. The piles should be properly slanted and roofed, so that rain will run off and not soak the lumber. To pile lumber closely, without proper circulation of air throughout the piles, results in some cases in warping, sap-stain, and, ultimately, decay. Then, too, it is almost impossible for the stock in the center of the pile ever to become properly dry.

At best, however, air drying is a matter of months, even with softwoods, while proper kiln drying can be accomplished within one to three weeks or so, depending on the thickness of the stock. As a rule, hardwoods both kiln-dry and air-dry more slowly.

Air-dried stock should be shipped in the same manner as kiln-dried and handled in the same way at the factory, except that it must be kiln-dried to the proper moisture content before it is conditioned in the shop.

The principles given briefly in the foregoing paragraphs, together with their application and underlying reasons, are brought out in detail in the following pages.

WOODS USED FOR AIRPLANE CONSTRUCTION.

The most important wood for aircraft construction is spruce, including red, white, and Sitka spruce (*Picea rubens* Sarg., *P. canadensis* (Mill.) B. S. P., and *P. sitchensis* (Bong.) Trautv. and Mayer), but of these Sitka spruce, on account of its much larger size and the consequently greater quantity of clear lumber that can be obtained, is paramount. By far the greatest proportion of the lumber entering into the construction of most present-day airplanes is spruce or one of its substitutes. The combination of strength properties with light weight found in spruce is not duplicated in any other wood. Most of the beams in the directing surfaces are preferably of spruce or a soft wood, as are many of the struts, and these parts account for the bulk of the timber in an airplane.

An excellent substitute for spruce is Port Orford cedar (*Chamaecyparis lawsoniana* (Murr.) Parl.), which is slightly heavier. Unfortunately the supply of this splendid wood is decidedly limited. Douglas fir (*Pseudotsuga taxifolia* (Lam.) Br.), though much heavier than spruce, is an extensively used substitute. Other woods which can play some part in this way or may be used for special purposes where a softwood is needed are western white pine (*Pinus monticola* Dougl.), sugar pine (*P. lambertiana* Dougl.), western hemlock (*Tsuga heterophylla* (Raf.) Sarg.), white fir (*Abies concolor* (Gord.) Parry), amabilis fir (*A. amabilis* (Loud.) Forbes), noble fir (*A. nobilis* Lindl.), yellow or tulip poplar (*Liriodendron tulipifera* Linn.), basswood (*Tilia americana* Linn.), incense cedar (*Libocedrus decurrens* Torr.), and western red cedar (*Thuja plicata* Don.). Certain parts of an airplane frame as a rule are made from hardwoods. In such parts great strength and toughness are requisite. Here, commercial white ash[1] stands supreme. For example, it is unsurpassed for longerons ·in those fuselages not constructed wholly or mostly of veneer. Black ash (*Fraxinus nigra* Marsh), which does not possess sufficient stiffness for use ·in highly stressed parts, can be distinguished from white ash (*2; 30*, p. 47; *68*, p. 62).[2] White oak,[3] hard maple (*Acer saccharum* Marsh), and

---

[1] Commercial white ash includes white ash (*Fraxinus americana* Linn.), green ash (*F. lanceolata* Borkh.), blue ash (*F. quadrangulata* Michx.), and Biltmore ash (*F. biltmoreana* Beadle).
[2] Serial numbers (italic) in parentheses refer to "Literature cited" at the end of this bulletin.
[3] White oak as used here includes white oak (*Quercus alba* Linn.), bur oak (*Q. macrocarpa* Michx.), cow oak (*Q. michauxii* Nutt.), and post oak (*Q. minor* (Marsh) Sarg.).

rock elm[4] are sometimes used instead of white ash. Hickory,[5] so far, has been principally used for tail skids. The two finest woods for propellers are black walnut (*Juglans nigra* Linn.) and true mahogany (*Swietenia mahagoni* Jacq.), also known as Central American mahogany. Other species commonly used are yellow birch (*Betula lutea* Michx. f.), sweet birch (*B. lenta* Linn.), African mahogany (*Khaya senegalensis* A. Juss.), black cherry (*Prunus serotina* Ehrh.), hard maple, white oak, and yellow poplar. However, a number of other woods are occasionally utilized, and in the future a wide variety of species will probably be admitted. European designers even now are less exacting in this respect, sometimes using two species of wood in the same propeller, which on the whole is considered poor practice in this country.

TABLE 1.—*Distribution of wood in airplanes, showing the service requirements and the adaptation thereto of the different grades of the several species.*

Designation of assembly and name of part.	Spruce.	Douglas fir.	Port Orford cedar.	Basswood.	Tulip poplar.	White pine.	White fir.	Western hemlock.	White ash.	White oak.	Hard maple.	Rock elm.	Hickory.
Main and center planes, ailerons, stabilizer, elevator, rudder, and fins:													
Beams, solid	A	A	A	....	A	A	A	A					....
Beams, box	A	A	A	....	A	A	A	A					....
Filler blocks	C	C	C	C	C	C	C	C					....
Fillet strips	B	B	B	B	B	B	B	B					....
Panel blocks—													
Brace blocks													
Corner blocks	C	C	C	C	C	C	C	C	C	C	C	C	C
Spacer blocks													
Reinforcing blocks													
Rib webs, solid	B	B	B	B	B	B	B						....
Rib webs, compression (solid)	A	A	A	A	A	A	A	A					....
Compression struts	A	A	A	....	A	A	A						....
Cap strips	A	A	A	A	A	A	....						....
Trailing edge—													
Straight	B	B	B	....	B	B	B	B					....
Bent									A	A	A	A	A
Entering edge—													
Straight	B	B	B	....	B	B	B	B					....
Bent									A	A	A	A	A
Gussets	B	B	B	....	B	B							....
Masts	A	A	A	....	A	A							....
Stringers	B	B	B	....	B	B	B	B					....
Interplane struts	A	A	A	....					A	A	A		....
Center section struts	A	A	A	....					A	A	A		....
Fuselage:													
Longerons—													
Straight	A	A	A	....					A	A	A	A	....
Bent									A	A	A	A	....
Struts, vertical, and horizontal—													
High stress	A	A	A	....	A	A	A	A	B	B	B	B	....
Low stress	B	B	B	....	B	B	B	B					....
Struts, diagonal	B	B	B	....	B	B	B	B					....
Supports, heavy	A	A	A	....	A	A	A	A	A	A			....
Supports, light	B	B	B	B	B	B	B	B	B				....
Brace blocks	B	B	B	B	B	B	B	B	B	B	B	B	....
Stiffeners	B	B	B	B	B	B	B	B	B	B	B	B	....
Cleats									C	C	C	C	....
Furring strips	B	B	B	B	B	B	B	B					....
Floor and seat boards	C	C	C	C	C	C	C	C					....
Cradle slats	C	C	C	C	C	C	C	C					....
Seat rail	A	A	A	A	A	A	A	A					....
Tail post	A	A	A	....					A	A	A		....
Tail skid									A	A	A	A	A
Landing chassis:													
Struts	A	A	A	....					A	A	A	A	....
Stream lining	C	C	C	C	C	C	C	C					....

[4] Rock elm includes rock elm (*Ulmus racemosa* Thomas) and the more dense stock of both white elm (*U. americana* Linn.) and slippery elm (*U. pubescens* Walt.).

[5] The true hickories include mockernut hickory (*Hicoria alba* (Linn.) Br.), shellbark hickory (*H. laciniosa* (Michx. f.) Sarg.), pignut hickory (*H. glabra* (Mill.) Br.), and shagbark hickory (*H. ovata* (Mill.) Br.).

Table 1, which is an adaptation of specification 15037-B of the Bureau of Aircraft Production, shows where the various woods may be used in an airplane and the quality desired. The symbol A indicates a grade of wood of the very highest quality and free from all injurious defects; grade B demands a quality of wood similar to grade A in all respects except that a little tolerance is allowed in regard to straightness of grain and specific gravity; wood of grade C is used in parts where little strength is needed and may contain various defects, provided the piece is strong enough for the purpose intended.

These woods are not the only ones used for airplanes, but they are the most important. Others are mentioned here and there in this bulletin. It can be predicted that, with a growing scarcity of the more desirable species and an increase in our knowledge of the properties of other species, woods little or not at all used at present will become of importance. For a full discussion of this entire subject, the reader is referred to other sources (*60; 69*, p. 34-40).

GENERAL DEFECTS OF AIRPLANE WOODS.

It is impossible to thoroughly understand wood without a working knowledge of its structure and mechanical properties. This is more difficult to attain than with most other materials of construction, for wood, instead of being a relatively simple and more or less homogeneous compound, is a highly complex organic structure whose chemical composition is even now none too well understood. The discussion in the following pages will be much clearer to the reader provided he has such knowledge. There are a number of valuable publications which may be referred to in this connection (*30, 45, 47, 48, 68, 69*).

Besides decay, there are other defects which reduce the strength of timber, and these must be given due consideration. Wood may be inherently weak because of its structure, it may be injured by some process of manufacture, or the trouble may be due to faulty design or assembly. Such defects in relation to airplane woods have been discussed in various publications (*42; 46; 68*, p. 15-20; *69*, p. 11-22), but a review of the more important of these is essential here, since by the uninitiated some of them are confused with decay.

GRAIN.

One of the most common defects in airplane woods is an excessive slope of diagonal or spiral grain. Since any deviation from straight grain is accompanied by a reduction in strength, the requirements in this respect are very exacting, a deviation from straight grain of more than 1 inch in 20 inches rarely being allowed for any highly stressed portion of an airplane, although this may be reduced to 1 inch in 12 in portions of less severe stress. A discussion of the methods to be employed in detecting this defect, together with its effect on strength, may be found in several publications (*31; 42*, p. 8-14; *68*, p. 15-16; *69*, p. 11-20).

SPECIFIC GRAVITY.

Brashness or brittleness in wood is another common defect. These synonymous terms denote a lack of toughness in wood to which they are applied. Brash wood is usually low in strength, and when tested by bending fails with a short break instead of a splintering fracture. This is one indication of decay, but not all wood showing such defect is decayed. Too often when wood appears to be somewhat brash and develops less than the normal strength, instead of making a serious attempt to determine the real source of the difficulty the cabalistic term " dry-rot " is uttered, and the case is settled, often resulting in the loss of good material, while the trouble goes on unchecked. Even if the wood be decayed, it most probably is not dry-rot, which term to the pathologist embraces a definite type of decay caused by a certain fungus. Let us consider a few of the more important causes of brashness, aside from decay, in aircraft woods.

The primary requisite of wood for use in airplanes is that it must be of specific gravity high enough to give the necessary strength. It has long been known that an increase in strength of any species of wood goes with an increase in specific gravity, and it has finally become possible accurately to express this relation for the various strength properties, so that if the specific gravity of a given piece of wood is known it is possible quite accurately to derive its strength under various stresses (41). No matter how perfect a piece may be in other respects and free from all other defects, if it is below the minimum specific gravity it should not be used. These minimum figures have been carefully worked out for the more important airplane woods (68, p. 21; 69, p. 26). Wood of low specific gravity is naturally somewhat brittle, and for this reason is often erroneously considered as slightly decayed. While the actual specific gravity of the wood substance in various species is practically the same (13), having a value of 1.54, the porous nature of the wood is such that most commercial species range from 0.3 to 0.6. In other words, only one-fifth to three-fifths of a unit volume of wood is occupied by wood substance; the remainder is air.

It is self-evident that a density or specific gravity determination of every individual piece of wood to be used for a primary member in an airplane is out of the question. Neither is it necessary. The most reliable index of specific gravity, without making an actual test, is the ratio of spring wood to summer wood per annual ring. This is best seen on the cross or end section after it has been smoothed off with a sharp knife or a high-speed miter saw. In the softwoods the summer wood is the darker of the two bands composing each annual ring, as is shown in Figure 1, which illustrates cross sections from two wing beams of Douglas fir, one of average and the other of low specific gravity. In the ring-porous hardwoods (ash, for example) the summer wood appears more solid and very much less porous than the spring wood, but in the diffuse-porous hardwoods (such as birch) this is often very difficult to determine. For Douglas fir a minimum specific gravity of 0.47 has been established for high-stressed members, but this can probably be reduced to 0.45 with perfect safety when used as a substitute for spruce. As a rule, wood of this species with less than 6 or more than 30 annual rings per inch, measured radially on the cross section, falls below the minimum specific gravity. The former usually comes from the center of the tree, where the wood is rapid growing and brash, while the latter is the slow-grown soft " yellow fir " so characteristic of the outer layers of very old trees. If each annual ring is composed of approximately one-third or more of summer wood the piece possesses the necessary strength. In those pieces with very narrow annual rings, in which the summer wood is indicated by a mere dark line at the outer edge of each annual ring, the wood is very soft and weak, often having a specific gravity as low as 0.34 (Fig. 1).

Sometimes the proportion of material of low specific gravity in Douglas fir airplane lumber is exceedingly high. The writer has seen several consecutive carload lots of selected wing-beam stock at one factory in which from 25 to 50 per cent of the pieces in each car were below the minimum specific gravity. The stock was cut from old

FIG. 1.—Cross sections of wing beams of Douglas fir of average and low specific gravity. The large proportion of summer wood, indicated by the dark bands, in the piece of good specific gravity (on the right) in comparison with that in the piece with low specific gravity (on the left) is plainly shown.

slow-grown trees, which yield the " yellow fir " so much preferred by the trade, but which invariably contain a large percentage of material of low specific gravity not suitable for aircraft or any other type of construction where high strength is requisite.

The same general relations hold good in Sitka spruce. Here, again, if the annual rings are too few or too many per inch, they indicate wood of low density. The minimum specific gravity for this species is established at 0.36.

It is often difficult to approximate the specific gravity by visual examination of the proportion of summer wood per annual ring in the case of those pieces close to the minimum density permitted in softwoods. There is considerable chance for error even with Douglas fir, but with spruce this is increased, owing to the fact that the summer wood and spring wood merge into each other, not being sharply delimited as in Douglas fir. With experience it is quite feasible to judge with accuracy the relative specific gravity of many of the pieces, leaving the doubtful ones for an actual test or to be worked up along with those below the minimum into parts less highly stressed. In making tests to determine the specific gravity it is not necessary to use the time-consuming immersion method. The pieces can be cut fairly regularly, oven dried, and the volume ascertained by measuring to the nearest half millimeter or to the nearest sixty-fourth of an inch. The weight should be obtained as usual. The writer has tested this method extensively and found the limit of error rarely over 0.01. In most cases the result will not vary from that obtained by the immersion method. This method can not be used on irregularly shaped pieces, however.

In the ring-porous hardwoods, such as ash, it is very easy to determine the relative proportions of spring and summer wood in each annual ring. Here the condition is the reverse of that found in the softwoods. About three-fifths or more summer wood per annual ring in the case of white ash is necessary to give the strength required by the minimum specific gravity of 0.56. Wood with few annual rings to the inch in white ash has a high specific gravity, and this, as a rule, decreases as the number of rings per inch increases. Wood with 20 to 25 annual rings or more to the inch is usually worthless if strength is a requisite. The relations just discussed are fairly constant throughout the ring-porous hardwoods, such as white oak, rock elm, and hickory.

A large proportion of summer wood is not always an indication of strength in white ash. The notable exception to this rule is pumpkin ash, so called by the trade. This ash has remarkably broad bands of summer wood in the annual rings. These rings are often half an inch broad and contain only one or two narrow lines of pores in the spring wood, but the specific gravity of the wood is low, and when tested in static or impact bending it breaks with a brash, brittle failure under a light load. It can readily be detected by cutting with a knife, yielding softly without the resistance offered by good ash. When finished it has a waxy white, cream, or light-brown color in tangential section and can be readily dented with any hard blunt instrument. In cross section the pores in the summer wood sometimes appear as small brown, rather indistinct spots.

Pieces may be found with almost the same appearance as pumpkin ash which when tested with a knife prove to be hard and tough, with a good specific gravity; or, again, both hard and soft wood may be found in the same board.

As nearly as can be ascertained from hearsay evidence, this pumpkin ash is not confined to a particular tree species, but may be found in any of the white-ash group when grown under swampy conditions in the southern part of the range. It does not necessarily occur, but when it does the central portion of the butt logs or even the entire trunk may be composed of such wood. Pumpkin ash has been assigned by botanists as the common name for one definite tree species (*Fraxinus profunda* Bush), but the name as applied in the lumber trade denotes white-ash wood having the characteristics above described without regard to species.

It is quite difficult to judge the specific gravity of diffuse porous ardwoods by visual examination except in those pieces patently ery low or very high. Actual specific-gravity determinations will ave to be used to a greater extent when handling this class of woods.

In examining a piece of wood of any considerable length to deter- ine its specific gravity, care must be used to examine it throughout. ieces in which the grain is not perfectly straight may have high pecific gravity in one portion and a low density in another, as at- ested by the percentage of summer wood. This is due to the fact hat trees may not develop wood of the same or nearly the same spe- ific gravity throughout their life. Such a condition is not at all ncommon in white-ash longerons, and it must be remembered that ny given piece of wood is no stronger than its weakest portion.

As a general rule, airplane timber should be purchased under speci- cations so worded in regard to the ratio of spring wood and summer ood per annual ring and number of annual rings per inch of radius as to reject at the source of supply most of the stock of low specific gravity.

COMPRESSION WOOD.

Occasional pieces of wood of unusual growth are encountered. The annual rings are very broad, with an abnormally large proportion of summer wood per annual ring, and there is little contrast between the spring wood and the summer wood. The specific gravity is very much higher than that of normal material. The abnormal growth is supposed to be due to the fact that the tree or portion of the tree from which the piece came had been under some long-continued un- usual stress or had been in an unusual position. The term " com- pression wood " is usually applied to material of this nature. The writer remembers particularly a spruce wing beam with six annual rings per inch of radius, 75 per cent or more of summer wood per annual ring, and a specific gravity of 0.85. Since the usual specific gravity of spruce used is about 0.40, it can readily be seen that the weight of this wing beam was more than double the normal. Com- pression wood is not confined to spruce, but may be found in other soft woods. This type of wood is not desirable. Its strength proper- ties are uncertain, and its shrinkage does not correspond to that of normal wood, the longitudinal shrinkage being several times as great, while the radial and tangential shrinkage is very much less. The excessive weight is also a factor that must be considered in a deli- cately balanced machine.

STEAMING AND BENDING.

Wood may be rendered brittle or otherwise injured by steam bend- ing if this is not properly done. It is necessary to bend certain parts of an airplane frame in this way in order to obviate the ini- tial stresses which would result if these members were simply sprung into place. This should not be attempted on thoroughly air-dry or kiln-dry material, because wood once dried is weaker when brought back to a higher moisture content, and in addition such material has a tendency to spring back after the clamps are removed if it was not thoroughly resoaked. As a rule, wood with less than 18 per cent of moisture based on oven-dry weight should not be steamed and bent.

Too high temperatures in the steam box will make wood brittle, seriously weakening it. Steaming should be accomplished at atmospheric pressure and for a period not to exceed six hours. Higher pressure means higher temperatures and weakened wood. Most hardwoods are more or less discolored by this process, assuming a dead-gray color, but this does not indicate injury. White oak may change to a blackish brown. White ash becomes a dead-gray color, on which a bluish gray discoloration may appear. Elm also takes on this gray shade to some extent. The change in color is very much less noticeable in the soft woods.

Soft woods should not be steamed and bent, because they are very susceptible to injury by this process. When tested, the bent portion will be very weak and brash. A close examination will reveal numerous slight compression failures on the inner curve of the bend. Spruce is particularly subject to this type of injury.

SEASONING.

It is well established that a decrease in the moisture content of wood after the fiber saturation point is reached results in marked progressive increase in the strength of wood, accompanied by a decided shrinkage (63). The fiber saturation point is the condition at which the cell walls are completely saturated, or, in other words, have absorbed the maximum percentage of water which they can hold, but the cell cavities are empty. For two reasons, then, to increase the strength and to prevent subsequent shrinkage when the pieces have been worked to size or even assembled, it is essential that airplane timber be dried or, as it is commonly termed, seasoned. This may be done by air drying, that is, natural seasoning in the air, or by kiln drying, that is, seasoning with artificial heat (4, 12, 64, 65, 66, 70).

As a result of improper seasoning, particularly that which occurs unevenly or too rapidly, checks, which are small longitudinal splits, may occur in the wood. Almost invariably these are on the tangential face, since wood as a rule shrinks about twice as much in the direction of the annual rings as it does radially or across them. The longitudinal shrinkage (with the grain) is so slight that it usually has no effect. Checks are decidedly weakening, but fortunately are easy to recognize.

Airplane wood is usually kiln dried, because the seasoning process can be better controlled than in air drying; it is more rapid, a lower moisture content can be attained, and there is less tendency for kiln-dried wood to shrink and swell with subsequent changes in the humidity of the air. Extensive tests have been made on the effect of artificial seasoning (73). Kiln drying when not properly done is a source of serious injury. Temperatures that are too high or proper temperatures that are combined with humidity that is too low may markedly weaken a charge of lumber, particularly if these conditions are maintained for some time. The detection of such injury, when not severe, is very difficult. Hence, it is highly important that self-recording instruments showing temperatures and relative humidities at all times be properly installed in the kilns and that these be calibrated from time to time. In pronounced cases the lumber will readily reveal its brittle nature when picked with a knife blade.

In all cases where it can not be determined satisfactorily by other methods, representative pieces should be selected for impact bending. This test above all others most readily reveals brittleness in wood. But the test must be made, or at least the results and breaks reviewed, by some one experienced in this method of testing and thoroughly conversant with the mechanical properties of wood.

COMPRESSION FAILURES.

Compression failures may be due to abnormal stresses on the standing tree (from a wind of unusual velocity, for example), to shocks in felling the trees, or to injury during the process of manufacture. Figure 2 shows a compression failure, probably caused when the tree was felled, in a section from an unfinished wing beam of Sitka spruce. As an example of injury during the course of manufacture, it might be mentioned that when a large number of wing beams, improperly piled, are transported on a car or wagon the weight and jar sometimes cause such failures in beams near the bottom of the pile.

The smaller compression failures are not easy to detect. They appear as small whitish wrinkles or irregular lines across the face of the piece, at right angles to the grain. A hand magnifier is often necessary to bring out the finer failures dis-

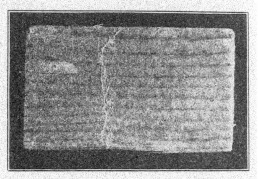

Fig. 2.—Section from an unfinished wing beam, showing a compression failure in Sitka spruce which probably occurred when the tree was felled.

tinctly. The more pronounced failures appear as rather rounded ridges resulting from the "buckling" of the wood fibers under stress.

Compression failures are quite detrimental to the strength of wood, particularly as regards bending strength and shock-resisting ability. Material showing compression failures must not be used in parts where strength is required. One visible small compression failure usually indicates the presence of others.

Members with a small cross section are sometimes subjected to a rough test which makes the wood appear to be brash. It is well known that beams when placed in static bending characteristically fail first in compression, that is, in the fibers between the center (neutral plane) and the top of the beam. Hence, when a spruce longeron, for example, is supported at both ends and a load applied in the center, slight and practically invisible compression failures may result. Such failures appear as tiny whitish lines or wrinkles on the surface of the wood. If the member is then turned over and the load again applied until failure occurs, the break will be sharp and straight across with no splintering, typical of a compression break. This test should not be applied to softwood longerons, particularly spruce, since the resulting breaks will nearly always be short and sharp and may be confused with breaks in brash wood. By turning the member over after the first weight is applied, the compression side, already partially failed, becomes the tension side under the new load; and when the new compression side fails, the tension side, already fractured squarely across, fails with it. To test the resiliency of such members, apply the load on one side only, and do so with moderation.

SHAKES.

Shakes are long tangential cracks or separations in the wood fiber. They are the result of an actual rupture of the wood due to wind, felling stresses, or other causes and are exceedingly detrimental to strength. Old shakes which have occurred while the tree was still standing are often stained and readily visible to the naked eye. This is also true where lumber has been exposed to the weather and dirt has filtered into the cracks. But where they are neither discolored nor opened up the rupture is not so easily detected.

PITCH POCKETS.

Pitch seams or pockets are lens-shaped cavities or openings between the annual rings. They contain resin or pitch either in solid or liquid form; hence the name. These defects result from injury to the living tree, but the cause of injury is as yet unknown. Pitch pockets may indicate more serious wounds. They are very common in Douglas fir, but may be found in other resin-producing softwoods, including spruce.

While pitch pockets reduce the strength of wood, the reduction is not as serious as is generally supposed. General specifications regarding the presence of these defects have been worked out for wing beams of spruce and Douglas fir (*69*, p. 21).

WORM HOLES.

Worm holes are caused by the larvæ of three main types of woodboring insects. The powdery or granular matter, the excrement or frass of either the adults or the "worms," or larvæ, with which these galleries or burrows are usually filled, need not be confounded with decay, since there is no difficulty in separating the two defects. In decay the transition from the soft, spongy, or friable wood to the normal hard material is gradual, while in the worm holes, usually circular or somewhat flattened when seen in cross section, the line between the firm wood and the frass or finely excreted wood is very sharp.

(1) Ambrosia beetles or "pinworms." The small adult beetle bores into the green saw log or green lumber and deposits its eggs. The larvæ hatching from these eggs extend other burrows at an angle from the parent galleries. Moisture is necessary for this type of insect. There may be a blackish discoloration extending around the galleries, particularly those in the sapwood. This is the result of the activity of a wood-staining fungus which does not cause decay in the wood and therefore need not be considered as weakening the material.

(2) Borers. The adults of borers, as a rule, require bark under which to lay their eggs. The larvæ hatching from these eggs burrow under the bark through the sapwood and sometimes into the heartwood; the holes are often large.

(3) Powder-post beetles. Powder-post beetles cause the most dangerous type of defect, and their presence may be detected by fine, powdery droppings coming from the wood. The eggs are laid either in the pores of the wood or under the bark, depending upon the type of insect causing powder post.

white wood of these species, whereas in darker woods the streaks would pass unnoticed.

Burns or scorches in wood may occur from the use of high-speed saws if the saws are not set properly to provide sufficient clearance. Improperly set planing knives will produce the same effect. Usually such burns, appearing on the face of the piece as dark-brown to blackish blotches, are very superficial and can be planed off. The injurious effect is negligible. Deep burns, extending through a piece one-eighth or even one-fourth of an inch in thickness are rarely encountered and are usually confined to particularly susceptible woods, such as the white pines.. These may result when a high-speed sander stops suddenly. The wood is injured and can not be used for highly stressed parts. Burns usually occur in the remanufacture of dry lumber and not on green lumber in the mills.

DISCOLORATIONS CAUSED BY WOUNDS.

The term "wounds" as applied to trees includes not only those scars by which the bark is removed from living trees, exposing the sapwood or heartwood with the death of the cambium over the exposed surface, but also those injuries by which the cambium is temporarily damaged but not killed. The cambium, which is very susceptible to injury, is the very narrow layer of delicate growing tissue of a tree situated at the junction of the living bark and sapwood. When this tissue is injured or killed, a healing or callusing process immediately begins which causes a dip or wave in the grain. Consequently, irregularity of grain in a timber often indicates proximity to a wound.

Wounds in living trees result from a variety of causes, among which may be mentioned fire, lightning, insects, birds, and man. All such injuries are usually accompanied by a discoloration of the wood, particularly the sapwood. Such discolorations are most intense in the hardwoods, especially in the sapwood of such species as white ash, hickory, maple, birch, and tulip poplar.

When the wood of a living tree is exposed to the air it dries out and changes color. In softwoods the change is to a grayish brown or dead-gray color, while in hardwoods the change ranges from a deep brown to almost black, most noticeable in the sapwood. This color change is an oxidation process. Although the wood is not weakened by this change, wound wood of this type should be avoided, owing to the fact that during its exposure to the air it often becomes infected by wood-destroying fungi and may be weakened by incipient decay.

LIGHTNING WOUNDS.

The general appearance of lightning injury is readily recognized. Spike tops and stag heads, together with the spiral wounds existing for many feet along the trunks of the trees, are unmistakable.

Besides such wounds, the cambium is very susceptible to electrical discharge and may be affected for some distance down the tree without any outward visible indications. This irritation to the cambium results in the formation of a layer of cells changed in both shape and structure from the normal. Often in the conifers an unusually large number of resin cells or resin ducts are formed within this injured

portion. In a short time the cell formation returns to normal. Ulti- .
mately, as the growth of the tree proceeds, these lightning rings,
always following one definite annual ring, are deep within the wood,
extending completely or partially around the circumference over a
varying distance. When the tree is worked up for lumber certain of
the boards may have such lightning rings extending completely
through, both in width and length. Such a. board then consists of
two layers of wood held together by a zone of abnormal structure
forming a plane of cleavage. Checking often occurs along this line,
since the continuity of the medullary rays may be interrupted. Such
checks are striking, since they invariably are tangential, following
an annual ring on end section or radial face but not visible on the

tangential face. This
is not at all an un-
common defect in air-
plane timber. An ab-
normal number of
resin ducts may be
found in the annual
ring following many
types of mechanical
injury, but for prac-
tical purposes there is
no difference between
such so-called trau-
matic resin ducts and
the abnormal ducts
formed as a result of
lightning injury.

It is self-evident
that wood with these
lightning rings must
be used with discre-
tion. Even though
the lightning ring
does not check on dry-
ing, when a mem-
ber with this defect is
put under severe
strain and stress a

Fig. 4.—Section from a finished interplane strut, showing
a small lightning injury in Sitka spruce.

serious check may develop. Of course, every member showing a
lightning ring need not be considered valueless. Such a defect in
the stream line of a strut, for example, would be trifling, while a
much shorter ring in the butt or inner bay of a wing beam, particularly if in the same plane as the bolts, would be serious. The same
ring in the tip of such a beam could be overlooked.

The detection of lightning rings in rough lumber is exceedingly
difficult, unless accompanied by small wounds, which is sometimes
the case. Then such wounds must be scrutinized closely for the
presence of a lightning ring. Two or more of these wounds, which
resemble sapsucker wounds, occurring on the same annual ring
and connected by a lightning ring, are sometimes found. Figure 4
shows one of these wounds on an interplane strut, in this case not of

are not subject to these pith-ray flecks, but a somewhat similar injury in western hemlock known as black check results from the work of a different insect (*11*).

CHEMICAL DISCOLORATIONS.

The sapwood of many species of wood is subject to discolorations, varying widely in appearance but fundamentally the same, which are the result of chemical action (*3*). Sapwood is rich in organic compounds and also contains certain soluble ferments which facilitate the oxidation of such compounds. Under favorable temperature conditions, for example, when green sapwood is exposed to the oxygen of the air, these ferments, known as oxidizing enzyms, act on the organic compounds in the sapwood. The result of their action, which is an oxidation process, is a discoloration of the sapwood, with the colored substance most noticeable upon microscopic examination in those cells mainly concerned in the storage and transportation of food.

Hot, humid weather is most favorable for this staining. Cool, dry weather retards it or prevents it entirely. Logs immersed in water are not affected. Light is not necessary for this reaction, as it takes place just as readily in darkness. The stain is confined to the immediate surface layer, and the wood is not weakened. The most practical method of prevention, if this is considered necessary, is by dipping the green sap boards into boiling water for a few minutes as they come from the saw.

HARDWOODS.

Birch, maple, and cherry stain a reddish yellow or rusty color. The wood of alder becomes very intensely red or red-brown on freshly cut surfaces, often within an hour or so after the surface is exposed (*40*). In the case of red alder (*Alnus oregona* Nutt.), if the wood dries and remains white, the red color will appear upon the addition of water in the presence of air, provided the temperature is favorable. A bluish stain often occurs in red gum (*Liquidamber styraciflua* Linn.).

The European linden (*Tilia europaea*, Linn.) is subject to a striking discoloration (*39*), which probably also occurs on basswood in this country. When freshly sawed boards are so closely piled that they dry slowly, a more or less apparent dirty green color appears in from 8 to 10 days. Under very favorable conditions the color is exceedingly bright and intense. The color varies between wide limits, from yellow-green or brown-green through all possible gradations to the purest moss green. Only the outer layers of the wood are colored. Usually the stain extends to a depth of one thirty-second of an inch or rarely to a depth of one-eighth of an inch. The staining, although it is the result of a chemical reaction (an iron-tannin reaction), is not dependent on temperature, since it occurs just as readily in winter as in summer. Too much moisture hinders the reaction, but a certain degree of moisture is essential. If the boards are dried quickly no staining results.

SOFTWOODS.

Coniferous woods are not so commonly subject to this type of discoloration, but there are a few examples. The ends of incense-cedar logs sometimes have a decided brownish red stain on the sapwood. This is of no importance, because it does not occur on sawed lumber except so faintly as to be almost invisible.

A very unsightly discoloration known as brown-stain (*43*, p. 305–307), which, however, does not weaken the wood, often occurs on sugar pine, but is frequently not noticeable until the lumber has been finished. This appears in the sapwood as a streaky, dirty, light to dark brown or brownish black discoloration, and may be superficial or very deep. It is quite striking against the faint yellowish white sapwood in finished lumber. The discoloration occurs on green sap lumber upon exposure to the air and may appear during air drying or kiln drying. In the last instance it is known as kiln burn, but it does not differ from the brown-stain and is probably sometimes due to defective circulation in the kiln. Brown-stain is particularly bad in lumber cut in early spring. Hot, humid weather and poor circulation of air in the lumber piles favor the staining, while cool, dry weather and proper piling tend to prevent it. This brown stain is an oxidation process similar to the others, but whether it can be prevented by the hot-water treatment is doubtful, since the discoloration often extends deeply into the lumber.

The wood of sugar pine in dead trees, standing or down, may be affected by a very brilliant orange stain which occurs in spots or as a solid color, but more often is seen as narrow to broad streaks parallel to the grain of the wood. It is found in both heartwood and sapwood. The exact cause of this discoloration is unknown, but it is probably the result of chemical reaction, since no fungous mycelium has been found associated with it. While the wood is apparently not weakened, the presence of this stain indicates that the lumber came from dead trees, and it should be closely watched for signs of decay and insect borings.

DISCOLORATIONS CAUSED BY FUNGI.

From an economic standpoint by far the most important discolorations in wood are caused by fungi. Fungi are very simple plants which can not live on the simple food elements of the soil and air and build up complex organic matter, as is done by the green plants with which we are familiar, but must have organic matter already prepared in order to sustain life. This they find in the material built up by green plants; hence they may attack living plants, or dead portions of such plants, or any dead vegetable matter. Some live on animal matter, but these do not concern us. The development of fungi is dependent upon a supply of oxygen, of which there is always sufficient in the air, a certain degree of moisture, a suitable range of temperature, and the necessary food substances. The maximum and minimum of these requirements vary widely with different fungi.

The fungous plant consists of very fine threads (hyphæ), which are invisible to the naked eye unless they occur in mass. Individual hyphæ require magnification by a compound microscope. Collectively, the hyphæ are termed mycelium. The hyphæ usually live in the tissues of the substance on which the fungus is growing. The fruiting bodies or sporophores, which vary in size from those so small as to be invisible to the naked eye except in a mass to others quite large and conspicuous, appear on the surface after the hyphæ have developed vigorously. The fruiting bodies bear the spores, which are microscopically small reproductive bodies of relatively simple structure. The spores, being very light, are borne about by air currents. If they alight in a suitable place under proper conditions, germination takes place and hyphæ develop.

Fungi growing on wood may be roughly divided into two groups, depending on the habit of growth of hyphæ. In the first group are placed those fungi whose hyphæ live on the substances contained in the various cells of the wood, while to the second group belong those whose hyphæ attack the actual wood substance of the cell walls and destroy it. The first group is principally represented by the sap-staining or discoloring fungi, so called because they produce various discolorations which are confined to the sapwood. To the second group belong the wood-destroying fungi.

SAP-STAIN.

DESCRIPTION.

Sap-stain, which has been extensively studied (*23, 27, 38, 50, 51*), even though it may render wood very unsightly does not reduce its strength for practical purposes. The discoloration is normally limited to the green sapwood, because as a rule there is neither sufficient food material nor moisture in the dry dead heartwood for the development of the fungus. The discoloration is usually most intense in the medullary rays, since in these tissues the bulk of the food material is found. The stain is produced in two ways, either by a reflection of the color of the hyphæ through the cell walls of the wood or by an actual color solution excreted by the hyphæ, which stains the wood itself. These stains vary in color from blue or blackish to reddish, the former being the most common. Since these fungi do not attack the cell walls in which the strength of the wood reposes, except to a negligible extent, discolored wood is not appreciably weakened. This has been determined by comparative mechanical tests on stained and unstained wood (*41; 56*, p. 13–14; *72*, p. 17).

Although the strength of the wood fibers is not impaired by such stains, the wood is objectionable in places where color is a factor. In a highly varnished interplane strut, for example, a stained streak is unpleasant to the eye. Furthermore, it may lead to a strong prejudice against the airplane having such a member, because while by the uninitiated a dangerous defect not readily apparent is passed unnoticed, an unsightly though harmless discoloration is considered to indicate a serious weakness. Where the discoloration is to be covered up or painted there is no reason to exclude it.

It must be remembered that the conditions which promote the development of the fungus discoloration are highly favorable to the development of true wood-destroying fungi. These conditions are a comparatively high humidity and warm weather. Sap-stain is at its worst during warm wet weather, when the humidity of the air is relatively high and lumber dries slowly. It is at such periods that the most severe staining may occur if the lumber is not properly handled. The climate of the Pacific Northwest is usually exceedingly favorable for the development of wood-staining and wood-destroying fungi during the spring and summer months. It is from this region that the three most important airplane woods—Sitka spruce, Douglas fir, and Port Orford cedar—are obtained.

Wood containing very severe sap-stain therefore should be carefully examined for the presence of wood-destroying fungi. If decayed, the wood will be brash and may be softer and less tough when the fibers are picked with a knife. If any doubt exists after an inspection, the decision should be based on a microscopical examination or a mechanical test by a qualified expert.

The most important of these stains from an economic standpoint is blue-stain, caused by various species of Ceratostomella, which may be found on almost any hardwood or softwood. Softwoods are more commonly affected, and certain species are particularly susceptible. This is due both to the character of the wood and to the climatic conditions of the region where the species occurs. The discoloration may be more or less superficial, occurring as spots or streaks. If the staining is severe, however, the entire sapwood will be affected, so that it can not be surfaced off. The fungi causing these stains are not readily seen, but sometimes if a deeply stained, almost black piece is inspected with a hand magnifying glass, innumerable bristles with a bulbous base will be observed. These are the fruiting bodies, containing an enormous number of spores, which are exuded and are carried about by air currents. Falling on green sap lumber they sprout, the hyphæ develop, and more blue-stain results. Under favorable conditions blue-stain may develop with surprising rapidity, appearing on lumber within a day after sawing.

Other colors, such as black, brown, gray, red, pink, and violet, are caused by species of Hormodendron, Hormiscium, Graphium, Penicillium, and Fusarium. These discolorations are not nearly so common as blue-stain.

Certain other discolorations of sapwood are produced by fungi belonging to the molds, of which the green mold on fruits or in certain cheeses is an example. Usually such stains are superficial and readily surface off. They occur on both hardwoods and softwoods. The bluish or blackish stains are difficult to separate by visual inspection from the true blue-stain.

CONTROL.

Considerable study has been devoted to the development of methods of prevention and control of sap stains caused by fungi (1, 25, 72). Naturally most of this work has been concentrated on blue-stain, and the following paragraphs are most directly applicable to it, but will probably also apply fairly well to the others. Blue-stain may be checked after it has started, but the stain can not be eradicated unless it is so superficial that it can be planed off. Therefore, the keynote of all treatments must be prevention.

Unfortunately, there is no one principle that can be applied to the prevention of this discoloration. Staining may take place at any time after the trees are felled or, in the case of dead timber, while they are still standing. Hence, in logging operations in regions where blue-stain is of importance, the logs should be removed from the woods as soon as possible after the trees are felled and bucked (cut up into log lengths). The practice of leaving logs lying in the woods for months can not be too strongly condemned, as this not only causes blue-stain but also promotes the growth of wood-destroying fungi. ' Furthermore, the inevitable attacks of wood-boring insects assist greatly in the spread of blue-stain and decay. When the trees are bucked the narrow space left by the saw kerf between the logs as they are lying end to end affords an ideal situation for the development of the blue-stain fungi. Such logs often stain deeply, while those with the ends fully exposed remain entirely free from discoloration. As soon as the logs are in the mill pond danger from staining is over for the time being, since the oxygen supply is so reduced that the fungi can not develop.

The greatest danger of all is encountered during the process of drying the rough lumber as it comes from the saw. The best method of preventing blue-stain is by kiln drying. If the stock checks easily, so that low temperature and high humidities must be maintained over a considerable period, some of the other staining fungi such as molds, may develop. But these can be checked by raising the temperature in the kiln to about 160° F. or slightly more for an hour by turning live steam into the kiln. When this is done, care must be taken to keep the air saturated while steaming and to reduce the humidity gradually after steaming. When the stock has once been dried properly the moisture content has been so reduced that there is no more danger from staining, provided it is kept dry. A dispute that arose over the efficiency of a dry kiln was immediately settled by the fact that the blue-stain fungi had resumed vigorous growth the day after the stock was removed from the kiln. This could not have occurred if the lumber had been properly dried.

All airplane lumber should be kiln-dried immediately, since this not only prevents blue-stain, but also stops the growth of wood-destroying fungi, prevents future checking, and greatly reduces weight without in any way injuring the lumber, provided temperatures that are too high are avoided.

In case kiln drying is impossible, treatment with antiseptic solutions is of considerable value. As it comes from the saws the green lumber is dipped into a hot or cold chemical solution. The solutions most commonly employed are sodium carbonate or sodium bicarbonate in water. Neither is 100 per cent effective under optimum conditions for staining, but they aid materially in checking discoloration. These two chemicals, however, color the treated wood a decided yellow or brownish. Sodium fluorid, although it does not stain the lumber and is slightly better for blue-stain, is not so effective against certain molds as the two solutions first mentioned. This chemical is seldom used. It must be remembered that the strength of the solutions must necessarily vary with the conditions. The more favorable the conditions for blue-stain, the stronger the solutions should be.

After being dipped in any of these solutions the lumber must be carefully open piled, that is, with spaces between the boards to insure good ventilation. Narrow cross strips or "stickers" chemically treated should be used, to prevent staining at the points where the boards and cross strips meet. Detailed instructions as to the proper methods of piling lumber may be consulted elsewhere (4, p. 17–21).

Salt is of little or no value in preventing blue-stain in comparison with the other chemicals. The application of salt after blue-staining has well started is almost a waste of money. In fact, the application of wet salt or a strong salt solution may prove detrimental in the long run, for if the lumber is dried after such treatment the affinity of the salt for water may cause the moisture content to remain much higher than normal.

Mercuric chlorid in a 0.1 per cent solution is exceedingly effective against blue-stain, but on account of its highly poisonous nature and extremely corrosive action when in contact with many metals it is little used.

Shipping green stock closely piled in closed box cars during the spring and summer months is almost certain to result in severe staining. Indeed, the writer has seen some stock handled in this way which stained even in winter. On the other hand, any measures taken to prevent staining, such as open piling in gondolas or on flat cars, will almost certainly result in severe checking. Of the two evils, checking is by far the most serious in airplane stock, since checked lumber is greatly reduced in strength, while the stained lumber is only somewhat unsightly. Shipping green lumber in the close hold of a vessel, particularly if tropical seas are to be traversed, is an invitation to swift and sure disaster as far as sap staining is concerned. It is doubtful whether dipping in any chemical solution now used, except possibly mercuric chlorid, would be effective under such severe conditions.

But, to repeat, the most effective measure to employ against blue-stain is speed in drying the wood. Get the logs from the woods to the saw with the greatest rapidity and the lumber from the saw directly into the dry kiln.

SAP-STAIN ON SOFTWOODS.

Certain species are peculiarly susceptible to sap-stain. This is due both to the character of the wood and to the climatic conditions of the region where the species grows. Western white pine, spruce, and southern yellow pine, the last-named wood including longleaf pine (*Pinus palustris* Mill.), shortleaf pine (*P. echinata* Mill.), and loblolly pine (*P. taeda* Linn.), are very subject to sap-stain, especially blue-stain, while true fir and cedar are not so easily affected. Douglas fir occupies an intermediate position.

Besides blue-stain, a red stain has been very commonly found on Sitka spruce airplane lumber. It occurred abundantly in the East on stock in cars just arrived from the Pacific coast and also developed on material along the Atlantic coast which had arrived unstained at the port of embarkation but was held over awaiting shipment. The stain appeared as terra-cotta or brick-red spots on the rough lumber, varying from very faint to a pronounced color. In the stock worked up in the factories in this country it was found that the stain was superficial, usually surfacing out during remanufacture; but reports from abroad indicate that the fungus developed very intensively by the time the lumber reached European ports, and the discoloration penetrated deeply into the sapwood. The appearance of the wood is not marred to the same extent that it is by blue-stain, and as far as is known no reduction in strength results. The fungus causing the discoloration is as yet unknown.

Blue-stain is very severe on the white pines and is particularly noticeable because of their white wood. Plate I, left part, shows a section from a sugar-pine rib web in which the sapwood is stained to some extent. The small, darker, bluish black spots are the ends of the medullary rays, in which, as before stated, the fungous mycelium is most abundant. The longer streaks are the resin ducts.

Certain fungi (*Penicillium* spp.), stain the sapwood of the pines an orange-red to a crimson-red color. Another fungus (*Fusarium roseum* Link) is responsible for a pink to lilac color in the same woods. The color is produced by means of a pigment secreted by the hyphæ, which actually dyes the wood.

A wood-staining fungus (*Zythia resinae* (Fr.) Karst.) has been reported in Europe (*9*) as working on finished pine lumber after the wood has been oiled. The discoloration was characterized by violet. to dirty red or even dark grayish brown flecks beneath the oiled surface of the wood. The spots were covered with minute pustules varying from violet, orange, and brown to black. These constitute the spore-producing bodies. The discolored areas extend within the wood as streaks closely associated with the medullary rays and resin ducts. The report does not state whether the discoloration was confined to sapwood. Apparently the wood was not reduced in strength. As far as is known, this stain has not yet been found in the United States.

SAP-STAIN ON HARDWOODS.

Hardwoods are not as subject to the stains caused by fungi as are softwoods. In hardwoods, when sap-stain does occur, the discoloration is most intense in the medullary rays and large pores or vessels. In a wood such as yellow birch, in which these vessels are not too closely crowded, the stain, if not too severe, appears in longitudinal section as very narrow bluish black lines or streaks following the grain of the wood. This stain will not necessarily be confined to the surface layers, but may extend entirely through the sapwood. Of all the hardwoods, however, red gum seems to be the most susceptible to stains caused by fungi.

BROWN-OAK DISCOLORATIONS.

A somewhat different discoloration than those previously described, in that it is confined to heartwood only, is the "brown oak" (*18, 19*) found in Great Britain. This is also known as "red oak" and "foxiness," but the name first given is most commonly accepted. Instead of the normal heartwood, certain trees of the common European oak have a dull-brown to rusty brown or even rust color in the heartwood. In some cases the color is uniform, while again longitudinal streaks of normal-colored heartwood may alternate with those of the brown color. When these brown streaks contain black patches this type of wood is known as "tortoise-shell" oak. This discoloration originates in the heartwood of living trees, the normal heartwood changing first to a faint yellow color, which continues to deepen until the brown stage is attained. The color change is caused by a fungus, but so far as known the infected wood is not weakened.

The hyphæ attack the cell walls very slightly, presumably living on the tannin, of which oak wood contains a high percentage. The value of the wood for veneers is very much enhanced. The writer has no record of this discoloration being found on oaks in this country.

DECAY DISCOLORATIONS.

The hyphæ of wood-destroying fungi living within the wood feed on the various substances composing the cell walls. They use certain constituents of the cell walls, neglecting others, with the result that these walls are broken down, the wood being thus greatly weakened and more or less destroyed. It is the breaking down of the wood and the change in its physical and chemical qualities that is termed decay. The degree of decay is determined by the energy of growth of the fungus, the length of time it has been at work, and the type of wood it attacks. Some fungi attack many different kinds of wood, while others are limited in their choice. Owing to their less exacting moisture requirements, wood-destroying fungi are able to live on heartwood as well as sapwood. The fruiting bodies, usually quite large, are found on the surface in the form of brackets, crusts, or mushrooms or toadstools. They are not developed until the hyphæ have been at work for some time; consequently, the presence of fruiting bodies indicates serious decay.

Two types of wood-destroying fungi may be recognized, (1) those mainly attacking the heartwood, rarely the sapwood, of standing living trees, and (2) those principally confining their activities to the manufactured product, such as sawed lumber, crossties, and poles. The former type may continue their work of destruction after the tree has been cut down and worked up into lumber. The latter, attacking the manufactured product, usually invade the sapwood first, since it is far richer in stored food, generally has a higher moisture content than the heartwood, and is not so inherently resistant to decay. Fungi causing this type of decay are often very abundant in yards where the lumber is closely piled on damp earth, with little or no aeration under the piles, and much accumulated wood débris scattered throughout the yard. Unfortunately, such conditions are all too prevalent in mill yards. Sanitary yards both at the mills and the factories are badly needed. Humphrey (28) gives a complete account of the life history and habits of these fungi, the damage caused by them, and methods for their control.

CONDITIONS AFFECTING DECAY.

All conditions which favor sap stains are equally favorable to wood-destroying fungi. Furthermore, the latter can attack wood with a lower moisture content, so the fact that wood does not sapstain is no indication that fungi causing decay may not be present. The discolorations caused by the latter in sapwood are not so pronounced as sap-stain; consequently, they are much harder to detect.

Moisture in wood.—Dry lumber will not decay. The most efficient method to prevent decay is to air-dry or kiln-dry lumber immediately and then keep it dry by proper methods of storage. Placing dry lumber in the open, exposed to rain, or in damp sheds can not be too strongly condemned. If the lumber becomes moist again, it is just as liable to decay as before. To be sure, kiln drying is much better than air drying, since the high temperatures employed in the former process are probably fatal to the hyphæ of some decay-producing fungi, while under the latter conditions the fungi may merely remain dormant until suitable moisture conditions are again restored. However, since wood-destroying fungi are common around and in yards and wood-working factories, the chances are that kiln-dried lumber will be reinfected, and if it becomes moist again decay will begin.

Shipping green or even partially air-dried lumber on long voyages through tropical seas in the hold of a vessel offers a chance for a heavy loss through decay. The close humid air of the ship's hold becomes a perfect forcing chamber for wood-destroying fungi when warm latitudes are reached. Shipments of Douglas fir leaving the Pacific coast perfectly sound have contained a considerable percentage of decayed lumber when unloaded at a South African port (*36*, p. 36). Indirect reports indicate that the same condition resulted during the World War in some shipments of Sitka spruce routed to Europe through the Panama Canal and the Mediterranean Sea.

Durability of wood.—Resistance to decay, or as it is termed "durability," is a factor that should no longer be neglected in selecting woods for airplane construction. Airplanes are being more and more exposed to unfavorable weather conditions as their use extends, conditions which in some instances are highly favorable to decay. Furthermore, certain conditions created by the construction of an airplane promote decay. For example, in the interior of the wings the relative humidity may be much higher than that of the surrounding air, and there is often considerable condensation of moisture. In addition, the temperature is slightly higher. All these factors are favorable to the development of wood-destroying fungi.

Within any species durability increases with the increase in specific gravity. Consequently, the fact that only wood with high specific gravity is used for aircraft not only increases strength but serves to increase durability. However, it is well known that different species vary widely in their durability. Unfortunately, spruce is not at all durable. Neither are basswood and birch. Douglas fir is fairly durable, as is also white oak. But the cedars are remarkable for their inherent durability, and among these Port Orford cedar compares favorably with spruce in all its strength properties and is only slightly heavier. Consequently, this wood can not be too highly recommended for use in aircraft where resistance to decay must be considered. Sapwood must not be used under such circumstances, for no matter what the species is it decays easily.

Contrary to existing belief, the resin content of wood is of slight importance in relation to durability (*74*, p. 153–154; *75*, p. 66–68). Resin itself has no poisonous effect on the growth of fungous hyphæ, and its only beneficial effect in increasing durability is its waterproofing action on wood. This is so slight, however, if the normal resin content of softwoods is considered, as to be practically negligible. If wood is rendered more durable through a sufficient increase in its resin content to have a decided waterproofing effect, it is usually completely resin soaked or contains pitch streaks which make it unsuitable for painting or contact with fabric coverings.

INCIPIENT DECAY.

It is a simple matter to recognize well-advanced rot or typical decay. Here the changes in the wood structure due to the longer action of the wood-destroying fungus are so profound as to be very plainly apparent, but the earlier stages of decay, termed incipient decay, immature decay, or advance rot, are often far from easy to detect (6, 7). In some cases detection is practically impossible without a microscopical examination of the wood.

Specific gravity is not a reliable index of decay. It has been suggested that decay in any piece of wood will be immediately reflected in a lowering of the specific gravity. But this can not be detected unless the specific gravity of the piece was known before decay commenced, a manifest impossibility in most cases. Incipient decay does not cause a sufficient reduction in the specific gravity to bring the heavier pieces of wood below the minimum set for the species. The writer has tested pieces of yellow birch, white ash, and Douglas fir with conspicuous incipient decay and found the specific gravity of the affected pieces to be from 0.05 to 0.2 higher than the minimum permissible. The same condition will exist in all species. Douglas fir with pronounced white cellulose pockets characteristic of the final stage of red-rot or conk-rot has been found in some cases to have a higher specific gravity than the minimum of 0.45. Of course, when sound such wood had a high specific gravity.

Wood is weakened by incipient decay, the degree depending on the stage of the decay and somewhat on the species of fungus at work. Furthermore, if infected material is merely air dried the hyphæ may remain dormant, ready to continue their work of destruction again if suitable conditions arise. The chalky quinine fungus (*Fomes laricis* (Jacq.) Murr.), which normally causes decay in the heartwood of various coniferous trees, either living or dead, has been found causing decay in the roof timbers of cotton weave sheds (5). Undoubtedly this originated from timbers containing incipient decay of this species placed in the roofs at the time they were built, where the high temperature and humidity which prevails in such sheds soon resulted in renewed activity of the fungous hyphæ and their spread to adjoining sound timbers. The rose-colored Fomes (*Fomes roseus* (Alb. and Schw.) Cke.), which is common on dead trees and is sometimes found on living trees in the coniferous forests of the Pacific Northwest, has been found to be very destructive to timbers in basements with high humidity and poor ventilation in the Northeastern States (26, p. 28). As a general rule, infected wood must not be used.

It is extremely doubtful whether incipient decay in one of the laminations of ply wood can be considered an important defect. In the first place, the reduction in strength would be negligible. Furthermore, there would be but little danger of the fungus ever resuming its activities, because the high degree of heat and humidity to which the ply wood is subjected during various stages of its manufacture must kill the vegetating hyphæ. However, this does not prevent reinfection and subsequent damage if conditions for decay by the Indian paint fungus (*Echinodontium tinctorium* E. and E.). This is found on the true firs in the western United States, being especially prevalent and severe on white fir (*37*). It is also exceedingly serious on western hemlock (*71*).

In white fir the first indications of this decay on a radial or tangential section are light-brown or golden tan spots or larger areas of discoloration in the light-colored heartwood, which may be accompanied by small but clearly distinct radial burrows, resembling somewhat very shallow insect burrows without the deposit of excrement. These burrows are not easily detected in cross section. Next, rusty reddish streaks appear following the grain. Throughout this stage the wood appears firm and strong, but in reality is so greatly weakened that boards may separate along the annual rings when dried. The discoloration intensifies, the wood becomes soft, showing a decided tendency to separate along the spring wood in the annual rings, and finally the typical stage is reached, in which the wood is brown, with pronounced rusty, reddish streaks and becomes fibrous and stringy. Hence, the name stringy brown-rot is applied to the decay. The incipient decay usually extends from 2 to 6 feet beyond the typical decay. Plate VI shows the incipient decay.

In western hemlock the incipient decay is much harder to detect, because the initial discoloration above described so closely approximates the pale-brown, slightly tinged with red, color of the normal heartwood. The wood first assumes a faint yellowish color, which is sometimes intensified by the presence of small, hardly discernible brownish areas. These areas later develop into the typical decay. The extension of the incipient decay beyond the typical decay varies from 1 to 5 feet. For the sake of safety 2 feet should be added beyond the last recognizable yellowish discoloration in order to eliminate all incipient decay.

TYPES OF DECAY IN LIVING HARDWOOD TREES.

Hardwood trees are subject to very serious decays. One of the most important from our standpoint is the white heartwood rot (*58*) so commonly found in commercial white-ash stock, caused by the ash Fomes (*Fomes fraxinophilus* (Pk.) Sacc.). This fungus attacks the heartwood of living trees and produces a very characteristic rot. On cross section the first indication of the decay is a light brownish discoloration, often difficult to distinguish from the normal grayish brown or reddish brown heartwood. This discoloration is most apparent in the broad bands of summer wood. Next, there is a bleaching of the spring wood, during which it turns to a straw color, and then small white spots or specks appear. On the radial (edge-grain) and tangential (slash-grain) faces these appear as small whitish spots, streaks, or blotches, usually following the grain, but some may be at right angles to it if the decay follows a medullary ray. The whitish color becomes more marked, until the entire spring wood is affected and appears disintegrated. Then the fibers fall apart. The summer wood passes through the same process, but much more slowly, thus during the earlier stages of the typical decay causing a banded appearance. The completely rotted wood is whitish or straw colored, very soft, and spongy, readily absorbing water. A section from a white-ash longeron with this incipient decay is illustrated in Plate I, right side.

Apparently mycelium does not occur in the brown discolored wood in advance of the white spots. It would seem that the wood is not weakened until the white spots are found, and the wood with the brown discoloration alone need not be rejected. It is an excellent hint for close scrutiny of an affected piece, however. The incipient decay is somewhat obscured in rough lumber, but is usually readily apparent on smooth surfaces. This stage does not extend many feet beyond the typical decay, and on long boards the latter will most likely also occur. Once the presence of the typical decay is ascertained it is a relatively simple matter to determine the limits of the incipient stage.

Areas in which the wood failed to change color upon transition from heartwood to sapwood (see p. 16) can be differentiated from the initial stages of white-rot by their larger size, by the straw-yellow color as opposed to the whitish of the decay, by the sharp line between the two colors, and by the fact that the spots are much larger, without becoming soft and spongy, than would be the case with the decay.

Sweet birch and yellow birch are subject to a white heart-rot (*32*) which, although very·similar to the foregoing, is caused by a different fungus, the false tinder fungus (*Fomes igniarius* (L.) Gill.). The first indication of the incipient decay is a brown discoloration, not very apparent against the reddish brown heartwood. Next, faintly paler streaks or spots appear, which finally become a yellowish white, strikingly apparent against the dark background. This stage is illustrated by Plate VII. In the center of these streaks small spots are found in which the yellowish white wood appears to have collapsed. Usually the long axis of these spots is parallel to the grain, but in some it may be at right angles to it. The wood up to this time appears firm and hard. Next the white streaks merge, the wood becomes soft, and finally the entire affected portion of the heartwood is reduced to a yellowish white fibrous mass composed principally of cellulose, the result of the delignification by the fungous hyphæ. As in the white-rot of ash, hyphæ are not found in the brown discoloration. Hence, no reduction in the strength of the wood may be expected until the very first indications of the whitish streaks or spot, which may be found as much as 8 feet in advance of the typical decay.

One of the most common decays (*24*) on oaks and also on certain poplars (Populus) is the heart-rot caused by the oak fungus (*Polyporus dryophilus* Berk.). The incipient decay of this whitish piped rot in white oak has a water-soaked appearance in the unseasoned wood, but when dry the discoloration becomes hazel to tawny in color. The discoloration may extend from 1 to 10 feet in advance of any other indication of the decay. The next stage of the decay, which is best seen on a radial face, is characterized by whitish spots or streaks, usually following the medullary rays, which produce a mottled appearance of the wood. This mottling is the result of a delignification process; that is, the lignin is removed from the wood, leaving only the cellulose. In the final stages the decayed wood is firm, with a white, stringy appearance, and the delignification is practically complete.

A somewhat similar rot in oaks (*34*) is the honeycomb heart-rot (*Stereum subpileatum* B. and C.). As in the whitish piped rot, the first indication of this decay in white oak is a slight water-soaked appearance of the fresh heartwood, and when dry this "soak" becomes a tawny color. Next, light-colored isolated areas appear in the tawny discolored wood, and pronounced delignification occurs. This is indicated by the appearance of very small irregular whitish patches in the light-colored areas. These patches develop into small pits with their long axes parallel to the grain of the wood, and they increase in number until the affected wood is completely occupied. The pits are from one thirty-second to one-fourth of an inch wide by one-fourth to five-eighths of an inch long, and lined with cellulose fibers. At this stage the appearance of the decay is similar to the red-rot in softwoods previously described. Later the cellulose lining may disappear. The wood is probably not weakened by this decay until the light-colored areas appear in the tawny discoloration.

An incipient decay is sometimes encountered in African mahogany, the cause of which is unknown to the writer. This decay appears as light-yellow, brown, or merely lighter brown closely crowded spots or flecks on the reddish-brown heartwood. These flecks vary from one-sixteenth to one-quarter of an inch long and are several times longer than broad, the long axis corresponding with the direction of the grain in the wood. Such wood is weakened.

TYPES OF DECAY IN LOGS AND LUMBER.

In addition to the wood-destroying fungi which normally attack living trees, and which may continue to decay the wood after the tree is cut, there are fungi which grow only or principally on wood in the form of logs or lumber. Owing to their destructiveness, some of these deserve more than passing mention. Although it is true that damage caused by such fungi is due to improper handling of the timber during the course of manufacture and utilization, unfortunately such improper handling does occur and must be reckoned with.

Softwood logs and lumber.—One of the most important of these fungi is that which causes dry-rot in stored logs or lumber and in timber in structures (*22*). The term "dry-rot" is loosely applied to cover almost any type of decay, but it is correctly applicable only to the work of the dry-rot fungus (*Merulius lacrymans* (Wulf.) Fr.). This decay is more common on coniferous woods than on hardwoods. The incipient decay appears as a yellow-brown discoloration not easy to detect. Wood with typical decay is yellow to brown in color, much shrunken and cracked, and is so badly disintegrated that it can be easily crushed to a powder. Both sapwood and heartwood are attacked.

Another common decay on logs and sawed lumber, particularly on railroad ties, is the brown-rot (*62*) caused by the brown Lenzites (*Lenzites sepiaria* (Wulf.) Fr.), which is practically confined to coniferous wood. The typical decay is brown, friable, and easily reducible to a powder. In the early stages of decay infected wood is darker in color than the normal. Sometimes the early spring wood of the annual rings may be completely decayed, while the summer wood is scarcely affected. In this condition the wood separates readily along the annual rings.

Hardwood logs and lumber.—Certain fungi (*Polystictus versicolor* (L.) Fr., *Stereum hirsutum* (Willd.) Pers., and others) cause a sap rot very difficult of detection in its incipient stage. The typical decay is very light in weight, white in color, rather soft, and easily broken in the hands. But since the first indication of this decay is a faint whitening of the diseased wood and white is the normal color of most sapwoods, it is apparent that the initial stages may be readily overlooked. At the same time the wood is decidedly reduced in strength. The decay is most common on hardwoods, but also occurs to some extent on softwoods. Fortunately none of the fungi causing this white sap-rot attack living trees of the species which furnish airplane timber.

Red-gum logs when left in the woods for any considerable time are subject to a very serious sap-rot (*59*) caused by the smoky Polyporus (*Polyporus adustus* (Willd.) Fr.). The heartwood is comparatively durable. Boards cut from diseased logs are very characteristic and striking in appearance. Normally, red-gum sapwood is a light yellowish white, commonly with a reddish tinge. The sapwood in a decayed board has a number of various-colored streaks or lines irregularly distributed from the end of the board toward the middle. These streaks are light orange at first, but in the more advanced decay are a very light straw color (in fact, almost white) and are intermingled with lines and patches of bluish gray and the normal-colored sapwood. Black zigzag lines may extend from the ends of the board for a distance of 2 inches or more parallel to the grain. The general consistency of sapwood with this incipient decay, which may extend 2 or 3 feet in advance of the typical decay, is firm and solid. Sapwood with the typical decay is badly broken down, being soft and pulpy and without firmness.

This and other sap rots may be prevented by shortening the drying period in the woods. Coating the ends with hot coal-tar creosote immediately after the logs are cut is also effective. Where possible, all freshly cut logs, particularly those cut during the spring and summer, when the rot develops best, should be peeled. Sap rots similar to those found in the red gum are found in tupelo gum (*Nyssa sylvatica* Marsh) and in maple.

DECAY IN FINISHED AIRPLANES.

Little information about decay in finished airplanes is available. In the past there has been very small chance for airplanes to decay, because the completed machines rarely ever were stored, and their life in use was a relatively brief one; but since the conclusion of the World War immense quantities of airplane material have been placed in storage, and the average life of the machines has been materially increased by changes in construction. Under average conditions there should be practically no damage to finished airplanes by decay. When in use there is little danger from this source, owing to the fact that when not actually in flight the machines are properly housed. The wooden parts in the interior of the wings and around the engine are most susceptible. In these places there is an increased temperature and relative humidity. Keeping the machines in a dry place when not in use will suffice in most climates. There is more danger in humid tropical or semitropical regions, particularly to seaplanes.

Serious loss can easily result to machines through improper handling while being stored or shipped. Airplanes are usually knocked down for storing and shipping; that is, the machine is taken apart, and the individual assemblies, such as the wings, tail surfaces, and fuselage, are handled separately. When shipped, these parts are carefully wrapped in heavy paper and packed in solid crates. If these crates are left out in the air, cracks open up between the boards, water may get in, and then the trouble commences. Once damp, it is almost impossible for the mass of paper wrappings to dry out unless the crate is completely unpacked. Varnish or dope does not prevent the taking up of moisture, so that the wood soon attains a moisture content sufficient for the growth of molds and wood-destroying fungi, while the other conditions within the crate, such as lack of air circulation with the resulting high humidity and the higher temperatures, are ideal for the development of these organisms. Even before the wood is decayed the elements of the ply wood are very likely to separate, owing to the action of moisture and molds on the glue. Even water-resistant glues can not permanently withstand such conditions.

There is no cure for decay, once it has started. The damaged part can be replaced and further destruction prevented, but the constant aim should be not to let decay begin. Material should not be kept in packing cases any longer than is necessary. The practice of leaving packing cases containing airplanes or spare parts in the open for several months can not be too severely condemned.

When put in storage, the parts should be removed from the cases and placed on racks, so that a complete circulation of air is possible around each unit or piece. The storage houses should be equipped with a forced-ventilation system, so that air of the proper humidity can be constantly circulated through the piles of material. The relative humidity should be maintained at 60 which will keep the wood at a moisture content of about 11 per cent, low enough to prevent decay, mold, or sap-stain.

Circumstances will arise where planes are in use or while being shipped when it will be impossible to maintain proper conditions to prevent deterioration. In the warm climate and high humidity of tropical or semitropical regions in particular this will be true. It is advisable to have planes for use under such conditions constructed from a durable wood such as Port Orford cedar. Where this can not be done, methods should be employed to make the other species more durable.

Wood may be moisture-proofed by the application of aluminum leaf. This not only prevents decay, since the wood is kept dry, but protects the glue joints from the action of moisture and mold.

As a last resort, the wood could be treated with preservatives to prevent decay. These liquids are most effective when forced into the wood under pressure. Consequently the completed individual wood parts would have to be treated before assembly. Sodium fluorid could be used on parts to be glued, while coal-tar creosote could be applied to the others. The most highly efficient of all, mercuric chlorid, is unfortunately a deadly poison, corrodes metal, and is very difficult to handle. The subject of preservative treatment is one about which little is known as applied to airplanes.

Little information is available as to what fungi actually cause decay in finished airplanes or as to the types of decay found. Undoubtedly the fungi most concerned are those commonly attacking the manufactured product, such as the dry-rot fungus, the brown Lenzites, or the rose-colored Fomes. Fungi decaying the heartwood of living trees are not commonly found. When they do appear, this is practically proof positive that the manufacturer used wood with incipient decay in the fabrication of the wooden parts.

SUMMARY.

Among the softwoods or conifers the most valuable for airplane construction are red, white, and Sitka spruce, the last being most important on account of its large size and the consequently greater proportion of clear lumber that can be obtained. A splendid substitute for spruce, and its superior where durability must be considered, is Port Orford cedar. However, the supply of this wood is limited. Douglas fir, which is much heavier than spruce and therefore not so desirable, is also extensively used. In those parts of an airplane frame requiring great strength and toughness, hardwoods are used. White ash is best, but white oak, hard maple, and rock elm may be substituted. Hickory is principally used for tail skids. Black walnut and true mahogany are unsurpassed for propellers, but yellow birch, sweet birch, African mahogany, black cherry, hard maple, and white oak are acceptable substitutes. As the supply of timber diminishes in the future, a wider variety of woods will be acceptable for airplane construction.

All wood is subject to defects, of which one of the most serious is decay; but other defects which reduce the strength of timber must be recognized. Among these can be mentioned spiral and diagonal grain, specific gravity that is too low or too high, brashness caused by excessive temperatures during steaming or kiln drying, compression failures, shakes, pitch pockets, and insect galleries.

Decay in its incipient stage is often not readily recognized; but wood with incipient decay must not be used in airplane construction, since infected wood may be reduced in strength. Furthermore, the decay may continue if suitable conditions arise. The first indication of decay is usually a discoloration of the infected wood, but not all discolorations result from decay. Marked discoloration of the wood, particularly the sapwood, usually accompanies pith-ray flecks and wounds made by lightning and sapsuckers. Conditions favorable for decay also promote sap stains. These discolorations of the green sapwood of various softwoods and hardwoods occur in two ways: (1) By an oxidation of the organic compounds in the cells of the sapwood when exposed to the air and (2) by the attack of sap-staining fungi, the hyphæ of which feed on the organic compounds in the cells of the sapwood without attacking the cell walls except to a negligible extent. The discolorations are confined to the sapwood as a rule, but occasionally the sap-staining fungi, may discolor the heartwood slightly. For practical purposes wood so discolored is not reduced in strength.

The discolorations resulting from incipient decay may be found in the sapwood or heartwood. Incipient decay extends for varying distances beyond the typical decay. In cutting out this defect it is advisable to leave a margin of safety of at least 2 feet in a longitudinal direction beyond the last visible evidences of the incipient decay, in order to remove all infected wood. This margin of safety is particularly important with brown or red-brown friable decays, since infected wood may be dangerously weakened by them while the incipient stage is still practically invisible.

Many decays other than those described in this paper are found in living trees, in logs, and in manufactured timber, but the examples cited include both the most important decays and the principal types. For most purposes it is sufficient to recognize incipient decay as distinguished from other discolorations or defects without determining the causal fungus.

FIG. 1.—SECTION FROM A RIB WEB, SHOWING BLUE-STAIN IN SUGAR PINE.

The dark-blue specks are the ends of the medullary rays. The pale orange colored wood at the right is unstained heartwood.

FIG. 2.—SECTION FROM A WHITE-ASH LONGERON.

The brownish discoloration with the small white streaks indicates incipient white heartwood rot.

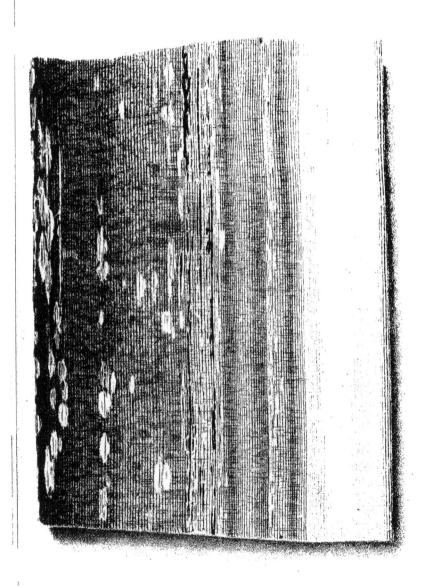

SECTION OF THE HEARTWOOD OF DOUGLAS FIR.

The typical decay here shown is caused by the ring-scale fungus. The light-colored wood at the right is sound sapwood.

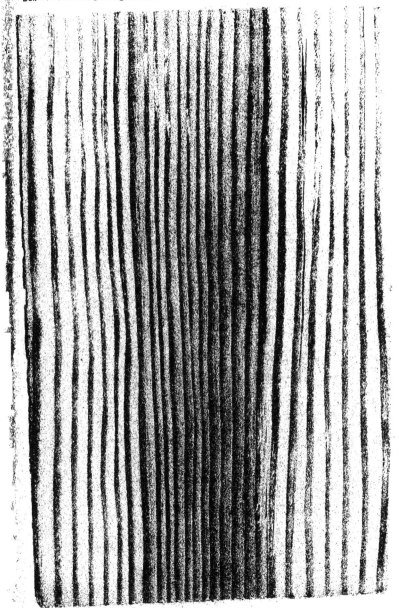

INCIPIENT DECAY IN DOUGLAS FIR CAUSED BY THE RING-SCALE FUNGUS.

The white spots are the beginning of the formation of cellulose pits in the central discolored zone, indicating decay.

A. HOEN & CO BALTO

DECAY COMMON IN THE HEARTWOOD OF PINE, LARCH, AND DOUGLAS FIR.
This typical decay, with the characteristic conspicuous white mycelium felts, is caused by
the chalky quinine fungus.

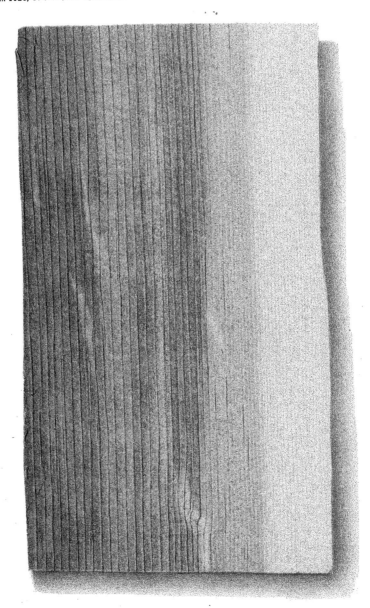

INCIPIENT DECAY IN THE HEARTWOOD OF WESTERN YELLOW PINE.

The discoloration indicates the presence of decay caused by the chalky quinine fungus.
The pale orange colored wood at the right is sound heartwood.

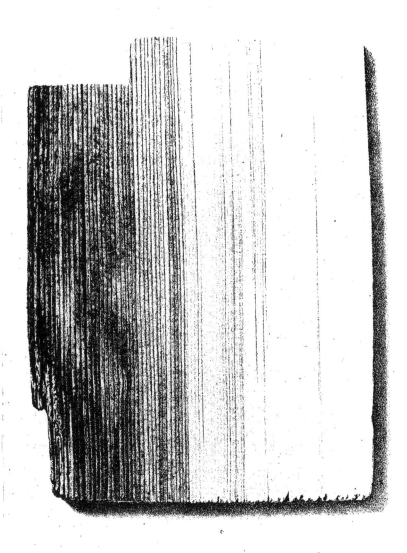

INCIPIENT DECAY IN THE HEARTWOOD OF WHITE FIR.

This golden brown discoloration indicates decay caused by the Indian-paint fungus. Note the contrast in color with the normal white wood.

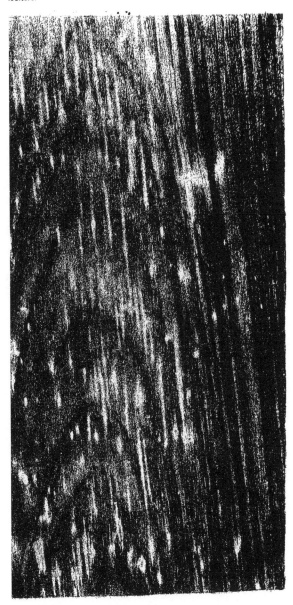

CTION OF YELLOW-BIRCH PROPELLER STOCK.
ent decay here shown is caused by the false tinder fungus.

LITERATURE CITED.

(1) ANONYMOUS.
    1919. Dipping treatment for prevention of sap stain. *In* Timberman, v. 20, no. 7, p. 35, illus.

    1919. How to distinguish black ash from commercial white ash lumber. *In* Tech. Notes (U. S. Forest Serv., Forest Products Lab.) No. D–11.

(3) BAILEY, IRVING W.
    1910. Oxidizing enzymes and their relation to "sap stain" in lumber. *In* Bot. Gaz., v. 50, p. 142–147.

(4) BETTS, HAROLD S.
    1917. The seasoning of wood. U. S. Dept. Agr. Bul. 552, 28 p., 18 fig., 8 pl.

(5) BLAIR, R. J.
    1919. Fungi which decay weaveshed roofs. (Abstract.) *In* Phytopathology, v. 9, p. 54–55.

(6) BOYCE, J. S.
    1918. Advance rot and latent defects in aeroplane timber. *In* Aerial Age Weekly, v. 7, p. 674–675, 691. Bibliography, p. 691.

(7)   1918. Detection of decays, advance rots and other defects in wood. *In* Bur. Aircraft Production, Inspection Manual, QT–16, 6 p.

(8)   1920. The dry-rot of incense cedar. U. S. Dept. Agr. Bul. 871, 58 p., 3 fig., 3 pl. Literature cited, p. 57–58.

(9) BRICK, C.
    1911. Zythia resinae (Fr.) Karst. als unangenehmer Bauholzpilz. *In* Jahresber. Angew. Bot·, Jahrg. 8, 1910, p. 164–170. Bibliographical footnotes.

(10) BROWN, H. P.
    1913. Pith-ray flecks in wood. U. S. Dept. Agr., Forest Serv. Circ. 215, 15 p., 6 pl. References, p. 14–15.

(11) BURKE, H. E.
    1905. Black check in western hemlock. U. S. Dept. Agr., Bur. Ent. Circ. 61, 10 p., 5 fig.

(12) DUNLAP, FREDERICK.
    1906. Kiln-drying hardwood lumber. U. S. Dept. Agr., Forest Serv. Circ. 48, 19 p., 4 fig.

(13)   1914. Density of wood substance and porosity of wood. *In* Jour. Agr. Research, v. 2, p. 423–428.

(14) EXNER, WILHELM FRANZ.
    1912. Die technischen Eigenschaften der Hölzer. *In* Handbuch der Forstw. Aufl. 3, Bd. 2, p. 342–442, 3 fig. Tübingen. Bibliographical footnotes.

(15) FUCHS, GILBERT.
    1905. Über das Ringeln der Spechte und ihr Verhalten gegen die kleineren Forstschädlinge. *In* Natürw. Ztschr. Land-u. Forstw., Jahrg. 3, p. 317–341, 7 fig., pl. 7. Bibliographical footnotes.

(16) GLOVER, H. M.
    1919. Spruce red wood. *In* Indian Forester, v. 45, p. 243–245.

(17) GREENE, CHARLES T.
    1914. The cambium miner in river birch. *In* Jour. Agr. Research,
        v. 1, p. 471–474, pl. 60–61.

(18) GROOM, PERCY.
    1915. "Brown oak" and its origin. *In* Ann. Bot., v. 29, p. 393–408.

(19)   1920⁻ Brown oak. *In* Quart. Jour. Forestry, v. 14, p. 103–109.

(20) GROSSENBACHER, J. G.
    1910. Medullary spots: A contribution to the life history of some
        cambium miners. N. Y. Agr. Exp. Sta. (Geneva) Tech. Bul. 15,
        p. 49–65, 5 pl. Bibliographical footnotes.

(21)   1915. Medullary spots and their cause. *In* Bul. Torrey Bot. Club, v.
        42, p. 227–239, pl. 10–11.

(22) HARTIG, ROBERT.
    1902. Der echte Hausschwamm . . . Aufl. 2. vii, 105 p., 33 fig. (partly
        col.). Berlin.

(23) HEDGCOCK, GEORGE GRANT.
    1906. Studies upon some chromogenic fungi which discolor wood. *In*
        Mo. Bot. Gard. 17th Ann. Rpt., p. 59–114, illus., pl. 3–12.
        Bibliographical footnotes.

(24) ———— and LONG, W. H.
    1914. Heart-rot of oaks and poplars caused by Polyporus dryophilus.
        In Jour. Agr. Research, v. 3, p. 65–78, pl. 8–10. Literature
        cited, p. 77.

(25) HOWARD, N. O.
    1922. The control of sap-stain, mold, and incipient decay in green
        wood, with special reference to vehicle stock. U. S. Dept.
        Agr. Bul. 1037, 55 p., 26 fig., 2 pl. Literature cited, p. 52–55.

(26) HOXIE, F. J.
    1915. Dry-rot in factory timbers. 107 p., 70 fig. Boston.

(27) HUBERT, ERNEST E.
    1921. Notes on sap-stain fungi. *In* Phytopathology, v. 11, p. 214–224,
        4 fig., pl. 7. Literature cited, p. 223–224.

(28) HUMPHREY, C. J.
    1917. Timber storage conditions in the Eastern and Southern States
        with reference to decay problems. U. S. Dept. Agr. Bul. 510,
        43 p., 41 fig., 10 pl. Bibliographical footnotes.

(29) KHAN, A. HAFIZ.
    1919. Red wood of Himalayan spruce (*Picea morinda* Link). *In*
        Indian Forester, v. 45, p. 496–498.

(30) KOEHLER, ARTHUR.
    1917. Guidebook for the identification of woods used for ties and
        timbers. U. S. Dept. Agr., Forest Serv., 79 p., 8 fig., 31 pl.,
        11 maps.

(31)   1918. The "grain" of wood with special reference to the direction of
        the fibers. *In* Bur. Aircraft Production, Inspection Manual,
        QT–13, 8 p., 12 fig.

(32) LINDROTH, J. IVAR.
    1904. Beiträge zur Kenntnis der Zersetzungserscheinungen des Birken-
        holzes. *In* Naturw. Ztschr. Land-u. Forstw., Jahrg. 2, p. 393–
        406, 7 fig. Bibliographical footnotes.

(33) LONG, WILLIAM H.
    1914. A preliminary note on the cause of "pecky" cypress. (Ab-
        stract.) *In* Phytopathology, v. 4, p. 39.

(34)   1915. A honeycomb heart-rot of oaks caused by Stereum subpileatum.
        In Jour. Agr. Research, v. 5, p. 421–428, pl. 41. Bibliographi-
        cal footnotes.

(35) McATEE, W. L.
1911. Woodpeckers in relation to trees and wood products. U. S.
Dept. Agr., Biol. Survey Bul. 39, 99 p., 44 fig., 12 pl. Bibliography, p. 55–56.

(36) MacMILLAN, H. R.
1916. Timber trade of South Africa. In Timberman, v. 17, no. 8, p.
34–39.

(37) MEINECKE, E. P.
1916. Forest pathology in forest regulation. U. S. Dept. Agr. Bul. 275,
63 p. Bibliographical footnotes.

(38) MÜNCH, ERNST.
1905–1906. Die Blaufäule des Nadelholzes. In Naturw. Ztschr. Land-
u. Forstw., Jahrg. 5' p. 531–573; Jahrg. 6, p. 32–47, 297–323,
33 fig. Bibliographical footnotes.

(39) NEGER, F. W.
1910. Die Vergrünung des frischen Lindenholzes. In Natürw. Ztschr.
Forst u. Landw., Jahrg. 8, p. 305–313, 2 fig.

(40) 1911. Die Rötung des frischen Erlenholzes. In Natürw. Ztschr. Forst-
u. Landw., Jahrg. 9, p. 96–105, 2 fig.

(41) NEWLIN, J. A., and WILSON, T. R. C.
1919. The relation of the shrinkage and strength properties of wood
to its specific gravity. U. S. Dept. Agr. Bul. 676, 35 p., 9 fig.
(partly fold.).

(42) OAKLEAF, H. B. (revised by BOYCE, J. S.).
1918. Important defects in wood. In Bur. Aircraft Production, Inspection Manual, QT–10a, 18 p., 10 figs.

(43) PRATT, MERRITT B.
1915. The deterioration of lumber. Calif. Agr. Exp. Sta. Bul. 252, p.
301–320, 8 fig.

(44) RECORD, SAMUEL J.
1911. Pith flecks or medullary spots in wood. In Forestry Quart., v.
9, p. 244–252, illus. References cited, p. 251–252.

(45) 1914. The mechanical properties of wood . . . Ed. 1. xi, 165 p., 52
fig., front. New York. Bibliography, p. 145–160.

(46) 1918. Defects in airplane woods. In Sci. Amer., v. 119, p. 212, 218–
219, illus.

(47) 1919. Identification of the economic woods of the United States . . .
Ed. 2. ix, 157 p., 15 fig., 6 pl. New York. References, p.
109–117. Bibliography, p. 119–125.

(48) ROTH, FILBERT.
1895. Timber: An elementary discussion of the characteristics and
properties of wood. U. S. Dept. Agr., Div. Forestry Bul.
10, 88 p., 49 fig.

(49) RUDELOFF, M.
1897–1899. Untersuchung über den Einfluss des Blauwerdens auf die
Festigkeit von Kiefernholz. Sonderabdruck aus den Mitt. K.
technischen Versuchsanstalten, 1897, p. 1–46, 55 fig.; 1899, p.
209–239, 9 fig.

(50) RUMBOLD, CAROLINE.
1911. Blue stain on lumber. In Science, n. s. v. 34, p. 94–96.

(51) 1911. Über die Einwirkung des Säure- und Alkaligehaltes des Nähr-
bodens auf das Wachstum der holzzersetzenden und holzver-
färbenden Pilze; mit einer Erörtung über die systematischen
Beziehungen zwischen Ceratostomella und Graphium. In
Naturw. Ztschr. Forst- u. Landw., Jahrg. 9, p. 429–466, 22 fig.
on 3 pl.

(52) Schramm, W. H.
    1906. Zum Vergrauen der Holzer. *In* Jahresber. Angew. Bot., Jahrg. 4,
        1906, p. 140–153. Bibliographical footnotes.

(53)   1907. Zu den Farbenangaben bei Hölzern. *In* Jahresber. Angew. Bot.,
        Jahrg. 4, 1906, p. 154–163. Bibliographical footnotes.

(54)   1907. Zur Holzvergilbung. *In* Jahresber. Angew. Bot., Jahrg. 4, 1906,
        p. 116–139. Bibliographical footnotes.

(55) Schrenk, Hermann von.
    1900. Some diseases of New England conifers. U. S. Dept. Agr., Div.
        Veg. Phys. and Path. Bul. 25, 56 p., 3 fig., 15 pl. Bibliographi-
        cal footnotes.

(56)   1903. The "bluing" and the "red rot" of the western yellow pine,
        with special reference to the Black Hills Forest Reserve.
        U. S. Dept. Agr., Bur. Plant Ind. Bul. 36, 40 p., 14 pl. (partly
        col.).

(57)   1903. The brown-rot disease of the redwood. *In* U. S. Dept. Agr.,
        Bur. For. Bul. 38, p. 29–31, pl. 10–11.

(58)   1903. A disease of the white ash caused by Polyporus fraxinophilus.
        U. S. Dept. Agr., Bur. Plant Ind. Bul. 32, 20 p., 1 fig., 5 pl.

(59)   1907. Sap-rot and other diseases of the red gum. U. S. Dept. Agr.,
        Bur. Plant Ind. Bul. 114, 37 p., 8 pl.

(60) Sparhawk, W. N.
    1919. Supplies and production of aircraft woods. National Advisory
        Commit. for Aeronautics Rpt. No. 67, 62 p., 23 maps. (Pre-
        print from 5th Ann. Rpt.)

(61) Spaulding, Perley.
    1906. Studies on the lignin and cellulose of wood. *In* Mo. Bot. Gard.
        17th Ann. Rpt., p. 41–58, pl. 1–2 (col.). Bibliographical
        footnotes.

(62)   1911. The timber rot caused by Lenzites sepiaria. U. S. Dept. Agr.,
        Bur. Plant Ind. Bul. 214, 46 p., 3 fig., 4 pl. Bibliography, p.
        31–37.

(63) Tiemann, Harry Donald.
    1907. The strength of wood as influenced by moisture. U. S .Dept.
        Agr., Forest Serv. Circ. 108, 42 p., 6 fig. Bibliographical foot-
        notes.

(64)   1912. Principles of drying lumber at atmospheric pressure and humid-
        ity diagram. U. S. Dept. Agr., Forest Serv. Bul. 104, 19 p.,
        2 fig. (1 fold.).

(65)   [1917]. The Kiln Drying of Lumber ... xi, 316 p., 54 fig. in text
        and on pl., 8 pl. (1 fold.). Philadelphia, London.

(66)   1917. The theory of drying and its application to the new humidity-
        regulated and recirculating dry kiln. U. S. Dept. Agr. Bul.
        509, 28 p., 3 fig.

(67) Tubeuf, C. von.
    1897. Die Zellgänge der Birke und anderer Laubhölzer. *In* Forstl.
        Naturw. Ztschr., Jahrg. 6, p. 314–319, 3 fig.

(68) U. S. Dept. Agr., Forest Products Laboratory.
    1918. Information for inspectors of airplane wood. Bur. Aircraft
        Production, Inspection Dept., 72 p., 52 fig., 2 pl. Washington,
        D. C.

(69)   1919. Wood in aircraft construction. Reprinted from Aircraft De-
        sign Data, Bur. Construction and Repair, Navy Dept., 149 p.,
        82 fig. Washington, D. C.

(70) Wagner, Joseph B.
    1917. Seasoning of Wood ... xiii, 274 p., 101 fig. (1 fold.). New
        York. Bibliography, p. 251.

(71) WEIR, JAMES R., and HUBERT, ERNEST E.
1918. A study of heart-rot in western hemlock. U. S. Dept. Agr. Bul. 722, 39 p., 13 fig. Bibliographical footnotes.

(72) WEISS, HOWARD F., and BARNUM, CHARLES T.
1911. The prevention of sap stain in lumber. U. S. Dept. Agr., Forest Serv. Circ. 192, 19 p., 4 fig.

(73) WILSON, T. R. C.
1920. The effect of kiln drying on the strength of airplane woods. National Advisory Commit. for Aeronautics Rpt. No. 68, 69 p., 22 fig., 9 pl., 27 tables. (Preprint from 5th Ann. Rpt.)

(74) ZELLER, SANFORD M.
1917. Studies in the physiology of the fungi.—III. Physical properties of wood in relation to decay induced by Lenzites saepiaria Fries. In Ann. Mo. Bot. Gard., v. 4, p. 93–164, 1 fig., 11 charts (partly double), pl. 9–13. Bibliography, p. 154–155.

(75)   1920. Humidity in relation to moisture imbibition by wood and to spore germination on wood. In Ann. Mo. Bot. Gard., v. 7, p. 51–74, 5 fig., pl. 1. Literature cited, p. 72–73.

DEFECTS OF WOOD REFERRED TO IN THIS BULLETIN, ARRANGED BY SPECIES.

ORGANIZATION OF THE UNITED STATES DEPARTMENT OF AGRICULTURE.

Secretary of Agriculture_____ HENRY C. WALLACE.
Assistant Secretary_____ C. W. PUGSLEY.
Director of Scientific Work_____ E. D. BALL.
Director of Regulatory Work_____
Weather Bureau_____ CHARLES W. MARVIN, Chief.
Bureau of Agricultural Economics_____ HENRY C. TAYLOR, Chief.
Bureau of Animal Industry_____ JOHN R. MOHLER, Chief.
Bureau of Plant Industry_____ WILLIAM A. TAYLOR, Chief.
Forest Service_____ W. B. GREELEY, Chief.
Bureau of Chemistry_____ WALTER G. CAMPBELL, Acting Chief.
Bureau of Soils_____ MILTON WHITNEY, Chief.
Bureau of Entomology_____ L. O. HOWARD, Chief.
Bureau of Biological Survey_____ E. W. NELSON, Chief.
Bureau of Public Roads_____ THOMAS H. MACDONALD, Chief.
Fixed-Nitrogen Research Laboratory_____ F. G. COTTRELL, Director.
Division of Accounts and Disbursements__ A. ZAPPONE, Chief.
Division of Publications_____ JOHN L. COBBS, Jr., Chief.
Library_____ CLARIBEL R. BARNETT, Librarian.
States Relations Service_____ A. C. TRUE, Director.
Federal Horticultural Board_____ C. L. MARLATT, Chairman.
Insecticide and Fungicide Board_____ J. K. HAYWOOD, Chairman.
Packers and Stockyards Administration____⎱CHESTER MORRILL, Asistant to the
Grain Future-Trading Act Administration__⎰ Secretary.
Office of the Solicitor_____ R. W. WILLIAMS, Solicitor.

This bulletin is a contribution from—

Bureau of Plant Industry_____ WILLIAM A. TAYLOR, Chief.
    Office of Investigations in Forest Pa-   HAVEN METCALF, Pathologist in
      thology.   Charge.
52

UNITED STATES DEPARTMENT·OF AGRICULTURE

BULLETIN No. 1129

Washington, D. C.　　▼　　November 27, 1922

A PHYSICAL AND CHEMICAL STUDY OF MILO AND FETERITA KERNELS.

By George L. Bidwell, Leslie E. Bopst, and John D. Bowling, *Cattle Food and Grain Investigation Laboratory, Miscellaneous Division, Bureau of Chemistry.*

CONTENTS.

PURPOSE OF INVESTIGATION.

The grain sorghums are a comparatively new crop in the United States, where they have been grown for only 25 or 30 years (2).[1] At first their use was largely restricted to the feeding of farm animals. These grains, however, are now being used in increasing quantities for human food .and various industrial purposes, and are receiving attention from manufacturers of alcohol and starch.. ·Feterita and milo, which contain on an average 65 per cent of starch, seem to be especially suitable as raw material for the manufacture of high-grade starch by commercial processes.

As a basis for a process utilizing nonsaccharine sorghums in the manufacture of starch and feeding stuffs, and to provide data for engineers who may be called upon to design machinery for their treatment, the Bureau of Chemistry has conducted a study on the physical characteristics and the chemical composition of milo and feterita kernels and the various parts into which they might be separated by milling. This study is a continuation of similar work done on the kafir kernel, the results of which are published in United States Department of Agriculture Bulletin 634. Milo and feterita. have the same botanical characteristics and the kernels very much the same structure as the kafir kernel (Fig. 1). The data on corn and kafir herein reported are taken from Bulletin 634.

[1] The numbers in parentheses throughout this bulletin refer to the bibliography on page 8.

12343°—22

PHYSICAL PROPERTIES OF KERNELS.

Fifty kernels of milo and 50 kernels of feterita were measured with a micrometer in three directions. [2] As the kernels lay on a flat surface, the vertical diameter was called the thickness, the distance from the hilum to the opposite end the length, and the dimension at right angles to these the width. The maximum, minimum, and average dimensions are given in Tables 1 and 2.

TABLE 1.—*Measurements of 50 kernels of dwarf milo.*

Dimensions.	Maxi-mum.	Mini-mum.	Aver-age.
	Milli-meters.	*Milli-meters.*	*Milli-meters.*
Thickness	3.12	2.31	2.88
Width	5.05	2.69	4.47
Length	5.13	2.81	4.42

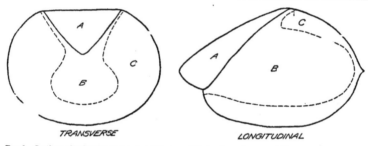

FIG. 1.—Sections of kafir kernels showing (*A*) germ, (*B*) starchy endosperm, (*C*) horny endosperm.

One thousand kernels of milo weighed 33.9 grams. Therefore, one kernel weighs on an average 0.0339 gram. Calculated from the measurements recorded in Table 1, the average volume of these kernels is 29.8 cubic millimeters and the surface of such a kernel is 48.3 square millimeters.

TABLE 2.—*Measurements of 50 kernels of dwarf feterita.*

Dimensions.	Maxi-mum.	Mini-mum.	Aver-age.
	Milli-meters.	*Milli-meters.*	*Milli-meters.*
Thickness	3.12	2.28	2.76
Width	4.82	3.83	4.18
Length	4.85	3.76	4.39

One thousand kernels of feterita weighed 32.7 grams. Therefore, one kernel weighs on an average 0.0327 gram. Calculated from the measurements recorded in Table 2, the average volume of these

---

[2] The feterita and milo used in this work were obtained from the Office of Cereal Investigations, Bureau of Plant Industry, U. S. Department of Agriculture, and were identified under the following numbers: Dwarf Milo C. I. 332 and Feterita C. I. 182.

kernels is 25.5 cubic millimeters and the surface of such a kernel is 44.9 square millimeters.

Table 3 gives the proportions of the component parts of the kernel.

TABLE 3.—*Proportion of component parts of kernels.*

Kernels.	Bran.		Germ.		Endosperm.	
	Proportion of kernel separated.	Average volume in kernel (calculated).	Proportion of kernel separated.	Average volume in kernel (calculated).	Proportion of kernel separated.	Average volume in kernel (calculated.)
	Per cent.	Cubic millimeters.	Per cent.	Cubic millimeters.	Per cent.	Cubic millimeters.
Corn	7.4	....	11.5	....	81.1	....
Kafir	6.1	1.02	10.0	1.68	83.9	14.10
Milo	5.5	1.63	11.1	3.30	83.4	24.80
Feterita	6.6	1.68	7.3	1.86	86.1	21.93

The calculations in Table 3 are based on the assumption that the different parts of the kernel have the same specific gravity. On this assumption the thickness of the milo bran would average 0.033 millimeter, while that of the feterita bran would be 0.037 millimeter. It is realized that there are differences in the specific gravity of these tissues, but they are too small to affect the conclusions here drawn.

CHEMICAL COMPOSITION OF KERNELS.

Table 4 gives a comparison of the composition of the whole kernels of the kafir, milo, and feterita, on a water-free basis.

TABLE 4.—*Comparison of composition of kafir, milo, and feterita kernels on a water-free basis.*

Kernels.	Proportion of kernel.	Ash.	Ether extract.	Protein.	Crude fiber.	Nitrogen-free extract.	Starch.	Pentosans.
	Per cent.	Per cent.	Per cent.	Per cent.	Per cent.	Per cent.	Per cent.	Per cent.
Kafir	100	1.80	4.10	12.70	1.80	79.60	61.90	3.30
Milo	100	1.89	3.47	13.99	1.93	78.72	68.52	3.95
Feterita	100	1.79	3.06	16.69	2.22	76.24	64.16	3.38

In these comparisons the greatest differences are observed in the protein and starch content. The other results show little variation.

In Tables 5, 6, 7, and 8 comparisons are made between the parts of the corn and kafir kernel and the corresponding parts of the milo and feterita kernel.

TABLE 5.—*Comparison of corn hulls and kafir bran with milo and feterita brans.*

Material.	Proportion of kernel.	Ash.	Ether extract.	Protein.	Crude fiber.	Carbohydrates.	Starch.	Pentosans.
	Per cent.	Per cent.	Per cent.	Per cent.	Per cent.	Per cent.	Per cent.	Per cent.
Corn hulls	7.4	0.79	0.89	3.96	....	94.36	....	18.40
Kafir bran	6.1	2.00	6.80	4.80	16.20	70.20	....	21.35
Milo bran	5.5	3.07	4.33	7.08	15.36	70.16	1.60	15.79
Feterita bran	6.6	2.95	5.74	6.85	13.56	70.90	3.89	

In studying these results it will be noted that the amount of ash and ether extract in the corn hulls is decidedly lower than that in the bran of kafir, milo, or feterita. These determinations in the kafir, milo, and feterita appear to resemble one another fairly closely.

TABLE 6.—*Comparison of corn and kafir horny endosperm with milo and feterita horny endosperm.*

Horny endosperm.	Proportion of kernel.	Ash.	Ether extract.	Protein.	Crude fiber.	Carbohydrates.	Starch.	Pentosans.
	Per cent.	Per cent.	Per cent.	Per cent.	Per cent.	Per cent.	Per cent.	Per cent.
Corn	55.6	0.44	1.15	11.85	....	86.56	....	....
Kafir	48.9	.30	.70	14.50	....	83.80	68.80	0.70
Milo	54.7	.56	.15	15.11	0.70	83.49	72.24	.69
Feterita	61.1	.71	.33	19.75	2.12	77.09	60.36	2.12

The most noticeable differences among these results are in the comparatively high fat content of the corn and the comparatively high protein content of feterita.

TABLE 7.—*Comparison of corn and kafir starchy endosperm with milo and feterita starchy endosperm.*

Starchy endosperm.	Proportion of kernel.	Ash.	Ether extract.	Protein.	Crude fiber.	Carbohydrates.	Starch.	Pentosans.
	Per cent.	Per cent.	Per cent.	Per cent.	Per cent.	Per cent.	Per cent.	Per cent.
Corn	25.5	0.26	0.24	7.84	....	91.66	....	....
Kafir	35.0	.30	.80	11.66	....	86.44	70.40	1.90
Milo	28.7	.71	.28	8.91	0.80	89.29	82.50	4.35
Feterita	25.1	.96	.64	10.61	2.38	85.41	75.84	4.66

These results show a marked similarity, the protein content being slightly higher in the kafir than in the other grains.

TABLE 8.—*Comparison of the corn and kafir germ with the milo and feterita germ.*

Germ.	Proportion of kernel.	Ash.	Ether extract.	Protein.	Crude fiber.	Carbohydrates.	Starch.	Pentosans.
	Per cent.	Per cent.	Per cent.	Per cent.	Per cent.	Per cent.	Per cent.	Per cent.
Corn	11.5	9.90	34.84	19.80	....	35.46	....	....
Kafir	10.0	13.20	31.50	19.30	3.80	32.20	....	6.10
Milo	11.1	9.46	19.92	20.84	9.11	40.67	1.53	8.57
Feterita	7.3	11.35	25.45	21.70	8.54	32.96	2.16	6.95

In Table 8 notice is immediately taken of the low ether extract of the milo germ. The other results show a great similarity.

A general consideration of all the tables shows that the protein content of the feterita is higher than that of the other grains. The horny endosperm in each case has more protein than the starchy endosperm. The germs of these sorghums are very similar in composition.

MALTING OF KAFIR, MILO, AND FETERITA.

While the work just reported was in progress the question of the diastatic power of malts made from these sorghums arose. For some time little attention has been paid to grains other than barley for malting purposes, as this grain has served the brewing industry satisfactorily. However, it was thought that a comparison of the diastatic power of barley with that of the sorghums, kafir, milo, and feterita might be of value.

MALTING PROCESS (5).

The grain was washed free from chaff, weed seeds, and other foreign material, covered with clean, fresh water, and allowed to stand for 12 hours, the water being replaced once or twice during this period. The water was then removed and the grain was allowed to stand for an additional 12 hours. This entire operation was repeated for such a time as was required to bring about complete steeping. The grain was considered thoroughly steeped when it could be crushed between the thumb and fingers and the inside was not hard or glassy, but soft and chalklike.

SPROUTING.

After the water had been removed the steeped grain was allowed to germinate at a temperature of 15.5° C. In about six days the sprouts which had been developing inside the seed coat forced their way out at the end of the grain opposite the rootlet. The germination was continued for from 8 to 14 days, or until the sprouts were about three or four times the length of the grain.

DRYING.

All moisture possible was expelled, at first at room temperature and finally at 40° C. It was found especially advantageous to observe the following precautions (4). To prevent molding as much as possible, the grain after being washed and soaked for one hour in water was allowed to stand for one-half hour in 0.24 per cent solution of formaldehyde, after which the steeping in water already described was continued. The grain was germinated between approximately sterile damp towels to prevent molding and drying, the towels being replaced every other day.

COMPARISON OF TEMPERATURE, TIME OF STEEPING, AND TIME OF GERMINATION OF GRAIN SORGHUMS.

A comparison of the temperature, time of steeping, and time of germination of the grain sorghums investigated is shown in Table 9.

TABLE 9.—*Comparison of temperature, time of steeping, and time of germination of grain sorghums.*

Malt.	Time of steeping.	Time of germination.	Average daily temperature during germination.
	Hours.	*Days.*	*°C.*
Kafir	30	14	17
Milo	30	8	20
Feterita	22	10	20

The difference in the time of steeping shown in Table 9 is due to the capacity of the various grains to absorb water, this capacity being governed principally by the hardness and compactness of the grain. The interior starchy portion of the kafir and milo kernels is harder and more glassy than that of the feterita, and consequently requires a longer time for the complete absorption of water. The time of germination varies in each case, but is governed to a large extent by the temperature. The grain required a shorter time for germination in cases where the temperature was higher.

DIASTATIC POWER OF MALTED GRAIN SORGHUMS.

After the malting was completed the finished malt was analyzed by the following methods:

Preparation of sample.—After the malt had been thoroughly mixed and a uniform sample taken, it was ground to pass a 20-mesh sieve.

Moisture.—Two grams of the ground malt was accurately weighed in a covered weighing dish and dried at 60° C. in a vacuum to constant weight.

Diastatic power (3).—Twenty-five grams of ground malt was extracted with 500 cubic centimeters of distilled water (free from ammonia, nitrates, etc.) for 3 hours at 21° C. and filtered. The first 100 cubic centimeters of the filtrate was rejected. Then 100 cubic centimeters of a 2 per cent starch solution (soluble starch prepared according to Lintner) was treated with 1 cubic centimeter of the malt extract of diastase solution for 1 hour at 21° C., 50 cubic centimeters of Fehling solution was added, and the whole was heated rapidly to 98° C. It was next placed in a boiling water bath for seven minutes, and, without being diluted, the cuprous oxid was filtered immediately, dried, and weighed. The weight of cuprous oxid was calculated to copper by the following factor: $\frac{Cu_2}{Cu_2O} = 0.8882$. The weight of copper found minus the weight of copper reduced by 100 cubic centimeters of the 2 per cent starch solution (determined by a blank on this amount carried through the regular procedure) was divided by 0.441 (gram of copper in 50 cubic centimeters of Fehling solution), and this result, multiplied by 100, gave the Lintner value.

Acidity.—Fifty grams of ground malt was digested with 300 cubic centimeters of distilled water at 15.5° C. for three hours. The acidity of the filtered extract was measured by titrating against N/20 sodium hydroxid and calculated to percentage of lactic acid.

A comparison of the diastatic power of some of the malted grain sorghums with that of a barley is shown in Table 10.

TABLE 10.—*Comparison of the diastatic powers of barley, kafir, feterita, and milo malts.*

Malt.	Moisture.	Diastatic power.		Acidity as lactic acid.	
		Moisture basis.	Dry basis.	Moisture basis.	Dry basis.
	Per cent.	Degrees.	Degrees.	Per cent.	Per cent.
Barley	6.73	162.4	174.1	0.176	0.189
Kafir	6.88	9.5	10.2	.221	.227
Feterita	5.22	35.0	36.9		
Milo	5.97	35.3	37.5		

The sample of barley malt shown in Table 10 is of exceptionally high diastatic power, being much higher in diastase than the ordinary dried brewing malts, which range between 20° and 40° Lintner, and therefore can not be taken as an average representative of that type. From the standpoint of the brewer, the color, flavor, and percentage of soluble material play a very important part, and the diastatic power is sacrificed to some extent to bring about these factors through the action of heat during drying. The grain sorghums shown in Table 10 were malted under conditions that would give the highest possible diastatic power, the other requirements of a good brewing malt being sacrificed to obtain this property.

The acidity of the kafir malt was determined as a check on the malting process for the purpose of showing that the acidity was not high enough to have any effect upon the diastatic power.

The results obtained show conclusively that the sorghums investigated do not meet the requirements of a green malt. The diastatic power of these sorghums, with the exception of kafir, is comparable with that of dried malts, when malted under conditions that would give the highest possible diastatic power. When subjected to temperatures that would give the color and flavor required in a dried malt, however, this diastatic power would be too low for all practical brewing purposes.

SUMMARY.

On the whole, the kafir, corn, milo, and feterita resemble one another in composition and appearance. The proximate constituents of the kernels of these four sorghums indicate their value as food for man and domestic animals, and show the possibility of their being used as raw products in certain important commercial operations having for their purpose the manufacture of starch, sirup, alcohol,

and oil, when proper machinery and processes have been devised.
It has been found, however, that it would probably be impracticable
to use them commercially for malting purposes.

BIBLIOGRAPHY.

(1) BIDWELL, G. L.   A physical and chemical study of the kafir
    kernel.   U. S. Dept. Agr. Bul. 634, 6·PP.   1918.
(2) CHURCHILL, O. O., and WRIGHT, A. H.   The grain sorghums.
    Okla. Agr. Exp. Sta. Bul. 102, 68 pp.   1914.
(3) SHERMAN, H. C., KENDALL, E. C., and CLARK, E. D.   Studies
    on amylases.   I. An examination of methods for the deter-
    mination of diastatic power.   In J. Am. Chem. Soc. (1910),
    32: 1076.
(4) STEWART, ROBERT, and STEPHENS, JOHN.   The effect of formalin
    on the vitality of seed grain.   Utah Agr. Exp. Sta. Bul. 108,
    10 pp.   1910.
(5) WENTE, A. O., and TOLMAN, L. M.   Potato culls as a source of
    industrial alcohol.   U. S. Dept. Agr. Farmers' Bul. 410, 'p.
    19–23.   1910.

This bulletin is a contribution from—

Bureau of Chemistry ....WALTER G. CAMPBELL, *Acting Chief.*
Miscellaneous Division..................J. K. HAYWOOD, *Chief.*

UNITED STATES DEPARTMENT OF AGRICULTURE

DEPARTMENT BULLETIN No. 1130

Washington, D. C. ▼ January 26, 1923

SIGNIFICANCE OF WHEAT HAIRS IN MICROSCOPICAL EXAMINATION OF FLOUR.

By George L. Keenan, *Microanalyst, Microchemical Laboratory, Bureau of Chemistry.*

CONTENTS.

PURPOSE OF METHOD.

Since the publication of United States Department of Agriculture Bulletin 839, "The Microscopical Examination of Flour," further study has suggested that the number of wheat hairs present in a weighed portion of the sample might be of value in classifying it.

Heretofore the grading of a flour by the original method has depended upon a count of the bran particles and hairs in a weighed portion of the sample. In practice, however, the identification of bran particles appears to be a more difficult task for the untrained eye than the recognition of wheat hairs or fragments of hairs. The bran particles occur in the flour in such a variety of forms that an analyst unaccustomed to the differentiation of histological sections under the microscope may encounter difficulties in obtaining consistent bran-particle counts. The wheat hairs and hair fragments, on the other hand, are readily identified and the quantity present in a sample has been found to be indicative of the flour grade.[1]

METHOD.

The method employed, which is similar to the one described in Department Bulletin 839, with some modifications, is as follows:

Carefully weigh out upon an accurate balance a 5-milligram portion of flour and transfer the weighed portion to the center of a microscope slide the surface of which has been ruled with lines running lengthwise and 1 millimeter apart. The flour having been transferred to the slide, mix about 4 drops of chloral hydrate solution (1:1) with the flour by means of a preparation needle. After making a uniform mixture of the flour and the chloral hydrate solution, apply a cover-glass 22 millimeters square and gently warm the slide on the hot

---

[1] The term "grade" is here used in a general way, to classify the assembled types of flour.

16243—23

plate until the preparation is properly cleared. The clearing is complete when the preparation becomes transparent. Then transfer the slide to the stage of the microscope and allow it to remain until no movement is evident in the mount when viewed under the microscope. .Count the hairs and hair fragments. The magnification giving approximately 180 diameters here employed was obtained by the use of compensating ocular 12 × and 16-millimeter apochromatic objective. If apochromatic objectives are not available, an achromatic objective with an ordinary eyepiece giving the same magnification is satisfactory.

COUNTING THE HAIRS.

The counting of a slide consists in the methodical enumeration of all the hairs and hair fragments in the mount (Fig. 1). By means

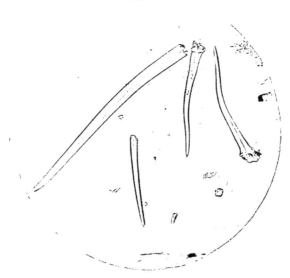

FIG. 1.—Wheat hairs (×180).

of the mechanical stage on the microscope, no difficulty is encountered in thoroughly and accurately covering the entire mount. Each hair and hair fragment is given a value of 1, the final number being taken as the value for the flour in question.

SOURCES OF VARIATION IN METHOD.

Department Bulletin 839 contains a full discussion of tests conducted to determine the sources of variation in such a method. It is evident that the variation in the counts made by two analysts is greater in the case of bran particles than in the case of hairs.

EXAMINATION OF MILL STOCKS.

Modern milling processes consist essentially in releasing the floury endosperm from the wheat grain, purifying it of bran substance, and eventually reducing it to what is known as flour. Any manipulation in the various steps of milling leading to the removal of an insufficient quantity of the bran material will eventually reveal itself in the finished flour. The method already described has been devised to detect such irregularities.

The break rolls in a mill are designed to crush the wheat kernel so that the inclosed endosperm may be released and later reduced to the fineness of flour on the smoother rolls. The general practice in milling is to make as little break flour as possible. When made to any extent, break flour invariably contains a large quantity of offal, consisting of hairs, hair fragments, and bran particles. The middlings

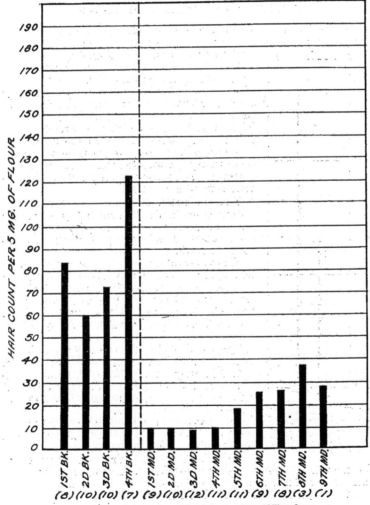

Fig. 2.—Average hair counts on 35 break flours and 74 middlings flours.

(granular particles of endosperm), on the contrary, are relatively free from hairs and bran particles after proper purification.

To illustrate these differences in break stocks and middlings stocks, a composite chart (Fig. 2) has been constructed. It is based on data obtained from 35 break flours and 74 middlings flours, the hair count being the average on all samples examined for each grade.

The break flours in each instance show a much higher hair count than any of the middlings stocks. The hair count of the middlings stock begins to increase with the fifth middlings, indicating that the first four middlings are much cleaner than the succeeding ones in the series.

EXAMINATION OF COMMERCIAL FLOURS.

Commercial grades of flour generally fall into four more or less sharply defined classes known as "patents," "straights," "clears," and "low grades." As a rule the so-called patent flours are limited to those which are composed of the first-class flour streams, most often those ground from purified middlings stocks. However, stocks other than first-class middlings are often passed into patent flours. When this is the case the proportion of offal in the flour increases. In Figure 3 the hair count of patent flours made from middlings stocks only is compared with that of patent flours containing lower-grade stocks in addition to middlings stocks.

The average hair count on 13 samples of patent flours made from middlings only is 13; the average hair count on 13 samples of patent flours made from lower-grade stocks in addition to middlings is 28.

When only one grade of flour is manufactured in the mill, it is commercially designated as a straight flour. It usually consists of all the flour that can be obtained from the wheat grain with the exception of some low-grade flour. Such a flour naturally contains more offal than a patent flour.

The so-called clear flours usually contain the lower grades of middlings and break flours, although they may contain the purer middlings from the tail of the mill. Naturally, the offal content of such flour is higher than that of patent and straight flours.

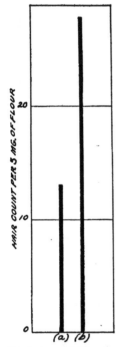

FIG. 3.—Average hair counts on patent flours made from middlings only and on those made from middlings and lower grade stocks. (a) Middlings only; (b) middlings and lower grade stocks.

The low-grade flour is made from low-grade stocks, the better stocks in the mill having been already diverted into the higher grades.

Table 1 shows the hair counts obtained on the samples of commercial flours examined. As might be expected, there is a variation in the counts for the different classes, doubtless due to the lack of uniformity in milling procedure.

Figure 4 illustrates the differences between the four so-called commercial grades of flour, based on the average hair count obtained for all samples examined under each grade. According to the manufacturers, these flours had been milled from hard, blended, and soft wheats, respectively, and the results obtained have been classified under these three general classes of wheat.

TABLE 1.—*Hair counts obtained on commercial samples of flour.* [1]

Sample No.	Patent flours.			Straight flours.			Clear flours.			Low-grade flours.		
	Hard wheat.	Blended wheat.	Soft wheat.	Hard wheat.	Blended wheat.	Soft wheat.	Hard wheat.	Blended wheat.	Soft wheat.	Hard wheat.	Blended wheat.	Soft wheat.
1	34	17	10	34	26	40	45	61	72	91	132	27
2	9	21	25	55	22	31	147	65	68	129	131	257
3	15	40	11	45	28	38	114	73	32	131	94	145
4	23	27	32	33	18	58	133	40	39	112	183	261
5	12	19	1	25	36	26	43	96	40	155	141	219
6	30	13	34	39	40	60	178	45	44	88	76	139
7	10	37	17	31	31	70	49	49	143	301	61	124
8	16	25	12	51	38	54	57	47	167	335	59	80
9	19	15	22	61	47	27	71	142	30	264		
10	9	18	29	87	30	71	93	98	66	163		
11	28	13	19	65	28	81	71	44	99	238		
12	31	13	26	19	29	40	102	67	164			
13	28		30	26	26	22	204		155			
14	24			47	37	34	140					
15	13			61	45	39	196					
16	39			17	47	34	124					
17	36			22	58	38	67					
18	2				37		68					
19	33						39					
20	2						119					
21	26						136					
22	14						62					
23	4						184					
24	10						102					
25	11						223					
26	12						126					
27	21						77					
28	15						98					
29	20						50					
30	20						166					
31	5						132					
32	9											
33	45											
34	13											
35	13											
36	8											
Average	18	21	20	42	34	44	110	68	86	182	109	156

[1] As the flours examined were milled under different conditions the counts vary with the milling practices at the various mills.

The average hair count on all patent flours examined was 19; on all straight flours, 40; on all clear flours, 88; and on all low-grade flours, 149. The average hair count obtained for each grade shows how distinctive the classification of these flours can be made by the method here described. With the exception of the hard-wheat clear flour and the soft-wheat low-grade flour, there is no indication that one grade overlaps another. The exception noted emphasizes the fact that grading practices in various mills lack uniformity. In other words, the same grade of flour from two mills might show a variation in the hair count as a result of the variations in the composition of the finished flour.

EXAMINATION OF EXPERIMENTAL SERIES OF FLOUR.

A study was also made of samples of flour whose composition, in so far as the mill streams entering into them is concerned, was definitely known.

Table 2 shows the hair counts obtained on these samples. These counts are more uniform and consistent than those for the commercial flours examined (Table 1). The results have been plotted in Figure 5.

An examination of the results obtained on the experimental series of flours, as compared with those obtained on the commercial flours, justifies the statement previously made that but little uniformity exists in grading finished flours in different mills. In other words, there is less overlapping between grades in the experimental flours than there is in commercial flours.

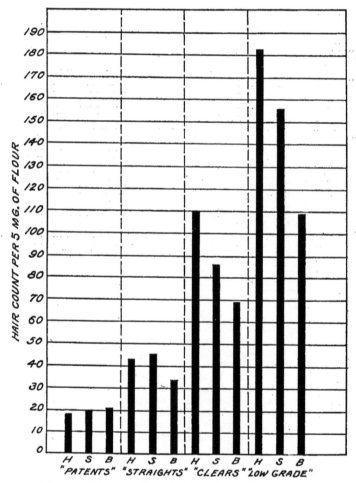

Fig 4.—Average hair count on 61 patent, 56 clear, 52 straight, and 16 low-grade flours.

TABLE 2.—*Hair counts obtained on experimental samples of flour.* [1]

Sample No.	Types of flour.				
	70 per cent.	97.5 per cent.	90 per cent.	27.5 per cent.	2.5 per cent.
1	13	28	26	45	129
2	13	29	22	49	131
3	18	26	28	47	112
4	12	39	31	65	....
5	9	29	28	51	....
6	....	30	34	40	....
Average	13	30	28	49	124

[1] As these flours were made under the supervision of the Bureau of Chemistry, their constituent streams were known. A description of the streams composing them is given in Department of Agriculture Bulletin 839.

SUMMARY.

Experimental data secured by the Bureau of Chemistry have shown in a general way the existence of a significant relationship between the wheat-hair count and the flour classified according to milling practices. Reliable information on the quality of the mill streams composing any finished flour was available only in the case of the experimental samples of flour. Consequently, any suggestion as to the tolerance to be applied in a method of this kind would be justified only when definite information concerning the milling process, such as the streams employed in composing a flour and the cleaning of the wheat, is at hand.

The data obtained on the experimental samples of flour, however, indicate the possibility of making an interesting classification based on the hair count alone. It is possible, of course, that the number of hairs or hair fragments from the brush of the wheat grain might differ materially, according to the variety of wheat used and the milling operations employed. Nevertheless, an examination of a large number of samples representing a great variety of milling practices indicates that flours made from purified middlings material show a low hair count, while flours containing lower-grade mill stocks show a higher hair count.

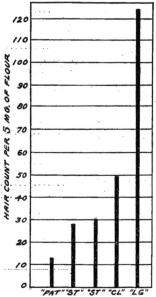

FIG. 5.—Average hair count on a 70 per cent patent, 90 and 97.5 per cent straight, 27.5 per cent clear, and 2.5 per cent low-grade flour.

ORGANIZATION OF THE UNITED STATES DEPARTMENT OF AGRICULTURE.

Secretary of Agriculture	HENRY C. WALLACE.
Assistant Secretary	C. W. PUGSLEY.
Director of Scientific Work	E. D. BALL.
Director of Regulatory Work	
Weather Bureau	CHARLES F. MARVIN, *Chief.*
Bureau of Agricultural Economics	HENRY C. TAYLOR, *Chief.*
Bureau of Animal Industry	JOHN R. MOHLER, *Chief.*
Bureau of Plant Industry	WILLIAM A. TAYLOR, *Chief.*
Forest Service	W. B. GREELEY, *Chief.*
Bureau of Chemistry	WALTER G. CAMPBELL, *Acting Chief.*
Bureau of Soils	MILTON WHITNEY, *Chief.*
Bureau of Entomology	L. O. HOWARD, *Chief.*
Bureau of Biological Survey	E. W. NELSON, *Chief.*
Bureau of Public Roads	THOMAS H. MACDONALD, *Chief.*
Fixed Nitrogen Research Laboratory	F. G. COTTRELL, *Director.*
Division of Accounts and Disbursements	A. ZAPPONE, *Chief.*
Division of Publications	JOHN L. COBBS, Jr., *Chief.*
Library	CLARIBEL R. BARNETT, *Librarian.*
States Relations Service	A. C. TRUE, *Director.*
Federal Horticultural Board	C. L. MARLATT, *Chairman.*
Insecticide and Fungicide Board	J. K. HAYWOOD, *Chairman.*
Packers and Stockyards Administration	CHESTER MORRILL, *Assistant to the*
Grain Future Trading Act Administration	*Secretary.*
Office of the Solicitor	R. W. WILLIAMS, *Solicitor.*

This bulletin is a contribution from—

Bureau of Chemistry	WALTER G. CAMPBELL, *Acting Chief.*
Microchemical Laboratory	B. J. HOWARD, *in Charge.*

8

UNITED STATES DEPARTMENT OF AGRICULTURE

DEPARTMENT BULLETIN No. 1131

| Washington, D. C. | PROFESSIONAL PAPER | February 13, 1923 |

THE FORMATION AND PATHOLOGICAL ANATOMY OF FROST RINGS IN CONIFERS INJURED BY LATE FROSTS.

By Arthur S. Rhoads, formerly *Assistant in Forest Pathology, Office of Investigations in Forest Pathology, Bureau of Plant Industry.*

CONTENTS.

INTRODUCTION.

Various writers have shown that an abnormal or pathologic parenchyma tissue may occur as an interruption of the normal course of the wood elements in the growth rings of coniferous trees, resulting from a variety of widely different causes, which may either directly or indirectly influence the growth of the cambium. Among these causes may be enumerated mechanical injuries of any kind; attacks by various cryptogamic and phanerogamic parasites which stimulate the woody tissue to an abnormal development; abnormal physiological conditions of growth and nutrition which per se produce a like effect; premature defoliation; and injuries resulting from such meteorological causes as lightning, frost, and drought. The last-mentioned three forms of injury have rather distinctive anatomical characteristics which are scarcely recognized in this country and additional knowledge of these is highly desirable.

Owing to its close resemblance to the disturbances in the wood caused by certain forms of lightning injury which he was studying, the writer was impelled to investigate also the pathological anatomy of late-frost injury. The present bulletin is therefore designed as a contribution to our knowledge of the pathological anatomy of late-frost injury in the conifers.

The material used as a basis of this study was collected by the writer in connection with his field work in various parts of northern Idaho, northeastern Washington, and northwestern Montana and was supplemented by material collected later in the District of Columbia and in Missouri. The photomicrographs were made by the writer from his own sectional preparations.

18163—22——1

REVIEW OF THE LITERATURE.

Despite the great mass of literature on the subject of frost injury, there are but few descriptions of the pathological effect of the injury on the structure of the wood. In fact, the effect on forest growth of temperatures below the freezing point, or frost, is seldom considered, except in so far as it causes injuries the external manifestations of which are readily apparent.

The so-called frost rings, or "moon rings," as they sometimes are called when extending only a part of the way around the stem, occurring in young trees as a result of the action of frost, have been mentioned by various European writers, but it is only rarely that their structure and origin have been studied from the standpoint of their pathological anatomy, and illustrations of this abnormality are rare.

Mayr (5, p. 36)[1] states that the stimulating action of a mild late frost on the annual ring already in a state of cambial activity exerts itself in such a way that in place of the elongated tracheids a short-celled parenchyma arises. According to Mayr (5, p. 37), this abnormal wood may occur either on only one side of the stem or extend entirely around it, depending upon the way in which the cold air strikes the plant. In either case internal healing ensues, proceeding from the parenchyma cells of the wood, which fill up possible cavities with wound parenchyma, while a new cambium is developed in the bark from the bast parenchyma remaining alive. In addition, Mayr states that if the frost has killed the bast together with the cambial layer, then the entire plant part dies.

Hartig (2) investigated the action of a May frost on the shoots of young trees of *Pinus sylvestris*. He describes in detail the formation of zones of parenchyma tissue, which constitute the so-called frost ring, in the growth ring developing during the year of the injury. He likewise describes the peculiar permanent distortion of the injured young shoots, a circumstance occasioned by their loss of turgor and consequent drooping after the freezing, followed by an effort to redirect their shoots upward. In many cases, however, the whorls of shoots were killed outright.

Hartig also investigated the formation of similar frost rings in young trees of *Picea excelsa*, *Larix europaea*, and *Chamaecyparis lawsoniana*, but he illustrates their formation only in *Pinus sylvestris* and *Picea excelsa*. He states that frost-ring formation was so frequent in a spruce 2 meters high that he counted 10 frost rings in a section about 15 years old, so that 25 rings were to be counted in a casual macroscopic examination. The frost-ring formation extended down into the stem parts, which were 10 to 12 years old. In the larch the frost rings occurred only in its youth, as in the spruce, and were found only in the youngest to the 4-year-old axes; in the Lawson cypress, however, frost rings still occurred in the older axial parts, and such ring formation was noted also in the interior of the phloem. Hartig gives the same account later in his textbook of plant diseases (3).

---

[1] Serial numbers (italic) in parentheses refer to "Literature cited" at the end of this bulletin.

Petersen (*9*) describes and illustrates the zone of parenchyma tissue or frost ring which resulted in a double-ring formation in beech trees which had suffered from frost on May 17 and 18 in Holland.

Tubeuf (*14*, pl. 31, fig. 1), in an article upon the pathological anatomy of spruce trees that were dying back from the top in consequence of drought injury, evidently for the sake of comparison, illustrates a portion of a frost ring in a small tree of *Picea excelsa*. However, he makes no allusion in the text to frost injury, which would seem to be due to his apparent failure to publish the concluding part of the article.

Sorauer, who was able to add the action of frost to the causes which bring about the formation of false annual rings (*12*, p. 320), later gives the details of an extensive study to determine the effects of early and late frosts on the mature and immature wood of a large number of fruit and forest trees (*13*). He found that eruptions in the vascular cylinder are generally manifested either in radial clefts within the medullary rays or in tangential cracks within the cambial region. In addition, many cavities appear in the pith and the bark parenchyma. The separated tissue within the cambium region gradually heals over, after presenting the appearance of a ring growth of two years. Sorauer discusses the formation of double rings from the activity of frost and gives the same account of this in the last edition of his manual of plant diseases (*12*) as well as a detailed account of the injurious action of frost injury in general upon plant tissue. Here (p. 577) he describes the brown circular zones, or "frost lines," frequently occurring in fruit trees after spring frosts and composed of collapsed, misshapen cells. The occurrence of this phenomenon was also investigated experimentally in artificial freezing experiments.

Graebner (*1*), who investigated the action of late frosts on oak, beech, spruce, and fir, makes no mention of frost-ring formation as such, but does mention a wound-parenchyma formation that can be followed back into the 2-year-old and 3-year-old wood.

Neger (*7*) investigated a tip blight of *Picea excelsa* with which two ascomycetous fungi were associated; however, they were found only on shoots that had been injured by frost. Sections of the stems, taken both through the dead tips and through the still living stems, showed a more or less broad zone of parenchyma wood or frost ring occurring in the beginning of the 1913 growth ring. Since this parenchyma zone followed immediately upon the summer wood of the 1912 growth ring and was not preceded by normal spring-wood tracheids, it was assumed that a late frost was not involved, but rather an early frost occurring in the fall of 1912. While the frost of 1912 did not come particularly early, relatively low temperatures occurred in comparison with other years, following upon a cold wet summer, which greatly retarded the maturation of the axial growth of that year. This injury therefore was considered to be more nearly due to the action of the winter frost upon immature wood. Tubeuf (*15*) had previously briefly described and illustrated a tip blight of *Picea excelsa* due to the same causes, but he does not go into the pathological anatomy of the injured shoots. According to Neger, the frost injury had the effect of suspending or at least

reducing the bark pressure, with the result that a zone of parenchyma wood was developed as the first growth in the following
spring instead of the normal tracheidal wood, in so far as the stem
had remained living and continued its annual ring formation. In
his textbook, which appeared later, Neger (8) briefly describes frost
rings and reproduces an illustration of one caused by this winter
frost.

Somerville (11) describes an abnormal zone of parenchyma tissue
that is very closely related to frost rings, if not actually identical
with them. This abnormal zone occurred in the early-spring wood
of a large percentage of young conifers whose wood he had occasion to examine. All of the species examined, including *Larix leptolepis, Pseudotsuga douglasii* (=*P. taxifolia*), *Tsuga albertiana*
(=*T. mertensiana*), *Cedrus deodara, Thuja plicata*, and *Picea
sitchensis*, exhibited more or less of the injury.

Somerville describes the abnormal wood formation only for *Larix
leptolepis*. He says that the abnormal wood formed in the early
part of 1912 is easily distinguished by the naked eye. On a cross
section it appears as a narrow brown ring, while on a radial section
it forms a thin brown streak. A microscopic examination shows
that the medullary rays are seen to pursue a most irregular course
and to consist of much elongated and swollen cells. The rays frequently are discontinuous with those of the previous ring. The intervening cells, many of which have walls much thickened, instead
of getting smaller as one proceeds outward, have a tendency to become larger. A radial section along the junction of the normal
summer wood and the abnormal spring wood of 1912 shows that
the abnormal zone of tissue is largely composed of irregularly
shaped parenchymatous cells with simple pits and rectangular transverse walls. It will thus be seen that the foregoing description of
Somerville's abnormal wood formation agrees closely with Neger's
description of frost rings, especially since they occur following immediately upon the summer wood of the preceding growth ring.

Somerville, however, states that the cause would appear to be the
excessive heat and drought of the summer and fall of 1911, which
seriously affected the growth of many trees, notably the Japanese
larch. He says:

This climatic condition evidently so upset the normal function of the cambium that when the wood of 1912 came to be formed it was found to deviate
greatly from the usual type.

However, from a consideration of Somerville's description and
illustrations of the injury, together with the fact that it occurred
also in the spring wood of other years, the writer is inclined to regard this injury as the result of frost rather than of drought. This
view appears to gain credence when it is considered that, inasmuch
as the drought occurred during the summer of 1911, it would seem
likely that the injury to the cambium must have occurred in ample
time to have registered in the latter part of the 1911 ring, whereas
it did not register until the beginning of the growth ring of the
following year.

Mix (6) describes and illustrates the formation of a zone of parenchyma wood in apple trees varying in age from 2 to 8 years, following an injury to the cambium due to freezing while in the dormant

condition. Macroscopically the injury appeared as a brown line between two annual rings. A microscopic examination showed that the wood first formed in the spring following the injury was a comparatively narrow zone of parenchyma wood, that the normal xylem was soon laid down outside of this zone, and that the remainder of the growth ring was normal. The medullary rays, which had become enlarged and spread out tangentially, could be traced into this parenchyma zone. Mention is made of a yellowish brown amorphous substance occurring in the intercellular spaces. While Mix was unable to definitely determine the exact nature of this substance, the writer, from his investigation of this group of substances (10), would regard the brown color as a sign of humification and the brown substance itself as a huminlike compound originating as a decomposition product of the cell contents of the cells killed by frost. The type of frost injury which Mix described is closely related to that described by Neger (7) in *Picea excelsa*.

GENERAL SYMPTOMS AND MACROSCOPIC APPEARANCE.

During the field season of 1921 the writer repeatedly observed in frost localities on cut-over lands in Washington, Idaho, and Montana areas of coniferous reproduction on which a large percentage of the young trees showed the effect of repeated late frosts, both externally and internally.

In unusually severe cases the young growth had been killed back until the trees had developed an abnormally compact bushy form.[2] Such a growth form, which was by no means common in such native trees as *Thuja plicata*, *Tsuga heterophylla*, *Pseudotsuga taxifolia*, *Larix occidentalis*, *Picea engelmanni*, *Abies lasiocarpa*, and *Tsuga mertensiana*, was rarely observed in *Pinus contorta*, *P. ponderosa*, and *P. albicaulis*.[3] It was extremely common, however, in *Abies grandis* (Pl. I, A). The greater tendency of young trees of *Abies grandis* to assume this compact bushy form after injury by late frost is due to the great readiness with which this species develops compensatory shoots. Since the recovery of any given species from frost injury depends largely upon its ability to retain dormant buds which give rise to such compensatory shoots, it should rank very high in both *Abies grandis* and *A. concolor*.

In the cases of less severe injury the trees did not develop any particularly compact bushy form and often did not appear unusual in any way, yet the same frost rings occurred in the wood, although less frequently and perhaps only in the wood increment of but a single year. Where such frost rings occurred, however, it could be detected upon close examination in practically all cases investigated by the writer that the original terminal shoot of the stem in question had been killed back by frost after the initiation of its growth, and that in some cases the same had happened one or more times to the volunteer shoots. In this connection the writer wishes to state that he has never observed in any of the coniferous species studied

---

[2] The writer wishes to make it clear that he does not consider all cases of the brooming of young conifers to be due to late-frost injury, since this abnormal form of growth may be induced by parasitic fungi alone. In the latter case, however, the formation of frost rings does not occur within the zones of annual increment.
[3] Host names for American species follow the usage in the publications of George B. Sudworth, of the United States Forest Service.

by him any pronounced permanent distortion of the living shoots which would indicate injury by late frost, except in the case of *Pinus densiflora* Sieb. and Zucc., a Japanese species which will be considered later.

In every case where the terminal growth had been killed, a narrow brownish zone of abnormal tissue, or frost ring, could be traced from the base of the dead shoot down the stem for a distance of several inches, or often for several feet in the case of saplings. This zone of abnormal tissue, which has the appearance of a brownish stripe in sections of the stem, usually occurred in the immediate beginning of the growth ring or else a short distance beyond the outer limit of the growth ring of the preceding year. In the latter case it gave the appearance of a double ring formation, especially when the growth rings were rather narrow. As a rule, the action of late frost manifests itself in a closed ring, although occasionally the zone of injury appears only on one side of the stem. In no case of late-frost injury observed by the writer was any external sign of mechanical injury to the bark visible.

Measurements of the linear extent of the frost rings were made in only a few instances where larger trees were involved, since this point was not deemed of any particular importance. In general, it may be said that in the smaller trees they usually extend down to or nearly to the ground line. In the larger trees, however, they terminate rather abruptly as the older and therefore better protected portion of the stem is reached. While the writer has observed the occurrence of frost rings in the outer growth rings of saplings of *Larix occidentalis* and *Pseudotsuga taxifolia* 2 inches in diameter, he has not observed their occurrence in coniferous stems of larger size at the time of the injury. Frost-ring formation, however, often occurs in larger stems of fruit trees that are subject to various forms of frost injury. The latter in general, however, perhaps due in part to the cultural practices employed, are more susceptible to frost injury than the coniferous trees. Detailed stem-analysis data are recorded for four saplings of *Larix occidentalis* from an area in which frost rings were found to be especially numerous, as mentioned below.

STEM ANALYSIS OF LARIX OCCIDENTALIS SAPLINGS WITH FROST RINGS, CUT AT IONE, WASH., AUGUST 24, 1920.

Tree No. 1.—The tip of the original leader formed in 1918 had been killed and was dead down to an elevation of 223 centimeters above the ground, at which point a 2-year-old volunteer had developed subsequent to the injury, giving the sapling a total height of 278 centimeters. A conspicuous brownish zone of parenchyma wood, located in the 1919 growth ring and developed very soon after the initiation of the growth of that year (Pl. II, *C*), could be traced down the stem to an elevation of 65 centimeters above the ground, at which point it was no longer apparent under a hand lens. A section of the wood at this point showed under the microscope practically no distortion of the wood elements.

Tree No. 2.—Another sapling, with a height of 365 centimeters and with no evidence of any external injury or dead terminal shoot, showed upon dissection a similar brownish zone of parenchyma formed shortly after the beginning of the 1919 growth ring. This line of parenchyma could be traced from the apex of the 1918 growth, at an elevation of 300 centimeters, down the stem to an elevation of 175 centimeters, below which point it was no longer in evidence.

Tree No. 3.—In this case the original leader had been killed, and a volunteer leader 2 years old had been put out at a height of 158 centimeters, just below the dead tip of the 1918 growth. A brownish zone of parenchyma, formed shortly after the beginning of the 1919 growth ring, was traceable down the stem directly from the base of the volunteer leader, at an elevation of 158 centimeters to an elevation of 30 centimeters above the ground. In these first three trees there was no evidence of any frost injury in the growth rings of any year other than those enumerated.

Tree No. 4.—The original leader of this sapling had been killed, and a 2-year-old volunteer had been established at a height of 237 centimeters just below the dead tip of the 1918 growth, giving the tree a height of 300 centimeters. A conspicuous brownish zone of parenchyma, developed shortly after the beginning of the 1919 growth ring, could be traced from the apex of the growth of this year, at the base of the dead 1918 tip, at an elevation of 237 centimeters, down the stem to an elevation of 75 centimeters. At this point a faint zone of parenchyma also showed in the beginning of the 1918 growth ring and could be traced up the stem to an elevation of 200 centimeters, a point just below the apex of the 1918 growth, where the stem had a diameter of but 2 millimeters. Beyond this point the injury was not evident with a hand lens, but only in sections examined under the microscope. By means of a microscopic examination this zone of parenchyma formation could be traced up to an elevation of 211 centimeters, at which point the stem, consisting of only the 1918 growth, was but 1 millimeter in diameter, or practically to the apex of the growth ring of that year.

Through the kindness of J. A. Larsen, director of the Priest River Experiment Station in Idaho, the writer was enabled to examine and procure material for the study of a number of nonindigenous conifers that showed the effects of repeated late-frost injury. The trees had been grown to the transplant stage in California and planted some years previously on an open bench at the experiment station. The stock in question comprised young trees of *Pinus lambertiana, Pseudotsuga taxifolia, Chamaecyparis lawsoniana,* and *Sequoia washingtoniana,* all of which except *Pseudotsuga taxifolia* are nonindigenous to Idaho. All of these trees, especially the two species mentioned last, exhibited an abnormally compact and bushy form and owing to the repeated injury contained frost rings in practically every growth ring. At the time of the examination all of the two species last mentioned, as well as a large number of the first two species, were dead, due probably to the combined action of the repeated late-frost injury and recent drought injury.

The young shoots, however, are by no means always killed back by late frost. Not infrequently the shoots injured by frost may remain alive throughout and still record the injury within their tissues in the usual manner. In this form of late-frost injury the terminal shoots as well as the corresponding lateral shoots sometimes exhibit more or less of a characteristic permanent distortion, which is accompanied by a frost-ring formation in the wood. While not observed in any of the western frost-injured conifers which the writer studied, this type of injury has been described by Hartig (2) for *Pinus sylvestris* and has been observed by the writer in a row of young trees of *Pinus densiflora,* a Japanese species of dwarf bushy pine grown in a nursery on the Mall, in Washington, D. C. For the correlation of this form of injury with late frost and the observations on the behavior of the trees immediately after the freezing the writer is indebted to R. H. Colley and G. F. Gravatt, of the Office of Investigations in Forest Pathology.

From March 27 to 29, 1921, there occurred a general cold wave, coming after a period of abnormally warm weather, which was very destructive to the active vegetation over a large part of the country east of the Mississippi River. On the day following this freeze, March 30, it was observed that large numbers of the 1921 shoots along this entire row of *Pinus densiflora* trees, which was the outermost row on one side of the nursery, had wilted and drooped, due to loss of turgor. On a row of trees of *Taxus baccata* near by in the same nursery it was observed that a large number of the new shoots, which averaged half an inch in length, were killed outright.

On September 30 the writer had the opportunity to observe these trees. The entire row of *Pinus densiflora* trees showed numerous cases of permanent deformation of the terminal and many of the lateral shoots of the last whorl, but all had remained living and had regained to a large extent their normal erect position, although not without leaving more or less of an S-shaped kink in their stems (Pl. III). In all cases which the writer examined, such shoots exhibited a frost ring in the beginning of the 1921 growth ring, which could be traced readily down the stem for several inches from the base of the last whorl, although it was scarcely to be distinguished. even with a hand lens, from the outer limit of the 1920 growth ring, owing to its close coincidence (Pl. IV, *A*). The frost ring likewise was traceable macroscopically on sections cut with a keen microtome knife, though better microscopically, for a distance of several centimeters above the bases of the deformed terminal and lateral shoots of the last whorl, where it appeared in the first wood elements bordering upon the pith and in the outer cells of the pith. It was lacking in those few lateral branches of the last whorl that sometimes escaped injury by reason of their lack of development at the time of the freeze. In the far less numerous cases of frost injury in *Taxus baccata*, however, there was no evidence of any deformation of the young shoots, such as occurred in *Pinus densiflora*, but the young terminal shoots were killed outright and replaced by one or more volunteer shoots. In all such cases, where the terminal shoot had been killed by late frost, a frost ring could be traced down the stem for several inches below the base of the dead terminal shoot in the beginning of the 1921 growth ring.

A row of trees of *Pinus montana* var. *uncinata*, a more hardy appearing species planted next to the row of *Pinus densiflora*, showed no single external symptoms of frost injury, and none of the shoots which the writer cut into showed any frost rings. On the other hand, with the exception of the two species mentioned, there was no evidence of any deformation or killing of the shoots by frost on any of the other conifers, of which a large variety were in the nursery.

ANATOMICAL STRUCTURE OF THE FROST RINGS.

As is well known, when living plant tissue is frozen the water is withdrawn from the cells, solidifying to ice in the intercellular spaces or other tissue gaps. Upon the initiation of the freezing the water from the still living cambial wood passes out between the wood and the bark and forms an ice mantle there. The extraordinarily tender nature of the youngest cambial cells favors the separation of the tissue, and a loosening of the phloem is facilitated either by the stronger shrinkage of the frozen wood or by the expansion of the cortex due to the stress exerted by the ice formation beneath it. The lower the temperature falls the thicker the ice mantle becomes, and it compresses the tender cambial cells until their outlines are more or less indistinguishable, as is to be seen in Plate IV, *A*, *B*, and *C*.

FROST INJURY TO ABIES GRANDIS AND TSUGA HETEROPHYLLA.

A.—Young tree of *Abies grandis* repeatedly injured by late frosts, showing the abnormally compact and bushy form of growth as a result of the ready development of numerous compensatory shoots. This tree exhibited frost rings in practically every growth ring. (One-fifth natural size.) *B.*—Transverse section of a branch of a similar tree of *Tsuga heterophylla*, showing frost-ring formation, either partially or entirely around the stem, in every growth ring after the first one. (×10.)

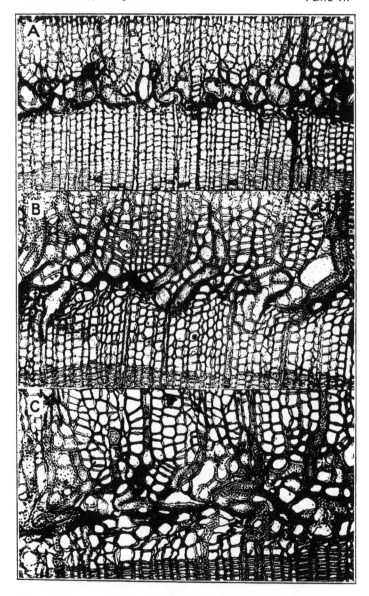

FROST INJURY TO THUJA PLICATA, PSEUDOTSUGA TAXIFOLIA, AND LARIX OCCIDENTALIS.

A.—Transverse section through frost ring in *Thuja plicata*, showing a pronounced distortion of the medullary rays. (×135.) *B.*—Transverse section through frost ring in *Pseudotsuga taxifolia*, showing the crumpling of the wood cells that were but slightly lignified at the time of freezing. (×135.) *C.*—Transverse section through frost ring in *Larix occidentalis* sapling (tree No. 1), at 146 centimeters above the ground, showing an extreme case of lateral displacement of the medullary rays. (×135.)

FROST INJURY TO PINUS DENSIFLORA.

Effect upon *Pinus densiflora* of a late March frost occurring after the development of many of the 1921 shoots had been initiated, showing the characteristic permanent distortion of the terminal shoot and three of the five lateral shoots. Photographed September 30. (Two-thirds natural size.)

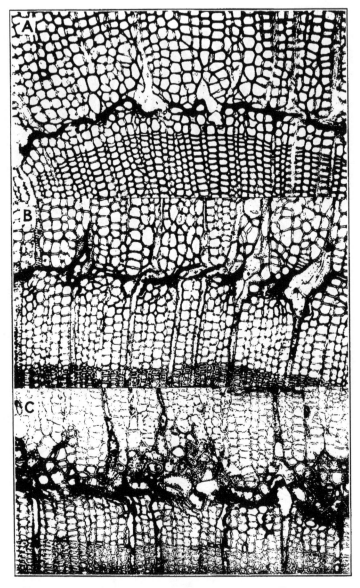

FROST RINGS OF PINUS DENSIFLORA, ABIES GRANDIS, AND TSUGA HETERO-
PHYLLA.

A.—Transverse section of stem of *Pinus densiflora* taken 10 centimeters below the 1921 whorl of branches, showing a slight frost ring formation in the 1921 growth. (×135.) *B.*—Transverse section of *Abies grandis*, showing a more pronounced frost-ring formation, with the characteristic lateral displacement of the medullary rays and their proliferation. (×135.) *C.*—Transverse section through a frost-ring formation in *Tsuga heterophylla*, showing the formation of a broad zone of parenchyma wood (×135.)

FROST INJURY TO PINUS MONTICOLA AND PINUS ALBICAULIS.

A.—Transverse section through a stem of *Pinus monticola*, showing the termination of the preceding annual ring (at the outer margin of the resin canal at bottom of picture) and three frost rings occurring in the early portion of the succeeding growth ring. (×135.) *B.*—Transverse section through a frost ring in *Pinus albicaulis*, showing the crumpling of the wood cells that were but slightly lignified at the time of freezing and the formation of a radial cleft (at the left) which has become filled by large-celled parenchyma. (×135.)

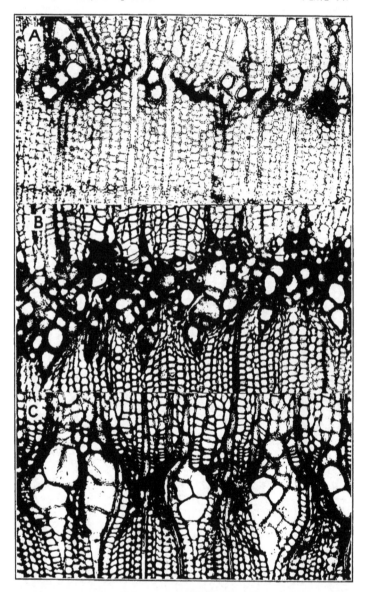

FROST INJURY TO TSUGA MERTENSIANA, CHAMAECYPARIS LAWSONIANA, AND
SEQUOIA WASHINGTONIANA.

A.—Transverse section through frost ring in *Tsuga mertensiana*, showing the outer face of a preceding growth ring at bottom and a large number of well-lignified tracheids developed before the
freezing; also a radial cleft (at upper left-hand corner) filled up with large-celled parenchyma.
(×135.) *B.*—Transverse section through a frost ring occupying a median position in a growth
ring of *Chamaecyparis lawsoniana*, showing an unusually broad zone of dark-brown parenchyma
and radial clefts also filled up with large-celled parenchyma. (×135.) *C.*—Frost ring occurring
at the outer limit of a summer-wood formation in *Sequoia washingtoniana*, showing a series of
radial clefts subsequently filled up with large-celled parenchyma. (×135.)

The already thick-walled but still unlignified cells collapse also, their walls presenting a crumpled appearance (Pl. II, *B;* Pl. V, *B*).

After the thawing, the cell tissue that has been compressed does not expand to its previous form and size, but remains permanently distorted. In the cases of the more severe injury there begins at the periphery of the wood formed before the injury a more or less broad zone of large-celled parenchyma, which is distinguished by its greatly thickened simple-pitted walls and by the dark-brown color of the walls and the cell contents. This zone of parenchyma tissue quickly passes over into tracheidal tissue, which at first is usually somewhat larger celled than that developed before the frost injury, but which quickly becomes typical. In this manner the frost injury results in the formation of a false ring, especially if it occurs after the development of several spring-wood tracheids (Pl. IV, *B;* Pl. V, *A;* Pl. VI, *A* and *B*).

As may be seen from the accompanying reproductions of photomicrographs, the frost rings exhibit great dissimilarity in structure, according to the degree of intensity of the frost action and the susceptibility of the wood tissue at the time of its occurrence.

The medullary rays, which extend through the frost ring and stretch in accordance with the stress exerted upon them, naturally suffer most from the displacement of the tissue. Their deformation varies according to the severity of the injury, but in general is very characteristic. On the inner side of the frost ring the rays widen out abruptly, often becoming 2-seriate or 3-seriate instead of uniseriate (Pl. IV, *B*; Pl. II, *B*). The rays apparently are stimulated to lateral broadening by the diminution of the pressure normally exerted by the adjoining wood elements, caused by the crushing together of the young wood elements. This broadening ensues immediately in the region of the frozen young wood and reaches its greatest extent within the region which, in the frozen condition, was filled by ice. In addition to broadening out laterally, the rays usually are also more or less sharply displaced, often undergoing a knee-shaped bending (Pl. II, *A* and *C*). Within any one stem the medullary rays are usually, although by no means always, displaced uniformly either to the one side or to the other. As the wood ring enlarges after the thawing, the medullary rays are brought into an oblique position and later grow out again in their original direction, continuing in equal number in the newly formed wood and causing the wood tissue to appear as though a fault had occurred in it. The lateral displacement of the medullary rays apparently depends upon the circumstance that their stretching during the ice formation remains preserved after the thawing. This lateral expansion and displacement of the medullary rays is by far the most conspicuous and characteristic feature of late-frost injury and is a constant feature of all injuries to wood by late frost. In at least the more severe cases of injury the frost ring is further accentuated by a more or less broad zone of brownish parenchyma tissue.

There also may arise after the thawing a series of radial gaps or clefts, occurring with variable frequency and conspicuousness within the tracheidal tissue, where it had been stretched apart previously by the excessive tangential contraction. With subsequent growth, these tissue gaps become filled with large-celled parenchyma derived from the new cambial formation (Pl. V, *B*; Pl. VI, *B* and *C*.) An unusually striking example of this radial cleft formation occurred in the frost rings observed in stems of *Sequoia washingtoniana*, where clefts were present not only in the early formed portion of the growth ring but also at the outer limit of the summerwood formation (Pl. VI, *C*). In the latter case the frost rings appeared to lie between the summer wood of one growth ring and the spring wood of the next, so that there was no sharp demarcation between the two annual rings except where the frost ring did not extend completely around the stem. Still other stems from the same material, which had been injured by frost near the close of the growing season and had died without subsequent growth, exhibited the same radial clefts at the periphery of the xylem, but in this case the clefts were still open and free from any occlusion by parenchyma cells. Such tissue disturbances result in a very pronounced false ring formation.

A large part of the phenomena which come to light in frost injuries to young stems, however they may vary, can be traced to simple mechanical processes. Sorauer (*12*) has proved experimentally that processes of loosening are initiated in the cell membranes by the action of frost; and this explains the formation of this parenchyma zone instead of the normal wood elements as the result of a weakening of the compressing influence exerted by the bark girdle on the youngest tissue, that is, the cambium. According to Sorauer, the frost, without necessarily forming ice crystals in the intercellular spaces, contracts the tissue in direct proportion to the thinness of the walls of the tissue. The bark suffers considerably more than the wood, which, reached later, cools down less easily and contracts less. The tangential contraction is greater than the radial. As Sorauer states, this difference acts like a one-sided strain and exerts itself in the direction of the circumference of the trunk, to which the different layers of the bark will respond to a different degree when the bark as a whole is very young. Consequently, with the action of the frost there must take place everywhere within a woody axis a preponderance of tangential strain over radial contraction, and under certain circumstances this must increase to a radial splitting of the tissue. With an equal degree of contraction at all points in the bark, the cells lying nearest the periphery and most elongated in the direction of the circumference of the trunk will be the most displaced. As Sorauer also states, if one considers that the outer cells of the primary bark, because of the greater coarseness of their walls, are not as elastic as the underlying thinner walled ones, it is clear that when the strain ceases in them the permanent stretching, caused by the incomplete elasticity, will be the greatest there. After the action of the frost, which continues but a short time in late frosts, has stopped, the tissue that has become stretched is not sufficiently elastic to contract again to its original volume, and the cells retain their distended and distorted form. In this way each frost action leaves behind an excessive lengthening of the peripheral tissue layers in proportion to the adjacent layers which lie more toward the inside. The bark body as a whole is therefore larger and either does not have room enough on the wood cylinder, so that in places it is raised up from it, or it at least decreases its constricting influence on the cambial elements of the wood cylinder. The cambial zone responds to this with the formation of parenchyma wood, as may be seen in every wound in which the bark is raised. If the bark girdle closes together again into a connected layer the cambial cylinder by growth in thickness must again resist the constricting effect of the bark and on this account again forms normal wood elements.

In sections containing frost rings that when viewed macroscopically appear to be only one-sided, it can be recognized in a microscopic examination that, as a rule, a lesser disturbance has occurred on the other side of the stem (Pl. II, *B*). However, a disturbance of the wood tissue by no means always extends entirely around the stem, the same often being purely local and consisting of numerous isolated groups of parenchyma elements. The frost rings occasioned by late frost vary greatly in their position within the growth ring, but usually occur early in the spring wood, either in the immediate beginning or after the formation of a few normal tracheids. On the other hand, they may not be formed until late in the growth ring when the frost must necessarily occur during the summer. Frost rings in the latter position are comparatively rare, however.

More than one frost ring may occur within the wood of any one growth ring, depending upon whether or not the frost occurs more than once after the spring growth has been initiated. Two frost rings within one annual ring are fairly common, and the writer has observed the occurrence of three frost rings in the spring-wood zone of an annual ring in *Pinus monticola* (Pl. V, *A*) and in *Picea engelmanni*.

Frost-ring formation may occur in the wood from the action of either late or early frosts during the course of the growing season or from the freezing of the cambium during the winter when the tree is dormant. The frost rings, therefore, may register at any point within the growth ring, the relative position of the frost ring within the growth ring signifying the time at which the injury occurred.

According to Hartig (*2*, p. 4), frost rings arise through late-frost injury only when the cambial activity has already commenced and at least some few cells have been cut off toward the interior, if, therefore, the annual ring formation has been initiated. It has been the writer's experience with late-frost injury that, while the number of spring-wood tracheids that intervene between the outer limit of the summer wood of the preceding annual ring and the frost ring is usually fairly uniform on any radius, the frost rings sometimes appear to abut directly on the summer wood of the preceding growth ring, although groups of normal spring-wood tracheids usually intervene in places. The formation of at least some normal spring-wood elements would therefore appear to be a diagnostic feature of late-frost injury.

In the case of late frost occurring unusually late in the season, the frost rings may register in the median or outer portion of the growth ring (Pl. VI, *B*). In the case of early frosts occurring late in the season, at a time when the annual accretion of wood has not matured, or in the case of frost injury occurring during the dormant period of the year, the resulting frost ring registers in the immediate beginning of the next growth ring, often tending to obscure the normally sharp demarcation between the two rings (Pl. VI, *C*).

In general, it appears that frost injury occurring shortly after the initiation of active growth causes a greater distortion of the wood elements than that occurring when the growth ring is practically mature or when the tree is dormant.

Frost rings are often confusing to those who have occasion to engage in age determinations or stem analyses of trees. The frost-ring formation, however, usually occurs within such close limits of the beginning of the annual ring formation that, macroscopically at least, the parenchyma zone appears to coincide more or less closely with the outer limit of the preceding growth ring. Frost-ring formation should prove confusing in age counts only when it occurs late in the season after a considerable portion of the growth ring has been formed. Moreover, since only the younger stems appear to be susceptible to frost-ring formation, it is believed that in conifers at least, false ring formation from this source need be expected chiefly only in the first several growth rings formed in the life of the tree.

As may be expected from their structure, frost rings constitute a plane of weakness in the wood, since there is no strong bond between the wood formed before the injury and the parenchyma wood formed immediately after it. In chopping off a face on stems containing one or more frost rings in order to follow their linear extent, the wood frequently splits peripherally along the plane of these zones of abnormal wood. In future years it seems likely, as Somerville (11) states for the abnormality which he describes, that they may lead to the formation of ring shakes within the trees.

The writer's investigation of the pathological anatomy of late-frost injury confirms those of Mayr, Hartig, and Sorauer in all particulars except the occurrence of the chains of pathologic resin canals, which Mayr (4) suggests may be caused by frost and which Hartig (2) found sometimes associated with the frost rings.

Mayr (4, p. 29), in a discussion of the chains of abnormal or pathologic resin canals sometimes found in the wood of Abies firma and Tsuga, suggests that they may be caused by late frost, which, he states, is of fairly common occurrence. However, he observed that such chains of resin canals may also be found in the hard summer-wood zone of the annual ring, where late frost is excluded as a cause. Although not considered by Mayr, a number of other types of injury could easily have been responsible for this pathologic resin-canal formation.

Hartig (2, p. 7) states that he has repeatedly found that the wound parenchyma developing in the frost ring contained resin canals, so that a more or less complete ring of them was recognizable in the frost zone. Despite the writer's particular consideration of this point and his extensive investigations on pathologic resin-canal formation in general, which will appear shortly, he has never observed the formation of chains of pathologic resin canals as the result of frost injury. While zones of pathologic resin canals do occasionally coincide with the frost rings in a stem, the writer has always traced their origin to some mechanical wound. It is by no means impossible, however, for such zones of pathologic resin canals to arise schizogenously within the broad aggregates of parenchyma wood comprising the frost ring.

Hartig (*2*, p. 7) likewise mentions the occurrence of chains of abnormal resin canals, which he regards as due to the action of late frost, throughout the entire circumference of the phloem of stems of *Chamaecyparis lawsoniana* 2 centimeters thick, at a slight distance from the cambial layer. He states that these arise by the medullary rays stretching and becoming broadened laterally through cell division and that between each two rays the delicate-walled tissue composed of sieve tubes and parenchyma was crowded apart. He assumes that here also the tissue gaps are not closed after the thawing of the ice, and finds that the surrounding living cells become enlarged more or less into these gaps and become converted into resin-secreting cells, pouring large quantities of resin into them. As a result of this formation a festoon of large resin beads appears from the bark on the ends of cut-off shoots. The writer, however, did not observe any formation of chains of pathologic resin canals in the phloem of the frost-injured material of *Chamaecyparis lawsoniana* studied by him.

SUMMARY.

The pathological anatomy of late-frost injury has been studied in detail by the writer in *Pinus albicaulis, P. contorta, P. densiflora, P. lambertiana, P. monticola, P. ponderosa, Picea engelmanni, Larix occidentalis, Pseudotsuga taxifolia, Abies grandis, A. lasiocarpa, Tsuga heterophylla, T. mertensiana, Thuja plicata, Chamaecyparis lawsoniana, Sequoia washingtoniana,* and *Taxus baccata;* also in apple and pear trees.

The young shoots injured by late frost may either wilt through loss of turgor and after again directing their points upward usually become permanently distorted, or, as generally happens, they may be killed outright and replaced by one or more volunteer shoots. The structural disturbance initiated by the action of late-frost injury is not confined to the shoots then developing, but extends down the stem for distances varying from several inches to several feet below the base of the injured shoots, or as far as the cambium has been injured by the freezing without entailing the death of the stem. The healing proceeds internally and results in the formation of a brownish zone of parenchyma wood, or frost ring, within the growth ring, developing at the time of the injury.

Late-frost injury results in very characteristic disturbances in the tissue of the growth ring forming at the time of the injury. The abnormal tissue of the frost ring varies greatly, according to the severity of the injury, and may be characterized by various combinations of such features as the crumpling of the wood cells that were but slightly lignified at the time of the injury, a marked broadening or proliferation of the medullary rays, a strong lateral displacement of the medullary rays together with a marked broadening or proliferation, the presence of radial clefts subsequently filled up by large-celled parenchyma, and more or less broad zones of wound parenchyma. The displacement of the medullary rays is occasioned by their stretching and lack of elasticity; the radial clefts, to the preponderance of the tangential contraction over the radial contraction; and the interpolated zone of parenchyma wood, to a transitory weakening of the compressing influence exerted by the bark girdle on the cambium, due to the disrupting action caused by the freezing.

Frost-ring formation may occur in the wood from the action of either late or early frost during the course of the growing season or from the freezing of the cambium during the winter when the tree is dormant. The frost rings, therefore, may register at any point within the growth ring, the relative position of the frost ring within the growth ring signifying the time at which the injury occurred.

Frost rings arise through late frost only when the cambial activity has already commenced and some new xylem cells have been differentiated. As a rule, there is a definite zone of spring-wood tracheids intervening between the outer limit of the summer wood of the preceding annual ring and the frost ring. In the case of early frosts the frost ring may either register late in the summer wood of the growth ring or not until the immediate beginning of the ensuing growth ring. Frost injury occurring during the dormant period likewise is recorded as a frost ring in the immediate beginning of the ensuing growth ring.

Young trees injured by repeated frosts often develop an abnormally compact and bushy form, especially in *Abies grandis* and other species, which readily form compensatory shoots. Frost injury that results in the killing of the young shoots often detracts greatly from the straight axial growth of the trees and, where frequently repeated, may render the tree absolutely valueless for commercial purposes. In addition, late-frost injury may render young conifers more susceptible to weakly parasitic fungi than they would be otherwise.

Late-frost injury, when occurring late in the season after any considerable portion of the growth ring has been formed, results in a false or double ring formation, which is often confusing in age determinations. Frost-ring formation from late-frost injury has not been observed by the writer in coniferous stems larger than 2 inches in diameter, although it often occurs in larger stems of fruit trees that are subject to various forms of frost injury.

As may be expected from their structure, frost rings constitute a plane of weakness in the wood, which may not only predispose to the formation of circular shake in the standing tree, but may require the manufactured wood to be discriminated against for use in small pieces where great strength is required.

LITERATURE CITED.

(1) GRAEBNER, PAUL.
 1909. Beiträge zur Kenntnis nichtparasitärer Pflanzenkrankheiten an
 forstlichen Gewächsen. 3. Wirkung von Frösten während der
 Vegetationsperiode. *In* Ztschr. Forst. u. Jagdw., Jahrg. 41, Heft
 7, p. 421–431, 5 fig.

(2) HARTIG, ROBERT.
 1895. Doppelringe als Folge von Spätfrost. *In* Forstl. Naturw.
 Ztschr., Jahrg. 4, Heft 1, p. 1–8, 6 fig., pl. 1.

(3) 1900. Lehrbuch der Pflanzenkrankheiten . . . Aufl. 3, ix, 324 p.,
 280 fig. Berlin.

(4) MAYR, HEINRICH.
 1890. Monographie der Abietineen des Japanischen Reiches . . .
 viii, 104 p., 7 col. pl. München.

(5) 1894. Das Harz der Nadelhölzer, seine Entstehung, Vertheilung, Be-
 deutung und Gewinnung. 96 p., 4 fig., 2 col. pl. Berlin.

(6) MIX, A. J.
 1916. The formation of parenchyma wood following winter injury to
 the cambium. *In* Phytopathology, v. 6, no. 3, p. 279–283, 3 fig.

(7) NEGER, F. W.
 1916. Ueber eine durch Frühfrost an Nectria cucurbitula Fr. und
 Dermatea eucrita (Karst.) verursachte Gipfeldürre der Fichte.
 In Naturw. Ztschr. Forst. u. Landw., Jahrg. 14, Heft 3/4, p. 121–
 127. 4 fig.

(8) 1919. Die Krankheiten unserer Waldbäume und wichtigsten Gar-
 tengehölze . . . viii, 286 p., 234 fig. Stuttgart.

(9) PETERSEN, O. G.
 1905. Nattefrostens Virkning paa Bøgens Ved. *In* Denmark. Forst-
 lige Forsøgsvaesen, Bd. 1, p. 49–68, 12 fig.

(10) RHOADS, ARTHUR S.
 1917. The black zones formed by wood-destroying fungi. Tech. Pub.
 8 (v. 17, no. 28), N. Y. State Coll. Forestry, 61 p. incl. 6 pl. Literature cited, p. 46–49.

(11) SOMERVILLE, WILLIAM.
 1916. Abnormal wood in conifers. *In* Quart. Jour. Forestry, v. 10,
 no. 2, p. 132–136, 10 fig. on 3 pl.

(12) SORAUER, PAUL.
 1886–1909. Handbuch der Pflanzenkrankheiten. Theil 1, Die nicht-
 parasitären Krankheiten. Aufl. 2, xvi, 920 p., 61 fig., 19 pl. Berlin. 1886. Aufl. 3, xvi, 891 p., 208 fig. Berlin. 1909. Bibliographical footnotes.

(13) 1906. Experimentelle Studien über die mechanischen Wirkungen des
 Frostes bei Obst- und Waldbäumen. *In* Landw. Jahrb., Jahrg. 35,
 Heft 4, p. 469–526, pl. 9–13 (partly col.).

(14) TUBEUF, CARL VON.
 1906. Pathologische Erscheinungen beim Absterben der Fichten im
 Sommer 1904. *In* Naturw. Ztschr. Land. u. Forstw., Jahrg. 4,
 Heft 11, p. 449–466, 6 fig., pl. 26–32; Heft 12, p. 511–512.

(15) 1913. Absterben der Gipfeltriebe an Fichten. *In* Naturw. Ztschr.
 Forst. u. Landw., Jahrg. 11, Heft 8, p. 396–399, 1 fig.

15

ORGANIZATION OF THE UNITED STATES DEPARTMENT OF AGRICULTURE.

Secretary of Agriculture_____ HENRY C. WALLACE.
Assistant Secretary_____ C. W. PUGSLEY.
Director of Scientific Work_____ E. D. BALL.
Director of Regulatory Work_____
Weather Bureau_____ CHARLES F. MARVIN, Chief.
Bureau of Agricultural Economics_____ HENRY C. TAYLOR, Chief.
Bureau of Animal Industry_____ JOHN R. MOHLER, Chief.
Bureau of Plant Industry_____ WILLIAM A. TAYLOR, Chief.
Forest Service_____ W. B. GREELEY, Chief.
Bureau of Chemistry_____ WALTER G. CAMPBELL, Acting
                                              Chief.
Bureau of Soils_____ MILTON WHITNEY, Chief.
Bureau of Entomology_____ L. O. HOWARD, Chief.
Bureau of Biological Survey_____ E. W. NELSON, Chief.
Bureau of Public Roads_____ THOMAS H. MACDONALD, Chief.
Fixed-Nitrogen Research Laboratory_____ F. G. COTTRELL, Director.
Division of Accounts and Disbursements_____ A. ZAPPONE, Chief.
Division of Publications_____ JOHN L. COBBS, Jr., Chief.
Library_____ CLARIBEL R. BARNETT, Librarian.
States Relations Service_____ A. C. TRUE, Director.
Federal Horticultural Board_____ C. L. MARLATT, Chairman.
Insecticide and Fungicide Board_____ J. K. HAYWOOD, Chairman.
Packers and Stockyards Administration_____⎫ CHESTER MORRILL, Assistant
Grain Future Trading Act Administration____⎭   to the Secretary.
Office of the Solicitor_____ R. W. WILLIAMS, Solicitor.

This bulletin is a contribution from the—

Bureau of Plant Industry_____ WILLIAM A. TAYLOR, Chief.
    Investigations in Forest Pathology_____ HAVEN METCALF, Pathologist in
                                              Charge.

16

UNITED STATES DEPARTMENT OF AGRICULTURE

DEPARTMENT BULLETIN No. 1132

| Washington, D. C. | PROFESSIONAL PAPER | March 21, 1923 |

THE RESULTS OF PHYSICAL TESTS OF ROAD-BUILDING ROCK FROM 1916 TO 1921, INCLUSIVE.

Prepared in the Bureau of Public Roads.

CONTENTS.

INTRODUCTION.

This bulletin gives the results of tests of all rock made by the Bureau of Public Roads from January 1, 1916, to January 1, 1922, classified alphabetically according to location. It supplements United States Department of Agriculture Bulletin 370, "Results of Physical Tests of Road-Building Rock," and replaces United States Department of Agriculture Bulletin 670, "Results of Tests of Road-Building Rock in 1916 and 1917." The results of tests of approximately 5,300 samples are now avilable in the two bulletins, and these tests re resent road-building material from practically all parts of the United States and some parts of Canada, Haiti, the Dominican Republic, and Porto Rico. Reference to Table 1, in which the results of tests made subsequent to January 1, 1916, are tabulated, will show that a test of crushing strength has been made on a number of samples, and a column of test results not found in Bulletin No. 370 is added t ereby. Tests of crushing strength made prior to 1916 are recorded in Table 2. This quality of rock is not determined ordinarily when making examinations of their suitability for road building, but it is employed often when considering rock for use as paving blocks or as railroad ballast. A brief description of this test as made by the Bureau of Public Roads is given on page 46.

TABLE 1.—*Results of physical tests of road-building rock from the United States, Haiti, and Canada—January 1, 1916, to January 1, 1922.*

ALABAMA.

Serial No.	Town or city.	County.	Name of material.	Crushing strength, pounds per square inch.	Weight per cubic foot.	Absorption, pounds per cubic foot.	Per cent of wear.	French coefficient of wear.	Hardness.	Toughness.
13387	Anniston	Calhoun	Lime.	(?)	170	0.22	6.8	5.9	14.7	4
13388	do.	do.	Magnesium limestone	(?)	174	.64	6.0	6.7	17.3	9
13389	Anniston (near)	do.	Limestone	(?)	169	.27	4.8	8.3	14.7	9
13390	Anniston	do.	Siliceous dolmite	(?)	175	.30	4.6	8.7	17.3	6
13506	do.	do.	Sandstone	(?)	154	1.33	6.1	8.5	19.1	10
13507	do.	do.	Limestone	(?)	89	.16	4.7	6.5	15.3	8
13508	do.	do.	do.	(?)	172	.68	11.6	8.5	(?)	
13509	do.	do.	do.	(?)	140	.12	5.4	3.4	16.0	6
16712	do.	do.	Blast furnace slag	(?)	179	.57	2.4	7.4	17.0	12
20081	do.	do.	Slag	(?)	149	1.68	11.5	16.6	13.3	7
13510	Camp McClellan	do.	Dolomite	(?)	175	.38	5.0	3.5	16.0	8
13504	Weavers Cave	do.	do.	(?)	172	.89	7.2	8.5	(?)	
14450	(¹)	(¹)	Quartzite schist.	(?)	164	.38	4.4	9.5	18.7	19
20821	(¹)	Colbert	Thin limestone.	(?)	144	1.19	4.7	9.1	15.7	5
10138	Bridgeport	Jackson	Oolitic limestone.	(?)	168	.21	4.4	8.5	15.7	5
20354	Lim Rock	do.	Limestone.	(?)	168	.16	4.4	9.1	16.3	7
16112	(¹)	do.	Crystalline limestone.	(?)	174	.57	3.8	10.5	15.3	8
16113	(¹)	do.	...limestone.	(?)	166	.34	6.2	6.5	18.0	6
9985	Birmingham	Jefferson	Limestone.	(?)	168	.55	5.0	8.0	15.3	6
18721	Ensley	Lee	Slag.	(?)	137	4.44	14.7	2.7	(?)	
19981	O...(near)	do.	Marl.	(?)	162	2.56	25.3	1.6	(?)	
16196	A...	Limestone	do.	(?)	146	4.10	10.7	3.7	(?)	
16188	do.	do.	Dolomite marble.	(?)	168	.60	4.4	9.1	14.7	7
16189	do.	do.	Crystalline limestone.	(?)	165	.79	5.3	7.6	13.3	5
16074	Hartsella (near)	do.	do.	(?)	168	.81	5.0	11.8	16.3	6
16072	Lacon (near)	do.	do.	(?)	168	.50	3.4	11.4	15.3	8
16073	do.	do.	do.	(?)	168	.45	3.5	10.5	15.3	9
12757	(¹)	Morgan	Limestone	(?)	166	.11	3.8	7.4	14.5	9
12758	(¹)	do.	do.	(?)	167	.38	6.4	6.7	13.3	7
12812	(¹)	do.	do.	(?)	167	.19	6.0	6.7	13.3	6
11506	Gantts Quarry	Talladega	Marble.	(?)	169	.29	5.9	6.8	9.7	4

No.	County	Locality	Kind of rock							
14119	Cochise	Douglas	Copper slag	(²)	217	0.58	6.5	7.3	0.0	9
15296	Coconino	Grand Canyon	Calcareous sandstone	(²)	134	8.41	23.3	1.7	18.7	2
15297	...do...	...do...	Siliceous limestone	(²)	153	4.20	7.9	5.1	13.7	6
15298	...do...	...do...	Chert	(²)	120	2.28	13.7	2.9	(²)	6
15299	...do...	...do...	Dolomite	(²)	162	2.28	5.0	8.0	15.0	
13977	Gila	Globe	Copper slag	(²)	221	1.28	3.2	12.5		(²)
13978	...do...	...do...	...do...	(²)	220	1.43	3.1	12.9	15.0	(²)
14746	Greenlee	Clifton	...do...	(²)	216	1.75	6.8	8.9	18.0	9
15190	Pima	Tucson (west of)	Siliceous limestone	(²)	207	.37	4.5	8.9	15.5	27
11642-A				(²)	166	.48	5.4	7.4		5

ARKANSAS.

No.	County	Locality	Kind of rock							
17696	Baxter	Cotter	Argillaceous dolomite	(²)	163	3.96	6.1	6.6	14.0	5
17475	Cleburne	Heber Springs	Argillaceous sandstone	(²)	(²)	(²)	(²)	10.0	(²)	9
16777	Conway	Morrillton	Sandstone	(²)	155	2.10	4.0	11.4	17.7	11
17710	...do...	...do...	Feldspathic sandstone	(²)	156	3.18	3.5	10.3	13.7	(²)
16383	Faulkner	Springfield	...do...	(²)	164	.80	3.9	11.8	19.3	14
20391	...do...	Beryl	Sandstone	(²)	155	2.01	3.4	(²)	17.3	25
12261	...do...	Conway	Ferrugineous sandstone	(²)	159	.18	(²)	15.4	17.3	13
19118	...do...	...do...	Sandstone	(²)	161	1.62	2.6	12.9	13.7	9
19119	...do...	...do...	...do...	(²)	159	3.91	3.1	6.7	16.7	9
19453	...do...	...do...	Feldspathic sandstone	(²)	156	2.50	6.0	9.3	17.3	11
19752	...do...	Conway (near)	Sandstone	(²)	157	2.57	4.3	10.0	18.0	9
20012	...do...	...do...	...do...	(²)	154	2.89	4.0	9.3	18.0	13
20168	...do...	...do...	...do...	(²)	160	1.36	4.3	18.2	19.0	14
20169	...do...	...do...	...do...	(²)	158	2.09	2.2	12.5	17.7	14
20170	...do...	...do...	...do...	(²)	163	.79	2.2	18.2	18.7	13
20659	...do...	Mayflower (north of)	...do...	(²)	159	1.98	2.2	12.5	17.3	10
19916	...do...	...do...	...do...	(²)	162	1.27	2.7	14.8	15.3	19
19418	...do...	Mayflower (near)	...do...	(²)	160	1.35	2.8	14.3	13.3	17
19117	...do...	Wooster	...do...	(²)	154	2.45	3.2	12.5	18.3	8
9946	...do...	...do...	...do...	(²)	150	3.19	5.3	7.5	17.3	13
28652	...do...	(¹)	...do...	(²)	156	2.12	3.7	10.8	17.7	16
18419	...do...	(¹)	...do...	(²)	158	1.84	2.9	13.8	18.3	15
861	...do...	(¹)	...do...	(²)	162	1.47	3.7	10.8	15.7	9
10632	...do...	(¹)	...do...	(²)	152	3.16	4.7	8.5	17.0	11
20335	...do...	(¹)	...do...	(²)	163	1.40	5.1	10.8		11
18386	Franklin	(¹)	...do...	(²)	158	2.26	10.4	7.8	8.3	3
14422	Independence	Penters Bluff	Crystalline limestone	(²)	166	.60	10.8	3.8	153	
14483	...do...	...do...	Chert	(²)	157	2.08	5.4	3.7		7
14585	...do...	...do...	limestone	(²)	166	.57	10.5	7.4		3
4586	...do...	...do...	...do...	(²)	167	.69		3.8	7.3	

¹ Exact locality not known. ² Test not made.

TABLE 1.—*Results of physical tests of road-building rock from the United States, Haiti, and Canada—January 1, 1916, to January 1, 1922*—Continued.

ARKANSAS—Continued.

Serial No.	Town or city.	County.	Name of material.	Crushing strength, pounds per square inch.	Weight per cubic foot.	Absorption, pounds per cubic foot.	Per cent of wear.	French coefficient of wear.	Hardness.	Toughness.
11511	Pfeiffer	Independence	Marble	[2]	163	1.06	[2]	[2]	14.0	5
19056	Cabin Creek	Johnson	Feldspathic sandstone	[2]	157	2.37	3.2	12.5	16.3	13
9829	Lamar	do	do	21,980	159	1.97	[2]	[2]	18.7	13
14665	do	do	do	[2]	156	2.51	3.5	11.4	[2]	[2]
14959	do	do	do	[2]	[2]	[2]	[2]	[2]	18.0	11
15443	do	do	do	[2]	155	3.27	5.0	8.0	17.0	11
16510	do	do	do	[2]	156	2.57	3.8	10.5	17.3	13
17253	do	do	do	[2]	155	2.69	3.4	11.8	10.7	11
20819	Black Rock	Lawrence	Dolomite	[2]	156	5.98	4.9	6.8	13.0	7
17902	Sloan	do	Limestone	[2]	171	1.24	4.9	8.2	19.0	6
19532	Rusellville (near)	Pope	Feldspathic sandstone	[2]	160	1.43	3.2	12.5	19.3	13
12993	Little Rock	Pulaski	Quartzite	[2]	165	.38	3.3	12.1	19.0	26
12994	do	do	do	[2]	165	.27	3.3	12.1	18.5	23
14293	do	do	Porphyritic syenite	[2]	163	.20	3.7	10.8	16.3	12
14280	Little Rock (16 miles west of).	do	Sandstone	[2]	157	1.76	6.4	6.3	16.3	10
12320	[1]	do	Feldspathic sandstone	[2]	162	.96	2.5	16.0	18.9	32
14279	do	do	Sodalite syenite	[2]	156	1.23	5.0	8.0	18.7	8
9838	Fort Smith	Sebastian	Sandstone	[2]	150	5.00	6.5	6.2	15.3	6
10436	Gillham	Sevier	Feldspathic quartzite	[2]	164	.42	2.3	17.4	19.0	32
13295	White Cliffs	do	Argillaceous limestone	[2]	[2]	2.40	13.9	2.9	0.0	[2]
16657	Williford	Sharp	Dolomite	[2]	169	.89	3.6	11.1	14.7	16
17908	do	do	do	[2]	177	[2]	3.7	14.0	[2]	[2]
16488	Fayetteville	Washington	Weathered chert	[2]	[2]	1.65	2.2	7.4	15.3	[2]
20923	do	do	Argillaceous limestone	[2]	168	4.01	5.4	[2]	15.3	7
15466	Plainview	Yell	Feldspathic sandstone	[2]	152	[2]	4.7	8.5	[2]	6

CALIFORNIA.

Serial No.	Town or city.	County.	Name of material.	Crushing strength, pounds per square inch.	Weight per cubic foot.	Absorption, pounds per cubic foot.	Per cent of wear.	French coefficient of wear.	Hardness.	Toughness.
11527	San Francisco	San Francisco	Marble	[2]	176	0.35	[2]	[2]	12.0	6
11373	San Jose	Santa Clara	Feldspathic quartzite	[2]	172	.32	1.8	22.2	18.7	18
14496	Kennett	Shasta	Copper slag		221	1.09	4.9	8.2	17.7	9

[1] Exact locality not known.   [2] Test not made.

Serial No.	Locality	County	Kind of rock	Weight per cubic foot	Cementing value	Toughness	Hardness	French coefficient of wear	Per cent of wear
9757	do....	do....	do....	165	1.08	(a)	(a)	17.2	7
9758	do....	do....	do....	165	.41	4.1	9.8	19.3	13
9759	Atlanta (near)	do....	do....	168	.30	3.8	10.5	19.3	13
9760	Atlanta (near)	do....	do....	165	.40	4.7	11.4	18.3	9
9761	do....	do....	Gneissoid granite.	165	.34	(a)	8.5	18.6	7
9762	do....	do....	Biotite gneiss.	172	1.03	(a)	(a)	14.7	4
9763	do....	do....	Hornblende schist.	184	.77	5.0	(a)	19.0	7
9764	Atlanta....	do....	Gneissoid granite.	162	.85	3.4	8.0	19.3	8
9765	...ta (near)	do....	Biotite gneiss.	165	.18	4.4	11.8	18.7	6
9766	...ta (near)	do....	Granite gneiss.	165	.36	4.4	9.1	18.0	9
9767	do....	do....	Hornblende biotite gneiss.	175	.26	5.3	9.1	16.7	6
13914	do....	do....	Granite.	(a)	.27	4.1	7.5	18.0	9
10396	Fairmount (¼ mile south).	Gordon.	Limestone.	169	.08	5.7	9.8	14.7	5
10397	Fairmount (near).	Gordon.	do....	170	.71	5.2	7.0	15.3	6
10559	Grayson (2 miles).	Gwinnett.	Biotite granite.	158	.67	5.5	7.7	18.0	5
10561	Grayson (southwest of).		Gneissoid granite.	162	.67		7.3	17.5	4
10563	Grayson (3 miles south-west of).		Granite.	162	.78			18.3	6
10562	Langley Quarry.	do....	do....	162	.82	6.7	6.0	17.5	4
10547	Lawrenceville.	do....	Biotite hornblende schist.	83	.60	(a)	(a)	15.7	5
10553	Lawrenceville (near).	do....	Granite gneiss.	159	.62	4.4	9.0	17.0	5
10554	Lawrenceville (1½ miles east of).	do....	Granite.	165	.33	5.9	6.8	19.2	6
10555	Lawrenceville (1½ miles east of).	do....	do....	162	.86	(a)		12.7	4
10556	Lawrenceville (12 miles northeast of).	do....	Hornblende schist.	196	.65	6.6	6.1	(a)	6
10557	Lawrenceville (6 miles southeast of).	do....	Granite.	162	.72	4.9	8.2	18.4	5
10558	Lawrenceville (near).	do....	do....	162	.61	4.6	8.7	13.0	13
10550	Lawrenceville (4 miles west of).	do....	do....	190	.32	3.4	11.8	18.0	
10560	MacElveny Shoals....	do....	Gneissoid granite.	162	.71	5.2	7.7	18.2	.4
10564	Roseburg....	do....	Biotite gneiss.	162	.69	5.6	7.1	13.9	.6
10565	Snellville (near).	do....	do....	162	.73	5.5	7.3	17.7	.3
10566	Snellville (2 miles south-east of).	do....	do....	162	.73	4.0	10.0	13.3	6
10546	Jefferson (4 miles north).	Jackson.	do....	163	.65	5.6	7.1	18.3	5
10556	Jefferson (3 miles east of).	Aug.	Hornblende schist.	90	.04	(a)	(a)	17.0	4
10545	Holders Siding (near).	do....	Hornblende gneiss.	165	.48	4.0	10.0	18.3	7
10543	Prendergrast.	do....	Olivine diabase.	184	.09	3.6	11.1	19.0	16
10544	Taimo....	do....	do.... gneiss.	161	1.13	7.6	5.2	(a)	5
10897	Robertsville (1½ miles northeast).	Jones.	Argillaceous sandstone.	105	19.08	12.2	3.2	(a)	
16655	Dublin (near).	Laurens.	Chert.	150	4.03	8.2	4.9	20.0	7
10384	Marietta-Rockwell road.	Milton.	do.... gneiss.	167	.56	6.6	6.1	13.0	8
10385	do....	do....	do....	163	.59	6.9	5.8	13.8	6
10858	Columbus (4 miles north).	Muscogee.	Hornblende gneiss.	179	.25	4.5	8.9	16.7	5
10859	Columbus....	do....	do.... gneiss.	179	.45	5.0	8.0	13.7	5
10864	Columbus (8 miles north of).		G... gneiss.	163	.83	4.3	9.3		7

a Test not made.

TABLE 1.—Results of physical tests of road-building rock from the United States, Haiti, and Canada—January 1, 1916, to January 1, 1922—Continued.

GEORGIA—Continued.

Serial No.	Town or city	County	Name of material	Crushing strength, pounds per square inch.	Weight per cubic foot.	Absorption, pounds per cubic foot.	Per cent of wear.	French coefficient of wear.	Hardness.	Toughness.
10831	Columbus (east of)	Milton	...te gneiss	(³)	165	.36	3.9	10.2	18.7	7
10890	Fortston (2 miles south)	do	Biotite granite	(³)	168	.40	4.2	9.5	19.3	8
10861	Fortston (4 miles south)	do	Biotite gneiss	(³)	167	.48	3.7	10.8	18.7	10
10862	Fortston (1 mile south)	do	do	(³)	164	.89	5.3	7.6	18.7	9
10863	...an (3½ miles north)	do	do	(³)	163	.50	3.6	11.1	18.7	9
10865	do	do	H ...le gneiss	(³)	163	.58	3.7	10.8	18.7	10
11518	Marblehill	Pickens	Marble	(³)	169	.09	15.7	2.5	11.3	2
11513	Tate	do	do	(³)	169	.17	13.2	3.0	9.3	2
11514	do	do	do	(³)	169	.33	12.0	3.3	10.3	3
11515	do	do	do	(³)	169	.40	17.0	3.4	3.9	2
11516	do	do	do	11,340	171	.37	10.6	3.8	10.3	3
11517	do	do	do	8,735	169	.40	(³)	(³)	8.6	3
17757	do	do	do	(³)	168	.47	12.5	3.2	11.3	3
15378	... (near)	Tbot.	D ...se	(³)	187	.32	1.7	23.5	18.7	27

IDAHO.

Serial No.	Town or city	County	Name of material	Crushing strength, pounds per square inch.	Weight per cubic foot.	Absorption, pounds per cubic foot.	Per cent of wear.	French coefficient of wear.	Hardness.	Toughness.
10462	St. Anthony	Fremont	Basalt	(³)	159	4.17	7.2	5.6	16.7	4
17329	Filer	Twin Falls	Olivine basalt	(³)	175	1.34	4.6	8.7	16.3	12

ILLINOIS.

Serial No.	Town or city	County	Name of material	Crushing strength, pounds per square inch.	Weight per cubic foot.	Absorption, pounds per cubic foot.	Per cent of wear.	French coefficient of wear.	Hardness.	Toughness.
15938	Olive Branch	Alexander	Chert	(³)	148	1.97	9.7	4.1	(³)	(³)
18739	Irondale	Cook	Slag	(³)	126	1.17	19.9	2.0	(³)	(³)
11224	McCook	do	Dolomite	(³)	158	2.33	6.0	6.7	(³)	(³)
11220	Thornton	do	do	(³)	157	2.27	6.8	5.9	(³)	(³)
11872	do	do	Argillaceous dolomite	(³)	162	2.43	5.5	7.3	13.6	6
14426	South Chicago	do	Slag	(³)	141	3.48	9.1	4.4	14.3	6
16039	do	do	Dolomite	(³)	159	3.12	4.5	8.9	14.0	7
12236	Whitehill Quarry	Johnson	Siliceous limestone	(³)	195	.54	4.9	8.2	14.7	12
9750	Aurora	Kane	Smelter slag	(³)	221	.17	2.2	18.2	(³)	(³)

Lab. No.	Locality	County	Kind of rock							
2367	Kankakee	Kankakee	Dolomite	11,180	158	2.12	8.4	4.8	16.0	5
11790	Lehigh	do	Argillaceous dolomite	(2)	157	3.08	7.6	5.7	14.3	7
197	do	do	Dolomite	(2)	162	2.60	4.6	8.7	12.7	7
208	Fox Township	do	do	(2)	159	1.67	4.9	8.2	13.3	8
11133	Coniac	Kendall	Argillaceous limestone	(2)	156	2.73	12.9	3.1	(?)	(2)
1230	Alton	Livingston	Limestone	(2)	166	.93	5.9	6.8	12.7	4
14949	do	Madison	Fossiliferous limestone	35,320	166	1.19	6.0	6.7	18.3	10
19451	(1)	Union	Argillaceous limestone	22,570	167	.37	3.5	11.4	16.3	9
002	Cobden		Limestone	(?)	168	.27	4.0	10.5	16.0	10
	do (near)		Smelter slag	(?)	212	.00	7.3	5.5	18.7	7
10772	Aurora (near)	Will	Dolomite	8,130	168	1.18	4.9	8.2	15.1	8
9827	Joliet		Slag	(?)	149	2.54	10.1	4.0	(?)	(2)
18861	do									

INDIANA.

Lab. No.	Locality	County	Kind of rock							
132	Henryville	Clark	Dolomitic limestone	(2)	177	1.06	3.5	11.4	17.0	13
98	(1)	do	Argillaceous dolomite	(2)	150	5.23	10.3	3.9	.0	3
182	Brazil	Clay	Limestone	(2)	174	.66	4.3	9.3	17.3	11
0 8	Milltown	Crawford	do	(2)	167	.66	3.3	12.1	16.3	11
019	do	do	do	(2)	168	.60	3.6	11.1	15.0	7
11021	do	do	do limestone	(2)	167	1.17	3.5	11.4	15.3	11
192	do	do	do	(2)	168	.37	3.0	13.3	15.3	6
183	do	do	do lime	(2)	168	.61	4.5	8.9	16.7	7
184	do	do	do	(2)	158	2.78	4.4	9.1	15.7	4
105	do	do	limestone	(2)	161	2.59	5.2	7.7	14.7	8
89	St. Paul	Bar.	do	(2)	168	2.01	4.5	8.9	14.0	5
0 1	do	do	Limestone	(2)	168	1.01	4.0	9.1	13.3	6
11778	do	do	Limestone	(2)	166	1.62	4.7	10.0	12.3	6
4571	Delaware	Delaware	Dolomite	11,250	169	1.43	5.8	8.5	15.7	12
195	Schnellville	Dubois	do limestone	11,980	135	5.82	3.8	6.9	6.7	4
198	St. Anthony	do	tone	(2)	139	6.77	10.2	7.5	10.7	9
189	do	do	do	706	166	.12	10.7	3.9	12.0	6
183	New Paris	Elkhart	do limestone	(2)	164	2.43	4.0	3.7	13.3	4
1374	Floyds Knobs	Floyd	do lime	(2)	132	9.64	4.7	10.0	3.7	3
15375	do	do	do sandstone	(2)	134	9.75	11.8	8.5		7
196	do	do	do	26,420	163	2.10	10.9	3.4	14.0	(2)
53	Huntington	Huntington	Di	(2)	161	5.78	4.10	3.7		9
194	do	do	Argillaceous dolomite	(2)	159	4.30	7.1	9.7	15.3	9
9811	do	Jennings	Dolomite	(2)	167	2.08	5.0	5.6	15.3	4
1947	do	do	lime	49	49	6.90	3.9	10.2	12.0	6
195	do	do	Di	24,150	162	3.67	8.1	4.9	12.3	11
126	do	do	Arg dolomite	27,90	164	1.45	4.8	8.3	14.7	6
117	do	do	Dol mite	15,330	166	1.00	5.7	7.0	13.3	11
123	do	do	do dolomite	14,30	141	2.27	4.5	8.9	8.0	6
12389	Bad.	Lawrence	limestone	(2)	143	7.75	10.9	3.6	.0	5

2 Not made.

TABLE 1.—*Results of physical tests of road-building rock from the United States, Haiti, and Canada—January 1, 1916, to January 1, 1922—Continued.*

INDIANA—Continued.

Serial No.	Town or city.	County.	Name of material.	Crushing strength, pounds per square inch.	Weight per cubic foot.	Absorption, pounds per cubic foot.	Per cent of wear.	French coefficient of wear.	Hardness.	Toughness.
10256	Bloomington (east of)	Monroe	Limestone	(2)	(2)	(2)	(2)	(2)	12.0	4
10257	...do...	...do...	Argillaceous limestone	(2)	(2)	(2)	(2)	(2)	14.6	5
10403	...do...	...do...	Limestone	(2)	185	1.03	4.8	8.3	14.7	7
9860	Greencastle	Putnam	...do...	(2)	168	.66	(2)	(2)	16.7	5
11818	...do...	...do...	...do...	(2)	167	.66	6.9	5.8	15.3	5
10717	...do...	...do...	...do...	(2)	160	1.07	7.3	5.5	9.0	3
10519	Fillmore	...do...	Argillaceous limestone	(2)	159	2.22	(2)	(2)	11.2	6
10520	...do...	...do...	...do...	(2)	162	2.00	(2)	(2)	12.0	6
10020	...do...	...do...	...do...	(2)	159	3.81	4.5	8.9	15.3	9
9935	Elberfeld	Warrick	Limestone	(2)	165	2.89	6.2	6.5	15.0	9
14730	Bluffton	Wells	Dolomite	(2)	170	.41	5.6	7.1	15.7	8
10693	Monon	White	...do...	(2)	166	1.24	5.4	7.5	13.5	7
10094	(1)	(1)	Limestone	(2)	148	8.75	8.9	4.5	.0	5
	(1)	(1)	Argillaceous limestone	(2)	(2)	(2)	(2)	(2)	(2)	3

IOWA.

Serial No.	Town or city.	County.	Name of material.	Crushing strength, pounds per square inch.	Weight per cubic foot.	Absorption, pounds per cubic foot.	Per cent of wear.	French coefficient of wear.	Hardness.	Toughness.
13913	Brandon	Black Hawk	Limestone	(2)	161	0.36	4.7	8.5	15.0	4
11783	Dubuque	Dubuque	Argillaceous dolomite	(2)	169	1.55	5.7	7.1	15.0	7
13903	Stone City	Jones	Dolomite	(2)	132	11.81	14.5	2.7	0.0	4
11614	Council Bluffs (near)	Mills	Limestone	(2)	166	.43	6.4	7.4	15.7	6
15961	(1)	Story	Dolomite	(2)	(2)	(2)	3.4	6.3	(2)	2
15962	(1)	...do...	Limestone	(2)	(2)	(2)	(2)	11.8	(2)	(2)

KANSAS.

Serial No.	Town or city.	County.	Name of material.	Crushing strength, pounds per square inch.	Weight per cubic foot.	Absorption, pounds per cubic foot.	Per cent of wear.	French coefficient of wear.	Hardness.	Toughness.
9599	Fort Scott (7 miles west of)	Bourbon	Limestone breccia	7,380	47	5.11	12.5	3.2	5.0	3
15939	Sedan	Chautauqua	Argillaceous limestone	(2)	55	3.64	9.2	4.4	(2)	4
11683	Lawrence	Douglas	...do...	(2)	54	4.40	7.6	3.7	8.7	6
11684	...do...	...do...	...do...	(2)	52	3.97	6.1	5.3	14.7	4
11687	Lawrence (near)	...do...	...do...	(2)	38	2.40	9.3	6.6	4.0	4
11689	Lecompton	...do...	Cherty limestone	(2)	57	1.01	31.8	4.3	8.7	5
11681	Junction City	Geary	Argillaceous limestone	(2)	19	12.30	1.0	1.3	12.0	3
11682	...do...	...do...	Cherty limestone	(2)	34	10.22	(2)	3.1	14.0	2

Laboratory number	Locality	County	Kind of rock								
11695	....do	Geary	Argillaceous limestone	(²)	149	5.44	13.7	2.9	14.3	(²)	7
11696	....do	....do	do	(²)	164	1.51	5.6	7.0	11.3		5
11686	Tonganoxie	Leavenworth	do	(²)	156	2.91	7.6	5.3	15.7		6
11692	Neeley	....do	Limestone	(²)	155	2.60	8.3	4.8	4.3		4
9780	Beloit	Mitchell	Argillaceous limestone	(²)	143	6.71	18.2	2.2	(²)		3
11694	Council Grove	Morris	Chert	(²)	153	2.45	4.6	8.7	11.7	(²)	2
11693	Council Grove (near)	....do	Argillaceous limestone	(²)	153	3.67	9.1	4.4	16.7		8
11677	Helmick	....do	do	(²)	132	8.85	11.5	3.5	2.7		3
11678	....do	....do	do	(²)	122	9.19	30.1	1.3	.0		3
11679	....do	....do	do	(²)	143	6.59	15.0	2.7	.0		7
11680	....do	....do	do	(²)	134	9.25	19.5	2.1	18.7		
14882	Woodruff (2½ miles west of)	Phillips	Sandstone	(²)	144	1.77	5.7	7.0			
14711	(¹) of).	Riley	Dolomite	(²)	174	2.20	4.0	10.0	15.3	(²)	10
11676	Levis	Shawnee	Limestone	(²)	165	1.35	5.1	7.8	13.3		8
11685	....do	....do	do	(²)	156	3.14	7.7	5.2	16.5		6
11685	Topeka	....do	Argillaceous limestone	(²)	152	4.72	8.7	4.6	10.3		6
11690	....do	....do	do	(²)	151	4.99	7.7	5.2	12.0		5
11691	....do	....do	do	(²)	144	7.76	7.2	5.6	13.3		3
11697	....do	....do	do	(²)	160	2.42	6.7	6.0	13.0		6

KENTUCKY.

Laboratory number	Locality	County	Kind of rock								
16746	Jackson	Breathitt	Feldspathic sandstone	(²)	153	4.62	8.6	4.7	0.0	(²)	5
11343	Princeton (near)	Caldwell	Cherty limestone	(²)	164	.48	4.5	8.9	16.7		8
16192	....do	....do	Limestone	(²)	167	.47	6.0	7.8	(²)		11
12754	Grayson (near)	Carter	Argillaceous limestone	(²)	167	.18	5.1	7.8	15.0		6
17060	Olive Hill	....do	Limestone	(²)	169	.15	17.6	2.3	15.3		8
17075	....do	....do	Ferrugineous sandstone	(²)	(²)	(²)	4.5	8.9	15.3		6
17003	....do	....do	Limestone	(²)	167	.61	4.5	8.2	14.0		4
17158	....do	....do	Limestone	(²)	167	.65	6.1	6.3	12.7		4
10134	....do	Fayette	Argillaceous limestone	(²)	168	.19	5.5	5.7	(²)		6
10136	....do	....do	do	(²)	168	.17	5.0	7.6	14.0		5
16537	Nicholasville	Jessamine	Limestone	(²)	171	1.14	5.3	4.0	.7		4
17257	....do	....do	do	(²)	167	1.15	9.9	4.2	.0		5
17061	East Bernstadt	Laurel	Limestone	(²)	143	4.62	9.5	4.9	8.0		4
16778	Bradenburg	Meade	Feldspathic sandstone	(²)	169	7.34	8.1	6.7	16.7		5
17011	Harrodsburg	Mercer	Argillaceous limestone	(²)	169	.28	6.0	11.8	13.0		13
17658	....do	....do	Crystalline limestone	(²)	170	.20	3.4	7.4	3.3		7
17073	Livingston	Rockcastle	Limestone	(²)	147	2.20	5.8	6.9	(²)		11
19599	Morehead	Rowan	Siliceous dolomite	(²)	163	5.22	5.2	7.7	(²)		7
16313	(¹)	....do	Feldspathic sandstone	(²)	167	5.09	4.7	8.5	14.2		6
16416	Elkton	Todd	Calcareous sandstone	(²)	147	.63	(²)	(²)	13.7		10
10451	Cerulean Springs (near)	Trigg	Limestone	(²)	163	.45	(²)	(²)	15.5		
9829	(¹)	(¹)	Argillaceous limestone	(²)	165	1.31					
9830	(¹)	(¹)	Argillaceous limestone	(²)	165	.82					

¹ Exact locality not known. ² Test not made.

TABLE 1.—*Results of physical tests of road-building rock from the United States, Haiti, and Canada—January 1, 1916, to January 1, 1922*—Continued.

LOUISIANA.

Serial No.	Town or city.	County.	Name of material.	Crushing strength, pounds per square inch.	Weight per cubic foot.	Absorption, pounds per cubic foot.	Per cent of wear.	French coefficient of wear.	Hardness.	Toughness.
11241	New Orleans	Orleans	Argillaceous sandstone	(²)	128	11.35	19.1	2.1	14.7	6
18145	Florien	Sabine	Sandstone	(²)	135	6.29	7.0	5.7	16.3	9
20927	(¹)	(²)	Granite	28,810	163	.47	4.0	10.0	19.3	8

MAINE.

Serial No.	Town or city.	County.	Name of material.	Crushing strength, pounds per square inch.	Weight per cubic foot.	Absorption, pounds per cubic foot.	Per cent of wear.	French coefficient of wear.	Hardness.	Toughness.
11483	Auburn	Androscoggin	Biotite gneiss	(²)	170	0.58	4.4	9.1	18.0	8
12755	Portland	Cumberland	Sericite schist	(²)	170	.18	4.1	9.8	17.3	14
12756	...do	...do	Granite	(²)	166	.24	3.8	10.5	18.0	10
10219	North Jay	Franklin	...do	21,260	164	.84	2.7	14.8	19.3	7
11416	...do	...do	Biotite granite	25,090	(²)	(²)	(²)	(²)	17.3	11
12283	...do	...do	Granite	(²)	163	.69	4.4	9.1	19.0	9
9997	Mnt Desert	Hancock	...do	19,780	165	.21	3.4	11.8	19.7	9
10233	...do	...do	...do	19,220	162	.90	4.1	9.8	18.7	8
10234	...do	...do	...do	24,700	160	.67	3.2	12.5	18.7	12
6304	...do	...do	...do	(²)	164	.51	3.3	12.1	17.3	12
0968	Ship Harbor	...do	...do	28,650	165	.21	(³)	(³)	19.3	18
0969	...do	...do	...do	26,500	163	.31	(³)	(³)	18.7	13
190	...do	...do	...do	32,450	164	.42	(³)	(³)	19.3	16
17439	Swans Island	...do	Biotite granite	36,530	163	.55	3.4	11.8	18.7	13
13862	(¹)	...do	salite	(²)	(²)	(²)	3.7	10.8	18.7	10
11327	Hallowell	Kennebec	...do	25,380	162	.78	3.0	13.2	18.7	8
1486	...do	...do	...do	27,760	163	.72	3.2	12.5	18.7	7
11408	Litchfield	...do	Biotite gneiss	(²)	168	.40	4.0	10.0	19.3	6
11468	Nw	...do	Mica schist	(²)	164	.47	4.1	9.8	15.0	8
11215	Camden	Knox	Biotite quartzite	18,040	172	.22	3.4	11.8	16.7	11
17022	Clark Island	...do	Biotite granite	24,915	168	.63	2.6	15.4	19.0	12
123	...do	...do	...do	22,315	168	.65	2.6	11.8	18.0	11
724	...do	...do	...do	30,825	169	.53	2.5	16.0	18.7	10
9996	Long die	...do	Granite	17,540	168	.22	3.3	12.1	19.2	13
10249	...do	...do	Biotite granite	22,500	165	.86	3.0	13.3	19.3	8
10250	...do	...do	Granite	22,330	166	.82	3.4	11.4	19.3	10
13868	...do	...do	Biotite granite	(²)	(²)	(²)	3.5	11.8	18.7	10
9706	Rockland	...do	Marble	(²)	175	.40	4.3	9.3	17.0	4

¹ Exact bility not known.   ² Test not made.

No.	Locality	Kind of rock	County							
11411	Rockport	Granite	do.	31,580	(²)	(²)	(²)	(²)	18.0	8
9781	St. George	do.	do.	18,780	(²)	(²)	(²)	(²)	(²)	12
9865	...do...	do.	do.	17,150	(²)	(²)	(²)	(²)	18.8	9
11418	...do...	Biotite granite	do.	25,180	(²)	(²)	(²)	(²)	18.0	10
19944	Vinal Haven	do.	do.	(²)	165	.57	3.1	12.9	19.3	13
10019	...do...	do.	do.	21,650	165	.25	3.1	12.9	19.3	14
13854	...do...	Granite	do.	32,090	(²)	(²)	(²)	12.1	18.7	11
11414	...do...	Biotite granite	do.	(²)	165	.43	3.3	11.8	18.7	13
19212	...do...	do.	do.	33,485	(²)	(²)	3.4	11.4	18.0	11
13855	...do...	do.	do.	(²)	165	(²)	3.4	11.8	18.0	14
13866	State Point	Biotite gneiss	do.	(²)	165	.89	9.5	4.2	17.3	10
11406	Bowdoinham	...do...	Sagadahoc	(²)	169	1.63	7.1	5.6	(²)	3
11421	...do...	Gneissoid granite	do.	(²)	163	1.74	12.4	3.2	17.0	(²)
11422	...do...	Biotite gneiss	do.	(²)	163	1.79	11.4	3.5	18.0	(²)
11404	Richmond	Granite	do.	(²)	163	.76	4.1	9.8	17.0	5
11405	...do...	Biotite gneiss	do.	(²)	170	1.41	8.4	4.8	18.0	5
11407	...do...		do.						17.3	3

MARYLAND.

No.	Locality	Kind of rock	County							
16350	Ashland[1]	Blast furnace slag	Baltimore	(²)	162	2.04	6.7	6.0	(²)	6
16851	do.	do.	do.	(²)	138	9.91	19.0	2.1	15.3	6
16852	do.	do.	do.	(²)	166	3.52	6.5	6.7	(²)	13
16853	do.	do.	do.	(²)	175	.97	4.6	8.7	17.3	11
14167	Baltimore	Copper blast furnace slag	do.	(²)	203	.57	5.5	7.3	15.3	12
14179	do.	do.	do.	(²)	205	.95	5.5	7.7	18.7	5
14193	do.	do.	do.	(²)	199	.72	3.1	12.9	12.3	8
20319	do.	Feldspathic quartzite	do.	(²)	169	.21	(²)	5.2	14.0	6
11556	Bare Hills	Tale rock	Baltimore	(²)	161	1.02	7.7	7.8	15.0	15
20558	Butler	Lime gneiss	do.	(²)	168	.56	5.1	7.1	15.0	7
19028	Cockeysville (near)	Marble	do.	(²)	163	.19	5.6	11.4	17.0	5
11335	Raspeburg	Hornblende schist	do.	(²)	186	.41	3.5	6.0	17.0	6
11336	do.	Hornblende gneiss	do.	(²)	165	.89	6.7	5.8	11.0	6
20116	Sparks	Biotite gneiss	do.	(²)	169	1.24	6.9	4.8	19.3	4
20167	do.	Biotite granite	do.	(²)	170	1.26	8.4	5.3	17.3	8
18639	Texas	Marble	do.	(²)	172	.22	7.6	4.0	18.3	10
14846	Towson	do.	do.	(²)	175	.38	9.9	9.5	18.0	(²)
19508	do.	Micaceous marble	do.	(²)	165	.21	4.2	8.2	16.0	17
20114	do.	Gneissoid granite	do.	(²)	172	.57	5.4	7.4	16.7	9
15387	Port Deposit	Marble	Cecil	(²)	169	.30	4.9	14.3	(²)	10
12802	do.	Hornblende white schist	do.	(²)	163	.01	2.8	(²)	17.3	5
20318	do.	Biotite gneiss	do.	(²)	183	.57	(²)	15.3	18.3	11
15161	Sykesville-Rising Sun	Hypersthene granite	Frederick	(²)	(²)	2.02	3.0	13.8	18.0	(²)
10105	Frederick	Lime	do.	(²)	169	.25	2.9	15.4	16.0	6
6196	do.	Siliceous limestone	do.	(²)	172	.14	2.6	9.8	16.7	19
12630	Lime Kiln	Argillaceous limestone	do.	(²)	170	.11	4.1	9.8	16.0	21
9692	do.	Altered gabbro	Harford	(²)	189	.18	2.6	9.8	16.0	
12360	Belair (near)	Amphibolite	do.	(²)	190	.17	2.8	14.3	18.7	
14348	...do...		do.							

¹ Exact locality not known.   ² Test not made.

TABLE 1.—*Results of physical tests of road-building rock from the United States, Haiti, and Canada—January 1, 1916, to January 1, 1922*—Continued.

MARYLAND—Continued.

Serial No.	Town or city.	County.	Name of material.	Crushing strength, pounds per square inch.	Weight per cubic foot.	Absorption, pounds per cubic foot.	Per cent of wear.	French coefficient of wear.	Hardness.	Toughness.
20191	Havre de Grace	Harford	Hornblende schist	(²)	185	.18	2.9	13.8	17.7	16
13669	Kingsville (near)	do.	Amphibolite	(²)	191	.41	4.0	10.0	17.3	10
10021	North Laurel	Howard	do.	(²)	200	.46	3.5	11.4	17.7	8
20316	Savage	do.	do.	(²)	190	.48	(²)	(²)	17.7	14
20388	...do.	do.	do.	(²)	190	.23	1.5	26.7	19.3	30
17458	(¹)	do.	Hornblende gneiss	(²)	167	.78	4.6	8.7	19.3	8
12607	Bethesda (near)	Montgomery	Mica gneiss	(²)	168	.33	3.4	11.8	18.5	9
10101	Dickerson	do.	Diabase	(²)	(²)	(²)	1.4	28.6	15.4	21
12766	...do.	do.	do.	(²)	181	.12	2.6	15.4	(²)	(²)
14264	...do.	do.	Epidote hornblende gneiss	(²)	187	.24	(²)	(²)	18.7	20
11152	Halpine	do.	Biotite granite	(²)	198	.65	3.1	12.9	16.0	11
11153	...do.	do.	Diabase	(²)	171	.42	3.1	12.9	18.7	13
13728	(¹)	Prince Georges	Diabase	(²)	(²)	(²)	1.6	25.0	(²)	(²)
1342	Cavetown	Washington	Marble	(²)	171	.29	3.6	11.1	16.0	9
14424	Weverton	do.	Quartzite	(²)	167	.31	3.1	12.9	(²)	(²)

MASSACHUSETTS.

Serial No.	Town or city.	County.	Name of material.	Crushing strength, pounds per square inch.	Weight per cubic foot.	Absorption, pounds per cubic foot.	Per cent of wear.	French coefficient of wear.	Hardness.	Toughness.
10016	Great Barrington	Berkshire	Marble	(²)	175	0.37	5.6	7.1	15.3	4
11508	Lee	do.	Dolomitic marble	(²)	179	.31	7.2	5.6	11.2	2
10288	Otis	do.	Granite	18,260	166	.71	2.6	15.4	18.0	9
15457	Pittsfield (west)	do.	Marble	(²)	172	.65	5.1	7.8	13.3	7
12473	Windsor	do.	Quartzite	(²)	164	.24	3.9	10.3	18.7	12
11017	Acushnet	Bristol	Chlorite gneiss	(²)	167	.44	2.4	16.6	19.0	17
9770	Fall River	do.	Biotite gneiss	(²)	178	.27	2.7	14.8	18.2	17
10247	Seekonk	do.	Feldspathic sandstone	(²)	167	.76	4.0	10.0	18.7	12
15178	...do.	do.	do.	(²)	165	1.21	4.3	9.3	18.7	14
15179	...do.	do.	Siliceous slate	(²)	164	1.84	3.9	10.3	(²)	(²)
11413	Beverly	Essex	Hornblende granite	28,580	(²)	(²)	(²)	(²)	19.3	9
12289-A	...do.	do.	Biotite syenite	(²)	(²)	.87	(²)	(²)	17.0	24
12289-B	...do.	do.	Hornblende granite	(²)	181	.87	(²)	(²)	19.0	15
20878	Danvers	do.	Diorite	(²)	186	.35	2.8	14.3	18.3	10
9649	Gloucester	do.	Granite	19,580	165	.32	3.7	10.8	19.7	10
9650	...do.	do.	...do.	18,125	165	.35	4.4	9.1	19.7	10
19958	Essex	do.	...do.	(²)	163	.51	4.8	8.3	18.7	8

Lab. No.	Locality	County	Kind of rock	Crushing strength	Weight per cu. ft.	Cementing value	French coef. of wear	Toughness	Hardness	Per cent of wear
18650	Dover (near)	Jones	Fossiliferous limestone	(²)	150	3.85	10.6	3.8	13.7	(²)
12883	Pollocksville	do.	Shell limestone	(²)	(²)	(²)	16.9	2.4	17.0	(²)
20043	Osgood	Lee	Siliceous slate	(²)	174	.34	2.8	14.3	15.0	11
19996	Sanford		Altered basalt	(²)	180	.26	2.9	13.8	16.0	23
18044	Bugno	Madison	Dolomite	(²)	181	.25	3.5	11.4	18.3	11
11397	Ashford	MacDowell	Dolomitic marble	(²)	178	.41	4.5	8.9	38.0	8
250	Old Fort		Altered granite porphyry	(²)	169	.44	4.3	9.3	18.7	9
4514	(¹)	Mecklenburg	Weathered granite	(²)	163	.37	2.3	8.9	18.3	8
4515	(¹)		Quartzite	(²)	166	.54	2.9	17.4	18.3	(²)
4516	(¹)		Uralite diabase	(²)	182	.80	3.7	10.8	18.0	14
5285	(¹)		Altered mite granite	(²)	134	.65	2.8	10.8	18.0	26
16869	Mitchell	Mitchell	Granite gneiss	(²)	168	.37	3.7	10.5	12.7	9
17485	Swift Island Ferry	Montgomery	Amphibolite	(²)	185	.98	3.8	4.1	18.3	17
12888	Castle Hayne	New Hanover	Limestone	(²)	152	4.88	9.8	15.4	18.0	5
19419	Franklinville	Randolph	Altered rhyolite tuff	(²)	171	.27	2.6	14.3	18.7	18
19909	do.		Fragmental rhyolite	(²)	171	.15	2.8	18.2	18.3	24
19980	Ashboro		Hornblende epidosite	(²)	191	.47	2.2	11.8	19.3	14
20527	Stacey	Rockingham	Granite	39,170	163	.61	2.9	13.8	18.7	10
20528	do.		do.	41,410	165	.29	4.6	8.7	19.3	9
9892	Rowan	Rowan	do.	34,860	162	.41	2.0	20.0	19.0	10
10306	Granite Quarry		do.	28,340	164	.22	11.4	11.4	19.0	11
15009	Granite Quarry (near)		Gneissoid granite	20,030	163	.57	(²)	12.1	19.3	15
11415	Granite Qarry		Granite	23,580	164	.51	3.3	14.3	19.3	7
13972	Salisbury		do.	17,800	162	.43	2.8	12.1	18.0	10
10412	do.		do.	26,400	164	.43	3.3	7.7	18.3	9
10413	(¹)		do.	37,820	162	.44	5.2	18.2	17.3	7
10770	(¹)		Biotite gneiss	12,290	163	.55	2.2	12.1	18.7	10
11200	(¹)		Biotite granite	13,680	166	.61	3.3	5.6	18.0	9
20119	(¹)		Granite	23,990	166	.56	7.1	7.8	18.3	11
11706	Harris (near)	Rutherford	do.	(²)	162	.61	5.1	7.4	18.7	6
12116	Harris		do.	(²)	164	.71	5.4	8.7	14.0	4
11420	Mount Airy	Surry	Biotite gneiss	(²)	162	.79	4.6	8.0	17.7	11
13527	do.		do.	26,375	165	.59	5.0	8.8	18.3	6
14891	do.		do.	(²)	169	1.31	4.1	9.5	17.7	7
20·20	do.		Siliceous slate	(²)	166	.55	7.0	9.5	12.3	8
20802	Penrose	Transylvania	Gneissoid granite	(²)	165	.65	4.2	8.2	18.0	4
19924	(¹)		do.	(²)	166	.52	4.2	13.3	17.7	8
19925	(¹)		do.	(²)	173	.60	4.9	11.1	17.7	9
19926	(¹)		Biotite granite	(²)	163	.72	3.0	10.0	18.0	7
19927	(¹)		do.	35,140	167	.51	3.6	10.8	13.0	10
15442	Monroe	Union	Siliceous slate	(²)	162	.79	4.0	14.3	18.0	7
15078	Graystone	Vance	Gneissoid granite	31,050	170	.45	3.4	8.2	18.7	6
15474	do.		do.	(²)	165	.56	2.8	12.5		7
15079	do.		Biotite granite	(²)	163	.47	4.9	23.5		6
4244	Henderson (near)		do.	(²)	186	.38	3.2	8.2	18.0	8
19787	Cary	Wake	Biotite granite	(²)	168	.65	4.9		18.7	(²)
14175	Raleigh (near)		do.							19
15012	do.		Olivine diabase							9
16004	Raleigh		Hornblende granite							

¹ Exact locality not known.   ² Test not made.

NORTH CAROLINA—Continued.

Serial No.	Town or city.	County.	Name of material.	Crushing strength, pounds per square inch.	Weight, per cubic foot.	Absorption, pounds per cubic foot.	Per cent of wear.	French coefficient of wear.	Hardness.	Toughness.
19654	Rollsville	Wake	Biotite granite	21,790	167	.53	7.0	5.7	18.0	7
11402	Wendell	do	do	(²)	164	1.04	4.3	9.3	17.3	4
14174	....do	do	do	(²)	(²)		(²)	(²)	17.0	5
16256	Manson	Warren	Gneissoid granite	21,920	164	.76	4.2	9.5	18.0	6
11566	Neverson	Wilson	Granite		165	.34	5.4	7.4	18.7	9
19405	Bald Mountain	Yancey	Altered rhyolite	21,920	163	.02	2.9	13.8	19.2	28
19406	....do	do	do	60,725	166	.12	3.0	13.3	18.3	15

OHIO.

Serial No.	Town or city.	County.	Name of material.	Crushing strength, pounds per square inch.	Weight, per cubic foot.	Absorption, pounds per cubic foot.	Per cent of wear.	French coefficient of wear.	Hardness.	Toughness.
16722	Liberty Township	Adams	Limestone	(²)	173	0.60	5.5	7.3	11.0	5
14016	Delphos	Allen	Argillaceous dolomite	(²)	169	.20	4.8	8.3	16.2	6
14018	...do	do	Dolomite	(²)	174	1.04	5.1	7.8	15.3	9
14019	...do	do	do	(²)	171	.89	4.4	9.1	14.7	9
14772	...do	do	Argillaceous dolomite	(²)	170	.70	4.8	8.3	15.3	13
9884	Lima	do	Dolomite	(²)	165	2.67	3.2	12.5	14.7	7
10025	...do	do	Argillaceous limestone	(²)	168	2.77	3.7	11.4	14.7	12
10026	...do	do	do	(²)	168	1.96	3.6	10.8	16.0	11
10027	...do	do	do	(²)	169	2.26	3.6	21.1	15.0	11
10305	...do	do	Limestone	(²)	166	1.80	3.7	9.5	14.7	9
15216	...do	do	Argillaceous dolomite	(²)	166	1.86	6.2	10.8	.0	7
20055	Somerset	Belmont	Sandstone	(²)	142	1.84	26.6	6.5	14.7	2
19379	...do	do	do	(²)	135	7.48	24.2	1.5	.0	2
20449	Union Township	do	do	(²)	136	6.28	24.6	1.7	44.0	4
20054	Warren	Butler	Feldspathic sandstone	(²)	141	2.33	4.1	1.6	(²)	
9953	Middletown	do	Bbc open-hearth slag	(²)	209	2.74	20.4	9.8	(²)	6
9854	...do	do	do	(²)	190	.20	6.9	1.7	12.7	7
19625	Lewis	Brown	Limestone	(²)	169	.63	7.2	5.8	10.7	6
20099	Perry	do	Argillaceous lime	(²)	169	.20	6.4	6.3	11.7	5
20921	...do	do	do	(²)	166	2.06	4.3	9.3	11.3	3
20922	Sterling	Clark	do	(²)	150	2.19	19.6	2.0	(²)	5
16660	Springfield	Clermont	Limestone	18,575	141	7.30	5.5	7.3	13.0	6
17062	Miamiville	do	Miss sandstone	(²)	171	.17	5.3	7.6	11.3	6
19140	Stonelick	do	do	(²)	168	.58	10.0	4.0	11.7	6
16728	(¹)	do	do	(²)	69	.78	6.6	6.1	13.3	6
20129	(¹)	do	do	(²)	171	.47	5.2	7.6	13.2	4
10516	Farmer	Clinton	do	(²)	171	1.66				

No.	County	Locality	Material								
10517	do	do	Siliceous limestone	(²)	167	.49	6.6	6.1	13.7	(²)	5,5
14524	Richland	do	Argillaceous dolomite	(²)	157	3.48	9.4	4.3	13.3	(²)	5
15096	Columbiana	Leetonia	Blast-furnace slag	(²)	111	8.42	16.2	2.5	(²)	(²)	
12890	Cuyahoga	Berea	Sandstone	(²)	124	7.41	(²)	(²)	(²)	(²)	9
18718		Cleveland	Slag	(²)	141	4.09	15.6	2.6	(²)		6
18730		do	do	(²)	136	5.12	21.0	1.9	2.7		8
12891		Euclid	Sandstone	(²)	139	6.55	(²)	(²)	(²)		9
15464	Defiance	(¹)	Shale	(²)	157	.45	10.0	4.0	15.8		10
15215	Delaware	Defiance	Argillaceous limestone	(²)	163	4.93	5.3	7.6	15.0		8
20394		Delaware	do	(²)	168	1.52	3.5	11.4	12.9		6
1131-		Troy	Limestone	(²)	167	1.38	3.0	13.3	15.9		4
13073	Erie	Sandusky	do	14,615	169	1.07	4.8	8.5	12.4		6
13074		do	do	(²)	166	1.56	4.7	10.3	13.3		7
19783	Franklin	Franklin	Argillaceous limestone	(²)	167	.70	12.1	3.3	(²)		
16347		Columbus	Blast-furnace slag	(²)	139	5.44	2.0	10.0	14.7		6
17079		do	Limestone	(²)	165	1.44	4.3	9.3	(²)		7
16340		do	Argillaceous limestone	(²)	167	1.39	5.4	7.4	15.2		
16418		Marble Cliff	do	25,900	162	1.14	(²)	(²)	15.3	(²)	3
10536		do	do	(²)	(²)	(²)	4.7	8.5	.0		10
15888	Gallia	Springfield	Limestone	26,285	166	1.52	4.5	8.9	15.0		15
17411	Hardin	Dunkirk	Sandstone	(²)	166	1.50	23.7	1.7	15.3		10
19327		Kenton	Argillaceous dolomite	(²)	142	7.18	3.4	11.8	17.0		
11329		do	Dolomite	(²)	167	2.17	2.7	14.8	(²)		5
11202		do	do	(²)	167	2.08	2.5	16.0	14.0		6
11225	Highland	Fairfield	do	(²)	164	2.35	3.9	13.0	19.3		5
16417		do	do	(²)	168	2.12	13.5	3.0	12.7		6
20519		do	do	(²)	166	2.35	14.2	2.8	12.7		10
20520		Homer	Argillaceous dolomite	(²)	154	4.45	7.1	5.6	12.7		7
2521		Paint	Dolomite	(²)	160	2.86	7.4	5.4	12.7		5
14525		do	do	(²)	169	1.35	12.5	2.3	13.3		6
19141		do	do	(²)	161	2.92	11.6	3.4	3.7		5
19142		(¹)	Argillaceous dolomite	(²)	160	3.90	6.5	6.2	13.7		5
19730	Holmes	Salt Creek Township	Dolomite	(²)	165	1.78	5.3	7.5	3.7		4
16939	Huron	Bellevue	do	(²)	163	1.00	6.9	5.8	13.7		6
19929		Huron	Limestone	(²)	164	3.91	4.9	8.2	6.0		9
11198		do	Feldspathic sandstone	(²)	156	4.89	6.3	6.3	10.3		
13095	Jackson	Clarksfield	Slag	7,910	157	5.85	7.5	5.3	(²)		6
11203		Jackson	Blast furnace slag	(²)	176	7.75	4.5	8.9	(²)		11
18717	Jefferson	Island Creek	Sandstone	(²)	156	.39	10.3	3.9	(²)		14
20566	Lawrence	Ironton	Blast furnace slag	(²)	146	2.78	18.2	2.2	(²)		
20348		do	do	(²)	181	4.30	5.8	6.9	(²)		
9854		do	do	(²)	148	1.73	7.2	5.6	15.3		
15906	Lorain	Lorain	Slag	(²)	153	4.08	7.1	5.6	16.0		
15997		do	Blast furnace slag	(²)	136	3.97	8.6	4.7	18.0		
18728		Lorain	Slag	(²)	123	5.89	16.8	2.4			
14833	Lucas	do	Dolomite	(²)	123	5.71	24.3	1.6			
18731		Toledo	Slag	(²)	172	.49	6.1	6.6	12.7		6
13093		do	Argillaceous dolomite	(²)	135	3.51	15.7	2.5	16.3		11
18865		Waterville	Slag	(²)	168	2.36	3.3	12.1	16.3		14
9800		do	Argillaceous dolomite	(²)	168	2.04	2.8	14.3			
9983		do	Dolomite								

¹ Exact locality not known.   ² Test not made.

TABLE 1.—*Results of physical tests of road-building rock from the United States, Haiti, and Canada—January 1, 1916, to January 1, 1922—Continued.*

OHIO—Continued.

Serial No.	Town or city.	County.	Name of material.	Crushing strength, pounds per square inch.	Weight per cubic foot.	Absorption, pounds per cubic foot.	Per cent of wear.	French coefficient of wear.	Hardness.	Toughness.
13179	Waterville	Lucas	Slate	(?)	171	.40	8.6	4.6	16.0	14
13397	do	do	do	(?)	165	.23	4.0	10.0	16.0	19
16747	do	do	do	(?)	163	2.07	6.9	6.5	4.3	6
11097	Whitehouse	do	Siliceous limestone	(?)	161	2.90	6.2	6.6	9.3	6
19289	do	do	Argillaceous limestone	(?)	160	3.49	6.1	2.1	7.0	6
18737	Brier Hill	Mahoning	Slag	(?)	135	5.16	19.5	3.1	(*)	(*)
16290	Youngstown	do	do slag	(?)	201	3.07	12.8	2.0	(*)	(*)
17501	do	do	do	(?)	(*)	(*)	20.1	1.6	(*)	(*)
17505	do	do	do	(?)	(*)	(*)	26.0			
10637	Piqua	Miami	Dolomite	9,810	156	2.53	10.3	3.9	11.0	4
10538	do	do	do	15,150	178	.97	4.8	8.3	15.0	13
10535	Centerville	Montgomery	do lime	(?)			(*)	(*)	10.9	3
19350	Deerfield	Morgan	Sandstone	(?)	138	8.54	16.7	2.4	13.3	3
19352	do	do	Argillaceous limestone	(?)	168	.74	6.2	6.5	12.7	0
16922	Malta	do	Limestone	(?)	168	.26	6.5	6.2	15.3	6
17389	do	do	do limestone	(?)	164	1.32	4.7	8.5	14.7	7
19351	do	do	do	(?)	162	1.64	5.9	6.8		8
16171	do	do	Feldspathic sandstone	(?)	143	6.78	7.7	5.2	.0	4
16173	do	do	do	(?)	138	7.61	10.5	3.8	.0	4
19377	Stock	Noble	Ferruginous sandstone	(?)	142	6.92	11.9	3.4	.0	7
19378	do	do	do limestone	(?)	168	.23	6.0	6.7	16.0	5
19793	Allen	Ottawa	Dolomite	(?)	162	3.15	9.4	4.3	13.3	7
9973	do	do	do	13,360	162	(*)	5.5	7.3	12.0	9
9945	Rocky Ridge	Perry	Chert	(?)	175	.41	5.4	7.4	£2.0	
19452	Thorn Township	Pickaway	do	(?)	152	1.95	7.4	5.4	(*)	9
15217	Circleville	do	Dolomitic marble	(?)	164	2.82	4.4	9.1	14.7	9
10639	New Paris	Preble	Dolomite	16,480	167	1.12	3.4	11.8	16.7	6
12258	Woodville	Sandusky	do	(?)	160	4.14	7.5	5.3	17.0	7
13888	do	do	do	(?)	159	3.85	5.8	6.9	16.0	7
16647	do	do	do	(?)	162	3.53	5.8	6.9	(*)	(*)
19781	Bascom	Seneca	Argillaceous limestone	16,565	161	3.71	7.9	5.1	8.7	4
11330	Bloomville	do	Dolomite	(?)	166	2.22	3.6	11.1	12.5	6
19831	Clinton Township	do	do	(?)	160	2.90	5.4	7.4	12.7	7
19782	Liberty	Trumbull	do	(?)	165	2.72	7.5	5.3	11.0	7
18732	Hubbard	do	Slag	(?)	137	5.63	13.0	3.1	(*)	(*)
18734	MacDonald	do	Blast furnace slag	(?)	125	5.80	15.4	2.6	(*)	5
20578	Dover	Tuscarawas	slag	(?)	120	7.67	18.0	2.2	12.7	10
11328	do	Van Wert	Argillaceous limestone	27,570	169	1.76	3.8	10.5	13.6	

No.	Locality	County	Kind of rock							
14771	...do...	...do...	Dolomite	(²)	166	2.07	5.0	8.0	15.7	8
9947	Bowling Green	Wood	...do...	(²)	165	1.38	7.5	5.3	12.2	6
10346	Lockey	...do...	...do...	(²)	162	3.68	5.0	5.5	12.0	6
9883	North Baltimore	...do...	Argillaceous dolomite	(²)	168	2.61	5.0	8.0	16.0	10
9957	...do...	...do...	Dolomite	(²)	168	2.08	4.0	10.0	14.3	14
15947	...do...	...do...	Argillaceous dolomite	(²)	168	2.57	4.6	8.7	(²)	(²)
19446	(¹)	...do...	Feldspathic sandstone	(²)	156	2.80	4.3	9.3	14.7	8

OKLAHOMA.

No.	Locality	County	Kind of rock							
19366	Springtown	Atoka	Chert	(²)	158	1.75	4.6	8.7	15.7	9
19367	...do...	...do...	...do...	(²)	161	.82	4.0	10.0	19.3	16
14997	Armstrong (near)	Bryan	Fossiliferous limestone	(²)	164	1.49	6.3	6.4	13.3	6
16134	Armstrong(near)	...do...	Limestone	(²)	166	1.46	4.9	8.2	15.7	6
15118	do (near)	...do...	...do...	(²)	153	5.08	6.4	6.3	.07	5
16170	do	...do...	Arg. sandstone	(²)	158	3.69	6.1	6.6	14.7	6
16136	Durant (near)	...do...	Cal. sandstone	(²)	154	5.32	6.8	5.9	11.3	7
16135	Durant (near)	...do...	Fossiliferous	(²)	167	1.20	4.9	8.2	14.7	7
19348	Troy	Johnston	Diabase	(²)	189	.09	4.0	10.0	18.7	20
19349	...do...	...do...	Granite	(²)	163	.57	10.3	3.9	18.0	8
20583	Bromide	...do...	Lime	(²)	163	1.94	5.9	6.8	15.3	8
17738	(¹)	Kay	Argillaceous limestone	(²)	145	6.28	8.2	4.9	12.0	4
17057	Gowen	Latimer	Sandstone	(²)	143	5.02	15.8	2.5	(²)	
18228	Salina	Mayes	Chert	(²)	(²)	(²)	4.8	9.3	(²)	
18229	...do...	...do...	...do...	(²)	(²)	(²)	5.7	8.3	(²)	
18230	...do...	...do...	...do...	(²)	(²)	(²)	5.6	7.0	.7	
19098	Okmulgee	Okmulgee	Ferruginous sandstone	(²)	102	5.61	4.1	2.6	15.7	4
15957	Hartshorne	Pittsburg	do	(²)	168	.49	3.8	9.8	(²)	5
17875	...do...	...do...	do	(²)	163	1.32	4.2	10.5	(²)	7
15510	Barnett	Tulsa	...do...	(²)	163	3.03	5.7	9.5	13.3	6
15790	Lost City	...do...	...do...	(²)	161	2.50	7.4	7.0	11.0	5
16588	Tulsa	...do...	...do...	(²)	159	2.63	8.2	5.4	12.3	5
16826	...do...	...do...	...do...	(²)	166	.66	6.1	4.9	12.0	6
16825	Sands Springs	...do...	...do...	(²)	163	1.59	6.0	7.8	13.0	6
15788	...do...	...do...	...do...	(²)	161	1.93	5.8	6.7	12.7	5
15789	Tulsa	...do...	...do...	(²)	64	1.07	5.7	6.9	14.7	5
14914	(¹)	Washington	ous limestone	(²)	165	1.16	7.1	7.0	14.0	5
11640	Dewey	...do...	...do...	(²)	166	1.10	5.3	5.6	11.3	12
11641	...do...	...do...	do	(²)	164	1.14	5.3	7.6	18.3	13
16060	(?)	(?)	...do...	(²)	159	1.88	1.7	7.6	18.3	
16062	(?)	(?)	do	(²)	155	2.28	4.9	23.5		
16060	(?)	(?)	...do...	(²)	156	1.72	2.3	17.4		

OREGON.

No.	Locality	County	Kind of rock							
18224	La Grande (near)	Baker	Basalt	(²)	174	1.62	3.4	11.8	18.7	18
18223	Nelsons	Malheur	Marble	(²)	166	.69	5.9	6.8	16.7	7

¹ Exact locality not known. ² Test not made.

TABLE 1.—*Results of physical tests of road-building rock from the United States, Haiti, and Canada—January 1, 1916, to January 1, 1922*—Continued.

PENNSYLVANIA.

Serial No.	Town or city	County	Name of material	Crushing strength, pounds per square inch.	Weight per cubic foot.	Absorption, pounds per cubic foot.	Per cent of wear.	French coefficient of wear.	Hardness.	Toughness.
9786	Granite	Adams	Gabbroitic diabase	23,435	(?)	(?)	(?)	(?)	15.2	14
16012	York Springs	do	Diabase	(?)	189	0.53	1.8	22.2	18.7	34
14582	Carnegie	Allegheny	Lead slag	(?)	238	.38	4.3	9.3	17.3	14
8729	Duquesne	do	Slag	(?)	140	3.78	13.7	2.9	(?)	(?)
16077	Parkers Landing	Armstrong	Limestone	19,470	161	.88	4.2	9.5	15.3	6
10104	Birdsboro (near)	Berks	Diabase	(?)	188	(?)	1.7	23.5	18.7	13
14468	Birdsboro	do	do	(?)	141	.35	(?)	(?)	18.7	10
8863	do	do	Slag	(?)	170	3.24	9.5	4.2	(?)	(?)
14642	Douglas Township	do	Altered slate	(?)	114	.32	1.9	21.1	18.7	28
8862	Temple	do	Slag	(?)	165	8.08	18.8	2.1	(?)	(?)
8221	Tuckertown (near)	do	Siliceous limestone	(?)	160	.12	3.7	10.8	15.7	10
11733	Yardley (near)	do	Granite gneiss	16,330		.21	4.0	10.0	18.3	15
13129	Tyrone	Blair	Sandstone	(?)		.13	3.3	12.1	18.7	12
5989	do	do	Chert	(?)	(?)	(?)	3.0	13.3	(?)	(?)
5987	Rock Hill	Bucks	Hypersthene diabase	(?)	(?)	(?)	2.3	17.4	18.0	(?)
11409	Quakertown	do	Diabase	34,040	(?)	(?)	(?)	(?)	18.3	10
12166	do	do	Hypersthene diabase	(?)	191	.17	2.8	14.3	(?)	25
14150	Johnstown	Cambria	Open-hearth slag	(?)	186	2.02	11.0	3.6	(?)	(?)
14151	do	do	Slag	(?)	128	6.88	18.9	2.1	(?)	(?)
12908	(?)	do	Sandstone	(?)	152	1.48	7.4	5.4	15.3	9
13174	(?)	do	do	(?)	153	.27	6.7	6.0	18.3	8
13178	Lehigh Gap	Carbon	Quartzite	(?)	152	.27	8.2	4.9	16.7	7
2477	do	do	Feldspathic quartzite	(?)	165	.42	3.3	12.1	18.7	17
2478	Palmerton	do	Spigel slag	15,090	178	.35	3.3	14.3	18.7	16
11261	Summithill	do	Feldspathic sandstone	(?)	123	7.52	13.1	3.1	18.0	10
14943	Devault	Chester	Dolomitic marble	(?)	163	.83	4.7	8.5	14.0	5
9087	do	do	Dolomite	(?)	176	.70	7.7	5.2	14.0	8
14294	Howellville	do	Marble	(?)	177	.51	4.0	10.0	(?)	(?)
17919	do	do	do	(?)	173	.36	4.3	9.3	14.0	5
12767	Berwick	Columbia	Sandstone	(?)	175	.31	4.6	8.7	14.0	14
12181	Catawissa	do	Feldspathic sandstone	(?)	164	.35	4.8	8.3	18.7	17
12186	do	do	do	(?)	167	.38	2.8	14.3	19.3	25
12361	Conewago	Dauphin	Diabase	(?)	166	.41	3.2	12.5	18.0	20
10357	Erie	Delaware	Biotite gneiss	(?)	188	.35	2.8	14.3	18.0	9
8866	(?)	Erie	Slag	(?)	135	2.35	16.5	2.4	(?)	(?)
9773	Connellsville	Fayette	Siliceous limestone	(?)	168	.46	2.8	14.3	17.7	13
8727	Dunbar	do	Slag	(?)	129	6.33	14.5	2.8	(?)	(?)
13933	Point Marion	do	Feldspathic sandstone	(?)	151	3.53	10.3	3.9	11.0	6

No.	Locality	County	Kind of rock								
1590	Fayetteville	Franklin	Quartzite	(²)	158	.85	4.9	8.2	19.0	11	7
12379	Union Furnace	Huntingdon	Marble	(²)	173	.33	3.9	10.3	15.7	7	3
15440	Donaghmore	Lebanon	Blast-furnace slag	(²)	123	8.50	8.8	4.5	(²)	(²)	
14999	Emaus	Lehigh	...d diorite	(²)	175	.77	5.8	6.9	(²)	(²)	
8740	Hockendauqua	do	Slag ... slag	(²)	134	5.65	13.1	3.1	12.3	7	
15441	do	do	Slag ... slag	(²)	130	5.70	17.1	2.3	(²)	3	
8867	do	do	Diorite	(²)	121	5.10	19.5	2.1	18.0	10	
5351	(¹)	do	Diorite	(²)	184	.91	5.0	8.0	16.7	13	
11225	Duryea	Luzerne	Feldspathic ...ite	36,000	167	.41	3.4	11.8		19	
11352	White Haven	do	a ...te	20,380	(²)	17	(²)	15.4	18.3	16	
8104	do	do	...the	21,160	169	44	2.6	15.4	18.2	9	
10672	Irey Shore	Lycoming	...is limestone	22,460	166	27	2.6	4.5	14.7	8	
19239	Rio Bluff	do	do	(²)	168	10	7.3	6.6	16.2	6	
10518	...ville	do	...ne	(²)	168	18	6.6	5.3	15.3	5	
2929	Montoursville (near)	...mery	...d ...e	(²)	169	30	7.5	17.4	17.3	24	
12261	...n Lane	do	...is ...e	(²)	169	38	2.3	9.5	18.0	10	
8587	do		...ne marble	(²)	172	26	4.2	8.2	15.3	7	
3939	Ivy ...	...d	Slag	(²)	177	54	4.9	12.8	19.0	11	
17921	...e	d	Slag	38,949	168	4.83	3.2	8.1			
8735	...n (near)	...n	Dolomite	18,990	133	04	14.4	7.5	15.0	10	
2688	...n (near)		...e	21,440	174	14	4.9	2.6	14.7	7	
12690	do			(²)	171	28	5.2	6.5	11.8	8	
2691	do		...t ... free slag	(²)	167	5.19	6.2	2.4	12.3	3	
15439	do		Slag ...	(²)	139	6.15	20.2	3.6			
8736	do		...e	(²)	129	1.98	11.9	6.1	15.7	8	
5264	...in	...m	Blast-furnace slag	(²)	174	4.42	6.1	4.3	13.7	3	
10137	66th ...		Feldspathic ...e	(²)	145	43	9.3	16.7	19.5	13	
12234	...ia (near)		...te	(²)	166	53	2.4	12.1	19.0	7	
10429	Mint Carmel	Northumberland	...te	21,530	163	58	3.3		18.7	10	
9812	Holmesburg	Philadelphia	...e ...iss	25,930	165	(²)	(²)		18.7	12	
1410	do	do	do	(²)	(²)	(²)	(²)		18.7	7	
3907	do		...te	(²)	165	1.04	4.9	8.2	16.0	10	
14785	Matamoras	Pike	Feldspathic ...te	25,250	170	63	5.2	8.0	16.7	12	
11190	Shohola	do	d... ...s	24,790	158	34	3.6	12.5	16.7	7	
10345	Confluence	Somerset	...s	(²)	169	35	2.3	11.1	17.7	19	
14691	(¹)	(¹)	Siliceous limestone					17.4			

RHODE ISLAND.

No.	Locality	County	Kind of rock							
19418	Cranston	Providence	Granite gneiss	(²)	167	0.37	3.1	12.9	18.7	10
10248	East Providence	do	Feldspathic sandstone	(²)	168	.59	3.6	11.1	18.0	12
10171	Lincoln	do	Granite gneiss	(²)	170	.17	3.9	10.3	18.7	12
10467	Westerly	Washington	Granite gneiss	31,450	161	.37	3.9	10.3	18.7	9
11398	do	do	Biotite granite	18,260	162	.37	2.4	16.7	19.3	11
12445	do	do	Granite	(²)	162	.56	(²)	(²)	13.7	15

¹ Exact locality not known. ² Tests not made.

TABLE 1.—Results of physical tests of road-building rock from the United States, Haiti, and Canada—January 1, 1916, to January 1, 1922—Continued.

SOUTH CAROLINA.

Serial No.	Town or city.	County.	Name of material.	Crushing strength, pounds per square inch.	Weight per cubic foot.	Absorption, pounds per cubic foot.	Per cent of wear.	French coefficient of wear.	Hardness.	Toughness.
15453	Trenton	do	Biotite granite	(²)	164	0.74	3.2	12.5	(²)	(²)
10531	Rion (near)	do	do	25,540	165	.59	4.4	9.1	18.3	8
14765	Rion (near)	do	do	20,100	164	(²)	3.5	11.4	18.0	12
11417	Winsboro	do	do	22,970	(²)172	.69	(²)		18.0	7
10129	Greenville	do	Hornblende gneiss	(²)	165	.68	8.0	5.0	17.0	6
10131	Greenville (17 miles from)	d	do	(²)	165	.82	8.4	4.4	18.7	8
20015	Travelers Rest	d	do	(²)	167	.91	9.1	4.4	17.7	6
20188	do	d	do	(²)	(²)	(²)	4.1	9.8	(²)	
20321	do	d	Granite	(²)	164	.52	4.8	8.3	17.7	5
14457	Cayce	Lexington	do	33,090	163	.51	3.5	12.9	18.3	13
19652	Leesville	McCormick	gneiss	37,680	166		3.1	12.8	13.7	13
14298	McCormick (4 miles east)	McCormick	do	(²)	171	2.82	10.6	3.8	16.7	8
14301	Beverly	do	gneiss	(²)	163	.34	9.8	4.1	(²)	
10130	Columbia (near)	Rand	gneiss	21,500	166	.99	4.1	12.9	17.7	4
11647	Columbia (near)	do	do	(²)	165	.18	6.4	12.9	18.0	8
19682	Spartanburg	do	Quartz	(²)	165	.57	6.3	6.3	18.5	
15153	Lockhart	Union	do	(²)	189	.64	2.4	5.9	19.0	10
12803	Rock Hill	York	gabbro	(²)	188	.10	3.2	12.5	18.0	17

SOUTH DAKOTA.

Serial No.	Town or city.	County.	Name of material.	Crushing strength, pounds per square inch.	Weight per cubic foot.	Absorption, pounds per cubic foot.	Per cent of wear.	French coefficient of wear.	Hardness.	Toughness.
19068	Bijou Hills	Brule	Opaline sandstone	(²)	144	1.76	(²)	(²)	18.0	10
17874	(¹)	Gregory	Calcareous sandstone	(²)	140	3.92	7.4	5.4	17.7	9
17872	Gregory	do	Tuffaceous limestone	(²)	144	5.66	14.2	2.8	6.7	6
18101	Piedmont (west of)	Meade	Dolomitic limestone	(²)	159	3.05	7.1	5.6	9.3	5
10108	Dell Rapids	Minnehaha	Quartzite	(²)	165	.41	2.8	14.3	19.3	17
18885	Dell Rapids	Minnehaha	Quartzite	51,700	166	0.07	2.5	16.0	18.7	20
19596	do	do	do	(²)	(²)	(²)	(²)	(²)	(²)	
10894	Sioux Falls	do	Olivine diabase	(²)	163	.27	1.4	28.6	19.3	17
10895	do	do	do	36,280	190	.37	2.7	14.8	18.7	18
9894	do	do	Quartzite	(²)	170	.30	2.3	17.4	18.7	17
10096	Rowena	do	do	(²)	164	.28	2.7	14.8	19.3	17
13729	(¹)	do	do	(²)	(²)	(²)	(²)	(²)	19.7	30
13730	Colome (near)	Tripp	Sandstone	(²)	149	1.06	9.3	4.3	16.3	6
16017	do	do	do	(²)	148	1.52	8.6	4.7	(²)	
16018	Colome	do	Siliceous limestone	(²)	144	4.19	24.8	1.6	5.3	5
16019	do	do	Tuffaceous limestone	(²)	138	6.12	10.9	3.7	(²)	7

¹ Exact locality not known.   ² Test not made.

No.	Locality	County	Kind of rock		Weight per cubic foot	Per cent of wear	Hardness	Toughness	French coefficient of wear	Cementing value
9992	Maryville	Blount	Argillaceous limestone	(²)	168	0.40	3.8	10.5	16.7	6
9993	do	do	Limestone	(²)	168	.30	4.3	9.3	15.7	5
16326	Harrogate (near)	Claiborne	Dolomite	(²)	174	.92	3.2	12.5	16.0	14
10327	do	do	do	(²)	171	1.86	3.6	11.1	16.3	7
10292	New Tazewell	do	Siliceous limestone	(²)	172	1.84	4.2	9.5	13.3	8
10446	New Tazewell (near)	do	Dolomite	(²)	170	1.20	4.1	9.8	13.3	9
10581	do	do	Siliceous dolomite	(²)	145	1.93	4.1	3.7	13.2	9
10483	Jamestown	Fentress	Sandstone	(²)	168	3.97	10.8	10.3	15.0	4
12703	Chattanooga (near)	Hamilton	Limestone	(²)	168	.11	3.9	3.6	16.0	10
12740	do	do	Argillaceous limestone	(²)	169	.20	4.2	8.8	16.0	9
13064	Chattanooga	do	limestone	(²)	168	.08	4.5	8.8	15.7	8
15986	Erin	Houston	Siliceous sinter	16,030	90	21.32	43.1	9	(²)	2
11521	Asbury	Knox	Marble	(²)	169	.23	6.0	6.7	13.3	3
11519	Knoxville	do	do	(²)	169	.13	5.7	5.7	13.6	5
11520	do	do	do	9,230	168	.11	7.3	7.3	13.0	4
11522	do	do	do	(²)	168	.17	6.2	6.5	13.0	3
11523	do	do	do	(²)	168	.20	5.5	7.3	13.0	3
11524	do	do	do	23,000	178	.47	5.0	9.8	16.0	11
9887	Mascot	Lawrence	Dolomite	(²)	168	.25	6.1	6.6	15.6	8
16275	Iron City	Loudon	Agrillaceous limestone	(²)	178	.41	4.0	10.0	12.6	3
11526	Amaro	Monroe	Marble	(²)	167	.46	6.3	6.4	17.3	8
10315	Madisonville	do	Ferruginous sandstone	(²)	171	.77	8.3	4.8	16.7	9
10316	do	do	Siliceous limestone	(²)	171	.33	4.2	9.5	17.3	9
10317	do	do	Limestone	(²)	174	1.36	6.0	6.6	15.7	8
10318	do	do	do	(²)	158	2.05	3.3	12.1	9.7	5
16323	do	do	Crystalline limestone	(²)	165	.64	4.9	8.2	12.9	18
10414	(¹)	do	Siliceous-dolomite	(²)	168	2.65	4.5	8.8	13.2	5
17507	Clarksville (near)	Montgomery	Limestone	(²)		1.64	4.3	6.3	17.3	5
19913	Livingston (near)	Overton	do	(²)	170	.17	3.5	10.3	(²)	12
9734	Byrdstown	Pickett	Argillaceous dolomite	(²)	170	.84	6.9	7.3	12.3	13
9735	do	do	do	(²)	175	.29	6.6	5.8	15.3	(²)
16897	Copperhill	Polk	Smelter slag	(²)	169	.49	2.5	16.0	17.3	5
11525	Luttrell	Union	Marble	(²)			5.7	7.0	15.3	4
14840	Brayesville	Washington	Limestone	(²)						16
14464	Johnson City	do	Siliceous limestone	(²)						5
14841	Washington College	do	Limestone	(²)						

TEXAS.

No.	Locality	County	Kind of rock		Weight per cubic foot	Per cent of wear	Hardness	Toughness	French coefficient of wear	Cementing value
16633	Blanket	Brown	Argillaceous limestone	(²)	162	1.42	6.7	6.0	(²)	5
18686	New Braunfels	Comal	Limestone	(²)	160	2.44	5.5	7.3	11.3	6
20092	do	do	do	(²)	161	1.21	5.5	7.3	12.0	6
13880	El Paso	El Paso	Lead slag	(²)	222	1.60	7.1	5.6	(²)	(²)
15004	(¹)	do	Smelter slag	(²)	224	.80	4.8	8.3	(²)	(²)
15005	do	do	Lead smelter slag	(²)	212	.65	9.8	4.1	(²)	(²)
17633	Fredericksburg	Gillespie	Limestone	(²)	(²)	(²)	6.9	5.8	(²)	(²)

¹ Exact locality not known. ² Test not made.

TABLE 1.—Result of physical tests of road-building rock from the United States, Haiti, and Canada—January 1, 1916, to January 1, 1922—Continued.

TEXAS—Continued.

Serial No.	Town or city	County	Name of material	Crushing strength, pounds per square inch.	Weight per cubic foot.	Absorption, pounds per cubic foot.	Per cent of wear.	French coefficient of wear.	Hardness.	Toughness.
10044	(¹)	Grayson	Clay lime	(²)	134	12.80	(²)		.0	2
12488	Longview	Gregg	Ferruginous shale	(²)	153	9.74	25.8	1.6	9.0	3
12489	...do	...do	Ferruginous do	(²)	178	4.89	13.7	2.8	13.5	6
12496	...do	...do	Ferruginous	(²)	150	7.31	13.9	2.9	11.3	3
12491	Gladewater	...do	...do	(²)	143	9.06	16.6	2.4	3.8	4
16590	(¹)	Harrison	...do	(²)	165	4.72	21.0	1.9	(²)	11
16828	Groesbeck	Limestone	Siliceous limestone	(²)	158	1.32	6.0	6.7	19.3	8
17497	Limestone	Llano	lime	(²)	164	.38	2.5	17.4	13.0	21
17442	Llano	...do	lime	(²)	135	.98	6.9	6.9	(²)	9
11347	Bowie	Montague	Quartz conglomerate	(²)	148	6.62	21.6	1.9	15.3	6
19458	Mineral Wells	Palo Pinto	...do limestone	(²)	162	2.39	4.3	9.3	13.3	5
19397	...do	Schleicher	...do	(²)	147	4.34	12.4	3.2	12.0	4
19398	...do	...do	Limestone	(²)	150	5.11	7.9	5.1	17.3	11
17080	Friendship	Smith	Ferruginous sandstone	(²)	166	5.62	27.3	1.5	17.6	5
17074	Starville	...do	...do	(²)	177	8.47	5.7	7.0	13.0	9
17020	San Angelo	Tom Green	Limestone conglomerate	(²)	155	.41	5.7	7.1	18.7	29
17943	...do	...do	Dolomite	(²)	155	1.21	4.8	8.3	14.3	4
13106	Austin	Travis	Nephalite basalt	(²)	195	4.65	2.8	14.3		
11395	Waco	Wise	Limestone	(²)	169	.30	5.7	7.0		

UTAH.

Serial No.	Town or city	County	Name of material	Crushing strength, pounds per square inch.	Weight per cubic foot.	Absorption, pounds per cubic foot.	Per cent of wear.	French coefficient of wear.	Hardness.	Toughness.
14250	Price	Carbon	Limestone	(²)	168	0.47	4.9	8.2	16.7	6
14251	Price (near)	...do	Argillaceous limestone	(²)	166	.91	4.5	8.9	15.3	7
14257	Price	...do	...do	(²)	156	3.28	5.8	8.6	15.3	7
14258	...do	Emery	Calcareous sandstone	(²)	161	2.15	6.3	6.4	14.7	8
14252	Castle Dale	...do	Limestone conglomerate	(²)	154	3.95	17.3	2.3	(²)	(²)
14253	...do	...do	Argillaceous limestone	(²)	168	.48	4.7	8.5	16.0	6
14254	Castle Dale (near)	...do	Calca reus lime	(²)	161	2.08	3.3	12.1	15.3	19
14249	Emery (near)	...do	Limestone	(²)	162	2.16	7.1	5.6	16.0	12
14867	Polson Spring Bench	...do	Argillaceous limestone	(²)	144	5.93	7.3	5.5	12.0	3
15281	...do	...do	...do	(²)	139	4.66	8.4	4.8	10.7	5
14968	(¹)	...do	Limestone	(²)	166	.87	8.7	8.5	16.0	7
14255	...do	Salt Lake	Calcareous sandstone	(²)	166	1.79	7.6	5.3	14.7	7
13999	Garfield	...do	Copper slag	(²)	210	1.03	4.9	8.2	(²)	(²)
15107	...do	...do	...do	(²)	202	.27	5.0	8.0	(²)	(²)
15109	...do	...do	...do	(²)	208	1.37	6.6	60	18.0	13
14643	Midvale	...do	Lead slag	(²)	221	.97	4.7	8.5	14.7	7

No.	Locality	County	Kind of rock	Crushing strength	Weight per cubic foot	Water absorbed	Per cent of wear	French coefficient	Hardness	Toughness
12190	Hardwick	Caledonia	Biotite granite	(2)	165	1.11	(2)	(2)	17.0	8
10848	Burlington	Chittendon	Siliceous dolomite	40,700	163	.26	3.7	11.1	16.7	13
11503	do	do	Siliceous marble	(2)	177	.78	(2)	(2)	17.6	24
11191	Darby	do	Siliceous limestone	16,050	171	.46	3.0	13.3	17.3	9
11488	Dor	Rutland	Serpentine marble	12,720	171	.22	(2)	(2)	18.0	6
11489	do	do	Black marble	8,755	171	.17	4.6	8.7	16.7	16
11490	do	do	Marble	11,045	170	.26	5.9	6.8	14.3	9
11491	do	do	do	7,750	167	.32	16.9	(2)	11.0	3
11492	do	do	do	6,945	168	.55	7.2	2.4	(2)	(2)
11493	do	do	do	9,520	167	.56	9.3	4.6	(2)	2
11494	do	do	do	7,105	168	.31	10.6	4.3	(2)	2
11495	do	do	do	7,380	168	.41	(2)	3.8	(2)	2
11496	do	do	do	7,110	168	.39	6.4	(2)	(2)	3
11497	do	do	do	8,770	168	.46	7.8	6.3	(2)	3
11498	do	do	do	10,120	168	.52	7.8	5.1	(2)	3
11499	do	do	do	9,010	168	.32	4.8	8.3	(2)	3
11500	do	do	do	2,300	168	.28	7.3	5.5	(2)	4
11501	do	do	do	8,730	168	.36	(2)	(2)	(2)	3
11502	do	do	do	(2)	168	.41	2.8	14.3	(2)	4
11528	do	do	do	(2)	165	.45	(2)	(2)	7.3	9
9673	Barre	Washington	Biotite granite	(2)	165	.37	(2)	(2)	19.0	11
12209	do	do	do	(2)	165	.47	(2)	(2)	18.0	11
12200	Bethel	Windsor	Granite	(2)	164	.52	(2)	(2)	18.0	11

VIRGINIA.

No.	Locality	County	Kind of rock	Crushing strength	Weight per cubic foot	Water absorbed	Per cent of wear	French coefficient	Hardness	Toughness
10253	Charlottesville	Albemarle	Granite gneiss	(2)	171	0.75	5.4	7.4	17.3	5
12863	do	do	Mica schist	(2)	166	4.13	4.1	9.8	18.0	6
15887	Charlottesville (near)	do	Amphibolite	(2)	182	1.47	6.8	5.9	15.0	7
19332	Hatton	do	Altered diabase	(2)	187	.19	4.4	9.1	17.4	12
13299	Ivy	do	Amphibolite	(2)	194	.28	3.0	13.3	18.0	24
13712	do	do	Biotite gneiss	(2)	176	.86	4.6	8.7	17.0	8
20582	Mecharus River (near)	do	do	(2)	178	.46	4.7	8.5	17.0	8
14131	Ivins River (near)	do	Sericite schist	(2)	177	.74	5.4	7.4	(2)	6
9161	(1)	do	Biotite gneiss	(2)	168	.77	17.5	2.3	18.3	(2)
20581	Wills Crossing	do	do	(2)	178	.42	5.6	7.1	18.7	6
9926	(1)	do	Hornblende gneiss	(2)	181	.57	5.1	7.8	16.3	7
9927	(1)	do	Biotite gneiss	(2)	193	.98	3.5	11.4	17.6	9
9928	(1)	do	Sericite schist	(2)	175	.62	5.3	7.5	18.3	7
13376	(1)	do	Biotite gneiss	(2)	165	.69	5.0	8.0	18.7	7
13298	(1)	do	do	(2)	173	1.21	5.4	7.4	16.7	3
16454	(1)	do	Gneiss	(2)	176	.77	6.2	6.5	(2)	7
20197	(1)	do	Granite gneiss	(2)	169	.61	5.8	6.9	18.3	12
10172	Clifton Forge		Siliceous limestone	(2)	166	.48	2.5	16.0	17.6	10

1 Exact locality not given.   2 Tests not made.

VIRGINIA—Continued.

Serial No.	Town or city	County	Name of material	Crushing strength, pounds per square inch	Weight per cubic foot	Absorption, pounds per cubic foot	Per cent of wear	French coefficient of wear	Hardness	Toughness
17332	Long Dale	Alleghany	Slag	(²)	152	1.86	12.0	3.3	(²)	7
20890	...do	...do	Blast furnace slag	(²)	124	3.34	(²)	(²)	16.0	7
14570	Lynchburg	Amherst	Amphibolite	(²)	188	.81	5.3	7.6	16.7	10
20634	Falls Church (near)	Arlington	...granite	(²)	162	.55	2.7	14.8	18.7	11
20190	Basic City	Augusta	Slate	(²)	163	.37	6.4	6.3	17.0	8
20192	Craigsville	...do	Slate	(²)	172	.22	4.5	8.9	14.7	4
14881	Lone Fountain	...do	Limestone	(²)	169	.22	5.8	6.9	16.5	19
16776	...do	...do	Limestone	(²)	174	.34	2.8	14.3	16.7	19
13499	...do	...do	...dolomite	(²)	175	.09	3.1	12.9	16.5	16
13842	Staunton	...do	Limestone	(²)	176	.62	3.5	13.8	15.3	17
20558	...do	...do	Siliceous dolomite	(²)	175	.41	3.5	11.4	17.7	12
20639	...do	...do	Dolomite	(²)	175	1.05	2.9	11.8	15.7	8
20640	...do	...do	...do	(²)	172	.81	4.4	8.2	14.0	18
20637	...do	...do	Limestone	(²)	168	.24	4.9	10.0	16.3	(²)
19978	West Virginia	...do	...phic quartzite	(²)	168	.35	4.0	11.4	(²)	15
19979	...do	...do	Sandstone	(²)	162	1.46	3.5	11.4	16.0	11
19915	()	...do	Siliceous limestone	(²)	174	.31	3.5	13.0	16.0	24
19916	()	...do	...phic sandstone	(²)	163	1.25	3.1	12.9	18.0	6
19917	()	...do	...do	(²)	178	.45	6.3	12.4	15.7	4
19918	()	...do	Sandstone	(²)	168	.34	5.5	8.0	15.3	9
15187	()	...do	...ne	(²)	169	.51	5.9	7.3	15.3	10
15188	()	...do	...do	(²)	168	.52	4.9	8.2	18.7	7
16641	()	...do	...te	(²)	172	.48	2.7	14.8	17.3	9
13990	Lynchburg (west of)	Bedford	...andesite	(²)	175	0.31	10.0	4.0	16.0	14
14224	Major	...do	Hornblende gneiss	(²)	188	.43	6.6	7.2	(²)	8
16227	()	...do	Hornblende chist	(²)	187	.73	10.3	3.9	16.7	12
16228	()	...do	Amphibolite	(²)	192	.82	4.4	9.1	15.0	10
16640	()	...do	Siliceous dolomite	(²)	187	.68	4.8	8.3	16.3	5
16686	()	...do	...do	(²)	176	.32	6.2	9.5	17.2	10
13906	Blue Ridge	Botetourt	Limestone	(²)	174	.17	4.2	12.1	16.3	23
14449	...do	...do	Dolomite	(²)	195	.39	3.3	7.3	(²)	12
19956	Bornack	...do	Argillaceous dolomite	(²)	177	.27	5.5	6.2	16.7	9
13724	Buchanan (near)	...do	Siliceous dolomite	(²)	173	.65	5.0	6.7	18.0	7
15111	Buchanan ()	...do	Calcareous slate	(²)	176	.23	6.0	10.2	16.7	9
16648	Salt Petre Cave	...do	Dolomite	(²)	170	.50	3.9	3.3	(²)	
15452	...do	...do	Quartz	(²)	178	.33	12.0			
15655	Bocock (near)	Campbell	Sericite gneiss	(²)	165	.77				
14651	Bocock (near)	...do	Hornblende epidosite	(²)	165	.35				
11179	Halsey (near)	...do	Quartzite schist	(²)	198	1.34				
9891	Lone Jack Station	...do		(²)	159					

No.	Locality		Rock								
904	do.		Aplitic granite.	20,200	165	.53	5.4	7.4	18.7		7
11551	do.		Quartz.	(?)	162	.71	10.9	3.7	(?)	(?)	14
10344	Lynchburg.		Quartzite.	25,885	190	1.20	4.3	9.3	18.6		8
11251	Lynchburg (near).		Quartz.	(?)	165	.20	4.8	6.9	(?)	(?)	6
11362	Lynchburg.		Hornblende gneiss.	(?)	178	.80	10.3	3.9	19.3		8
12364	do.		Biotite schist.	(?)	196	1.60	6.8	5.5	16.0		7
16307	do.		Dolomitic marble.	(?)	172	.24	6.9	8.8	(?)		9
16763	do.		Hornblende schist.	(?)	196	.52	13.5	5.8	17.0		9
12834	(?)		do.	(?)	184	.27	4.4	3.0	16.3		5
9819	Cliffview.		do.	(?)	181	.71	15.8	9.1	18.3		14
9820	do.		Mica gneiss.	(?)	196	1.16	5.9	2.5	14.3		5
9197	Woodlawn.		do.	(?)	165	1.04	3.0	6.8	17.0		7
10198	(?)		Biotite gneiss.	(?)	163	.28	3.9	13.3	19.3		17
1964	do.		do.	(?)	169	.87	15.7	10.3	18.7		12
18106	Boyce.		do.	(?)	166	.13	6.4	2.5	(?)		
13193	(?)		do.	(?)	168	.05	4.7	6.3	15.0		7
0115	Boston.		Sericite gneiss.	(?)	196	.84	5.4	8.5	19.0		5
19358	do.		Feldspathic sandstone.	(?)	165	.36	4.9	7.4	17.3		8
19359	do.		do.	(?)	167	.57	3.5	8.2	17.7		7
19361	do.		Mica schist.	(?)	168	.50	2.8	11.4	18.0		13
19365	do.		do.	(?)	162	.42	2.9	14.2	18.0		15
20077	do.		Feldspathic stone.	(?)	162	.37	5.4	13.8	18.0		12
11394	Clintwood.		Feldspathic sandstone.	(?)	158	3.14	5.0	7.4	(?)		6
16190	do.		Feldspathic sandstone.	(?)	158	2.47	8.2	8.0	17.3		7
16191	do.		gneiss.	(?)	158	3.03	3.6	4.9	11.3		6
19211	Hampton.		Sericite gneiss.	(?)	155	.69	5.4	11.1	19.3		13
20907	Run.		Amphibolite.	(?)	176	.66	4.0	7.4	15.7		9
0908	Fairfax.		Amphibolite.	(?)	169	1.15	4.1	10.0	18.3		17
17231	do.		Amphibolite.	(?)	174	1.32	9.1	4.4	6.3		6
189	do.		epidote schist.	(?)	185	.72	3.4	9.8	14.0		7
17700	do.		epidote schist.	(?)	187	.51	4.2	11.8	17.7		18
18409	do.		do.	(?)	187	.60	6.0	9.5	16.0		7
19494	do.		do.	(?)	182	1.22	8.9	6.7	13.7		5
19495	do.		schist.	(?)	177	2.04	6.5	4.5	8.0		4
19496	do.		Ferruginous stone.	(?)	180	1.74	16.0	6.2	(?)	(?)	
896	do.		schist.	(?)	175	1.06	12.4	2.5	(?)	(?)	
9824	do.		schist.	(?)	143	6.30	12.9	3.2	.0		6
19617	do.		Amphibolite.	(?)	138	1.23	13.1	3.1	6.3		6
19618	do.		amphibolite.	(?)	184	2.92	10.2	3.0	12.0		5
9819	do.		beta.	(?)	185	1.22	5.9	3.9	.0		5
1011	Herndon.		beta.	(?)	167	2.32	3.8	6.8	(?)		11
19724	do.		Diabase.	(?)	191	.41	6.1	10.5	17.7		9
9809	Fairfax.		Sericite gneiss.	(?)	176	.43	2.5	6.6	15.3		12
0936	do.		Amphibolite.	(?)	192	.33	9.8	16.0	18.3		6
16729	(?)		Mica gneiss.	(?)	172	1.85	2.8	4.1	(?)		15
895	Marshall.			(?)	197	.26	6.6	14.3	18.7		8
15382	do.		granite.	(?)	162	2.16	6.1	6.6	18.0		10
1680	Midland (near).		do.	(?)	164	.65	3.8	10.5	18.7		7
16226	The Plains.		Altered basalt.	(?)	175	.81	3.0	13.3	17.3		28
13195	do.		do.	(?)	188	.50	2.4	16.6	18.3		12
13196			do.	(?)	186	.69	7.9	5.6	16.0		

1 Exact locality not known. 2 Test not made.

TABLE 1.—*Results of physical tests of road-building rock from the United States, Haiti, and Canada—January 1, 1916, to January 1, 1922—Continued.*

VIRGINIA—Continued.

Serial No.	Town or city.	County.	Name of material.	Crushing strength, pounds per square inch.	Weight per cubic foot.	Absorption, pounds per cubic foot.	Per cent of wear.	French coefficient of wear.	Hardness.	Toughness.
15767	The Plains	Faquier	Calcareous talc schist	(²)	180	.81	3.9	10.3	16.7	21
15768	...do	...do	Chlorite talc schist	(²)	177	1.52	10.7	3.7	(²)	(²)
15769	...do	...do	Chlorite schist	(²)	181	.72	11.7	3.4	(²)	24
15770	...do	...do	Chlorite epidote schist	(²)	184	.52	3.2	12.5	17.3	
16308	...do	...do	Hornblende epidote schist	(²)	185	.40	9.9	4.1	(²)	22
16309	...do	...do	Chlorite epidote schist	(²)	184	.72	5.2	7.7	(²)	
16310	...do	...do	Hornblende epidote schist	(²)	190	.42	6.2	6.5	(²)	
16312	...do	...do	Chlorite epidote schist	(²)	187	.44	6.4	6.3	(²)	31
16626	...do	...do	...do	(²)	183	.39	4.4	9.1	(²)	8
17086	...do	...do	...do	(²)	193	.24	5.3	7.5	15.7	
18042	...do	...do	Talc epidote schist	(²)	193	.67	7.9	5.1	(²)	26
18043	...do	...do	...do	(²)	193	.78	4.6	8.7	17.7	
18144	...do	...do	Epidote amphibolite	(²)	189	.32	2.2	18.2	17.7	12
18893	...do	...do	Amphibolite	(²)	188	.33	2.8	14.3	17.3	
18894	...do	...do	...do	(²)	187	.20	3.3	12.1	(²)	
9919	Warrenton	...do	...do	(²)	181	.76	4.6	8.7	(²)	11
9920	...do	...do	Epidote chlorite schist	(²)	185	2.44	5.9	6.7	14.7	19
10304	...do	...do	...do	(²)	202	.63	8.5	12.4	18.3	
13197	(¹)	...do	Epidosite	(²)	194	.54	1.8	22.2	18.3	10
14460	(¹)	...do	...do	(²)	187	1.32	6.0	6.7	17.0	7
15896	(¹)	...do	Chlorite epidote schist	(²)	168	.48	4.8	8.3	11.7	10
20996	Floyd	Floyd	Hornblende mica gneiss	(²)	181	2.81	10.6	3.8	18.3	10
13765	Shores	Fluvanna	Schist	(²)	185	.33	2.4	16.7	15.0	
15485	Strathmore	...do	Mica schist	(²)	164	.19	4.3	12.1	(²)	7
19099	(¹)	...do	Quartz	(²)	169	.02	3.9	5.3	(²)	3
13194	Winchester (near)	Frederick	Limestone	(²)	171	.10	7.5	4.8	15.3	14
14583	...do	...do	...do	(²)	173	.28	8.4	11.4	15.3	5
14579	...do	...do	Dolomite	(²)	158	3.16	3.5	4.5	16.7	15
14880	...do	...do	Calcus slate	(²)	176	.21	8.9	13.3	.0	
14969	...do	...do	Dolomite	(²)	165	.89	3.0	12.9	17.3	
11246	Bluff City	Giles	Siliceous dolomite	(²)	175	.33	3.1	11.1	(²)	9
11248	...do	...do	...do	(²)	177	.52	3.6	12.5	16.3	13
14463	Pembroke	...do	...do	(²)	175	.30	8.2	14.8	17.3	6
11412	Ripplemeade	...do	Biotite granite	19,270	164	(²)	2.7		18.0	10
16988	Forest Hills	Henrico	...do	(²)	(²)	.47	3.4	11.8	17.3	5
16519	Richmond (near)	...do	Limestone	(²)	167	.94	6.9	5.8	18.0	7
14584	Dryden	Lee	Minus limestone	(²)	168	.30	5.7	7.0	(²)	

Laboratory number	Exact locality	County	Kind of rock	Classification	Weight per cubic foot	Water absorbed	French coefficient	Per cent of wear	Hardness	Toughness
20123		do.	Limestone	(a)	169	.20	5.8	6.9	15.3	3
20124		do.	do.	(a)	170	.28	5.4	7.4	15.3	6
12878	Stickleyville	do.	Argillaceous limestone	(a)	167	.17	9.1	4.4	14.3	8
12879		do.	Limestone	(a)	165	.17	5.4	11.4	13.3	8
12880		do.	Ferruginous sandstone	(a)	167	.31	5.3	7.5	8.0	8
13176		do.	Limestone	(a)	169	.01	6.1	6.4	16.0	4
13917		do.	do.	(a)	168	.34	6.0	6.5	16.7	5
13918		do.	Argillaceous limestone	(a)	169	.30	6.4	6.6	15.7	11
13641	(1)		Limestone	(a)	168	.21	3.7	7.4	15.7	9
19723	Albie		Altered basalt	(a)	181	.26	3.3	10.8	17.7	20
20641		do.	Altered diabase	(a)	177	.73	3.1	12.1	18.0	12
20642		Loudoun	Altered basalt	(a)	180	.35	1.9	12.9	18.3	34
19722		do.	Basalt	(a)	187	.24	2.2	20.9	18.7	
16047	Areola	do.	(Gabbroitic diabase)	(a)	(a)	(a)		18.2		(a)
16048	Belmont Park	do.	Amphibolite	(a)	178	.49	2.3	17.4	17.3	10
10009	Hamilton (1 mile east)	do.	the epidote schist	(a)	188	1.20	3.9	10.3		8
15489	Leesburg	do.	the limestone	(a)	172	.92	12.3	3.3	13.7	6
15490		do.	Marble	(a)	175	(a)	6.3	-6.4	17.3	10
20514		do.	Lime conglomerate	(a)	151	.39	4.8	8.3	17.0	10
15457	Luckets	do.	uns sandstone	(a)	187	2.82	3.8	10.5	15.7	17
15488		do.	Conglomerate	(a)	175	.63	3.4	11.8		(a)
16031		do.	Limestone conglomerate	(a)	174	.28	5.8	9.8		(a)
16257		do.	do.	(a)	175	.33	4.1	9.8	18.7	9
16414		do.	Sericite schist	(a)	168	.35	4.3	9.3	19.0	7
17097		do.	Quartzite	(a)	165	.50	5.9	6.8	19.3	8
18762		do.	Sericite gneiss	(a)	168	.25	6.7	6.0	17.7	12
18789		do.	Limestone conglomerate	(a)	175	.36	6.2	6.5	16.7	
14197	Point of Rocks (near)	do.	Basalt	(a)	180	.33	5.7	7.0		10
14198	(1) do.	do.	Feldspathic sandstone	(a)	161	.39	4.5	8.9	18.3	8
14294	Between Blacksburg and Newport,	Montgomery		(a)	185	1.73	3.2	12.5	18.3	14
15152	Arrington (near)	Nelson	Amphibolite	(a)	165	1.42	3.5	11.4	18.3	11
15903		do.	Quartz	(a)	171	.13	7.8	5.1	16.3	11
15904		do.	Altered gneiss	(a)	192	1.60	9.3	4.3	16.3	13
15905		do.	Amphibolite	(a)	171	.61	2.7	14.8	16.3	11
12835	Byrans Mill	(1)	Biotite gneiss	(a)	164	.20	6.5	6.2	12.7	5
20322	Barboursville (near)	Orange	Micaceous sandstone	(a)	182	1.61	12.6	3.3	8.0	5
20323		do.	Talc amphibolite	(a)	165	1.21	12.0	3.3	15.3	6
20324	Barboursville (near)		Micaceous sandstone	(a)	148	1.17	7.6	5.3	8.3	4
15944	Compton	Page	Feldspathic sandstone	(a)	167	5.55	18.0	2.2	14.3	5
14099	Luray	do.	Argillaceous limestone	(a)	170	.75	5.4	7.4	14.0	6
14384	New Design (near)	Pittsylvania	Biotite gneiss	(a)	65	.21	4.5	8.9	18.0	
13071	(1)	do.	Quartz	(a)	172	.20	13.8	2.9	(a)	(a)
13529		do.	Biotite gneiss	(a)	163	.49	4.2	9.5	18.7	10
19943		do.	Sandstone	(a)	166	.68	2.8	14.3	18.7	17
19987		do.	do.	(a)	178	.43	2.7	14.8	17.3	15
10298	Buckland	Prince William	Diabase	(a)	178	1.75	(a)	(a)	17.3	16
15366	Occoquan (near)	do.	Altered granite	(a)	163	1.06	4.7	8.5	19.3	8

1 Exact locality not known.   a Classification not known.   2 Test not made.

TABLE 1.—*Results of physical tests of road-building rock from the United States, Haiti, and Canada—January 1, 1916, to January 1, 1922*—Continued.

VIRGINIA—Continued.

Serial No.	Town or city.	County.	Name of material.	Crushing strength, pounds per square inch.	Weight per cubic foot.	Absorption, pounds per cubic foot.	Per cent of wear.	French coefficient of wear.	Hardness.	Toughness.
20317	Occoquan (near)	Prince William	ite gneiss	(²)	170	1.06	(²)	(²)	18.3	8
15919	Draper	Pulaski	ous l imestone	(²)	168	.35	5.3	7.5	15.3	(²)
16025	do	do	g ous lime	(²)	170	.24	5.4	7.4	15.3	7
16026	do	do	Siliceous clay lime	(²)	165	.20	4.6	8.7	14.7	11
15786	Draper (near)	Rappahannock	Limestone nist.	(²)	167	.71	6.8	5.9	15.0	7
4988	Glenbar (near)	do	Biotite serie nist.	(²)	176	.64	5.1	7.8	16.0	7
15980	Scrabble	do	Feldspathic (me.	(²)	164	.60	4.0	10.0	17.7	12
15960	do	do	ered gneiss	(²)	165	.81	4.9	8.2	18.0	8
14461	Sperryville (near)	do	Altered agtite	(²)	163	.70	3.8	10.5	18.3	12
15963	Woodville	do	Bio gneiss	(²)	171	.34	5.0	8.0	17.0	10
15964	do	do	do	(²)	173	.68	5.5	7.5	17.7	8
19542	do	do	Biotite sericite schist	(²)	175	.38	7.2	5.6	10.0	7
19961	Roanoke	cke	Dolomite	(²)	176	.43	3.0	13.3	15.3	11
20580	(¹)	(¹)	do	(²)	173	.78	7.0	5.7	13.7	4
11549	Buena Vista (near)	Rockbridge	ine ous ite	(²)	170	.78	2.4	14.8	18.3	23
11550	do	do	ous lim ite	(²)	168	.20	2.4	16.7	17.0	11
13041	Glasgow	do	us lim	(²)	165	.19	4.7	8.5	16.3	9
13042	do	do	ine lim.	(²)	175	.20	6.4	6.3	12.7	17
13043	Glasgow (ar)	do	ne lim.	(²)	182	.24	3.0	13.3	(²)	5
17929	Natural Bridge	do	g do	(²)	177	.09	5.2	7.1	2.7	11
17935	do	do	Argill eous	(²)	175	.33	4.4	9.1	18.0	12
14017	Iron Ridge	do	Sili eous dolomite	(²)	169	.19	2.8	14.1	18.9	11
15512	do	do	Siliceous lim tone	(²)	169	.14	3.8	10.5	18.3	14
15513	do	do	do	(²)	169	.26	3.0	13.3	18.7	17
16223	(¹)	do	do	(²)	175	2.10	6.0	6.7	13.3	5
17092	(¹)	do	do	(²)	171	.23	5.7	7.0	12.6	5
16513	Harrisonburg	Rockingham	Argillaceous limestone	(²)	169	.08	5.7	12.1	(²)	13
12789	Balton	do	Dolomite	(²)	175	.15	3.9	10.3	16.7	21
11719	do	do	lime nia	(²)	169	.74	3.9	11.1	17.3	13
12788	Hansonville	do	lime	(²)	171	.08	5.8	6.9	16.7	14
12840	(¹)	Sott.	ous lime	(²)	168	.38	4.1	9.7	15.3	8
10930	Gates City	Shenandoah	eous lme	(²)	172	.32	4.6	8.7	16.0	13
20889	Strasburg Junction	Smyth	do	(²)	173	.81	6.7	6.0	15.7	4
16011	Atkins	do	Dolomite	(²)	173	.38	2.8	14.3	18.0	7
16110	do	do	us lime	(²)	174	.67	4.7	8.6	16.3	7
16262	do	do	Siliceous lomite	(²)	167	9.02	5.6	7.1	(²)	10
16507	do	do	do	(²)	174	.74	5.8	6.9	(²)	9
16509	do	do	Dolomite	(²)	174	.58	5.4	7.4	13.7	7
16589	do	do	Limestone	(²)	169					5

20896	Lopez Island	San Juan	Volcanic sandstone	(?)	(?)	(?)	(?)	3.0	13.3	19.3	(?) 7
20882	Sinclair Islet	Skagit	Altered basalt	(?)	(?)	(?)	(?)	4.6	8.7	13.7	(?) 10
20884	...do...	...do...	...do...	(?)	(?)	177	0.92	3.7	10.8	16.0	24
10209	Cook (3 miles north)	Skamania	Basalt					2.6	15.4	18.3	

WEST VIRGINIA.

13896	B.....ian	Barbour	Sandstone	(?)	147	2.60	7.7	5.2	17.3	(?)	7
1088	B.....naton (east of)	Be....ley	Argillaceous limestone	(?)	172	.19	4.9	8.2	16.0		10
10075	...do...	...do...	...do...	(?)	168	.32	5.6	7.1	(?)	(?)	4
0046	Berkeley Station	...do...	Limestone	(?)	168	.27	6.3	6.4	16.0		6
0085	Blairton (near)	...do...	Argillaceous limestone	(?)	168	.19	5.1	7.8	16.7		5
10064	...do...	...do...	Limestone	(?)	168	.23	5.9	6.8	16.0		4
10070	Bker Hill	...do...	...do...	(?)	168	.24	5.1	7.8	16.0		10
0049	Butts Sare	...do...	Feldspathic sandstone	(?)	140	3.45	7.2	5.6	18.7		4
0085	...do...	...do...	L.....ne	(?)	172	.52	4.6	8.7	16.7		4
10077	Dartsville	...do...	...do...	(?)	168	.31	5.0	8.5	15.0		8
009	Falling Water	...do...	...do...	(?)	68	1.27	4.7	7.1	16.7		
0082	Falling Water (near)	...do...	...do...	(?)	168	.59	5.6	8.5	16.7		
0083	Falling Water	...do...	Chert and limestone, mixed	(?)	(?)	(?)	4.7	7.5	(?)	(?)	4
10074	Ferrell Ridge	...do...	Limestone	(?)	168	1.61	6.2	6.5	14.0		12
	...do...	...do...	....eous limestone	(?)	172	.46	6.5	6.2	15.7		

[1] Exact l.....ality not known.   [2] ....lts not known.

TABLE 1.—*Result of physical tests of road-building rock from the United States, Haiti, and Canada—January 1, 1916, to January 1, 1922*—Continued.

WEST VIRGINIA—Continued.

Serial No.	Town or city.	County.	Name of material.	Crushing strength, pounds per square inch.	Weight per cubic foot.	Absorption, pounds per cubic foot.	Per cent of wear.	French coefficient of wear.	Hardness.	Toughness.
10073	Hedgesville (east of)	Berkeley	Feldspathic sandstone	(²)	165	.62	2.8	14.3	16.7	19
10062	land (west of)	do	Sandstone	(²)	144	3.19	16.6	2.4	19.3	2
10067	Jones Springs	do	Siliceous limestone	(²)	168	.31	4.4	9.1	17.3	9
10081	do	do	...limestone	(²)	168	.37	5.7	7.0	14.0	4
10080	Kile Georgetown	do	Argill...ous ...	(²)	175	.37	6.5	6.2	18.7	10
10064	...rg (south of)	do	Dol mite	(²)	178	.31	3.6	11.1	16.3	10
10086	do	do	Limestone	(²)	168	.56	5.8	6.9	18.0	5
10102	Martinsburg	do	do	(²)	(²)	(²)	5.2	7.7	16.7	6
11708	do	do	do	(²)	170	.19	5.9	6.8	14.0	3
14263	do	do	do	(²)	169	.15	(²)	(²)	14.7	6
14265	do	do	do	(²)	170	.08	7.3	14.4	14.7	3
14266	do	do	D... mite	(²)	169	.09	9.0	4.5	14.0	3
19991	Nip in	do	Limestone	(²)	173	.58	4.8	5.5	17.3	8
10071	Springmills	do	do	(²)	168	.43	4.9	8.2	16.0	3
10072	Tomahawk	do	Siliceous limestone	(²)	168	.27	4.2	9.5	15.0	8
10078	Tomahawk (north of)	do	Sandstone	(²)	168	.27	4.5	8.9	18.3	15
10087	Van Clarksville (south of)	Fayette	Argillaceous limestone	(²)	156	1.66	7.9	5.1	(²)	(²)
10076	Kingston	Grant	Feldspathic sandstone	(²)	168	.36	5.0	8.0	17.0	9
14358	Scherr	g ... limestone	... limestone	(²)	156	3.06	9.3	4.3	14.3	9
10611	Port Springs	...ier	...	(²)	166	.60	5.4	9.8	(²)	(²)
9972	Renick	do	Argillaceous limestone	(²)	168	.24	4.1	10.5	15.7	9
9925	Roncevert	do	Limestone	(²)	168	.66	3.8	9.3	16.3	8
11925	Wite Spur Springs	d...	Feldspathic sandstone	(²)	188	.18	4.3	12.5	16.7	11
11715	(¹)	...e	do	(²)	164	.84	3.2	13.3	18.7	14
11763	Wardensville	Hardy	...e	(²)	165	.82	3.0	13.3	18.7	14
17866	Clarksburg	Harrison	Arg ... limestone	(²)	170	.15	4.9	8.2	13.3	4
14496	Kearneysville	Jefferson	Dolomite	(²)	154	4.34	2.7	8.5	10.0	8
10103	do	do	Feldspathic sandstone	(²)	(²)	(²)	4.8	14.8	14.0	6
15988	do	do	...ne	(²)	169	(²)	4.6	8.3	(²)	(²)
16209	(¹)	Kanawha	Arg ... limestone	(²)	177	.12	4.5	8.7	14.7	6
11609	Charleston (near)	do	Dolomite	(²)	155	.40	4.6	8.9	16.7	6
12728	(¹)	Cabin	Feldspathic sandstone	(²)	157	4.67	12.2	8.7	3.0	7
13706	Hamlin	Logan	do	(²)	153	3.88	4.7	3.3	12.0	5
13908	Hamlin (near)	Marion	Sandstone	(²)	156	4.98	8.7	4.6	12.0	3
13992	Logan	Mercer	...us a ...le	(²)	169	3.90	8.6	4.7	3.3	7
14625	Ridesville	Monongalia	c ...us a ...ne	(²)	163	.86	7.5	5.3	13.3	9
13396	Princeton		...ne	(²)	156	.50	4.3	9.3	16.0	8
16384	Greer		Sandstone	(²)	168	2.80	3.9	10.3	(²)	8
9966			Argillaceous limestone			.73	4.7	8.5	15.7	

Lab. No.	Locality	County	Kind of rock		Weight per cubic foot	Per cent of wear	French coef. of wear	Hardness	Toughness	Cementing value
9967	do	do	do	(³)	168	.59	4.7	8.5	15.7	9
9968	do	do	do	(³)	168	.73	4.8	8.3	14.0	9
9969	do	do	Siliceous limestone	(³)	168	.56	3.0	13.3	16.7	10
15812	Union	Monroe	do	(³)	170	.20	5.3	7.5	16.3	8
15813	do	do	do	(³)	171	.27	4.6	8.7	16.0	9
15814	do	do	Quartzite	(³)	170	.19	2.9	13.8	17.3	13
14733	Berkeley Springs (near)	Morgan	Blast furnace slag	(³)	164	.41	2.6	15.4	19.3	22
14710	Wheeling	Ohio	Sandstone	(³)	130	6.96	7.0	4.9	(²)	(²)
10343	Albright (near)	Preston	Ferruginous sandstone	(³)	154	1.88	8.1	10.0	17.3	5
10349	do	do	Argillaceous limestone	(³)	160	2.40	5.7	7.0	15.3	9
20894	Irondale	do	do	(³)	162	2.38	11.7	9.1	16.7	4
20895	do	do	do	(³)	166	1.35	11.6	3.4	2.7	6
14320	Hurricane	Putnam	Feldspathic sandstone	(³)	153	4.47	3.1	8.4	(²)	7
12787	Nitro	Raleigh	do	(³)	152	2.16	3.8	12.9	15.0	6
11472	Beckley	do	Sandstone	(³)	156	3.07	4.5	10.5	15.3	7
14133	Beckley (near)	do	Feldspathic sandstone	(³)	159	2.62	31.6	8.9	17.2	(²)
14134	do	do	Sandstone	(³)	153	3.03	3.6	7.8	(²)	4
16326	Beckley	do	Feldspathic sandstone	(³)	151	3.47	8.0	1.3	16.7	5
11736	Colt	do	Quartz	(³)	152	3.23	8.0	4.9	11.3	7
11545	Cherry Glade	do	Sandstone	(³)	159	3.14	4.8	5.0	16.7	8
16203	Cranberry	do	Feldspathic sandstone	(³)	155	2.19	4.2	8.3	17.3	5
11546	Daniels	do	Sandstone	(³)	158	2.24	9.5	9.5	13.3	7
11544	Ghent	do	do	(³)	150	2.32	4.4	4.2	16.3	10
11471	Price Hill	do	do	(³)	152	3.60	6.4	6.3	18.0	6
16464	Lester (near)	do	do	(³)	156	2.74	4.4	9.1	18.0	6
16487	Prosperity	do	do	(³)	156	1.96	4.9	8.2	17.7	10
11547	Shady Springs	do	do	(³)	155	2.44	4.2	9.3	14.8	8
11473	Surveyor	do	do	(³)	156	2.74	3.4	11.8	16.6	9
16146	do	do	do	(³)	160	2.64	6.1	6.6	16.5	4
14176	Sylvia	do	do	(³)	154	1.69	3.9	10.3	2.0	9
11130	Trap Hill District	Roane	Feldspathic sandstone	(³)	156	3.69	12.3	3.4	10.7	6
10036	Spencer (near)	do	Micaceous sandstone	(³)	156	3.52	8.9	4.5	15.0	9
12571	do	do	do	(³)	165	4.22	4.4	9.1	17.7	20
13806	do	do	do	(³)	152	1.78	4.7	8.5	11.7	5
14245	do	do	Sandstone	(³)	154	1.32	3.9	10.3	14.3	10
19978	Blueville	Taylor	Feldspathic sandstone	(³)	167	2.62	9.2	4.3	16.3	6
13296	Fetterman	do	Siliceous	(³)	168	3.91	3.7	10.8	9.0	5
10509	Davis	Tucker	Argillaceous limestone	(³)	154	.05	5.0	8.0	6.7	3
10510	do	do	Feldspathic sandstone	(³)		.12	7.8	5.1		4
13887	Middlebourne (near)	do	do	(³)	144	4.15	19.1	2.1		
14281	Littleton (east of)	do	do	(³)	151	6.22				
14282	do	do	do	(³)		4.64	10.6	3.8		

¹ Exact locality not known.   ² Test not made.

TABLE 1.—*Result of physical tests of road-building rock from the United States, Haiti, and Canada—January 1, 1919, to January 1, 1922*—Continued.

WISCONSIN.

Serial No.	Town or city.	County.	Name of material.	Crushing strength, pounds per square inch.	Weight per cubic foot.	Absorption, pounds per cubic foot.	Per cent of wear.	French coefficient of wear.	Hardness.	Toughness.
14132	Brillion	Calumet	Dolomite	(?)	173	0.98	4.6	8.7	12.5	4
11971	Springdale	Dane	do	(?)	172	1.27	3.7	10.8	16.0	12
18746	Knowles	Dodge	do	(?)	169	1.30	5.2	7.7	13.7	7
18744	do	do	do	(?)	172	1.01	3.8	10.5	14.7	8
9999	Berlin	Green Lake	do	(?)	165	.16	1.9	21.3	19.0	25
13743	Kewaunee	Kewaunee	Dolomite	(?)	175	.63	4.3	9.3	16.0	8
13168	Buffalo	Marquette	And syenite	(?)	167	.13	2.2	18.2	19.3	30
18713	Liberty Bluff (near)	do	Sandstone	19,495	157	1.48	17.0	2.4	18.7	7
14676	Montello	do	Granite	(?)	164	.25	2.4	16.7	18.7	16
13537	do	Milwaukee	Siliceous stone	(?)	166	2.15	6.0	6.7	15.3	9
10014	do	do	Argillaceous limite	(?)	168	2.11	3.7	10.8	11.7	8
11129	do (near)	do	do lime	16,700	168	2.01	3.8	10.5	15.3	11
11367	do	do	Dolomite	20,370	163	3.20	2.1	19.0	14.0	8
12615	(?)	do	Argillaceous dolomite	(?)	166	2.84	4.0	10.0	13.3	7
12616	(?)	do	do	(?)	161	2.42	6.4	6.3	12.0	7
12617	(?)	do	Dolomite	(?)	164	3.21	4.5	8.9	11.3	10
12618	(?)	do	Argillaceous do	(?)	175	.14	6.5	6.1	16.0	6
12619	(?)	do	do sandstone	(?)	167	2.66	3.7	10.8	14.3	10
10086	Wells	Monroe	Dolomite	(?)	162	2.79	4.8	8.3	18.0	5
9970	Blackcreek	Outagamie	Argillaceous dolomite	(?)	178	.58	4.6	8.7	14.7	9
9971	do	do	Dolomite	(?)	175	.53	4.1	9.8	15.3	8
10022	Belgium	Ozaukee	Argillaceous dolomite	(?)	175	1.15	7.4	5.5	14.3	8
11625	Mequon	do	Dolomite	22,750	174	1.09	3.4	11.8	12.3	7
11638	do	do	do	(?)	178	1.13	5.6	7.1	15.0	7
29916	Stevens Point	Portage	Sandstone	27,715	167	2.39	4.3	9.3	18.7	10
11447	Redgranite	Waushara	Granite	(?)	165	.33	1.4	28.5	19.3	14
10159	Grand Rapids	Wood	Sandstone	(?)	153	1.91	3.3	12.1	19.3	5
10028	(?)	(?)	Dolomite	(?)	168	1.05	7.1	5.6	13.3	6

No.	Locality	Region	Kind of rock							
13920	Burnt River	Ontario Province	Siliceous limestone	(²)	174	0.68	3.1	12.9	15.7	11
16923	Dundas	do	Dolomite	(²)	(²)	(²)	4.1	9.8	15.0	13
16924	do	do	do				4.7	9.3	14.0	13
17922	do	do	do		177	.67	3.6	11.1		(²)
17923	do	do	do	33,650	173	1.31	3.2	12.5		(²)
20390	do	do	Argillaceous dolomite	27,195	171	.99	3.6	11.1	15.0	13
20391	do	do	Dolomite	25,380	162	1.52	4.9	8.2	14.0	6
20392	do (north of)	do	do		174	.74	3.7	10.8	16.0	10
11648	Ottawa (east of)	do	Argillaceous dolomite		166	3.05	4.8	8.8	13.7	4
11649	do	do	Limestone	30,225	167	.56	4.9	8.3	12.0	4
20667	Ottawa	do	Argillaceous dolomite	27,485	170	1.82	4.5	8.9	14.3	10
20568	do	do	Dolomite	20,500	166	1.61	5.8	6.9	14.3	10
20569	do	do	do	16,740	165	1.77	4.9	8.4	13.3	4
20577	Walkerton	do	Limestone	(²)	164	.67	7.4	5.4	13.3	13
9746	Windmill Point	do	Cherty limestone	(²)	165	.41	3.9	16.7	18.0	13
11650	Hull (near)	Quebec Province	Diabase	(²)	194	.54	2.4	18.2	18.0	13
10017	Montreal	do	Nephelite syenite	(²)	156	.60	2.2	18.2	18.7	13
10332	Wellesley Island	do	Biotite granite	(²)	165	.28	2.9	13.8	18.0	10

DOMINICAN REPUBLIC.

No.	Locality	Region	Kind of rock							
15864	Santo Domingo (near)	Santo Domingo Province	Crystalline limestone	(?)	143	5.01	24.0	1.7	(²)	(²)
15865	do	do	Fragmental basalt	(?)	177	.97	3.5	11.4	18.7	11
15866	South shore of Sāma Bay (near Boca del Infierno).	do	Tufaceous limestone		155	3.01	11.2	3.6	(²)	(²)
15867	Sanchez-Samana Cross-roads.	Samana Province	Crystalline limestone	(?)	170	.27	(?)		8.5	6.
16101	Santo Domingo (near)	Santa Domingo Province	Tufus limestone	(?)	178	4.13	6.3	6.4	10.7	5
16103	La Vega Highway, kilometer 30.	do	Tufus basalt	(?)	179	1.14	3.5	11.4	16.7	8
16104	La Vega Highway, kilometer 34.	do	Andesite	(?)	177	1.26	3.9	10.3	13.7	10

HAITI.

No.	Locality	Region	Kind of rock							
19740	Acul Samedi (near)		Quartz diorite	(?)	171	0.58	2.8	14.3	18.0	15
19737	Cape Haitien		Weathered chert	(?)	146	4.05	9.1	4.4	17.7	22
19742	Limbe (near)		Serpentine	(?)	188	1.13	5.8	6.9	18.7	7
19744	Pont Beudet		Limestone	(?)	165	1.11	4.4	9.1	14.7	(³)

¹ Exact locality not known.   ² Test not made.

CRUSHING STRENGTH OR COMPRESSION TEST.

This test is made upon a cylindrical test specimen 2 inches in diameter and 2 inches high. Both ends of the specimen, which have been sawed at right angles to the axis of the cylinder, are carefully ground to plane surfaces. The cylinder then is crushed in a 200,000-pound Universal testing machine at a speed of 0.1 inch per minute. A small 2-inch spherical bearing block is placed between the moving head of the machine and the specimen. The average of at least two determinations is reported as the crushing strength, calculated in pounds per square inch. Crushing strength tests are made only when specifically requested.

INTERPRETATION OF RESULTS OF PHYSICAL TESTS.

To interpret the results of the physical tests of road-building rock, the Bureau of Public Roads has adopted a table of general limiting test values for broken stone for the various types of road construction. For general reference, these limiting values, together with comments upon limits shown, are given in Table 3. By comparing the results of tests on a sample of rock with the limits shown in the table a general idea of the types of road construction for which it is best suited may be obtained. It must be emphasized, however, that these values represent average conditions only. For any given material a number of factors such as type of stone, character and volume of traffic, and the character of available material will influence the interpretation to be given the results of the tests. Table 4 contains the total number of rock samples received from the various States which have been tested between January 1, 1916, and December 31, 1921.

TABLE 2.—*Results of compression tests of rock, made prior to Jan. 1, 1916.*

ARKANSAS.

Serial No.	Locality.	County.	Name.	Crushing strength pounds per square inch.
6331	Bald Knob	White	Sandstone	19,860

CONNECTICUT.

9791	Oneco	Windham	Biotite granite	16,635

ILLINOIS.

4422	Embarras	Coles	Limestone	17,300
5509	Thornton	Cook	Dolomite	23,060
6053	do	do	do	16,880
8711	Hillside	do	Argillaceous dolomite	15,730
4660	Tunnel Hill	Johnson	Sandstone	19,150
7509	Reevesville	do	Argillaceous limestone	25,780
7510	do	do	do	28,400
4764	Kankakee	Kankakee	Dolomite	20,610
5550	do	do	do	17,710
6088	do	do	Argillaceous dolomite	20,830
6165	do	do	Dolomite	11,660
6865	do	do	do	13,500
7298	do	do	Argillaceous dolomite	25,850
7299	do	do	do	20,000
7300	do	do	do	19,008

TABLE 2.—*Results of compression tests, of rock, made prior to Jan. 1, 1916*—Continued.

ILLINOIS—Continued.

Serial No.	Locality.	County.	Name.	Crushing strength, pounds per square inch.
7301	Kankakee	Kankakee	Argillaceous dolomite	19,700
7302	....do	....do	Dolomite	17,050
7871	Lehigh	....do	Argillaceous dolomite	16,700
4421	Alton	Madison	Limestone	15,100
7422	Brookville	Ogle	Argillaceous dolomite	18,640
7423	....do	....do	....do	18,180
5549	Anna	Union	Limestone	19,510

INDIANA.

Serial No.	Locality.	County.	Name.	Crushing strength
5534	Logansport	Cass	Limstone	20,350
4655	Greensburg	Decatur	Dolomite	17,960
4658	St. Paul	....do	Limestone	18,400
4690	Westport	....do	Dolomitic limestone	20,000
4659	St. Paul	....do	....do	20,510
5088	....do	....do	Limestone	19,800
4197	Mitchell	Lawrence	Argillaceous dolomite	12,250
5027	Bedford	....do	Limestone	6,900
5029	....do	....do	....do	6,450
3368	Greencastle	Putnam	....do	16,000
5737	Osgood	Ripley	....do	14,470
4657	Wabash	Wabash	Dolomitic limestone	18,790

IOWA.

Serial No.	Locality.	County.	Name.	Crushing strength
5525	Cedar Rapids	Linn	Dolomite limestone	19,950
5526	La Grande	Marshall	....do	14,850

KENTUCKY.

Serial No.	Locality.	County.	Name.	Crushing strength
5552	Princeton	Caldwell	Dolomitic limestone	23,860
7688	Cedar Bluff	....do	Argillaceous limestone	25,720
5921	Limestone	Carter	Limestone	14,900
5922	Carter	....do	Siliceous limestone	13,400

MAINE.

Serial No.	Locality.	County.	Name.	Crushing strength
7438	Swans Island	Hancock	Biotite granite	18,400
8745	Vinal Haven	Knox	Granite	20,020
8768	St. George	....do	....do	22,800
8769	Vinal Haven	....do	....do	20,930
8781	St. George	....do	....do	18,780
9865	....do	....do	....do	17,150
9996	Long Cove	....do	....do	17,540
9445	Vinal Haven	....do	Biotite granite	21,220
10366	St. George	....do	....do	27,050
7439	Frankford	Waldo	....do	20,600

MARYLAND.

Serial No.	Locality.	County.	Name.	Crushing strength
5611	Mount Savage Junction.	Alleghany	Siliceous limestone	34,930
4884	Frederick	Frederick	Limestone	17,580
5694	Havre de Grace	Harford	Gneissoid granite	34,410
5695	....do	....do	Sericite gneiss	20,090
5696	....do	....do	Gneissoid granite	21,670
5697	....do	....do	Amphibolite	34,380
5698	....do	....do	Gneissoid granite	35,210
5699	....do	....do	....do	22,190

TABLE 2.—*Results of compression tests of rock, made prior to Jan. 1, 1916*—Continued.

MASSACHUSETTS.

Serial No.	Locality.	County.	Name.	Crushing strength, pounds per square inch.
6891	Rockport	Essex	Biotite granite	22,370
6892	....do	....do	....do	23,610
6893	....do	....do	....do	22,670
6894	....do	....do	....do	21,600
8796	....do	....do	....do	23,830
5671	Westfield	Hampden	Altered diabase	32,850
8862	Westford	Middlesex	Granite	13,980
8874	....do	....do	....do	17,000
8875	....do	....do	....do	16,250
5988	West Auburn	Worcester	Mica gneiss	21,950

MICHIGAN.

9593	Calcite	Presque Isle	Limestone	10,300

MINNESOTA.

5524	Stockton	Winona	Argillaceous dolomite	16,000

MISSOURI.

6375	Rochefort	Boone	Limestone	13,900
6377	Sweeney	Cooper	Argillaceous limestone	14,900

NEW YORK.

6457	(1)	Clinton	Plagioclase gneiss	18,500
6458	(1)	....do	Pyroxene gneiss	20,500
8011	(1)	Dutchess	Dolomite	34,450
5544	Camelo	....do	....do	29,050
5872	Akron Junction	Erie	Cherty limestone	16,700
6056	....do	....do	....do	31,180
8577	Gloversville	Fulton	Biotite gneiss	14,580
4157	Alexandria Bay	Jefferson	Granite	21,600
8833	....do	....do	....do	26,180
8932	....do	....do	....do	14,150
9129	....do	....do	....do	14,390
9130	....do	....do	Gneissoid granite	17,600
7437	....do	....do	Granite	27,200
8012	(1)	Rockland	Gabbroitic diabase	31,300
8013	(1)	....do	Siliceous dolomite	22,200

NEW HAMPSHIRE.

8872	Melford	Hillsboro	Granite	15,050
9010	....do	....do	Biotite granite	16,640
9011	....do	....do	....do	14,870
9012	....do	....do	....do	18,230
9031	Concord	Merrimack	Granite	16,600
9036	....do	....do	....do	13,420
9037	....do	....do	....do	13,900
8870	....do	....do	....do	15,100

NORTH CAROLINA.

8396	(1)	Forsythe	Granite	13,140
8397	(1)	....do	Hypersthene gabbro	11,880
8682	Spencer Mountain	Gaston	Feldspathic quartzite	31,520
8881	Gastonia	....do	Quartzite	17,100
8576	Mooresville	Iredell	Biotite granite	26,000
5373	(1)	McDowell	Sanstsone	22,600

¹ Exact locality not known.

TABLE 2.—*Results of compression tests of rock, made prior to Jan. 1, 1916*—Continued.

NORTH CAROLINA—Continued.

Serial No.	Locality.	County.	Name.	Crushing strength, pounds per square inch.
9038	Wilson	Wilson	Granite	16,070
5956	Stacey	Rockingham	Granite gneiss	23,220
5496	Sansbury	Rowan	Granite	33,750
6071	Bostic	Rutherford	Biotite gneiss	16,100
5497	Mount Airy	Surry	Granite	18,400
7433	....do	....do	....do	15,200
8901	....do	....do	....do	5,100
9048	....do	....do	....do	16,440
8419	Granita (near)	Wake	Biotite granite	14,160
3807	Wise	Warren	Granite	18,240
3808	....do	....do	....do	18,560
5374	(1)	Yancey	Quartzite	12,900

OHIO.

4694	Osborne	Clark	Dolomitic limestone	8,690
4695	Springfield	....do	Dolomite	18,960
9282	Cleveland	Cuyahoga	Granite	31,790
9283	....do	....do	....do	27,900
9284	....do	....do	....do	24,790
9285	....do	....do	....do	26,990
9459	....do	....do	....do	24,900
4378	Sandusky	Erie	Limestone	19,400
5554	....do	....do	....do	21,850
5753	Castalia	....do	Dolomitic limestone	18,530
6055	....do	....do	Limestone	20,810
5505	Marble Cliff	Franklin	....do	16,750
5506	....do	....do	....do	12,350
5630	Columbus	....do	Ferrugineous sandstone	21,800
4693	Patterson	Hardin	Dolomite	11,360
5553	Dunkirk	....do	....do	26,200
4707	Hillsboro	Highland	Cherty limestone	15,590
8347	Clarksfield	Huron	Calcareous sandstone	9,490
4656	Big Springs	Logan	Argillaceous limestone	16,380
6054	Vulcan	Lucas	Siliceous limestone	25,480
6057	Holland	....do	Argillaceous limestone	19,430
8402	Toledo, 10 miles west of	....do	Dolomite	11,600
6052	White Rock	Ottawa	....do	16,620
5556	Bloomville	Seneca	Limestone	20,250
5555	Middleport	Van Wert	Dolomite	25,200

OKLAHOMA.

3388	Granite	Greer	Granite	18,000

PENNSYLVANIA.

5602	Hyndman	Bedford	Impure limestone	24,150
5603	....do	....do	Siliceous limestone	21,860
5632	Birdsboro	Berks	Altered diabase	39,215
8724	Juniata	Blair	Argillaceous limestone	15,480
8725	(1)	....do	....do	20,880
8625	Hazard	Carbon	Blast-furnace slag	9,000
7973	(1)	Chester	Pyroxene quartzite	31,800
7978	(1)	....do	Mica schist	23,500
7979	(1)	....do	....do	23,900
5578	Salona	Clinton	Argillaceous limestone	18,710
7844	(1)	Dauphin	Siliceous limestone	26,500
8306	(1)	....do	Limestone	8,510
8427	(1)	....do	....do	19,250
8465	(1)	....do	Siliceous dolomite	9,640
8049	(1)	Elk	Ferruginous sandstone	14,150
5771	Indian Creek Station	Fayette	Calcareous sandstone	37,740
6097	Bidwell	....do	Limestone	13,450

1 Exact locality not known.

TABLE 2.—*Results of compression tests of rock, made prior to Jan. 1, 1916*—Continued.

PENNSYLVANIA—Continued.

Serial No.	Locality.	County.	Name	Crushing strength, pounds per square inch.
9347	Connellsville	Bedford	Impure limestone	26,050
5604	Water Street	Huntingdon	Feldspathic sandstone	22,330
5557	Walford	Lawrence	Limestone	27,500
6153	Porter Township	Lycoming	Argillaceous limestone	28,580
6154	....do	....do	....do	26,860
6155	....do	....do	....do	18,610
6156	....do	....do	....do	22,930
6157	....do	....do	Limestone	21,900
6158	....do	....do	....do	14,160
7980	Port Allegheny	McKean	Feldspathic sandstone	9,680
8022	(¹)	(¹)	Ferruginous sandstone	12,130
8023	(¹)	(¹)	....do	14,000
8024	(¹)	(¹)	....do	12,480
3243	Mcspadden	Somerset	Sandstone	26,000
5830	Prompton	Wayne	Feldspathic sandstone	26,340
5605	Blairsville intersection	Westmoreland	Siliceous limestone	32,560
7428	York	York	Dolomitic marble	27,400

RHODE ISLAND.

8867	Westerly	Washington	Granite	11,740
8868	....do	....do	....do	20,300
8869	....do	....do	....do	20,750

SOUTH CAROLINA.

8389	Williamstown	Anderson	Granite	12,990
5568	Rion	Fairfield	....do	29,180
5586a	....do	....do	....do	25,790
5586b	....do	....do	....do	19,240
5586c	....do	....do	....do	33,880

TENNESSEE.

5597	Quarry	Carter	Limestone	22,750
5502	Straw Plains	Jefferson	....do	21,730
5504	....do	....do	....do	28,340
5503	....do	....do	Dolomite	38,070
6533	Knoxville	Knox	Marble	17,970

VERMONT.

5543	East Wallingford	Rutland	Altered diabase	16,800
8853	Barre	Washington	Granite	19,560

VIRGINIA.

8804	Albert	Bedford	Granite gneiss	13,820
6796	(¹)	Dinwiddie	Granite	13,150
4900A	Broad Run	Fauquier	Quartz	28,400
4900B	....do	....do	Epidosite	28,000
5923	Strathmore	Fluvanna	Chlorite epidote schist	13,210
5678	Eggleston (near)	Giles	Dolomite	45,690
5924	Boscobel	Goochland	Granite gneiss	13,550
6615	Korah Station	Henrico	Biotite granite	20,300
5925	Greenway	Nelson	Feldspathic quartzite	16,500
5492	Nokesville	Prince William	Ferruginous sandstone	17,780
5920	Greenlee	Rockbridge	Dolomitic marble	36,900
5382	Bluff Water Station	Rockingham	Limestone	21,450
5385	....do	....do	....do	40,850
5375	St. Paul	Russell	....do	17,600
7217	Burkes Garden	Tazewell	Dolomitic sandstone	21,500

¹ Exact locality not known.

TABLE 2.—*Results of compression tests of rock, made prior to Jan. 1, 1916*—Continued.

WEST VIRGINIA.

Serial No.	Locality.	County.	Name.	Crushing strength, pounds per square inch.
5365	Berkeley	Berkeley	Limestone	23,350
5917	Renick	Greenbrier	Crystalline limestone	21,300
5918	Frazier	....do	Limestone	17,450
5919	Snow Flace	....do	...do	13,550
7475	Green Spring (east of)	Hampshire	Siliceous limestone	34,400
7476	....do	....do	Quartzite	15,050
6109	Spring Hill	Kanawha	Sandstone	12,400
9132	Fairmont	Marion	...do	5,420
9133	....do	....do	...do	5,720
9134	....do	....do	...do	6,080
5610	Sturgisson	Monongalia	Siliceous limestone	22,440
5612	....do	....do	Limestone	17,910
5613	....do	....do	Argillaceous limestone	14,300
5614	....do	....do	Calcareous sandstone	29,840
5615	....do	....do	Impure limestone	19,650
5616	....do	....do	Argillaceous limestone	24,850
8447	Parkersburg	Wood	Feldspathic sandstone	11,910

WISCONSIN.

5523	Pebbles	Fond du Lac	Dolomite	32,600
3448	Amberg	Marinette	Biotite granite	20,000
8656	Lannon	Waukesha	Dolomite	23,020

TABLE 3.—*General limiting test values.*

Type of construction.	French coefficient of wear.	Toughness.
Water-bound macadam	7 or over	....
Bituminous macadam	7 or over	....
Bituminous concrete	8 or over	8 or over.
Cement concrete	7 or over	....
Water-bound base course	5 or over	....

Granites, gneisses, schists, sandstones, and quartzites should not, in general, be used in the wearing course of water-bound macadam roads. Shales and slates should never be used in this connection.

For further details and explanation of results in this table and also for tests on all materials to January 1, 1916, see U. S. Department of Agriculture Bulletin 370.

TABLE 4.—*Geographical distribution of samples tested from January 1, 1916, to January 1, 1922.*

State.	Number of samples.	State.	Number of samples.
Alabama	31	Illinois	21
Arizona	10	Indiana	45
Arkansas	55	Iowa	6
California	3	Kansas	27
Colorado	16	Kentucky	23
Connecticut	21	Louisiana	3
Delaware	9	Maine	46
District of Columbia	2	Maryland	44
Florida	12	Massachusetts	127
Georgia	131	Michigan	21
Idaho	2	Minnesota	8

TABLE 4.—*Geographical distribution of samples tested from January 1, 1916, to Januar 1, 1922*—Continued.

State.	Number of samples.	State.	Numbe of sam- ples.
Mississippi	6	South Dakota	1
Missouri	16	Tennessee	
Montana	9	Texas	
Nebraska	8	Utah	1
New Hampshire	19	Vermont	
New Jersey	21	Virginia	2
New Mexico	7	Washington	
New York	43	West Virginia	
North Carolina	93	Wisconsin	
Ohio	123	Canada	1
Oklahoma	33	Dominican Republic	
Oregon	2	Haiti	
Pennsylvania	75		
Rhode Island	6	Total	1,6
South Carolina	19		

UNITED STATES DEPARTMENT OF AGRICULTURE

DEPARTMENT BULLETIN No. 1133

Washington, D. C.   ▼   February 28, 1923

THE FREEZING TEMPERATURES OF SOME FRUITS, VEGETABLES, AND CUT FLOWERS.

By R. C. WRIGHT, *Physiologist*, and GEORGE F. TAYLOR, *Associate Physicist, Office of Horticultural and Pomological Investigations, Bureau of Plant Industry.*

CONTENTS.

INTRODUCTION.

There is an ever-increasing demand from those interested in the growing, shipping, and handling of produce for exact data on the free n points, or the temperatures at which various products freeze.g

The extent of damage due to the freezing of produce in transit naturally varies from year to year, but it is usually very heavy, aggregating frequently several hundreds of thousands of dollars during a year. This in general applies not only to such products as apples and potatoes, most of which are grown in the North and harvested and shipped in the late fall and winter, but to products which are grown in the South and Southwest during the winter and shipped to the northern markets. This latter group includes citrus fruits, strawberries, tomatoes, lettuce, string beans, cabbage, cauliflower, eggplant, etc. Cars of these food products often leave the shipping point under refrigeration and in 24 to 36 hours may pass into a zone of freezing temperatures. As they approach the more northern markets they may be exposed to temperatures ranging several degrees below zero. Under some conditions when harvested in warm weather some of these products may be precooled—that is, rapidly cooled to a refrigerating temperature, either immediately before or directly after they are placed in the car for shipment, in order to delay maturity and consequent deterioration. Where precooling is practiced, it is, of course, very important to know the temperatures to which the product can be lowered with absolute safety.

NOTE.—This bulletin gives the results of a portion of the work carried on under the projects "Factors affecting the storage life of vegetables" and "Factors affecting the storage life of fruits."

21854—23

Knowledge of the exact freezing points of fruits and vegetables is of importance also to the commercial cold-storage man. In most cases fruits and vegetables other than dried or prepared products when placed in cold storage are alive, and the problem is to keep them alive and healthy throughout their storage period. Since various fruits and vegetables freeze at different temperatures, there is more or less doubt in the minds of those interested as to the proper and safe temperatures at which to hold these various products in storage. One of the problems in the storage of many of these products is to hold them at a temperature low enough to slow down the living processes in order to prolong their storage life and yet not allow them to be damaged by actual freezing. Of course, some products, such as berries, may be purposely kept at a freezing temperature and used at once on thawing out, but this subject comes under the head of freezing storage and will not be discussed here. It is therefore essential in commercial work of this kind that accurate data be at hand on the temperatures to which these products can be exposed without injuring their keeping qualities or market value. It should be borne in mind, however, that freezing or freezing injury does not always occur when fruit or vegetable products are exposed to temperatures at or below their true freezing points. This is shown in the studies on Irish potatoes reported in a previous publication,[1] where tubers were cooled as much as 10° F. below their freezing points and again warmed without apparent injury. The commonly known fact that some kinds of products may be actually frozen and then thawed out under certain conditions with no apparent injurious effects constitutes further evidence on this point. On the other hand, some commodities are injured if stored at temperatures well above their actual freezing points. It is evident, therefore, that temperatures just above the freezing point can not be regarded as safe for all types or varieties of fruits and vegetables. It is also noticeable that there are some variations in the freezing points of fruits or vegetables of the same variety and from the same lot, as is shown in the tables that follow. Furthermore, it is quite probable that different individuals of the same variety and strain when grown under different conditions will have somewhat different average freezing points. Attention is therefore called to the fact that the freezing points given in the following tables should be considered as danger points; that is, at or near these temperatures, either above or below them, there is a possibility that the product will be in danger of injury by freezing if exposed for a sufficient length of time. These are temperatures at which it is unsafe to hold produce which is to be used for food if it is desired to maintain it for any length of time in a living condition.

The determinations of the freezing points of a number of fruits and vegetables have been made by the Bureau of Plant Industry in connection with its cold-storage investigations. By freezing point is meant the temperature at which ice crystals begin to form within the product, either fruit or vegetable.

Some 10,000 of these determinations have already been made on many varieties of commercially grown fruits and vegetables, and

---

[1] Wright, R. C., and Taylor, George F. Freezing injury to potatoes when undercooled. U. S. Dept. Agr. Bul. 916, 15 p., 1 fig., 1 pl. 1921. Literature cited, p. 15.

work is being continued. It has been found in some cases that the freezing points of some varieties are liable to slight variations from year to year, even though the same strain grown in the same locality is used. These variations, however, are probably of more importance in the study of the exact causes and results of freezing injury than from the point of view of the commercial cold-storage and produce man, for the variation of a fraction of a degree hardly warrants any change in the treatment of the produce. It therefore seems advisable to publish the results of these investigations from time to time as obtained, because of the need for such information and because there is no comprehensive publication on the subject.

The method of determining freezing points has been described in former papers,[2] and a repetition of this description is not required here.

FREEZING POINTS OF FRUITS.

Where several varieties of one kind of fruit were investigated the results are given separately to allow comparisons to be made. All temperatures are expressed in degrees Fahrenheit.

Apples.—Freezing-point determinations were made for a number of authentic varieties of summer or early apples and of fall and winter varieties, most of which were grown on the Arlington Experiment Farm. The tabulated results given by varieties are shown in Table 1. These results show considerable varietal differences among both summer and winter apples. The average of all summer varieties is practically the same as that of winter varieties, the former being 28.44° F. while the latter is 28.51° F. These results show very little difference between the freezing points of eastern-grown and western-grown fruit.

Cherries.—Freezing-point determinations were made for seven varieties of cherries grown on the Arlington Experiment Farm. The average of all varieties was 27.81° F. (Table 1.)

Grapes.—Results were obtained from the freezing of seven varieties of grapes, all of which were grown on the Arlington Experiment Farm. The average freezing point of all the varieties was 28.16° F. (Table 1.)

Oranges.—The average freezing point of the six varieties of oranges studied was 28.03° F. (Table 1.)

Peaches.—Freezing-point determinations were made for 11 varieties of peaches grown near Leesburg, Va., in the Loudoun orchard of the American Fruit Growers (Inc.). Peaches in the hard-ripe stage were utilized for these tests. The average freezing point of all varieties when hard ripe was found to be 29.41° F. (Table 1.)

Plums.—Freezing points were obtained for four varieties of plums that were grown in California and purchased on the market and for one variety (Red June) grown at the Arlington Experiment Farm. The variety with the lowest freezing point is Tragedy, with a freezing temperature of 27.21° F. The average freezing point of all varieties is 28.53° F. (Table 1.)

[2] Taylor, George F.   Some improvements on the needle type thermocouple for low-temperature work. *In* Jour. Ind. and Eng. Chem., v. 12, p. 797–798, 1 fig.   1920.
   Wright, R. C., and Harvey, R. B.   The freezing point of potatoes as determined by the thermoelectric method.   U. S. Dept. Agr. Bul. 895, 7 p., 1 fig.   1921.   Bibliographical footnotes.
   Wright, R. C., and Taylor, George F.   Freezing injury to potatoes when undercooled.   U. S. Dept. Agr. Bul. 916, 15 p., 1 fig., 1 pl.   1921.   Literature cited, p. 15.

TABLE 1.—*Average and extreme freezing points of fruits.*

Fruit and varieties.	Temperatures (° F.) Aver. age.	Extremes. Mini- mum.	Extremes. Maxi- mum.	Fruit and varieties.	Temperatures (° F.). Aver- age.	Extremes. Mini- mum.	Extremes. Maxi- mxm.
Apples, summer varieties:				Oranges—Continued.			
Yellow Transparent..	27.72	27.29	28.16	Washington Navel...	28.42	28.30	28.68
Red Astrachan	28.58	28.25	28.70	Valencia (California).	27.01	26.90	27.60
Early Ripe	29.18	28.82	29.47	Satsuma (Owari variety)	28.18	27.93	28.68
Red June	29.59	29.29	29.71				
Sweitzer	27.38	27.32	27.41	Average	28.03	27.86	28.34
Shoemaker	28.46	27.93	28.03				
Benoni	28.83	28.49	29.00	Peaches (hard ripe):			
Early Joe	27.81	27.60	28.49	Belle	29.82	29.50	30.28
Martha (crab)	26.70	26.62	26.76	Elberta	29.72	29.43	30.00
				Stevens	28.65	28.25	28.90
Average (not including the crab apple)	28.44	28.12	28.62	Edgemont	29.40	29.30	29.50
				Williams	29.56	29.10	30.00
Apples, fall and winter varieties, eastern grown:				Bilyeu	28.00	28.35	28.96
Baldwin	29.04	28.84	29.43	Smock	29.28	29.05	29.57
Ben Davis	28.61	28.21	28.96	Salwey	29.57	29.10	29.80
Delicious	28.48	28.16	29.10	Hiley	30.02	29.90	30.24
Grimes	28.97	28.82	29.05	Carman	29.57	29.30	29.95
Jonathan	28.22	27.79	28.69	Champion	29.06	28.73	29.95
Paragon	28.50	28.45	28.55				
Rambo	28.55	28.34	28.90	Average	29.41	29 09	29.74
Stayman Winesap	28.51	28.02	28.91				
Winesap	28.23	27.93	28.72	Plums:			
Yellow Newtown	28.00	27.80	28.20	Burbank	29.26	29.05	29.80
York Imperial	28.34	28.10	28.50	Wickson	29.53	29.19	29.75
				Tragedy	27.21	26.76	27.41
Average	28.49	28.22	28.82	Red June	28.13	27.79	28.44
Apples, fall and winter varieties, western grown:				Average	28.53	28 20	28.8c
Delicious	28.36	27.98	28.86	Strawberries:			
Gano	28.55	28.26	29.05	American	29.70	29.66	29.75
Grimes	28.60	28 26	29.05	Big Late	30.03	29 25	30.05
Jonathan	28.35	28.02	28.72	Big Joe	29.98	29.78	30.19
Rome Beauty	28.92	23.72	29.38	Brandywine	29.96	29.85	30 36
Esopus (Spitzenberg)	28.69	28.26	29.05	Chesapeake	30.29	29 94	30 32
Winesap	28.24	27.93	28.35	Dunlap	29.82	29 24	29.99
				Excelsior	29.94	29.28	30 04
Average	28.53	28.20	28.92	Early Ozark	29 82	29 66	30.13
				Early Jersey Giant	29.82	29.43	30 22
Cherries:				Gandy	29 24	28.85	29.55
Early Richmond	27.94	27.60	28.35	Glen Mary	30.08	29.53	30 16
Montmorency	28.10	27.79	28.58	Howard 17 (*Premier*)	30.23	29.58	30.38
St. Medard	28.09	27.60	23.58	Hustler	30.48	30.41	30.60
Royal Nouville	28.16	27.95	28.50	Klondike	29.59	29 28	29 90
Gloire de France	27.65	27.37	28.21	Kellog (*Kellog's Pride*)	30 13	29.78	30.48
Mecker	26.88	26.76	27.69	Late Jersey Giant	30.25	30.13	30.26
Bigarreau (unknown variety)	27.83	27.83	27.83	Lupton	28 84	28.82	29.10
				Rewastico	30 05	30.08	30.13
Average	27.81	27.56	28.25	Stevens	30.18	29.37	30.42
				Sample	30 38	29.63	30.48
Grapes:				Superb	30.46	29.85	30.81
New Concord	28.39	27.93	28.68	Twilley	29.22	28.96	29.53
Ambrosia	28.21	27.83	28.63				
Dracut Amber	27.88	27.77	28.10	Average	29.93	29.56	30.13
Moores Early	28.28	28.15	28.62				
Captivator	27.86	27.14	28.05	Blackberries:			
Campbell (black)	27.96	27.77	28.00	Jumbo	29.09	28.71	29.30
Mericadel	28.54	28.40	28.54	Eldorado	29.21	28.76	29.54
				Crystal White	28.40	28.12	28.63
Average	28.16	27.85	28.37	Logan (*Loganberry*)	29.51	29.32	29.75
				Raspberries:			
Oranges:				Ranere (*St. Regis*, red)	30.41	30.12	30.5C
Temple	28.64	28.34	28.82	Columbia (black)	28.76	28.24	28.79
Pineapple	27.72	27.60	27.83	Cranberries:			
Florida Seedling	28.20	28.10	28.43	Searl	28.20	27.93	28.44
				Gebhart Beauty	28.30	26.00	26.60
				Mammoth	26.70	26.40	25.90
				Metallic	25.60	24.8	25.80

TABLE 1.—*Average and extreme freezing points of fruits*—Continued.

SUMMARY OF AVERAGES.

Fruit and varieties.	Temperatures (°F.)			Fruit and varieties.	Temperatures (°F.).		
	Average.	Extremes.			Average.	Extremes.	
		Minimum.	Maximum.			Minimum.	Maximum.
Apples:				Grapefruit................	28.36	28.00	28.50
Summer varieties....	28.44	28.12	28.62	Lemons..................	28.14	27.89	28.47
Fall and winter......	28.51	28.21	28.87	Oranges.................	28.03	27.86	28.34
Bananas (Jamaica):				Peaches (hard ripe)......	29.41	29.09	29.74
Green..{Peel........	29.84	29.76	29.92	Pears (Bartlett):			
Green..{Pulp........	30.22	30.10	30.58	Hard ripe............	28.46	28.06	28.70
Ripe...{Peel........	29.36	29.15	29.53	Soft ripe............	27.83	27.20	28.00
Ripe...{Pulp........	26.00	25.45	26.50	Pears (unknown Japan-			
Blackberries:				ese variety)...........	29.39	29.34	29.53
Black varieties.......	29.15	28.73	29.42	Japanese persimmons			
White varieties......	28.40	28.12	28.63	(Tanenashi)...........	28.33	28.07	28.63
Logan (Loganberry)..	29.51	29.32	29.75	Plums..................	28.53	28.20	28.85
Cherries..................	27.81	27.56	28.25	Raspberries:			
Cranberries..............	26.70	26.28	26.93	Red varieties.........	30.41	30.12	30.50
Currants................	30.21	30.18	30.25	Black varieties.......	28.76	28.24	28.79
Gooseberries.............	28.91	28.70	29.18	Strawberries............	29.93	29.56	30.13
Grapes (eastern)........	28.16	27.85	28.37				

Strawberries.—Freezing-point determinations were obtained for 22 authentic varieties of strawberries grown at the Maryland Agricultural Experiment Station. The greatest difference was found between the Lupton, which froze at 28.84° F., and the Hustler, at 30.48° F. The average for all varieties was 29.93° F. (Table 1.)

Blackberries, raspberries, and cranberries.—Three varieties of blackberries were frozen, viz, Jumbo, Eldorado, and Crystal White. The two black varieties froze at 29.09° and 29.21° F., respectively, while the white variety froze at 28.4° F. Logan blackberries (eastern grown), froze at 29.51° F. One variety each of red and black raspberries was frozen. The Ranere (*St. Regis*) froze at 30.41° F., while the Columbia froze at 28.76°. Four varieties of cranberries were frozen. Considerable differences were found in the freezing points of some of these varieties. While the Searl variety froze at 28.2° F., the Metallic froze at 25.6°. The results for Gebhart Beauty and Mammoth are intermediate, being 26.3° and 26.7 F., respectively.

Miscellaneous fruits.—A number of other fruits and berries were investigated, but only one variety was available in each case. The results are therefore not given separately, but are included in the summary of Table 1 covering the average freezing points of all the fruits studied.

FREEZING POINTS OF VEGETABLES.

While several different kinds of vegetables have been used in the freezing-point determinations, those on which the most extensive variety studies have been centered are Irish potatoes, sweet potatoes, and tomatoes.

Potatoes.—Freezing-point determinations were made on 18 different authentic varieties of potatoes. Bulletins 895 and 916 of the United States Department of Agriculture give the results of this study in detail, so they will not be discussed here. The average freezing points of all varieties was 28.92° F. (Table 2.)

TABLE 2.—*Average and extreme freezing points of potatoes, sweet potatoes, tomatoes, and other vegetables.*

Kind and variety.	Temperatures (° F.).			Kind and variety.	Temperatures (° F.).		
	Aver- age.	Extremes.			Aver- age.	Extremes.	
		Mini- mum.	Maxi- mum.			Mini- mum.	Maxi- mum.
Potatoes:				**Tomatoes (ripe)—Contd.**			
Triumph	29.20	29.00	29.33	Greater Baltimore	30.62	30.20	30.81
Early Prospect	28.80	28.72	29.30	Columbia	30.31	30.29	30.77
Irish Cobbler	29.67	29.60	29.72	Delaware Beauty	30.02	29.95	30.33
First Early	29.00	28.88	29.00	Livingston's Globe	30.58	30.32	30.88
New Early Standard.	28.97	28.74	29.12	Livingston's Acme	30.46	30.41	30.74
Ehnola	29.17	29.01	29.30	Greenhouse varieties—			
Spaulding No. 4	29.33	29.21	29.32	Carter's Sunrise	30.58	30.06	30.85
Green Mountain	28.50	28.38	28.55	Stirling Castle	30.54	30.41	30.60
Gold Coin	28.63	28.40	28.70				
Rural New Yorker	28.70	28.46	28.75	Average	30.38	30.20	30.67
Russet Rural	28.32	28.30	28.48				
U. S. Seedling No.				**Tomatoes (green):**			
38774	28.77	28.65	28.83	Bonny Best	30.57	30.38	30.83
Up-to-date	29.10	29.10	29.10	Earliana	30.24	29.77	30.58
Producer	28.70	28.73	28.79	John Baer	30.53	30.48	30.58
Oregon White Rose	28.71	28.60	28.80	Early Michigan	30.70	30.53	30.77
British Queen	29.27	29.22	29.30	Red Rock	30.58	30.34	30.67
Garnet Chile	28.16	28.00	28.28	Stone	30.15	30.10	30.38
American Giant	29.64	29.48	29.68	Greenhouse varieties—			
				Carter's Sunrise	30.29	30.20	30.59
Average	28.92	28.80	29.02	Stirling Castle	30.11	29.90	30.15
Sweet potatoes:				Average	30.40	30.21	30.57
Big Stem	28.05	27.48	28.72				
Dooley	28.46	27.93	28.91	**Sweet corn:**			
Early Carolina	28.59	28.40	28.96	Crosby	29.07	28.82	29.43
Georgia	28.05	27.79	28.58	Country Gentlemen	29.11	28.63	29.43
Gold Skin	28.47	28.21	28.63	Howling Mob	28.00	27.89	28.16
Improved Big Stem	28.76	28.26	29.00	Golden Bantam	29.61	29.25	29.85
Miles	28.34	28.16	28.54				
Nancy Hall	28.10	27.54	28.35	Average	28.95	28.65	29.22
Mullihan	27.64	27.46	27.93				
Pierson	28.68	28.02	28.72	**Onions:**			
Porto Rico	28.34	27.87	28.68	Yellow Danvers	30.10	29.61	30.17
Pumpkin	28.98	28.68	29.09	White Globe	30.20	29.75	30.41
Red Brazil	28.40	28.30	28.63	Texas Bermuda	29.96	29.71	30.13
Red Bermuda	28.17	27.96	28.63				
Red Jersey	28.52	28.30	28.77	Average	30.09	29.69	30.24
Southern Queen	28.56	28.25	28.82				
Triumph	28.43	28.26	28.72	**Lettuce:**			
Yellow Belmont	28.57	28.49	28.82	May Queen	30.49	30.38	30.60
Yellow Jersey	28.97	28.26	29.05	Way Ahead	31.54	31.25	31.77
Yellow Strasburg	28.72	28.30	29.00	Prize Head	31.57	31.45	31.77
Average	28.44	28.10	28.72	Average	31.20	31.03	31.38
Tomatoes (ripe):				**Carrots:**			
Bonny Best	30.60	30.48	30.68	Danvers	29.61	29.43	29.66
Olney Special	30.59	30.34	30.67	Chauntenay	29.53	29.42	29.70
Earliana	30.52	30.43	30.77				
John Baer	30.57	30.24	30.90	Average	29.57	29.42	29.68
Landreth	30.45	30.34	30.72				
Early Michigan	30.67	30.19	30.85	**Peas:**			
Marvel	30.03	29.90	30.38	Early Alaska	28.93	28.26	29.19
Bloomdale	29.99	29.90	30.53	Hosford's Market			
Red Rock	30.55	30.48	30.62	Garden	30.93	30.73	30.99
Trucker's Favorite	30.06			Laxtonian	30.23	30.03	30.56
New Glory	29.78	29.63	30.38				
Stone	30.31	30.10	30.58	Average	30.03	29.67	30.25

SUMMARY OF AVERAGES.

	Aver- age.	Mini- mum.	Maxi- mum.		Aver- age.	Mini- mum.	Maxi- mum.
Beans (snap)	29.74	29.65	30.06	Lettuce	31.20	31.03	31.38
Cabbage (Early Jersey Wakefield)	31.18	31.06	31.34	Onions (dry)	30.09	29.69	30.24
Carrots	29.57	29.42	29.68	Peas (green)	30.03	29.67	30.25
Cauliflower	30.08	29.95	30.15	Potatoes	28.92	28.80	29.02
Corn, sweet	28.95	28.65	29.22	Potatoes, sweet	28.44	28.10	28.72
Eggplant	30.41	30.17	30.69	Tomatoes (ripe)	30.38	30.20	30.67
Kohl-rabi	30.02	29.74	30.22	Turnips	30.23	30.16	30.48

Sweet potatoes.—The results of freezing 20 more or less common varieties of sweet potatoes are presented in Table 2. The varieties with the lowest freezing points are Big Stem and Georgia, both of which froze at 28.05° F. The highest freezing points were found with Pumpkin and Yellow Jersey varieties, which froze at 28.98° and 28.97° F., respectively. The average of all varieties was 28.44° F.

Tomatoes.—The freezing temperatures of 19 commercially grown varieties of tomatoes were determined and are presented in Table 2. These tomatoes were all grown under the same conditions at the Arlington Experiment Farm. Determinations were made on both ripe and practically full-grown green specimens, such as are usually picked for shipment from the Southern States to the northern markets. With the ripe tomatoes the lowest freezing point (29.78° F.) was found in connection with the New Glory variety. The Early Michigan variety froze at 30.67° F., which represents the highest freezing point of all the varieties studied. There was no appreciable difference in the average freezing points of ripe and green tomatoes, the averages being 30.38° and 30.40° F., respectively.

Sweet corn.—The freezing point of sweet corn varied considerably with the age of the product. There was also considerable variation between varieties. Four varieties were studied. (See Table 2.)

Miscellaneous vegetables.—The freezing points of three varieties of onions, three varieties of lettuce, two varieties of carrots, and three varieties of peas, and of at least one variety each of beans, cabbage, cauliflower, eggplant, kohl-rabi, and turnips are also presented in the body or in the summary of Table 2.

FREEZING POINTS OF CUT FLOWERS.

Requests have been received for information on the freezing points of such cut flowers as are commonly held in cold storage or shipped in quantities. Determinations were made for peonies, roses, and Easter lilies, and these are presented in Table 3. Results are shown for both petals and leaves. With peonies and roses the petals freeze at temperatures higher than do the leaves. Rose petals froze at 30.04° F., while peony petals did not freeze until a temperature of 29.05° was reached. In the case of Easter lilies the leaves froze before the petals, the latter not succumbing until the temperature reached 27.50° F.

TABLE 3.—*Average freezing points of the petals and leaves of cut flowers.*

Scope of inquiry.	Peony.		Rose.		Easter lily.	
	Petals.	Leaves.	Petals.	Leaves.	Petals.	Leaves.
Number of determinations	12	8	6	6		
Freezing point........° F..	29.05	28.39	30.04	28.27	27.50	29.20

RECAPITULATION.

Freezing or freezing injury does not always occur when fruit or vegetable products are exposed to temperatures at or below their actual freezing points. Under certain conditions many of these products can be undercooled; that is, cooled to a point below the true freezing temperature of each and again warmed up without freezing and without apparent injury. Certain products under certain conditions may be actually frozen and then thawed out without apparent injury, while, on the other hand, some products are injured if stored at temperatures well above their actual freezing points. Evidence seems to show that different individuals of the same variety and strain when grown under different conditions will have somewhat different freezing points, and that there are also some variations in the freezing points of products of the same variety and from the same lot.

In view of these facts the freezing points given in this bulletin should be considered only as danger points at or near which, either above or below, there is a possibility of freezing injury if exposed for a sufficient length of time. These are temperatures at which it is unsafe to hold produce for any length of time, as serious danger of frost injury exists.

Fruits.—The average of the freezing points of 9 varieties of summer apples was found to be 28. 44° F., while the average for 14 varieties of fall and winter apples was 28.49° and 28.53° F. for eastern-grown and western-grown fruit, respectively, showing very little difference between the results for apples of the same varieties.

The freezing points of 7 varieties of cherries averaged 27.81° F.; 7 varieties of grapes, 28.16°; 6 varieties of oranges, 28.03°; 11 varieties of peaches, 29.41°; 4 varieties of plums, 28.53°; 22 varieties of strawberries, 29.93°; blackberries, 29.15°; white blackberries, 28.4°; Logan blackberries, 29.51°; red raspberries, 30.41°; black raspberries, 28.76°; cranberries, 26.7°; green bananas, peel 29.84°, pulp 30.22°; ripe bananas, peel 29.36°, pulp 26°; currants, 30.21°; gooseberries, 28.91°; grapefruit, 28.36; hard-ripe Bartlett pears, 28.46°; soft-ripe Bartlett pears, 27.83°; Japanese pears (unknown variety), 29.39°; and Japanese persimmons (Tanenashi), 28.33°.

Fruits freezing above 30° F. are green bananas (pulp), currants, and red raspberries. Those freezing between 29° and 30° F. are green bananas (peel), ripe bananas (peel), blackberries, Logan blackberries, peaches, Japanese pears, and strawberries. Those freezing between 28° and 29° F. are apples, blackberries (white), gooseberries, grapes, grapefruit, lemons, oranges, Bartlett pears (hard ripe), Japanese persimmons (Tanenashi), plums, and raspberries (black). Those freezing between 27° and 28° F. are cherries and Bartlett pears (soft ripe). Cranberries and ripe bananas (pulp) freeze between 26° and 27° F.

Vegetables.—The average freezing point of 18 varieties of potatoes was 28.92° F.; for 20 varieties of sweet potatoes, 28.44°; and for 19 varieties of tomatoes (ripe), 30.38°. The freezing points of other vegetables investigated were beans (snap), 29,74°; cabbage, 31.18°; carrots, 29.57°; cauliflower, 30.08°; sweet corn, 28.95°; eggplant, 30.41°; kohlrabi, 30.02; lettuce, 31.2°; onions (dry), 30.09°; peas (green), 30.03°; and turnips, 30.23°.

Two vegetables froze above 31° F., viz, cabbage and lettuce. Those freezing between 30° and 31° F. were cauliflower, eggplant, kohl-rabi, onions, peas, tomatoes, and turnips. Those freezing between 29° and 30° F. were beans and carrots. Sweet corn, potatoes, and sweet potatoes froze between 28° and 29° F.

Cut flowers.—Determinations of the freezing points of the petals and leaves of Easter lilies, peonies, and roses show that Easter lily petals freeze between 27° and 28° F.; rose leaves and peony leaves, between 28° and 29°; peony petals and Easter lily leaves, between 29° and 30°; and rose petals, between 30° and 31°.

UNITED STATES DEPARTMENT OF AGRICULTURE

DEPARTMENT BULLETIN No. 1134

Washington, D. C.	PROFESSIONAL PAPER	April 26, 1923

SELF-FERTILIZATION AND CROSS-FERTILIZATION IN PIMA COTTON.

By THOMAS H. KEARNEY, *Physiologist in Charge of Alkali and Drought Resistant Plant Investigations, Bureau of Plant Industry.*

CONTENTS.

INTRODUCTION.

The three principal types of cotton grown in the United States—upland (*Gossypium hirsutum*), sea island (*G. barbadense*) and Egyptian [1]—hybridize freely among themselves when opportunity is afforded for cross-pollination. The first or conjugate generation of the hybrid between any two of these types is extremely fertile and vigorous, but in hybrids of upland with sea-island or with Egyptian cotton degenerate and more or less sterile forms occur in large numbers in the later generations (*29*).[2] On the other hand, so far as is known, the perjugate generations of crosses between varieties of the same type are little, if any, inferior in fertility to the parents. The high degree of compatibility between types so distinct as Egyptian and upland makes the frequency of natural cross-fertilization under given conditions a problem of much importance in breeding work with this plant and in maintaining supplies of pure seed of the agricultural varieties.

---

[1] The Egyptian type of cotton as it now exists appears to constitute a distinct botanical species, although it is supposed to have originated through hybridization (*27, p. 289*).
[2] Serial numbers (italic) in parentheses refer to "Literature cited" at the end of this bulletin.

22421—23——1

Evidence is presented in this bulletin that although the cotton flower is admirably adapted to cross-pollination most of the ovules usually are self-fertilized. The percentage of vicinists, or natural hybrids, produced when two distinct varieties or types are grown side by side ordinarily is not large, although the occurrence of only a small initial percentage may, of course, seriously impair the purity of the stock. In the Egyptian type of cotton, particularly, self-fertilization has been found to predominate greatly over cross-fertilization. Investigations of the structure and later ontogeny of the flower, of the deposition of self pollen and of foreign pollen upon the stigmas, and of the competition of like and unlike pollens, here described, contribute to an explanation of the predominance of self-fertilization. Other aspects of the subject treated are the local and seasonal differences in the relative completeness of fertilization and the effect upon fertility of continued self-fertilization.

Most of the data and conclusions relate to the Pima variety of the Egyptian type of cotton, but comparison with upland cotton has been made in numerous instances. With very few exceptions the experiments were performed at Sacaton at the Pima Indian Agency in southern Arizona during the eight-year period from 1914 to 1921. Acknowledgment is made of the cordial cooperation of S. H. Hastings, formerly superintendent of the Cooperative Testing Garden at Sacaton, and of C. J. King, the present superintendent.

Many of the experiments from 1914 to 1919, inclusive, were performed by Walton G. Wells, during that period assistant cotton breeder in the Office of Alkali and Drought Resistant Plant Investigations, Bureau of Plant Industry. Walter F. Gilpin, assistant cotton breeder in the same office, who assisted in the work during 1917 and 1919, performed many of the experiments during the years 1920 and 1921. Others who have aided in the investigations are H. G. McKeever, Rolla B. Wade, Harvey Thackery, F. Ben Clark, Roy W. Nixon, George C. Powell, George J. Harrison, Robert D. Martin, C. J. King, W. W. Ballard, Max Willett, R. H. Manthey, R. H. Peebles, and C. A. Bewick.

Plates I, II, III, IV, and V are from photographs by W. F. Gilpin. Plates VI and VII are from photographs by Harold F. Loomis, of the Office of Crop Acclimatization and Adaptation Investigations, Bureau of Plant Industry.

VICINISM, OR NATURAL HYBRIDIZATION, IN COTTON.

In considering the evidence regarding the occurrence of vicinists, or natural hybrids, the published results of other investigators will be reviewed, and the data of experiments performed in Arizona will be presented.

DATA ON VICINISM IN LITERATURE.[1]

Webber, as the result of his experience in South Carolina and other Southeastern States, observes (48, p. 370):

In several instances varieties have been grown in single rows with other varieties all around them of such a kind that crossing where it occurred could be easily detected in the progeny. Plants grown from seed matured under

---

[1] The accounts of experiments concerning vicinism in cotton rarely state whether or not the rows were thinned; and, if so, whether the removal of the extra plants was managed so as to avoid discrimination in favor of the more vigorous hybrid individuals.

such circumstances show but few crosses, indicating that the majority must have been self-fertilized. Judging from the observations thus far made, it would seem that ordinarily only from 5 to 10 per cent of the seeds are normally cross-fecundated.

Balls, on the basis of his investigations in Egypt, states (6, p. 27):

The vast majority of individuals in any cotton crop yet studied are heterozygous in several characters, and the amount of crossing which takes place between cotton plants growing in a field so producing this heterozygous condition ranges from 5 to 25 per cent, by experimental evidence.

The same investigator, in a later publication (7, p. 222), remarks: "In 1905 we found that some 6 to 10 per cent of the ovules in a field of Egyptian cotton were cross-fertilized instead of being selfed;" and he points out that in general culture the apparent percentage of vicinists is usually larger than the actual percentage, owing to the stronger hybrid plants being retained when the fields are thinned. Certain progenies are mentioned (8, p. 119) in which the percentages of natural hybrids ranged from 25 to 35.

Allard (2) planted easily distinguishable varieties of upland cotton (Keenan, Okra Leaf, Red Leaf) in alternate rows in northern Georgia and found that progenies grown from at least 20 per cent of the bolls borne by plants of the Keenan variety contained one or more hybrids. Some of the bolls yielded only hybrids, indicating that the flowers from which these bolls developed had produced only abortive or self-sterile pollen.

Shoemaker (43), working in north-central Texas, found that when plants of the Triumph variety of upland cotton were scattered through a plat of an "okra-leaf" upland strain, so that each Triumph plant was entirely surrounded by plants of the other type, 47 per cent of the Triumph bolls, seed from which was planted the following year, yielded hybrids, although these in no case amounted to as much as 50 per cent of the entire progeny of the boll. The proportion of hybrids in the entire population grown from bolls collected on the Triumph plants was 10.9 per cent. No correlation could be observed between the position of the boll on the plant and the extent of the cross-fertilization observed, from which this investigator concluded that "the insects which did the crossing must have worked regularly through the season."

McLendon (39, pp. 162–167), in Georgia, grew Willett's Red Leaf and Hastings Big-Boll (a green-leafed variety of upland cotton) in alternate rows and planted seed from the Hastings plants. In a resulting population of 4,467, 87 (1.9 per cent) of the individuals proved to be vicinists.

Ricks and Brown (1, pp. 4, 15, 17), in Mississippi, found that when green-leafed varieties of upland cotton were grown in rows alternating with rows of Willett's Red Leaf, the percentages of natural hybrids produced by the resulting seed ranged from 4.9 to 11.1. From table 9 of the publication cited (p. 17) it may be deduced that of the bolls borne on plants of Lone Star and of Trice 36 and 44 per cent, respectively, gave progenies which contained one or more hybrids with Red Leaf.

In regard to the prevalence in India of natural cross-fertilization of cotton, Gammie (19, pp. 2, 3), from observations at Poona, concluded that it is a very rare occurrence. Evidence to the contrary is given by Leake (*35*), by Kottur (*34*), and by Thadani (*46*). Kottur states that at Dharwar when two pure strains, one having a long leaf and the other a short leaf, were grown side by side, 6 per cent of vicinists occurred in the progeny of the short-leaf strain.

The distance to which pollen may be carried under natural conditions is a subject of much practical importance. Shoemaker (*43*) observed that where Triumph and Okra Leaf cottons were grown 2 rods apart,[4] a planting from the seed of the former yielded about 1 per cent of hybrids. This would indicate that a relatively slight distance affords a fair degree of protection against cross-pollination.

Balls (*8*, pp. 19, 123), in Egypt, found that whereas under ordinary field conditions the number of vicinists ranged from 5 to 10 per cent, in his breeding plat, where numerous different types of cotton were grown in close proximity, the percentage rose to as high as 50 or even 100. He observed that hybrids were occasionally produced with Willett's Red Leaf when the plants of the latter were 50 meters distant from the plants which produced the hybridized seed, with dozens of other cotton plants intervening.

Ricks and Brown (*1*), in Mississippi, found that seed gathered from plants of the Cleveland variety of upland cotton which were situated in the middle of a 4-row plat of this variety, the plat being separated by 10 rows of corn from a row of Willett's Red Leaf cotton, produced 0.8 per cent of Cleveland × Red Leaf hybrids, as compared with 4.9 per cent where the two varieties were grown in adjacent rows and 18.5 per cent where they were grown in alternate hills.

EXPERIMENTS IN ARIZONA.

VICINISM BETWEEN VERY DISTINCT TYPES.

A plat of cotton of the Egyptian type was grown by the writer at Yuma, Ariz., in 1907 in close proximity to a plat of upland cotton. Seed from the open-pollinated flowers of the Egyptian plants was planted in 1908, and of the resulting population of approximately 3,000 individuals 8.2 per cent were hybrid.

Under the direction of O. F. Cook, Egyptian and Kekchi (upland) cottons were planted in alternate rows by Argyle McLachlan near Yuma in 1909. The population grown in 1910 from the seed produced by the Kekchi plants contained 5 per cent of hybrids.[5]

Open-pollinated bolls were collected at Sacaton in 1919 from three adjacent rows of cotton, there having been a row of Pima (Egyptian), bordered on one side by a row of the Lone Star (upland) variety and on the other by a row of the Holdon (upland) variety. The seed obtained from each row was planted in 1920, and the percentages of first-generation hybrids were determined, as given in Table 1.

---

[4] Although the point is not mentioned in the work cited, Dr. Shoemaker has informed the writer that to the best of his recollection there were several rows of Triumph cotton between the plants of that variety from which seed was gathered and the row of Okra Leaf cotton.
[5] Argyle McLachlan in letter to O. F. Cook, July 9, 1910.

TABLE 1.—*Hybrids in populations from open-pollinated seed produced by adjacent rows of Egyptian and upland varieties of cotton at Sacaton, Ariz., in 1920.*

Variety from which seed was obtained.	Plants.	F₁ hybrids.	
		Number.	Per cent.
Pima (Egyptian)...	585	17	2.9±0.5
Lone Star (upland)...	448	23	5.1±.7
Holdon (upland)...	437	49	11.2±1.0

That these percentages of hybrids correspond closely to the actual percentages of ovules which were cross-fertilized by pollen of the other type is indicated by the following facts: The seeds were planted four to the hill and no thinning was done. Comparison of the percentages of hybrids in the hills containing one, two, three, and four plants, respectively, showed that while each successive increase in the number of plants was accompanied by a decrease in the percentage of hybrids, the differences were not significant, even as between hills containing one plant and hills containing four plants. Hence, it may be concluded that little, if any, natural selection in favor of the hybrid plants had taken place during germination and the seedling stage of growth.[6]

The difference in the percentages of hybrids between the progenies of the Pima and of the Lone Star plants is apparently not significant, but the percentage of hybrids in the progeny of Holdon is nearly four times as great as in the progeny of Pima, and the difference is 7½ times its probable error. So far as this evidence goes, it would seem that when Egyptian and upland cottons are grown in close proximity, the former yields a smaller percentage of vicinists than the latter. It should be noted, however, that during the latter half of the summer the upland plants showed a much greater decline in the rate of flowering than did the Pima plants, and this would favor the production of a higher percentage of upland × Pima than of Pima × upland hybrids.

The extent of vicinism occurring when upland plants are located in the midst of a field of Egyptian cotton is indicated by the results of an experiment performed at Sacaton in 1920 and 1921. Fifty plants of Acala (upland) cotton were grown in 1920 in the middle section of the central row of a 7-row plat of Pima cotton. Adjacent to this plat, on both sides, were several other plats which contained only Pima cotton. The rows contained about 400 plants each, so that the upland cotton was completely surrounded by the Egyptian. The arrangement of the planting is shown in Figure 1.

---

[6] Data given elsewhere in this bulletin indicate that seeds produced by Pima flowers which had been cross-pollinated with upland pollen germinate somewhat better than Pima × Pima seeds, although the difference in the germination did not exceed 4.1±1 per cent and was therefore too small to affect materially the percentage of hybrids yielded by seed from naturally pollinated flowers on the Pima plants. To illustrate: If the proportion of germination of the seeds resulting from cross-fertilization of Pima ovules with upland pollen was only 4 per cent higher than that of seeds from Pima ovules fertilized with Pima pollen and if the population grown from seed produced by naturally pollinated Pima flowers contained 10 per cent of hybrids, the actual percentage of hybridized (Pima × upland) ovules would have been 9.6 per cent.

Bolls were gathered in the fall from all 50 of the Acala (upland) plants and from each of the 50 plants, opposite to these, in Pima rows 1, 2, 3, 4, 6, 8, 10, 15, and 20, on the west and rows 1′, 2′, 3′, 4′, 6′, 8′, 10′, 15′, and 20′ on the east of the upland. Each lot of seed was thoroughly mixed, and a representative sample was planted in

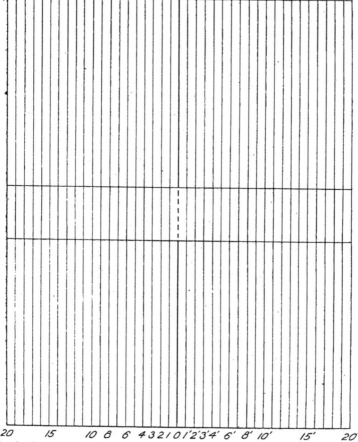

20   15   10 8   6   4 3 2 1 0 1′2′3′4′ 6′ 8′ 10′   15′   20′

FIG. 1.—Planting plan of an experiment to determine the extent of vicinism resulting when plants of the Acala variety of upland cotton were located in the midst of a field of the Pima variety of Egyptian cotton. The middle section of the central row (row O), indicated by the dotted portion of the line, contained the upland plants, the remainder of this row and the rest of the field having been planted to Pima. Horizontal lines inclose the portions of the Pima rows from which seed was harvested for determination of the percentage of vicinists.

1921 in order to determine the percentages of vicinists. No thinning was done, all seeds which germinated having been allowed to develop. The results are stated in Table 2, in which the populations grown from each pair of Pima rows having the same cardinal number and its prime, both east and west of the Acala section, are combined as one array.

TABLE 2.—*Vicinists yielded in 1921 by seed from plants of Acala cotton located in the midst of a field of Pima cotton and by seed from those portions of successive Pima rows which were opposite to and on both sides of the section of Acala cotton, at Sacaton, Ariz., in 1920.*

Variety from which seed was obtained.	Plants.	F_1 hybrids.		Variety from which seed was obtained.	Plants.	F_1 hybrids.	
		Number.	Per cent.			Number.	Per cent.
Acala (upland),[1] row 0.. {	671 (714)	93 (136)	13.9±0.9 (19.1)	Pima (Egyptian)—Con.			
Pima (Egyptian):				Rows 6 and 6'......	579	1	0.2
Rows 1 and 1'......	635	9	1.4± .3	Rows 8 and 8'......	456	0	0
Rows 2 and 2'......	615	2	.3	Rows 10 and 10'...	[2] 600	0	0
Rows 3 and 3'......	685	4	.6	Rows 15 and 15'...	[2] 600	0	0
Rows 4 and 4'......	609	0	.0	Rows 20 and 20'...	[2] 600	0	0

[1] Through an oversight, the seed from the Acala plants was planted in a plat in which upland cotton had been grown in 1920. There were numerous volunteer plants, many of them first-generation upland × Egyptian hybrids which could not be distinguished from the hybrids belonging to this experiment unless they occurred outside the rows and hills of the 1921 planting. Consequently, it was deemed best to count as vicinists belonging to this experiment only F_1 plants which grew in hills with plants of Acala, excluding such F_1 plants as occurred singly in a hill, even though their alignment and spacing distance conformed to that of the 1921 experiment. The figures obtained by including such plants are, however, given in parentheses. It is probable that the first percentage given in the table is lower and the second higher than the true percentage of vicinists yielded in this experiment.

[2] Estimated.

The percentage of vicinists yielded by the section of Acala plants was at least ten times greater than that yielded by the Pima plants which grew on either side of them (rows 1 and 1'). A considerably higher percentage in the former case would be expected (1) because the Acala was surrounded on all sides by Pima and (2) because during the latter part of the season the Pima plants were flowering more profusely than the Acala. But these factors alone do not seem adequate to explain the much greater proportion of vicinism in the case of the upland. It will be noted that no vicinism was detected in the Pima cotton situated farther away from the Acala than rows 6 and 6'.

A 7-row plat of Pima cotton was grown at Sacaton in 1920 adjacent to a 7-row plat of Durango (upland). Each row of each variety was harvested separately. Each resulting lot of seed was thoroughly mixed, and a portion of each lot was planted in 1921 in order to determine the percentages of vicinists. No thinning was done, all plants which germinated having been allowed to develop. The results are stated in Table 3.

TABLE 3.—*Vicinists yielded in 1921 by plantings of seed from successive rows in adjacent plats of Pima and Durango cottons grown at Sacaton, Ariz., in 1920.*

[No. 1 designates the adjacent row of each of the two varieties and No. 7 the row of each variety which was most remote.]

Row.	Plantings of seed from Pima (Egyptian) rows.			Plantings of seed from Durango (upland) rows.		
	Plants.	F_1 hybrids.		Plants.	F_1 hybrids.	
		Number.	Per cent.		Number.	Per cent.
No. 1................	270	9	3.3±0.7	255	6	2.4±0.6
No. 2................	386	8	2.1± .4	313	10	3.2± .7
No. 3................	346	10	2.9± .6	288	2	.7± .3
No. 4................	252	4	1.6± .5	313	2	.6± .2
No. 5................	365	2	.5± .2	233	7	3.0± .8
No. 6................	355	3	.8± .3	286	2	.7± .3
No. 7................	361	5	1.4± .4	288	4	1.4± .5
Total...............	2,335	41	1.8± .2	1,976	33	1.7± .2

The results of this experiment are exceptional, practically the same total percentage of vicinists having been yielded by seed from the Egyptian and from the upland plants, and the percentage yielded by seed from the row of each variety which was most distant from the plat of the other type (row 7) having been not significantly lower than that yielded by the row that was nearest (row 1).

Seed was gathered in 1920 from each of a number of rows in a field of Pima (Egyptian) cotton at Buckeye, Ariz., which was separated from a field of upland cotton by a rather wide road bordered by a row of trees. Each lot of seed was thoroughly mixed, and a portion of that from each row was planted in 1921 in order to determine the percentages of vicinists. No thinning was done, all seeds which germinated having been allowed to develop. The results are stated in Table 4.

TABLE 4.—*Vicinists yielded in 1921 by plantings of seed collected in 1920 from several rows of Pima cotton situated in close proximity to a field of upland cotton at Buckeye, Ariz.*

[No. 1 designates the outside row, nearest the upland field.]

Row.	Plants.	F_1 hybrids.		Row.	Plants.	F_1 hybrids.	
		Number.	Per cent.			Number.	Per cent.
No. 1	284	6	2.1	No. 20	143	1	0.7
No. 2	314	2	.6	No. 30	138	1	.7
No. 3	305	1	.3	No. 40	136	3	2.2
No. 5	287	4	1.4	No. 50	285	5	1.8
No. 10	291	0	0				
No. 15	189	0	0	Total	2,372	23	1.0

It is interesting to note that the most distant row (No. 50) yielded a percentage of vicinists not materially lower than that yielded by row No. 1, which was nearest the field of upland cotton. It seems, however, that pollinating insects which had left one field and crossed a wide road bordered by trees would be as likely to alight at a considerable distance within the second field as at the edge of it.

VICINISM BETWEEN VARIETIES OF THE SAME TYPE.

The cases of vicinism in Arizona thus far discussed have been between widely different types of cotton. It will be interesting to consider a case involving two related varieties belonging to the same general type but sufficiently uniform and sufficiently distinct to make the recognition of accidental hybrids between them fairly certain. A row of Pima cotton was grown side by side with a row of Gila cotton, both varieties belonging to the Egyptian type,[7] at Sacaton, Ariz., in 1916. In this case there was no appreciable difference in the height of the plants and the duration of the flowering period. Seed from the open-pollinated Pima flowers was planted in 1917. The hills were thinned to one plant, the thinning having been done in such manner as to avoid selection. The total number of plants after thinning was 302, of which 5 were certainly, and 2 more were doubtful first-generation Pima × Gila hybrids. The

---

[7] These varieties are described by Kearney (27), and the characters of hybrids between them are discussed by Kearney and Wells (30).

indicated maximum proportion of hybrids was therefore 2.3 per cent. Taken in connection with the low percentages of hybrids produced by seed from open-pollinated flowers of Pima cotton grown adjacent to upland cottons (Tables 1, 2, and 3) these data indicate a strong tendency to self-fertilization in the Pima variety.

VICINISM NOT A COMPLETE MEASURE OF CROSS-FERTILIZATION.

The percentage of recognizable vicinists does not afford an adequate expression of the relative frequency of cross-fertilization as compared with self-fertilization, for the plants produced by ovules which have been fertilized with pollen from other plants of the same variety are usually not distinguishable from the plants resulting from self-fertilization. In order to determine the actual percentage of ovules which have been cross-fertilized, a single individual of one variety should be isolated among plants of another and readily distinguishable variety, allowing only one flower to open daily on the isolated mother plant. In such case only recognizable hybrids would be produced by all seeds from ovules not fertilized with pollen of the same flower.

The conditions outlined in the preceding paragraph were met in an experiment begun at Sacaton, Ariz., in 1920. In the central row of a 7-row plat of Acala (upland) cotton 8 plants of Pima (Egyptian) were so located that from 5 to 10 Acala plants intervened between each 2 Pima plants. Eight plants of Acala cotton were similarly located in a plat of Pima. Only one flower was allowed to open daily on each of the isolated plants, any additional flower buds due to open on the same day having been removed before the corolla expanded. It is believed that under these conditions all or very nearly all of the ovules were either strictly self-fertilized or were cross-fertilized by pollen of the other type. Consequently, the total cross-fertilization which took place should be indicated by the percentages of first-generation hybrids in the progenies of these plants.

The seed produced by each of the isolated individuals was planted in 1921. No thinning was done, all seeds which germinated having been allowed to develop. The percentages of hybrids were determined after the plants had developed sufficiently to make identification certain. The results are stated in Table 5.

TABLE 5.—First-generation hybrids in the progenies of Pima and of Acala plants which had been grown isolated in a plat of the other variety and on which only one flower had been allowed to open daily, at Sacaton, Ariz., in 1920.

Progeny.	Pima (Egyptian) plants.			Progeny.	Acala (upland) plants.		
	Number.	F_1 hybrids.			Number.	F_1 hybrids.	
		Number.	Per cent.			Number.	Per cent.
No. 1	263	4	1.5±0.5	No. 1	219	64	29.2±2.1
No. 2	340	26	7.6±1.0	No. 2	283	98	34.6±1.9
No. 3	211	33	15.6±1.7	No. 3	197	66	33.5±2.3
No. 4	259	30	11.6±1.3	No. 4	225	48	21.3±1.8
No. 5	157	47	29.9±2.5	No. 5	285	64	22.4±1.7
No. 6	234	28	12.0±1.4	No. 6	223	75	33.6±2.1
No. 7	212	11	5.2±1.0	No. 7	260	73	28.1±1.9
No. 8	242	52	21.5±1.8	No. 8	123	18	14.6±2.1
Total	1,918	231	12.0± .5	Total	1,815	506	27.9± .7

There was much more variation in the percentage of hybrids
among the progenies of the Pima plants than among the Acala progenies, one of the Pima progenies having yielded a somewhat higher
percentage than most of the Acala progenies. If the eight progenies of each variety are taken as a single population, however,
it is seen that the percentage of cross-fertilized ovules was more
than twice as great as in the upland variety as in the Egyptian variety.
The results of this experiment indicate that on the average 88 per
cent of the ovules in Pima (Egyptian) cotton and 72 per cent in
Acala (upland) cotton were autogamically fertilized.

These types of cotton differ less in height of plant and rate of
flowering in early summer than later in the season, when the Pima
plants become much taller than the Acala and produce relatively
a greater number of flowers. In order to determine whether these
differences are reflected in different degrees of cross-fertilization of
the early and late flowers, dated tags were attached to all flowers
which opened on the isolated plants. The progeny of each individual was planted in three sections, representing as many periods
during which the flowers had opened—July 1 to 21, July 22 to
August 11, and August 12 to September 3. The number and percentage of F_1 hybrids from seed produced by flowers which opened
during each period were determined for each variety, these data
being presented in Table 6.

TABLE 6.—*First-generation hybrids yielded in 1921 by seed representing different
flowering periods which was produced by the isolated plants of Pima and
of Acala cotton, at Sacaton, Ariz., in 1920.*

Period.	Progenies of 8 Pima (Egyptian) plants.			Progenies of 8 Acala (upland) plants.		
	Number.	F_1 hybrids.		Number.	F_1 hybrids.	
		Number.	Per cent.		Number.	Per cent.
July 1 to 21	311	63	20.2±1.5	646	166	25.7±1.2
July 22 to August 11	793	136	17.2±.9	462	120	26.0±1.4
August 12 to September 3	815	32	3.9±.5	706	220	31.2±1.2

The difference between the two varieties in the percentage of hybrids from seed produced by flowers of the first period probably was
not significant, but flowers of the second and third periods yielded
significantly greater percentages of hybrids in the case of Acala than
in the case of Pima plants. The very marked decline during the last
period (August 12 to September 3) in the relative cross-fertilization
of the flowers borne by the isolated Pima plants is probably to be
attributed to a diminished flower production of the Acala plants
which surrounded them. The isolated Acala plants, on the other
hand, showed a slight increase in the percentage of cross-fertilization during the same period, indicating that no corresponding reduction had taken place in the rate of flowering of the Pima plants by
which they were surrounded.

The fact that the Pima and the Acala flowers which opened during
the period from July 1 to 21, when both types of cotton were in full

blossom, yielded approximately equal percentages of hybrids points to the conclusion that the higher percentages of vicinists usually obtained from seeds produced by upland plants than from seeds produced by Egyptian plants when the two types are grown side by side is due partly to the earlier slowing down of the rate of flowering in the case of upland cotton. Evidence presented in another part of this bulletin indicates, however, that there may be an intrinsic difference in the liability to cross-fertilization of the two types.

CONCLUSIONS REGARDING THE PREPONDERANCE OF SELF-FERTILIZATION.

There is much variation in the percentages of vicinists, or natural hybrids, formed when two distinct types of cotton are grown in proximity, as is shown by the results obtained by other investigators and by the writer. This is to be expected in view of the many variable factors involved, such as local differences in the number and kind of pollinating insects and differences in the habit of growth and period of flowering of the varieties. The proportion of vicinists rarely exceeds 20 per cent, however, and is usually much smaller. The available information in regard to vicinism therefore points strongly to the conclusion that in cotton self-fertilization greatly predominates over cross-fertilization. It should not be inferred, however, that because most of the ovules normally are self-fertilized, such cross-fertilization as occurs is negligible in its effect upon the uniformity of a variety.

As a rule, the percentage of vicinists decreases rapidly as the distance between the seed-bearing and the pollen-bearing parents increases, but the data at hand do not permit a conclusion to be drawn as to the degree of isolation necessary to eliminate the danger of cross-pollination. This is doubtless affected by the nature of the varieties grown, by local and seasonal variations in the insect population and in the flowering of other plants, and by topography, weather, and other factors.

The percentage of recognizable vicinists produced under natural conditions does not measure the proportion of cross-fertilization occurring, for the reason that many of the ovules are cross-fertilized by pollen from other plants of the same variety. An experiment was performed at Sacaton, Ariz., in which this source of error was eliminated by growing scattered plants of one type in a field of another type and allowing only one flower to open daily on each of the isolated plants, seed from which was planted the following season. Plants thus treated yielded 12 per cent of hybrids in the case of Pima (Egyptian) and 28 per cent in the case of Acala (upland). It is believed that these percentages correspond very closely to the percentages of cross-fertilized ovules.

The results of this experiment indicated that in Pima 88 per cent and in Acala 72 per cent of the ovules were self-fertilized. Other evidence has been obtained at Sacaton that upland × Egyptian are more numerous than Egyptian × upland vicinists. That this is due partly to an earlier decline in the flowering rate of upland as compared with Egyptian cotton is suggested by the fact that seeds produced by flowers of Pima and of Acala cotton which opened during a period when both types were blossoming freely yielded approximately the same percentage of vicinists.

STRUCTURE OF THE FLOWER IN RELATION TO POLLINATION.

The large and showy cotton flower with its reproductive organs so placed as to be readily accessible to all kinds of insects (Pls. I and II) would seem to be admirably adapted to cross pollination, especially as the abundant secretion of nectar attracts large numbers of pollen-carrying insects. The transfer of pollen is favored by the fact that even during the height of the blossoming period the number of flowers opening daily on the individual plant rarely exceeds three and is usually only one.[8] Yet the evidence presented in the preceding pages indicates a strong preponderance of self-fertilization. In seeking an explanation of this apparent anomaly the structure and the later ontogeny of the flower will be considered.

The description which follows is based upon the Pima variety, but applies in all essential particulars to other varieties of the Egyptian type. The points of structure relative to pollination in which the flower of upland cotton (*Gossypium hirsutum*) differs from that of Egyptian cotton will be mentioned for comparison.

POSITIONAL RELATIONS OF THE REPRODUCTIVE ORGANS.

Egyptian cotton, like other members of the genus Gossypium, has the ovary and style inclosed in a sheath or tube formed by the coalescent bases of the filaments of the stamens, and the pistil projects above the summit of this so-called staminal column (Pl. I, Fig. 1; Pl. II, Fig. 1). There is no sharp differentiation between stigmas and style, the latter beginning to increase in diameter and to become pubescent below the summit of the staminal column, but under normal conditions pollen is deposited in quantity only on the exserted portion of the pistil, and for convenience the term "stigmas" will be used in referring to this portion only. The erect and usually somewhat spirally twisted stigmas (Pl. I, Fig. 1) are coherent except very near the apex and are slightly enlarged upward. The stigmatic surface is not viscid but is densely pubescent, and this together with the spiny surface of the pollen grains secures their adhesion to the stigmas. Unlike the condition in many of the Malvaceæ, the stigmas do not become spreading or reflexed after the flower opens but remain erect. There is no evidence that the flower is protandrous, as is the case in most of the Malvaceæ.[9] The stigmas from the apex to a little below the point where they emerge from the staminal column are homogeneous in texture and pubescence, and pollen grains adhere to and doubtless germinate upon all parts of their surface.

Reference to Plate I, Figure 1, and to Plate II, Figure 1, shows that in Pima cotton the stigmas project far beyond the summit of the staminal sheath, averaging in length, at 8 a. m., or about 1¼ hours after the corolla has begun to open, 10 millimeters, or one-

---

[8] Darwin (*13*, p. 389), evidently having in mind plants on which numerous flowers are in anthesis at the same time, states "Insects usually search a large number of flowers on the same plant before they fly to another, and this is opposed to cross-fertilization."
[9] Knuth (*33*, p. 206). According to K. Schumann (*42*, p. 32) all Malvaceæ are protandrous.

COTTON FLOWERS IN VERTICAL SECTION, SHOWING THE POSITIONS OF THE STIGMAS AND STAMENS.

FIG. 1.—Egyptian cotton, Pima variety, characterized by stigmas which greatly surpass the relatively short stamens and by having the basal portion of the stigmas closely screened by the uppermost stamens. FIG. 2.—Upland cotton, Acala variety, characterized by stigmas which barely surpass the relatively long stamens and by having no portion of the stigmas closely screened by the stamens.

Photographed by W. F. Gilpin.

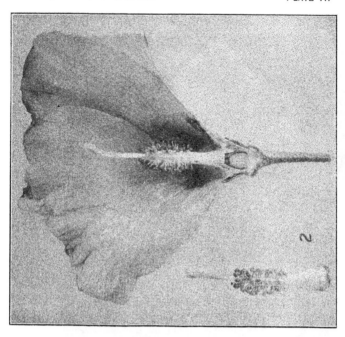

COTTON FLOWERS IN VERTICAL SECTION.

Fig. 1.—Pima variety of Egyptian cotton. Fig. 2.—Sea island cotton, showing characters of the reproductive organs similar to those of Pima, except that the stigmas are longer and less densely screened at the base by the upper stamens.

Photographed by W. F. Gilpin.

third of the total length of the pistil exclusive of the ovary.[10] At the same hour the short uppermost stamens are found to extend on the average 2.5 millimeters above the summit of the staminal sheath. Consequently, at the time of opening of the corolla, approximately one-fourth of the total length of the stigmas is surrounded by the uppermost stamens. Owing to the density of the mass of surrounding stamens, this part of the stigmas probably is screened effectively against the access of foreign pollen. The erect or semierect position of the filaments of the upper stamens brings their anthers into close contact with the base of the stigmas, and automatic self-pollination is thus effected.

Trelease (47, p. 322), whose observations doubtless were made upon upland cottons, states:

The reproductive organs are so placed that on the expansion of the corolla pollen has usually been deposited on the stigmas, self-fertilization being thus secured.

Robson (41) observes that " fertilization in the majority of cotton flowers is effected from the section of the stigma nearest the ovary."

The adaptation of the cotton flower both to self-fertilization and to cross-fertilization is described as follows by Kottur (34, pp. 52, 53):

The entire surface of the style that projects beyond the staminal column is stigmatic; and this has been proved by cutting the stigma and fertilizing it only at the base. Again, in the majority of flowers the filaments of the upper anthers are sufficiently long to touch the base of the stigma. All these conditions are quite favorable for self-fertilization. The anthers are in contact with the stigma and they shed their pollen as soon as the flower opens. But, on the other hand, we have in most cottons a very attractive corolla. The quantity of honey and pollen in the flower is profuse and invites the insects that roam in search of them. All these favor natural crossings. We have thus one set of conditions favoring self-fertilization and another set favoring cross-fertilization; but the former occurs as a rule and the latter as an exception in all varieties of Indian cotton under observation at Dharwar.

The stamens of Pima cotton change their position very slightly, if at all, during the day. Observation as late as 3 p. m., when the corolla was beginning to wilt, showed the filaments of the uppermost stamens to be still erect and the anthers as though glued to the stigmas by the masses of extruded pollen.

In sea-island cotton (Gossypium barbadense) the positional relations of the reproductive organs (Pl. II, Fig. 2) are much the same as in Egyptian cotton, but the anthers do not form as dense a girdle around the base of the stigmas, which is probably somewhat more accessible to foreign pollen.

Most varieties of upland cotton (Gossypium hirsutum) are characterized by much shorter stigmas and by longer filaments of the stamens than in Egyptian cotton (Pl. I, Fig. 2). Measurements made in 1918 upon fully open flowers of the Pima (Egyptian) and Holdon (upland) varieties gave the means stated in Table 7, which show that in a typical upland cotton the stamens are much longer and the stigmas are much shorter, both absolutely and relatively, than in the Egyptian type as represented by the Pima variety.

[10] Measurement of 100 Pima cotton flowers at 8 a. m. showed the mean length of the pistil from the summit of the ovary to be 30.5±0.33 millimeters and the mean length of the stigmas (portion outside the staminal sheath) to be 10.2±0.35 millimeters. The mean projection of the stamens above the summit of the sheath in the same flowers was 2.5±0.16 millimeters.

TABLE 7.—*Measurements of the reproductive organs in Pima and Holdon cottons.*

Variety.	Number of plants on which flowers were measured.	Number of flowers measured.	Mean length of parts (millimeters).			Relative length of stigmas (percentage of pistil length).
			Stamens.[1]	Pistil.[2]	Stigmas.	
Pima (Egyptian).................	21	83	5.0±0.01	36.3±0.29	9.8±0.21	27.0±0.45
Holdon (upland).................	19	84	8.0± .03	26.5± .14	3.1± .08	11.7± .48
Differences....................			3.0± .03	9.8± .32	6.7± .22	15.3± .65

[1] Measured from the base of the filament to the apex of the anther. The average length of 10 stamens per flower was taken as the unit in computing these means. Stamens from near the middle of the staminal column were measured. The uppermost stamens are much shorter. Measurement in 1921 of 5 upper and 5 middle stamens per flower in 5 flowers, each from a different plant of Pima cotton, gave the following means Uppermost stamens, 2.4±0.04 millimeters; middle stamens, 4.3±0.05 millimeters.
[2] Measured from the bottom of the corolla (hence somewhat below the summit of the ovary) to the apex of the stigmas.

Examination in 1920 of the flowers of 20 varieties of upland cotton growing at Sacaton, Ariz., showed that, shortly after the corolla begins to open, the upper stamens are erect. In 16 varieties they were from slightly shorter than to slightly longer than the stigmas, while in 4 varieties the stigmas exceeded the stamens by lengths not greater than 5 millimeters.[11] In most of the upland varieties, therefore, the whole or the greater part of the length of the stigmas is surrounded by the stamens, and the erect position of the latter during the first hour or so after the opening of the flower brings the anthers into contact with the stigmatic surface. Unlike the condition in Egyptian cotton, there is a limited power of movement, for later in the day the filaments become more nearly horizontal. It was observed in 1921 that in the Acala variety at 3 p. m. most of the uppermost filaments diverged at angles of 20° to 45°, although even at this hour occasional anthers remained in contact with the stigmas. The entire length of the stigmas in upland cottons is at all times, however, much more accessible to foreign pollen than is the interstamen section of the Egyptian stigmas.

If one overlooks the receptive character of the entire surface of the pistil outside the staminal sheath and the possibility of a high degree of fertilization by self-pollen automatically discharged upon the basal portion of the stigmas, the assumption is likely to be made that varieties of cotton having long stigmas are not well adapted to self-fertilization. Meade (40) drew this conclusion from the results of an experiment with upland cottons performed by him at San Antonio, Tex., in which flowers of a short-style variety (Acala) and of a longer styled variety (Durango) were artificially pollinated, the stigmas having been thoroughly smeared with their own pollen. Comparing these artificially pollinated flowers with naturally pollinated flowers of the same varieties in respect to the percentages of bolls set, the variety having long stigmas showed a mean increase of 11.0±2.2 per cent from artificial pollination, as compared with an increase of only 5.3±2.4 per cent in the variety having short stigmas,

[11] It is possible that the stigmas were abnormally short in some of the upland cottons grown at Sacaton in 1920, among which were several of the long-staple varieties. According to Meade (40) in many of the long-staple upland varieties the stigmas often exceed the anthers by 15 millimeters.

but the difference between the increases in the two cases was less than twice its probable error.

The converse proposition, that the ovules of flowers with short stigmas are less likely to be cross-fertilized than those of flowers having long stigmas, would seem to be self-evident. It was not borne out, however, by the results of an experiment performed by Balls (8, pp. 118, 119) who compared two strains derived from an Egyptian-upland cross, one of which had the stigmas so short as to be surpassed by the uppermost anthers, while the other had stigmas which greatly surpassed the anthers. No difference was found between the two strains in the percentage of hybrids resulting from natural cross-pollination. Apparently in this case short stigmas offered no effective obstacle to the access of foreign pollen. It is of interest in this connection to note that the Lone Star variety of upland cotton, in which the stigmas normally are exceeded by the upper stamens, produced at Sacaton, Ariz., 5 per cent of vicinists when grown in a row adjacent to a row of Pima (see Table 1, p. 5). The probable explanation is that both in the hybrids compared by Balls and in the Lone Star variety the density of the screen formed by the stamens was not sufficient to protect the short stigmas from access of foreign pollen.

FLOWER STRUCTURE IN RELATION TO CROSS-FERTILIZATION.

In Pima cotton the deposition of foreign pollen upon the basal portion of the stigmas presumably is prevented by the density of the surrounding girdle of stamens (Pl. I, Fig. 1; Pl. II, Fig. 1). An experiment was performed in 1919 with the object of determining the effectiveness of this protection. The material consisted of a row of Pima plants having on one side a row of the Holdon variety and on the other side a row of the Lone Star variety, the populations being the same as in the vicinism experiment (Table 1), Flower buds of all three varieties were opened before anthesis, and the extra-staminal portion of the stigmas, if any, was excised, after which the flowers were left exposed to the visits of insects. In the Lone Star variety the stigmas usually are exceeded by the stamens; hence little or no excision was necessary in this case. In the Holdon variety the portion excised was much shorter than in the case of Pima.

The seed produced by the treated flowers of the three varieties was planted in 1920. The population from seed borne by the Pima plants was much larger than the upland populations, for the reason that the proportion of the treated flowers which failed to set bolls was much larger in the upland cottons [12] than in Pima, and the quantity of seed produced was consequently much greater in the latter case. Early in July, when the plants were well enough developed to show their characters clearly, counts were made of the number of hybrids in the three populations. The rows were not thinned, so that all plants which survived the germination and seedling stages were counted.[13] The results are given in Table 8.

---

[12] This does not indicate that the excision of the extrastaminal part of the stigmas had been more injurious to the upland than to the Egyptian flowers, as the rate of boll shedding at Sacaton, Ariz., is always much higher with upland than with Egyptian cotton.

[13] Data given on page 5 indicate that there had been no natural selection in the earlier stages of growth which would affect the percentages of hybrids.

TABLE 8.—*First-generation hybrids in progenies grown at Sacaton, Ariz., in 1920, from seed produced by flowers the stigmas of which, had been excised in the bud at the level of the uppermost stamens.*

Variety of which seed was produced by excised flowers.	Total plants.	F₁ hybrids.	
		Number.	Per cent.
Pima (Egyptian)	172	0	0
Lone Star (upland)	19	9	47.3±7.7
Holdon (upland)	54	1	1.8±1.2

Reference to Table 1 shows that a population grown from seeds produced by unmutilated naturally pollinated flowers of the Pima plants used in the present experiment contained approximately 3 per cent of hybrids, while the data given in Table 8 show that excision of the extrastaminal portion of the stigmas had prevented cross-fertilization of the Pima flowers. This might have been explained on the ground that the removal of a portion of the corolla in the process of excising the stigmas had rendered the flowers unattractive to insects, were it not for the fact that cross-fertilization occurred in similarly treated flowers of the two upland varieties. It seems probable, therefore, that in Pima cotton the basal portion of the stigmas is effectively screened by the surrounding stamens against the access of foreign pollen, whereas in upland cottons no portion of the stigmas is inaccessible to such pollen.

An anomalous result of the experiment is the much higher percentage of hybrids in the population derived from treated flowers of the Lone Star variety than in the corresponding Holdon population, whereas in the vicinism experiment, involving untreated naturally pollinated flowers on the same plants (Table 1), Holdon yielded more than twice as high a percentage of hybrids as Lone Star, and the difference was five times its probable error.

ONTOGENY OF THE FLOWER IN RELATION TO POLLINATION.

Only the last stages in the ontogeny of the flower are of importance in relation to pollination. The time and rate of opening of corolla and anthers, the condition of the pollen from shortly before the flower opens until it has begun to wilt, and the duration of receptivity of the stigmas will be considered in this connection. 'The final stages in the development of the flower are illustrated in Plate III.

OPENING OF THE COROLLA.

The bud remains tightly closed during the night preceding anthesis, the petals beginning to separate at the apex usually about an hour after sunrise. During the next hour or so the opening of the corolla proceeds slowly, but thereafter the aperture widens rapidly, with a slowing down in the rate shortly before the maximum diameter is attained. Accurate data as to the rate of opening were obtained from an experiment performed in 1919. During three periods of five days each (July 29 to August 2, August 18 to August 22, and September 11 to September 15) 20 flowers were tagged daily, and the aperture of the corolla was measured at half-hour intervals. The mean diameter of the aperture for each half hour is stated in Table

FLOWERS OF PIMA COTTON IN LATE STAGES OF DEVELOPMENT.

Fig. 1.—At 5 p. m. of the day preceding anthesis, showing the corolla and anthers still tightly closed. This is the condition of the flower buds at the time emasculation is performed. Fig. 2.—At 7.30 a. m. of the day of anthesis, showing the corolla in an early stage of expansion and the anthers partly open. Fig. 3.—At 9.30 a. m., showing the corolla almost fully expanded and the anthers wide open.

Photographed by W. F. Gilpin.

PLATE IV.

FLOWER BUDS OF PIMA COTTON.

The successive stages of the process of emasculation during the evening preceding anthesis:
Intact buds (bottom); bud with corolla removed, showing the tightly closed anthers (middle);
anthers removed, flower ready for pollination (top).

Photographed by W. F. Gilpin.

9, the probable error having been computed from the departures of the daily means of 20 flowers from the mean of the daily means. The half-hour means for the day when the opening was most rapid

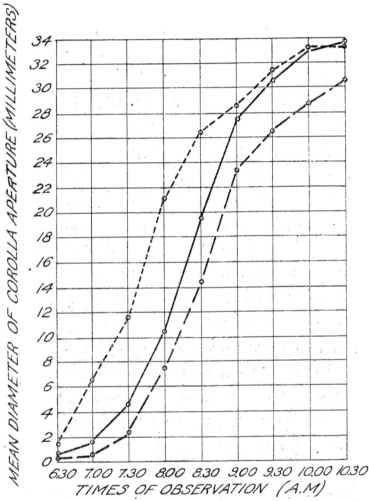

Fig. 2.—Average, maximum, and minimum rates of expansion of the corolla of Pima cotton, as indicated by the mean aperture of the corolla at half-hour intervals during the morning, this having been determined by measurement of 20 flowers on each of 15 days during the period from July 29 to September 15, 1919. The mean hour of sunrise during this period was 5.26. The dotted and broken lines indicate the rates on the days when expansion was most rapid and least rapid, respectively, and the solid line indicates the average rate of expansion for all 15 days.

and for the day when it was least rapid are also given in the table. The average, maximum, and minimum rates of expansion are shown graphically in Figure 2.

22421—23——3

TABLE 9.—*Measurements of the aperture of the corolla of Pima cotton at successive half-hour intervals during three periods of five days each in 1919.*

Hour of measurement.	Daily mean diameter (millimeters).			Hour of measurement.	Daily mean diameter (millimeters).		
	Average for the 15 days.	For the day when the rate of opening was—			Average for the 15 days.	For the day when the rate of opening was—	
		Most rapid (Aug. 18).[1]	Least rapid (Aug. 2).[2]			Most rapid (Aug. 18).[1]	Least rapid (Aug. 2).[2]
6.30 a. m.....	0.6±0.03	1.3±0.13	0.4±0.04	9.00 a. m.....	27.3±0.60	28.7±0.58	23.3±0.66
7.00 a. m.....	1.6± .18	6.6± .48	.7± .12	9.30 a. m.....	30.7± .40	31.2± .53	26.7± .63
7.30 a. m.....	4.7± .39	11.7± .42	2.2± .38	10.00 a. m.....	32.9± .47	33.2± .55	28.8± .55
8.00 a. m.....	10.6± .69	21.0± .67	7.6± .75	10.30 a. m....:	33.7± .43	33.2± .55	30.3± .65
8.30 a. m.....	19.6± .90	26.3± .56	14.3± .85	11.00 a. m.....	(³)	33.2± .55	31.5± .71

[1] Sky clear at and after sunrise.
[2] Sky partly cloudy at and after sunrise.
[3] Omitted in the general average because data were not determined on several days.

The time of sunrise in Arizona in 1919 was 5.11 on July 29 and 5.42 on September 15, the mean for the period having been 5.26. The data given in Table 9 show that as a rule expansion of the corolla had barely commenced at 6.30, or about one hour after sunrise. It is evident that in general the opening of the corolla proceeded most rapidly during the hour 8 to 9, the average increase in aperture during this hour having amounted to one-half of the mean diameter when the corolla ceased to open farther. As the period during which the measurements were made comprised 48 days and as the time of sunrise was 31 minutes later at the end than at the beginning of this period, a progressive retardation of the opening of the corolla might have been expected. In fact, however, the average rate of opening was practically the same during each of the five-day periods.

Records were kept for each morning of the experiment of the shade temperature, relative humidity, and degree of cloudiness at hourly intervals beginning at 6.30 a. m., the object having been to ascertain whether differences in the rate of opening of the corolla on different days bore any relation to these meteorological factors. No evidence of a general correlation was detected, except that on cloudy mornings the rate of opening was somewhat slower and more gradual, the curve showing a less abrupt rise between the hours 7 to 9 than on mornings of full sunshine.

Simultaneous observations of the rate of opening of the corolla in the Pima variety of Egyptian cotton and in the Acala variety of upland cotton on several mornings in July and August, 1920, indicated that as a rule the opening begins a few minutes earlier and proceeds somewhat more rapidly in Acala than in Pima, notwithstanding the fact that the Pima flowers, which are borne on longer fruiting branches, are more exposed than the Acala flowers to the early rays of the sun.

Observations made in 1921 afforded data as to the relative earliness of opening of the corollas of Pima and of upland varieties, the first appearance of an aperture having been taken as the criterion. On August 11, 50 flowers of Pima and 24 flowers of King (upland) were examined. Of these flowers 60 per cent showed an aperture as early as 6.30 in the case of King, but not until 7.15 in the case of

Pima; 90 per cent showed an aperture at 7.05 in the case of King, but not until 8.05 in the case of Pima. Similar observations on August 12 on 50 flowers each of Pima and of the Durango, Acala, and Lone Star varieties of upland cotton indicated, on the contrary, the more rapid appearance of an aperture in Pima than in the upland varieties. The hours at which an aperture had appeared in 50 and in 90 per cent of the flowers examined are shown in Table 10.

TABLE 10.—*First appearance of an aperture in the corollas of 50 flowers of each of four varieties of cotton grown at Sacaton, Ariz., as observed on August 12, 1921.*

Aperture present—	Time of opening (a. m.).			
	Pima (Egyptian).	Upland varieties.		
		Durango.	Acala.	Lone star.
In 50 per cent of the flowers	7.15	7.40	7.50	....
In 90 per cent of the flowers	7.50	8.10	8.25	8.55

While the several observations gave contradictory results as to the relative earliness of the first appearance of an aperture in Pima and in upland varieties, it appears that the further expansion of the corolla proceeds more rapidly in upland than in Pima. Comparing the Pima and Acala varieties it was observed that in the former expansion begins with a very minute aperture at the apex of the bud, which enlarges gradually, whereas in Acala the initial aperture is larger and the petals separate much more rapidly. The greater length of the Pima petals and the fact that they are more tightly wrapped in the bud probably explain this difference.

The flower of both Egyptian and upland cottons is of brief duration. On sunny days in July and August the corolla begins to wilt and change color by midafternoon, and before sunset the wilting has proceeded so far that the corolla is closed or nearly so and the pistil is becoming flaccid. Abscission of the style in the Pima variety normally takes place within 36 hours after the beginning of anthesis. Observations on 50 Pima flowers in 1922 showed that in every case the style had separated from the ovary by 2 p. m. of the day following anthesis, or 31 hours after the commencement of anthesis. The mean number of hours from the commencement of anthesis to the abscission of the style was 29 ± 0.08.

OPENING OF THE ANTHERS AND DISCHARGE OF POLLEN.

Examination of flower buds of Pima cotton late in the afternoon preceding the opening of the corolla (Pl. III, Fig. 1) shows, as a rule, the anthers tightly closed and the pistil free from pollen grains. At this stage the pollen can not be extracted easily from the anthers. Occasional flowers have been observed in which a few of the anthers were open sufficiently in the evening to show the pollen grains, but in none of these cases was pollen found upon the stigmas under conditions making it certain that the discharge had not taken place as a result of rupturing the anthers in the process of cutting away the corolla. In the early morning, however, when the corolla is still closed or is open at the apex to the extent of not more than 1 or 2 millimeters, as is usually the case in July and August up to about 7 a. m., the anthers are found to be partly open, so as to expose the pollen. The rapidity with which both corolla and anthers open depends to some extent upon the position of the flower on the plant, which determines how early it is exposed to the rays of the sun. The condition of the sky also is doubtless a factor in the earliness of opening.

On July 25, 1920, during the half hour from 5.30 to 6 a. m. 25 Pima flowers which had the corolla still closed, although in some cases the petals were beginning to loosen at the tip, showed the anthers to be partly open in all of the flowers. Pollen grains in greater or less number were already present on the interstamen region of the stigmas in all but one flower, but some of this pollen may have been deposited in the act of opening the bud. That this was probably the case is indicated by further observations during the same summer, in which extreme care was taken to avoid the discharge of pollen upon the stigmas while opening the bud. Ten flowers were examined at about 7 a. m. on each of six days during the period from August 3 to August 14. At the time of observation the corolla was closed or was open to an extent of not more than 1 or 2 millimeters, while the anthers were at least half open and were extruding pollen. Pollen was found upon the interstamen region of the stigmas in about half of the flowers, but the number of grains there present was very small, frequently not exceeding one or two.

When the natural opening of the corolla is delayed the discharge of pollen also is retarded.[14] On July 25, 1917, 10 closed or nearly closed flowers were examined at 8 a. m. (hence nearly three hours after sunrise), and four of these had no pollen on the stigmas, even on the portion surrounded by the uppermost anthers. Examination, on July 30, 1920, of a few buds which were still closed at 8 a. m. showed that self pollen was just beginning to be deposited upon the stigmas in appreciable quantity. On August 19, 1921, fully 90 per cent of the flowers were open sufficiently between 7.30 and 8 a. m. to admit insects. Of the belated buds, which were either tightly closed or were just beginning to loosen at the tip, 20 were opened during this half hour, taking every precaution to avoid further discharge of pollen, and the number of grains present on the stigmas was determined as accurately as could be done without touching the anthers. The counts showed numbers of grains present on the lower half of the stigmas as follows: In 8 flowers, 6 grains or fewer; in 5 flowers, 6 to 12 grains; in 7 flowers, more than 12 grains. Of the buds examined 65 per cent had no more than a dozen grains of pollen present on the stigmas.

In upland cottons the opening of the anthers may or may not precede that of the corolla. Five flowers each of some 20 upland varieties were examined at Sacaton, Ariz., in 1920. In six varieties some of the flowers had the anthers still closed after the corolla had begun to expand. In the other varieties the opening of the anthers was keeping pace with the expansion of the corolla in most of the flowers. Examination of 10 closed or barely opening flower buds

---

[14] Cook (*11*, p. 204) states that "in cool moist weather the anthers sometimes fail to open, so that no pollen is available." An instance of complete failure to set bolls from this cause was observed in Guatemala.

of the Acala variety of upland cotton, on each of six dates from August 3 to August 14, 1920, showed that at about 7 a. m. discharge of pollen had begun in only one-third of the flowers. A comparison was made of the relative rates of opening of the corolla and anthers in Pima and Acala cottons on August 9, 1920. It was observed at 7 a. m. that in Pima the corollas were open only 1 or 2 millimeters, but the anthers were well open; while on near-by Acala plants the corollas were open from 5 to 10 millimeters, but the anthers were still closed or were just beginning to split.

Further observations were made at Sacaton, Ariz., in 1921. At 7.30 to 8 o'clock on the cool, cloudy morning of July 27, upland flowers of which the corollas were already open to an extent of 5 to 10 millimeters had the anthers in most cases either still closed or split only sufficiently to disclose but not to discharge the pollen grains. Only one of the eight varieties examined showed the discharge of pollen in some of the flowers before the corolla had commenced to expand, while in all closed buds of Pima cotton, which were examined at the same time, the anthers were wide open, and in many of them the discharge of pollen upon the stigmas had begun. On the other hand, on August 12 at 7.30 to 7.45 a. m. examination of closed buds of the Acala variety showed that the anthers were partly open in all cases and that a few pollen grains were present on the stigmas in 7 of the 10 buds examined.

Observations upon upland cotton have shown that dehiscence of the anthers and discharge of pollen before the petals have begun to unfold are more likely to occur in belated flowers than in flowers which have not been retarded in their opening. Thus, on August 9, 1921, a warm, sunny morning, when most of the flowers of upland varieties were already open at 8.15 o'clock, approximately two-thirds of the buds which still remained closed had the anthers partly open. In many of these buds a few grains of self pollen were already present on the stigmas. Closed buds of Pima cotton examined during the same half hour had the anthers much more fully open than in the upland varieties, and in nearly every case the stigmas had received self pollen in greater or less quantity. On the following morning, with similar weather conditions, observations were made on the Lone Star and Acala varieties of upland cotton and on Pima cotton during the half hour from 8.10 to 8.40, when most of the flowers of the three varieties were partly open. Of the still closed buds of Lone Star, 20 were opened carefully, and 9 of these were found to have the anthers partly open and a few grains of pollen on the stigmas. In the remaining 11 buds the anthers were still closed or were beginning to split but were not yet discharging pollen. Of six closed flowers of the Acala variety, four had the anthers partly open and a few grains of pollen present on the stigmas. Ten unexpanded Pima flowers had the anthers much wider open than in the upland varieties, and in most but not all of these a little pollen was present on the stigmas.

It may be concluded from these observations on the comparative rate of opening of the corolla and anthers in Pima and upland cottons that in Pima the opening of the anthers and the discharge of pollen somewhat precede the expansion of the corolla, while in upland as a rule the corolla and anthers begin to open almost simultaneously. In case the opening of the upland corolla has been retarded, however, the anthers often begin to open and to discharge pollen before the petals commence to unfold. It seems clear that even in Pima cotton no considerable quantity of pollen ordinarily is deposited upon the stigmas before the expansion of the corolla has begun.

Other investigators have noted that different species of Gossypium differ in the rate of opening of the anthers. A statement by Fyson (*18*, p. 5) implies that in India the anthers of American upland cotton (*Gossypium hirsutum*) open and discharge their pollen earlier than do anthers of Asiatic species (*G. herbaceum*, etc.). Smith (*44*), in the West Indies, observed that sea-island cotton (*G. barbadense*) opens its anthers earlier in the day than does a native cotton of the American upland type.

VIABILITY OF THE POLLEN IN DIFFERENT STAGES OF DEVELOPMENT.

The viability of the pollen during the hours immediately preceding and following the opening of the corolla is of interest in relation to the phenomena of pollination. The rapidity and completeness with which the pollen grains eject their contents at different stages in the ontogeny of the flower were tested by immersing them in a 5 per cent aqueous solution of cane sugar, although apparently ejection takes place with equal readiness in water.

The discharge of protoplasm by the pollen grain in these media takes place in the manner described as "pseudogermination" by Andronescu (*4*), the contents being ejected with explosive suddenness in a very long slender thread, which immediately becomes twisted into a tangled spiral. Andronescu's illustration of the process in Zea (*4*, pl. 2) represents very well the phenomenon as it occurs in Gossypium. It is uncertain in what degree the rate of pseudogermination at different hours of the day is correlated with that of normal germination upon the stigmas. It will be shown, however, that in cotton little or no pseudogermination takes place in the evening preceding the opening of the corolla and that it increases in rapidity and completeness during the following morning, reaching a maximum intensity at noon and then gradually declining to a very low minimum long before sunset. It seems at least probable that normal germination follows a similar course and that the vigor of pseudogermination is indicative of the viability of the pollen (*4*, p. 16). The phenomenon will be referred to in this bulletin as "ejection," thus avoiding the cumbersome term "pseudogermination."

Observations were made with a binocular microscope. The pollen was immersed in the sugar solution as soon as possible after detaching the flower from the plant. The criteria of viability used were (1) the number of seconds after immersion until active ejection ceased and (2) the percentage of the total number of grains in the field of the microscope which discharged their protoplasm during the period of active ejection. An "index of viability," which integrates rapidity and completeness of ejection at different hours, was obtained by dividing the percentage of the total grains ejected by the number of seconds required to complete active ejection and multiplying the quotient by 100.

The condition of the pollen on the day preceding anthesis will be considered first. Pollen from Pima buds was collected on several occasions at from 3 to 6 p. m., and its reaction in a solution of cane sugar was observed. After immersion during one to five minutes a small percentage of the grains ruptured and their contents oozed out slowly, the phenomenon having been very different from the explosive ejection of a long thread which was observed in pollen grains collected in the morning from open flowers.

The viability of the pollen of Pima cotton during the day of anthesis was tested on July 26, 1917, and on July 25 and August 5, 1919. As the results show close agreement, only those of August 5 will be considered in detail, parallel tests with the Durango variety of upland cotton having been made on that date. Pollen of each variety was collected at half-hour intervals from 6 a. m. (hence before the corollas had opened) until 10.30 a. m. and at intervals of one hour thereafter until 3.30 p. m., with a final collection at 5.30 p. m. Shortly before the first collection was made the sky was cloudy, but during the remainder of the day there was

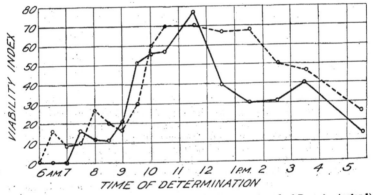

FIG. 3.—Indexes of viability of the pollen of Pima (Egyptian) and of Durango (upland) cotton at successive time intervals during the day of anthesis. The curve for Pima is indicated by a solid line and that for Durango by a dotted line. Both curves show a low viability early in the morning, a rapid increase beginning at 8.30 or 9 o'clock, and a gradual decline after midday.

full sunshine. The tests were made upon one flower of each variety up to 10.30 a. m. and thereafter on two flowers of each variety, the average of the viability indexes of the two flowers having been used in plotting the curves.

Endeavor was made to select only flowers which were so located on the plant as to have been exposed to full sunlight up to the time of collection. This object was realized in the case of Pima but not in the case of Durango, owing to the limited number of flowers available. However, no flowers of Durango were taken later in the day which had not been so exposed during several hours, and the earliest flowers in the most exposed situations were selected. The Durango anthers tended to become exhausted of pollen earlier in the day than the Pima anthers, probably because the shallow, flaring corolla of upland cotton attracts more of the large pollen-carrying insects.

The indexes of viability of the two varieties at different hours are shown by curves in Figure 3. The percentage of grains ejected, one of the factors in computing the index, was merely estimated, except in a few cases when the total number of pollen grains in the field of the microscope was small. The more rapid decline in viability during the afternoon shown by the Pima pollen was probably caused by the fact, already noted, that the flowers of this variety were more exposed to the direct rays of the sun than the Durango flowers.

Pollen has been found to retain its viability much longer in flowers which have been inclosed in paper bags to prevent cross-pollination than in open flowers. On July 26, 1917, buds due to open that morning were bagged at 6 a. m., and the viability of the pollen was tested in sugar solution at 6 p. m. of the same day and at 6 a. m. of the day following. The results are given in Table 11.

TABLE 11.—*Prolongation of the viability of the pollen in cotton flowers bagged at 6 a. m. July 26.*

Hour of testing.	Number of flowers.	After immersion until ejection—		Estimated ejection.	Viability index.
		Began.	Ceased actively.		
		Seconds.	*Seconds.*	*Per cent.*	
6 p. m., July 26	2	37	105	75	71
6 a. m., July 27	1	35	270	40	15

Whereas in the case of unbagged flowers the proportional ejection of pollen at 6 p. m. of the day of anthesis was estimated at only 3 or 4 per cent, pollen from bagged flowers at the same hour ejected with great vigor, and the percentage of grains ejected was almost as high as in the case of pollen from uninclosed flowers shortly before noon of the day of anthesis. At 6 a. m. of the day following anthesis the po en from bagged flowers ejected more slowly and less completely. ll It seems probable, therefore, that even in bagged flowers the pollen loses its viability during the day following anthesis.[15]

It may be deduced from the curves shown in Figure 3, which are based upon an index integrating the percentage of pollen grains which eject their contents and the rapidity with which ejection is completed, that under conditions at Sacaton, Ariz., the viability of the pollen of Pima (Egyptian) and of Durango (upland) cotton is low during the early morning hours, begins to increase rapidly at about 9 o'clock, and begins to decline at or shortly after midday. If the index of viability based upon the rapidity and completeness of ejection in a sugar solution indicates the capacity for normal germination, it would be concluded that pollen which reaches the stigmas before 8 or 9 a. m. will germinate more slowly and less completely than pollen which arrives later in the morning. It should be noted, however, that while at earlier hours a much longer time was required for the ejection to take place, the percentages of the total number of grains which finally ejected their contents were in some cases relatively high. Thus, in the case of Pima cotton, ejection

---

[15] Pollen longevity in the snapdragon and in maize is the subject of a recent publication by H. E. Knowlton (*32*), who summarizes (p. 755–759) the results of other investigators with various plants and points out (p. 786) that pollen may retain its capacity to germinate when no longer able to effect fertilization.

finally took place in about 70 per cent of the grains collected at 6.30 a. m. on July 26, 1917, and in about 65 per cent of those collected at 6 a. m. on July 25, 1919. A test of Durango pollen on August 5, 1919, showed ejection at 6.30 a. m. in about 75 per cent of the total number of grains. It also seems probable that pollen discharged at an early hour may continue to mature after it has reached the stigmas.

DEGREE OF MATURITY OF POLLEN AS AFFECTING FERTILIZATION.

An experiment was performed in 1921 to ascertain whether fertilization can be effected by immature pollen placed upon the stigmas many hours in advance of the time of anthesis. Pima flower buds were emasculated in the evening, pollen squeezed from the anthers of the same flower was placed upon the stigmas, and the flowers were kept inclosed in bags until the stigmas had withered and there was no longer danger of accidental cross-fertilization. Only 1 of 25 flowers thus treated produced a boll which reached maturity. This boll contained five ripe seeds. A second boll was retained longer than 10 days but finally dropped, the exact date not having been ascertained. The remaining 23 flowers shed their undeveloped bolls within 10 days of the date of pollination, this being apparently the average number of days from anthesis to shedding for Pima cotton in Arizona (*31*), p. 15). The results of this experiment are of practical interest as showing that when flowers are emasculated the evening before anthesis for the purpose of making hybrids, every precaution should be used to prevent self pollen from reaching the stigmas, fertilization with such pollen being possible, although evidently not frequent.

The methods used in emasculating and bagging flowers in this and in experiments subsequently described are illustrated in Plates IV and V.

In order to ascertain whether fertilization is affected by deferring pollination several hours after it would take place normally, 240 Pima flower buds were emasculated late in the afternoon preceding anthesis during the period from July 22 to August 2, 1921, 20 buds having been treated on each day of the experiment. Other flower buds were bagged at the same time to supply the pollen required. Half of the flowers were pollinated at 8 o'clock the following morning and the others at about 5 p. m. In open flowers the anthers would have been practically empty of pollen, and the stigmas would have been losing their turgidity at the latter hour, but it has been shown that bagging tends to prolong the freshness of the flower.

The number of bolls which matured and the number of seeds in each boll were determined, and from these data were computed the percentage of bolls matured and the mean number of seeds per boll, as stated in Table 12. The difference in the percentage of bolls matured was in favor of the deferred pollination, but was less than three times the probable error. On the other hand, early pollination yielded a somewhat higher mean number of seeds per boll, and this difference was approximately three times its probable error. It may be concluded that in bagged flowers the pollen retains its ability to effect fertilization practically unimpaired up to 5 p. m. of the day of anthesis.

22421—23——4

TABLE 12.—*Comparison of morning and evening pollination of cotton flowers, showing the percentage of bolls matured and the mean number of seeds per boll.*

Time of pollination.	Flowers treated.	Percentage of bolls matured.	Mean number of seeds per boll.
Flowers pollinated at 8 a. m.	120	89.2±1.93	14.5±0.23
Flowers pollinated at 5 p. m.	120	95.0±1.35	13.4± .26
Difference		5.8±2.35	1.1± .35

Another experiment was performed in 1921 with the object of ascertaining whether the pollen in bagged flowers remains viable as long as 26 hours after anthesis would have begun under normal conditions. Pima flower buds were emasculated in the evening of August 5 and pollinated on August 6. Of the 100 buds emasculated 50 were pollinated at 1 p. m. with pollen from flowers which had been bagged on August 5 at the time the emasculation was done. The other 50 were pollinated at 9 a. m. with pollen from flowers bagged in the bud on August 4 which at the time of pollination were about 26 hours past the normal time of the beginning of anthesis. In these old flowers when collected for use in pollination, the petals were wilted and the pollen was very loose in the anthers. The relative fertilization obtained from the two pollinations, as shown in Table 13, indicates that although the flowers had been protected by inclosure in bags, much of the pollen had lost its ability to effect fertilization 26 hours after the normal time of the beginning of anthesis.

TABLE 13.—*Results obtained by pollination with old and with fresh pollen, showing the percentage of bolls matured and the mean number of seeds per boll.*

Pollination with pollen from flowers in which anthesis normally would have begun—	Flowers treated.	Percentage of bolls matured.	Mean number of seeds per boll.
6 hours previously (fresh pollen)	49	85.7±3.44	12.6±0.41
26 hours previously (old pollen)	50	38.0±4.63	6.4± .58

DURATION OF THE RECEPTIVITY OF THE STIGMAS.

It has been mentioned that in uninclosed cotton flowers at Sacaton, Ariz., the stigmas show a perceptible loss of turgor before sunset of the day of anthesis. The results of the experiment summarized in Table 12 indicate, however, that when the flowers have been protected by bagging, the stigmas show no appreciable loss of receptivity, as measured by the degree of fertilization attainable, as late as 5 p. m. In order to determine whether the stigmas retain their receptivity for a still longer period when the flowers are inclosed, 100 Pima flower buds were emasculated and bagged during the evening of August 3, 1921, and were cross-pollinated with fresh pollen from Pima plants, half of them at 1 p. m. of the day following emasculation and half at 8 a. m. of the second day. It proved somewhat difficult to extract pollen from the anthers of the

PLATE V.

INCLOSING A COTTON FLOWER IN A PAPER BAG TO PREVENT ACCIDENTAL CROSS-POLLINATION.

In order to attach the bag a slit is made in it nearly to the middle, so as to straddle the fruiting branch, and the bag is then tightly closed underneath the branch by means of a loop in a piece of insulated wire.

Photographed by W. F. Gilpin.

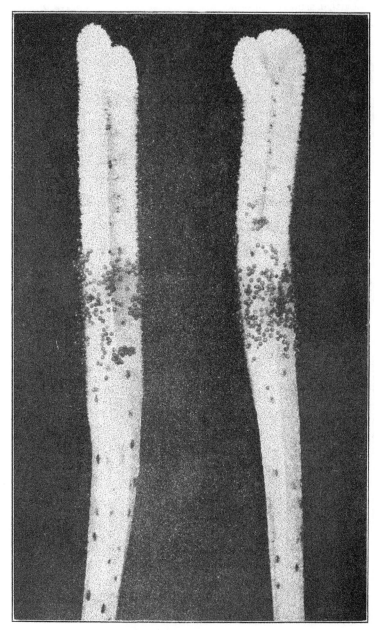

STIGMAS AND UPPER PORTION OF THE STYLE OF BAGGED FLOWERS OF PIMA COTTON.

These parts, dissected at about 3 p. m. of the day of anthesis from flowers which had been bagged to exclude insects, show the locus of automatic deposition of self pollen. The position of the lowest pollen grains indicates the height to which the sheath of the staminal column extended. The upper half of the stigmas is entirely free from pollen. (Magnified 10 times.)

Photographed by H. F. Loomis.

PLATE VII.

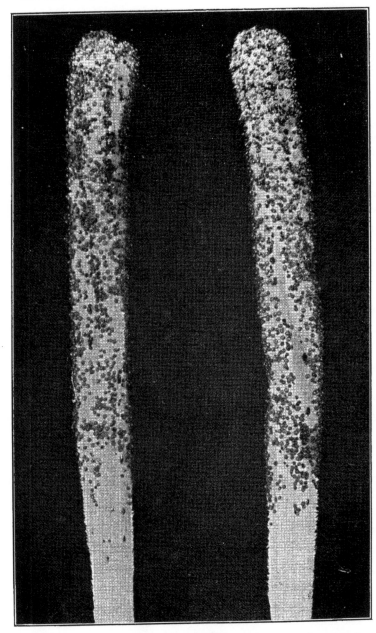

STIGMAS AND UPPER PORTION OF THE STYLE OF UNINCLOSED FLOWERS OF PIMA COTTON.

These parts were dissected at about 3 p. m. from uninclosed, naturally pollinated flowers. The whole stigmatic surface is covered with pollen grains. (Magnified 10 times.) Photographed by H. F. Loomis.

pollen-bearing flowers as early as 8 a. m., but it is believed that in every case the quantity applied was sufficient to have insured thorough pollination under normal conditions.

The resulting data, as given in Table 14, show that the stigmas had retained their receptivity in only a few of the flowers the pollination of which was deferred until the second day. Those which remained receptive, however, were as well fertilized as the flowers pollinated on the day of anthesis.[16]

TABLE 14.—*Results obtained by pollinating Pima cotton flowers on the day of anthesis and on the following day, showing the percentage of bolls matured and the mean number of seeds per boll.*

Time of pollination.	Flowers treated.	Percentage of bolls matured.	Mean number of seeds per boll.
1 p. m. of the day of anthesis	50	90.0±2.86	13.7±0.32
8 a. m. of the day following anthesis	48	8.3±2.70	[1] 13.2±3.05

[1] Omitting one of the four bolls matured which contained only a single seed, the mean number of seeds in the remaining bolls was 17.3±1.79.

LOCUS OF POLLEN DEPOSITION IN RELATION TO SELF-FERTILIZATION AND CROSS-FERTILIZATION.

Numerous examinations of flowers of Pima cotton when the corolla is still closed or is just beginning to expand have shown that if the flower is opened with sufficient care pollen is rarely found upon the stigmas at a height of more than 2 millimeters above the uppermost anthers, to which height the grains probably can be thrown by automatic discharge. A similar condition is found in flowers which have been bagged to prevent cross-pollination, even when the corolla has opened to a degree which in unbagged flowers would permit the ready access of pollen-carrying insects. As about 2.5 millimeters of the length of the stigmas is surrounded by the uppermost stamens, the portion upon which self pollen is automatically discharged therefore does not exceed, as a rule, 5 millimeters, or about half the average total length of the stigmas. The girdle of self-pollen grains deposited upon the stigmas at the height of the uppermost anthers, hence just above the summit of the staminal sheath, is shown in Plate VI. It has been pointed out that this zone, on which is lodged the great bulk of the automatically discharged self pollen, is so closely screened by the uppermost stamens with their short filaments as to be practically inaccessible to foreign pollen.

On the other hand, in flowers which open under natural conditions in a locality like Sacaton where pollinating insects are abundant, the entire surface of the stigmas usually becomes covered with pollen during the morning (Pl. VII). There can be little doubt that in this type of cotton, pollen which is found upon the upper half of the

[16] In Pima cotton the style normally drops off within 36 hours after the beginning of anthesis. A much longer duration of receptivity of the stigmas has been noted in other plants. Dorsey states (14, p. 116) that in the plum the "stigma remains receptive for a maximum period of about one week." It is reported by Anthony and Harlan (5, p. 528) that the stigmas of barley retained their receptivity during five days following emasculation, although the degree of fertilization effected diminished rapidly after the second day.

stigmas has been conveyed there by insects, whether it originated in the same or in other flowers, and that pollen which is lodged upon the basal quarter of the stigmas has been self-deposited.

The question suggests itself whether the rate of growth of the tubes from pollen grains deposited at different loci on the stigmas may be an important factor in determining the relative frequency of self-fertilization and of cross-fertilization. There is a considerable difference in the distance to the ovary to be traversed by the tubes from self-pollen grains automatically deposited near the base of the stigmas and by the tubes from insect-carried pollen grains deposited higher on the stigmas, the maximum difference, corresponding to the average length of the stigmas, being about 10 millimeters. This might be expected to give the self pollen a decided advantage in the time required for the pollen tubes to reach the ovary and to account, at least in part, for the observed preponderance of self-fertilization in Egyptian cotton.

Fertilization in Gossypium, according to Balls (8, p. 12), "is normally completed within 30 hours after the first opening of the flower, i. e., by the afternoon of the following day." An experiment was performed at Sacaton, Ariz., in 1921, in an endeavor to determine the length of time required to effect fertilization, or rather penetration of the ovary by the pollen tubes. Flower buds of Pima cotton were emasculated in the evening before anthesis and were pollinated at 1 p. m. the following day with pollen of the same variety. The pollen was deposited in some of the flowers at the apex and in others at the base of the stigmas. The pistils of approximately equal number of these flowers were then excised at the summit of the ovary at 8 p. m. of the day of pollination and at 5, 7, 9, and 11 a. m., and 1 p. m. of the following day.[a] A record was kept of the number of bolls which matured and of the number of seeds per boll, from which were computed the data given in Table 15.

TABLE 15.—*Degrees of fertilization attained in Pima cotton flowers pollinated at the apex and at the base of the stigmas, the pistils having been excised at various intervals following pollination.*

Pistil excision.		Apical pollination.			Basal pollination.		
Hour excised.	After pollination (hours.)	Flowers treated.	Percentage of bolls matured.	Mean number of seeds per boll.	Flowers treated.	Percentage of bolls matured.	Mean number of seeds per boll.
8 p. m.	7	45	0		45	0	
5 a. m.	16	45	66.7±4.7	11.4±0.49	45	46.7±5.0	8.1±0.63
7 a. m.	18	45	77.8±4.2	14.7± .34	45	46.7±5.0	12.8± .45
9 a. m.	20	45	80.0±4.0	16.9± .23	45	68.9±4.7	12.7± .31
11 a. m.	22	45	82.1±3.9	16.5± .19	45	84.4±3.6	13.6± .28
1 p. m.	24	37	83.8±4.1	16.8± .18	40	87.6±3.5	15.1± .13

Fertilization did not occur in either the apically or the basally pollinated flowers of which the pistils were excised at 8 p. m. on the day of pollination. It is therefore evident that in this case more than

[a] Her{bert-Nilsson (22) describes results obtained by this method of excising the style in computing the rate of pollen-tube development in Oenothera, which he found to average 4.5 millimeters per hour in mid-July. Fertilization did not occur in flowers of which the styles were excised earlier than 19 hours after pollination. This investigator also obtained evidence "that the pollen tubes of O. gigas grew slower in the styles of O. lamarckiana than O. lamarckiana's own pollen tubes."

7 hours were required for penetration of the ovary by the pollen tubes.[a] Considering for the moment only the apically pollinated flowers, it is shown that at 5 a. m., or 16 hours after the pollen was deposited, the tubes had reached the ovaries of two-thirds of the flowers in number sufficient to fertilize on the average more than half of the mean number of ovules, which is 21. A slower rate of development of some of the tubes is indicated by the much more nearly complete fertilization of flowers in which the pistils were not excised until 9 a. m.

Some of the tubes doubtless had penetrated the ovary earlier than 5 a. m., but in estimating the mean rate of growth it may be assumed that the period of 16 hours represents the average length of time required. The further assumption is made, although proof is lacking, that germination began as soon as the pollen reached the stigmas. In the case of pollen applied at or near the apex of the stigmas, which average in Pima cotton one-third the length of the pistil exclusive of the ovary, it may be assumed that most of the grains germinated within 2 millimeters of the apex of the stigmas, or 28 millimeters above the base of the style, the average total length of stigmas and style being 30 millimeters. A growth of 28 millimeters in 16 hours indicates a mean rate of 1.75 millimeters per hour.[b] Self pollen automatically deposited at or near the base of the stigmas would be located on the average about 6 millimeters nearer the ovary, and tubes starting from this locus might be expected to penetrate the ovary 3½ hours in advance of the tubes from grains of foreign pollen starting near the apex of the stigmas. This would seem to give self pollen a decided advantage over foreign pollen, provided the conditions at both loci are equally favorable for the germination and development of the pollen.

Comparison of the rates of fertilization by apically and by basally deposited pollen, as stated in Table 15, indicates, however, that the base of the stigmas affords less favorable conditions for pollen development than the apex. For each interval after pollination, fertilization, as measured by the mean number of seeds per boll, was significantly less complete in the basally than in the apically pollinated flowers, and in the flowers excised at the latest hour, 1 p. m., the mean difference in favor of apical pollination amounted to 1.7±0.22. The mean number of seeds per boll from basally pollinated flowers which had the pistils excised at 1 p. m. (24 hours after the pollen was deposited) was not significantly greater than the mean number from apically pollinated flowers which had the pistils excised at 7 a. m. (only 18 hours after the pollen was deposited).

Another experiment performed in 1921 yielded additional indications that pollen germinates and develops under relatively unfavorable conditions when deposited at the base of the stigmas. Pima

[a] In a similar experiment performed in 1920, however (see Table 24), a few bolls matured from Pima flowers of which the stigmas and style were excised 7½ hours after pollination, and these bolls contained relatively large numbers of seeds. Additional experiments performed in 1922, the complete data of which were not available in time for inclusion in this paper, gave convincing evidence that in Pima cotton within 8 hours after deposition of pollen on the stigmas the tubes can penetrate the ovary in number sufficient to fertilize more than half of the ovules.

[b] The fact that, in experiments performed in 1922, a few but comparatively well-fertilized bolls developed from apically pollinated flowers of Pima cotton of which the stigmas and style had been excised 8 hours after deposition of the pollen, indicates that in exceptional cases the average hourly growth rate may attain 3.5 millimeters.

flower buds were emasculated the evening before anthesis, other buds
having been bagged at the same time to supply pollen. On the following morning approximately equal numbers of the emasculated
flowers were pollinated (1) near the apex of the stigmas, (2) near
the base, and (3) on the whole stigmatic surface. Record was kept
of the number of bolls which matured from the several treatments
and of the number of seeds in each boll, from which were computed
the data given in Table 16.

TABLE 16.—*Degrees of fertilization in Pima cotton resulting from pollination of
the apical and of the basal portion of the stigmas and of the whole stigmatic
surface.*

Locus of pollination.	Flowers treated.	Percentage of bolls matured.	Mean number of seeds per boll.
Near the apex of the stigmas	94	80. 8±2. 73	14. 7±0. 28
Near the base of the stigmas	98	89. 8±2. 04	9. 7± . 29
Upon the whole length of the stigmas	100	98. 0± . 94	14. 1± . 22

A higher percentage of bolls matured from flowers pollinated near
the base of the stigmas than from flowers pollinated near the apex,
but the difference is not significant. On the other hand, the mean
number of seeds per boll resulting from basal pollination was much
smaller than that resulting from apical pollination, the difference
having been 5.0±0.40 (more than 12 times its probable error).
Pollination of the whole stigmatic surface yielded a significantly
higher percentage of bolls matured than did either partial pollination, but did not show a significant difference in the mean number
of seeds per boll as compared with pollination of the apical portion
only. It may be inferred from this fact that a difference between
the two halves of the stigmas is responsible for the inferior fertilization from basally deposited pollen, the extent of the area receiving
pollen having been approximately the same in the apical and basal
pollinations.

The data given in Tables 15 and 16 indicate [17] that when flowers of
Pima cotton are emasculated and are pollinated artificially the basal
region of the stigmas is a less favorable medium for the germination
or development of pollen than is the apical region.[18] Care was taken
in these experiments to apply as nearly as practicable equal quantities of pollen at both loci, but it was noted that the pollen adhered
more closely to the stigmatic surface when apically deposited than
when basally deposited. This was probably a factor in the superior
fertilization from apical pollination. It is doubtful, however,
whether this factor is operative in equal degree under natural conditions, for, with the stamens present, the close contact of the upper

[17] Additional and conclusive evidence that when emasculated flowers of Pima cotton
are pollinated artificially better fertilization results with apical than with basal deposition of the pollen was obtained from two experiments in 1922, the complete data of
which were not available in time to be included in this bulletin.
[18] Meade (*40*, p. 282) concluded from the results of his investigation of pollination in
upland cottons, referred to under the heading "Structure of the flower in relation to
pollination," that "most of the flowers with long stigmas projecting above the stamens
do not become completely self-fertilized, as the anthers and stigmas are too widely
separated." If limitation of pollen deposition to the basal region, as would be the case
in flowers having long stigmas when pollinating insects are scarce, results generally in
inferior fertilization, Meade's conclusion is probably well founded.

anthers with the base of the stigmas would favor the retention there of a greater number of pollen grains than in the case of emasculated flowers. Nevertheless, in experiments which afforded a comparison of the fertilization resulting from (a) automatic self-pollination in flowers that were not emasculated but in which the pollen was confined to the lower halves of the stigmas and (b) artificial pollination of emasculated flowers in which the bulk of the pollen was deposited on the upper halves of the stigmas, the latter treatment gave significantly better fertilization in six out of seven comparisons. On the other hand, data given in Table 16, which were fully confirmed by the results of an experiment performed in 1922, indicate that flowers receiving pollen on the upper halves of the stigmas only are fully as well fertilized as flowers receiving pollen on the whole stigmatic surface. It is probable, therefore, that apart from conditions affecting the adhesion of the pollen, there is a qualitative difference between different parts of the stigmas and that penetration of the tissues is effected more readily at the apex than at the base.

If in Pima cotton under natural conditions the pollen germinates and develops better at the apex of the stigmas than at the base, this probably more than offsets any advantage which the automatically deposited self pollen might derive from its nearness to the ovary. The structure of the flower in other types of cotton in which self-fertilization predominates increases the probability that the locus of pollen deposition is not a factor of much importance in determining the predominance of self-fertilization. In many varieties of upland cotton the uppermost stamens equal or even surpass the stigmas, so that the entire length of the latter is accessible to automatically discharged self pollen. The whole stigmatic surface is also accessible to insect-carried foreign pollen, no part of it being screened by a dense mass of stamens, as in the Egyptian cottons. Examination of open flowers of upland cotton when growing in close proximity to Pima shows the yellow pollen grains of the latter to be scattered over the whole surface of the stigmas, although usually most abundant near the apex.

RELATIVE EARLINESS OF ARRIVAL OF SELF-DEPOSITED AND OF INSECT-CARRIED POLLEN.

Especial interest in connection with the problem of the relative frequency of self-fertilization and of cross-fertilization attaches to the question whether there is an appreciable interval of time between the first arrival upon the stigmas of self pollen and of foreign pollen. There can be little doubt that if the stigmas greatly exceed the stamens, as is the case in Pima cotton, all pollen present upon the upper halves of the stigmas has been conveyed there by insects. When the pollen present on the stigmas is all of the same type it is impossible to determine what part of it has originated in the same flower and what part has been conveyed from other flowers by insects, but examination of flowers exposed to cross-pollination by a different type of cotton having readily distinguishable pollen showed that foreign pollen was being conveyed to the stigmas of most of the flowers. It may be assumed, therefore, that when pollen is present on the upper halves of the stigmas some of it has originated in other flowers.

OBSERVATIONS ON PIMA COTTON.

Examination in 1916 of numerous flowers, the corollas of which were open only 1 or 2 millimeters, showed none of them to have pollen present on the upper half of the stigmas. Flowers were examined in 1919 at intervals on July 27, beginning about two hours after sunrise, and on August 3, beginning about an hour after sunrise. Ten flowers were inspected at each interval on both dates. An endeavor was made to select in all cases flowers which had been fully exposed to the direct rays of the sun at and after sunrise and which should therefore have been favorably situated for the earliest possible opening of the corolla. Table 17 shows for each interval the percentage of the total number of flowers (10 in each case) in which an appreciable quantity of pollen was found upon the stigmas at a height sufficient to justify the conclusion that it must have been conveyed by insects.

TABLE 17.—*Rate of deposition of pollen on the upper portion of the stigmas in open-pollinated flowers of Pima cotton in 1919.*

Hour of observation.	Flowers having the upper portion of the stigmas pollinated (per cent).		Hour of observation.	Flowers having the upper portion of the stigmas pollinated (per cent).	
	July 27.	Aug. 3.		July 27.	Aug. 3.
6.30 a. m.		0	10.30 a. m.		50
7.30 a. m.	0	0	12.00 m.		40
8.00 a. m.	10		1.00 p. m.		50
8.30 a. m.	50	20	2.00 p. m.		70
9.30 a. m.	60	40	3.00 p. m.		90
10.00 a. m.	70				

On both dates, at the earliest hour of observation, the anthers of the flowers were discharging pollen, some of which presumably was reaching the lower half of the stigmas. Reference to Table 9 (p. 18) shows that at 8 a. m., the earliest hour when pollen was found in appreciable quantity upon the upper half of the stigmas, the average aperture of the corolla in Pima cotton is about 10 millimeters. A difference in the rapidity of pollination of the upper half of the stigmas on the two dates is indicated by the data in Table 17. Cross-pollination of 70 per cent of the flowers had taken place at 10 a. m. on July 27, and not until 2 p. m. on August 3. Yet the conditions would seem to have been more favorable to early pollination by insects on August 3, a clear sunny day, than on July 27 when the sky was overcast during the morning. The probable explanation is that on August 3 there was a marked scarcity of bees and other active pollen carriers in the cotton field.

Observations in 1920 indicated an earlier arrival of insect-carried pollen. On July 25, at 7.40 a. m., Pima flowers which were open about 10 millimeters were found to have numerous grains of pollen on the upper half of the stigmas, and in one flower, which had a corolla aperture of only 2.5 millimeters, much upland pollen was present. Most of the flowers examined on July 30, 1920, between 7.45 and 8 a. m. were already open from 5 to 20 millimeters and had numerous pollen grains on the upper half of the stigma, while in the few flowers which were still closed at this time, self pollen was just beginning to be deposited in the interstamen region. Most of the flowers examined on August 8 at 7.30 a. m. were open from 5 to 10 millimeters and had pollen present on the upper half of the stigmas. Of 10 closed buds which were examined at the same hour, 7 had a very few grains of self pollen on the interstamen section of the stigmas. On August 21 the opening of the corolla had been retarded by the coolness of the early morning (minimum temperature 62° F.), but at 8.40 a. m., of 30 flowers which were open from 5 to 10 millimeters, only 3 or 4 had the upper half of the stigmas free from pollen. Many flowers which were open only about 5 millimeters had the stigmas well pollinated at this hour.

Observations in 1921 indicated that bees sometimes enter Pima flowers and deposit pollen upon the stigmas when the orifice of the corolla is still minute and that they occasionally do so by pushing aside the loosened petals before any orifice has formed. It was noted, however, on August 16 that most of the flowers had not been entered until the orifice had reached a diameter of 2 or 3 millimeters, in which stage most of the flowers had pollen present upon the upper half of the stigmas. The readiness with which insects enter unopen corollas seems to be controlled in some degree by the weather, for on the cloudy morning of August 18, when as late as 8 a. m. many of the buds showed no distinct orifice, although the petals were well loosened at the apex, most of the flowers in this stage of anthesis had more or less pollen upon the upper half of the stigmas.

It is evident that at the same locality there is considerable variation on different days in the earliness of the arrival of insect-conveyed pollen in the flowers of Pima cotton. This is doubtless to be accounted for by variations in the weather and in the number, kind, and habits of the pollinating insects. The conclusion seems warranted, however, that as a rule many of the flowers are entered by pollen-conveying insects soon after the expansion of the corolla has begun.

Evidence has already been presented that the automatic deposition of self pollen upon the stigmas does not commence much in advance of the time when the petals begin to unfold and that the quantity deposited before the corolla has developed an orifice is usually very small. It is probable that as a rule the interval of time between the first arrival of self pollen and of foreign pollen does not exceed half an hour and that frequently foreign pollen begins to arrive before any considerable quantity of self pollen has been deposited upon the interstamen region of the stigmas.

OBSERVATIONS ON UPLAND COTTON.

It has been pointed out that when the two types are growing under similar conditions the corollas of upland varieties open somewhat more rapidly than those of Pima cotton. On the other hand, while in Pima the opening of the anthers always precedes that of the corolla, the anthers of upland varieties frequently do not begin to open until the expansion of the corolla has begun, while in some upland varieties the anthers are often still closed when the corolla is partly open. In the Cleveland and Dixie Triumph varieties on July 27, 1920, the anthers were observed to be still closed in flowers which had opened sufficiently to allow the stigmas to become well covered with foreign pollen. In most of the 20 upland varieties upon which observations were made in 1920, it appeared, however, that the first arrival upon the pistil of self pollen and of foreign pollen was virtually simultaneous.

In 1921 several instances were recorded of the occurrence of foreign pollen upon the stigmas of partly open upland flowers in which self-pollination had not yet taken place, the anthers being still closed. The presence of foreign pollen upon the stigmas was readily determined in these cases, as the upland varieties in 1920 and 1921 were grown in close proximity to Pima cotton, the bright-yellow pollen grains of which are easily distinguished from the whitish grains of the upland pollen. It may be concluded, therefore, that in upland cottons the interval between the beginning of automatic self-pollination and that of pollination by insects is at most a very brief one and that not infrequently foreign pollen reaches the stigmas in advance of self pollen.

DEPOSITION OF SELF POLLEN AND OF FOREIGN POLLEN BY INSECTS.

Evidence of the degree in which cross-pollination occurs in the two types of cotton was afforded in 1920 by examination of flowers borne by isolated plants of Pima (Egyptian) cotton distributed through a plat of Acala (upland) and of flowers borne by isolated Acala plants distributed through a plat of Pima in an experiment described on a preceding page, the object of which was to determine the percentages of natural hybrids or vicinists which would be produced under these conditions (Table 5). The isolated plants were separated from each other by several plants of the other variety, and only one flower was allowed to open daily on each isolated plant. It is therefore certain that most, if not all, of the pollen from other flowers which reached the stigmas of these plants was of the other type; hence, readily distinguishable from the self pollen. Observations on several days (July 30 to August 3) during a period when both types were producing flowers in approximately equal numbers gave the results stated in Table 18.

TABLE 18.—*Relative proportions of self pollen and of foreign pollen present on the upper portion of the stigmas of Pima and of Acala plants isolated among plants of the other type.*

[The figures indicate the number of flowers belonging to each category.]

Nature of the pollen present.	On the stigmas of—	
	Pima (Egyptian).	Acala (upland).
Self pollen only	6	1
Self pollen predominating	19	11
Approximately half-and-half	5	9
Foreign pollen predominating	4	4
Foreign pollen only	0	0
Total flowers examined	34	25

Since in Pima cotton the pollination of the upper portion of the stigmas is effected by insects, the data in Table 18 point strongly to the conclusion that much of the pollen conveyed to the stigmas by this agency originates in the same flower and that the preponderance of self-pollination is an important factor in the preponderance of self-fertilization in cotton. It would appear also that under like conditions as to climate and insect fauna upland cotton is more subject than Egyptian to cross-pollination, self pollen having predominated in 73 per cent of the Egyptian flowers and in only 48 per cent of the upland flowers. The latter conclusion is supported by the results of an examination at Sacaton, Ariz., in 1920, of flowers of Pima and of upland cotton which were growing in adjacent rows. There was much more Pima pollen on the stigmas of the upland flowers than of upland pollen on the Pima stigmas.

Further observations were made in 1921. The flowers examined were taken from adjacent rows of Pima and of upland, in every case from the side of the plant which faced a plant of the other type. They were collected in pairs, one flower of each type from opposite or nearly opposite plants. Pima flowers were preferred which were borne at approximately the same height above the ground as the upland flowers. The Pima plants were flowering somewhat more freely than the upland, but the difference in this respect was not great. The results are stated in Table 19.

TABLE 19.—*Flowers of Pima and of upland cottons having different quantities of pollen of the other type present on the stigmas.*

[The figures indicate the number of flowers belonging to each category.]

Type of cotton.	Flowers examined.	Pollen of other type on stigmas.			
		None.	Fewer than 10 grains.	Ten or more grains, but less than half of total pollen present.	Half or more than half of total pollen present.
Pima (Egyptian)	100	31	57	11	1
Upland	100	10	47	43	0

Of the total number of Pima flowers examined 31 per cent had no upland pollen present on the stigmas and 88 per cent had fewer than 10 grains of upland pollen. Of the total number of upland flowers only 10 per cent had no Pima pollen on the stigmas and only 57 per cent had fewer than 10 grains of Pima pollen. These percentages do not, however, fully indicate the difference between the two types, for of the flowers which were classed as having fewer than 10 grains of pollen of the other type on the stigmas, the number which had received very few grains (1 to 3) was much greater in the case of Pima than in the case of upland. There can be no doubt, therefore, that when both types of cotton are growing side by side and are flowering at approximately the same rate Pima pollen is conveyed to the upland stigmas in greater quantity than upland pollen to the Pima stigmas. This must be a very important factor in the observed greater prevalence of cross-fertilization in upland than in Pima cotton.

An answer to the question why Egyptian pollen is conveyed to the stigmas of upland cottons in greater quantity than upland pollen to the Egyptian stigmas is to be sought in a consideration of the habits of the pollen-carrying insects in relation to the ontogeny of the flower. At Sacaton, Ariz., the honeybee and at times wild bees of the genus Melissodes are the insects which enter most frequently the corollas of Pima cotton. It has been observed that many of the flowers are first entered when the petals are just beginning to unfold, occasionally even before there is an actual aperture at the apex of the corolla, under which conditions the bees almost invariably come into contact with the reproductive organs, taking up and depositing pollen. When the Pima corollas are in this early stage of expansion the anthers of upland cotton frequently are still closed or are just beginning to split, so that little, if any, pollen of this type is available for transfer to the Pima stigmas. On the other hand, many of the upland corollas at this time are quite as accessible as those of Pima to entry by the insects, and this accounts for the frequent deposition of Pima pollen upon the upland stigmas before any self pollen has reached the latter.

By the time the upland anthers have begun to discharge pollen freely most of the Pima corollas have opened to a degree which allows honeybees to reach the nectaries by crawling down the inside of the petals without touching the reproductive organs and to make their exit in the same manner. It is a relatively infrequent occurrence for the honeybees to touch stigmas or stamens in entering or leaving a well-opened Pima flower. On the other hand, the wild bees (*Melissodes* spp.) apparently do so regularly. It would be interesting to ascertain whether foreign pollen is conveyed in greater quantity to the Pima flowers during periods when Melissodes are visiting them in large numbers than when honeybees are the predominant visitors.

POLLEN-CARRYING INSECTS AT SACATON.

There is little doubt that natural cross-pollination in cotton is effected almost solely by the agency of insects. The nature of the pollen grains of Gossypium is unfavorable to their transportation by currents of air. Allard (*2*, p. 256), however, found that glass plates smeared with vaseline and exposed in cotton fields in northern Georgia collected considerable quantities of cotton pollen. On the other hand, Balls (*8*, p. 117), using the same method for the detection of wind-disseminated pollen in Egypt, obtained negative results.

No systematic study of the insects which visit cotton flowers has been attempted in connection with these investigations, but numerous specimens have been collected at Sacaton, Ariz., and notes have been made upon the efficiency as pollinators of those which most frequently enter the flowers. The writer is indebted for the identification of the specimens to Dr. L. O. Howard, Chief of the Bureau of Entomology, United States Department of Agriculture.[19]

---

[19] The several groups were identified by the following specialists: Hymenoptera, by S. A. Rohwer; Coleoptera, by E. A. Schwarz; Hemiptera, by Miss E. A. Wells and W. L. McAtee; Orthoptera, by A. N. Caudell; Lepidoptera, by H. C. Dyar; and Diptera, by J. M. Aldrich.

Various Hymenoptera are the most efficient carriers of cotton pollen at Sacaton, Ariz.,[20] as is probably the case wherever cotton is grown. The honeybee and wild bees (*Melissodes* spp.) are the most important cotton pollinators in this locality.

The honeybee (*Apis mellifica* L.) is very assiduous in its visits to cotton flowers, although sometimes preferring the extrafloral nectaries to those within the flower.[21] Nevertheless, this insect probably holds first rank at Sacaton, Ariz., as a conveyor of cotton pollen, especially among Pima flowers. As was noted on a preceding page, honeybees entering and emerging from the flowers when the petals are just beginning to unfold almost invariably come in contact with the reproductive organs. Later in the morning, when a sufficient aperture has developed, the bees usually crawl down the inside of the petals without touching the stigmas or stamens and make their exit in the same manner.[22] Occasionally, however, the honeybee touches the staminal column and stigmas even when the corolla is fully open, this being especially likely to happen when the insect is confused by the entrance of another individual.

At times wild bees of the genus Melissodes (*M. agilis agilis* Cress., *M. agilis aurigenia* Cress., *M. tristis* Ckll.) are even more efficient pollinators than honeybees. It was observed at Sacaton, Ariz., in 1921 that Melissodes were much more numerous in the cotton fields toward the close of the season than was the case earlier in the summer and that, unlike the honeybee they commonly crawl over the stigmas and staminal column of open flowers in order to reach the nectaries at the base of the corolla. Another bee, *Megachile parallela* Smith, is remarkable for the quantity of pollen it carries but is apparently a much less frequent visitor.

Large wasps of the genus Campsomeris, especially *C. dives* Prov., also frequent the cotton flowers. They apparently prefer upland varieties, which have a shallow, widely flaring corolla, to the Egyptian cotton with its deep and relatively narrow corolla. These insects carry much pollen from flower to flower. Their habits of grasping the stamens with their legs when entering and leaving the flower and of pressing the stamens against the stigmas while drinking from the intrafloral nectaries doubtless also contribute materially to self-pollination.

Other Hymenoptera which have been observed to carry cotton pollen at Sacaton, Ariz., are *Cerceris* sp.; *Dasymutilla ursula* Cress., and the carpenter bees (*Xylocopa arizonensis* Cress. and *X. varipuncta* Patt.)[23] A species of Pepsis seems to be more efficient in distributing pollen within the flower than in transferring pollen from one flower to another.

[20] Allard states (*2*, p. 254) that in northern Georgia *Melissodes bimaculata* Le P. and the honeybee are "the most abundant and constant visitors of cotton." Allard gives a list of insects observed to visit cotton flowers in that region, with interesting notes on the itineraries of honeybees and bumblebees among the cotton plants. In a later paper by the same author it is stated (*3*, p. 680) that of 129 observed entrances of insects into cotton flowers in the Georgia locality, 45 were by species of Melissodes and 45 by honeybees. It was noted that the wild bees were much more frequent visitors when the observations began, while later the honeybees increased the frequency of their visits.
[21] Seasonal variations in the habit of the honeybee in this respect were noted by Allard in Georgia (*2*, pp. 256, 257).
[22] The same habit was observed at Palestine, Tex., by Shoemaker (*43*).
[23] According to Shoemaker (*43*) bumblebees were the most active pollinators at Palestine, Tex., in September, but seemed to be more efficient in insuring thorough self-pollination than in effecting cross-pollination.

Species of Coleoptera which have been observed to visit cotton flowers and to carry more or less pollen on their bodies, but which are probably of minor importance as pollinators, are *Megilla maculata fuscilabris* Mulsant, *Diabrotica 12-punctata* Fabr., *D. balteata* Leconte, *D. trivittata* Mannerheim, *Collops vittatus* Say, *Phalacrus penicellatus* Say, and the fruit beetle (*Allorhina nitida* L.). The same remarks apply also to certain Hemiptera (*Zelus renardi* Kol., *Congus* sp., *Corizus hyalinus* Uhler, and *Apiomerus spissipes* Say) and to *Nemotelus trinotatus* Mel., of the order Diptera.

A small and very slender black beetle *Conotelus stenoides* Murray, which is extremely abundant at Sacaton, Ariz., sometimes effects its entrance to the flower as a result of an abnormal separation of the bases of the petals while the tip of the bud is tightly closed and occasionally makes its way into flowers which have been bagged to prevent cross-pollination. The small size and the smoothness of the body of this insect make it unlikely that it has any importance as a carrier of pollen from flower to flower. Another small beetle occasionally found in bagged flowers is *Notoxus calcaratus* Horn, and one of these insects having a single grain of pollen attached to its head was found in a flower thus inclosed. It is unlikely, however, that an appreciable quantity of pollen is transferred from flower to flower under these circumstances.[24]

The method of inclosing the flower in a paper bag, illustrated in Plate V, has proved very efficacious as a means of preventing cross-pollination. Many thousands of flowers have been " selfed " in this manner at Sacaton during the past eight years and none of the resulting progenies have given clear evidence of contamination from the access of foreign pollen. The efficacy of this method of excluding pollen transfer was tested by an experiment performed in 1915, in which 40 flower buds of Pima cotton were carefully emasculated and bagged in the ordinary manner the evening before the corolla was due to open. No artificial pollination was done, and none of the flowers developed a boll. The experiment was repeated in 1920, using 100 flowers, not one of which developed a boll.

RELATIVE COMPATIBILITY OF LIKE AND OF UNLIKE POLLEN.

The possibility suggests itself that pollen of another variety may be less compatible than self pollen or pollen of the same variety and that this, in addition to the preponderance of self-pollination, may be a factor in the greater prevalence of self-fertilization. To test this possibility, comparison was made of the degrees of fertilization attained when pollens of different degrees of relationship were applied separately to the Pima stigmas.

COMPARISON OF SELF-POLLINATION AND OF CROSS-POLLINATION WITHIN THE VARIETY.

An experiment was performed in 1921 in which some flowers were self-pollinated and others cross-pollinated on the same plants. Two Pima populations, the continuously open-pollinated stock and a

---

[24] Robson (*41*) observed in the West Indies that thrips enter the corolla before it has developed an orifice and concluded that cross-pollination may be effected by the agency of this insect.

family which has been strictly inbred (selfed) during seven generations, were used in this experiment. The treatments were as follows:

(A) Flower emasculated and bagged the evening before anthesis and pollinated the following morning with pollen from another flower on the same plant.

(B) Treatment similar to the above except that pollen from other plants of the same variety was used, these having been of the open-pollinated stock, not of the inbred family.

The use in treatment A. of pollen from another flower on the same plant insured self-fertilization unless somatic variation had occurred, and of this there was no indication.[25] The possibility that the pollination might have been less thorough in the self-pollinated than in the cross-pollinated flowers also was eliminated by this method. In addition to the percentages of bolls matured and the mean numbers of seeds per boll, determinations were made of the mean weights and the germination percentages of the seeds resulting from the two treatments. The data of this experiment are given in Table 20.

TABLE 20.—*Comparison of the results of self-pollination and of cross-pollination within the variety in an open-pollinated stock of Pima cotton and in a family which had been closely inbred during seven generations.*

[All flowers emasculated.]

Population.	Pollination.	Flowers treated.	Percentage of bolls matured.	Mean number of seeds per boll.	Mean weight of 100 seeds.	Percentage of germination.
Open-pollinated	Self	165	91.0±1.5	17.0±0.17	12.8±0.04	90.8±0.9
Do	Cross	162	85.8±1.8	16.7±.18	12.6±.08	88.2±1.0
Difference			5.2±2.3	.3±.25	.2±.09	2.6±1.3
Inbred	Self	155	92.9±1.3	17.2±.16	13.5±.05	86.8±1.0
Do	Cross	151	86.3±1.7	17.5±.18	12.6±.08	89.7±.9
Difference			6.6±2.1	.3±.24	.9±.09	2.9±1.3

The data given in Table 20 show little difference in the results of the two treatments in either population. The only differences that appear to be significant occurred in the inbred population in respect to the percentage of bolls matured and the mean weight of seeds, self-pollination having given the higher value in both cases. In the mean number of seeds, the real criterion of the relative completeness of fertilization, neither population showed a significant difference. The outcome of this experiment warrants the conclusion that within the Pima variety there is practically no difference in compatibility between self pollen and pollen from other plants.

[25] Emoto (*16*) tested species of Primula, Brassica, Hyacinthus, Freesia, etc., as to the comparative effects of autogamy (fertilization by pollen of the same flower), geitonogamy (fertilization by pollen from another flower of the same plant), and xenogamy (fertilization by pollen from another plant). The criteria used were fruitfulness, length, and width of the capsules, number of seeds per capsule, and germination of seeds. This author concluded that geitonogamy was superior to autogamy in very few cases. Darwin (*13*, p. 329) concluded from the results of his experiments with plants belonging to numerous families that "in very few cases did crossing different flowers of the same plant as compared with selfing a flower with its own pollen appreciably increase the number of seeds produced."

COMPARISON OF CROSS-POLLINATION WITH RELATED AND WITH UNRELATED POLLEN.

Flower buds on several Pima cotton plants in 1914 were emasculated and bagged in the evening and were pollinated the following morning, some with pollen from other plants of the same variety and others with pollen of the Gila variety of Egyptian cotton. The results, which show no significant difference in fertilization from the two pollinations, are given in Table 21.

TABLE 21.—*Fertilization of emasculated Pima flowers resulting from cross-pollination with pollen of the same variety and with pollen of the Gila variety of Egyptian cotton.*

Cross-pollination with—	Number of bolls matured.	Mean number of seeds per boll.
Pima (Egyptian) pollen	69	15.8±0.48
Gila (Egyptian) pollen	157	15.6± .36
Difference		.2± .60

A similar experiment was performed in 1917 on plants of a Pima family which had been strictly inbred during three successive generations. The cross-pollinations of emasculated flowers were made with pollen from (1) sister plants of the same inbred family, (2) plants of the continuously open-pollinated stock of the Pima variety, and (3) plants of the Gila variety. Table 22 gives the results of this experiment, which show that while a greater number of seeds per boll resulted from the application of pollen of another variety of the Egyptian type as compared with that from pollen of related and of unrelated plants of the same variety, the differences were not significant. It may be concluded, therefore, that within the limits of the Egyptian type there is no important difference in the compatibility of pollen derived from sister plants of a presumably homozygous strain, from unrelated plants of the same variety, and from another variety.

TABLE 22.—*Fertilization of emasculated Pima flowers resulting from cross-pollination with pollen from sister plants and from unrelated plants of the same variety and with pollen of the Gila variety.*

Cross-pollination with pollen from—	Flowers treated.	Percentage of bolls matured.	Mean number of seeds per boll.
Sister plants of the Pima variety	61	98±1.2	15.9±0.29
Unrelated plants of the Pima variety	90	99± .7	16.3± .19
Plants of the Gila (Egyptian) variety	31	97±2.1	17.1± .36

Experiments will be described next in which cross-pollination within the Pima variety was compared with cross-pollination with a wholly different type, the Acala variety of upland cotton. The results of such an experiment, performed in 1920, are presented in Table 23 (upper part) and indicate that the mean number of seeds per boll and the germination percentage of the seeds were significantly higher from flowers which had received pollen of the other type, the differences having been, respectively, six and four times the probable error. This outcome being somewhat unexpected the experiment was repeated in 1921. Five plants of an inbred (seven generations selfed) Pima family were used as mothers. Flowers were emasculated before anthesis and were cross-pollinated the following day, some with pollen from plants of the bulk Pima stock, others with pollen of Acala (upland). The flowers which received both pollinations were borne on the same plants. The results of this experiment are also presented in Table 23 (lower part).

TABLE 23.—*Fertilization of emasculated Pima flowers, some of which were cross-pollinated with pollen of the same variety and others with pollen of the Acala variety of upland cotton in 1920 and 1921.*

Season and character of pollination.	Flowers treated.	Percentage of bolls matured.	Mean number of seeds per boll.	Mean weight of 100 seeds (grams).	Percentage of germination.
Season of 1920:					
Pima pollen	45	80.0±4.0	12.9±0.45	12.5±0.26	92.5±0.9
Acala (upland) pollen	48	79.2±3.9	16.2± .29	12.6± .08	96.6± .5
Difference		.8±5.6	3.3± .53	.1± .27	4.1±1.0
Season of 1921:					
Pima pollen	175	86.3±1.7	17.5± .18	12.6± .08	89.7± .9
Acala (upland) pollen	176	93.1±1.3	17.6± .16	13.0± .10	93.0± .8
Difference		6.8±2.1	.1± .24	.4± .13	3.3±1.2

In 1921 application of pollen of a different type, Acala, resulted in a slight but possibly significant increase in the percentage of bolls matured, but did not effect more nearly complete fertilization, the mean number of seeds per boll having been practically the same as that obtained by cross-pollination within the variety. There were indications that fertilization by the more foreign pollen slightly increased the weight and percentage germination of the seeds, although the differences were scarcely significant.[a]

Considering the whole series of experiments in which pollens of different degrees of foreignness were compared as to their relative efficiency in fertilizing Pima flowers, it may be concluded that fertilization by the more foreign pollen is consistently neither better nor poorer than that effected by the more nearly related pollen. The conclusion holds good whether comparison is made (1) between pollen of the same plant or of a sister plant of an inbred family and pollen of unrelated plants of the same variety, or (2) between pollen of the same variety and pollen of another variety of the same type of cotton (Gila, Egyptian). On the other hand, comparison

[a] Two experiments performed in 1922, the detailed results of which were not available in time to be included in this bulletin, showed that bolls from Pima flowers pollinated with upland pollen (Lone Star variety) as compared with bolls from Pima flowers pollinated with Pima pollen, contained significantly greater mean numbers of seeds, the increases from extra-varietal pollination, in the two experiments, respectively, having been 9 and 15 per cent and having been 4.5 and 4.4 times the probable error of the difference. The reciprocal pollinations on Lone Star (upland), on the contrary, gave in both experiments a greater mean number of seeds per boll from the flowers pollinated with Lone Star pollen than from the flowers pollinated with Pima pollen, the decreases from extra-varietal pollination of Lone Star in the two experiments having been, respectively, 19.3 and 5.4 per cent, although the decrease was barely significant in the first experiment (difference 3.2 times its probable error) and was not significant in the second experiment. These results might be taken as indicating superior vigor of the Lone Star pollen but, when the two pollens were tested in sugar solution, the Pima pollen ejected somewhat more rapidly and completely than the Lone Star pollen.

of the fertilization of Pima flowers by Pima pollen and by pollen of a very different but still compatible type of cotton (upland), shows that in several cases somewhat better fertilization resulted from the foreign pollen. This is of especial interest in view of the fact that the pistils of the upland varieties used in these experiments (Acala and Lone Star) are much shorter than the Pima pistils.

RAPIDITY OF GERMINATION AND DEVELOPMENT OF DIFFERENT POLLENS.

Comparison of like and unlike pollens in respect to the rapidity of development of the tubes was the object of an experiment performed in 1920. Pima flower buds were emasculated in the evening and were thoroughly cross-pollinated the following day, some with pollen from other Pima plants, others with pollen of Acala (upland). The pistils were then excised at the summit of the ovary at successive intervals of time.

TABLE 24.—*Comparison of the rapidity of germination and development of different pollens, as shown by Pima flowers with pistils excised at successive intervals of time after pollination.*

Pistil excision.		Pollination with Pima (Egyptian) pollen.			Pollination with Acala (upland) pollen.		
Hour excised.	After pollination (hours).	Flowers treated.	Percentage of bolls matured.	Mean number of seeds per boll.	Flowers treated.	Percentage of bolls matured.	Mean number of seeds per boll.
8 p. m...................	7½	40	7.5±2.8	13.7±1.4	37	0	0
5 a. m...................	16½	39	61.5±5.2	11.5± .6	35	45.7±5.7	13.7±0.8
7 a. m...................	18½	35	63.0±5.5	13.5± .6	35	51.5±5.7	14.5±1.0
9 a. m...................	20½	36	91.8±3.0	15.7± .6	34	73.5±5.1	15.6± .6
11 a. m...................	22½	35	80.0±4.6	15.6± .5	39	95.0±2.4	15.0± .4
1 p. m...................	24½	26	92.3±3.5	14.4± .5	25	84.0±4.9	14.5± .7

The data of this experiment, as given in Table 24, indicate that the Pima and the upland pollen were equally efficient in fertilizing the Pima flowers. There was also no important difference between the two pollens in the rate of growth of the tubes, as indicated by the degrees of fertilization at successive intervals after pollination, except that of the flowers excised 7½ hours after pollination, three which had been pollinated with Pima pollen set bolls, while no bolls developed from flowers pollinated with Acala pollen which had been excised at this early hour.

POLLEN COMPETITION AS A FACTOR IN SELF-FERTILIZATION AND CROSS-FERTILIZATION.

Evidence was given on a preceding page that when the several pollens were applied separately to the Pima stigmas, approximately equal compatibility of self pollen, pollen from other plants of the same variety, pollen of another Egyptian variety, and pollen of another type of cotton (upland) was shown by the degree of fertilization effected. Fairly satisfactory evidence also was presented that the tubes of Pima and of upland pollen grow with approximately equal rapidity when these pollens are applied separately. It remains to consider whether, when different pollens are in competition on the stigmas of the same flower, selective fertilization occurs.

Balls (7, pp. 222, 223; 8, pp. 122–125), using "a method of mixed pollination, whereby the stigma of a flower received equal quantities of (1) self pollen from its own anthers and (2) pollen from another plant," found that the seed produced by Egyptian flowers receiving both self pollen and upland pollen yielded 10 hybrids out of 330 plants, or somewhat less than 3 per cent. The percentage was about the same with the reciprocal cross-pollination upland × self + Egyptian. On the other hand, when stigmas of Egyptian or of upland cotton were pollinated simultaneously with approximately equal quantities of self pollen and of pollen from Egyptian × upland F_1 plants, the resulting percentages of hybrids were 20 and 28, respectively. These results seem to indicate that pollen of the conjugate generation of a hybrid between very different types of cotton, when applied to the stigmas of one of the parent types, is better able to compete with the self pollen than is the pollen of the other parental type. Balls does not describe in detail the method used in this experiment; but if automatic self-pollination of the base of the stigmas was not prevented, this would account in part for the very low percentages of hybrids when pollen of the other type, in addition to self pollen, was applied.

Longfield Smith (44) performed experiments the object of which was to produce the largest possible number of F_1 hybrids with the least expenditure of labor. To this end the stigmas of unemasculated flowers of sea-island cotton and of cotton of an upland type, said to be native in St. Croix, were smeared at 7.30 to 8 a. m. with pollen of the other species. Sea island × St. Croix yielded from 30 to 40 per cent of hybrids, while the reciprocal cross-pollination yielded 70 per cent. The much greater percentage of hybrids obtained from the reciprocal was attributed by this experimenter to the earlier opening of the anthers in the sea-island than in the St. Croix flowers, which allowed automatic self-pollination to begin earlier in the former than in the latter. The very high percentages of hybrids obtained from unemasculated flowers of the St. Croix cotton in this experiment seem to indicate a decided "prepotency" of the foreign pollen.

The hitherto unpublished data of an experiment conducted by Argyle McLachlan, under the direction of O. F. Cook, at Yuma, Ariz., in 1910 and 1911 are also of interest in this connection. Flowers of Egyptian cotton (Yuma variety) were pollinated with pollen of the same variety and with upland pollen, and flowers of upland cotton (Triumph and Durango varieties) were pollinated with pollen of the same variety and with Egyptian pollen. The flowers to be pollinated were emasculated before their anthers had opened and were then inclosed in bags. The flowers which were to furnish the pollen were bagged before their corollas had opened. Pollination was done as soon as the anthers opened.[26] In some cases the two kinds of pollen were applied simultaneously, in other cases the second kind was applied after intervals of 15, 30, and 60 minutes, using

[26] The original records of this experiment apparently have been lost, but the results are stated in a memorandum prepared by Mr. McLachlan on August 9, 1911, from which Table 25 has been compiled. Further details in regard to the procedure followed were supplied from memory by Mr. McLachlan in a letter to the writer dated December 5, 1919.

for the first pollination in some cases pollen of the same variety, in other cases pollen of the other type. Progenies from the resulting bolls were grown in 1911. The percentages of hybrids obtained from the various pollinations are shown in Table 25.

TABLE 25.—*Hybrids resulting in 1911 from double pollinations of Egyptian and upland cotton flowers at Yuma, Ariz., in 1910.*

Method of pollination.	Egyptian as the female parent.		Upland as the female parent.	
	Plants grown.	Percentage of hybrids.	Plants grown.	Percentage of hybrids.
Both pollens applied simultaneously........................	164	18 ±2.0	158	32 ±2.5
Egyptian pollen applied first, upland pollen 15 minutes later...	184	8 ±1.3	142	56 ±2.8
Egyptian pollen applied first, upland pollen 30 minutes later...	146	14 ±1.9	160	24 ±2.3
Egyptian pollen applied first, upland pollen 60 minutes later...	151	13 ±1.8	121	59 ±3.0
Average for the Egyptian followed by upland pollination.	....	11.7±1.0	....	46.3±1.6
Upland pollen applied first, Egyptian pollen 15 minutes later..	118	5 ±1.4	107	51 ±3.3
Upland pollen applied first, Egyptian pollen 30 minutes later..	123	10 ±1.8	93	36 ±3.4
Upland pollen applied first, Egyptian pollen 60 minutes later..	166	7 ±1.3	107	47 ±3.3
Average for the upland followed by Egyptian pollination..	....	7.3± .9	....	44.7±1.9
Totals for the two types..............................	1,052	10.8± .6	888	42.3±1.1

The data given in Table 25 show no consistent differences in the percentages of hybrids depending upon whether pollen of the same or of the other variety was applied first or upon the length of the interval between the application of one and the other pollen. When Egyptian cotton was used as the female parent, deferring the application of the upland pollen until one hour after the Egyptian pollen was applied resulted in an apparent reduction in the percentage of hybrids as compared with that resulting from simultaneous application of the two pollens, but the difference was not significant. On the other hand, deferring the application of the Egyptian pollen until an hour after the upland pollen was applied, so far from increasing the percentage of hybrids, resulted in an apparently significant decrease as compared with the percentage from simultaneous application. With upland cotton as the female parent the percentage of hybrids when application of the Egyptian pollen was deferred one hour was significantly greater than in the case of simultaneous application of the two pollens, but a much greater and more significant increase in the percentage of hybrids resulted from deferring application of the upland pollen until one hour after the Egyptian pollen was applied. These results are inconsistent and seem inexplicable, but at any rate they increase the probability that the slight differences, under natural conditions, in the time of the arrival of self pollen and of foreign pollen, as noted on a preceding page, are of little consequence in determining the relative degree of self-fertilization and of cross-fertilization.

The total number (1,052) of Egyptian flowers which were double pollinated in the McLachlan experiment yielded 10.8±0.6 per cent of hybrids, and the total number (888) of upland flowers yielded 42.3±1.1 per cent of hybrids, the latter figure representing only a small departure from the 50 per cent to be expected if the two pollens compete upon equal terms. It would therefore seem that while Egyptian pollen is very strongly prepotent over upland pollen on the Egyptian stigmas, there is no corresponding prepotency of upland pollen on the upland stigmas.

EXPERIMENTS AT SACATON, ARIZ.

DEPOSITION OF THE TWO POLLENS NOT SIMULTANEOUS.

An experiment was performed in 1916 with the object of determining in what degree pollen of a distinct but related variety may compete with automatically deposited self pollen. Flower buds on several plants of Pima cotton were bagged early in the morning but were not emasculated. At about 10.30 o'clock the stigmas were thoroughly smeared with pollen of the Gila variety, which is also of the Egyptian type, and the bags were replaced. Seed from the resulting bolls was planted in 1917 and the plants were thinned in such manner as to avoid any selection. Of the 240 plants which remained after thinning 34, or 14.2 ± 1.5 per cent, were classed as hybrids (Pima $\times$ Gila F_1) and the remainder as pure Pima. We may therefore conclude that 86 per cent of the ovules had been self-fertilized in flowers which had received an abundance of foreign pollen.

In order to ascertain whether pollen of a very different type may compete better with self pollen than pollen of a related variety, an experiment was performed in 1919. Two flowers each on a number of plants of Pima (Egyptian) cotton were bagged in the evening, but were not emasculated, thus permitting automatic self-pollination to proceed in the normal manner. At about noon of the following day the stigmas of one flower on each plant were smeared with pollen of the Gila variety of Egyptian cotton, and the stigmas of the other flower were smeared with pollen of the Acala variety of upland cotton. In 1920, populations were grown from the seed resulting from each self + cross-pollination, all plants which developed having been left in place until the percentages of first-generation hybrids (Pima $\times$ Gila and Pima $\times$ Acala, respectively) had been determined. The results are stated in Table 26 (upper part).

TABLE 26.—*Hybrids resulting from seed produced by flowers of Pima cotton which, in addition to having been automatically self-pollinated, had been cross-pollinated with pollen of Gila and of Acala cotton, respectively, in 1919 and with pollen of Acala in 1920.*

Season and character of pollination.	Plants.	F_1 hybrids.	
		Number.	Per cent.
Season of 1919:			
Gila (Egyptian)	206	74	35.9 ± 2.3
Acala (upland)	287	96	33.4 ± 1.9
Difference			2.5 ± 3.0
Season of 1920:			
Acala (upland)	479	143	29.8 ± 1.4

The difference in the percentage of hybrids produced in 1919 by the two foreign pollens was not significant, and it is clear that pollen of another variety of the same species (Egyptian cotton) was not better able than pollen of a different species (upland cotton) to compete with the self pollen. The percentage of hybrids in both cases is very high in comparison with that of the 1916 experiment with Gila pollen.

In a similar experiment in 1920 a number of Pima flower buds were bagged but were not emasculated, so that automatic self-pollination was not interfered with. Early in the afternoon of the day of anthesis abundant pollen of the Acala variety of upland cotton was applied to the stigmas. The resulting seed was planted in 1921. No thinning was done, all seeds which germinated having been allowed to develop. The resulting percentage of F_1 hybrids, as also stated in Table 26, did not differ significantly from that yielded by seed resulting from the corresponding self + cross-pollination in the experiment of 1919.

The percentage of cross-fertilization in all three of these experiments was considerable, notwithstanding that both in time of arrival upon the stigmas and in nearness to the ovary the automatically deposited self pollen would seem to have had a marked advantage. The results therefore tend to confirm the evidence given on preceding pages that conditions at the base of the stigmas are relatively unfavorable for the germination of the pollen or penetration of the tubes.

DEPOSITION OF THE TWO POLLENS SIMULTANEOUS.

An experiment performed in 1919 was designed to determine what percentages of the ovules are fertilized by pollen of the same and of another variety when both sorts of pollen are applied as nearly as possible simultaneously and in as nearly as possible equal quantity. For this purpose a number of Pima cotton flowers were emasculated and bagged in the evening. During the following morning the stigmas were smeared with pollen of the same variety and with pollen of Acala (upland) cotton. Half of the flowers on each date received the upland pollen first, and the other half received the Pima pollen first, but the interval of time between the applications of the two lots of pollen was negligible. This method of applying the two pollens was adopted because of the impracticability of mixing them in approximately equal quantity. The comparative viability of the pollens used in this experiment was not determined, but pollen of Pima and of Acala from plants growing in the same field had been tested in a sugar solution three weeks previously and had shown no appreciable difference in viability.

The seeds obtained from each pollination were planted in 1920, four seeds to the hill, and the rows were not thinned. The number of first-generation Egyptian × upland hybrids in each lot was determined early in July, with the results given in Table 27. Comparison of the percentages of hybrids in hills containing, respectively, one, two, three, and four plants, showed no significant differences. This would indicate that the heterozygotes, in spite of the larger size which they soon attained, had had no special advantage during the germinating and seedling stages (see p. 5).

TABLE 27.—*Hybrids from seeds produced by emasculated flowers of Pima cotton when pollinated first with upland cotton and then with Pima pollen and vice versa.*

Pollination.	Plants.	F_1 hybrids.	
		Number.	Per cent.
Pima × upland + Pima.............................	134	33	24.6±2.5
Pima × Pima + upland.............................	160	21	13.1±1.8
As one array......................................	294	54	18.4±1.5

It will be noted that the percentage of hybrids produced was almost twice as great when the upland pollen was applied first as when the Pima pollen was applied first, and the difference amounted to about three and a half times its probable error, whereas in the double-pollination experiment performed by McLachlan (Table 25) the percentage of hybrids from flowers borne by Egyptian plants was somewhat higher when Egyptian pollen was applied first than when upland pollen was applied first. Possibly in the present experiment the stigmas were so well covered at the first application that many of the pollen grains of the second application were not in contact with the stigmatic surface. It would seem to be a fair assumption that the percentage of hybrids obtained by taking as one array plants resulting from the two treatments represents what would have been obtained if a mixture of both pollens in equal quantity had been applied.

The results of the McLachlan experiment showed that 89 per cent of the ovules of Yuma (Egyptian) cotton had been fertilized by pollen of the same variety when upland pollen was also present on the stigmas. In the present experiment 82 per cent of the ovules of Pima (Egyptian) cotton were fertilized by pollen of the same variety, although both pollens were applied as nearly as possible simultaneously and in equal quantity. The fact that even when upland pollen was applied first only about 25 per cent of the resulting plants were hybrids, makes it difficult to avoid the conclusion that on the stigmas of Egyptian cotton pollen of the same variety is strongly prepotent over upland pollen.

It is interesting to compare the percentages of hybrids obtained in the double-pollination experiment (Table 27) with the percentages, as given in Table 26 (1919 experiment), from flowers which had not been emasculated and had had the stigmas pollinated (1) with pollen of another variety of Egyptian cotton and (2) with upland pollen. Notwithstanding the fact that in the latter case automatic self-pollination of the basal or interstamen region of the stigmas was not interfered with, the percentage of hybrids which resulted from either cross-pollination was about twice as great as the average of the percentages from the two double cross-pollinations of emasculated flowers. This further corroborates the conclusion that pollen deposited at the base of the stigmas, as was the self pollen in the unemasculated flowers, is under less favorable conditions than pollen deposited nearer the apex, as was the foreign pollen in the same flowers. In the double pollination of emasculated flowers the pollen of both kinds was deposited over the same stigmatic area.

CONCLUSIONS REGARDING SELECTIVE FERTILIZATION.

The occurrence of selective fertilization in favor of the Pima pollen when this and upland pollen are present in approximately equal quantity on the Pima stigmas is interesting in view of the evidence given on preceding pages that the upland pollen, when applied separately, germinates at least equally well and penetrates the ovary with a rapidity equal to that of the Pima pollen. To account for selective fertilization it seems necessary, therefore, to assume that there is a partial-inhibition of the germination or subsequent development of the foreign pollen when pollen of the same variety is also present on the same stigmatic area.

Darwin (*13*, pp. 391, 392), although concluding that pollen from another plant of the same variety or from another variety of the same species "is often or generally prepotent over that from the same flower," obtained evidence that the reverse is true in the case of different (but presumably compatible) species.

If pollen from a distinct species be placed on the stigma of a castrated flower, and then after several hours pollen from the same species be placed on the stigma, the effects of the former are wholly obliterated, excepting in some rare cases.

The results here described are not in accordance with Darwin's findings, for in the experiments in which foreign pollen was applied to unemasculated Pima flowers, pollen "from another variety of the same species" (Gila) was not prepotent over the self pollen, and pollen of a distinct species (Acala) fertilized a considerable percentage of the ovules although applied several hours after self-pollination had begun. Acala pollen was also able to effect fertilization when applied simultaneously with self pollen to Pima flowers which had been emasculated.

Interesting results as to pollen competition in maize have been reported recently by Jones (*24, 25, 26*), who found that in the great majority of the combinations tested more of the ovules were fertilized by self pollen than by foreign pollen when the two kinds were in direct competition and that the "handicap placed upon the foreign pollen is proportional to the germinal unlikeness" (*25*, p. 283), notwithstanding the fact that the weight of the seeds resulting from cross-fertilization and the vigor of the plants grown from such seeds increased with the wideness of the cross. "In proportion as the cross-fertilization benefits the immediate progeny in its development the less effective is that pollen in accomplishing the union" (*25*, p. 271).

The results of the experiments with cotton described in this bulletin agree only partially with those obtained by Jones with maize. It is true that on the stigmas of emasculated flowers of Egyptian cotton, pollen of the same variety was found to be prepotent over pollen of a very distinct type (upland cotton) when the two kinds were in direct competition. On the other hand, when applied to the stigmas of unemasculated Pima flowers, pollen of another variety of the same type (Gila, Egyptian) was not more successful than pollen of another type (upland) in competing with the self pollen. Yet heterosis is far more pronounced in the cross Pima × upland than in the cross Pima × Gila. Furthermore, McLachlan's results (Table 25) indicate that on the stigmas of upland cottons pollen of a very different type (Egyptian) competes on nearly equal terms with pollen of the same variety.[27]

RELATIVE COMPLETENESS OF INSECT POLLINATION AT DIFFERENT LOCALITIES.

Observation in Arizona has shown that the number of efficient pollinating insects differs greatly in different localities.[28] Bees and other active pollinators are normally abundant among the cotton flowers at Sacaton throughout the summer, and the entire surface of the stigmas is almost invariably well covered with pollen soon after the corolla has opened. On the other hand, observations in the Salt River Valley, at distances of 25 to 40 miles from Sacaton, have shown that insect pollination of cotton there is often much less rapid and complete. The probable explanation is that in recent years an extensive and almost continuous acreage has been planted to cotton, and the insect population is not large enough to insure thorough pollination of all the flowers.

Thus, on July 18, 1919, in a field situated near Tempe in the heart of the cotton-growing district, no pollen grains were observed upon the extrastaminal portion of the stigmas at 9 a. m. and very few at 10 a. m. Late in the afternoon of July 20, 1920, inspection of the same field showed the extrastaminal portion of the stigmas to be free from pollen in most of the flowers, while the remainder bore only a few insect-transported grains. None of the flowers examined showed thorough pollination of the whole stigmatic surface. Two other centrally located fields, one at Phoenix and one near Tempe, which were examined at 5 p. m. on August 5 and at 4 p. m. on August 6, showed similarly deficient pollination. On the other hand, in fields situated on the outskirts of the valley, at Litchfield and at Goodyear, which were examined at noon on the same days, bees and other pollinators were abundant, and the stigmas of the cotton flowers were found to be well covered with pollen.

Experiments were made in 1920 with the object of comparing the relative degree of fertilization by natural pollination in fields where observation had shown, on the one hand, thorough pollination of the entire stigmatic surface and, on the other hand, a deficiency of pollen on the upper portion of the stigmas. It was sought also to ascertain whether in the latter case artificial pollination would increase the degree of fertilization, as compared with that of naturally pollinated flowers.

At weekly intervals during the month of August the stigmas of approximately 100 flowers were smeared with pollen from other Pima plants, and an approximately equal number of flowers were tagged and left to natural pollination. The only difference between the two treatments was the thorough cross-pollination of the entire stigmatic surface of the artificially pollinated flowers, neither lot

---

[27] Attempts made at Sacaton, Ariz., to determine whether selective fertilization occurs in upland cotton have been unsuccessful, owing to the loss by shedding of nearly all of the bolls from the treated flowers.

[28] A pronounced difference in the abundance of pollinating insects at different localities in Arizona was noted by Cook, McLachlan, and Meade (*12*, p. 34) : "At the time of our visits to the fields at Yuma and Sacaton there was a notable difference in the activity of the insects at the two places. Several species of large wild bees that were industriously visiting the flowers at Yuma in September were not seen at all at Sacaton."

having been bagged. These experiments were performed at Sacaton, Ariz., and in a field near Phoenix where observation had shown that even late in the afternoon the upper portion of the stigmas remained relatively free from pollen.

The percentages of bolls matured from each lot of flowers and the mean numbers of seeds per boll are stated in Table 28. The data are given for each day separately and for all four dates as one array.

TABLE 28.—*Results of natural and artificial pollination of unbagged flowers of Pima cotton at Phoenix and at Sacaton, Ariz., in 1920.*

Locality and date.	Naturally pollinated flowers.			Mean number of seeds per—		Artificially pollinated flowers.			Mean number of seeds per—.	
	Flowers treated.	Bolls matured.	Percentage of bolls matured.	Boll matured.	100 flowers treated.[1]	Flowers treated.	Bolls matured.	Percentage of bolls matured.	Boll matured.	100 flowers treated.[1]
Sacaton, Ariz.:										
Aug. 6....	95	88	92.7±1.8	15.1±0.21	1,400±33	94	82	87.2±2.3	15.1±0.24	1,316±40
Aug. 13...	96	91	94.8±1.5	14.6± .19	1,385±28	91	88	96.7±1.3	14.6± .24	1,411±30
Aug. 20...	91	88	96.7±1.3	16.1± .21	1,556±29	89	87	97.8±1.1	16.3± .18	1,595±25
Aug. 26...	95	93	97.9±1.0	17.7± .15	1,734±23	87	83	95.4±1.5	17.7± .15	1,689±30
All dates..	377	360	95.6± .7	15.9± .11	1,520±15	361	340	94.2± .8	15.9± .11	1,496±16
Phoenix, Ariz.:										
Aug. 6....	91	80	87.9±2.3	11.1± .34	975±39	98	93	94.9±1.5	15.8± .23	1,500±32
Aug. 13...	92	66	71.8±3.2	12.3± .44	883±50	89	85	95.5±1.5	17.3± .23	1,651±34
Aug. 20...	72	62	86.1±2.8	15.3± .29	1,317±50	95	72	75.8±3.0	16.7± .22	1,266±53
Aug. 26...	89	76	85.4±2.5	17.6± .23	1,501±48	94	90	95.8±1.4	17.9± .17	1,716±30
All dates..	344	284	82.6±1.4	14.0± .20	1,157±26	376	340	90.3±1.0	16.9± .10	1,526±19

[1] The probable error of this value was computed by the formula $\sqrt{(Ab)^2+(Ba)^2}$, A±a being the percentage of bolls matured and B±b being the mean number of seeds per boll.

Considering the combined results for the four dates, it appears that the fertilization of the naturally pollinated flowers at Phoenix was significantly inferior to that at Sacaton, the difference in the percentage of bolls matured having been 13±1.6 and the difference in the mean number of seeds per boll having been 1.9±0.23. At Sacaton it is evident that artificial pollination did not result in more nearly complete fertilization than was attained by natural pollination, neither the percentage of bolls matured nor the mean number of seeds per boll having differed significantly in the two lots of flowers. Artificial pollination at Phoenix, on the contrary, significantly increased the degree of fertilization, the increases over the results from naturally pollinated flowers having been for the entire period 7.7±1.7 in the percentage of bolls matured and 2.9±22 in the mean number of seeds per boll. In the mean number of seeds per 100 flowers, a value which integrates the percentage of bolls matured and the mean number of seeds per boll, the increase due to artificial pollination amounted to 32 per cent, indicating that a substantially greater crop both of seed and of fiber [29] might be expected if bees were abundant in the Salt River Valley cotton fields during the blossoming period.

[29] Evidence that the weight of fiber per boll is correlated with the number of seeds has been presented elsewhere (28).

SEASONAL VARIATIONS IN THE RELATIVE COMPLETENESS OF FERTILIZATION.

Comparison of the fertilization attained in different seasons can be made most effectively on the basis of the mean number of seeds per boll expressed as a percentage of the mean number of ovules. Counts made in 1921 on 250 3-celled and on 25 4-celled ovaries of Pima cotton showed the mean numbers of ovules to be 20.6±0.09 and 25.3±0.34, respectively. Since at Sacaton approximately 5 per cent of the Pima ovaries are 4-celled and practically all the others are 3-celled, the mean number of ovules in a random sample of ovaries should be 20.8. The frequency distributions for the number of ovules in the 3-celled and the 4-celled ovaries are given in Table 29.

TABLE 29.—*Frequency distributions of the number of ovules in 3-celled and in 4-celled ovaries of Pima cotton.*

Ovaries.	Number of ovules.															
	15	16	17	18	19	20	21	22	23	24	25	26	27	28	29	30
3-celled	5	8	11	16	24	41	52	44	35	14						
4-celled							1	3	3	4	3	2	4	1	3	1

Bolls from various lots of naturally pollinated flowers at Sacaton have been found to contain mean numbers of developed seeds as given in Table 30, which also states the mean numbers of seeds as percentages of the mean number of ovules when taken as 21.

TABLE 30.—*Mean numbers of seeds per boll from different lots of naturally pollinated flowers of Pima cotton at Sacaton, Ariz.*

[The mean numbers of seeds are stated also as percentages of the mean number of ovules.]

Year.	Plants.	Bolls.	Mean number of seeds.	
			Actual.	As percentage of the mean number of ovules.
1915	53	530	16.0±0.12	76
1916	81	810	16.9± .08	80
1917	82	820	17.7± .07	84
1918	85	850	16.5± .07	78
1919	200	200	16.5± .13	78
1920		95	14.2± .21	67
1920		91	15.0± .20	71
1920		360	15.9± .11	75
1921	100	[1] 100	18.6± .13	89
1921	30	560	17.3± .09	82

[1] 3-locked bolls only.

The mean percentage of ovules fertilized, as stated in Table 30, varied from 67 to 89. The fact that both lots of flowers in 1921 gave a significantly higher mean number of seeds than any of the three lots in 1920 indicates that there is considerable variation from year to year in the conditions for fertilization. Reference to Table 28 shows that the conditions vary also during the same season. Con-

sidering only the naturally pollinated flowers, the mean numbers of
seeds per boll and per 100 flowers were significantly greater during
the second half of August, 1920, than during the first half. Whether
the difference, which was much more pronounced at Phoenix than at
Sacaton, was caused by more favorable weather or by an increase
in the number of pollinating insects is uncertain.

The bolls upon which were computed the mean numbers of seeds
given in Table 30, with the single exception noted, were taken at
random, without reference to the number of locks. It has been
determined by a number of counts which have given practically the
same result, that at Sacaton the proportion of 4-locked bolls in Pima
cotton slightly exceeds 5 per cent,[30] practically all the others being

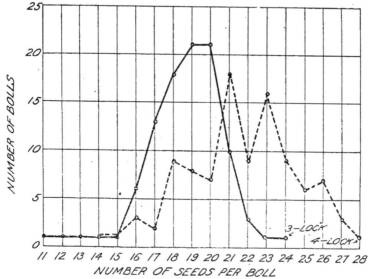

Fig. 4.—Frequency distributions of the number of seeds in one hundred 3-locked and 4-
locked bolls on well-grown plants of Pima cotton at Sacaton, Ariz., in 1921. The
bolls were collected in pairs, a 3-locked and a 4-locked boll from each plant. The
mean numbers of seeds were 18.6±0.13 for the 3-locked bolls and 21.7±0.19 for the
4-locked bolls. The frequency distribution for the 3-locked bolls, shown by the solid
line, is much more regular than that for the 4-locked bolls, shown by the dotted line.

3-locked, the number of bolls having two and five locks being negligible. It was found at Sacaton in 1921 by counts on 100 bolls of each
lock number taken from as many plants that the average number
of seeds per boll was 18.6±0.13 for the 3-locked bolls, and 21.7±0.19
for the 4-locked bolls.[31] The frequency distributions for the number
of seeds in the 3-locked and in the 4-locked bolls are shown in
Figure 4.

---

[30] Much higher percentages have been recorded at other localities. Counts made by
C. G. Marshall and W. B. Camp on 40 plants in a field of Pima cotton near Bakersfield,
Calif., in 1917, showed that in a total of 2,486 bolls 21.3 per cent were 4-locked. O. F.
Cook in 1920 counted bolls on 5 plants taken at random in a field near Porterville, Calif.,
and found that in a total of 62 bolls, 20 (or 32.3 per cent) were 4-locked.

[31] A greater difference in sea-island cotton in the mean numbers of seeds in 3-locked
and 4-locked bolls is indicated by data given by Harland (*21*, Table II, p. 152), which
show that the means for 3-locked and 4-locked bolls were 17.4 and 23.2, respectively.

THE INFERIOR FERTILIZATION OF BAGGED FLOWERS.

Bolls from flowers which have been inclosed in paper bags in order to prevent cross-pollination and which have not been pollinated by hand nearly always contain fewer seeds than bolls from open-pollinated flowers. For example, in 1915, the mean number of seeds per boll in 678 bolls from bagged flowers was found to be only 13.6 ± 0.34, as compared with a mean of 16 ± 0.12 in 530 bolls from open-pollinated flowers. In Table 31 are assembled the data from a number of experiments which afforded a close comparison of the relative fertilization of bagged and of open-pollinated flowers, both lots of flowers having opened during the same period and either on the same or on neighboring plants.

TABLE 31.—*Relative completeness of fertilization in bagged and in open-pollinated flowers of Pima cotton.*

Year and treatment of flower.	Number of bolls.	Mean number of seeds per boll.	Year and treatment of flower.	Number of bolls.	Mean number of seeds per boll.
Season of 1916:			Season of 1920:		
Bagged	743	10.9 ± 0.14	Bagged	80	10.7 ± 0.36
Open pollinated	707	$15.3 \pm .12$	Open pollinated	95	$14.2 \pm .21$
Difference		$4.4 \pm .18$	Difference		$3.5 \pm .42$
Season of 1919:			Bagged	634	$11.5 \pm .13$
Bagged	168	$13.9 \pm .23$	Open pollinated	360	$15.9 \pm .11$
Open pollinated	174	$16.6 \pm .25$	Difference		$4.4 \pm .17$
Difference		$2.7 \pm .34$	Season of 1921:		
Bagged	62	$16.5 \pm .25$	Bagged	129	$15.4 \pm .30$
Open pollinated	58	$18.2 \pm .22$	Open pollinated	560	$17.3 \pm .09$
Difference		$1.7 \pm .33$	Difference		$1.9 \pm .31$

The data in Table 31 indicate in every case very significant inferiority of the bagged flowers in relative completeness of fertilization. In seeking an explanation of this difference the following factors are to be considered:

(1) Exclusive self-pollination of the bagged flowers.
(2) Special environment created by inclosure of the flowers in paper bags.
(3) Pollination of only the lower half of the stigmatic surface in the bagged flowers.

Evidence was given on a preceding page that in Pima cotton self-pollination as compared with cross-pollination does not result in an inferior degree of fertilization. That inclosure of the flowers is not an important factor is indicated by the results of an experiment in 1921. On the same Pima plants a number of flowers were bagged before opening, and others were left unbagged. Neither lot was emasculated, and both were pollinated during the morning of the day of anthesis with pollen from other plants of the same variety, the whole stigmatic surface having been thoroughly covered with pollen. Presence or absence of the bags was therefore the only variable. The data given in Table 32 show that the bagged flowers were as well fertilized as those which were not inclosed.

TABLE 32.—*Fertilization of unemasculated Pima flowers of which the upper portion of the stigmas was thoroughly pollinated with pollen of the same variety, some of the flowers having been inclosed in paper bags and others having been uninclosed.*

Treatment.	Flowers treated.	Percentage of bolls matured.	Mean number of seeds per boll.
Bagged	170	88.3±1.7	17.2±0.16
Not bagged	170	89.4±1.6	17.0± .19
Difference	....	1.1±2.3	.2± .25

Since the absence of cross-pollination and the environment created by inclosure in bags do not seem to be responsible for the inferior fertilization of the bagged flowers, the third variable, locus of pollen deposition, remains to be considered. Table 33 gives the data of several experiments in which the results of pollinating only the lower halves of the stigmas, as in the case when the flower is bagged and left to automatic self-deposition, are compared with the results of pollinating the whole stigmatic surface. In all of these experiments the area of pollen deposition was the only variable, all flowers having been inclosed in bags but not emasculated, and the artificial pollination of the upper portion of the stigmas having been done either with pollen from the anthers of the same flower (experiments of 1916, 1917, and 1920) or with pollen from another flower on the same plant (experiment of 1921).

TABLE 33.—*Relative completeness of fertilization of Pima flowers in which pollen was confined to the lower halves of the stigmas and of flowers which received pollen on the whole stigmatic surface.*

Year and area pollinated.	Flowers treated.	Percentage of bolls matured.	Mean number of seeds per boll.	Year and area pollinated.	Flowers treated.	Percentage of bolls matured.	Mean number of seeds per boll.
Season of 1916:				Season of 1920:			
Lower	1,143	35.5±1.0	10.8±0.21	Lower	95	84.2±2.5	10.7±0.36
Whole	1,100	45.9±1.0	12.5± .18	Whole	97	86.6±2.3	11.2± .32
Difference	......	10.4±1.4	1.7± .28	Difference	......	2.4±3.4	.5± .48
Season of 1917:				Season of 1921:			
Lower	78	90.0±2.3	16.7± .40	Lower	137	94.2±1.4	15.4± .30
Whole	86	74.0±3.2	17.5± .39	Whole	176	90.4±1.5	17.5± .17
Difference	......	16.0±3.9	.8± .56	Difference	......	3.8±2.0	2.1± .34

The data in Table 33 show that there was in every case a higher mean number of seeds per boll from flowers of which the whole stigmatic surface was pollinated, although the differences were significant only in the experiments of 1916 and 1921. These data alone do not make it clear whether the inferior fertilization when pollen is confined to the lower half of the stigmas is due to the smaller size of the area pollinated or to less favorable conditions for pollen development in the basal region of the stigmas. Reference to Table 16 shows, however, that confining pollen to half of the stigmatic area when this was the apical half, did not result in diminished fertilization as indicated by the mean number of seeds per boll. It may be concluded, therefore, that the inferior fertilization of bagged flowers which receive pollen only on the lower half of the stigmas is due primarily to this region being relatively unfavorable to the germination or development of the pollen.

BOLL SHEDDING IN RELATION TO POLLINATION AND FERTILIZATION.

A general discussion of the phenomenon of boll shedding would be out of place in this bulletin. The physiological aspects of the subject have been treated by Balls (*8*, pp. 65–75), Lloyd (*37* and *38*), Ewing (*17*, pp. 21–37), and King (*31*, pp. 11–21). It may be well, however, to consider briefly such data as have been obtained at Sacaton, Ariz., concerning the relation between the shedding of bolls and fertilization. The observed percentages of boll shedding in Pima cotton at Sacaton, as recorded in Table 34, are in most cases much lower than have been reported by investigators of sea-island and upland cottons at other localities (*20*, p. 195; *17*, p. 21; *40*). In Pima cotton grown at Phoenix, Ariz., 40 miles distant from Sacaton, King (*31*, p. 19) recorded instances of bolls shed in 1919 ranging from 16.7 to 26.5 per cent.

TABLE 34.—*Boll shedding from flowers of Pima cotton naturally pollinated in different years at Sacaton, Ariz.*

Year of experiment.	Flowers recorded.	Flowers which failed to develop bolls (per cent).	Year of experiment.	Flowers recorded.	Flowers which failed to develop bolls (per cent).
1919	200	13.0±1.6	1920	377	4.4±0.7
1919	69	16.0±3.0	1921	999	10.3± .6
1920	98	3.0±1.2	1921	[1] 4,931	25.1± .4
1920	99	8.1±1.8			

[1] Flowers tagged daily during the period from July 11 to September 15.

It is unlikely that deficient pollination is a frequent cause of boll shedding in Pima cotton. Meade (*40*), working with upland varieties, found that "bolls failed to set unless at least 25 grains of pollen were applied to the stigmas; even with this number only one or two seeds matured in each lock." The records for flowers of Pima cotton which have been bagged to prevent cross-pollination show that the quantity of self pollen deposited automatically upon the basal portion of the stigmas is sufficient to insure, as a rule, the retention and maturation of 80 to 90 per cent of the bolls. In flowers naturally open pollinated at Sacaton, additional large quantities of pollen are conveyed to the stigmas by insects. It is probable that only in rare instances is the number of pollen grains which reach the stigmas fewer than 10 times the number of ovules (Pl. VII). Even where insect pollination is deficient, as in the field at Phoenix where the experiment in artificial pollination was performed, the data given in Table 28 show that the additional pollen applied by hand to the stigmas increased the proportion of bolls retained and matured by only about 9 per cent, while increasing the mean number of seeds per boll by 21 per cent.

Evidence also has been obtained that it is not requisite that many of the ovules be fertilized in order that bolls may be retained and matured. Thus, in 1917, among 71 bolls which matured from a lot of bagged flowers, 3 contained only 2 seeds, 6 contained only 3 seeds, 3 contained only 4 seeds, and 5 contained only 5 seeds. Hence, in 17 bolls (or 24 per cent of the number which reached maturity) fewer than one-fourth of the mean number of ovules had been. fertilized. Counts were made of the number of seeds in 633 bolls which matured from bagged flowers in 1920, and of these 2 contained only 1 seed, 7 contained only 2 seeds, and 14 contained only 3 seeds. Few of the bolls which mature from flowers naturally open pollinated show fertilization of less than half of the average number of ovules. Of 447 such bolls in 1920 only 22 (or 4.9 per cent) contained fewer than 10 seeds. On the other hand, of 633 bolls which matured from bagged flowers during approximately the same period 201 (or 31.7 per cent) contained fewer than 10 seeds.

It has been shown on preceding pages that the pollen of Pima cotton is highly viable and perfectly self-compatible. Evidence has been presented, also, that the number of pollen grains normally reaching the stigmas vastly exceeds the number of ovules and that fertilization of only a few of the ovules is necessary in order to insure retention and maturation of the boll. It may be concluded, therefore, that with this variety, under the conditions existing at Sacaton, deficient pollination and fertilization are not important factors in the shedding of bolls.

INBREEDING IN RELATION TO FERTILITY.

The effect upon cotton of continuous and strictly controlled self-fertilization appears to have been little investigated. Leake and Prasad (*36*, pp. 39–45), working in India with cottons of the Asiatic type, obtained indications that partial sterility, as expressed by the percentage of bolls retained, occurred in the first and later inbred generations and that this tendency could be overcome by subsequent cross-pollination. Different types apparently differed in their tendency to sterility. One type showed a marked tendency to imperfect development of the anthers in the second inbred generation which, however, disappeared in the third generation. In one strain self-pollination with pollen from another flower on the same plant resulted in the retention of a much smaller percentage of bolls than did cross-pollination with pollen from a sister plant; but in another strain of the same type no such difference was observed. The numbers of flowers dealt with in these experiments were too small to afford conclusive results.

A different conclusion was reached by Kottur (*34*), who also worked with the Asiatic type of cotton, in India. He found that sterile anthers, containing no pollen, are of common occurrence. In an unselected open-pollinated stock of the Kumpta variety, of which 500 flowers were examined, sterile anthers were found in all but 128, the proportion of empty anthers having been as high as 43 per cent of the total number in some of the flowers. Controlled self-fertilization during six successive generations did not increase this form of sterility. In fact, it is shown by Kottur's data that in the continuously self-fertilized strain the proportion of the flowers having more than 10 sterile anthers was only 13.6 per cent, as compared with 35.9 per cent in the open-pollinated stock. Kottur also observed that the rate of boll shedding was lower and that the percentage of ovules which failed to develop into seeds was no greater in the continuously self-fertilized than in the continuously open-pollinated population. Kottur states further that continuous self-fertilization in the Asiatic cottons (*Gossypium herbaceum* and *G. neglectum*) and in American upland cotton (*G. hirsutum*) did not induce sterility.

The effects of inbreeding in Pima cotton have been the subject of investigation at Sacaton, Ariz., the following criteria of fertility having been considered:

    Viability of the pollen.
    Number of ovules.
    Rate of flowering.
    Boll-shedding percentage.
    Size of the boll.
    Weight of seed cotton per boll.
    Number of seeds per boll.
    Weight of seeds.
    Viability of the seeds (germination percentage).
    Lint index (weight of fiber per 100 seeds).

Comparison with random samples of the continuously open-pollinated (hence, more or less cross-pollinated) stock has been used necessarily as the measure of fertility in the inbred populations, although it is realized that inbreeding may have been accompanied by segregation, plus or minus, in respect to some or all of these values. There was, however, no intentional selection in the development of the inbred families here dealt with.

POLLEN VIABILITY OF AN INBRED POPULATION.

A family resulting from strict self-fertilization during five successive generations was compared in 1919 with a continuously open-pollinated stock in regard to the viability of the pollen as measured by the rate of ejection of the contents of the grains and by the percentage of the total number ejected in a 5 per cent solution of cane sugar (see p. 22). Flowers were collected at 11 a. m., one from each of five plants in each population, and flowers of the inbred and of the open-pollinated stock were alternated in making the tests. The results, as given in Table 35, show no difference in the average viability of the pollen.

TABLE 35.—*Viability of the pollen from plants of a family of Pima cotton inbred during five generations compared with that from plants of a continuously open-pollinated stock of this variety.*

	Inbred family.			Open-pollinated stock.		
	After immersion until ejection—		Estimated ejection.	After immersion until ejection—		Estimated ejection.
Plant and flower.	Began.	Ceased actively.		Began.	Ceased actively.	
	Seconds.	*Seconds.*	*Per cent.*	*Seconds.*	*Seconds.*	*Per cent.*
No. 1	70	170	95	60	170	95
No. 2	65	110	100	60	170	100
No. 3	70	180	100	70	135	95
No. 4	85	155	98	65	120	100
No. 5	55	120	100	65	140	100
Average	69	147	98	64	147	98

It was observed that in three of the five flowers of the inbred population a few of the pollen grains were very small and did not eject their contents during the period of observation, which was about two and one-half minutes. Only one of the five flowers of the open-pollinated stock had an appreciable number of abnormally small grains, although in this case the proportion of such grains was fully as great as in any of the flowers of the inbred family. Further observations were therefore made upon the occurrence of sterile pollen grains in the inbred and in the continuously open-pollinated population. Examination of a number of flowers of the continuously open-pollinated stock showed that in most cases from 2 to 5 per cent of the pollen grains were very small and presumably sterile, 20 per cent of the pollen in one flower having been of this character. Counts made on pollen from five plants of each population, with the results given in Table 36, afforded no evidence of an increase in the proportion of sterile pollen grains having resulted from continuous self-fertilization.

TABLE 36.—*Flowers of a family of Pima cotton inbred during five generations compared with those of a continuously open-pollinated stock of this variety, showing the percentage of abnormally small and presumably sterile pollen grains.*

Plant and Flower.	Inbred family.			Open-pollinated stock.		
	Number of pollen grains.[1]		Percentage of sterile grains.	Number of pollen grains.[1]		Percentage of sterile grains.
	Total.	Sterile.		Total.	Sterile.	
No. 1	?	0	0	26	1	3.8
No. 2	56	1	1.8	?	0	0
No. 3	?	0	0	30	2	6.7
No. 4	14	2	14.3	36	1	2.8
No. 5	?	0	0	25	3	12.0

[1] The total number of grains in the field of the microscope was not determined if no abnormally small grains were present.

It would be expected that if continued inbreeding had impaired the viability of the pollen, fertilization in the inbred strain would be more nearly complete when the flowers are cross-pollinated than when they are self-pollinated. The data given in Table 20 show, however, that in a family which had been inbred during seven successive generations there was not a significant difference in the mean number of seeds per boll from the cross-pollinated and from the self-pollinated flowers and that a somewhat higher percentage of bolls matured from the self-pollinated than from the cross-pollinated flowers.

NUMBER OF OVULES IN AN INBRED POPULATION.

Counts were made in 1919 of the ovules in 20 ovaries of a family which had been strictly inbred by controlled self-fertilization during five generations and in 30 ovaries of a continuously open-pollinated stock, each ovary having been taken from a different plant. The counts were made upon 3-celled ovaries and yielded the mean and extreme numbers given in Table 37. It is obvious that controlled self-fertilization during five successive generations, as compared with continuous open pollination, had resulted in no reduction of the number of ovules.

TABLE 37.—*Count of the ovules in the 3-celled ovaries of a family of Pima cotton inbred during five generations compared with those of a continuously open-pollinated stock of this variety.*

Stocks compared.	Mean.	Maximum.	Minimum.
Inbred during five generations	21.0±0.33	24	14
Continuously open pollinated	20.8± .27	24	15

RATE OF FLOWERING, PERCENTAGE OF BOLL SHEDDING, SIZE OF BOLLS, AND NUMBER, WEIGHT, AND VIABILITY OF THE SEEDS IN AN INBRED POPULATION.

A family which had resulted from controlled self-fertilization during seven successive generations was compared in 1921 with a random sample of the continuously open-pollinated commercial stock of the Pima variety, the two populations having been grown in adjacent rows. A record was kept for 88 days of the number of flowers opening daily on every plant of both populations, and from these data were compiled the means given in Table 38, which indicate that there was no significant difference in the potential productiveness of the two populations.

TABLE 38.—*Daily mean number of flowers per plant in a Pima family strictly inbred during seven generations compared with that in a random sample of the continuously open-pollinated stock of this variety.*

Population.	Number of plants.	Mean number of flowers per plant, daily
Inbred	78	1.01±0.02
Open pollinated	84	.97± .02
Difference		.04±. 03

The percentages of bolls shed, the mean numbers of seeds per matured boll, the mean weights of seeds, and the germination percentages of the seeds were determined on 15 plants of each population, well-grown individuals which occupied opposite or nearly opposite positions in the two rows having been selected for comparison. Naturally pollinated flowers which had opened on the same days on both sets of plants furnished the material. This procedure eliminated sources of error which might have arisen from soil heterogeneity or from differences in the weather during the period of development of the flowers and bolls. The data, as given in Table 39 (upper part), show no significant differences between the two populations except in the mean weight of seeds, in which case the difference was in favor of the inbred population.

TABLE 39.—*Pima cotton strictly inbred during seven successive generations compared with a random sample of the continuously open-pollinated commercial stock of this variety.*

Population.	Flowers tagged.	Percentage of bolls shed.	Mean number of seeds per matured boll.	Mean weight of 100 seeds (grams).	Percentage of germination of the seeds.[1]
Inbred	296	11.8±1.3	17.2±0.12	13.6±0.04	90.8±0.8
Open pollinated	367	8.4±1.0	17.1± .12	13.4± .03	90.2± .9
Difference		3.4±1.6	.1± .17	.2± .05	.6±1.2

Population.	Boll dimensions.			Boll weight and lint index.		
	Number of bolls.	Length (millimeters).	Diameter (millimeters).	Number of bolls.	Seed cotton (grams).	Lint index.
Inbred	25	46.6±0.56	26.8±0.19	105	3.22±0.21	4.90±0.27
Open pollinated	25	45.7± .80	26.1± .19	115	3.04± .06	5.12± .03
Difference		.9± .97	.7± .27		.18± .22	.22± .27

[1] Determined for 500 seeds of each population.

Further comparison of the same populations was made in regard to the length and the greatest diameter of the bolls, the weight of seed cotton in the ripe boll, and the lint index. The determinations were made on bolls from naturally pollinated flowers on five plants in each population, individuals which occupied opposite positions in the two rows having been used and the bolls having been from flowers which had opened during the same period in both populations. Five bolls, judged to be full grown, although not yet open, were measured on each plant. The weight of seed cotton per boll and the lint index were determined separately on from three to five lots of five bolls each from each plant. The units from which were computed the means and probable errors, as given in Table 39 (lower part), were in all cases the averages for the individual plants. The results of this comparison show no significant differences between the two populations.

CONCLUSIONS IN REGARD TO THE EFFECTS OF INBREEDING.

No evidence was obtained that the fertility of Pima cotton had been impaired by strict inbreeding during five or seven successive generations. The inbred families were not inferior to the continuously open-pollinated stocks in viability of the pollen; number of ovules; daily flower production; percentage of bolls retained; size, weight, and seed content of the bolls; weight and viability of the seeds; and abundance of the fiber.[32]

The absence of superior fertility in the continuously open-pollinated populations is hardly surprising in view of the evidence

[32] This comparison of the naturally pollinated commercial stock of Pima cotton, a relatively uniform variety, with the closely inbred (self-fertilized) strain may be regarded as a comparison of restricted or "narrow" breeding with "line" breeding, to use Cook's evolutionary terminology (10, p. 9). The evidence here presented that the closest inbreeding during seven generations resulted in no diminution of fertility does not prove that such effect might not be shown eventually. From Cook's point of view, "though all forms of restricted descent lead ultimately to degeneration, the decline may be exceedingly slow and gradual if methods of line breeding are followed" (10, p. 38).

given on preceding pages that in cotton most of the ovules normally are self-fertilized. This would be expected to result in a degree of " immunity " to the supposedly injurious effects of continued inbreeding, comparable in some degree to that of wheat and other plants in which cross-fertilization rarely takes place under natural conditions.

The hypothesis of a direct physiological effect of inbreeding is rejected, however, by recent investigators (*9, 15, 23, 45*), who attribute the often injurious results to segregation of deleterious recessive factors or to elimination of favorable dominant factors upon which depends the vigor of heterosis. To quote Jones (*23*, p. 95), " whether good or bad results from inbreeding depends solely on the constitution of the organisms before inbreeding is commenced." As stated by East and Jones (*15*, pp. 139, 140) : " The only injury proceeding from inbreeding comes from the inheritance received. The constitution of the individuals resulting from a process of inbreeding depends upon the chance allotment of characters preexisting in the stock before inbreeding was commenced. If undesirable characters are shown after inbreeding, it is only because they already existed in the stock and were able to persist for generations under the protection of more favorable characters which dominated them and kept them from sight." Substantially the same idea is expressed by Stout (*45*, p. 124) as follows: " The accumulation of evidence that inbreeding is not necessarily injurious has led to the view that decreased vegetative and reproductive vigor in inbred stock is due to an inherently weak constitution existing before inbreeding was begun."

The assumption seems justifiable that in Pima cotton factors contributing to low fertility had been eliminated in large part in the ancestry of the plant which gave rise to the variety or by the subsequent selection and isolation which resulted in development of the present highly uniform commercial stock. The fertility of the latter may be regarded, therefore, as due to segregation rather than to heterosis.

SUMMARY.

The three principal types of cotton grown in the United States, upland, sea island, and Egyptian, although very different in their botanical characters, intercross readily, giving rise to hybrids which are extremely fertile in the first generation.

When any two of these types or any two varieties of the same type of which the hybrid offspring is easily distinguishable are grown in close proximity in a locality where pollinating insects are abundant, the proportion of vicinists (natural hybrids) in populations grown from the resulting seed seldom exceeds 20 per cent and is often much lower. Upland cotton usually produces more vicinists than Egyptian cotton when each type is equally exposed to cross-pollination by the other.

From the point of view of maintaining varietal purity, a very small proportion of vicinism must be regarded as a menace. A few accidental hybrids, unless they are promptly eliminated, will eventually contaminate the stock.

The percentage of recognizable vicinists does not indicate the total extent of cross-fertilization occurring under natural conditions, many of the ovules being fertilized by pollen from other plants of the same variety, but even when single plants of Egyptian or of upland cotton were scattered through a field of the other type and the conditions were so controlled as to make it highly probably that all seeds not derived from self-fertilization had resulted from cross-fertilization by pollen of the other type, the maximum number of vicinists in populations grown from these plants did not exceed 35 per cent. The average percentage of cross-fertilized ovules under these conditions was 12 in Pima (Egyptian) and 28 in Acala (upland).

The cotton flower is large and showy, and the reproductive organs are readily accessible to pollen-carrying insects attracted in large numbers by the abundant production of nectar and of pollen. One might therefore expect cross-fertilization to predominate over self-fertilization. The structure of the flower, however, is well adapted not only to cross-pollination by insects but to automatic self-pollination from the uppermost anthers. These are in contact with the base of the stigmas in Egyptian cotton and with practically the whole stigmatic surface in many varieties of upland cotton.

In the Egyptian type only the extrastaminal portion of the stigmas is accessible to foreign pollen, the basal region being effectively screened by the upper anthers. Experimental evidence was obtained that in the Pima variety cross-fertilization does not occur when the extrastaminal portion of the stigmas is excised. In upland cottons, on the other hand, the entire length of the stigmas is accessible to foreign pollen, and excision did not prevent cross-fertilization.

The corolla of Pima cotton commences to open about an hour after sunrise and continues to expand during the next four hours, the maximum aperture usually being attained about 10.30 a. m. In upland cottons an aperture first appears at about the same time as in Pima, but the subsequent expansion is more rapid. In both types the flower is of brief duration, the petals beginning to wilt and the pistils to lose their turgor before sunset on the day of anthesis.

The opening of the anthers and release of pollen in Pima cotton begin somewhat earlier than the expansion of the corolla. In upland cottons, as a rule, corolla and anthers commence to open almost simultaneously, although not infrequently the upland anthers are found to be still closed when the corolla is open sufficiently to admit insects. Even in Pima cotton, however, very little self pollen is deposited automatically upon the stigmas before the petals have begun to unfold.

The viability of the pollen of Pima (Egyptian) and of Durango (upland) cotton, as measured by the rate of ejection of the cell contents when the grains are immersed in a sugar solution, is low during the early hours of the morning, begins to increase rapidly between 8 and 9 a. m., and shows a gradual decline after midday. Inclosure of the flower in a paper bag greatly prolongs the period of viability.

Pollen extracted from the anthers and applied to the stigmas the evening before anthesis showed a very limited ability to effect fertilization. On the other hand, the viability of pollen collected from bagged flowers 26 hours after the beginning of anthesis, as indicated by the ability to effect fertilization, was still considerable, although greatly inferior to that of fresh pollen.

The style of the Pima cotton flower normally is lost by abscission within 36 hours after the beginning of anthesis. In bagged flowers it was found that fertilization could be effected 24 hours after the beginning of anthesis in fewer than 10 per cent of the flowers tested, the indication being that the stigmas do not remain receptive much longer than this even when the flowers are protected by inclosure in bags.

Self pollen being automatically deposited in Pima cotton upon that part of the stigmas which is nearest the ovary and foreign pollen being excluded from this zone by the dense girdle of stamens, the self pollen would seem to have a decided advantage in the distance to be traversed by the tubes in reaching the ovary. Computation from rather unsatisfactory data as to the average rate of growth of the pollen tubes suggests that, other things being equal, pollen tubes from self grains might reach the ovary $3\frac{1}{2}$ hours before penetration could be effected by foreign pollen deposited higher on the stigmas. Evidence has been obtained, however, that the conditions for pollen development are less favorable in the basal than in the apical region of the stigmas, and it is therefore to be doubted that the locus of pollen deposition is an important factor in the preponderance of self-fertilization in Pima cotton. The doubt is increased by the fact that in upland cottons, in which also self-fertilization preponderates, the whole stigmatic surface is accessible to both self pollen and foreign pollen.

The automatic deposition of self pollen upon the stigmas of Pima cotton does not begin long in advance of the first arrival of insect-carried pollen, and in upland cottons the first arrival of pollen from both sources seems as a rule to be virtually simultaneous. It may be concluded, therefore, that the time of arrival of the pollen does not determine the relative frequency of self-fertilization and of cross-fertilization.

By controlling conditions so as to prevent the access of foreign pollen not readily distinguishable from the self pollen, but so as not to interfere with natural cross-pollination, it was demonstrated that a large proportion of the pollen transferred to the stigmas by insects is derived from the anthers of the same flower. As much self pollen is also deposited automatically, preponderance of self-pollination would seem to be an important, if not the principal, factor in the preponderance of self-fertilization.

When the two types are growing side by side, the quantity of Pima pollen deposited upon the stigmas of upland cottons exceeds the quantity of upland pollen deposited upon the Pima stigmas, a fact which helps to explain the greater frequency of upland $\times$ Pima than of Pima $\times$ upland vicinists. The habits of the pollinating insects and the relative rates of opening of the corolla and anthers in the two kinds of cotton seem to account for this difference in cross-pollination. Many of the Pima flowers are entered by honeybees just as the petals begin to unfold and at a time when little upland pollen is available for transfer, the anthers of the upland flowers being for the most part still closed. In entering the Pima flower in this early stage of expansion the insect comes into contact with the stigmas and stamens, depositing and taking up pollen. Later in the morning, when upland pollen is available in quantity for transfer, the Pima corollas are open to a degree which allows the insects to enter and leave the flower without touching the reproductive organs. Insects coming from Pima flowers which have just begun to open are often loaded with pollen, the Pima anthers usually being well open when the expansioh of the corolla begins. As a result Pima pollen is frequently deposited in upland flowers before the anthers of the latter have opened.

Insect pollination of cotton at Sacaton, Ariz., is effected principally by Hymenoptera, the honeybee and wild bees of the genus Melissodes being the most important species. Certain Coleoptera and Hemiptera also have been observed to carry pollen, but these insects probably are of very minor importance as pollinators.

By applying the different kinds of pollen separately to different flowers it was sought to ascertain whether different degrees of fertilization in Pima cotton result from self-pollination as compared with cross-pollination within the variety and from cross-pollination within the variety as compared with cross-pollination with more foreign pollen. The results were negative so far as concerns cross-pollination within the Egyptian type, there having been no consistent differences in the degree of fertilization attained, whether the stigmas received self pollen, pollen from other plants of the Pima variety, or pollen of another variety of the Egyptian type. On the other hand, somewhat better fertilization of the Pima flowers was obtained in several cases with pollen of a very different type of cotton (upland) than with pollen of the same variety.

An experiment in which Pima flowers were pollinated, some with Pima and others with upland pollen, gave no satisfactory evidence of a difference in the relative growth rate of the pollen tubes of the two types.

Selective fertilization, in favor of the related pollen, has been found to occur when pollen of the same variety is in competition with pollen of another Egyptian variety or with pollen of upland cotton on the stigmas of Egyptian cottons. On the other hand, the results of an experiment performed by Argyle McLachlan indicated the absence of a corresponding prepotency of upland pollen on the upland stigmas, and as most of the ovules normally are self-fertilized in both types of cotton, it remains doubtful in what degree selective fertilization contributes to the greater frequency of self-fertilization.

As both Pima and upland pollen when applied separately to the stigmas of different Pima flowers appear to develop their tubes with equal rapidity and as the upland pollen is at least equally efficient in accomplishing fertilization, it seems necessary, in order to explain the fact of selective fertilization when the two pollens are in direct competition, to assume an inhibiting influence of pollen of the same variety upon the more foreign pollen.

In localities where bees are not numerous in the cotton fields comparatively little pollen reaches the upper part of the stigmas of Pima flowers. Under such conditions artificial pollination resulted in a marked increase in fertilization; whereas at Sacaton, Ariz., where the cotton flowers are much frequented by bees, artificial pollination did not affect the degree of fertilization.

The degree of fertilization resulting from natural pollination has been found to differ in different seasons and at different times in the same season, as well as at different localities.

Flowers inclosed in paper bags in order to exclude foreign pollen and left to automatic self-pollination are nearly always less well fertilized than open-pollinated flowers, but by artificial pollination

UNITED STATES DEPARTMENT OF AGRICULTURE

 BULLETIN No. 1135

Washington, D. C.   PROFESSIONAL PAPER   May 19, 1923

SPINNING TESTS OF COTTON COMPRESSED TO DIFFERENT DENSITIES.

By WILLIAM R. MEADOWS, *Cotton Technologist,* and WILLIAM G. BLAIR, *Specialist in Cotton Testing, Bureau of Agricultural Economics.*

CONTENTS.

IN TIMES of prosperity, when transportation and storage facilities are taxed to the limit, the conservation and utilization of space in freight cars and terminal warehouses becomes of paramount importance. A considerable saving in space and freight charges would be possible if a more compact and neater package were adopted for cotton.

PURPOSE OF TESTS.

Does compressing cotton to higher densities than 15 pounds per cubic foot injure the spinning value of the cotton? This is a much discussed question among cotton growers, merchants, brokers, and manufacturers. The spinning tests herein described were conducted for the purpose of arriving at conclusions in regard to this question as definite as could be determined by tests covering a single season's growth.[1]

---

[1] These spinning tests were conducted under the general supervision of William R. Meadows, cotton technologist, and under the direction of William G. Blair, specialist in cotton testing, who was assisted by H. B. Richardson, C. E. Folk, and E. S. Cummings, assistants in cotton testing. The Cleveland Big Boll was spun at the North Carolina State College of Agriculture and Engineering, Raleigh, N. C., and the other cottons were spun at the Clemson Agricultural College, Clemson College, S. C.

KINDS OF BALES.

At present there are five distinct types of bales: Flat, standard or railroad compressed, high density, round, and ginner's compress. The first three are of frequent occurrence, while the latter two have varied in amount of use.

Flat bale.—Most of the cotton ginned in this country on saw gins is put up in the form of a rectangular package known as the flat bale. (Pl. 1, Fig. 1.)   This bale has a density varying from 12 to 15 pounds per cubic foot.   It is covered with all the different types and grades of burlap, has six ties or hoops, and varies in weight anywhere from 300 to 750 pounds.

Standard or railroad compressed bale.—The standard or railroad compressed bale (Pl. I, Fig. 2) is made by applying great pressure to the ordinary flat bale from which the ties have been removed and to which patches have been added to cover the cuts in the burlap where samples were drawn.   Pressure is applied only to the top and bottom of the bale, thus allowing the cotton to spread slightly sidewise and endwise.   This spreading and the speed with which the bales are handled make a very irregular package.   A well-organized crew of press hands may compress as many as 120 bales per hour.   The density of this type of bale is from 22 to 28 pounds per cubic foot and varies with the amount of cotton in the bale.   The bale has usually eight ties when it leaves the compress.

High-density bale.—After the ties have been removed and patches added to cover the cuts in the burlap where samples were drawn, the flat bale is placed in the press, the side doors are raised, and steam pressure is applied to the bottom or movable platen.   The cotton is compressed between the top and bottom platens.   As the side doors prevent any side spreading of the bale, the cotton can spread only endwise.   The addition of the side doors makes the high-density bale (Pl. II, Fig. 1) more uniform in shape than the standard bale with the same pressure.   High-density bales are compressed at a much slower rate than are the standard density bales because of the use of the side-door attachment, the rate being about 70 bales per hour for the high-density compared with 120 bales per hour for the standard density.

It is an easy matter to detect the high-density bale because of its much more uniform shape and because of the nine ties fastened by a high-grade buckle.   The high-density attachment is used when cotton is to be exported or shipped by water.   The density of the bale is from 28 to 40 pounds per cubic foot, varying with the amount of cotton in the bale.

Round bale.—The round bale (Pl. II, Fig. 2) is made by taking the loose cotton from the gins and winding it in a continuous sheet around a core and at the same time applying pressure through other rolls, thus making a very compact cylindrical-shaped bale of small size.   This bale averages about 250 pounds in weight, has no ties, and is usually covered with a higher grade of burlap than any other type of bale with the possible exception of the Egyptian bale.   The density per cubic foot averages about 35 pounds.   This bale does not have an extensive domestic distribution, but some foreign firms specify this type of bale when ordering cotton shipped from this country.

Ginners' compress bale.—A ginners' compress bale (Pl. III) is made in exactly the same manner as the flat bale only greater pressure is applied. The gin box and apparatus are made more rugged to withstand the greater pressure when compressing the loose cotton to this higher density. This type of bale usually has six ties. Its density varies from 25 to 30 pounds per cubic foot, depending upon the amount of cotton in the gin box.

This type of bale was not included in this study because of the small number of gin compresses in use and inability to secure a pure strain of cotton from such a compress.

CONDITIONS OF THE TESTS.

The general conditions of the tests follow, and specific information regarding details of results are found under the descriptions of the separate tests.

VARIETIES OF COTTON TESTED.

The varieties of cotton tested consisted of pure strains of Cleveland Big Boll, Rowden, Delta, and Webber 49 grown by men of reputation for their plant-breeding work.

The Cleveland Big Boll, Delta, and Webber 49 cottons were grown during the season of 1920 under normal weather conditions up to the time of picking. At this time, the rainfall delayed the opening of the bolls so that the number of pickings was reduced.

The climatic conditions during the season of 1921, under which the Rowden cotton was grown, were normal for the first half of the season followed by an extended drought which seemed to have the effect of shortening the length of staple.

All of the bales of the same variety of cotton were picked at the same time, ginned on the same day on the same battery of gins, and compressed on the same day with the exception of the round bale of the Rowden variety which was ginned on a different gin than the rectangular bales.

The reason for securing pure strains and proceeding as described, was to eliminate as many variables as possible with each variety, thus placing the variable of compression to different densities upon a strictly comparative basis. The test on each variety is therefore a separate test.

Detailed information regarding the cotton selected for the tests is shown below.[2]

Variety.	Grown at—	Season.	Grade.	Staple.	Stored in bale.
				Inches.	Months.
Cleveland Big Boll	Hartsville, S. C	1920	Middling	1⁵⁄₈	6
Rowden	Wills Point, Tex	1921	Strict Middling	1	6
Delta	Scott, Miss	1920	Middling	1⅛	12
Webber 49	Hartsville, S. C	1920	Middling	1¼	9

[2] The cotton was classed by members of the board of examiners, a committee authorized to class cotton at the future exchanges under the provisions of the United States cotton futures act.

WASTE DETERMINATIONS.

Accurate weighings were made of the net amount of cotton fed to and delivered by each cleaning machine and of the net amount of waste discarded by each. From these weighings, the percentage of visible, invisible, and total waste was determined. The percentage of waste for each variety is in the description of each test.

MECHANICAL CONDITIONS.

The cotton from the bales of different densities of the same variety was run under mechanical conditions which conformed to average mill conditions for the length of staple used. No changes were made except those necessary to maintain the desired weight or sizing of the stock in process.

MOISTURE CONDITIONS.

The moisture conditions under which the cotton is machined affect its spinning properties in a number of ways. The amount of invisible waste varies with the amount of moisture in the cotton as well as with differences in the character of the cotton. The moisture content depends upon the weather conditions to which the cotton has been exposed before reaching the mill and upon the relative humidity under which it is machined. Controlling the relative humidity in the mill tends to bring the cotton to a certain moisture level and thus reduces the varying factor of invisible waste caused largely by fluctuations in the moisture content of the cotton. Controlling the humidity also makes possible more accurate weighings or sizings and thus gives more even running work. The cotton also spins and weaves better under proper humidity conditions.

The humidifiers were regulated by hand as closely as possible to give a relative humidity of 50 per cent in the picker room, 60 per cent in the card room, and 70 per cent in the spinning room. At Raleigh, N. C., there were no humidifiers in the picker room, but as damp weather prevailed at the time the stock was on the pickers the humidity was above the desired amount at this point. There was no way to dehumidify in any of the tests. On excessively moist or dry days, it was not always possible to maintain the humidity conditions at the desired level. The actual conditions which prevailed are given under each test.

Samples of the raw stock from the bale, finisher picker lap, card sliver, final processes of drawing and roving, and yarn were collected for moisture determinations. The results are included under each test.

BREAKING STRENGTH AND SIZING OF THE YARN.

The yarns were tested for strength and size in the cotton testing laboratory at Washington, which is equipped with a modern automatic humidity and temperature regulating system which controls the humidity at 65 per cent and prevents the temperature from falling below 70° F.

Twenty-four skeins of 120 yards from each number and twist of yarn were reeled and placed on a specially constructed rack and allowed to condition at least 24 hours under 65 per cent relative humidity before breaking and sizing. Each skein was then broken and sized in rotation. This method assures breaking and sizing the yarn of the different lots under identical moisture conditions.

FIG. 1.—FLAT OR UNCOMPRESSED BALE, TOP, SIDE, AND END VIEWS. DENSITY, 12 TO 15 POUNDS PER CUBIC FOOT. APPROXIMATE DIMENSIONS, 54 BY 27 BY 48 INCHES.

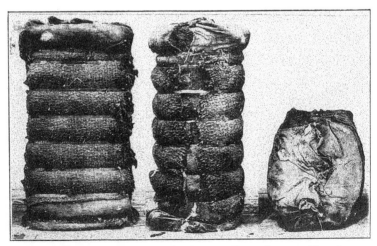

FIG. 2.—STANDARD OR RAILROAD COMPRESSED BALE, SHOWING TOP, SIDE, AND END VIEWS. DENSITY, 22 TO 28 POUNDS PER CUBIC FOOT. APPROXIMATE DIMENSIONS, 56 BY 28 BY 18 INCHES.

FIG. I.—HIGH-DENSITY BALE, TOP, SIDE, AND END VIEWS. DENSITY, 28 TO 40 POUNDS PER CUBIC FOOT. APPROXIMATE DIMENSIONS, 59 BY 24 BY 19 INCHES.

FIG. 2.—ROUND BALE, SIDE AND END VIEWS. DENSITY, 28 POUNDS PER CUBIC FOOT. APPROXIMATE DIMENSIONS, 35 BY 20 INCHES (DIAMETER).

PLATE III.

GINNER'S COMPRESS BALE, SHOWING TOP AND SIDE OF BALE. DENSITY, 25 TO 35 POUNDS PER CUBIC FOOT. APPROXIMATE DIMENSIONS, 52 BY 25 BY 20 INCHES.

IRREGULARITY OF YARNS.

The irregularity or the quality of the yarns was determined by three methods: By photographing the yarn, testing for evenness on a Moscrop single strand tester, and calculating the average deviation of the sizings and strengths obtained in the skein-breaking strength tests.

SPINNING TESTS OF CLEVELAND BIG BOLL COTTON OF FIFTEEN-SIXTEENTHS-INCH STAPLE.

The Cleveland Big Boll cotton was compressed into four bales: A flat bale, a standard or railroad compressed bale, a high-density bale, and a high-density bale compressed while wet. The latter bale was made by wetting a flat bale with water from a hose for a day and then compressing it to high density in the usual manner.

PERCENTAGE OF WASTE.

Table 1 gives the percentage of visible, invisible, and total waste obtained from the different types of bales.

TABLE 1.—*Percentage of waste from Cleveland Big Boll cotton of fifteen-sixteenths-inch staple; grade, Middling.*

Type of bale	Flat.	Standard.	High density.	High density wet.
PICKER WASTE.[1]	*Per cent.*	*Per cent.*	*Per cent.*	*Per cent.*
Opener-breaker motes and fly	0.96	1.20	0.98	1.50
Finisher motes and fly	.43	.52	.45	.66
Total visible	1.39	1.72	1.43	2.16
Invisible	.94	1.02	.96	1.46
Total visible and invisible	2.33	2.74	2.39	3.62
CARD WASTE.[2]				
Flat strips	2.59	3.00	2.69	3.17
Cylinder and doffer strips	.70	.83	.69	.88
Motes and fly	1.53	1.65	1.19	2.17
Sweepings	.10	.11	.09	.12
Total visible	4.92	5.59	4.66	6.34
Invisible	[3] .37	.09	.15	.62
Total visible and invisible	4.55	5.68	4.81	6.96
PICKERS AND CARDS.[1]				
Total visible	6.20	7.16	5.98	8.27
Total invisible	.58	1.11	1.11	2.06
Total visible and invisible	6.78	8.27	7.09	10.33

[1] Based upon net weight fed to bale-breaker.
[2] Based upon net weight fed to cards.
[3] Gain.

Referring to Table 1 and comparing the percentages of visible waste obtained from the different types of bales, it is seen that the flat bale and the high-density bale were practically equal in wastefulness. The standard or railroad compressed bale was about 1 per cent more wasty than either the flat or high-density bale, while the high-density bale compressed while wet was about 2 per cent more wasty.

The percentages of visible waste obtained from the bales of different compressions were:

Per cent.
Flat bale... 6.20
Standard or railroad compressed bale........................... 7.16
High-density bale... 5.98
High-density bale compressed wet.............................. 8.27

MOISTURE CONDITIONS.

Table 2 gives the average temperatures and relative humidities under which each type of bale was tested.

TABLE 2.—*Average temperatures and relative humidities during the testing of Cleveland Big Boll cotton of fifteen-sixteenths-inch staple.*

Type of bale	Flat.		Standard.		High density.		High density wet.	
	Temperature.	Relative humidity.	Temperature.	Relative humidity.	Temperature.	Relative humidity.	Temperature.	Relative humidity.
STAGE.	° F.	Per cent.	° F.	Per cent.	° F.	Per cent.	° F.	Per cent.
When opened...............	91	57	85	66	83	62	82	57
Finisher picker.............	93	57	89	59	84	56	92	56
Card......................	85	58	87	58	90	55	90	55
Drawing frames:								
59 grain sliver...........	83	61	85	62	89	57	90	56
73 grain sliver...........	.87	58	83	62	87	60	87	56
Roving frames:								
2.00 hank intermediate...	87	58	87	58	89	57	88	57
4.40 hank fine...........	88	57	88	57	89	56	90	56
5.40 hank fine...........	87	57	88	56	. 89	55	89	55
Spinning frame:								
16's yarn.................	91	56	91	56	89	55	89	55
22's yarn.................	84	.56	84	56	85	57	85	57

Table 3 gives the percentage of moisture regain of the cotton at the various stages of the manufacturing process.

TABLE 3.—*Percentage of moisture regain in the Cleveland Big Boll cotton at the different stages of the manufacturing process.*

Type of bale	Flat.	Standard.	High density.	High density wet.
STAGE OR SAMPLE.	Per cent.	Per cent.	Per cent.	Per cent.
From bale.......................................	6.04	7.12	7.12	6.95
Finisher picker lap...............................	4.82	6.61	6.10	5.76
Finisher picker lap during carding................	6.81	7.00	6.91	6.99
Card sliver.....................................	6.82	6.78	6.64	6.46
Finisher drawing:				
59 grain sliver...............................	7.35	7.06	6.15	6.15
73 grain sliver...............................	6.67	7.12	6.38	6.27
Roving frames:				
2.00 hank for 16's...........................	6.61	6.55	6.27	6.27
4.40 hank for 22's...........................	5.99	6.10	6.38	6.33
5.40 hank for 28's...........................	7.00	6.84	6.95	6.89
Ring spinning frame:				
16's yarn....................................	6.67	6.55	6.61	6.55
22's yarn....................................	6.78	6.78	6.78	6.72
28's yarn....................................	7.06	7.00	6.44	6.84

BREAKING STRENGTH OF YARNS.

The cotton of each compression was spun into 16's, 22's, and 28's yarn with twists equal to 4.25, 4.50, and 4.75 times the square root of the number spun. The average breaking strength of these yarns are shown in Table 4.

TABLE 4.—*Breaking strength in pounds per skein of 120 yards of yarn spun from Cleveland Big Boll cotton, fifteen-sixteenths-inch staple.*

No. of yarn.	New Draper standard.	Twist multiplier.	Type of bale.			
			Flat.	Standard.	High density.	High density wet.
	Pounds.		*Pounds.*	*Pounds.*	*Pounds.*	*Pounds.*
16's	120	4.25	109.1	101.2	110.3	94.8
		4.50	107.0	102.4	107.5	92.0
		4.75	106.8	102.6	107.5	93.5
		Average..	107.6	102.1	108.4	93.4
22's	87	4.25	73.3	70.7	74.5	64.7
		4.50	73.0	70.9	74.3	65.7
		4.75	72.7	70.6	73.1	65.0
		Average..	73.0	70.7	74.0	65.1
28's	69	4.25	54.7	53.2	54.5	47.3
		4.50	53.1	52.7	54.1	48.0
		4.75	52.4	51.9	54.9	48.0
		Average..	53.4	52.6	54.5	47.8

Referring to Table 4 and comparing the breaking strength of the yarn spun from the cotton of the different types of bales, it is seen that there is practically no difference between the strength of the yarns obtained from the flat bale and the high-density bale compressed under normal conditions. The standard bale produced yarns slightly weaker than those produced from either the flat or high-density bale compressed under normal conditions, while the high-density bale compressed while wet produced yarns about 12 per cent weaker.

None of the yarns broke as strong as the new Draper standard. This weakness may have been due to the excessive rainfall, which delayed the opening of the bolls and the picking of the cotton.

IRREGULARITY OF YARNS.

The following figures give the irregularity of the sizings and breaking strengths of the yarns from the different types of bales:

	Sizing (per cent).	Break (per cent).
Flat bale	1.97	3.72
Standard or railroad compressed bale	1.98	4.30
High-density bale	2.17	4.02
High-density bale compressed wet	2.22	4.18

These figures indicate that there is practically no difference in the irregularity of the sizings or strengths of the yarns from the different types of bales.

The results of the calculations of the irregularity of the yarns are verified by tests on the Moscrop single-strand tester. Figure 1 is a photograph of a chart made by this tester when breaking 22's yarn spun from cotton compressed to different densities.

Each dot in Figure 1 represents the breaking strength of a single strand of yarn 12 inches long. The greater the distance these dots are from a horizontal line, the more irregular the yarn.

Plate IV, Figure 1, is from a photograph of 22's yarn spun from the Cleveland Big Boll cotton which shows practically no difference in the quality of the yarn spun from the different types of bales.

MANUFACTURING PROPERTIES.

There was no noticeable difference in the running of the different types of bales.

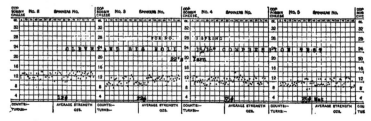

Fig. 1.—Irregularity of 22's yarn spun from Cleveland Big Boll cotton compressed to different densities.

SUMMARY OF TESTS.

The results of this test indicate that compressing cotton in a dry or normal condition does not injure its spinning value.

Compressing cotton to high density while wet increased the waste approximately 2 per cent, and it also caused a decrease in the breaking strength of the yarn of about 12 per cent.

SPINNING TESTS OF ROWDEN COTTON OF 1-INCH STAPLE.

The Rowden cotton was compressed into four types of bales: A flat bale, a standard or railroad compressed bale, a high-density bale, and a round bale.

PERCENTAGE OF WASTE.

Table 5 gives the percentage of visible, invisible, and total waste obtained from the different types of bales.

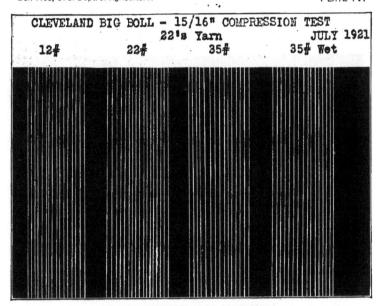

FIG. I.—PHOTOGRAPH OF 22'S YARN SPUN FROM CLEVELAND BIG BOLL
COTTON COMPRESSED TO DIFFERENT DENSITIES.

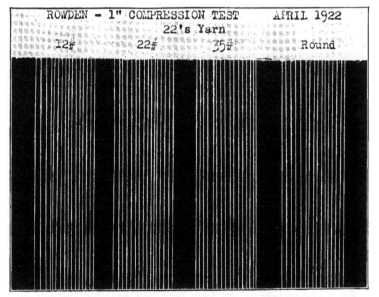

FIG. 2.—PHOTOGRAPH OF 22'S YARN SPUN FROM ROWDEN I-INCH COTTON
COMPRESSED TO DIFFERENT DENSITIES.

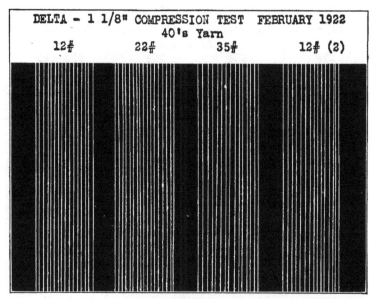

DELTA - 1 1/8" COMPRESSION TEST   FEBRUARY 1922
40's Yarn
12#   22#   35#   12# (2)

FIG. 1.—PHOTOGRAPH OF 40's YARN SPUN FROM DELTA 1⅛-INCH COTTON COMPRESSED TO DIFFERENT DENSITIES.

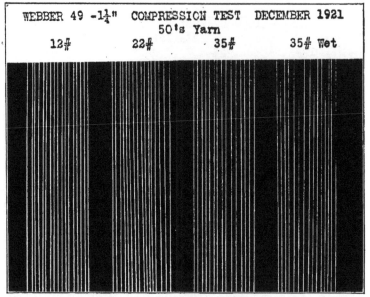

WEBBER 49 -1¼"   COMPRESSION TEST   DECEMBER 1921
50's Yarn
12#   22#   35#   35# Wet

FIG. 2.—PHOTOGRAPH OF 50's YARN SPUN FROM WEBBER 49 COTTON COMPRESSED TO DIFFERENT DENSITIES.

TABLE 5.—*Percentage of waste from Rowden cotton of 1-inch staple; grade, Strict Middling.*

Type of bale	Flat.	Stand-ard.	High density.	Round.
PICKER WASTE.[1]	*Per cent.*	*Per cent.*	*Per cent.*	*Per cent.*
Opener-breaker motes and fly	0.95	0.77	0.76	0.68
Finisher motes and fly	.89	.78	.92	.81
Total visible	1.84	1.55	1.68	1.49
Invisible	.85	.46	.77	.14
Total visible and invisible	2.69	2.01	2.45	1.63
CARD WASTE.[2]				
Flat strips	1.85	1.78	1.68	1.76
Cylinder and doffer strips	.77	.81	.82	.79
Motes and fly	2.50	2.40	2.35	2.50
Sweepings	.14	.05	.05	.05
Total visible	5.26	5.04	4.90	5.10
Invisible	.13	[3].58	[3].10	[3].32
Total visible and invisible	5.39	4.46	4.80	4.78
PICKERS AND CARDS.[1]				
Total visible	6.96	6.49	6.46	6.51
Total invisible	.98	[3].11	.67	[3].17
Total visible and invisible	7.94	6.38	7.13	6.34

[1] Based upon net weight fed to bale-breaker.
[2] Based upon net weight fed to cards.
[3] Gain.

Referring to Table 5 and comparing the percentages of waste obtained from the different types of bales, it is seen that there is practically no difference between the amount of visible waste discarded, the figures being:

Per cent.

Flat bale	6.96
Standard or railroad compressed bale	6.49
High-density bale	6.46
Round bale	6.51

MOISTURE CONDITIONS.

Table 6 gives the average temperatures and relative humidities under which each type of bale was tested.

TABLE 6.—*Average temperatures and relative humidities during the testing of Rowden cotton of 1-inch staple.*

Type of bale	Flat.		Standard.		High density.		Round.	
	Temper-ature.	Relative humid-ity.	Temper-ature.	Relative humid-ity.	Temper-ature.	Relative humid-ity.	Temper-ature.	Relative humid-ity.
STAGE.	*° F.*	*Per cent.*	*° F.*	*Per cent.*	*° F.*	*Per cent.*	*° F.*	*Per cent.*
When opened	67	49	71	50	71	53	70	42
Finisher picker	76	51	73	54	72	41	74	61
Card	73	58	73	61	71	58	74	59
Drawing frames:								
53 grain sliver	72	58	73	60	72	59	75	59
73 grain sliver	74	59	74	61	72	60	74	58
Roving frames:								
4.00 hank fine	73	59	73	59	73	59	73	59
4.40 hank fine	73	59	73	59	73	59	73	60
5.60 hank fine	73	59	72	59	73	59	73	60
7.23 hank fine	73	60	73	59	73	60	73	60
Spinning frame:								
16's yarn	79	73	74	73	79	73	81	71
22's yarn	77	72	75	71	77	72	73	72
28's yarn	73	70	75	71	73	70	72	69
36's yarn	81	73	78	70	81	73	76	71

Table 7 gives the percentage of moisture regain of the cotton at the various stages of the manufacturing process.

TABLE 7.—*Percentage of moisture regain in the Rowden cotton at the different stages of the manufacturing process.*

Type of bale	Flat.	Standard.	High density.	Round.
STAGE OR SAMPLE.	*Per cent.*	*Per cent.*	*Per cent.*	*Per cent.*
From bale	5.76	5.43	5.63	4.42
From bale-breaker	5.54	5.26	5.55	4.60
Finisher picker lap	5.57	5.65	5.26	5.26
Finisher picker lap during carding	5.19	5.57	4.90	5.50
Card sliver	5.32	5.57	4.95	5.82
53 grain finisher drawing	5.65	5.85	4.79	6.04
73 grain finisher drawing	5.82	5.87	5.45	5.79
Roving frames:				
4.00 hank, fine	5.76	5.81	5.09	5.54
4.40 hank, fine	6.10	6.10	6.43	6.38
5.60 hank, fine	6.43	6.49	6.49	5.76
7.23 hank, fine	5.93	6.15	5.09	6.10
Spinning frame:				
16's yarn	6.49	5.59	6.78	6.49
22's yarn	7.35	7.18	7.70	7.06
28's yarn	6.66	6.89	6.84	5.54
36's yarn	6.72	6.38	6.72	6.72

BREAKING STRENGTH OF YARNS.

The cotton of each compression was spun into 16's, 22's, 28's, and 36's yarn with twists equal to 4.25, 4.50, and 4.75 times the square root of the number spun. The average breaking strengths of these yarns are shown in Table 8.

TABLE 8.—*Breaking strength, in pounds, per skein of 120 yards of yarn spun from Rowden cotton, 1 inch staple.*

No. of yarn.	New Draper standard.	Twist multiplier.	Type of bale.			
			Flat.	Standard.	High density.	Round.
	Pounds.		*Pounds.*	*Pounds.*	*Pounds.*	*Pounds.*
16's	120	4.25	140.8	141.3	141.9	132.4
		4.50	133.8	142.8	137.7	131.1
		4.75	128.7	137.0	137.8	129.6
		Average..	134.4	140.4	139.1	131.0
22's	87	4.25	92.0	99.4	94.9	87.3
		4.50	92.7	97.5	94.1	89.3
		4.75	89.9	94.9	95.7	87.3
		Average..	91.5	97.3	94.9	88.0
28's	69	4.25	68.0	73.0	70.3	63.3
		4.50	67.4	72.9	71.3	64.4
		4.75	65.7	70.8	68.0	63.7
		Average..	67.0	72.2	69.9	63.8
36's	54	4.25	48.3	51.0	50.6	44.2
		4.50	47.6	50.9	50.5	46.2
		4.75	47.0	50.7	49.5	45.7
		Average..	47.6	50.9	50.2	45.4

Referring to Table 8 and comparing the breaking strength of the yarn spun from the cotton of the different types of bales, it is seen that the strongest results were obtained from the standard bale, followed in order by the high density bale, flat bale, and round bale.

All the 16's and 22's yarn broke stronger than the new Draper standard. All the 28's yarn, with the exception of that spun from the round bale, broke practically as strong as the standard strength for this number. The 36's yarn spun from all the types of bales was weaker than the standard strength for this number.

On an average, the yarns spun from the round bale were about 7 per cent weaker than the yarns spun from the other types.

IRREGULARITY OF YARNS.

The following figures give the irregularity of the sizings and breaking strengths of the yarns from the different types of bales:

	Sizing (per·cent).	Break (per cent).
Flat bale	1. 98	4. 15
Standard or railroad compressed bale	1. 93	3. 87
High-density bale	1. 91	3. 97
Round bale	2. 22	4. 66

These figures indicate that there is practically no difference in the irregularity of the sizings or strengths of the yarn spun from the first three types of bales but the yarn from the round bale was slightly more uneven.

The results of the calculations of the irregularity of the yarns are verified by tests on the Moscrop single-strand tester. Figure 2 is a photograph of a chart made by this tester when breaking 22's yarn spun from the Rowden cotton compressed to different densities.

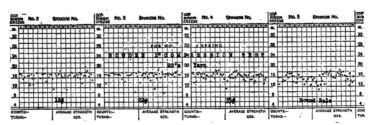

Fig. 2.—Irregularity of 22's yarn spun from Rowden 1″ cotton compressed to different densities.

Each dot of figure 2 represents the breaking strength of a single strand of yarn 12 inches long. The greater the distance these dots are from a horizontal line, the more irregular the yarn.

Plate IV, Figure 2, is from a photograph of 22's yarn spun from the Rowden cotton which shows practically no difference in the quality of the yarn spun from the different types of bales.

MANUFACTURING PROPERTIES.

There was no noticeable difference in running the rectangular bales. A mill attempting to run round bales continuously must use special opening equipment.

SUMMARY OF TESTS.

The results of this test show that compressing cotton does not affect the amount of waste discarded in the manufacturing process. On an average, the yarn spun from the round bale was about 7 per cent weaker than that spun from the other types of bales.

SPINNING TESTS OF DELTA COTTON OF 1 1-8 INCH STAPLE.

The Delta cotton was compressed into three types of bales: A flat bale, a standard or railroad compressed bale, and a high-density bale.

PERCENTAGE OF WASTE.

Table 9 gives the percenta e of visible, invisible, and total waste obtained from the different types of bales.

TABLE 9.—*Percentage of waste from Delta cotton of 1¼ inch staple; grade, Middling.*

Type of bale	Flat.	Standard.	High density.
PICKER WASTE.[1]	Per cent.	Per cent.	Per cent.
Opener-breaker motes and fly	1.00	0.95	0.86
Intermediate motes and fly	.93	1.17	1.16
Finisher motes and fly	.58	.94	.76
Total visible	2.51	3.06	2.78
Invisible	1.29	1.46	1.26
Total visible and invisible	3.80	4.52	4.04
CARD WASTE.[2]			
Flat strips	2.63	2.58	2.81
Cylinder and doffer strips	1.10	1.12	1.22
Motes and fly	2.04	1.99	2.17
Sweepings	.10	.12	.08
Total visible	5.87	5.81	6.28
Invisible	1.50	1.08	1.34
Total visible and invisible	7.37	6.89	7.62
PICKERS AND CARDS.[1]			
Total visible	8.15	8.61	8.81
Total invisible	2.74	2.49	2.55
Total visible and invisible	10.89	11.10	11.36

[1] Based upon net weight fed to bale-breaker.
[2] Based upon net weight fed to cards.

Referring to Table 9 and comparing the percentages of waste obtained from the different types of bales, it is seen that there is practically no difference between the amount of visible waste discarded, the figures being:

Per cent.
Flat bale... 8.15
Standard or railroad compressed bale...................... 8.61
High-density bale... 8.81

MOISTURE CONDITIONS.

Table 10 gives the average temperatures and relative humidities under which each type of bale was tested.

TABLE 10.—*Average temperatures and relative humidities during the testing of Delta cotton of 1⅛-inch staple.*

Type of bale	Flat.		Standard.		High density.	
	Tem-perature.	Relative hu-midity.	Tem-perature.	Relative hu-midity.	Tem-perature.	Relative hu-midity.
STAGE.	° F.	Per cent.	° F.	Per cent.	° F.	Per cent.
When opened	74	52	73	50	66	45
Finisher picker	72	51	72	45	72	50
Card	72	60	66	54	70	59
Drawing frames, 50 grain sliver	76	61	61	58	72	60
Roving frames:						
6.66 hank, fine frame	68	55	70	58	70	58
8.00 hank, jack frame	72	56	70	58	70	57
11.11 hank, jack frame	72	54	72	55	73	54
Spinning frame:						
30's yarn	69	63	74	68	69	63
40's yarn	75	65	77	68	75	65
50's yarn	72	69	75	64	75	64

Table 11 gives the percentage of moisture regain of the cotton at the various stages of the manufacturing process.

TABLE 11.—*Percentage of moisture regain in the Delta 1⅛-inch cotton at the different stages of the manufacturing process.*

Type of bale	Flat.	Standard.	High density.
STAGE OR SAMPLE.	Per cent.	Per cent.	Per cent.
From bale	5.95	7.05	6.26
From bale-breaker	6.22	6.59	6.04
Finisher picker lap	5.47	5.43	6.04
Finisher picker lap during carding	5.63	5.23	5.71
Card sliver	5.70	4.88	5.59
Finisher drawing sliver	6.58	5.18	5.87
Roving frames:			
6.66 hank, fine frame	5.04	5.93	5.37
8.00 hank, jack frame	6.38	6.32	6.38
11.11 hank, jack frame	5.76	6.10	6.26
Ring spinning frame:			
30's yarn	5.26	6.10	5.31
40's yarn	5.48	6.55	5.70
50's yarn	5.65	6.32	6.32

BREAKING STRENGTH OF YARNS.

The cotton of each compression was spun into 30's, 40's, and 50's yarn with twists equal to 4.25, 4.50, and 4.75 times the square root of the number spun. The average breaking strengths of these yarns are shown in Table 12.

Referring to Table 12 and comparing the breaking strength of the yarn spun from the cotton of the different types of bales, it is seen that there is practically no difference between the strength of the yarns spun from the different types of bales.

TABLE 12.—*Breaking strength in pounds per skein of 120 yards of yarn spun from Delta cotton, 1⅛-inch staple.*

No. of yarn.	New draper standard.	Twist multiplier.	Type of bale.		
			Flat.	Standard.	High density.
	Pounds.		*Pounds.*	*Pounds.*	*Pounds.*
30's...	64	4. 25	50. 5	51. 8	48. 5
		4. 50	51. 6	51. 3	48. 6
		4. 75	49. 6	49. 1	47. 3
		Average..	50. 6	50. 7	48. 1
40's...	48	4. 25	34. 0	35. 5	32. 7
		4. 50	33. 6	35. 0	32. 7
		4. 75	33. 8	34. 1	32. 2
		Average..	33. 8	34. 9	32. 5
50's...	39	4. 25	24. 3	24. 3	23. 6
		4. 50	24. 3	24. 3	23. 2
		4. 75	24. 2	23. 6	23. 0
		Average..	24. 3	24. 1	23. 3

None of the yarns broke as strong as the new Draper standard. This weakness is probably due to the excessive rainfall which delayed the opening of the bolls and the picking of the cotton.

IRREGULARITY OF YARNS.

The following figures give the irregularity of the sizings and breaking strengths of the yarns from the different types of bales:

	Sizing (per cent).	Break (per cent.)
Flat bale...	2. 06	4. 53
Standard or railroad compressed bale...................	1. 85	5. 18
High-density bale....................................	2. 60	5. 18

These figures indicate that there is practically no difference in the irregularity of the sizings or strengths of the yarns from the different types of bales.

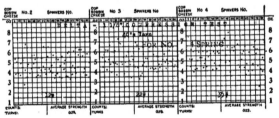

FIG. 3.—Irregularity of 40's yarn spun from Delta 1⅛″ cotton compressed to different densities.

The results of the calculations of the irregularity of the yarns are verified by tests on the Moscrop single-strand tester. Figure 3 is a photograph of a chart made by this tester when breaking 40's yarn spun from cotton compressed to different densities.

Each dot on Figure 3 represents the breaking strength of a single strand of yarn 12 inches long. The greater the distance these dots are from a horizontal line the more irregular the yarn.

Plate V, Figure 1, is from a photograph of 40's yarn spun from the Delta 1⅜-inch cotton which shows practically no difference in the quality of the yarn spun from the different types of bales.

MANUFACTURING PROPERTIES.

There was no noticeable difference in the running of the different types of bales.

SUMMARY OF TESTS.

The results of this test show that compressing cotton does not injure its spinning value.

SPINNING TESTS OF WEBBER 49 COTTON OF 1¼ INCH STAPLE.

The Webber 49 cotton was compressed into four bales: A flat bale, a standard or railroad compressed bale, a high-density bale, and a high-density bale compressed in a wet condition. The latter bale was made by wetting a flat bale with water from a hose for a day and then compressing it to high density in the usual manner.

PERCENTAGE OF WASTE.

Table 13 gives the percentage of visible, invisible, and total waste obtained from the different types of bales.

TABLE 13.—*Percentage of waste from Webber 49 cotton of 1¼-inch staple; grade, Middling.*

Type of bale	Flat.	Standard	High density	High density wet.
PICKER WASTE. [1]	Per cent.	Per cent.	Per cent.	Per cent.
Opener-breaker motes and fly	0.75	0.74	0.78	0.85
Intermediate motes and fly	.74	.81	.67	.75
Finisher motes and fly	.49	.56	.86	.87
Total visible	1.98	2.11	2.31	2.47
Invisible	1.75	2.13	1.33	2.36
Total visible and invisible	3.73	4.24	3.64	4.83
CARD WASTE. [2]				
Flat strips	2.95	2.93	3.27	3.85
Cylinder and doffer strips	1.08	1.10	1.22	1.20
Motes and fly	1.68	1.63	1.73	1.78
Sweepings	.06	.10	.10	.05
Total visible	5.77	5.76	6.32	6.88
Invisible	[4].35	.77	.42	[4]1.12
Total visible and invisible	5.42	6.53	6.74	5.76
PICKER AND CARDS. [1]				
Total visible	7.54	7.62	8.40	9.02
Total invisible	1.41	2.87	1.74	1.29
Total visible and invisible	8.95	10.49	10.14	10.31
COMBER. [3]				
Visible waste	16.72	16.68	15.83	16.92
Invisible waste	.32	[4].34	1.10	.53
Total visible and invisible	17.04	16.34	16.93	17.45
PICKER, CARDS, AND COMBER [1]				
Total visible waste	22.78	22.54	22.63	24.20
Total invisible waste	1.70	2.57	2.73	1.77
Total visible and invisible	24.48	25.11	25.36	25.97

[1] Based upon net weight fed to bale-breaker.
[2] Based upon net weight fed to cards.
[3] Based upon net weight fed to comber.
[4] Gain.

Referring to Table 13 and comparing the percentage of waste obtained from the different types of bales, it is seen that there was practically no difference in the amount of visible waste discarded from the flat, standard, and high-density bales compressed in a dry or normal condition, while the high-density bale compressed in a wet condition was about 2 per cent more wasty. The percentages of visible waste obtained from the different types of bales were as follows:

	Per cent.
Flat bale	22.78
Standard or railroad compressed bale	22.54
High-density bale	22.63
High-density bale compressed wet	24.20

MOISTURE CONDITIONS.

Table 14 gives the average temperatures and relative humidities under which each type of bale was tested.

TABLE 14.—*Average temperatures and relative humidities during the testing of Webber 49 cotton of 1¼ inch staple.*

Type of bale	Flat.		Standard.		High density.		High density compressed wet.	
	Temperature.	Relative humidity.	Temperature.	Relative humidity.	Temperature.	Relative humidity.	Temperature.	Relative humidity.
STAGE.	°F.	Per cent.	°F.	Per cent.	°F.	Per cent.	°F.	Per cent.
When opened	75	51	71	40	87	58	83	64
Finisher picker	75	44	73	46	83	63	87	58
Card	76	56	70	51	79	59	82	61
Comber	73	54	78	57	71	52	82	58
Drawing frames	70	52	75	57	66	51	82	55
Roving frames:								
7.30 hank, fine	72	56	71	55	71	55	72	56
10.00 hank, jack	72	58	72	58	71	57	72	57
12.00 hank, jack	72	58	72	57	71	57	72	57
Spinning frame:								
40's yarn	74	66	74	66	75	73	75	73
50's yarn	70	65	70	65	74	67	74	67
60's yarn	72	68	72	68	72	69	72	69

Table 15 gives the percentage of moisture regain of the cotton at the various stages of the manufacturing process.

TABLE 15.—*Percentage of moisture regain in the Webber 49 cotton at the different stages of the manufacturing process.*

Type of bale	Flat.	Standard.	High density.	High density. wet.
STAGE OR SAMPLE.	Per cent.	Per cent.	Per cent.	Per cent.
From bale	6.36	7.15	7.07	7.74
Finisher picker lap	4.17	5.57	6.67	6.27
Finisher picker lap during carding	6.06	5.53	7.79	7.72
Card sliver	5.78	5.40	6.84	6.85
Comber sliver	5.31	5.80	5.73	6.24
Finisher drawing sliver	5.54	6.15	5.59	6.21
Roving frames:				
7.30 hank, fine	6.38	6.67	7.07	7.41
10.00 hank, jack	5.26	4.98	6.15	6.21
12.00 hank, jack	5.87	6.15	6.60	6.6
Spinning frame:				
40's yarn	6.44	6.44	7.30	7.41
50's yarn	5.48	5.65	5.48	5.42
60's yarn	5.98	5.93	6.32	6.21

BREAKING STRENGTH OF YARNS.

The cotton of each compression was spun into 40's, 50's, and 60's yarn with twists equal to 4.00, 4.25, and 4.50 times the square root of the number spun. The average breaking strength of these yarns are shown in Table 16.

TABLE 16.—*Breaking strength in pounds per skein of 120 yards of yarn spun from Webber 49 cotton, 1¼ inch staple.*

No. of yarn.	New Draper standard	Twist multiplier.	Type of bale.			
			Flat.	Stand-ard.	High density.	High density wet.
	Pounds.		*Pounds.*	*Pounds.*	*Pounds.*	*Pounds.*
40's	61	4.00	44.2	45.7	46.7	47.0
		4.25	45.3	47.0	46.0	46.0
		4.50	44.2	45.7	45.7	46.2
		Average..	44.6	46.1	46.1	46.4
50's	48	4.00	35.0	36.5	36.4	34.5
		4.25	35.0	35.3	34.7	33.8
		4.50	34.0	34.7	34.6	33.2
		Average..	34.7	35.5	35.2	33.8
60's	39	4.00	25.9	26.3	25.8	25.9
		4.25	24.8	25.9	25.5	24.9
		4.50	25.5	25.6	24.8	24.5
		Average..	25.4	25.9	25.4	25.1

Table 16 shows that there is ract ca no difference between the strength of the yarns spun from the different types of bales. None of the yarns broke as strong as the new Draper standard.

IRREGULARITY OF YARNS.

The following figures give the irregularity in the sizings and breaking strengths of the yarns spun from the different types of bales:

	Sizing (per cent).	Break (per cent).
Flat bale	1.92	5.51
Standard or railroad compressed bale	2.02	4.96
High-density bale	1.98	4.73
High-density bale compressed wet	2.00	4.68

These figures indicate that there is practically no difference in the irregularity of the sizings or strengths of the yarns from the different types of bales.

The results of the calculations of the irregularity of the yarns are verified by tests on the Moscrop single-strand tester. Figure 4 is a photograph of a chart made by this tester when breaking 50's yarn spun from cotton compressed to different densities.

Each dot in this figure represents the breaking strength of a single strand of yarn 12 inches long. The greater the distance these dots are from a horizontal line, the more irregular the yarn.

Plate V, Figure 2, is from a photograph of 50's yarn spun from the Webber 49, 1¼ inch cotton which shows practically no difference in the quality of the yarn spun from the different types of bales.

MANUFACTURING PROPERTIES.

There was no noticeable difference in the running of any of the bales.

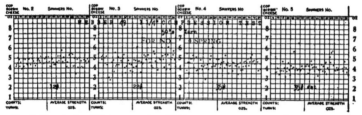

Fig. 4.—Irregularity of 50's yarn spun from Webber 49 cotton compressed to different densities.

SUMMARY OF TESTS.

The results of this test show that compressing cotton in a dry or normal condition does not injure its spinning value.

Compressed cotton to high density while wet increased the waste approximately 2 per cent, but did not materially affect the breaking strength.

CONCLUSIONS.

All of these tests showed that compressing cotton to standard or high density when in a dry or normal condition is not injurious to its spinning value.

Compressing wet cotton to high density either increases the percentage of waste or reduces the breaking strength of the yarn, or may do both.

Compressing cotton into a round bale with a hard core reduces the strength of the yarn about 7 per cent. If the round bale were to be run continuously in a mill, special opening equipment would be required.

ORGANIZATION OF THE UNITED STATES DEPARTMENT OF AGRICULTURE.

Secretary of Agriculture	HENRY C. WALLACE.
Assistant Secretary	C. W. PUGSLEY.
Director of Scientific Work	E. D. BALL.
Director of Regulatory Work	
Weather Bureau	CHARLES F. MARVIN, *Chief.*
Bureau of Agricultural Economics	HENRY C. TAYLOR, *Chief.*
Bureau of Animal Industry	JOHN R. MOHLER, *Chief.*
Bureau of Plant Industry	WILLIAM A. TAYLOR, *Chief.*
Forest Service	W. B. GREELEY, *Chief.*
Bureau of Chemistry	WALTER G. CAMPBELL, *Acting Chief.*
Bureau of Soils	MILTON WHITNEY, *Chief.*
Bureau of Entomology	L. O. HOWARD, *Chief.*
Bureau of Biological Survey	E. W. NELSON, *Chief.*
Bureau of Public Roads	THOMAS H. MACDONALD, *Chief.*
Fixed Nitrogen Research Laboratory	F. G. COTTRELL, *Director.*
Division of Accounts and Disbursements	A. ZAPPONE, *Chief.*
Division of Publications	JOHN L. COBBS, Jr., *Chief.*
Library	CLARIBEL R. BARNETT, *Librarian.*
States Relations Service	A. C. TRUE, *Director.*
Federal Horticultural Board	C. L. MARLATT, *Chairman.*
Insecticide and Fungicide Board	J. K. HAYWOOD, *Chairman.*
Packers and Stockyards Administration	⎱ CHESTER MORRILL, *Assistant to*
Grain Future Trading Act Administration	⎰ *the Secretary.*
Office of the Solicitor	R. W. WILLIAMS, *Solicitor.*

This bulletin is a contribution from—

Bureau of Agricultural Economics,	HENRY C. TAYLOR, *Chief.*
Division of Cotton	WM. R. MEADOWS, *in Charge.*

19

UNITED STATES DEPARTMENT OF AGRICULTURE

BULLETIN No. 1136

Washington, D. C. ▼ May 12, 1923

KILN DRYING HANDBOOK.

By Rolf Thelen, *In Charge, Section of Timber Physics, Forest Products Laboratory, Forest Service.*

CONTENTS.

PURPOSE.

The principal purpose of this bulletin is to present to the dry-kiln operator, in condensed and convenient form, the fundamental facts about the drying of wood which he must know in order to get the most satisfactory results with his kiln. The major portion of the bulletin deals with the kiln drying of lumber, but there are also included specific suggestions concerning the drying of other forms of wood. The general information is applicable to all kinds of drying.

No attempt has been made to present detailed data in substantiation of the information given. The conclusions are for the most part based on extensive investigations and experiments by the Forest Products Laboratory of the Forest Service, Department of Agriculture, Madison, Wis., tested out in commercial practice.

MOISTURE IN WOOD.

The purpose of drying or seasoning wood is to remove a certain amount of the moisture which is naturally present in it, and which if allowed to remain would interfere with its use for most construction purposes. The exact amount of moisture to be removed de-

NOTE.—Acknowledgement is made by the author to the members of the Section of Timber Physics, both past and present, who are largely responsible for the development of the practical technique of kiln drying described in this bulletin.

23241°—23——1

pends upon the quantity present and the purpose for which the wood is to be used. Rarely, except for test pieces, is it necessary or desirable to remove all the moisture, producing an oven-dry or bone-dry condition.

Moisture in wood is commonly called sap. There is no universally accepted definition of this word "sap," and its use causes much confusion. The moisture, or sap, in both sapwood and heartwood consists almost entirely of water. It does contain, however, small percentages of organic and mineral matter. In the sapwood these substances are principally sugars of various kinds, and in the heartwood they include tannins, coloring matter, and various other chemicals. For the purposes of this bulletin, sap will be considered to be water only.

Water occurs in wood in two distinct forms, spoken of as "free" water and "imbibed" water. The free water exists in the cell cavities and the imbibed water in the cell walls. Imagine each cell of the wood to be a small bucket of some porous or absorbent material. If this bucket is filled with water, a certain amount will be absorbed by the sides and bottom, in addition to the "pailful" inside the bucket. This pailful is free water, that absorbed by the walls is imbibed water, and the sum of the two represents all the water the bucket, or the cell, can hold. A portion or all of the free water can be removed from the cell without changing the amount of imbibed water in the walls; but when the bucket is empty further drying removes water from the walls themselves and they begin to dry out. This point at which the bucket becomes empty is called the "fiber-saturation point." It has a very important bearing upon the process of drying and will be discussed more fully later.

In most living trees there is some free water in both heartwood and sapwood. The amount varies considerably depending on a number of factors. Thus, sapwood almost always contains more moisture than heartwood. The butt may contain much more than the top, as is evidenced by the sinker stock of redwood and sugar pine. The season of year in which the trees are felled may have some influence upon the moisture in the sapwood, but this influence is not very important. There are a number of instances on record in which there was more moisture present in the sapwood in winter than in summer. The common conception is that the reverse is true.

Species and locality of growth have an important bearing upon the amount of moisture in the living tree. Species growing in swampy regions are apt to contain much more moisture and to be harder to dry than similar upland species. The oaks are an excellent illustration of this fact. On the other hand, certain species contain comparatively large amounts of water, even though growing under reasonably dry conditions. All of these variations must be taken into consideration in the drafting of drying schedules and in the actual drying operation.

MOISTURE DETERMINATION.

To dry stock successfully and to know when it has reached the proper dryness, it is essential that the operator be able to determine the amount of moisture in wood at any time. There are several methods by which the moisture content of wood may be determined, but the following is the one commonly used for moisture determinations on lumber.

Crosscut the board or stock at least 2 feet from one end, to avoid the effect of end drying, and then again about three-fourths inch from the first cut, thus securing a section as wide and thick as the original board and three-fourths inch long with the grain. Remove all loose splinters from the section and weigh it immediately on a sensitive scale. Record the weight, called "original weight." Place the section in a drying oven kept at a temperature of about 212° F., leaving it there until it no longer loses weight. This requires from 12 to 24 hours, sometimes longer. Leaving the sections in the oven longer than the required time produces an appreciable error in the result. Remove the section from the oven and again weigh it. This will be the "oven-dry" weight, the actual weight of the wood. The difference between the original and oven-dry weights is the weight of water originally in the section, and the moisture percentage is readily calculated.

Divide the difference between the two weights by the oven-dry weight, and to reduce to per cent multiply by 100. The formula is:

$$\frac{\text{Original weight—oven-dry weight}}{\text{oven-dry weight}} \times 100 = \text{moisture content in per cent.}$$

Thus, if the green weight is 180 and the oven-dry weight 150, a difference of 30, the moisture percentage will be $\frac{30}{150} \times 100 = 20$ per cent. The moisture content so determined is based on the oven-dry weight of the wood. It is, however, possible to base it upon the original weight. This system is occasionally used for moisture determinations by those who are accustomed to use it for other purposes. Its use is not recommended for wood sections, but it is occasionally necessary to convert moistures from one system to the other. The calculating and conversion formulas are given.

$$\text{Moisture content based on original weight, in per cent} = \frac{\text{original weight—oven-dry weight}}{\text{original weight}} \times 100.$$

In this system the original weight equals 100 per cent, whereas in the other the oven-dry weight equals 100 per cent.

To convert moistures from one system to the other, use the following formula:

$$\text{Moisture based on oven-dry weight} = \frac{\text{moisture based on original weight}}{1 - \text{moisture based on original weight}}.$$

BALANCES.

Any system of weights may be used, but the metric system is more convenient than the others and is preferred for this reason. The unit of this system is the gram, and weights are expressed as grams and decimal fractions thereof.

The choice of balance is a matter of personal preference and of first cost. For general use the balance should have a capacity of 1 kilogram (1,000 grams) and be sensitive to 0.1 gram. These requirements are met by the ordinary analytical type of balance in which the two pans are suspended from an overhead beam. Other types are the Harvard trip, which has the beam located under the pans and is provided with a scale beam and rider sensitive to 0.1 gram, and with a 10-gram capacity; the torsion balance, with beams below the pans; and the multiple-beam balance, with only one pan suspended from the beam, which is provided with sliding weights.

DRYING OVENS.

Several makes of drying ovens can be bought. All of these are electrically heated and provided with thermostatic control, which keeps the temperature accurately at the desired point. Steam-heated ovens are convenient and free from trouble and will be found excellent where high-pressure steam is continuously available. Ovens of this kind are usually homemade. The walls and doors can be of galvanized iron, made hollow with a 1½-inch space filled with mineral wool, and the heating element can be conveniently made of 1-inch or 1¼-inch pipe. Ventilators should be fitted to the top, and provision made under the steam pipes for the entrance of fresh air. The temperature is usually regulated by means of a reducing valve on the steam line and dampers on the ventilators. For each cubic foot of volume above the heating coils in the oven there should be at least 1½ square feet of heating surface and six square inches of ventilator area. Shelves should be provided for the moisture sections. Plate I illustrates one of the steam drying ovens used by the Forest Products Laboratory.   .

There are available various kinds of hot plates used in place of ovens for drying out moisture sections. It is customary to use very thin sections with these hot plates and to leave them on only a short time—15 to 45 minutes. These hot plates fill a need in that they are cheap and used by those who do not care to buy a regular oven, and in the hands of a skillful operator can be made to yield good results. They can not be recommended except as makeshifts.

It is very helpful, except in the simplest kinds of drying, to know how the moisture is distributed throughout the cross section of the board or stick, and for this purpose "moisture distributions" are made. The moisture section is cut in the usual manner, but instead of weighing it as a whole, it is cut or split so as to separate the core or center from the shell or outside, and separate moisture determinations are made on the core and shell. The latter will usually be in two or four pieces, which can be most conveniently weighed as a single unit. For thick stock it may be desirable to divide the sections into three units, a shell, an intermediate zone, and the core. The procedure is precisely the same as before, the pieces of the intermediate zone being weighed as a unit just as are those of the shell. To secure satisfactory results, these "moisture distributions" must be made accurately, and an analytical or torsion balance sensitive to 0.01 gram should be used. The capacity of this balance need not be over 100 grams. A larger balance should also be available for the heavier work of weighing regular moisture sections.

Figure 1 illustrates the method of cutting the moisture and distribution sections. While it is the usual practice to cut a full section and a distribution section whenever a distribution test is to be made, it is not absolutely necessary, since the average moisture content may

Steam Oven Used at the Forest Products Laboratory for Drying Moisture Sections. The Thermometer, Shelves, and a Portion of the Heating Coils Can Be Seen in the Open Sections.

FIG. I.—HEATER UNIT FOR EXTERNAL BLOWER.

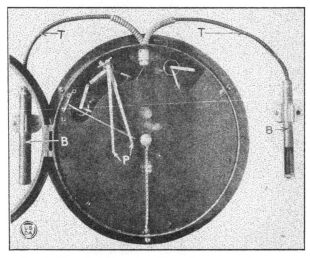

FIG. 2.—TWO-PEN EXTENSION TUBE RECORDING THERMOME-
TER SECTIONED AND WITH CHART REMOVED.

The bulbs *B* are connected to the instrument through the armored tubing *T*
entering at the top of the case. The pens *P* and pen arms are slightly to the
left of the center.

be secured with reasonable accuracy from the distribution section alone by assuming the original weights of all the pieces to be the original weight of the section, and similarly with the dry weight. The entire calculation will be as follows:

Shell.	Core.	Section.
Original weight $=60$	Original weight $=100$	Original weight $=160$
Oven-dry weight$=50$	Oven-dry weight$=80$	Oven-dry weight$=130$
Moisture$=\dfrac{10\times100}{50}$	Moisture$=\dfrac{20\times100}{80}$	Moisture$=\dfrac{30\times100}{130}$
$=20$ per cent	$=25$ per cent	$=23.1$ per cent

GENERAL PRINCIPLES OF DRYING WOOD.

The drying of wood is a very complex process, concerning many phases of which we are still uninformed. However, it is not essential that the operator understand all of the details of the movement of

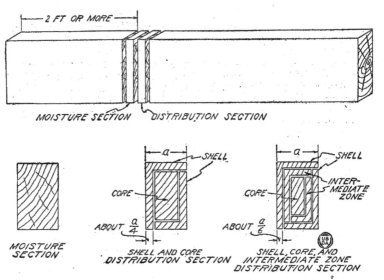

FIG. 1.—Method of cutting sections from board or plank for making moisture distribution determinations.

the moisture through the wood, and all of the attendant phenomena. Let him take it for granted, for the time being, that the moisture tends to distribute itself evenly through the wood, moving from the more moist regions to the drier ones.

This movement of moisture within the wood is affected by three controllable external factors—heat, humidity, and circulation. A constant application of these factors in proper proportion is essential to the successful drying of lumber to the moisture content required for a specific use. The regulation of the heat, humidity, and circulation is, in fact, the main problem in the successful operation of kilns.

HEAT IN THE KILN.

Heat is used in a kiln to produce rapid evaporation and to hasten the transfusion of moisture from the interior to the surface of the wood. The correct temperature to use is determined by the character of the wood and varies widely with different kinds of stock. Commercial kiln temperatures range from 100° to 250° F.

The use of temperatures above that of the surrounding atmosphere introduces a problem in the heating of buildings, and imposes an added burden upon the heating system, namely, to keep the kiln building hot and to replace the heat lost through the walls of the kiln. The higher the kiln temperature, the greater will be these heat losses. The amount of heat actually used in the evaporation of the moisture is only a small part of the total heat supplied; it is seldom over 40 per cent and frequently as low as 5 per cent, depending upon the kind of drying being done.

SOURCES OF HEAT.

Many methods have been used to heat kilns, and although most of them are obsolete or impractical, brief mention will be made of the principal ones.

Direct furnace heat.—Smoke and other products of combustion are led direct from an ordinary furnace into the kiln, from which they are exhausted by chimney or other suitable means. Kilns of this type are known as "smoke kilns." At one time it was thought that lumber dried in them was superior to steam-dried stock, but their use has been largely abandoned.

Indirect furnace heat.—As in an ordinary hot-air furnace, the air passes around the fire pot and radiators on its way to the kiln, and the products of combustion pass directly up the chimney instead of through the kiln.

Gas.—Occasionally natural or artificial gas is used to heat small dry kilns, the burners being arranged much as in an ordinary household gas oven.

Electricity.—Electric heat can be used in small kilns, although the cost of current is prohibitive, except possibly for experimental units.

Hot water.—Hot-water heat can readily be adapted to the heating of kilns which do not demand too high a temperature. A suitable hot-water supply would rarely be available, however, in the absence of steam.

Steam.—At present steam is almost universally used for heating dry kilns of all types, and a knowledge of its use is essential to intelligent kiln operation. It may be either high pressure, above 10 pounds per square inch, or low pressure, below 10 pounds. High-pressure steam is almost invariably live steam—that is, steam direct from the boilers; low-pressure steam is frequently exhaust steam, or that which has passed through engine, pump, or turbine on its way from the boilers to the kilns. High-pressure steam is much drier, as a rule, than low-pressure steam, principally because exhaust steam generally carries with it much water condensed in its passage through the engine or other unit in which it has done work. As the steam circulates through the kiln radiators the kiln air is heated and the contained lumber is dried accordingly.

PIPE COILS AND RADIATORS.

The form, construction, and arrangement of the kiln radiators is of importance. Those constructed of pipe coils are in most common use. Pipe coils are made of ordinary merchant pipe, extra heavy pipe of various kinds, and wrought-iron pipe, the last being particularly suitable for severe drying schedules. Among the advantages of pipe-coil radiators are low first cost, ease of manufacture and installation, ready adaptability to a great range of shapes and sizes, and ease of repair by the shop mechanic or millwright. There are several essentials which a good pipe coil must possess: First, it must be of such size and shape and so located that it can properly heat the air in the kiln; second, it must be mechanically strong and durable and provided with means for permitting the expansion and contraction of the individual pipes in the coil; third, it must provide for the ready escape of air and water of condensation from the entire system; fourth, it must provide for adjustment in the amount of heating surface to be used by cutting certain pipes in or out. As it is difficult to combine all these essentials in the highest degree in any one type of coil, different ones have been found best adapted for various special conditions.

A large portion of all pipe coils used for dry-kiln heating are located in the kiln proper, between or under the rails. These fall into two general classes, known as header and return-bend coils. In the former, a number of pipes spring from the same supply pipe or header and return to a similar drip pipe or header, usually but not always, located at the other end of the kiln. In the return-bend type, however, the pipes of each group are connected end to end by means of return bends or double-elbow fittings; steam enters at the front of the first or top pipe, and condensation is removed from the end of the last or bottom pipe. Figure 2 illustrates various types of header and return-bend coils.

PLAIN HEADER COIL.

The action of the two types of coils is quite different, especially when operated with a thermostat. When steam is turned on in a plain header coil with a header at each end of the kiln that end of the kiln nearest the supply header will heat up first; the other end will not heat until the front end has become hot and all the air has been exhausted from the coil. This uneven heating takes place each time the thermostat opens. If the heating surface is unduly large, as it may be when low temperatures are used, the thermostat will operate often, and there will be a marked difference in temperature between the two ends of the kiln. Another characteristic of the header system is that the large heating surface of the headers themselves causes an uneven distribution of heat by causing a "hot spot" at each header.

RETURN-BEND COIL.

In the return-bend type the top pipes in each group become hot first, since the steam must pass through them before reaching the lower ones. Each pipe runs the full length of the kiln, and heating will be practically uniform from end to end. The return-bend type also has disadvantages, among which are the first cost and the amount

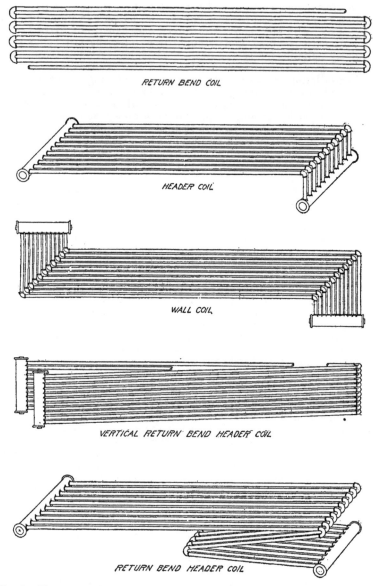

RETURN BEND COIL

HEADER COIL

WALL COIL

VERTICAL RETURN BEND HEADER COIL

RETURN BEND HEADER COIL

FIG. 2.—Pipe coils used for heating dry kilns. These are designed to provide for the expansion and contraction of the individual pipes and for the free flow of the condensed steam to the drain end. The wall coil may also be used as a horizontal coil, called "Z" coil.

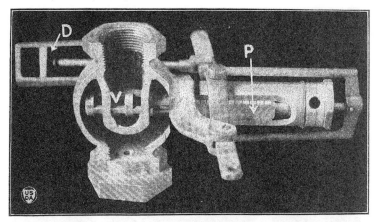

FIG. I.—A PISTON TYPE OF BALANCED REDUCING VALVE ESPECIALLY
ADAPTED TO SERVICE IN WHICH THE FLOW OF STEAM IS CONTINUOUS.

The low-pressure steam acts on the piston *P* in the cylinder and tends to close the valve *V*.
Loose weights hung on the horizontal lever counteract this tendency. The dashpot *D* steadies
the motion of the piston and valve, preventing bouncing.

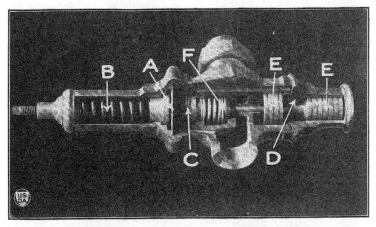

FIG. 2.—A REDUCING VALVE USED FOR A WIDE RANGE OF PRESSURES.

The reduced pressure operates the diaphragm *A* under the main adjusting spring *B*, thus opening
and closing a small pilot valve *C* concealed in the plug under the diaphragm. The pilot valve
controls the admission of high-pressure steam to the space *D* between the two pistons *E* in the
bottom of the body; this steam forces the pistons *E* up and so opens the main valve *F*. When
the pilot valve closes, the high-pressure steam on the main valve *F*, the low-pressure steam on
the larger piston, and the valve spring all act to close the main valve.

PLATE IV.

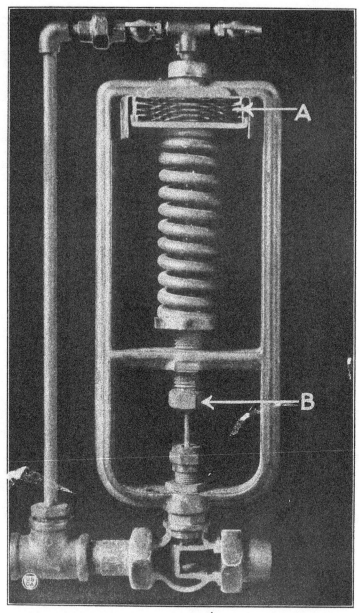

A REDUCING VALVE WITH A METAL BELLOWS (A) AND AN ADJUSTING SPRING IN PLACE OF RUBBER DIAPHRAGM AND WEIGHTS. THE LOW-PRESSURE STEAM ENTERS THE BELLOWS AT THE TOP. THE DESIRED PRESSURE IS SECURED BY TURNING THE ADJUSTING NUT (B).

of headroom which the vertical arrangement of the groups of pipe demands. This headroom must be sufficient not only for the pipes and the return bends, but also for at least 0.1 inch of the downward pitch per foot from the supply to the discharge end of each group. This pitch causes adjacent pipes to form a V with each other, and the headroom required for the pipes increases rapidly with the length of the kiln. For short kilns requiring accurate temperature control and even heat distribution the return-bend coil is specially adapted.

RETURN-BEND HEADER COIL.

Various modifications of the two types have been introduced, retaining the advantages of both and eliminating the disadvantages. Among these are the return-bend header coil, with horizontal headers and two or more layers of pipe connected with return bends; and the vertical header coil, with both headers at one end of the kiln and return bends or double elbows with a short run of pipe at the other end. These compromise types have merit and will operate advantageously under conditions to which they are adapted.

WALL COILS.

Several types of kiln use pipe-coil radiators on the side walls. These radiators do not need to differ materially from those located under the lumber, and the great amount of headroom available makes it a simple matter to get rid of the water of condensation from almost any type of coil. It also permits the use of return-bend coils in long kilns without the sacrifice of the pitch required for proper drainage.

Cast-iron radiators of various kinds have recently been introduced for use in dry kilns. They can be had in a wide range of sizes and shapes adapted to practically any space or heating requirement. This type of radiation is higher in first cost than some other types, but great durability is claimed for it on account of the resistance of cast iron to rust.

Blower kilns of several types have the heating units located outside of the kiln as shown in Plate II, Figure 1. These units are usually of the standard types used in blower systems for heating buildings. Practically all of these consist of compactly arranged groups of pipes or pipe coils made up into cast headers, which form the base of the heater. Sometimes special forms of cast-iron radiators are used. It is good practice to equip the heater with valves, so that various portions of it may be used as desired. Such heaters give little trouble, since their design permits unusually easy removal of air and water and the short pipes are free from difficulties caused by uneven expansion and contraction.

In addition to the heating equipment described, some kilns are equipped with ceiling coils. These usually consist of a few runs of pipe spaced a foot or more apart and hung a few inches below the ceiling. They are connected independently and are used most or all of the time. Their function is to replace the heat lost through the ceiling and so prevent the latter from acting as a condenser. During cold weather especially, and when high humidities are used, the ceiling is likely to accumulate a great deal of condensation, which drips down upon the lumber and prevents humidity control.

CONTROL OF KILN TEMPERATURE.

The proper measurement of the temperature in the kiln is essential to proper control and deserves much more time and attention than it usually receives. Temperature-measuring instruments or thermometers may be grouped in two classes, indicators and recorders. Indicating glass-stem thermometers for kiln work are almost invariably of the mercury-filled type, though sometimes alcohol-filled ones are used.

INDICATING THERMOMETERS.

There are many kinds of mercury thermometers available, and care must be used to select reliable instruments. The very cheap ones, with separate scales stamped on metal and attached to the case, are not accurate enough for kiln work and should be avoided. A number of better grades also have separate scales, but the highest-grade thermometers have the graduations etched on the glass stem. These can be obtained with or without a metal protecting case. Occasionally it is desirable to insert the thermometer through the kiln wall, with the bulb inside and the scale outside. Industrial-type thermometers are well adapted for this purpose. These have a brass extension tube surrounding the bulb and part of the stem, and a weatherproof brass casing with a glass face protecting the scale. The extension tubes can be made 3 feet or longer, and the stem fitted on at almost any desired angle. A right-angle stem is desirable where the extension tube projects horizontally into the kiln, because it permits the scale to be vertical and therefore most easily read.

An electrical-resistance thermometer has recently been developed for dry-kiln use. This thermometer has a special panel and connecting wires, so that the temperatures at a number of places can be read from the one instrument. The temperature is indicated by a pointer moving over a graduated dial.

RECORDING THERMOMETERS.

Recording thermometers used in kiln work are almost invariably of the extension-tube type provided with 1-day or 7-day charts. In recorders of this type the sensitive element or bulb is connected to the instrument by a capillary tube of suitable length. (See Pl. II, fig. 2.) This tube is usually protected by a flexible armor and ends in a spring capsule in the case. This capsule may be any one of several different types, all of which are flexibly constructed, so that changes in internal pressure produce a movement of the capsule which is usually transmitted through a series of levers to a pen arm, which moves across a slowly revolving chart and produces a graphic record of the temperature in the kiln. The chart is rotated by a clock movement which is wound whenever the chart is changed.

There are three types of recording thermometers, the difference being in the material used for filling the bulbs. These three types are commonly known as liquid-filled, gas-filled, and vapor-filled. The choice of type depends upon the accuracy desired and the conditions under which the thermometer is to be used.

In dry-kiln work the tube and the case of the thermometer are liable to be subjected to wide variations in temperature, which influence the accuracy of the instrument, especially in the case of the mercury-filled and gas-filled types. In these the record is influenced by the bulb temperature, the tube temperature, and the case temperature. Variations in any one of the three will change the reading of the instrument, except when compensation is made for variations in case temperature. The vapor-filled instrument is nearly free from this particular defect, since the bulb is partially filled with a volatile liquid, and the pressure of gas or vapor in the tube and the capsule is virtually the vapor pressure of the liquid in the bulb at the bulb temperature. If the bulb is large and filled with the proper amount of liquid, the thermometer is practically free from errors due to case and tube temperatures, and this type is recommended for dry-kiln work.

Charts recording temperature for one-week periods are satisfactory for most purposes. It is desirable to use charts at least 10 inches in diameter. The divisions on the charts of most vapor-filled instruments are not uniform, because the vapor pressure does not vary in direct proportion with the temperature. The divisions spread as the temperature rises. This drawback has been overcome by introducing a cam movement which compensates for the lack of uniformity and produces a uniform pen movement.

The temperature in the kiln is controlled by the use of auxiliary apparatus, such as valves and thermostats. The pipe leading from the steam main to the kiln is almost always provided with a simple globe or gate valve, by which the steam supply to the kiln may be turned on or shut off. This valve can also be used for hand control of the temperature in case no other means is available. The pressure in the steam main is usually higher than necessary to furnish the desired temperature in the kiln, and it then becomes desirable to place a reducing valve (Pls. III and IV) between the steam main and the kiln. With this the pressure may be reduced to almost any desired point; the variations in this reduced pressure are less than those in the high-pressure main. If the pressure reduction is very great, from 100 pounds down to 1 or 2 pounds per square inch, it may be necessary to install two reducing valves in tandem, the first one reducing to perhaps 10 pounds and the second making the final reduction. In an installation of this kind a steam receiver or a couple of lengths of pipe should be placed between the two reducers to provide a cushion, and thus prevent the first reducer from chattering. Reducing valves should always be so installed that they can be readily removed for repairs. Whenever a battery of kilns is run part time on exhaust steam and part time on live steam it is very desirable to have a reducer between the boilers and the exhaust-steam main to the kilns, so that the live steam may be supplied to this main at about the exhaust pressure. Steam-pressure gauges should invariably be provided so that the operator may always know just what pressure he has available.

The intelligent manipulation of reducing valves assists materially in maintaining good temperature control. The pressure to the kilns may be so adjusted that it is barely sufficient to keep the desired temperature with the steam-control valve wide open. Excessive temperature rises may thus be prevented and the coils kept full of steam most of the time. Under hand control this arrangement is unusually sensitive, since a comparatively large change in the setting of the hand valve makes only a small change in the amount of steam supplied. If the kiln is provided with automatic control, the control valve will usually be located next to the kiln. The use of automatic control valves is recommended for practically all kinds of kiln drying, because a more even temperature may be maintained, injury from excessive temperatures avoided, and loss of time from unnecessarily low temperatures prevented.

AUTOMATIC TEMPERATURE CONTROLS.

There are two classes of automatic temperature control in common use in dry kilns. These are known as self-contained and auxiliary operated. The self-contained thermostats are operated by means of the direct pressure of vapor or liquid upon the valve stem. The action is very similar to that of the recording thermometers already described. A large bulb in the kiln is connected by means of a capillary tube to a diaphragm or capsule in the head of the valve located in the steam line. The temperature variations in the kiln change the pressure inside the bulb, which in turn causes corresponding pressure changes in the capsule. This results in the opening and closing of the valve, the stem of which bears upon the capsule. The valve itself is usually of balanced type to provide ease of movement. A counter force or pressure is provided by means of an adjustable spring or sliding weights, and the instrument is set for the desired temperature by changing the tension of the spring or the position of the weights. (See Pl. V.) The principal advantages of the self-contained thermostat are that no auxiliary source of power is required for its operation and that the first cost is comparatively small. This type is not so sensitive as the auxiliary operated type. The manufacturers claim regulation within 2° of the temperature for which the instrument is set, but in kiln operation the variation is often much greater than that. The auxiliary operated instruments are supposed to control with a variation of only 1° and in kiln operation usually maintain this accuracy.

The auxiliary operated instruments using air as the operating medium are usually provided with a small bulb inserted in the kiln and connected to a capsule in the instrument by means of a capillary tube. (See Pl. VI.) The movement of the capsule top in response to temperature changes in the kiln is transmitted to a small valve connected on one side to a supply of air compressed to 15 pounds pressure and on the other side to a diaphragm-motor valve on the steam main. Sometimes a bimetallic system is used in place of the capsule to operate the air valve. This small air valve is so arranged, in instruments using direct-acting diaphragm valves, that as the temperature rises, air pressure is admitted to the head of the diaphragm-motor valve. This forces the diaphragm down, which closes the valve and shuts the steam off from the kiln. As the temperature falls, the air pressure is shut off, and a means of escape is provided for the air in the valve head. The valve then opens through spring action and admits steam to the kiln. Reverse-acting diaphragm valves are so constructed that the air pressure opens them and the springs close them. The air valve must be modified accordingly.

The advantage of the reverse-acting type is that a failure of the air supply causes the valves to shut, which prevents a dangerous rise in temperature. The same effect may be secured in a battery of

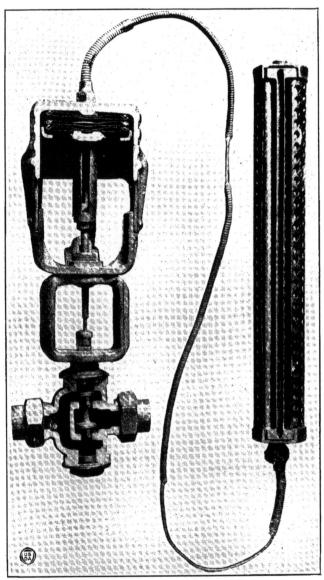

SELF-CONTAINED THERMOSTAT.

The large bulb at the right is connected through the armored tube to the bellows in the head of the valve. The lower part of the bellows is connected to the stem of the balanced steam valve, and the pressure in the bellows tends to close this valve. A weighted lever, not shown, acting through the slot below the bellows, opposes this pressure and keeps the valve open until the desired temperature is reached.

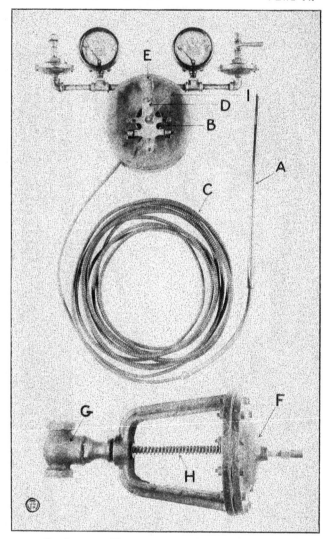

AIR-OPERATED THERMOSTAT AND DIAPHRAGM VALVE.

The bulb *A* is connected to the flexible capsule *B* through the armored capillary tube *C*. Changes in the temperature of the bulb cause changes in the pressure of the liquid or gas in the bulb. The capsule expands and contracts accordingly, and moves a pivoted lever *D*, which opens and closes a small air valve *E*. Air at about 15 pounds pressure enters the system from the left, passes to the head *F*, and closes the steam valve *G*, the stem of which is connected to the diaphragm in the head. When the air valve *E* closes, the air supply to the diaphragm is shut off, the pressure is relieved by leakage through the valve *E*, and the spring *H* opens the steam valve.

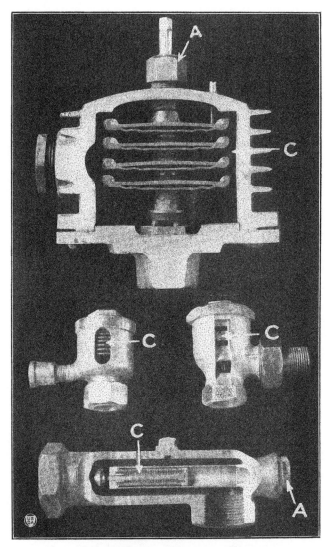

THERMOSTATIC AIR VALVES AND TRAPS.

In those illustrated the thermostatic element consists of a flexible capsule *C* and a volatile or nonvolatile liquid, the expansion of which shuts the valve. The capsules serve as springs to open the valves. The traps are provided with adjusting nuts *A* to compensate for variations in the steam pressure in the system.

direct-acting thermostats by putting a single reverse-acting valve in the steam main and connecting it direct to the air supply. Both types are equipped with dials indicating the proper temperature adjustment. Various combination instruments can be secured for different services. One type consists of a combination recording thermometer and reverse-acting air-operated thermostat. Other types are discussed below.

After the steam has passed through the various valves, it enters the steam coils proper. If the coils are in one unit, steam enters all. However, they may be divided into several groups, each group controlled by a gate or globe valve. In the latter case, enough groups should be turned on to produce a temperature only slightly in excess of that desired. Care must be exercised to select the different groups so that the kiln will be heated uniformly throughout.

When steam is first turned on, the coils are full of air and will not heat properly until the air has been removed. The use of air valves to remove the air depends upon the method employed in removing the water of condensation from the coils. An automatic thermostatic air valve should be provided near each trap unless it is of the thermostatic type, for which no air valve is needed.

Automatic air valves operate thermostatically. They remain open until a definite temperature is reached and then automatically close through the action of some element, such as a metal bar or a liquid-filled capsule, which expands with the heat. (See Pl. VII.) This action permits the cold air to be blown out of the coils and prevents the passage of the hot steam. Other things being equal, air valves should be placed near the bottom of the coil, since the air is heavier than the steam and consequently settles to the bottom. They should be mounted on fittings projecting from the top of the drip pipe, so that they will not become water bound.

THERMOSTATIC STEAM TRAPS.

Steam imparts its heat mainly through condensation. This condensed steam must be continuously removed from the heating coils, or they fill with water and become cold. Various devices are used to remove water from steam coils and several patented systems are in use. In most dry kilns steam traps which allow the escape of the water but trap the steam are used. They can be divided into two general classes, those depending upon temperature for their operation, and those depending upon the weight of the accumulated water. The first class is known as thermostatic. (See Pl. VII.) Most thermostatic traps have an operating bellows or diaphragm filled with some volatile liquid. One end of the bellows is attached to a valve stem and valve, and the motion of the bellows opens and closes the valve. The trap is connected to the lowest point in the heating system, so that the water will drain readily to it.

The coils are cold and full of air, and the trap is cold and open when steam is first turned on. The steam displaces the air which is driven out through the open trap. A certain amount of steam is condensed, and this hot water flows to and through the trap. Warmed by the water, the trap partly closes, owing to pressure from heat expansion inside the bellows, but remains partly open until all the air and water have been forced out and steam starts blowing through. The higher temperature of the steam causes a further expansion of the bellows and a complete shutting off of the trap. A screw adjustment is necessary so that the trap may be set for various steam temperatures, since the temperature of saturated steam increases with the pressure. After the trap has closed, condensed steam accumulates back of it, until the trap cools enough to allow it to open and blow out. It is desirable to locate the thermostatic traps and air valves in the operating room where they will be under better supervision and will be more sensitive, since they will cool more quickly than if they were located in the hot kiln.

Properly installed thermostatic traps are very useful in dry-kiln work, especially on coils built in groups. One installed on each group prevents trouble which arises when all the groups are operated by one trap. They also operate on coils which are controlled by auxiliary operated thermostats, allowing the coils to heat uniformly and thoroughly in a minimum time.

Several types of traps used on dry kilns are operated by the weight of the water of condensation. Among these are tilt, float, and bucket traps. The water of condensation flows into a receptacle within the trap and by its weight or buoyancy opens a valve that allows the water to be blown out, after which the valve returns to its closed position. Such traps do not, as a rule, provide for the escape of air from the coils, and for this reason automatic air valves or hand-operated pet cocks are fitted to them.

VACUUM PUMPS.

Kilns are sometimes equipped with a vacuum pump for the rapid removal of air and water from the coils. One is sufficient for a battery of kilns, each heating coil being connected through a thermostatic trap to the pump suction main. Dependence must be placed on the traps, since the pump will not work properly without them. Although the pump is very effective in removing air and water, especially on low-pressure systems, the rapid relief obtained by it is not needed in most kilns.

HUMIDITY IN THE KILN.

ABSOLUTE HUMIDITY.

Humidity or water vapor in the air is the most puzzling factor with which the average kiln operator must contend. The amount of water vapor in the atmosphere may be expressed in terms of the weight of water vapor for every unit volume of atmosphere. The unit of weight used is the grain and the unit of volume the cubic foot. The absolute humidity is the number of grains water vapor per cubic foot. This alone is no indication of the drying capacity of the air, since its capacity to hold water varies greatly with the temperature.

RELATIVE HUMIDITY.

Air containing the total number of grains of water vapor it can hold at a given temperature is saturated. The ability of air to dry any substance varies with the amount of additional moisture it can hold before becoming saturated. The amount of vapor in the air expressed in percentage of the amount held at saturation is called relative humidity, and is what is meant when the term "humidity" is used in this bulletin. The lower relative humidities represent dry air and the higher ones moist air. Air at a temperature of 125° F. can hold a maximum of 40 grains of water vapor per cubic foot. If an atmosphere at that temperature had only 10 grains of water per cubic foot it would have only ten-fortieths of the maximum amount of water vapor it could hold, or a relative humidity of 25 per cent. Air with 25 per cent relative humidity is comparatively dry. The relative humidity of air having 30 grains would be thirty-fortieths, or 75 per cent, and would be considered moist. Air at 155° F. can hold 80 grains per cubic foot, or twice as much water vapor as at 125°. At 155° air containing 10 grains of water per cubic foot would

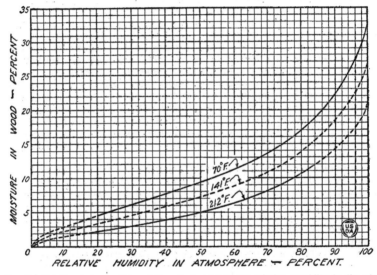

Fig. 3.—Relation between the moisture in wood and the relative humidity in the surrounding atmosphere at three temperatures. Solid lines are based on actual data.

be very dry, having a relative humidity of only 12½ per cent, and air containing 30 grains per cubic foot would still be moderately dry, having a relative humidity of 37½ per cent.

The amount of moisture in the air determines not only the rate but also the extent to which materials will dry. There is a definite balance between the humidity in the air and the moisture content of wood. All kinds of wood, if held long enough in an atmosphere of constant temperature and humidity, will come to the same moisture content. The time required for this adjustment varies with different species. The relation between humidity in the air and moisture in the wood is an important one, since it forms the basis for some drying schedules and determines the extent to which wood for use under specified conditions of temperature and humidity should be dried. Figure 3 presents curves showing the humidity-moisture relation at three temperatures. The middle curve has been interpolated, actual data having been secured for the outer ones only.

HUMIDITY MEASURING INSTRUMENTS.

Since the humidity in the air determines the drying characteristics at any given temperature, the control of humidity in the kiln is of prime importance. It is essential that the moisture be removed from the wood surface at the maximum safe drying rate. If the humidity is too low the wood will dry too fast and will be injured; if the humidity is too high the drying will be slow and expensive.

Humidity is measured by an instrument variously named a hygrometer, a psychrometer, or a wet and dry bulb thermometer. Modifications of the instrument adapted to dry-kiln use bear trade names, but the principle underlying all modifications is the same. A wet surface exposed to a breeze of nonsaturated air will be cooled a certain amount by the evaporation of water from the surface. The amount is constant for any given temperature and humidity. Knowing the amount of cooling, called wet-bulb depression, and the temperature of the air, the humidity can be determined by formula or by reference to a humidity chart. The wet and dry bulb thermometer consists of two separate thermometers, mounted on a panel. One, the dry bulb, registers the temperature of the air; and the other, the wet bulb, registers the air temperature minus the wet-bulb depression. The wet bulb is equipped with a silk or muslin wick dipped in a water reservoir. The wick surrounds the bulb of the thermometer and keeps it wet by drawing water from the reservoir. The evaporation of this water from the bulb produces the cooling or wet-bulb depression.

To obtain accuracy it is essential that the wicks be clean and that there be a brisk circulation of air over the wet bulb. A velocity of at least 15 feet per second is recommended by various authorities, but this is more than is needed, except for the most accurate work. With certain types of wet and dry bulb thermometers circulation is produced by whirling the entire instrument. Such instruments are known as sling psychrometers. Other instruments are provided with maximum-reading thermometers, so that they can be removed from the kiln and read outside. The mercury or fluid column in these thermometers must be shaken down before they are replaced in the kiln. They record only the maximum wet and dry bulb temperatures since they were last shaken down. If the temperature and humidity variations have been reasonably great during this time the readings will be deceptive.

Table 1 is a humidity chart for use with wet and dry bulb thermometers. It is based on the difference between the wet-bulb and dry-bulb temperatures. The dry-bulb temperatures are in the left-hand column and the difference between wet and dry bulb temperatures in the top row. The relative humidity is given at the intersection of the row and column. Suppose the dry bulb reads 140° F. and the wet bulb 130° F., the difference between them is 10°. By reading across the 140 row to column 10 the relative humidity will be found to be 75 per cent.

Most of the kiln humidity recorders are wet-bulb instruments with extension tubes. They differ from dry-bulb recorders (recording thermometers) in that the sensitve bulb in the kiln is provided with a wick and a water reservoir. Any type of recording thermometer

TABLE 1.—*Relative humidity table for use with wet and dry bulb thermometers.*

Difference between wet and dry bulb thermometers, in degrees Fahrenheit.

Temperature of dry bulb	1	2	3	4	5	6	7	8	9	10	11	12	13	14	15	16	17	18	19	20	21	22	23	24	25	26	27	28	29	30	31	32	33	34	35	36	37	38	39	40
60	94	89	85	80	75	69	65	58	53	48																														
70	95	90	86	78	76	72	68	64	59	55	51	47	43	40	37	33	29																							
80	95	91	87	83	79	75	71	68	64	61	57	54	50	47	44	41	38	35																						
90	96	92	88	85	81	77	74	71	67	65	61	58	55	52	49	47	44	41	39																					
100	96	92	89	86	83	80	76	74	71	68	65	62	60	57	55	52	50	48	46	43	41																			
102	96	93	89	86	84	80	77	75	72	69	66	64	61	59	56	54	52	49	47	45	43	41																		
104	96	93	90	87	84	81	78	75	72	70	67	65	62	60	58	55	53	51	49	47	44	42																		
106	96	93	90	87	84	81	78	76	73	70	68	65	63	61	59	57	54	52	50	48	46	44																		
108	96	93	90	87	85	82	79	76	74	71	69	66	64	62	60	58	56	53	51	49	47	45																		
110	96	93	90	88	85	82	79	77	74	72	69	67	65	63	61	58	56	54	52	50	48	46																		
112	96	93	91	88	85	82	80	78	75	72	70	68	66	64	62	59	57	55	53	51	49	47																		
114	97	93	91	88	85	83	80	78	75	73	71	69	66	64	62	60	58	56	54	52	50	48	26																	
116	97	94	91	88	86	83	81	78	76	74	71	69	67	65	63	61	59	57	55	53	51	49	35	26																
118	97	94	91	89	86	84	81	79	76	74	72	70	68	66	64	62	60	58	56	54	52	50	37	29																
120	97	94	91	89	86	84	82	79	77	75	73	71	68	66	64	62	60	58	57	55	53	51	38	29																
122	97	94	91	89	87	84	82	80	77	75	73	71	69	67	65	63	61	59	57	56	54	52	39	30	27															
124	97	94	92	89	87	85	82	80	78	76	74	72	70	68	66	64	62	60	58	57	55	53	40	31	28															
126	97	94	92	89	87	85	82	80	78	76	74	72	70	68	66	64	63	61	59	57	56	54	41	31	28	27														
128	97	94	92	90	87	85	83	81	79	77	75	73	71	69	67	65	64	62	60	58	57	55	42	32	29	28														
130	97	94	92	90	88	85	83	81	79	77	75	73	71	69	68	66	64	62	61	59	58	56	43	33	30	29	27													
132	97	94	92	90	88	86	84	82	80	78	76	74	72	70	68	67	65	63	62	60	58	57	44	34	31	30	28													
134	97	94	92	90	88	86	84	82	80	78	76	74	72	70	69	67	65	64	62	61	59	58	45	35	32	31	29	27												
136	97	95	92	90	88	86	84	82	81	79	77	75	73	71	69	68	66	64	63	61	60	58	46	36	33	32	30	28												
138	97	95	92	90	88	86	84	83	81	79	77	75	73	72	70	68	67	65	64	62	60	59	47	37	34	33	31	29												
140	97	95	92	91	89	87	85	83	81	80	78	76	74	72	71	69	67	66	64	63	61	60	48	38	35	34	32	30												
142	98	95	93	91	89	87	85	83	82	80	78	76	74	73	71	69	68	66	65	63	62	60	49	39	36	35	33	31												
144	98	95	93	91	89	87	85	84	82	80	79	77	75	73	72	70	68	67	65	64	62	61	50	40	37	36	34	32												
146	98	95	93	91	89	87	86	84	82	81	79	77	75	74	72	70	69	67	66	64	63	62	50	41	38	37	35	33												
148	98	95	93	91	89	88	86	84	83	81	79	78	76	74	73	71	69	68	66	65	63	62	51	42	39	38	36	34												
150	98	95	93	91	90	88	86	84	83	81	80	78	76	75	73	72	70	69	67	66	64	63	51	43	40	39	37	35												
152	98	95	93	92	90	88	86	85	83	82	80	78	77	75	73	72	70	69	68	66	65	63	52	44	41	40	38	36												
154	98	95	93	92	90	88	87	85	83	82	80	79	77	76	74	72	71	69	68	67	65	64	52	45	42	41	39	37												
156	98	95	93	92	90	88	87	85	84	82	81	79	78	76	75	73	71	70	68	67	66	64	53	46	43	42	40	38												
158	98	96	94	92	90	88	87	85	84	82	81	79	78	76	75	73	72	70	69	68	66	65	54	47	44	43	41	39												
160	98	96	94	92	90	89	87	86	84	83	81	80	78	77	75	74	72	71	69	68	67	65	54	48	45	44	42	40	27											
162	98	96	94	92	90	89	87	86	84	83	81	80	78	77	76	74	73	71	70	69	67	66	55	49	46	45	43	41	28											
164	98	96	94	92	91	89	87	86	85	83	82	80	79	77	76	75	73	72	70	69	68	66	55	50	47	46	44	42	29											
166	98	96	94	92	91	89	88	86	85	84	82	81	79	78	76	75	74	72	71	70	68	67	56	51	48	47	45	43	30											
168	98	96	94	93	91	89	88	86	85	84	82	81	80	78	77	75	74	73	71	70	69	67	56	52	49	48	46	44	31											
170	98	96	94	93	91	89	88	87	85	84	83	81	80	79	77	76	74	73	72	70	69	68	57	53	50	49	47	45	32											
172	98	96	94	93	91	89	88	87	85	84	83	82	80	79	78	76	75	73	72	71	70	68	57	54	51	50	48	46	33											
174	98	96	94	93	91	90	88	87	86	84	83	82	80	79	78	76	75	74	72	71	70	69	58	55	52	51	49	47	34											
176	98	96	94	93	91	90	88	87	86	85	83	82	81	79	78	77	75	74	73	72	70	69	58	56	53	52	50	48	35											
178	98	96	94	93	91	90	88	87	86	85	84	82	81	80	78	77	76	74	73	72	71	69	59	57	54	53	51	49	36											
180	98	96	94	93	92	90	89	87	86	85	84	82	81	80	79	77	76	75	73	72	71	70	59	58	55	54	52	50	37											
182	98	96	94	93	92	90	89	87	86	85	84	83	81	80	79	78	76	75	74	73	71	70	60	58	56	55	53	51	38											
184	98	96	94	93	92	90	89	88	86	85	84	83	82	80	79	78	77	75	74	73	72	70	60	59	57	56	54	52	39											
186	98	96	94	93	92	90	89	88	87	85	84	83	82	81	80	78	77	76	74	73	72	71	61	60	58	56	55	53	40											
188	98	96	94	93	92	90	89	88	87	86	84	83	82	81	80	79	77	76	75	74	72	71	61	61	59	57	56	54	41											
190	98	96	95	93	92	90	89	88	87	86	85	84	82	81	80	79	78	76	75	74	73	72	62	62	60	57	56	54	42											
200	98	96	95	93	92	90	89	88	87	86	85	84	83	82	80	79	78	77	76	74	73	72	63	63	60	58	57	55	43											

can be used equally well as a wet-bulb recorder, though sometimes it is necessary to change the shape or design of the bulb.

The wet-bulb temperature alone is of no value in determining humidity without the corresponding dry-bulb temperature. Hence, wet and dry recorders are set up side by side, or, as is much more convenient, combined in one instrument called a two-pen recorder, which records both temperatures on one chart. The space between the two represents the wet-bulb depression. For general use, two-pen recorders have the tubes and bulbs separate from each other, but when designed exclusively for use as wet and dry bulb recorders the extension tubes are frequently encased in a single protecting armor extending from the case of the instrument almost to the bulbs. The wick trough is made with two sets of brackets, one set for the wet bulb and one for the dry bulb. Instruments of this type are usually called recording psychrometers. The facts concerning recording thermometers apply to wet and dry bulb recorders.

CONTROL OF KILN HUMIDITY.

It is simpler to increase the humidity in a kiln than to decrease it. The universal method of increasing humidity is to inject steam into the kiln chamber.

Atmospheric air is usually drier than that in the wood-drying kiln and can be used only for dehumidification, a practice common with ventilated kilns. The moist air is drawn off through ventilating flues and the fresh air enters through intake flues or ducts. As the fresh air is heated its relative humidity falls while the dew point remains the same.

Moisture may also be removed from the air by condensation. The water vapor in the air condenses as it passes over a substance colder than the dew point of the air. Condenser pipes with cold water flowing through them are commonly used for this purpose. When cold water is not available, a refrigerator plant may be installed and brine circulated through the condenser pipes.

Cold-water sprays are also used to dehumidify air. The spray temperature must be below the dew point of the air passing through. If the sprays are powerful enough the air will be cooled to about the temperature of the water and will come out saturated at a temperature below its original dew point. In other words, the dew point will have been lowered. If the air be heated to its original temperature it will be drier than it originally was.

In the chemical laboratory air is dried by passing it through chemicals which have affinity for moisture. Principal among these are calcium chloride and sulphuric acid. Their use has not been developed for commercial wood drying.

The control of humidity is more difficult than temperature control, and greater attention must be given to the apparatus to secure satisfactory results. One principal reason is that a small difference in the wet-bulb temperature produces a comparatively large difference in humidity, and to secure good control requires an accurate instrument.

The controllers of greatest importance are those which depend partly or wholly upon a wet-bulb of one type or another. Temperature controllers of various types can be made into wet-bulb controllers by providing the bulb or sensitive element with a suitable wick and water supply. The Forest Products Laboratory has used with success air-operated wet-bulb controllers of both the extension bulb (vapor filled) and the bimetallic or differential expansion types. Self-contained thermostats can also be used, but their sensitiveness is not so great as that of the air-operated instruments. Wet-bulb controllers can keep the wet-bulb temperature constant. If the dry-bulb temperature is also kept constant, the humidity will remain constant. If it does not, however, the humidity will vary, even if the wet-bulb temperature is accurately controlled. To overcome this difficulty a differential type of self-contained humidity control has been developed. In this instrument there is a dry bulb as well as a wet bulb; the two bulbs are connected to their respective motor diaphragms on the body of a balanced steam valve so that an increase in the wet-bulb temperature will close the valve and an increase in the dry-bulb temperature will open it. Balance between the two is secured by a lever and sliding weights. This system provides for a constant difference between the vapor pressures in the wet and dry bulb motor diaphragms, no matter what the dry-bulb temperature may be. This results in an approximately constant difference between the wet and dry bulb temperatures.

A glance at the humidity table shows that, with a constant difference between wet and dry bulb temperatures, even quite a considerable variation in the dry-bulb temperature has but little effect upon the relative humidity.

To secure satisfactory service from wet-bulb thermostats, care and attention should be given especially to the wicks, which should be changed as often as they become hard and dirty.

Humidity controllers almost without exception operate valves controlling steam jets, just as temperature controllers operate valves upon the heating system. The same kind of valves are ordinarily used, each valve being adapted to the needs of the particular service it is to render. As the use of humidity controllers on steam-jet lines presupposes that the humidity will always need to be increased, means must be provided to insure this need. Ordinarily in ventilated kilns the fresh-air inlets and the moist-air vents are open sufficiently to require continuous humidification. If necessary in special cases, the controllers can be made to operate dampers of various sorts, and also to control the flow of water in condenser pipes. Control in the various kiln types will be considered more in detail later.

Several special types of temperature and humidity-control instruments have been designed or adapted for dry-kiln use. Among these are double-duty air-operated instruments which have two sensitive bulbs and extension tubes with but a single case, in which are housed the capsules and air valves. These instruments can be used for temperature and humidity control, or for temperature control and the removal of condensation from the heating coils. This latter use is not common in dry kilns.

The recorder regulator has already been mentioned under temperature control. This air-operated instrument provides for the control of either wet or dry bulb temperature and for a graphic record of the controlled temperature.

Time is an element in certain classes of control in which it is desirable to change the setting of the control instrument at definite intervals. To meet this need both single-duty and double-duty instruments are made with time attachments. These are usually in the form of clock-driven cams, upon which ride levers controlling the adjustment of the air valves. By providing a suitable assortment of cams and a sufficiently flexible system of gearing between the clock and the cam any desired drying schedule can be reproduced automatically.

AIR CIRCULATION IN THE KILN.

It is absolutely necessary to have a certain amount of circulation of air in a kiln to convey the heat from the steam coils or other source to the lumber and to carry away the evaporated moisture.

PRODUCTION OF CIRCULATION.

The simplest way to produce circulation is by means of chimneys or flues. This natural draft is caused by the difference in temperature of the outside air and the air in the kiln. The warm air in the kiln is lighter than the air outside and is continually escaping through the top. The cold outside air is drawn in at the bottom. There is always inleakage at the bottom and outleakage at the top of the kiln, no matter how well it may be built; and when the path of the air is made easy by providing chimneys and fresh-air intakes the circulation becomes quite brisk. The velocity in the chimneys may be 600 feet per minute or more, depending upon circumstances. A reasonable amount of draft may be secured through the chimneys, even though no air intake openings are provided. There may also be considerable draft through the intake when there are no chimneys, or when the chimney dampers are closed. Under such conditions the whole kiln acts as a chimney, and the leakage is sufficient to permit the escape or entrance of appreciable amounts of air.

Air intakes are usually placed at the bottom of the kiln and the outlets from the kiln to the chimneys at varying heights along the sides and in the ceiling. The chimneys usually, but not always, project above the roof. The higher the chimneys the more rapid will be the circulation.

It is sometimes considered advantageous to draw the air over a circuitous route through which the circulation will ordinarily not start of its own accord. This may be done by some special means to stimulate the circulation, such as the use of radiators, aspirators, or inspirators. The simplest form of radiator for this purpose is a single length of pipe running the full length of the chimney and fed with steam from the bottom. These radiators produce an upward draft of air in the chimneys by heating the air. They may be left on throughout the entire drying period if the added circulation is desirable. The heat given off by these radiators is lost, except in so far as it does useful work in producing circulation.

Condensers if properly located will assist materially in producing circulation, and will also reduce the humidity. If air is being continuously heated at one point in a confined space and continuously cooled at another point, there will be a continuous flow of heated air upward at the first point and a continous flow of cooled air downward at the second point. There will also be cross-circulation between the two points, the warmed air above flowing from the hot point to the cold one and cold air below flowing from the cold point to the hot one. Condensers may well act as the cooling agent and the steam coils as the suppliers of heat.

Water sprays, if cool enough, may likewise act as the cooling agent and, in conjunction with a suitable source of heat, produce a recirculating system. The water sprays, in addition to their cooling effect, may stimulate the circulation through the impact of the water particles upon the air. For this reason it is desirable that the sprays point downward, at a place where downward circulation is desirable and readily producible.

Water sprays may be used as either humidifiers or dehumidifiers at the time they are assisting in producing circulation. Water sprays are as a rule used only in recirculating kilns.

Steam sprays are used in many ways in kilns, and their maximum usefulness has not yet been developed. The mechanical or heat efficiency of these steam-jet blowers is not as great as that of high-grade fans, but often this fact is outweighed by other considerations.

The circulation in almost any ventilated kiln may be materially increased by the use of suitable steam jets in the intakes, the outlet flues, or both. Jets placed in the outlet flues increase the circulation through the exhaustion of air from the kiln, but if the jets are placed in the intakes, they not only induce circulation but humidify the air and preheat it by imparting some of the heat of the steam. Under most conditions the proper place for the jets is in the intakes.

Centrifugal blowers of various designs are used to produce circulation in kilns of many types. The volume of air moved per unit of time may be any desired amount within wide limits, and the direction of the circulation may be controlled and regulated to meet individual needs and conditions. Centrifugal blowers are located almost exclusively outside of the kilns and are usually arranged to recirculate the air.

Disk fans of several different types have been used for special drying problems. These fans may be either in or out of the kiln, depending upon individual design, and may be driven by shaft or belt or have direct connection to engine or motor.

MEASUREMENT AND CONTROL OF CIRCULATION.

For a particular drying condition it is possible to specify temperature and humidity, but the amount of circulation is not so easily specified. While it is true that rapid uniform circulation produces faster and more even drying and permits of better control of the drying conditions than slow, irregular circulation, it becomes increasingly difficult to secure uniformity as the speed of circulation increases; and there is an added expense to produce and maintain high circulation rates. Ventilated kilns with low rates of circulation have been in satisfactory operation for many years.

RATE OF CIRCULATION.

The Forest Products Laboratory recommends for all difficult drying work which demands uniform drying conditions a circulation of at least 25 feet per minute through the lumber piles. Where requirements are not so exacting much lower rates may be used. If only the removal of the moisture from the kiln through ventilation is desired, a very low rate may be ample. In fact, certain types of kilns are being successfully operated without any visible means of moisture removal, leakage being sufficient to keep the humidity below the desired point.

Generally high rates of circulation produce increased drying rates in wood as well as in many other substances, temperatures and humidities being the same; but actual data on the subject are meager and it is not possible at present to say how far it may be commercially feasible to go in the matter of very high circulation, and to what extent similar effects may be produced by other means.

TESTING CIRCULATION.

Much trouble in drying is caused by poor or nonuniform circulation, and it is frequently necessary to determine the amount of circulation and its direction as a preliminary to prescribing a remedy. The rate of circulation inside the average kiln is so low that most of the methods usually employed in the measurement of air velocities are not suitable. About the only method which has proved satisfactory is to watch the drift of smoke and, if desired, to time its movement over a known distance by means of a stop watch. One of the special advantages of this method is that it shows clearly the direction of movement. It is, of course, necessary for the operator to be inside the kiln during the test.

Tobacco, punk sticks, or rope may be used to provide the smoke, although it is difficult with these means to get a sufficient volume of smoke, and the fire risk is an objectionable feature. It is almost necessary, however, to use one of these methods in determining the circulation at an inaccessible point. A few punk sticks or a bit of rope can be tied to the end of a stick and poked into many places which could not otherwise be reached. Smoke from any burning substance, it must be remembered, tends to rise because of its higher temperature; hence the true circulation will not be indicated until the smoke has cooled to the temperature of the surrounding air.

A special form of smoke machine for dry-kiln work has been developed at the Forest Products Laboratory. This machine consists essentially of two small bottles and a few pieces of connecting tubing. One bottle is partly filled with hydrochloric acid and the other with ammonia. When air is blown through the bottles, fumes of the two chemicals are mixed, producing a dense fog or smoke which will drift readily with the air current.

To secure proper results in smoke tests, it is essential that all the doors be closed and that the kiln be operating in the normal manner.

For higher velocities, such as those usually occurring in the flues of ventilated kilns and in the interior of some types of forced circulation kiln, the Biram type of anemometer is suitable. This anemometer is in essence a disk fan mounted upon pivot bearings and provided with a revolution counter. This counter is ordinarily in the form of a dial and pointer, one revolution of the pointer usually representing an air movement of 100 feet. It is necessary to use a watch with the anemometer, to determine the time corresponding to a certain air movement. It is customary to let the anemometer run a definite number of minutes, and then to divide the number of feet recorded by the number of minutes, the quotient being the velocity expressed in feet per minute. It must be remembered that the velocity in any duct varies throughout the cross-section, being greatest at the center and least along the sides, and that a single reading will probably not represent a true average. For accurate results the cross-section of the duct should be divided into squares about equal to the diameter of the anemometer and a reading taken on each square. This will seldom be necessary, however, in ordinary work. In using anemometers in open places care must be exercised to set the anemometer with its axis truly parallel with the air movement. Otherwise it will register less than it should. Smoke may be used to indicate the direction of the air movement.

Anemometers are imperfect in that the speed of the fan is not truly proportional to the air velocity over the entire range of usefulness of the instrument, and it becomes necessary to apply a correction factor. This correction factor is determined by actual trial or calibration at the factory, and a curve showing the amount of correction to be applied at different velocities should accompany the instrument.

DRYING AND DRYING STRESSES.

MOISTURE GRADIENT.

The moisture in wood tends to equalize itself by flowing to areas of least moisture. If we desire to produce a flow of moisture in a piece of wood of uniform moisture content, we must first upset this uniform condition. This is done by removing some of the moisture from the surface by circulating air of proper temperature and humidity around the piece. As soon as evaporation from the surface commences, a "moisture gradient" has been established; that is, we have made the wood drier on the surface than in the interior, and have thereby started the movement of the moisture from the interior toward the surface. If we continue to remove the moisture from the surface through evaporation a moisture gradient will continue to exist. If the moisture be removed from the surface faster than it can transfuse from the interior, the moisture gradient will increase or become steeper, whereas if it be removed more slowly, the gradient will become less.

SHRINKAGE.

As the drying of green wood progresses the amount of free water in the cells gradually diminishes, and soon the cells near the surface have lost all their free water, i. e., they have reached the fiber-saturation point. It is at this point, which is a very definite one for most species, usually between 25 and 30 per cent moisture, that the changes in the properties of the wood begin to take place. As wood dries beyond the fiber-saturation point it begins to shrink, and it will continue to shrink as long as it loses moisture. In fact, this shrinkage is very nearly proportional to the amount of drying below the fiber-saturation point. Shrinkage is not uniform in all directions, however. The longitudinal shrinkage, parallel to the length of a board or vertical in a standing tree, is practically nothing, and may be neglected here. The tangential shrinkage, parallel to the circumference or rings or in a horizontal direction in the standing tree, is usually from one and one-half to three times as great as the radial shrinkage (horizontal in the standing tree, from the pith to the circumference, perpendicular to the rings and to the tangential direction). Shrinkage is more or less proportional to density or weight of wood; the heavier woods, as a rule, shrink more than the lighter ones.

Shrinkage is accompanied by a hardening of the wood, a reduction in its plasticity, and a reduction in the rate at which the moisture transfuses through it. There are also important changes in the mechanical properties. The wood becomes stronger under stresses, such as bending, tension, and compression, and also gains in stiffness. The increase in these properties as the wood is dried from the fiber-saturation point to zero moisture may be as much as several hundred per cent of the values in the green wood.

DRYING DEFECTS DUE TO UNEVEN SHRINKAGE.

Most of the defects ordinarily classed as drying defects would not exist if it were not for uneven shrinkage and the attendant stresses set up by it. Take the simplest case, a hypothetical one, in which a board dries without moisture gradient and with uniform radial shrinkage and uniform tangential shrinkage. If the board be radial (quarter-sawed or edge grain) or tangential (plain-sawed or flat grain), it will remain flat in drying, but after drying the radial board will be thinner and wider than the tangential one if they were both of the same width and thickness when green. If, however, the board is neither radial nor tangential, but has the grain running uniformly at an angle to the sides and edges, the difference between radial and tangential shrinkage will cause " diamonding," the sides and edges no longer being at right angles to each other. In a board partly quartered and partly slash grained the difference between radial and tangential shrinkage will cause the board to cup, the edges turning away from the heart.

CASEHARDENING.

As the outer surfaces of the board reach and pass the fiber-saturation point they begin to shrink. In order to shrink, however, they must squeeze together all of the green wood inside, since it has not yet reached the fiber-saturation point and is therefore not ready to shrink of its own accord. The first result is that the surface layers, in trying to squeeze the inside or core, create in it a state of compression and in themselves a corresponding state of tension, or pull. Imagine a rubber band stretched across a book or bundle of papers. The band is stretched and the book compressed or squeezed. The only difference is that the tension is put into the

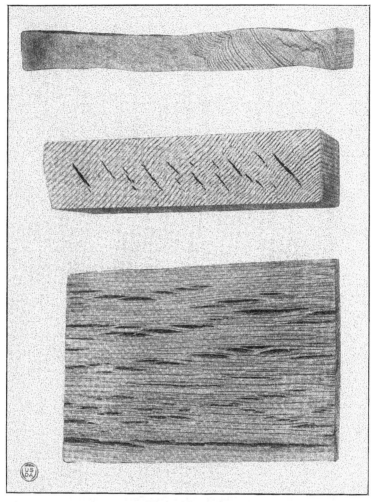

DRYING DEFECTS.

The upper board is a piece of redwood showing collapse; before drying the board was of uniform thickness.　The piece of Douglas fir plank in the center shows honeycomb.　The lower board is a resawed piece of badly honeycombed slash-sawed oak, showing the appearance of honeycomb on the tangential faces.

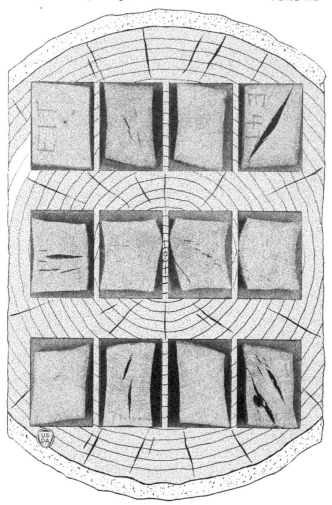

CROSS SECTION OF A SOUTHERN SWAMP OAK TREE CUT INTO BOL-
STER STOCK AND DRIED.

The black rectangles represent the green size and exact location of the pieces in the tree. The dried pieces exhibit in exaggerated form many of the common drying defects, such as checks, honeycomb, diamonding, and even cupping. The difference between radial and tangential shrinkage and the comparatively small shrinkage of some of the sapwood are illustrated.

rubber by actually stretching it, whereas the tension is produced in the outer layers of the wood by preventing it from shrinking. The same thing occurs if a piece of wet leather is prevented from shrinking as it dries.

This drying stress will increase as the drying progresses. The outer layers continue drying and shrinking and to them are continually being added other intermediate layers which are reaching the fiber-saturation point and are ready to shrink. Layers once in compression begin shrinking and place themselves in tension. Those layers still near the fiber-saturation point are more or less plastic and able to yield to stress without too much difficulty. The outer layers, however, having yielded at first, much like the rubber band, are now getting dry, and are becoming constantly less yielding. Eventually they become sufficiently stiff and there are enough of them so that they can successfully resist the stresses placed upon them by the drying, and they are in what is known as a "set" state. Further drying results in a reversal of stresses. The shrinkage of the inner layers or core is now opposed by the "set" exterior layers, and the result is that the inner layers are in tension and the outer layers in compression. If no special precautions are taken, it is to be expected that most kiln-dried stock will be in this state of stress when it is removed from the kiln. This condition is usually described as "casehardened."

CHECKING AND HONEYCOMBING.

It has been assumed that the stresses in the board were not sufficient to cause visible damage. If, however, the strength of the wood in tension across the grain is not sufficient to resist the tensile stresses in the surface layers during the early stages of drying, it will tear open, forming surface checks of varying size and depth. Likewise, if the inner layers are not strong enough to resist the tension placed upon them during the latter stages, they will rupture, causing "honeycomb" or "hollowhorn." Because radial shrinkage is less than tangential, and because a weak plane is produced where the rays and fibers cross, checks and honeycomb more often run radially than tangentially. It not infrequently happens that surface checks formed during the early stages of drying, or, in the case of partially air-dried stock, before entering the kiln, close up and disappear during the final drying. In fact, the effect caused by the shrinkage of the core may go still farther and result not only in closing the checks at the surface, but in actually deepening them and opening them up in the center, forming honeycomb. (See Fig. 4.)

WARPING, LOOSENING OF KNOTS, END CHECKING.

There are several other drying defects due to uneven shrinkage, such as warping and twisting, which are often caused by spiral or interlocked grain, by a difference in longitudinal shrinkage between sapwood and heartwood, and by various other irregularities in structure and in the drying. (See Pls. VIII and IX.) The loosening of knots is caused by the drying-out or exudation of cementing resins and gums and by the differentials in shrinkage caused by the fact that the axis of the knot or branch is at right angles to the axis of the tree. Thus the knot shrinks away from the wood lengthwise of the board, but does not shrink appreciably in the radial direction. End checking, which is caused by the very rapid drying from the end surfaces, is discussed more fully under "Drying schedules."

COLLAPSE.

One form of seasoning defect which occurs in the green wood is the actual collapse of rows of cells, just as a rubber tire collapses when the air is let out. This defect occurs only in a few species, such as redwood, western red cedar, swamp oak, and red gum. The remedy consists in the use of low temperatures at the beginning of the kiln run.

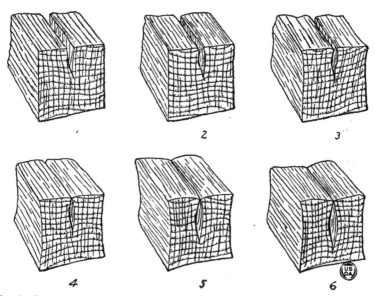

FIG. 4.—Development of a surface check into a honeycomb. 1, 2, and 3 show the check gradually closing up as the piece dries and shrinks. 4, 5, and 6 indicate how the tensile stresses deepen the bottom of the honeycomb as the casehardening becomes more severe. The depression along the center of the top, in 5 and 6, is typical of honeycomb.

STRESS DETECTION.

The detection and relief of the shrinkage stresses causing case-hardening, checking, and honeycombing is one of the most important of the kiln operator's duties, and one which requires skill and close application.

The usual method of detecting the presence of these stresses, commonly called casehardening stresses, is to cut a stress section from an average board. This stress section should be cut at least 2 feet from the end of the board, and should be about 1 inch long in the direction of the grain. It is then slotted as shown in Figure 5, the number of slots depending upon the thickness of the board and upon the preference of the individual operator. Often it is desirable to cut up several stress sections with varying numbers of slots. The direction in which the individual prongs turn and the relative lengths of the various prongs tell the story. If the outer prongs turn out, it is an indication of tension in the outer layers. If they turn in, there is compression in the outer layers. Cutting the section into prongs disturbs the balanced state and allows each prong or group of layers to make a new adjustment within itself. The compression side of each prong will immediately stretch and the tension side will contract, just as a spring under tension or compression will return to its original length when the deforming pressure is removed. In doing this the prong will be bent, the amount of the bend depending upon the thickness of the prong and upon the amount of stress originally present. The side which was originally in tension will become the concave side and the one originally in compression will become the convex one. The amount and distribution of the drying stresses can be judged by the relative bending

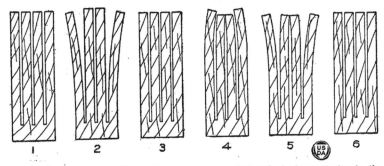

Fig. 5:—Typical stress sections. 1 represents a green board; 2 shows tension in the surface, typical of early stages in the drying; 3 shows drying has progressed farther and the shrinkage of the interior has balanced that of the surface; 4 shows typical casehardening; 5 reveals slight reversal of stresses by treatment to relieve case-hardening; 6 is the finished board free from stress. The changes in the length of the prongs have been exaggerated slightly for emphasis.

of the several prongs on each side, especially when the prongs all turn outward. When they turn inward the relative bending can not be judged so well, since they interfere with each other. In such cases it may be advantageous to cut the section into a larger number of prongs, thus reducing the amount of curve in each prong and permitting comparison of the relative lengths of the individual prongs. If they are thin enough there will be but little difference in stress between the two sides of each prong, and the state of stress will be indicated by the change in its length. All prongs in tension at the time of cutting will shorten, and those in compression will relieve themselves by lengthening. The top ends of all the prongs will form a curve, and the shape of this curve will indicate clearly the state of stress. If it is convex or high in the center, it indicates tension in the outer layers and compression in the core. If low in the center, the reverse is indicated.

So far only general indications at the time of sawing the sections have been considered. If they be now set aside in a warm place they will soon dry down to an approximately uniform moisture content, the actual amount depending upon the temperature and humidity of the surrounding atmosphere; and the changes in the moisture content of the section will be portrayed by changes in the length and curvature of the individual prongs. Loss of moisture on one side of a thick section will usually be most plainly indicated by a change of shape, the prong bending toward the side that has been drying. If the prong be in the center and there is an equal loss of moisture from both sides, the only indication will be a shrinkage in the length. In thin sections this is apt to be the case anyway, because their very thinness precludes much difference in moisture between the two sides. Under ordinary circumstances, except after special treatments, the drying of stress sections will cause a contraction or an inward turning, or both, to take place in all the prongs, the amount being proportional to the amount of moisture lost from each prong. The final shape of the section, then, is a criterion by which to judge the condition of the stock in the kiln after the drying has been completed. Caution must be used, however, since the sections dry without further stress and the stock in the kiln probably does not. The more nearly dry the stock is when the stress section is cut, the more reliable an indicator will it be in this respect.

Now that the meaning and function of stress sections have been explained, it is necessary to understand the significance of the story they tell and to learn how to correct matters if they are in need of correction.

STRESS REMEDIES.

RELIEF OF SURFACE TENSION.

The first evidence of stress in green stock in the kiln is a tension in the outer shell. This is shown in the stress section by an outward turning of the prongs, and may be considered a normal condition of affairs, more or less unavoidable. If this tension becomes too severe, surface checks will result. As it is easier to watch for surface checks than to cut stress sections, the condition of the stock in the early part of the run is usually judged by the presence or absence of surface checks. Excessive tension in the surface and surface checks are caused by too steep a moisture gradient; in other words, the moisture is being removed from the surface more rapidly than the rate of transfusion from the center to the surface. The remedy is to slow down the rate of evaporation by increasing the relative humidity of the air in the kiln. The effect of a definite increase in humidity will be apparent from a study of stress sections cut before and after the change in humidity.

PRELIMINARY STEAMING OF AIR-DRIED STOCK.

Air-dried or partially air-dried stock is frequently put into kilns for further drying. Its condition upon entering the kiln should be carefully determined so that suitable subsequent treatment may be accorded. If deep surface checks are present, the fact should be noted and recorded and the drying carried on with unusual care. Casehardening is frequently present in air-dried stock, and the surface is apt to be so dry that the transfusion of the moisture is badly hampered. For these reasons, and also to warm the stock through before drying commences, it is good practice to give it a preliminary steaming treatment. This is customarily continued for from 1½ to 2 hours for each inch of thickness, the temperature being about 15° above that at which the drying is to begin. The humidity should be kept at 100 per cent not only during the steaming but also during the subsequent cooling to the initial drying temperature. When the center of the stock is already in tension a high humidity treatment should be used instead.

RELIEF OF INTERNAL TENSION.

Assume that the stock has safely passed the first stages of drying and that the tension in the surface has passed its maximum and is now diminishing. During this period the stock is not usually liable to injury, and the only surface phenomenon is the probable closing up of any checks which may be in it. As soon as these checks have closed, or possibly even before, the tension in the surface will have disappeared and compression begun to develop. This compression will be accompanied by a corresponding tension in the core. If surface checks were originally present and have closed up, the increasing tension is apt to deepen them into honeycomb. If no surface checks were present, the stock can stand more of the internal tension which accompanies casehardening than it could otherwise. In any event, it is necessary to remedy the condition or relieve the stresses before they have reached a dangerous intensity. This is accomplished by softening the surface so that it will yield to the pull or tension of the core, thus allowing the whole piece to adjust itself by shrinkage. The amount of shrinkage is usually readily noticeable. The usual method of softening the surface is to subject the kiln charge to a steaming treatment at saturation or to a high humidity treatment at less than saturation. When the depth to which the layers in compression extend is small—that is, when the compression "zone" is shallow—steaming treatments at 100 per cent humidity are safe and satisfactory. They will produce a quick effect on the surface, which is desirable, moistening and softening only a shallow zone, which is then compressed or squeezed together by the tension or pull of the core. At the time the steaming is completed the surface will still be in compression and the core in tension, the amount of these stresses being, however, comparatively small and representing only the force required to squeeze together the wood in the compression zone, in its moistened and softened condition. Immediately after the steaming treatment, however, the surface layers will lose most of the moisture picked up during the treatment and will shrink accordingly, thus reducing all stresses and possibly even reversing them, putting the surface back into tension and preparing the stock for further shrinkage of the core.

PREVENTION OF REVERSE CASEHARDENING.

When the stock is reasonably dry and the compression zone comparatively deep, a steaming treatment may readily result in too severe an effect on the surface without enough effect toward the inner portion of the compression zone. If the treatment be continued long enough to penetrate the entire compression zone, the surface may have picked up so much moisture that the resultant great shrinkage will produce a permanent reverse casehardening, which the drying down to the desired final moisture content is not able to eliminate. This state of affairs must be avoided since reverse casehardening in dry stock can not be removed without softening up the entire piece again—a tremendously long and unsatisfactory process. It is better, therefore, to employ milder means as the stock becomes drier. Instead of steaming (100 per cent humidity), the humidity is kept at some lower point ranging usually between 60 and 85 per cent. The time required is considerably more, and the effect is correspondingly milder and more uniformly distributed through a deeper zone.

GENERAL RULES FOR STEAMING AND HIGH-HUMIDITY TREATMENTS.

It is not possible to lay down hard and fast rules for steaming and high humidity treatments; each operator will have to learn by experience just what can and must be done. The Forest Products Laboratory usually recommends that high humidity treatments be used when the core of the stock contains less than 18 per cent moisture. Above this point steaming at from 160° to 185° F. may be safely used, the period of steaming varying from one-half to three hours. These temperatures can be used advantageously also in high humidity treatments. The relative humidity will vary with the dryness of the stock. It may well be between 75 and 90 per cent when the core is between 15 and 18 per cent and between 65 and 75 per cent below that. The duration of high humidity treatments may be from 10 to 30 hours, sometimes shorter but seldom longer.

The degree to which steaming and high-humidity treatments should be used depends entirely upon the stock being dried and the purpose for which it is to be used. It may be laid down as a general rule that better results will be secured, and at less risk of damage, principally from honeycomb, if the stresses are relieved frequently by short, mild treatments than infrequently through long, severe treatments. In any event, the treatment given should be determined by the condition of the stock at the time.

Casehardening is not in itself a serious defect during the drying process, though, of course, it is undesirable and leads to various difficulties. In the finished stock, however, matters are different, and casehardening is of itself a serious defect, which results in cupping and warping, unequal shrinkage, and similar trouble, especially in resawing or in working deep patterns. It is essential, therefore, that casehardening be removed before the stock is taken from the kiln, and provision for a final treatment should be made in the drying schedule. While it is not customary to do this in the drying of most softwoods, it has been repeatedly shown that, especially for resaw stock, final relief of casehardening is very advantageous even in woods like the soft pines. There are, on the other hand, many cases, such as drying simply for shipping weight, where the financial advantage is questionable.

STEAMING TO KILL MOLDS AND WOOD-BORERS.

The kiln operator is frequently confronted with the necessity of handling stock showing evidences of decay, mold, stain, or the action of borers. Under ordinary drying conditions in the kiln, borers will be killed and the growth of decay, molds, and stains will be arrested, except possibly in the case of stains similar to the brown stain of western yellow pine. When drying is carried on at low temperatures and high humidities, however, conditions are favorable to the growth of many of these parasites, and sometimes they may cause trouble in the kiln. The growth of mold on heavy oak wagon stock during the early stages of the drying is not uncommon, and borers are occasionally found working in hickory wagon-axle stock in the kiln. The remedy usually applied is steaming for a period of about two hours at a temperature of about 180° F. This treatment may have to be repeated periodically in the case of molds, until the surface of the stock becomes dry enough to inhibit further growth.

DRYING SCHEDULES.

A drying schedule is a prescription or rule for the operation of the kiln during the drying period. Drying schedules are usually presented in the form of curves or tables showing the temperatures and humidities to be used at various stages of the drying, it being taken for granted that a kiln of suitable type, with ample and uniform circulation, etc., is available. Obviously, successful drying can not be accomplished if the kiln is incapable of doing the work required of it. The temperatures and humidities in drying schedules are based upon either the length of time the stock has been in the kiln or the current moisture content of the stock. The latter basis is used exclusively by the Forest Products Laboratory, since it is logical and of universal application.

KILN SAMPLES.

To use a drying schedule based upon the current moisture content of the stock requires a system by which this current moisture can be determined with ease and certainty. The best system so far developed depends upon the use of kiln samples. Kiln samples are short pieces of typical stock of known original moisture content, which are placed in different parts of the kiln and are periodically weighed to determine the loss of moisture. The current moisture content is computed from the original moisture content and the loss in weight, and is assumed to be the average moisture content of the stock represented by the samples.

Kiln samples are prepared as follows: Several boards, representing both fast drying and slow drying stock, are selected from the stock to be dried, and from each one or more samples about 2 feet long are cut. The sample should be cut not less than 2 feet from the end of the board, if possible, and the end 2 feet discarded. Each sample should be cut 2 inches longer than desired, a moisture section cut immediately from each end, and the moisture determination made. The average of these two moistures is assumed to be the average moisture content of the sample.

END COATINGS.

When the moisture sections have been weighed and placed in the oven the samples should be end coated. It has already been shown that wood dries out much faster from the end grain, and if the end surfaces were not protected in some suitable manner the samples would dry out from the ends, and since they are comparatively short they would soon become drier than the rest of the stock and would not represent an average.

A number of materials are being used to prevent or retard end drying under various conditions, and while some are excellent for the low temperatures encountered in air seasoning, comparatively few have proved suitable for kiln work. The most satisfactory end coating so far tested is a 213° coal-tar pitch. There are probably other pitches, asphalts, and similar materials which would serve the purpose, but additional research will be required to determine the relative efficiency of the many grades available. Materials with very high melting points are barred, since they can not be applied to the wood, and those with low melting points are unsuitable because they would flow off at the temperatures used in the kiln. Rosin and lampblack mixtures have been used with success, but their efficiency is not so great as that of coal-tar pitch, and their cost is considerably more. No coatings, liquid at ordinary temperatures, have proved so satisfactory as the hot dips.

The ends of the moisture samples are dipped into the melted pitch to a depth of about one-half to three-fourths inch. The pitch should be hot enough to produce a smooth coating approximately one-sixteenth inch thick, but not hot enough to cause any of the moisture in the wood to flash into steam and blow holes in the coating. A very thin coating is undesirable on account of lack of imperviousness, and a thick one is wasteful of pitch and at the same time causes an error in the current moisture determinations. As soon as a sample has been dipped it should be weighed immediately and the weight recorded. The average moisture content of the two moisture sections is assumed to be the moisture content of the sample. The oven-dry weight of the sample is found by multiplying the original weight of the sample by 100 and dividing by 100 plus the moisture content expressed in per cent. Thus, assume that the sample originally weighs 3.75 pounds and that the two moisture sections average 25 per cent moisture. Then the oven-dry weight of the sample equals $\frac{3.75 \times 100}{100 + 25}$, or 3 pounds. If the moisture content were expressed as a decimal instead of in the form of percentage, this formula would be still simpler; oven-dry weight equals $\frac{3.75}{1.25} = 3$. The kiln samples are placed in convenient parts of the various truck loads or piles of lumber and allowed to dry with the rest of the stock.

Whenever a current weight is taken, the current moisture content is always calculated on the basis of the calculated oven-dry weight, just as if the sample were a regular moisture section, and the moisture content of the load is assumed to be the average of the moisture contents of the various samples. If the work has been accurately done, this method will yield excellent results, but in any case a check should be made at the end of the run, by cutting moisture sections from the samples and comparing the actual moisture with the calculated moisture. Stress sections should also be cut from the samples. Extra samples should be placed in the kiln, so that current stress and moisture determinations may be made as desired.

The use of end coatings on samples is imperative; coating the ends of all of the stock in the kiln would be desirable in most kinds of difficult drying, but is not considered economical except in unusual cases, such as in the drying of heavy vehicle parts, gunstock blanks, and shoe-last blocks. The 213° pitch is recommended for this work as well as for the samples.

USE OF DRYING SCHEDULES.

The drying schedules presented on the following pages are intended to be used with kiln samples, the changes in temperature and humidity being made as the moisture content of the samples passes the various stages. All of the schedules are safe. It is possible to obtain good results with faster drying, but the use of schedules more severe than those recommended will require most careful judgment on the part of the kiln operator.

The schedules of widest application are the hardwood schedules, originally intended for furniture stock, and the softwood schedules, which provide for drying at higher temperatures. These two series supplement each other and are numbered consecutively, No. 000 of the softwood schedules being the most severe and No. 8 of the hardwood schedules being the mildest.

Preliminary steaming has been mentioned for the relief of air-drying stresses in partly dry stock. This treatment is also recommended for green stock, not to relieve stresses, but to warm the stock thoroughly before the drying operation begins. It is not necessary to steam green stock so long as partly seasoned stock, 1 hour per inch of thickness being sufficient. The temperature may be from 10 to 15° above the starting point of the schedule.

All of the drying schedules are equally applicable to green and to partially dried stock. The moisture of the stock as it enters the kiln determines where to start on the schedule. Start on the point of the schedule corresponding to that moisture content, disregarding everything above that point, just as if the previous drying had been done in the kiln in accordance with the upper part of the schedule.

HARDWOOD SCHEDULES.

The following instructions apply specifically to the hardwood schedules in Table 2. These are intended to be used on all lumber up to about 6/4 inches in thickness. Thicker stock can be dried by using a schedule one number higher (milder) for each added inch in thickness. It is intended that only one species and one thickness be dried at a time. The wet-bulb temperature is included in the schedule merely for the sake of convenience. Schedules 3 and 4 have been modified somewhat to conform to the other schedules in the group.

23241°—23——3

TABLE 2.—*Hardwood schedules 1 to 8.*

[D= dry-bulb temperature in degrees F.; W= wet-bulb temperature in degrees F.; H= per cent relative humidity.]

Moisture per cent.	Schedule 1.			Schedule 2.			Schedule 3.			Schedule 4.		
	D.	W.	H.	D.	W.	H.	D.	W.	H.	D.	W.	H.
Initial	140	132	80	135	128	80	130	123	80	125	118	80
40	145	135	75	140	130	75	135	126	75	130	121	75
30	150	137	70	145	133	70	140	128	70	135	123	70
25	155	136	60	150	132	60	145	128	60	140	123	60
20	160	135	50	155	131	50	150	127	50	145	122	50
15	165	127	35	160	124	35	155	124	40	150	120	40
10 to final	170	116	20	165	112	20	160	115	25	155	111	25

Moisture per cent.	Schedule 5.			Schedule 6.			Schedule 7.			Schedule 8.		
	D.	W.	H.	D.	W.	H.	D.	W.	H.	D.	W.	H.
Initial	120	113	80	115	109	80	110	105	85	105	101	85
40	125	116	75	120	111	75	115	109	80	110	104	80
30	130	119	70	125	114	70	120	111	75	115	107	75
25	135	121	65	130	116	65	125	112	65	120	109	70
20	140	120	55	135	116	55	130	112	55	125	110	60
15	145	119	45	140	115	45	135	111	45	130	109	50
10 to final	150	112	30	145	108	30	140	108	35	135	107	40

TABLE 3.—*Index of drying schedules to use with various hardwood species (up to 6/4 inch thick.)*

Species.	Hard-wood sched-ule.	Remarks.	Species.	Hard-wood sched-ule.	Remarks.
Ash	2		Holly, American	4	
Basswood	1		Hornbeam (iron-wood).	4	
Beech	3	Relieve stresses often.			
Birch	1		Locust	5	
Boxwood	5	Squares or quartered stock only.	Magnolia	4	
			Mahogany	4	
Butternut	2		Maple (hard and soft).	3	
Cherry, black	5				
Chestnut	2	Relieve stresses frequent-ly.	Oak, red and white	6	Northern highland stock.
			Do	7	Northern lowland stock.
Cotton gum (tu-pelo).	3		Do	7	Southern highland stock.
Cotton wood	2		Do	8	Southern lowland stock.
			Osage orange	5	
Elm	2		Persimmon	5	
Gum, red	2	Including "sap gum."	Poplar, yellow	1	
Gum, black	3		Sycamore	5	
Hackberry	2		Walnut, black	5	
Hickory	5		Willow	2	

SOFTWOOD SCHEDULES.

Because of large variations in the initial or "green" moisture content existing among the various softwoods, it has been found expedient to divide softwood schedules into several divisions, as shown in Table 4. The divisions of each schedule differ from one 'another only in the moisture contents at which the changes in temperature and humidity are to be made. It has also been found desirable to make specific recommendations for the drying of different grades and sizes of various species. Thus, while the basic principles in the construction and use of both hardwood and softwood schedules are identical, there is a slight difference in arrangement.

The softwood schedules are used as follows: Find in the species table (Table 5) the size and kind of stock to be dried and note the schedule and division given opposite it. Use this division without reference to any of the other divisions in the schedule. Suppose 4/4 Douglas fir is to be dried. The table shows two schedules, 000–IV and 00–IV, for 4/4 to 6/4 Douglas fir. The more severe one is for the ordinary run of stock and the milder one for wide flat-grain stock. There is also a general note at the foot of Table 4 stating that in drying vertical-grain flooring strips the temperature may be raised 10° F. higher than the schedule after the stock has dried down to 25 per cent. Therefore, if the 4/4 Douglas fir is flooring strips, use Schedule 000–IV, Table 4, raising the temperature to 200° F. at 25 per cent and to 210° F. at 13 per cent. If it is ordinary stock, use Schedule 000–IV without change, and if it is wide flat-grain stock, use 00–IV. These softwood schedules are not intended for use with low grades of stock. Schedules for low grades are being developed by the Forest Products Laboratory.

The initial entering-air humidity of 85 per cent given in the softwood schedules is an ideal which can be maintained only under the most favorable conditions. With fast-drying woods, the humidity of the air increases rapidly in its passage through the lumber and, unless the circulation be very rapid, air entering the lumber at 85 per cent humidity may become saturated before it leaves the pile. This causes uneven drying. Further, differences in temperature in various parts of the kiln cause comparatively wide variations in drying rate at high humidities. It is, therefore, impractical to use such high initial entering-air humidities in kilns which do not have very fast circulation and very uniform temperature throughout. Lower initial entering-air humidities must then be used in kilns with slow circulation and in kilns lacking uniformity in temperature. The slow circulation compensates in large measure for the lower entering-air humidity, since the humidity rises rapidly as the air passes through the pile, and only a small portion of the lumber is subjected to the low humidity.

In drying thin stock of a number of species, particularly southern pine and Douglas fir, it is possible to secure first-class results with lower initial entering-air humidities (as low as 70 per cent) even in kilns with extremely rapid circulation.

The operator will need to experiment more or less to determine the particular initial entering-air humidity which will give the best results w t the particular stock to be dried and the equipment available.i h

TABLE 4.—*Softwood schedules Nos. 0, 00, and 000.*

SCHEDULE 0.

Moisture content at which changes should be made.			Dry bulb.	Wet bulb.	Relative humidity.
Div. I.	Div. II.	Div. III.			
Per cent. Initial.	*Per cent.* Initial.	*Per cent.* Initial.	*° F.*	*° F.*	*Per cent.*
30	25	20	135	129	85
20	16	13	150	132	60
15	12	10	175	140	40
			175	130	30

SCHEDULE 00.

Moisture content at which changes should be made.				Dry bulb.	Wet bulb.	Relative humidity.
Div. I.	Div. II.	Div. III.	Div. IV.			
Per cent. Initial.	*Per cent.* Initial.	*Per cent.* Initial.	*Per cent.* Initial.	*° F.*	*° F.*	*Per cent.*
40	35	30	25	160	154	85
20	16	13	13	170	150	60
				180	135	30

SCHEDULE 000.

Per cent. Initial.	*Per cent.* Initial.	*Per cent.* Initial.	*Per cent.* Initial.	*° F.*	*° F.*	*Per cent.*
40	35	30	25	180	173	85
20	16	13	13	190	168	60
				200	150	30

Temperatures for vertical-grain flooring strips may be 10° higher than those in the schedule after the stock has dried to a moisture content of 25 per cent.

TABLE 5.—*Index of drying schedules for use with various species and thicknesses of softwood lumber.*

Species.	Size.	Softwood schedule.	Remarks.
Cedar, Port Orford	4/4–6/4	00–III	
	7/4–9/4	00–IV	
Cedar, western red	4/4–6/4	00–IV	Wide, clear (after sinkers are removed).
	4/4–6/4	0–III	Sinker.
	7/4–9/4	00–III	Free from sinkers.
	7/4–9/4	0–III	Sinker.
	10/4–12/4	0–III	
Cedar, white	4/4–6/4	00– II	Flat grain.
	7/4–9/4	00–III	
	10/4–12/4	0– II	
Cypress, bald	4/4–6/4	00– I	
	7/4–9/4	00– II	
	10/4–12/4	0– I	
Douglas fir	3–1/2–4–1/2	00–IV	Cross arms.
	4/4–6/4	000–IV	
	4/4–6/4	00–IV	Wide, flat grain.
	7/4–9/4	00–IV	
	10/4–12/4	0–III	

TABLE 5.—*Index of drying schedules, etc.*—Continued.

Species.	Size.	Softwood schedule.	Remarks.
Fir, balsam	4/4–6/4	000– I	Wide flat grain.
	7/4–9/4	000– II	Do.
	10/4–12/4	0– I	
Fir, lowland white	4/4–6/4	000– I	
	4/4–6/4	00– I	Do.
	7/4–9/4	000– II	
	7/4–9/4	00– II	Do.
	10/4–12/4	0– I	
Fir, noble	4/4–6/4	000–III	
	4/4–6/4	00–III	Do.
	7/4–9/4	000–IV	
	7/4–9/4	00–IV	Do.
	10/4–12/4	0–III	
Fir, white	4/4–6/4	000– I	
	4/4–6/4	00– I	Do.
	7/4–9/4	000– II	
	7/4–9/4	00– II	Do.
	10/4–12/4	0– I	
Hemlock (eastern)	4/4–6/4	00– I	Uppers.
	7/4–9/4	00– II	Do.
	10/4–12/4	0– I	
Hemlock, western	4/4–6/4	000– I	
	7/4–9/4	000– II	
	10/4–12/4	0– I	
Larch, western	4/4–6/4	00– II	Do.
	7/4–9/4	00–III	Do.
	10/4–12/4	0– II	
Pine, Norway	4/4–6/4	000– II	
	7/4–9/4	000–III	
	10/4–12/4	0– II	
Pine, southern yellow	4/4–6/4	000– I	
	7/4–9/4	00– I	
	10/4–12/4	0– I	
Pine, western yellow	4/4–6/4	000– I	
	7/4–9/4	00– I	
	10/4–12/4	0– I	
Pine, white (eastern and western)	4/4–6/4	00– II	Do.
	7/4–9/4	00–III	Do.
	10/4–12/4	0– II	
Redwood	4/4–6/4	00– I	Free from sinkers.
	4/4–6/4	0– I	Sinker.
	7/4–9/4	00– II	Free from sinkers.
	7/4–9/4	0– II	Sinker.
	10/4–12/4	0– I	
Spruce, Engelmann	4/4–6/4	00– II	
	7/4–9/4	00–III	
	10/4–12/4	0– I	
Spruce, red	4/4–6/4	00–III	
	7/4–9/4	00–IV	
	10/4–12/4	0–III	
Spruce, Sitka	4/4–6/4	000– II	
	4/4–6/4	00– II	Wide, flat grain.
	7/4–9/4	000–III	
	7/4–9/4	00–III	Do.
	10/4–12/4	0– II	
Spruce, white	4/4–6/4	000–III	
	4/4–6/4	00–III	Do.
	7/4–9/4	000–IV	
	7/4–9/4	00–IV	Do.
	10/4–12/4	0–III	
Tamarack	4/4–6/4	00– II	
	7/4–9/4	00–III	
	10/4–12/4	0– II	

The hardwood schedules and the softwood schedules together cover almost the entire temperature range commonly used in kiln drying. They range from an initial temperature of 105° F. in hardwood schedule 8, Table 2, to a final temperature of 210° F. for vertical-grain flooring strips in softwood schedule 000, Table 4. While most drying can be reasonably well done by the use of the proper one of these 11 schedules, it has been found advantageous to develop special schedules for certain purposes. A number of these follow.

COMMON GRADES OF DOUGLAS FIR.

The kiln drying of Douglas fir common is a problem quite different in several respects from most seasoning problems. One of the most important considerations is to keep the knots from falling out, and another is the fact that it is not necessary to dry the stock lower than about 15 per cent. This latter makes it much easier to keep the knots from falling out, but brings the added complication that it is very difficult to dry a load of mixed heart and sap to a uniform moisture content as high as 15 per cent. To prevent excessive shrinkage of the knots, it is necessary to maintain a high humidity throughout the drying. The maximum temperature is more or less definitely limited because it is undesirable to use temperatures high enough to melt the resin from around the knots. The need for reasonable uniformity in moisture content at the end of the run and the use of high humidity make it necessary to have a very rapid and uniform circulation readily reversible in direction, and an accurate control of temperature and humidity.

Douglas fir common schedules were developed in a semicommercial unit of the Forest Service internal-fan kiln, and this is the only type which can at present be safely recommended for this class of work. A constant temperature of 175° F. may be used throughout the entire drying period. In the case of 1 by 6, 1 by 8, 2 by 4, and 2 by 6 inch stock the humidity may be kept constant at 70 per cent. For 1 by 10, 1 by 12, 2 by 8, 2 by 10, and 2 by 12 inch stock, it is better to use a humidity of 80 per cent for the first half of the run, dropping then to 70 per cent. The drying time will vary considerably with the size and shape of the stock. For 1 by 8 inch material it should be about 32 hours, with a final average moisture content of 15 per cent.

AIRCRAFT STOCK.

It has been proved by many kiln runs and by many thousands of strength tests that the aircraft schedules given below, if carefully followed, will produce stock that is just as strong in every way as the most carefully air-seasoned stock. These schedules were prepared by the Forest Products Laboratory, and since 1917 they have been the standard for the Army and Navy air services. They are intended to be used on stock 3 inches or less in thickness. For thicker stock the temperature is to be lowered 5° F. for each inch increase in thickness.

TABLE 6.—*Aircraft Schedule I.*

Stage of drying.	Drying conditions.		
	Maximum dry-bulb temperature.	Minimum relative humidity.	Wet bulb.
	° F.	Per cent.	° F.
At the beginning..	120	80	113
After fiber saturation is passed (25 per cent).................	125	70	114
At 20 per cent moisture..	128	60	112
At 15 per cent moisture..	138	44	112
At 12 per cent moisture..	142	38	112
At 8 per cent moisture...	145	33	110
Final...	145	33	110

SPECIES FOR WHICH AIRCRAFT SCHEDULE I IS APPLICABLE.

Ash, white, blue, and Biltmore.
Birch, yellow.
Cedar, incense.
Cedar, northern white.

Cedar, western red.
Cedar, Port Orford.
Cypress, bald.
Pine, sugar.

Pine, white (eastern and western).
Spruce, red and white.
Spruce, Sitka.

TABLE 7.—*Aircraft Schedule II.*

Stage of drying.	Drying conditions.		
	Maximum dry-bulb temperature.	Minimum relative humidity.	Wet bulb.
	° F.	Per cent.	° F.
At the beginning..	105	85	100
After fiber saturation is passed (25 per cent).................	110	73	101
At 20 per cent moisture..	117	62	103
At 15 per cent moisture..	129	46	106
At 12 per cent moisture..	135	42	109
At 8 per cent moisture...	135	40	107
Final...	135	40	107

SPECIES FOR WHICH AIRCRAFT SCHEDULE II IS APPLICABLE.

Cherry, black.
Douglas fir.

Mahogany.
Oak, white, and red.

Walnut, black.
Maple (hard and soft).

OAK WHEEL BLANKS.

Several schedules have been developed for oak artillery-wheel stock—club-turned spokes and bent rims. Since oak is extremely variable in its drying characteristics, extreme care must be exercised in using these schedules. Steaming of bent rims must be done with caution, since over-steaming will relieve the set caused by the bending, thus allowing the stock to straighten out. Steaming for from 1 to 2 hours at 160 to 180° F. may be done periodically after the outer one-half inch has dried below 25 per cent.

TABLE 8.—*Drying schedule for 56-inch artillery wheel spoke blanks, oak, 2¾ by 2¾ by 26 inches.*

Moisture content.	Dry bulb.	Wet bulb.	Relative humidity.
Per cent.	*° F.*	*° F.*	*Per cent.*
80	105	100.5	85
60	106	100.5	82
40	107	100.5	79
30	110	101.5	74
25	115	102	63
20	120	102	54
15	131.5	104	40
10	142	106	30

TABLE 9.—*Drying schedule for 60-inch artillery wheel spoke blanks, oak, 3¾ by 3¾ by 26 inches.*

Moisture content.	Dry bulb.	Wet bulb.	Relative humidity.
Per cent.	*° F.*	*° F.*	*Per cent.*
80	100	96	85
60	101	96	82
40	102	96	80
30	105	97	75
25	110	98	64
20	115	99	55
15	127	101	40
10	140	103	29

TABLE 10.—*Drying schedule for 56-inch artillery wheel rims, bent oak, 3½ by 3½ by 56 inches.*

Moisture content.	Dry bulb.	Wet bulb.	Relative humidity.
Per cent.	*° F.*	*° F.*	*Per cent.*
70	90	83	75
65	95	88	75
60	100	93	75
55	105	97	75
50	110	102	75
35	115	105	70
30	120	105	60
20	130	106	45
15	140	108	35
10	150	107	25

TABLE 11.—*Drying schedule for 60-inch artillery wheel rims, bent oak, 3¾ by 3¾ by 60 inches.*

Moisture content.	Dry bulb.	Wet bulb.	Relative humidity.
Per cent.	*° F.*	*F°.*	*Per cent.*
70	85	78	75
65	90	83	75
60	95	88	75
55	100	93	75
50	105	97	75
35	110	100	70
30	115	100	60
20	125	102	45
15	135	104	35
10	145	104	25

WALNUT GUNSTOCKS.

Walnut for gunstocks is usually cut in the form of rough blanks, steamed to darken the sapwood, and then shipped to the gunmaker for drying. All stocks to be kiln dried should be end dipped in hot pitch before loading into the kiln. A schedule that has been used successfully in the drying of many thousand blanks is given in Table 12.

MAPLE SHOE-LAST BLOCKS.

Maple shoe-last blocks, end dipped and piled on stickers, can be dried successfully under hardwood schedule 7.

PENCIL CEDAR.

Pencil cedar, the southern juniper used for pencils and cedar chests, is quite difficult to dry and care must be used to prevent the shelling off of the streaks of sapwood which will result from too steep a moisture gradient and too severe casehardening. A special schedule (Table 13) has been prepared for the drying of 1-inch boards of this species; it covers about the same range as hardwood schedule 3.

The cedar oil present in this wood causes a variable error in making moisture determinations, since it is driven off with the moisture in the drying oven, resulting in a calculated moisture content higher than the actual. This error is usually not more than 2 or 3 per cent, though it may be as great as 5 per cent.

TABLE 12.—*Drying schedule for black walnut gunstock blanks.*

Moisture content.	Dry bulb.	Wet bulb.	Relative humidity.
Per cent.	° *F.*	° *F.*	*Per cent.*
Initial.	110	102	75
35	113	102	68
20	115	104	67
15	117	103	62
10	130	105	43
8 to final.	140	107	34

TABLE 13.—*Drying schedule for 1-inch pencil cedar.*

Moisture content (heart samples).	Dry bulb.	Wet bulb.	Relative humidity.
Per cent.	° *F.*	° *F.*	*Per cent.*
Initial.	140	128	70
20	150	127	50
15	155	124	40
10 to final.	160	115	25

PLYWOOD PANELS.

The drying of plywood panels is a special problem in which simplicity of control and operation are important. Panels can be dried successfully under widely varying conditions of temperature and humidity, largely because the original moisture content is low. However, the effect of the drying schedule upon the properties of the glue must be taken into consideration. It has been found possible to dry panel stock at a constant temperature and a constant humidity, the latter corresponding to a moisture content about 3 per cent below that to which the panels are to be dried. Thus, if the panels are to come down to 10 per cent, a humidity corresponding to about 7 per cent would be used. (See Fig. 3.) At a temperature of 125° F., which is considered suitable for this work, the humidity corresponding to 7 per cent moisture is about 43 per cent. A temperature of 125° F. and a humidity of 43 per cent will dry the average half-inch panel down to 10 per cent moisture in a few hours; and if the stock be left in the kiln considerably longer, no particular damage will result, since the drying rate below the desired 10 per cent will be increasingly slow.

BENT STOCK.

Bent stock of various kinds may be dried according to the lumber schedules applying to species and thickness, but caution must be exercised in the matter of steaming, since the excessive use of steam in the early stages of the drying is very apt to result in straightening out the stock.

SUPERHEATED-STEAM DRYING.

All of the schedules so far presented are adapted to use in "air" kilns. It is possible to accomplish drying in superheated steam, and several types of superheated-steam kilns are now in use. Live steam superheated by means of coils carrying high-pressure steam is turned into the kiln. The degree of superheat, or the temperature above the boiling point at atmospheric pressure, governs the drying rate, and no further humidity control is needed. Drying temperatures usually range between 225° and 240° F., depending upon the class of wood being dried and upon the boiling point at atmospheric pressure. Sometimes an unusual amount of air is mixed with the steam in the kiln, with the result that the drying capacity of the atmosphere is correspondingly increased. Such cases are indicated by a wet-bulb reading below the boiling point, and so a lower degree of superheat must be carried.

Species now being dried commercially by superheated steam are principally Douglas fir and western hemlock. Other species for which it may be suitable are western yellow pine, sugar pine, eastern white pine, southern yellow pines, most of the spruces, and some of the true firs. In some of these woods a certain amount of darkening of the surface, especially of the sapwood, may be expected.

DRYING PERIODS.

The extreme variability of the drying time with individual lots of stock and with different types of equipment, added to the variable time consumed in steaming and conditioning treatments, makes a tabulation of drying time of doubtful value. About the fastest drying time for lumber of which the Forest Products Laboratory has record is the drying of 1 by 4 inch Douglas fir flooring strips in 24 hours; the slowest, the drying of some southern oak wagon bolsters, which were in the kiln almost a year, and then were not drier than 15 per cent.

The average periods required to dry several common hardwoods are presented in Table 14. While these drying rates can readily be secured in kilns with high velocity of circulation, it does not necessarily follow that they can be duplicated under all conditions.

TABLE 14.—*Average drying time for 1-inch stock, green from the saw to 5 per cent moisture.*

Species.	Original moisture content.	Drying time.	Species.	Original moisture content.	Drying time.
	Per cent.	*Days.*		*Per cent.*	*Days.*
Yellow birch..................	80	21	Oak, red and white:[1]		
Red gum..................	100	26	Northern highland stock...	80	40
Sugar maple..................	80	23	Northern lowland stock. _ _ }	80	48
Mahogany..................	80	22	Southern highland stock...}		
Black walnut..................	80	30	Southern lowland stock....	80	56

· ₁ Plain sawed only; quartered takes about one-third longer with the same schedule.

Maple last blocks can be dried in about 60 days, and walnut gunstock blanks in about the same length of time. Heavy oak wagon stock takes from one and one-half to two months per inch of thickness to dry down to 15 per cent moisture. The common drying times for 1-inch softwoods, such as Douglas fir, the southern yellow pines, and the white pines, run from two to four days, there being exceptions in both directions. Quartered stock may usually take a higher schedule, and thus make up for some of its natural slowness in drying. It has already been mentioned that certain woods, like redwood, western red cedar, and cypress, are subject to collapse at high moisture and temperatures. The hardwoods, as a rule, are more plastic when hot and moist than the conifers, and in consequence are more easily bent. This fact is taken advantage of in the drying of red gum, for instance, which has a natural tendency to warp, but seems plastic enough at high temperatures to overcome this tendency, drying with but little trouble if properly " stickered."

FINAL MOISTURE CONTENT.

As has been stated, the final moisture content should be slightly lower than that which the finished product would naturally have after it had been in service for some time. The first thing to consider, therefore, is the ultimate use to which the finished product is to be put and the climatic conditions at the point of use. Whether the product is for use indoors or outdoors also is a determining factor. Sometimes it is desired to have the stock swell after it is put in service, and in these cases it is dried lower than it otherwise would be.

A study of the weather reports for various parts of the country shows that the average atmospheric temperature and humidity conditions vary greatly in the different regions and that they also have important seasonal variations in each place. The relative humidities for a number of cities are given in Table 15 to show these variations.

While it is not possible to lay down any hard-and-fast rules for proper final moistures, the information in Table 16, based on average conditions in the East and Middle West, may serve as a guide in the drying of stock for specific purposes.

TABLE 15.—*Mean relative humidities at various points in the United States.*

City.	Mean relative humidity, per cent.				
	Winter.	Spring.	Summer.	Fall.	Annual.
Cleveland, Ohio	77	72	70	74	73
Denver, Colo	54	51	49	46	50
El Paso, Tex	45	27	41	46	40
Galveston, Tex	84	82	79	78	81
Madison, Wis	82	80	71	75	74
Memphis, Tenn	74	69	75	71	72
New Orleans, La	79	75	78	77	77
New York, N. Y	73	70	74	75	73
Pensacola, Fla	80	77	79	75	78
Phoenix, Ariz	47	32	32	41	38
Portland, Oreg	84	72	67	79	75
San Diego, Calif	74	78	81	78	78
Spokane, Wash	82	61	47	67	64
Wilmington, N. C	78	78	83	81	80

TABLE 16.—*Final moisture content of stock for various uses.*

	Final moisture, per cent.
Furniture	5 to 7
Interior woodwork	6 to 8
Vehicle stock, except wheel and box parts	15 to 18
Vehicle wheel and box parts	8
Gunstocks	6 to 8
Aircraft (Army)	8
Aircraft (Navy)	12
Outdoor sporting goods (bats, golf sticks, tennis rackets, polo mallets, etc.)	10
Musical instruments	5 to 7
Softwoods for long freight shipments	12 or less
Miscellaneous outdoor material	12

NOTE.—Thoroughly air-dried wood ranges from 12 to 18 per cent moisture content, depending on local climatic conditions.

MOISTURE SPECIFICATION.

Much of the trouble experienced in the use of lumber results from improper seasoning, and many disputes arise from a misunderstanding of the use or meaning of broad and loose terms, such as " kiln dried " or " air dried," or even " thoroughly kiln dried " or " thoroughly air dried." These terms are so indefinite that they really are without significance. There is now no universally accepted standard moisture specification, and each purchaser must draw his own. A moisture or seasoning specification is fully as important as a grade specification—sometimes much more important—and it is essential that the purchaser know that he is getting stock properly seasoned for his use.

A number of wood users throughout the country are now specify-, ing the amount of moisture that the stock shall contain at the time of shipment or receipt, which is excellent in every way. It is not always enough, however, since there may be a vast difference as to seasoning between two lots of stock dried down to the same moisture. The specification should include a clause concerning the presence of drying stresses, based upon the use of stress sections. To be complete and accurate such a clause would be quite lengthy and cumbersome, and therefore more or less impractical. However, a simple statement that the wood shall be free from injurious drying stresses, while very broad, affords reasonable protection to the purchaser.

STORAGE OF KILN-DRIED STOCK.

Whenever possible, the stock should be cooled before it is removed from the kiln, since exposure of the hot stock to the cool air is liable to cause checking. All of the boards in the kiln are not of the same moisture content at the end of the drying period. It is therefore necessary that they be held in storage until both dry and moist boards have the same moisture content. The required time for storage varies with conditions. Where little accuracy is needed, as with softwood, the stock need be stored but a short time. One week is considered long enough for furniture stock, and two weeks are specified for aircraft stock. Careful conditioning in the kiln reduces the required time of storage.

Dimension stock and finished wood products which have to be stored should be held in the proper atmospheric conditions, or they will absorb or lose too much moisture. Later, when the stock is manufactured and put into actual use, this loss or gain may damage its serviceability. Stock taken from damp, unheated storerooms into heated shops is too moist for the best utility. The moisture is unevenly distributed not only in the individual pieces of stock but in the entire pile. The boards on the sides and top have a different moisture content from those in the pile. Products made from such stock may be end-checked or distorted. Short stock with large end surfaces warps when stored in a damp atmosphere. Such stock used in chair seats of the common saddle style, if dried too rapidly, shows end checks and open glue joints.

KILN TYPES.

Dry kilns for wood may be grouped in two general classes, commonly known as progressive and compartment. Progressive kilns are sometimes called "continuous" kilns, and compartment kilns are known as "box" or "charge" kilns. The differences between the two types depend on the method of handling the stock through the kiln. In the progressive kiln (Fig. 6), the stock enters at one end and moves progressively through to the other end, emerging, presumably dry, at the proper time. The stock is fed in and removed periodically, and the process is continuous. In the compartment kiln the entire kiln is loaded at one time, and the charge remains in place throughout the drying period. In the progressive kiln the temperature and humidity at any point remain constant, but the kiln is hotter and drier at the discharge end than at the receiving end; in the compartment kiln the temperature and humidity are as nearly uniform as possible throughout the kiln at any given time, and are changed from time to time as the stock dries.

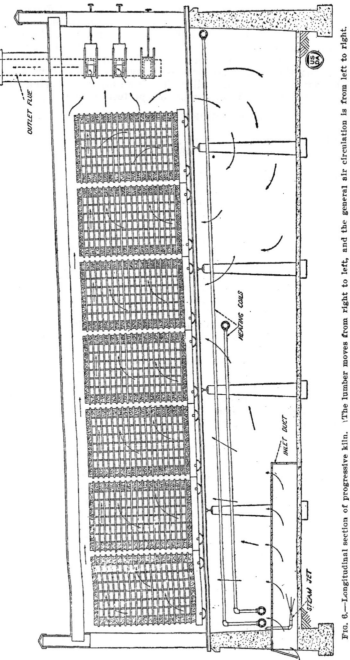

FIG. 6.—Longitudinal section of progressive kiln. (The lumber moves from right to left, and the general air circulation is from left to right.

Since the temperature and humidity vary from end to end in a progressive kiln, the circulation of air must, in part at least, be longitudinal; the circulation in a compartment kiln may be in almost any desired direction but is usually some kind of cross circulation.

The progressive kiln finds its greatest field of usefulness in those places where drying requirements are not exacting and quantities of the same class of stock are to be dried continuously. The compartment kiln is adapted to all classes of drying. The heat efficiency of the progressive kiln is generally greater than that of the compartment type, but its accuracy of control and its flexibility are much less.

PROGRESSIVE KILNS.

Almost all progressive kilns are of the natural-draft type, although a number of progressive blower kilns have been built. The air usually enters through ducts at the discharge or dry end of the kiln, is heated by steam coils under the lumber, and humidified by means of a steam jet. It then passes upward through the lumber, horizontally the length of the kiln, and finally out into the atmosphere at the green end through chimneys provided for this purpose. As it progresses through the kiln it becomes cooler and more moist, the cooling itself increasing the relative humidity and the moisture evaporated from the wood adding its share. Thus the severity of its action is automatically reduced as the air reaches the greener lumber. The extent of this reduction depends upon the individual kiln design, upon outside atmospheric conditions, and upon the kind, thickness, and initial moisture content of the stock being dried. The longer the kiln the more moist and the cooler will be the air at the green end. Very wet, easily dried stock, or a reduction of heating surface at the green end will have the same effect. A reduction of the rate of circulation may have a similar effect. To adjust conditions so that moisture and humidity are in accordance with the drying schedule throughout the length of the kiln is usually very difficult, since ordinarily the temperature and humidity can each be regulated at one point only. They can both be controlled at one end or at opposite ends, as seems best under the circumstances. Occasionally steam jets can be fitted along the length of the kiln to increase the humidity as the air moves toward the green end, and in some kilns vents are provided along the length so that some of the air can be exhausted before it reaches the green end. There is seldom any provision, however, for regulating the temperature along the length of the kiln.

The methods of producing circulation and ventilation vary considerably among the kiln manufacturers, just as details of the heating elements differ. The general principles and operation are, however, much more nearly alike than would appear at first sight.

Progressive kilns are always provided with tracks, and the lumber is rolled through on trucks or bunks. To provide for preliminary steaming, in many ventilated progressive kilns a steaming chamber can be formed by dropping a curtain between two trucks near the green end. Steaming in this curtained-off space is apt to upset the conditions in the kiln, increasing the humidity throughout. Furthermore, trouble may result if the steamed stock is not carefully cooled in saturated air to the drying temperature before the curtain is rolled up and drying resumed.

VENTILATED COMPARTMENT KILNS.

Ventilated compartment kilns also vary considerably in detailed design. Most of them, however, are arranged for cross circulation,

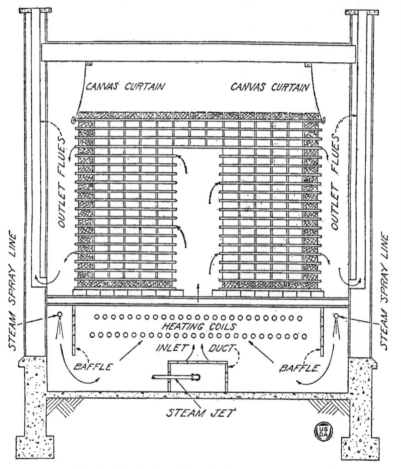

Fig. 7.—Cross section of ventilated compartment kiln.

and the fresh air is usually brought in at the bottom and distributed throughout the length of the kiln by means of ducts under the lumber. Ventilating flues are usually provided along the length of the kiln on both sides, and outlets to these made at various heights and in various manners, in accordance with the ideas of the individual manufacturer. The entire possible range of locations for these outlets is represented in commercial practice, at least one manufacturer drawing the air from under the lumber on the floor of the kiln, and another having the vents located in the roof. Almost as wide a range is to be found in the location of the inlet openings in the kiln; although the air may be brought into the kiln in ducts running along the floor, several kiln designers carry it up in risers at various points along the length of the kiln and deliver it at convenient heights above the rails. While it is usual to provide considerable outlet flue area, there is a wide difference in the amount of inlet area. One maker provides none at all, another allows about a square foot for a kiln 70 feet long, and a third insists upon at least 4 or 5 square feet for a similar kiln only 40 feet long.

The cross circulation in most ventilated compartment kilns depends largely on the draft of the chimneys or vents. It may be assisted by steam jets placed in air intakes or outlets, and even by the steam used in the kiln for humidification. If the circulation caused by the cooling of the air as moisture is evaporated from the wood can be made to augment the draft of the chimneys, the maximum circulation and the most satisfactory drying will be secured. Figure 7 shows the general construction of a ventilated compartment kiln. This figure is a composite representing no particular make of dry kiln. While it is not offered as a scale drawing for an ideal kiln, very good results can be obtained from kilns built upon the principles illustrated.

The principles of the kiln can best be understood by following the arrows which indicate the air flow. The air enters through the inlet duct, which has suitable openings along its length. The steam jet located in the inlet duct where it enters the kiln increases the rate of flow. The air from the duct passes over the heating coils and into the chimney or flue in the center of the lumber pile, thence outward and downward. Some is exhausted through the flue outlets and some returns past the steam-spray line and the baffles to the heating coils and around again. The downward-pointing steam sprays are always used for steaming and high-humidity treatments, and may be used to assist the steam jet or to act in its place during the drying period. The baffles prevent the air from rising in any passages except the chimney, thus assisting materially in producing and maintaining the desired air flow. They also prevent the steam from spraying against the lumber or the heating pipes. The floor boards under the lumber pile protect the lower layers from direct radiation and prevent the short-circuiting of the air through them.

WATER SPRAY AND CONDENSER KILNS.

The water-spray kiln was invented and developed at the Forest Products Laboratory. As ordinarily designed it embodies the principles of the condenser kiln, and the two may be described together. Figure 8 is a cross section of a typical water-spray kiln. The circulation is similar to that in Figure 7, although there are no intakes or outlets. The baffles at the bottom of the spray chambers prevent spray or mist from passing along with the air and thus increasing the humidity beyond the desired point. The condensers and the water sprays are located close together, and both serve to regulate the humidity and increase the circulation. The sprays and condensers are usually used for high and low humidity, respectively. When the sprays are in use the air is cooled to the dew point each

time it passes through the circuit; but with the condensers no attempt
is made to do this, and condenser water just sufficient to keep the
humidity down to the desired point is used. A kiln designed for the
use of condensers only, need have neither sprays nor baffles, and the
height of the condensers may be varied to meet individual requirements. Water-spray and condenser kilns require a supply of cold

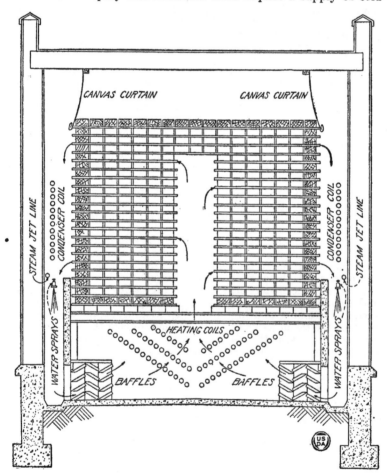

FIG. 8.—Cross section of water-spray compartment kiln.

water in addition to the steam or other source of heat. In the condenser kiln the water is ordinarily run out as waste after passing
through the coils, but in the water-spray kiln it is usually returned
from the spray chambers and recirculated by means of pumps,
enough cold water being added to bring the temperature down to
the desired point. The humidity in the water-spray kiln, when using
the sprays, is controlled by regulating the water temperature; and

since the air leaving the sprays and passing through the baffles is at its dew point, a recording thermometer is usally placed in the baffles. This thermometer shows the dew point rather than the wet-bulb temperature, and for convenient use in water-spray kilns, the drying schedules should be modified to show the dew-point temperature as well as the wet-bulb temperature.

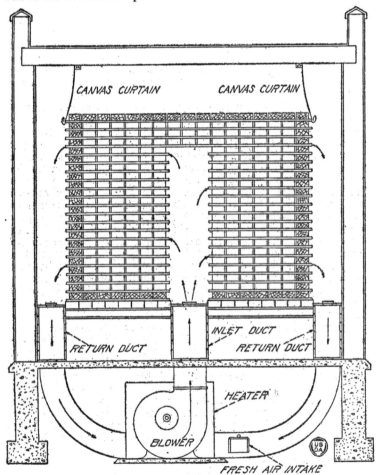

Fig. 9.—Cross section of blower compartment kiln.

BLOWER KILNS.

Fans or blowers are used in several types of kilns for forcing the circulation. Blower kilns for drying lumber are, almost without exception, of the recirculating compartment type, and those in commercial use are mostly of the external-blower type. Figure 9 is a diagrammatical cross section of a blower kiln and illustrates the path of the air through the system. The blower is usually placed outside the kiln in an operating room at one end, discharging and returning through ducts running the full length of the kiln. The heating units may be in a box located at the blower, or they may be arranged in almost any desired form in the kiln proper. Humidity may be increased by means of a steam jet located in the return duct and decreased by opening a fresh-air intake also in the return duct. One manufacturer prefers to decrease the humidity in his blower kilns by using canvas curtains to form the outer walls of the flues. Between these curtains and the side walls of the kiln are ventilated passages about a foot wide. Moisture transfuses through the curtains from the inside out, and is carried away on the ventilating current of air. This air may be drawn from the operating room and exhausted through a chimney.

The rate of circulation in blower kilns may be increased indefinitely, but beyond a certain point it is difficult to maintain unformity. A few forced-circulation kilns in which the circulation is produced by fans located in the kiln itself have been used for the drying of lumber and veneer; and several such types of kilns are being developed at the Forest Products Laboratory. In one of these the fans are all mounted on a single shaft running lengthwise of the kiln and driven by a motor located outside. Office fans and other self-contained motor-driven fans have also been used with considerable success. There are several points of special interest in this type of forced circulation, of which ease of installation and reversal of circulation are foremost. Periodical reversal of the circulation produces faster and more uniform drying. Humidity in these kilns may be controlled by any one of several methods, but usually steam alone is sufficient, as leakage keeps the humidity sufficiently low.

Figure 10 is a diagrammatical cross section of an internal-fan kiln of the compartment type, arranged for flat-end piling. The double-pointed arrows illustrate the path of the air through the lumber; the direction of air travel may be reversed at will by reversing the direction of rotation of the fan shaft. This shaft extends the length of the kiln and has fans mounted upon it at intervals of about 7 feet. These fans are so housed that when the direction of rotation is such that the air movement is upward through the central flue and downward along the side walls, the air enters the fans through suitable openings in the side walls of the housings and is deflected upward after passing through the fans. The double distributors serve to distribute the air uniformly along the width and length of the central flue, reducing the velocity appreciably at the same time.

Recent tests have shown that a very uniform, fast circulation of air may be obtained in this type of kiln with a surprisingly small power consumption.

SUPERHEATED-STEAM KILNS.

The superheated-steam kiln is comparatively simple in construction and operation. Provision must be made for high-pressure steam for heating coils and jets; the circulation must be reversed periodically; and the kiln must be designed for short travel of the steam through the lumber. One type of superheated-steam kiln was invented and developed at the Forest Products Laboratory. Figure 11 illustrates in a general way the principles of construction. The heating coils are conveniently mounted on the side walls, and a steam-jet line runs along the top and bottom of each wall. The two left lines operate simultaneously, and likewise the two right lines. The arrows indicate the direction of the circulation when the left lines are open. With the right lines open the circulation will be reversed.

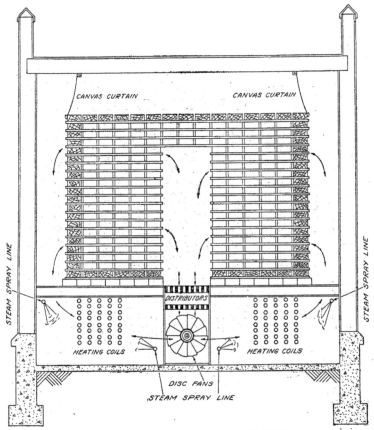

FIG. 10.—Cross section of internal-fan kiln. A number of disk fans are mounted at intervals upon a shaft extending the full length of the kiln.

PILING LUMBER FOR KILN DRYING.

Lumber to be kiln dried is usually piled in layers with strips or stickers between each two layers. Sometimes short stock, like spoke billets, handles, and shoe-last blocks, is simply dumped into the kiln without any attempt at orderly arrangement. This method is apt to produce irregular drying unless only small amounts are dried at a time. The piling and sticking of the lumber should provide suitable air passage between the boards in each layer and between layers, and furnish support to the lumber during drying so that it will be as straight as possible when dry.

For drying in a progressive kiln, the lumber is always loaded on trucks or bunks and run through the kiln on rails, which are usually pitched down toward the dry end, so that gravity will assist in moving the trucks. Large compartment kilns are usually provided

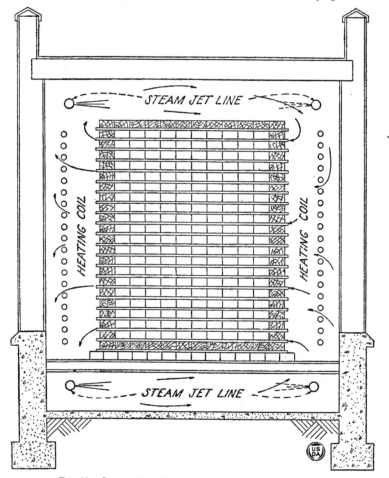

FIG. 11.—Cross section of superheated-steam compartment kiln.

with rails, so that the lumber can be run in on trucks; but many small kilns have no such provisions, and the lumber is piled on horses or other supports.

The two general kinds of piling used for lumber are vertical or edge piling, and horizontal or flat piling. Each of these may be divided into cross and end piling. In cross piling, the boards run crosswise of the kiln, and in end piling they run lengthwise of the kiln.

FLAT PILING.

Cross piling (Pl. X) is most suitable for kilns with longitudinal circulation, and end piling for kilns with cross circulation. This is determined by the arrangement of the stickers. In cross piling they extend lengthwise of the kiln, thus aiding longitudinal circulation. In the same way, end piling (Pl. XI) favors cross circulation. A large number of kilns are, nevertheless, being operated contrary to these principles, particularly cross-circulation ventilated compartment kilns with cross piling. These methods are not absolutely essential, but better results are obtained by following them.

The spacing of the boards in the layer has an important bearing upon circulation, especially in ventilated kilns, and manufacturers of this type frequently recommend a wide spacing. This assists in permitting a freer circulation, especially in cross-circulation kilns with cross piling. The amount of space to leave in any particular case is a matter of judgment and depends upon the circulation. Ordinarily 1-inch spaces do very well for almost all kinds of stock when there is ample circulation; when the circulation is poor, and uneven drying results, the spaces may be enlarged to 3 or 4 inches for wide boards. For narrow boards there is less need for widening the spaces.

The thickness of the stickers may vary with local conditions; however, they should all be straight and of uniform thickness. Seven-eighths-inch stickers are commonly used for most classes of stock, except in edge-stacking, when the requirements of the stacking machine may determine the thickness. If stickers are made about one and one-half times as wide as they are thick, they will lie flat and not tend to roll when the boards are laid on them.

The spacing between rows of stickers should be reasonably close. Four feet should be the maximum distance for most hardwoods and 6 feet for easily dried softwoods. If the boards show a tendency to twist and warp, a closer spacing should be used, and great care must be exercised in the actual piling. To obtain best results, material dried at one time should be of the same species and thickness and with moisture content as nearly uniform as circumstances permit. The supports for the lumber should be firm and even and arranged with one under each row of stickers. These rows should be kept perfectly vertical; otherwise there will be a tendency to warp the boards. The ideal is to have boards of only one length in each pile; but where this is impossible the piles should be made long enough to cut down the number of projecting ends, and the short boards should be brought flush alternately at both ends of the pile. In the case of cross-piled progressive kilns it is especially desirable that the piles should take up the full width of the kiln, so that there may be as little opportunity as possible for the short circuiting of the circulation around the lumber. For the same reason, the piles should extend the full length of the trucks.

VERTICAL PILING.

Under certain conditions vertical or edge piling is considered to be somewhat cheaper than flat piling, and is being used by a number of big mills in the softwood regions. (See Pl. XII.) Several different automatic stacking and unstacking machines have been developed for this work. While they differ in operation, the resulting piles are very much alike, except in the width and thickness of the stickers. The layers of boards and the stickers are vertical, and there is no space between the boards in each layer. As the lumber dries and shrinks there is a tendency for the piles to become loose and to lean. To avoid this trouble several take-ups have been devised. These take-ups are intended to squeeze the load together sidewise as the boards shrink and thus keep it always tight. A serious objection to most of them is that they increase the weight of the bunk very considerably; this is important where the bunks have to be handled by hand.

The principal direction of circulation with vertical piling must be upward or downward through the lumber. In ventilated kilns it is upward, in blower kilns either upward or downward, and in superheated steam kilns both upward and downward.

Vertical stacking would seem, at first sight, to permit much better circulation than flat piling. The unimpeded passage of the hot air from the heating coils underneath up through all the straight, open, vertical spaces between the layers of boards seems very simple. However, it is not so simple as it appears. Trouble is experienced in keeping the air in the lumber piles hot, it cools as soon as it strikes the lumber, and then begins to descend and interferes with the air trying to come up. Further, there is usually a space on either side of the kiln and other spaces between the trucks through which the air can rise more easily than through the piles. Another peculiarity which may cause trouble, especially in superheated steam kilns, is that the length of travel through the pile is comparatively great, causing a large difference in drying conditions between the entering air and leaving air sides of the pile. These points indicate why it is necessary with vertical piling to use a specially designed kiln instead of using a kiln designed for flat piling.

DETAILS OF KILN OPERATION.

The successful operation of dry kilns requires constant care and attention. The results secured depend in a large degree upon the operator, and he should be impressed with his responsibility to bend every effort to turn out perfect stock. The operator must first familiarize himself with the kilns under his supervision. Before making the first run in a kiln, he should make a careful inspection to assure himself that it is mechanically safe, that the heating coils, traps, etc., are in proper working order, and that the instruments have been checked, calibrated, and properly located.

INSPECTION OF KILN.

The kiln building should be kept tight and mechanically safe and sound. Interior surfaces should be painted with a good kiln paint. Doors should be kept in good repair and fitting tightly; poor doors allow a great deal of heat to escape and upset the drying conditions. Rails and rail supports should be inspected periodically and the fastenings checked over. Pipes should be kept in proper repair, and their pitch to the drain end maintained to allow free flow

HORIZONTAL CROSS PILING.

HORIZONTAL END PILING.

VERTICAL CROSS PILING.

of the condensed water to the traps. Suitable gratings or runways should be provided, so that the men entering the kiln can do so with safety and without walking on the pipes. The interior iron work and pipes should be protected by a good kiln paint, or the pipes can be painted while hot with a mixture of cylinder oil and graphite, if preferred. The coils should be inspected occasionally to make sure that they are all working, and the traps should be observed every day.

CALIBRATION AND ADJUSTMENT OF INSTRUMENTS.

Success in all except the easiest kind of kiln drying depends upon the accuracy of the instruments and apparatus used in the regulation of the kiln and in the determination of the moisture content. It is therefore essential that the apparatus be maintained in an accurate operating condition. Most important is the matter of temperature indicating, recording, and regulating instruments, since through them both temperature and humidity are determined and controlled.

THERMOMETERS.

The simplest and most satisfactory way to calibrate indicating and recording thermometers is to compare them at different temperatures within their range with a standardized or calibrated thermometer of known accuracy. Each operator should have at least one such standard thermometer. The type recommended is a 12-inch glass chemical thermometer, with graduations in degrees Fahrenheit etched on the stem, and having a range of 30° to 220° correct for ordinary purposes. Such a thermomoter can be purchased for about $3 list price; and a brass protecting sleeve or case, recommended for use in kilns, can be had for about $1.50.

The usual laboratory method of calibration by comparison with a standard thermometer consists in immersing the standard and the thermometers to be calibrated in a vessel of water, which is constantly stirred to keep the temperature uniform throughout. The water is gradually heated, and the thermometers are read at intervals of a few degrees. The difference between the reading of any thermometer and the standard at any temperature is the error of that thermometer, and a correction of this amount must be applied to the reading to give the correct temperature. If the standard reads higher, call the correction plus (+) and add it to the reading of the thermometer, and vice versa. This method is applicable to glass-stem thermometers and other portable types. Wet-bulb thermometers are calibrated this way also, the wicks being removed during calibration. Once every six months should be sufficient for the calibration of glass thermometers.

Recording thermometers require more attention than other types on account of the comparative ease with which they may become deranged. They should be calibrated in water, as described for glass thermometers, the bulb and about a foot of the tube being immersed. This calibration will give a good idea of how the error, if any, varies throughout the operative range of the instrument. After calibration the instrument should be mounted in place in the kiln and then checked up at several points in its range by comparison with the standard thermometer hung close beside its bulb. These comparisons can well be made during the run, if care be taken to read the instruments only after the temperature has been practically constant for 10 minutes, to allow the recorder bulb to overcome its natural lag. A full correction curve can then be plotted for the entire range, and the pen arm of the recorder adjusted to reduce this correction to the minimum. For making this adjustment there is usually provided a small screw at or near the pen-arm pivot, the turning of which moves the pen over the scale.

Wet-bulb recorders should be calibrated similarly, preferably without the wick, and double-pen instruments should have both bulbs calibrated, dry, at the same time. An occasional check with a wet and dry bulb thermometer will show whether the wet bulb is really recording the wet-bulb temperature. It must be kept in mind that a reasonable amount of circulation past the bulb is necessary to secure enough evaporation to bring the bulb temperature clear down to the actual wet-bulb temperature.

. Recorders should be calibrated in place at least once every two months, and oftener if they show a tendency to fluctuate abnormally. They should be handled carefully, in accordance with the manufacturer's instructions, special care being taken in changing charts not to bend the pen arm, and when filling the pen not to spill ink down the pen arms. Instruments should be returned to the manufacturer when other than the clock mechanism needs repair. Competent jewelers can keep the clocks in order.

Although recorders can be obtained in weatherproof cases which need no special protection from the elements, it will be found advantageous to mount them in the operating room in some place which is readily accessible and as free from temperature changes as possible.

THERMOSTATS.

Thermostats do not as a rule require any calibration except to determine whether in the case of the wet bulb there is enough circulation past it to insure proper depression. This can be done by comparison with a wet-bulb thermometer placed right at the regulator bulb. It should be read first without fanning and again after vigorous fanning. The drop in temperature will indicate the extent to which the regulator bulb represents the actual wet-bulb temperature.

It is necessary, however, to give the thermostat regulators occasional attention. In self-contained instruments which have a stuffing box on the valve stem a small quantity of oil and graphite applied occasionally on the stem at the box will help to reduce friction and make the instrument more accurate. The stuffing box should be tightened only enough to prevent leakage. In the air-operated type the small valves in the regulator head must be kept free from the oil which is apt to be carried by the air. An occasional washing of the head, by disconnecting the air lines and pouring gasoline through it, will keep the parts clean and prevent sticking.

DRYING OVEN.

The drying oven needs no particular attention, except to make sure that it is maintaining a temperature of 212° F. and not varying over 2° or 3°. Variations in the oven temperature will make an appreciable difference in the moisture-content determinations. Steam ovens are easily regulated by means of a reducing valve in the steam main, and electric ovens by an adjustable thermostat operating on the heating circuit.

SCALES AND BALANCES.

Scales for weighing samples and sections should be sensitive to the smallest quantity which they are intended to weigh; if they are not, they should be repaired or returned to the factory. The absolute accuracy of the scales is not, however, of paramount importance, so long as all the readings are in proportion. Thus, suppose that a scale is 5 per cent in error; this error will apply just as much to the original and the current weights as to the oven-dry weight, and the moisture percentages will be just the same. This assumes, of course, that all the weighings are made on the same scale. This illustration is given simply to show that it is not absolutely necessary to have a set of standard weights for calibrating the scales. It is necessary, however, to be assured that the indicated weights are always in proportion. If, for instance, one sample weighs twice as much as another, the scales must show this. Specifically, this means that all of the weights and the poise must be in proper proportion. This can be readily determined on platform scales by any scheme which allows the same piece or quantity of material to be weighed with the different loose weights and the poise. To illustrate: A 200-pound silk scale has a single poise and beam graduated to 2 pounds by hundredths of a pound and loose counterpoise weights of 100, 50, 20, 10, 10, 5, 3, and 2 pounds respectively. This scale can be checked up as follows: Balance the beam accurately, set the poise at 2 pounds, and place just enough weight on the platform to balance. Then return the poise to zero and put the 2-pound loose weight on the counterpoise. The beam should balance again. If it does not, it can be brought to balance by adding to or removing weight from the platform and then weighing again with the poise. Having checked the 2-pound weight against the poise, check the 3-pound weight by putting enough additional weight on the platform to balance at 3 pounds with the poise set at 1 pound and the 2-pound weight on the counterpoise. Remove the 2-pound weight, return the poise to zero, and place the 3-pound weight on the counterpoise. This scheme of comparisons may be continued through the entire capacity range of the scale. It is most convenient, in securing the final balance of the beam at the different weights, to use a pan of shot, sand, or water.

Balances using loose weights can be checked simply by interchanging the contents of the two pans. If they were in balance in the first place and remain so, the balance arms must be of equal length. If the arms are not of equal length, the balance can still be used, by always placing the weights on the same pan. The individual loose weights may be checked against each other by placing the same nominal weight on each pan.

STEAM GAUGES.

Steam-pressure gauges, if used simply to give a general idea of the amount of pressure available or to check the operation of a reducing valve, need not be very accurate. However, the operator

should know how to calibrate them so that he may do so when
necessary. There are two general methods in common use; in one
the gauge is compared directly with a standard test gauge and in
the other the pressure to which the gauge is subjected is actually
weighed by means of standard weights placed on a piston of known
diameter.

In both cases the test pressure is produced by means of a small
hand pump filled with oil, and provided with connections for the
gauges. Pressures throughout the range of the gauge being tested
are produced and the errors noted. Adjustment can be made by
pulling the gauge hand from its pivot and putting it back again in
the proper position. Testing equipment of this sort is carried by all
boiler inspectors. If none is available, comparisons can often be
made with other gauges, such as those on the boilers, and a fair
idea of the accuracy obtained.

LOCATION OF INSTRUMENT BULBS.

The drying schedules in this bulletin are based on the assumption
that the temperature and humidity are measured and controlled at
some point where the air enters the lumber pile. The conditions at
such points are the most severe, since the air becomes cooler and more
moist as it travels through the lumber.

Only a thorough examination by means of the smoke test and
thermometers hung in different parts of the kiln will determine
where the recorders and regulator bulbs must be hung to be exposed
to conditions which correspond to those of the entering air. Corrections can then be made in the setting or reading of the instruments. It is usually necessary, in single-width progressive kilns and
in other single-width cross-piled kilns, to hang the bulbs on the wall,
since it is not considered worth while to remove and replace them
each time the kiln charge is moved. Further, the circulation is
frequently such that no definite "entering air" side can be determined.

In compartment kilns, such as the one in Figure 7, the bulbs can
be placed in the central flue, and this is the proper place for them.
They should be at least 15 feet from the end of the kiln and 6 feet
above the heating coils, unless they are shielded from direct radiation.

In the water-spray kiln illustrated in Figure 8, the thermostat
and dry-bulb recorder bulbs should be located in the entering air
flue and the dew-point thermometer in one of the baffle boxes. In
the external blower kiln, the bulbs can be located on the side of
the pile at which the air enters. When the heating coils are in the
kiln, the bulbs must also be located in the kiln and on the entering-
air side of the pile.

In the superheated-steam kiln illustrated in Figure 11 the bulbs
can be located in the center of the top passage, as indicated, or in
the center of the lower passage. These locations are best, because
they are free from direct radiation, out of the way, and subject to
the same conditions, no matter which pair of jet lines happens to be
open. The instruments, however, if so placed should be carefully
checked against standard thermometers located on the entering-air
side and properly shielded from direct radiation, since the tem-

perature will undoubtedly be higher there than in the upper and lower passages.

PLACING OF SAMPLES.

The placing of samples is of prime importance, and a large number, 10 or 12, should be used for each run until the behavior of the kiln is well determined. Samples should be so placed in the piles of lumber that they will receive exactly the same drying treatment as the lumber itself. They should be located on both entering-air and leaving-air sides of the piles, high, low, and halfway up, so that the relative drying effects can be determined. In case of erratic circulation or trouble from uneven drying, samples can also be placed in the middle of the piles; on these there will be no intermediate weighings possible. In progressive kilns, or any type operating at high temperatures, the obtaining of intermediate weights on any of the samples is often a difficult matter. When the kiln has been loaded steaming can start immediately. A full supply of high-pressure steam should be available, so that the steaming temperature may be reached quickly and full saturation of the air assured. Care must be used to prevent possible injury to the instruments as the kiln is heated; the steaming temperature will probably be higher than that for which the regulators are set, and if these are of the liquid-filled type the excessive pressure developed may strain the bulbs or diaphragms or cause the valve to stick on its seat.

After the drying conditions have been established a study should be made of the circulation. This study can well be supplemented by the use of a number of wet and dry bulb hygrometers scattered throughout the kiln, preferably near the various samples. The readings of these will give a good idea of the relative drying conditions at these points. The readings should be tabulated and the relative humidity determined. The variations in the relative humidity are a good indicator of the variations to be expected in the drying rate throughout the kiln. In progressive kilns the matter is more difficult, and more reliance must be placed upon circulation tests and upon the moisture content of the samples in the dry stock. If wet and dry bulb hygrometers are used in progressive kilns to determine uniformity of drying, they should all be placed on a single truck at a time, since variations from end to end are to be expected.

The samples should be weighed frequently enough so that there will be at least 5 determinations for the kiln run; in the case of runs extending over more than 10 days, the samples should be weighed every day. The moisture per cent should be calculated immediately, and a chart should be maintained, showing graphically the loss of moisture day by day. On this same chart may be plotted the daily temperatures and humidities. This can then be compared with the drying schedule and differences noted and corrected. If preferred, the temperature and humidity of the schedule may be plotted on the same sheet, thus giving a useful comparison between the schedule and the actual run. (See Fig. 12.)

KILN RECORDS.

In addition to this chart, it is desirable to keep a permanent record of the details of each run. Forms for this purpose are provided by some of the kiln companies and can well be used wherever they are applicable. It frequently happens, however, that the operator prefers to make up his own form, possibly combining chart and tabulations on the same sheet.

The runs for compartment kilns should each be numbered and all the data on each run kept together. For progressive kilns the records can be kept by days for each kiln, and other modifications can be made to suit. All of the following information should be provided for on the form: (1) Company name; (2) operator's name; (3) run number; (4) kiln number; (5) thickness and species

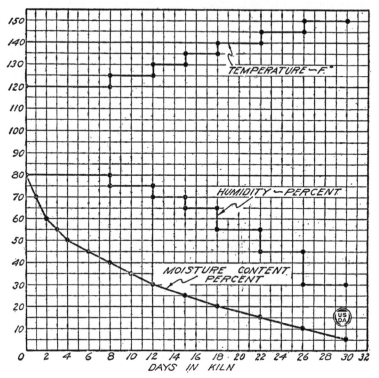

Fig. 12.—Hardwood Schedule 5 plotted against an average drying time of 30 days.

or kind of stock; (6) amount on each truck; (7) locality in which stock was grown; (8) date of arrival at yard, condition, and time of seasoning when ready for kiln; (9) appearance of stock as to seasoning defects; (10) use to which put; (11) final moisture content desired; (12) original and final weights and moisture content of moisture section from samples; (13) original weight, moisture content, and calculated dry weight of each sample; (14) running record of current weights and calculated moisture content for each sample; (15) weights and moisture content of each moisture section cut from the samples at the end of the run; (16) running record of temperatures and humidities taken once or twice a day at least; (17) corrections on recording and indicating thermometers used in the run; (18) running record of appearance of stock, stress determinations, and steaming and high humidity treatment; (19) final condition of stock.

The charts from the recorders, with run number, dates, and corrections plainly indicated on each, should be filed with each run report, and final-stress sections can frequently be kept to advantage, at least until the stock has been worked up. To make the marking of kiln samples simpler, it is suggested that each one bear the run number and an additional individual serial number. Thus, if there are four samples in run 32, they should be numbered 32–1, 32–2, and 32–3, 32–4, respectively. Moisture sections cut from the sample should bear the sample number and also an individual identifying number or letter. The two sections first cut from 32–1 might be 32–1A and 32–1B and the final section 32–1C.

ESSENTIAL APPARATUS.

In order to work effectively, every operator should have certain apparatus described in this handbook, and a suitable room or office in which to keep and use it. The following list represents the minimum compatible with efficient work:

One standard-grade etched-stem glass chemical thermometer, 30° to 220° F., graduated in degrees.

Six wet and dry bulb hygrometers, 60° to 220° F., graduated 2 degrees.

One balance or trip scale for weighing moisture sections, capacity 1 kilogram (1,000 grams=2.2 pounds, about) sensitive to 0.1 gram, with sliding poise on arm for weights up to 5 grams. Brass weights, 1 gram to 1,000 grams in box.

One platform scale or balance for kiln samples. Platform balance capacity 100 pounds, sensitive to 1/100 pound. Beam graduated to 1/100 pound; or—

Solution scale, capacity 20 kilograms, sensitive to 1 gram; 2 scale beams, one graduated to 100 grams in 1-gram units, the other graduated to 1,000 grams in 100 gram units; counterpoise and loose weights.

One drying oven (electric or steam) inside dimensions at least 10 by 12 by 10 inches. Thermostatic control on electric oven sensitive to 2° F. To operate at 212° F.

One 10-inch slide rule.

One smoke box with concentrated ammonia and hydrochloric acid.

Two flash-lamps; spare batteries and lights.

One gas plate and kettle for heating pitch.

Miscellaneous tools, such as saw, screw drivers, hammer, rule, etc.

AIR SEASONING.

It is not within the province of this bulletin to discuss the air seasoning of wood, except in so far as a knowledge of it is essential to the kiln operator. Much of the lumber dried in kilns, especially hardwood lumber, is first air dried, either at the sawmill or the manufacturing plant, and the quality of the finished product depends in no small measure upon the care taken in the preliminary air seasoning.

The following general rules apply in piling the stock in the yard for seasoning:

Foundations for piles should be firm and solid, level in one direction and properly pitched in the other, well above the ground and free from weeds and decay.

Stickers should be of uniform size, not over 2 inches wide nor less than seven-eighths inch thick, free from decay, and planed on two sides. The practice of using boards from the pile for stickers should be avoided.

Care and accuracy in piling are essential. Boards of only one length should be piled together. The pile should pitch forward about 1 inch per foot. There should be a row of stickers over every foundation sill (about 4 to 6 feet for hardwoods and 6 to 8 feet for softwoods), and these rows should run up parallel to the front of the pile. Front and rear rows of stickers should be flush with the ends of the boards.

All piles should be carefully roofed, preferably with a double layer of boards projecting over the pile, front and rear. Roofs should be fastened down to prevent the wind from blowing them off.

UNITED STATES DEPARTMENT OF AGRICULTURE

BULLETIN No. 1137

Joint Contribution from the Bureaus of Plant Industry and
Entomology, in Cooperation with the Illinois, Indiana, and
Wisconsin Agricultural Experiment Stations.

Washington, D. C.   PROFESSIONAL PAPER.   March 22, 1923

SYMPTOMS OF WHEAT ROSETTE COMPARED WITH THOSE PRODUCED BY CERTAIN INSECTS.[1]

By Harold H. McKinney, *Assistant Pathologist, Office of Cereal Investigations, Bureau of Plant Industry,* and Walter H. Larrimer, *Scientific Assistant, Office of Cereal and Forage Insect Investigations, Bureau of Entomology.*

CONTENTS.

INTRODUCTION.

Shortly after wheat rosette was brought to the attention of plant pathologists, certain workers advanced the idea that the disease was due to an infestation of the Hessian fly (*Phytophaga destructor* Say) on account of certain characters manifested by the diseased plants which resemble those of plants infested with the larvæ or puparia of this insect. Although this view was not held by entomologists who were familiar with the situation, it was considered desirable that the latter group of workers should cooperate in the investigations in order that the possibilities of an insect cause might not be overlooked.

The writers have made observations and conducted experiments with wheat rosette and also with a number of maladies of wheat caused by insects which in certain stages of their development might be confused with wheat rosette.

During 1920–21 careful observations were made on wheat plants growing in soil infested with the causal agent of wheat rosette. Three plats of Harvest Queen (white-chaffed Red Cross) wheat were sown at intervals during the fall. These plats were 5 feet

[1] This bulletin deals with the disease previously designated 'take-all and so-called take-all which occurs in Illinois and Indiana.

23244—23

wide and 2 rods long. On November 11, after the adult Hessian flies had ceased to fly, determinations of the percentage of fly infestation were made in all the plats by W. B. Cartwright, of the Bureau of Entomology. In the early part of the following spring observations were made in the same plats by Dr. R. W. Webb, of the Bureau of Plant Industry, to determine the percentage of rosette infestation. The results of these observations of infestation are given in Table 1.

TABLE 1.—*Infestations of Harvest Queen wheat by the Hessian fly in the fall of 1920 and by rosette in the spring of 1921 on plats near Granite City, Ill.*

Date of sowing.	Plants showing infestation (per cent).	
	Hessian fly, in the fall.	Rosette, in the spring.
September 21	2.5	93.6
October 4	0	85.6
October 11	0	96.0

Since rosette develops very early in the spring, before the spring emergence of the Hessian fly adults, it is obvious that any possible connection between this insect and rosette can involve only the fall infestation of the Hessian fly. It will be noted from Table 1 that there is no direct correlation between the percentage of fall Hessian fly infestation in any of the plats and the percentage of rosette in the same plats the following spring. The fall fly infestation was insignificant or absent, while the percentages of rosette were very high. It is therefore quite evident that some other factor than the Hessian fly is the prime cause of wheat rosette.

While all evidence indicates that the disease in question is not caused by an insect, particularly the Hessian fly, it is recognized that under certain conditions there is a possibility of confusing the symptoms of the disease with certain of those produced by the Hessian fly, the wheat strawworm (*Harmolita grandis* Riley), and to a less extent the wheat stem maggot (*Meromyza americana* Fitch). It therefore seems advisable to give the chief points of similarity and difference between the symptoms of the maladies under discussion.

The insects discussed in this paper have long been recognized as important wheat pests, and details of their respective life histories will not be included. Osborn (*2*),[2] Webster (*5*), and many others have recorded the life history of the Hessian fly. Phillips (*3*) has given similar information concerning the wheat strawworm, and Webster (*4*) has discussed the life history of the wheat stem maggot.

SYMPTOMS OF WHEAT ROSETTE.

A complete description of the symptoms of wheat rosette has been given by the senior writer in another publication (*1*).

FALL PERIOD.

Field symptoms.—As this disease is interpreted at the present time there are apparently no field symptoms in the fall. During the past two seasons a highly susceptible variety of wheat growing

---

[2] Serial numbers (italic) in parentheses refer to "Literature cited" on page 8 of this bulletin.

on soil of extremely high infestation appeared to be in a perfect state
of health during the autumn. While certain fungi infect the outer
tissues of the subterranean tiller parts and the subcrown internode,[3]
the general field appearance of the plants was far better than that of
varieties not known to develop wheat rosette.

Plant symptoms.—While the characteristic plant symptoms of the
disease do not develop in the fall, close observations and tiller counts
seem to indicate that the excessive development of tillers, which is
so characteristic of the disease in the spring, commences to a certain
extent in the autumn. However, since other important symptoms are
not associated with this fall condition, its importance as a fall symptom and as an indicator of the development of the disease in the
spring is still a question.

SPRING PERIOD.

Field symptoms.—The first positive indications of the disease
become evident early in the spring after the growth of the healthy
plants is well started. In the fields but slightly infested, distinct
patches of badly dwarfed plants show here and there without regard
to the type or condition of the soil (Pl. I). Such patches may vary
in size from those containing but a few diseased plants to areas
many feet in diameter. Often these patches are almost circular in
shape, while others are irregular. It is not uncommon to find diseased plants occurring singly intermixed with healthy plants. In
cases where spotting occurs, the edges of such spots are usually more
sharply defined than the margins of spots caused by unfavorable soil
conditions, especially poor drainage. In the rosette-spotted areas
most of the plants are diseased and therefore stunted right up to
the edge of the spot. In spots caused by local unfavorable soil conditions all the plants usually decrease in height gradually from the
edge toward the center.

In fields more severely infested it is not uncommon to find a large
proportion or in some cases all of the field involved. In such cases
most of the plants may be affected. There is no case on record, however, where all plants in a large area have developed the disease.
Investigations have shown that apparently there are resistant strains
in the most susceptible varieties.

A striking characteristic of fields affected by the disease in the
early spring is the comparative freedom from blank spaces or areas
due to dead plants. Practically all plants are intact, even though
diseased. Later in the spring, however, under certain conditions such
plants may die. During seasons of heavy rainfall diseased plants
may be washed out of the soil, causing blank areas in the field, but
this condition is rather unusual.

Plant symptoms.—Plants affected by rosette remain dormant in
the spring after healthy plants commence their spring growth. The
fall tillers of the diseased plants usually do not " shoot." or if they do
the process is delayed and of short duration. The leaves of diseased
plants are dark blue-green in color. They are rather broad and stiff.
Thus far, no parasites or external lesions have been found consistently
associated with the vital tissues of diseased plants during this period.

---

[3] The term subcrown internode is used to designate the elongated region which under
certain conditions develops between the seed and the crown of the plant.

A little later in the spring an excessive number of tillers becomes strikingly evident, giving the diseased plants a rosette appearance (Pl. II, *B*). Later, the underground portion of the older tillers develops a brown, rotted condition (Pl. I, *C*).

SUMMER PERIOD.

Field symptoms.—In case of badly infested wheat fields,. those plants which escape or resist rosette develop and form a thin stand of grain, and the diseased plants under usual conditions slowly recover by sending up straggling secondary tillers. In the case of the early death of diseased plants, the thick tufts of plant remains will be found on the ground usually until after harvest, except during seasons of heavy rainfall, when these plants are practically all washed away.

Recovering diseased plants do not ripen until after the healthy plants; hence, as the healthy plants turn in color at maturity the diseased areas show up conspicuously as green spots in the ripening, healthy grain.

Plant symptoms.—In the case of diseased plants which do not recover, their dead remains, consisting of low compact tufts of tillers and leaves, will be found in place on the ground except where they have been washed away. Plants which recover consist of a number of straggling secondary culms coming up from the stool of dead fall tillers and leaves. Such secondary culms may or may not produce heads. In some cases remarkable recovery occurs, especially on rich moist soil, but usually very small imperfectly filled heads develop. Frequently, plants are found in which only part of the tillers are diseased. In such cases the healthy tillers usually develop normally, resulting in a plant consisting of a few normal tillers with dead fall tillers at the base and perhaps a few secondary tillers attempting to attain maturity.

SYMPTOMS PRODUCED BY THE HESSIAN FLY.

FALL PERIOD.

Field symptoms.—A wheat field infested with the Hessian fly is of a shade of green darker than normal, with a certain bristling appearance due to the stiff and upright leaves of the infested plants. As the season advances, the seemingly healthy appearance gives way to a more or less ragged, sickly stage, described by the farmer as "going back."

Under certain conditions seemingly dependent upon the response of the wheat plant to soil variations, there may be a decided field spotting due to fly infestation. These spots or patches are usually associated with such conditions as soil color, type, topography, and exposure.

Plant symptoms.—In the case of an infested plant, the central shoot is usually absent, and the leaves are broad, short, more or less stiff, and of a dark-green color (Pl. II, *E*). By stripping down the leaf sheath, the larva or the puparium (flaxseed) can easily be found near the base of the plant (Pl. III, *E*). The presence of a single small larva or a flaxseed is sufficient to have caused the characteristic appearance of the wheat plant. An infested plant may produce a few normal tillers or it may be killed, depending upon the degree of infestation. In the latter case, as the season advances the plant

SYMPTOMS OF WHEAT ROSETTE.

A typical spot in a field caused by the rosette of wheat. Note the dwarf and leafy appearance of the diseased plants in the lower right-hand portion of the picture as compared with the surrounding tall, healthy plants.

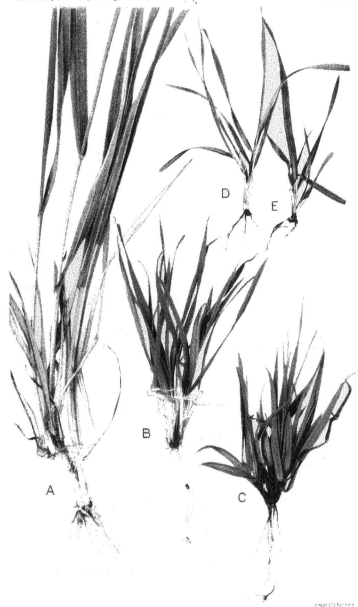

PLANTS OF WINTER WHEAT SHOWING THE EFFECTS OF ATTACKS OF THE ROSETTE
AND THE HESSIAN FLY, RESPECTIVELY, COMPARED WITH HEALTHY PLANTS.

A, Healthy plant in the spring; *B* and *C*, plants of the same age as *A*, showing early and
advanced stages, respectively, of the rosette; *D*, healthy plant as it appears in the late
autumn; *E*, plant of the same age as *D*, infested by the Hessian fly.   Note the similarities
in color but the differences in the extent of tillering in plants affected by the two maladies
compared with the corresponding healthy plants.

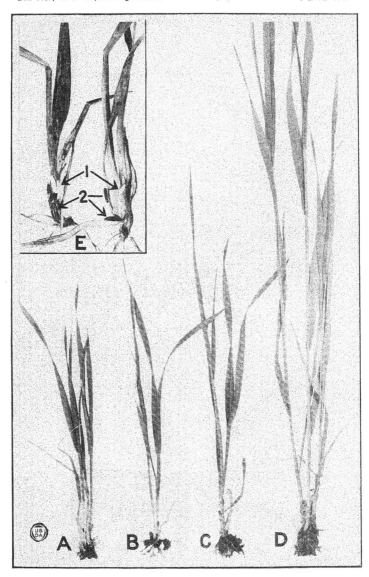

WHEAT PLANTS INFESTED BY THE HESSIAN FLY COMPARED WITH AN UNINFESTED PLANT.

A, *B*, and *C*, Spring-wheat plants infested by the Hessian fly; *D*, healthy plant of the same age for comparison. The infested plants are much dwarfed and show the same dark-green color in comparison with the healthy plant as is shown in Plate II, *D* and *E*. *E*, Winter-wheat plants infested by the Hessian fly, showing larvæ (1) and puparia (2) (flaxseeds) of the insect. The leaf sheaths have been stripped away.

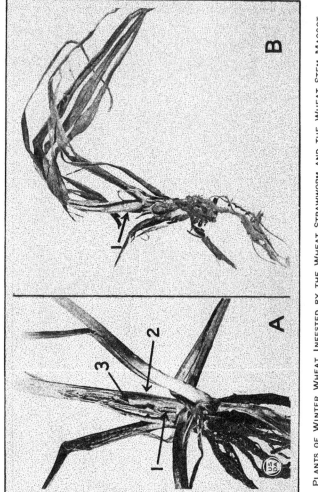

PLANTS OF WINTER WHEAT INFESTED BY THE WHEAT STRAWWORM AND THE WHEAT STEM MAGGOT.

A, An infested winter-wheat plant early in the spring, showing the larva (1) of the wheat strawworm (*Harmolita grandis* Riley). Note the rather elongated, bulblike swelling (2) and the cavity (3) in the infested tiller. *B*, An infested winter-wheat plant early in the spring, killed by the attacks of the larva (1) of the wheat stem maggot (*Meromyza americana* Fitch).

rapidly decays, leaving the flaxseeds·more or. less free in or on the surface of the soil. This condition persists until the emergence of the principal spring brood of the fly.

SPRING PERIOD.

Field symptoms.—In the case of extremely heavy infestation the previous fall, practically all the plants may be killed. Varying degrees of infestation give the field a more or less ragged, bunchy appearance, and numerous blank spaces or areas may be evident. As the principal spring generation begins to get in its work, the general color of the field becomes a dark green, and growth is retarded in accordance with the severity of the infestation.

Plant symptoms.—The effect of infestation on small plants in the spring is practically the same as in the fall, and larvæ and flaxseeds are located at relatively the same place on the culms. On larger plants the larvæ or the flaxseeds may be found higher up on the stem, but they may easily be found by stripping down the leaf sheath. The culm may be killed or not, depending on its size and the number of larvæ or flaxseeds present.

SUMMER PERIOD.

Field symptoms.—A thin stand with fallen straw, depending on the severity of the infestation, usually marks an infested field in summer. A light infestation may escape notice.

Plant symptoms.—Culms that have become weakened at the location of the flaxseeds usually fall over before harvest. Culms that were heavily infested may ·have been killed or prevented from producing a head, but in any case the flaxseeds may be found as the cause.

COMPARISON BETWEEN THE SYMPTOMS OF WHEAT ROSETTE AND THOSE CAUSED BY THE HESSIAN FLY.

Since rosette is not apparent in the autumn and since it becomes evident in the spring before the emergence of the adult Hessian fly, there is very little chance to confuse the two maladies during these periods.

In the late spring there is a possibility of confusion, especially if plants affected by rosette show, in addition, the spring infestation of the Hessian fly.

In the latter part of the spring, fields affected by rosette sometimes show blank areas caused by the diseased plants being washed out of the soil by unusually heavy rains. Such fields are practically indistinguishable from those suffering from a severe attack of the fly, when the infestation of either is general over the field. Owing to the fact, however, that spring fly infestation has never been noted to occur in localized areas or spots in the field, as is commonly the case with wheat rosette, such field spotting observed at any time during the growing season practically precludes fly injury as the sole cause, even though all the affected plants may have been washed away.

In the case of plant symptoms, fly infestation causes a reduction rather than an increased number of tillers, as is the case in plants affected by rosette. While plants affected by the latter malady often show fly infestation, it will usually be found that many near-by plants affected by rosette show no evidence of such infestation. In the case of plants suffering from fly injury, the larva or flaxseed of the insect or the empty flaxseeds will be found at the base of the plant, usually under the first leaf sheath.

SYMPTOMS PRODUCED BY THE WHEAT STRAWWORM.

FALL PERIOD.

The wheat strawworm passes the fall and winter in the old stubble or straw, so of course it has no effect upon the fall growth of winter wheat.

SPRING PERIOD.

Field symptoms.—Almost invariably the infestation by the wheat strawworm occurs in a field bordering on old stubble or in a field which the previous year was in wheat the stubble of which was poorly plowed. In the first case the stand is thinner and plants shorter next to the old stubble field, and this difference gradually shades off to normal as the distance from the edge of the field increases. This is due to the inability of the wingless form of the insect to travel far, and for this reason most of the infestation occurs within a strip 30 yards wide bordering on the old stubble.

Plant symptoms.—Plants infested by the strawworm resemble those infested by the Hessian fly except that in the former case tillering up to this time has been normal. The larvæ develop at the base of the plant, causing a bulblike swelling to appear at that point. The infested culms are always killed, and frequently all the culms are infested. The swelling usually serves to identify the injury caused by this insect, and of course the larvæ or pupæ of the insect itself (Pl. IV, *A*) are inside the stem, while in the case of the Hessian fly the larva or flaxseed is merely under the leaf sheath.

SUMMER PERIOD.

Field symptoms.—The thin stand along the old stubble field is all that serves to mark an infested field in summer. The second generation of the insect has enabled it to spread throughout the whole field.

Plant symptoms.—The decaying remains of tillers infested earlier in the season are about all that marks the plants which have been infested. The larval form of the second generation in the straw at this time is difficult to locate except by splitting the infested straw.

COMPARISON BETWEEN THE SYMPTOMS OF WHEAT ROSETTE AND THOSE CAUSED BY THE WHEAT STRAWWORM.

Wheat rosette is not confined to the vicinity of old wheat stubble fields, as is the case with the strawworm infestation. If the former malady occurs near such a stubble field its presence can be distinguished by means of the bulblike swelling on plants infested with the insect; also the latter plants develop the normal number of tillers in contrast with the excessive tillering caused by rosette. The dead and decayed culms in late spring or autumn killed by the first generation of the strawworm will still be recognizable by their bulbous growth containing the refuse left by the larvæ of this generation.

SYMPTOMS CAUSED BY THE WHEAT STEM MAGGOT.

FALL PERIOD.

Field symptoms.—A field infested by the wheat stem maggot has very much the same appearance as if infested by the Hessian fly. The stem maggot is not usually so prevalent as the fly, and instances of extreme infestation are more rare. The color of an infested field is a darker green than normal, and when severely infested the ragged, sickly appearance comes on earlier than if infested by the Hessian fly.

Plant symptoms.—An infested plant has the center shoot discolored or dead and the other leaves broader and darker green than normal. The larva, difficult to find when small, occurs at the base of the stem, where it lacerates the tender tissues with its mouth hooks and feeds upon the juices.

SPRING PERIOD.

Field symptoms.—Depending upon the severity of the infestation, gaps in the drill row caused by the dead plants mark a field infested by the wheat stem maggot in spring; but there are so many other causes of this same appearance that it can not be taken as characteristic of this insect.

Plant symptoms.—The infested culms, and frequently the entire plant, if able to withstand the injury during the fall, usually die during the winter. Therefore, in the spring these dead and more or less disintegrated plants contain the full-grown larvæ or pupæ of the insect (Pl. IV, *B*).

COMPARISON BETWEEN THE SYMPTOMS OF WHEAT ROSETTE AND THOSE CAUSED BY THE WHEAT STEM MAGGOT.

As in the case of the fall infestation of the Hessian fly, the symptoms produced by an infestation of wheat stem maggot in the autumn will not lead to confusion with rosette, even though the plants affected by the two maladies resemble each other in certain respects. There is practically no chance for confusing the troubles in the spring, because the spring infestation of the maggot does not cause symptoms which resemble the fall symptoms in any way.

CONCLUSIONS.

The insect injuries described in this bulletin may usually be diagnosed with certainty, on account of the presence in some stage of the insect on the affected plant. However, in the late stages of these disorders it is sometimes difficult to find any trace of the insect, and in such cases the infested fields and affected plants are difficult or impossible to distinguish from fields and plants affected by rosette.

The symptoms of rosette can not be distinguished with certainty after the spring period, and it is safer not to diagnose the disease positively after early spring, especially if heavy rains have washed out many diseased plants.

In the early spring the disease manifests itself by a retarded development of the plants, followed by excessive tillering and a dark blue-green coloration, the leaves being broad and stiff and the whole plant having a bunchy rosette appearance. At this time, when the disease is not complicated with insect infestations the drill rows do not have any blank spaces.

LITERATURE CITED.

(1) McKINNEY, H. H.
    1923. Investigations on the rosette disease of wheat and its control.
        In Jour. Agr. Research, v. 23, no. 10. [In press.]
(2) OSBORN, HERBERT.
    1898. The Hessian fly in the United States. U. S. Dept. Agr., Div.
        Ent. Bul. 16, n. s., 58 p., 8 fig., front., 2 pl. Bibliography, p. 48–57.
(3) PHILLIPS, W. J.
    1920. Studies on the life history and habits of the jointworm flies of
        the genus Harmolita (Isosoma), with recommendations for control.
        U. S. Dept. Agr. Bul. 808, 27 p., 8 fig., 6 pl.
(4) WEBSTER, F. M.
    1903. Some insects attacking the stems of growing wheat, rye, barley,
        and oats. U. S. Dept. Agr., Div. Ent. Bul. 42, 62 p., 15 fig.
(5)   1920. The Hessian fly and how to prevent losses from it. U. S. Dept.
        Agr., Farmers' Bul. 1083, 16 p., 13 fig.

ORGANIZATION OF THE UNITED STATES DEPARTMENT OF AGRICULTURE.

UNITED STATES DEPARTMENT OF AGRICULTURE

DEPARTMENT BULLETIN No. 1138

| Washington, D. C. | PROFESSIONAL PAPER | February 10, 1923 |

VITAMIN B IN THE EDIBLE TISSUES OF THE OX, SHEEP, AND HOG.

I. VITAMIN B IN THE VOLUNTARY MUSCLE.
II. VITAMIN B IN THE EDIBLE VISCERA.

By Ralph Hoagland, *Senior Biochemist, Biochemic Division, Bureau of Animal Industry.*

CONTENTS.

VITAMIN B IN THE DIET.

Vitamin B, also known as the antineuritic vitamin, is one of those chemically unidentified substances which are absolutely necessary for the growth and maintenance of man and animals. The disease known as beriberi, formerly rather common among the rice-eating people of the East, is due to the consumption of a diet made up very largely of polished rice, which is very deficient in this vitamin. On the other hand, natives who subsist largely on the unpolished cereal do not contract beriberi, and the disease may be cured simply by substituting unpolished for polished rice in the diet. A less-marked deficiency of vitamin B in the diet results in retarded growth and other disorders. Birds fed a diet very deficient in vitamin B lose weight rapidly and develop polyneutritis, while young rats make but slight, if any, growth on such a diet. Since the chemical identity of vitamin B or of any of the other vitamins is not known, the only reliable method for the estimation of the vitamin content of a foodstuff is by animal experimentation. This method has its limitations, but when feeding tests are carried on with the greatest care and the results are interpreted with caution, fairly accurate, relative vitamin values may be assigned to the foods tested.

Considering the fact that practically all our knowledge concerning vitamins has been acquired only during the last decade, we have a very considerable amount of information regarding the values of the important foodstuffs in terms of vitamins A, B, and C. The data are far from sufficient, however, for the purpose of assigning other than tentative values to many of our staple food products. Meat, for example, one of our most important foodstuffs, has been assigned a rather low value as a source of the three vitamins; but a careful review of the literature indicates that only a limited number of investigations have been carried on to determine the vitamin content of this food, and that practically all the work has been done with beef and horse meat. The validity of the work which has been done is not questioned, but it is too limited in amount to justify the statement that meat in general is poor in vitamins. Certain animal organs, on the other hand, particularly the heart, liver, and kidney, have been found to be relatively rich in the three vitamins.

Additional information regarding the vitamin content of meat, which should include not only beef, but veal, mutton and lamb, and pork as well, is much to be desired, as well as data concerning the vitamin content of the edible organs and other tissues of the meat food animals. It is the purpose of this bulletin to report the results of investigations that have been carried on to determine the vitamin-B content of the voluntary muscle and the edible organs of the ox, sheep, and hog.

I. VITAMIN B IN THE VOLUNTARY MUSCLE OF THE OX, SHEEP, AND HOG.

IMPORTANCE OF MEAT AS A FOOD.

Meat long has been and still is one of the most important articles of food in the dietary of the American people. In pounds, its per capita consumption for the year 1922 (1) [1] was as follows: Beef, 57.7; veal, 8.3; mutton and lamb, 6.1; and pork, excluding lard, 72.8; a total of 144.9 pounds per year, or 0.4 pound per day. According to Langworthy and Hunt, (2) (1910) meat forms, together with poultry, 16 per cent of the aggregate American dietary as compared with 18 per cent for dairy products, 25 per cent for fruits and vegetables, and 31 per cent for cereals and their products. Meat also furnishes 30 per cent of the protein and 59 per cent of the fat in the dietary. Even more striking is the relatively large expenditure for meat as compared with other classes of foods. Sherman (3) (1918) states that as a result of a dietary study of 2,567 workingmen's families, the United States Bureau of Labor Statistics found that the average expenditure for meat, poultry, and fish amounted to 33.8 per cent of the total sum expended for foods.

PREVIOUS INVESTIGATIONS WITH MEAT.

Eykman (4) (1906) reports that he cured polyneuritic fowls with raw meat, but the kind and quantity fed are not stated.

Watson and Hunter (5) (1906) carried on feeding tests with rats to ascertain the effect of exclusive horseflesh and ox-flesh diets, respectively, upon very young and mature animals. When horseflesh was fed to very young rats the result was invariably fatal. Young rats 2 to 3 months old did somewhat better on the diet, but

---

[1] Italic figures in parentheses refer to Literature cited. p. 46.

part of them died early in the test, while the others did fairly well, though their growth was retarded. Ox flesh gave rather better results. A part of the very young rats died early, while the remainder grew fairly well but did not attain normal weight. Young rats 2 to 3 months old did well on the diet, reaching greater weights than the controls.

Cooper (6) (1912) appears to have been the first to study systematically the antineuritic properties of muscle (beef). Five lots of pigeons of five birds each were fed polished rice, and in addition the birds in the several pens were fed daily 2, 4, 6, 10, and 20 grams each, respectively, of fresh beef. The results of this test indicate that the daily addition of 20 grams of fresh beef to the rice diet was necessary in order to prevent the development of polyneuritis in pigeons during a period of 50 days. The average weight of the pigeons receiving 20 grams each of beef daily was slightly greater at the close of the test than at the start; but the addition of less than 20 grams of beef daily to the diet was only sufficient either to delay the occurrence of the symptoms of the disease or to reduce their severity.

Osborne and Mendel (7) (1917) found that a diet containing 20 per cent of dried ox muscle as the sole source of vitamins and protein, and otherwise adequate, did not induce growth in young rats. The addition of butterfat to the ration did not improve its quality; but when dried yeast was added, normal growth took place. A ration containing 5 per cent of water-soluble solids of fresh beef, which would correspond to 28.9 per cent of dried muscle, did not induce normal growth in rats, although somewhat better results were obtained than with the ration that contained 20 per cent of dried muscle.

Cole (8) (1917) fed a dried-meat powder prepared from the lean meat of South American cattle to young rats, the meat amounting to 26.8 per cent of the ration. The meat was the sole source of protein and vitamins. The rats made satisfactory growth during a 14-day period and the author concludes that the product contains a good supply of the accessory food factors.

Voegtlin and Lake (9) (1919) studied the antineuritic properties of beef when fed to dogs, cats, and rats. Two cats were maintained for 180 days in perfect health on an exclusive diet of beef that had been heated for 3 hours at 120° C. Two pregnant cats fed the same ration developed polyneuritis in 45 and 110 days respectively. The authors call attention to the great difference in the susceptibility of dogs, cats, and rats to polyneuritis when fed the same ration. When fed exclusively on beef that had been heated for 3 hours at 120° C. in the presence of sodium carbonate, cats developed polyneuritis as early as the eighteenth day, dogs at a month to 6 weeks, and rats lived for at least 110 days without showing symptoms of the disease.

McCollum, Simmonds, and Parsons (10) (1921) investigated the nutritive value of ox muscle when fed to white rats. Two lots of rats were fed rations in which the vitamins were furnished exclusively in 25 per cent of dried raw and 25 per cent of dried cooked muscle, respectively. In both lots growth ceased at the end of about four weeks. Five per cent of butterfat was then added to each of the rations and there was a marked response in growth. In another test, rats fed a ration containing 20 per cent of ox muscle and vitamin A in the form of 3 per cent butterfat made fair but not normal growth. Another lot of rats fed exclusively on ox muscle made little growth, had no young, and died early. Rats fed a ration consisting of ox muscle, calcium carbonate, sodium chlorid and 3 per cent butterfat grew at practically the normal rate and appeared healthy. When rats were fed a ration containing 50 per cent ox muscle and 3 per cent butterfat, they made normal growth. Rats were raised to the third generation on this diet with reasonable success. Another lot of rats, fed for a period exclusively on ox muscle, made but little growth. The addition of sodium chlorid and calcium carbonate to the diet was followed by a slight response in growth. Rats fed a ration containing 50 per cent ox muscle, sodium and potassium chlorids, calcium carbonate, dextrin, and butterfat made normal growth and the second and third generations were raised successfully on this diet.

EXPERIMENTAL WORK.

METHODS EMPLOYED.

The purpose of the experiments reported in Part I of this paper was to ascertain the antineuritic properties of the voluntary muscle of the ox, sheep, and hog when fed to pigeons in connection with polished rice. The pigeons used were of the homer type, healthy, mature birds weighing between 300 and 400 grams being selected. Four or five birds were fed each ration at the start, but occasionally a bird would have to be removed during the test on account of an injury.

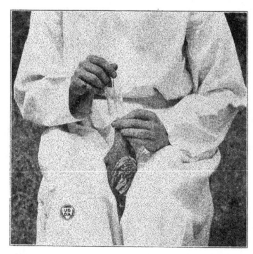

Fig. 1.—Method of feeding the pigeons.

The pigeons were weighed individually before feeding on the first day of the test and at approximately weekly intervals thereafter, always before feeding. Each bird was fed daily, except Sunday, a ration amounting to 5 per cent by weight of the initial weight of the pigeon. Forced feeding was practiced throughout the experiments. The ration was fed into the crop of the pigeon through a Gooch funnel having a bowl 1½ inches in diameter and a stem 3 inches long with an inside diameter of ¼ inch, a glass rod being used as a plunger.

When proper care is used, very few birds'are injured by this method of feeding. The method is illustrated in Figure 1.

The meat used in these tests was of the best quality. It was purchased in the local market and no information was available regarding the feeding of the animals from which the meat had been derived. The muscle tissue was trimmed as free as practicable from fat and connective tissue, ground fine, and mixed with water and toluol to form a semifluid mass which was spread out in a thin layer on shallow trays and dried in a forced current of air at a maximum temperature

Fig. 2.—Pigeon with acute polyneuritis, showing lack of control of muscles in the wings, legs, and neck.

Fig. 3.—The same pigeon as in Fig. 2, 24 hours later, after having been fed 15 grams of dried smoked ham. The bird is a little unsteady on its feet but shows no acute symptoms of the disease.

of 60° C. Drying was carried on in a simple oven designed by the writer, its capacity being 5 kg. of fresh tissue to air dryness in 24 hours. The dried tissue was ground fine and stored in stoppered bottles until needed. The moisture content of the dry tissue ranged from 4 to 8 per cent.

The rice used was the ordinary polished rice of commerce. It was ground medium fine and, unless otherwise stated, was heated two hours in an autoclave at 130° C. before being used.

The term "survival period" as used in this paper denotes the period between the start of the experiment and (1) the development of positive symptoms of polyneuritis, (2) death due apparently to polyneuritis, or (3) the close of the test.

It is not necessary to describe the symptoms of polyneuritis in pigeons, as they have been fully stated by other writers. The symptoms of acute polyneuritis are unmistakable. However, even on a polished-rice diet, not all birds develop this type of the disease, but some may exhibit a chronic form, usually first indicated by the regurgitation of food, later by inability to empty the crop, weakness in the legs, etc., followed by general prostration, partial paralysis, difficult breathing, collapse, and death. As a rule, polyneuritic pigeons were promptly fed dried yeast, to which treatment most, but not all, cases responded favorably. Usually birds with the acute type of the disease yielded to treatment more readily than those with the chronic form.

TESTS WITH POLISHED RICE.

Feeding tests were carried on with three pens of pigeons on an exclusive rice diet in order to establish a basis for comparison with pigeons fed on rations containing various proportions of muscle in addition to rice. The results of these tests are shown in Table 1.

TABLE 1.—*Results of feeding polished rice to pigeons.*

Ration.	Pigeon No.	Survival period.	Change in weight.	Result.
PEN 1.		*Days.*	*Per cent.*	
Rice not heated	73	19	−20.7	Polyneuritis.
Do	70	21	−15.0	Do.
Do	72	35	−17.8	Very thin, weak, end of test.
Do	74	35	−31.7	Do.
Average		27.5	−21.3	
PEN 2.				
Rice heated 2 hours at 130° C	79	17	−20.0	Polyneuritis.
Do	77	21	−23.3	Do.
Do	76	30	−39.3	Do.
Do	78	35	−36.9	Very thin, weak, end of test.
Average		25.6	−23.9	
PEN 3.				
Rice heated 2 hours at 130° C	66	9	−5.8	Polyneuritis.
Do	38	11	−13.0	Do.
Do	64	18	−23.3	Do.
Do	67	18	−19.9	Do.
Do	69	21	−22.4	Do.
Average		15.4	−16.9	
Average, pens 2 and 3		20.5	−23.4	
Average, pens 1, 2, and 3		22.8	−22.7	

The data presented in Table 1 do not require a detailed discussion. Attention is called to the difference in the survival period of birds in a single pen on the same ration. The average survival period of the birds in pens 2 and 3, getting heated rice, is seven days less than that of the pigeons in pen 1 on the unheated-rice ration; but the loss in weight is about the same. The survival period of the birds in pen 3 is 12 days less than that of pen 1. In addition to these results, the writer has found that when an animal tissue, like liver, normally of high antineuritic value is heated in an autoclave for two hours at 130° C. its protective properties are practically destroyed. For these reasons all the polished rice which was used in subsequent experiments as a base in the rations with muscle, was heated two hours at 130° C. in an autoclave. The change in weight of the pigeons in pens 1, 2, and 3 is shown graphically in Figure 4, at the end of this paper. The marked and rapid decrease in the weights of the birds is at once apparent.

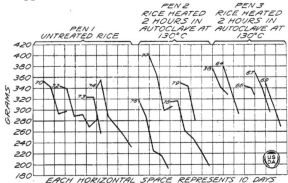

FIG. 4.—Variations in weight of pigeons resulting from feeding polished rice. The numbers opposite beginnings of lines refer to Pigeon Nos. of tables.

The graphs presented in Figures 4 to 45, inclusive, are based upon the weights of the pigeons recorded at approximately weekly intervals during the experiments, except that the weight of any bird suffering from a congestion of food in its crop, an early symptom of polyneuritis, was not recorded. Since most pigeons that develop polyneuritis suffer from this condition of the crop, it was found to be inadvisable to weigh each bird at the time it developed polyneuritis. For this reason, then, the graph of a pigeon usually indicates a shorter period than the survival period for the same bird recorded in the table. Occasionally a graph may indicate a slightly longer period than the survival period shown in the table. In such cases the crop of the bird was normal and the last weighing was made a few days after the development of the disease. The percentage change in weight of each pigeon, as indicated in the tables, is based upon the initial weight and upon the last normal weight as shown in the graph for the same bird. The graphs are presented distinctly for the purpose of showing at a glance the rate and extent of the change in weights of the pigeons during the experiments, and not for the purpose of indicating the survival periods of the birds.

TESTS WITH OX MUSCLE.

The results of the feeding tests with ox muscle are shown in Tables 2, 3, and 4, and the changes in the weights of the birds are shown graphically in Figures 5, 6, 7, 8, 9, and 10.

Pens 4 and 5 (Table 2) were fed rations containing 25 and 15 per cent, respectively, of muscle derived from the round of the carcass of a single fat steer. The slight difference in the average survival periods of the two pens of birds is not material. There was practically no difference in the average loss in weight of the two pens of birds. By referring to Table 1 it will be noted that the average survival period of the birds in pens 2 and 3, which were fed autoclaved rice alone, was 20.5 days, or practically the same as that of pens 4 and 5 on the ox-muscle rations.

TABLE 2.—*Experimental feeding of dried ox muscle and polished rice.*

Meat ration.	Pigeon No.	Survival period.	Change in weight.	Result.
PEN 4.		*Days.*	*Per cent.*	
25 per cent round No. 553..........	80	14	−12.0	Polyneuritis.
Do............................	75	17	−15.4	Do.
Do............................	68	19	−18.0	Do.
Do............................	85	20	−24.7	Do
Do............................	90	24	−8.4	Do.
Average......................	....	18.8	−15.7	
PEN 5.				
15 per cent round No. 553..........	96	12	−4.1	Do.
Do............................	98	14	−5.5	Do.
Do............................	97	17	−16.3	Do.
Do............................	48	19	−10.9	Do.
Do............................	95	45	−35.0	Died, inanition
Average......................	....	21.4	−14.4	
PEN 6.				
25 per cent chuck No. 568..........	8	13	−5.0	Polyneuritis.
Do............................	10	24	−11.4	Do.
Do............................	9	26	−8.7	Do.
Do............................	7	37	−20.6	Do.
Average......................	....	25	−11.4	
PEN 7.				
25 per cent sirloin No. 569..........	13	20	−2.5	Do.
Do............................	11	23	−11.6	Do.
Do............................	12	25	−16.0	Do.
Do............................	14	55	−25.5	Alive, very thin, end of experiment.
Average......................	....	30.8	−13.9	
PEN 8.				
25 per cent round No. 589 dried at room temperature.	32	13	−10.4	Polyneuritis.
Do............................	33	24	−22.4	Do.
Do............................	31	25	−9.7	Do.
Do............................	35	55	−36.0	Alive, very thin, end of test.
Average......................	....	29.2	−19.6	

Pen 6 was fed a ration containing 25 per cent of muscle taken from the shoulder of another fat carcass of beef. The slightly longer survival period and smaller loss in weight indicate a somewhat higher antineuritic value for this sample of muscle than for that fed to pens 4 and 5.

Pen 7 was fed a ration which contained 25 per cent of muscle taken from the loin of another fat carcass of beef. The survival period of this pen of birds was slightly longer than that of pen 6 getting 25 per cent of muscle from the round, but this difference is due to the survival of pigeon 14 in pen 7 at the end of the test, although it was in very poor condition at that time. The three other birds in this pen developed polyneuritis on the twentieth, twenty-third, and twenty-fth days. In reality, there was probably no material difference in the antineuritic value of the muscle from the loin as compared with that of the muscle from the shoulder.

The muscle fed to pen 8 was taken from the round of another fat carcass of beef and dried at room temperature (25° to 30° C.). The result obtained with this pen is very similar to that described for pen 7. On the other hand, pen 4, fed a ration containing 25 per cent of muscle from the round of another carcass, the tissue being dried

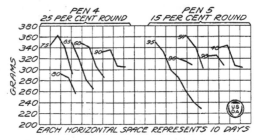

Fig. 5.—Dried ox muscle; changes in weights of pigeons fed.

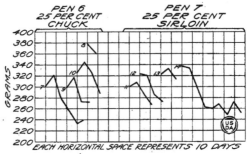

Fig. 6.—Dried ox muscle; changes in weights of pigeons fed.

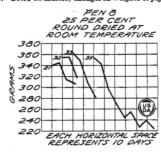

Fig. 7.—Dried ox muscle; changes in weights of pigeons fed.

at 60° C., had a much shorter survival period, 18.8 days as compared with 29.2 days for pen 8. This difference is probably due to the fact that pen 8 contained one very resistant bird, No. 35, while in pen 4 all the birds developed polyneuritis by the twenty-fourth day. The three other birds in pen 8 developed polyneuritis by the twenty-fifth day. Apparently the muscle dried at room temperature had no greater antineuritic value than that dried at 60° C.

23833—23——2

Pens 9 and 10 were fed rations containing 15 and 25 per cent, respectively, of ox tongue. Approximately a dozen tongues were used in preparing this lot of dried tissue. The results are similiar to those obtained with pens 7 and 8. Pen 9 contained one of the very resistant types of birds, No. 79, which materially lengthened the survival period of the pen to 32 days, that of the three other birds in the pen being 24 days. If allowance is made for this bird, it appears that there was no material difference in the antineuritic values of the rations containing 15 and 25 per cent, respectively, of ox tongue. The details are shown in Table 3 and Figure 8.

TABLE 3.—*Experimental feeding of dried ox tongue and polished rice.*

Meat ration.	Pigeon No.	Survival period.	Change in weight.	Result.
PEN 9.		*Days.*	*Per cent.*	
15 per cent ox tongue No. 611.......	77	18	−3.3	Polyneuritis.
Do.............................	78	25	−21.3	Do.
Do.............................	76	30	−9.6	Do.
Do.............................	79	55	−34.2	Very thin, weak, end of test.
Average.....................	....	32	−17.2	
PEN 10.				
25 per cent ox tongue No. 611.......	73	21	+5.9	Polyneuritis.
Do.............................	74	21	+10.6	Do.
Do.............................	75	25	−5.7	Do.
Do.............................	72	49	−16.7	Do.
Average.....................	....	29	−1.5	

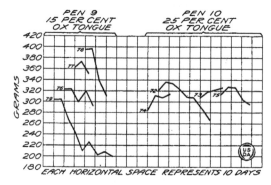

FIG. 8.—Dried ox tongue; changes in weights of pigeons fed.

Pens 11 to 14, inclusive, were fed muscle tissue derived from veal calves. The hind quarters from two carcasses of the best grade of medium-weight veal were used. The results from these tests are very similar to those obtained in feeding the same percentages of muscle from the mature ox. The average survival period of all the pigeons fed calf muscle was 27.9 days, while that of the birds receiving muscle from the mature ox was 26.6 days. The slight difference is not material. The results are shown in Table 4 and Figures 9 and 10.

TABLE 4.—*Experimental feeding of dried calf muscle and polished rice.*

Meat ration.	Pigeon No.	Survival period.	Change in weight.	Result.
PEN 11.		Days.	Per cent.	
15 per cent calf muscle No. 667......	18	19	−18.0	Polyneuritis.
Do............................	19	19	−10.9	Do.
Do............................	17	20	−12.2	Died.
Do............................	20	21	−18.3	Polyneuritis.
Average......................	....	19.8	−14.9	
PEN 12.				
25 per cent calf muscle No. 667......	23	18	−10.7	Polyneuritis.
Do............................	63	19	−20.8	Do.
Do............................	22	26	−26.8	Died.
Do............................	24	55	−20.3	Very thin, active, end of test.
Average......................	....	29.5	−19.7	
PEN 13.				
15 per cent calf muscle No. 725......	98	23	−21.7	Polyneuritis
Do............................	203	24	−20.0	Do.
Do............................	204	30	−30.2	Do.
Do............................	56	47	−26.5	Do.
Average......................	....	31	−24.6	
PEN 14.				
25 per cent calf muscle No. 725....	248	17	−2.7	Polyneuritis.
Do............................	282	28	+1.4	Do.
Do............................	270	32	−18.3	Do.
Do............................	274	49	−15.8	Severe keratomalacia.
Average......................	....	31.5	−8.9	

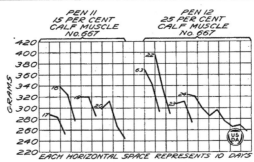

FIG. 9.—Dried calf muscle; changes in weights of pigeons fed.

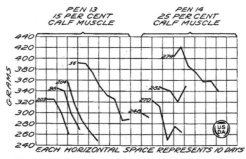

FIG. 10.—Dried calf muscle; changes in weights of pigeons fed.

FEEDING TESTS WITH SHEEP MUSCLE.

The results of the feeding test with sheep muscle are shown in Table 5. Each sample of muscle was derived from a single hind saddle of lamb, i. e., the two hind quarters. Sample 680 used in the rations fed to pens 15 and 16 represents a fairly fat, medium-weight carcass; sample 716 was taken from a light carcass of the same quality; while sample 719 represents an extra-fat, heavy-weight carcass of superior quality.

TABLE 5.—*Experimental feeding of dried sheep muscle and polished rice.*

Meat ration.	Pigeon No.	Survival period.	Change in weight.	Result.
PEN 15.		*Days.*	*Per cent.*	
15 per cent lamb muscle No. 680....	50	15	−14.0	Polyneuritis.
Do.............................	49	17	−20.9	Do.
Do.............................	52	22	−16.7	Do.
Do.............................	51	24	−22.3	Do.
Average......................	....	19.5	−18.5	
PEN 16.				
25 per cent lamb muscle No. 680....	56	20	−5.1	Do.
Do.............................	55	29	−20.8	Do.
Do.............................	53	41	−33.2	Do.
Average......................	....	30	−19.7	
PEN 17.				
25 per cent lamb muscle No. 716....	44	25	−17.7	Do.
Do.............................	83	28	−20.1	Do.
Do.............................	200	34	−6.9	Do.
Do.............................	6	47	−22.9	Very thin at close of test.
Average......................	....	33.5	−16.9	
PEN 18.				
25 per cent lamb muscle No. 719....	30	32	+0.5	All birds in normal condition at close of test.
Do.............................	97	32	+8.2	
Do.............................	99	32	+5.1	
Average......................	....	32	+4.6	
PEN 19.				
15 per cent lamb tongue No. 619..	62	18	−13.3	Polyneuritis.
Do.............................	16	18	−11.9	Do.
Do.............................	198	24	−20.3	Do.
Do.............................	28	35	−12.4	Do.
Average......................	....	23.8	−14.5	
PEN 20.				
25 per cent lamb tongue No. 619....	37	25	−9.9	Do.
Do.............................	63	32	−4.9	Do.
Do.............................	24	55	−7.6	Fair condition at close of test.
Do.............................	61	55	−3.5	Do.
Average......................	....	41.8	−6.5	

The result of the test with pen 15 indicates that the ration containing 15 per cent of lamb muscle, No. 680, had a very low antineuritic value, about the same as that of the autoclaved polished rice fed to pens 2 and 3. The antineuritic value of the ration which contained 25 per cent of the same lot of lamb muscle was somewhat higher as measured by the survival periods of the two pens of birds, but the loss in weight was about the same.

Pen 17, getting a ration which contained 25 per cent of lamb muscle No. 716, yielded results very similar to those obtained with pen 16.

The results of the test with pen 18, which was fed a ration containing 25 per cent of lamb muscle No. 719, are of particular interest.

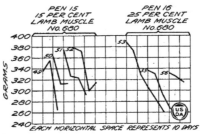

Fig. 11.—Dried lamb muscles; changes in weights of pigeons fed.

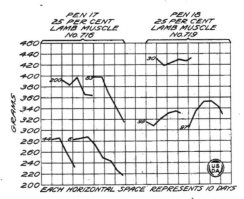

Fig. 12.—Dried lamb muscle; changes in weights of pigeons fed.

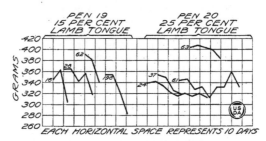

Fig. 13.—Dried lamb tongue; changes in weights of pigeons fed.

Not one of these pigeons developed polyneuritis, and all were in normal condition on the thirty-second day when the test was concluded because the supply of this lot of lamb muscle was exhausted. Although the survival period of this pen is recorded as 32 days, this value should not be compared with those of the other pens, since the possible length of the test was 55 days. It has been observed that, as a rule, if pigeons maintain their weight and are in good condition after feeding 32 days on a ration, they will not develop the disease during an additional 23-day period. Each of the three pigeons in this pen gained in weight, the average being 4.6 per cent.

Pens 19 and 20 were fed rations which contained 15 and 25 per cent of lamb tongue No. 619. This sample was prepared from approximately 50 lamb tongues. The result obtained from pen 19 was about the same as that from pen 15, getting 15 per cent of lamb muscle No. 680, and indicates a low antineuritic value. Pen 20, getting 25 per cent of lamb tongue, yielded rather better results than pen 19, the survival period being 41.8 days as compared with 23.8, and the loss in weight only 6.5 per cent as compared with 14.5. Two birds in pen 20 were in fair condition at the close of the test, while all the pigeons in pen 19 had developed polyneuritis. The change in weights of t e pigeons on the lamb-muscle rations are shown in Figures 11, 12, andhl3.

TESTS WITH HOG MUSCLE.

RESULTS WITH UNCOOKED FRESH MUSCLE.

The feeding tests with hog muscle yielded the most interesting results of all of the experiments. The first lot of tenderloin, No. 681, which was purchased frozen, consisted of the tenderloin muscle from approximately 20 hogs. The results with uncooked fresh muscle are seen in Table 6 and Figures 14, 15, and 16.

In pen 21, pigeon 33 developed an infection of the eye early in the test and died on the forty-third day without any symptoms of polyneuritis. The data for this bird are excluded from the average for the pen. The three other birds were in good condition at the close of the test and each had gained in weight, the average being 3.1 per cent.

The birds in pen 22, on the ration containing 25 per cent of the same lot of tenderloin, were all in fine condition at the close of the test. One pigeon, No. 38, lost 3.2 per cent in weight, but by referring to Figure 14 it will be noted this bird was gaining in weight after an earlier loss. The average gain in weight for the pen was 7.1 per cent.

Pens 23 and 24 were fed rations containing 15 and 25 per cent of muscle obtained from four fresh pork hams representing the same number of hogs. The hams weighed from 8 to 10 pounds each. Every pigeon in each of these pens was in fine condition at the close of the test and each had gained very considerably in weight, the gains ranging from 10 to 20.6 per cent. The average gain for pen 23 was 13.6 per cent and for pen 24 it was 16.8 per cent.

Pens 25 and 26 were fed rations containing 15 and 25 per cent of another lot of frozen pork tenderloin, No. 702. Every bird but one in these pens was in fine condition at the close of the test and had gained in weight from 5.2 to 14.8 per cent. The one bird, No. 183, was in fair condition and had lost only 1.6 per cent in weight. The average gain in weight for each of the two pens was 10.1 and 11.0 per cent, respectively.

TABLE 6.—*Experimental feeding of dried uncooked hog muscle and polished rice.*

Meat ration.	Pigeon No.	Survival period.	Change in weight.	Result.
PEN 21.		*Days.*	*Per cent.*	
15 per cent tenderloin No. 681......	[1] 33	43	−11.7	Died.
Do...............................	34	55	+3.9	Good condition at close of test.
Do...............................	35	55	+2.4	Do.
Do...............................	36	55	+3.0	Do.
Average.......................		55	+3.1	
PEN 22.				
2 5 per cent tenderloin No. 681......	37	55	+11.8	Fine condition at close of test.
Do...............................	38	55	−3.2	Do.
Do...............................	39	55	+15.8	Do.
Do...............................	40	55	+4.0	Do.
Average.......................		55	+7.1	
PEN 23.				
15 per cent fresh ham...............	83	55	+14.7	Do.
Do...............................	200	55	+10.4	Do.
Do...............................	55	55	+18.9	Do.
Do.	30	55	+10.5	Do.
Average.......................		55	+13.6	
PEN 24.				
25 per cent fresh ham...............	65	55	+19.9	Do.
Do...............................	34	55	+20.6	Do.
Do...............................	199	55	+10.0	Do.
Average.......................		55	+16.8	
PEN 25.				
15 per cent tenderloin No. 702......	165	55	+14.4	Do.
Do...............................	193	55	+13.1	Do.
Do...............................	58	55	+14.4	Do.
Do...............................	183	55	−1.6	Fair condition at end of test.
Average.......................		55	+10.1	
PEN 26.				
25 per cent tenderloin No. 702......	93	55	+14.8	Fine condition at close of test.
Do...............................	15	55	+15.0	Do.
Do...............................	87	49	+5.2	Do.
Do...............................	80	55	+9.1	Do.
Average.......................		53.5	+11.0	

[1] Data for this bird excluded from average.

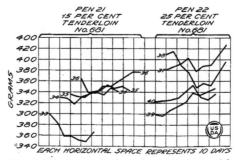

FIG. 14.—Dried hog muscle; changes in weights of pigeons fed.

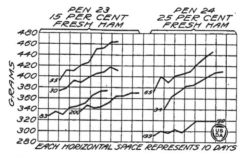

FIG. 15.—Dried hog muscle; changes in weights of pigeons fed.

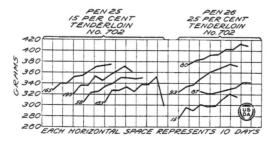

FIG. 16.—Dried hog muscle; changes in weights of pigeons fed.

RESULTS WITH UNCOOKED CURED, AND SMOKED MUSCLE.

Since most hams are not sold fresh, but are cured and smoked and sold as smoked hams, a feeding test was carried on with this class of hams in order to ascertain the effect of curing and smoking upon the antineuritic value of the product. Pens 27 and 28 were fed rations containing 15 and 25 per cent of muscle from two mild-cured smoked hams. Each and every bird in the two pens was in fine condition at the close of the test and had gained in weight; the gain for pen 27 was 6.3 per cent; that for pen 28 was 9.7 per cent. By referring to Table 6, pens 23 and 24, and to Table 7, pens 27 and 28, it will be noted that the antineuritic properties of the muscle from the fresh hams are very similar to those of the smoked hams. The birds getting the fresh-ham muscle made rather larger gains in weight, which indicates a slight advantage for the fresh hams.

Pens 29 and 30 were fed rations containing 15 and 25 per cent of muscle from hog tongues. The lot of muscle used represents approximately 50 hogs. One bird was removed from pen 29 early in the test on account of an injury to its neck; the three other birds were in good condition at the close of the test. The pen suffered a loss of 4.7 per cent in weight. The birds in pen 30 were all in fine condition at the close of the test and the average gain in weight was 9.6 per cent.

The results of this series are seen in Table 7, and the change in weights of the pigeons in pens 27 to 30, inclusive, is shown in Figures 17 and 18.

TABLE 7.—*Experimental feeding of dried, uncooked hog muscle and polished rice.*

Meat ration.	Pigeon No.	Survival period.	Change in weight.	Result.
PEN 27.		*Days.*	*Per cent.*	
15 per cent smoked ham	59	55	+5.3	Fine condition at close of test.
Do	45	55	+8.3	Do.
Do	58	55	+10.6	Do.
Do	88	55	+0.9	Do.
Average		55	+6.3	
PEN 28.				
25 per cent smoked ham	515	55	+12.4	Fine condition at close of test.
Do	130	55	+5.7	Do.
Do	56	55	+8.0	Do.
Do	176	55	+12.7	Do.
Average		55	+9.7	
PEN 29.				
15 per cent hog tongue	84	55	−1.7	Good condition at close of test.
Do	86	55	+0.6	Do.
Do	87	55	−12.9	Do.
Average		55	−4.7	
PEN 30.				
25 per cent hog tongue	80	55	+12.3	Fine condition at close of test.
Do	81	55	+17.3	Do.
Do	82	55	+10.1	Do.
Do	83	55	−1.3	Do.
Average		55	+9.6	

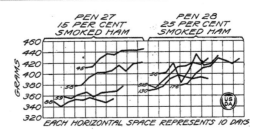

FIG. 17.—Dried smoked ham; changes in weights of pigeons fed.

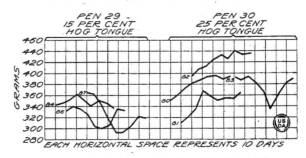

FIG. 18.—Dried hog tongue; changes in weights of pigeons fed.

THE EFFECT OF COOKING UPON THE ANTINEURITIC PROPERTIES OF HOG MUSCLE.

Since but very little pork is eaten in raw condition in this country, it is important to know the effect of cooking upon the antineuritic properties of hog muscle. Two experiments were carried on, one with tenderloin, the other with ham. The pork tenderloins, which weighed about one-fourth pound each, were baked 40 minutes at 200° C. in an oven. The meat was cooked just right for serving and then ground and dried in the usual manner. The cooked ham used in the feeding tests was the boneless, pressed ham of the kind which is sold sliced in retail markets. The method followed in cooking this type of hams is as follows: The cured hams are boned out, trimmed free of excess fat, and placed in metal containers in which they are pressed into the desired shape by means of a hydraulic press. The

TABLE 8.—*Experimental feeding of dried cooked hog muscle and polished rice.*

Meat ration.	Pigeon No.	Survival period.	Change in weight.	Result.
PEN 31.		*Days.*	*Per cent.*	
15 per cent baked tenderloin No. 722.	[1] 45	42	+7.1	Fine condition at end of test.
Do.	51	55	+15.0	Do.
Do.	59	55	+13.2	Do.
Do.	188	55	+4.1	Do.
Average.		55	+9.9	
PEN 32.				
25 per cent baked tenderloin No. 722.	15	55	+14.1	Do.
Do.	30	55	+11.0	Do.
Do.	56	55	+11.8	Do.
Do.	176	55	+14.5	Do.
Average.		55	+12.9	
PEN 33.				
15 per cent cooked ham No. 721.	[2] 58	35	+8.8	Removed, account injury.
Do.	65	55	+1.0	Fine condition at close of test.
Do.	193	55	+4.5	Do.
Do.	839	55	−1.0	Do.
Average.		55	+1.5	
PEN 34.				
25 per cent cooked ham No. 721.	207	55	+10.5	Do.
Do.	2,193	55	+6.1	Do.
Do.	287	55	+.3	Do.
Average.		55	+5.6	

[1] This pigeon substituted for an injured bird on thirteenth day.
[2] Data for this bird excluded from average.

hams, still in the containers, are then deposited in a cabinet-shaped steam cooker, where they are cooked for from 7 to 8½ hours by means of steam at a temperature of approximately 150° F., never higher than 160° F. At the end of the period the hams are chilled in a spray of cold water.

The results of feeding the cooked muscle are shown in Table 8, and the change in weight of the birds in Figures 19 and 20.

Pens 31 and 32 were fed rations containing 15 and 25 per cent of cooked tenderloin. At the end of the test not a bird in either pen had developed polyneuritis and all had gained in weight and were in better condition than at the start. These results are equally as favorable as those secured in feeding the two lots of uncooked tender-loin, as shown in Table 6.   Pens 33 and 34 were fed rations containing 15 and 25 per cent of cooked ham.   One bird, No. 58, in pen 33 was removed on the thirty-fifth day on account of an injury, but it had gained 8.8 per cent in weight at the time.   The other birds were in fine condition at the end of the test.   The average gain in weight was 1.5 per cent.   The birds in pen 34 were in fine condition at the close of the test and the average gain in weight was 5.6 per cent.   By referring to Table 6, it will be noted that the average gains in weight of pens 23 and 24, respectively, getting raw ham, were somewhat higher than those of pens 33 and 34 which were fed corresponding percentages of cooked ham.   This indicates a slightly lower anti-neuritic value for the cooked ham.

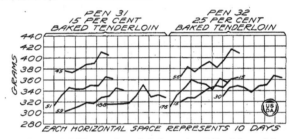

Fig. 19.—Dried hog muscle, cooked; changes in weights of pigeons fed.

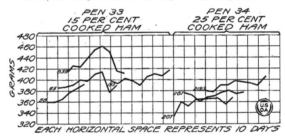

Fig. 20.—Dried ham, cooked; changes in weights of pigeons fed.

DISCUSSION OF RESULTS.

Since the identity of the antineuritic vitamin and the B-growth vitamin, though highly probable, is not yet proved, information on the subject is of interest.   In the experiments which are reported in this paper it has been noted that, as a rule, though with a few excep-. tions, a marked decline in weight precedes the development of poly-neuritis.   Occasionally, however, a pigeon will lose over a third of its initial weight without developing the disease; on the other hand, if a bird maintains its weight, it is only rarely that it develops poly-neuritis.   These relations may be clearly seen by comparing the charts and tables in Part I of this paper.   These facts are simply another indication of the close relationship that is known to exist between the antineuritic and the B-growth vitamins.

The wide difference which was found in the antineuritic properties of the ox and sheep muscle on the one hand and the hog muscle on the other is surprising. The most reasonable explanation is that this variation is due to a difference in the antineuritic properties of the rations fed to the animals. This view is supported by the work of various investigators who have studied the effect of the character of the ration upon the vitamin content of milk—Dutcher and associates (11) (1920); Drummond and associates (12) (13) (1920) (1921); and Kennedy and Dutcher (14) (1922). Unfortunately we have no data as to the effect of the character of the feed consumed upon the antineuritic properties of the muscle of either the ox, sheep, or hog. It is possible, also, that the hog may have the peculiar function of storing up a larger proportion of the vitamin in its tissues than do the other animals named.

It is hardly necessary to state that, while the experiments which have been reported in this paper indicate that ox muscle has a much lower antineuritic value than hog muscle, it, of course, does not follow that beef has a low nutritive value. Rather, meat has a high nutritive value regardless of its vitamin content, and the presence of one or more of the vitamins in considerable quantities simply enhances the value of meat as a food. Naturally, if meat were the sole source of vitamin B in the diet, or even the most important source, then pork would be preferred to beef; on the other hand, if an ample supply of the B vitamin is furnished by other foods, then the relative antineuritic properties of beef, pork, and mutton become a matter of minor importance.

SUMMARY OF PART I.

The results of experiments to determine the antineuritic values of ox, hog, and sheep muscle when fed to pigeons may be summarized as follows:

1. *Ox muscle (mature ox).*—The samples of ox muscle examined had relatively low antineuritic values when used in rations to the extent of 25 per cent. This percentage would correspond to 3.75 grams of the dried tissue in the daily ration of a pigeon weighing 300 grams.

2. *Ox muscle (calf).*—The average antineuritic value of the samples tested was practically the same as the average value of the samples from the mature ox.

3. *Sheep muscle (lamb).*—Two samples of muscle had relatively low antineuritic values; one had a fair value (tongue); and the fourth had a reasonably high value, 25 per cent of the dried muscle in the ration protecting a pen of pigeons against polyneuritis and loss in weight during a period of 32 days.

4. *Hog muscle.*—The antineuritic values of the samples of uncooked hog muscle tested were very much higher than those of the ox or sheep muscle. Fifteen per cent of each of the samples tested was sufficient in a ration to protect a pen of pigeons against polyneuritis for a period of 55 days, and in only one instance did a pen of the birds lose slightly in weight, the other pens gaining from 3.1 to 16.8 per cent.

5. *Effect of cooking upon the antineuritic value of hog muscle.*—Baked tenderloin had practically the same value as the uncooked muscle, but cooked ham had a slightly lower value than the raw product. However, 15 per cent of cooked ham in a ration protected a pen of pigeons against polyneuritis and loss in weight during a period of 55 days.

II. VITAMIN B IN THE EDIBLE VISCERA OF THE OX, SHEEP, AND HOG.

IMPORTANCE OF EDIBLE VISCERA AS FOOD.

In the commercial slaughter of cattle, sheep, and hogs in this country, practically every edible part of the animal for which there is a market is saved for food purposes. The dressed carcass, of course, represents the largest proportion of the total food value of the animal; but the edible by-products, in packing-house parlance called "edible offal," are an important source of food. The edible viscera, or internal organs, make up the bulk of the edible by-products. In addition to their other nutritive properties, it has been observed that several of the internal organs are rich in vitamins.

In Tables 9 to 12, inclusive, which follow, are shown the yields of blood and edible viscera obtained in the commercial slaughter of several grades of cattle, sheep, and hogs.[1] Potentially, all the products named are available as food, but in practice some of them are saved only in limited quantities on account of the restricted demand for the same, or because it is not profitable to save them. Also there must be deducted from the total yields of the products named those products which have been condemned as unfit for food in accordance with the meat-inspection law. However, even after such corrections have been made, the quantity of edible viscera and blood saved for food purposes represents a very material percentage of the dressed weight of the ox, the sheep, and the hog.

TABLE 9.—*Average yield of edible viscera and blood from cattle.*

Item.	Canner cows, 128 head.		Medium steers, 71 head.		Prime steers, 65 head.	
	Average weight.	Per cent of dressed weight.	Average weight.	Per cent of dressed weight.	Average weight.	Per cent of dressed weight.
	Pounds.	*Per cent.*	*Pounds.*	*Per cent.*	*Pounds.*	*Per cent.*
Average live weight	805.0		1,134.0		1,375.0	
Average dressed weight (chilled)	382.0		640.0		801.0	
Blood	30.0	7.85	55.0	8.59	80.0	9.99
Liver	9.0	2.35	10.0	1.56	14.3	1.79
Heart	2.8	.73	3.8	.59	4.4	.55
Lungs	6.0	1.57	6.7	1.05	7.0	.87
Spleen	2.0	.52	2.2	.34	2.2	.27
Kidneys	2.0	.52	2.3	.36	2.5	.31
Stomach (edible part)	15.5	4.06	19.0	2.97	19.0	2.37
Brains	.8	.21	1.0	.16	1.0	.12
Tongue (trimmed)	3.4	.89	4.5	.70	5.8	.72
Pancreas			1.2	.19	1.3	.16
Thymus			.3	.05	.3	.04
Total viscera and blood	71.5	18.70	106.0	16.56	137.8	17.19

[1] The data from which these tables have been prepared were kindly furnished by one of the large meat-packing establishments located in Chicago.

TABLE 10.—*Average yield of edible viscera and blood from calves.*

Item.	1 lot of 33 calves.		1 lot of 20 calves.	
	Average weight.	Per cent of dressed weight.	Average weight.	Per cent of dressed weight.
	Pounds.	*Per cent.*	*Pounds.*	*Per cent.*
Average live weight	137.00	....	240.00	....
Average dressed weight	95.00	....	155.00	....
Blood	5.50	5.79	6.60	4.26
Liver	2.70	2.84	3.60	2.32
Heart	1.00	1.05	1.30	.83
Lungs	2.00	2.10	2.90	1.87
Spleen	.50	.53	.70	.45
Kidneys	.60	.63	1.20	.77
Stomach	3.00	3.15	6.60	4.26
Brains	.50	.53	.60	.39
Tongue	1.10	1.16	1.70	1.10
Thymus	.50	..53	.60	.39
Pancreas	.05	.05	.06	.04
Total viscera and blood	17.45	18.36	25.86	16.68

TABLE 11.—*Average yield of edible viscera and blood from sheep.*

Item.	1 lot of 20 sheep.		1 lot of 20 sheep.		1 lot of 20 sheep.	
	Average weight.	Per cent of dressed weight.	Average weight.	Per cent of dressed weight.	Average weight.	Per cent of dressed weight.
	Pounds.	*Per cent.*	*Pounds.*	*Per cent.*	*Pounds.*	*Per cent.*
Average live weight	83.00	....	99.00	....	111.00	....
Average dressed weight	38.10	....	52.10	....	57.00	....
Blood	3.20	8.40	3.80	7.29	4.50	7.89
Liver	1.30	3.41	1.40	2.69	1.80	3.16
Heart	.40	1.05	.40	.77	.50	.88
Lungs	1.10	2.89	1.20	2.30	1.10	1.93
Spleen	.20	.53	.20	.38	.20	.35
Kidneys	.20	.53	.20	.38	.20	.35
Stomach	3.50	9.19	3.90	7.48	4.50	7.89
Brains	.20	.53	.20	.38	.30	.53
Tongue	.40	1.05	.50	.96	.50	.88
Thymus	.06	.16	.07	.13	....	....
Total viscera and blood	10.56	27.74	11.87	22.76	13.60	23.86

TABLE 12.—*Average yield of edible viscera and blood from hogs.*

Item.	Average of several tests.		Average of several tests.		Average of several tests.	
	Weight.	Per cent of dressed weight.	Weight.	Per cent of dressed weight.	Weight.	Per cent of dressed weight.
	Pounds.	*Per cent.*	*Pounds.*	*Per cent.*	*Pounds.*	*Per cent.*
Average live weight	200.0	....	300.0	....	400.0	....
Average dressed weight	148.0	....	228.0	....	308.0	....
Blood	6.0	4.05	7.9	3.46	10.0	3.25
Liver	2.8	1.89	3.5	1.53	4.0	1.30
Heart	.6	.41	.7	.31	.8	.26
Spleen	.2	.13	.5	.22	.5	.17
Kidneys	.4	.27	.5	.22	.8	.26
Stomach	1.1	.74	1.3	.57	1.8	.58
Brain	.3	.20	.3	.13	.3	.10
Tongue	.8	.54	1.0	.44	1.3	.42
Total viscera and blood	12.2	8.23	15.7	6.88	19.5	6.34

PREVIOUS INVESTIGATIONS WITH EDIBLE VISCERA.

Cooper (6) (15), (1912) (1914) studied the antineuritic properties of a number of animal tissues in feeding tests with pigeons. Ox liver had the highest value, the daily addition of 0.9 grams of the dry tissue to the ration of pigeons being sufficient to protect them against polyneuritis for 50 days. The following quantities of each of the other tissues tested had like values: Ox heart, 1.7 grams; ox cerebrum, 1.2 grams; ox cerebellum, 2.4 grams; and sheep cerebrum, 1.6 to 3 grams.

McCollum and Davis (16) (1915) report that the addition of dried pig heart or kidney to the "fat-free diet" of rats that were declining in weight greatly stimulated growth, the kidney having greater value than the heart.

Eddy (17) (1916) found that the water-soluble portion of an alcoholic extract of sheep pancreas was capable of inducing marked growth in rats that had previously been fed a vitamin-free diet.

Osborne and Mendel (18) (1918) studied the value of dried pig heart, liver, kidney, and brain in the diets of young rats as a source of vitamins A and B, as well as of protein. They found that 19 per cent of pig heart in the ration as the sole source of protein and vitamins A and B induced normal growth in rats. Similar results were obtained with a ration containing 22 per cent of pig kidney. Rats made normal growth on a ration that contained 32.5 per cent of pig brain as a source of vitamin B, vitamin A being supplied in the form of butterfat. Ten per cent of pig brain did not supply sufficient vitamin B for growth. Seven per cent of pig liver, in an otherwise adequate diet, did not furnish sufficient vitamin B for growth; but when 10 per cent of liver was added, satisfactory growth took place.

McCollum, Simmonds, and Parsons (10) (1921) found that 25 per cent of dried ox liver or of ox kidney in a ration furnished an ample supply of vitamins A and B for growth and reproduction in white rats. Rats receiving 20 per cent of ox kidney in the ration also grew and reproduced normally, but those getting 20 per cent of ox liver did not do so well. One lot of rats that was fed solely on dried ox blood declined rapidly in weight and at the end of two weeks the ration was changed to contain 50 per cent of dried ox muscle. The rats then grew at about half the normal rate.

EXPERIMENTAL WORK.

The method of procedure followed in these experiments was practically the same as that employed in the tests with muscle tissue described in Part I. The various tissues studied were obtained in fresh conditions from local meat-packing establishments and were dried in the manner previously described. The dry tissue was used in all tests and the polished rice was first ground and then heated four hours at 120° C. in an autoclave before being used in the rations.

TESTS WITH OX LIVER.

The results of the feeding tests with ox liver are presented in Table 13. Three pens of pigeons were fed rations which contained 5, 15, and 30 per cent, respectively, of ox liver. By comparing the survival periods and the changes in weight of the three pens of pigeons, it is apparent that neither 5 nor 15 per cent of ox liver in the ration was sufficient to protect the birds against polyneuritis for any considerable time, but that 30 per cent of ox liver was sufficient to protect three pigeons for at least 105 days. Each of the three pigeons had gained in weight and was in fine condition at the close of the test, but the fourth bird getting the same ration developed polyneuritis on the ninety-third day. The changes in weight of the pigeons are shown in Figure 21.

TABLE 13.—*Experimental feeding of dried ox liver and polished rice.*

Liver ration.	Pigeon No.	Survival Period.	Change in weight.	Result.
PEN 35.		*Days.*	*Per cent.*	
5 per cent ox liver............	110	44	−15.3	Polyneuritis.
Do............	114	39	−28.2	Do.
Do............	115	45	−17.0	Do.
Do............	117	40	−22.9	Do.
Average............	....	42	−20.9	
PEN 36.				
15 per cent ox liver............	116	55	−14.8	Fair condition at end of test.
Do............	118	40	−10.8	Polyneuritis.
Do............	119	37	−1.8	Do.
Do............	121	45	−10.0	Do.
Average............	....	44	− 9.4	
PEN 37.				
30 per cent ox liver............	120	105	+19.3	Fine condition at end of test.
Do............	123	105	+ 9.9	Do.
Do............	124	105	+ 2.4	Do.
Do............	214	93	− .1.3	Polyneuritis.
Average............	....	102	+ 7.6	

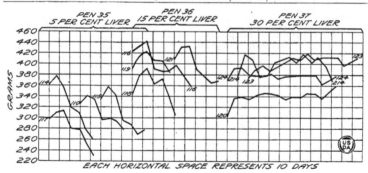

FIG. 21.—Dried ox liver; changes in weights of pigeons fed.

TESTS WITH CALF LIVER.

The results of the feeding tests with calf liver are shown in Table 14. Three pens of pigeons were fed rations which contained 5, 15, and 30 per cent, respectively, of calf liver. On taking into consideration both the survival periods of the pigeons and their changes in weights, it is evident that the ration which contained 5 per cent calf liver had the lowest antineuritic value, followed in turn by those containing 15 and 30 per cent of the tissue. The changes in the weights of the birds are seen in Figure 22.

TABLE 14.—*Experimental feeding of dried calf liver and polished rice.*

Liver ration.	Pigeon No.	Survival period.	Change in weight.	Result.
PEN 38.		*Days.*	*Per cent.*	
5 per cent calf liver	46	19	−28.1	Polyneuritis.
Do	52	50	−39.2	Very thin, end of test.
Do	57	50	−41.5	Do.
Average		39.7	−36.3	
PEN 39.				
15 per cent calf liver	138	28	−7.8	Polyneuritis.
Do	140	74	−23.6	Do.
Do	141	65	−28.3	Do.
Do	1 143	48	−28.8	Died, pneumonia.
Average		55.7	−19.9	
PEN 40.				
30 per cent calf liver	62	55	−13.7	Polyneuritis.
Do	65	55	+16.0	Do.
Do	139	65	−4.4	Do.
Do	145	89	−2.5	Do.
Average		66	−1.2	

1 Data for this pigeon excluded from average.

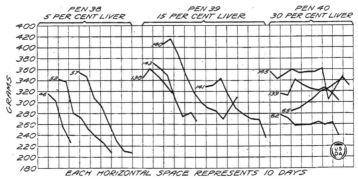

FIG. 22.—Dried calf liver; changes in weights of pigeons fed.

TESTS WITH LAMB LIVER AND HOG LIVER.

In Table 15 are presented the results of the feeding tests with lamb liver and hog liver. The ration containing 15 per cent of lamb liver had a very low antineuritic value, the average survival period of the pen of birds being only 21 days and the loss in weight 11.4 per cent. The ration which contained 25 per cent of lamb liver had a considerably higher antineuritic value, the survival period for the pen being 62 days out of a possible 70 days. One pigeon developed polyneuritis on the thirty-eighth day, one died from an injury on the sixty-eighth day, and the three other birds completed the test.

The results of the tests with hog liver were more favorable than those with lamb liver. The pen of pigeons getting 15 per cent of hog liver in their feed showed a survival period of 62 days out of a possible 70. One bird developed polyneuritis on the thirty-seventh day, but the three others finished the test either in good or in fine condition. The pen showed a gain in weight of 4 per cent. The pigeons that were fed 25 per cent of hog liver in their ration all completed the 70-day test in fine condition with an average gain in weight of 12.1 per cent. Figures 23 and 24 show the changes in weights of the pigeons on the lamb-liver and hog-liver diets.

TABLE 15.—*Experimental feeding of dried lamb and hog liver with polished rice.*

Liver ration.	Pigeon No.	Survival period.	Change in weight.	Result.
PEN 41.		*Days.*	*Per cent.*	
15 per cent lamb liver	164	20	−14.3	Polyneuritis.
Do	165	22	−12.9	Do.
Do	166	16	−9.9	Do.
Do	167	24	−10.2	Do.
Do	168	24	−9.7	Do.
Average		21	−11.4	
PEN 42.				
25 per cent lamb liver	159	70	−2.3	Fine condition end of test.
Do	160	38	−12.8	Polyneuritis.
Do	161	70	+18.3	Fine condition end of test.
Do	162	70	−15.6	Fair condition end of test.
Do	1 163	68	−7.4	Died, injury.
Average		62	−3.1	
PEN 43.				
15 per cent hog liver	155	37	−3.6	Polyneuritis.
Do	156	70	−1.6	Good condition end of test.
Do	157	70	+9.8	Fine condition end of test.
Do	158	70	+11.3	Do.
Average		62	+4.0	
PEN 44.				
25 per cent hog liver	149	70	+16.2	Do.
Do	150	70	+8.4	Do.
Do	151	70	+14.8	Do.
Do	308	70	+8.8	Do.
Average		70	+12.1	

1 Data for this pigeon excluded from average.

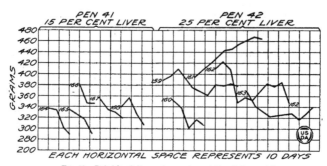

FIG. 23.—Dried lamb liver; changes in weights of pigeons fed.

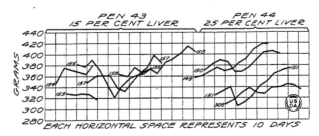

FIG. 24.—Dried hog liver; changes in weights of pigeons fed.

TESTS WITH OX HEART AND HOG HEART.

Four pens of pigeons of four birds each were fed rations containing 15 and 25 per cent of ox heart and of hog heart, respectively, during a period of 55 days. There was not a single case of polyneuritis and every bird had gained in weight, the percentages ranging from 2.7 to 21.1. The average gains for the pens of birds ranged from 6.9 to 14.3 per cent, the pigeons getting the ox-heart rations making slightly larger gains than the others. The high antineuritic value of ox heart and hog heart is evident. Figures 25 and 26 show the changes in the weights of the pigeons fed ox heart and hog heart.

TABLE 16.—*Experimental feeding of dried ox heart and hog heart with polished rice.*

Heart ration.	Pigeon No.	Survival period.	Change in weight.	Result.
PEN 45.		*Days.*	*Per cent.*	
15 per cent ox heart	19	55	+12.3	Fine condition end of test.
Do	20	55	+21.1	Do.
Do	21	55	+15.0	Do.
Do	22	55	+5.5	Good condition end of test.
Average		55	+13.5	
PEN 46.				
25 per cent ox heart	15	55	+12.1	Fine condition end of test.
Do	16	55	+16.7	Do.
Do	17	55	+19.1	Do.
Do	18	55	+9.2	Do.
Average		55	+14.3	
PEN 47.				
15 per cent hog heart	27	55	+4.6	Do.
Do	28	55	+10.3	Do.
Do	29	55	+9.8	Do.
Do	30	55	+2.7	Do.
Average		55	+6.9	
PEN 48.				
25 per cent hog heart	23	55	+15.0	Do.
Do	24	55	+9.8	Do.
Do	25	55	+12.2	Do.
Do	26	55	+12.5	Do.
Average		55	+12.4	

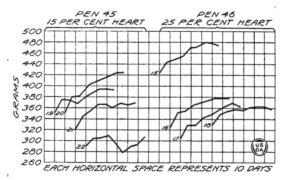

FIG. 25.—Dried ox heart; changes in weights of pigeons fed.

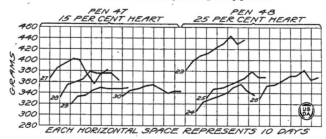

FIG. 26.—Dried hog heart; changes in weights of pigeons fed.

TESTS WITH LAMB HEART.

The results of the tests with lamb heart are presented in Table 17. None of the birds fed the ration which contained 15 per cent lamb heart developed polyneuritis during the test period of 63 days; one bird lost 7.4 per cent in weight, while the two others gained 3.7 and 2.7 per cent, respectively. Three pigeons were fed a ration containing 25 per cent lamb heart; one developed polyneuritis on the thirty-fourth day, even though it had gained 8.5 per cent in weight; the two other birds were in fine condition at the close of the test on the sixty-third day. Figure 27 shows the changes in weight of pigeons that were fed lamb heart.

TABLE 17.—*Experimental feeding of dried lamb heart and polished rice.*

Heart ration.	Pigeon No.	Survival period.	Change in weight.	Result.
		Days.	*Per cent.*	
PEN 49.				
15 per cent lamb heart.....................	2	63	+3.7	Fine condition end of test.
Do....................................	134	63	−7.4	Do.
Do....................................	176	63	+2.7	Do.
Average................................	....	63	−0.3	
PEN 50.				
25 per cent lamb heart.....................	82	63	+17.5	Do.
Do....................................	838	63	+10.5	Do.
Do....................................	284	34	+8.5	Polyneuritis.
Average................................	....	53	+12.2	

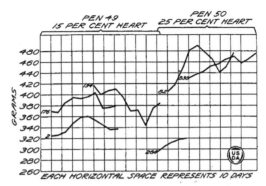

FIG. 27.—Dried lamb heart; changes in weights of pigeons fed.

TESTS WITH OX KIDNEY AND HOG KIDNEY.

The results of the feeding experiments with ox kidney and hog kidney are presented in Table 18. Fifteen per cent of ox kidney in a ration was sufficient to protect three pigeons against polyneuritis for a period of 63 days, and all the birds were in good condition at the close of the test. The average change in weight of the birds on this ration was a loss of 4 per cent. The ration containing 25 per cent of ox kidney also protected three pigeons against polyneuritis during a period of 63 days and the birds were in good condition at the close of the test. The average change in weight of the birds was a gain of 6.3 per cent. A fourth pigeon in the pen died on the fifty-first day from an unknown cause. It apparently was in normal condition on the previous day.

TABLE 18.—*Experimental feeding of dried ox and hog kidney with polished rice.*

Kidney ration.	Pigeon No.	Survival period.	Change in weight.	Result.
PEN 51.		Days.	Per cent.	
15 per cent ox kidney....................	28	63	−6.6	Good condition end of test.
Do....................................	29	63	−0.9	Do.
Do....................................	35	63	−4.5	Do.
Average............................	....	63	−4.0	
PEN 52.				
25 per cent ox kidney....................	24	63	+4.5	Do.
Do....................................	25	63	+7.6	Do.
Do....................................	26	63	+5.8	Do.
Do....................................	[1] 27	51	+1.0	Died.
Average............................	....	63	+6.3	
PEN 53.				
15 per cent hog kidney....................	65	63	−3.6	Good condition end of test.
Do....................................	66	63	−3.5	Do.
Do....................................	67	63	+7.2	Do.
Average............................	....	63	+0.03	
PEN 54.				
25 per cent hog kidney....................	37	63	+7.8	Do.
Do....................................	61	63	+11.5	Do.
Do....................................	62	63	+2.6	Do.
Do....................................	63	63	+13.6	Do.
Average............................	....	63	+8.9	

[1] Data for this pigeon excluded from average.

The rations containing 15 and 25 per cent, respectively, of hog kidney, each protected pigeons against polyneuritis for a period of 63 days and all the birds were in good condition at the end of the test. The birds getting the ration that contained 15 per cent hog kidney maintained their weight, and those getting 25 per cent hog kidney in their feed gained an average of 8.9 per cent. On comparing the results of the tests with ox kidney and hog kidney it appears that they have practically the same antineuritic value.

Figures 28 and 29 show the changes in the weights of the pigeons fed the ox- and hog-kidney rations.

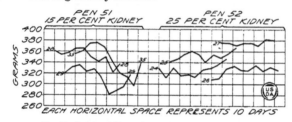

FIG. 28.—Dried ox kidney; changes in weights of pigeons fed.

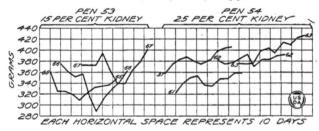

FIG. 29.—Dried hog kidney; changes in weights of pigeons fed.

TESTS WITH OX SPLEEN AND HOG SPLEEN.

In Table 19 are presented the results of the feeding tests with ox spleen and hog spleen. Fifteen per cent of ox spleen in a ration was sufficient to protect three out of four pigeons against polyneuritis during a test period of 57 days, but the fourth bird developed the disease on the fifty-second day. The average loss in weight of the birds was 13 per cent. Twenty-five per cent of ox spleen protected four pigeons for 57 days and the average loss in weight was 15.6 per cent.

The feeding tests with hog spleen yielded results very similar to those obtained with ox spleen. Fifteen per cent of hog spleen protected three pigeons against polyneuritis for 57 days, but one bird developed the disease on the forty-ninth day. Twenty-five per cent of hog spleen protected three pigeons for 57 days, but one bird, No. 67, was greatly emaciated at the close of the test. Another bird, No. 83, died on the forty-fourth day without having shown any characteristic symptoms of polyneuritis. Every pen of pigeons on the ox-spleen and hog-spleen diets lost considerably in weight, the percentages ranging from 13 to 20.4. Figures 30 and 31 show the changes in the weights of the pigeons fed the ox- and hog-spleen rations.

TABLE 19.—*Experimental feeding of dried ox spleen and hog spleen with polished rice.*

Spleen ration.	Pigeon No.	Survival period.	Change in weight.	Result.
PEN 55.		*Days.*	*Per cent.*	
15 per cent ox spleen..........................	2	57	−23.4	Fair condition end of test.
Do..	5	57	−5.0	Good condition end of test.
Do..	42	52	−0.4	Polyneuritis
Do..	45	57	−23.0	Fair condition end of test.
Average...................................	....	56	−13.0	
PEN 56.				
25 per cent ox spleen..........................	64	57	−6.3	Fair condition end of test.
Do..	74	57	−12.8	Do.
Do..	77	57	−24.6	Do.
Do..	99	57	−18.7	Do.
Average...................................	....	57	−15.6	
PEN 57.				
15 per cent hog spleen........................	65	49	−12.0	Polyneuritis.
Do..	66	57	−14.5	Fair condition end of test.
Do..	68	57	−28.0	Poor condition end of test
Do..	71	51	−6.2	Fair condition end of test.
Average...................................	....	55	−15.2	
PEN 58.				
25 per cent hog spleen........................	29	57	−0.6	Good condition end of test.
Do..	35	57	−12.6	Fair condition end of test.
Do..	67	57	−47.9	Very poor condition end of test.
Do..	[1] 83	44	−17.0	Died.
Average...................................	....	57	−20.4	

[1] Data for this bird excluded from average.

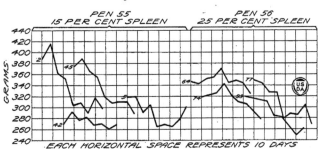

FIG. 30.—Dried ox spleen; changes in weights of pigeons fed.

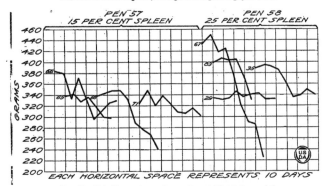

FIG. 31.—Dried hog spleen; changes in weights of pigeons fed.

THE EFFECT OF HEATING UPON THE ANTINEURITIC VALUE OF OX LIVER, HEART, AND
KIDNEY.

Since liver, heart, and kidney are, of course, not used in a raw
condition as human food, it is important to know the effect of cooking
upon the antineuritic value of these tissues. In Table 20 are presented the results of feeding experiments with pigeons to test the
effects of heating upon the antineuritic properties of ox liver. The
changes in weight are shown in Figures 32 and 33.

TABLE 20.—*Effect of heating ox liver on its antineuritic value.*

Liver ration.	Pigeon No.	Survival period.	Change in weight.	Result.
PEN 59.		*Days.*	*Per cent.*	
30 per cent ox liver heated 2 hours at 100° C.	91	18	−18.5	Polyneuritis.
Do.	92	20	−6.0	Died.
Do.	93	20	−18.0	Polyneuritis.
Do.	94	35	−17.9	Thin, active, end of test.
Average		23	−15.1	
PEN 60.				
30 per cent ox liver heated 2 hours at 124° C. in autoclave.	86	25	−16.8	Polyneuritis.
Do.	88	23	−13.9	Do.
Do.	89	17	−17.6	Do.
Do.	556	24	−23.7	Do.
Average		22	−18.0	
PEN 61.				
30 per cent ox liver heated 2 hours at 130° C. in autoclave.	81	25	−24.3	Do.
Do.	82	32	−34.7	Do.
Do.	83	30	−44.9	Do.
Do.	84	35	−27.7	Fair condition end of test.
Average		31	−32.9	
PEN 62.				
25 per cent fried ox liver	169	70	−4.2	Do.
Do.	170	43	−9.8	Polyneuritis.
Do.	171	65	−25.4	Do.
Do.	172	48	−2.9	Do.
Do.	173	70	−1.5	Fair condition end of test.
Average		59	−11.0	
PEN 63.				
25 per cent ox liver baked 30 minutes at 186° C.	4	42	−12.1	Polyneuritis.
Do.	5	55	+3.7	Fine condition end of test.
Do.	6	55	+1.6	Do.
Average		51	−2.3	

Pen 59 was fed a ration which contained 30 per cent of liver that
had been heated two hours in live steam at 100° C. The liver was
first dried in the usual way and then spread out in a thin layer in
pans and heated in an Arnold sterilizer for two hours and again
dried. The result of the feeding test with the ration containing 30
per cent of this lot of liver indicates that the antineuritic value of
the tissue had been largely destroyed. One pigeon developed polyneuritis on the eighteenth day, another on the twentieth day, a third
died on the same day without positive symptoms of polyneuritis,
while the fourth bird was in fair condition on the thirty-fifth day
when the test was concluded.

Pen 60 was fed a ration containing 30 per cent of ox liver that had been heated two hours in an autoclave at 124° C. The previously dried liver was spread out in a thin layer in pans and heated in an autoclave under the conditions stated, and then dried in the usual way. The result of the feeding test with this lot of liver indicated that the antineuritic properties of the tissue had been practically destroyed. The four pigeons on this ration developed polyneuritis on the seventeenth, twenty-third, twenty-fourth, and twenty-fifth days, respectively. The average survival period was 22 days, and the average loss in weight was 18 per cent.

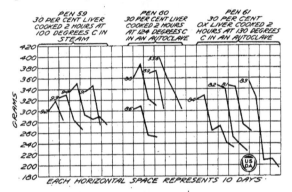

FIG. 32.—Cooked ox liver; changes in weights of pigeons fed.

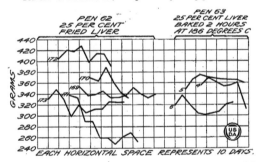

FIG. 33.—Fried and baked ox liver; changes in weights of pigeons fed.

Pen 61 was fed a ration which contained 30 per cent of ox liver that had been heated 2 hours at 130° C. in an autoclave. The antineuritic properties of this lot of liver were largely destroyed by the method of cooking used.

Pen 62 was fed a ration containing 25 per cent of ox liver that had been fried in the manner customary in its preparation for the table. The fried liver was ground and dried. This pen of pigeons was fed for a period of 70 days and the average survival period was 59 days. Three pigeons developed polyneuritis on the forty-third, forty-eighth, and sixty-fifth days, respectively, while two birds finished the test in fair condition. By comparing the results obtained from this pen of birds with those from pens 59 to 61, inclusive, it is apparent that frying caused a much smaller destruction of the antineuritic vitamin in ox liver than the other methods of heating. By comparing the results obtained from pen 62, Table 20, with those from pen 37, Table 13, it appears that the fried liver had an appreciably lower antineuritic value than the uncooked product.

Pen 63 was fed a ration which contained 25 per cent of ox liver that had been baked 30 minutes in an oven at 186° C. The liver was sliced as for frying and then baked in a gas oven until cooked through. The cooked liver was ground and dried. One bird in this pen developed polyneuritis on the forty-second day, but the other two were in good condition on the fifty-fifth day when the test was concluded. The baked liver appeared to have practically the same antineuritic value as the fried product.

The effect of cooking on the antineuritic values of ox heart and kidney is shown in Table 21, and the changes in the weights of the pigeons fed are seen in Figure 34. The heart was washed free of blood and then cooked in boiling water for 75 minutes and finally baked for

TABLE 21.—*Effect of cooking upon the antineuritic value of ox heart and kidney.*

Heart and kidney rations.	Pigeon No.	Survival period.	Change in weight.	Result.
PEN 64.		*Days.*	*Per cent.*	
15 per cent cooked ox heart...............	68	59	− 3.2	Good condition end of test.
Do...............................	69	37	−18.0	Polyneuritis.
Do...............................	70	22	−12.1	Do.
Do...............................	71	59	+ 1.9	Good condition end of test.
Average...................		44	− 7.9	
PEN 65.				
15 per cent cooked ox kidney...............	41	20	− 4.6	Polyneuritis.
Do...............................	42	50	−21.7	Do.
Do...............................	43	24	−12.3	Do.
Do...............................	44	56	−31.3	Very thin end of test.
Average...................		38	−17.5	
PEN 66.				
25 per cent cooked ox kidney...............	45	54	−10.0	Polyneuritis.
Do...............................	46	56	−18.8	Fair condition end of test.
Do...............................	47	56	−16.0	Do.
Do...............................	48	56	− 7.2	Do.
Average...................		56	−13.0	

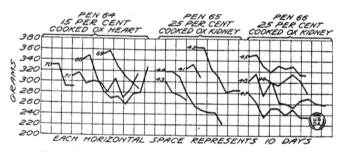

FIG. 34.—Cooked ox heart and ox kidney; changes in weights of pigeons fed.

40 minutes at 210°–220° C. The cooked heart was then ground and dried. Pen 64 was fed a ration containing 15 per cent of the cooked ox heart. Two pigeons developed polyneuritis, one on the twenty-second day, the other on the thirty-seventh day, and the other two birds were in good condition at the close of the test on the fifty-ninth day. By comparing the result of this test with that secured from feeding the ration that contained 15 per cent of uncooked ox heart, pen 45, Table 16, it is evident that the method employed in cooking the ox heart materially lowered its antineuritic value.

The ox kidney was cooked in the following manner: The fresh kidneys were split open, trimmed as free as practicable from fat and connective tissue, cut into small cubes, and then washed thoroughly in cold water. The kidney was then placed in a kettle, covered with water, and heated to boiling. The water was poured off, fresh water was added, and boiling was continued for an hour when the kidney was sufficiently tender to eat. The water was poured off and the cooked kidney was ground and dried is the usual manner. Pens 65 and 66 were fed rations which contained 15 and 25 per cent, respectively, of the cooked ox kidney. The ration containing 15 per cent of the cooked ox kidney had a rather low antineuritic value. Three pigeons developed polyneuritis on the twentieth, twenty-fourth, and fiftieth days, respectively, and one bird was in very poor condition at the close of the test on the fifty-sixth day. The ration that contained 25 per cent of the cooked kidney had a fair antineuritic value. One pigeon developed polyneuritis on the fifty-fourth day; the three others were in fair condition at the close of the test on the fifty-sixth day. The pen of birds suffered an average loss in weight of 13 per cent, which is an indication of a deficiency of the antineuritic vitamin in the ration.

TESTS WITH OX BRAINS AND LAMB BRAINS.

The results of the feeding test with ox and lamb brains are reported in Table 22. The ration containing 15 per cent of ox brains had a very low antineuritic value, three of the birds having developed polyneuritis by the nineteenth day and the fourth bird was in poor condition at the close of the test period of 55 days. The average survival period was 26 days and the loss in weight 9.7 per cent. The ration which contained 25 per cent of ox brains had a fair antineuritic value, the average survival period being 41 days and the loss in weight 6.7 per cent. Two birds developed polyneuritis on the twenty-fifth and thirtieth days, respectively; the other two were in good condition at the close of the test.

Lamb brains had practically the same antineuritic value as ox brains. One bird in pen 70 died on the twenty-second day of the test on account of an injury. The changes in the weights of the pigeons getting the ox-and-lamb brains ration are shown in Figures 35 and 36.

TABLE 22.—*Experimental feeding of dried ox brains and lamb brains with polished rice.*

Brain ration.	Pigeon No.	Survival period.	Change in weight.	Result.
PEN 67.		*Days.*	*Per cent.*	
15 per cent ox brains.....................	39	13	−9.7	Polyneuritis.
Do..................................	40	16	−13.4	Do.
Do..................................	41	55	−13.7	Poor condition end of test.
Do..................................	42	19	−2.1	Polyneuritis.
Average.............................	....	26	−9.7	
PEN 68.				
25 per cent ox brains.....................	35	55	−9.3	Good condition end of test.
Do..................................	36	30	−12.5	Polyneuritis.
Do..................................	37	55	−3.6	Good condition end of test.
Do..................................	38	25	−1.4	Polyneuritis.
Average.............................	....	41	−6.7	
PEN 69.				
15 per cent lamb brains...................	20	26	−6.6	Do.
Do..................................	21	15	−4.0	Do.
Do..................................	22	41	−11.0	Do.
Do..................................	[1] 23	35	−29.6	Died.
Average.............................	....	29	−12.8	
PEN 70.				
25 per cent lamb brains...................	16	55	+0.9	Good condition end of test.
Do..................................	17	25	−11.8	Polyneuritis.
Do..................................	18	55	+4.8	Good condition end of test.
	[1] 19	22	+0.8	Died account injury.
Average.............................	....	45	−2.0	

[1] Results from this bird excluded from average.

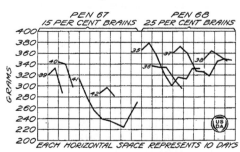

FIG. 35—Dried ox brains; changes in weights of pigeons fed.

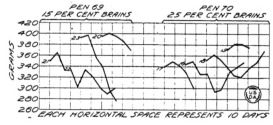

FIG. 36—Dried lamb brains; changes in weights of pigeons fed.

TESTS WITH OX LUNGS AND LAMB LUNGS.

In Table 23 are presented the results of the feeding tests with ox lungs and lamb lungs. The ox lungs appeared to have a fair antineuritic value. Two of the pigeons which were fed the ration containing 15 per cent of ox lungs were in good condition at the close of the test; one bird developed polyneuritis on the forty-second day; and the other died at the same time. The ration containing 25 per cent of ox lungs had a somewhat higher antineuritic value. Two of the pigeons were in good condition and two were in fair condition at the close of the test.

TABLE 23.—*Experimental feeding of dried ox lungs and lamb lungs with polished rice.*

Lung ration.	Pigeon No.	Survival period.	Change in weight.	Result.
PEN 71.		*Days.*	*Per cent.*	
15 per cent ox lungs	6	55	−5.9	Good condition end of test.
Do	22	42	−13.1	Polyneuritis.
Do	34	55	−9.0	Good condition end of test.
Do	72	42	−17.4	Died.
Average		49	−11.4	
PEN 72.				
25 per cent ox lungs	21	55	−15.1	Good condition end of test.
Do	85	55	−26.4	Fair condition end of test.
Do	92	55	−16.3	Good condition end of test.
Do	95	55	−18.8	Fair condition end of test.
Average		55	−19.2	
PEN 73.				
15 per cent lamb lungs	50	33	−18.3	Polyneuritis.
Do	51	55	−20.9	Very thin end of test.
Do	57	21	−2.6	Removed account extreme weakness.
Do	59	21	−6.3	Polyneuritis.
Average		33	−12.0	
PEN 74.				
25 per cent lamb lungs	52	50	−27.2	Died.
Do	54	55	−12.0	Poor condition end of test.
Do	55	55	−14.6	Do.
Do	100	45	−31.3	Died.
Average		51	−21.3	

Lamb lungs appeared to have a rather lower antineuritic value than the ox lungs tested. The ration containing 15 per cent of lamb lungs protected four pigeons against polyneuritis for an average period of only 33 days, and the ration which contained 25 per cent of the tissue protected four birds for an average period of 51 days. Two birds getting the latter ration died of inanition on the forty-fifth and fiftieth days, respectively, after having suffered severe losses in weight, but without showing any characteristic symptoms of polyneuritis. The two surviving birds were in poor condition at the close of the test.

The changes in the weights of the pigeons during the test are shown in Figures 37 and 38.

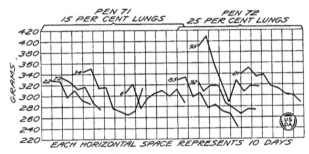

FIG. 37—Dried ox lungs; changes in weights of pigeons fed.

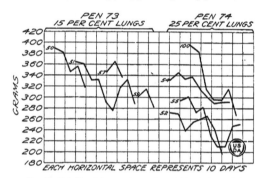

FIG. 38—Dried lamb lungs; changes in weights of pigeons fed.

TESTS WITH CALF PANCREAS AND HOG PANCREAS.

In Table 24 are presented the results of the feeding tests with calf pancreas and hog pancreas. Calf pancreas appears to have a rather low antineuritic value. The rations containing 15 and 25 per cent, respectively, of the tissue had practically the same value, the average survival period and the loss in weight being practically the same for the two pens of pigeons getting these rations.

Hog pancreas appears to have a slightly higher antineuritic value than calf pancreas. The pigeons that were fed the ration containing 15 per cent of hog pancreas showed an average survival period of 29 days and a loss in weight of 23.2 per cent; while the birds that received 25 per cent of hog pancreas in their food showed an average survival period of 41 days and a loss in weight of only 9.6 per cent. Two birds receiving this ration were in good condition at the close of the test on the fifty-fifth day.

The changes in the weights of the pigeons during the test are shown in Figures 39 and 40.

TABLE 24.—*Experimental feeding of dried calf pancreas and hog pancreas with polished rice.*

Pancreas ration.	Pigeon No.	Survival period.	Change in weight.	Result.
PEN 75.		*Days.*	*Per cent.*	
15 per cent calf pancreas....................	73	37	−34.9	Died, inanition.
Do..	75	47	−38.3	Polyneuritis.
Do..	69	35	−11.3	Do.
Do..	86	24	−44.3	Died, inanition.
Average...............................	....	36	−32.2	
PEN 76.				
25 per cent calf pancreas....................	8	32	−32.3	Polyneuritis.
Do..	81	55	−42.9	Very thin, weak, end of test.
Do..	89	25	−24.5	Polyneuritis.
Do..	96	30	−36.8	Died.
Average...............................	....	36	−34.1	
PEN 77.				
15 per cent hog pancreas....................	26	17	−11.6	Polyneuritis.
Do..	79	52	−50.3	Died, inanition.
Do..	82	10	−5.1	Polyneuritis.
Do..	87	35	−25.9	Do.
Average...............,...............	....	29	−23.2	
PEN 78.				
25 per cent hog pancreas....................	80	17	−6.2	Do.
Do..	98	55	−10.1	Good condition end of test.
Do..	181	55	−1.9	Do.
Do..	192	38	−20.3	Died.
Average...............................	....	41	−9.6	

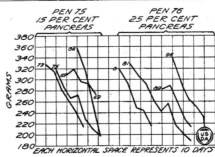

FIG. 39.—Dried calf pancreas; changes in weights of pigeons fed.

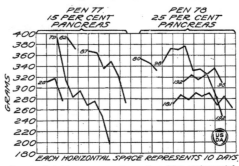

FIG. 40.—Dried hog pancreas; changes in weights of pigeons fed.

TESTS WITH CALF THYMUS AND HOG CHITTERLINGS.

The thymus gland of the calf is the true sweetbread. Chitterlings are that part of the intestinal tract of the hog used as food; and the product used in these tests was cooked chitterlings. In Table 25 are reported the results of the feeding tests with the above-named tissues. The ration containing 15 per cent of calf thymus had a low antineuritic value, the average survival period being only 23 days, and the ration which contained 25 per cent of the tissue had only a fair value, the average survival period of the birds being 34 days.

The chitterlings tested had a fair antineuritic value. All the pigeons which were fed the ration containing 15 per cent of the chitterlings developed polyneuritis by the thirty-ninth day, and the three birds that received 25 per cent of the tissue in their feed all developed polyneuritis by the fifty-second day. The fourth bird in this pen died a few days after the start of the test from an unknown cause. It appears that the calf thymus and hog chitterlings tested had practically the same antineuritic value.

The changes in the weights of the pigeons during the test are shown in Figures 41 and 42.

TABLE 25.—*Experimental feeding of dried calf thymus and hog chitterlings with polished rice.*

Thymus and chitterlings rations.	Pigeon No.	Survival period.	Change in weight.	Result.
PEN 79.				
		Days.	*Per cent.*	
15 per cent calf thymus	92	15	−7.3	Polyneuritis.
Do	93	35	−24.4	Died.
Do	94	26	−19.6	Polyneuritis.
Do	95	14	−14.3	Do.
Average		23	−16.4	
PEN 80.				
25 per cent calf thymus	88	25	−14.2	Removed account badly infected eyes.
Do	89	55	−24.5	Fair condition end of test.
Do	90	35	+.7	Polyneuritis.
Do	91	22	+6.6	Do.
Average		34	−7.9	
PEN 81.				
15 per cent chitterlings	9	19	−10.3	Polyneuritis.
Do	10	15	−6.7	Do.
Do	11	39	−34.3	Do.
Do	70	19	−15.4	Do.
Average		23	−16.7	
PEN 82.				
25 per cent chitterlings	13	17	−.6	Polyneuritis.
Do	15	46	−22.4	Do.
Do	16	52	−14.8	Do.
Average		38	−12.6	

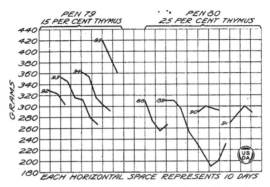

FIG. 41.—Dried calf thymus; changes in weights of pigeons fed.

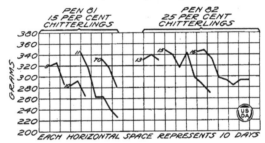

Fig. 42.—Dried hog chitterlings; changes in weights of pigeons fed.

TESTS WITH TRIPE AND HOG STOMACH.

Tripe is prepared from the walls of the first and second stomachs of the ox. It is partially cooked during preparation for food purposes. Hog stomachs are commonly used either as containers for certain sausage products or in the preparation of sausage. Both the tripe and the hog stomachs used in these tests had been cooked according to the regular commercial practice. The results of the feeding tests with tripe and hog stomach are presented in Table 26. From a glance at this table it is at once apparent that each of the products has a very low antineuritic value. It is of interest to note that of the 16 pigeons that were fed the rations containing tripe and hog stomach, 14 developed polyneuritis by the twenty-ninth day of the test, one on the forty-second day, and one died on the twentieth day without showing positive symptoms of polyneuritis. It may be noted also that the average loss in weight of each of the several pens of pigeons was large, ranging from 16.9 to 21.8 per cent.

The changes in the weights of the pigeons during the tests are shown in Figures 43 and 44.

TABLE 26.—*Experimental feeding of dried cooked tripe and hog stomach with polished rice*

Tripe and stomach rations.	Pigeon No.	Survival period.	Change in weight.	Result.
PEN 83.		Days.	Per cent.	
15 per cent tripe................	1	24	−24.5	Polyneuritis.
Do................	2	19	−13.1	Do.
Do................	3	29	−28.8	Do.
Do................	4	19	−11.9	Do.
Average................		23	−19.6	
PEN 84.				
25 per cent tripe................	86	13	−11.7	Do.
Do................	6	20	−20.0	Died.
Do................	7	17	−11.8	Polyneuritis.
Do................	8	19	−24.2	Do.
Average................		17	−16.9	
PEN 85.				
15 per cent hog stomach................	25	42	−30.2	Do.
Do................	26	28	−23.0	Do.
Do................	27	20	− 5.8	Do.
Do................	28	20	−12.0	Do
Average................		28	−17.8	
PEN 86.				
25 per cent hog stomach................	29	28	−21.7	Do.
Do................	30	17	−24.2	Do.
Do................	31	25	−11.6	Do.
Do................	32	28	−29.6	Do.
Average................		25	−21.8	

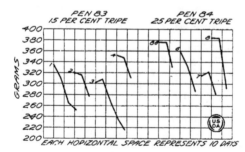

FIG. 43.—Dried cooked tripe; changes in weights of pigeons fed.

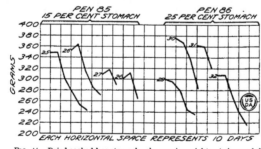

FIG. 44.—Dried cooked hog stomach; changes in weights of pigeons fed.

TESTS WITH OX BLOOD AND CALF BLOOD.

Information regarding the vitamin content of blood is of interest, not only on account of its importance as a food, but also because blood acts as a carrier of vitamins to the tissues.

Samples of defibrinated blood were obtained fresh from a local meat-packing establishment. The serum, which was separated from the corpuscles by means of a centrifuge, was only slightly colored with hemoglobin. The corpuscles were washed several times with normal salt solution. The whole defibrinated blood, the serum, and the corpuscles were dried in the usual way. The results of the feeding tests with these products are shown in Table 27.

The ration containing 15 per cent of ox blood had a very low antineuritic value, the average survival period of the pen of birds getting this ration being only 17 days, while the average loss in weight was 17.6 per cent. The calf blood had a slightly higher value, the average survival period being 31 days, but the loss in weight was 35 per cent. The ox-blood corpuscles had a lower antineuritic value than the whole blood, the average survival period of the two birds getting this ration being only 10 days, while the loss in weight was 23.6 per cent. The very short survival period of the pigeons receiving the ration containing 15 per cent of corpuscles suggests that the presence of this constituent in the ration actually hastened the development of polyneuritis, since it is unusual for pigeons to develop polyneuritis in so short a time, even on a ration consisting entirely of autoclaved polished rice. More experimental evidence is needed to determine this point. The ox-blood serum had a somewhat higher antineuritic value than the whole blood, and a considerably higher value than the corpuscles. However, the serum must be considered as having a low antineuritic value as compared with most

TABLE 27.—*Experimental feeding of dried ox blood and calf blood with polished rice.*

Blood ration.	Pigeon No.	Survival period.	Change in weight.	Result.
PEN 87.		*Days.*	*Per cent.*	
15 per cent ox blood	43	12	−19.9	Polyneuritis.
Do	44	19	−19.8	Do.
Do	45	20	−13.2	Do.
Average		17	−17.6	
PEN 88.				
15 per cent calf blood	46	21	−44.2	Extreme inanition.
Do	47	55	−39.9	Do.
Do	48	17	−20.8	Polyneuritis.
Average		31	−35.0	
PEN 89.				
15 per cent ox-blood corpuscles	5	9	−16.7	Do.
Do	6	11	−30.4	Do.
Average		10	−23.6	
PEN 90.				
15 per cent ox-blood serum	14	35	−30.1	Died.
Do	15	14	−13.2	Polyneuritis.
Average		25	−21.7	

of the other animal products that have been tested. Figure 45 shows the changes in weight of the pigeons fed the blood rations.

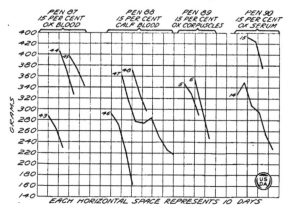

FIG. 45.—Dried ox and calf blood; changes in weights of pigeons fed

SUMMARY OF PART II.

In order to facilitate the interpretation of the results of the experiments reported in Part II of this bulletin Table 28 has been prepared in which are set forth the average data for each pen of pigeons fed. As has been stated before, the antineuritic value of a ration fed to pigeons must be judged, not only by the survival period of the birds, but also by the changes in their weights; and that basis for judgment has been followed here.

The results of the experiments to determine the relative antineuritic properties of the edible viscera and blood from the ox, sheep, and hog may be summarized as follows:

I. ANTINEURITIC VALUES OF DIFFERENT ORGANS AND BLOOD FROM THE OX, HOG, AND SHEEP, RESPECTIVELY.

The ox.—The heart had the highest value, followed closely by the kidney, and the liver. The other products had considerably lower values in the following order: Spleen, lungs, brain, calf thymus, calf pancreas, tripe, serum, ox blood, calf blood, and ox-blood corpuscles.

The hog.—The heart and liver had practically the same value and the kidney a slightly lower value. The spleen, pancreas, chitterlings, and stomach, in order, had much lower values.

The sheep.—The heart had the highest value, followed closely by the liver. The brain and lungs, in order, had much lower values.

II. ANTINEURITIC VALUES OF THE SAME ORGAN FROM THE OX, SHEEP, AND HOG.

Hog liver had the highest antineuritic value, but there was not much difference in the values of ox, calf, and lamb liver.

The heart, kidney, spleen, brain, lungs, pancreas, stomach, and blood, respectively, each had practically the same antineuritic value regardless of source.

III. EFFECT OF HEATING UPON THE ANTINEURITIC PROPERTIES OF OX LIVER, HEART, AND KIDNEY.

The results of the tests which have been reported in this bulletin are summarized in Table 29. The data indicate that ox liver, heart, and kidney suffered material reduction in their antineuritic properties on cooking, the extent of the damage depending upon the temperature and time of cooking. However, fried and baked ox liver and cooked ox heart and kidney still had very fair antineuritic values.

TABLE 28.—*Summary of antineuritic properties of edible viscera (from the ox, sheep, and hog), fed with polished rice.*

Pen No.	Ration.	Test period.[1]	Survival period.	Change in weight.
		Days.	*Days.*	*Per cent.*
35	5 per cent ox liver	55	42	−20.9
36	15 per cent ox liver	55	44	−9.4
37	30 per cent ox liver	105	102	+7.6
38	5 per cent calf liver	75	40	−36.3
39	15 per cent calf liver	75	56	−19.9
40	30 per cent calf liver	75	66	−1.2
41	15 per cent lamb liver	70	21	−11.4
42	25 per cent lamb liver	70	62	−3.1
43	15 per cent hog liver	70	62	+4.0
44	25 per cent hog liver	70	70	+12.1
45	15 per cent ox heart	55	55	+13.5
46	25 per cent ox heart	55	55	+14.3
47	15 per cent hog heart	55	55	+6.9
48	25 per cent hog heart	55	55	+12.4
49	15 per cent lamb heart	63	63	−0.3
50	25 per cent lamb heart	63	53	+12.2
51	15 per cent ox kidney	63	63	−4.0
52	25 per cent ox kidney	63	63	+6.3
53	15 per cent hog kidney	63	63	+0.03
54	25 per cent hog kidney	63	63	+8.9
55	15 per cent ox spleen	57	56	−13.0
56	25 per cent ox spleen	57	57	−15.6
57	15 per cent hog spleen	57	55	−15.2
58	25 per cent hog spleen	57	57	−20.4
67	15 per cent ox brains	55	26	−9.7
68	25 per cent ox brains	55	41	−6.7
69	15 per cent lamb brains	55	29	−12.8
70	25 per cent lamb brains	55	45	−2.0
71	15 per cent ox lungs	55	49	−11.4
72	25 per cent ox lungs	55	55	−19.2
73	15 per cent lamb lungs	55	33	−12.0
74	25 per cent lamb lungs	55	51	−21.3
75	15 per cent calf pancreas	55	36	−32.3
76	25 per cent calf pancreas	55	36	−34.1
77	15 per cent hog pancreas	55	29	−23.2
78	25 per cent hog pancreas	55	41	−9.6
79	15 per cent calf thymus	55	23	−16.4
80	25 per cent calf thymus	55	34	−7.9
81	15 per cent hog chitterlings	55	23	−16.7
82	25 per cent hog chitterlings	55	38	−12.6
83	15 per cent tripe	55	23	−19.6
84	25 per cent tripe	55	17	−16.9
85	15 per cent hog stomach	55	28	−17.8
86	25 per cent hog stomach	55	25	−21.8
87	15 per cent ox blood	55	17	−17.6
88	25 per cent ox blood	55	31	−35.0
89	15 per cent ox-blood corpuscles	55	10	−23.6
90	15 per cent ox-blood serum	55	25	−21.7

[1] The term "test period" indicates the duration of a feeding test which includes a number of pens of pigeons, and the term is not synonymous with "survival period" which has already been defined. The survival period of a pigeon must be considered in relation to the length of the test period as well as to the change in weight of the bird in order to appraise the antineuritic value of the ration fed. In the earlier work with animal tissues, test periods of different length were employed, but in recent work an eight-week test has been adopted as standard.

ORGANIZATION OF THE U. S. DEPARTMENT OF AGRICULTURE.

Secretary of Agriculture	HENRY C. WALLACE.
Assistant Secretary	C. W. PUGSLEY.
Director of Scientific Work	E. D. BALL.
Director of Regulatory Work	
Weather Bureau	CHARLES F. MARVIN, Chief.
Bureau of Agricultural Economics	HENRY C. TAYLOR, Chief.
Bureau of Animal Industry	JOHN R. MOHLER, Chief.
Bureau of Plant Industry	WILLIAM A. TAYLOR, Chief.
Forest Service	W. B. GREELEY, Chief.
Bureau of Chemistry	WALTER G. CAMPBELL, Acting Chief.
Bureau of Soils	MILTON WHITNEY, Chief.
Bureau of Entomology	L. O. HOWARD, Chief.
Bureau of Biological Survey	E. W. NELSON, Chief.
Bureau of Public Roads	THOMAS H. MACDONALD, Chief.
Fixed Nitrogen Research Laboratory	F. G. COTTRELL, Director.
Division of Accounts and Disbursements	A. ZAPPONE, Chief.
Division of Publications	JOHN L. COBBS, Jr., Chief.
Library	CLARIBEL R. BARNETT, Librarian.
States Relations Service	A. C. TRUE, Director.
Federal Horticultural Board	C. L. MARLATT, Chairman.
Insecticide and Fungicide Board	J. K. HAYWOOD, Chairman.
Packers and Stockyards Administration	} CHESTER MORRILL, Assistant to the
Grain Future Trading Act Administration	} Secretary.
Office of the Solicitor	R. W. WILLIAMS, Solicitor.

This bulletin is a contribution from

Bureau of Animal Industry	JOHN R. MOHLER, Chief.
Biochemic Division	M. DORSET, Chief.

48

UNITED STATES DEPARTMENT OF AGRICULTURE

DEPARTMENT BULLETIN No. 1139

Washington, D. C.	PROFESSIONAL PAPER	April 14, 1923

STORAGE OF WATER IN SOIL AND ITS UTILIZATION BY SPRING WHEAT.

By O. R. Mathews, *Assistant Agronomist*, with Introduction by E. C. Chilcott, *Agriculturist in Charge, Office of Dry-land Agriculture Investigations, Bureau of Plant Industry.*

CONTENTS.

INTRODUCTION.

The work of the Office of Dry-Land Agriculture Investigations covers many stations and consequently a wide range of soils and climatic conditions. It has been continuous at these stations for a relatively long term of years. It consequently offers exceptional opportunity for the generalization of data and the drawing of conclusions based on the average conditions of soil, location, and season. This possibility of generalization does not preclude or interfere with the recognition of the extremes of individual conditions, but makes it possible to assign to them their relative importance in the make-up of the whole.

The water-storage capacity of a soil and the depth to which crops are able to use the stored water are matters of prime importance. Other conditions being equal, the soil that will hold the greatest quantity of water within reach of plant roots should show the most material benefits from methods of cultivation calculated to conserve and accumulate soil moisture. It usually happens in the Great Plains, however, that the water-storage capacity of the soil is only partially used. During the greater portion of the time on most soils the quantity of water held in the soil is limited by the amount of water available for storage rather than by a lack of storage capacity.

25323°—23——1

The present study is not intended primarily to establish the maximum depth to which a wheat crop is capable of feeding. The purpose is rather to determine and present the actual depth to which the wheat crop has utilized the soil in a series of seasons, on a wide range of soils, and under radically different cultivation methods. The data are classified to show whether this depth was limited by the depth of the soil itself, by the quantity of water available for storage, by the physiological limitations of the crop, or by the character of the season.

The material was obtained in connection with the preparation of United States Department of Agriculture Bulletin No. 1004, entitled "Use of Water by Spring Wheat on the Great Plains," by John S. Cole and O. R. Mathews. All the members of the technical staff of the Office of Dry-Land Agriculture Investigations from 1906 to date have contributed to the publication by the data they have obtained at the stations where they have been located.

E. C. CHILCOTT,
Agriculturist in Charge.

SOURCES OF INFORMATION.

At the time the work of the Office of Dry-Land Agriculture Investigations was inaugurated it was recognized by those in charge that a measure of the water content of the soil would be of great value in interpreting crop yields. For this reason frequent determinations of soil moisture were made at the stations then in operation, on plats receiving different cultural treatments. This work has been carried on continuously at these stations and at all stations where experiments have been subsequently started by the office mentioned except one, where the character of the soil prohibits soil sampling by the usual method. Moisture determinations have been made on all of the principal crops, but at the stations where wheat grows well it has been considered the basic crop and has been sampled more regularly than any other. It should not be inferred, however, that wheat is the most important crop at all the stations from which data are presented. At some of them it is, in fact, of little importance, but even at these certain data have been obtained on it for purposes of comparison. The moisture reactions of spring wheat and winter wheat have been found to be somewhat different. Spring wheat alone is considered in this publication, as more moisture determinations have been made with it than with winter wheat. Some of the stations having the best soil-moisture records have been necessarily omitted because the major part of their work has been with winter wheat.

The data presented consist of moisture determinations at 17 stations in different portions of the Great Plains on three plats of spring wheat, known as plats A, B, and C or D. The moisture history of these three plats constitutes a total of 135 crop years, after omitting years when some factor, such as hail, was responsible for crop damage and years when the number of samples taken was not great enough to determine the changes in moisture content of the plats.

The plats indicated by the same letter receive the same cultivation at all stations. They represent systems of tillage so different that they should show maximum differences in their moisture relations.

Wheat is grown continuously on plat A. No cultivation is given the plat in the fall after a wheat crop is removed or in the spring until nearly time for seeding, when it is given a shallow plowing and usually one harrowing. No effort is made to control weed growth or to enable the plat to take up or conserve moisture. The plowing is usually only about 3 inches deep and the harrowing after plowing represents a minimum of cultivation in preparing a seed bed. This plat was originally designed to serve as a contrast to other plats receiving thorough cultivation for the purpose of storing water.

Wheat is likewise grown continuously on plat B. This plat is given a deep plowing, usually 8 inches, as early in the fall as possible after the wheat crop is removed. It may be either worked down immediately or left rough for a period, depending upon whether it seems advisable to conserve the moisture already in the soil or to leave the ground rough in order to catch precipitation more readily. No expense is spared in either the number or character of operations necessary to keep the ground free from weeds and in good tilth. The plat usually receives two double diskings and one or more harrowings. It represents what should be the greatest efficiency in storing moisture between harvest and seeding, and indicates the maximum results from the use of moisture-conservation methods where a crop is grown every year.

Wheat is grown on land alternately cropped and fallowed on plats C or D. One of these plats is in crop each year and the other in fallow. By the use of two plats it is possible to obtain a record each year of wheat grown on fallowed land. The fallow plat is plowed in the spring to a depth of about 8 inches. It is kept free from weeds during the summer and fall, and an effort is made to maintain the surface of the soil in condition to take up moisture readily. These plats represent the approximate maximum that may be expected in moisture storage, when a year's crop is sacrificed in order to accumulate moisture for a crop the following year. Unpublished experiments in methods of fallow conducted by the Office of Dry-Land Agriculture Investigations have shown this to be one of the most efficient methods of fallowing. Plat C or D in this bulletin always refers to each plat in the year when wheat is grown.

RANGE OF MOISTURE CONTENT OF SOILS.

The quantity of water that may be held within any unit of soil is subject to a definite limitation. When the moisture content of any section of soil increases to a point where the molecular attraction of the moisture for the soil particles is exceeded by the pull of gravity, there is a movement of water downward through the soil. It is in this manner that water falling upon the surface of a soil is conducted to the lower depths. Each successive layer of soil must become wet to a certain degree before water can reach the layer below. The addition of water in any considerable quantity to any foot section of soil necessitates that all of the soil above must have been wet enough to permit the passage of water through it. The condition of a soil holding all of the moisture that it is capable of holding against the pull of gravity is called its "field carrying capacity." Burr describes this condition of the soil as follows:

The maximum water-holding capacity of a soil is the amount of water that soil will retain against the pull of gravity. When water is added to a soil in sufficient amount the film of water around each soil particle becomes thickened and the small spaces between the soil particles filled with water. In the addition of water a point is reached where the attraction of gravity overcomes the force that holds the water to the soil particles, and the water is drawn downward into the lower soil. If no more water is added a point is reached where the pull of gravity is equalled by the force that holds the water to the soil and there is no further movement except by the slow action of capillarity. The amount of water in the soil at this time is termed " maximum water-holding capacity " or " saturation point." [1]

It will be noted that Burr used the term " maximum water-holding capacity." This term describes the condition of the soil accurately, but has been used by other investigators in a different sense; therefore the term " field carrying capacity " is preferred.

The fact that the moisture content of a soil must be at its field carrying capacity before water is conducted to the lower depths does not indicate that it remains in that condition for any long period of time. The water held within a soil is removed by direct evaporation, by the action of plants, and to a limited extent may be transported by vaporization and recondensation.

The field carrying capacity of each individual foot section of soil at the 17 stations included in this publication has been determined for every foot section that has been wet often enough to permit accurate determination of the point. It has been determined by averaging the moisture content of each individual foot section of soil every time it has been wet enough to permit moisture to move through it into the foot section below.

The averages show that the field carrying capacity of a soil depends upon the physical character of the soil and bears a linear relation to its moisture equivalent and other physical constants. It is a little lower than the moisture equivalent as described by Briggs and McLane.[2]

The moisture equivalent of each foot section of soil in the plats from which data are here presented has been determined.

Loss of water from the soil takes place in various ways, but the principal loss in a soil upon which a wheat crop is growing is the water taken up by the roots of the crop and transpired by the plant tissues. Not all of the water in the soil is removed, as there is always a residue not available to plants. A soil whose moisture content is at a point where plant roots can no longer remove water is in a condition termed its " minimum point of exhaustion." This condition is described by Burr as follows:

The minimum point of exhaustion of water from the soil by the plant is the point at which the force exerted by the plant in obtaining water is equalled by the attraction of the soil for the water. At this point the plant can obtain no more water from the soil and will suffer until water is supplied.[1]

The minimum point of exhaustion of a soil bears a direct relation to the wilting coefficient as determined by Briggs and Shantz.[3] Al-

[1] Burr, W. W. The storage and use of soil moisture. Nebraska Agr. Exp. Sta. Research Bul. 5, 88 pp., illus. 1914.
[2] Briggs, Lyman J., and McLane, John W. The moisture equivalent of soils. U. S. Dept. Agr., Bur. Soils Bul. 45, 23 pp., 1 fig., 1 pl. 1907.
[3] Briggs, Lyman J., and Shantz, H. L. The wilting coefficient for different plants and its indirect determination. U. S. Dept. Agr., Bur. Plant Indus. Bul. 230, 83 pp., 9 figs., 2 pls. 1912. Bibliographical footnotes.

way, McDole, and Trumbull[5] have recognized the wilting coefficient of a soil as the dividing line between wetness and dryness and have pointed out the possibility of distinguishing by observation whether the moisture content of a soil is appreciably above or below that point. In at least the first few foot sections of a soil the minimum point of exhaustion is considerably lower than the wilting coefficient, and the soil when at or near the minimum point can be recognized as dry.

The minimum point has been determined for each foot section of the soil studied by an average of determinations made while the crop was suffering for water, the water content of the soil not being reduced. The point varies with the character of the soil and to some extent with the distance from the surface.

A soil in which the moisture content is at the minimum point is spoken of in this bulletin as dry. One in which the moisture content is at the field carrying capacity is spoken of as filled with water, and one in which the moisture content is between the minimum point and the field carrying capacity is spoken of as partly filled. All water held above the minimum point is termed "available water."

The range between the field carrying capacity and the minimum point of exhaustion in a uniform soil becomes gradually less as the distance from the surface increases. In such a soil the sixth foot section, for example, even when filled with water, contains considerably less water available to plants than the first or second foot of soil. The range between the minimum point and the field carrying capacity is particularly small in the lower depths of some of the heavier soils. In a few of these it is often difficult to determine whether or not moisture available to the wheat crop is present in the fifth and sixth foot sections.

MANNER OF STUDY.

The moisture determinations made on the wheat plats consist of measurements of the water content of each individual foot of soil to a depth great enough to include the zone of feeding of the crop. The depth varies from 2 to 6 feet with the different soils. The moisture content is expressed as a percentage of the weight of water-free soil.

The records at most stations have been kept long enough to permit the establishment of the field carrying capacity and the minimum point of exhaustion for most foot sections of soil under conditions ordinarily obtaining in these plats in the field. At stations with a shorter record the fewer determinations combined with the known moisture equivalent and wilting coefficient of the soils have permitted a close estimation of these factors. With the carrying capacity and minimum point of exhaustion of a soil established, a determination of the water content of any foot section enables one to determine whether available water is present in the soil and whether the water-storage capacity of the soil is being fully utilized.

---

[5] Alway, F. J., McDole, G. R., and Trumbull, R. S. Interpretation of field observations on the moistness of the subsoil. Jour. Amer. Soc. Agron., v. 10, No. 7/8, pp. 265–278. 1918.

There is an experimental error in sampling, depending largely upon the lack of uniformity of the soil. Different soils vary greatly in this respect. Almost all soils in the Great Plains become less uniform in character and structure as distance from the surface in-

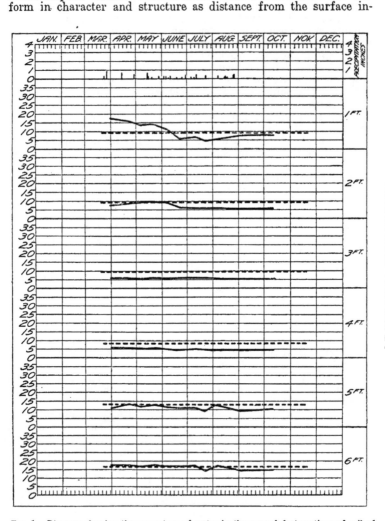

FIG. 1.—Diagram showing the percentage of water in the several foot sections of soil of plat B in wheat at Williston, N. Dak., at each date of sampling in 1910.

creases. Thus, any single sampling can not be taken as giving an exact measure of the water content of a plat, but must be considered as giving a close approximation, the closeness depending upon the uniformity of the soil. In all of the years and stations under study there have been only a few moisture determinations that have been considered as not providing a true indication of the moisture content of the plat.

The object of this study is not to determine the exact quantity of water used from each foot section of soil each year, but rather to determine the extent to which the moisture-storage capacity of the soil has been utilized and the extent to which the stored water has been removed at harvest.

The moisture content of each foot of soil of each plat at every determination during the season has been charted. By a study of the diagram it can be determined quickly and with a considerable degree of accuracy whether available moisture has been present in any foot of soil during the growing season and whether the available moisture in any foot of soil has been removed.

Figure 1 shows the moisture content of each individual foot of plat B at Williston, N. Dak., in 1910. The successive determinations of the moisture content of each foot have been connected by lines. The resulting curves give a good history of the moisture content of each foot of soil for the season; the dotted lines represent the wilting coefficients of the several foot sections.

The soil in the first foot at the time of the initial determination was at its field carrying capacity. This moisture content was not maintained by rainfall, and by harvest, July 26, the moisture of the first foot had been reduced to the minimum point of exhaustion. The second foot of soil possessed only a small quantity of available moisture, and this supply was exhausted long before harvest. There is no evidence to indicate that any available moisture was present below the second foot, and results from other plats and from this plat in other years show that it was dry as far as water available to crops is concerned. A point worthy of note is the fact that the minimum point of exhaustion of the soil in the lower depths more nearly approximates the wilting coefficient than in the upper depths. The greater experimental error in the fifth-foot and sixth-foot depths is indicated by the broken curves of those sections. The fact that the crop suffered severely for lack of water was noted several weeks before harvest. The extent of drought injury is indicated by the low yield of 1.3 bushels per acre.

The depth to which the crop used water that year was less than 2 feet. The storage capacity of the first foot of soil was all utilized and that of the second foot only partly utilized.

CLASSIFICATION OF DATA.

· The presence of available moisture in the soil each year and the extent to which the moisture present has been used are divided into five classes, which are indicated by symbols. These symbols are designed to show at a glance the moisture history of any foot section of soil for a season. The condition represented by each symbol is as follows:

(1) A condition where the soil has been filled with water to its field carrying capacity at some time during the growing season and where all of the

available moisture has been removed by harvest time. This represents full use of water and soil and is indicated by the symbol F.

(2) A condition where available moisture was present in the soil during the growing season and where the moisture content was reduced but not exhausted at harvest. It is indicated by the symbol PW and represents partial utilization of the moisture in the soil and the presence of available water in the soil at harvest. In some cases, particularly in the first foot, it may indicate a condition where all of the available water has been removed at some time before harvest but where precipitation near harvest time has again raised the moisture content above the minimum point.

(3) A condition where the soil was only partly filled with moisture and all of the available water was removed by harvest. This is indicated by the symbol PD and represents partial use of water and a soil dry at harvest.

(4) A condition where available moisture was present in the soil but was not used. It is designated by the symbol OW representing zero use, although water was present. In a very few cases, particularly in the first foot of soil, it indicates a year with so much rain near harvest time that the soil at harvest is at its field carrying capacity.

(5) A condition where no moisture has been used and no available moisture has been present in the soil during the growing season. This is designated by the symbol OD, representing zero use of water and a dry soil.

It is apparent that there is no definite line of demarcation between these classes. In some cases the classification of a foot section of soil might have been changed by a moisture determination at some date when none was made. In general, however, the designations give a very close approximation of the status of any foot section of soil for the season, and the large number of cases makes up to a great extent for the lack of refinement of data.

. Making application of these symbols to the data illustrated in Figure 1, the first foot section would be classified as F; the second as PD; and the third, fourth, fifth, and sixth sections as OD.

In Table 1 these symbols are used to indicate the moisture history of each foot of soil each year at each of the 17 stations. The yield in bushels per acre is given for each plat each year, to indicate to what extent drought injury has reduced the yield of the different plats, as practically all low yields were the result of drought injury. As stated before, years when some factor, such as hail, was responsible for a low yield are not included. Years when the moisture determinations were so infrequent as to leave a material doubt as to the classification of the different foot sections of soil are likewise omitted.

It must be understood that close comparisons can not be made between corresponding plats at different stations in any one year. The stations are in most cases rather widely separated and subject to local conditions of rainfall and other climatic factors. In many cases the differences between two stations, even in one State, during the same season may be greater than those between different seasons at one station. Each station must be considered as a unit both in soil and climate in this study.

No attempt will be made to describe the soil of the different stations further than is necessary to indicate the facility of its penetration by water and roots. Peculiarities that inhibit the soil from functioning in these respects are perforce noted.

A brief summary of the soil utilization at each station will be made, and points of special interest considered.

TABLE 1.—*Yield of wheat on each plat and designation of the extent to which each foot section of soil functioned at 17 field stations in the Great Plains area for the 14-year period from 1907 to 1920, inclusive.*

[KEY TO SYMBOLS OF WATER USE.—F=full use; PW=partial use, with water remaining in the soil at harvest; PD=soil dry at harvest, but only partial use because never filled to capacity; OW=no use, although water was present; OD=no use, and (or because) soil was dry.]

Station, plat, and foot section of soil.	Yield per acre (bushels) and symbol showing use of water.													
	1907	1908	1909	1910	1911	1912	1913	1914	1915	1916	1917	1918	1919	1920
Assinniboine:														
Plat A, yield											3.5		1.5	7.2
Section 1											F		PD	F
Section 2											PD		PD	PD
Section 3											PD		OD	OD
Section 4											OD		OD	OD
Plat B, yield											3.8		1.0	7.5
Section 1											F		PD	F
Section 2											PD		OD	PD
Section 3											OD		OD	OD
Section 4											OD		OD	OD
Plat C or D, yield											11.7		2.2	10.5
Section 1											F		PD	F
Section 2											F		PD	F
Section 3											F		PD	PD
Section 4											PW		PD	OD
Section 5											OW		PD	OD
Section 6											OD		OD	OD
Huntley:														
Plat A, yield						11.0	16.0	18.3	24.5	5.8	7.8	1.5	0	8.2
Section 1						F	F	F	F	PD	F	F	PD	F
Section 2						OD	F	PD	F	OD	F	PD	OD	F
Section 3						OD	PD	OD	PD	OD	F	OD	OD	F
Section 4						OD	OD	OD	OD	OD	PD	OD	OD	OD
Section 5						OD	OD							
Section 6						OD	OD							
Plat B, yield						7.8	11.8	20.2	25.3	7.8	6.8	5.7	0	7.0
Section 1						F	F	F	F	F	F	F	PD	F
Section 2						OD	PD	PD	F	OD	F	F	OD	F
Section 3						OD	OD	OD	OD	OD	F	PD	OD	F
Section 4						OD	OD	OD	OD	OD	PD	PD	OD	OD
Section 5						OD	OD							
Section 6						OD	OD							
Plat C or D, yield						22.6	19.5	36.5	13.5	11.3	18.8	.7		6.8
Section 1						F	F	F	F	F	F	PD		F
Section 2						F	F	F	F	F	F	PD		F
Section 3						F	F	F	F	PD	F	OD		F
Section 4						PD	OD	PD	OD	PD	PD	OD		OD
Section 5						OD	OD							
Section 6						OD	OD							
Sheridan:														
Plat A, yield											6.5		.5	16.2
Section 1											F		F	F
Section 2											F		PD	F
Section 3											PD		OD	F
Section 4											PD		OD	PD
Section 5											OD		OD	OD
Section 6											OD		OD	OD
Plat B, yield											5.3		0	20.5
Section 1											F		PD	F
Section 2											F		OD	F
Section 3											PD		OD	F
Section 4											OD		OD	PD
Section 5											OD		OD	PD
Section 6											OD		OD	OD
Plat C or D, yield											3.3		5.3	23.5
Section 1											F		F	F
Section 2											F		F	F
Section 3											PD		F	F
Section 4											OD		F	F
Section 5											OD		F	PW
Section 6											OD		PD	PW

TABLE 1.—*Yield of wheat on each plat and designation, etc.*—Continued.

Station, plat, and foot section of soil.	Yield per acre (bushels) and symbol showing use of water.													
	1907	1908	1909	1910	1911	1912	1913	1914	1915	1916	1917	1918	1919	1920
Williston:														
Plat A, yield				1.7	2.7	25.2	16.8	23.8	19.3	23.2				
Section 1				F	F	PW	F	F	F	PW				
Section 2				OD	PD	F	F	F	F	F				
Section 3				OD	OD	F	PD	F	PD	PD				
Section 4				OD	OD	PD	OD	OD	PD	PD				
Section 5				OD	OD	OD	OD	OD	OD	OD				
Section 6				OD	OD	OD	OD	OD	OD	OD				
Plat B, yield				1.3	2.8	23.8	11.7	22.5	14.5	24.3				
Section 1				F	F	F	PD	F	F	PW				
Section 2				PD	PD	F	PD	F	PD	F				
Section 3				OD	OD	F	PD	F	PD	PD				
Section 4				OD	OD	PD	OD	OD	OD	OD				
Section 5				OD	OD	OD	OD	OD	OD	OD				
Section 6				OD	OD	OD	OD	OD	OD	OD				
Plat C or D, yield			30.6	4.2	7.6	39.7	16.5	19.4	27.7	28.0				
Section 1			F	F	F	F	F	F	F	PW				
Section 2			F	F	F	F	F	F	F	F				
Section 3			F	F	PD	F	F	F	F	F				
Section 4			F	F	PD	F	F	F	PW	PW				
Section 5			PW	F	PD	PW	PW	F	PW	OW.				
Section 6			OW	PW	PD	OW	OW	PW	PW	OW				
Dickinson:														
Plat A, yield	37.0	24.3	26.8	17.4	5.7	(1)	13.5	10.5	25.8	16.7	5.5		0	15.6
Section 1	PW	F	F	F	F		F	PD	PW	PW	F		PD	PD
Section 2	PW	F	PW	F	PD		F	OD	PW	PW	PD		PD	PD
Section 3	PW	F	PW	PD	OD		PD	OD	PW	PW	PD		PD	OD
Section 4			PW	PD	OD		PD	OD	OW	PW	PD		OD	OD
Section 5			OW	PD	OD		OD	OD	OW	PW	PD		OD	OD
Section 6			OW	PW	OW		OW	OW	OW	OW	PD		OD	OD
Plat B, yield	31.6	17.7	25.2	18.2	1.4	(1)	20.5	8.9	28.7	21.0	2.7		1.3	12.8
Section 1	PW	F	PW	F	F		F	F	PW	PW	F		PD	PD
Section 2	PW	F	PW	F	PD		F	OD	PW	PW	PD		PD	PD
Section 3	PW	PD	PW	PD	OD		F	OD	PW	PW	PD		OD	OD
Section 4			PW	PD	OD		PD	OD	OW	PW	PD		OD	OD
Section 5			OW	OW	OW		PD	OD	OW	PW	PD		OD	OD
Section 6			OW	OW	OW		PD	OD	OW	OW	PW		OD	OD
Plat C or D, yield	28.3	33.8	35.7	26.8	23.3	(1)	27.0	20.1	38.7	22.8	12.3		5.2	21.1
Section 1	PW	F	PW	F	F		F	F	PW	PW	F		PD	PD
Section 2	PW	F	PW	F	F		F	PW	PW	PW	F		PD	PD
Section 3	PW	F	PW	F	F		F	PW	PW	PW	F		PD	PD
Section 4			PW	F	F		PD	PW	OW	PW	PW		PD	PD
Section 5			OW	PW	PW		PW	PW	OW	OW	PW		PD	OD
Section 6			OW	OW	PW		PW	OW	OW	OW	PW		PD	OD
Mandan (main field):														
Plat A, yield									30.5	19.2	15.3	12.7	7.5	1.5
Section 1									PW	PW	F	F	F	PD
Section 2									PW	F	PD	F	F	PD
Section 3									PW	F	PD	PD	F	OD
Section 4									OW	PW	PW	PW	PD	OD
Section 5									OW	OW	OW	PW	PD	OD
Section 6									OW	OW	OW	PW	PD	OD
Plat B, yield									32.1	18.5	14.8	15.3	5.3	1.0
Section 1									PW	PW	F	F	F	PD
Section 2									PW	F	PD	PD	F	OD
Section 3									PW	F	PD	PD	PD	OD
Section 4									PW	PW	PD	PD	PD	OD
Section 5									OW	OW	OW	OW	PD	OD
Section 6									OW	OW	OW	OW	PD	OD
Plat C or D, yield									39.3	21.8	17.2	32.0	15.7	9.5
Section 1									PW	PW	F	F	F	F
Section 2									PW	F	F	F	F	F
Section 3									PW	F	F	F	F	F
Section 4									PW	PW	PW	F	F	F
Section 5									PW	PW	PW	OW	OW	PW
Section 6									OW	PW	OW	OW	OW	PW
Edgeley:														
Plat A, yield	4.1	13.3	28.3	4.0	.7	35.0	16.3	11.3	34.8	[2]5.5	8.3		.5	8.8
Section 1	F	F	F	F	F	PW	F	F	PW	PW	F		F	F
Section 2	PD	F	F	PD	F	PW	PW	PW	PW	PW	PW		F	PW
Plat B, yield	7.0	15.3	23.3	5.2	.5	27.0	12.1	9.2	26.2	[2]3.8	7.5		1.8	9.2
Section 1	F	F	F	F	F	PW	F	F	PW	PW	F		F	F
Section 2	PD	F	F	F	F	PW	PW	PW	PW	PW	PW		F	PW
Plat C or D, yield	9.9	16.0	27.0	5.7	.7	30.3	16.8	13.0	40.3	[2]6.8	4.5		.3	3.8
Section 1	F	F	F	F	F	PW	F	F	F	PW	F		F	F
Section 2	F	F	F	F	F	PW	PW	F	PW	PW	PW		F	PW

[1] Damaged by hail.
[3] Yield on all plats at Edgeley reduced by rust in 1916.

TABLE 1.—*Yield of wheat on each plat and designation, etc.*—Continued.

Yield per acre (bushels) and symbol showing use of water.

Station, plat, and foot section of soil.	1907	1908	1909	1910	1911	1912	1913	1914	1915	1916	1917	1918	1919	1920
Belle Fourche:														
Plat A, yield			23.8	0		0	6.2	4.0	56.5	10.6	4.4	8.5		29.2
Section 1			F	F		F	F	F	F	F	F	F		F
Section 2			F	PD		PD	PD	OD	F	F	F	PD		F
Section 3			F	OD		OD	OD	OD	OD	OD	OD	OD		F
Plat B, yield			23.3	0		0	7.9	4.8	57.7	10.8	2.8	9.8	0	28.7
Section 1			F	F		F	F	F	F	F	F	F	PD	F
Section 2			F	PD		PD	PD	PD	F	PD	PD	PD	OD	F
Section 3			F	OD		OD	OD	OD	OD	OD	OD	OD	OD	F
Plat C or D, yield			32.2	5.0	0	0	16.8	15.8	57.2	18.7	11.1	35.0	6.2	29.2
Section 1			F	F	PD	F	F	F	F	F	F	F	F	F
Section 2			F	F	PD	PD	F	F	F	F	F	F	F	F
Section 3			F	F	OW	OD	F	F	OD	F	F	F	F	F
Ardmore:														
Plat A, yield						3.3	8.8		49.2	18.0	7.5	27.7	3.3	23.8
Section 1						F	PD		PW	F	F	F	F	F
Section 2						PD	PD		PW	F	F	PW	PD	F
Section 3						OD	OD		PW	F	F	PW	PD	F
Section 4									OW	PD	PD	PW	PD	PW
Section 5										OD				
Section 6										OD				
Plat B, yield						3.2	7.3		49.5	17.5	5.5	24.2	3.0	20.0
Section 1						F	PD		PW	F	F	F	F	F
Section 2						PD	OD		PW	F	F	PW	PD	F
Section 3						OD	OD		PW	F	PD	PW	PD	F
Section 4									OW	F	PD	PW	PD	PW
Section 5										PW				
Section 6										PW				
Plat C or D, yield						6.5	3.4		45.0	15.8	8.7	37.0	10.3	23.7
Section 1						F	F		PW	F	F	F	F	F
Section 2						F	F		PW	F	F	F	F	F
Section 3						F	F		PW	F	F	PW	F	F
Section 4						PD	PD		OW	PD	PW	PW	PW	F
Section 5										PW				
Section 6										PW				
Archer:														
Plat A, yield						10.3	6.8	26.8	2.3	15.6		3.5		
Section 1							F	F	PD	F		F		
Section 2						PD	F	F	PD	F		F		
Section 3						OD	OD	F	OD		PD	PD		
Section 4						OD	OD	PD	OD	PD		OD		
Plat B, yield							7.5	23.7	2.4	13.6		2.5		
Section 1							F	F	PD	F		F		
Section 2							F	F	F	F		F		
Section 3							PD	PD	PD	F		OD		
Section 4							OD	PD	OD	PD		OD		
Plat C or D, yield						10.1		25.7	2.8	14.9		7.1		
Section 1							F	F	F	F		F		
Section 2							F	F	F	F		F		
Section 3						PD	F	F	F			F		
Section 4						OD	PD	OD	F		PD			
Scottsbluff:														
Plat A, yield					.5	8.7	12.0	5.7	[1]5.0	5.5	9.2	3.7		12.3
Section 1					F	F	F	F	F	PD	F	F		F
Section 2					PD	PD	PD	PD	F	PD	F	PD		F
Section 3					PD	PD	PD	PD	F	PD	F	PD		F
Section 4					OD	OD	PD	PD	PD	PD	F	OD		F
Section 5					OD	OD	OD	OD	OD	OD	PD			PD
Section 6											OD			
Plat B, yield					.5	6.3	7.8	6.7	16.2	5.7	7.0	6.7		14.0
Section 1					F	F	F	F	F	PD	F	F		F
Section 2					PD	PD	PD	F	F	PD	F	PD		F
Section 3					PD	PD	F	F	F	PD	F	PD		F
Section 4					OD	OD	OD	OD	PD	PD	F	OD		OD
Section 5					OD	OD	OD	OD	OD	OD	OD			
Plat C or D, yield						22.5	17.3	11.7	[1]12.5	11.2	18.7	21.3		19.3
Section 1						F	F	F	F	PD	F	F		F
Section 2						F	F	F	F	F	F	F		F
Section 3						F	F	F	F	F	F	F		F
Section 4						PD	F	F	F	F	F			F
Section 5						OD	PD	OD	PD	PD	PD			F
Section 6							PD	OD	OD	OD	OD			

[1] Damaged by hail.

TABLE 1.—*Yield of wheat on each plat and designation, etc.*—Continued.

Station, plat, and foot section of soil.	Yield per acre (bushels) and symbol showing use of water.													
	1907	1908	1909	1910	1911	1912	1913	1914	1915	1916	1917	1918	1919	1920
North Platte:														
Plat A, yield	24.5	22.7	23.0	6.8	0	12.8	2.0	6.0	22.7	17.2	4.2	.....	15.5	16.5
1..	F	F	F	F	F	F	F	F	OW	PD	F		F	F
2..	F	PD	F	PD	PD	F	PD	PD	OW	PD	PD		F	F
3.. Section	F	PD	F	PD	OD	F	OD	OD	PW	PD	PD		PD	F
4..	.....	OD	PD	PD	OD	PD	OD	OD	PW	PD	PD		PD	F
5..	.....	OW	PD	PD	OD	PD	OD	OD	PW	PD	PD		OD	PD
6..	.....	OW	OW	PD	OD	OD	OD	OD	PW	PW	PD		OD	OW
Plat B, yield	26.0	27.3	15.3	6.7	0	11.2	1.8	5.2	22.8	17.5	5.2	.....	13.0	18.8
1..	F	F	F	F	F	F	F	F	OW	PD	F		F	F
2..	F	F	F	PD	PD	F	PD	F	PW	PD	PD		PD	F
3.. Section	F	PD	PD	PD	OD	F	OD	OD	PW	PD	PD		PD	F
4..	.....	OD	OD	PD	OD	PD	OD	OD	PW	PD	OD		OD	F
5..	.....	OW	OW	OW	OW	PD	OD	OD	PW	PD	OD		OD	F
6..	.....	OW	OW	OW	OW	PD	OD	OD	OW	OW	OW		OW	F
Plat C or D, yield	31.8	40.5	18.0	18.3	0	10.5	10.0	15.2	27.8	19.7	18.7	.....	16.7	21.2
1..	F	F	F	F	F	F	F	F	OW	F	F		PW	F
2..	F	F	F	F	PD	F	PD	F	PW	F	F		PW	F
3.. Section	F	F	F	F	PD	F	PD	PD	PW	F	F		F	F
4..	.....	F	F	F	OW	F	PD	PD	PW	F	F		F	F
5..	.....	PW	PW	F	OW	F	OW	OD	PW	PW	PW		PW	F
6..	.....	PW	PW	PW	OW	F	OW	OD	PW	PW	PW		PW	PW
Akron:														
Plat A, yield	.....	17.3	14.3	11.3	2.9	21.3	4.8	22.2	26.3	9.3	.....	.....	.....	.....
1..		F	PW	F	PD	PW	F	F	PW	F				
2..		F	F	PD	OD	F	PD	F	F	F				
3.. Section		F	PD	PD	OD	F	OD	PD	F	PD				
4..		.....	OD	OD	OD	PD	OD	OD	PW	PD				
5..		.....	OD	OD	OD	PD	OD	OD	PW	OW				
6..		.....	OD	OD	OD	OD	OD	OD	OW	OW				
Plat B, yield	.....	14.0	10.3	6.2	4.1	20.7	.8	12.2	25.8	3.8	.....	.....	.....	.....
1..		F	PW	F	PD	F	PD	F	PW	PD				
2..		F	F	PD	F	F	OD	F	F	OD				
3.. Section		F	PD	PD	F	PD	OD	PD	PD	OD				
4..		.....	OD	OD	OD	OD	OD	OD	OD	OD				
5..		.....	OD	OD	OD	OD	OD	OD	OD	OD				
6..		.....	OD	OD	OD	OD	OD	OD	OD	OD				
Plat C or D, yield	.....	.....	18.5	8.5	4.7	16.0	5.7	14.2	33.8	12.3	.....	.....	.....	.....
1..			PW	F	PD	F	F	F	PW	PD				
2..			F	F	PD	F	F	F	F	F				
3.. Section			F	F	F	PD	F	F	F	F				
4..			F	PW	PD	OD	PD	OD	F	PD				
5..			OW	PW	PD	OD	PD	OD	PW	PW				
6..			OW	PD	PD	OD	OD	OD	OW	OW				
Garden City:														
Plat A, yield	.....	.....	2.1	2.5	0	3.5	(1)	1.5	17.5	0	0	.....	0	0
1..			F	F	PD	F	.....	F	F	F	F		F	F
2..			PD	F	PD	F	.....	F	F	PD	PD		F	PD
3.. Section			OD	PD	PD	PD	.....	PD	PD	OD	OD		F	OD
4..			OD	OD	OD	OD	.....	OD					PD	OD
5..			OD	OD	OD	OD	.....	OD					OD	OD
6..			OD	OD	OD	OD	.....	OD					OD	OD
Plat B, yield	.....	.....	3.2	5.2	0	6.3	(1)	4.3	12.6	0	0	.....	0	0
1..			F	F	PD	F	.....	F	F	F	F		F	F
2..			PD	F	PD	F	.....	F	F	PD	PD		F	F
3.. Section			OD	PD	PD	OD	.....	PD	PD	OD	OD		F	PD
4..			OD	OD	OD	OD	.....	PD					F	PD
5..			OD	OD	OD	OD	.....	OD					OD	OD
6..			OD	OD	OD	OD	.....	OD					OD	OD
Plat C or D, yield	.....	.....	6.7	7.7	0	9.3	(1)	5.3	21.6	5.0	0	.....	1.1	7.0
1..			F	F	PD	F	.....	F	F	F	F		F	F
2..			F	F	F	F	.....	F	F	F	F		F	PW
3.. Section			PD	F	F	F	.....	F	F	F	F		F	PW
4..			PD	F	PD	PD	.....	PD	F	F	F		F	PW
5..			OD	PD	PD	PD	.....	PD	F	PD	PD		OD	PW
6..			OD	OD	OD	OD	.....	OD	PD	OD	PD		OD	PW

1 Damaged by hail.

TABLE 1.—*Yield of wheat on each plat and designation, etc.*—Continued.

Station, plat, and foot section of soil.	Yield per acre (bushels) and symbol showing use of water.													
	1907	1908	1909	1910	1911	1912	1913	1914	1915	1916	1917	1918	1919	1920
Dalhart:														
Plat A, yield		[1]	0	[1]	0	[1]	0	7.8	......	[1]	0			
Section 1			PD		PD		PD	F			F			
Section 2			OD		PD		OD	F			PD			
Section 3			OD		OD		OD	F			OD			
Section 4			OD		OD		OD	PD			OD			
Section 5			OD		OD		OD	PD			OD			
Section 6			OD		OD		OD	OD			OD			
Plat B, yield		[1]	4.0	[1]	0	[1]	0	9.0		[1]	0			
Section 1			PD		PD		PD	F			F			
Section 2			PD		PD		PD	F			PD			
Section 3			PD		OD		OD	F			OD			
Section 4			PD		OD		OD	F			OD			
Section 5			OD		OD		OD	PD			OD			
Section 6			OD		OD		OD	OD			OD			
Plat C or D, yield		[1]	10.5	[1]	0	[1]	1.3	12.4		[1]				
Section 1			F		F		F	F						
Section 2			PW		F		F	F						
Section 3			F		F		F	F						
Section 4			F		F		F	F						
Section 5			F		OW		PW	F						
Section 6			PW		OW		OW	OW						
Amarillo:														
Plat A, yield					7.3	6.3	0	11.0	12.4	3.5	1.7	0		
Section 1					F	F	PD	F	F	PD	F	PD		
Section 2					PD	F	OD	F	F	PD	PD	PD		
Section 3					OD	F	OD	PD	F	OD	OD	OD		
Section 4					OD	PD	OD	OD	OD	OD	OD	OD		
Section 5					OD	OD	OD	OD	OD	OD	OD			
Section 6					OD	OD	OD	OD	OD	OD	OD			
Plat B, yield					10.0	8.5	0	12.8	11.0	7.0	3.8	3.2		
Section 1					F	F	PD	F	F	PD	F	F		
Section 2					PW	F	OD	F	F	PD	F	F		
Section 3					PD	F	OD	PD	F	PD	PD	PD		
Section 4					OD	PD	OD	PD	F	PD	OD	OD		
Section 5					OD	OD	OD	OD	PD	OD	OD	OD		
Section 6					OD	OD	OD	OD	OD	OD	OD			
Plat C or D, yield					19.0	9.5	9.3	13.8	11.6	4.7	3.5	2.8		
Section 1					F	F	PD	F	F	PW	F	F		
Section 2					F	F	F	F	F	F	F	F		
Section 3					F	F	PD	F	F	F	F	F		
Section 4					F	PD	PD	PD	F	F	PD	PD		
Section 5					PD	PD	OD	OD	F	PW	OW	OW		
Section 6					OD	OD	OD	OD	OW	PW	OW			
Tucumcari:														
Plat A, yield								13.5	5.6	0	0			
Section 1								F	F	F	F			
Section 2								PW	F	PD	PD			
Section 3								PD	F	OD	OD			
Section 4								PD	F	OD	OD			
Section 5								OD	PD	OD	OD			
Section 6									PD	OD	OD			
Plat B, yield								14.4	5.2	.9	0			
Section 1								PW	F	F	F			
Section 2								PW	F	F	PD			
Section 3								F	F	PD	OD			
Section 4								PD	F	OD	OD			
Section 5								OD	PD	OD	OD			
Section 6									PD	OD	OD			
Plat C or D, yield								14.7	6.2	1.3	0			
Section 1								PW	F	F	F			
Section 2								PW	F	F	F			
Section 3								PW	F	F	PD			
Section 4								PW	F	PD	OD			
Section 5								OW	PD	OD	OD			
Section 6									PD	PW	OD			

[1] Damaged by hail.

CONDITIONS AT INDIVIDUAL STATIONS.

The soil at Assinniboine is glacial till and offers no serious physical difficulty to the penetration of moisture or plant roots. All the years for which moisture determinations are given were years of low precipitation, and in these years even in the fallow plats available moisture has never been present in the sixth foot. Neither plat A nor B has had the third foot filled with moisture. It will be noted that in two years out of three plat A has been moist to a greater depth than plat B. All of the available moisture has been removed from the soil on all plats all years except from plat C or D in 1917. In that year the crop, in spite of its need for water, was not able to use all the water from the fourth foot and was unable to remove any moisture from the fifth foot. This year represents a case where the demands of the crop for water were so heavy that the crop roots were unable to extend themselves and take up moisture rapidly enough to maintain life in the crop. The wheat suffered a forced ripening even while available water was present at a depth that could have been reached by the wheat roots under conditions less adverse.

At Huntley the full storage capacity of the soil has never been utilized. This has been due in a large measure to the high water-holding capacity of the soil, which has prevented the limited rainfall at this station from penetrating to any great depth. In addition, there seems to be an increased difficulty of water penetration in the lower depths. That there is no impervious layer of soil that prohibits moisture movement has been shown on other plats which have become wet to a depth of at least 6 feet. All of the available moisture has been removed each year from all plats. Plats A and B have shown very little difference in water storage. Plat C or D has stored the most moisture, but has never stored moisture to a depth where it could not be utilized.

The soil at Sheridan has been easily penetrated by moisture and by roots. Little difference is shown between plats A and B in water storage, and neither of these plats has been wet deep enough to utilize fully the moisture-storage capacity of the soil. Plat C or D has carried available moisture in all 6 feet in two of three years. In 1919 the wheat crop removed all available water from all foot sections of this plat, but the yield was seriously reduced by drought injury. In 1920, when the crop was not seriously injured by drought, it used but did not exhaust the water content of the fifth and sixth foot sections.

At Williston the A and B plats have never had available moisture present below the fourth foot. That this has been due to lack of precipitation rather than to difficulty of soil penetration is indicated by the fact that plat C or D has each year had available water present in all 6 feet of soil. The moisture in plats A and B has always been exhausted by harvest in all depths below the first foot. In a few cases there has been enough rain before harvest to raise the content above the minimum point at that time, though all available moisture had been exhausted earlier in the season. There is little difference between plats A and B in the quantity of water stored, but the difference seems to favor plat A. Plat C or D has each year had available moisture in all foot sections. The extent to which the moisture has been utilized varies to some extent in different years. In the four years of heaviest production the soil-moisture content of the fifth foot section was not reduced to the minimum point. In the two years of low production all of the available moisture was removed from the fifth foot and use was made of the water in the sixth foot. In 1911 the sixth foot of soil was dry at harvest. The indications are that the soil at lower depths is most completely utilized when the crop suffers for moisture.

At Dickinson there has been a great opportunity to study moisture penetration and depth of feeding of crops. The soil at the station is open and water penetrates freely, and the precipitation in some years has been so high that under all the methods of cultivation the soil has been wet to a depth of at least 6 feet. At this station neither plat A nor B has shown to advantage over the other in respect to moisture stored in the soil. These two plats furnish a striking illustration of the fact that roots will not penetrate a dry soil, even though there may be available water below. In 1919 plat A used all of the available moisture in the first 5 feet of soil but not in the sixth foot. In the same year plat B exhausted the available moisture in the first 4 feet, but did not secure that from the fifth and sixth foot sections. The moisture present in the soil in the spring of 1911 and that added by precipitation during the growing season moistened the soil to a depth of less than 2 feet. In spite of severe drought injury no moisture was used below that depth. The dry layer in the third and fourth foot sections prevented the roots from extending to moisture in the fifth and sixth foot sections. The crops of both plats were destroyed by hail in 1912, but the soil did not become wet that year to a depth greater than the fourth foot. In 1913, both plats stored moisture to a depth of 4 feet. This was enough to wet all of the dry layer in plat B, but the fifth foot in plat A still remained dry, as it was left by the crop in 1910. The roots of the wheat crop on plat B in 1913 were able to draw upon the available water in the fifth and sixth foot sections, but in plat A the roots were not able to reach the available water in the sixth foot on account of the dry layer in the fifth foot. The soil in plat C or D shows a deeper storage of moisture in dry years than in plat A or B. In all years except 1920 the plat has held available water in each foot of soil at all depths. In the two years of heaviest production no water was used from below the fourth foot, although there was water present in the fifth and sixth foot sections.

The soil at Mandan is easily penetrated by moisture. In 1915, it was wet in all plats to a depth of more than 6 feet. The moisture in the fifth and sixth foot sections of plats A and B was not all removed until the very dry summer of 1919, in spite of the fact that the wheat growing on these plats had suffered from drought injury in the three years preceding. The water of the first 4 feet is utilized freely, but evidently the stress of a long-continued demand for water is precedent to its complete utilization at lower depths.

Edgeley is a striking example of a shallow soil. At this station the soil is a heavy clay that changes into undecomposed shale at a depth of about 2 feet. Even in the second foot pieces of undecomposed shale distributed through the soil are frequent enough to reduce seriously the quantity of available moisture that can be held. The depth of penetration of plant roots seems to be limited to 2 feet. The quantity of rain between harvest and seeding has been large enough to wet thoroughly all the soil on all plats practically every year. This limitation of storage capacity has had the effect of eliminating differences between different cultivation methods in the quantity of moisture conserved. Edgeley is the only station included with such a limited water-storage capacity that it has been practically all utilized each year by all methods of cultivation.

The soil at Belle Fourche is a heavy clay which changes to open partially decomposed shale in the fourth foot. In this soil there is no layer that prohibits moisture penetration, but the soil at the depth of about 2 feet is compact and swells so much when wet that water movement through it is very slow.[6]

Penetration by roots is likewise difficult, and even when available moisture has been present in the lower depths the feeding depth of the wheat crop has been limited to a little less than 3 feet. Evidently the roots penetrate into the third foot only as necessity requires, and they have not been able to reach a depth greater than 3 feet before death or the ripening of the crop occurs. For practical purposes there is no need of considering the soil below the third foot. In spite of the limited water-storage capacity of the soil, there have been only two years when plats A and B have been filled to capacity. There has been practically no difference between the two plats in this respect. Plat C or D has been wet to capacity in all but two years. Belle Fourche represents a station where the demands of the crop for water have been so heavy that the soil moisture has been exhausted in all plats each year at harvest. The only exception is plat C or D in 1911. In that year climatic conditions were so adverse that the crop on the other plats did not germinate and on this plat suffered from drought and heat almost from the time it came up. It made such a limited growth that the roots were not able to extend to a depth of more than 2 feet.

The soil at Ardmore is a heavy clay that changes into fine sand in the fifth and sixth foot sections. The moisture results show that changes in the water content occur below a depth of 4 feet, but the difficulty in sampling the fifth and sixth foot sections has been so great that sampling has been limited to 4 feet in all but one year. As far as the first 4 feet of soil is concerned, there has been practically no difference in the moisture status of plats A and B. The extent to which plat C or D is superior to plats A and B in moisture stored can not be determined, as changes in moisture content evidently have occurred below the fourth foot. The quantity of water used from below the fourth foot, however, can not be large, as plat C or D is little superior to the other plats in point of yield.

Archer represents a station with a soil depth of approximately 4 feet. Below the fourth foot is a bed of gravel that prohibits sampling to a greater depth. It is doubtful whether moisture has penetrated deeper than 4 feet on plats A and B, and in only one year is it probable that water was stored at a depth lower than 4 feet on plat C or D. Plats A and B have approached each other very closely in water stored, utilization of water, and yield. Plat C or D has been little superior to plats A and B in storing moisture. This is re-

---

[6] Mathews, O. R. Water penetration in the gumbo soils of the Belle Fourche Reclamation Project. U. S. Dept. Agr. Bul. 447, 12 pp., 4 fig. 1916.

flected in the yield. All available water has been removed from all foot sections of soil in all years under study.

The soil at Scottsbluff is sandy in character. It is easily penetrated by water in the upper depths, but evidently becomes increasingly difficult of penetration in the lower depths. Plat B has never had available water present below a depth of 4 feet, and plat A only once. The maximum depth of penetration of plat C or D has been 6 feet, and this depth has been reached but once. On this soil all available water has been removed from all plats each year. Plats A and B have exhibited only minor differences in the extent to which they have utilized the storage capacity of the soil. Plat C or D has been superior to the others in water stored and in yield. The soil is evidently porous enough to allow root development sufficient to remove all moisture penetrating into it under ordinary conditions.

The soil at North Platte is probably the most uniform of any at these stations on the Plains. It is open and porous and offers a maximum opportunity for penetration of water and roots. The precipitation at this station has been high enough at different times to wet the soil thoroughly to a depth greater than 6 feet. Determinations of soil moisture to a depth of 15 feet have been made at this station, but spring wheat has shown no evidence of feeding to a depth greater than 6 feet. The station record comprises about an equal number of good and poor years. The fact that roots will not penetrate a dry layer of soil to obtain water in moist lower depths is illustrated by plat A in 1908 and by plat B in 1908, 1909, 1911, 1917, and 1919. These two plats exhibit some differences in their moisture relations in individual years, but on an average they show about the same water storage and water utilization. Plat C or D has stored much more moisture than plats A and B. In all years except 1914 it has carried available moisture to a depth of 6 feet, and there is evidence that on several occasions water has penetrated beyond the sixth foot. This water has been lost to the wheat crop, as the roots of wheat do not penetrate the seventh foot section, even in this favorable soil. The season of 1915 at North Platte was one of the wettest on record at any station. All three of the plats contained as much moisture in the first foot at harvest as they had at any time during the growing season, and all foot sections of soil on all plats had available water at harvest. The use of water in the fifth and sixth foot sections of soil has been usual on plat C or D, but only on one occasion has all of the available water been used from these units. Plat C or D in 1911 shows the result of severe climatic conditions in limiting the depth of feeding. In that year the weather was so hot and dry and the demands of the crop for moisture so excessive that the crop died before it was able to extend its roots to the available water in the fourth, fifth, and sixth foot sections.

Under natural conditions and under some conditions of cultivation there is considerable run-off from the soil at Akron. After water penetrates the surface the character of the soil does not definitely limit further penetration or development of the roots. Plat A has shown on an average a deeper water penetration than plat B. In

1911 plat B was moist to a greater depth than plat A, but in all other years when a difference has existed it has favored plat A. The margin of difference was greatest in 1912, 1915, and 1916. Plat C or D generally, but not always, has been moist to a greater depth than the continuously cropped plats. On all the plats the depth of feeding has generally been limited by the depth to which moisture has been present. However, even when moisture has been present in the fifth and sixth feet it has not been entirely used up except in extremely dry years.

At Garden City the character, distribution, and quantity of precipitation have had the effect of limiting the penetration of moisture. Even the fallow plat has rarely been moist to a depth of 6 feet. In plats A and B no available water has been present below the fourth foot. The difference between plats A and B in moisture stored distinctly favors plat B. The storage of moisture in plat C or D has been consistently greater than in plats A and B. All the available moisture was removed from all plats except plat C or D in 1920. The greater storage of water on plat C or D is reflected in a consistently higher yield.

At Dalhart there has been a slight difference between plats A and B, favoring plat B both in water storage and in yield. Neither plat has fully utilized the storage capacity of the soil at any time, and on both plats all of the available moisture in the soil has been removed each year by harvest time. Plat C or D has been filled with available moisture to a depth of 6 feet each year. Crop requirements for water have been so heavy that each year the wheat has suffered for water before harvest. In spite of this all the available moisture in the fifth foot section has been removed only twice in four years, while the moisture present in the sixth foot has never been entirely removed. In three of the four years presented no water was removed from the sixth foot by the crop.

The soil at Amarillo is not easily penetrated by water. In spite of the high precipitation at this station, water has never reached a depth greater than 4 feet in plat A or 5 feet in plat B. At this station there has frequently been a difference between the two in water storage, and in every case where a difference has existed it has been in favor of plat B. The soil in plat C or D did not become wet to a depth of 6 feet until 1915. The crop has never been able to remove all of the water added to the sixth foot of soil that year. In nearly every year plat C or D has stored water to a depth greater than plats A and B, but the difference in most cases has not been large. The soil at Amarillo is an example of one that holds very little available moisture in the lower depths. It is in many cases very difficult to tell whether or not available moisture is present.

The soil at Tucumcari is sandy in the upper foot sections, and moisture is readily taken into it. In the lower depths the soil is of a clay texture, and water penetrates it with difficulty. When wet it holds only a small quantity of available moisture. The wheat crop was able to use all the water to a depth of 6 feet in one year (1915). In the year 1914 the highest yields recorded at this station were obtained on all three plats. In that year no water was used from below the fourth foot on any plat, though available water was present in the fifth foot of plat C or D. There has been very little difference between plats A and B in water stored. Plat C or D has always stored considerably more water than the other two plats.

AVERAGE OF RESULTS FOR ALL STATIONS.

The data from the individual stations demonstrate that the storage and use of water by the wheat crop are somewhat different at the individual stations. There are, however, enough points in common between the different stations to permit general deductions to be made from the data as a whole.

For this purpose the water content and use at all stations, as indicated by the symbols, are brought together in a composite table. It must be recognized that this composite table shows a greater percentage of water use in the lower depths than actually exists. The data on the fifth and sixth foot sections of soil are largely from stations where water has been used to that depth. The inclusion of the lower depths at stations like Edgeley, Belle Fourche, Huntley, and Scottsbluff would greatly increase the number of cases where no water was used in these foot sections, the soil being either wet or dry.

The data from the individual foot sections of soil at the different stations are grouped together in Table 2. In the upper part of the table the data are presented by cases, the figures under each symbol indicating the number of times that symbol was used in Table 1 for the purpose of indicating the water relations of that plat at the depth indicated. In the lower part of the table these figures are reduced to percentages in order to make the different foot sections of soil more directly comparable. For example, plat A has 135 determinations of the first foot and only 72 of the sixth foot. A comparison of the two sections in regard to the proportion of the time a particular symbol has been used is more readily made when they are expressed as percentages.

TABLE 2.—*Recapitulation of Table 1, showing the number of times each symbol was used in describing the use of water in each foot section of each plat.*

[The first part of the table records the number of cases studied; in the second part these are expressed as percentages of the totals.]

Symbol use at depth indicated (foot sections of soil).	Instances of the use of each symbol as indicating the water relations on plats A, B, and C or D																	
	F.			PW.			PD.			OW.			OD.			Total.		
	A.	B.	C or D.	A.	B.	C or D.	A.	B.	C or D.	A.	B.	C or D.	A.	B.	C or D.	A.	B.	C or D.
Times used:																		
1..	101	98	107	14	14	15	19	22	10	1	1	1	0	0	0	135	135	133
2..	58	57	107	14	17	18	52	47	8	1	0	0	10	14	0	135	135	133
Section..... 3..	30	27	90	8	8	11	39	45	14	0	0	1	45	42	3	122	122	120
4..	5	9	45	11	7	18	28	26	29	3	3	2	56	57	11	103	102	105
5..	0	3	11	5	3	23	14	11	18	6	13	13	56	52	16	81	82	86
6..	0	1	1	4	1	21	5	5	10	14	17	23	49	48	27	72	72	82
Relation to total, per cent:																		
1..	75	73	80	10	10	11	14	16	8	1	1	1	0	0	0	.....	.....	.....
2..	43	42	80	10	13	14	39	35	6	1	0	0	7	10	0	.....	.....	.....
Section..... 3..	24	22	75	7	7	9	32	37	13	0	0	1	37	34	3	.....	.....	.....
4..	5	9	43	11	7	17	27	25	28	3	3	2	54	56	10	.....	.....	.....
5..	0	4	13	6	4	32	17	13	21	7	16	15	69	63	19	.....	.....	.....
6..	0	1	1	6	1	26	7	7	12	19	24	28	68	67	33	.....	.....	.....

The differences in the number of cases in the different foot sections are in a large measure the result of the limitation of sampling due to the limitation of depth of feeding in certain soils. If the samples had all been taken to a depth great enough to make the table entirely symmetrical, the condition of the sixth foot would have been expressed by the symbols OW or OD in nearly all of the 63 cases when determinations were made in the first foot section but not in the sixth.

Consideration of the table will be confined largely to the portion where the results are expressed as percentages. The most striking feature of the table is the closeness with which plats A and B approximate each other. In the first foot of soil both were filled to capacity, and all of the water was used about three-fourths of the time. About 10 per cent of the time the soil was not entirely filled with water at any time during the growing season, but all available water was used. In only 1 per cent of the time, which represents the year 1915 at North Platte, was the soil filled with water at harvest. There has never been a case where no available water was present in the first foot during the growing season. In one year, 1911, at Belle Fourche, very little available moisture was present in the first foot of plats A and B. This year was necessarily omitted in Table 1, as the soil was so dry that the wheat did not come up.

Summing up the results for the first foot, it is found by adding the percentages under the symbol PD to those under the symbol F that the available water in both plats A and B was entirely depleted at harvest in 89 per cent of the cases studied; the water content was reduced but not entirely exhausted (the condition represented by the symbol PW) in 10 per cent of the cases; and the soil was still full of water at harvest time (classed as the condition OW) in 1 per cent of the cases.

The second foot section of plats A and B, when compared with the first, shows a sharp reduction in the number of times full use of water was made (F). This is accounted for by the great increase in the percentage of cases when the soil was only partly filled with moisture and all of it used (PD) and in the appearance of a few cases where the soil was dry all the season (OD). The proportion of the time that moisture present in the soil was only partly used (PW) remains nearly constant.

Summing up the results for the second foot section, it is found that it was dry at harvest 89 per cent of the time on plat A and 87 per cent of the time on plat B. This is the sum of the percentages under symbols F, PD, and OD. The moisture content was reduced but not exhausted in 10 per cent of the cases on plat A and in 13 per cent of the cases on plat B. This condition is represented by the symbol PW. There was only 1 per cent of the time on plat A when the moisture content of the soil was not reduced when available moisture was present. This is the condition shown by the symbol OW. All of the available water in the second foot of the two plats was removed practically the same proportion of the time as in the first foot. The aggregate quantity of water obtained by the wheat crop from the second foot must have been considerably less than that obtained from the first foot, as it has been filled with water less frequently.

The third foot section of soil, when compared with the second, shows a material reduction in the full use of water on plats A and B. In this section the soil has been filled to capacity and all the water used (F) only about 25 per cent of the time. This is accounted for by a marked increase in the proportion of cases when no available water was present (OD). There is a slight reduction in the percentage of time the available water was only partly used (PW). Little change is shown in the percentage of cases when the soil was only partly filled with water and all available water used (PD). The reduction in the number of times the soil moisture was reduced but not exhausted (PW) probably represents the fewer number of times that rains near harvest affected the water content of the soil to this depth.

Summing up the results for this foot section, the soil was dry at harvest (F, PD, and OD) 93 per cent of the time on both plats A and B. In the remaining 7 per cent of the cases the water content of the soil was reduced but not exhausted (PW). Thus, it is found that there is no great difference in the first 3 feet of soil in the percentage of the time that harvest finds them without available water, but that the actual use of water is progressively less as the distance from the surface increases, because of the limitation in the extent to which the soil is filled with moisture.

In the fourth foot section of plats A and B the soil has been filled with water and all the water used (F) less than 10 per cent of the time, partly filled with water and all used (PD) in about 25 per cent of the cases, and it has been dry all the season (OD) about 55 per cent of the time. There is little change in the proportion of cases where the moisture has been reduced but not exhausted (PW). A few cases appear on each plat where available water was not reduced (OW).

The percentage of the time when no water was available at harvest remains nearly as high as in the upper 3 feet of soil. But the great proportion of the time that this foot section has been dry or only partly filled with water makes it far less valuable than the third section in supplying moisture to the wheat crop.

Below the fourth foot available water has been present in the soil of these plats in only one-third of the cases. Full use practically ceases, and the number of times the soil has been partly filled with water and all of it used is reduced. On the other hand, the proportion of the time no use is made of available water rises.

Considering the fact that the soil at depths below 4 feet has been moist only infrequently, that the quantity of moisture held when the soil is filled to capacity is not great, and that the wheat crop has been able to use all the available water present only about half the time in the fifth foot and one-third of the time in the sixth foot the conclusion must be drawn that the fifth and sixth foot sections of soil on land continuously cropped to wheat are generally without value so far as crop production is concerned.

In plats A and B it was found that the limitation of the depth to which water was used in the upper sections at least depended so much upon the depth to which moisture was present in the soil that other factors were obscured. In the C or D plat the soil has been wet to a greater depth, as a rule, and it has been possible to compare the individual sections of soil in their water relations without lack of moisture being the determining factor.

In the first foot plat, C or D closely approaches the other plats in its moisture relations. The chief difference has been a slightly greater number of cases where the soil was filled with moisture and all available moisture used (F), and a correspondingly lesser number of cases where the soil was only partly filled with water and all the water used (PD). The soil was dry at harvest practically the same proportion of the time as on the other plats.

The data for the second foot of plat C or D almost duplicate those from the first foot. This seems to indicate that the second foot of soil is normally filled with roots when moisture is present and that water is used as freely from this section as from the soil above it. The difference shown between the second foot of plat C or D and that of the other two plats appears to be solely due to the quantity of moisture present in the soil.

The third foot of soil evidently differs but little from the first and second in regard to the demands which the wheat crop has made upon it for moisture and the extent to which it has responded. It is only slightly lower in the proportion of time that the soil has been filled with water and the water all removed by harvest. This decrease is accounted for by the fact that the soil has not always been moist to a depth of 3 feet even in fallow. The same decrease in the proportion of the time the available water has not all been used is found in this plat as in plats A and B.

In the fourth foot full use of water has taken place only 43 per cent of the time. That this is due to lack of penetration of water rather than to other factors is indicated by the greater percentage of cases, as compared with the upper sections, when the soil was dry or partly dry. There is, however, a small increase in the number of times the available moisture has been only partly exhausted (PW) and a corresponding decrease in the percentage of the time all available moisture has been removed from the soil before harvest.

In the fifth and sixth foot sections full use of the soil is not frequent. There is a marked increase in the proportion of the time the available water has been only partly used (PW) and in the number of times no use has been made of available moisture (OW). There are, too, an increasing number of cases where no available moisture has been present (OD). In the fifth foot sections available water has been present in the soil 81 per cent of the time. In 47 of this 81 per cent the water has been unused or only partly used before harvest. In the sixth foot section available moisture has been present 67 per cent of the time. Only 13 of this 67 per cent represent cases where all available moisture was removed from the soil. The remainder of the time the available water was only partly removed or not used at all.

As a whole, there is a greater use of water in the lower depths of plat C or D than in the other two plats. This is largely due to the fact that water has been present in the fifth and sixth foot sections more frequently. The quantity of water used by the crop from these depths in an average year must be small, since full use of water is so infrequent.

COMPARISON OF CULTURAL METHODS.

The conservation and use of moisture in plats on which different cultural practices have been employed, are sufficiently comparable at the different stations to allow definite deductions to be made.

For the average of all stations, plats A and B show no notable differences in the quantity of moisture conserved. The differences at individual stations are only minor. In the northern section of the Great Plains the advantage of one or the other at the stations where one is superior favors plat A. This is without doubt due to the fact that in most years there is a better opportunity to obtain moisture by holding the winter snow than by conserving the moisture that falls after harvest. The soil at harvest has been shown to be dry approximately 90 per cent of the time; therefore, cultivation at that time usually conserves no moisture, because none is present. By preventing weed growth, fall plowing is better able than spring plowing to conserve the moisture that falls between harvest and winter. However, the moisture that falls after harvest is not usually all used up on land not fall cultivated. The season between harvest and freezing is not long, and the demand of plants for moisture at that time is not high. Where there is sufficient precipitation after harvest to induce weed growth, there is usually enough so that the moisture supply is not exhausted by the time freezing kills the weeds.

In years with a heavy precipitation after harvest, plat B usually conserves more moisture than plat A. The greater number of times that plat A possesses the higher moisture content in the spring shows the superiority of catching snow over retaining fall precipitation in conserving moisture at the northern stations.

At the southern stations the difference between the two methods in conserving moisture when a difference exists has been in favor of plat B. In this region there is little snow; consequently, the superiority of plat A in catching snow is of little importance. There is also an earlier harvest and a later fall than at the northern stations. This gives plat B a longer period for moisture storage and also gives the weeds on plat A a greater chance to remove the moisture that falls after harvest. In spite of this, the difference between the two plats in the quantity of moisture stored has generally been small.

That the greater depth of plowing practiced on plat B has not increased the root development of this plat over that of plat A is indicated by the fact that the two plats have been practically duplicates in the utilization of the moisture present.

Unfortunately, the slight superiority of one plat over the other in moisture storage in different sections of the Great Plains is such that it is not possible to benefit greatly from it in farm practice. The. southern stations, where plat B has conserved more moisture than plat A, are particularly subject to soil blowing during the winter months. This operates against the use of fall cultivation on an extended scale.

At the northern stations, where plat A has been slightly superior to plat B, there is a practical limit to the spring work that can be done without unduly delaying seeding. In that region the earlier seeding that may be practiced on fall plowing frequently more than makes up for any superiority of spring plowing in the quantity of moisture conserved.

Certainly the greater quantity of moisture stored by either method in any section is not enough to counterbalance other factors such as timeliness of work, control of weeds, and prevention of soil blowing.

Plat C or D has been markedly superior to the other two plats in moisture storage at all stations except those with a limited water-storage capacity. At Edgeley, it will be remembered, the soil is so shallow that practically all of it has been filled to capacity for all methods of cultivation each year between harvest and seeding; consequently, little difference between methods has existed. At some other stations, such as Archer and Ardmore, the difference in favor of plat C or D has been small. The superiority of C or D over A and B in individual years has depended upon the quantity of rainfall as well as the character of the soil. The demand of the wheat crop for moisture differs in the several portions of the Plains,[7] and a given quantity of stored water may be of more value at one station than another. When translated into bushels of yield 4 inches of water stored at Assinniboine would probably be much more valuable than the same quantity of water at Amarillo. The superiority of plat C or D over the other plats in conserving moisture must be considered in terms of increase in bushels per acre to determine the value of fallowing as a farm practice.

Alternate cropping and summer fallowing practiced in these experiments has in all but the driest years stored moisture in the entire zone of natural development of the roots of the wheat crop. It is evident from this that any extension of the fallow period for the purpose of increasing the quantity of moisture stored would not often be effective in increasing the yields of wheat. The more likely result in most years would be the storage of moisture at a depth where its recovery by the wheat crop would be extremely doubtful.

The three plats taken together indicate that moisture is the controlling factor in crop production in the Great Plains and that differences in yield generally are due to differences in the water supply. Plats A and B have produced yields almost or quite equal to those on plat C or D in years when they have contained the same quantity of water.

GENERAL CONCLUSIONS.

Under dry-farming conditions there is present in the soil no ground water or other source of free water. Below the zone of a few feet near the surface, which the present study shows may be wetted and dried during the cycle from harvest to harvest, the soil is either dry or does not contain water above its field carrying capacity. Under these conditions no water moves upward through appreciable distances to replace the water removed by the roots. Water is supplied to the roots only by such part of the soil as they occupy, and only that part of the soil suffers exhaustion or reduction of its water content.

The development of the roots of the wheat plant is indicated by the depth and extent to which the soil water is used. The usual depth of development is indicated by the results given in detail in Table 1 and summarized in Table 2. It appears that at stations

---

[7] Cole, John S., and Mathews, O. R.   Use of water by spring wheat on the Great Plains. U. S. Dept. Agr. Bul. 1004, 34 p., 10 fig.   1923.

where the character of the soil permits easy penetration of water and plant roots, the natural zone of development of wheat roots is the first 4 feet of soil. In many years, particularly on plats A and B, lack of moisture prohibits root growth to that depth, but where moisture is present in the first 4 feet of soil the evidence at hand points to a nearly uniform utilization of moisture within these 4 feet. The use of water below the fourth foot section of soil depends primarily upon the character of the season. In years when moisture is present in all 6 feet of soil, little or no use of water below the fourth foot is shown if there is at all times a supply of available moisture present in the first 4 feet. Development of any considerable number of roots in the fifth and sixth foot sections of soil seems to be made only under stress of a shortage of moisture, either temporary or continued. The extent to which the moisture in these depths is used depends largely upon the length of time that the crop suffers for moisture without drying up or ripening prematurely. The complete utilization of water at these depths seems to require a fair growth of crop and an extended period of time when the crop needs water but does not actually die or come to a forced maturity. The quantity of available moisture held in the fifth and sixth foot sections of soil is usually small, and its complete or nearly complete utilization necessitates conditions so severe that the yield of the crop is almost always seriously compromised. So far as actual benefit to the crop in ordinary years is concerned, the moisture held in the soil below the fourth foot is of no importance. In a few years the moisture at these lower depths has maintained life in a crop and has enabled it to take advantage of favorable conditions later in the season.

In exceptionally severe years, such as 1911 at Belle Fourche and North Platte, the demands for moisture by the wheat crop have been so excessive that the plants dried up without feeding deeply because the roots could not extend themselves rapidly enough to obtain a supply of moisture sufficient to maintain life. The limitation of root development was caused not by lack of water or by lack of demand for water, but by a demand for water so great that it could not be met. This condition is rare, but an approximation of it late in the life of the crop has often been responsible for a forced ripening without the roots reaching their fullest development.

The fact that moisture is normally exhausted in the first 4 feet of soil does not indicate that the moisture is exhausted simultaneously in the different foot sections. In general, the several foot sections are reduced to the minimum point successively in the order of their distance from the surface. There is very little margin between the first and second foot sections of soil in the time at which they become dry. The principal reason for this is doubtless that the roots become well disseminated through at least this much soil before the wheat reaches a stage of growth where its demands for moisture become heavy. There is, in addition, the fact that the exhaustion of the moisture content of the first foot of soil is frequently delayed by precipitation. Reduction of soil moisture in the third and fourth foot sections commences before the moisture in the first 2 feet of soil is exhausted. However, the minimum point is reached distinctly later in the third foot section than in the second and distinctly later in the fourth than in the third.

The fact that all the available moisture present is utilized about the same proportion of the time in each of the first 4 feet of soil indicates that when water is present the roots of the wheat crop usually completely occupy the soil to about that depth before the plants reach maturity.

This does not indicate that water held at lower depths is not usually valuable. In most years all available moisture within reach of the roots of grain crops is needed, and the plat that carries the greater quantity of moisture in the zone of normal development of roots generally makes the higher yield.

The value of moisture-storage capacity in a soil depends largely upon the precipitation. Thus, at Williston, where the soil is of sufficient depth to permit the storage of moisture to a depth of 6 feet, plats A and B have only occasionally been filled with moisture to a depth of 3 feet, and in some years the second foot of soil has not been filled to its carrying capacity. In spite of its greater moisture-storage capacity, it is doubtful whether, in the aggregate, more moisture has been stored in these plats than in the corresponding plats at Edgeley, where the shallow soil has been filled to capacity each year. Stations like Dickinson, that combine a high storage capacity with a relatively large precipitation, are able to utilize moisture to a greater extent.

Another evident fact is that the utilization of a large soil mass is not essential to a high yield. The yield depends more upon the maintenance of a constant supply of available moisture at a depth where it can be easily absorbed by the roots than it does upon the mass of soil involved. The highest yields recorded at any station were produced at Belle Fourche in 1915, when the soil was at no time wet to a depth greater than 2 feet. At the same station in 1920, when all the soil was filled to capacity with moisture and the crop prospects were even better than in 1915, the yield was reduced below that of 1915 because the available moisture was exhausted too long a time before harvest. Yields of wheat on the shallow soil at Edgeley under favorable conditions have been as high or higher than at stations where a much greater soil mass has been occupied by the roots.

SUMMARY.

With knowledge of the field carrying capacity and the minimum point of exhaustion of each soil unit the soil-moisture data have been utilized to classify into five groups the extent to which each foot section of soil has functioned each year in the production of spring wheat by three distinct cultural methods at 17 field stations on the Great Plains.

On land producing a crop each year differences in cultural methods are not sufficient to cause major differences in the depth to which water is stored and from which it is recovered. Alternate fallowing and cropping results, on the average, in the utilization of a somewhat greater volume of soil.

The depth to which available water is stored may be limited by the shallowness of the soil. When not limited by soil character the surface 6 feet of soil may function in the growth of spring wheat. Except on soils of limited storage capacity, the depth to which water is stored in the Great Plains is more often determined by the quantity and character of the precipitation than by the storage capacity of the soil.

Available water, when present in the soil, is removed with about the same degree of frequency from each of the first 4 feet. The aggregate quantity of water contributed by each foot section becomes progressively less with increasing distance from the surface, both because each successive foot section is less frequently filled with water and because the quantity of available water that may be held in each successive unit is less. The fifth and sixth foot sections hold still less available water, and the full use of their limited capacity is not frequent. They contribute very little to the total quantity of water used by the crop, but under certain conditions this contribution may be important.

In about 90 per cent of the years covered by these investigations the soil within the zone of normal root development was dry at harvest time.

The utilization of a large soil mass is not essential to a high yield. The yield depends more upon the maintenance of a constant supply of available moisture to the depth at which it can be easily obtained than upon the mass of soil involved.

ORGANIZATION OF THE UNITED STATES DEPARTMENT OF AGRICULTURE.

Secretary of Agriculture_____ HENRY C. WALLACE.
Assistant Secretary_____ C. W. PUGSLEY.
Director of Scientific Work_____ E. D. BALL.
Director of Regulatory Work_____
Weather Bureau_____ CHARLES F. MARVIN, Chief.
Bureau of Agricultural Economics_____ HENRY C. TAYLOR, Chief.
Bureau of Animal Industry_____ JOHN R. MOHLER, Chief.
Bureau of Plant Industry_____ WILLIAM A. TAYLOR, Chief.
Forest Service_____ W. B. GREELEY, Chief.
Bureau of Chemistry_____ WALTER G. CAMPBELL, Acting Chief.
Bureau of Soils_____ MILTON WHITNEY, Chief.
Bureau of Entomology_____ L. O. HOWARD, Chief.
Bureau of Biological Survey_____ E. W. NELSON, Chief.
Bureau of Public Roads_____ THOMAS H. MacDONALD, Chief.
Fixed Nitrogen Research Laboratory_____ F. G. COTTRELL, Director.
Division of Accounts and Disbursements_____ A. ZAPPONE, Chief.
Division of Publications_____ JOHN L. COBBS, Jr., Chief.
Library_____ CLARIBEL R. BARNETT, Librarian.
States Relations Service_____ A. C. TRUE, Director.
Federal Horticultural Board_____ C. L. MARLATT, Chairman.
Insecticide and Fungicide Board_____ J. K. HAYWOOD, Chairman.
Packers and Stockyards Administration_____⎤CHESTER MORRILL, Assistant
Grain Future Trading Act Administration_____⎦ to the Secretary.
Office of the Solicitor_____ R. W. WILLIAMS, Solicitor.

This bulletin is a contribution from the—

Bureau of Plant Industry_____ WILLIAM A. TAYLOR, Chief.
Office of Dry-Land Agriculture Investigations_ E. C. CHILCOTT, Agriculturist in Charge.

28

UNITED STATES DEPARTMENT OF AGRICULTURE

DEPARTMENT BULLETIN No. 1140

| Washington, D. C. | PROFESSIONAL PAPER | March 29, 1923 |

THE DETERIORATION OF FELLED WESTERN YELLOW PINE ON INSECT-CONTROL PROJECTS.[1]

By J. S. Boyce, *Pathologist, Office of Investigations in Forest Pathology, Bureau of Plant Industry.*

CONTENTS.

INTRODUCTION.

During the past 15 years extensive insect-control measures have become necessary in various localities in the western United States in order to check epidemics of the western pine beetle (*Dendroctonus brevicomis* Lec.) and the mountain-pine beetle (*Dendroctonus monticolae* Hopk.) on western yellow pine (*Pinus ponderosa* Laws.), lodgepole pine (*Pinus contorta* Loud.), western white pine (*Pinus monticola* Dougl.), and sugar pine (*Pinus lambertiana* Dougl.). Briefly, control consists in felling and barking the infested trees (or burning the bark in the case of *Dendroctonus brevicomis*), in order to destroy the overwintering stages of the beetles. The trees usually are limbed well into the top but are not cut into log lengths.

The attacks of the western pine beetle on western yellow pine have been widespread, and consequently the most extensive control projects have been concentrated on this tree species. At present control work is under way in the yellow-pine regions of British Columbia and central California, while a large project was begun in the spring of 1922 in the Klamath Lake region of southern Oregon.

The southern Oregon–northern California project begun in the spring of 1922 necessitated the felling of about 16,000 merchantable western yellow pines, with an occasional sugar pine, comprising ap-

---

[1] This study was made in cooperation with the Klamath Forest Protective Association at Klamath Falls, Oreg. Without the yearly records of the association giving the location of felled trees, the study would have been impossible. The writer is indebted to J. F. Kimball, secretary-treasurer, and to H. H. Ogle, of the same association, for valuable assistance in obtaining the field data.

proximately 16,000,000 feet board measure, over an area roughly of 200,000 acres. Further work in the next three or four years will probably involve cutting an additional 20,000,000 feet of merchantable timber on adjoining areas. These trees must be left on the ground until such time as they can be reached by logging operations. The rate of deterioration of this felled timber then becomes of paramount importance. It is in connection with this project that the study reported here was made.

METHOD OF COLLECTING DATA.

Local control work has been carried on in this region for some years by the Klamath Forest Protective Association, and records of this association were available, giving the general location of trees felled yearly since 1915. From these records, felled trees were relocated and examined during November, 1921.

Each tree was opened up sufficiently with ax and saw to permit scaling in 16-foot logs with the Scribner decimal C scale, according to standard commercial practice. Logs two-thirds or more unmerchantable by volume were culled. Diameter measurements were taken to the nearest inch, and length measurements to the nearest tenth of a foot. The gross scale where given is the actual merchantable volume in the trees at the time of felling, determined when this study was made. In making the measurements of decay, the subsequent advance of decay present in the living tree at the time of felling was disregarded. In the region in which the trees were studied the decays in living yellow pine seem to advance very slowly or not at all after an infected tree is felled. Characteristically, western yellow pine is a sound species, and the normal loss through decay in stands of living trees does not exceed 2.5 per cent and may be much less. The only two kinds of decay found in the trees examined which were there at the time of felling were rots caused by the ring-scale fungus (*Trametes pini* (Thore) Fr.) and brown cubical butt-rot caused by the velvet-top fungus (*Polyporus schweinitzii* Fr.). Two trees had been infected with the first-named rot, with a slight loss resulting. Brown cubical butt-rot had also been present in two trees, but there was little indication left of the decayed wood, which had been almost completely destroyed by fire when the bark removed from the trees was burned.

Data were obtained on a total of 100 trees, all western yellow pine, near Bly, Klamath Falls, and Keno, in Klamath County, Oreg., at elevations around 6,000 feet above sea level. The site conditions were essentially the same for all the localities. These trees varied from 16 inches to 43 inches in diameter outside bark at stump height, and the usual stump height ranged from 2½ to 3 feet.

RATE OF DETERIORATION.

These felled trees deteriorate with extreme rapidity, far more rapidly than the casual observer is led to believe. The heat from burning the bark and from the sun's rays results in a pronounced drying of the outer sapwood to depths averaging one-half inch. This outer layer, being too dry to decay, remains hard and sound for several years, and if tested superficially leads to the belief that the tree is sound throughout, when as a matter of fact it may be commercially a complete loss through decay. Table 1 shows the rate of deterioration.

TABLE 1.—*Rate of deterioration of felled western yellow-pine trees in Klamath County, Oreg.*

When cut.	Seasons of exposure.	Volume (board feet).			Percentage of cull.	Trees with merchantable volume.		Average diameter inside bark stump (inches).	Number of trees (basis).
		Gross.	Cull.	Net.		Number.	Percentage of total.		
1	2	3	4	5	6	7	8	9	10
April, 1921............	1	6,400	810	5,590	13	6	100	24	6
December, 1920......	1	11,350	2,060	9,290	18	12	100	23	12
February, 1920.......	2	11,610	7,360	4,250	63	11	79	23	14
November, 1919......	2	8,080	6,120	1,960	76	6	75	21	8
Spring of 1919........	3	15,870	12,900	2,970	81	10	62	24	16
Spring of 1918........	4	2,650	1,790	860	68	3	100	23	3
April, 1917............	5	35,510	28,960	6,550	82	7	44	31	16
Spring of 1916........	6	13,270	12,060	1,210	91	2	14	23	14
Spring of 1915........	7	11,470	10,710	760	93	1	9	25	11

In Table 1 the expression "seasons of exposure" means the number of growing seasons that have elapsed since the trees were felled. It is, of course, during the growing season that the greatest deterioration occurs, although loss continues throughout the year. This is shown by the fact that the trees cut in April, 1921, and exposed for one season show a loss of 13 per cent, while those cut in December, 1920, also exposed for one season but with four additional months in winter and early spring, show a loss of 18 per cent. The same relation holds for the trees exposed for two seasons but cut at different times.

The important feature of Table 1 is the enormous increase in the cull percentage after the first season. This increase is from 13 and 18 per cent for the first season to 63 and 76 per cent for the second season and is so great that from an economic standpoint felled trees must be utilized before they pass into the second season of exposure. This means that the bulk of the trees cut on a control project must be regarded as a loss, since it is at present commercially impossible so to adjust logging operations that trees scattered over a large area can be picked up in a single season.

After the second season deterioration increases steadily, until by the end of the seventh season there is little merchantable volume to be obtained, and this only in an occasional tree much larger than the average or with some other abnormal condition. For example, the merchantable volume in the trees cut in 1916 came from two trees only, as is shown in column 7 of Table 1. One of these was a large tree with a diameter inside bark at stump height of 37 inches, while the other, though 11 inches smaller in the same dimension, had an unusually resinous butt log. The 760 feet board measure in the 1915 trees came from the first three logs in a 43-inch tree.

The criticism may be made that Table 1 is based on insufficient data. An examination of the table will show that the trees are well distributed by seasons of exposure except in the case of those cut in 1918, of which there are only three, all that could be obtained. The basis for this class is insufficient. The cull percentage shows a steady increase and the percentage of total trees with merchantable volume a steady decrease except in the 1918 trees. This points to a sufficient basis for the other classes. Then, too, during the course of the field work the similarity in condition between trees exposed for the same number of seasons was quite apparent.

Figure 1, which is a diagrammatic smoothed curve based on Table 1, illustrates the rate of deterioration of the down timber.

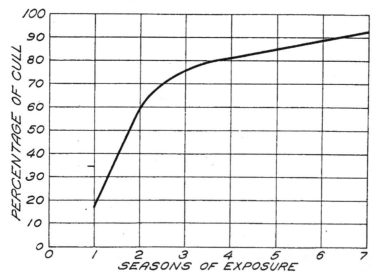

FIG. 1.—Diagrammatic smoothed curve, illustrating the rate of deterioration of felled western yellow pine.

CAUSES OF DETERIORATION.

In Table 1 sap-stain is not considered a defect. While this discoloration does degrade the lumber, discolored wood can still be used for a variety of purposes. In this region blue-stain caused by the fungus *Ceratostomella* sp. is most common, while a brown stain, of which the causal fungus is probably *Alternaria* sp.[2] is sometimes found. Staining is practically confined to the sapwood, rarely penetrating the heartwood. The extent of the stain in a tree is easily misjudged. As previously pointed out, there is a very dry outside layer of sapwood, too dry to stain, and a hasty examination may show bright wood, but deeper chopping will reveal the stain. By the end of the first season all the sapwood with the exception of the outer layer was heavily stained in the trees examined. In the upper portions of the trees, where the bark had been left on, this outer layer, since it had been kept moist, was also stained. The discoloration

[2] Hubert, Ernest E. Some wood stains and their causes. *In* Hardwood Rec., v. 52, no. 11, p. 17–19, illus. 1922.

first began along the checks and then spread over the entire sapwood. If stained sapwood is considered a defect the loss for Table 1 after one season of exposure would amount to 78 per cent in the trees cut in April, 1921, and 67 per cent in the trees felled in December, 1920. This difference may be mere chance or it may indicate that the winter-felled trees for some unknown reason were less susceptible to discoloration by the time that climatic conditions in spring or summer favorable for staining arrived. Observations made on windthrown yellow pine in this region showed that heavy staining began in July. To avoid sap-stain as much as possible trees should be logged before that time.

That the principal causes of deterioration were relatively few and well defined is shown in Table 2.

The most important cause of cull in the trees exposed for one season was checks. Checks were confined mostly to the sapwood but in some cases extended deep into the heartwood.

TABLE 2.—*Causes of deterioration of felled yellow-pine trees in Klamath County, Oreg.*

When cut.	Seasons of exposure.	Cull (percentage of gross volume.)					
		Checks.	Sap-rot.	Heart-rot.	Broken in felling.	Burned.	Borers.
1	2	3	4	5	6	7	8
April, 1921................	1	13.7	....	....	....	0.3	....
December, 1920............	1	16.2	1.5	....	0.2	0.3	....
February, 1920............	2	16.9	24.6	....	....	21.9	....
November, 1919............	2	11.5	57.3	....	3.7	3.2	....
Spring of 1919.............	3	....	59.4	9.6	1.2	11.1	....
Spring of 1918.............	4	....	63.4	4.2	....	....	1.9
April, 1917...............	5	1.4	53.2	15.0	.5	9.6	....
Spring of 1916.............	6	3.9	63.7	14.1	.8	8.3	....
Spring of 1915.............	7	.3	57.0	30.3	....	5.8	....

Checking usually began and was most severe on the side of the trunk exposed to the direct rays of the sun. Exceptions to this rule were found where particularly intense heat had caused severe checking when the bark was burned. Normally the loss through checking in any one tree resulted from several or numerous checks, but in a very spiral grained tree a single deep check twisting around the tree sometimes caused all the loss. Considering column 3 of Table 2 it would seem that the loss through checking decreases with the length of exposure after the second season, while it is self-evident that this loss should increase slightly or remain about the same. The explanation is that as sap-rot becomes more severe the checks become obscure or disappear completely, and in scaling the loss from this source is then difficult to separate from that caused by sap-rot.

There was little sap-rot during the first season. In fact, the entire 170 board feet given in Table 2 were obtained from a single tree. But by the end of the second season the loss from this cause was heavy and continued so. After that time sap-rot was the most important factor in deterioration. In poles and young thrifty standards with wide sapwood, sap-rot by amounting to two-thirds or more of the gross volume often caused the loss of the entire tree. It followed then that poles and young thrifty standards were subject to much more rapid deterioration than large trees, in which the ratio of sapwood to heartwood is inverted.

The upper side of the trunk decayed most rapidly, and the under side, the portion resting on the ground, much more slowly. This is probably explained by the retarding effect on the development of wood-destroying fungi from the excessive moisture content, lessened oxygen supply, and lower temperature of the wood of the under side as compared with the upper side. Decay first appeared along the checks, but avoided the dried outer layer of sapwood. Tongues of decay extended down from the ends of the checks. The decay then spread from the checks, finally involving the entire sapwood with the exception of the outer layer. Where the bark was left on in the top, the outer layer also decayed. Barking the tree somewhat retards decay, but not enough to be of practical importance, while on the other hand it promotes checking.

Generally it was impossible to determine the exact kind of decay in the different trees, but where this was done it was found that a white cellulose pocket rot [3] caused by *Polyporus anceps* Pk. was most common, while a brown friable rot caused by the brown Lenzites (*Lenzites sepiaria* (Wulf.) Fr.) and a yellow-brown friable rot caused by *Fomes pinicola* (Fr.) Cke. occasionally occurred.

Heart-rot was not found in the trees until the third season of exposure. Decay first appeared as tongues running in from the sapwood or following in along deep checks. The white cellulose pocket rot was most common.

A negligible amount of loss resulted from breaks, usually in the top, when the trees were felled.

A more important source of cull was fire at the time the trees were felled and bucked. This sometimes did considerable damage. When the bark was burned, trees with open wounds were very likely to burn out along the scar and for some distance in advance. Fire scars, particularly in pitchy butts, were common starting points for destructive burns. Felling trees across one another or leaving limbs resting on the trunk resulted in additional loss from fire.

The loss caused by wood-boring insects was negligible. Ambrosia beetles did not attack the trunk from which the bark had been removed, while the round-headed and flat-headed borers did not attack the trees until sap-rot was well started.

From the foregoing discussion of Table 2 it is apparent that while checks caused some loss (and in a lesser degree so did fire), decay, particularly the very rapid decay of the sapwood, is responsible for most of the deterioration in these trees.

CONCLUSIONS.

The facts brought out in this bulletin should not be considered as of value for local application only. The climatic conditions of the Klamath Lake region, characterized by a small yearly precipitation, with a long summer drought, often beginning in the late spring and extending well into the fall, and low winter temperatures, are

---

[3] This decay has also been called western red-rot. According to Dr. J. R. Weir, *Polyporus ellisianus* Murr. as known in the West is the same as *P. anceps* Pk.

exactly similar to those of a great part of the yellow-pine belt of eastern California, Oregon, and Washington, and not markedly at variance with conditions in other western yellow-pine regions in North America.

These results should prove generally applicable, with minor variations, on control projects in western yellow pine. Timber averaging smaller than that studied here will deteriorate more rapidly, while the deterioration in larger timber will, of course, be slower.

The felled and barked trees were completely sap-stained by the end of the first season of exposure. If sap-stain is considered a defect serious enough to make discolored wood worthless for lumber, there is such a large loss the first season that utilization by midsummer is imperative. However, as a rule, stained lumber is only degraded and not culled.

Deterioration is very rapid and is chiefly caused by decay, particularly the very rapid decay of the sapwood, followed more slowly by the breaking down of the heartwood. The resulting loss is so high by the end of the second season that felled trees must be utilized by the beginning of the second season, or else the volume of merchantable wood obtained is so small as to be of little commercial importance. Consequently, the timber in most of the trees cut on a control project becomes a complete loss, since under present economic conditions it is usually not possible to utilize scattered trees over a large area within such a limited period of time.

ORGANIZATION OF THE UNITED STATES DEPARTMENT OF AGRICULTURE.

Secretary of Agriculture _____ HENRY C. WALLACE.
Assistant Secretary _____ C. W. PUGSLEY.
Director of Scientific Work _____ E. D. BALL.
Director of Regulatory Work _____
Weather Bureau _____ CHARLES F. MARVIN, Chief.
Bureau of Agricultural Economics _____ HENRY C. TAYLOR, Chief.
Bureau of Animal Industry _____ JOHN R. MOHLER, Chief.
Bureau of Plant Industry _____ WILLIAM A. TAYLOR, Chief.
Forest Service _____ W. B. GREELEY, Chief.
Bureau of Chemistry _____ WALTER G. CAMPBELL, Acting Chief.
Bureau of Soils _____ MILTON WHITNEY, Chief.
Bureau of Entomology _____ L. O. HOWARD, Chief.
Bureau of Biological Survey _____ E. W. NELSON, Chief.
Bureau of Public Roads _____ THOMAS H. MACDONALD, Chief.
Fixed Nitrogen Research Laboratory _____ F. G. COTTRELL, Director.
Division of Accounts and Disbursements _____ A. ZAPPONE, Chief.
Division of Publications _____ JOHN L. COBBS, Jr., Chief.
Library _____ CLARIBEL R. BARNETT, Librarian.
States Relations Service _____ A. C. TRUE, Director.
Federal Horticultural Board _____ C. L. MARLATT, Chairman.
Insecticide and Fungicide Board _____ J. K. HAYWOOD, Chairman.
Packers and Stockyards Administration _____ ⎱CHESTER MORRILL, Assistant to
Grain Future Trading Act Administration _____ ⎰ the Secretary.
Office of the Solicitor _____ R. W. WILLIAMS, Solicitor.

This bulletin is a contribution from the—

Bureau of Plant Industry _____ WM. A. TAYLOR, Chief.
   Investigations in Forest Pathology _____ HAVEN METCALF, Pathologist in Charge.

8

UNITED STATES DEPARTMENT OF AGRICULTURE

DEPARTMENT BULLETIN No. 1141

Washington, D. C. ▼ May, 1923

EVAPORATION OF FRUITS.[1]

By JOSEPH S. CALDWELL, *Plant Physiologist, Office of Horticultural and Pomological Investigations, Bureau of Plant Industry.*

CONTENTS.

EXTENT AND CHARACTER OF THE FRUIT-DRYING INDUSTRY.

THE TERMS " dried fruit " and " evaporated fruit " are popularly used to designate all fruits preserved by reduction of their moisture content to such a point that spoilage does not occur. In the trade the term " dried fruit " is applied to any product in which moisture reduction has been brought about by exposure of the fresh material to the heat of the sun, while products made by driving off the surplus moisture by the use of artificial heat are known as " evaporated " fruits; less frequently as dehydrated or desiccated fruits. While the processes of sun drying and drying with artificial heat in evaporating devices are widely different, the differences in the

---

[1] This bulletin is of interest to fruit growers who have such quantities of surplus fruit as to require the employment of large-scale factory methods for its utilization. It is intended to serve as a rather complete nontechnical handbook of information in regard to methods of evaporating fruits which are applicable to farm conditions.

This bulletin supersedes Farmers' Bulletin 903, " Commercial Evaporation and Drying of Fruits,' by James H. Beattie and H. P. Gould. Much of the material in that publication is reproduced, with revision, in this bulletin. New sections dealing in considerable detail with the construction of the driers, the arrangement of the equipment, the practical details of handling the various fruits, and the choice of fruits to be used for evaporating purposes have been added.

quality of the products obtained are relatively slight, it is possible to apply both processes to any of the fruits ordinarily dried, and the extent to which one or the other method is employed in preserving any given fruit is determined by the climatic conditions prevailing during the period in which the drying must be done. By reason of the possession of an exceedingly favorable combination of dry atmosphere, continuous sunshine, and practical absence of rain or dew during the drying season, California has developed sun drying on a large scale and is the only State which has done so.

The fruits which are dried in commercial quantities in the United States are prunes, raisins, apricots, apples, peaches, pears, blackberries, Logan blackberries, and raspberries, with very small quantities of figs and cherries. Among these, prunes rank first in point of average annual production, which approximates 400,000,000 pounds. Of this total, sun-dried prunes, made only in California, make up almost or quite 50 per cent; the remainder are evaporated prunes produced by the States of Oregon, Washington, and Idaho, which rank in the order given in the quantities produced. Commercial drying of peaches, apricots, pears, and figs is practically wholly confined to California, and the method employed is exclusively sun drying, the average annual production approximating 62,000,000 pounds of peaches, 30,000,000 pounds of apricots, 19,000,000 pounds of figs, and 6,900,000 pounds of pears for the five-year period from 1915 to 1919, inclusive. Raisin making is likewise an industry peculiar to California, and the use of other methods than sun drying has been practically unknown up to a very recent period. The annual production of raisins in California has increased from 125,000,000 pounds in 1910 to 395,000,000 pounds in 1919, with an average production for the 10 years, 1910 to 1919, inclusive, of 225,400,000 pounds. Practically all the dry berries coming into the market are machine evaporated, raspberries being produced in New York and Oregon, while evaporated Logan blackberries were formerly produced in considerable quantities in Oregon. The increasing popularity of the Logan blackberry for canning and juice-making purposes has operated alike to extend commercial plantings and to reduce the quantities dried.

By reason of the late maturity of the varieties used for the purpose, the commercial production of dried apples is carried on exclusively in evaporators. Trustworthy figures as to annual production since the year 1909, in which the total was 44,568,000 pounds, are not available, but the average probably does not greatly exceed 50,000,000 pounds. This total is made up of contributions from a much wider area than is the case with any other fruit. Approximately 70 per cent of the total production comes from western New York. California has recently considerably increased her production, which has risen from an average of 6,800,000 pounds for the years 1910 to 1916 to a maximum of 25,000,000 pounds for 1919. By far the greater part of this total originates in the Pajaro district of Sonoma and Santa Cruz Counties. Oregon ranks next in point of production. Washington has only recently become a producer, but is at the present time very rapidly increasing her annual output, as is likewise the case in lesser degree with Idaho. Missouri, Arkansas, Pennsylvania, Illinois, North Carolina, Virginia, and West Virginia also produce variable quantities of evaporated apples, their average combined production being somewhat less than that of California. In so far as available figures enable a conclusion to be reached, it would appear that the evaporated-apple industry is growing in importance in the States of the Pacific Northwest, less rapidly in Arkansas and the Virginias, little if at all in New York, and is decreasing in quantity of output in the other producing States.

As a commercial practice sun drying no longer exists outside of California, but has there attained the rank of a primary industry, practically all the fruit used for the purpose being grown specifically for drying and without intention to offer it for sale in the fresh condition. As a consequence, varieties specially suited to drying purposes have been developed or selected and are planted to the exclusion of others. While a portion of the prune crop of the Pacific Northwest is sold fresh or evaporated according as market conditions may determine, by far the greater portion is grown specifically for drying, individual growers or groups of growers constructing such drying equipment as their acreage may require. With this exception evaporation is at the present time distinctly an industry developed by fruit growers as an adjunct to their chief business of producing fruit for market, and its relation to that business is that of a stabilizer or safety valve. In direct proportion as it has been developed in any given territory it serves to increase orchard returns by converting low-grade and unmarketable portions of the crop into salable products and to maintain fresh-fruit prices by absorbing a portion of the marketable grades in years of overproduction. As a consequence of this safety-valve relation to the fresh-fruit industry, the material coming into the evaporators has not been grown with reference to its special fitness for drying purposes, but varies widely from year to year in character and quality as well as in total volume. For these reasons the drying industry, unlike that of canning, in only a few exceptional cases has been engaged in by large commercial concerns making it their sole business and having definite acreages of material of specified varieties grown under contract for the purpose. The product of such plants constitutes only a very small percentage of the total output. The drying of fruits as practiced at the present time is therefore peculiarly a farm industry, carried on by fruit growers themselves as a part of the routine of harvesting and disposing of the crop. The plants in which the work is done are mainly small, their size being most frequently determined by the size of the owner's orchard, and there is great diversity in the drying apparatus, the accessory equipment, and the details of the drying methods employed, with a consequent absence of definite standardization of the product. This would be expected in view of the fact that 252,289 farms reported the production of dried fuits in the census of 1919.

It is the purpose of this bulletin to describe in detail the types of artificially heated evaporators found by the test of actual use to be best suited to specific purposes, to describe model installations of labor-saving machinery, and to give somewhat full discussion of improved methods of handling the various fruits in preparation for drying as well as during the drying process. The drying installations described are of the most modern character, but are of such moderate size and cost as to be suited to the means and needs of the largest possible number of fruit growers. They are purposely so planned as to be capable of enlargement or alteration to meet the needs of a particular case.

PRINCIPLES INVOLVED IN DRYING FRUITS.

The purpose in view in drying any food material is to reduce its moisture content to such a point that the growth of organisms therein will no longer be possible, and to do this with a minimum of alteration in the food value, appearance, and palatability of the product. The necessity for avoiding changes in physical appearance and chemical composition, other than actual loss of water, puts very definite limitations upon the means which may be employed to bring about drying and makes an understanding of certain principles a prerequisite to successful work.

It is obviously of advantage that drying be brought about as rapidly as possible, since rapid drying minimizes opportunity for the growth of organisms and for the spontaneous chemical changes which set in as soon as the interior of the fruit is exposed to the air and since a short drying period increases the working capacity of the drying apparatus. There are three possible ways in which drying may be accelerated, namely, by passing currents of air over the material, thus giving a large volume of air for absorbing and carrying away moisture, by raising the temperature and consequently the moisture-absorbing capacity of the air, and by employing air which has previously had all moisture removed from it by passing through an air-drying apparatus. A theoretically perfect method of drying would, of course, combine all three means of hastening the process, and while such methods are in use in certain industries, they are impracticable for drying fruit because of their high cost.

Consequently, practical drying methods rely upon the use of heated air, with some means of maintaining the air in circulation over and through the product.

The moisture-carrying capacity of the air is a function of its temperature, and is practically doubled by every increase of 27 degrees in temperature. Consequently, the application of a relatively moderate degree of heat brings about a very great increase in its capacity to absorb moisture. This is evident from a consideration of the fact that raising the temperature of a quantity of air 108 degrees, from 60° to 168° F., for example, results in a sixteenfold increase in its moisture-carrying capacity. The temperature employed is consequently the most significant factor in determining the drying rate, and it is advisable to employ the highest temperature which can be used without injury to the material. But the use of extreme temperatures in drying fruits is impossible for three reasons. The various fruits contain 65 to 88 per cent of water when prepared for drying. If such water-filled material were suddenly exposed to dry air having a temperature approaching that of boiling water, the rapid expansion of the fluids of the tissues would burst the cell membranes, thus permitting the loss of many of the soluble constituents of the fruit by dripping. Some decomposition of the sugars of the fruit would also occur at such temperatures, and the caramel formed would injure both the flavor and the appearance of the dry product. Furthermore, the very rapid drying of a thin layer at the surface of the material would occur, and this dry layer would retard the movement of water outward to the surface from the interior of the material, thus slowing down the drying process. The maximum temperature which can be employed without producing these injurious effects varies considerably with the different fruits, since it depends in every case upon the physical structure and chemical composition of the particular fruit, but it is in all cases very considerably below the boiling point of water.

There must also be a careful adjustment between the amount of heat applied and the volume of air passing through the apparatus. The heat required to convert the water evaporated from the liquid condition to vapor is very considerable; the evaporation of 1 pound of water absorbs a quantity of heat which would reduce the temperature of 65,000 cubic feet of air by 1° F., or 1,000 cubic feet by 65° F. It would seem at first glance that the greatest efficiency in a drying apparatus would be effected by allowing the heated air to expend most of its heat in vaporizing water and to permit it to become saturated before allowing it to escape from the drier. This is not the case, for several reasons. Air at any given temperature takes up water vapor quite rapidly until it has absorbed about half the quantity it is capable of carrying at that temperature, after which absorption goes on at a rapidly diminishing rate. At the same time the air is losing heat through the vaporization of water, every reduction of 27° F. resulting in the loss of half its moisture-carrying capacity, this loss also operating to reduce the rate of absorption of moisture. Consequently, it is not practicable to secure saturation of the air before allowing it to escape, as this would make the drying exceedingly slow. The best practice aims at permitting the air to vaporize and absorb such an amount of moisture as will reduce its temperature by not more than 25° to 35° F. during its passage through the apparatus, thus effecting rapid drying at the expense of the loss of about half of the theoretical drying efficiency of the heat used. As a matter of fact this heat is not wholly lost, since the expansion and resulting buoyancy of the warm air maintains a current through the apparatus, if provision for its escape at the highest part of the drier is made. Without such provision, the air can not escape and will quickly become saturated, with the result that the escape of water vapor from the material is stopped and the fruit is cooked in its own juices. In most evaporators in common use the construction is of such a type that the air is admitted at the lowest portion of the apparatus and is allowed to escape at the highest point, the arrangement of material in the interior being such as to offer a minimum of obstruction to its flow upward. In other types, the air movement is made independent of gravity by placing fans in the air inlets or outlets or in both. Some driers of this type have the defect that the air movement is so rapid that the air can take up only a portion of the moisture it is capable of carrying, thus giving a low return for the fuel employed. Other driers obtain greater efficiency from the heat used by the employment of devices for the recirculation of the air, which is forced to pass repeatedly over the material before being discharged from the apparatus. As contrasted with driers in which the circulation is wholly dependent upon the buoyancy of the warm air, driers of this type gain somewhat in capacity as a result of the shorter time required for drying a given quantity of material, but are more expensive to construct and operate, are dependent for successful operation upon a source of power for driving the fans, and require a higher class of labor because of their more complicated character. In practice their efficiency is often lowered by reason of the fact that the rate of air movement is excessive, causing rapid drying of the surface of the material and thus retarding the escape of moisture from the interior of the product.

Whatever the type of drier employed may be, it is essential to success that drying be continuous and that the temperature be maintained fairly uniform throughout the process. The flesh of the various fruits is an excellent medium for the growth of a great variety of microorganisms, including both bacteria and fungi. As soon as the material is opened up to the air it becomes subject to attack by these organisms, which are present in great numbers in the form of spores upon the skins of fruit and in the dust of the workroom, with the result that considerable numbers become scattered over the surfaces of the prepared fruits. As long as the temperature of the material is maintained fairly high and the escape of moisture from the surface goes on uninterruptedly, the conditions are unfavorable for the growth and multiplication of these organisms, but if the temperature is permitted to drop and moisture accumulates upon the surface of the material, the spores germinate, the organisms multiply rapidly, and fermentation or souring of the material begins. For this reason material should never be prepared and allowed to stand before being placed in the drier, and the drying should be completed without interruption.

Other conditions prerequisite to success in drying have to do with the selection and preparatory treatment of the material to be dried, and these determine the quality of the product to an even greater degree than does the type and manner of operation of the drier. Drying will not make an inferior article better, nor does it ever produce products indistinguishable from fresh. When conducted with the greatest care and the employment of the best methods known, dried products undergo perceptible modifications which do not affect their food value, but, nevertheless, make it easy to distinguish them. In order that these alterations, which affect texture and flavor in some degree, may be at a minimum, the materials used should be in prime condition, fully ripe, free from decay, and should be handled throughout their preparation with scrupulous regard for cleanliness. With most of the fruits usually dried, chemical changes which modify the color and appearance of the fruit set in as soon as the flesh is exposed by peeling and slicing. The application of such a degree of heat as can be used without injury to the material does not arrest these changes, but, on the contrary, it causes them to go on at a much more rapid rate than would be the case at ordinary air temperature until most of the water of the fruit has been driven off. This is particularly true of the oxidation of pigments and the changes in tannin occurring in such fruits as the apple, pear, apricot, and peach, which are responsible for the appearance of brownish discoloration of the flesh of these fruits when peeled. While such discoloration does not injuriously affect the palatability or the food value of the fruits in which it occurs, the purchasing public has learned to discriminate against such fruit, and the existing grades for commercial dried fruits consider color as being as important as any other single character in determining the market value. Consequently, the maker who desires to command for his product a ready market at top prices must employ suitable means for preserving the color of his fruit. These methods are considered in connection with the preparatory treatment recommended for the various fruits.

Success in drying, therefore, depends upon the employment of sound, ripe fruit of unimpaired table quality, the use of suitable means for preventing oxidation and other chemical changes in the material during the drying process, the employment of a drying temperature so regulated that the material may not be injured by excessive heating and so maintained that opportunity for fermentation and spoilage is avoided, and the provision of an adequate circulation of air to carry away the escaping moisture. Failure to give proper attention to any one of these factors will result in the production of an inferior grade of product or in the total loss of the material used.

COMMUNITY DRYING PLANTS.

In many communities in which the growing of fruit is not a primary industry, the aggregate quantity of unmarketable fruit may be such as to make advisable the construction of a community drying plant to which every grower in the vicinity may bring his surplus to be worked up. A number of considerations, which should be kept clearly in mind when the project of a community or cooperative evaporator is under discussion, may be briefly mentioned.

It must first be definitely ascertained whether the quantity of unused fruit is actually such as will justify the necessary expenditure. This information can only be obtained by a careful canvass of the district and a tabulation of the results. The making of such a canvass is a task calling for conservatism and the exercise of good judgment, for the reason that unintentional but gross overstatement of the unmarketed and unused portion of the fruit crop which could be used as evaporator stock is the rule rather than the exception. It must be borne in mind that in the case of apples, only mature, reasonably sound fruit of fair size will make a marketable dry product and that estimates which include premature drops, specked and decayed fruit, and small-sized cider apples are worse than useless because misleading. The canvass should take into account all fruits grown in the district, and should secure such detailed information as will give a clear idea not only of the total quantities of the various fruits grown, but also of the sequence in which they must be handled at the drier, the length of time over which the ripening of each will extend, the maximum quantity per day which the plant will be required to accommodate, and the extent of plantings not yet in bearing which will contribute to the stock of raw material when fruiting begins, if such plantings exist. The distribution of the material over the district should also be studied, in order that the drier may be located with reference to the sources of heaviest supply.

With this data in hand it is possible to determine the size and type of evaporator needed to care for the materials to be dried. As these will in most cases be rather varied, the evaporator must be of a general-purpose type; that is, its construction must be such that materials such as apples, peaches, plums and prunes, berries, sweet corn, and beans may be dried with equal satisfaction. Such a general-purpose evaporator must necessarily be one of the types employing trays. While a very considerable number of patented evaporators are to be found on the markets, the cash investment necessary to secure such machines is such as to be prohibitive in the case of many communities in which fruit growing is not a primary business. Consequently, there is very great need for simple, inexpensive drying equipment which can be constructed by an ordinary workman at the place where needed and will give satisfactory results when operated by intelligent amateurs. Of such driers as meet this requirement, the tunnel evaporator, described in a subsequent section, is in many respects the most satisfactory. For this reason, the construction of an evaporator of this type, and the nature and amount of equipment which will be required for handling the various fruits, are discussed with special fullness in the section on " The prune tunnel evaporator," page 24.

BUILDINGS AND EQUIPMENT FOR DRYING.

The evaporator buildings and accessory equipment described in the following pages are of two types. The kiln evaporator is designed specially for the handling of apples in large quantities, and is more widely used for that purpose than all others combined, but it is not well adapted to the drying of other fruits. For this reason, the building of a kiln evaporator in a district which is devoted to general fruit growing would be ill advised. The prune tunnel evaporator, on the other hand, is a general-purpose evaporator which may be employed for drying other materials as well as apples and is consequently better fitted to the needs of a farm or community which may have occasion to dry peaches, prunes, berries, or other fruits. For this and a number of other reasons, which will be pointed out in a subsequent section, a tunnel or modified tunnel drier should be built wherever a community drying plant is needed.

THE KILN EVAPORATOR.

The driers used in the farm apple-drying industry of the United States are at the present time almost exclusively of the kiln type. This type of drier first came into use for the drying of fruits in the eastern portion of the United States about 30 years ago, having been derived with some modification from a type of drier long in use in the British Empire and subsequently in the United States for the drying of hops. Its use was at first confined to the drying of raspberries, the drying of apples being at that time conducted in cabinet evaporators. This type was rather rapidly displaced by the kiln drier in that portion of western New York which produces the larger part of the commercial output, and from that territory its use has gradually extended until it is now almost exclusively employed in all districts in which evaporated apples are commercially produced, with the exception of the Pacific Coast States. In Washington, Oregon, and Idaho driers primarily intended for use with prunes are used to some extent in drying apples, although kilns are employed where apples are the chief fruit to be dried. In California, local conditions, such as an ample supply of Asiatic labor, have resulted in the retention of driers of the cabinet, or stack, type even when apples are the only fruit dried. The widespread and increasing use of the kiln drier has been brought about by the low first cost of the kilns, the relatively large capacity, the large extent to which labor-saving machinery may be made to replace handwork, and to a certain degree because their construction and operation are well understood by fruit growers and by the labor available in the apple-growing districts.

A kiln evaporator plant consists of a two-story building divided into two portions, one of which contains workrooms in which the fruit is received and prepared for drying, with storage rooms for fresh and dry fruit, the other containing the kilns or drying rooms. The individual kiln is the unit of structure, and plants of any desired capacity are obtained by constructing a series of such units.

THE INDIVIDUAL KILN.

The individual kiln consists of a structure two stories in height, the first, or ground, floor being occupied by a furnace inclosed in a concrete or masonry room for distributing the heat, as shown in Figure 1, and the second floor, which is of slat construction, serving as the drying floor. The walls extend above the drying floor far enough to give sufficient headroom for working in the kiln and support the roof, which is fitted with ventilators for removing the moisture-laden air as it rises from the material being dried.

The ground plan and cross section of a typical kiln are illustrated in Figure 1. It will be noted that the kiln is 20 by 20 feet, the standard dimensions of a kiln of this type. The distance from the furnace floor to the drying floor is usually 16 feet and should never be less than 14 feet, as uniform distribution of heat to the drying floor can not be obtained with a height less than this. In order to give sufficient headroom for the storage room or workroom on the second floor along the side of the kiln, the roof on one side is not as steep as on the other side. The roof is so constructed that the ridge is in the middle of the kiln, with the ventilators along the ridge.

Foundation.—The foundation walls for the kiln may consist of any suitable material, their depth being determined by the nature of the subsoil and the character of the building material to be used for the superstructure. Concrete is the best foundation material, as, when once properly set, it is impossible for water to get under it and cause damage by freezing. Whatever the material used, the foundation walls should be of sufficient size to support the building without settling, as even slight settling throws the machinery out of alignment and causes leaks in the heating apparatus and in the hopper. If the walls of the kiln are to be of frame construction, the foundation is usually 2½ feet above the surface of the ground, in order to make room for the air vents, to have the floors of the preparation room sufficiently high to prevent decay, and to give ample room for the circulation of air beneath it, as part of the air supply for the kiln must pass under this floor. When the walls of the kiln are of stone, brick, or masonry of any sort, the foundation is carried up only to the surface of the ground or far enough above to make it level, and the walls are started directly on this. The air ducts, described later, are placed in the walls below the level of the workroom floor. If the ground upon which the building stands is firm and dry the earth itself may form the floor of the furnace room. If the location or soil is such that trouble from seepage is to be expected, the furnace room should be floored with a layer of concrete resting upon broken stone.

Walls.—The walls of most of the dry kilns are constructed of wood. Concrete, concrete blocks, hollow tile, brick, or stone makes a more durable structure, but the first cost is considerably higher. Wood kilns demand frequent repairs, are short lived, and take a higher rate of insurance than kilns made of other material. The most economical material to use must be determined by local condi-

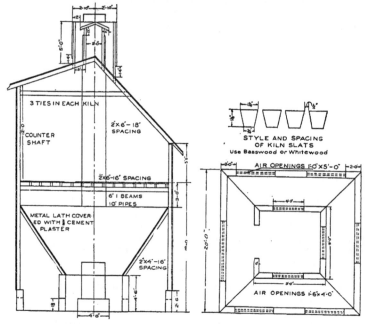

Fig. 1.—Cross section and ground plan of a kiln. When the kilns are built in rows the furnace rooms are not separated, but the furnaces have separate inclosures and hoppers for distributing the heat. The drying floors are separated by walls.

tions; if concrete is cheap in a particular locality, that may be the best material. The details of the construction of the kiln must be determined by the material used for the walls, but the interior dimensions remain the same irrespective of the kind of material selected. In the usual type of wood construction, the walls are made by setting 2 by 6 inch studding 16 inches apart, measured center to center. On the outside of the studding a layer of sheathing boards is placed diagonally. A layer of building paper is then applied, and the siding placed on the outside of this. When cement blocks are used, the wall, as a rule, is made 8 inches thick. The same dimension is used for hollow tile or brick. When stone is used, the walls must be 10 to 12 inches thick. Whatever the material used, the doors, windows, and other openings are the same size and the interior dimensions of the kiln are the same.

Roof and ventilators.—The roof is always of frame construction, consisting of 2 by 6 inch rafters spaced 24 inches apart and covered with sheathing and an asphaltum roofing paper. Metal roofing is not well adapted to kilns, as the sulphur fumes used in bleaching the apples soon corrode the metal. The method of constructing the roof is shown in Figure 1. The type of ventilator used on practically all modern kilns is shown in the same figure. The ventilators are always placed at the peak of the roof, so that the moisture-laden air will be quickly removed.. This type of ventilator has been found to be wind and rain proof. No matter which way the wind blows the kiln is sure to draw. The wind passes through the opening between the roof and the outside wall of the ventilator and causes suction, which tends to create a draft from the interior of the kiln. Rain on the

Fig. 2.—Drying plant at Victor, N. Y., equipped with modern ventilators.

roof of the ventilator falls between the outside and inside walls of the ventilator, strikes the main roof, and runs off. Figure 2 shows a drying plant equipped with ventilators of this type. Other styles of ventilators are used, but are not as efficient as the type just described.

Heating apparatus.—Cast-iron, hard-coal furnaces are universally used in apple kilns throughout the Eastern States. These furnaces have a grate of 5 to 8 square feet and are capable of supplying heat for a standard 20 by 20 foot kiln. Such furnaces are of very heavy construction, weighing 1,500 to 1,800 pounds, and consequently they maintain a fairly uniform temperature with only occasional attention from the fireman. The products of combustion pass through sheet-iron pipes arranged in rows under the floor and finally into the chimney. Three systems of piping are in use, all of which are illustrated in Figure 3. The difference in these systems consists in the extent

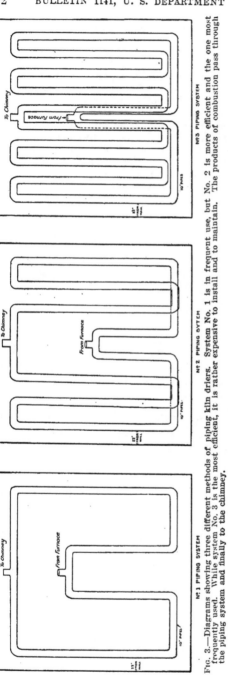

Fig. 3.—Diagrams showing three different methods of piping kiln driers. System No. 1 is in frequent use, but No. 2 is more efficient and the one most frequently used. While system No. 3 is the most efficient, it is rather expensive to install and to maintain. The products of combustion pass through the piping system and finally to the chimney.

and the distribution of the pipes under the drying floor. In all these systems a section of double-thickness Russia iron pipe, 10 inches in diameter and 4½ feet long, is placed on top of the furnace. This reaches a point about the same distance from the drying floor. The course of the hot gases in the different systems may be followed by referring to the illustration. The outside row of pipes is placed about 22 inches from the wall of the kiln. The whole piping system is given a gradual rise from the furnace to the flue and is held in place by wires or chains attached to the joists. Openings fitted with covers are provided at several points, in order that the piping may be cleaned out without taking it down. At the point where the pipe enters the flue the pipes are about 2 feet below the joists of the drying floor. Some furnaces are fitted with two openings for pipes, and with this type of furnace one opening is used for each side of the kiln and the pipes are joined with a tee just before entering the chimney. The second system illustrated is used to a greater extent than any of the others, for the reason that the third system, while giving greater radiating surface, is very difficult to keep free from soot. In the Pacific Coast States and in parts of the South the absence of supplies of hard coal makes the use of other fuel necessary. Wood is generally used. The furnaces employed are usually heavy stoves of the box type, fitted with special linings, although brick or stone furnaces lined with fire brick and covered with heavy sheet-iron tops are also successfully used. When wood is the fuel used, especial care must be taken to keep all joints of piping and furnace tight, as the volatile resins of the wood may otherwise impart a disagreeable flavor to the fruit. It is impracticable to use soft coal, on account of the soot and smoke.

Chimneys.—As it is the practice to build the kilns in rows, it is the usual custom to build a 2-flue chimney in the wall between two kilns to serve both furnaces. The chimneys have two 8 by 10 inch flues and must be carried above the highest part of the building, so there will be a good draft. Near-by trees which are higher than the building may cause much difficulty in securing a good draft, and this point should be borne in mind in determining the location of the plant.

Distributing hopper and air ducts.—Drying in these kilns depends on passing heated air through the material which is spread on the drying floor. It is necessary to have suitable openings, so that cold air can be admitted at the bottom of the kiln, be heated by being passed over the furnace and its piping, and, after passing through the material to be dried, discharged through the ventilators at the top of the building. The sizes and location of the ducts for the inlet of the air are shown in Figure 1. These ducts are $1\frac{1}{2}$ feet high by 5 feet long, and are four in number, two on each side of the kilns. When the kilns are built in rows, two air ducts are placed in each side wall and the partition walls between the furnace rooms of the individual kilns are omitted. This is brought out in Figure 4. To give more uniform results, the furnace is set in a square concrete or masonry inclosure. This is a comparatively recent improvement in kiln construction. It consists of a concrete inclosure 9 feet square and $4\frac{1}{2}$ feet high directly in the middle of the furnace room. This has three openings, each 18 inches by 4 feet, on three sides of the inclosure, and the fourth side has a portion 4 feet wide cut away to serve as a fire door. The upper portion of this opening is covered with a sheet-iron door. On top of this wall a hopperlike structure is built, the bottom corresponding to the top of the concrete inclosure and the top meeting the side walls of the kiln at a point 3 feet below the drying floor and 13 feet from the ground. The frame of this hopper is of 2 by 4 inch scantling, covered on the inside with metal laths and three-eighths of an inch of cement plaster. The sides of the hopper are made perfectly tight, so that no air can reach the drying floor without entering the bottom of the hopper through the air ducts. This prevents unequal drying on the sides of the kiln as a result of wind, and at the same time the hopper prevents loss of heat by radiation through the side walls. Many operators believe that properly constructed hoppers reduce the fuel consumption by at least 15 to 20 per cent. The details of construction are shown in Figure 1.

The drying floor.—The drying floor carries considerable weight and must be strong. The usual type of construction is to have two wood or steel beams set into the side walls of the kiln and spaced evenly. The joists are placed at right angles to these girders and are set back

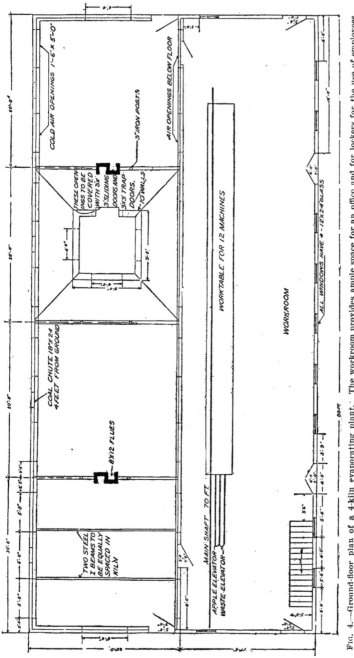

FIG. 4.—Ground-floor plan of a 4-kiln evaporating plant. The workroom provides ample space for an office and for lockers for the use of employees, as well as room for storing sufficient fruit for a day's run.

into the wall at either end. The salts that make the drying floor proper are of whitewood or basswood, 1½ inches thick, 1¼ inches wide on the upper side, and three-fourths of an inch on the side next the joist. In cross section they are keystone shaped. They are placed one-fourth of an inch apart with the narrow side down, in order that the openings between them may not be clogged with material lodging in them. The floor strips should run at right angles to the side of the kiln containing the door, so that it will be easy to handle the product with shovels. Basswood or whitewood is used for making kiln slats, for the reason that these woods do not warp or split under heat and are free from resins or other constituents which could give foreign odors or tastes to the product. After the floor is in place it is oiled three times at intervals of a week with lard oil, paraffin oil, or a mixture of equal parts tallow and boiled linseed oil, applied very hot, in order thoroughly to impregnate the slats. This prevents sticking of the fruit. After the kiln is in use, a few oilings each season will keep it in good condition, but it should be thoroughly scrubbed with strong hot soapsuds twice a week during the season.

THE KILN-DRYING PLANT.

Several individual kilns constitute a drying plant. As it is necessary to have enough drying capacity to keep the machinery and help employed, the number of kilns in a plant varies, but economic considerations would generally forbid the construction of a plant having less than four kilns, since installations of power-driven equipment in a smaller plant would be almost as expensive as in a four-kiln plant. A plant of this size is large enough to keep the operators busy, and plants larger than this increase the fire risk without adding much to the economy. A plan sometimes followed when a larger capacity than is offered by the four-kiln plant is desired is to erect two sets, separated by a space of 75 to 100 feet, with an overhead bridge connecting them. One set of machinery and one workroom serve for both, yet the fire risk is considerably reduced.

Location of the plant.—The drying plant is, of course, located near extensive orchards. Each 20 by 20 foot kiln will evaporate from 100 to 150 bushels of apples every 24 hours, a four-kiln plant operated continuously for a working season of 60 days evaporating 20,000 or 25,000 bushels of apples if peels and cores are also dried, or a somewhat larger quantity if these are disposed of in other ways. If the venture is to be profitable, sufficient fruit must be available to keep the plant busy for the maximum period.

Arrangement of the plant.—When a four-kiln unit is used the kilns are usually arranged in a row with the work and storage rooms along one side. The first-floor plan of such a plant is shown in Figure 4. The structure is 80 feet long and the kiln portion 20 feet wide. The workroom portion is 17½ feet wide and 80 feet long. The furnace floor is dirt at the ground level, while the workroom floor is on top of the foundation. Air inlets in the outer wall permit the air to pass freely beneath the workroom floor to the air inlets of the furnace rooms. Steps lead down from the workroom to the furnace room. Usually one end of the workroom is partitioned off and used as an office, for supplies, or sometimes as bins. Frequently the bins are built outside the kiln in a row along the main building, as shown in Figure 5.   In other cases the bins are covered, as shown in Figure 6.

Fig. 5.—A large drying plant with the storage bins located along the side of the workroom.

Both these illustrations show typical drying plants.   Figure 5 is one of all-wood construction, and Figure 6 is one with stone walls up to the drying floor and the remainder of wood.

Fig. 6.—A drying plant with the storage bins under cover.   The building is of frame construction with the exception of the walls of the kiln up to the drying floor, which are of stone.   This plant has a capacity of 400 to 600 bushels of fresh fruit during each 24 hours.

The workroom on the second floor is taken up with the bleacher, the slicer, and a space for conditioning the evaporated material.   It may also have bins where fruit is stored and delivered by gravity to the worktable below. The bleacher is swung from the rafters $6\frac{1}{2}$ feet above the floor, so that there is headroom to enter the kilns. It discharges fruit directly into the hopper of the slicer which stands immediately beneath the end of the bleacher. The plan of the second floor and the location and size of the bleacher are shown in Figure 7. The floor of the conditioning room is level with the drying floors of the kilns, in order to facilitate handling the material. The floors of the workrooms should be made of a good quality of dressed, matched flooring, carefully laid to facilitate cleaning. As they are required to bear considerable weight, they may well be double. A stairway is provided between the first and second floors. The loca-

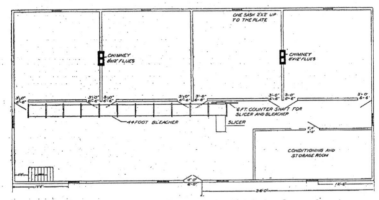

FIG. 7.—Second-floor plan of a 4-kiln drying plant. The drying floor and workroom are on the same level. The bleacher is hung from the rafters with sufficient headroom for passing into the kiln.

tion of the windows and doors and the size of the various openings are shown in Figures 4 and 7.

THE APPLE-DRYING WORKROOM AND ITS EQUIPMENT.

Equipment necessary in the workroom.—The essential equipment of the workroom of an apple-drying plant includes a washing tank with an adequate supply of fresh water, a grader, a worktable equipped with belt conveyors for carrying pared apples and waste, peeling machines, elevators for carrying pared apples and waste to the second floor, elevated bins with gravity chutes for supplying unpared apples to the worktable, the bleacher (a closed box with a slat-and-chain conveyor and a stove for burning sulphur), the slicer, a chopper for working up apples too small or soft to be profitably made into pared stock, shafting, belting, pulleys, and an electric motor or a gasoline engine to operate the machinery, low, broadwheeled hand trucks for moving prepared fruit from the slicer to the kilns and from kilns to the conditioning room, a conditioning room screened to exclude insects and provided with partitions or bins for keeping the various grades of stock separate, baskets, trimming knives, wooden shovels, tools for adjusting and repairing machines, and a supply of spare parts of such equipment as is subject to wear or breakage (pulleys, link chain, paring-machine gears, knives, and coring spoons), a supply of reliable thermometers reading to 212° F., a box press for use in packing the dried fruit, a box-nailing machine, a supply of box shook, mops, pails, and brooms, and means for heating water for cleaning.

The arrangement of the equipment of the workroom is exceedingly important. The drying plant is a factory having a relatively short working season and handling bulky, highly perishable material upon which there is a relatively narrow margin of profit. Successful operation demands that the plant shall run at full capacity throughout the working season and that a high degree of efficiency of the labor employed be obtained by substituting automatic power-operated conveyors and elevators for hand labor in moving the bulky material from place to place in the plant and by assigning every employee a definite task which will keep him fully employed without wasted effort and without necessity for constant supervision. This can not be accomplished if the arrangement of the equipment is haphazard, as the unnecessary labor and the mutual interference of employees with one another which is unavoidable in badly planned workrooms results in a reduction of 10 to 30 per cent in the output of the plant or in a corresponding increase in the cost of production.

The arrangement of the workrooms and their equipment here described is the result of a study of a considerable number of evaporators, and it combines the best features and the most efficient labor-saving devices found in the course of that study with the results of experience in planning and equipping a number of plants. A number of evaporators equipped in this manner have been in successful operation for several seasons, and all the recommendations made have been subjected to the test of actual use. The primary purpose in view has been to make such an arrangement of the equipment as will carry the raw material through the plant along the shortest possible route and secure its rapid, uninterrupted passage through the various stages of preparation. Power-operated labor-saving devices have been employed wherever possible, for the reason that these are coming into practically universal use in the newer plants, and any drier which does not employ them will find that its higher costs of production constitute a very heavy handicap.

As the reasons for the arrangement of the various portions of the equipment will be most easily grasped by following the course of the fruit through the processes of preparation, they are described in that order.

Receiving, washing, and grading the fruit.—Whether fruit is stored in bins or received directly from wagons, a means of washing and grading the fruit is necessary. Washing is a prerequisite to the making of clean, high-grade stock, and the rapid wear of machines by sand and grit carried on unwashed stock is a consideration not to be forgotten by any operator to whom cleanliness does not make a sufficiently strong appeal. A grader which will separate fruit into several sizes is also essential, as paring machines, while capable of adjustment to peel apples of almost any size, must be adjusted to fruit of definite size if they are to do their best work. Some means of keeping the operators of paring machines supplied with fruit at all times is also a necessity.

The washing tank should be located outside and at one end of the building, at a distance of 10 to 12 feet. It should be so placed that fruit may be unloaded directly into it and should be sufficiently large to receive an ordinary wagonload at one time. A length of 6 feet, with a breadth and depth each of 4 feet, is a good size. The tank should be placed with the end, rather than the side, toward the building. It should be provided with a faucet for supplying water, and a large plug should be placed near the bottom to facilitate draining and cleaning.

From the washing tank the apples should be carried by a power-driven bucket-and-chain conveyor to the grader on the second floor of the building. This conveyor, like all others used in apple-drying plants, is made of a standard separable-link chain obtainable in a great variety of sizes and styles of links suited to various purposes. For making conveyors to carry materials in a horizontal plane, the type of link employed is one to which a hardwood slat is attached, the slats forming a flexible belt. For lifting materials vertically, or up an incline, the belt is made up of slats, as in the first case, but at intervals of 12 to 18 inches there are inserted special links to which "buckets" made of two wooden pieces of suitable width, nailed together to form an L-shaped trough, are attached. Link-belt chain of suitable sizes is carried by practically all the larger supply houses, and the wooden parts are readily made and attached by an ordinary workman. The conveyor runs in a flat trough 10 or 12 inches wide and 4 or 5 inches deep, supported by a trestle, and the belt returns beneath the trough. The upper end of the conveyor passes through the wall of the building at a point 8 to 10 feet above the second-floor level and delivers directly into the hopper of the grader. The lower end extends almost to the bottom of the tank, thus enabling the conveyor to remove practically all apples from the tank without attention, while at the same time acting as a stirrer to assist the washing. The inclination of the conveyor to the building prevents the dropping of fruit, while the open construction of the buckets allows the fruit to drain thoroughly before entering the building.

All that is necessary by way of grading is that the fruit be separated into sizes, each of which shall contain fruits varying not more than one-half inch in diameter, as paring machines are so constructed that they may be adjusted to handle fruit with this amount of variation in size. A good plan is to adjust the grader to separate into five sizes, the first of these consisting of fruits measuring $3\frac{1}{2}$ inches or more in diameter, the second of those measuring 3 to $3\frac{1}{2}$ inches, the third of $2\frac{1}{2}$ to 3 inches, the fourth of $2\frac{1}{4}$ to $2\frac{1}{2}$ inches, and the fifth including all fruits measuring less than $2\frac{1}{4}$ inches. These last are run into a separate bin to be pressed for juice or made into chops, as they are too small to be profitably worked up into white stock. The other sizes should be kept separate, so that each size may be delivered to machines adjusted for peeling that particular size. This may be accomplished by placing the storage bin in the corner of the second-floor workroom and placing the grader directly over it, so that the fruit of each size drops into a separate compartment, or by placing the grader at one side of the bin and arranging chutes through which fruit may roll into the various compartments. The bin should be large enough to contain stock for a day's run; dimensions of 20 by 8 feet with a height of 6 feet will permit this, yet give sufficient room for placing the grader above it.

A very simple device serves to deliver fruit automatically from the bin to the paring machines. Each compartment of the bin is provided with a false flooring inclined from all sides of the compartment to the center, thus forming a flattened hopper. From the center of each hopper a wooden chute 10 inches square passes through the floor, runs with a downward inclination of 1 or 2 inches per foot of length across the ceiling of the first-floor workroom to a point above the paring table, and descends vertically to end in a box placed beside the paring machine. A sliding door near the lower end of the chute enables the operator of the machine to fill the box as it becomes empty. If desired, the main chute may be divided, so as to

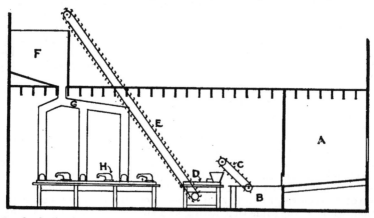

FIG. 8.—Sectional side view of an apple evaporator, showing a belt conveyor from the grader to the storage bin and chutes from the bin to the paring table. *A*, Apple bin with elevated floor and sliding door delivering into *B*, the washing tank; *C*, conveyor lifting apples from the washing tank into the hopper of *D*, the grader; *E*, a second conveyor receiving apples from the grader and carrying them to *F*, the apple bin on second floor; *G*, chutes from the second-floor bin to the paring table; *H*, parers.

supply two or more machines from one compartment. As the chutes are near the ceiling and over the worktable, they are out of the way. This arrangement has the obvious advantages that there need be no stoppage of machines because the supply of fruit is exhausted, the workroom is not obstructed by boxes of fruit waiting to be worked up, and the time of two or more men which would otherwise be spent in getting fruit ready for paring and distributing it by hand to the paring table is saved. The only expenditure of power is that necessary for running the elevator and grader. The entire arrangement is made clear by Figure 8.

The worktable.—The table at which the peeling and trimming are done is located in the first-floor workroom in the position indicated in Figure 4. It is placed 6 feet from the wall separating the workroom from the furnace rooms, thus giving ample room for passage behind it without interference with those working at the table. In a 4-kiln plant the table should be 54 feet long, thus allowing 4½ feet of space for each of 12 paring machines. This number of machines is larger than is necessary to keep the plant running at capacity, but it is advisable to provide at least 2 machines for use when others are temporarily stopped for repairs, while the additional table space will be extremely useful as a workbench for repair work. The paring table should be 4½ feet wide. Many operators employ 4-foot tables, but the additional width is of advantage in various ways. The framing of the table should be of 2 by 4 inch stuff, substantially braced, and the supporting legs of 4 by 4 inch material, spaced 4½ feet apart, so as not to be in the way of operators at the machines, and spiked to the floor. The table should be 42 inches high at the inner and 35 inches high at the opposite or outer side, where the trimmers work. This gives the table top, which is made of 2-inch boards, an inclination of 2 inches per foot of width toward the side at which the trimmers work, in order that peeled apples dropping from the forks of the paring machines may roll across the table to the trimmers' side, where a 4-inch strip nailed to the edge of the table and projecting 2 inches above it serves to arrest them. The height of the table is such that both parers and trimmers may stand at their work or sit on stools, as they may prefer.

The paring machines are placed along the higher side of the table, each machine being given a total working space of 4½ feet. Each machine is leveled and raised a few inches above the surface of the table by placing wooden blocks of suitable thickness solidly fastened to the table, beneath each leg, thus giving additional clearance for waste under the machine. It is also a good plan to place a short bit of board under each machine in such position as to form a sharply inclined plane upon which apples drop as they are pared, as the additional impetus thus given will aid materially in carrying them across the table. The chutes for delivering apples from the bin above are so placed that each delivers into a box placed at the left and about 12 inches from the machine it supplies. The main power shaft is suspended from the joists directly above the paring table and each machine is driven directly from it.

The table is supplied with two conveyors running throughout its length—one beneath it for removing peels and cores, the other, which is raised 6 inches above it, for carrying pared and trimmed fruit. Each conveyor consists of a wooden trough 8 inches wide and 5 inches deep, with a chain-and-slat belt of the type already described. In some plants successful use is made of belts of water and oil proof material supplied at intervals of 12 or 18 inches with cross cleats of some nonresinous hardwood, but such belts usually give more or less trouble through their tendency to slip, and their use is not recommended. At either end of the table the conveyors run over pulleys supplied with take-ups for adjusting the tension and return beneath the table. The conveyor for waste is placed 12 inches below the table, beneath and a little toward the inner side of the paring machines, and an opening 8 inches square is cut in the top of the table under each machine, permitting peels and cores to drop directly upon the belt beneath. A similar opening is cut on the opposite side of the table between each pair of trimmers. An inch strip nailed along the upper edge of this opening keeps apples from rolling into it, and a short inclined trough carries trimmings, which are pushed into it occasionally as they accumulate, into the waste conveyor.

The conveyor for pared and trimmed apples occupies the center of the table and is raised on posts, so that there is a clearance of 6 inches between its bottom and the top of the table. Pared apples drop from the machines and roll down the incline beneath the conveyor to the opposite side, where they are arrested by the edging strip. The trimmers then remove any bits of peel or other imperfections and toss the trimmed apples upon the conveyor. The elevation of the conveyor above the table keeps peels and waste out of it and also permits ready inspection and easy detection of careless work on the part of any trimmer. Details of construction of the table and arrangement of its equipment will be clear from an inspection of Figure 9.

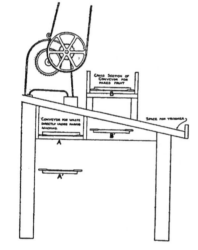

FIG. 9.—A section through the worktable.

At the end of the paring table the conveyors for apples and waste deliver into parallel elevators which carry them to the second floor.

These elevators are inclined 15 or 20 degrees from the vertical and are of the link-belt slat-and-bucket type already described. The conveyor for pared apples extends through the floor and nearly to the ceiling of the second story, where it delivers the fruit into a hopper from which it drops into the bleacher; that for peels and cores extends only far enough above the floor level to deliver the waste into a large box mounted on a hand truck, on which it is rolled into the kilns. In case peels and cores are not dried, but are pressed for cider or otherwise disposed of, the elevator to the second floor is not constructed, and the waste is taken directly from the end of the paring-table conveyor to be pressed or discarded as the case may be.

The bleacher.—The purpose of treatment of the fruit with the fumes of sulphur is primarily to prevent discoloration by oxidation in the air and also to bleach or remove such discoloration as has already occurred prior to the treatment. For this latter purpose sulphuring is not wholly effective, and for this reason it is imperative that fruit reach the bleacher in the shortest possible time after paring. For the further reason that contact of iron with the pared flesh greatly accelerates the rate at which discoloration occurs and also makes it impossible to remove it, the conveyors, elevators, and even the bleacher itself are so constructed that metal does not come in contact with the pared fruit. Bleaching was at one time carried out in sulphuring cabinets or boxes, in which the pared or sliced fruit was exposed in trays or shallow boxes to the action of fumes. This method was laborious; a longer time elapsed and as a result considerable discoloration occurred after paring and slicing and before exposure to the fumes, while it was difficult or impossible to secure uniform penetration of the fumes into the compact layers of slices. In consequence, all modern evaporators employ power-driven bleachers of the type here described.

A power bleacher is essentially a long, tightly constructed wooden box, 2 to 3 feet in width, 3 feet in height, and of a length proportional to the size of the plant, 5 feet of length being commonly provided for each 100 bushels of apples to be handled in an 8-hour or 9-hour working day, so that a plant of 600 bushels maximum daily capacity will require a 30-foot bleacher. Operators usually purchase the metal parts only from supply houses, which can furnish them for bleachers of any desired capacity, and build the box and wooden parts at the plant. The bleacher is suspended by hangers from the ceiling of the second-floor workroom, near the walls of the kilns, and high enough to be out of the way of workmen. Pared and trimmed apples are brought up by the elevator from the paring table and delivered into a hopper at one end of the bleacher, from which they drop to an endless belt conveyor, made of two lengths of link chain carrying hardwood slats, which occupies the bottom of the box and extends through its length, moving over a series of steel rollers placed 12 to 18 inches apart, to distribute the load and prevent sagging. By means of a worm gear this belt is made to move very slowly, so that 30 to 40 minutes are required for fruit to pass through the bleacher. The bleached fruit drops through a short chute directly into the hopper of the slicer, which is placed beneath the outlet end of the bleacher. Sulphur is burned in a heavy iron pan placed in a chamber provided for it at the apple-inlet end, or less commonly in a special sulphur stove placed on a wall bracket or suspended beneath the bleacher, the sulphur fumes being led into the bleacher by a short length of terra-cotta or heavy cast-iron pipe. Provision is made for their escape at the opposite end of the bleacher by a flue of terra-cotta pipe heavily cemented at the joints and extending well above the roof. The apple inlet and outlet are provided with curtains of heavy canvas, weighted to keep them in place and prevent the escape of the intensely irritating fumes into the room. For the same reason the box is built of well-seasoned matched lumber and all cracks are carefully filled with white lead, as are the joints about the pipe connections. The top of the bleacher is provided with hinged doors near either end to permit access to the interior, and these should be made to fit tightly. Figure 10 gives a clear idea of the construction of the bleacher, portions of the side wall and end being represented as cut away in order to show the interior construction.

The slicer.—Several power slicers, differing rather widely in construction, but alike in that they are durable and do satisfactory work, are on the market. The essential features are that the machine be strongly constructed, that it will not readily get out of the order, that it has a daily capacity equal to or greater than the expected maximum demand upon it, and that it be capable of delivering a high percentage of perfect rings when operating at full capacity.

The slicer should be placed at the outlet end of the bleacher, so that the sulphured apples may drop directly into it. Both bleacher and slicer are driven by belts from a short countershaft placed above the inlet end of the bleacher and driven by a belt from the main drive shaft on the first floor. The machine should be raised sufficiently above the floor to permit a broad-wheeled hand truck, carrying a box 12 or 15 inches deep and having one side hinged so as to drop down, to be placed directly beneath the chute down which the slices pass. When the box becomes filled the truck is replaced by another, and the loaded truck is rolled into the kiln, the side dropped, and the contents spread upon the kiln floor. The lowered side of the box forms an incline down which the fruit runs without injury, which is an advantage, as the freshly sliced rings are easily broken, and unnecessary or rough handling at this time lowers the grade of the fruit by increasing the percentage of broken pieces. The loading of the kiln floor is begun at the corner farthest from the door, each truck load being spread as uniformly as possible to a depth of 5 or 6 inches by means of a broad-bladed wooden shovel and a wooden rake.

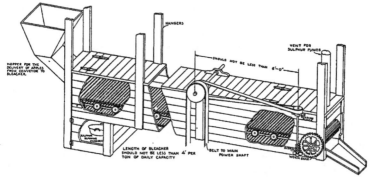

FIG. 10.—An apple bleacher.

In this arrangement of equipment the fruit passes rapidly through the various stages of preparation, a given apple reaching the bleacher within 1½ to 2 minutes after it is placed upon the paring machine, thus eliminating the discoloration resulting from standing in the air. All transfers of the bulky material from floor to floor or about the building are accomplished by automatic power conveyors or by gravity, the hand labor involved being reduced to the actual operations of feeding peeling machines, trimming, and spreading the sliced fruit on the kiln floor. This work does not require great physical strength and is almost universally performed by women and girls.

THE PRUNE TUNNEL EVAPORATOR.

The term "tunnel evaporator," or "prune tunnel," as employed throughout the Pacific Northwest, designates a drying apparatus of a definite type, universally employed in the prune-growing districts of Oregon, Washington, and Idaho for the curing of that fruit. As it exists to-day it is the sole survivor from the early years of the prune industry of at least a score of devices for drying prunes, most of which were patented, as was the earliest form of the tunnel drier. It

owes its survival and present popularity to the fact that it originally
embodied two or three principles essential to the successful drying
of prunes, and the expiration of the patents has resulted in gradual
modifications and improvements at the hands of users.[2]

In contrast with the kiln, which is intended for use with apples
and is not well adapted to the drying of most other fruits, the tunnel
evaporator is an excellent general-purpose drier. The distinctive
features of its operation which adapt it to the drying of prunes make
it equally well suited to the handling of peaches, apricots, berries,
apples, and pears, and it is quite generally employed for drying these
fruits wherever they are commercially dried in prune-growing territory. That it has not come into use in districts in which apples alone
are dried is due to the larger expenditure of labor involved in drying
apples on trays.

In its essential features the drying chamber of the tunnel evaporator consists of a long, narrow compartment, with the floor and ceiling inclined uniformly from end to end, with a furnace placed below
the floor at the lower end. The room is cut into a series of narrow
chambers, the " tunnels," by parallel partitions extending from floor
to ceiling. Warm air is admitted to each tunnel through an opening
in the floor at the lower end and escapes through a ventilating shaft
at the opposite end. The two ends of the tunnel have doors opening
the full width and height. The material to be dried is spread on
trays which are inserted on parallel runways at the upper end of the
tunnel, pushed gradually along as the drying proceeds, and removed
dry at the lower end. The inclination of the tunnel, aided by an
arrangement of the trays to be presently described, facilitates uniform
flow of air over the trays in all parts of the tunnel.

DETAILS OF CONSTRUCTION OF THE TUNNELS.

Tunnels are generally built in groups of three, heated by a single
furnace. The prevailing size of the individual tunnel has been 20
feet in length by 6½ in height and 3 in width. For reasons which
will be stated in considering the operation of the tunnel evaporator,
it is strongly recommended that the length be increased to 23 feet,
leaving the other dimensions unchanged. The floor and ceiling are
inclined, as already stated, the inclination that gives the best results
being one of 2 inches per foot of length. Walls and ceilings are of
wood or galvanized iron, and the floor should be of galvanized iron,
in order to reduce the fire risk. At the lower end of the tunnel an
opening in the floor 3 by 3 feet in size admits heated air from the
furnace room beneath. This opening is provided with a sliding door
of sheet iron which can be closed when ashes are being removed from
the furnace, in order to keep dust from rising into the tunnel. The
ventilating shaft is located at the opposite higher end of the tunnel,
extends entirely across the series of tunnels, and is 2 feet in width.
A ventilator of the type already described in the section on the
kiln evaporator, page 11, is very effective. The ventilating shaft
should extend 6 or 8 feet above the roof of the building, and the

---

[2] The tunnel evaporator in one of its earlier forms came into somewhat general use in
France under the name of the American, or Ryder, evaporator about 1890, and a somewhat improved form was patented in France under the name of the Tritschler evaporator
prior to 1893. (Nanot, Jules, and Tritschler, L. Traité Pratique du Séchage des Fruits
et des Légumes, p. 83–91, fig. 12–13. Paris, 1893.

partitions between individual tunnels should extend upward 3 or 4 feet into it, in order that winds may not interfere with the air movement through a part of the group of tunnels. The doors are made to fit accurately and are supplied with latches which close them tightly to prevent air leakage. Their height and width are equal to the inside dimensions of the tunnel, and they must swing back far enough to clear the opening completely.

In most tunnel evaporators the trays are supported by wooden runways made of strips 1 inch square, nailed to the partitions parallel with the floor of the tunnel, and extending from one end of it to the other. The strips are placed 3½ inches apart from center to center, and the upper edges are planed smooth and carefully lined up with a straightedge in order that trays may be pushed along the runways with a minimum of effort. The lowest runways are placed 4 inches above the floor, while the last pair is 6 inches below the ceiling. This arrangement gives 18 tiers of trays. Each tier will accommodate 5 trays, each 3 by 4 feet in size, or a total of 90 trays, with a drying surface of 1,080 square feet for each tunnel. When properly spread, each tray will accommodate about 25 pounds of fresh apples or prunes, 16 to 20 pounds of berries, or 12 to 15 pounds of peaches or apricots. The capacity of a tunnel, therefore, ranges from approximately 2,250 pounds of prepared apple slices to about half this weight of prepared apricots or peaches at a single char e.

In a number of large plants the labor involved in handling trays is somewhat reduced by substituting trucks with a skeleton frame upon which trays are loaded for the runways just described. The trucks are made of such height as just to clear the tunnel ceiling and are provided with low wheels which run upon light iron tracks. They have not come into very general use for the reason that it is difficult to construct a truck which permits the trays to be "banked" or "offset" in the manner described in the section on the operation of the tunnel evaporator, while it is impossible to secure uniformity of drying at different levels of the truck unless this arrangement can be made.

THE CONSTRUCTION OF TRAYS.

The best type of tray is one made of wire netting and 3 by 4 feet in size, as larger trays can not be conveniently handled when loaded. The wire netting should be the best grade of galvanized screening obtainable, with meshes one-fourth inch square; a screen with one-fifth inch meshes is preferable if berries are to be handled. The frame should be made of wooden strips 1 inch square and should be double, that is, four strips should be nailed together to form a rectangular frame; a strip of metal box strapping or a piece of heavy wire should then be drawn tightly across the frame at the middle and nailed in place, and the wire netting is then nailed to the frame. A second strip of box strapping is then nailed in place over the first, and the edges of the netting are folded back and hammered down so that they do not project beyond the frame. A second set of wooden strips are now nailed to the first, thus giving a tray which can be used either side up. The box strapping reinforces the middle of the tray and prevents sagging of the wire, while there are no projecting ends of wire to injure the hands of workmen or cause difficulty in moving the trays along the runways.

The number of trays provided should be 40 or 50 per cent greater that the capacity of the tunnels. This will enable the day force to spread a sufficient number of trays of fruit to keep the tunnels filled during the night. The night attendant can keep the fires going, remove trays as the fruit becomes dry, and keep the tunnels filled, but he should not be expected to perform these tasks properly if no surplus trays are provided and his time is largely occupied with unloading and reloading trays.

THE OPERATION OF THE TUNNEL EVAPORATOR.

The construction of the tunnel gives it several features to which it owes its superiority over other commonly used types. Fruit is exposed in thin layers to fairly rapid air currents which flow freely over both upper and lower surfaces of the layers, instead of being forced to pass through a single thick layer of fruit, as is the case in the kiln, or through many superposed trays, as is the case in cabinet driers. Fruit is exposed at the beginning of the drying process to air of relatively low temperature and high humidity, thus avoiding injury from overheating, but is automatically transferred without rehandling into air of lower moisture content and higher temperature as the drying proceeds. The operation of loading the drier is continuous, since trays which have become dry are constantly being removed, thus permitting insertion of fresh material as rapidly as it is prepared and keeping the apparatus working at capacity. This is accomplished by an arrangement of the trays upon the runways. which the following description will assist in making clear.

Freshly prepared fruit is introduced only at the higher end of the tunnel. In charging the tunnel with fruit for the first time a rather moderate fire is started in the furnace, and trays are inserted one after another on the lowest runway and pushed down until the front edge of the foremost tray is just flush with the air inlet in the tunnel floor. If the tunnel is 23 feet in length as recommended in an earlier paragraph, the runways will hold five 4 by 3 foot trays. leaving the 3-foot opening of the air inlet unobstructed. The second runway is next loaded with five trays, but these are pushed down until the edge of the foremost tray projects 2 inches beyond that of the one on the first runway. The other runways are loaded in similar fashion, each tier of trays being made to project at its lower end 2 inches beyond that just beneath it[3] and consequently leaving a corresponding free space at the upper end of the runways.

When the tunnel is filled the edges of the tiers of trays project over the warm-air inlet, thus forming a series of baffle plates which break up the ascending column of warm air and force it to enter the spaces between the trays. Since the successive trays with their loads of material form partitions through which the air can not readily pass, it necessarily flows between the trays, thus coming into contact with the fruit above and below until it reaches the upper end of the tunnel, where its free escape into the ventilator is facilitated by the fact that the edge of each tray projects 2 inches beyond its neighbor next above. The movement of the warm air is also aided by the upward

---

[3] As a matter of convenience a diagonal line should be drawn or marked with paint on the side walls at either end of the tunnel, to indicate the proper position of the trays.

inclination of the trays. In consequence there is a rapid and un-impeded air movement throughout the whole apparatus.

The temperature of the air falls rapidly as it passes through the tunnel, as a result of the heat expenditure in vaporizing water, while the amount of water vapor carried by it of course increases. The difference in temperature at opposite ends of the tunnel is usually from 25° to 30° F. In consequence, the fruit at the lower end of the tunnel dries rapidly, while the rate of drying decreases steadily with decrease in air temperature toward the upper end. When the tunnel is first charged with fruit the trays nearest the air inlet become dry, while those next them still contain much moisture, and those at the upper end are scarcely well started to dry. While this delays start-ing, it is of advantage once operation is well under way. The dry

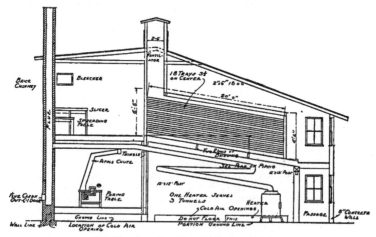

Fig. 11.—A section through the tunnel drier.

trays are removed at the lower end, the whole series moved down the length of one tray, and trays of fresh fruit inserted in the spaces thus made at the upper end. The heat supplied is now increased until the temperature at the lower end of the tunnel becomes as high as is safe to employ in completing the drying, since the fruit nearest the air inlet has lost the greater part of its moisture. The operation now becomes continuous; an exposure of one to three hours to the maximum temperature completes the drying of the fruit on the trays directly exposed to it, and as they are removed the whole series is moved down by the insertion of fresh trays at the upper end.

For maximum efficiency, it is essential that the baffle-platelike ar-rangement of the trays over the air inlet, termed by operators "bank-ing" or "offsetting." be carefully maintained and that the trays on each runway be pushed closely together, so that the air is forced to move between successive tiers of trays. By so doing a uniform dis-tribution of air movement through all parts of the drier, with a cor-responding uniformity of the rate of drying, is effected. Until the device of banking came into use, the runways were completely filled from top to bottom, with the result that entrance and exit of air were greatly hindered, air movement was mainly through, rather than over, the trays, and great differences in temperature and in the drying rate between the upper and the lower portions of the tunnel existed, with the result that it was necessary to shift the trays from the upper runways to lower positions in order to hasten the drying. These defects of the older tunnel driers are entirely remedied by the expedient of giving the tunnel 3 feet of additional length and offsetting, or banking, the trays.

THE FURNACE ROOM.

For a group of three tunnels heated by a single furnace, as is the prevailing practice, the furnace room has a width equal to that of

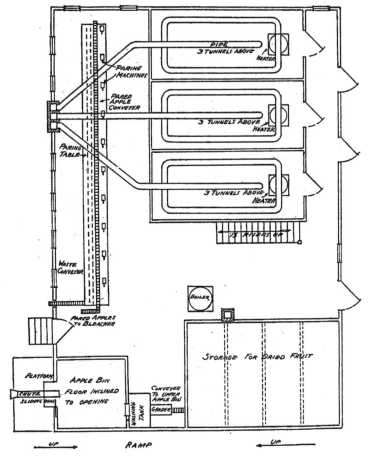

FIG. 12.—First-floor plan of the tunnel drier.

the group of tunnels and a length 2 feet greater. This additional 2 feet of length is given at the lower end of the tunnels and permits the furnace to be placed directly beneath the opening in the floor of the central tunnel, as shown in Figures 11 and 12. The height to the floor at this point should be 8 feet; as the ceiling of the furnace room is formed by the tunnel floors, which are inclined 2 inches per foot of length, the height of the ceiling at the opposite end of the room is 11 feet 10 inches. The walls of the furnace room may be of stone, brick, concrete, or metal lath and plaster; they should not be of wood, by reason of the nearness of the side walls to the furnace and the consequent danger of fire. Two air inlets 4 feet in length and 12 inches in height are provided in each of the side walls just above the ground level, with single inlets of the same size in the end walls and beneath the door of the furnace room.

The furnace is placed immediately beneath the floor opening of the central tunnel. The prevailing type of furnace in use in prune-growing districts where wood is the only available fuel is a large box stove, known as a hop-kiln furnace, equipped with heavy linings and of such size as to take 4-foot lengths of cordwood. Brick furnaces lined with fire brick are also used to some extent, and hard-coal furnaces of the type used in apple kilns may be employed where coal is available. Whatever the type of furnace, it is fitted with a length of heavy 10-inch or 12-inch pipe which rises to within about 4 feet of the floor level immediately beneath the center of the floor opening of the middle tunnel. It is fitted with a tee to which two lines of pipe are attached. These are utilized for heating the two lateral tunnels. Each line is carried from the tee to the center of the opening of the tunnel, where a drum 18 or 24 inches in diameter is sometimes used to give increased radiating surface. From this point the line of pipes is carried parallel with the side wall of the furnace room and beneath the floor of the tunnel to the opposite end of the room, where the two lines may be brought together before entering the chimney. The pipe is given an upward inclination toward the flue equal to that of the floor, and it is usually placed 18 to 20 inches below the sheet-iron floor. This arrangement of the pipes makes them effective in heating the side tunnels.

A MODIFIED TUNNEL EVAPORATOR.

A modified form of the tunnel evaporator which has been developed at the Oregon Agricultural Experiment Station [4] has, it is claimed, a considerable advantage over the ordinary form in point of economy of fuel and increase in capacity for a plant of a given size. Its distinctive feature is an arrangement whereby the air is repeatedly reheated and recirculated over the fruit. This is accomplished by cutting an opening 2 feet square in the floor of each tunnel at its upper end and building a duct leading from this opening to a housing surrounding a fan, which is so placed in front of the furnace that it forces a current of air over the furnace and piping and into the air inlets at the lower ends of the tunnels. The air intakes in the walls of the furnace room and the ventilator at the upper end of the tunnels are provided with trapdoors, which may be closed or opened to any desired degree at will, and similar provision is made for admitting fresh air into the housing surrounding the fan. The furnace and piping are examined and made tight by cementing or stripping the joints. When the fan is started the trapdoors in the ventilator are

[4] Weigand, Ernest H. Improved Oregon tunnel drier. *In* Better Fruit, v. 17, no. 7, p. 7–8. illus. 1923.

tunnels to the storage room, and their use saves much time which would otherwise be spent in transferring loaded trays about the plant by hand.

SMALL DRIERS OR EVAPORATORS.

Many persons produce quantities of fruit which are insufficient to justify the erection of an evaporator of the capacity here described, but which are of such quantity and value as to demand that provision of a small drying outfit capable of caring for the surplus be made. Farmers' Bulletin 984, Farm and Home Drying of Fruits and Vegetables, describes a number of inexpensive driers having capacities ranging from 100 to 2,000 pounds of fresh fruit daily. These evaporators are of such types that they can easily be built by any one who can use ordinary tools, and their construction and operation, the accessory equipment needed, and the preparatory treatment of the various fruits are fully described. As that bulletin is available for the use of individuals or groups of growers having small quantities of materials to be dried, it is unnecessary to describe small driers here.

TREATMENT OF THE VARIOUS FRUITS.

APPLES.

FRUIT SUITABLE FOR EVAPORATING.

There is an increasing demand for evaporated apples of the highest quality. The tendency has sometimes been to make quantity at the expense of quality. But prices are governed not only by the supply but also by the grade. The cleanest, whitest fruit, that is well cored, trimmed, bleached, ringed, and dried, is most in demand. Carelessness in any particular injures the product.

Primarily, the economic usefulness of an apple evaporator is through its utilization of grades of fruit which can not be marketed to good advantage in a fresh state, and it is these grades that are most often evaporated. But the magnitude of the crop also influences the grade of the evaporated product in a decided way. In seasons of abundant crops and low prices for fresh fruit, large quantities of apples that would ordinarily be barreled are evaporated, and the grade of stock produced is correspondingly improved. On the other hand, in years of scanty crops, when all apples that can possibly be shipped are in demand at high prices, only the very poorest fruit is evaporated, thus lowering the average grade of the output.

It is clear, however, that the quality of the product as a whole is improving from year to year. Better methods of production, competition between producing districts, stricter grading rules for fresh fruit which result in much fruit having superficial blemishes but otherwise good, as well as fruit lacking in color, being sent to the evaporators, and an increased demand for the better grades of dried fruit on the part of consumers are causes which have played a part in producing this improvement.

The commercial grading of evaporated apples is based primarily on appearance rather than on dessert quality, and the fact that one variety may make a better flavored product than another is not considered. As a rule, a product of high commercial grade can be made from any sort which has a firm texture and bleaches to a satisfactory degree of whiteness. For the reason that they meet these requirements in a fair degree and are also available in relatively large quantities, a few varieties furnish by far the greater part of the commercial evaporated apples produced in this country. As a result of the fact that the Baldwin is the most important variety in the New York evaporator district, it furnishes the bulk of the output of that territory, Northern Spy supplying most of the remainder. In the Ozark region, Ben Davis is the variety principally used, while York Imperial is most used in the Virginia and West Virginia evaporators. In the apple district centering about Watsonville and Sebastopol, Calif., Yellow Bellflower is the principal variety used for drying, with Yellow Newtown ranking next. In the Washington and Oregon apple-growing districts no one variety can be said to lead; Jonathan, Winesap, Stayman Winesap, Esopus, Yellow Newtown, Grimes Golden, Rome Beauty, Ben Davis, Arkansas Black, Delicious, Wagener, and a number of other varieties contribute to the total in amounts varying with their relative importance in the various districts.

Studies of some 250 varieties of apples with reference to their comparative suitability for drying purposes and the market and table quality of the products which can be made from them have been carried on in the Bureau of Plant Industry. Some results of this work may be of service as a guide in the choice of raw material for those who intend to place their product upon the commercial markets. In what is said it should be understood that market quality, that is to say, the color and general appearance of the product, rather than the table quality, is the primary consideration governing the statements made.

In general, early varieties are unsatisfactory for evaporating purposes. The small size of the fruit of many varieties tends to lower the grade in which the product will sell. More difficulty is encountered in controlling discoloration during drying than is the case with late varieties, and the product is prone to "go off" in color and flavor rather rapidly in storage. By reason of the low content of solids the yield of dry product is lower than with late varieties, and the table quality is less satisfactory. For these reasons the drying of summer and early-autumn varieties with the intention of marketing the fruit through the usual commercial channels should be undertaken with considerable caution.

Among the autumn or winter varieties, the following may be recommended as making "white stock" of good market appearance and color: Ben Davis, Bentley, Black Ben, Bismarck, Brackett, Baldwin, Bughorn, Benoni, Carson, Catline, Doctor, Delicious, Dickey, Evening Party, Fallawater Sweet, Granny Smith, Gano, Imperial Rambo, Ingram, Jersey Sweet, Klickitat, Lawver, London Pippin, McIntosh, Monmouth, Milam, Munson, Pewaukee, Rome Beauty, Ralls, Santa, Statesman, Sierra Beauty, Springdale, Shannon, Shone, Stayman Winesap, Sutton, Talbert, Vandevere Improved, White Doctor, White Pippin, Winesap, Wolf River.

A second group differs from the first in that the varieties placed in it have a sufficient amount of pigmentation in the flesh to give the dry product a slight golden color, often very attractive. In some markets such fruit sells at slightly lower price than clear white stock, in others no such distinction is made. The light-golden stock group includes: Arkansas Black, Annette, Beach, Barnes Best, Butter, Red, Camak, Collins, Fameuse, Golden Russet, Gravenstein, Holland, Illinois Favorite, Kittagskee, Kinnard, Loy, Wolseley, Missouri Pippin, Maiden Blush, Martin, Main, Northwestern Greening, Northern Spy, Pinnacle, Paragon, Red Canada, Rabun, Sweet Orange, Scott Winter, Swaar, Steward Golden, Stark, Tompkins King, Vanhoy, Western Beauty, Winter John, York Imperial, Yellow Skin, and Yellow Bellflower.

A third group comprises apples which are more heavily pigmented and which in consequence yield rather distinctly dark golden dry stock. While marketable, such stock is discriminated against by most dealers either by offering lower prices or by assigning the fruit to a lower grade. Some of the dark golden stock varieties are Abernathy, Akin, Arctic, Arkansas (*Mammoth Black Twig*), Babbitt, Barry, Baker, Buckingham, Black Gilliflower, Buckskin, Clayton, Colorado Orange, Collins Keeper, Fink, Ferdinand, Gold Medal, Golden Noble, Golden Pippin, Haycock, Hendrick, Imperial, King David, Mason Orange, Peck, Pink, Peter, Rubicon, Ribston Pippin, Smokehouse, Schroder, Twofaced, Traders Fancy, Terry, Whinery, Walbridge, Washington Strawberry, and Zoar.

PREPARING THE FRUIT FOR EVAPORATION.

Paring.—The sizing and distributing system described in the section on the workroom automatically supplies any given paring machine with fruits which do not vary more than half an inch in diameter. It is necessary to adjust the machines to fruit of the particular size supplied. This is done by shifting the attachment of the coil spring on the knife head inward or outward until the tension is such that the knife takes off a thin uniform paring, without tendency to skip or to cut so deeply as to choke the knife. It may also be necessary to loosen the coring spoon and move it slightly in or out, in order to make it cut cleanly through the fruit, yet throw the pared and cored apple clear of the parings. One person should have entire charge of the adjustment and repair of machines, and when once properly adjusted no tinkering with the machines by others should be permitted.

The operator should be instructed to place every apple upon the fork stem end first, so that the paring is begun at the calyx, and to aim at securing perfect removal of the core by the spoon. All standard power-operated machines are supplied with pulleys of such a size as to run the machines at the rate of 30 apples per minute. An inexperienced operator will find difficulty in feeding a machine at this rate. It is better policy to insist upon careful work and to have operators gradually acquire the necessary speed than to slow down the machines at first and subsequently raise them to standard speed.

Trimming.—In paring the fruit more or less skin is usually left around the stem and calyx of the apples and any irregular places that may occur. There will be worm holes, decayed spots, and other blemishes which will detract from the appearance of the product if allowed to remain. Even bruises are objected to by the most exacting operators. Hence all such defects are cut out as soon as the fruit is pared if the highest grade of product is expected. This is done with a narrow, straight-backed, sharp-pointed knife, having a blade not more than 2½ to 3 inches long, as the use of a longer blade leads to wastefulness in trimming.

In order that high-grade fruit be produced, it is absolutely essential that the number of trimmers be sufficient to prevent the accumulation of pared fruit on the tables. Usually two trimmers are able to care for the fruit pared by one machine, but if the fruit be exceptionally small or of poor quality, a third may be needed. In any case it is necessary to keep the trimming table clear and to get pared fruit into the bleacher without delay, as fruit which has become discolored from standing in the air does not regain its original whiteness in the bleaching process.

Bleaching.—The fumes of burning sulphur are employed not only to make the fruit white where the freshly cut surfaces have become discolored by contact with the air, but to prevent further discoloration after it is sliced. Sulphuring also renders the fruit more readily permeable to moisture and consequently accelerates the drying somewhat. It also acts as a deterrent to insects which otherwise might deposit their eggs upon the fruit, either during the drying or subsequently in storage.

There have never been definite standards governing the bleaching as to the time required, quantity of sulphur necessary to accomplish the desired end, etc. The aim is to treat until enough of the fumes have been absorbed by the apples to prevent discoloration after they are sliced and exposed to the air. If it is found that the fruit is not retaining its clean, white appearance with the treatment that is being given, either the length of time that the fruit is kept in the bleacher is increased or more sulphur is burned in the customary time for bleaching. Due caution should be exercised, however, in this connection, inasmuch as the bleaching of desiccated fruits with sulphur fumes is open to criticism. The sale of fruit containing sulphurous acid in any considerable quantity is prohibited by the pure-food laws of some States, as well as being restricted in some of the foreign markets. Under the Federal pure-food law, restrictions are also established with a view to limiting the sulphur-dioxid content to reasonable bounds. (See p. 62.)

The usual practice is to start the sulphur fumes by putting a few live coals into the receptacle used for the purpose, then adding a small piece or two of stick brimstone. Before this has all been vaporized, more is added. This is continued as long as the bleacher is in operation, sufficient heat being generated to vaporize the sulphur without the further addition of burning coals.

When apples are dried whole, without slicing or quartering, they require less bleaching than if they are to be sliced, inasmuch as the interior of the fruit does not come in contact with the air.

The allotted time for bleaching, in a large number of evaporators from which information has been obtained, varies from 20 minutes to 1½ hours. The usual time appears to be about 45 minutes. In experimental work carried on in the laboratories of the Bureau of Plant Industry, in which lots of apples of approximately 100 varieties have been subjected to bleaching for various periods of time and with varying quantities of sulphur, it has been found that exposure to the fumes in a tight bleacher for 30 to 40 minutes, employing sulphur at the rate of 3 to 4½ pounds per ton of fruit, has been sufficient to preserve the color of the dry product under proper storage conditions for periods of 12 to 20 months. It is clear that the wide variations in the quantity of sulphur employed and in the time of exposure necessary which are reported by operators are due to such factors as variations in the completeness of combustion of the sulphur, the construction of the bleachers, or the care with which the work is done rather than to regional or varietal differences in the fruit employed. It is clear that in some cases the quantities of sulphur employed are excessive and the bleaching period unnecessarily long; a reduction in both respects to the minimum necessary to produce the desired effect would eliminate a ground for criticism of the product and at the same time effect a slight economy in production.

As a result of the criticism which has been directed against the practice of sulphuring, considerable effort has been devoted to attempts to find satisfactory substitutes for the sulphur treatment, and a very considerable number of treatments have been proposed by various workers. Those which have been most strongly recommended substitute for treatment with sulphur fumes, a short treatment by dipping into a solution. Among other substances employed are rather dilute solutions of sodium bisulphite, potassium bisulphite, sodium chlorid (common salt), sodium bicarbonate (baking soda), acetic and tartartic acids, and hydrochloric acid. A somewhat detailed study of these and a number of other proposed treatments has been made in the laboratories of the Bureau of Plant Industry, with the general result that none of these treatments can be recommended as an effective substitute for sulphuring. The employment of sodium or potassium bisulphite solution merely changes the method by which sulphurous acid is introduced into the fruit for one which is no more effective and even more difficult to apply with uniformity. The other treatments mentioned vary somewhat in the degree to which they prevent discoloration during the actual drying process, but are alike in that they do not prevent slow spontaneous oxidation and consequent darkening in storage unless used in such concentrations as to give readily perceptible flavor to the fruit. For this reason, and for the further reason that they confer no protection against the deposition on the fruit of the eggs of insects, it is scarcely possible that any of these treatments will displace sulphuring as a commercial practice.

Slicing, quartering, etc.—After bleaching, the next step in preparing the fruit is slicing, unless instead of being sliced it is quartered or dried whole, as is done to a limited extent.

The slices are one-fourth inch thick, and in the largest degree possible should be cut at right angles to the hole made through the axis of the apple when the core is removed by the parer, thus producing the rings, which is the form most desired. Other things being equal, that fruit is sliced the best which contains the largest proportion of rings, and this point is given more or less weight in grading the finished product.

To secure a high percentage of perfect rings, the slicer should have a capacity considerably greater than the maximum demand made upon it; the slicing knives must be kept in perfect condition; and the chute from the bleacher must be so placed that equal distribution of fruit to the two sides of the turntable occurs. It is impossible to do perfect work if fruit is delivered so rapidly that two or more apples are carried by a single cup, as the fruits can not then move freely enough to turn into proper position for slicing before reaching the knives. When it is desired to evaporate apples in quarters or sixths they are run through machines which cut them accordingly, the cutting being done in the opposite direction from the slicing; that is, in a direction parallel to the axis of the apple instead of at right angles to it.

If they are to be dried whole they are transferred from the bleacher directly to the drying compartment without further treatment.

EVAPORATING THE FRUIT.

When the fruit has been placed in the drying compartment of an evaporator, of whatever type it may be, it has reached the most critical stage in the whole process of evaporation, and it is here that the greatest care and skill are required to insure the best possible results.

Capacity of floor space and trays.—In the case of kiln evaporators, the sliced fruit is evenly spread on the floor to the depth of 4 to 6 inches. A kiln 20 feet square will hold the slices of 100 to 125 bushels of fresh fruit, depending upon the amount of waste in the apples and the exact depth to which they are spread on the floor.

If the fruit is in quarters or is dried whole it may be somewhat thicker on the floor, since in these forms it does not pack down so closely as the slices do and hence does not impede the circulation of hot air through it if the depth is somewhat increased.

In other types of evaporators where the fruit is handled on trays the slices are seldom placed much more than 1 inch in depth. A tray 3 by 4 feet in size will hold about 25 pounds of slices, equivalent to three-fourths of a bushel of whole fruit.

The fruit is generally put on the floor of the kiln as fast as it is sliced, and the fire is started in the furnace below as soon as the floor is filled or, in many cases, before it is entirely covered.

Oiling the floors and trays.—It is a common practice to treat the floor of kilns occasionally with tallow or a mixture of equal parts of tallow and boiled linseed oil to prevent the fruit from sticking to it. This is done several times during the season, as conditions appear to make it advisable. Another practice with the same end in view is to scrub the floors thoroughly twice a week with water, using with it some one of the scouring soaps. This is preferred by some operators, who claim that oil or tallow discolors the fruit.

At each filling of the trays, where these are used, the surface of the wire netting is lightly wiped over with a cloth moistened in lard. This prevents the fruit from sticking to the netting and keeps it clean.

Temperature to be maintained.—There is no general agreement among operators as to the temperatures which give the best results in drying apples, and wide variations in practice exist without giving rise to any apparent differences in the appearance and market quality of the product. The prevailing method among operators of the kiln evaporator is so to regulate the fires for five or six hours after loading the kiln that a temperature of 150° to 160° F. will be registered by a thermometer placed in a cleared spot on the kiln

floor. By reason of the rapid escape of moisture, the actual temperature of the layer of fruit will be much lower, the difference varying with the efficiency of the ventilators, but usually being 20 to 30
degrees. After five or six hours the fruit is turned and opened up
so that the air passes through it more readily, and the fires are so
regulated that the temperature, measured in a bare spot on the floor
as before, rises to 165° to 175° F., but is not allowed to exceed the
last-named figure. It is maintained as nearly constant as possible
until the fruit has lost approximately two-thirds of its water, when
the firing is somewhat slackened and the drying completed at a floor
temperature of 150° to 160° F.

The practice just described can be commended in the light of experimental results obtained in the laboratories of the Bureau of
Plant Industry. The reduction in temperature as the fruit approaches dryness is especially to be advised, for the reason that the
temperature of the fruit, which is at first far below that of the surrounding air, gradually rises as drying proceeds and approaches that
of the air when nearly dry. Hence caramelization of the contained
sugar and breaking down or volatilization of flavoring substances,
with resulting injury to the color and flavor of the product, is more
likely to occur as the process nears completion. In work in which
the temperature is under accurate control and can be quickly altered
at will, temperatures considerably higher than those named have been
employed in the earlier part of the drying without injury, but with
the imperfect control of temperature and ventilation found in actual
practice, the upper limits mentioned should not be exceeded. Some
operators aim at maintaining a uniform temperature of 150° to
155° F. throughout the entire process, and a few operate at still lower
temperatures. Such practice materially lengthens the time required
for drying and cuts down the working capacity of the kiln without
producing a corresponding improvement in the quality and appearance of the product.

In drying apples in the tunnel evaporator, most operators maintain
an air temperature of 165° to 175° F. directly over the air inlet at
the lower end of the tunnel, while the temperature at the base of the
ventilating shaft will be 20 to 25 degrees lower. In consequence the
freshly introduced fruit is subjected to a temperature of 145° to
150° F. at the outset, and this is progressively increased as the drying
proceeds.

Turning the fruit.—To prevent the fruit from burning and from
sticking to the floor by remaining in contact with it too long and
to insure the most uniform drying that is possible, the fruit, in
the case of the kiln driers, is turned occasionally. The interval between turnings varies with different operators, with the condition of
the fruit, and with the degree of heat which is maintained. Some
operators do not turn the fruit until five hours have elapsed after
the furnace has been started, and this is to be commended as causing
less breaking of rings, although it is a more common practice to
make the first turning within two to three hours after the drying is
begun, or even sooner. After the first five or six hours it is generally
turned every two hours, and more frequently as the fruit becomes
drier, until perhaps it may require turning every half hour when
nearly dry.

The objects to be obtained by turning must be kept in mind and the fruit handled accordingly. It should be examined from time to time and turned often enough to prevent scorching or sticking and to insure uniform drying.

The instrument used in turning the fruit is a broad-bladed wooden shovel, with the handle so attached that the user may stand erect. A steel shovel can not be used, as contact with metal would discolor the fruit. The operator in charge of the kiln keeps a pair of rubber overshoes in a convenient place to be worn only when working in the kilns. Slipping these on, he begins turning the fruit by working along one wall parallel with the slats of the floor, throwing the fruit from a strip the width of his shovel back upon that next to it. On the return trip he fills this strip with the loosened fruit, leaving an exposed path which is filled as he returns, and so on until the opposite wall is reached, when he covers his path by walking backwards and drawing the fruit uniformly into the space. Stepping upon the drying fruit is thus avoided. Some operators employ movable walkways, consisting of a long board with short legs attached, which may be used to reach any part of the kiln from the door without disturbing the intervening fruit. When the fruit has lost most of its moisture, a long-handled wooden rake is of advantage for loosening any masses which are not drying properly.

A practice followed by some operators is of sufficient practical value to warrant mention. As the fruit in a kiln becomes nearly dry it is thrown to one side so as to leave one-half or three-fourths of the floor free. The loading of this area with fresh fruit then begins and is completed as soon as the dry lot is removed. Since the temperatures employed for beginning and finishing the drying are essentially the same, this practice permits continuous operation of the kilns.

In the case of other types of evaporators in which the fruit is handled on trays, no turning is required, although it may be necessary to open up compact masses if the spreading has been poorly done. Sometimes the relative positions of the trays are changed to make the drying more uniform, but if the offset arrangement of the trays in the tunnel is properly maintained this should be unnecessary. The absence of necessity for stirring or turning is one reason why the fruit dried on trays is generally of rather better quality than that from kilns. The repeated turning on the kiln floor is likely to crush and break the fruit more or less unless the turning is carefully done and the first turning is postponed until the fruit has lost enough of its moisture to be somewhat leathery, while in that which remains practically undisturbed on the racks the rings are maintained in better condition. The fruit also dries more quickly and is often more attractive in appearance.

The same general principles must be observed in tending the fruit where steam heat is used in place of direct hot air from furnaces.

Time required for drying.—The time necessary for drying fruit depends upon several factors. The more important are: Type of evaporator, depth to which fruit is spread, method of preparing (whether sliced, quartered, or whole), temperature maintained, conditions of the weather, and to a certain extent the construction of the evaporator.

The application of these several factors to the point in question readily follows. A good kiln evaporator should dry a floor of slices loaded to a depth of 5 to 6 inches in about 12 hours, 10 to 18 hours being the range of variation. Where the fruit is handled on trays, the time required is much shorter, but conditions are quite different from the kilns, as the fruit is seldom more than 1 or 1½ inches thick on the trays. For slices 5 hours is considered a reasonable time, with a range of 4 to 8 hours.

It is estimated that quarters will require from 18 to 24 hours in the average kiln, while the time for whole apples will range from 36 to 48 hours.

If the atmospheric conditions are heavy and damp, the drying is retarded. Under some conditions it is hardly possible to dry the fruit thoroughly. During windy weather, also, it is more difficult to regulate the heat, especially if the walls are poorly constructed and if hoppers about the furnaces are not employed, so that the draft of cold air into the furnace room can not be controlled. This applies especially to kilns heated by furnaces. It is claimed that steam-heated evaporators are less subject to the influence of climatic conditions.

When is the fruit dry?—Perhaps there is no step in the entire process that requires better trained judgment than to determine when the fruit is sufficiently dried to meet the requirements. Like several other steps in the process, it is largely a matter of experience, though there are certain general features which are capable of being reduced to words.

The fruit should be so dry that when a handful of slices is pressed together firmly into a ball the slices will be " springy " enough to separate at once upon being released from the hand. In this condition there will be no fruit, or only an occasional piece, that has any visible moisture on the surface. In a slice of average dryness it should not be possible to press any free juice into view in a freshly made cross section of it. In general, the fruit as it is handled should feel soft and velvety and have a pliable texture. This is a critical stage, since the slices may seem to possess these characteristics in the proper degree while warm, but after they are removed from the evaporator and have become cold they may be so dry as to rattle unless the removal has been very accurately timed.

The foregoing should represent as nearly as possible the average condition, but it can not be expected to be absolutely uniform throughout. Some slices—they should constitute only a very small percentage—will still plainly possess some of the juice of the apple; others—likewise, properly only a small proportion—will be entirely too dry, possibly dry enough to be brittle.

The curing or conditioning room.—When a quantity of fruit is considered dry enough it is removed from the kiln and put in a pile on the floor of the curing room. (Fig. 14.) Every day or two the pile should be thoroughly shoveled over to make uniform the changes which take place. Thus managed, the pile in a few days will become thoroughly homogeneous. The pieces that were too dry will have absorbed moisture, the superfluous moisture of other pieces will have disappeared, and the entire mass may be expected to reach the condition above described. When this condition has been reached, the batch may be added to the general stock in the storage room.

The conditioning room may be, and in most plants actually is, a portion of the second-floor workroom. It should be partitioned off from the remainder of the room, the windows and door should be provided with tight-fitting, closely woven screens to exclude insects, and the windows should be curtained to keep out direct sunlight, which would cause more or less discoloration of the fruit. If several varieties of apples are being handled, bins or compartment must be provided, in order that the fruit made from each variety may be kept separate from the rest, particularly if the products differ considerably in color. The room should be provided with a stove or other source of heat, in order that it may be kept at a temperature of 65° to 75° F. during the conditioning of the fruit.

If space permits, the conditioning room may also serve as a storage room in which the dried stock remains until it is boxed and sold. It is obviously bad business practice to store the dry fruit in the evaporator, as the danger of loss of the entire season's product by fire is con-

Fig. 14.—A pile of evaporated apples going through the sweating process in a curing room connected with a New York evaporator.

siderable. A much better practice is to employ a separate building located at some distance from the drier as a storeroom and to transfer dry stock to it as soon as conditioning is completed. Whatever the location of the storage room, the suggestions as to its construction given on page 57 should be followed.

HANDLING THE WASTE.

In the usual grades of apples taken to the evaporator there are many specimens that are too small to pare or which for other reasons can not be profitably used in this way. In the case of some of the larger evaporators which are operated in connection with vinegar factories, these apples, as well as all parings and trimmings, are sent to the presses for "vinegar stock," but in the smaller ones these portions are usually dried. When this is done the small fruit separated by the sizer is sliced without paring or coring, in a root cutter or chopper, and spread on the kiln floor. The depth of loading and the handling during drying is identical with that given for white stock. When peels and cores are dried, the fact that they do not pack closely makes it possible to load the floor much more deeply than with white stock, and less turning is necessary during drying. Chops and waste are usually dried to a considerably lower moisture content than white stock, and are quite frequently packed into burlap bags as soon as they are taken from the kiln. It is generally estimated that about one-third as much space is required to dry the parings and trimmings as is demanded for the "white fruit."[5]

"Waste" and "chops" are generally bleached, but are never passed through the bleacher which is used for the white fruit. Where they are dried in kilns, which is usually the case, a common way of bleaching is to burn the sulphur in the furnace room after the stock has been spread on the floor.

It is generally estimated that the waste from a given quantity of apples will pay the cost of the fuel for evaporating that quantity of fruit; that is, putting it on a bushel basis, the waste from a bushel will pay for fuel to evaporate both the white fruit and the waste from that bushel. While in some instances, when the price of such stock is low, this estimate may be too high, it not infrequently happens that it more than pays for the fuel.

PEACHES.

ECONOMIC CONSIDERATIONS.

At the present time an important economic factor enters into the general proposition of drying or evaporating peaches in the widely distributed peach-producing regions of the country.

For a number of years, which extended from the late seventies to the early nineties, large quantities of peaches were evaporated in Delaware and perhaps in some of the other older peach-growing regions. Twenty years or more ago one of the largest peach growers in the Fort Valley section of Georgia undertook to evaporate some of his fruit; but after operating a season or two the effort was abandoned as impracticable under existing conditions. For the past 25 years, however, practically no peaches have been evaporated for commercial purposes in this country outside of California. The reasons for this are largely economic. The peach-growing regions in the humid parts of the country are located more advantageously, as a rule, than are the peach-growing sections of California, with regard to the large consuming centers for the fresh fruit. This fact, of course, has to do with the logical working out of the best methods of disposing of the crop in different regions.

It is also true that the drying of peaches in California on a commercial scale is confined to a few varieties which are especially high in their solid content and hence give a larger yield of dry product than do the varieties grown in the humid regions.

Perhaps the most potent factors in the economics of the case, and especially at the present time, are relative cost of drying and relative selling price of the product. In all humid regions the first cost of the evaporator and the cost of fuel must be added to the expense of operation, in comparison with drying in California, since in that State peaches are dried, with few if any exceptions commercially.

---

[5] "White fruit" is a general term used by operators and dealers to denote the grades used for culinary purposes, in distinction from "waste," which comprises the parings and trimmings, and "chops," which are composed of the apples that are too small to pare or are otherwise defective.

by exposure to the sun. The cost of handling may be more under California methods, but probably the difference is not great. As a fuel cost, roughly estimated, about 1 cord of wood or a ton of hard coal is required to produce a ton of dried fruit.

Whether in an earlier day the varieties available for drying constituted a factor favorable to some regions and adverse to others is unimportant now. The variety factor is fundamental at the present time. In California, the Muir and Lovell are planted on an extensive scale expressly for drying. These ripen in good sequence with each other and are yellow freestones with rather dry, fine-grained, firm flesh, characteristics which are essential in a good drying peach.

In the earlier day when peaches were being evaporated in the East, such sorts as Early Crawford, Foster, Oldmixon Free, Moore, Late Crawford, Stump, and others were used. It is obvious that the dried product as a whole would lack the uniformity that is now demanded by the trade. However, within the past 25 years the Elberta has come very largely to the fore in all humid peach-growing regions. So important is it, relatively, that in many of the peach-growing centers it is the only variety shipped in relatively large quantities for use in the fresh state.

While the Elberta is dried to a very limited extent in California, the quantity handled in this way is negligible compared with the Muir and Lovell. The Elberta has some characteristics of a good drying peach, but it may be questioned whether the dried fruit would be of sufficiently high grade and attractive enough in appearance to compete successfully with the dried fruit from the Pacific coast when placed on the market in large quantities. It follows, in view of the very extensive production of the Elberta in most peach-growing centers in the humid regions, in comparison with other sorts, that the great bulk of the fruit available for drying in those regions is of the Elberta variety. Under normal conditions the annual average of 30,000 tons, more or less, of dried peaches from California supplies the market demand. It appears evident that should a large quantity of Elbertas from other sections be dried, new demands or new markets for the product would have to be developed if the growers who dry their fruit are to profit thereby.

DETAILS OF DRYING.

The kiln type of evaporator, which as previously noted is largely used in drying apples, is not suited to peaches, the characteristics of the fruit being such that it can not be handled well in the large bulk that is necessary to make the use of a kiln economical. Any of the cabinet or tunnel types where the fruit is spread in a thin layer on trays may be used in evaporating peaches.

The fruit to be evaporated should be of a uniform degree of maturity and fully ripe, otherwise the finished product will lack uniformity. Immature fruit does not make a good dried product. Moreover, the rate of drying is governed in part by the size of the pieces; hence it is an advantage if the fruit that is placed on any one tray is fairly uniform in size. For this reason all fruit should be passed over a sizer adjusted to separate it into three or four sizes.

The first step in the actual preparation of the fruit is to split it
open to remove the pit. This is done by cutting completely around
the peach in the line of the suture with a sharp knife. The cut needs
to be complete, since any tearing of the flesh will be apparent in the
evaporated product, making it less attractive in appearance than it
otherwise would be.

If the fruit is to be peeled,[6] the paring should be done before the
fruit is cut open for the removal of the pit. Paring is done by hand,
as a rule, when the practice is followed, sharp, straight-backed knives
with blades $2\frac{1}{2}$ to 3 inches long being satisfactory for this purpose.
Paring machines have been designed for peeling peaches, but they
do not appear to be much used.

A much more economical method is to employ a lye solution for
peeling, as is the practice in the commercial canning of peaches. A
solution of proper strength is made by dissolving 1 pound of ordinary concentrated lye (containing 96 per cent sodium hydrate). in
10 to 16 gallons of water. The solution must be actually boiling.
Fruit contained in a suitable crate or basket is plunged into the boiling solution and allowed to remain 60 to 90 seconds, the exact time
necessary depending upon the variety and degree of ripeness of the
fruit. It is then transferred to cold fresh water and agitated to
wash off the loosened peels and to free the fruit from the lye, after
which it is split and stoned, any blemishes or adhering bits of peel
being trimmed off by the splitters. The equipment necessary for lye
peeling is identical with that for dipping prunes, described on
page 51.

After the pits are removed the fruit is treated to the fumes of burning sulphur in much the same manner that apples are treated and for
the same purpose. The fruit should pass to the bleacher with the
least possible delay after it is split open, in order to prevent discoloration. Because of the character of the fruit, however, it should not
be handled in large bulk during the bleaching process, as is the practice with apples. The best method is to place the trays on which the
fruit is to be dried upon the worktable, and have the women who
split and stone the fruit lay the separated halves, stone cavity up,
closely side by side in a single layer upon the trays. Two women
may spread the prepared fruit upon one tray placed between them.
As rapidly as the trays are filled they are transferred to a bleacher
of the type described on page 34.

Experimental data obtained in the laboratories of the Bureau of
Plant Industry indicate that color and appearance of practically all
of the more important commercial varieties of peaches can be as well
preserved by exposure for 30 to 35 minutes to the fumes of sulphur
burned at the rate of 6 to 8 pounds per ton of whole fruit as by the

---

[6] Practically all evaporated peaches found on the market are dried without peeling.
While there is a considerable demand from consumers for a peeled evaporated peach,
producers have hesitated to attempt making such a product because of a practical difficulty. When fruit is peeled and treated with the fumes of burning sulphur for a prolonged period, juice escapes from the tissues into the stone cavity and to the outer
surface and drips away. As this juice is rich in sugar and flavoring substances, the
weight and quality of the product is lowered by its loss. This loss does not occur when
the peel is not removed, as the liquid can not pass through it. Experiments in the
laboratories of the Bureau of Plant Industry have shown that when sulphuring is continued only for a sufficient time to secure preservation of color, peeled peaches can be
treated without any loss of juice. Operators consequently have it in their power to
produce a peeled sulphured dry peach of good quality, provided they guard against excessive exposure of the fruit to sulphur fumes.

use of larger quantities or more prolonged exposure, or both. When
the fruit is peeled, so that penetration occurs from both surfaces
rather than from the stone cavity alone, the time of exposure may be
reduced to 20 to 25 minutes. With the drier firm-fleshed varieties,
such as the Lovell, Muir, Salwey, and a few others which are grown
for drying purposes in California, somewhat more prolonged treatment is necessary to insure good penetration, but there is no question
that exposures for 3 to 10 hours are needless and productive of no useful result. The operator should determine by experiment the minimum time which will give satisfactory results with his particular
equipment and raw material and carefully avoid overexposure and
excess in the use of sulphur.

HANDLING PEACHES IN THE EVAPORATOR.

The bleaching completed, the fruit is ready to be placed in the
evaporator. Care must be exercised in transferring the fruit in
order that the halves may remain cup side uppermost, thus preserving any juice which may have collected in the stone cavities during
sulphuring.

The temperature at the outset should not be allowed to exceed 140°
F., and it may be increased to 165° F. for finishing. As the trays
are pushed down to the lower end of the tunnel, the fruit should be
turned over or stirred to promote uniformity in drying.

The length of time required to dry the fruit will vary with the
equipment, the efficiency with which it is managed, the weather conditions at the time evaporation is being carried on, probably to some
extent the weather conditions during the development of the fruit,
and more especially the weather conditions during the few weeks immediately prior to picking. The variety is also a very definite factor
in the time required for drying. Beers Smock and other comparatively dry-fleshed sorts may be in condition for removal in 5 to 7
hours; others, under the same conditions of operation, in 6 to 8
hours, while very juicy varieties may need to remain in the evaporator
from 12 to 15 hours. Obviously, however, such sorts as the latter are
not desirable for drying, unless they possess other qualities which
give them some peculiar value.

Good judgment, which develops only with experience, is necessary
to determine just when the fruit is in a proper state of dryness to be
withdrawn from the evaporator. In general, the fruit should possess
the same physical properties as apples when evaporated. It should
not be possible to bring free moisture to the surface upon squeezing
a freshly cut surface tightly between the fingers; the fruit should
have a velvety, springy, pliable texture, and when a double handful
is tightly pressed together the pieces should immediately fall apart
when the hands are relaxed.

· When the fruit comes from the evaporator, as in the case of apples,
there will be some pieces that obviously contain too much moisture;
others will be so dry and hard that they will rattle when they are
handled. By placing them in a pile of considerable size and working them over several times during a period of a week or two, as is
done with apples (see p. 43) the entire lot may be brought to a uniform moisture content. When this stage is reached the fruit is transferred to the storage room, where it remains until it is packed for the
market.

APRICOTS. -.

The dried apricots found in the markets are wholly a California product, as the fruit is not dried in commercial quantities elsewhere. For the convenience of the occasional operator who may desire to evaporate small quantities, an outline of the method to be followed is given here.

The treatment of apricots is essentially that given to peaches. The fruit is graded into three sizes for the sake of securing uniformity in drying, split and stoned, placed upon trays, stone cavities uppermost, as closely as possible, precisely as recommended for peaches. The sulphuring of the fruit must be begun as promptly as possible and is continued for two to two and one-half hours if it is desired to secure a uniformly translucent golden-yellow dried fruit, although one hour's treatment will give sufficiently thorough penetration to prevent discoloration. The same precautions are necessary in the handling of trays, in order to avoid loss of juice, as are recommended in the case of peaches. The temperatures to be employed are those recommended in the case of peaches, as are the criteria for determining when the fruit is dry and the subsequent treatment in the conditioning room.

PEARS.

The drying or evaporation of pears in the humid regions has not received sufficient attention to establish any definite methods or rules of practice. Dried pears form one of the smaller though important products in the dried-fruit industry of California, where the drying is very largely by exposure to the sun rather than through the use of artificial heat. Of the varieties more commonly grown in the humid regions the Bartlett and the Seckel are the only ones which make a product of such quality as to compete in the markets with the California sun-dried pears, which are almost wholly composed of the Bartlett variety.

Usually the fruit is cut lengthwise into halves, pared, the stem and calyx removed but the core left in. If the fruit is very large it may be quartered or cut into other smaller sections to facilitate drying.

Bleaching is necessary, as with apples and peaches, in order to secure an attractive-looking dried product. For equally good results it is necessary to continue the bleaching for a considerably longer period than with apples and to use larger quantities of sulphur; an exposure of one to one and one-half hours, using sulphur at the rate of 8 to 10 pounds per ton of fruit, is believed to be sufficient. If the fruit is placed in a weak salt solution (1 per cent) as soon as it is peeled and kept there until it is spread on trays, the time of exposure to sulphur fumes may be reduced to 20 to 30 minutes.

The same general qualities described in connection with apples and peaches will indicate when a lot of fruit is ready to be taken from the evaporator, and upon removal it is handled in the same way.

CHERRIES.

Cherries occupy very much the same place as pears, so far as commercial drying in humid regions is concerned, and they are hardly more important in those regions where sun drying prevails. However, both sweet and sour cherries are dried by artificial heat as well as in the sun to a limited extent.

The fruit may be pitted or not before drying, but the best product is made when pitting precedes drying, though of course large quantities of juice are lost in the operation unless some provision is made for saving and utilizing it in some way. No bleaching is necessary. In other respects they may be handled much as raspberries are handled. The evaporation of this fruit is discussed on a later page (see p. 54).

PRUNES.

The question " What is a prune? " is frequently asked. The answer is simple. A prune is merely a plum having certain varietal qualities not possessed by other plums. The final, distinguishing quality or character is ability to dry without fermenting while the pit still remains in the fruit. If a plum can not be dried without fermenting unless the pit is removed (as is true of most varieties) it is not a prune. Therefore it may be said that all prunes are plums, but not all plums are prunes. As a matter of fact, all of the prunes of commercial importance belong to the *domestica* or European group of plums. None of the native or Japanese varieties are dried for market purposes, though there are certain native plums which are used locally in this way to a limited extent.

The commercial drying of prunes in this country is carried on in Oregon and California, and to some extent in certain localities in Washington and Idaho. The quantity dried in other States is so small as to be negligible. In Oregon, Washington, and Idaho the drying is done in evaporators, while in California sun drying is largely practiced, though evaporators are rapidly coming into general use.

Most of the dried prunes offered to the trade consist of two varieties—the *Italian*, grown largely in Oregon and Washington, and the *Agen*, or, as it is much more commonly called, the *French* or *Petite*, grown in California. A few other varieties are dried in small quantities, but they are unimportant as compared with the ones named.

Prunes for drying, like other fruits, should be fully ripe. The common practice is to permit them to remain on the trees until they drop of their own accord or fall with a very light tapping of the branches with poles. The fruit is then gathered from the ground and placed in lug boxes or other convenient receptacles and taken to the evaporator. Sometimes the fruit that drops naturally is picked up at three or four different times, and then poles are used to complete the harvest. Since the sugar content of prunes increases rapidly in the last week or 10 days prior to their fall from the tree, to allow them to ripen and fall of their own accord obviously gives a higher yield of better quality product than is obtained when they are shaken from the trees. For this reason, and also because ripe fruit checks very much more readily than immature fruit, the prunes which have fallen of their own accord should be kept separate from the less mature fruit.

While the details of handling the fruit at the evaporator vary considerably with different operators, a composite course is about as here described.

SIZING THE FRUIT.

The fruit is emptied from lug boxes or other receptacles upon the grader, set to separate the fruit into four or five sizes, which are kept apart through the subsequent treatment. Sizing well repays the labor, since more uniform checking in the dip and greater uniformity in drying, with a corresponding decrease in the percentage of "bloaters" and "frogs"[7] is thereby secured.

DIPPING THE FRUIT.

The fruit is dipped in a lye solution, the object of which is to remove the wax from the fruit and to produce a very fine checking of the skin. If this is not done, the moisture in the fruit can not escape readily, and the fruit in drying will not assume the shrunken condition that is desirable. Instead, many "frogs" or "chocolates," as they are variously called, i. e., fruits which do not assume the desired shrunken condition, will result. Such fruits have to be graded out and are worthless, or nearly so, as dried prunes.

The lye solution is made by dissolving ordinary high-grade caustic soda or caustic potash in water. The strength at which it is used varies from a pound in 10 or 12 gallons of water to a pound in 25 or 30 gallons of water, depending upon the variety (some requiring a stronger solution than others to accomplish the end in view), the ripeness of the fruit (fully ripe, fallen fruit requiring shorter treatment than that which has been shaken or beaten from the trees), the temperature at which the solution is maintained, the length of time the fruit is immersed, etc.

Ordinarily the lye solution is maintained at the boiling point, the tank in which it is contained being placed over a furnace or supplied with steam coils in such manner as to maintain the desired temperature, as described in the section on equipment, page 33.

When the solution is maintained at this high temperature, it is necessary to hold fully ripe fruit in the solution only a few seconds, though the time varies to some extent with different varieties. The operator soon learns to determine by the appearance of the fruit the necessary length of time under the temperature and other conditions that are being maintained. If the solution is too strong, or if the fruit is immersed for too great a length of time, the slight checks in the skin will become definite cracks in the fruit. This should be avoided, as fruits which are definitely cracked will lose much of their sugar by dripping and consequently will not make a desirable dried product.

Immediately after dipping, the fruit should be transferred to a bath of clear water and rinsed free from lye. The wash water should

---

[7] The terms "bloaters," "frogs," and "chocolates" are variously used to denote fruits that do not dry properly, but remain plump and retain certain other undesirable characteristics. "Bloaters" (California Exp. Sta. Bul. 114) have been designated as large, fully ripe fruits which ferment slightly in drying, producing a small amount of gas which prevents them from shrinking. "Frogs" are usually small, poorly developed fruits which for some reason will not respond properly to the lye solution. The skin does not become checked, and they do not dry properly. If a tree is very heavily overloaded and the fruit correspondingly small and poorly developed, much of the fruit from it is likely to "frog" when dried.

be constantly renewed, or two vessels of wash water should be provided, as suggested on page 34, as the fruit carries considerable quantities of lye into the wash water.

In addition to the dipping, the fruit, in some instances, is passed over a perforator, which in brief is an inclined plane provided with very small pin points, in order to slightly puncture the skin of the fruits as they pass over it. The pricking of the skin in this way serves the same purpose as the checking of the skin mentioned above in connection with the dipping. Where the perforator is used it is not necessary to carry the dipping quite as far as where it is not used, though the lye solution should completely remove the bloom from the fruit. While formerly much used, perforators are now rather generally discarded, because the breaking off of needles in the fruit was not an infrequent occurrence, and when lye dipping is properly done, perforation is unnecessary.

Combination machines are on the market which include equipment for dipping, washing, perforating, and sizing the fruit, and in which the fruit is automatically passed from one operation to the next. Where extensive operations are concerned, such an equipment is essential, but smaller, more simple equipment involving all handwork serves the purpose very well for small-scale activities.

The foregoing paragraphs describe the methods of checking the fruit at present in use. It has been shown by investigators at the Oregon Agricultural Experiment Station [8] that it is possible to dispense entirely with the use of lye and to secure satisfactory checking by the use of boiling water alone. It is necessary that the water be actually boiling, hence the tank used should be large enough so that the water will not be cooled below the boiling point by the vessel of fruit. The treatment requires 20 to 60 seconds, the exact time depending upon the ripeness of the fruit. By reason of its greater simplicity and economy, and its equal effectiveness, hot-water dipping should entirely replace the use of lye.

After dipping, the fruit is spread on trays of the type already described on page 26. A single layer of fruit only should be placed on the tray, but care should be taken to fill it completely, as partially filled trays interfere with proper distribution of the air currents. It is then ready to be placed in the evaporator.

HANDLING PRUNES IN THE EVAPORATOR.

It is obvious from the foregoing that an evaporator of the kiln type is not suitable for use in drying prunes. Any of the types in which the fruit is placed in thin layers on trays or racks as described above can be used. As a matter of fact, the tunnel type has at the present time almost completely displaced stack, cabinet, and various other types of driers which were formerly used for the drying of prunes. Figure 15 shows the exterior of a tunnel evaporator in Oregon. The dipper and other equipment used in preparing the fruit for drying is housed in the annex with a shed roof.

Considerable must be left to the operator's judgment with regard to the temperature at which the evaporator should be maintained. If it is too high in the beginning there is danger of the fruit bursting

[8] Lewis, C. I., Brown, F. R., and Barss, A. F. The evaporation of prunes. Oreg. Agr. Exp. Sta. Bul. 145, 36 p., 28 fig. 1917.

open, in which case the loss of sugar by dripping will seriously lower the quality of the dry product. As nearly as can be stated in definite terms it is safe to start with a temperature of 130° to 140° F., gradually raising it until the fruit is finished at 155° to 165° F.

As with other fruits, the time required in which to dry prunes varies with conditions, but from 24 to 30 hours is a conservative average.

The fruit is dry when the skin is well shrunken in the manner familiar to all users of prunes. The texture should then be firm but springy and pliable enough to yield readily when pressed in the hand. The drying should not continue until the individual fruits rattle as they are brought in contact with one another in handling. It is true, however, that when the bulk of the fruit has

Fig. 15.—-Exterior view of a prune evaporator in Oregon. The dipper and sizer are placed in the annex with shed roof. The compartments in which the fruit is dried are in the main part of the building.

reached the proper degree of dryness some specimens will be too dry while others will contain an excess of moisture, as is the case with other fruits. The condition is equalized in the same manner as with apples and peaches, by placing the prunes in a pile when they come from the evaporator, and working them over from time to time until uniformity of product is reached. This may require from several days to two or three weeks.

Instead of piling the fruit in bulk, it may be put in boxes of convenient capacity to handle and poured from one to another every day for a time while the fruit is curing or conditioning. Before the fruit is conditioned, however, the " bloaters " and " frogs " should be removed.

In drying, prunes shrink in weight on an average about three to one, i. e., about 3 pounds of fresh fruit are required to make 1 pound of the dried product.

The treatment given the Silver prune, which is dried in a small way in some sections, is identical with that of other prunes, with the addition that the fruit is sulphured to preserve the color. The sulphur treatment is given after the fruit has been dipped and spread on the trays. The fruit is left in the sulphuring chamber only 15 to 20 minutes and is then at once transferred to the drier.

SMALL FRUITS.

The small fruits are evaporated or dried to a limited extent only, with the exception of the Logan blackberry, which is a commercial factor in the fruit industry of the Pacific coast, and black raspberries, which are dried on a more or less extensive scale, principally in New York. Other small fruits, such as red raspberries, blackberries, strawberries, and blueberries, and perhaps still others, are dried sometimes for home use, but they are rarely seen in the market. These fruits may be dried by essentially the same methods as the more important ones above mentioned. These methods are briefly described here.

BLACK RASPBERRIES.

In some sections, the kiln type of evaporator is largely used in drying raspberries. The ones built in recent years have been constructed in general according to the plans described and illustrated in the first part of this bulletin, but the older evaporators do not have the hopper above the furnace. Evaporators of the tunnel and other types are also used, in which the fruit is handled on racks or trays with galvanized-wire netting bottoms.

Before the fruit is placed in the kiln, the floor is usually covered with muslin, burlap, or some other kind of loosely woven fabric, for the purpose of preventing the fruit from dropping through the spaces between the strips of which the floor is made, or sometimes galvanized-wire netting with $\frac{1}{8}$-inch mesh is used instead of a fabric.

As with all other fruits, raspberries for drying should be fully ripe. Much of the fruit is harvested by batting—a method whereby a wire hook is used to draw the canes into the desired position, allowing them to be lightly beaten with a wooden paddle which knocks the fruit into a device so arranged as to readily catch it as it drops. An expert hand picker under favorable conditions will hardly average more than 125 quarts a day, while in harvesting by the batting method $7\frac{1}{2}$ or 8 bushels is a fair average.

The manner of operating an evaporator in which raspberries are being dried is substantially the same as when other fruits are being handled. Where an evaporator of the kiln type is used, the fruit is spread on the floor from 4 to 5 or 6 inches deep, depending largely on the variety. Firm berries, such as the Ohio, can be placed considerably deeper than the softer, more juicy sorts, such as the Farmer. Where evaporators other than those of the kiln type are used the raspberries are spread in a thin layer on the trays, a tray 3 by 4 feet in size carrying about 11 or 12 quarts of fruit. The temperature should be 135° to 140° F. at the outset of drying and may be increased to 150° to 155° F. as the fruit becomes almost dry.

As it begins to dry, the fruit passes through a soft stage, which, however, lasts for only a comparatively short time. After this stage is passed and as soon as it can be done without mashing the individual fruits, the contents of each tray should be turned over occasionally to insure as far as possible uniformity in drying. Turning may be done with a small wooden-toothed rake or wooden scoop. In the tunnel evaporator, turning is postponed until the fruit has reached the lower end of the tunnel.

The length of time required to hold the fruit in the evaporator depends upon the same general factors that determine the time for other fruits—the weather conditions, type and management of the evaporator, and the variety of the berry. Some varieties dry quicker than others under the same conditions. Then, too, first pickings of the fruit frequently contain more moisture; hence, they require a longer time in which to dry than the later ones, particularly if the end of the berry season is accompanied by a drought, as is frequently the case. Employing the temperatures here recommended, it is possible to dry berries in the tunnel evaporator in six to eight hours, the trays being spread with 1 quart of berries to the square foot. On the kiln, a layer of berries 4 to 5 inches in depth will require 10 to 12 hours.

Under some conditions, the rate of drying and consequently the length of time the fruit remains in the evaporator, is made a matter of convenience to some extent. For example, the conditions in one region where large quantities of black raspberries are dried are such that it is convenient to place the fruit which is harvested during the day on the kiln floor late in the afternoon. The furnace is at once started, running the heat at once as high as the operator thinks the fruit will stand. The fruit is turned early the next morning and again in the middle of the forenoon, and by 3 or 4 o'clock in the afternoon it is ready to go to the curing room, the heat having been allowed to subside somewhat during the latter portion of the time. Upon the removal of the fruit, the kiln is again ready for another "run" with the fruit harvested during the day. While it might be possible to dry the fruit in a shorter period of time, this program is a convenient one under some conditions.

It is estimated that a ton of hard coal will dry about a ton of berries, but the quantity varies from half a ton to 2 tons of coal to a ton of fruit, depending on the variety, condition of the fruit, and other factors.

Experience alone will enable the operator to tell with certainty when the fruit is dry enough to be removed from the evaporator. When this stage is reached, some of the fruit will be dry enough to rattle; there will also be fruits (the proportion should be very small) obviously containing too much moisture. The bulk of the fruit should be of such a texture that it will stick to the hand somewhat if squeezed tightly, while yet the individual fruits can not be forced into a mushy condition; or another test may be to carry the drying as far as possible without reaching the point where the fruit will rattle as it is handled over on the trays. The fruit is then removed from the trays and conditioned in the same manner as apples and other fruits by being placed in bulk on a smooth, clean, tight floor where it is handled over each day with a scoop or other suitable implement for a period of perhaps two or three weeks. During this time the fruit is becoming uniform throughout with regard to moisture, and the drying progresses to the point where the fruit can be stored safely without danger of spoiling.

The curing room should be an airy, well-ventilated place. The fruit, if handled in bulk, may be placed in piles from 6 to 18 inches deep. However, some advantages are claimed for the method of handling the fruit in boxes having a capacity of a bushel or so, during the period of curing. In this way the fruit can be aerated thoroughly by pouring the contents of one box into another.

The variety, condition of the fruit, and other factors influence the shrinkage in drying. It requires, on an average, a little over 3 quarts, or about 4 pounds, of black raspberries to make 1 pound of the dried product. In a rainy season it may require 4 quarts to make a pound of dried fruit, while near the end of the season, when the berries are small, 2 quarts of fresh fruit will yield a pound of the dried product. Other estimates put the shrinkage at about $2\frac{1}{2}$ pounds of the Ohio variety to a pound of dried fruit, while it requires about $3\frac{1}{2}$ pounds of the Farmer for 1 pound of the dried product. Four or five quarts of red raspberries are required for a pound of evaporated fruit. Red raspberries, however, are rarely dried.

LOGAN BLACKBERRIES.

The Logan blackberry is grown extensively only in the Pacific Coast States, and naturally it is in those States that particular attention has been given to the utilization of the fruit. Lewis and Brown, of the Oregon Experiment Station, have reported results of investigations in evaporating it. In that State both stack (or prune tower) and tunnel types of evaporators have been used in drying the berry, with preference for the latter, provided that the tunnels do not exceed 20 to 23 feet in length.

In drying Logan blackberries in the tunnel evaporator, the furnace should be so regulated that the air temperature at the upper end of the tunnel does not exceed 130° F., while that at the lower end does not rise above 150° or 155° F. Employing the temperatures named, the time required for drying ranges from 16 to 20 hours, varying with the weather conditions. As these berries are considerably larger and more juicy than black raspberries, it is readily understood why they do not dry as quickly as the latter.

The manner in which Logan blackberries are handled will affect the weight of the dried product, but on an average 1 pound of dried fruit is made from $4\frac{1}{2}$ to $5\frac{1}{2}$ pounds of fresh fruit.

It is advised to remove the fruit from the evaporator while it is still hot; otherwise the berries will stick to the trays. When cool the fruit is transferred to the conditioning room and stirred daily for 10 days to 3 weeks, after which it may be stored in bulk in the same manner as other fruits.

OTHER SMALL FRUITS.

Strawberries, blackberries, blueberries, huckleberries, and other small fruits are sometimes dried in very limited quantities. No special mention of details is needed in this connection, since the methods already described for black raspberries and Logan blackberries may be used in handling other fruits of similar character.

STORING THE DRIED PRODUCTS.

In many plants the storage room is a part of the evaporator building adjacent to the conditioning room, or even continuous with it. This arrangement is permissible if it is the practice in the plant to pack and dispose of the fruit as rapidly as it is made. It is exceedingly bad practice if the run of the entire season is to be completed before packing and shipping begins or if the fruit is to be held for a favorable market after the close of the drying season. The value of the product for a season may be considerably greater than that of the building and its equipment, and the risk of loss from fire is therefore very considerable. There is also great danger of infestation of the entire stock of dry product by insects when fruit is stored adjacent to the workroom, since these pests are attracted by the drying fruit and may easily gain access to the storage room through doors carelessly left open, or through defective screens or cracks in partitions. For these reasons it is strongly advised that the storage room be located in a separate building, far enough from the evaporator to minimize the fire risk.

Whatever its location, special care should be taken in building the storage room to make floors, walls, and ceiling perfectly tight, as cracks permit entrance of insects and provide shelter for them after they have entered. While some operators make all walls double, this is not necessary if a good grade of properly seasoned matched lumber is used and due care is taken in putting it on. The windows and doors must be provided with accurately fitted screens of heavy, close-meshed mosquito screening; those of the windows should be fastened immovably in place, while those of the doors should be provided with springs to insure prompt closure. The windows should be fitted with shades made of a good grade of opaque material, and as direct sunlight causes discoloration of dried fruits, the shades should be kept down except when work in the room is actually in progress. Adequate provision for ventilation must be made. This can usually be had by partially raising windows along one side of the room while those on the opposite side are lowered from the top. If for any reason this is not possible, floor and ceiling ventilators should be provided. They should be permanently screened and fitted with tightly closing doors, in order that the room may be made practically air-tight when it is necessary to fumigate it. Sudden and extreme changes of temperature and humidity, either upward or downward, should be guarded against by closing the ventilating openings tightly for a sufficient time to permit the room temperature slowly to adjust itself to the changed conditions outside. If the fruit has been sufficiently dried and properly conditioned before being brought into the storage room, such fluctuations of atmospheric humidity and temperature as will occur in the storage room in the course of 3 to 12 months will not noticeably affect it. The fruit at the surface of the mass, if properly cured, will slowly take up moisture during prolonged periods of rainy weather, but will lose the added moisture when dry weather again sets in, the greater part of the mass remaining unaffected.

The room should be provided with a sufficient number of bins to make it possible to store the different varieties and grades of dried stock separately. If the room can be made of sufficient size to permit the work of packing to be done inside it and to allow the storing of the packed boxes until the fruit is finally sold, it will be highly advantageous, as much of the insect infestation of dried fruits is due to exposure of the boxes after they have been packed.

PREPARING EVAPORATED FRUITS FOR MARKET.

While the packing of dried fruits for the trade is conducted largely as a business which is distinct from evaporating or drying and a large proportion of the product passes out of the hands of the operator before it is packed for shipment, it should help the one who makes the product to know in a general way how it is handled by the packer. Some of the methods in use are here briefly described.

PACKING EVAPORATED APPLES.

GRADING.

In handling evaporated apples, three grades are generally recognized, which are commonly. designated as " fancy," " choice," and " prime." Two other grades, which in reality are special grades, are also sometimes recognized, viz, " extra fancy," and a lower grade than prime—usually called prime with some distinguishing prefix, frequently the name of a locality.

The standards demanded for these various grades are about as follows:

" Fancy " is a very white, clean stock, free from all pieces of skin and other objectionable portions which should be removed in trimming, and with a good proportion of the slices in rings.

" Choice " denotes a grade intermediate between " fancy " and " prime," not quite clean enough for " fancy," yet more nearly free from imperfections than the " prime " grade demands.

" Prime " must be a good stock, well cured, and of a generally attractive appearance. It must be comparatively white and mostly free from undesirable portions, but stock having a small percentage of such defects is usually put in this grade.

" Extra fancy," as the name implies, is a fancy grade that is exceptionally fine. It must possess all the qualities mentioned in describing that grade in a marked degree. At least 85 per cent of the slices should be rings.

So-called " facing stock " is obtained by selecting perfect rings of large size and perfect color from extra-fancy stock.

The grade below " prime " is the stock that has been so carelessly handled and is so unattractive in appearance that it can not maintain the standard of " prime." It is packed for an entirely different and much poorer class of trade than any of the other grades.

METHODS OF PACKING.

Evaporated apples are in suitable condition to pack when they have passed through the curing period and the individual pieces have all acquired a uniform degree of moisture.

The package largely used in marketing evaporated applies is a wooden box which holds 50 pounds of fruit when the contents are firmly pressed into it. Pasteboard cartons, holding 1 pound, or half a kilo (1.1 pounds) for certain export trade, are also more or less used.

In packing, the side of the box intended for the top or face is packed first, as in packing fresh fruit in boxes or barrels. The first step in packing, therefore, is to face this side.[9] The facers are slices which are perfect rings. These are usually selected from a quantity of fruit which contains a relatively large proportion of them; they are then placed on thin boards which are slightly smaller than the top of the box, inside measure, overlapping one another in rows, lengthwise of the board. Figure 16 shows such a board of facers. The facers are put in place by inserting the board on which they are arranged into the box, which is first lined with paraffin paper, and then with a dexterous movement of the hand flipping the layer of rings against the inner face, or the bottom, which is to become the top of the box.

After facing, the box is filled by placing over it a bottomless box provided with cleats to hold it in place, setting the whole on the scales, and filling loosely with fruit to the required weight. The box is then transferred to the platform of a box press, and the fruit is forced down until the upper box can be lifted off and the bottom nailed on. The cartons usually are filled by hand. Figures 17 and 18 show 50-pound boxes of dried apples as they appear upon being opened.

FIG. 16.—A "board" of facers.

Experiments have shown that lining the boxes completely with double layers of paraffin paper, the sheets being so placed that the joints in the first layer are covered by the second, greatly reduces the danger of insect infestation by making it impossible for moths to gain access to the fruit after it is packed. As the cost of such lining is slight, it should come into more general use than is the case at present.

PACKING PEACHES, APRICOTS, AND PEARS.

Dried peaches, apricots, and pears are usually packed in wooden boxes holding 25 pounds. They are packed, as a rule, without any special attention to grading. The package is faced, in effect, much the same as described above in packing evaporated apples, though the pieces are placed by hand rather than by a facing board.

If they have been well dried and contain the proper amount of moisture, the pieces are pliable when they are ready to come from the curing room where the moisture has become uniform throughout

---

[9] During the war period the practice of facing packages of evaporated fruit was discontinued, but it has now been generally resumed, at least for the better grades of fruit.

during the curing, or sweating, process. In this condition the product may be packed for the trade without further treatment.

However, if the fruit has become so dry that the individual pieces are not pliable, they will not pack well in the boxes. To put the fruit in good condition to pack it may be treated in several different ways with the end in view of making it pliable so that it will compress readily into the boxes.

The method most commonly employed in the past consists of dipping the fruit in water long enough to moisten the outside. The water used may be cold, tepid, or in some cases it is used boiling hot. Sometimes a little salt is added. The fruit is then spread 2 or 3 inches deep on trays and lightly sulphured, after which it is dried slightly before packing if considered necessary. It is sufficient, commonly,

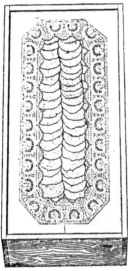

Fig. 17.—A 50-pound box of "fancy" evaporated apples with cover removed.

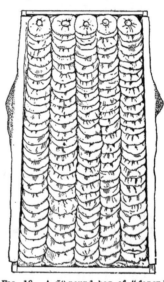

Fig. 18.—A 50-pound box of "fancy" evaporated apples with cover and paper lace removed.

to permit the fruit to remain in a dark room for 24 hours after dipping if it has not absorbed too much water in the dipping. This treatment usually softens the fruit enough to make it pack well and is said also to prevent the development of any insect larvæ or eggs or of fungous diseases with which the fruit may have become infected while in the curing room.

A good deal of care needs to be exercised in sulphuring the fruit at this time—just before it is packed. It is claimed that most of the complaints which have been made in regard to the sulphuring of these fruits are due to excessive treatment just before they are packed rather than to that which they receive before they are dried, and it is clear that an excessive treatment with sulphur has often been employed to prevent fermentation in fruit to which large quantities of water have been added by soaking prior to packing.

Experimental data obtained in the laboratories of the Bureau of Plant Industry indicate that treatment of the fruit with live, dry steam in preparation for packing is in every way preferable to dipping in water. The fruit is loosely spread on trays to a depth of 2 or 3 inches, the trays are inserted into a tight box built like an ordinary sulphuring box, and steam is turned in through a perforated pipe at the bottom of the box. A treatment of 2 to 4 minutes will raise the temperature of the fruit to 180° F., which will destroy any insect larvæ or eggs which might be present and will at the same time render the fruit sufficiently pliable to permit it to be readily packed. The absorption of moisture is very slight, less than one-half of 1 per cent, and as the steaming itself sterilizes the product, sulphuring is neither necessary nor desirable.

PACKING PRUNES.

As in the case of other fruits, the packing of prunes should not be begun until the fruit has remained in the conditioning room, with frequent stirring, for 2 or 3 weeks.

Prunes are graded as to size before they are packed, the different grades being designated as 30's to 40's, 50's to 60's, 90's to 100's, etc., the figures indicating the approximate number of fruits in a pound; thus " 40's to 50's " means a grade in which 40 to 50 fruits average a pound in weight.

In packing, the boxes are faced as in the case of other dried and evaporated fruits. The fruit is prepared for packing in various ways, all of which have the same objects in view, which are the softening of the individual fruits so they will pack well when compressed, the improvement of the appearance of the fruit, and the guarding against the development of insects.

The fruit is softened by dipping in solutions variously made up according to the preferences of individual packers. Some use a solution made by dissolving common salt in water at the rate of 1 pound to 20 gallons; glycerin, 1 pound to 25 gallons, is also used; many operators employ a solution containing 1 pound of glycerin and 8 ounces to 1 pound of salt in 30 gallons of water.

The salt solution is cleansing and leaves the skin bright and attractive. The glycerin gives a gloss to the skin. The solution is usually kept hot while dipping is in progress and should preferably be kept at the boiling point. The fruit should remain in the solution only long enough to become heated sufficiently to make it pliable enough to pack.

In one method of dipping, the fruit is passed through a revolving cylinder processor placed in a horizontal position and in the bottom of which the dipping solution is carried. The interior of the cylinder is so constructed that as it revolves it carries the prunes around with it. Thus they are in the solution only a portion of the time required to pass the length of the cylinder, which occupies but a very few minutes. Steam is constantly passed into the cylinder, so that when the fruit is not in the solution it is in a hot steam bath. Passing out of this apparatus, the fruit is placed for a short time where the surplus moisture drains away, and the fruit is then packed, commonly while still hot.

The dipping and heating of the fruit not only softens it so that it packs well, but it destroys any organisms with which the fruit may have become infected in the curing room.

LAWS RELATING TO EVAPORATED AND DRIED FRUITS.

Food Inspection Decision 176, issued by authority of the Secretary of Agriculture on May 28, 1918, contains a definition and standard for evaporated apples, approved by the joint committee on definitions and standards, which is as follows:

Evaporated apples are evaporated fruit made from peeled, cored, and sliced apples and contain not more than 24 per cent of moisture as determined by the official method of the Association of Official Agricultural Chemists.

As this decision is adopted as a guide in the enforcement of the food and drugs act, it takes precedence over the earlier standard of not more than 27 per cent of moisture, and evaporated apples will be considered as "adulterated," if found to contain more than 24 per cent. The official method of determination of moisture content above referred to consists in drying a sample of the material to constant weight in a current of hydrogen or in a vacuum oven.

The pure food laws of many States also apply in regard to the presence of sulphurous acid, sulphites, or other perservatives in food products. In addition, most of the food laws contain definitions of adulteration which include a statement regarding the presence of a filthy, decomposed, or putrid vegetable substance.

A California statute, approved March 20, 1903, requires that all fruit, green or dried, contained in boxes, barrels, or packages, and offered for shipment in the State, be so labeled as to designate the county and immediate locality in which the fruit was grown, but a decision of the supreme court of the State declares this law to be unconstitutional.

The Board of Food and Drug Inspection under the pure-food law enacted at the first session of the Fifty-ninth Congress relative to the quantity of sulphur dioxid permissible in evaporated or desiccated fruits ruled under date of March 5, 1908, in food-inspection decision 89, amending decision 76, that—

No objection will be made to foods which contain the ordinary quantities of sulphur dioxid, if the fact that such foods have been so prepared is plainly stated upon the label of each package.

An abnormal quantity of sulphur dioxid placed in food for the purpose of marketing an excessive moisture content will be regarded as fraudulent adulteration, under the food and drugs act of June 30, 1906.

The attention of all interested persons, especially exporters, should further be called to the fact that "the Governments of Prussia and Saxony, in order to unify the practices of inspectors of desiccated fruits, have issued decrees fixing the limit of sulphurous acid in desiccated fruits at 0.125 per cent." [10]

The presence of sulphurous acid in desiccated fruits, and also of zinc in fruit dried on galvanized-wire racks, has frequently been criticized in foreign markets and has been the source of unfavorable judgment, resulting in more or less agitation favoring laws restricting or prohibiting the sale of such fruit.

---

[10] Notice to exporters of desiccated fruits. (Food Inspection Decision 7.) *In* U. S. Dept. Agr., Bur. Chem., Food Inspection Decisions 1 to 25, p. 17. 1916.

PUBLICATIONS OF THE UNITED STATES DEPARTMENT OF AGRICULTURE OF INTEREST IN CONNECTION WITH THIS BULLETIN.

AVAILABLE FOR FREE DISTRIBUTION BY THE DEPARTMENT.

Muscadine Grape Sirup. (Farmers' Bulletin 758.)
Home Uses for Muscadine Grapes. (Farmers' Bulletin 859.)
Fresh Fruits and Vegetables as Conservers of Other Staple Foods. (Farmers' Bulletin 871.)
Homemade Fruit Butters. (Farmers' Bulletin 900.)
Farm and Home Drying of Fruits and Vegetables. (Farmers' Bulletin 984.)
Unfermented Grape Juice: How to Make It in the Home. (Farmers' Bulletin 1075.)
Home Canning of Fruits and Vegetables. (Farmers' Bulletin 1211.)
Farm Manufacture of Unfermented Apple Juice. (Farmers' Bulletin 1264.)
Raisins, Figs, and Other Dried Fruits and Their Use. (Separate 610 from Yearbook, 1912.)
Business Essentials for Cooperative Fruit and Vegetable Canneries. (Separate 705 from Yearbook, 1916.)
Control of Dried-Fruit Insects in California. (Department Bulletin 235.)

FOR SALE BY THE SUPERINTENDENT OF DOCUMENTS, GOVERNMENT PRINTING OFFICE, WASHINGTON, D. C.

Methods Followed in the Commercial Canning of Foods. (Department Bulletin 196.) Price, 10 cents.
Studies on Fruit Juices. (Department Bulletin 241.) Price, 5 cents.
Studies in the Clarification of Unfermented Fruit Juices. (Department Bulletin 1025.) Price, 5 cents.
Apple Sirup and Concentrated Cider: New Products for Utilizing Surplus and Cull Apples. (Separate 639 from Yearbook, 1914.) Price, 5 cents.
Unfermented Apple Juice. (Chemistry Bulletin 118.) Price, 5 cents.
The Value of Peaches as Vinegar Stock. (Chemistry Circular 51.) Price 5 cents.

63

ORGANIZATION OF THE
UNITED STATES DEPARTMENT OF AGRICULTURE.

Secretary of Agriculture_____ HENRY C. WALLACE.
Assistant Secretary_____ C. W. PUGSLEY.
Director of Scientific Work_____ E. D. BALL.
Director of Regulatory Work_____
Weather Bureau_____ CHARLES F. MARVIN, Chief.
Bureau of Agricultural Economics_____ HENRY C. TAYLOR, Chief.
Bureau of Animal Industry_____ JOHN R. MOHLER, Chief.
Bureau of Plant Industry_____ WILLIAM A. TAYLOR, Chief.
Forest Service_____ W. B. GREELEY, Chief.
Bureau of Chemistry_____ WALTER G. CAMPBELL, Acting Chief.
Bureau of Soils_____ MILTON WHITNEY, Chief.
Bureau of Entomology_____ L. O. HOWARD, Chief.
Bureau of Biological Survey_____ E. W. NELSON, Chief.
Bureau of Public Roads_____ THOMAS H. MACDONALD, Chief.
Fixed Nitrogen Research Laboratory_____ F. G. COTTRELL, Director.
Division of Accounts and Disbursements___ A. ZAPPONE, Chief.
Division of Publications_____ ELWIN L. POWELL, Acting Chief.
Library_____ CLARIBEL R. BARNETT, Librarian.
States Relations Service_____ A. C. TRUE, Director.
Federal Horticultural Board_____ C. L. MARLATT, Chairman.
Insecticide and Fungicide Board_____ J. K. HAYWOOD, Chairman.
Packers and Stockyards Administration___ ⎤CHESTER MORRILL, Assistant to the
Grain Future Trading Act Administration⎦ Secretary.
Office of the Solicitor_____ R. W. WILLIAMS, Solicitor.

This bulletin is a contribution from the—

Bureau of Plant Industry_____ WILLIAM A. TAYLOR, Chief.
    Office of Horticultural and Pomologi-
    cal Investigations_____ L. C. CORBETT, Horticulturist in
                                           Charge.
64

UNITED STATES DEPARTMENT OF AGRICULTURE

DEPARTMENT BULLETIN No. 1142

Washington, D. C. ▼ March, 30, 1923

THE BARRIER FACTORS IN GIPSY MOTH TREE-BANDING MATERIAL.

By M. T. SMULYAN, *Specialist, Gipsy Moth and Brown-Tail Moth Investigations, Bureau of Entomology.*

CONTENTS.

INTRODUCTORY AND HISTORICAL.

Gipsy moth tree-banding material is a greasy and semiviscid substance, with an odor resembling that of tar, which is being used for tree-banding by the Bureau of Entomology in its control work against the gipsy moth (*Porthetria dispar* L.). It is a domestic product, originated in 1915, by members of the staff of the Bureau of Chemistry, United States Department of Agriculture, as a result of a request made by A. F. Burgess, in charge of the gipsy moth and brown-tail moth suppression work for the Bureau of Entomology. It was developed as a substitute for the German "raupenleim" (*1, p. 132*),[1] a product which had been in use, experimentally, in this country since 1891–92.[2] About that time it was brought to the attention of the gipsy moth authorities by Prof. B. E. Fernow, then Chief of the Division of Forestry, United States Department of Agriculture, who knew of its use against the gipsy and nun[3] moths and other insects in the European forests (*3, p. 129*).[4] The material closely resembles the raupenleim which it has now replaced. As manufactured at present, the gipsy moth tree-banding material is composed of coal-tar neutral oil,[5] hard coal-tar pitch, rosin oil, and ordinary commercial hydrated lime (*2, p. 3–4*).[6] The odor and the viscosity of the material, the characteristics or elements which are of chief concern here, become more pronounced with rising temperature, and in a warm and more or less confined atmos-

---

[1] Numbers in parentheses (italic) refer to "Literature cited," p. 15.
[2] Other importations were made in 1893 (*3, p. 129*); 1909, and 1912 (*1, p. 131–132*).
[3] *Liparis monacha* L.
[4] In Europe it has also been used to cover the egg masses of insects to prevent hatching (*3, p. 125; 4, p. 787*).
[5] A distillate substantially free from bases or phenols.
[6] For further details see U. S. Department of Agriculture Bulletin 899.

phere, as in a room, the odor is quite pungent, irritating the mucous
membrane to a considerable degree.[7]

REASONS FOR INVESTIGATION.

In the course of the preparation and use of the tree-banding material, as well as of the last of the raupenleim, by members of the
gipsy moth force, the question as to what constitutes the barrier factor
in the band arose; that is to say: What element or elements in the band
halted the caterpillars in their attempted ascent to the foliage? Was
it the exhalation, or odor (chemical property) of the material; or
was it its softness, or viscidity (physical property)? Since the bands
did not function as well in cooler weather or as they aged, was their
decline in power or efficiency at such times due to their decreased viscosity, or firmer consistency; or was it due to the lessened odor?
These questions had a practical bearing on the development of an
efficient barrier, and attempts were made to obtain the desired information by means of field observations. These, however, were not
successful; indeed, they served only to develop decided differences
of opinion. Nor was there any help to be had from European
sources. Mr. L. H. Worthley, for instance, who spent the summer of
1912 in Europe investigating gipsy moth conditions for the Bureau
of Entomology, reported, on his return, that the forest authorities of
Saxony and Bavaria regarded the odor as the effective element, or
factor, in the band. But this information lacked applicability; for,
aside from the fact that these foresters dealt exclusively with raupenleim, a material possessing a somewhat stronger or more pungent
odor than the gipsy moth tree-banding material, their views were
based largely, if not entirely, on the behavior of another species of
insect, namely, the nun moth. It was possible, certainly conceivable,
that the two species might differ in their reaction; and an investigation of the literature on the subject disclosed the propriety of the
assumption, for, according to Judeich and Nitsche (*4, p. 845, 888*),
such a difference of behavior exists, at least in the case of the nun
and pine [8] moths, the caterpillars of the former, according to these
authors, avoiding or shunning the raupenleim to a far higher degree
than those of the latter. The uncertainty, it might be added, was
somewhat further increased, in view of the further statement of
Judeich and Nitsche (ibid.) that "Die Nonnenraupen vermeiden jede
Berührung des Leimes * * *," by the statement of Ratzeburg
(*9, p. 52*) to the effect that some of the caterpillars of the nun moth
will brave the odor of tar. Because, therefore, of the lack of definite
knowledge and the uncertainty and of the practical bearing that such
knowledge had on the elaboration of an efficient barrier, it was
deemed advisable to investigate the matter.

THE PROBLEM.

That the odor of the material exercises a restraining influence
could not be doubted. Neither, on the other hand, could one with a

---

[7] The term "odor" is used here in the common or ordinary (and older) sense, inclusive of the irritating quality of the material as perceived by the nasal mucous membrane.
Properly speaking, of course, the latter property of materials is not generally olfactory
(*5, p. 165, 169*). In this connection the writer wishes to thank Prof. G. H. Parker, professor of zoology, Harvard University, for the courtesy of allowing him to read portions
of his forthcoming book dealing with the chemical sense in vertebrates and for other suggestions.
[8] *Bombyx pini* L. (" der Kiefernspinner ").

knowledge of the habits and behavior of insects and the action of banding materials in general doubt that the soft and semiviscid condition of the material acts as a bar. As it presented itself to the writer, therefore, the problem seemed to be really a matter of determining the relative values of the two factors; that is, which of the two is primary and will by itself constitute the effective, or the more effective, barrier against the gipsy moth caterpillars. As to procedure, the problem appeared to be a matter of devising a material with an odor like or very similar, and similar in degree of pungency, to the gipsy moth tree-banding material which would readily solidify or stiffen without materially losing in the process its odor-emitting quality, and this was to be used against the caterpillars in the form of firm or more or less solid, odorous bands, in connection with odorless check bands, both viscous and solid.

EXPERIMENTAL WORK.

The basal solid ingredient which suggested itself as possibly best meeting the requirements for such a material was ordinary white wheat flour. Flour is itself odorless, possesses the property of readily becoming firm, or of solidifying after being mixed with ordinary liquids, and is very easily obtained. Furthermore, it can very easily, by merely mixing with water, be made into a soft and somewhat pasty odorless material which can be utilized for check bands.

Accordingly, such flour[9] was mixed with coal-tar neutral oil or with a mixture of coal-tar pitch and coal-tar neutral oil, and placed in the form of bands on sheets of white paper laid on a horizontal surface and also around peeled upright wooden stakes. White paper and peeled stakes were used merely to facilitate observation. The caterpillars tested included all stages, beginning with the second. Soft and semiviscid odorless bands, made of flour and water, of flour and molasses, and of molasses alone, were used as checks.

In summarizing the results of these tests, it may be said that the stiff or solid odorous bands, while exercising a repellent and restraining influence to a considerable degree, proved no absolute bar to the caterpillars. The soft and semiviscid odorless bands, on the other hand, were never crossed, although they were approached with far less hesitation and were, on the whole, touched more often and were even eaten. The bands on the horizontal surface were crossed more readily than those placed in the form of rings on the upright stakes, and, in general, the bands were less effective against the larger or more advanced stages of the caterpillars. The latter statement applies more particularly to the horizontal bands. The caterpillars— the larger ones in particular—seemed to have some difficulty in maintaining a " foothold " on the bands on the stakes, but this seems to have been due, in part at least, to the yielding and somewhat friable nature of the bands.

SERIES I.

The following illustrations, taken from numerous experiments or tests, will show in a detailed way the behavior of the caterpillars with reference to the stiff or solid odorous band series.

---

[9] Putty, as a substitute for flour, was later also used but proved less satisfactory.

EXPERIMENT A.

(Day dull and rather cool.)

ELEMENTS.

Caterpillar.

Fourth stage; not very far advanced, rather small for the stage.

Bands (horizontal).[10]

1. Flour paste band made of wheat flour and water, about $\frac{7}{8}$ inch high, $1\frac{1}{4}$ inches wide, $5\frac{1}{2}$ inches long. **2.** Solid band made of flour and water (hardened), $\frac{1}{4}$ inch high, $1\frac{3}{4}$ inches wide, 6 inches long, sides practically vertical. **3.** Solid band made of flour and coal-tar neutral oil (at rate of $1\frac{3}{4}$ ounces flour and $\frac{5}{8}+$ ounce oil), $\frac{1}{4}$ inch high, $1\frac{1}{2}$ inches wide, $5\frac{1}{2}$ inches long. **4.** Solid band made of flour and coal-tar neutral oil (at rate of 2 ounces flour and $1+$ ounce oil), $\frac{7}{8}$ inch high, $1\frac{7}{8}$ inches wide, $4\frac{1}{2}$ inches long, sides vertical. **5.** Solid band made of flour and coal-tar neutral oil (at rate of 2 ounces flour and $1\frac{1}{2}$ ounces oil), about $\frac{1}{4}$ inch high, $1\frac{7}{8}$ inches wide, and $5\frac{1}{4}$ inches long, sides vertical.

All on sheets of white paper.

TESTS.

Band 1: 9.25 a. m.

The caterpillar was placed five distinct times on the sheet of paper 6 inches from and facing the band, and during about one-half hour made 16 attempts to cross the band, but backed out or turned away each time it came more or less in contact with the band.

Band 2: 9.55 a. m.

The caterpillar was placed twice 6 inches from the band, and *crossed each time* without very much hesitation.

Band 3, *with marked coal-tar neutral oil odor,* somewhat damp to touch: 10.25 a. m.

The caterpillar was placed 6 inches from and facing the band. It approached within 2 inches of the band, then turned at an angle and went around the end of the band.

The caterpillar was placed again in the same position. It stopped short and turned somewhat at an angle when about 2 inches from the band but soon resumed a straight course, swung upon the band on reaching it, and *crawled across.*

The caterpillar was placed a third time. It stopped short and turned away from the band when within about $\frac{1}{4}$ inch of it and after crawling along it for a short distance, about $\frac{1}{4}$ inch away from it, it veered abruptly and crawled away.

Placed a fourth time, the caterpillar stopped and swung its head three times when about $\frac{1}{4}$ inch from the band, then continued, and on reaching the band (at a slight angle) it swung upon it with the first pair of legs, but after lingering on the band 2 or 3 seconds it swung off and crawled away.

Band 4, *with marked odor,* somewhat damp to touch: 11 a. m.

The caterpillar was placed 6 inches from and facing the band. It paused when about $4\frac{1}{2}$ inches away and again at a distance of $\frac{1}{4}$ inch and swung its head two or three times; stretched forward when about $\frac{1}{8}$ inch away and apparently came in contact with the band; then turned and crawled away.

The caterpillar was placed again. It paused when about $2\frac{1}{4}$ inches away and again at about $\frac{1}{4}$ inch, then stretched toward the band and after some hesitation swung upon it (with the first pair of legs) and *hesitatingly crawled up and across.*

When placed a third time, the caterpillar got to within about $\frac{1}{8}$ inch of the band, swung its head several times, turned and crawled away.

Placed for the fourth time, the caterpillar approached within about $\frac{7}{8}$ inch of the band and turned away, but soon swung back, and after getting upon the band with the first pair of legs, swung down and crawled away.

Being placed for the fifth time, the caterpillar stopped about $\frac{1}{8}$ inch from the band and swung its head two or three times, then resumed, and on reaching the band presently at a slight angle, it swung on with the first pair of legs,

---

[10] The gipsy moth tree-banding material band used on trees in the control work against the gipsy moth is $1\frac{3}{8}$ inch wide and $\frac{3}{32}$ inch thick, and is rectangular in form (*2, p. 10*).

but swung down almost immediately. It turned toward the band again, however, after crawling along it for a short distance, about ¼ inch away, and, on reaching it, swung on a second time and hesitatingly *crawled up and across.*

Band 5, *odor quite marked,* somewhat damp to touch: 11.40 a. m.

The caterpillar was placed 6 inches from and facing the band. It hesitated when about ⅛ inch from it, then went to it and swung on with two pairs of legs, but swung down after lingering on it a few moments. Then it moved along the band nearly to the end, at a distance of about ¼ inch, when it suddenly swung away still farther and crawled away.

Placed again, the caterpillar turned out of a straight course slightly, when about ⅜ inch from the band, and again when about ⅛ inch away; it then stretched toward the band and brushed it with its mouth parts, following which it swung away and crawled off the sheet of paper.

The caterpillar was placed a third time. It paused when within ⅛ inch of the band, then moved closer, swung on with two pairs of legs, and brushed the band with its mouth parts three times in succession. Then it swung down and crawled away.

Placed the fourth time, the caterpillar turned at right angles when about ¼ inch from the band and crawled away.

When placed the fifth time, the caterpillar approached within about ⅛ inch of the band, hesitated, stretched forward, and got on the band with the first pair of legs. After getting on a little farther, it swung off and crawled away—11.50 a. m.

For the sixth time the caterpillar was placed (1.25 p. m.). It turned when close to the band and crawled away.

At the seventh placing the caterpillar swung upon the band with the first pair of legs, then swung off; soon after it swung up with two pairs and swung off, but very soon after swung on a third time and *crawled hesitatingly across.*

EXPERIMENT B.

(Day more or less bright and fairly warm.)

ELEMENTS.

Caterpillar.

Fifth stage; quite well along, fairly large.

Bands (horizontal).

1. Flour paste band made of flour and water, $\frac{1}{16}$ to $\frac{1}{12}$ inch high, 1¼ inches wide, 6 inches long. **2.** Solid band made of flour and water (hardened), ¼ inch high, 1½ inches wide, 6 inches long, sides practically vertical. **3.** Solid band made of flour and a mixture of coal-tar pitch and coal-tar neutral oil (at the rate of 2 ounces flour and 1½ ounces pitch and oil mixture), ¼ to $\frac{5}{16}$ inch high, about 1½ inches wide, 5 inches long, sides vertical.

All on sheets of white paper.

TESTS.

Band 1: 2.35 p. m.

The caterpillar was placed nine distinct times on the sheet of paper, 5 inches from and facing the band. During the course of 42 minutes it made 15 attempts to cross the band, but backed out or turned away each time it came more or less in contact with it.

Band 2: 3.25 p. m.

The caterpillar was placed 5 inches from the band, as in the preceding test. It turned at an angle when about 2 inches from the band and crawled around the end.

The caterpillar was placed again. It swung upon the band with the first pair of legs and after some slight hesitation *crawled up and then across.*

Placed a third time, the caterpillar turned out of a straight course somewhat when about 3 inches from the band; then got to the band and touched it with its mouth parts several times in quick succession; *then crawled up slowly and across.*

Band 3, *with strong odor,* somewhat damp to touch: 4.15 p. m.

The caterpillar was placed 5 inches from the band, as before. It turned away slightly on reaching and touching the band with its mouth parts three or four times in rapid succession, but soon turned back and, after touching it as before, turned and crawled away, shaking its head nervously.

The caterpillar was placed again. It paused and shook its head when about ½ inch from the band, then hesitatingly and nervously moved to the band and touched it lightly with its mouth parts two or three times in rapid succession, brushed it with two pairs of legs, and turned away. It turned toward the band again, however, soon after, and swung up to the top with two pairs of legs, but after touching it with its mouth parts and swinging its head several times it swung down and crawled away.

Placed a third time, the caterpillar hesitated about ¼ inch away, then moved to the band and after touching it with its mouth parts lightly and brushing it w th two pairs of legs, swung down. It repeated this shortly after and crawled away.

Placed a fourth time, the caterpillar began to hesitate when about ¾ inch from the band. but finally reached it and continuing hesitatingly *crawled up and across*, swinging its head constantly while on the band.

The caterpillar was placed a fifth time. It swung upon the side of the band ·with its first pair or two pairs of legs and touched it lightly and rapidly with its mouth parts two or three times and swung down, but soon afterwards it moved toward the band again and after a slight pause swung up a second time (with two pairs of legs). After a few moments it started to swing off, but swung back almost immediately and after some further hesitation crawled up *and then across*—4.45 p. m.

Experiment C.

(Day bright and warm.)

ELEMENTS.

Caterpillar.

Fourth stage; fairly well along, medium size for the stage.

Bands (rings on stakes).

1. Flour paste band made of flour and water, 1¼ inches wide, ⅟₁₆ inch thick. **2.** Solid band made of flour and water (hardened), 2 inches wide, ¼ to ⅝ inch thick, bottom plane nearly flat. **3.** Solid band made of flour and coal-tar neutral oil (at rate of 2 ounces flour and 1 ounce oil), 1¼ inches wide, ⅟₁₆+ inch thick, bottom plane practically flat.

All on peeled upright stakes, 20 inches high and about 2¼ inches in circumference, lower edge of bands about 8½ inches from platform to,which stakes were fixed.

TESTS.

Band 1: 1.45 p. m.

The caterpillar crawled up each of the four distinct times that it was placed at the base of and facing the stake, and during the course of 35 minutes made 40 attempts to cross the band. but backed out or turned away each time it came more or less in contact with it.

Band 2: 2.45 p. m.

The caterpillar was placed twice at the foot of the stake, as before. It crawled up *and crossed* the band without hesitation each time.

Band 3, *with marked odor:* 3.20 p. m.

The caterpillar was placed at the foot of the stake, as before. It seemed to hesitate slightly about ½ inch below the band, but with that exception moved right up to the band and paused; then, after crawling somewhat, swung upon the band and started upward. It progressed slowly, however, and when on with the anter'or half of the body fell over backward, but clung to the stake with the last pair of prolegs. On swinging back to the band it resumed its upward climb. As before, its progress was slow; it was constantly working its legs and mouth parts and constantly applying the latter to the band: scratching up the surface. It persevered, however, and finally *crossed the band,* coming to rest about 1½ inches above it. Nearly two minutes was occupied in crossing.

The caterpillar was placed again. It crawled up slowly, came to rest about one-half inch below the band, and did not become active again for about four minutes, when it swung its head two or three times and moved up to within one-third inch. Here it rested for two minutes, and on being touched at the anal end with a small camel's-hair brush started upward again. On reaching the band it swung upon it with the first pair of legs, but after touching it with its mouth parts a number of times in rapid succession it swung off. It swung up a second time soon afterwards and swung down again after behaving as above. Very soon after it swung on a third time, but after touching the band with its mouth parts several times in quick succession, as before, it swung down again and came to rest about 1½ inches below the band. It remained thus. for four minutes, when, following application of the brush to the anal end, it turned round and crawled down the stake.

Placed a third time, the caterpillar paused and turned out of a straight course about one-fourth inch below the band and on reaching it swung upon it with the first pair of legs. It turned downward on swinging off and came to rest with its head about 2 inches below the band. It fell off the stake a few minutes later when its anal end was touched with the brush.

Placed once more, the caterpillar came to rest about two-thirds inch below the band. On being touched with the brush, about two minutes later, it moved up to within one-half inch and became motionless again, remaining thus for several minutes, except for swinging its head three times. It became active again on being touched once more with the brush, and on reaching the band it swung on with the first pair of legs. After swinging off and crawling somewhat, it swung on and off a second time. It swung on and off a third time soon after, and immediately afterwards swung on a fourth time, and continuing upward worked its way up, by degrees, *and across*—4.10 p. m. It took it a minute to cross.

In both instances, in which the band was crossed, the crossing was accomplished by a pawing-like motion of the legs and constant motion of the mouth parts, and by the continual application of the latter to the band.

Well defined as were the results of this series of tests, of which the above are examples, they were nevertheless not altogether satisfying. The fact is that the solid odorous bands, though strongly charged with odor, were not—and could not be made—as strong in this respect as the gipsy moth tree-banding material bands, owing to the limited capacity of the flour to absorb and to hold the liquid banding material ingredients. The results were indicative, indeed, but hardly conclusive.

SERIES II.

To obtain more conclusive results, another series of tests was initiated in which the odor condition was like or more nearly like that in the gipsy moth tree-banding material. Actual gipsy moth tree-banding material bands were used here, the bands being bridged (covered) with strips of medium-meshed cheesecloth (29 by 34 threads per square inch) of various widths. This combination fulfilled the conditions in an excellent manner; the soft, or viscid, quality of the material was eliminated and the odor apparently was not to any great extent interfered with. This was particularly true in the case of narrow bridges. As in the first series, horizontal bands on white paper, as well as ring bands around peeled vertical stakes, were used. Bands made of ordinary white flour and water (flour paste), of flour and molasses, of molasses alone, and of a commercial sticky tree-banding material were used as checks. and they served very satisfactorily. The ingredients of the gipsy moth tree-and n material could not be used in the making of an odorless bandi g

The following typical illustrations, Experiments A, B, and C, show the behavior of the caterpillars in this series:

EXPERIMENT A.

(Day bright. fairly warm.)

ELEMENTS.

1. Caterpillar.

Fourth stage; good size for stage, pretty well advanced, pretty well fed, active.

2. Odorous band (horizontal).

Gipsy moth tree-banding material, $1\frac{1}{2}$ inches high, $2\frac{1}{4}$ inches wide, 6 inches long, sides vertical, on a sheet of white paper. Band br'dged about in middle with strip of cheesecloth (medium mesh, 29 by 34 threads per square inch) 1 inch wide; cloth fitting closely to band at all poin s and extending from base of one side to base of opposite side. *Odor of band strong,* irritating writer's nasal membrane at a distance of 2 or more feet.

3.·**Strip of stiff white paper** 4 inches long and 1 inch wide.[11]

4. Paste band (horizontal).

Flour paste band made of white wheat flour and water, $\frac{1}{20}$ to $\frac{1}{16}$ inch high, 1 inch wide, 3 inches long, on a strip of paper like and of the same dimensions as 3.

TESTS.

The caterpillar was placed on the paper 6 inches from and facing the odorous band (2) at 2.43 p. m. It made straight for the band for about 2 inches, then turned at a diagonal, and con inuing in the same general direction went around the end of the band. It approached within 2 inches of the band.

Second placing (as before) : The caterpillar turned out of a stra ght course 3 inches from the band, and when within $\frac{1}{2}$ inch of it veered away still more (now parallel to the band), and, crawling along the band at that distance— its longer hairs brushing the band—'t crawled away.

Third placing: The results were similar to those just described.

Fourth placing: The results were similar to those last described.

Fifth placing: The caterpillar turned out of a straight course about 4 inches from the band and went around the end. It approached within 1 inch of the band.

Sixth placing: The caterpillar turned out of a straight course abou' 4 inches from the band, veered off still more when about $1\frac{3}{4}$ inches away, and crawled off the sheet of paper parallel to the band at the lat er distance.

Seventh placing: The caterpillar moved straight to within about $\frac{1}{8}$ inch of the band and hesitated, then continued to the band and apparently touched it—with the mouth parts as well as with the first pair of legs—then turned away. It repeated the procedure soon after on the adjoining side of the bridge, and crawled away.

Eighth placing: The caterpillar paused about $\frac{1}{2}$ inch from the band, then moved closer and swung upon the side with two pairs of legs, but swung off after touching it with its mouth parts, and after another pause backed slowly away. Soon it moved up to the band again and af er touching it with its mouth parts turned away nervously. Soon after this it approached close to the band a third time, but turned away apparently wi'hout touching it; then crawled away.

N'nth placing: The caterpillar began to turn out of a straight course about 1 inch from the band but turned toward it again when the strip of paper (3) was placed in its way (the paper being held at one end of the longer axis and interposed in the way of the caterpillar with the shorter axis either vertical or at an angle to the horizontal plane of the sheet of white paper on which the caterpillar was crawling). After some hesitation the caterp llar swung upon the side of the band with the first pair of legs, and after touching the band wi:h its mouth parts, swung off and crawled away, crawling across the interposed strip of paper.

Tenth placing: The caterpillar turned at an angle about 3 inches from the band, but veered back somewhat when the strip of paper was placed·in its way. It crawled right over the strip of paper, however, when about $1\frac{3}{4}$ inches from the band, and crawled away, rearing and swinging its head.

Eleventh placing: The caterpillar turned out of a straight course about 3 inches away and stopped for a few seconds when the strip of paper was interposed, then to within $\frac{1}{2}$ inch of the band—guided by means of the strip of paper—and paused. Following another pause, about $\frac{1}{4}$ inch away, it turned and crawled away over the strip of paper.

---

[11] This strip of paper, identical with that on which the paste band was placed, was used, as will be seen below, in the same manner as 4, and was designed as a check upon the latter—to make sure it was the soft and viscid quality of the band that forced the caterpillar on the bridged odorous band rather than the mere object or obstacle placed in its way.

Twelfth placing: The caterpillar turned out of a straight course about 4 inches from the band and stopped for a few seconds when the strip of paper was interposed. Being guided by means of the strip of paper it got to within ½ inch of the band, though constantly trying to turn out of the course. Following a pause it started to turn away again, but the strip of paper arrested it once more. Then it reached the band, but turned away almost immediately. It is impossible to say whether it touched the band. Crawling upon the strip of paper it reached over to the band and got on it with two pairs of legs, but after touching it with its mouth parts turned away. Getting over on the opposite side of the strip of paper, it crawled off and away.

Thirteenth placing: The caterpillar began to turn out of a straight course about 1½ inches from the band, but was arrested by the strip of paper. Following a pause it continued hesitatingly toward the band; when about ½ inch from it (*opposite the bridge*), it crawled up the strip of paper and stretched toward the bare part of the band; it turned away, however, and getting over on the opposite side of the strip of paper it crawled off and away.

Fourteenth placing: The caterpillar started to turn out of its course about 1½ inches from the band after it had stopped and reared and swung its head three or four times, but turned in the direction of the band again when the strip of paper was placed in its way. It stopped again about ¼ inch away (*opposite the bridge*), and then turned and crawled upon the strip of paper, the edge of the farther end of which rested against the band at one side of the bridge. On getting closer to the band it swung on the bare part of the latter and apparently touched it twice, then over on the bridged part and swung off almost immediately. It reached forward toward the band again soon after, hesitatingly, but swung away again. It is impossible to say whether it touched. Turning around, it got over on the opposite side of the strip of paper, and finally crawled off and away.

Fifteenth placing: The caterpillar halted and started to turn away when within about 1¼ inches (*opposite the bridge*), but turned in the direction of the band again when the strip of paper was interposed. It crawled upon the strip of paper, however, when about ½ inch from the band, and when close to the latter swung upon it (the bare part) and apparently touched it twice lightly, then swung in the opposite direction and landed on the bridged part. After brushing the cloth three times with the first pair of legs and mouth parts it swung over on the bare part again and then back to the strip of paper, then crawled over, hesitatingly, on the opposite side of the latter and crawled down and away.

Sixteenth placing: The caterpillar was stopped from turning out of its course about 2 inches from the band by means of the strip of paper. After some hesitation on its part, during which it started to crawl up the side of the paper rather than to continue in the direction of the band, it started toward the latter, the strip of paper keeping it in its course. It stopped again about 1 inch away (*opposite the bridge*), and on resuming crawled up the strip of paper, but when within ½ inch of the band it stopped once more. Finally it turned away, and after some hesitation got on the opposite side of the paper and crawled off and away.

Seventeenth placing: The caterpillar stopped and turned at a right angle about ½ inch from the band, and turned completely around and started to crawl in the opposite direction when the strip of paper was placed in its path. It turned completely around a second time when the strip of paper was again interposed, but kept right on, crawled upon the strip of paper when it was interposed a third time, and crawled off it and away, after getting, hesitatingly, to the opposite side of the same. (The edge of the farther end of the strip of paper rested against the band each time it was interposed, and always at either of adjoining sides of the bridge, so that up to the time it crawled upon the strip of paper the caterpillar was constantly opposite the bridged portion of the band.)

Eighteenth placing: The caterpillar was placed once more 6 inches from the band[12] (now 4.17 p. m.). It stopped (*opposite the bridge*), reared once or twice, and started to turn out of its straight course, about 1½ inches away, but turned in the direction of the band again on touching the *paste band* (4) which was placed in its way (horizontally). On reaching the band (which it had approached hesitatingly) it swung upon the bridge with all legs, and from here, after some hesitation, over on the bare part, but swung back to the bridge almost immediately and started slowly upward (the cloth now being thoroughly

---

[12] Unless otherwise stated or implied, the term "band" refers to the odorous band.

moist and dark, as it had been for some time, saturated with the banding material). Continuing nervously the caterpillar *crossed the band* and crawled away. It got off the bridge, on bare material, once, when on top of the band, but with no more than two pairs of legs, and drew back quickly.

Nineteenth placing: The caterpillar hesitated, reared, and started to turn out of its course about 5½ inches from the band, but on touching the paste band with the first pair of legs, it turned toward the band again. It did not advance, however, but reared, swung its head, and backed up. Then, swinging to one side, it started to crawl out of a straight course again (in the opposite direction from that in the former attempt), but on touching the paste band, which had been placed in its way again, with the first pair of legs at least, it turned once more toward the band and when within about 4½ inches of it, stopped. It now swung its head and turned to one side, and on touching the paste band, which was waiting for it, it swung in the opposite direction and started to turn away still farther from the band. On being interrupted by the paste band again, it turned once more toward the band, and, after some hesitation, started forward. Stopped about ½ inch away (*opposite the bridge*), and after rearing and swinging its head, it turned at a right angle and started crawling parallel to the band. On touching the paste band it turned completely around and started in the opposite direction, but on touching the interposed paste band again it turned in the direction of the band once more. On reaching the band it hesitatingly swung upon the bridged portion, and, after brushing the cloth with its legs, it swung over on the bare part. Then, after touching here once or twice, it swung off the band altogether. It swung back, however, on touching the edge of the paste band, which was waiting for it, then over on the bridge with the first pair of legs, and after touching here with its mouth parts, it swung to the bare part again, then back to the bridged portion, then *up, hesitatingly and nervously, and to the opposite side and down the latter*—4.55 p. m. The caterpillar got off the bridge, on bare material, soon after reaching the top of the band, but with no more than two pairs of legs, and drew back quickly.

EXPERIMENT B.

(Day bright and warm.)

ELEMENTS.

1. Caterpillar.

Fifth stage; medium size for stage, fairly well advanced, pretty well fed, active.

2. Odorous band (horizontal).

Gipsy moth tree-banding material, as in Experiment A, except ¼ inch longer (6¼ inches long), *with strong odor.* Bridge moist and dark.

3. Strip of stiff white paper 4 inches long and 1 inch wide.

4. Molasses-flour band (horizontal).

Molasses-flour mixture (molasses and white wheat flour), $\frac{1}{20}$ inch high, 1 inch wide, 3 inches long, on a strip of paper like and of same dimensions as 3; of about the same consistency as the commercial sticky tree-banding material used in these experiments—somewhat more viscid than the flour paste used in Experiment A.

TESTS.

The caterpillar was placed on the sheet of paper 6 inches from and facing the odorous band (2) at 1.51 p. m. It halted 5½ inches away and reared twice, repeated this movement 4½ inches away, and reared again two or three times at a distance of 4 inches. Then it turned slowly around and crawled away, rearing from time to time as it did so.

The caterpillar was placed again as before. It hesitated and turned its head somewhat from side to side at the start, and stopped and reared three times about 4½ inches away; repeated this at a distance of 3½ inches, and stopped and reared again when within about 2¾ inches. Finally it turned at a right angle and crawled away.

When placed the third time the caterpillar hesitated and reared three distinct times during the first 4 inches of its course toward the band, then turned out of its course somewhat and made its way, hesitatingly, to within ¼ inch. Here it stopped, reared, stretched forward, and brushed the bare part of the band with the first pair of legs and mouth parts. As it turned away the strip of paper (3) was placed in its way (as in Experiment A), whereupon it turned completely around and began to crawl in the opposite direction (parallel to the band). As the strip of paper was again interposed it stopped altogether (*opposite the bridge*). It backed up finally, turned, and began crawling in the direction away from the band, but as it came close to the strip of paper, which was interposed again, it turned at an angle and started (diagonally) toward the band—the strip of paper guiding it in that general direction. It got upon the strip of paper, however, when about $\frac{3}{4}$ inch from the band, and soon got off again, but after a pause got on once more and after getting over on the opposite side it crawled off it and away.

At the fourth placing, the caterpillar halted at the very start and had to be prodded (one-half minute later) to get it started again. It responded very slowly. It swung its head slightly, and, turning at right angles, started to crawl away (parallel to the band). It executed another right-angled turn as the strip of paper was placed in its way (now facing away from the band), and still another, when the paper was interposed as it started to crawl directly away from the band, being now parallel to the band. It halted and finally came to rest when the strip of paper was placed in its way a third time. It began to crawl about $1\frac{1}{2}$ minutes later, and as the strip of paper was placed in its way it turned in the direction opposite from the band; very soon after, when the strip of paper was interposed again, it turned at right angles (parallel to the band again) and started to crawl away once more. This time it crawled upon the interposed strip of paper and after crawling on it a short distance toward the band, it got on the opposite side and finally crawled off it, pausing and swinging its head before crawling away. At no time was the caterpillar nearer than 5 inches to the band.

The caterpillar was placed a fifth time. It started to turn out of its course at once and was redirected. Finally, after a good deal of hesitation throughout, it approached within $1\frac{1}{2}$ inches of the band.[13] It turned at right angles here and started crawling parallel to the band, but on getting some of its legs into the molasses-flour band (4), which was placed in its way (horizontally), it turned in the direction opposite from the band; soon after—after touching the molasses-flour band as before—it turned at right angles a third time, and after crawling somewhat (parallel to the band) and touching the interposed molasses-flour band again (three times) it turned once more away from the band. It turned at right angles a fifth time, soon after, because of the molasses-flour band (bringing it parallel to the band again), and on touching the molasses-flour band again it came once more turned in the direction of the band. It swung upon the side of the band, on finally reaching it, then down, but swung back on it on touching the molasses-flour band (which was waiting for it at the foot of the band), and landed at the foot of the bridge on finally swinging off a second time. It swung upon the bridge soon after and *crawled up and finally across to the opposite side*—tumbled off in going down latter side. Once, while on top of the band, it got partly off the cloth with some of its legs on bare material, but soon got back.

Placed a sixth time, the caterpillar swung upon the side of the band on finally reaching it (having crawled very slowly and hesitatingly from within about 1 inch), and after lingering a few moments swung down. It swung on and off again shortly afterwards, and after a pause started crawling parallel to the band (at a distance of about $\frac{3}{4}$ inch); on touching the molasses-flour band, which was placed in its way, it stopped and backed up. On resuming and touching the same a second time it turned at right angles and started crawling directly away from the band. It turned the other way again, however, on touching the molasses-flour band a third time (now parallel to the band again), and on touching it a fourth time it turned and headed directly toward the band. It swung up on the side on reaching it and finally got on with its whole body but soon tumbled off, landing at the foot of the bridge. Then it swung upon the latter (on the side of the band) with some of its legs, and after brushing it with these it swung over on the uncovered part but soon swung back to the cloth, then again to the bare part, then off entirely and started crawling parallel to the band; on touching the molasses-flour band it turned and commenced crawling directly away from the band. It turned at right angles again, however, on touching the molasses-flour band again, twice (now parallel to the band again), and after touching again shortly after, three times in succession, it turned and headed directly toward the band once more. It swung up again

---

[13] See footnote on p. 9.

on the side of the band and off, slowly, landing again at the foot of the bridge, then up again on the bridge and continuing upward, slowly, along the edge of the cloth, *reached the top; then, slowly, crawled to the opposite side and finally down the latter*—4 p. m.   The caterpillar got off the cloth somewhat—on bare material—two or three times, on its way across and down the opposite side. It apparently never got into the molasses-flour band with more than the first pair of legs and often only with the mouth parts.

Similarly, by means of flour-paste and molasses-flour bands, caterpillars were forced to cross even higher gipsy moth tree-banding material bands with narrower bridges—½ inch and ¼ inch wide.

EXPERIMENT C.

(Day bright and very warm.)

ELEMENTS.

1. Caterpillar.

Fifth stage; rather small for the stage. pretty well advanced. well fed.

2. Odorous band (ring on stake).

Gipsy moth tree-banding material, good $\frac{1}{16}$ inch thick and 2 inches wide, around a peeled stake 2¼ inches in circumference and 21 inches high, lower plane of band 6 inches from platform to which stake was fixed; lower plane of band quite flat, upper somewhat less so. *With very strong odor.* Band bridged with strip of cheesecloth (medium mesh, 29 by 34 threads per square inch) ⅓ inch wide; cloth fitting closely to band at all points and extending from inner circle of lower plane to inner circle of upper—not extending beyond band. Cloth stained dark by material, and odor over it almost as strong as over unbridged part.

3. Strip of stiff white paper 4 inches long and 1 inch wide.

4. Paste band (horizontal).

Flour paste made of flour and water, $\frac{1}{20}$ inch high, 1 inch wide, and 3 inches long, on a strip of paper like and of same d'mensions as 3: paste somewhat more viscid, or sticky, than gipsy moth tree-banding material.

TESTS.

The caterpillar was placed on the stake 4 inches below and facing the odorous band (2) (11.42 a. m.). It did not begin to crawl until it was prodded, then crawled right up to the band, except that it swung its head when about 2½ inches and again when 2 inches below it, and swung on with the first pair of legs, but after touching it with its mouth parts swung hastily off. This was soon repeated, and shortly after it swung on and off again, after touching it, hesitatingly, with its mouth parts twice. Soon, however, it swung on the band a fourth time, and after touching it as before swung hastily off; then turned downward and crawled down the stake. It rubbed its mouth parts against the stake several times as it swung off the band and turned downward.

The caterpillar was placed again as before and crawled to within about 3 inches below the band, after being redirected upward at the very start, and reared and swung its head violently three times. It repeated this once or twice 2 inches below, thence crawled cautiously and when close to the band stretched upward and got on it with the first pair of legs, but swung down to about ¾ inch below, after touching it with the mouth parts twice in quick succession. Then, after circling nearly one-half the stake, it reached the band again and swung on again, hesitatingly. with the first pair of legs, but swung down again quickly after touching it again with the mouth parts; then turned and crawled slowly down the stake.

Placed a third time, the caterpillar swung its head and hesitated at the very start, but continued upward, swinging its head frequently, and when about 1½ inches below the band slowed down still more and became still more hesitant. Finally, when close to the band, it reached up to it with the first pair of legs, and after touching it twice in quick succession with the mouth parts also, it turned away. Soon afterwards it swung on a second time with the first pair of legs, hesitatingly (near the edge of the bridge), and after touching it with the mouth parts swung over on the bridge, then off the band altogether. After a pause it swung on a third time, thence over on bare material; after touching the latter with the mouth parts it swung off altogether and turning around started downward. It paused about ⅓ inch below the band when the strip of paper (3) was placed in its way, horizontally (in horizontal relation to stake), then got on the paper and finally on the writer's hand and arm.

The caterpillar was placed a fourth time. It began rearing and swinging its head quite violently when about 3 inches below the band, and at 2 inches below reared and swung its head so violently as to turn almost completely around. It did not advance, however, on swinging back to its former position on the stake; instead it reared, swung round as before, and started downward, the interposed strip of paper failing to check it or to cause it to turn upward again.

The caterpillar was placed a fifth time. It hesitated noticeably at the start and swung its head two or three times when about 1 inch from the band, thence crawled slowly and when close to the band reached up and touched it with the first pair of legs and mouth parts, following which it swung down. This was repeated soon after, and again soon after that, touching it three times instead of once. After a pause about 1 inch below the band, it got to the band again, slowly, and swinging on as before touched it twice, then swung down and crawled downward, coming to rest finally on the strip of paper, which was placed in its way (about 3 inches below the band), and which it approached without hesitation. On becoming active soon afterwards it turned around, got to the stake again, and started to crawl up it, but swung down almost at once, and, turning round, crawled the full length of the strip of paper to the writer's hand.

When placed a sixth time the caterpillar hesitated at the start, crawled up slowly, and stopped altogether about 1 inch below the band (*opposite the bridge*). On resuming soon after (at a diagonal), it got to the band (bare part) and swung up toward it but swung quickly down—touching it lightly if at all. Then it got around nearer to the bridged part and swung up, close to the latter, with the first pair of legs, and after touching the bare material with its mouth parts swung over on the bridge. Touching here (on the cloth) once or twice, it swung off the band altogether. It swung back, however, on the bridge, and, continuing upward, along the edge, *crawled up and across*. (The cloth was moist—saturated—and the difference in odor between the bridged and bare parts of the band was slight.)

The caterpillar was placed a seventh time. It moved up slowly, and when about ¾ inch below the band [14] reared and swung the fore part of its body three times, seemingly as if it might turn downward each time. This was repeated about ¼ inch farther up; then the caterpillar crawled hesitatingly to the band and reached up with the first pair of legs, but on touching it also with its mouth parts it swung down quickly and turned downward. It turned upward again, however, after getting twice into the flour-paste band (4) (which was placed in its way in the same manner as 3) with its mouth parts—for several seconds the first time and for two seconds the next—but soon turned downward and on getting into the paste band again, with the first pair of legs as well as with the mouth parts, it turned upward once more. After two or three pauses and some swinging of the head, it reached the band (on the opposite side from the bridge). It swung on with the first pair of legs, but on touching it with the mouth parts it swung quickly down again. It swung on and off, as above, at short intervals, at different points on the band, six more times—touching it thrice, several times before swinging down—following which, the eighth time, it swung upon the bridged part, and in this instance *it continued upward—hesitatingly, and so crawled across*, continuing to the top of the stake (1.13 p. m.). The caterpillar got off the cloth slightly, on bare banding material, at least four times, twice on each side, while crossing.

Previous to this, caterpillars were, in the same manner, compelled to cross similar bands, with bridges respectively 1 inch, ¾ inch, and ¼ inch wide.

SERIES III.

Finally, in a third and last series, caterpillars in several instances were forced, by means of flour-paste (flour and water) and flour-molasses bands, into and on much higher (higher than themselves), and in some cases wider, naked (horizontal) gipsy moth tree-banding material bands; and in two cases where the banding material was rather firm the caterpillars actually crossed the bands. On the other hand, efforts in the reverse process; as a check measure, to compel

---

[14] See footnote on p. 9.

caterpillars to cross paste bands by means of interposed gipsy moth tree-banding material bands were unsuccessful. In one instance,. indeed, the caterpillar finally crossed the gipsy moth tree-banding material band. In the latter instances the two types of bands were of the same dimensions as regards height and width; about $\frac{1}{16}$ inch and 1 inch, respectively.

SUMMARY AND CONCLUSIONS.

That the two factors of (1) odor, and (2) soft and semiviscid condition, operate together in enabling the gipsy moth tree-banding material to halt the caterpillars in their efforts to ascend to the foliage, was clearly demonstrated by the qualitative tests described in this paper. The first series, in which the solid odorous bands were used, could not be considered conclusive, for physical or technical reasons (p. 7), but it indicated clearly that the first element, namely, odor, exercises at least a restraining influence. The second series, in which bands made of actual gipsy moth tree-banding material were used, demonstrated satisfactorily that the soft and semiviscid, or viscous, condition of the material is the basic or primary factor. The odor restrained, indeed, but when acting alone did not completely check; whatever "dislike" or "fear" it inspired was overcome sooner or later.[15] This series approximated closely to actual conditions, especially in the case of the narrowly bridged bands, in which the odor, after the strips of cloth became saturated with the material, was but little if at all interfered with or masked; indeed, the total odor emitted by some of these bands was far greater than would have been emitted, under the same conditions, by the smaller-sized "standard" band,[16] the odor being strong enough in the warm and rather confined atmosphere of the laboratory to irritate to a considerable degree, at a distance of about 2 feet, the nasal membrane of the writer. The various check bands used, namely, flour paste, flour-molasses, molasses, and also a commercial sticky tree-banding material, served very well, and if the last three were somewhat more viscid or "gluey" than the bands made from the gipsy moth tree-banding material, this fact was offset by the greater odor given off by the large size of the latter bands.

The caterpillars, it should be added, seemed to "dislike" or "fear" the odorless and nonirritating check bands in proportion as they were viscid, or "sticky," and they reacted to these very often, especially to the more viscid, fully as promptly as to the gipsy moth tree-banding material bands. This fact is further evidence of the importance of the viscid factor in the banding material, and is of value, obviously, in the elaboration of an efficient barrier band not only against gipsy moth caterpillars but also against any species of similar behavior. An illustration of the practical operation of this fact is perhaps seen in the efficiency of newly applied or newly combed bands of a commercial sticky tree-banding material, the odor or exhalation of which is weaker and otherwise less repellent than that of the gipsy moth tree-banding material, especially on warm days. An atmosphere consisting of, or heavily charged with, the exhalation or volatilized portion of the latter material, as in a container, will disable a cater-

---

[15] In nature, in response to such stimuli as light (positive heliotropism), and more especially, hunger, h "fear" would probably be overcome speedily.
[16] See footnote on p. 4.

pillar in a comparatively short time, even on days of moderate temperature. In case of actual contact, however, injury may be from an additional source—from the penetration of the material through the skin.[17]

The irritation or " burning " caused by the gipsy moth tree-banding material, as a result of contact, may therefore aid in repelling the caterpillars, especially if contact is with delicate and sensitive parts, such as the mouth parts. Again, since the latter are organs of taste, and in certain adult Lepidoptera at least the tarsi also act as such (*7, p. 202–203; 8, p. 80–81*), the sense of taste may be a factor. These considerations, however, should not affect the conclusion that *the viscous, or physical, condition is the more important, or primary, barrier factor in the band* as it ordinarily functions, which may be said to have been clearly demonstrated and which is borne out, so far as can be judged, by observations in the field. Indeed, since the head, the head appendages, and the legs of caterpillars seem to be well adapted for receiving olfactory stimuli (*6, p. 76*), we may perhaps also see in the rather rapid withdrawal of such parts the action of odor and thus additional evidence, or a confirmation of the other and more obvious conclusion, namely, that the two factors, i. e., the soft or semiviscid or viscous condition of the material, and the odor, or exhalation, of the material, are the chief factors which make the gipsy moth tree-banding material the efficient barrier that it is.

LITERATURE CITED.

(1) BURGESS, A. F., and GRIFFIN, E. L.
　　1917. A new tree-banding material for the control of the gipsy moth. *In* Jour. Econ. Ent., v. 10. no. 1, p. 131–135, pl. 6–7.
(2) COLLINS, C. W., and HOOD, Clifford E.
　　1920. Gipsy moth tree-banding material : how to make, use, and apply it. U. S. Dept. Agr. Bul. 899, 18 p., 4 fig., pl. 1–7.
(3) FORBUSH, E. H., and FERNALD, C. H.
　　1896. The gipsy moth (*Porthetria dispar* Linn.). Mass. State Bd. Agr. Rept., p. xli+495+c, 35+2 fig., 66 pl., 5 maps.
(4) JUDEICH, J. F., and NITSCHE, H.
　　1895. Lehrbuch der mitteleuropäischen forstinsektenkunde, Bd. II (Wien), p. xxii+737–1421, fig. 216–352, Taf. V–VIII.
(5) LUCIANI, L.
　　1917. Human physiology. Vol. IV. The sense organs. Trans. by F. A. Welby ; ed. by G. M. Holmes, p. x+519+4, 217 fig. London.
(6) McINDOO, N. E.
　　1919. The olfactory sense of lepidopterous larvae. *In* Ann. Ent. Soc. Amer., v. 12, no. 2, p. 65–84, 53 fig.
(7) MINNICH, D. E.
　　1921. An experimental study of the tarsal chemoreceptors of two nymphalid butterflies. *In* Jour. Exp. Zoöl., v. 33, no. 1, p. 173–203, 6 fig.
(8) ———.
　　1922. The chemical sensitivity of the tarsi of the red admiral butterfly, *Pyrameis atalanta* Linn. *In* Jour. Exp. Zoöl., v. 35, no. 1, p. 57–81, 3 fig.
(9) RATZEBURG, J. T. C.
　　1840. Die forst-insekten. Zweiter theil. die falter. p. v+252, Taf. I–XVI. Berlin.

---

[17] Severe " burning " may result if the material is placed upon and is allowed to penetrate the human skin.

ORGANIZATION OF THE UNITED STATES DEPARTMENT OF AGRICULTURE.

Secretary of Agriculture----------------- HENRY C. WALLACE.
Assistant Secretary---------------------- C. W. PUGSLEY.
Director of Scientific Work-------------- E. D. BALL.
Director of Regulatory Work-------------
Weather Bureau--------------------------- CHARLES F. MARVIN, Chief.
Bureau of Agricultural Economics-------- HENRY C. TAYLOR, Chief.
Bureau of Animal Industry--------------- JOHN R. MOHLER, Chief.
Bureau of Plant Industry---------------- WILLIAM A. TAYLOR, Chief.
Forest Service-------------------------- W. B. GREELEY, Chief.
Bureau of Chemistry--------------------- WALTER G. CAMPBELL, Acting Chief.
Bureau of Soils------------------------- MILTON WHITNEY, Chief.
Bureau of Entomology-------------------- L. O. HOWARD, Chief.
Bureau of Biological Survey------------- E. W. NELSON, Chief.
Bureau of Public Roads------------------ THOMAS H. MACDONALD, Chief.
Fixed Nitrogen Research Laboratory------ F. G. COTTRELL, Director.
Division of Accounts and Disbursements-. A. ZAPPONE, Chief.
Division of Publications---------------- JOHN L. COBBS, JR., Chief.
Library--------------------------------- CLARIBEL R. BARNETT, Librarian.
States Relations Service---------------- A. C. TRUE, Director.
Federal Horticultural Board------------- C. L. MARLATT, Chairman.
Insecticide and Fungicide Board--------- J. K. HAYWOOD, Chairman.
Packers and Stockyards Administration--⎫CHESTER MORRILL,
Grain Future Trading Act Administration-⎭ Assistant to the Secretary.
Office of the Solicitor----------------- R. W. WILLIAMS, Solicitor.

This bulletin is a contribution from

Bureau of Entomology-------------------- L. O. HOWARD, Chief.
   Gipsy Moth and Brown-Tail Moth In-
   vestigations------------------------ A. F. BURGESS, Entomologist in
                                 Charge.

16

UNITED STATES DEPARTMENT OF AGRICULTURE

DEPARTMENT BULLETIN No. 1143

Washington, D. C. ▼ April 10, 1923

DRY-LAND PASTURE CROPS FOR HOGS AT. HUNTLEY, MONT.

By A. E. SEAMANS, *Assistant Agronomist, Office of Dry-Land Agriculture Investigations, Bureau of Plant Industry.* [1]

CONTENTS.

INTRODUCTION.

The transition from cattle-range conditions to grain farming has been comparatively rapid in the Plains area of Montana.

Relatively high yields of wheat from low-priced land during the first few years when this change was taking place were a mighty stimulant toward the rather general adoption of this one-crop system of agriculture.

The experience of the older agricultural States has shown that a combination of live stock and crop farming formed the basis of a more permanent agriculture than where either grain or live stock was produced singly. Diversified farming as opposed to single-crop farming has frequently been demonstrated as a superior system of agriculture for the semiarid as well as for the humid sections of the country. There is ample reason to suppose that, in general, the dry-farming districts of Montana will prove to be no exception to this experience; and, furthermore, there have been numerous instances where the grain and forage returns from dry farms have been profitably marketed through live stock.

Live-stock production to a greater or less degree in connection with grain farming not only affords the dry-land farmer another direct source of income, but enables him to utilize profitably grain

[1] The results reported in this bulletin are from experiments conducted under a cooperative arrangement between the Montana Agricultural Experiment Station, the Office of Western Irrigation Agriculture and the Office of Dry-Land Agriculture Investigations, Bureau of Plant Industry, and the Bureau of Animal Industry, United States Department of Agriculture.

The following men from the Animal Husbandry Division of the Bureau of Animal Industry have been in charge of the animal-husbandry work at this station and have had the actual care of the hogs during the years specified: C. V. Singleton, 1917-1918; R. E. Gongwer, 1919-1920; and R. E. Hutton, 1921. George W. Morgan, who was in charge of the dry-land work at the Huntley, Mont., Experiment Farm from 1913 to 1915, outlined and conducted the experiments here reported during the season of 1915.

and forage crops which of themselves are of secondary importance but which fit in well with approved 'crop rotations and agricultural systems. For example: Experiments have shown, and practical farmers have found, that in many parts of the dry-land sections of the State the yields of small grains grown after corn are almost as large as on summer fallow, and the net returns are correspondingly greater when the corn crop can be profitably used. Corn generally has a greater value when fed to live stock than when harvested and sold as grain. The return of fertility to the land through the medium of manure is recognized as a factor in establishing a system of permanent agriculture.

Where animals are produced, raised, and prepared for market on the farm it is generally essential that some sort of pasture be a part of the scheme. The open range or other native-grass pasture answers this purpose in many cases for cattle and sheep. In the more thickly settled communities pasture will often have to be confined to cultivated crops. Where this is the case, hogs will more often be used than any of the other meat-producing animals.

With this phase of dry-land farming in mind, a series of hog-pasturing experiments was outlined and begun at the Huntley, Mont., Experiment Farm in 1915.

PURPOSE AND OUTLINE OF THE EXPERIMENTS.

The principal purpose of the experiments was not so much to determine the value of the several crops pastured from the standpoint of profit in pork production as to collect agronomic data bearing on the following points:

(1) The seasons at which the different crops become available for grazing by hogs and the length of time each crop will furnish palatable forage.

(2) The carrying capacity or number of hogs per acre these crops will support.

(3) The possibility of fitting together or matching up these crops, by means of a rotation or otherwise, so that their respective pasture periods will form continuous grazing over a considerable season.

(4) The agronomic effect of manure, the result of pasturing, on the yield of crops.

(5) The economic merits of pasturing these crops as contrasted with the usual methods of harvesting them.

While these five points are of primary importance in this work, the behavior of the animals themselves in point of gain or loss in weight is important as an indicator of the palatability and the quantity of forage produced. For this reason the results of pasturing are presented in pounds of gain.

The plats used in the pasturing experiments were 1 acre in area. They were 620 feet long and 70.3 feet wide. A 7-foot alley separated the plats on their long sides, and a 20-foot road bounded them on the ends. Suitable fencing, shelter, and water facilities were provided for the animals on each plat.

Pigs of the Duroc-Jersey breed were used in this work whenever obtainable, and the animals were placed on the pasture as soon as the forage was ready.

Individual hog weights were taken frequently enough during the pasture season to compare the conditions of the animals with the depletion of the forage and to form a basis from which to calculate the grain supplements to be fed. These weighings usually took place at intervals of 10 to 14 days or oftener as conditions demanded. The initial and final weights used were generally the average of weighings made on three consecutive days.

The annual crops used were arranged in the form of a rotation and grown as follows: Winter rye seeded in disked pea stubble, followed by corn on spring plowing, followed by beardless barley (Success variety) on disked corn ground, followed by peas on fall-plowed barley stubble. To obtain estimates of yield and for the ultimate determination of the effect of pasturing on yield this rotation was duplicated. The crops in the duplicate rotation were grown by the same cultural methods but allowed to mature and were harvested by machinery in the ordinary manner.

In this rotation pasturing began with the winter rye. Usually 10 fall pigs were used on this pasture. They were placed on the rye in the spring at as early a date as the conditions of season and pasture would permit. This was usually early in May when the rye was from 5 to 8 inches high. The crop was pastured until it was either exhausted, had become unpalatable, or had to be abandoned in order that the pigs could be turned into the acre of peas at a time when they might receive the greatest benefit from this crop. While on the rye plat the hogs were fed once daily a ration of corn equal to 2 per cent of the live weight of the animals.

The plat of peas was grazed off in the same manner as the rye. Theoretically, peas are a grain crop, and pigs should require no corn supplement, but under conditions as actually experienced in the field it seemed advisable for one reason or another to continue the 2 per cent corn ration.

From the plat of peas the hogs were moved to the plat of Success barley. This crop was usually headed out and the grain either matured or approaching maturity. The barley is supposed to constitute a straight grain ration, on which hogs should approach a finished condition.

A small lot of spring pigs was used to harvest the standing corn on the fourth plat in the rotation.

The perennial crops pastured were alfalfa and brome-grass. Two 1-acre plats of each crop were grazed off in these experiments. On one plat of each crop the forage was grown in rows 2 feet apart, while in the second plat the forage was sown broadcast. With the exception of brome-grass in rows each of the perennial pasture plats was duplicated by plats from which the crop was harvested as hay by machinery.

Plats of sweet clover for pasture and harvest were seeded in 1916 and 1919, but on account of dry seasons there was no stand, and consequently this crop has not been used as pasture.

The perennial pastures were seeded in 1916, and pasturing began in 1917. The first year both fall and spring pigs were used to harvest these crops, but since then the grazing has been done by fall pigs only. These were placed on the fields as early in the spring as practicable and maintained there as long as the conditions of the forage and animals would permit. While on pasture the hogs were fed a 2 per cent supplementary ration of corn and were weighed about every two weeks. At the end of the pasture period they were removed to the feed lot for fattening.

RESULTS IN 1915.

Seasonal conditions affect dry-land crop production so profoundly as to materially affect both the conduct of the experiment and its results. It therefore seems best to present the details of the experiment year by year. This allows opportunity for brief discussions of the seasons and explanation of apparent deviations or omissions from the outlined program.

The pasturing work in 1915 was of a preliminary character and was confined to the rotation of annual crops. The land used was broken from native sod the previous fall and all the crops were planted in the spring. This being the case, White Smyrna barley, a bearded variety, was used in place of winter rye. The season was cool, the rainfall was abnormally heavy, and all crops made yields considerably above the average. The hogs used were fall pigs of the Duroc-Jersey and Poland China breeds and were borrowed from neighboring farmers for the work.

Nine hogs, totaling 1,366 pounds, were placed on July 14 on the plat of White Smyrna barley, where they remained until July 30, a period of 16 days. At the time the pasturing began the barley was in the soft-dough stage. From the actions of the animals and the small gains made it was readily seen that the crop was unpalatable because of its beards, and the hogs were removed to the plat of Success barley. While on the White Smyrna barley a total gain of only 40 pounds for the lot was made. The check plat of this crop yielded 43.8 bushels of thrashed grain per acre.

Seven fall p s having a combined weight of 986 pounds were put on the plat of peas on July 17, when the grain was in the dough stage, and remained on it until August 3. During this period of 17 days the lot made a total gain of 280 pounds, or about 2.4 pounds per pig per day. The check plat yielded 8.4 bushels of thrashed peas per acre, but as much of the grain was lost by shelling out during harvest the actual yield was somewhat higher. No supplementary ration was fed with the peas.

The plat of Success barley was stocked on July 17 with eight pigs weighing 1,224 pounds. On July 30 the nine pigs from the White Smyrna barley plat were added. At this time these pigs weighed 1,406 pounds.

The total lot of 17 pigs was removed from the Success barley plat on August 11. Thus, the crop carried eight pigs for a period of 25 days and nine pigs for a period of 12 days. The first lot of eight pigs made a total gain of 129 pounds, or an average daily increase of 0.65 of a pound each. The lot of nine pigs added on July 30 made a total gain of 90 pounds, or 0.83 of a pound per pig per day. The harvested plat yielded 33.2 bushels of grain per acre.

The plat of corn was harvested by 10 spring pigs weighing 1,115 pounds. This lot was placed on the corn on September 29 and remained there until October 24. A total gain of 480 pounds was made in the 25-day period. This is 1.92 pounds a day for each pig. One of the animals suffered from rheumatism toward the last of the season and did not gain as rapidly as the others. The plat of corn husked out by hand yielded 33 bushels of grain per acre.

The experience of 1915 was valuable in working out the relationship these crops have to one another in regard to cultural methods, growth, season of pasture, and palatability. Methods of handling the hogs and the technic in regard to taking the individual weights were also developed.

RESULTS IN 1916.

RYE.

The first season when the pasturing work was conducted according to the outlined program was in 1916. Some difficulty in procuring suitable hogs was experienced. Ten Duroc-Jersey pigs having a total weight of 1,171 pounds [2] were purchased locally by the Montana Agricultural Experiment Station and placed on the plat of rye on May 6. At this date the rye was jointing and was generally somewhat farther advanced than was considered most desirable for pasturage. The crop grew too fast to be held in check by the pigs, and by May 21 they were confining their grazing to small areas where the rye had been closely pastured and new growth was continually appearing. The unpastured rye was clipped with a mower to induce new growth over the whole plat. Timely showers started this growth, which was pastured until June 30, when the hogs were transferred to the plat of peas.

A total gain of 339 pounds was made by the hogs during the 55 days on rye pasture. While on the rye pasture a ration of corn weighing 2 pounds for each 100 pounds of hogs was fed. The total was 1,480 pounds of corn, or 4.37 pounds of corn for every pound of gain in weight of the animals. The average daily gain per pig was 0.62 of a pound.

The check plat of rye thrashed out 19.2 bushels of grain per acre.

The results of the rye pasturing for the season indicated that the forage is much more palatable while young. When the crop begins to head the pigs will not eat it but will confine their grazing to areas that have been kept pastured closely and where a new growth of rye is continually appearing. If sufficient moisture is available, a new growth of forage may be induced by mowing the rye when it gets beyond the palatable stage. There seems to be little doubt that the pigs were held on the rye pasture too long for the best results. A 2 per cent ration of corn proved to be about right as a grain supplement for the rye pasturage.

PEAS.

From the rye pasture the pigs were moved directly to the acre of field peas. The crop at this time was well advanced toward maturity, the grain being in the hard-dough stage. As the crop appeared to be insufficient to carry the hogs until the barley was ripe, the 2 per cent ration of corn was continued. The peas with corn supplement carried the 10 pigs for a period of 20 days, the lot being removed on July 20. During this time a total gain of 270 pounds was made, and 636 pounds of corn were fed as a supplement. This feeding ratio is 2.36 pounds of corn for each pound of gain, while each animal made an average daily increase of 1.35 pounds in weight. The plat was completely bare of vegetation when the animals were removed.

Peas on the check plat yielded 10.9 bushels per acre of grain of poor quality.

The experience of this year indicated that an acreage of peas double that of rye could be used satisfactorily. This would permit

---

[2] After the grazing was well under way it was found that one of the animals had been bred before she was purchased. The actual weights of this animal while on rye, peas, and barley pastures have not been used in the calculations, but a weight equal to that of the average of the other nine pigs has been substituted for the actual weights of this animal.

leaving the rye at an earlier stage of its growth and pasturing the peas when they were not so mature, and the increased acreage would more completely fill the gap between rye and barley. With more forage containing an increased total weight of grain, it is possible the corn ration could be dispensed with. Peas appear to be very palatable, both grain and vines being consumed.

BARLEY.

The 10 pigs were moved on July 20 from the plat of peas to the plat of Success barley where they remained until August 7, a period of 18 days. At the beginning of the period the barley was in the hard-dough stage, but many of the plants along the edge of the plat were still comparatively green. It was observed that these green plants were consumed by the pigs before grazing the mature barley. During the first 10 days of the period a total gain of 42 pounds was made, but during the last 8 days the animals lost in weight to such an extent that the returns for the entire period on barley showed a loss of 14 pounds for the lot. Though the barley was all eaten, it was clearly evident that much of it was not digested by the animals and therefore not assimilated.

The crop on the acre check plat yielded 9.7 bushels of thrashed grain per acre.

There seems to be ample evidence that the barley was too mature to be of the greatest benefit to the hogs. This crop approximated a full grain ration, and it is possible that some roughage, such as alfalfa hay, should be fed along with the barley pasturage when the crop is so far advanced. If hogged-off when in a greener stage, there would probably be no need for a supplement.

The total increase in weight of the 10 pigs for the rye, peas, and barley pastures was 595 pounds during the 92-day period, and the corn fed totaled 2,116 pounds. At the end of the period the hogs were not in a finished condition, but they had developed large frames and fattened readily in the feed pens.

CORN.

A lot of four spring-farrowed pigs weighing 435 pounds was placed on the acre of corn on September 30. At this time the corn was nearly ripe, and the pigs consumed it readily. When the animals were removed at the end of a 9-day period, the corn was well cleaned up, and the pigs had made a gain of 71 pounds, or 1.97 pounds per pig per day.

The acre check plat husked out 16.5 bushels of corn of poor quality.

The ratio of corn consumed (using the yield of the check plat as the basis for figuring the yield of the pastured plat) was 13 pounds of corn to a pound of gain. As the corn consisted of a very large percentage of small ears, or nubbins, distributed throughout the entire plat, considerable energy had to be expended to find them. There seems to be little doubt that more satisfactory gains would have been obtained if the animals had been removed from the corn at an earlier date rather than left on the plat until all the corn had been found.

A small quantity of alfalfa hay was given the hogs while on the corn pasture, but they apparently ate very little of it.

RESULTS IN 1917.

RYE.

In 1917 a scarcity of suitable hogs for this pasturing work allowed but six Duroc-Jersey fall pigs to be used on the rye plat. [3] These began the grazing period on May 11 at an initial weight of 499 pounds. At this date the rye was about 6 to 7 inches high and well tillered. The forage appeared to be very palatable and was eaten readily by the animals during the early part of the season. The small number of pigs to the acre was not sufficient to keep the pasturage grazed down. By June 19 a large part of it had become too coarse to be palatable and the animals were confining their feeding to small areas where the rye had been kept short and new growth was appearing. The coarse forage was clipped, and a new growth came on immediately. This was consumed, but the gains made from it did not equal those made earlier in the season. The animals were removed on July 17. A total weight of 762 pounds was recorded on this date, showing a gain of 263 pounds for the 67-day period, or an average of 0.65 of a pound per pig per day. The corn fed totaled 910 pounds for the period, or a ratio of 3.46 pounds of corn per pound of gain.

The poor growth of the rye toward the end of the period would have justified removing the hogs at least 10 days earlier.

Rye on the check plat yielded 10.4 bushels per acre.

PEAS.

The crop of peas was seriously affected by a cold wet spring, which so reduced germination that the stand was estimated at about 30 per cent. The forage was further reduced by a hailstorm on July 4, that stripped pods and leaves from the vines and beat them into the ground.

The pigs were held on the rye pasture longer than the forage warranted in order to give the peas a chance to recover. On July 17 the plat was stocked with six pigs from the plat of rye. At this date the few peas remaining on the vines were in the-green-pea stage and therefore younger than was the case in 1916. The percentage of grain to vines was very small, and the 2 per cent ration of corn was again deemed advisable to supplement the pasturage.

The six pigs harvested the plat in 22 days and were immediately removed to the acre of beardless barley. A total gain of 174 pounds was made. This was at the rate of 1.32 pounds per pig each day and was made on a corn ratio of 1 pound of gain for each 2.06 pounds of corn fed.

The acre check plat returned 2.3 bushels of thrashed peas. An estimate made at the time of harvest was to the effect that about 50 per cent of the peas had been beaten from the vines and could not be gathered for thrashing.

In spite of the hailstorm and other factors the 1 acre of peas with the corn supplement furnished continuous grazing for six pigs for the 22 days between the rye and barley pastures.

[3] One of these animals was found to be with pig after the experiment started and was removed from the plat at the end of 61 days. A weight equal to the average of the other five hogs is used for this animal in all calculations made for rye. This hog was replaced by another on the pea and barley pastures. This substitution accounts for the discrepancy of 21 pounds in the weight of the lot at the end of the rye and the beginning of the pea pasture.

BARLEY.

The barley plats were somewhat affected by the hailstorm but recovered more completely than did the peas.

The lot of hogs from the peas weighed 915 pounds when placed on the barley plat on August 8. The grain was well filled at this time, but the crop was not nearly as mature as in 1916. That it was more palatable than during the previous year was evidenced by the way the animals consumed the entire plants, rather than limiting themselves to the grain. There were not enough pigs to harvest the whole acre while it was in this stage, so the forage was rather well matured by the end of the season. Though the hogs were kept on the plat until all the grain was consumed, it was apparent that they were getting little benefit from the matured barley and they were removed on August 22.

A total gain of 60 pounds was made during the 14-day pasture period. This was an average daily gain of 0.71 of a pound per pig.

The check plat yielded 16.2 bushels of mature grain per acre. Using this yield as an estimate of the grain consumed it appears that 12.95 pounds of barley were required for 1 pound increase in weight.

Rye, peas, and barley pastures returned a combined total of 497 pounds gain in weight for six pigs in a period of 103 days. A total of 1,268 pounds of corn was fed as a supplement to the rye and pea pasturage. As was the case in 1916, the animals were not in a finished condition at the end of this season but had made a good growth and fattened readily in the dry lot.

CORN.

Six spring pigs, totaling 442 pounds, were placed on the acre of corn on September 28. The corn was well ripened and was of a better quality than in 1916, though the yield was somewhat less. It required 17 days to hog-off the corn, and the animals were removed on October 15. During this period the total increase in the weight of the lot was 103 pounds, or 1.01 pounds per day for each pig.

The acre check plat yielded 9.6 bushels of corn of good quality. Using this yield as a basis of calculation the gains were made at the rate of 5.22 pounds of corn per pound of gain. The corn crop was not large enough to finish the animals to a marketable size and condition.

ALFALFA AND BROME-GRASS.

The alfalfa and brome-grass crops were seeded in 1916 in 1-acre plats. One plat of each was planted in rows 2 feet apart and one with rows 6 inches apart. In this bulletin the first is referred to as the row plat and the second as the broadcast plat. Good stands were obtained, and excellent pasturage was available in the spring of 1917. A sufficient number of fall pigs was not available for grazing off these plats efficiently, but five pigs having a total weight of 438 pounds were given access to the 2 acres of alfalfa on May 16. On the same date five similar pigs, totaling 427 pounds, were placed on the 2 acres of brome-grass. A 2 per cent ration of corn was fed each lot daily.

Both lots were carried on their respective pastures for a period of 56 days, being removed on July 11. The forage on each plat having made more growth during this period than the small number of pigs could consume, all plats except the brome-grass in rows were mowed. The 2 acres of alfalfa yielded 1,632 pounds of fair quality hay. The acre of broadcast brome-grass appeared to be more unpalatable than the row plat and was harvested at the same time as the alfalfa plats. This brome-grass plat yielded 1,880 pounds of good quality hay. The row plat of brome-grass, though much of the forage grew tall and was not eaten, seemed to furnish a greater quantity of acceptable grazing around the crowns of the plants, and the hogs confined themselves to this plat almost exclusively after the first two weeks of the season.

The gain of the fall pigs on alfalfa amounted to 232 pounds, or 0.83 of a pound per pig per day. The brome-grass pigs gained 190 pounds for the same period, or 0.68 of a pound per pig per day. The alfalfa pigs made their increase at the rate of 2.78 pounds of corn per pound of gain, while the brome-grass pigs required 3.2 pounds of corn for each pound of gain.

The comparison seemed to favor the alfalfa pasture, though actually most of the brome-grass grazing was done on the 1 acre of brome-grass in rows.

The check plat of alfalfa seeded broadcast was cut on June 29 and yielded 1,850 pounds of hay per acre, while the broadcast plat of brome-grass returned 2,560 pounds of hay per acre. No check plats of these crops in rows were available.

After removing the fall pigs from the pastures on July 11 the plats were restocked with spring pigs. Ten pigs were placed on each of the crops. The total hog weight for the 2 acres of alfalfa was 356 pounds and for the 2 acres of brome-grass 357 pounds.

As but little growth was made on the broadcast alfalfa plat after it was mowed, the spring pigs confined themselves to the row plat entirely. The dry season enabled the animals to keep the new growth grazed off fairly close over the whole acre, but the tendency to continually pasture certain areas was the same as that experienced with the rye pasture. On August 8 one pig was removed from the experiment because of sickness, and from that time until the experiment closed on September 28 nine pigs were used. During the 79-day period a total of 249 pounds of gain was made. This averaged about 0.34 of a pound per day for each animal. The corn consumed was 767 pounds, or 3.09 pounds of corn for each pound of gain. For the greatest and most economical gains the pasture season should have closed about three weeks earlier.

As was the case with the alfalfa, the row plat of brome-grass was pastured by the spring pigs in preference to the broadcast plat.

The row plat of brome-grass was mowed on July 24 and yielded 944 pounds of coarse hay. The subsequent new growth was pastured close by the 10 pigs for a period of 25 days, when they were removed. A gain of 32 pounds was made, or an average daily gain of 0.13 of a pound per pig. Shelled corn weighing 231 pounds was fed during this time, or a ratio of 7.22 pounds of corn for each pound of gain. A greater income from the pasture would have been secured if the hogs had been removed a week earlier.

The season's observations on alfalfa and brome-grass as hog pastures indicated that both crops were very palatable. It seems reasonable to suppose that placing a larger number of pigs on these crops early in the season would bring more profitable returns than the summer pasturing and also leave the pastures themselves in better shape.

The row plats of each crop furnished a more continuous growth of palatable forage than the broadcast plats.

RESULTS IN 1918.

RYE.

On May 7, 1918, 10 pure-bred Duroc-Jersey fall pigs, having a combined weight of 964 pounds, were turned on the rye pasture. The forage averaged about 6 inches in height on this date, and it was in good condition for grazing. June 5 found the animals confining their pasturing to the more closely grazed areas, while rye on the neglected areas grew tall and coarse. This was cut with a mower as it was beginning to head out. Though some new growth was induced from the clipped plants, the season was such that this growth was smaller than in former years, and the animals had little difficulty in keeping the whole acre pastured close. The hogs were removed from the plat on June 25. The total gain made during the 49-day period was 227 pounds, or an average daily increase of 0.46 of a pound per hog. The corn fed was 1,078 pounds, or 4.75 pounds of corn for each pound of gain in hog weight.

The check plat of rye made 10.1 bushels per acre.

PEAS.

The hogs from the rye plat were moved to the plat of peas on June 25. On this date a light hailstorm did some damage to the peas by stripping the young pods from the vines. The total weight of the animals when the pea pasturing was started was 1,191 pounds. As the forage was green and succulent, the corn ration was continued. At the end of a 14-day period the peas had been entirely cleaned up, and the hogs were placed on the acre of barley.

A gain of 229 pounds was made by the 10 pigs on peas. This is at the rate of 1.64 pounds per day for each pig. The total corn fed was 364 pounds, or a ratio of 1.59 pounds of corn for each pound of gain.

Peas which were harvested and thrashed yielded 5.6 bushels for the acre. It was estimated that about 50 per cent of the grain from this plat was lost because of the hailstorm.

A greater acreage of peas could have been used to advantage in 1918, as in former years.

BARLEY.

The barley crop had begun to dry up when it was stocked by the 10 pigs from the pea plat on July 9. The lot at this time weighed 1,420 pounds. At the end of the first 14-day period it was obvious that the pigs would not make satisfactory gains on the crop, and they were removed. In addition to the grain being of poor quality, the crop had become badly mixed with bearded varieties of barley which the pigs refused to eat.

The maturity of the barley made it seem advisable to supply a roughage ration with the pasturage, so alfalfa hay was fed in racks. A total of 52 pounds of hay was consumed during the 14 days. When the pigs were removed from the barley on July 23 they weighed 1,420 pounds, which was the same as their initial weight on this plat.

The check plat of barley made 3 bushels per acre of poor-quality grain.

The continuous pasture of rye, peas, and barley made a total gain of 456 pounds. A total of 1,442 pounds of corn was fed while the animals were on the rye and pea pastures.

CORN.

The quality of corn pastured was rather poor, and the yield was small. Six spring pigs weighing 442 pounds were placed on the plat of corn on September 6. Twelve days were required to complete the harvesting of the crop. The total gain made was only 54 pounds, or 0.75 of a pound per pig per day. During this experiment the hogs were supplied with alfalfa hay, but consumed only 8 pounds during the 12 days.

The check plat of corn yielded 8 bushels per acre. Using this yield as a basis for estimating the grain produced on the pastured plat, it required 8.3 pounds of corn to make a pound of gain.

ALFALFA.

A scarcity of fall pigs did not permit pasturing the entire acre plats of alfalfa to the best advantage, so the plats were divided and only half an acre was used in each case. For comparison the returns are reduced to an acre basis.

The broadcast plat was stocked at the rate of eight pigs to the acre and the row plat at the rate of six pigs per acre. This difference seemed advisable, as the longer grazing period given the row plat in 1917 resulted in the killing out or damaging of the forage to a greater degree than was experienced on the broadcast plat. This damage seemed to be confined entirely to the continuously grazed areas of the year before.

The alfalfa was about 7 inches high when the grazing began, and it seemed to be making a good growth.

The initial weight of the six hogs on the row plat was at the rate of 532 pounds per acre, and the eight hogs on the broadcast plat had an acre weight of 702 pounds. The animals remained on both plats until the forage became unpalatable, owing to the coarseness of the growth and the drought which hindered new growth. Both lots were removed on July 9, after a pasture period of 63 days. The lot on the row plat made an increase of 296 pounds per acre, or 0.78 of a pound per day per pig, while the lot on the broadcast plat gained an acre total of 348 pounds, or an average daily gain of 0.69 of a pound per pig. The ratio of corn fed to gain was 3.01 pounds of corn to 1 pound of gain on the row plat, and 3.3 pounds of corn to 1 pound of gain on the broadcast plat. The row plat made a greater daily gain per pig and did this on a lower corn ratio than the broadcast plat, but the latter made the greater gain per acre.

Contrary to expectations, however, the forage on the row plat seemed to suffer more from drought than did that on the broadcast plat. The ground between the rows of alfalfa was packed hard by tramping, and in many places the soil was deeply cracked. This condition was absent on the broadcast plat.

The unpastured halves of each plat were cut for hay and yielded 1,224 pounds per acre for the row plat and 1,800 pounds per acre for the broadcast plat. The acre check plat seeded broadcast made 1,254 pounds per acre.

BROME-GRASS.

Owing to the small number of hogs available for the work, the brome-grass pastures were reduced to half an acre each, as had been done with the alfalfa plats. Each half acre of brome-grass was supplied with four fall pigs on April 30. This was a week earlier than the alfalfa pastures were stocked, but was warranted by the earlier and more rapid spring growth made by the brome-grass. On this date the grass was 8 inches high. Hogs on the row plat weighed 764 pounds per acre, while those on the broadcast plat had an acre weight of 778 pounds. The forage carried each lot until July 9, a period of 70 days. At this time the pasturage was so coarse and unpalatable that satisfactory gains were not being made. The grass on the row plat was tall and coarse, while that on the broadcast plat was short and dry.

Pigs on the row plat returned an acre gain of 350 pounds, or a daily gain of 0.63 of a pound per pig. The broadcast plat yielded 374 pounds of gain per acre, or a daily average of 0.67 of a pound per pig. The corn consumed on each plat was 1,344 pounds. This was a ratio of 3.84 pounds of corn per pound of gain for the row plat and 3.59 pounds of corn per pound of gain for the broadcast plat. The results were somewhat in favor of the broadcast brome-grass.

The unpastured halves of each plat were cut for hay on June 15. From the row plat 1,392 pounds of hay per acre were obtained, while the broadcast plat yielded 720 pounds of hay per acre. The check plat of brome-grass sown broadcast yielded 664 pounds of hay.

RESULTS IN 1919.

RYE.

Conditions in 1919 were favorable for starting the pasture work about two weeks earlier than heretofore. Ten fall pigs with a total weight of 1,103 pounds were placed on the acre of rye on April 25, when the crop was about 7 inches high. The animals took to the forage readily and during the early part of the period made good gains. The season was very dry, and the growth of rye was checked to such an extent that the 10 pigs were able to keep the whole plat eaten off uniformly. This was the first year the plat did not need to be clipped to prevent the unpastured plants from maturing.

At the end of 56 days the hogs were removed and placed on the plat of peas. The gains made amounted to 287 pounds, which was an average daily increase of 0.51 of a pound for each animal. The corn fed was 1,403 pounds, or a ratio of 4.89 pounds of grain per pound of gain.

The check plat made 3.6 bushels per acre.

PEAS.

The crop of peas was severely damaged by drought, and but little forage was produced. The 10 pigs were placed on the plat on June 20 when they weighed 1,390 pounds. The peas were in the green-pea stage and were readily eaten.

The small crop cut the pasture period to seven days, the pigs being removed on June 27. A gain of 77 pounds was made by the lot during this period. The average daily increase was 1.1 pounds per day per pig and was made with the aid of 207 pounds of corn supplementing the forage, a ratio of 1 pound of gain to 2.69 pounds of corn.

The check plat of peas dried up before harvest, and no yield was obtained.

A total gain of 364 pounds was made on the rye and pea plats during the combined periods amounting to 63 days. A total of 1,610 pounds of corn was consumed.

BARLEY AND CORN.

The barley and corn plats dried up before making grain, and neither of these crops was grazed. No yields were obtained on the check plats.

ALFALFA.

As the effects of overpasturing in 1917 were still in evidence, the acre of alfalfa in rows was stocked on May 9 with only four fall pigs. These pigs had a total weight of 318 pounds. On the same date seven fall pigs weighing 530 pounds were placed on the broadcast plat of alfalfa. The forage on both plats was about 6 inches high at this time. Both lots made good gains during the first half of the season, but drought and hot weather reduced the average, as the growth of alfalfa was checked.

The pigs were removed from both pastures on June 27. The gain made on the row plat amounted to 130 pounds, or 0.66 of a pound per pig for each day of the 49-day period. On the broadcast plat the pigs increased in weight 188 pounds. This was an average daily gain of 0.55 of a pound for each animal. The pigs on the row plat received 376 pounds of corn, or 2.89 pounds of corn for each pound of gain. The pigs on the broadcast plat made 1 pound of gain on 3.21 pounds of corn, a total of 604 pounds of corn being fed. While the row plat by reason of the poor stand supported a smaller number of pigs and made a smaller gain per acre than the broadcast plat, each pig in it made a greater daily gain on a lower ratio of corn.

Alfalfa on the check plat was too small to be harvested, and so no yield was obtained.

BROME-GRASS.

Six fall pigs were put on each acre of brome-grass on April 25. The grass at this time was 7 inches high and was readily eaten by the animals.

The pigs on the row plat had a combined weight of 582 pounds, while those on the broadcast plat totaled 579 pounds.

Drought during the latter part of the grazing season curtailed the growth of forage and reduced the gains made by the hogs. Both lots were removed on June 14, after having been on the pastures 50 days. During this period the lot on the row plat gained 144 pounds, while that on the broadcast plat gained 191 pounds. The former averaged 0.48 of a pound daily for each animal, while the latter averaged 0.64 of a pound per day. The hogs on the row plat consumed 653 pounds of corn, or 4.53 pounds of corn for each pound of gain. The lot on the broadcast plat received the same weight of corn and made gains at the ratio of 1 pound to each 3.42 pounds of corn fed.

Both plats were grazed off close at the end of the season, and the severe drought prevented the forage making any growth after the pigs were removed. During the season there appeared to be no difference in drought resistance between the two plats.

The check plat of brome-grass dried up before the crop was tall enough to mow, so no yields were obtained.

Acre plats of alfalfa, brome-grass, and sweet clover seeded in rows and broadcasted were planted on April 10. These plats were intended to be used to replace the present pastures the next season. The young plants on these plats were completely killed by drought.

RESULTS IN 1920.

RYE.

A late spring in 1920 delayed opening the pasture season on rye until May 28. The rye at this time averaged about 12 inches in height and was well jointed. Because of the advanced stage of the crop and the late season 15 fall pigs were used instead of 10. These pigs weighed 1.627 pounds when placed on the pasture.

The forage grew too fast to be controlled by grazing, and by June 11 the hogs had confined their feeding to small closely pastured areas, and the rest of the crop was heading. After clipping with a mower on June 11 sufficient moisture was available to send out a new growth of rye. Some of this grew to a height of 4 inches before the entire plat was cleaned up. When the stock was removed on July 9 no forage remained.

During the 42-day period a gain of 270 pounds was made by the pigs. The gain per animal averaged 0.43 of a pound per day. The corn ration fed totaled 1,512 pounds, which was at the rate of 5.6 pounds of corn for each pound of gain.

Rye on the check plat was somewhat damaged by a hailstorm on July 4, and when thrashed on August 23 it yielded but 14.1 bushels of grain per acre.

PEAS.

When placed on the acre of peas on July 9 the 15 pigs from the rye plat weighed 1,897 pounds.

The hailstorm which damaged the check plat of rye on July 4 reduced a very promising pea crop by at least one-half. Practically all the peas were stripped from the vines and many of the vines themselves killed.

During the first two weeks of the pasture period a total gain of 158 pounds was made, but during the last 7 days a loss of 11 pounds was recorded for the lot. The 21-day period, therefore, showed a gain of only 147 pounds, or 0.47 of a pound per pig per day. Corn weighing 800 pounds was consumed, or 5.44 pounds of corn for each pound of gain. This was practically double the corn ratio and about half the average daily gain recorded for the plat in previous years and shows to some extent the value the seed in the peas may have as a part of the pea pasture.

The acre check plat of peas yielded 2.2 bushels of grain. A large percentage of this yield was made up from second-growth pods, the first pods having been destroyed by hail.

BARLEY.

New barley seed of the Success variety was secured for the pasturing work in 1920. The resulting crop was very satisfactory, no bearded barley whatever appearing in the stand.

The 15 hogs from the pea plat were moved to the plat of barley on July 30. The crop was in the soft-dough stage and just beginning to turn. The forage appeared to be very palatable and was readily eaten. During the first few days the animals seemed to find the leaves and straw satisfactory grazing.

By August 10 the barley had been consumed and the pigs were removed. A total gain of 135 pounds was made during the 11 days, or an average daily gain of 0.82 of a pound per pig. The acre check plat yielded 5.7 bushels of thrashed. grain. Taking this yield as representative of that on the pastured plat, it required 2.01 pounds of barley to produce a pound of gain.

The yield of both barley plats was somewhat reduced by the hailstorm of July 4. It appeared that the pastured plat was not as severely damaged as the harvested one.

The three crops added 552 pounds of gain to the initial weight of the 15 pigs in a period of 74 days. Corn fed during the periods on rye and peas totaled 2,312 pounds.

CORN.

A comparatively large yield of corn was available for hogging-down in 1920. The grain was nearly mature when six spring pigs were given access to the plat on September 18. The pigs weighed 387 pounds on this date and were in good condition to make rapid gains. A pasture period of 41 days was required to harvest the corn. During this time the pigs put on a total of 248 pounds, an individual gain of 1.01 pounds daily. As a supplement to the corn fed, the hogs consumed 79 pounds of alfalfa hay fed in racks.

The check plat of corn yielded 14.4 bushels of grain to the acre. Assuming this yield to be representative of that on the pastured plat, each pound of gain required 3.25 pounds of corn. When the hogs were removed from the plat on October 29 they were not in a finished condition.

ALFALFA.

Stands on both the row and broadcast seeded alfalfa plats had been considerably reduced by the drought and pasturing of 1919. The late spring did not permit turning the hogs into the alfalfa fields until May 28. At this time the alfalfa on each plat was about 10 inches high. Though somewhat higher than usual for pasturing, the alfalfa having had plenty of moisture was very succulent and readily eaten by the pigs.

The stand on the row plat appeared to be less than on the broadcast plat. The row alfalfa was therefore allotted four animals while the broadcast plat received six.

As the season advanced the areas where the alfalfa had died out became very weedy, and the plats had to be mowed to keep the weeds from maturing. The pigs were removed on July 9, as it was evident that further grazing would be injurious to the pasture and produce expensive gains in weight.

A total gain of 105 pounds was made by the four pigs on the row alfalfa plat during the 42-day period. This averaged a daily gain of 0.63 of a pound for each animal. The lot of six pigs on the broadcast plat made a gain of 142 pounds, or 0.56 of a pound a day each. Corn totaling 302 pounds was fed to the pigs on the row plat, and 450 pounds of corn were consumed by the animals on the broadcast plat. Gains were produced on the row plat at the rate of 2.88 pounds of corn per pound of gain, while on the broadcast plat 3.17 pounds of corn were required to produce a pound of gain.

An acre of row alfalfa seeded in 1918 and cut for hay this season yielded 2,260 pounds. The acre check plat of broadcast alfalfa cut for hay yielded 1,146 pounds.

BROME-GRASS.

The brome-grass pastures suffered more severely during 1919 than did the alfalfa. An estimate of the stand of each plat made previous to starting the grazing season indicated a stand survival of but 60 per cent on each plat. The spring growth of grass was also considerably behind the alfalfa, being, on May 28, only 8 inches high and very sickly looking.

On this date two grade Poland China pigs were placed on each brome-grass plat. This breed was used in place of Duroc-Jersey because of the scarcity of fall pigs of the latter breed.

The number of animals used was not sufficient to keep down the growth of vegetation, and both plats were soon covered with a rank growth of weeds. Both plats were mowed to control the weeds. The pigs were removed from both pastures on July 9.

The hogs on the row plat, starting with an initial weight of 170 pounds, gained 50 pounds during the 42 days on pasture, an average of 0.6 of a pound each per day. They received 166 pounds of corn, or 3.32 pounds of corn for each pound of gain.

The lot on the broadcast plat weighed 169 pounds to start with and gained 76 pounds, or 0.9 of a pound a day for each animal. During the 42 days on pasture 169 pounds of corn were fed. This was equal to 2.22 pounds of corn for each pound of gain.

The check plat of broadcasted brome-grass yielded 568 pounds of weedy hay.

RESULTS IN 1921.

RYE.

Winter rye in the pasture experiment did not come up until April 20 and was not ready for grazing until June 9. The forage was about 10 inches high and thinly scattered over the plat. The estimated stand was 50 per cent.

Ten pigs having a weight of 1,262 pounds were placed on the plat on June 9 and remained there until July 14, a period of 35 days. Owing to the thin stand of rye and the droughty conditions during the season, the 10 pigs had little difficulty in controlling the forage over the entire acre.

A gain of 286 pounds was recorded for the lot, or a daily gain of 0.82 of a pound per pig. The corn fed totaled 984 pounds, or 3.44 pounds of corn for each pound of gain.

The yield of the check plat of rye was somewhat reduced by a hailstorm on May 31, but it yielded 5 bushels per acre when thrashed.

PEAS.

The crop of peas was destroyed by hail on May 31, and no results were obtained either by pasturing or by harvesting with machinery.

BARLEY.

The lateness of the rye-pasturing season and the loss of the pea crop necessitated moving the 10 pigs directly from the rye to the barley plat. The barley had been somewhat injured by hail on May 31, but the crop had made considerable growth before the pigs were turned onto it on July 14. The grain was in the soft-dough stage and because of drought was maturing rapidly.

Though the pigs consumed all the grain on the plat with apparent relish, the light yield and poor quality resulted in only small gains.

The pigs were removed on July 28, after a pasture period of 14 days. A gain of 21 pounds was made by the lot, each pig averaging only 0.15 of a pound per day.

The check plat of barley yielded 6.4 bushels per acre of thrashed grain of poor quality.

CORN.

The corn on both the pasture rotation and the harvest rotation died of drought before making grain, and no yields were obtained.

ALFALFA.

A scarcity of fall pigs and the poor condition of the alfalfa pastures necessitated using half-acre areas. The areas having the best stand of alfalfa were fenced off and used for grazing. Both the broadcast and row plats were stocked on May 19 at the rate of six pigs per acre. The lot placed on the row plat totaled 772 poun s per acre, while that on the broadcast plat weighed 728 pounds per acre.

The alfalfa on each plat, though somewhat thinner as to stand than desirable, was about 6 inches high and seemed to be making a good growth. Though the season was dry, the crop made continuous grazing for a period of 70 days. The pigs were removed on July 28.

The pigs on the row plat increased 436 pounds per acre, or at the rate of 1.04 pounds per day each and at the ratio of 1 pound of gain to 3.04 pounds of corn. The pigs on the broadcast plat made a total gain of 402 pounds per acre, which averaged 0.96 of a pound per pig per day. This lot had a ratio of 3.3 pounds of corn fed for each pound of gain.

No alfalfa was obtained from the check plats because of drought

BROME-GRASS.

In order to use areas having fairly uniform stands of brome-grass for pasturing, one-half acre of the row plat was used and one-fourth acre of the broadcast plat. When the pigs were placed on these plats on May 19, the brome-grass averaged 6 inches in height. The stand on each plat was thinner than was desirable.

The row plat was stocked at the rate of six pigs per acre, with an initial weight of 732 pounds. The lot on the broadcast plat was at the rate of eight pigs per acre, totaling 1,012 pounds. The row plat produced continuous grazing for a period of 70 days, but on the broadcast plat the hogs had to be removed at the end of 62 days.

A gain of 0.74 of a pound per day for each animal, or 310 pounds per acre for the lot, was made on the row plat, while the individual daily average of the pigs on the broadcast plat was 0.9 of a pound, or a total of 436 pounds per acre.

Corn fed to the row-plat hogs totaled 1,246 pounds to the acre, or 4.02 pounds of corn for a pound of gain. The pigs on the broadcast plat received an acre total of 1,412 pounds of corn, or 3.24 pounds of grain for each pound of gain.

No yields were obtainable from the check plat of brome-grass because of the drought.

The duplicate perennial pastures seeded in 1919 and fallowed in 1920 were reseeded in the spring of 1921.

STUDY OF THE RESULTS WITH DIFFERENT CROPS.[4]

The data on pasturing the four crops, rye, peas, barley, and corn, in the 4-year rotation for the years from 1916 to 1921, inclusive, are assembled in four tables, one for each crop. The averages at the bottom of each table were determined for the number of years the crops were actually pastured, exclusive of 1915.

[4] For information on the pasturing of irrigated crops with hogs and the feeding of hogs while on pasture and in the feed lot, see the published reports of the work of the Huntley experiment farm, Bureau of Plant Industry, for the years 1913 to 1921, inclusive, by Dan Hansen, Farm Superintendent.

Rye has been pastured every year since 1915. The detailed results are given in Table 1. The average pasture period was from May 14 to July 4, a period of 51 days, for an average of 10.2 pigs per acre. These pigs with an average initial weight of 1,104 pounds gained an average of 279 pounds, or 0.58 of a pound a day for each animal. Corn averaging 1,228 pounds was fed to supplement the pasture. This averaged 4.42 pounds of corn for each pound of gain.

TABLE 1.—*Results obtained by pasturing 1 acre of winter rye with fall pigs at Huntley, Mont., each year from 1916 to 1921, inclusive.*

Year.	Number of pigs.	Pasture period.			Weights of animals and feed (pounds).						Yield of check plot (bushels).
					Hog weights.				Corn consumed.		
		Date on.	Date off.	Days.	Initial.	Final.	Gain.	Daily gain per pig.	Total.	Per pound of gain.	
1916........	[1]10	May 6	June 30	55	1,171	1,510	339	0.62	1,480	4.37	19.2
1917........	[2]6	May 11	July 17	67	499	762	263	.65	910	3.46	10.4
1918........	10	May 7	June 25	49	964	1,191	227	.46	1,078	4.75	10.1
1919........	10	Apr. 25	June 20	56	1,103	1,390	287	.51	1,403	4.89	3.6
1920........	15	May 23	July 9	42	1,627	1,897	270	.43	1,512	5.60	14.1
1921........	10	June 9	July 14	35	1,262	1,548	286	.82	984	3.44	5.0
Average, 6 years.	10.2	May 14	July 4	51	1,104	1,383	279	.58	1,228	4.42	10.4

[1] One of these pigs was pregnant during the pasture season. A weight equal to the average of the other nine is taken for this animal in the above calculations.
[2] At the end of 61 days one pig was removed because of pregnancy. A weight equal to the average of the other five is used for the removed animal in these calculations.

The average yield of rye on the check plot was 10.4 bushels per acre.

Peas were pastured every year since the experiments were started except in 1921, in which year the crop was destroyed by hail. As the work in 1915 was of a preliminary nature and the pasture was not continuous with the other crops in the rotation, the results for that year are not considered in the assembled data, which are given in Table 2.

TABLE 2.—*Results obtained by pasturing 1 acre of peas with fall pigs at Huntley, Mont., each year from 1916 to 1920, inclusive.*

Year.	Number of pigs.	Pasture period.			Weights of animals and feed (pounds).						Yield of check plot (bushels).
					Hog weights.				Corn consumed.		
		Date on.	Date off.	Days.	Initial.	Final.	Gain.	Daily gain per pig.	Total.	Per pound of gain.	
1916........	[1]10	June 30	July 20	20	1,510	1,780	270	1.35	636	2.36	10.9
1917........	[2]6	July 17	Aug. 8	22	741	915	174	1.32	358	2.06	2.3
1918........	10	June 25	July 9	14	1,191	1,420	229	1.64	364	1.59	5.6
1919........	10	June 20	June 27	7	1,390	1,467	77	1.10	207	2.69	0
1920........	15	July 9	July 30	21	1,897	2,044	147	.47	800	5.44	2.2
Average, 5 years.	10.2	July 2	July 19	17	1,346	1,525	179	1.18	473	2.83	4.2

[1] One sow was with pig. Weight for this animal was calculated as in the rye pasture (Table 1).
[2] Five pigs from the rye plat and one from the brome-grass plat.

The average for the five years from 1916 to 1920, inclusive, was 10.2 hogs per acre on peas from July 2 to July 19, a total of 17 days. At the beginning of this period the total weight averaged 1,346 pounds. An average increase in weight of 179 pounds was obtained. This was at the rate of 1.18 pounds per day for each pig. The supplementary corn ration averaged 473 pounds, or 2.83 pounds of corn for a pound of gain.

The check plat of peas yielded nothing in 1919, because of drought, and the crop was killed out by hail in 1921. The average yield of the peas from 1916 to 1920, including the zero yield of 1919, was 4.2 bushels per acre.

At no time did the 1 acre of peas furnish sufficient forage to carry the 10 pigs from the period of best grazing on the rye to that on barley.

Beardless barley (Success variety) has been pastured every year since 1916 with the exception of 1919, when the crop was killed by drought. The results are presented in Table 3.

TABLE 3.—*Results obtained by pasturing 1 acre of barley with fall pigs at Huntley, Mont., each year from 1916 to 1921, exclusive of 1919.*

Year.	Number of pigs.	Pasture period.			Weights of animals and feed (pounds).						Yield of check plat (bushels).
					Hog weights.				Barley consumed.[1]		
		Date on.	Date off.	Days.	Initial.	Final.	Gain.	Daily gain per pig.	Total.	Per pound of gain.	
1916........	[2] 10	July 20	Aug. 7	18	1,780	1,766	−14	−0.08	462	....	9.7
1917........	6	Aug. 8	Aug. 22	14	915	975	60	.71	777	12.95	16.2
1918........	10	July 9	July 23	14	1,420	1,420	0	0	142	....	3.0
1919 [3]....											
1920........	15	July 30	Aug. 10	11	2,044	2,179	135	.82	272	2.01	5.7
1921 [4].....	10	July 14	July 28	14	1,548	1,569	21	.15	305	14.52	6.4
Average, 5 years.	10.2	July 22	Aug. 5	14	1,541	1,582	40	.35	392	....	8.2

[1] Weight of grain from the check plat.
[2] The weight of one of these pigs was calculated as was done for the rye pasture (Table 1).
[3] The crop dried up before the pasture season, and no hogs were put on the plat.
[4] Hogs were moved from the rye plat directly to the barley plat because of the destruction of the pea plat by hail.

The pasture period averaged from July 22 to August 5, a total of 14 days, for an average of 10.2 pigs. The average initial weight of these pigs was 1,541 pounds, and the gains made averaged 40 pounds. The daily gain per pig each year averaged 0.35 pound.

The low gains were due chiefly to low yields of grain and the unpalatability of the forage.

Barley on the check plat averaged 8.2 bushels per acre for the five years when a crop was produced.

Using the yield of barley that might have been harvested as a basis of calculation, it required from 2.01 pounds of barley in 1920 to 14.5 pounds in 1921 to make a pound of gain. In 1916 there was a loss in weight on the barley pasture, and in 1918 no gains were made.

No corn was produced in either 1919 or 1921. With these exceptions corn has been pastured each year. For reasons stated above, the returns for 1915 have not been included in the assembled data

(Table 4). An average of 5.5 spring pigs has been used. It took these pigs an average period of 20 days, extending from September 20 to October 10, to harvest the acre. The average total weight of these pigs was 426 pounds at the beginning of the period, and they gained an average of 119 pounds. The average daily gain per pig for the four years was 1.19 pounds per day.

TABLE 4.—*Results obtained by pasturing 1 acre of corn with spring pigs at Huntley, Mont., in 1916, 1917, 1918, and 1920.*

Year.	Number of pigs.	Pasture period.			Weights of animals and feed (pounds).						Yield of check plat (bushels).
					Hog weights.				Corn consumed.[1]		
		Date on.	Date off.	Days.	Initial.	Final.	Gain.	Daily gain per pig.	Total.	Per pound of gain.	
1916........	4	Sept. 30	Oct. 9	9	435	506	71	1.97	924	13.00	16.5
1917........	6	Sept. 28	Oct. 15	17	442	545	103	1.01	538	5.22	9.6
1918........	6	Sept. 6	Sept. 18	12	442	496	54	.75	448	8.30	8.0
1919 [2]											
1920........	6	Sept. 18	Oct. 29	41	387	635	248	1.01	806	3.25	14.4
Average, 4 years.	5.5	Sept. 20	Oct. 10	20	426	545	119	1.19	679	7.44	12.1

[1] Yield of check plat.   [2] Corn dried up before making grain.

The average yield of the check plat was 12.1 bushels per acre. With this yield as a basis, the pigs averaged 1 pound of gain for each 7.44 pounds of corn eaten. An average of 57 pounds of alfalfa hay was fed with the corn.

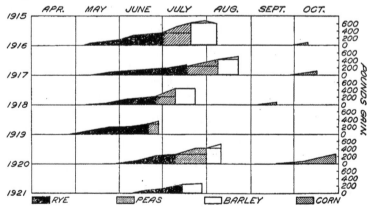

FIG. 1.—Diagram showing graphically the period in each year during which pigs were pastured on rye, peas, barley, and corn and the gain made while on each crop and between each weighing, arranged to show the combined gain on rye, peas, and barley.

Figure 1 presents graphically the data obtained from this rotation each year. The base line of each figure represents the initial weight of the hogs. The increase in height of the figure represents the increase in weight of the hogs as the season progresses. In other words, the gain in height of the figure represents the gain in hog weights above the first weight of the season. Thus, in 1917 the pigs were placed on the rye plat on May 11 and increased steadily in weight until at the end of the barley period, August 22, a total gain of 497 pounds had been made. The rise of peas above rye shows the gain made on peas, and the rise of barley over peas indicates the gain made on barley.

Besides the increase in weight for each crop, the diagram shows the period during which each crop was pastured.

TABLE 5.—*Results obtained by pasturing 1 acre of alfalfa with pigs at Huntley, Mont., each year from 1918 to 1921, inclusive.*

Kind of plats and year.	Number of pigs.	Pasture period.			Weights of animals and feed (pounds).						Yield of check plat.
					Hog weights.				Corn consumed.		
		Date on.	Date off.	Days.	Initial.	Final.	Gain.	Daily gain per pig.	Total.	Per pound of gain.	
Cultivated rows:											
1918....	6	May 7	July 9	63	532	828	296	0.78	890	3.01	....
1919....	4	May 9	June 27	49	318	448	130	.66	376	2.89	0
1920....	4	May 28	July 9	42	303	408	105	.63	302	2.88	2,260
1921....	6	May 19	July 28	70	772	1,208	436	1.04	1,326	3.04	0
Average	5	May 16	July 11	56	481	723	242	.78	724	2.96	753
Plats sown broadcast:											
1918....	8	May 7	July 9	63	702	1,050	348	.69	1,148	3.30	1,254
1919....	7	May 9	June 27	49	530	718	188	.55	604	3.21	0
1920....	6	May 28	July 9	42	458	600	142	.56	450	3.17	1,146
1921....	6	May 19	July 28	70	728	1,130	402	.94	1,326	3.30	0
Average	6.8	May 16	July 11	56	605	875	270	.69	882	3.25	600

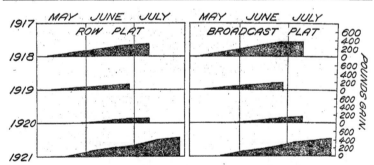

FIG. 2.—Diagram showing graphically the period in each year during which pigs were on alfalfa in rows and alfalfa sown broadcast and the gains made on each pasture and between weighings.

The data obtained on the alfalfa pastures are presented in Table 5 and shown graphically in Figure 2. This has been reduced to an acre basis for each year. Some preliminary pasturing was done with fall and spring pigs on alfalfa, but the data given in the table and the figure are for the years from 1918 to 1921, inclusive. During these years the average number of pigs used was 5 for the row plat and 6.8 for the broadcast plat. Both plats had the same pasture period, averaging 56 days from May 16 to July 11.

On the row plat the average daily gain per pig for each of the four years averaged 0.78 of a pound. A supplementary ration of corn was fed. The 4-year average ratio is 2.96 pounds of corn per pound of gain.

The lots on the broadcast plat made an average daily gain of 0.69 of a pound. This required an average of 3.25 pounds of corn for each pound of gain.

TABLE 6.—*Results obtained by pasturing 1 acre of brome-grass with pigs at Huntley, Mont., each year from 1918 to 1921, inclusive.*

Kind of plats and year.	Number of pigs.	Pasture period.			Weights of animals and feed (pounds).						Yield of check plat.
					Hog weights.				Corn consumed.		
		Date on.	Date off.	Days.	Initial.	Final.	Gain.	Daily gain per pig.	Total.	Per pound of gain.	
Cultivated rows:											
1918....	8	Apr. 30	July 9	70	764	1,114	350	0.63	1,344	3.84	....
1919....	6	Apr. 25	June 14	50	582	726	144	.48	653	4.53	....
1920....	2	May 28	July 9	42	170	220	50	.60	166	3.32	....
1921....	6	May 19	July 28	70	732	1,042	310	.74	1,242	4.02	....
Average	5.5	May 11	July 8	58	562	776	214	.61	851	3.92	....
Plats sown broadcast:											
1918....	8	Apr. 30	July 9	70	778	1,152	374	.67	1,344	3.59	664
1919....	6	Apr. 25	June 14	50	579	770	191	.64	653	3.42	0
1920....	2	May 28	July 9	42	169	245	76	.90	169	2.22	568
1921....	8	May 19	July 19	61	1,012	1,448	436	.90	1,412	3.24	0
Average	6	May 11	July 5	55	635	904	269	.78	895	3.11	308

The brome-grass pasture results are shown in Table 6 and Figure 3. When reduced to an acre basis, the row plat has carried an average of 5.5 pigs for a period of 58 days from May 11 to July 8. These pigs have made an average daily gain of 0.61 of a pound. The ratio is 1 pound of gain for each 3.92 pounds of corn.

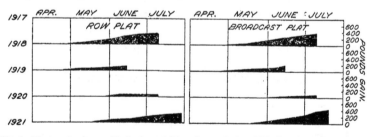

FIG. 3.—Diagram showing graphically the period in each year during which pigs were on brome-grass in rows and brome-grass sown broadcast and the gains made on each pasture and between weighings.

Six pigs were carried on the broadcast plat for an average of 55 days. This period was from May 11 to July 5. An average daily gain of 0.78 of a pound per pig was made on this plat. Corn fed amounted to an average of 3.11 pounds of grain for each pound of gain.

UNITED STATES DEPARTMENT OF AGRICULTURE

DEPARTMENT BULLETIN No. 1144

Washington, D. C.	▼	March 20, 1923

COST OF MILK PRODUCTION ON FORTY-EIGHT WISCONSIN FARMS.[1]

By S. W. MENDUM, *Junior Economist, Bureau of Agricultural Economics.*

CONTENTS.

NOTE.—The writer wishes to express his appreciation of the patience and courtesy of the cooperating farmers in making reports, and to thank a number of other men and women who have helped in the preparation of the bulletin.

The purpose of this study was to observe the management of a number of herds kept under ordinary farm conditions and to measure the more important factors of cost, with a view to determining the nature and degree of changes in management which may be expected to result in a more favorable relation between income and expense as prices of materials and of products change. Information was gathered through regular reports submitted by the farmers, supplemented by personal observations. The determination of an average cost figure was urgently solicited by farmers, with a view to influencing prices paid by consumers and factories, but for reasons apparent to all who are familiar with cost data, this figure is of only minor significance.

Milk production is only a part of the farm business on most Wisconsin dairy farms. Besides milk production, there are the herd itself, other classes of productive livestock, the corn, small grains, and hay grown to feed the livestock, and a variety of special crops grown for sale. Each of these other enterprises contributes more or less to the farm income, and entails its share of the farm expense. These shares are variable and not always well defined. Moreover, there are wide differences in the amount and value of land, buildings, equipment, and labor devoted to the several farm enterprises.

---

[1] The data for this bulletin were gathered by the writer under a cooperative arrangement between the Bureau of Agricultural Economics, United States Department of Agriculture, and the University of Wisconsin. The Wisconsin Division of Markets also assisted in the field work.

26543—23——1

It would be desirable if these various enterprises could be made to stand on their own merits, and to some extent they do, but the decision with respect to the management of any one of them does not depend solely on the fact of a figured profit or loss in any season or period of years, but rather on how it fits in the general farm operations. An enterprise will be continued as long as it pays better than any other which could be substituted for it, and as long as it contributes to the net income of the farm, either directly or indirectly.

As indicated above, the typical dairy farm has several activities more or less closely related to each other, a fact which tends to obscure the relations between the income and expenses for each and affects the decisions which will be made from time to time as costs and prices change.

The chief element in the cost of producing milk is feed, with labor next, the two together constituting two-thirds or more of the total cost. The remainder consists of a number of smaller incidental charges. In order to simplify the discussion as much as possible these are taken up separately. With the same purpose in view, milk production is considered primarily as an independent enterprise, then in its relations to the whole farm business. That the figures may be most generally usable, they are given as quantities to which anyone may apply prices or cost rates for any given time or locality. On the average, these basic factors of cost do not change so much or so frequently as do prices, although they show a wide range, suggesting the possibility of important changes in financial results to be brought about by changes in management.

The figures presented were obtained through the cooperation of 48 farmers during the calendar year 1920. These farms were divided into five groups, according to similarity in the more important factors of location, markets, feeds, herd management, and the like. Group A is made up of 12 farms in the eastern part of Sheboygan County; group B includes 8 farms in the eastern part of Columbia County; group C includes 11 farms west and south of Milwaukee in the Milwaukee milk district; group D is made up of 8 farms also in the Milwaukee milk district, but lying in a compact group to the north, most of them in Ozaukee County; group E includes, besides 7 farms in the southeast corner of Marathon County, 2 other farms of similar characteristics, but in other counties. (See Table 1.) The farms range in size from 17 acres to 240 acres, the size of herds from 3 cows and 1 heifer to 28.7 cows and accompanying stock cattle; in production from 13,000 pounds average per cow, including dry time and discards, down to 2,830 pounds per cow for the year. Some of the herds were purebred, but most of them were grade herds, with or without some pure-bred animals.

TABLE 1.—*General characteristics of the farms studied.*

	Group A (Sheboygan County).	Group B (Columbia County).	Group C (Milwaukee County).	Group D (Ozaukee County).	Group E (Marathon County.)	All farms.[1]
Number of records............	12	8	11	8	9	48
Average area..........acres...	75	145	107	59	106	97
Crop area...............do...	55	98	74	49	45	64
Pasture area...........do....	14	43	30	9	49	28
Horses, per farm....number..	3	4	4	3	3	3
Land value, per acre..,........	$200	$120	$150	$150	$70	$137
Land value, per farm........	$15,000	$17,500	$16,000	$8,800	$7,400	$13,300
Buildings, value per farm.....	$4,600	$7,800	$8,000	$4,500	$3,100	$5,600
Machinery, value per farm [2]...	(9) $1,490	(6) $2,250	(5) $1,700	(8) $1,275	(9) $1,470	(37) $1,590
Number of cows, per farm....	13.1	18.5	14.2	9.6	10.2	13.1
Milk produced, per farm, pounds.....................	128,606	128,926	95,215	60,123	56,655	96,103
Average milk produced per cow, pounds................	9,820	6,940	6,700	6,290	5,570	7,320
Winter production..per cent..	46.5	59.4	58.2	49.2	46.2	51.9
Summer production ....do....	53.5	40.6	41.8	50.8	53.8	48.1

VARIATIONS OBSERVED IN THE FACTORS SHOWN.

In size of farm:						
Largest............acres..	150	210	171	79	240	240
Smallest........do....	17	72	58	26	32	17
In number of cows:						
Largest herd...........:	18.4	28.7	28.2	12.6	23.8	28.7
Smallest herd.............	7.4	7.5	5.2	4.2	3.0	3.0
In average production, pounds per cow:						
Highest herd.............	13,000	8,370	8,050	9,350	6,320	13,000
Lowest herd.............	8,050	4,950	4,170	5,220	2,830	2,830

[1] The rates in this column in all tables are weighted averages figured from totals.
[2] Figures in parentheses show the number of farms reporting.

The quantities of feed and labor used, the number of cows in the herd, and the amount of milk produced were reported each month, together with price of feeds and of milk. A financial record was also kept, from which the data for figuring the other costs were obtained. The observations were made by working farmers for their own herds. Although they did not go into the more minute details, the farmers were conscientious in their observations of the main elements. For this reason it would seem possible for any farmer with little difficulty to check for his own farm any of the facts and conclusions here presented.

FEED REQUIREMENTS AND CONSUMPTION.

Naturally the kinds and amounts of feed supplied to cows for milk production vary greatly. Not only are the kinds and qualities of feeds on different farms numerous, but the number is multiplied by all the kinds and grades that may be purchased.

Henry and Morrison, in "Feeds and Feeding," tabulate analyses of nearly 350 feeding stuffs used in the United States. Twenty-six different concentrates, nine kinds of dry roughage, and eight kinds of succulent roughage, besides pasture, were reported as fed to a group of cows in association work in Wisconsin. Of course, these different feeds have different values for milk production—values which are more or less accurately reflected in the usual schedules of prices for the various components, materials, and mixtures.

Obviously all these different materials must be reduced to fairly definite relations to some standard if feeding animals is to be anything short of pure guesswork. Profitable feeding is a fine art, but an art developed on a basis of countless experiments to determine, by chemical analyses and by physical measurements, the relative values of different feeds for production and the feed requirements of cows of different capacities. The standards thus established serve as a means of reducing the different feeding practices to a common basis for comparison, and as a rough guide to the prices which may be offered or demanded for feeds of various kinds.

Armsby's feeding standards, as given in Henry and Morrison's "Feeds and Feeding," 1917 edition, have been used in the calculations of feed values and feed requirements for this study, the principal unit of measurement being the therm of net energy. Digestible protein must not be overlooked, however, in compounding rations or in comparing the values of concentrates, especially the cereal and oil-mill by-products which are used to balance rations.

The quantities of grain, hay, silage, and fodder fed to herds in the five groups are shown in Table 2. The term "grain" includes, besides the home-grown corn, oats, and barley, the various purchased mill feeds, brewers' grains reduced to a dry basis, and beans. The hay fed was mostly clover, with some alfalfa. Silage includes, in addition to corn silage, pea silage, with small amounts of soiling crops on a dry-matter basis. "Fodder" was mostly cornstalks, including little or no grain. Besides the feeds thus supplied, the cows had pasture in varying amounts and of varying qualities. The term "pasture" covers all the feed the cows gather for themselves during the summer, from wild or rough land unsuitable for crop production, from meadows or fields definitely set aside for the purpose, and from the aftermath of the other fields. Thus, pasture is an exceedingly variable quantity, both in the amount of feed provided and in the number of cows it will support and the time it will provide feed. It is unfortunate that pasture can not be more clearly defined and directly measured, as it plays a very important part in the management of dairy herds.

In order to approximate the amount of feed supplied by pasture and to explain the relations between feed consumption and milk production, the feeding standard and analysis of feeds mentioned above were used in calculating the feed requirements of the cows and for comparing the amounts of feed supplied in the several areas. The pasture season may begin in April and may continue into December. For present purposes the year was divided into two periods of six months—the winter season November 1 to May 1, and the "summer," or pasture season, from May 1 to November 1. Many farmers do not turn the cows out to pasture until the latter part of May and are obliged to resume feeding by the middle of July. The practice varies, of course, with the amount of feed supplied by pasture and the number of animals to be fed. The price of feeds and of milk affect the use of pasture; in 1920, with feed high in price and falling milk prices, many farmers did not resume feeding as early as they would under normal conditions.

The estimated annual feed requirements of the cows included in the study, due allowance being made for differences in size of the cows, the quantity of the milk produced and its quality, were computed according to the Armsby feeding standard (see Table 2). The net energy values of the average quantities used of the different feeds were then computed. The feed contribution of pasture was computed as the difference between the net energy required and the net energy supplied by the feeds supplementing pasture during the 6 months from May 1 to November 1. This calculation assumes that the cows maintained approximately the same body weight during the year, which, however, is not strictly true. On this basis, pasture supplied nearly one-fourth of the estimated feed requirements of the cows and somewhat less than that proportion of the total net energy supplied during the year.

TABLE 2.—*Feed consumption per cow and per 100 pounds of milk produced on 48 Wisconsin farms, 1920, together with the computed net energy values of this feed.*[1]

	Group A.	Group B.	Group C.	Group D.	Group E.	All farms.
Number of farms............................	12	8	11	8	9	43
Average production per cow, pounds......	9,820	6,940	6,700	6,290	5,570	7,320

ANNUAL FEED CONSUMPTION, PER COW (IN ADDITION TO PASTURE).

	Group A.	Group B.	Group C.	Group D.	Group E.	All farms.
Grain, pounds.............................	2,987	7,914	1,854	1,484	1,056	1,990
Hay, pounds..............................	2,045	2,581	2,743	2,358	2,372	2,430
Silage, etc., pounds.......................	8,496	7,993	7,640	9,140	3,948	7,591
Fodder, pounds...........................	852	124	448	1,527	393	595

NET ENERGY VALUES OF FEED SUPPLIED PER COW.

	Group A.	Group B.	Group C.	Group D.	Group E.	All farms.
Estimated requirement (year total), therms	4,850	4,085	4,304	3,772	3,949	4,490
Reported fed, therms......................	4,576	3,618	3,870	3,849	2,375	3,750
Pasture supplied, therms..................	859	1,248	961	914	1,574	1,053
Total provided, therms.............	5,435	4,866	4,831	4,763	3,949	4,803
Per cent of total required supplied by pasture	17.7	30.6	22.3	24.2	40.0	23.5

FEED SUPPLIED (IN ADDITION TO PASTURE) PER 100 POUNDS MILK.

	Group A.	Group B.	Group C.	Group D.	Group E.	All farms.
Grain, pounds.............................	30.4	27.6	27.7	23.6	19.0	27.2
Hay, pounds..............................	20.8	37.2	40.9	37.5	42.6	33.2
Silage, etc., pounds.......................	86.5	110.1	119.3	145.4	71.4	103.7
Fodder, pounds...........................	8.7	1.8	6.7	24.3	7.0	8.1

VARIATIONS OBSERVED IN RATE OF FEEDING GRAIN.

	Group A.	Group B.	Group C.	Group D.	Group E.	All farms.
In quantity of grain fed per cow:						
Largest, pounds.....................	5,454	2,614	3,053	3,146	1,807	5,454
Smallest, pounds....................	1,265	1,144	735	763	209	209
In grain fed per 100 pounds milk:						
Highest, pounds	43.5	39.6	45.2	34.3	28.5	45.2
Lowest, pounds......................	16.7	21.1	12.0	14.3	5.9	5.9

[1] The net energy values and standard requirements used in the computations for this and other tables in this bulletin are those published in "Feeds and Feeding," edition previously referred to. In his book, "Nutrition of farm animals" (1917), Dr. H. P. Armsby discusses the whole problem of feeding cows in minute detail, making a revision of the standard net energy requirements for milk production of approximately 10 per cent less than the figure used in these computations, based on the earlier tables. As these older tables are probably much more generally available to farm readers through "Feeds and Feeding," and Professor Eckles's book, "Dairy Cattle and Milk Production," and his research bulletins published by the Missouri Agricultural Experiment Station, the computations have been made on that basis rather than according to the modified standard.

It is evident that high-producing cows need more feed than low-producing cows. It is conceivable that production may be limited by lack of sufficient feeds of the proper kind. How far it is possible to increase production by supplying more feed is a question which can be answered only by trial, but it was acknowledged by some of the farmers reporting that their cows gave, in 1920, less milk than usual because of restricted grain feeding owing to relative prices of feeds and milk. The higher yields must usually be obtained by increased use of concentrates. Cows use digestible protein and net energy for two purposes; first, to maintain their bodies, and, second, for producing milk or flesh. The protein and net energy devoted to the first purpose are called the maintenance requirements and the feed supplying them the " maintenance ration." Whatever digestible protein and net energy there may be in the ration above the maintenance requirements are devoted to production. Milk production

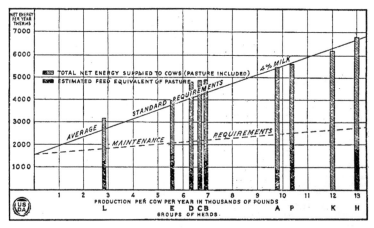

FIG. 1.—Computations of the net energy supplied to cows as reported by farmers compared with standard requirements show a very intimate relation between quantity of feed and quantity of milk produced, a relation which liberal feeders turn to their advantage.

may be limited by the amount of digestible protein supplied, and as the annual yield increases more attention must be given to this factor (as feeders recognize by adding more grain), especially the high-protein concentrates for their best cows. Total amount of feed, even of a well-balanced ration, may be a limiting factor in milk production. The amount of milk produced is the basis for feeding cows individually instead of giving the same amount to each. Some feeders still persist in the latter practice.

The relation between the maintenance requirements, total requirements, and milk production at rates up to 13,000 pounds per year is indicated in Figure 1. The upright bars show the production per cow in nine cases; H represents the highest herd; L, the lowest herd; A, B, C, D, and E, the averages of the groups into which the farms are divided; K, a single cow reported by Professor Eckles; and P, 120 cows taken from the Register of Production (Circ. 129 of the Wisconsin Agricultural Experiment Station). The full length of the bars shows the net energy values ·of the feed supplied in the respective cases, including the allowance for pasture as above noted. The solid part of the bars shows the net energy attributed to pasture.

The higher-producing cows are unusally larger than the lower-producing cows, and require more for maintenance, but the difference is not very great; in fact, some high-producing cows may be smaller than their lower-producing sisters. The total net energy requirements increase more rapidly after maintenance is provided; the requirements for production increase uniformly with increase in milk yield of the same quality; milk rich in butter fat, however, requires a higher rate per pound of milk than low test milk. (The net energy requirements for milk production is given by Armsby as 0.3 therm for each pound óf 4 per cent milk. The revised standard for 4 per cent milk is given as 0.265 therm per pound of milk, which is 10 per cent less than the figure used in these computations as noted above. Similar reductions are given for milk of other butter fat tests.)

The comparative economy of high-producing cows in a dairy enterprise is widely recognized. In this regard, tests conducted under comparable conditions, as in cow-testing association work, are conclusive. Considering the whole farm business, however, under different conditions, the case is not so clear, complicated as it is by varying prices and amount of feeds. The feeds consumed per 100 pounds of milk are shown in Table 1, together with the number of therms of net energy reported fed, including the allowance for pasture. The unit requirements shown in the table can hardly be used for single months or shorter periods, as they vary widely throughout the year according to practice and production, each of the items ranging from nothing up to a high figure per 100 pounds. Their unit requirements will nevertheless apply reasonbly well to different years because feeding habits do not change rapidly.

While the higher-producing cows consume the larger quantities of feed, particularly of grain, the difference is not so great when reduced to a unit basis, as is indicated in the case of grain in Figure 2, showing the average annual production of each of the herds and the number of pounds of grain fed per 100 pounds of milk produced.

The problem of feeds is presented in this detail to develop the method of calculating the feed equivalent of pasture, and to reiterate the advantage of adequate feeding of cows. Within the limits observed on these farms and up to the point where cows begin to show marked evidence of putting on flesh, production seems to increase with the quantities of feed supplied, financially as well as physiologically.

The prices used in figuring the cost of feed in 1920 were as follows:

Grain, $60 per ton; hay, $25; silage, $10; fodder, $15, and pasture $15 per cow for the season, with local variations.[2] At these rates the feed cost of milk was $2.02 per 100 pounds. These were the prices most commonly named, and they represent market values at the farm rather than actual cost. The actual cost of growing the crop is difficult to work out from data ordinarily available. Moreover, the

---

[2] For the Marathon group (Group E) the price of grain was $75 a ton and of pasture $9 a head for the season.

farmer feels that he ought to get through his cows as much as he would receive by selling his grain and hay.

One trouble with using market prices for feeds is that the home-grown feeds are not put to the test of sale agreement between interested parties as to grade. Much of the feed used for livestock is not marketable, or if marketable would be docked in price. Hay, however, has a relatively high market price because so much of it is fed out at home that the surplus is seldom more than enough to meet the demand of deficit areas. Then, too, the memory of high prices received persists, and it is common to assume that all the available supply might have been sold at those prices if it had not been fed, which of course is contrary to the experience of the most optimistic speculators. Then there is the expense of getting the feeds to market and the important consideration of maintaining fertility of the land through use of farm manure.

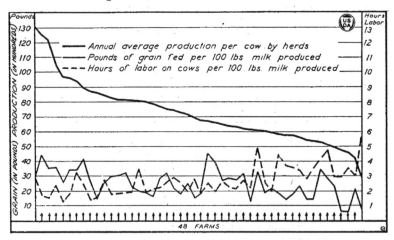

Fig. 2.—The higher producing cows usually get a higher proportion of concentrates in their rations than the others. The high producers are economical of labor.

Some farmers had to pay, in 1920, as high as $100 a ton for a part of their feed (in bag lots). Most of the purchased grain fed during the year was bought at prices above $60 per ton—even bran nearly touching that figure. Oats and corn would have sold for more than this for a considerable time. Although the price dropped sharply in the fall, and farmers perhaps did not get $60 per ton for their feed through the cows, it is felt that $60 is a reasonable figure to use.

Hay is figured at $25 per ton, though some hay was purchased at $30 and quotations for alfalfa went even higher. It takes a high price to make it worth while for a farmer to sell hay, especially if his farm is heavily stocked. Hay at $25 in the barn will ordinarily show a profit over cost of growing. This is approximately its conversion value compared with grain at $60 per ton.

Silage at $10 per ton is high or low according to the yield per acre. At ordinary yields, common practice and going rates for labor, corn silage cost very close to $10 per ton for the 1919 crop, most of which was fed in 1920. The 1920 crop also was made with high-priced labor. The pea silage bought cost about $2.50 per ton, plus the labor of getting it, which, while considerable in amount, was .done at odd times. The beets and the pea-vine silage fed were placed on the same basis as corn silage. Silage does not have a market value, but is assigned its value in various ways, sometimes from the price of corn, sometimes from cost of putting it up, sometimes from values of some feed which it will replace. Occasionally silage is sold at auction, but the price paid at a sale is not a very good indication of value, depending as it does on the necessities of the bidders and the cost of moving it to the place where it will be fed. Corn fodder has about twice as much dry matter per ton as silage, and nearly twice as much net energy, but is subject to somewhat greater waste, and is not highly rated where hay is abundant. If it may be contended that the prices used are too high for home-grown feed, it can hardly be denied that if all the feed needed had been purchased the total feed cost would have exceeded the amount figured. At any rate, such other prices as may seem fitting may be applied by anyone who wishes to take exception to those used.

In 25 cases where the cash paid out for feed for cattle was accounted for separately, the range was from $45 to $2,200, with an average somewhat more than $600 per farm. The average total feed cost for cows per farm at the rates given above is as follows: Group A, $2,345; Group B, $2,548; Group C, $2,131; Group D, $1,397; Group E, $1,001; all farms, $1,937. This compares with a general average of $2,569 per farm as the value of the milk produced. The average offset for manure is $278 per farm, ranging from $158 in Group E to $414 in Group B. (See manure credit below.) In special cases the manure may be worth more than this—when the quantity of concentrates fed is large, the need of the land great, and the management of the manure such as to avoid ordinary losses of plant-food value.

MANURE CREDIT.

The value of the manure produced on a dairy farm is considerable. It is generally shown as a credit or offset to cost. It is not a cash item, as it might seem to be at first glance from its usual position in the cost statements. It is closely associated with the prices or cost of feeds. If the farmer buys feed, he brings fertility to his farm; if he feeds his own crops he retains part of the fertility on his farm and can better afford to figure his feed as costing less than market price (less cost of marketing) than he can to part with his crops. The price a farmer gets for any feed he sells includes some payment for the plant food contained in the feed sold. Similarly, the price he pays for feed bought includes some payment for the fertility thus secured. The value placed on this is variable, and is somewhat obscured by the primary considerations leading to sale, or by the more direct use as feed in the case of purchases. While the fact is widely recognized, consciously or unconsciously, that some allowance for the plant food saved to the farm or brought to it properly may be made, there is more or less disagreement as to the amount of the allowance which should be made. This difference arises from different needs of different farms and alternative sources of plant food.

The amount of manure recovered and drawn to the fields is about 1 ton a month for each cow. The feeding season is about 7 months; the other 5 months the cows are outdoors most of the time. The estimated value of manure on Wisconsin farms in 1920 is $2.25 a ton for that produced during the feeding season and about half that price for the manure left on the fields and pastures, together amounting to $21.25 for the year for each cow.[3] At this rate the credit to milk production on account of manure is 29 cents per 100 pounds for the farms studied.

LABOR APPLIED TO MILK PRODUCTION.

The man labor spent on cows and milk per cow averaged 171 hours per cow for the year, or 28 minutes a day. This covers milking, feeding, caring for the barns, utensils, and the like. It does not include hauling manure away from the barn, delivering the milk, or care of the young stock. One farmer with a large herd spent 368 hours per cow of direct labor on cows, while the least work reported was 116 hours per cow. Five farms spent as little as 20 minutes a day per cow on care of cows, and only four farms spent more than 45 minutes per cow. Five farmers used milking machines part of the year and by use of them were able to reduce the labor to a low point, but several other farmers not equipped with machines spent very little more time on their cows than those using machines. The total labor on the dairy herd averaged 2,706 hours per farm for the year, of which 2,251 hours was for cows. The labor requirements by groups of farms is shown in Table 3.

TABLE 3.—*Labor requirements. Hours of labor per farm, per cow and per 100 pounds of milk produced, together with variations observed, on 48 Wisconsin dairy farms in 1920.*

	Group A.	Group B.	Group C.	Group D.	Group E.	All farms.
Number of farms............................	12	8	11	8	9	48
Average production, per cow, pounds.....	9,820	6,940	6,700	6,290	5,570	7,320
LABOR REQUIREMENTS (HOURS).						
Total per farm, cattle....................	2,808	3,305	2,838	2,433	2,112	2,706
Cow work only, per farm..................	2,328	2,721	2,377	2,094	1,714	2,251
Cow work per cow........................	178	146	167	219	169	171
Cow work per hundredweight of milk.....	1.81	2.11	2.50	3.48	3.03	2.34
VARIATIONS OBSERVED.						
In labor per cow per year:						
Highest farm, hours.................	368	221	276	304	215	368
Lowest farm, hours.................	116	118	116	146	141	116
In labor per hundredweight of milk:						
Highest farm, hours.................	2.84	2.95	4.73	4.96	5.85	5.85
Lowest farm, hours.................	1.23	1.75	1.90	2.57	2.24	1.23

Of the total labor applied to the dairy herd, 85 per cent was spent on the cows, 5 per cent on delivering milk to factory or shipping point, and 10 per cent on caring for the young stock. Half the

---

[a] A. R. Whitson, head of the department of soils, University of Wisconsin, is the authority for the price here used and the allowance of half this value during pasture season.

farmers hired their milk hauled; most of those selling in Milwaukee paid for hauling. Some of the labor of milk production was performed by women and children, but such labor was converted to the equivalent of man labor.

There is considerable variation in the amount of work accomplished in an hour on the different farms. Pressure of other work has much to do with this factor. On the whole, the amount of work required is proportional to the number of cows in the herd, small herds receiving very little more time per cow than the large herds. The higher-producing herds, with one exception, where official testing was done, required no more time than the lower-producing herds. The man labor required to produce 100 pounds of milk was materially less, in most cases, for the higher-producing herds than for the lower-producing herds. The lowest requirement reported was 1.23 hours, the highest 5.85 hours. (See the broken line in Fig. 2.)

The amount of time spent on cows is affected by a number of things, the more important among them being the convenience of the stable, location of feed storage, character of equipment, personal characteristics of the owner, and distribution of production. The amount of time devoted to cows on a given farm does not increase materially with increased yield. Milking takes a little longer where yield is high, as there is more feed to handle and a few more cans to wash, but doubling production does not by any means double the work required. Any tendency to increase labor requirements of the higher-producing cows is offset by the effect of yield on the rate per 100 pounds. (See Fig. 2.)

Most of the labor on cows on these farms was performed by the farmer or his family, only 14 of the 48 employing hired men regularly. Fifteen herds were handled by partnerships, or by fathers and sons. Under these conditions it is difficult to determine an average rate of wages for the purpose of figuring the labor cost of milk. Farm wages were high in 1920; many paid $75 a month and board to hired men, a cost of about $100 per month. The monthly duty of a hired man varies considerably, but runs between 250 hours (40 cents an hour) and 300 hours (33⅓ cents an hour). In view of wages paid other workers, 40 cents an hour would appear to be a reasonable figure to use in calculating the cost of milk. On this basis the labor cost of milk in 1920 was 94 cents per 100 pounds (2.34×40). Only 48 per cent of these 48 farmers, 54 per cent of the cows, and 56 per cent of the milk would come within this figure. Hauling milk to the factory or receiving station is not included, and a hauling charge ranging from 10 to 25 cents per 100 pounds, according to amount sold and distance hauled, must also be met.

If feed is figured at market prices at the farm and the costs other than labor are considered as fixed in the computation, we find, as will be seen later, that the balance left for labor was not, on the average, large enough to pay 40 cents an hour. But, even if it had been, half the farmers spent more than the average amount of time on their milk production, and therefore accepted less than the average rate (40 cents an hour) for their labor; while those who, by doing their work more quickly or because of the high production of their cows, required less than the average time per 100 pounds, got more than the average rate. Similarly, if labor and other costs are figured at

a uniform rate, some farmers find that they got full market price
for their feed, while others fell far short of it.

OTHER COSTS—INCIDENTALS, OVERHEAD.

Feed and labor make up by far the largest part of the cost of producing milk, but in addition to these major costs there are other items
which must be considered in figuring total costs, such as cow cost,
bull service, buildings, equipment, bedding, and general expenses
(items of irregular amount and occurrence, such as insurance, vet-
erinary expense, cow testing, and organization dues).

While it is true that these overhead expenses are higher for pure-
bred herds than for grade herds, and for high-producing herds than
for low-producing herds, they do not vary regularly with production,
nor do they bear any close and necessary relation to feed and labor
costs on any given farm or group of farms. The Pearson formula[4]
assigns 25 per cent of the total cost to these items. A study of costs
in New Hampshire in 1911 showed them to form about 10 per cent.
In western Washington in 1917–1920 they were found to be 20
per cent. In northwestern Indiana they were nearly 23 per cent.
In these latter studies the overhead costs were largely offset by the
credits. At what figures these costs will settle in any period under
observation is determined by the prices and valuations of the sundry
items involved, and having been once estabilshed they maintain the
given relations only if prices rise and fall together and in the
same proportions. It is possible by modifying operations to reduce
the proportion of overhead expense to total costs, and particularly
to reduce this item in the cost of 100 pounds of milk by increasing
production.

COW COST.

Cow cost is based on the fact of depreciation, whether caused by
death (which entails practically the total loss of the value of the
animal), by culling, or by price changes. It also includes an allowance for interest on the investment in cows, which, however, is not a
loss. Cow cost is a very variable figure at best.

On these farms, 775 different cows were used to maintain an average for the year of 630.25 cows. There were 621 cows on these 48
farms January 1, 1920, appraised at $165 each; 24 cows were pur-
chased at an average of $195; 130 heifers freshened for the first time
during the year, valued at $125 each; 112 cows were sold for $150
each; 13 died and were practically a total loss; and there were left
on the farms at the end of the year 650 cows, valued at $130 each.
This gives a depreciation of 18 per cent for the year, or $35.20 per
head for the average number kept, or 48 cents per 100 pounds of
milk. This depreciation was unusually large, owing to the high
price of cows in the fall of 1919, which established the value at the
beginning of the year, while at the end of the year appraisal was
unduly low because of discouragement over milk prices, resulting in

---

[4] In the course of the controversy over prices for fluid milk in the Chicago milk district
in 1917 Prof. F. A. Pearson, then of the University of Illinois, brought out a statement
of the unit requirements for producing milk to be used in computing a fair price to producers for fluid milk under changing costs of labor and feeds. See Bulletin 216, University of Illinois.

no demand for surplus stock, everybody wishing to cut down herds, with no purchasers in sight. The changes in values and in number of cattle are shown for each of the groups of farms in Table 4.

TABLE 4.—*Changes in values and numbers of cattle on 48 Wisconsin dairy farms during 1920.*

	Group A.	Group B.	Group C.	Group D.	Group E.	All farms.
Number of farms..........................	12	8	11	8	9	48
Average production per cow (pounds).....	9,820	6,940	6,700	6,290	5,570	7,320

AVERAGE VALUE OF CATTLE, 1920.

	Group A.	Group B.	Group C.	Group D.	Group E.	All farms.
Cows, Jan. 1.........................each..	$192	$187	$170	$95	$123	$165
Cows, Dec. 31.........................do....	190	115	125	65	120	130
Cows purchased.......................do....	193	108	159	87	263	195
Cows sold.............................do....	175	165	150	69	140	150
Other cattle, Jan. 1.................do....	130	106	126	45	85	104
Other cattle, Dec. 31................do....	157	97	92	37	93	100
Other cattle purchased.............do....	286	66	89	43	277	208
Other cattle sold....................do....	46	32	39	18	47	38
Increase in value of other cattle per farm..	534	794	[1] 664	181	323	[2] 493

NUMBERS OF ANIMALS (GROUP TOTALS), 1920.

	Group A.	Group B.	Group C.	Group D.	Group E.	All farms.
Cows, Jan. 1...............................	164	143	156	75	83	621
Cows, Dec. 31.............................	154	150	168	79	99	650
Cows bought..............................	7	2	3	3	9	24
Cows sold.................................	37	25	16	13	21	112
Heifers brought in........................	22	34	29	15	30	130
Cows died.................................	2	4	4	1	2	13
Different cows............................	193	179	188	93	122	775
Other cattle, Jan. 1......................	69	116	98	47	70	400
Other cattle, Dec. 31.....................	86	116	122	43	65	432
Purchased................................	25	5	10	5	10	55
Born......................................	162	136	148	77	100	623
Sold......................................	134	94	113	60	59	460

[1] Data available for only 10 farms.　　　　　[2] Basis is 47 farms.

The average value of cows of the better herds was practically the same at the end of the year as at the beginning. This would perhaps lead to the conclusion that there had been no depreciation, which was apparently the case in the Sheboygan County herds. In the other groups, however, the young cows did not increase in value to the same extent, the cows sold did not bring so near their inventory valuations, and the valuations at the end of the year were much smaller than at the beginning of the year. In figuring the depreciation, the young cows added to the herd were appraised at 75 per cent of the average value of the cows in the herd at the beginning of the year. The charge to the herd on account of heifers is made in order to separate the milk production enterprise from the cost and returns on account of young stock. The average value of the young cows so added was $339 per farm, or $125 per head, which approximates the cost of raising a 2-year-old heifer of the quality of the average cows in the herds.

The death risk is rather small, in this case a little more than 2 per cent. There is a further appreciable loss, but variable, due to accidents and culling, where the loss is partial, as in the case of cows sold to the butcher or to other dairymen. Even when condemned for tuberculosis the cows are not a total loss. Cows culled from the best herds may be attractive purchases for herds of lower standards of production, and the shrinkage in value may thus be distributed over a number of farms, but ultimately the cow will find her way to the butcher or will die on some farmer's hands. Breeders probably suffer less from depreciation than farmers who buy their stock, because they have young stock increasing in value.

Normal depreciation has not been of sufficient importance to attract strict analytical study. As an indication of the scope of the problem, it may be remarked that besides the 18 per cent here estimated under conditions acknowledged to be unusual, a rate of depreciation of 26 per cent in one year has been observed in one herd of over 300 cows, where the rearing of young stock was not a part of the farm business and so did not obscure the figures, and of about 11 per cent in another herd of 40 cows where all the factors involved were kept strictly separated. In each of these latter cases, the cows were forced and used up much faster than dairy farmers usually find economical. In times of rising prices there may be an increase in the value of cows more than enough to offset physical depreciation.

On the whole, from the year-after-year viewpoint, it would seem fair to allow a minimum of 6 per cent for depreciation instead of the 18 per cent claimed for 1920, and 6 per cent interest, both based on the valuation at the first inventory. At this rate there would be a charge of $19.80 per head, or 27 cents per 100 pounds of milk for these cows. If the full depreciation claimed by these farmers were allowed, the cow cost would be 62 cents per 100 pounds, of which 14 cents is for interest.

BULL SERVICE.

Bulls vary widely as to their value and the size of the herd they head. So far as milk production alone is concerned, bull service as a cost is just short of negligible. Except for his influence on the young stock, one bull will do as well as another, and the prevalence of grade and scrub bulls throughout the State indicates that many farmers fail to appreciate the bull's influence on the value of the stock. Frequently bulls are kept on farms for convenience only, and, except for convenience (occasionally contagious abortion in a neighborhood may be the deciding factor), keeping a bull is not warranted on a large number of farms. By cooperative ownership some farmers have been able to secure all the advantages of the use of a high-class pure-bred bull in improving their young stock. Occasionally a farmer with a small herd is obliged to maintain a bull because of inability to secure service locally at a reasonable fee.

Bull service does not count as an offset to cost of keep on the farms under discussion. Under ordinary circumstances in Wisconsin the difference between the cash received for veal calves and the current market value of the milk fed to them is sufficient to meet the cost of keeping an ordinary grade bull, especially in view of a general tendency to include the bull's feed and care with the feed and care of cows in farm calculations. Any costs incident to higher valuations are properly assigned to the cost of the offspring and do not therefore affect the cost of milk.

BUILDING COST·(RENT).

This item varies from farm to farm (see Table 1), and close examination reveals no direct relation between it and the cost of 100 pounds of milk. The better herds are usually kept in the more pretentious barns. Many an old barn, however, shelters a first-class herd, and many an otherwise profitable herd is rendered unprofitable by excessive investment in buildings and equipment. The building cost per cow is lowest when the barn is full and production is high; for a given farm it is the same regardless of the number of cows kept or of their rate of production. Suppose a barn with fixed equipment is worth $4,000 in its present condition and will house 15 cows. This would indicate a rent of $300 a year at 7½ per cent of valuation, at the lowest calculation. If the barn were full of 10,000-pound cows the cost per 100 pounds would be 20 cents, while if they were 7,000-pound cows the cost would be 28.5 cents; a reduction from 15 to 10 cows of the higher grade would raise the cost to 30 cents per 10 pounds while reducing to ten 7,000-pound cows would make it nearly 43 cents.

Since barns are commonly built to provide for the cattle, horses, crop storage, and frequently for hogs and machinery as well, it is more bother than most farmers are willing to take to apportion the cost of the buildings to the different purposes served, to say nothing of a general hesitation about assigning a value which is largely an estimate, or observing the actual cost over any extended period of time.

Assuming $2,500 as an average estimated· valuation of the share of the buildings devoted to the cows and storage of the necessary feed, and 7½ per cent as a minimum allowance, the rent is $187.50, or 20 cents per 100. pounds of milk for the average herd.

EQUIPMENT.

The equipment used in milk production, beyond the items usually considered as a part of the barn, is limited in amount. It includes pails, cans, strainers, scales, feed carts, a few cream separators, and an occasional milking machine. The investment in equipment, excepting the milking machines, averages about $50, on the farms studied, and entails an annual expense of· about $12 replacements, which, together with the interest, warrants an allowance of 1¼ cents per 100 pounds of milk.

GENERAL EXPENSE.

The reports on this item were not complete in all respects, but judging from those which were complete, an allowance of 5½ cents per 100 pounds, or about $50 per farm for the year would be necessary to meet general expenses not provided for otherwise.

PRODUCTION AND PRICES.

Cows naturally produce more milk in summer than in winter, but milk and dairy products are wanted all through the year in about the same quantities. This creates the deficit and surplus problem, so vexing to manufacturers and distributors, and is reflected in the prices paid. Winter milk is at a premium, and summer milk returns a price determined by the quantity offered and the speculator's judgment regarding the probable price of the stored products later in the year.

The distribution of the production of the 48 farms reporting is shown in Figure 3. Over half the milk was produced in five months, March to July, inclusive. August, September, and October were the months of lowest production. Pasture stimulates the milk flow of cows freshening in the early winter, and there is further increase in the spring owing to the large numbers of cows freshening at that time. One reason for the spring freshening is to avoid the necessity for the heavier feeding required to sustain the milk flow in winter. August is a trying month for cows, chiefly on account of failing pastures, and once they are allowed to fall off in yield they can not often economically be brought back in the fall. Grass pasture, so far as milk cows are concerned, is about exhausted by the

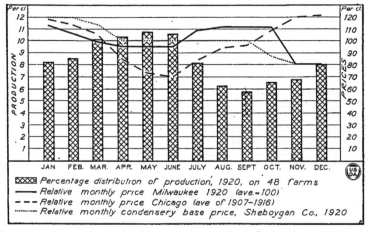

Fig. 3.—Spring was the season of maximum production on these farms in 1920. Failure of milk prices to follow the normal course in the autumn was marked and had a depressing influence on production.

middle of July, and supplementary feed is necessary unless fresh pasture is available, or the aftermath of the fields[5] is sufficient. Grain feeding was not resumed as promptly in 1920 as usual on account of the high price of feed and discouraging outlook for milk prices.

The average price of milk for 1920 for the Sheboygan County group was $2.33 per 100 pounds, the range being from $1.81 to $3.13; for the Marathon County group from $2.11 to $2.94, average $2.67; for the Columbia County group $2.30, with a range from $2.12 to $2.46, while the Milwaukee producers averaged $3.15 net at the farm. The range in price in any locality is caused not so much by difference in schedule prices paid by the factories as by the distribution of the production and the butter-fat test of the milk.

As between the Milwaukee price and prices outside Milwaukee, the higher price paid is due in no small measure to the activities of the

---

[5] Aftermath is secured from grain and crop fields as well as from hay fields.

Milwaukee Milk Producers' Association, which looks after the interests of its members, bargaining with the distributors with respect to price and taking care of all the surplus. Milk is sold at a uniform price per can (of 8 gallons) delivered in Milwaukee. All producers get the same price except for the cost of hauling to the city. Two cents per 100 pounds is paid into the association fund by each member to help meet unavoidable manufacturing losses. Market milk usually commands a higher price than factory milk, because of additional requirements and because no by-products are returned. Condensaries also pay somewhat higher prices than cheese factories for the latter reason. Outside the Milwaukee area practically all the milk is sold by test. Producers of high-test milk in the Milwaukee area usually plan to sell cream or have a special trade.

Price quotations commonly available need considerable interpretation because of differences in practice. Condensaries usually quote a base price per 100 pounds of 4 per cent milk. Creameries and cheese factories pay for butter fat according to test, and quote prices as so many cents per pound of butter fat. Thus, comparisons with whole milk are made by a simple multiplication, usually neglecting the skim milk or whey value. However, unless the milk tests 4 per cent the farmer does not get the quoted price. Comparatively few get the quoted price, for if cows are milking heavily, especially if they are Holsteins, the test is likely to be less than 3.5 per cent. Some factories pay a straight rate per pound of fat as shown by the test, others deduct from or add to the base price a fixed number of cents per pound for every tenth of 1 per cent by which the milk tests less or more than 4 per cent. This may have the effect of penalizing the farmer with low-test milk. Many condensaries maintain collecting routes and charge for hauling, saving the farmers the cost of making daily trips. These are perfectly straightforward and open practices, but they mean that many farmers do not and can not get for their milk the prices that quotations would indicate.

The differences between quoted prices and what a farmer gets for his milk are likely to be still more marked when several months are averaged. The common average of monthly quotations reflects the true average, in which alone the farmer is interested, only when the sales of milk are the same for each month. To illustrate: A common average price of $3.624 was quoted in 1919 by a condensary. One of its patrons, using his actual monthly prices in the common way, found his average was $3.31, with a range from $2.55 to $4.05. But even with good Guernsey cows he did not get the base price for more than 6 per cent of his milk; 65 per cent was sold in five months at $2.55 to $2.91 while the quoted price ran from $3.29 to $3.40 in these same months. His true average price for the year, before deducting hauling, was $3.09, netting $233 less on his total sales than his " average " price led him to suppose.

Other practices have been noted, all aiming to avoid unfavorable discussions among patrons about prices. In short, each producer must know definitely what he gets for his milk and why he does not get more.

The normal price movement by months is also shown in Figure 3 as the relative monthly prices 1907–1916 in Chicago. The highest prices are usually paid in December and January; lowest prices in May, June, and July. The 1920 prices did not follow the normal course. Instead of going up in the fall they went down. The high prices in late summer are partly explained by the success of producers in bargaining, with high cost as the basic argument, which distributors considered, but following the fall in grain prices, milk prices could not be sustained.

The spread in prices is some inducement to winter production, and those who produce in winter receive higher average prices for their milk than those who follow the normal practice. But the spread in prices is not commonly held to be sufficient to offset the extra cost of feeding for winter milk production, above roughing the cows through the winter and turning them out all summer where pasture is abundant. The chief arguments, however, for winter production are that the total yield for the year is increased by having the cows freshen in the fall, and that there is a better distribution of the farm labor over the year. Many who follow this practice say " it is easier to produce milk in the winter." There is more time to care for the cows, feeding can be controlled more definitely, there is not so much milking to do in hot weather and harvest time, and the production of cows suffers less from heat, flies and shrinking pastures. With the higher producing cows, year-around feeding is necessary, so that the time of freshening is not a significant factor in feed consumption. There may be some increase in " opportunity cost of feed," by which is meant that the farm price of feeds increases from harvest time on, and feeds might have been sold at increased prices instead of being fed, but the necessary supplies are definitely set aside on a dairy farm for the stock and the question of possible sale is disposed of early in the season. Purchased feed is also provided for on the same basis. The record of 120 cows in the Register of Production,[6] selected without regard to any factor other than date of freshening, were examined to determine the effect of time of freshening on production and on feed supply. The records of the cows freshening in each month of the year were taken. There was no significant difference in the average production, and very little difference in the character of the feed consumed. The fall-fresh cows were fed a little more grain than the cows freshening later in the winter, but the April and June fresh cows consumed more than the average. Of the 421 cows listed, only 142 freshened between March 1 and September 1.

Storage of butter, cheese, condensed milk, milk powder, and ice cream materials, tends to keep the winter price of milk below and the summer price above the points they would naturally reach without storage facilities. This is of benefit both to the consumer, who can have as much as he desires at all times, and to the producer, who, on account of the tendency of production to concentrate in the low price months, gets a higher price for his year's product.

Though the cost of milk is higher in winter than in summer, it is more nearly uniform than prevalent methods of figuring indicate. The tendency to figure cost of feeding dry and nearly-dry cows as part of the cost of winter milk is practically unavoidable. It results in a cost figure, which would mean a prohibitive price of dairy

---

[6] Wisconsin Agricultural Experiment Station Circular 129.

products or would spell loss to producers at winter prices of feed and usual prices paid for milk. It does not lay enough emphasis on the value of pasture as feed, and reconciles the producer to an unduly low price of milk in summer. " Pasture is cheap feed," farmers say; no grain is needed and less work is required; so low prices in summer are accepted with a shrug of the shoulders. Yet the cost of carrying cows through the winter is part of the cost of producing milk on pasture. Thus, though winter prices do not go so high as cost figures would indicate, summer prices do not go so low. A more nearly uniform price throughout the year, as urged at times, would tend to increase the concentration of production in the summer and would defeat its purpose. Only in the market-milk zone can anything approaching uniform price be effective, and then only when distributors are relieved of the burden of surplus milk, and on condition that milk from outside the normal territory for the city supply be kept off the city market, conditions which practically can not be met in the present state of organization of producers and of their control over production.

Adjustment of prices in favor of producers is a slow matter, requires continuous effort, and has not yet been wholly satisfactory with respect to price. Pooling plans have met with some measure of success in times of rising prices, but their story is not yet fully told; some of them have recently caused financial loss to participants. Still this kind of effort warrants the support of every producer. The individual producer must look to his own devices for improving his situation with regard to current costs and prices. Each needs to analyze his own results to determine current relations between his costs and prices, and proceed to make the adjustments necessary. These adjustments will usually be in the direction of adequate feeding, prompt and thorough culling, constructive breeding, and keeping expenses as low as possible.

In the matter of individual items of expense, one must bear in mind that low expense does not necessarily mean low cost if thereby production is restricted. Most dairy farms are provided with silos, although occasionally a farmer is found who does not yet believe in the silo. Most of these who do not have silos will have them when they can spare the funds necessary to build them. Silos are investments rather than expenses, and pay good returns. Silage as feed is itself relatively cheap and makes other feeds more effective. Drinking cups call for a considerable outlay, but the effect on production is so marked that more than one farmer has said that he would not be without them if he had to install a new set each year. In one case observed, a barn housing only six cows was provided with cups.

The matter of justifying the remodeling of stables to provide more light and air, concrete floors, swinging stanchions, which add to the health and comfort of the cows, is more difficult, as is also the question of outlay for litter carrier, feed cart, chutes for hay, and other labor-saving devices, the return from which is distributed over a long time and is indirect. It is impossible to relate losses from tuberculosis directly to poor accommodations for cows, but there is small room for doubt that a relation between the two exists. Many a farmer suffers a daily drain because of poor arrangement of his buildings and equipment, caused by the gradual development of his business and often not to be altered without rebuilding, but a tax none the less on his effort. As pointed out the judicious additional expenditure for high protein feeds to balance the ration, and for any kind of feed to maintain production as pastures fail has an effect on the year's return greatly in excess of its relation to the immediate cost. There is also the further means of reducing costs by careful scrutiny of the relative values of the feeds available, buying those which provide digestible nutrients at the lowest figures. In this way the dairyman produces at the lowest possible feed cost, and guards against paying excessive prices.

The constant examination of conditions is not a guaranty against loss, but is effective insurance against ordinary failure to make ends meet.

SUMMARY OF COSTS.

From this discussion it appears that the cost of producing milk in 1920 on the 48 farms in question was $3.30 per 100 pounds, with a modified allowance for depreciation, or $3.57 per 100 pounds with depreciation as observed. This figure includes an allowance of 19 cents per 100 pounds for interest, which some authorities maintain should not be displayed as an element of cost, though they agree that the price of the product must ordinarily be sufficient to cover it.

TABLE 5.—*Average cost of producing milk on 48 Wisconsin farms, 1920.*

Item.	Average cost per 100 pounds.	Per cent of net total cost.
Feed	$2.02	
Allowance for manure	.29	
Net cost of feed	1.73	53
Labor	.94	28
Hauling	.09	3
Other costs:		
Cow cost $0.27		
Building use .20		
Equipment use .015		
General expenses .055	.54	16
Net total cost	3.30	100
Deducting interest	.19	
Cost not including interest	3.11	
Average price of milk	2.65	
Opportunity loss	[1] 0.65	

[1] Or $0.46 without interest.

To offset a part of this loss some of the farmers took whey back from the factory for hog feeding, while others had skim milk for calf feeding. No fair estimate of the amount of this offset was obtained. Its value to a farmer depends on the use to which he puts it, and while it might be argued that farmers should use all the by-product in reduction of cost of the main product, cheese factory patrons do not always care to feed as large a number of hogs as the whey from their milk will feed, nor is it always possible to do so without changing their farm plans. Those who skim at the farm can make good use of the skim milk for calf feeding, and often have some left over for hogs. Of the 48 farmers reporting, 27 sold whole milk, 12 sold to cheese factories and 9 sold cream.

The computed cost of 100 pounds of milk and the value of the milk produced on the farms studied is shown in Table 6. The value of the milk fed to calves and of that used by the farm family varies materially. Neither value is generally considered of much significance. The quantity sold is usually the figure used by farmers when they think of quantities at all, except for records of individual cows. In this study the quantities sold, fed to calves, and used by the farm family were reported separately each month. The proportion of the total quantity produced used on the farm varied from about 1½ to 15 per cent. In the months of lowest production, in a few cases practically all of the milk was used on the farm.

TABLE 6.—*Cost of 100 pounds of milk and average value of milk produced on 48 Wisconsin dairy farms in 1920.*

	Group A.	Group B.	Group C.	Group D.	Group E.	All farms.
Number of farms..............	12	8	11	8	9	48
Average production per cow, pounds....................	9,820	6,940	6,700	6,290	5,570	7,320

VALUE OF MILK PRODUCED, 1920.

	Group A.	Group B.	Group C.	Group D.	Group E.	All farms.
Cash sales, per farm...........	$2,691.00	$2,690.00	$2,713.00	$1,742.00	$1,343.00	$2,281.00
Calf milk.....................	233.00	305.00	222.00	112.00	70.00	194.00
Family supply.................	73.00	73.00	64.00	39.00	99.00	71.00
Total, at market price..	2,997.00	3,068.00	2,999.00	1,893.00	1,512.00	2,546.00
Average price per 100 pounds .	2.33	2.38	3.15	3.15	2.67	2.65

COMPUTED COST OF 100 POUNDS OF MILK, 1920.

	Group A.	Group B.	Group C.	Group D.	Group E.	All farms.
Feed..........................	$1.80	$2.07	$2.19	$2.32	$1.82	[1] $2.02
Manure—credit.................	.24	.32	.32	.34	.28	.29
Net cost of feed..........	1.56	1.75	1.87	1.98	1.54	[1] 1.73
Labor at 40 cents per hour.....	.68	.84	1.00	1.39	1.21	.94
Hauling milk sold..............	.08	.14	.07	.02	.18	.09
Cow cost.....................	$0.24	$0.31	$0.30	$0.18	$0.24	$0.27
Building use..................	.12 .41	.20 .56	.28 .65	.25 .54	.18 .53	.20 .54
Equipment and general........	.05	.05	.07	.11	.11	.07
Total cost...............	2.73	3.29	3.59	3.93	3.46	3.30
Claimed depreciation..........	.02	1.00	.45	.52	.29	.48

[1] This is 8 cents per 100 pounds larger than a strict weighted average. For prices used in computations see page 7.

OTHER CONSIDERATIONS.

In separating one enterprise for particular study from a number of closely related, interdependent enterprises it is necessary to make some more or less arbitrary divisions of costs and benefits, to which many may take exception. There is opportunity for argument on every item of milk cost, especially in the feed and labor items. Competition is the ruling factor, with farmers bidding against each other and consumers paying as little as they are obliged to pay. It is not so much a question of what milk costs as of what farmers are willing to take for their milk. Just as a long period of rising prices was necessary to attract enough milk to glut the market in the fall of 1920, so a period of low prices will be necessary to discourage the less-favorably situated dairymen to the point of giving up milk production, and they seem likely to persist, partly because milk production seems to pay better than other alternatives and partly because they are willing to take less for their milk and therefore less for their services than others. This is what makes it so hard for dairymen to agree on a price and to hold together when a price is set. No price can be established on " cost of production," for, once a price is made, costs are immediately altered either by increasing production or decreasing or increasing costs of materials, or, more than likely, a combination of these alternatives. During the process of adjustment some dairymen are bound to suffer loss.

Some farmers concerned in this study were able to produce milk at a cost less than the price received by virtue of unusually high production or of unusually low expenses, or of a combination of the two, resulting in low unit costs. Most of them also had other enterprises which contributed to the annual income. Farm income exceeded farm outlay, but out of that margin had to come the living of the family and the maintenance of the farm buildings, equipment, live stock, and supplies. Many dairymen had to draw on these supplementary sources of income in 1920 to make up for deficits in the main line.

The supplementary sources of income are different in the different areas. The farmers in the Sheboygan County group sold crops, hogs, and poultry products in about equal amounts. The Columbia County group sold peas for canning, and hogs. The Milwaukee district groups sold truck crops and potatoes. The Ozaukee County group sold potatoes, sugar beets, and poultry. The Marathon County group sold some crops, hogs, and logs. A few farms reported no income except from the dairy enterprise. The receipts from crops varied from nothing up to about $4,000, hogs up to $1,400, poultry and eggs up to $975. The average increase in cattle other than cows was $493. The expenses incurred in producing these items were not separated. With the exception of the cattle, these supplementary sources of income do not warrant figuring an average, as an average would give only a vague and distorted idea of them. The crop inventory at the end of the year was in most cases larger in quantity than on January 1, but smaller in value, the price shrinkage amounting to several hundred dollars on many farms if compared with the crop value figured at prices in effect January 1, 1920.

The larger farms offered greater opportunity for employing the labor available, had larger incomes and larger expenses. As far as milk production is concerned, there does not seem to be any correlation between size of farm and cost of milk. Recession of inventory values absorbed a large part of such income as might be figured.

ORGANIZATION OF THE UNITED STATES DEPARTMENT OF AGRICULTURE.

Secretary of Agriculture	HENRY C. WALLACE.
Assistant Secretary	C. W. PUGSLEY.
Director of Scientific Work	E. D. BALL.
Director of Regulatory Work	
Weather Bureau	CHARLES F. MARVIN, Chief.
Bureau of Agricultural Economics	HENRY C. TAYLOR, Chief.
Bureau of Animal Industry	JOHN R. MOHLER, Chief.
Bureau of Plant Industry	WILLIAM A. TAYLOR, Chief.
Forest Service	W. B. GREELEY, Chief.
Bureau of Chemistry	WALTER G. CAMPBELL, Acting Chief.
Bureau of Soils	MILTON WHITNEY, Chief.
Bureau of Entomology	L. O. HOWARD, Chief.
Bureau of Biological Survey	E. W. NELSON, Chief.
Bureau of Public Roads	THOMAS H. MCDONALD, Chief.
Fixed Nitrogen Research Laboratory	F. G. COTTRELL, Director.
Division of Accounts and Disbursements	A. ZAPPONE, Chief.
Division of Publications	JOHN L. COBBS, Jr., Chief.
Library	CLARIBEL R. BARNETT, Librarian.
States Relations Service	A. C. TRUE, Director.
Federal Horticultural Board	C. L. MARLATT, Chairman.
Insecticide and Fungicide Board	J. K. HAYWOOD, Chairman.
Packers and Stockyards Administration	CHESTER MORRILL, Assistant to
Grain Future Trading Act Administration	the Secretary.
Office of the Solicitor	R. W. WILLIAMS, Solicitor.

This bulletin is a contribution from the

Bureau of Agricultural Economics	HENRY C. TAYLOR, Chief.
Farm Management and Cost of Production	H. R. TOLLEY, in Charge.

23

UNITED STATES DEPARTMENT OF AGRICULTURE

DEPARTMENT BULLETIN No. 1145

| Washington, D. C. | ▼ | May 10, 1923 |

MIGRATION RECORDS FROM WILD DUCKS AND OTHER BIRDS BANDED IN THE SALT LAKE VALLEY, UTAH.

By ALEXANDER WETMORE, *Assistant Biologist, Division of Biological Investigations, Bureau of Biological Survey.*

CONTENTS.

INTRODUCTION.

The Bear River marshes at the north end of Great Salt Lake, Utah (Pl. I, Fig. 1), a region highly attractive to wild ducks and other waterfowl, are known as one of the great centers where such birds gather in the West, so that information regarding the migratory movements of the large numbers of birds that visit this region is of interest and importance. In the period from 1914 to 1916, the writer, while engaged in the study of an alkali poisoning prevalent among waterfowl in the Salt Lake marshes, had opportunity to band and release a considerable number of ducks and other birds (Pl. I, Fig. 2), a fair proportion of which were killed subsequently in other regions.

Reports already published [1] have dealt with the so-called duck sickness, and have detailed methods by which a considerable number of the birds affected were cured. Before such individuals were set at liberty each was marked with a numbered band, and record made

---

[1] Reports made on the author's investigations of the duck sickness in Utah are contained in bulletins of the United States Department of Agriculture as follows: No. 217, Mortality among Waterfowl around Great Salt Lake, Utah (Preliminary Report), 10 p., 3 pls., 1915; and No. 672, The Duck Sickness in Utah, 25 p., 4 pls., 1918. Other reports based in part on investigations then made are contained in Bulletin No. 793, Lead Poisoning in Waterfowl, 12 p., 2 pls., 1919; and No. 936, Wild Ducks and Duck Foods of the Bear River Marshes, Utah, 20 p., 4 pls., 1921.

NOTE.—This bulletin is a report on a study of the migratory movements of waterfowl and other birds, based on banding operations carried on in Utah from 1914 to 1916. It is for the information of sportsmen, ornithologists, and others interested in bird migration and the protection of game birds.

of the number, the species of bird, and the date of release. In addition to wild ducks, numbers of young of other marsh birds were marked in a similar manner before they were able to fly. The release of these banded birds was given publicity, and reports on bands recovered have been received from widely scattered sections in the United States and even from Canada and Mexico. An account of these records is presented in detail in this bulletin.

Bands were placed on 1,241 individuals of 23 species of birds of large or medium size belonging to various families, the majority on wild ducks of 9 species. The bands used were of two kinds, both made of aluminum and manufactured originally for use in marking poultry. In each style a serial number was stamped on one side. The reverse of one was marked, " Notify U. S. Dept. Agt., Wash. D. C.," and of the other, " Notify Biological Survey, Washington, D. C."

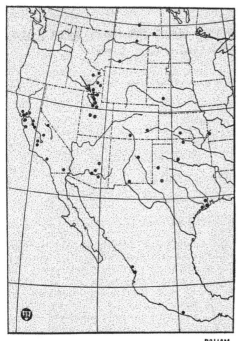

In the case of birds that had been at liberty for more than a year the bands returned were badly worn, and those received after two years' wear had become thin and friable. One band more than four years old was recovered, but it is probable that on most birds that survived beyond a period of three years the bands had become worn until they were broken and lost. To be used successfully, therefore, bands for water birds should be twice as thick as those ordinarily used for poultry.

B2118M

FIG. 1.—Map of the western United States showing migrations of ducks and other wild birds banded in the Salt Lake Valley, Utah, in three years, 1914–1916, return records to 1923. The place of banding and release is marked by a cross (position indicated by an arrow). Localities where banded birds were later recovered are indicated by round dots, a single dot in some cases representing several returns.

The thicker bands are now being employed by the Biological Survey in its extensive bird-banding operations.

All birds banded as a basis for the present study were released near the Duckville Gun Club, at the mouth of Bear River, Utah, save for a few that in 1916 were given to the State fish and game commission for exhibition at the annual State fair in Salt Lake City; these were subsequently released near Geneva, Utah, on the shore of Utah Lake. Of the 1,241 birds that were banded, 182 returns have been received, or somewhat more than 14 per cent.

Of the whole number banded, 994 were ducks, of which 174 were recovered. The number of returns from birds of this group, a little more than 17 per cent, indicates the results that may be obtained from work in banding birds of this family.

In .considering these records it is to be borne in mind that many of the birds banded at the mouth of Bear River, Utah, were individuals that had not bred there. Drake pintails and a few mallards begin to come in to that region after the first week in June and continue to gather, perhaps from points far distant, from then until late in fall. Migration out to other points begins about the first week in September, and there is a constant shifting of the waterfowl population during the fall as birds arrive from the north or leave for other points. The Bear River bays begin to freeze about Thanksgiving time, and in normal years by December 1 ducks are forced out of this region, although an occasional open winter may permit their sojourn until in January or later. A few remain to winter in Utah in sloughs or channels kept open by spring water, but the majority perform extended flights to other regions. Some of the wintering mallards pass a short distance northward into the Snake River drainage in Idaho.

Returns from all the records cover a vast area (see Fig. 1) extending from western Missouri and Kansas west to California, and from southern Mexico (Guerrero) to Saskatchewan, Canada. A study of the results indicates one general line of flight to the west from the Salt Lake Valley to California, a route followed by green-winged teals and shovelers and part of the mallards and pintails. Another line of flight, taken by a group of birds that includes cinnamon teals, redheads, pintails, and mallards, crosses to the Great Plains region and thence south into Texas. Indications are that some of the birds last mentioned fly north and east to cross the divide separating Snake River from the headwaters of the Missouri and follow down east of the foothills of the Rocky Mountains; that all pursue such a route is doubtful, since there is nothing to prevent a direct flight to the east or southeast across any of the mountain passes. There is also a third general migration southward over the Rocky Mountain Plateau, probably by a comparatively small number of birds, that carries the snowy herons and some of the ducks through the scattered lakes and ponds. found in central and southern Utah, New Mexico, and Arizona.

MIGRATION AND OCCURRENCE RECORDS.

✓ Following is a list of species from which there have been no returns, with figures to indicate the number of individuals banded and set at liberty:

	Banded.
Western grebe	4
Pied-billed grebe	4
California gull	1
Ring-billed gull	1
Baldpate, or American widgeon	14
Ruddy duck	2
American bittern	1
Black-crowned night heron	7
Avocet	6
Black-necked stilt	4
Marbled godwit	1

Species from which returns have been received are as follows, the numbers in the first column following each indicating the number of individuals banded, and in the second the number recovered and reported upon:

	Banded.	Returned.
Double-crested cormorant	1	1
Mallard	72	22
Gadwall	17	4
Green-winged teal	336	49
Cinnamon teal	45	5
Shoveler, or spoonbill	48	9
Pintail	221	34
Redhead	239	51
White-faced glossy ibis	104	1
Great blue heron	11	4
Snowy heron	83	4
American coot	18	1

MALLARD.

In comparison with some of the other species of ducks, the number of mallards handled was comparatively small, as only 72 were banded and released during the three seasons in which this work was carried on. Of these, 22—a little more than 30 per cent—were killed and reported subsequently (see Table 1). Seven were secured near the mouth of Bear River within a few miles of their place of release, 6 of them, and possibly 7, during the fall in which they had been marked. The other 15 individuals divide into two main groups, one of birds that remained until late fall or winter in the same general region as the mouth of Bear River, and the other of birds that made extended migrations to other regions.

In October two mallards marked during the preceding month were taken on Bear River near Tremonton, not far in an air line from the mouth of the stream. During November these ducks may wander more extensively, as, though several were taken during this month near the mouth of Bear River and one a short distance from Tremonton, others were reported in the sloughs near Great Salt Lake, west of Salt Lake City, and on Utah Lake, near Provo. In addition to these, late in November one was secured near Logan, Utah, and another on Snake River, in Fremont County, Idaho. Records for December are more widely scattered. One bird was killed on Bear River, near Collinston, December 13, and another on the Logan River, in Cache Valley, December 28. In the same month a drake was shot far to the south, on the Sevier River, north of Delta, Utah. During January one was taken near Pebble, Bannock County, Idaho, on the 14th, and another near Stone, in the same State, on the 19th. The latter bird was free from June 17, 1915, to January 19, 1917.

From this account it would seem that a number of mallards remain in ponds and channels kept open by the inflow of spring water after more extensive bodies of water are closed by ice. Such birds pass north in suitable localities as far as the Snake River in Idaho.

Return records from other States are notable more for their wide scattering than for anything else. One banded bird secured near Bishop, in Owens Valley, Calif. (in the Great Basin), on October 16, does not necessarily indicate an early migration from the Salt Lake Valley, for it had been at liberty for two years, so that there is no certainty that it had come from Utah the year it was killed.

A second bird was taken about March 1 in southeastern New Mexico, and a third on December 28, west of Houston, Tex. Part of the mallards from Salt Lake Valley, therefore, go west into California and part into the drainage basins leading into the western part of the Gulf of Mexico.

TABLE 1.—*Record of returns for banded mallards.*

Date released.[1]	Date recovered.	Place recovered.	
		State.	Locality.
Sept. 16, 1914	Fall, 1914[2]	Utah	Mouth of Bear River.[3]
Sept. 25, 1914	....do	....do	Do.
Sept. 17, 1916	Nov. 28, 1916	....do	Do.
Sept. 28, 1916	Nov. 12, 1916	....do	Do.
Do	....do	....do	Do.
Oct. 23, 1916	Nov. 15, 1916	....do	Do.
Sept. 16, 1914	Dec. 28, 1914	....do	On Logan River, Cache Valley, near Logan.
Sept. 23, 1914	Oct. 9, 1914	....do	2 miles east of Tremonton.
Sept. 25, 1914	Nov. 29, 1914	....do	At Utah Lake, 3 miles southwest of Provo.
Sept. 5, 1915	Nov. 7, 1915	....do	2 miles south of Thatcher.
Sept. 14, 1915	Nov. 26, 1915	....do	5 miles southwest of Logan.
Aug. 27, 1916	Dec. 31, 1916	....do	On Sevier River, 7 miles north of Delta.
Sept. 7, 1916	Oct. 9, 1916	....do	3 miles southwest of Tremonton.
Sept. 28, 1916	Dec. 13, 1916	....do	On Bear River, near Collinston.
Sept. 29, 1916	Nov. 10, 1916	....do	West Lakes near Salt Lake City.
Sept. 23, 1914	Jan. 14, 1915	Idaho	Pebble, Bannock County.
Sept. 24, 1914	Nov. 15, 1914	....do	On Snake River, Fremont County.
June 17, 1915	Jan. 19, 1917	....do	Near Stone.
Sept. 24, 1914	Oct. 16, 1916	California	9 miles south of Bishop.
Sept. 25, 1914	Mar. 1, 1915[4]	New Mexico	Newman Ranch, near Newman, 35 miles northeast of El Paso, Tex.
Sept. 23, 1914	Dec. 28, 1915	Texas	25 miles west of Houston.

[1] All banded and released at the mouth of Bear River, Utah.
[2] This bird and the one following were killed some time after November 1, of the year in which marked.
[3] The band of one other mallard killed here late in the fall of 1915 was lost, so that information as to date of banding is not available.
[4] Approximate date.

GADWALL.

Only 17 gadwalls were banded during the course of this work, but of these, returns came from 4 individuals (see Table 2). As all were killed in the immediate vicinity of the mouth of Bear River during the year in which they were released (except possibly in one instance), they offer nothing in regard to possible lines of migration of the species. Only one of the records is worthy of comment— an individual that was given its freedom August 27, 1916, and was killed below Willard, Utah, about October 12, 1916. Others lived at liberty only a comparatively short time.

TABLE 2.—*Record of returns for banded gadwalls.*

Date released.[1]	Date recovered.	Place recovered.	
		State.	Locality.
Sept. 11, 1915	Oct. 1, 1915	Utah	Mouth of Bear River.[3]
Do	Oct. 1-8, 1915	....do	Do.
Aug. 27, 1916	Oct. 12, 1916[2]	....do	Below Willard.

[1] All banded and released at the mouth of Bear River, Utah.
[2] The band taken from one gadwall killed in the fall of 1915 was lost before the number was recorded. This bird may have been released during 1915 or may have been one of three marked the previous year.
[3] Approximate date.

GREEN-WINGED TEAL.

PL. II, FIG. 1.

Of the total number of birds banded, 336, or slightly more than one-fourth, were green-winged teals, and 49 of these have been reported by hunters (see Table 3). Among 23 of these birds killed

TABLE 3.—*Record of returns for banded green-winged teals.*

Date released.[1]	Date recovered.	Place recovered.	
		State.	Locality.
Sept. 16, 1914	Oct. 7, 1914[2]	Utah	Mouth of Bear River.
Sept. 23, 1914	Nov. 24, 1914	....do	Do.
Do	Nov. 26, 1914	....do	Do.
Sept. 24, 1914	Oct. 10, 1914[2]	....do	Do.
Do	....do[2]	....do	Do.
Sept. 26, 1915	Oct. 20, 1916	....do	Do.
Sept. 28, 1915	Oct. 1-8, 1915	....do	Do.
Sept. 2, 1916	Oct. 1, 1916	....do	Do.
Sept. 7, 1916	Nov. 1, 1916[2]	....do	Do.
Sept. 11, 1916	Nov. 17, 1916	....do	Do.
Do	Oct. 20, 1916	....do	Do.
Do	Oct. 25, 1916	....do	Do.
Sept. 17, 1916	Oct. 20, 1917[2]	....do	Do.
Sept. 20, 1916	Oct. 2, 1916	....do	Do.
Do	Oct. 21, 1916	....do	Do.
Sept. 25, 1916	Oct. 20, 1916	....do	Do.
Sept. 29, 1916	Oct. 9, 1916	....do	Do.
Do	Oct. 4, 1916	....do	Do.
Sept. 30, 1916	Oct. 10, 1916	....do	Do.
Oct. 3, 1916	Nov. 16, 1916	....do	Do.
Oct. 15, 1916	Oct. 29, 1916	....do	Do.
Oct. 23, 1916	Nov. 20, 1916[2]	....do	Do.
Oct. 24, 1916	Oct. 31, 1916	....do	Do.
Sept. 16, 1914	Dec. 21, 1914	....do	New Moon Gun Club, near Salt Lake City.
Sept. 26, 1915	Dec. 21, 1915	....do	Near mouth of Jordan River.
Sept. 11, 1916	Oct. 20, 1916	....do	Sloughs west of Salt Lake City.
Sept. 20, 1916	Nov. 17, 1916	....do	Junction of Mill Creek and Jordan River, near Salt Lake City.
Oct. 10, 1916[3]	Oct. 12, 1916	....do	Utah Lake, near Geneva.
Sept. 30, 1916	Nov. 1, 1916	....do	North channel at mouth of Weber River.
Oct. 23, 1916	Nov. 13, 1916	....do	Mouth of Weber River.
Sept. 20, 1916	Jan. 28, 1917	California	Yolo County, 5 miles from Sacramento
Sept. 23, 1914	Jan. 17, 1915	....do	Big Lake, 1 mile from Clarksburg, Yolo County.
Sept. 2, 1916	Jan. 27, 1917	....do	Near Rutherford.
Sept. 16, 1914	Oct. 16, 1916	....do	Harvey Gun Club grounds, at junction of Cordelia and Suisun Sloughs.
Do	Jan. 17, 1915	....do	Near Gustin, Merced County.
Sept. 30, 1916	Jan. 28, 1917	....do	Near Ingomar, Merced County.
Do	Jan. 27, 1918	....do	Near Los Baños.
Sept. 29, 1916	Dec. 10, 1916	....do	7 miles southeast of Los Baños.
Sept. 11, 1916	Dec. 16, 1916	....do	8 miles southeast of Los Baños.
Sept. 14, 1915	Jan. 10, 1917[2]	....do	Near Los Baños.
Oct. 3, 1916	Dec. 2, 1916	....do	Near Brito, Merced County.
Sept. 30, 1916	Jan. 28, 1917	....do	Do.
Oct. 23, 1916	Dec. 10, 1916	....do	Mouth of Pajaro River near Watsonville, Santa Cruz County.
Sept. 7, 1916	Dec. 27, 1916	....do	Near Maricopa, Kern County.
Sept. 16, 1916	Dec. 12, 1916	....do	Near Porterville.
Sept. 26, 1915	Jan. 16, 1916	....do	12 miles northwest of Wasco, Kern County (section 13, township 25 south, range 23 east).
Sept. 23, 1914	Jan. 6, 1916	....do	Semitropic.
Aug. 20, 1916	Dec. 20, 1916	....do	On holdings of Chico Land & Water Co., Orange County, 33 miles below Los Angeles.
Sept. 16, 1914	Nov. 17, 1915	....do	Gun club of Christopher Land & Water Co., between Santa Ana and Sunset Beach, Orange County.
Sept. 28, 1915	Dec. 19, 1915	Arizona	Near Miami.
Sept. 30, 1916	March, 1917	Colorado	Near Sanford, Conejos County.

[1] All banded and released at the mouth of Bear River, Utah, unless otherwise indicated.
[2] Approximate date.
[3] Released near Geneva, Utah, on Utah Lake.

near their place of release (near the mouth of Bear River), 21 were taken during the fall in which they were set free, after periods varying from a few days to more than a month. Two, however, survived for slightly more than a year, only to be taken in this same region. Seven others were reported from Utah, 2 from the mouth of the Weber River, and 4 from the marshes along the Jordan River or the sloughs west of Salt Lake City. One, set at liberty on Utah Lake, was killed in the same vicinity two days later. All 7 were taken during the fall in which they were banded.

It would appear that the majority, or at least many, of the green-winged teals found in fall in the Salt Lake Valley pass in migration to California, as 19 of the return records came from that State. Several were secured in the southern Sacramento Valley and others farther south in the marshes of the San Joaquin River in Merced and Fresno Counties. None were found north of Sacramento, but to the south records come from as far down as Semitropic and Wasco, in Kern County, in the interior; and from Orange County, south of Los Angeles, on the coast. A coastal record of interest is that from Watsonville, Santa Cruz County, south of San Francisco Bay. Several birds were secured in the famous ducking grounds in the vicinity of Los Baños. One of these individuals was taken as early as November 17, and all others during the months of December and January.

Elsewhere, one bird was recorded from near Miami, in south-central Arizona, in December, and one near Sanford, in southern Colorado, in March. Two of the ducks under discussion enjoyed their liberty for 24 and 27 months, respectively, before they were killed. Others were retaken during the winter following their release.

To summarize the data presented, it would appear that the majority of the green-winged teals leave Utah to winter in California, a few are found in Arizona, and a few returning north in spring pass through Colorado, at least along the upper courses of the Rio Grande.

CINNAMON TEAL.

Five return records were received from 45 banded individuals of the cinnamon teal, a small number, but one that includes notes of considerable interest. One released October 3, 1916, was taken in the same vicinity three days later. Another, banded September 2, 1916, was more fortunate, as it was not captured until October 1, 1917, more than a year later, when it was shot 3 miles north of the Duckville Gun Club, in the same marshes in which it had been set free: its travels during that year may be only conjectured. One banded September 1, 1916, was taken November 4, 1916, near the mouth of the Weber River, and another, marked September 4, 1916, was secured subsequently at the Rudy Duck Club in the marshes at the mouth of the Jordan River, on October 6, 1916. The fifth record is that of a bird released September 16, 1914, and recovered January 20, 1915, at Mainer Lake, Brazoria County, Tex., a short distance west of Galveston.

Though the slender evidence available indicates a migration of
this species from northern Utah to the Gulf coast of Texas, it is
probable that with further data some birds marked in the same
region will be recovered in California. Normally, the majority of
the cinnamon teals leave the region around Great Salt Lake before
the 1st of October, so that only straggling individuals are found
later, after the opening of the shooting season.

TABLE 4.—*Record of returns for banded cinnamon teals.*

Date released.[1]	Date recovered.	Place recovered.	
		State.	Locality.
Oct. 3, 1916.........	Oct. 6, 1916........	Utah..............	Mouth of Bear River.
Sept. 1, 1916........	Nov. 4, 1916.......	...do..............	Near mouth of Weber River.
Sept. 2, 1916..,.....	Oct. 1, 1917.........	...do..............	Bear River marshes, 3 miles north of Duckville Gun Club.
Sept. 4, 1916........	Oct. 8, 1916.........	...do..............	Marshes at mouth of Jordan River.
Sept. 16, 1914.......	Jan. 20, 1915........	Texas..............	Mainer Lake, Brazoria County, west of Galveston.

[1] All banded and released at the mouth of Bear River, Utah.

SHOVELER, OR SPOONBILL.

The percentage of returns on banded shovelers, or spoonbills, was
slightly higher than in the case of the cinnamon teal, as from a total
of 48 birds released 9 were subsequently reported (see Table 5).
Six of these were killed in the Bear River marshes (several in South
Bay, one on the Salt Creek marshes, and one on the Chesapeake
Bay) from a few days to several weeks after they had been banded.
One was captured at the mouth of the Weber River, and another at
the mouth of the Jordan, near Salt Lake City. The remaining bird
was taken near Vallejo, Calif., nearly 14 months after it had been
released. From this slight evidence it appears that some spoonbills
migrate from Utah to pass the winter in California.

TABLE 5.—*Record of returns for banded shovelers.*

Date released.[1]	Date recovered.	Place recovered.	
		State.	Locality.
Sept. 29, 1914.......	Oct. 17, 1914.......	Utah..............	Mouth of Bear River.
Sept. 1, 1916........	Oct. 12, 1916.......	...do..............	Do.
Sept. 25, 1916.......	Oct. 7, 1916........	...do..............	Do.
Sept. 28, 1916.......	Oct. 1, 1916.........	...do..............	Do.
Do...........	Oct. 8, 1916.........	...do..............	Do.
Do...........	Oct. 7, 1916.........	...do..............	Do.
Do...........	Oct. 21, 1916........	...do..............	Mouth of Weber River.
Sept. 29, 1916.......	Oct. 20, 1916 [2].....	...do..............	Mouth of Jordan River.
Sept. 1, 1916........	Oct. 23, 1917.......	California.........	Near Vallejo.

[1] All banded and released at the mouth of Bear River, Utah.
[2] Approximate date.

coast in Texas. The spring migration carries the latter individuals northward through the plains again, eastward as far as western Missouri and north at least into southern Canada. Spring records in the Missouri Valley drainage ceased after 1915, as in the following year spring shooting in the United States was prohibited by Federal law, and no further returns came from ducks killed at this season.

It may be noted that only a small part of the pintails found early in the fall in the Salt Lake Valley nest there, as the species is only moderately common as a breeder in that region. Migrants from other regions, probably to the northward, arrive early, even in June, and continue to gather in suitable areas until fall.[2]

Banding records furnish some idea as to the average length of life of a pintail after it reaches maturity. Of birds banded in September, 1914, one was taken in April and one in November, 1916, one in January, 1917, and one in December, 1917. Of those marked from August to October, 1916, one was shot in December, 1917, two in January and one in November, 1918, while one was fortunate enough to escape until the last of November, 1920, a period of slightly more than four years.

REDHEAD.

Domestic ties in the redhead family are as loose perhaps as among any of the North American ducks. Several females may use one nest for their eggs, and when ducklings appear they are self-reliant little chaps that as often as not start off on adventurous explorations of their own, with no regard for the movements of their mother. The parent may forsake her charges when they are less than half grown, and it is the rule for them to be left to their own devices at an early age. Though like some other children in their lack of respect for parental guidance and opinion, young redheads are gregarious and seek others of the season's hatching, so that they ordinarily travel in company. These inexperienced birds, as they passed the duck pens where birds convalescent from the duck sickness were confined, came over in search of company, and clambered out on shore in an attempt to join the ducks in the cages. Trapping them when they were still unable to fly was an easy matter, so that in 1915 and 1916 many were captured and 239 were banded and released. Fifty-one of these have been reported by hunters (see Table 7), more than half, 28 to be exact, being taken in the Bear River marshes, all during the fall of their release.

Most of the birds were marked in August and September. Two of the returns came during the month of September, one from a bird found dead from the duck sickness, and one from an individual drowned accidentally at the duck pens. Twenty-two were killed during October, a number potted by hunters as they passed in boats up or down the river, others shot at points on the bays in the delta of the

---

[2] See U. S. Dept. Agr. Bull. No. 936, pp. 7–8.

stream or near the river below Corinne. Two were secured on November 5 and two on November 12.

Among 16 other records for Utah, 6 came from the vicinity of Bear River above its mouth, or its larger tributaries within a radius of 50 miles. Five of these returns were secured between October 1 and 17 of the year of their release. A single individual shot November 22 near Honeyville was reported as thin and poor, and may have been diseased or injured in some way. One was killed near the Hot Springs, north of Ogden, on November 18, and 1 near the mouth of the Weber River, on October 29. From a little farther south 3 were reported from Syracuse, near the border of Great Salt Lake, 2 birds shot in company on October 14, and 1 on October 20; 2 were shot on October 2 in the sloughs west of Salt Lake City and another in the same vicinity about the middle of November. In the Narrows of the Jordan River, 20 miles south of Salt Lake City, 1 was killed December 24, 1915, while another was recorded from the Sevier River, near Gunnison, Utah, October 1.

Three marked redheads were secured in eastern Idaho, all in or near the drainage of Snake River. Two of these were shot on October 1 and 15, respectively, and 1 was taken in Bingham County on December 8, more than two years after it was released.

Scattered records from east of the Rocky Mountains have considerable value, as they indicate a line of flight to a winter range. One bird released September 27, 1916, was killed about November 27, near Ordway, in the drainage of the Arkansas River, on the plains of eastern Colorado. Another, banded October 23, 1916, was secured near O'Donnell, Dawson County, western Texas, on November 22. A third, set at liberty August 20, 1916, was killed near Nashville, Kingman County, south central Kansas, April 21, 1917, probably while in northward migration. The last of these distant records, one without apparent connection with the others, is that of an individual released between August 27 and September 27, 1916, and killed January 25, 1919, on the Florence Reservoir, near Florence, Ariz., in the Gila River Basin.

The majority of redheads on the Bear River marshes leave in fall migration between the 1st and 10th of September, and after that only stragglers are found. Indications from returns of banded birds are that the line of flight is eastward, probably to a wintering ground on the Gulf coast of Texas, though no returns have actually come from that region. It is possible that part of these birds travel northward to the drainage area of the Missouri and then swing southward over the plains, since two records come from eastern Idaho at the proper season to support such belief. Release of young birds late in September, after the bulk of the species has left, may induce more or less aimless wandering among some and account for part of the scattered returns. There is a distinct movement southward along the eastern shore of Great Salt Lake, however, for a distance of 60 miles, that may be an indication of a second line of southward flight. December records for Utah and Idaho are perhaps from injured individuals unable to perform extended flights.

TABLE 7.—*Record of returns for banded redheads.*

Date released.[1]	Date recovered.	Place recovered.	
		State.	Locality.
Aug. 15, 1915	Oct. 2, 1915	Utah	Mouth of Bear River.
Sept. 3, 1915	Oct.1–8, 1915	...do	Do.
Sept. 14, 1915	....do	...do	Do.
Sept. 20, 1915	Oct. 17, 1915	...do	Do.
Sept. 25, 1915	Oct. 3, 1915	...do	Do.
Do	Oct. 1–8, 1915	...do	Do.
Do	....do	...do	Do.
Do	....do	...do	Do.
Do	Oct. 1, 1915	...do	Do.
Sept. 28, 1915	Oct. 1–8, 1915	...do	Do.
Do	....do	...do	Do.
Do	October, 1915	...do	Do.
Aug. 25, 1916	Oct. 7, 1916	...do	Do.
Sept. 2, 1916	Oct. 20, 1916	...do	Do.
Sept. 4, 1916	Oct. 10, 1916	...do	Do.
Do	October, 1916	...do	Do.
Sept. 7, 1916	Oct. 2, 1916	...do	Do.
Do	Oct. 8, 1916	...do	Do.
Sept. 8, 1916	Nov. 12, 1916	...do	Do.
Do	Sept. 28, 1916	...do	Do.
Do	Oct. 22, 1916	...do	Do.
Do	Sept. 29, 1916	...do	Do.
Sept. 27, 1916	Oct. 5, 1916	...do	Do.
Do	Oct. 2, 1916	...do	Do.
Do	Nov. 12, 1916	...do	Do.
Do	Oct. 21, 1916	...do	Do.
Oct. 15, 1916	Nov. 5, 1916	...do	Do.
Oct. 21, 1916	....do	...do	Do.
Aug. 22, 1915	Oct. 1, 1915	...do	4 miles west of Logan.
Sept. 7, 1916	Nov. 22, 1916	...do	Near Honeyville.
Do	Oct. 11, 1916	...do	Salt Creek, near Tremonton.
Sept. 17, 1916	Oct. 7, 1916 [2]	...do	3 miles east of Tremonton.
Sept. 4, 1916	Oct. 8, 1916	...do	Near Bear River City.
Do	Oct. 17, 1916	...do	Do.
Sept. 17, 1916	Nov. 18, 1916	...do	Near Hot Springs, Boxelder County.
Sept. 4, 1916	Oct. 29, 1916	...do	Mouth of Weber River.
Do	Oct. 20, 1916	...do	Near Syracuse, Davis County.
Sept. 7, 1916	Oct. 14, 1916	...do	Do.[2]
Do	....do	...do	Do.
Aug. 28, 1916	Oct. 2, 1916	...do	Sloughs west of Salt Lake City.
Sept. 4, 1916	....do	...do	Do.
Aug. 27, 1916	Nov. 14, 1916	...do	Vicinity of Magna, near Salt Lake City.
Aug. 22, 1915	Dec. 24, 1915	...do	Narrows of Jordan River, 20 miles south of Salt Lake City.
Aug. 15, 1915	Oct. 1, 1915	...do	3 miles west of Gunnison.
Aug. 27, 1916	Oct. 1, 1916	Idaho	Mud Lake, near Hamer.
Aug. 20, 1916	Dec. 8, 1918	...do	Tanner Field Lake, Bingham County.
Sept. 4, 1916	Oct. 15, 1916	...do	Blackfoot Swamp, 12 miles north of Soda Springs.
Sept. 27, 1916	Nov. 27, 1916	Colorado	Ordway Lakes, near Ordway.
Aug. 20, 1916	Apr. 21, 1917	Kansas	Near Nashville, Kingman County.
Oct. 23, 1916	Nov. 22, 1916	Texas	Near O'Donnell, Dawson County.
Fall, 1916 [4]	Jan. 25, 1919	Arizona	Florence Reservoir, near Florence.

[1] All banded and released at the mouth of Bear River, Utah.
[2] Approximate date.
[3] This bird and the one following were banded and released at the same time and when killed were still in company.
[4] Released between August 27 and September 27.

RETURNS FROM OTHER BIRDS.

Records of five species of other families of birds may be considered briefly.

An immature double-crested cormorant that was banded on July 3, 1915, was shot near the Jordan River, 12 miles northwest of Salt Lake City, on October 10 of the same year.

Of 11 great blue herons marked in 1916 while in the nest, a return came from one bird, an individual banded July 3, 1916, and killed November 1, 1916, 4 miles southwest of Billings, Mont. The indicated northward movement after the breeding season is in accordance with similar habits recorded for little blue herons and egrets in the East.

An American coot, one of 18 marked on August 20, 1916, was shot on December 5 about 75 miles south, near Lehi, Utah. As this species is not hunted extensively in the West, nothing was heard from others.

Though 104 young white-faced glossy ibises were banded in rookeries where they nested in company with snowy herons, return has come from but 1 individual. This bird, marked July 3, 1916, and found sick on the shores of Tulare Lake, Calif., on October 22, 1922, indicates a migration movement from the Salt Lake Valley toward the southwest.

The snowy heron nests in colonies in the lower Bear River marshes, and on July 3 and 14, 1916, 83 nestlings were marked with bands. In March, 1917, a peon at Mexcaltitan, Territory of Tepic, Mexico, brought a bit of aluminum to a Japanese labor contractor, saying that he had found it on the leg of a heron that he had killed and eaten. The band had been preserved out of curiosity, as the peon was unable to read, but chance had brought a return on one of the snowy herons that was marked in Utah the previous year. About June 1, 1917, another snowy heron killed on the Papagayo Lagoon, in Guerrero, Mexico (long. 99° 48′ W., lat. 16° 48′ N.), was reported through the State Department by the American consul at Acapulco. A third record is of a snowy heron found on the San Pedro River, in northwestern Cochise County, Ariz., on April 13, 1919; and a fourth is furnished by a heron recovered at Escuinapa, Sinaloa, Mexico, on January 20, 1923.

These dates indicate that the breeding snowy herons of the Salt Lake Valley winter on the west coast of Mexico. Their route northward may follow the Colorado River, or birds may scatter in an inland flight that carries them more or less directly northward. In Utah it was observed that though part of the snowy herons arrived early, others continued to join the breeding colonies until late in June, observations that coincide with the late date at which one from this region was secured in Guerrero.

PUBLICATIONS OF THE UNITED STATES DEPARTMENT OF AGRICULTURE RELATING TO GAME BIRDS AND THE DISTRIBUTION AND MIGRATION OF BIRDS.

FOR FREE DISTRIBUTION BY THE DEPARTMENT.

Bird Migration. (Department Bulletin 185.)
Eleven Important Wild-duck Foods. (Department Bulletin 205.)
Propagation of Wild-duck Foods. (Department Bulletin 465.)
The Duck Sickness in Utah. (Department Bulletin 672.)
Food Habits of Seven Species of American Shoal-water Ducks. (Department Bulletin 862.)
Wild Ducks and Duck Foods of the Bear River Marshes, Utah. (Department Bulletin 936.)
Migration Records from Wild Ducks and Other Birds Banded in the Salt Lake Valley, Utah. (Department Bulletin 1145.)
Game Laws for 1922. (Farmers' Bulletin 1288.)
The Great Plains Waterfowl Breeding Grounds and Their Protection. (Yearbook Separate 723.)
Federal Protection of Migratory Birds. (Yearbook Separate 785.)
Conserving Our Wild Animals and Birds. (Yearbook Separate 836.)
Instructions for Bird Banding. (Department Circular 170.)
Directory of Officials and Organizations Concerned with the Protection of Birds and Game, 1922. (Department Circular 242.)
Annual Report of the Governor of Alaska on the Alaska Game Law, 1922. (Department Circular 260.)
Migratory Bird Treaty, Act, and Regulations. (Biological Survey Service and Regulatory Announcement No. 48.)

FOR SALE BY THE SUPERINTENDENT OF DOCUMENTS, GOVERNMENT PRINTING OFFICE, WASHINGTON, D. C.

Mortality Among Waterfowl Around Great Salt Lake, Utah. (Department Bulletin 217.) Price, 5 cents.
Lead Poisoning in Waterfowl. (Department Bulletin 793.) Price, 5 cents.
Game as a National Resource. (Department Bulletin 1049.) Price, 10 cents.

15

ORGANIZATION OF THE UNITED STATES DEPARTMENT OF AGRICULTURE.

Secretary of Agriculture_____ HENRY C. WALLACE.
Assistant Secretary_____ C. W. PUGSLEY.
Director of Scientific Work_____ E. D. BALL.
Director of Regulatory Work_____ ——————.
Weather Bureau_____ CHARLES F. MARVIN, Chief.
Bureau of Agricultural Economics_____ HENRY C. TAYLOR, Chief.
Bureau of Animal Industry_____ JOHN R. MOHLER, Chief.
Bureau of Plant Industry_____ WILLIAM A. TAYLOR, Chief.
Forest Service_____ W. B. GREELEY, Chief.
Bureau of Chemistry_____ WALTER G. CAMPBELL, Acting Chief.
Bureau of Soils_____ MILTON WHITNEY, Chief.
Bureau of Entomology_____ L. O. HOWARD, Chief.
Bureau of Biological Survey_____ E. W. NELSON, Chief.
Bureau of Public Roads_____ THOMAS H. MACDONALD, Chief.
Fixed Nitrogen Research Laboratory_____ F. G. COTTRELL, Director.
Division of Accounts and Disbursements___ A. ZAPPONE, Chief.
Division of Publications_____ JOHN L. COBBS, Jr., Chief.
Library_____ CLARIBEL R. BARNETT, Librarian.
States Relations Service_____ A. C. TRUE, Director.
Federal Horticultural Board_____ C. L. MARLATT, Chairman.
Insecticide and Fungicide Board_____ J. K. HAYWOOD, Chairman.
Packers and Stockyards Administration___⎱CHESTER MORRILL, Assistant to the
Grain Future Trading Act Administration⎰ Secretary.
Office of the Solicitor_____ R. W. WILLIAMS, Solicitor.

This bulletin is a contribution from—

Bureau of Biological Survey_____ E. W. NELSON, Chief.
  Division of Biological Investigations_____ E. A. GOLDMAN, in Charge.
  16

▽

UNITED STATES DEPARTMENT OF AGRICULTURE

 BULLETIN No. 1146

WASHINGTON, D. C.   PROFESSIONAL PAPER   April 5, 1923

THE INFLUENCE OF COPPER SPRAYS ON THE YIELD AND COMPOSITION OF IRISH POTATO TUBERS.

By F. C. Cook, *Physiological Chemist, Insecticide and Fungicide Laboratory, Miscellaneous Division, Bureau of Chemistry.*

CONTENTS.

PURPOSE OF INVESTIGATION.

For years Bordeaux sprays have been applied to the potato plant to control fungous diseases, particularly in the northern parts of the country where the late blight (*Phytophthora infestans*) frequently causes serious losses. In those parts of the Central and Southern States where potatoes are grown the only spray ordinarily applied is an arsenical to control the Colorado potato beetle. Arsenicals are usually added to the Bordeaux sprays. The formulæ of Bordeaux sprays may vary in different localities. A 5–5–50 spray is one in which 5 pounds of copper sulphate and 5 pounds of lime are used and the spray is made to 50 gallons with water.

The fact that potato plants treated with Bordeaux spray give larger yields of tubers than those which do not receive such applications has been established by a series of experiments extending over many years at the Vermont, Maine, and New York agricultural experiment stations. The influence of the copper sprays on the composition of the tubers, however, has received no detailed study in this country. In view of the importance of the potato crop it is surprising that practically no detailed analyses of potato tubers grown in the United States are available.

27475°—23——1

When in 1917 it was found that the solids, starch, and nitrogen contents of tubers from copper-sprayed potato plants were greater than those of tubers from unsprayed plants, an investigation was begun in the Bureau of Chemistry to determine the effect of Pickering sprays, barium-water sprays, and standard Bordeaux sprays as compared with that of noncopper sprays on the yield and on the composition of potatoes grown in different localities. The distribution of copper in the tubers, roots, stems, and leaves of the various sprayed and unsprayed potato plants was studied also.

RESULTS OF PREVIOUS INVESTIGATIONS.

YIELD OF POTATOES.

Giddings (20),[1] of the West Virginia station, fund that in 1909 three applications of Bordeaux increased the yield of potatoes 53.5 per cent and that in 1910 four applications increased the yield 39.3 per cent.

In New York Stewart and his associates (46, 47, 48) have conducted an extensive series of experiments to show the benefits of Bordeaux spraying. In discussing the results obtained at the New York station in 1911 Stewart stated: "There was no late blight whatever, only a very little early blight and very little flea-beetle injury. The unsprayed rows were affected by no disease of any consequence except tip burn and even of that there was only a moderate amount, * * * yet spraying increased the yield at the rate of 93 bushels per acre. Plainly we have here a striking example of the beneficial influence of Bordeaux in the absence of disease and insect enemies."

In 1912 Lutman (32) published data from Vermont showing that a greater yield of tubers was obtained from copper-sprayed potato plants at various stages of growth than from the unsprayed plants. Plants which received a Pickering spray, a Bordeaux spray in which part of the copper sulphate had been replaced by iron sulphate, and a commercial spray containing copper also gave higher yields than the check plants. The increased yield seemed to be in proportion to the amount of copper present in the spray. The application of a spray containing silver did not increase the yield. Lutman suggested that the Bordeaux mixture acts as a stimulant, bringing about an increase in the quantity of starch produced daily.

Clinton (8) in 1915 reported that homemade Bordeaux sprays used on potatoes in Connecticut uniformly increased the yields. The average increase for the sprayed plants during the 13 years that the tests were carried on was 36 bushels an acre.

In 1916 Lutman (33) reported the results he obtained in 1912 from using 5–5–50 Bordeaux and 2½–2½–50 Bordeaux on potatoes in Vermont. He concluded that "the amount of copper sulphate and lime used did not appear to be important providing the mixture was fairly strong. A little difference appeared in favor of the 5–5–50 combination over the 2½–2½–50. Frequent and early sprayings did not seem favorably to affect the yield of tubers. Some of the plants were sprayed ten times but they produced little or no larger crops than did those plants sprayed less often." He stated further that the use

---

[1] Italic figures in parentheses refer to literature cited at end of bulletin.

of Bordeaux under field conditions increases the yield of tubers from potato plants by preventing tip burn·and flea-beetle injury. He believed that the yields are not increased when plants which are not troubled by tip burn or flea beetle are sprayed. According to this investigator, Bordeaux mixture seems in the long run to be neither beneficial nor harmful, but it is unnecessary to apply it to plants grown in the greenhouse or to those in regions where neither tip burn nor flea beetles are a factor in potato growing and where neither early nor late blight occurs.

Babcock (4) reported in 1917 that spraying potatoes thoroughly with a 4–4–50 Bordeaux mixture in Ohio when the plants were about 8 inches high and every 10 days to two weeks thereafter materially increased the yield, even in years when there were no disease epidemics.

Erwin (16) reported a difference in yield in favor of the Bordeaux-sprayed plots, indicating a definite response to the use of Bordeaux spray in Iowa. When tip burn was generally present and early blight practically absent the yields were higher on the sprayed plots, indicating that the plants had been stimulated and benefited by the Bordeaux application.

In 1919 Leiby (29) published data obtained in North Carolina showing an average gain of 51.6 bushels an acre, representing 64.2 per cent, as a result of the use of a 3–4–50 Bordeaux plus lead arsenate spray on potatoes. Bordeaux alone produced an increased yield of 35 bushels an acre.

During a 10-year period in New York an average gain of 60 bushels an acre was obtained by spraying with Bordeaux. At the Vermont station during 20 years, which covered all seasonal variations, an average gain of 105 bushels of potatoes an acre was effected by the use of Bordeaux. Experiments at the Maine station extending over a period of years showed that spraying with Bordeaux gave increased yields of tubers, even in years when no late blight was prevalent.

COMPOSITION OF POTATOES.

Although no detailed analyses of potatoes grown in the United States are available, the results of several analytical studies of European varieties have been reported.

Kreusler (26) gives the results of analyses of large, medium, and small tubers grown in Germany. They had the same general composition, the only difference being the presence of slightly more crude fiber and solids in the small than in the large tubers. The medium-sized tubers had more crude fiber than the large tubers but the same proportion of solids.

Appleman (2), who investigated the changes in Irish potatoes during storage, gives data on the moisture, total sugar, and starch contents.

Girard (21) in 1889 reported the changes taking place in tubers in France during growth. The sucrose content dropped from 1.48 to 0.02 per cent and the dextrose content from 0.67 per cent to none. Protein increased from 1.36 to 1.98 per cent, ash from 0.86 to 1.46 per cent, starch from 8.4 to 16.38 per cent, and cellulose from 0.84 to 1.66 per cent. The insoluble nitrogen dropped from 1.66 to 0.19 per cent and the insoluble ash from 0.16 to 0.06 per cent.

Pott (37) showed that the water content decreased, while the total nitrogen, starch, and crude fiber contents increased in the tubers as they matured.

Prunet (39) considered that during growth the nutritive substances are uniformly distributed in the tuber, but after full size has been reached there is a movement of these substances toward the apical buds.

Jones and White (24) in 1899 reported some experiments made on Delaware and White Star varieties of potatoes in Vermont. From analyses of tubers from both Bordeaux-sprayed and unsprayed plots, they concluded that the variations in yield were of more importance than variations in composition. The unsprayed tubers showed the presence of more water and ash than the sprayed tubers. As all of the tubers matured the solids and nitrogen-free extract decreased somewhat, while the ash, protein, and crude fiber increased slightly.

Stewart, Eustace, and Sirrine (46) in 1902 reported that one lot of tubers from Bordeaux-sprayed plants gave higher solids and starch results than a corresponding lot from unsprayed vines.

Woods (51) of the Maine station in 1919 published analyses showing that tubers from Bordeaux-sprayed potato vines averaged 19.1 per cent starch and that tubers in the same field from unsprayed vines averaged 17.5 per cent starch. The dry matter in the tubers from the sprayed portions of the field was also 1½ per cent higher than that in the tubers from the unsprayed portions.

PLANTS IN GENERAL.

Sorauer (45) observed that swellings were formed on the leaves of potato plants by the action of copper salts. Sections of these growths showed that they were composed of parenchyma cells so strongly hypertrophied as to break the epidermis.

Frank and Krüger (19) in 1894 obtained a definite improvement in growth by treating potato plants with a 2 per cent Bordeaux spray. The effect of the copper was most marked on the leaves and was chiefly indicated by physiological activity rather than morphological changes. The leaves were thicker and stronger and their life was lengthened. The chlorophyll content was apparently increased and correlated with this was a rise in the assimilating capacity, more starch being formed. A rise in transpiration also occurred. A subsidiary stimulation took place in the tubers, as the greater quantity of starch produced required space for its storage. The ratio of tuber formation on treated and untreated plants was 19 : 17 and 17 : 16. These investigators held that the action was catalytic, that is, an increase in photosynthesis resulted from the presence of copper.

Rumm (40) in 1895 noted that grape foliage sprayed with Bordeaux showed thickened leaves of a blue-green color which outlived the leaves of the unsprayed vines. After measuring leaves from sprayed and unsprayed vines Rumm presented data showing that the thickness of the leaf, the epidermis, the palisade tissue, and the parenchyma was increased in the case of the sprayed vines. These data suggest that copper was taken into the growing leaf where it produced certain morphological changes.

Lodeman (31) found that the thickness of plum leaves and prune leaves was increased by the application of Bordeaux spray.

Working with a large number of greenhouse plants, Zucker (*52*) concluded that plants sprayed with Bordeaux have greater resistance to etiolation than the unsprayed plants. The sprayed plants also showed an increase of chlorophyll and an increased power of assimilation, and their shoots lived longer. All of the sprayed plants transpired more than the unsprayed plants or those sprayed with lime alone.

Harrison (*22*) found that Bordeaux-sprayed plum, peach, and pear leaves were slightly thickened and that a marked development of chlorophyll granules occurred in their cells.

According to Chuard and Porchet (*6*), copper spray causes a slight increase in the sugar content of matured fruits. Injection of solutions of copper salts into the tissues of such plants as the grapevine produced more vigorous growth, more intense color, and greater persistence of the leaves. The copper seemed to act as a stimulant to all the cells of the organism. Other metals, such as cadmium and iron, are said to give a similar effect. Injecting small quantities of copper salts into the branches of a currant bush caused an acceleration in the maturation of the fruit identical with that obtained by the application of Bordeaux to the leaves. If the quantity of copper introduced into the vegetable organism was increased, the toxic action of the metal was brought into play. These investigators attribute the stimulus, as shown by the earlier maturation of the fruit, to a greater activity of all the cells of the organism and not to an excitation of the chlorophyll functions alone.

Treboux (*49*), in 1903, demonstrated the harmful effect of solutions of copper salts on leaves, measuring the activity of photosynthesis by a determination of the rate of emission of bubbles of oxygen.

Kanda (*25*) undertook to ascertain whether copper had a stimulating action on plants. He found that very small amounts of copper sulphate were toxic to peas grown in distilled water.

Schander (*41*) believes that the copper in a Bordeaux spray penetrates the leaf to a very small extent, perhaps less than one in a hundred million parts, and that the copper there produces changes in assimilation and in transpiration. He considers that the shading effect of the Bordeaux spray on the leaves is beneficial to the absorption of carbon dioxid.

Ewert (*17*) states that in the morning Bordeaux-sprayed potato plants contain more starch than the unsprayed plants, not because they are making more starch, but because they are unable to get rid of it as rapidly. The starch is piled up in the chlorophyll bodies as the minute amount of copper absorbed checks the diastase action. Bordeaux spraying, shading the plants with cloth, and a combination of the two procedures diminish the yield of tubers. This author demonstrated by its effect on diastase that copper is present in the sprayed leaf in minute amount and concludes that the organic life of the plant is hindered rather than stimulated by the application of Bordeaux sprays.

Von Schrenk (*50*), working with cauliflower, also observed that swellings were formed on the leaves owing to the action of copper salts.

Amos (*1*) studied the effect of Bordeaux mixture on the assimilation of carbon dioxid by the leaves of plants to determine whether any stimulation resulted. He found a diminished assimilation by the sprayed leaves for a time. This effect, however, gradually disappeared. It is suggested that the stomata are blocked by the Bordeaux mixture, so that less air is diffused into the intercellular spaces and less carbon dioxid comes into contact with the absorption surfaces. This then is a mechanical and not a physiological action that reduces assimilation.

Duggar and Cooley (14) showed that potted potato plants when sprayed with Bordeaux transpire more water than unsprayed plants.

Duggar and Cooley (14), using potted potato plants, studied the effects of surface films on the rate of transpiration. The use of Bordeaux and other films increased the rate of transpiration. The plants treated with weak Bordeaux (2–3–50) were in good condition at the close of the test, while those sprayed with stronger Bordeaux (4–6–50) showed injury from too much transpiration. These investigators stated that it does not follow that the same results will be obtained in the open.

After measuring the cells of Bordeaux-sprayed and unsprayed potato leaves, Lutman (33) concluded that in general the leaves from the Bordeaux-sprayed plants had thicker palisade and pulp parenchymas than those from the check plants. He believed also that the number of chlorophyll bodies was increased in the sprayed leaves. An increased turgor is probably the immediate cause of these unusually large cells. He considered that a small quantity of copper enters the leaf and that a chemical combination takes place between the chlorophyll and the copper. The chlorophyll is less easily removed from sprayed plants, showing that it has been rendered less soluble. Greenhouse tests and experiments conducted for one year in Germany by Lutman showed no stimulation effects. Lutman considers that in this country the physiological effects of Bordeaux on the potato are quite as important as its fungicidal effects. The physiological effect observed in Vermont is ascribed to lessened tip burn and flea-beetle injury and not to a stimulation and daily increase of starch formation as suggested earlier by him.

Edgerton (15) decided that Bordeaux applied in Louisiana delayed the ripening of tomatoes, while any increase in yield was uncertain. Pritchard and Clark (38) concluded that treatment with copper sprays increased the yield of tomatoes in Virginia, Maryland, Indiana, and New Jersey.

In some of Montemartini's experiments (36) one side of a plant was sprayed while the other was not. Leaves sprayed in the morning with dilute copper sulphate solution and removed and measured in the evening had a greater dry weight per unit area than the untreated leaves. When leaves were treated at night and removed in the morning they had a lower dry weight per unit area than the untreated leaves. According to Montemartini, these results indicate that the treatment stimulated the formation and translocation of organic matter.

Ball (5) has definitely established the fact that the potato leafhopper causes "burning" of potato leaves, to which the term "hopperburn" has been applied. He states also that it has long been recognized that spraying with Bordeaux mixture reduces tip burn, probably because it acts as a partial repellent against the leafhoppers.

Dudley and Wilson (*13*) report that the potato leafhopper is one of the most important enemies of the potato in the United States. Bordeaux repels the leafhopper and therefore effectively controls the potato leafhopper and hopperburn. According to Fenton and Hartzell (*18*), the leafhopper can be effectively controlled and hopperburn can be prevented by covering the potato plants with Bordeaux spray. This spray keeps the adult insects from laying their eggs on the plants and kills many of the young insects.

EXPERIMENTAL PROCEDURE.

Three kinds of sprays containing copper were used in the experimental work reported here: (*a*) Ordinary Bordeaux spray, prepared by mixing milk of lime and copper sulphate solutions; (*b*) Pickering spray, prepared by mixing a saturated solution of limewater with a dilute solution of copper sulphate; and (*c*) a bariumwater spray, prepared by mixing barium hydroxid with a dilute copper sulphate solution. These sprays are discussed fully in United States Department of Agriculture Bulletin 866.

The yield data were obtained from the two middle rows of a 4-row plot. Care was taken to select for these experiments plants which were as free as possible from late blight, mosaic, leaf roll, etc. The tubers from six plants receiving the same treatments were placed in a sack and immediately taken to the laboratory for analysis. For each analysis six medium-sized tubers were selected from the sample and the analyses were made the day on which the tubers were dug. All of the samples were run through a Herles press which gives a very finely divided product. All determinations were made in duplicate, the average figures being recorded in the tables. With the exception of the 1921 data, which include detailed analyses, only solids, starch, and total nitrogen determinations are reported.

Solids, ash, insoluble ash, sugars, total nitrogen, and phosphorus were estimated by the methods of the Association of Official Agricultural Chemists (*3*). Starch was determined by the Herles method (*23*) which depends upon the conversion of the insoluble starch to a soluble starch by means of hydrochloric acid and a reading of the percentage of soluble starch in the polariscope. Copper (*9*) was estimated on 10 grams of the dried sample by the colorimetric procedure, using potassium ferrocyanid. Soluble nitrogen, soluble phosphorus, ammonia nitrogen, coagulable nitrogen, and nitrogen as monoamino and amid nitrogen were estimated on water extracts of the finely-divided samples of tubers as previously outlined by the writer (*10*). The pH data were obtained on the water extracts of the tubers, using the colorimetric procedure of Clark and Lubs (*7*).

RESULTS OF EXPERIMENTAL WORK.
CHANGES IN COMPOSITION OF TUBERS DURING GROWTH.

During the season of 1921 tubers from four varieties of potatoes grown at Presque Isle, Me., were analyzed. Some of the plants had been sprayed with copper sprays, while others had not. The tubers were analyzed at various periods during their growth in order to determine when the influence of the copper sprays was exerted, and also to show the changes that take place in the composition of American-grown tubers during their development. These data are given in Table 1.

Table 1.—Data on tubers from sprayed and unsprayed potato plants, Presque Isle, Me., 1921.

Date of digging	Serial No.	Variety	Treatment	Solids	Starch	Sugars		Sugars to starch ratio	Ash	Insoluble ash	Proportion of total ash that is insoluble	pH of water extract	Nitrogen (N)					Percentage of total nitrogen as—				Undetermined material (fiber, etc.)
						Reducing as dextrose	Sucrose						Total	Soluble	Coagulable	Mono-amino and amid	Ammonia	Soluble	Coagulable	Mono-amino and amid	Ammonia	
				P.ct.	P.ct.	P.ct.	P.ct.		P.ct.	P.ct.	P.ct.		P.ct.	P.ct.	P.ct.	P.ct.	P.ct.	P.ct.	P.ct.	P.ct.	P.ct.	P.ct.
July 26	25	Irish Cobbler	Bordeaux	16.75	9.95	0.39	1.04	1- 7.0	0.95	0.129	13.2	6.2	0.319	0.212	0.027	0.078	0.0030	66.5	8.5	21.4	0.94	2.99
Do	26	do	Pickering	15.56	9.60	.38	1.28	1-14.4	.95	.137	14.6	6.2	.303	.207	.030	.078	.0033	68.3	9.9	25.7	1.09	2.01
Do	27	do	Check	15.21	9.25	.51	1.41	1- 4.8	.93	.147	15.8	6.5	.286	.198	.023	.112	.0027	69.2	8.0	25.6	.94	1.88
Aug. 15	35	do	Bordeaux	18.16	12.40	.10	.96	1-12.4	.87	.085	16.8	6.4	.289	.246	.112	.112	.0025	85.1	38.7	38.4	.90	2.51
Do	36	do	Pickering	18.28	10.70	.20	.98	1- 9.2	.83	.081	10.5	6.4	.286	.246	.106	.104	.0040	85.0	37.1	36.4	1.40	3.85
Do	37	do	Check	18.70	11.60	.24	1.05	1- 9.0	.81	.077	10.3	6.0	.269	.235	.101	.104	.0028	87.4	37.5	38.7	1.04	3.75
Sept. 17	51	do	Bordeaux	22.67	16.90	trace	.37	1-45.4	.93	.100	10.8	6.0	.347	.292	.102	.149	.0030	84.1	29.4	42.9	.86	3.00
Do	52	do	Pickering	20.86	15.90	..do..	.44	1-36.1	.99	.102	10.3	6.0	.333			.134	.0044			40.2	1.02	2.12
Do	53	do	Check	20.86	15.90	..do..	.38	1-44.2	.96	.085	8.9	6.0	.336			.134	.0034			39.9	1.31	3.91
Aug. 2	28	Early Rose	Bordeaux	16.98	9.20	.29	1.50	1- 5.1	.89	.103	11.6	6.3	.282	.230	.068	.090	.0028	82.1	24.3	32.1	1.00	3.88
Do	29	do	Check	16.05	8.25	.33	1.75	1- 4.9	.86	.106	12.3	6.3	.252	.226	.065	.084	.0030	89.5	25.8	33.3	1.19	3.38
Aug. 19	40	do	Bordeaux	17.27	10.85	.15	.72	1-12.6	.82	.137	15.7	6.4	.297	.263	.062	.134	.0034	88.5	23.0	43.6	1.14	3.50
Sept. 14	41	do	Check	14.44	10.80	.14	.62	1-13.1	.87	.133	16.7	6.4	.269	.230	.079	.112	.0030	85.5	24.8	41.6	1.12	3.89
Do	49	do	Bordeaux	18.77	12.50	.07	.31	1-33.9	.79	.070	8.9	6.3	.319	.292	.073	.180	.0028	91.5	24.1	56.8	.88	3.70
Do	50	do	Check	19.28	13.15	.02	.29	1- 8.1	.76	.092	10.1		.308	.272	.055	.172	.0026	87.3	17.9	50.8	.86	3.33
Aug. 3	30	Early Ohio	Bordeaux	18.64	11.40	.12	1.38	1- 5.1	.94	.092	9.8	6.5	.286	.269	.047	.095	.0032	89.8	16.4	30.8	1.04	2.89
Do	31	do	Check	16.72	12.75	.49	.97	1-11.8	.91	.098	10.8	6.3	.300	.257	.084	.087	.0030	86.0	27.5	30.4	1.05	2.74
Aug. 18	38	do	Bordeaux	18.90	12.80	.17	1.10	1- 9.8	.83	.086	10.1	6.1	.305	.263	.084	.120	.0028	86.2	26.3	40.6	.93	3.90
Do	39	do	Check	18.54	14.45	.17	.05	1-46.5	.88	.073	7.5	6.3	.375	.345	.076	.127	.0026	92.0	27.8	41.6	.85	4.13
Sept. 13	48	do	Bordeaux	22.49	8.80	.05	.29	1-40.1	.93	.077	8.3	6.3	.364	.336	.101	.133	.0048	76.7	23.5	35.5	.69	2.46
Do	47	do	Check	21.44	9.90	.04	.23	1- 6.4	.92	.074	8.9	6.4	.301	.231	.068	.141	.0040	77.5	24.1	38.7	1.33	4.28
Aug. 9	32	...Min	Bordeaux	14.93	10.05	.23	1.15	1- 8.0	.92	.080	8.8	6.5	.285	.221	.067	.090	.0036	83.1	22.6	24.1	1.24	3.26
Do	33	do	Barium	16.89		.30	1.16	1-18.5	.84	.074	8.6	6.4	.221	.221	.067	.070	.0030	80.9	22.5	22.9	1.05	3.25
Do	34	do	Check	17.71	12.70	.27	1.17	1-16.5	.69	.066	10.6	6.5	.258	.238	.073	.067	.0036	83.1	24.1	37.0	1.19	2.94
Aug. 23	42	do	Bordeaux	18.44	12.30	.11	.54	1-23.1	.71	.078	9.3	6.2	.283	.230		.104	.0024	83.3	17.9	30.8	.85	2.86
Do	43	do	Pickering	18.02	12.60	.11	.66	1-25.1	.78	.095	11.0	6.2	.319	.258	.073	.120	.0022	80.9	20.5	34.6	.69	3.43
Do	44	do	Check	20.83	13.80	.06	.57	1-16.9	1.00	.088	9.5	6.0	.347	.252	.062	.120	.0024	72.6	23.0	42.8	.69	3.24
Aug. 29	45	do	Barium	20.86	13.90	.16	.66	1-22.1	.95	.094	9.1	6.2	.317	.252	.061	.119	.0024	79.5	21.7	37.6	.81	3.40
Do	46	do	Check	20.12	12.90	trace	.37	1-37.0	.97	.088	9.7	6.2	.364	.297	.073	.149	.0060	81.6	19.3	40.9	1.89	2.55
Sept. 20	54	do	Bordeaux	18.81		..do..	.97	1-26.9	.79	.087	11.0	6.1	.378	.319	.079	.164	.0035	84.4		40.6	.96	3.99
Do	55	do	Barium	18.57	12.90	..do..	.48	1-55.4	.81	.082	10.1	6.1	.336	.348	.034	.180	.0024	97.1	43.4	50.6	.64	2.53
Do	56	do	Pickering	17.53	12.30	..do..	.24	1-40.0	.92	.085	9.3	6.2	.333	.297	.107	.127	.0041	89.2	32.1	38.1	1.24	
Do	57	do	Nickel				.31										.0034				1.02	
Do	58	do	Check																			

The proportion of solids in most cases showed a gradual increase during the growth of the tubers. With the exception of the Green Mountain sample, the proportion of solids was higher in the tubers from copper-sprayed plants than in those from the unsprayed plants at the time of the first analysis, that is, when the tubers were less than an inch in diameter. This indicates that the effect of the copper was exerted very early in their development.

The solids for all the tubers from the Bordeaux-sprayed plants averaged 18.63 per cent; for all those from the unsprayed plants, 17.87 per cent; for all those from barium-water-sprayed plants, 19.58 per cent; and for all those from Pickering-sprayed plants, 18.29 per cent.

The following average ash figures were obtained for all the samples analyzed: Tubers from unsprayed vines, 0.87 per cent; tubers from Bordeaux-sprayed plants, 0.88 per cent; and tubers from Pickering-sprayed plants, 0.85 per cent. The percentage of the total ash found as insoluble ash decreased in most cases during the growth of the tubers.

The pH data obtained on the water extracts of the tubers showed no significant change.

The proportion of total nitrogen, which increased during the growth of all four varieties of tubers, was somewhat higher for the tubers from copper-sprayed plants than for those from the unsprayed plants. The percentage of nitrogen was higher for the tubers from copper-sprayed plants than for those from the unsprayed plants at the time of the first analyses, showing again that the action of the copper on the metabolic activities of the plant was exerted very early.

The percentage of insoluble nitrogen in the tubers showed a tendency to decrease during growth. The percentage of soluble nitrogen increased during growth. The percentage of coagulable nitrogen increased during growth in the case of the Irish Cobbler, the Early Ohio, and the Early Rose varieties, but not in the Green Mountain variety. The monoamino and amid nitrogen, which includes the nitrogen not precipitated by phosphotungstic acid, showed a marked increase for all four varieties during growth. The average percentage was slightly higher in the tubers from copper-sprayed plants than in those from the unsprayed plants. The ammonia nitrogen content showed no regular change.

During tuber development the percentage of starch increased somewhat more rapidly than the percentage of solids. A larger percentage of starch was usually found in the tubers from copper-sprayed plants from the first analysis to the last than in the check tubers. The average data for the content of starch in the tubers were: Bordeaux-sprayed, 12.24 per cent; check, 11.73 per cent; barium-sprayed, 12.67 per cent; and Pickering-sprayed, 12.36 per cent.

The sugars, calculated as dextrose and sucrose, were present in the young tubers in relatively large proportions. At the time the tubers had reached maturity the dextrose had practically disappeared and the quantity of sucrose had markedly decreased. The unsprayed tubers of the three early varieties contained a higher percentage of sugars in the first stages of development and usually a lower percentage at maturity than the tubers from copper-sprayed plants.

This means that the copper sprays may in some way accelerate the transformation of sugar to starch during the active stages of growth. The Green Mountain tubers did not show this tendency. The ratio of sugars to starch decreased greatly during growth, the percentage of sugars decreasing while the percentage of starch increased. The ratio of sucrose to dextrose increased during the growth of the tubers, the dextrose practically disappearing at maturity. At the time the first and second analyses were made the three early varieties of potatoes contained a higher percentage of dextrose plus sucrose than the late variety (Green Mountain). This higher sugar content may be characteristic of early varieties and may be associated with the rapid growth which these varieties make. The unsprayed tubers, with the exception of the Green Mountain, usually showed a higher ratio of sugar to starch than the tubers from the copper-sprayed plants.

It is evident that marked changes take place in the potato during development. Apparently these changes are influenced in some way by the copper sprays, higher percentages of solids, starch, and nitrogen usually following the application of copper sprays to potato vines.

These data may be of value in determining when a potato is mature. It appears that the sugar to starch ratio, as suggested by Appleman (2), as well as the ratio of protein to amid nitrogen and the percentage of total nitrogen as amid nitrogen, is of value. The percentage of starch in terms of total solids may be used. Apparently certain changes in the ash constituents may be applied to solve the question.

EFFECT OF COPPER SPRAYS ON YIELD AND COMPOSITION OF TUBERS.

1917 AND 1918 DATA (MAINE).

In 1916 and again in 1917 potato plants which received copper sprays gave higher yields than those which received no copper spray. It was therefore thought that the copper sprays might influence the composition of the tubers as well as the yield. Late blight was severe in 1917 in this locality but was slight in 1916 and 1918. During the season of 1917 Green Mountain potatoes were sprayed at Presque Isle, Me., using 5–5–50 Bordeaux, Pickering sprays containing various amounts of copper, and a barium-water-copper-sulphate spray containing 0.7 per cent of copper sulphate. Duplicate determinations for solids were made on four samples of tubers from (a) 5–5–50 Bordeaux-sprayed vines (1.25 per cent copper sulphate); (b) Pickering-sprayed vines (0.64 per cent copper sulphate); and (c) unsprayed vines grown in the same field. All of the vines were sprayed seven times during the season, lead arsenate being used on all of the plants.

The four samples of tubers from the Bordeaux-sprayed vines averaged 21.45 per cent solids; those from the Pickering-sprayed vines, 21.49 per cent solids; and those from the check vines, 20.65 per cent solids. Similar results were obtained with this variety of potatoes in Maine during the season of 1918.

Arlington Experimental Farm, Va.—The 1919 experiments at the Arlington Experimental Farm of the Department of Agriculture were conducted on the Early Rose and Irish Cobbler varieties of potatoes. All plots were sprayed four times, lead arsenate being applied to both unsprayed and copper-sprayed plots. The field was uniformly fertilized, using 4–8–4 mixture which was applied at the rate of 1,200 pounds to the acre. The tubers were analyzed the day they were dug.

TABLE 2.—*Yield and composition of tubers from copper-sprayed and unsprayed (check) potato plants, Arlington Experimental Farm, 1919.*

Variety.	Treatment.	Yield from 2 rows, each 100 feet long.	Solids.	Nitrogen.
		Pounds.	*Per cent.*	*Per cent.*
Early Rose	No copper spray (check)	50.0	13.96	0.293
Do	Bordeaux 4–4–50 (1 per cent copper sulphate)	87.6	14.30	.272
Do	Pickering spray (0.5 per cent copper sulphate)	90.3	15.83	.325
Irish Cobbler [1]	No copper spray (check)	124.0	16.41	.346
Do	Bordeaux 4–4–50 (1 per cent copper sulphate)	134.0	18.14	.347
Do	Pickering spray (0.5 per cent copper sulphate)	123.0	18.57	.364

[1] Average of 3 determinations given in each case.

The data in Table 2 indicate that the copper sprays increased the yield for the Early Rose variety and the solids content of tubers of both varieties in a locality where late blight is unknown and where Bordeaux or other copper sprays are not employed generally.

Seven States.—The yield and composition of tubers from Bordeaux-sprayed and unsprayed plants in seven States (Virginia, Maine, Minnesota, Pennsylvania, New York, Connecticut, and New Jersey) are recorded in Table 3. The analytical data are average figures for 62 samples. Data for Pickering-sprayed plots are included with the Arlington Experimental Farm results. The tubers analyzed were from sprayed and unsprayed potato plants grown in the various States under the direction of plant pathologists and were sent to the writer by express the day on which they were dug. Arsenical sprays were used on all plots.

The average increase in yield per acre of potatoes was 25 per cent. The average increase of solids in the tubers was from 20.77 per cent, in the tubers from the check plots, to 21.99 per cent in those from Bordeaux-sprayed plants, an increase of 5.9 per cent. The average figures for pounds of solids of the tubers per acre were 2,591 for the noncopper-sprayed and 3,430 for the copper-sprayed plants, an average increase of 32.4 per cent or 48 bushels, due apparently to the use of copper sprays. It is important to note that the tubers from Virginia, Maine, and Minnesota, where practically no late blight occurred, showed the same general results as those from the other four States, where more or less late blight was noted. This means that prevalence of late blight was apparently not the important factor or necessarily a factor at all. The potato plants grown in

TABLE 3.—*Yield and composition of tubers from copper-sprayed and check potato plants from seven States, 1919.*

Source.	Number of samples analyzed.	Variety.	Treatment.	Solids.	Nitrogen.	Yield of tubers per acre.	Solids of tubers per acre.	Remarks on condition of plants.
				Per cent.	Per cent.	Pounds.	Pounds.	
Arlington Experimental Farm, Va.	4	Irish Cobbler[1] and Spalding Rose.	Unsprayed (check)	15.80	0.33	5,275	833	No late blight present on any of the sprayed or unsprayed vines.
	4	...do...	Bordeaux sprayed[3]	17.18	.33	6,120	1,051	
	4	...do...	Pickering sprayed[3]	17.89	.35	5,741	1,027	
Presque Isle, Me.	1	Green Mountain.	Unsprayed (check).	26.05	.35	18,315	4,771	No late blight until Sept. 1 on either plot; after Sept. 1 traces of blight; all killed Sept. 12 by frost.
St. Paul, Minn.	1	...do...	Bordeaux sprayed.	26.96	.38	19,305	5,205	
	1	Early Ohio.	Unsprayed (check).	19.25	.40	7,448	1,434	Seed from unsprayed crop of 1918; no late blight present.
	1	...do...	Bordeaux sprayed.	22.79	.48	12,015	2,738	Seed from sprayed crop of 1918; no blight present.
State College, Pa.	1	Heath's Late Beauty.	Unsprayed (check).	20.89	.36	13,750	2,873	Vines had severe late blight and died early.
	1	...do...	Bordeaux sprayed.	22.02	.36	18,550	4,084	Vines had slight late blight and died early.
Bath, N. Y.	2	Scott's Magnum Bonum,[1] and Dibble Russet.	Unsprayed (check).	23.99	.41	12,700	3,046	Vines blighted Sept. 15; nearly dead from late blight when dug.
	2	...do...	Bordeaux sprayed (3 sprayings).[3]	25.32	.37	12,700	3,215	Vines moderately blighted; killed by frost Oct. 7.
	2	...do...	Bordeaux sprayed (6 sprayings).	25.61	.40	15,900	4,072	Vines slightly blighted; killed by frost Oct. 7.
Mt. Carmel, Conn.	8	8 different varieties.	Unsprayed (check).	20.92	.40			All the check and sprayed vines died early in the season from late blight, before the spray could exert any beneficial action. Tubers held in cellar in Connecticut for 2 weeks, and in storage in District of Columbia for 3 or 4 days before analysis.
	8	...do...	Bordeaux sprayed.	20.44	.40			
New Jersey	11	Irish Cobbler[2] and American Giant.	Unsprayed (check).	18.50	.34			A little early blight and tip burn present.
	11	...do...	Bordeaux sprayed.	18.90	.36			
		Average.	Unsprayed (check).	20.77	.37	11,498	2,591	Average increase of yield per acre, 25 per cent.
		...do...	Bordeaux sprayed.	21.99	.39	14,378	3,430	Average increase of solids per acre, 32.4 per cent.

[1] Figures given are averages of separate analyses of an equal number of samples of the 2 varieties.
[2] Average figures for separate analyses of 5 samples of Irish Cobbler and 6 of American Giant.
[3] Results not included in average.

Connecticut were well infected with late blight before any Bordeaux spray was applied. All the plants died early; consequently, it is not surprising that the tubers showed no effect of the Bordeaux spray, probably because they were formed before the first spray was applied and were therefore too far advanced to derive any benefit from the sprays. The New Jersey results for solids were not higher for the tubers from the copper-sprayed than for those from the unsprayed plants in the case of all samples examined, although the average figures were higher for the tubers from the Bordeaux-sprayed plants. A discussion of the use of Bordeaux spray on potatoes in New Jersey by Lint (30) is interesting in this connection. He considers the climate, cultivation, and fertility of the field to be important factors in determining to what extent Bordeaux is beneficial to the potato. According to this author, Bordeaux prolongs the life of the vines and affords the best control of flea beetle, although increased yield of tubers does not consistently result from the application of Bordeaux to potato plants in New Jersey.

It has been the writer's experience that an occasional sample of tubers from a check plot will run higher in solids, starch, and nitrogen than a sample from a Bordeaux- or other copper-sprayed plot. This is the exception to the rule, however, and may be due to the inclusion among the tubers selected for analysis of a potato or several potatoes that are not hard and firm. Sometimes one of the tubers in a hill is a little softer than the rest, probably because the food supply has been limited or checked in some way. In work of this kind average figures are undoubtedly the only criterion.

1920 DATA.

Arlington Experimental Farm, Va.—In the spring of 1920 experiments were carried out at Arlington Experimental Farm, using Irish Cobbler, Early Ohio, and Early Rose varieties of potatoes. Spalding Rose, Gold Coin, Irish Cobbler, and McCormick potatoes were grown in the fall. A 4-4-50 Bordeaux spray, a Pickering spray, a 10-10-50 Bordeaux, and a 0-4-50 spray were used. The check plots and all the copper-sprayed plots received a lead arsenate spray. The figures reported in Table 4 are the averages for 53 sets of tubers separately analyzed.

TABLE 4.—*Yield and composition of tubers from sprayed and unsprayed potato plants, Arlington Experimental Farm, Va.; August and October, 1920.*

Variety.	Treatment.	Yield from 2 rows, each 100 feet long.	Composition of tubers.		
			Solids.	Starch.	Nitrogen.
Early potatoes (August):		*Pounds.*	*Per cent.*	*Per cent.*	*Per cent.*
Irish Cobbler [1].......	4-4-50 Bordeaux.................	357	19.91	14.20	0.372
Do [2].............	Check (no copper).................	321	19.59	13.70	.368
Do [1].............	Pickering spray..................	340	20.64	14.50	.383
Do [1].............	10-10-50 Bordeaux...............	341	20.42	14.70	.367
Do [1].............	0-4-50 spray (no copper)...........	350	19.85	13.90	.356
Early Ohio [1].........	4-4-50 Bordeaux................	217	19.17	13.90	.412
Do [1].............	Check (no copper)................	216	19.28	13.90	.410
Do.............	Pickering spray.................	211	19.44	14.70	.433
Early Rose [1].........	4-4-50 Bordeaux................	245	20.18	14.38	.367
Do [1].............	Check (no copper)................	228	18.97	13.60	.326
Do [1].............	Pickering spray.................	229	20.86	14.83	.364

[1] Average of 2 sets.   [2] Average of 4 sets.

TABLE 4.—*Yield and composition of tubers from sprayed and unsprayed potato plants, etc.—Continued.*

Variety.	Treatment.	Yield from 2 rows, each 100 feet long.	Composition of tubers.		
			Solids.	Starch.	Nitrogen.
Late potatoes (October):		Pounds.	Per cent.	Per cent.	Per cent.
Spalding Rose.......	0–4–50 spray (no copper).............	153	19.36	16.80	0.406
Do..............	Pickering spray....................	221	21.48	19.20	.397
Do..............	4–4–50 Bordeaux...................	250	21.45	....	.430
Do..............	Check (no copper).................	248	19.81	....	.409
Gold Coin..........	4–4–50 Bordeaux...................	242	22.09	17.00	.485
Do..............	0–4–50 spray (no copper)..........	232	21.12	....	.461
Do..............	Pickering spray....................	296	23.80	17.90	.457
Do..............	Check (no copper).................	294	19.52	14.50	.444
Irish Cobbler [2].......	4–4–50 Bordeaux...................	303	22.69	17.20	.413
Do [1]............	0–4–50 spray (no copper)..........	245	20.14	15.13	.400
Do [1]............	10–10–50 Bordeaux.................	291	22.43	17.15	.444
Do [2]............	Pickering spray....................	261	21.92	16.73	.443
Do [2]............	Check (no copper).................	288	20.66	15.68	.429
McCormick [1].......	Check (no copper).................	245	21.72	15.85	.430
Do [1]............	0–4–50 spray (no copper)..........	237	21.36	15.50	.419
Do [1]............	Pickering spray....................	259	21.88	15.90	.456
Do [1]............	4–4–50 Bordeaux...................	241	21.32	15.50	.436
Do [1]............	10–10–50 Bordeaux.................	226	21.47	15.75	.457

[1] Average of 2 sets.   [2] Average of 3 sets.

The 10–10–50 Bordeaux spray showed no particular advantages over the 4–4–50 Bordeaux spray or the Pickering spray in either the early or late tests. The vines receiving the 0–4–50 spray, which contained no copper but did contain lime, usually showed yield results lower than those of the checks, but the results of the analyses of the tubers usually agreed rather closely with those obtained for tubers from the check plants. The yield data are variable, but on an average are higher for the copper-sprayed than for the check plants. The data for solids, starch, and nitrogen are generally higher for the copper-sprayed than for the lime-sprayed or check plants. This indicates that copper is the essential constituent of the spray.

Maine, New York, New Jersey, and Pennsylvania.—Thirty-three samples of tubers from Bordeaux-sprayed plants from Maine, Pennsylvania, and New Jersey and from Bordeaux-sprayed and Bordeaux-dusted and unsprayed potato vines in New York (Table 5) were examined. All of the plants were sprayed with an arsenical. Sander's Bordeaux dust was used. The sprays and dusts were applied five times during the season.

TABLE 5.—*Composition of tubers from sprayed and unsprayed potato plants, Maine, Pennsylvania, New Jersey, and New York, 1920.*

Source.	Variety.	Treatment.	Composition of tubers.		
			Solids.	Starch.	Nitrogen.
			Per cent.	Per cent.	Per cent.
Maine..........	Irish Cobbler............	5–5–50 Bordeaux............	20.45	15.95	0.367
Do..........	.....do....................	Check (no copper)..........	18.39	13.80	.353
Do..........	Spalding Rose..........	5–5–50 Bordeaux............	18.23	13.80	.356
Do..........	.....do....................	Check (no copper)..........	18.13	13.95	.319
Do..........	McCormick..............	5–5–50 Bordeaux............	21.70	16.80	.371
Do..........	.....do....................	Check (no copper)..........	20.91	16.00	.356
Do..........	Early Rose.............	5–5–50 Bordeaux............	21.65	17.00	.316
Do..........	.....do....................	Check (no copper)..........	21.93	16.95	.339

TABLE 5.—*Composition of tubers from sprayed and unsprayed potato plants, Maine, Pennsylvania, New Jersey, and New York, 1920*—Continued.

Source.	Variety.	Treatment.	Composition of tubers.		
			Solids.	Starch.	Nitrogen.
			Per cent.	*Per cent.*	*Per cent.*
Pennsylvania....	Blight Proof	5–5–50 Bordeaux...........	25.55	20.80	0.395
Do........	.....do....	Check (no copper)...........	21.92	17.30	.353
Do........	Dibble Russet...........	5–5–50 Bordeaux...........	21.79	16.75	.362
Do........	.....do....	Check (no copper)...........	23.36	18.53	.334
Do........	Blight Proof Union Co..	5–5–50 Bordeaux...........	24.42	21.04	.340
Do........	.....do....	Check (no copper)...........	19.80	15.20	.363
New Jersey......	American Giants [1].....	4–4–50 Bordeaux...........	18.20	12.73	.334
Do........	.....do[1].	Check (no copper)...........	18.33	12.35	.290
New York.......	Variety 9 (Wilkes).....	4–4–50 Bordeaux...........	23.12	19.50	.274
Do..........	.....do....	Bordeaux dust...........	22.96	19.00	.311
Do..........	.....do....	Check (no copper)...........	23.16	19.10	.297
Do..........	Variety 9 (White).....	4–4–50 Bordeaux...........	22.74	18.60	.412
Do..........	.....do....	Bordeaux dust...........	22.74	18.40	.403
Do..........	.....do....	Check (no copper)...........	22.35	18.20	.367
Do..........	Heavyweight (Edwards)...............	Bordeaux dust...........	23.80	18.90	.401
Do..........	.....do....	Check (no copper)...........	21.72	17.30	.356
Do..........	Goldson...........	4–4–50 Bordeaux...........	28.16	22.30	.455
Do..........	.....do....	Bordeaux dust...........	26.42	21.00	.478
Do..........	.....do....	Check (no copper).........	26.62	21.40	.416
Do..........		4–4–50 Bordeaux...........	24.03	19.60	.236
Do..........		Check (no copper)...........	20.34	15.40	.290
Do..........	Dibble Russet (Slayton).	Bordeaux dust...........	27.61	22.75	.348
Do..........	.....do....	Check (no copper)...........	27.37	22.80	.347

[1] Average of 2 sets.

For the New York data several varieties of potatoes grown near Bath and one variety from Geneva were analyzed. From the limited number of samples tested it is impossible to state definitely whether Bordeaux dust has the same favorable effect on the potato plant as Bordeaux spray has, although the results in Table 5 are not particularly favorable to the dust, with the exception of those for the Heavyweight variety. Average figures for three sets grown in New York gave 24.67 per cent of solids for tubers from Bordeaux-sprayed plants, 24.04 per cent for tubers from Bordeaux-dusted plants, and 24.04 per cent for tubers from unsprayed plants. The average starch results for these three sets are 20.13 per cent for tubers from plants receiving Bordeaux spray, 19.47 per cent for those from plants treated with Bordeaux dust, and 19.57 per cent for those from the check plants. The average nitrogen data for the three sets are: Tubers from Bordeaux-sprayed plants, 0.38 per cent; tubers from Bordeaux-dusted plants, 0.397 per cent; and tubers from unsprayed plants, 0.36 per cent. Comparing all five dusted plots with the five corresponding checks gives an average of 24.71 per cent solids against 24.24 per cent, and comparing all four Bordeaux-sprayed plots an average of 24.51 per cent solids against 23.12 per cent for the checks. In general, the results for the New York tubers were higher when Bordeaux spray was used than when no spray was used.

Data were secured for four varieties of potatoes grown in Maine, two varieties from Pennsylvania, one variety having been grown in two different places, and one variety from New Jersey. Three of the four samples of tubers from Maine were higher for Bordeaux and they averaged 20.51 per cent solids from the Bordeaux-sprayed plants and 19.84 per cent from the check plants. Two of the three sets of tubers from Pennsylvania were higher for the Bordeaux samples and the average solids content for the three sets was 23.92 per cent from the Bordeaux-sprayed plants, as compared with 21.69 per cent for the tubers from the check vines. The two samples of the American Giant variety from New Jersey had practically the same content of solids and the tubers from the Bordeaux-sprayed vines had but slightly higher contents of starch and nitrogen.

The average results for the tubers from the four States show that the general effect of the copper sprays is to increase the solids content of the tubers.

1921 DATA.

Presque Isle, Me.—The 1921 experiments were conducted at Presque Isle, Me., to determine the influence of Bordeaux, Pickering, and barium-water sprays, all containing copper, on the yield of tubers. The data were compared with data obtained from check or noncopper-sprayed plants in each case. All of the plants received an arsenical spray.

TABLE 6.—*Yield from 3 varieties of potatoes, Presque Isle, Me., 1921.*

Variety.	Front plots.			Rear plots.			Total.[3]
	Plot No.	Spray used.	Yield.[1]	Plot No.	Spray used.	Yield.[1]	
Aroostook farm:			*Pounds.*			*Pounds.*	*Pounds.*
Early Rose.....	2	Bordeaux..........	[2]128	1	Check (no copper)...	[2]107	....
Early Ohio.....	4	.....do .....,......	[2]106	3	.....do	[2]99	....
Irish Cobbler...	5A	Check (no copper)..	868	5B	.....do	724	1,592
Do.........	6	Bordeaux..........	864	7	Pickering...........	780	1,644
Green Moun-	8A	Check (no copper)..	1,020	8B	Check (no copper)...	821	1,841
tain.							
Do.........	9	Bordeaux..........	1,070	10	Barium..............	850	1,920
Do.........	11A	Pickering..........	1,046	11B	.....do	909	1,955
Kneeland farm:							
Green Moun-	1A	Bordeaux..........	723	1B	Bordeaux..........	636	2,751
tain.							
Do.........	2A	Proprietary spray..	639	2B	Proprietary spray...	707	2,682
Do.........	3A	Check (no copper)..	583	3B	Check (no copper)...	532	2,376
Do.........	3C	Barium spray.:.....	671	3D	Barium spray.......	733	2,859
Do.........	4A	Bordeaux..........	732	4B	Bordeaux..........	660	....
Do.........	5A	Pickering..........	664	5B	Pickering...........	716	2,760
Do.........	6A	Check (no copper)..	648	6B	Check (no copper)...	613	....
Do.........	6C	Barium spray......	744	6D	Barium spray.......	711	....
Do.........	7A	Proprietary spray..	625	7B	Proprietary spray..:	711	....

[1] Yield from 2 rows, 300 feet long, in case of Aroostook farm potatoes; yield from 2 rows, 225 feet long, in case of Kneeland farm potatoes.
[2] Yields from 50 hills each.
[3] Yield from 2 plots in case of Aroostook farm; yield from 4 plots in case of Kneeland farm.

From the data from the Aroostook farm and from the Kneeland farm (Table 6) it is evident that the copper-sprayed plants generally gave an increased yield of tubers. In 1921 there was no late blight (*Phytophthora infestans*) in northern Maine. The reason for using copper sprays in this locality is to control this fungus. Increased yields seem to follow the application of these sprays in seasons when no late blight was prevalent.

PROPORTION OF TUBERS TO VINES PLUS TUBERS.

The weights of vines and tubers were determined at Presque Isle, Me., at the time the analyses of the tubers reported in Table 1 were made. As a rule, eight healthy potato plants were pulled and the potatoes under them dug. The dirt was shaken from the vines and the adhering roots, and the soil was wiped from the tubers. The vines and tubers were then weighed together and separate weighings of the tubers were made. From these data the percentage of tubers in terms of the total weight of the vines plus tubers was calculated.

TABLE 7.—*Weight of potato vines and tubers, Presque Isle, Me., 1921.*

Variety.	Date weighed.	Bordeaux-sprayed.			Pickering-sprayed.			No copper spray (check).		
		Vines.	Tubers.		Vines.	Tubers.		Vines.	Tubers.	
		Lbs.	Lbs.	Per ct.	Lbs.	Lbs.	Per ct.	Lbs.	Lbs.	Per ct.
Irish Cobbler	July 26[1]	7.50	3.00	28.5	7.25	2.50	25.6	9.75	2.50	20.4
Do	Aug. 15[2]	5.25	5.75	52.3	7.00	7.00	50.0	5.25	5.25	50.0
Do	Sept. 17[3]	3.50	8.50	70.8	3.25	9.00	73.5	2.50	11.25	[6]81.8
Early Rose	Aug. 2[1]	6.00	2.75	31.4				6.00	2.75	31.4
Do	Aug. 19[2]	6.75	6.75	50.0				6.75	6.75	50.0
Do	Sept. 14[3]	6.25	13.75	68.8				4.75	13.00	[6]73.2
Early Ohio	Aug. 3[1]	6.50	2.75	29.7				8.25	2.50	23.3
Do	Aug. 18[2]	7.25	6.75	48.2				8.25	8.00	49.2
Do	Sept. 13[3]	4.25	8.25	66.0				4.00	8.00	[6]66.7
Green Mountain	Aug. 23[1]	10.75	4.00	27.1	[4]11.50	[4]5.00	[4]30.3	8.50	2.75	24.4
Do	Aug. 23[2]	7.00	5.50	44.0	5.25	4.00	43.2	5.75	4.00	41.0
Do	Aug. 29[2]				[4]4.25	[4]4.00	[4]48.5	5.00	5.00	50.0
Do	Sept. 20[3]	3.38	7.38	68.6	[4]4.00	[4]8.75	[4]68.6	2.25	7.25	[6]76.3
Do	Sept. 21[3]				4.00	10.50	72.4			
Do	...do				[5]3.00	[5]9.50	[5]76.0			

[1] Date of first analysis.
[2] Date of second analysis.
[3] Date of last analysis.
[4] Barium-sprayed.
[5] Nickel-sprayed.
[6] The check vines at time of last analyses were dead or partly dead and therefore lighter than the vines of the copper-sprayed plants. These figures are not comparable with the other data.

The data presented in Table 7 show that when the potato vines were growing, that is, while they were green, a higher proportion of tubers to vines plus tubers was usually found in the copper-sprayed than in the unsprayed plants. At the time the first weighings were made, as soon as the tubers were about an inch in diameter, the influence of the copper sprays was shown. The results in Table 7 indicate that the stimulating effect of the copper is largely shown by the increased weights of tubers rather than by increased weights of the vines and that it is exerted early in their development. As the tubers are the storehouse for the starch formed in the leaves, the percentage of starch in the tubers would naturally increase. At the time the last analyses of the tubers were made the unsprayed vines had partly dried and therefore were lighter than the corresponding vines for the copper-sprayed plants. The data for these samples are not directly comparable with the rest of the data.

INFLUENCE OF STRENGTH AND NUMBER OF APPLICATIONS OF COPPER SPRAYS ON COMPOSITION OF TUBERS.

Several samples of tubers grown in New Jersey during the season of 1920 were analyzed for solids and nitrogen. Some of the plots from which samples were taken had received a 10–10–50 Bordeaux spray; others had received a 5–5–50 Bordeaux spray; a third plot had been treated with a 2½–2½–50 spray; while some of the plots had received no copper spray. The results for solids and nitrogen in the tubers from copper-sprayed plants were: 10–10–50 spray, 17.9 per cent solids and 0.38 per cent nitrogen; 5–5–50 spray, 18.5 per cent solids and 0.34 per cent nitrogen; 2½–2½–50 spray, 20.1 per cent solids and 0.33 per cent nitrogen. The check tubers contained 18.3 per cent solids and 0.33 per cent nitrogen. The tubers from the plots receiving the 2½–2½–50 spray were highest, and those from the 10–10–50-sprayed plots were lowest in solids.

These results suggest the possibility that a certain proportion of copper in a spray gives the maximum stimulating effect in this locality and that a spray containing a greater proportion of copper may have a toxic rather than a stimulating effect. Tubers grown at Arlington Experimental Farm in 1920 from vines that were sprayed with a 10–10–50 Bordeaux spray (p. 13) seemed to have no advantages over the tubers from plants sprayed with a 4–4–50 Bordeaux. It is, of course, probable that the stimulating effect of the copper varies with the climatic conditions, variety of potatoes used, etc. Tubers from vines in New Jersey sprayed with a 5–5–50 spray eight times during the season were compared with tubers from vines sprayed only four times with Bordeaux spray of the same strength. The average data for four sets were 18.6 per cent of solids and 0.37 per cent of nitrogen in the tubers from vines sprayed eight times and 19.1 per cent of solids and 0.35 per cent of nitrogen for the tubers from vines sprayed only four times. These variations are small and may not be due to the differences in the spray applications. These data also indicate that too much copper may have reached the vines by the eight applications, whereas the amount of copper present in the four applications was nearer the quantity required to give the best protective effect or a maximum stimulation to the plants.

INFLUENCE OF ENVIRONMENT ON COMPOSITION OF TUBERS.

The following data were obtained during the 1919 season. Early Rose tubers grown in Connecticut contained 21.59 per cent solids and 0.38 per cent nitrogen and the same variety grown at Arlington Experimental Farm contained 15.83 per cent solids and 0.33 per cent nitrogen. Irish Cobbler tubers grown in Connecticut contained 22.28 per cent solids and 0.43 per cent nitrogen, while the same variety grown at Arlington Experimental Farm contained 18.57 per cent solids and 0.36 per cent nitrogen. Dibble Russets from New York contained 25.38 per cent solids and 0.39 per cent nitrogen and the same variety grown at Mt. Carmel, Conn., contained 21.24 per cent solids and 0.30 per cent nitrogen. Early Ohio tubers from Minnesota contained 22.79 per cent solids and 0.48 per cent nitrogen and the same variety from Connecticut, 20.52 per cent solids and 0.48 per cent nitrogen. These results again suggest that the composition of the tubers is influenced by the environment.

Although these tubers were not grown from the same stock, the results in each case seem to indicate that a northern tuber is higher in solids than a southern tuber. This may explain why a northern grown potato is a better seed potato than one grown in the South. The data also show that there is a decided variation in the percentage of solids in tubers of different varieties grown in the same locality. In this connection it is interesting to recall the findings of LeClerc and Yoder (27) who, working with wheat in four different parts of the United States, concluded that environment rather than heredity is the major factor in determining the physical and chemical characteristics of the wheat crop.

COPPER CONTENT OF VINES, STEMS, ROOTS, AND TUBERS OF SPRAYED AND UNSPRAYED PLANTS.

Copper is widely distributed in nature. Apparently all plants and animals contain small amounts of this metal.

In 1816 Meissner (*35*) reported that copper was present in the ash of various plants in small quantities. Dieulafait (*12*) in 1880 showed that the amount of copper present in vegetation was largely determined by the nature of the soil.

Lehmann (*28*), in 1895 and 1896, estimated the copper in wheat, rye, barley, oats, maize, buckwheat, potatoes, beans, linseed, apricots, pears, breads, cocoa, and chocolate. He found that only in the plants grown in soil relatively high in copper does any appreciable amount of copper get into the plant. The species of plant is apparently of less importance than the copper content of the soil in determining the amount of copper found in the plant. In wheat and buckwheat the copper was chiefly in the stems and leaves, little being found in the fruits and seeds. Therefore a high copper content in the soil does not necessarily mean that much copper is present in the grain and seed. The form in which the copper exists in plants is not known. Lehmann gives data showing that the quantity of copper in any species of plant varies with the individuals of the species, even when grown on the same soil in the same year, and under similar conditions.

MacDougal (*34*) examined microscopically and analyzed various parts of a tree which had grown in copper-bearing soil. He found metallic copper in relatively large quantities throughout the tissues, indicating an absorption of copper by the tree over a period of years.

TABLE 8.—*Copper in tubers from copper-sprayed and noncopper-sprayed plants.*

[Parts per million.]

Variety.	Place grown.	Copper in dry tubers from vines treated with [1]—				
		Calcium arsenate (no copper).	Bordeaux spray.	Pickering spray.	Lead arsenate (no copper).	Check (no copper).
Spalding Rose	Arlington Experimental Farm, Va.	8	11	15		
Irish Cobbler	....do	11	13	9		
Do	....do	11	15	14		
Do	....do	14	16	15		
Average	....do	11	14	13		
American Giant	New Jersey		15		11	
			9		10	11
					10	
Early Ohio	Minnesota		10			13
Green Mountain	Presque Isle, Me.		10			9
Magnum Bonum	New York		11			10
Dibble Russet	....do		[2] 8			7
			[3] 8			
	Pennsylvania		8			10
Average			10			10

[1] All of the copper-sprayed plants received an arsenical spray as well.
[2] Sprayed twice.
[3] Sprayed 6 times.

Some of the tubers from copper-sprayed and from unsprayed potato plants grown at Arlington Experimental Farm during the season of 1920 were analyzed for copper (Table 8). The average figure for tubers from copper-sprayed plants grown at Arlington was 13.5 and for those from plants receiving no copper, 11 parts of copper per million. Average figures for tubers grown in other localities were 10 parts of copper per million for those from both the Bordeaux-sprayed and unsprayed vines. The writer (*11*) has shown that tubers contain only traces of copper, while the roots, stems, and leaves of potato plants contain appreciable quantities.

During the season of 1921 three separate samples of leaves, stems, and roots from four varieties of potatoes were analyzed for copper. At the time of each analysis nine plants were dug and immediately taken to the laboratory, where they were washed in water. The plants were next dipped in 4 per cent hydrochloric acid for 30 seconds and then held in water for 5 minutes. This process was repeated three times. The plants were finally placed in a large tub, covered with water, and allowed to remain overnight. The next day all of the plants were thoroughly rinsed in running water and then in distilled water, after which they were dried in the air. The leaves were used for analysis directly. The stems and roots of all the samples were carefully scraped with a knife to remove the outer layers of plant tissue. The scraped samples were then washed in distilled water to remove any possible copper contamination during the scraping process. Five grams of the dried sample were used for copper analysis by the colorimetric method. The acid and water treatments apparently removed all the external copper from the plants, as the results for copper in the roots are higher than those for copper in the leaves.

TABLE 9.—*Copper in leaves, stems, and roots of Bordeaux-sprayed and unsprayed potato plants, 1921.*

(Parts per million on the dry basis.)

Date of digging.	Variety.	Leaves.		Stems		Roots.	
		Sprayed plants.	Unsprayed plants.	Sprayed plants.	Unsprayed plants.	Sprayed plants.	Unsprayed plants.
Aug. 2..	Early Ohio	5.6	5.0	3.4	2.6	6.7	3.8
Do...	Early Rose	13.0	10.0	6.6	4.0	18.4	7.6
Do...	Irish Cobbler [1]	11.0	9.0	9.3	8.9	21.5	16.9
Do...	Green Mountain [2]	8.0	7.4	4.6	5.8	7.5	8.0
Aug.18..	Early Ohio	10.6	12.0	9.4	8.1	16.2	9.9
Do...	Early Rose	9.6	9.6	6.0	8.0	8.6	10.4
Do...	Irish Cobbler	12.0	8.0	7.6	10.2	8.4	8.0
Do...	Green Mountain [2]	11.4	10.6	7.0	7.0	10.1	8.6
Sept. 13.	Early Ohio	17.3	10.0	14.0	11.2	26.0	13.8
Do...	Early Rose	13.0	9.0	5.0	8.5	19.4	9.1
Do...	Irish Cobbler	11.0	9.0	8.1	6.3	8.3	9.0
Do...	Green Mountain	9.0	6.8	6.3	4.4	9.1	6.6

[1] Sprayed with Pickering spray.   [2] Sprayed with barium-water spray.

The data for the leaves, stems, and roots, given in Table 9, show certain variations, but in the majority of the samples the corresponding figures for the copper-sprayed were higher than those for the unsprayed samples. The roots held the most and the stems the least copper for all four varieties of potato plants. The three early varieties of potato plants contained more copper than the Green Mountain, a late variety. An appreciable quantity of the copper was present in all of the check plants.

GENERAL DISCUSSION.

In the case of copper sprays it is generally recognized that a small quantity of copper is gradually rendered soluble either by the juices of the plant or by the carbon dioxid of the air, and this copper thus rendered soluble may protect the plant and may stimulate its metabolic activities. The intensity of action of the copper compounds varies with the kind of plant used and with the quantity of copper applied. This difference in the ability of plants to withstand the action of copper sprays was illustrated by the drastic effect of Pickering sprays (9) on the grape and apple compared with its favorable action on the potato and cranberry. The influence of environment, soil, climate, etc., must also be considered in this connection, as a Bordeaux spray may be used on a certain plant in one section of the country but can not be used without severe injury on the same plant in another locality. The data show that increased growth and tuber formation of the potato following the use of copper sprays may be secured. The fact that a certain amount of hopperburn was present in most of the fields where these tests were conducted is recognized. It was not severe in any case and practically none was observed on the plants at Arlington Experimental Farm. Some of the increased yield of tubers from copper-sprayed potato plants was undoubtedly due to the action of the copper sprays in controlling potato leafhoppers and thereby reducing hopperburn. It is difficult to explain it all on the basis of protective action alone.

Analyses of grapes from copper-sprayed and from unsprayed vines reported by the writer (9) showed that the composition of the grape had apparently been altered by the application of the copper sprays. Evidently copper sprays alter the composition of the potato and the grape and there is no reason to believe that their action is restricted to these two plants.

Several theories have been advanced to explain the increased yield of tubers from Bordeaux-sprayed potato plants:

(a) Bordeaux spray increases the transpiration rate of potato plants, according to Lutman, Duggar, and others. This effect would apparently be an advantage in wet seasons or wet localities but a disadvantage in dry seasons or dry localities. Differences in humidity cause differences in the transpiration of plants, and this may react on the growth of the plant and the composition of the tubers.

(b) It is possible that changes in the rate of respiration or in the general metabolism of potato plants may follow the application of copper sprays. A small quantity of copper may be absorbed by the plant and stimulate it to increased activity. There are several examples of stimulation brought about by a small amount of a substance which in large quantities is toxic. There is evidence that copper stimulates some plants and the fact that stimulation can not be shown to exist does not prove that it is not there. Analyses of the leaves, vines, and roots of sprayed and unsprayed potato vines in most cases showed a higher proportion of copper in the leaves, stems, and roots of the sprayed potato plants than in those of the unsprayed plants.

(*c*) Variations in sunlight or stimulation resulting from the application of copper sprays may influence the photosynthetic processes.

(*d*) The copper sprays protect the vines which are thus kept freer from tip burn, disease, and insect injury. Vines treated in this way are therefore more vigorous and their tubers may show an increase in solids, as well as in yield. It is now recognized that potato leafhoppers are the direct cause of hopperburn and that Bordeaux mixture repels the hoppers. Bordeaux spray is a protection against potato leafhoppers, flea beetles, and other insects, as well as against fungous diseases. It is not clear why the tubers should be higher in solids unless it is simply taken for granted that a vigorous plant produces a tuber higher in solids than a less vigorous plant. There is a possibility that the protective effect of Bordeaux is the only effect produced, but copper salts have such a pronounced effect on all living tissue that a stimulation is generally suspected and even accepted by many investigators in this field.

Some suggestions from the recent work of Sherman and his co-workers are of interest in this connection. They studied the effects of certain antiseptics upon the activity of amylases (*42*), all of which were very sensitive to copper sulphate. They also studied the influence of certain amino acids upon the enzymic hydrolysis of starch (*43*), finding that glycine, alanine, phenyl alanine, or tyrosine caused an undoubted increase in the rate of hydrolysis of starch by purified pancreatic amylase, commercial pancreatin, saliva, or purified amylase. The favorable effect is not due to any influence on hydrogen ion concentration nor to a combination of the amino acid with the product of the enzymatic reaction. The addition of 1 per cent of these amino acids was shown to be a very effective means of protecting the enzyme from the deleterious effect of copper sulphate and may even serve to restore to full activity any enzyme which has been partially inactivated by copper. Arginine and cystine have a favorable influence upon the hydrolysis of starch by purified pancreatic amylase, while histidine and tryptophane do not (*44*). The effect of histidine and tryptophane differs from that of all the other amino acids studied, possibly because of their heterocyclic structure or their position in the protein complex which doubtless constitutes either the enzyme itself or an essential part of it.

There is evidence that a somewhat larger quantity of copper is present in copper-sprayed potato plants than in the unsprayed plants, and also that the proportion of amino and amid nitrogen in potato plants increases during growth. Data showing that copper had a favorable effect on the yield and composition of tubers were obtained. Possibly the amino acids protect the cell activity from any toxic action of the copper, thus permitting the copper to exert a stimulating effect on the cells.

It is recognized that it would be desirable to have data showing the normal variation for the different varieties of tubers under the same conditions, but time did not permit the securing of such data. Analyses of several hundred tubers, both copper-sprayed and check, were obtained and the average data from this large number of tubers should overcome individual variation.

The results reported in this paper appear to establish the fact that copper sprays not only increase the yield of potatoes in various sections of the country, but favorably influence their composition.[2]   Bordeaux sprays, Pickering sprays, and barium-water sprays seemed to give the increased yield and increased solids of the tubers which apparently depend on the presence of copper in the spray.   In addition to plant-disease control and insect control, the copper appears to exert a stimulating action on the potato plant.

Bordeaux and other sprays containing copper are usually applied to the potato to control the late blight.   In some States such a spray is applied as a repellent to the flea beetle and the potato leafhopper, thereby reducing the injury to the foliage from these two insect pests and at the same time lessening tip burn and hopperburn.   The importance of the effect of copper sprays on the yield of potatoes, in addition to their control of diseases and insects, has not been generally recognized or at least emphasized.   Nor has the fact that tubers from copper-sprayed plants may be stored more satisfactorily—that is, with less loss from rot—than tubers from noncopper-sprayed plants been widely advertised.   When, in addition, an increased yield of potatoes and a higher proportion of solids in them follow the application of copper sprays, important additional reasons for their more general use become evident.

SUMMARY.

Tubers from copper-sprayed potato plants at the time they were large enough for analysis (about one inch in diameter) were usually higher in solids, starch, and nitrogen than the tubers from unsprayed vines.   The starch content increased approximately 50 per cent as the tubers matured, while the dextrose disappeared and the sucrose was materially reduced.   The early varieties of potatoes showed a decrease in their sugar content to accompany an increased starch content in the copper-sprayed tubers during the early stages of development.   The proportion of insoluble ash decreased during the growth of the tubers, although the total ash content remained constant.   The total nitrogen increased.   The figures for soluble, coagulable, and particularly the monoamino and amid nitrogen increased as the tubers matured.

The proportion of tubers to green vines appeared to be higher for the copper-sprayed than for the unsprayed plants.

Average data for seven States obtained in 1919 showed the food value of an acre of copper-sprayed potatoes to be 839 pounds more than that for an acre of noncopper-sprayed potatoes.   Two factors, increased yield (48 bushels an acre) and an increase of solids (5.6 per cent), are involved.

Some results obtained at Arlington Experimental Farm, Va., comparing a 10–10–50 Bordeaux and a 5–5–50 Bordeaux, suggest that the former spray has no advantage over the latter and may possibly furnish too much copper for the maximum stimulating or protective effects.   Results from New Jersey, where a 4–4–50 Bordeaux spray was applied eight times, compared with results where the same spray

---

[2] Attention is called to the experiments of Gray and Ryan, Monthly Bull. Dept. Agr. State of California, Chemical Number, vol. 10, no. 1, pp. 11–33, 1921.   They showed that the acidity of oranges was reduced by the arsenical spray.

was applied four times, show that the tubers were lower in solids in the former than in the latter case, suggesting again that too much copper may have reached the plant for the best results in the absence of any late blight.

Tubers from several varieties of potatoes grown in a northern State were higher in solids than tubers of the same varieties grown in a State farther south.

A larger yield of potatoes was secured from copper-sprayed than from check or noncopper-sprayed vines. Late blight (*Phytophthora infestans*) is eliminated as a necessary factor in the case.

When a lime spray containing no copper was used at Arlington Experimental Farm, Va., the yields of tubers were decreased. Pickering-limewater spray and a barium-water spray gave practically the same increase in yield and in solids of the tubers as a Bordeaux spray. The copper in the spray seems to be the essential factor.

LITERATURE CITED.

(1) AMOS, A.
    The effect of fungicides upon the assimilation of carbon dioxide by green leaves. J. Agr. Sci., 2 (1907) : 257–266.
(2) APPLEMAN, C. O.
    Changes in potatoes during storage. Md. Agr. Exp. Sta. Bull. 167 (1912) : 327–334.
(3) ASSOC. OFFICIAL AGR. CHEMISTS.
    Official and tentative methods of analysis, 417 pp. Washington, D. C., 1920.
(4) BABCOCK, D. C.
    Potato diseases. Ohio Agr. Exp. Sta. Bull. 319 (1917) : 121–136.
(5) BALL, E. D.
    The potato leafhopper and the hopperburn. Phytopath., 9 (1919) : 291–293.
(6) CHUARD, and PORCHET, E.
    L'action des sels de cuivre sur les végétaux. Arch. sci. phys. nat., 14 (1902) : 502–5.
(7) CLARK, W. M., and LUBS, H. A.
    The colorimetric determination of hydrogen ion concentration and its applications in bacteriology. J. Bact., 2 (1917) : 1–34.
(8) CLINTON, G. P.
    Report of the botanist for 1915. Conn. Agr. Exp. Sta. 39th Ann. Rpt. (1915) : 421–487.
(9) COOK, F. C.
    Pickering sprays. U. S. Dept. Agr. Bull. 866 (1920) : 47 pp.
(10) —— ——.
    Composition of tubers, skins, and sprouts of three varieties of potatoes. J. Agr. Research, 20 (1921) : 623–635.
(11) —— ——.
    Absorption of copper from the soil by potato plants. J. Agr. Research, 22 (1921) : 281–287.
(12) DIEULAFAIT.
    Sur la présence normale du cuivre dans les plantes qui vivent sur les roches de la formation primordiale. Compt. rend., 90 (1880) : 703–705.
(13) DUDLEY, J. E., and WILSON, H. F.
    Combat potato leafhopper with Bordeaux. Wis. Agr. Exp. Sta. Bull. 334 (1921) : 31 pp.
(14) DUGGAR, B. M., and COOLEY, J. S.
    The effects of surface films on the rate of transpiration: Experiments with potted potatoes. Ann. Mo. Bot. Gard., 1 (1914) : 351–356.
(15) EDGERTON, C. W.
    Delayed ripening of tomatoes caused by spraying with Bordeaux mixture. La. Agr. Exp. Sta. Bull. 164 (1918) : 1–16.

(16) ERWIN, A. T.
    Bordeaux spray for tip burn and early blight of potatoes. Iowa Agr.
    Exp. Sta. Bull. 171 (1917) : 61–75.
(17) EWERT, R.
    Der wechselseitige Einfluss des Lichtes und der Kupferkalkbrühen auf
    den Stoffwechsel der Pflanze. Landw. Jahrb., 34 (1905) : 233–310.
(18) FENTON, F. A., and HARTZELL, A.
    Control of the potato leafhopper. Iowa Agr. Exp. Sta. Circ. 77 (1922) :
    4 pp.
(19) FRANK, B., and KRÜGER, F.
    Ueber den Reiz, welchen die Behandlung mit Kupfer auf die Kartof-
    felpflanze hervorbringt. Ber. botan. Ges., 12 (1894) : 8–11.
(20) GIDDINGS, N. J.
    Potato spraying in 1909 and 1910. W. Va. Agr. Exp. Sta. Rpt., 1909–10,
    pp. 18–19.
(21) GIRARD, A.
    Recherches sur la culture de la pomme de terre industrielle. Dévelop-
    ment progressif de la plante. Compt. rend., 108 (1889) : 602–604.
(22) HARRISON, F. C.
    The effect of spraying Bordeaux mixture on foliage. Ont. Agr. Coll.
    23d Ann. Rpt. (1897) : 125–128.
(23) HERLES, F.
    Volumetric starch estimation in potatoes. 8th Internat. Congress Ap-
    plied Chem., 26 (1912) : 5–10.
(24) JONES, C. H., and WHITE, B. O.
    Report of the chemists. Vt. Agr. Exp. Sta. 13th Ann. Rpt. (1899–
    1900) : 374–390.
(25) KANDA, M.
    Studien über die Reizwirkung eininger Metallsalze auf das Wachsthum
    höherer Pflanzen. J. Coll. Sci. Imp. Univ. Tokyo, 19, Art. 13 (1904) :
    1–37.
(26) KREUSLER, U.
    Chemisch-physiologische Untersuchungen über das Wachsthum der
    Kartoffelpflanze bei kleinerem und grösserem Saatgut. Landw.
    Jahrb., 15 (1886) : 309–379.
(27) LECLERC, J. A., and YODER, P. A.
    Environmental influences on the physical and chemical characteristics
    of wheat. J. Agr. Research, 1 (1914) : 275–291.
(28) LEHMANN, K. B.
    Hygienische Studien über Kupfer. Arch. Hyg., 24 (1895) : 1–17; 27
    (1896) : 1–7.
(29) LEIBY, R. W.
    The spraying of Irish potatoes. N. C. Dept. Agr. Bull. 40 (1919), no.
    3, 38 pp.
(30) LINT, H. C.
    Report of potato scab experiments, 1915. N. J. Agr. Exp. Sta. 36th
    Ann. Rpt. (1915) : 375–394.
(31) LODEMAN, E. G.
    The spraying of orchards, apples, quinces, plums. N. Y. Cornell Agr.
    Exp. Sta. Bull. 86 (1895) : 47–76.
(32) LUTMAN, B. F.
    Plant diseases in 1911, potato spraying experiments in 1911. Vt. Agr.
    Exp. Sta. Bull. 162 (1912) : 33–45.
(33) ————.
    Some studies on Bordeaux mixture. Vt. Agr. Exp. Sta. Bull. 196
    (1916) : 1–80.
(34) MACDOUGAL, D. T.
    Copper in plants. Botan. Gaz., 27 (1899) : 68–69.
(35) MEISSNER, W.
    Versuche über den Kupfer-Gehalt einiger Pflanzenaschen. J. Chem.
    Physik. (Schweigger), 17 (1816) : 340–54.
(36) MONTEMARTINI, L.
    Nuove osservasioni sopra l'azione eccitante del solfato di rame sulle
    piante. Rev. patol. veg., 10 (1920) : 36–40.
(37) POTT, E.
    Handbuch der tierischen Ernährung und der landwirtscaftlichen
    Futtermittel, vols. 1 and 2. Paul Parey, Berlin, 1904.

(38) Pritchard, F. J., and Clark, W. B.
     Effect of copper soap and of Bordeaux soap spray mixtures on control
     of tomato leaf spot. Phytopath., 9 (1919) : 554–564.
(39) Prunet, A.
     Recherches physiologiques sur les tubercules de la pomme de terre.
     Rev. gén. botan., 5 (1893) : 49–64.
(40) Rumm, C.
     Zur Kenntnis der Giftwirkung der Bordeauxbrühe und ihrer Bestand-
     teile auf Spirogyra longata und die Uredosporen von Puccinia
     coronata. Erwin Nägale, Stuttgart, 1895.
(41) Schander, R.
     Über die physiologische Wirkung der Kupfervitriolkalkbrühe. Landw.
     Jahrb., 33 (1904) : 517–584.
(42) Sherman, H. C., and Caldwell, Mary L.
     A study of the influence of arginine, histidine, tryptophane and cystine
     upon the hydrolysis of starch by purified pancreatic amylase. J. Am.
     Chem. Soc., 43 (1921) : 2469–2476.
(43) ——— and Walker, Florence.
     The influence of certain amino acids upon the enzymic hydrolysis of
     starch. J. Am. Chem. Soc., 43 (1921) : 2461–2469.
(44) ——— and Wayman, Marguerite.
     Effect of certain antiseptics upon the activity of amylases. J. Am.
     Chem. Soc., 43 (1921) : 2454–2461.
(45) Sorauer, P.
     Einige Beobachtungen bei der Anwendung von Kupfermitteln gegen
     die Kartoffelkrankheit. Z. Pflanzenkrankh., 3 (1893) : 32–36.
(46) Stewart, F. C., Eustace, H. J., and Sirrine, F. A.
     Potato-spraying experiments in 1902. N. Y. Geneva Agr. Exp. Sta.
     Bull. 221 (1902) : 235–263.
(47) ———.
     Potato-spraying experiments, 1902–1911. N. Y. Geneva Agr. Exp. Sta.
     Bull. 349 (1912) : 99–139.
(48) Stewart, F. C., French, G. T., and Sirrine, F. A.
     Potato-spraying experiments in 1910. N. Y. Geneva Agr. Exp. Sta.
     Bull. 338 (1910) : 115–151.
(49) Treboux, O.
     Einige stoffliche Einflüsse auf die Kohlensäureassimilation bei sub-
     mersen Pflanzen. Flora, 92 (1903) : 56–58.
(50) Von Schrenk, H.
     Intumescences formed as a result of chemical stimulation. Mo. Bot.
     Gard. 16th Ann. Rpt. (1905) : 125–148.
(51) Woods, C. D.
     Potato studies. Maine Agr. Exp. Sta. Bull. 277 (1919) : 17–32.
(52) Zucker, A.
     Beitrag zur direkten Beeinflussung der Pflanzen durch die Kupfer-
     vitriol-Kalkbrühe. Alfred Müller & Co., Stuttgart, 1896.

UNITED STATES DEPARTMENT OF AGRICULTURE

DEPARTMENT BULLETIN No. 1147

| Washington, D. C. | ▼ | June 9, 1923 |

CHEMICAL, PHYSICAL, AND INSECTICIDAL PROPERTIES OF ARSENICALS.

By F. C. Cook, *Physiological Chemist, Insecticide and Fungicide Laboratory, Miscellaneous Division, Bureau of Chemistry*, and N. E. McIndoo, *Insect Physiologist, Fruit Insect Investigations, Bureau of Entomology.*[1]

CONTENTS.

PURPOSE OF INVESTIGATION.

A study of the chemical, physical, and insecticidal properties of arsenicals on the market was undertaken in order to gain a better understanding of them, to be able, if possible, to improve them, and to produce new arsenicals for insecticidal purposes. The results of this investigation, which was conducted by the Bureau of Chemistry and the Bureau of Entomology of the United States Department of Agriculture, are here reported.

ARSENICALS STUDIED.

Paris green and lead arsenate, which have been standardized and found reliable for many years, have constituted the principal insecticides used against external chewing insects. However, during the past few years, the use of calcium arsenate has steadily increased, owing in part to the discovery that it is effective in combating the boll weevil. The manufacture of calcium arsenate, although well beyond the experimental stage in most factories, probably will not be completely standardized for several years. Because of the importance and recent large-scale production of calcium arsenate, many of the results in this bulletin deal with comparisons of calcium arsenate and acid lead arsenate.

---

[1] The following assisted in this work: R. Elmer, W. A. Gersdorff, R. Jinkins, B. Neuhausen, and A. Schultz, Junior Chemists, Insecticide and Fungicide Laboratory, Bureau of Chemistry, and W. A. Hoffman. Scientific Assistant, and W. B. Wood, Entomological Assistant, Bureau of Entomology.

27476°—23—Bull. 1147——1

The arsenicals analyzed in this investigation, many of which were used in the entomological tests (pp. 26–50), were obtained on the market in 1916. The samples were used as purchased, with the exception of the paste products which were dried before being used. Samples of the following arsenicals were studied: Arsenious oxid (4 samples), arsenic oxid (2 samples), acid lead arsenate (18 samples), basic lead arsenate (2 samples), calcium arsenate (9 samples), zinc arsenite (2 samples), Paris green (2 samples), mixture of calcium and lead arsenates (2 samples), sodium arsenate (2 samples), potassium arsenate (1 sample), London purple (1 sample), and magnesium arsenate (1 sample). Several samples of acid and basic lead arsenate and of calcium arsenate, and one of barium arsenate, one of aluminum arsenate, and one of copper barium arsenate mixture were prepared in the laboratory, analyzed, and tested on insects.

Various names are applied to the arsenicals here designated as (a) acid lead arsenate, (b) basic lead arsenate, (c) arsenious oxid, and (d) arsenic oxid. Some of these names are incorrect because they are based on erroneous analyses or interpretations of composition, for example, ''neutral lead arsenate'' for a basic lead arsenate. Some are considered not to be in good usage, according to modern chemical writing, for example, ''arsenious acid'' for arsenious oxid. Arsenious oxid dissolved in water forms arsenious acid. The same relation exists between arsenic oxid and arsenic acid. Other names, although correct, are unnecessarily involved, for example, ''hydroxylead arsenate'' for basic lead arsenate. The terms selected for use in this bulletin are both scientifically correct and commonly applied to arsenicals. Their names, with the synonyms, are as follows:

(a) Acid lead arsenate ($PbHAsO_4$).
 Ordinary lead arsenate.
 Hydrogen lead arsenate.
 Diplumbic arsenate.
 Dilead arsenate.
 Diplumbic hydrogen arsenate.
 Bibasic arsenate.
(b) Basic lead arsenate ($Pb_4(PbOH)$ $(AsO_4)_3$. H_2O).
 Triplumbic arsenate (T. P. arsenate).[2]
 Neutral lead arsenate.[2]

(b) Basic lead arsenate—Continued.
 Trilead arsenate.[2]
 Nonacid lead arsenate.
 Hydroxy-lead arsenate.
 Lead ortho arsenate.[2]
(c) Arsenious oxid (As_2O_3).
 Arsenic.
 White arsenic.
 Arsenious anhydrid.
(d) Arsenic oxid (As_2O_5).
 Arsenic pentoxid.
 Arsenic anhydrid.

CHEMICAL PROPERTIES OF ARSENICALS.

OXIDS OF ARSENIC.

Arsenious oxid (As_2O_3), commonly called white arsenic or simply arsenic, is the basis for the manufacture of all arsenicals. In the United States arsenious oxid is a by-product from the smelting of lead, copper, silver, and gold ores, being recovered from the flue dust and fumes. The arsenious oxid first sublimed is impure, owing to the presence of carbon and sometimes of sand. The impure oxid may then be resublimed to give a relatively pure oxid, consisting of approximately 99 per cent of arsenious oxid and a trace of arsenic oxid (As_2O_5). Between 11,000 and 12,000 tons of arsenious oxid were produced in the United States in 1920, more than half of which was

---

[2] These names are incorrect, having been used when basic lead arsenate was considered to be trilead arsenic.

used for insecticide purposes. Canada, Mexico, England, Germany, France, Japan, and Portugal produce large quantities of arsenious oxid.

There are three forms of arsenious oxid: (a) The amorphous, vitreous, or glassy form; (b) the ordinary crystalline ("octahedral") form; and (c) the orthorhombic crystalline form. The amorphous form changes spontaneously into the crystalline form on standing. The trade usually recognizes two grades of arsenious oxid, the light and the heavy forms, although they are the same chemically.

The literature contains conflicting statements concerning the solubility of arsenious oxid in water. Because of the slowness with which arsenious oxid goes into solution, many weeks being required to dissolve even a small sample of the solid, it is probable that in all of the reported results equilibrium had not been reached. The varying percentages of crystalline and amorphous material present in the samples tested, the amorphous form being more soluble than the crystalline forms, may possibly help to account for these discrepancies.

With the exception of Paris green, the arsenites are prepared by combining arsenious oxid and the base.

As a rule, arsenates are made by the direct action of arsenic acid in solution on a metallic oxid. The arsenic acid used for this purpose is manufactured from arsenious oxid by oxidation, usually by means of nitric acid, but sometimes by other oxidizing agents.

The analytical results here reported are based on the weights of the original samples. The methods of analyses used were in general those of the Association of Official Agricultural Chemists (1).[3]

Table 1 gives the analytical results on the six samples of arsenious and arsenic oxids selected to represent the arsenical materials used in the manufacture of arsenicals.

TABLE 1.—Composition of arsenious oxid (As_2O_3) and arsenic oxid (As_2O_5) used in manufacturing arsenicals.

Sample No.	Material analyzed.	Moisture.	Total arsenious oxid (As_2O_3).	Total arsenic oxid (As_2O_5).	Water-soluble arsenious oxid (As_2O_3).[1]	Water-soluble arsenic oxid (As_2O_5).[1]
		Per cent.	Per cent.	Per cent.	Per cent.	Per cent.
9	Laboratory arsenious oxid	0.20	99.80	....	17.77	....
19	Commercial arsenious oxid	.99	99.01	....	24.56	....
27	....do	.71	99.29	....	38.00	....
37	....do	.15	99.22	....	30.26	....
10	Laboratory arsenic oxid (solid arsenic acid)	....	....	77.27	....	77.27
16	Commercial arsenic oxid (dissolved arsenic acid)	....	....	66.10	....	66.10

[1] Determined by the A. O. A. C. method for Paris green.

Attention is called to the wide variation in the data obtained for water-soluble arsenious oxid in the different samples of arsenious oxid. This is undoubtedly due to differences in the size and structure of the crystals present in the samples tested.

Traces of arsenious oxid (0.008 per cent) and nitric acid (0.02 per cent) were found in the commercial sample of arsenic acid (No. 16).

[3] Italic numbers in parentheses refer to literature cited.

All samples of commercial arsenic acid are likely to contain traces of arsenious oxid and nitric acid. Arsenic acid solutions containing from 56 to 66 per cent of arsenic oxid have a specific gravity of from 1.8 to 2. Solid arsenic acid containing from 75 to 80 per cent of arsenic oxid has recently been placed on the market.

BASES USED IN PREPARING ARSENICALS.

The oxids of lead, zinc, calcium, and magnesium are the bases most used in manufacturing arsenicals. Litharge is the commercial lead oxid and lime the commercial calcium oxid. Zinc oxid (ZnO) and lead oxid (PbO), ordinarily employed in the manufacture of zinc arsenite and lead arsenate, are more expensive than calcium oxid (CaO) (in the form of lime) and magnesium oxid (MgO) used in manufacturing calcium arsenate and magnesium arsenate. Table 2 gives the results of the analyses of the five bases and the copper oxid (CuO) and barium hydroxid (Ba(OH)$_2$) which were used in this investigation.

TABLE 2.—*Composition of bases in arsenicals.*

Sample No.	Material analyzed.	Moisture.	Oxid.	Carbon dioxid (CO$_2$).	Undetermined material, by difference.
		Per cent.	*Per cent.*	*Per cent.*	*Per cent.*
11	Lime (laboratory)............................	6.54	84.00 (CaO)......	9.02	0.44
12	Lead oxid (laboratory).......................	.00	99.13 (PbO).....	Trace.	.87
20	Lead oxid (commercial)......................	.02	97.88 (PbO).....	1.64	.46
22	Zinc oxid (commercial)......................	.17	100.00 (ZnO).....	.00	....
63	Magnesium oxid (laboratory)................	.99	77.16 (MgO).....	21.89	....
65	Copper oxid (laboratory).....................	.00	98.75 (CuO).....	.10	1.15
67	Barium hydroxid (laboratory)...............	14.58	66.73 (BaO).....	14.91	3.78

ACID LEAD ARSENATES.

F. C. Moulton, chemist for the Massachusetts gypsy moth committee, is credited with the discovery in 1892 of the insecticidal properties of lead arsenate. The use of arsenate of lead as an insecticide, first recommended in October, 1893 (*21*), has greatly increased during the past few years. Thirty-one United States patents for its production have been issued.

The principal lead arsenate is acid lead arsenate (PbHAsO$_4$), an acid salt, so-called because of the presence of hydrogen (H) in its molecule. It has the following theoretical composition, As$_2$O$_5$ (33.13 per cent), PbO (64.29 per cent), and water of constitution (2.58 per cent).

In the early procedure for preparing acid lead arsenate, solutions of lead acetate or of lead nitrate were precipitated by sodium hydrogen arsenate (Na$_2$HAsO$_4$). The tendency is to produce acid lead arsenate when lead nitrate is used and the more basic form when the acetate is used. McDonnell and Smith (*27*) obtained acid lead arsenate of practically theoretical composition by precipitating lead nitrate or lead acetate by an excess of monopotassium arsenate. A method frequently employed in manufacturing this arsenate is to mix arsenic acid (H$_3$AsO$_4$) and litharge (PbO) in the presence of a small amount of nitric acid. Other processes, however, are used. The fact that acid lead arsenate is a comparatively stable compound and is but slightly soluble in water, offers an explanation as to why it burns foliage only very slightly when properly applied. McDonnell and Graham (*26*) found that long-continued exposure to constantly changing water brings about decomposition, both lead and arsenic being dissolved,. the arsenic, however, at a relatively greater rate, leaving the residue more basic than the original acid lead arsenate. According to McDonnell and Smith (*27*), the specific gravity of acid lead arsenate crystals is 6.05.

The chemical data on 10 samples of powdered lead arsenates and on 9 samples of paste lead arsenate, the latter being dried in the laboratory before analysis, are reported in Table 3. Of the powdered arsenate samples 1 apparently was a basic lead arsenate and 9 were acid lead arsenates. Of the paste lead arsenate samples, 1 apparently was a basic lead arsenate and 8 were acid lead arsenates. These samples, which were obtained from various manufacturers in this country, include most of the leading brands. The results of the analyses, therefore, are representative of the composition of the commercial lead arsenates on the market in 1916.

TABLE 3.—*Composition of powdered and paste commercial lead and calcium arsenates.*

Sample No.	Material analyzed.	Moisture.	Arsenic oxid (As₂O₅).		Oxid.	Carbon dioxid (CO₂).	Water of constitution and impurities by difference.
			Total.	Water-soluble.			
		Per cent.	*Per cent.*	*Per cent.*	*Per cent.*	*Per cent.*	*Per cent.*
1	Powdered acid lead arsenate....	0.32	30.86	0.31	64.88 (PbO)	0.54	3.40
2	....do..............................	1.43	31.55	.24	62.95 (PbO)	.15	3.92
13	....do....	.21	32.29	.32	64.23 (PbO)		3.27
14	....do.....	.17	32.00	.30	63.42 (PbO)		4.41
35	....do....	.30	31.24	.38	64.35 (PbO)		4.11
38	....do....	.14	32.47	.45	64.29 (PbO)		3.10
39	....do....	.20	32.93	.67	63.92 (PbO)		2.95
40	....do....	2.06	32.76	.45	63.70 (PbO)		1.48
70	....do....	.45	31.59	.22	63.00 (PbO)		4.96
28	Powdered basic lead arsenate...	.35	24.80	.43	72.23 (PbO)		2.62
3	Paste acid lead arsenate, dried..	.10	31.95	.34	64.57 (PbO)	Trace.	3.38
4	....do....	.12	32.30	.42	64.50 (PbO)		3.08
29	....do....	.19	30.38	.53	65.21 (PbO)		4.22
43	....do....	.11	32.07	.11	65.01 (PbO)		2.81
44	....do....	.11	33.17	.22	63.82 (PbO)		2.90
47	....do....	.11	32.51	.22	64.67 (PbO)		2.71
48	....do....	.22	33.09	.67	63.41 (PbO)		3.28
49	....do:....	.12	32.98	1.73	63.13 (PbO)		3.77
21	Paste basic lead arsenate, dried.	.11	23.00	.50	73.99 (PbO)		2.90
6	Paste calcium arsenate, dried..	.28	43.35	.70	38.86 (CaO)	2.74	14.77
7	Powdered calcium arsenate.....	1.58	43.35	.38	44.08 (CaO)	1.83	9.16
24	....do....	1.33	49.40	2.74	40.57 (CaO)	.98	7.72
32	....do....	.31	41.82	.22	42.61 (CaO)	1.64	13.62
34	....do....	9.56	38.16	1.92	37.38 (CaO)	4.34	10.56
56	....do....	7.71	39.19	.55	42.79 (CaO)	4.04	6.27
57	....do....	11.30	40.49	.08	44.03 (CaO)	1.05	3.13
58	....do....	.99	47.83	.25	46.16 (CaO)	1.70	3.32
59	....do....	6.07	45.37	2.32	41.48 (CaO)	2.43	4.65

The results in Table 3 show that in most cases the chemical composition of the commercial samples of acid lead arsenates closely approaches the theoretical composition. The manufacture of lead arsenate has become standardized to such an extent that different batches, or "runs," of the product vary but little from the theoretical figures. Acid lead arsenates are sold in both dry and paste form, the paste containing usually from 45 to 50 per cent of water.

The two most important determinations to be made on lead arsenates are the total arsenic oxid and the water-soluble arsenic oxid. The total arsenic oxid of an acid lead arsenate usually varies from 31 to 33 per cent, and the water-soluble arsenic oxid is less than 0.3 per cent in a good grade of commercial acid lead arsenate.

Robinson and Tartar (37) reported analytical results on commercial lead arsenates and described various tests used to determine the forms in which the lead and the arsenic are combined, as well as the extent to which these forms exist in such substances.

In acid lead arsenate the ratio by weight of arsenic oxid to lead oxid is theoretically 1 to 1.94. According to the results of the analysis (Table 3), however, this ratio is somewhat higher in commercial lead arsenates, showing that a slight excess of lead oxid (litharge) had been used in their manufacture in order to make sure that no uncombined arsenic acid would be left in the product. A small amount of carbon dioxid, which had been introduced in the litharge, was found in the acid lead arsenates tested. This is of no practical significance. In all but three of the powdered samples the moisture content was less than 0.35 per cent. The water of constitution of acid lead arsenates is theoretically 2.58 per cent. The results by difference show differences slightly greater than the theoretical figures, but in no case are they of any magnitude. The percentages of arsenic oxid and lead oxid, together with the low percentage of water-soluble arsenic oxid, indicate that the commercial acid lead arsenates examined were good and stable products.

BASIC LEAD ARSENATE.

The early investigators recognized "basic," or "sub," arsenate of lead and applied the term "neutral lead arsenate" to $PbHAsO_4$, which is the present commercial acid lead arsenate. They also applied the term "neutral lead arsenates" to lead pyroarsenates, which are not commercial products, and therefore will not be discussed here. McDonnell and Smith have printed a report on pyroarsenates (27). As a result of another investigation on basic lead arsenates, these authors (28) report the existence of a basic arsenate having optical and crystallographic properties similar to those of mimetite, from the analytical data apparently hydroxy mimetite, containing one molecule of water of crystallization. One or two manufacturers of insecticides sell, generally on special order, what is commercially called "T. P." arsenate.

Basic lead arsenate may be prepared as follows: Produce basic lead acetate by the action of acetic acid on lead or lead oxid, usually litharge. Then mix it with arsenic acid, thus forming basic lead arsenate. Basic lead arsenate may also be made by the reaction of sodium arsenate, litharge, and nitric acid, or by the action of ammonia on acid lead arsenate. It has the following theoretical composition: As_2O_5 (23.2 per cent), PbO (75 per cent), and water of constitution and crystallization (1.8 per cent). The specific gravity of this substance was found by McDonnell and Smith (28) to be 6.86.

Only two samples (Table 3, Nos. 28 and 21) of commercial basic lead arsenate (a powder and a paste) were secured on the market. While these showed somewhat greater variations from the theoretical than did the acid lead arsenates, both are relatively pure compounds.

solubility in water and yielded only 3.01 per cent of arsenic oxid soluble in water saturated with carbon dioxid.

London purple, originally a by-product in the manufacture of aniline dyes, is now made directly to a limited extent. It consists of arsenite of lime and arsenate of lime, with the addition of a dye. Table 4 gives the composition of the material used in the investigation. The analyses of four additional samples showed the following variations: Arsenious oxid, 18.30 to 29.38 per cent; arsenic oxid, 0.07 to 11.49 per cent; water-soluble arsenious oxid, 0.48 to 5.30 per cent; and water-soluble arsenic oxid, 0.07 to 2.46 per cent. One sample showed 24.91 per cent of calcium oxid, 2.70 per cent of magnesium oxid, and 11.25 per cent of ferric oxid and silicon dioxid. London purple, therefore, is of uncertain composition and contains varying amounts of water-soluble arsenious oxid and arsenic oxid. On account of its variable character and its tendency to burn foliage, the addition of lime is recommended when it is used as a spray.

Calcium and lead arsenates combined (samples 36 and 8) were analyzed and tested on insects. The demand for a mixed calcium and lead arsenate is limited. It is held by some that lead arsenate adheres to foliage better than calcium arsenate, so that the presence of a little lead arsenate in the mixture increases the adhesive properties. The use of calcium carbonate in the mixture reduces the percentage of arsenic present and permits the product to be sold more cheaply.

Sodium arsenate was formerly on the market in two grades, a 45 per cent and a 65 per cent arsenic oxid product. During the past three or four years it has been difficult to obtain sodium arsenate in commercial quantities. In preparing sodium arsenate containing 45 per cent of arsenic oxid, nitrate of soda (Na_2NO_3), arsenious oxid (As_2O_3), sodium carbonate (Na_2CO_3), and salt ($NaCl$) are roasted together. In preparing the 65 per cent grade the salt is omitted. The two commercial samples (Nos. 31 and 41) correspond to these two grades, although sample 41 contains about 60 per cent of arsenic oxid. Sample 31 contains 28.44 per cent of sodium chlorid, sample 41, 6.14 per cent, and sample 25, 0.096 per cent. Calculating the results for these two samples and for sample 25 (prepared in the laboratory) to a moisture-free basis, sample 25 contains 60 per cent, sample 31 about 47 per cent, and sample 41 about 64 per cent of arsenic oxid. All the arsenic present in sodium arsenate is water soluble. Sodium arsenate is sometimes added to Bordeaux mixture to produce a combined fungicide and insecticide. The excess lime of Bordeaux combines with the arsenic oxid of the sodium arsenate, forming insoluble calcium arsenate. The amount of sodium arsenate added and the amount of the excess lime of the Bordeaux are the factors which determine whether all of the soluble sodium arsenate is converted into the insoluble calcium arsenate.

Potassium arsenate.—Sample 26 is a laboratory product containing 59.39 per cent of arsenic oxid, all of which is soluble in water. No commercial samples of potassium arsenate are now available.

MISCELLANEOUS EXPERIMENTAL ARSENICALS.

The analytical results on three samples of lead arsenates and four samples of calcium arsenates made in the laboratory are given in Table 5.

TABLE 5.—*Composition of lead and calcium arsenates prepared in the laboratory.*

Sample No.	Material analyzed.	Moisture.	Arsenic oxid (As_2O_5).		Lead oxid (PbO).	Calcium oxid (CaO).	Carbon dioxid (CO_2).	Water of constitution and impurities, by difference.
			Total.	Water-soluble.				
		Per cent.	*Per cent.*	*Per cent.*	*Per cent.*	*Per cent.*	*Per cent.*	*Per cent.*
17	Acid lead arsenate..........	0.02	33.09	0.19	63.80	....	....	3.09
68	.....do.....................	.10	33.25	.00	63.67	....	....	2.98
18	Basic lead arsenate..........	.06	23.40	.27	74.66	....	....	1.88
45	Calcium meta-arsenate.......	.03	79.63	Trace.	....	18.45	0.00	1.89
46	Monocalcium arsenate........	.23	69.09	61.67	....	19.92	.10	10.66
42	Tricalcium arsenate..........	1.06	52.05	.46	....	40.07	-.96	5.86
69	.....do.....................	2.30	42.84	.17	....	44.89	5.73	4.24

Lead arsenates.—The two samples of acid lead arsenate (Nos. 17 and 68) contained percentages of arsenic oxid very close to the theoretical (33.11). They were prepared by mixing lead nitrate and arsenic acid, according to the procedure of McDonnell and Smith (*27*). The percentage of lead oxid in the two samples is a little lower than the theoretical. Basic lead arsenate (sample 18) was prepared by the action of ammonia on acid lead arsenate. There is slightly more arsenic oxid and slightly less lead oxid in this sample than is called for by the theoretical figures. Both the acid and basic lead arsenates were made from pure lead oxid and crystallized arsenic acid; consequently they are extremely pure.

Calcium arsenates.—A calcium meta-arsenate ($Ca(AsO_3)_2$) (sample 45) was prepared according to directions obtained from C. M. Smith of the insecticide and fungicide laboratory. The theoretical percentage of arsenic oxid for such a product is 80. No moisture or carbon dioxid was present in the sample, as the product had been ignited. Although high in arsenic oxid, the product is so insoluble that its insecticidal properties would undoubtedly be low. A monocalcium arsenate ($CaH_4(AsO_4)_2$) (sample 46) was also prepared according to Smith's directions. Its theoretical composition is as follows: Arsenic oxid (71.4 per cent), calcium oxid (17.41 per cent), and water of crystallization and water of constitution (11.19 per cent). This compound is very soluble in water and can not be considered a commercial possibility as an insecticide. Two samples of tricalcium arsenate were prepared. The composition of sample 42 approached the theoretical composition of tricalcium arsenate ($Ca_3(AsO_4)_2.2H_2O$) as determined by Robinson (*35*), 38.7 per cent of calcium oxid, 53 per cent of arsenic oxid, and 9.3 per cent of moisture and water of constitution. Sample 69 was prepared by using equal weights of lime and arsenic oxid, which gave a compound with an excess of lime, having slightly more than 4 equivalent parts of calcium oxid to 1 part of arsenic oxid, and containing but 0.17 per cent of water-soluble arsenic oxid. Calcium arsenate of this composition was recommended by Haywood and Smith (*18*) as suitable for commercial manufacture.

Barium arsenate seems to have been used first by Kirkland (*20*) in 1896. The next year Kirkland and Burgess (*21*) tested barium arsenate against certain insects. Smith (*48*) in 1907 also used a barium arsenate. Its preparation is not described by any of these investigators. A sample of barium arsenate (sample 71, Table 4) was prepared by adding a solution of arsenic acid to a solution of barium hydroxid with constant stirring. The details were as follows: Dissolve 546 grams of barium hydroxid ($Ba(OH)_2.8H_2O$), containing 240 grams of barium, in 3 liters of water to which 300 cubic centimeters of commercial arsenic acid, containing 0.4 gram of arsenic oxid per 1 cubic centimeter, has been added. After this mixture has been thoroughly stirred, the precipitated barium arsenate soon settles. Then wash the precipitate several times by decantation, filter it on a Büchner filter, dry and pulverize it, and finally pass it through a 100-mesh sieve. The theoretical composition of tribarium orthoarsenate ($Ba_3As_2O_8$) is as follows: Barium (59.7 per cent) and arsenic oxid (33.32 per cent); that is, the ratio of arsenic oxid to barium is 1 to 1.8. The ratio for the sample made in the laboratory was 1 to 1.9, showing the presence of a slight excess of barium. Its insecticidal value is discussed on page 38.

Copper barium arsenate mixture (sample 74, Table 4) was made as follows: A solution containing 360 grams of copper sulphate was mixed with 275 grams of arsenic oxid. No precipitate resulted. A dilute solution of barium chlorid was added and then barium hydroxid until the solution was but slightly acid. The mixture of copper and barium arsenate and barium sulphate was then thoroughly stirred and allowed to settle. The precipitate was washed several times by decantation and then was separated by filtering on a Büchner filter. The precipitate was finally dried, ground, and passed through a 100-mesh sieve. Its adhesive and fungicidal properties have not been tested, but its insecticidal powers are discussed on pages 38 to 46.

Aluminum arsenate (sample 73, Table 4) was prepared by mixing a solution of aluminum sulphate with arsenic acid. The precipitate was washed, filtered, and dried. The insecticidal results of this product are discussed on pages 38 to 42.

Copper arsenate was prepared by mixing a solution of copper sulphate with arsenic acid and then adding ammonia. The percentage of water-soluble arsenic oxid in this product was so high that no additional tests were made with the sample.

Zinc arsenate has been prepared by several investigators. The sample prepared in this study was made by mixing a solution of zinc chlorid with arsenic acid. Its physical properties did not seem to warrant further study.

COMBINATIONS OF ARSENICALS WITH FUNGICIDES AND OTHER MATERIALS.

In order to reduce the cost of spraying, various combinations of arsenicals with fungicides are frequently made. The arsenicals are also mixed with other substances, like glue and casein, to increase the length of time the arsenicals will adhere to the foliage or fruit.

While some of these combinations are frequently made, very little exact knowledge as to the chemical changes which take place in them is available. Accordingly, an investigation was undertaken to obtain information on the changes which occur in some of the important combinations involving arsenicals. One pound of powdered acid lead arsenate per 50 gallons of water is recommended as satisfactory for most commerical spraying. Acid lead arsenate at this rate and other arsenicals in corresponding amounts, depending on their arsenious or arsenic oxid contents, were used in the tests.

Thus amounts of the arsenicals containing equivalent percentages of arsenious or arsenic oxid were taken in each case.

In all the tests the mixtures of the arsenicals and other material were agitated in flasks by rotating in a water bath which was maintained at a constant temperature of 35° C. All were made in triplicate, but only the average figures are reported in the tables. The soluble arsenic (that found in the filtrates) was determined by the modified Gutzeit test (47) or by the Gooch-Browning method (1).

ARSENATES AND LIME-SULPHUR.

Ruth (38) made a study of the chemical changes resulting when acid lead arsenate and lime-sulphur were mixed. He found (a) a decrease of lime and sulphur in the solution, (b) an increase of thiosulphate sulphur in the solution and in the residue, (c) an increase of sulphite in the solution, (d) formation of lead sulphid, and (e) the formation of a compound containing arsenic and sulphur, but insoluble in the lime-sulphur solution. Robinson (35), after agitating mixtures of lead arsenate and lime-sulphur for three days, allowed them to settle and then poured off the clear liquid. He found that 25 per cent of the lime and more than 35 per cent of the sulphur had been precipitated and that 5 per cent of the arsenic had become soluble. Robinson and Tartar (37) tested mixtures of lime-sulphur and lead arsenates (4.8 grams of arsenate per 1,000 cubic centimeters of lime-sulphur, diluted 1 to 30). When basic lead arsenate was used little change occurred, but when acid lead arsenate was used an increase of soluble arsenic and a decrease of total soluble sulphur and polysulphid sulphur resulted. They concluded that the efficiency of the lime-sulphur had been reduced 25 per cent, and that the arsenic rendered soluble might injure foliage. Fields and Elliott (15) present data showing that less than five parts per million of arsenic oxid by weight was made soluble when solutions of lime-sulphur were mixed with either acid or basic lead arsenates.

In the present investigation standard commercial lime-sulphur solution was diluted (1 to 30) with recently boiled and cooled distilled water. Control flasks (500 cubic centimeters volume), completely filled with this diluted solution, were securely closed with stoppers and paraffin and agitated for 1-hour and 91-hour periods. Other flasks, filled with the diluted solution of lime-sulphur, to each of which 1.2 grams of powdered acid lead arsenate (sample 39) had been added, were similarly treated. Series of three flasks were removed, and the solutions were filtered immediately on removal from the bath. The results obtained with lead arsenate are given in Table 6.

TABLE 6.—*Composition of lime-sulphur solution and of the filtrates from mixtures of lead arsenate or calcium arsenate and lime-sulphur solution.*

Material analyzed.	After having been shaken for—	Composition (grams per 500 cubic centimeters).					
		Total lime (CaO).	Total sulphur (S).	Sulphid sulphur (S).	Thio-sulphate sulphur (S).	Sulphate sulphur (S).	Arsenic oxid (As$_2$O$_4$).
SERIES 1:							
Lime-sulphur solution....	1 hour.....	1.9680	4.9430	4.5190	0.1960	0.0035	0.0002
	91 hours...	2.0520	4.9290	4.5060	.2030	.0069	.0002
Filtrates from mixtures of lead arsenate and lime-sulphur solution........	1 hour.....	1.8050	4.4770	4.1620	.2020	.0029	.0270
	19 hours...	....	4.2670	4.0450	.1990	.0055	.0205
	43 hours...	....	4.2560	3.9080	.1980	.0036	.0199
	91 hours...	1.8030	4.2790	3.7110	.1970	.0076	.0200
SERIES 2:							
Lime-sulphur solution....	1 hour.....	1.9800	5.2500	4.7800	.3200	.0089	.0002
	21 hours...	1.9900	5.2500	4.7500	.3200	.0099	.0002
	5 days.....	2.0400	5.2000	4.7000	.3300	.0077	.0003
Filtrates from mixtures of calcium arsenate and lime-sulphur solution...	1 hour.....	2.0400	5.1000	4.7500	.3200	.0089	.0008
	21 hours...	2.0600	5.0500	4.6800	.3300	.0087	.0005
	5 days.....	1.9600	5.1000	4.7000	.3600	.0108	.0010

Using the analytical data on the lime-sulphur solution as controls, the analytical results on filtrates from a mixture of lead arsenate and lime-sulphur solution show the following: (a) The total lime in solution was reduced 10 per cent after having been shaken for either 1 hour or 91 hours; (b) the total sulphur in solution was reduced 9.5 per cent after 1 hour and 14 per cent after 19, after 43, and after 91 hours; (c) the sulphid sulphur was reduced 8 per cent after 1 hour and 18 per cent after 91 hours; (d) the thiosulphate sulphur remained unchanged after each period; (e) the sulphate sulphur increased slightly, although the same increase was observed in the control; and (f) 5.2 per cent of the total arsenic oxid of the lead arsenate used was rendered soluble. From these results, it is apparent that chemical changes have occurred. The mixture is therefore chemically incompatible.[5] Some of the sulphur in lime-sulphur solution probably united with the lead of the lead arsenate and produced lead sulphid, which could be seen as black particles in the mixture. The arsenic oxid group, liberated by the decomposition of the lead arsenate, was then free to combine with the lime in the lime-sulphur solution, probably forming calcium sulph-arsenate. The formation of insoluble tricalcium arsenate took place only to a limited degree.

Robinson (*34*) in examining mixtures of calcium arsenates and lime-sulphur found that no reaction took place in such mixtures. His tests with "dry lime-sulphur" mixed with calcium arsenate showed the presence of no soluble arsenic, but those with "soluble sulphur" mixed with calcium arsenate showed that it was present. Lovett (*24*) also reported that no changes take place when calcium arsenate is mixed with lime-sulphur solution.

Experiments similar to the lead arsenate tests were performed, using calcium arsenate (sample 57) in place of the acid lead arsenate. A series of 500 cubic centimeter flasks were filled with lime-sulphur solution diluted 1 to 30. Nine of the flasks were used as controls; to each of the others 1 gram of calcium arsenate was added. The solutions were agitated for periods of 1 hour, 21 hours, and 5 days. They were immediately filtered and the filtrates were tested.

---

[5] The term "compatible" is here used only in the chemical sense.

The data given in Table 6 (series 2) show that no detectable changes took place when calcium arsenate and lime-sulphur were mixed. The small amount of arsenic found in the filtrates was the water-soluble arsenic originally present in the calcium arsenate and amounted to 0.2 per cent of the total arsenic oxid in the calcium arsenate.

In brief, it is evident that chemical changes take place when acid lead arsenate and lime-sulphur are mixed. This mixture is therefore incompatible chemically. When calcium arsenate is mixed with lime-sulphur no soluble arsenic is formed in the case of high-grade products. Therefore this arsenate, when mixed with lime-sulphur, would seem to be a satisfactory insecticide. Field experience, however, shows that it often injures the foliage sprayed.

Such a mixture is chemically compatible and has been recommended by Quaintance and Siegler (*32*), Sanders (*40*), and others, who, however, do not claim that it is always free from burning properties.

No experiments with basic lead arsenate and lime-sulphur were performed. Bradley (*5*), in 1909, used basic lead arsenate in combination with lime-sulphur, and found 0.28 and 0.43 per cent of soluble arsenic. He considered that there was no danger of the formation of excessive amounts of soluble arsenic in such mixtures. Bradley and Tartar (*6*), who used both acid and basic lead arsenates in combination with lime-sulphur, found eight times more soluble arsenic with acid lead arsenate than with basic lead arsenate. Both forms of lead arsenate were more soluble in saline water than in pure water. Alkaline carbonates exerted a decomposing action, especially on acid lead arsenate.

ARSENATES AND BORDEAUX MIXTURE.

Fields and Elliott (*15*) stated that very little soluble arsenic is present when Bordeaux mixture is combined with lead arsenate. They found in both the acid and the basic lead arsenates only from 1 to 3 parts of soluble arsenic per million.

Since combinations of arsenicals with Bordeaux mixture are frequently made, it was considered important to determine whether or not chemical changes take place in these combinations. Tests were therefore conducted in which 4–3.67–50 Bordeaux mixture was prepared, dried, and passed through a 100-mesh sieve. Four-gram samples of the dry Bordeaux were placed in each of a series of 300 cubic centimeter flasks and to each flask were added portions of one of the four arsenicals in the following amounts: 0.8 gram of acid lead arsenate (sample 39); 0.667 gram of calcium arsenate (sample 57); 0.69 gram of sodium arsenate (sample 25); and 0.47 gram of Paris green (sample 64). Mixtures of the various arsenicals alone and of Bordeaux alone in distilled water were prepared and tested under the same conditions as the mixtures of the arsenicals and Bordeaux. The flasks were agitated at a temperature of 35° C. for periods of 1 hour, 1 day, and 3 days. The mixtures were filtered immediately and the filtrates were tested for copper by the colorimetric test with potassium ferrocyanid (*12*) and for lead by the lead sulphid color test as used by W. D. Lynch, of the insecticide and fungicide laboratory. The analytical data are given in Table 7.

No copper was found in any of the filtrates. The filtrates from the acid lead arsenate Bordeaux mixtures contained the following percentages of the total lead present in the sample: For the one-hour period, 3 per cent; for the one-day period, 7 per cent; and for the three-day period, 7.6 per cent. The results for water-soluble arsenic in the combinations are lower than those for water-soluble arsenic in the arsenicals alone. It is evident that the excess lime of the Bordeaux combined with part of the soluble arsenic present in the arsenates, forming insoluble calcium arsenate.

The results show that Bordeaux mixture and the arsenates of lead and calcium, as well as Paris green, are compatible, that a soluble arsenate, such as sodium arsenate, may be used in quantities large enough to act as an insecticide in combination with ordinary Bordeaux mixture, and that the excess lime of the Bordeaux will combine with the soluble arsenic to form insoluble calcium arsenate.

ARSENATES AND KEROSENE EMULSION.

As kerosene emulsion is occasionally used in combination with acid lead arsenate and may be used with calcium arsenate, a series of experiments was undertaken to determine whether detectable chemical changes take place in these combinations.

A kerosene emulsion was prepared according to the following directions:[6] One liter of commercial kerosene oil and 1 ounce of sodium fish-oil soap in water were mixed, and the resulting emulsion was diluted to 10 liters.

A series of 300 cubic centimeter flasks were filled with this emulsion and 0.8 gram of acid lead arsenate (sample 39) or 0.667 gram of calcium arsenate (sample 57) was added to each of the flasks, with the exception of the control flasks. Mixtures of the arsenates alone and of the emulsions alone were used for controls. The mixtures were agitated at 35° C. for periods of one hour, one day, and three days. They were filtered immediately and the filtrates were tested for arsenic. The average figures only are recorded in Table 7.

TABLE 7.—*Soluble arsenic in filtrates from combinations of arsenicals with Bordeaux mixture and with kerosene emulsion.*

Sample No.	Material analyzed.	Total arsenic (As) in sample taken.	Soluble arsenic (As) found after standing for—			Percentage of total arsenic (As) found soluble after standing for—		
			1 hour.	1 day.	3 days.	1 hour.	1 day.	3 days.
		Grams.	Grams.	Grams.	Grams.	Per cent.	Per cent.	Per cent.
25	Sodium arsenate............	0.1709			0.1650			96.55
64	Paris green..............	.1938			.0066			3.41
57	Calcium arsenate...........	.1753			.00034			0.20
39	Acid lead arsenate.........	.1709			.0048			2.81
61	Bordeaux mixture				.00006			
—	Sodium arsenate (25) plus Bordeaux (61)............	.1709	0.00095	0.00001	.00001	0.56	0.00	.00
—	Paris green (64) plus Bordeaux (61)...............	.1938	00113	.00053	.00046	.58	.27	.24
—	Calcium arsenate (57) plus Bordeaux (61)............	.1753	.00003	.00005	.00000	.02	.03	.00
—	Acid lead arsenate (39) plus Bordeaux...............	.1709	.00051	.00030	.00018	.30	.18	.11
—	Calcium arsenate (57) plus kerosene emulsion.........	.1753	.0018	.0095	.0122	1.03	5.42	6.96
—	Acid lead arsenate (39) plus kerosene emulsion........	.1709	.0332	.0768	.0740	19.43	44.94	43.30

[6] Taken from U. S. Dept. Agr. Farmers' Bull. 958, p. 28.

27476°—23—Bull. 1147——3

The amount of arsenic made soluble was much larger when acid lead arsenate was combined with kerosene emulsion than when calcium arsenate was combined with it. The same amount of arsenic was rendered soluble in one day as in three days in the case of the acid lead arsenate. When calcium arsenate was used, 1.5 per cent more of the total arsenic was made soluble the third day than the first day. It is evident that the lead and the lime of the arsenates combined with the fatty acids to produce soaps, leaving the corresponding amounts of arsenic in a soluble condition. The results show that less decomposition occurred in the case of calcium arsenate mixed with kerosene emulsion than in the case of acid lead arsenate and kerosene emulsion. Both mixtures are chemically incompatible.

ARSENATES AND FISH-OIL SOAP.

Combinations of acid lead arsenate with fish-oil soap are sometimes made. Because of the large quantity of calcium arsenate now being manufactured, it seemed advisable to test combinations of calcium arsenate and of acid lead arsenate with fish-oil soap in order to determine how much arsenic might be made soluble.

Fish-oil soap solutions of two strengths, 1 and 2 pounds of soap per 50 gallons, were prepared. The fish-oil soap was the same kind as that used in making the kerosene emulsion. A series of 300 cubic centimeter flasks were filled with the soap solution. No arsenical was added to some of the flasks which were used as controls, but 0.8 gram of acid lead arsenate (sample 39) or 0.667 gram of calcium arsenate (sample 57) was added to the others. A one-day period was taken for agitating the solutions, because the results with kerosene emulsion showed that in one day the reactions were practically complete for the lead arsenate and much retarded in the case of the calcium arsenate.

TABLE 8.—*Arsenic rendered soluble on combining lead or calcium arsenates with fish-oil soap.*

Sample No.	Material analyzed.	Arsenic (As) present in sample taken.	Arsenic (As) rendered soluble after standing for 1 day.	
		Grams.	*Grams.*	*Per cent.*
57	Calcium arsenate [1].................................	0.1753	0.0003	0.17
39	Acid lead arsenate [2]...............................	.1717	.0032	1.86
—	Calcium arsenate plus fish-oil soap (1 pound to 50 gallons).	.1753	.0503	28.69
—	Acid lead arsenate plus fish-oil soap (1 pound to 50 gallons)..	.1717	.1475	85.90
—	Calcium arsenate plus fish-oil soap (2 pounds to 50 gallons)..	.1753	.0667	38.05
—	Acid lead arsenate plus fish-oil soap (2 pounds to 50 gallons).	.1717	.1703	99.18

[1] Calcium arsenate at the rate of 0.93 pound per 50 gallons.
[2] Lead arsenate at the rate of 1.11 pounds per 50 gallons.

The results obtained (Table 8) follow the trend of the results secured with kerosene emulsion (Table 7) in that they show that more arsenic was rendered soluble when acid lead arsenate was used than when calcium arsenate was used. They also show that the greater the quantity of fish-oil soap used the larger the amount of soluble arsenic formed. All of the arsenic was made soluble when acid lead arsenate was mixed with the soap at the rate of 2 pounds per 50 gallons. The lead soaps are more readily formed than the lime soaps, for which reason more arsenic was left in a free or soluble form when acid lead arsenate was used·than when calcium arsenate was used. Based on the results of chemical analyses, both of these mixtures are incompatible.

ACID LEAD OR CALCIUM ARSENATES AND NICOTINE SULPHATE SOLUTIONS.

Mixtures of acid lead arsenate and of calcium arsenate with a solution of nicotine sulphate were prepared and analyzed. A 1–800 dilution of a 40 per cent solution of nicotine sulphate was made. In the first series 500 cubic centimeter flasks were filled with this dilute nicotine sulphate solution and 1.2 grams of acid lead arsenate (sample 39) or 1 gram of calcium arsenate (sample 57), containing 13 per cent of free calcium oxid, was added to each of the flasks, with the exception of the controls. Results of the analyses of the lead and calcium arsenates used are given in Table 3. After agitating the different solutions for periods of one hour, one day, and three days they were immediately filtered and the filtrates were analyzed for arsenic and nicotine. Nicotine was determined by the official silicotungstic acid method (1). A second series of tests, using two commercial calcium arsenate samples (Nos. 32 and 59) and a pure tricalcium arsenate prepared by C. M. Smith, was made. Sample 32 contained 9.99 per cent, sample 59, 5.23 per cent, and sample 464 no free calcium oxid. In this series 0.6 gram of the calcium arsenate was placed in each of a series of 300 cubic centimeter flasks, which were made to volume with the dilute nicotine sulphate solution. These solutions were agitated for one hour and for three days.

TABLE 9.—*Results of combining acid lead arsenate or calcium arsenate with nicotine-sulphate solutions.*

Material analyzed.	Soluble nicotine after agitating for—			Soluble arsenic oxid (As₂O₅) after agitating for—		
	1 hour.	1 day.	3 days.	1 hour.	1 day.	3 days.
500 cubic centimeter volume tests:	*Grams.*	*Grams.*	*Grams.*	*Per cent.*	*Per cent.*	*Per cent.*
Nicotine-sulphate solution............	0.2748	....	0.2820	0.00	....	0.00
Acid lead arsenate (39) plus nicotine sulphate........................	.2748	0.2780	.2763	.45	0.34	.60
Calcium arsenate (57) plus nicotine sulphate........................	.2778	.2815	.2815	.44	.52	.50
Acid lead arsenate (39)................	.0000	.0000	.0000	.60	....	....
Calcium arsenate (57).................	.0000	.0000	.0000	.80	....	....
300 cubic centimeter volume tests:						
Nicotine-sulphate solution...........	.1740	....	....	.00	....	.00
Calcium arsenate (32) plus nicotine sulphate........................	.1750	....	....	1.15	....	1.09
Calcium arsenate (59) plus nicotine sulphate........................	.1760	....	....	11.04	....	11.50
Calcium arsenate (464) plus nicotine sulphate........................	.1740	....	....	10.39	....	11.86
Calcium arsenate (32).................	....	....	....	.27	....	.27
Calcium arsenate (59).................	....	....	....	2.09	....	2.22
Calcium arsenate (464)................	....	....	....	3.34	....	3.57

The results (Table 9) show that acid lead arsenate (sample 39) when combined with nicotine sulphate gives no increase of soluble arsenic and that the amount of soluble nicotine is not altered. This mixture is therefore chemically compatible.

When calcium arsenates are combined with nicotine sulphate solutions, soluble arsenic oxid may be produced, depending on the sample of calcium arsenate used and on the quantity of nicotine sulphate present in the mixture. The percentage of soluble arsenic oxid will be low if there is enough excess lime in the calcium arsenate to combine with the SO_4 of the nicotine sulphate. If sufficient excess lime is not present, the SO_4 combines with some of the CaO of the calcium arsenate, liberating soluble arsenic oxid. Calcium arsenate (sample 57) contained 13.16 per cent of free calcium oxid, and when combined with nicotine sulphate only 0.5 per cent of free arsenic oxid was found. Calcium arsenate (sample 32) contained 9.99 per cent of free calcium oxid, and when combined with nicotine sulphate 1.15 per cent of soluble arsenic oxid was found.

When the free lime in the calcium arsenates was low or absent entirely there was a marked rise in the percentage of soluble arsenic oxid. For example, sample 59, containing 5.23 per cent of free calcium oxid, and sample 464, containing no free calcium oxid, gave practically 12 per cent of soluble arsenic oxid. Sample 6 (3.68 per cent free calcium oxid) and sample 58 (9.06 per cent free calcium oxid) gave, respectively, 6.67 and 2.28 per cent of soluble arsenic oxid after being agitated for 1 hour with nicotine sulphate solution in the proportions given. These mixtures, therefore, are chemically incompatible, and the only way that such a combination should be made is to use a high-grade calcium arsenate containing at least 10 per cent of excess calcium oxid and using a proportion of nicotine sulphate no higher than that used in these tests.

The lime of calcium arsenate decomposes the nicotine sulphate, leaving free nicotine, but does not change the amount of nicotine present. The results given in Table 9 show that the percentage of soluble nicotine was not altered by the presence of calcium arsenates.

A few tests made in the insecticide and fungicide laboratory in which free nicotine solution was mixed with acid lead arsenate or with calcium arsenate showed that these combinations were chemically compatible. Results obtained on combining nicotine sulphate solutions with Bordeaux mixture were reported by Safro (39) and Wilson (52), who claimed that such mixtures were compatible.

PHYSICAL PROPERTIES OF ARSENICALS.

A commercial calcium arsenate and a commercial acid lead arsenate were selected for a series of tests on the adhesive properties of these substances on sprayed foliage, which was extended over three seasons (1917, 1918, and 1919). For each 50 gallons of water 1 pound of powdered acid lead arsenate or an equivalent amount of calcium arsenate, based on the arsenic oxid content, was used. The sprays were applied to potato and apple leaves with a power sprayer. At various periods after the sprays had been applied leaves were gathered for analysis. The leaves were dried and samples of approximately 5 grams each were digested with nitric and sulphuric acids and analyzed for arsenic by the modified Gutzeit (47) method. The results (Table 10) by this method do not warrant in all cases the expression to the degree of accuracy which the figures may imply, but this is the common way of expressing results where small amounts of a substance are present.

TABLE 10.—*Arsenic on potato and apple leaves sprayed with lead or calcium arsenates.*

Year and locality.	Spray used.	Average number of samples.	Arsenic (As) found.	
			Per square meter of leaf surface.	On dry leaves.
1917.	POTATO LEAVES.		*Milligrams.*	*Parts per million.*
Washington, D. C.	Acid lead arsenate	7	5	140
Do.	Calcium arsenate	8	3	50
Presque Isle, Me.	Acid lead arsenate	2	80	1,460
Do.	Calcium arsenate	2	56	1,270
Greenwood, Va.	Acid lead arsenate	2	16	50
Do.	Calcium arsenate	2	19	70
1918.				
Washington, D. C.	Acid lead arsenate	3	....	170
Do.	Calcium arsenate	3	....	60
Greenwood, Va.	Acid lead arsenate	2	....	180
Do.	Calcium arsenate	2	....	270
1919.				
Arlington, Va.	Acid lead arsenate	5	....	260
Do.	Calcium arsenate	5	....	210
1917.	APPLE LEAVES.			
Greenwood, Va.	Acid lead arsenate	2	40	510
Do.	Calcium arsenate	2	9	120
1918.				
Greenwood, Va.	Acid lead arsenate	4	....	130
Do.	Calcium arsenate	4	....	260

The results of the tests for all three years show an average of 286 parts per million of arsenic on the dry leaves receiving the lead arsenate spray and an average of 219 parts per million of arsenic on the dry leaves receiving the calcium arsenate spray. The 1917 and 1919 results show that a larger percentage of arsenic of acid lead arsenate adhered to the leaves than of the arsenic of the calcium arsenate. The 1918 results are practically the same for the two arsenates.

Lime was used with certain of the arsenates in some of the 1918 tests (Table 11). Potato vines were sprayed with a commercial calcium arsenate and a commercial acid lead arsenate alone and with the addition of lime to each. Zinc arsenite and calcium meta-arsenate were used without the addition of lime. Two calcium arsenates, one with a molecular ratio of 3 CaO to 1 As$_2$O$_5$ and the other with one of 4 to 1, were tested, with and without the addition of lime. In these two cases both 2 ounces and 4 ounces of lime per 10 gallons of spray were used. The arsenious or arsenic oxid contents of the sprays were made the same in all cases, with the exception of calcium meta-arsenate. From the data in Table 11 it is evident that the lime was of no advantage in increasing the amount of arsenic adhering to the leaves.

TABLE 11.—*Arsenic on potato leaves sprayed with arsenicals with and without the addition of lime.*[1]

Sample No.	Material used.	Total arsenic oxid (As₂O₅) in dry arsenical.	Arsenical used per 10 gallons.	Arsenic (As) on dry leaves.
		Per cent.	*Ounces.*	*Parts per million.*
24	Calcium arsenate..................	49.40	2	240
24A	Sample 24 plus lime (2 ounces)...........	49.40	2	340
40	Acid lead arsenate.................	32.76	3½	530
40A	Sample 40 plus lime (2 ounces)...........	32.76	3½	580
23	Zinc arsenite........	² 41.49	2½	540
86	Calcium meta-arsenate..............	79.60	2½	830
87	Calcium arsenate.................	55.00	2	290
87A	Sample 87 plus lime (2 ounces)...........	55.00	2	270
87B	Sample 87 plus lime (4 ounces)...........	55.00	2	290
88	Calcium arsenate.................	42.80	2½	360
88A	Sample 88 plus lime (2 ounces)...........	42.80	2½	280
88B	Sample 88 plus lime (4 ounces)...........	42.80	2½	380

[1] Equal percentages of As₂O₃ and As₂O₅ were used for all the sprays.
[2] As₂O₃.

During the season of 1920 potato plants were sprayed at Arlington, Va., using (a) dry acid lead arsenate, (b) dry "suspender" [7] acid lead arsenate, (c) zinc arsenite, and (d) Paris green. The sprays were made to contain the same percentage of arsenious or arsenic oxid and were applied four times during the season, using a power sprayer. Nine duplicate sets of 50 leaves each were collected on the same days throughout the season from each plot of the various sprayed vines. These leaves (900 in all from each plot receiving a different spray) were analyzed for arsenic, with the following average results, expressed as parts of arsenic per million of dried potato leaves: Paris green, 155; "suspender" acid lead arsenate, 195; zinc arsenite, 203; and acid lead arsenate, 210.

The physical properties of arsenicals have been studied to some extent since the time they were first prepared, but no complete study has been reported. This may be due in part to the difficulties encountered in measuring those physical properties which contribute toward making a satisfactory product for dusting or spraying. Wilson (53) in 1919 gave data on the burning, suspensibility, and adhesiveness of Paris green, zinc arsenite, acid and basic lead arsenates, and calcium arsenate.

A series of tests was performed, using commercial powdered arsenicals (Table 12), to obtain comparative data on the apparent density and suspensibility of these products. The apparent density of a powder here described is based on the number of grams occupying a volume of 1,000 cubic centimeters and the suspensibility on the volumetric readings of 30 grams of powder which had settled after having been shaken for one minute with approximately 500 cubic centimeters of water and having stood for 10 and for 60 minutes.

[7] "Suspender" lead arsenate is a trade name applied to a powdered lead arsenate containing some added organic substance for the purpose of keeping the arsenate in suspension when mixed with water.

TABLE 12.—*Physical properties of commercial powdered calcium and lead arsenates and zinc arsenite.*

Sample No.	Material examined.	Total arsenic oxid (As₂O₅) in powders.	Apparent density.[1]	Suspension properties after standing for [2]—	
				10 minutes.	60 minutes.
		Per cent.	*Grams.*	*Cubic centimeters.*	*Cubic centimeters.*
59	Calcium arsenate	45.37	254	245	200
58	....do....	47.83	257	188	115
97	....do....	40.38	364	365	145
98	....do....	41.40	365	380	120
24	....do....	49.40	422	170	140
57	....do....	40.49	532	245	57
56	....do....	39.19	567	170	71
85	Acid lead arsenate	31.89	247	230	167
39	....do....	32.93	249	270	132
83	....do....	31.50	284	110	123
84	....do....	32.90	306	265	135
38	....do....	32.47	369	146	90
82	....do....	32.75	747	88	60
23	Zinc arsenite	[3]41.49	355	165	77

[1] Weight of powder occupying a volume of 1,000 cc. without being jarred.
[2] Based on volumetric readings of 30 grams of powder, shaken with 500 cc. of water and allowed to stand.
[3] Arsenious oxid (As₂O₃).

In Table 12 the calcium and acid lead arsenates are arranged according to their apparent densities, the lightest ones first. The lightest powders usually remained suspended for the longest time (60-minute test) and the heavy powders settled most rapidly. More than 90 per cent of all the arsenicals tested passed a 40-mesh sieve after having been shaken for five minutes. These results are of no value and therefore are not given. It is believed that the fineness of powdered arsenicals, which are generally amorphous, can not be correctly determined by this test, since fine powders pack in a 40-mesh sieve. The fineness of relatively coarse arsenicals, such as arsenious oxid, can be determined by sieving.

Microscopical examinations of the various arsenicals were made. A large number of samples of powdered calcium and acid lead arsenates and one of zinc arsenite were blown from a dust gun. These dusts, collected on six or more microscopic slides placed at varying distances from the dust gun, were photographed. Then, using a high-power lens of the microscope, drawings were made by the aid of the camera lucida which made possible the determination of slight differences in the size of particles but did not ve satisfactory information on the dusting or spraying properties of these products.

Several samples of powdered lead arsenate and Paris green, examined under a magnification of 100 diameters, appeared to be amorphous. The samples of calcium arsenate contained a few small crystals, although the samples on the whole appeared to be largely without crystalline shapes. Four samples of arsenious oxid were examined under the microscope. Samples 19 and 27 consisted chiefly of small octahedral crystals; sample 37 contained somewhat larger crystals.

COMPARATIVE TOXICITY OF ARSENICALS.

RESULTS OF PREVIOUS INVESTIGATIONS.

CALCIUM ARSENATE.

Bedford and Pickering (*3*) and Smith (*48*) appear to have been the first to use calcium arsenate as an insecticide. In 1907 all three of these men tried it as a substitute for lead arsenate. Bedford and Pickering found it practically as efficient as acid lead arsenate on fruit trees in England. Against the army worm in New Jersey, however, Smith did not find it satisfactory.

Between 1907 and 1912, calcium arsenate apparently was not further tested as an insecticide, but during the seasons of 1912, 1913, and 1914, the office of fruit insect investigations of the Bureau of Entomology, United States Department of Agriculture, began to test it, as a result of which a commercial calcium arsenate was put on the market. Since 1915 the use of this arsenate in the field has steadily increased. In 1914 a commercial calcium arsenate in combination with lime-sulphur gave very satisfactory control of the codling moth (*45*).

Scott (*46*), who, during the seasons of 1913 and 1914, used calcium arsenate, states that for spraying apple and shade trees, it may be used with the same degree of efficiency and safety as acid lead arsenate.

Sanders (*40*), using acid lead and calcium arsenates of equal arsenic contents, found the lead salt slightly superior in killing power, but the calcium salt more desirable for use with sulphid sprays.

Sanders and Kelsall (*42*) state that when calcium arsenate is used alone it may under some conditions burn foliage, but that when used in combination sprays with Bordeaux mixture or lime-sulphur, it is as safe as any known arsenical. In sodium sulphid sprays it is much the safest of all arsenicals. It adheres fairly well to foliage and remains in suspension.

Coad (*9*) used various arsenicals, as dusts, against cotton boll weevils. He found acid lead arsenate much more toxic than basic lead arsenate and a high-grade calcium arsenate still more effective. Coad and Cassidy (*10* and *11*) recommend a high-grade calcium arsenate above all other arsenicals for controlling the cotton boll weevil, and they enumerate some of the physical and chemical properties that such an arsenical should have.

Ricker (*33*), testing poison baits against grasshoppers, determined that calcium arsenate, used in direct competition with Paris green and crude arsenious oxid, gave equally good results.

BARIUM ARSENATE.

Barium arsenate seems to have been used first by Kirkland (*20*), who tested it in Massachusetts against the larvæ of the gypsy moth, fall webworm, and *Datana ministra*, securing satisfactory results in each case. Kirkland and Burgess (*21*) say:

The experiments with barium arsenate in 1896 gave so good results that we were hopeful that this insecticide would prove superior to lead arsenate. Its killing effects on larvæ in confinement are certainly superior to those of arsenate of lead. In the field spraying operations it was found that the poison did not adhere to the foliage for a sufficiently long time to kill the larvæ.

Smith (*48*) did not find barium arsenate satisfactory against one species of army worm.

Brittain and Good (*7*) used barium arsenate in 1917 against the apple maggot, but did not recommend it because of its tendency to burn the foliage.

MISCELLANEOUS SPRAY MIXTURES.

Kirkland and Burgess (*21*) determined in field experiments on the gypsy moth that acid lead arsenate is slightly better than basic lead arsenate.

Wilson (*51*) reported that zinc arsenite killed tent caterpillars (*Malacosoma erosa* and *M. pluvialis*) more quickly and stayed in suspension better than the basic lead arsenate. The basic lead arsenate, while slow in its action, finally killed the insects. The same arsenic content was not used for both sprays. Lime-sulphur mixed with arsenicals retarded the action of the arsenicals. Lime-sulphur used alone was not of much value as a stomach poison.

Robinson and Tartar (*36*) conducted tests with tent caterpillars (*M. pluvialis*) on sprayed foliage in an open part of an insectary, using an equal arsenic content. The acid lead arsenate killed more quickly than did the basic lead arsenate which, however, although slow, proved satisfactory because it killed all the caterpillars tested.

Tartar and Wilson (*50*), also using tent caterpillars, determined that acid lead arsenate (2–200) was more efficient than the basic form (2–100). The acid lead arsenate had an arsenic content of about 33 per cent, while the basic form had one of only 25 per cent.

Sanders and Brittain (*41*), reporting tests on the toxic value of certain arsenicals, both alone and in combination with fungicides, against the brown tail moth, tent caterpillar, cankerworm, tussock moth, and fall webworm in the field, report that calcium arsenate is inferior to both acid and basic lead arsenates, and that barium arsenate is still more inferior. Basic lead arsenate is inferior to acid lead arsenate in all combinations except with Bordeaux mixture. They think that Bordeaux mixture does not inhibit the action of the basic form as much as it does that of the other arsenicals used.

Lovett and Robinson (*24* and *25*) used the tent caterpillar (*M. pluvialis*) throughout their experiments to determine the toxic values and killing efficiency of the arsenates. Instead of examining all the larvæ daily to determine the exact number dead, they counted the dead ones that dropped daily from the sprayed foliage in the laboratory. These men also carried on preliminary field experiments with calcium arsenate. They summarize their results as follows:

Lead hydrogen [acid lead] arsenate has a higher killing efficiency at a given dilution than either calcium or basic lead arsenate. It requires a longer period of time to kill the nearly mature caterpillars than the small forms. All of the arsenic devoured by the insects in feeding upon sprayed foliage is not assimilated, but a portion passes through the intestinal tract in the excrement. The percentage amount of the arsenic assimilated depends upon the arsenate used; lead hydrogen arsenate was assimilated readily and most of the arsenic was retained in the tissues while much of the basic lead arsenate was found in the excrement. It requires approximately 0.1595 milligram of arsenic pentoxid to kill 1,000 small tent caterpillars, and approximately 1.84 milligram of arsenic pentoxid to kill 1,000 nearly mature tent caterpillars, irrespective of the particular arsenate used as a spray.

Howard (*19*), experimenting with the spotted cucumber beetle in the field, used equal amounts (by weight) of several arsenicals. The average mortality on the fifth day, based upon the results of two seasons' work, is as follows: Zinc arsenite, 24 per cent; acid lead arsenate, 17 per cent; Paris green, 16. per cent; Bordeaux-lead arsenate, 14 per cent; and calcium arsenate, 1 per cent.

Sanders and Kelsall (*43*) give comparative figures for the toxicity of several arsenicals. On the basis of one-half pound of metallic arsenic to 100 gallons of liquid, they obtained the following percentages of dead fall webworms on the eighth day: Sodium arsenate, 52; Paris green, 72; acid lead arsenate, 36; zinc arsenite, 60; calcium arsenate, 44; and white arsenic (As_2O_3), 60. On the same arsenic-content basis, but with the addition of Bordeaux mixture (10–10–100) to the spray materials, they obtained the following percentages of dead tussock-moth caterpillars on the eighth day: Sodium arsenate, 60; Paris green, 64; calcium arsenate, 48; and white arsenic, 60.

Wilson (*53*), using five arsenicals against the potato beetle in the field and laboratory, presents their rates of toxicity graphically as follows: Paris green, 80 per cent; zinc arsenite, 65 per cent; acid lead arsenate, 60 per cent; calcium arsenate, 50 per cent; and basic lead arsenate, 20 per cent. He did not use the same arsenic content in any two of them.

EXPERIMENTAL WORK.

In comparing the toxicities of the various arsenicals, fed to several species of insects, equal percentages of the two oxids of arsenic (As_2O_3 and As_2O_5) were used in the spray mixtures.

PREPARATION OF SPRAY MIXTURES.

Suspensions or solutions of each of the arsenicals used were prepared on the basis of the presence of 0.076 gram of arsenious or arsenic oxid per 100 cubic centimeters of distilled water. This proportion is at the rate of 1 pound of dry or 2 pounds of paste acid lead arsenate to 50 gallons of water, it being assumed that 32 per cent is the average arsenic oxid content of a dry acid lead arsenate. On the basis of equal percentage, the mixtures made by using arsenious oxid contained 16.2 per cent more metallic arsenic than did those containing arsenic oxid. Each mixture, however, had either an arsenious or arsenic oxid content of 0.076 per cent. All the laboratory samples used in 1919 and 1920 were pulverized and passed through a 100-mesh sieve before being mixed with water, but the commercial samples were used as purchased. When properly prepared, the arsenical mixtures were placed in clean mason jars having rubbers and tops. Each jar was then thoroughly shaken to dissolve, if possible, and to distribute the arsenical, and subsequently the mixtures were sprayed on foliage which was eaten by insects.

APPLICATION OF SPRAY MIXTURES.

In all, seven species of insects were tested: Silkworms (*Bombyx mori* L.), two species of fall webworms (*Hyphantria cunea* Dru. and *H. textor* Harr.), and tent caterpillars (*Malacosoma americana* Fab.), belonging to Lepidoptera; the Colorado potato-beetle larvæ (*Leptinotarsa decemlineata* Say), belonging to Coleoptera; grasshoppers (mostly *Melanoplus femur-rubrum* De G.), belonging to Orthoptera; and honeybees (*Apis. mellifica* L.), belonging to Hymenoptera. An atomizer was used in all the spraying experiments.

Silkworms.—Silkworm larvæ were fed leaves treated as follows: Mulberry leaves were sprayed with the various mixtures, the control leaves being sprayed with tap water only. After having been dried in the air the leaves were cut into small strips which were then placed in small wire-screen cages. An effort was made to put approximately the same quantity of food in each cage, so that a rough comparative estimate of that consumed could be made. In 1919 about 50 normal silkworms in the second instar (varying in length from 7 to 12 millimeters, with an average of 10 millimeters, and not ready to molt) were put in each cage, but in 1920 silkworms in the third instar (18 to 30 millimeters long, average 25 millimeters) were employed. Counts were made daily except on Sundays, the cages being cleaned and treated food being renewed at the same time. No disease was noticed among these larvæ.

Webworms.—The webs were collected in the fields from a variety of plants on Monday. At the laboratory these webs containing webworms were kept in large cages with a small amount of food until Tuesday noon, when the larvæ, which were then very hungry, were well mixed according to size (all instars but first one). Tuesday morning approximately the same quantity of mulberry foliage was placed in each of several wide-mouthed bottles containing water. It was then sprayed, and, when dry, a bottle with contents was placed in a large battery jar, 8 inches in diameter by 12 inches high. Tuesday afternoon approximately the same number of webworms were placed in each jar, and thereafter the sprayed food was renewed daily. Thus by starting each set of experiments on the same day of the week, the days (Sundays) on which no records were taken always fell on the fifth, twelfth, and nineteenth days of the tests. Very little disease or parasitism was noticed among these larvæ.

Tent caterpillars.—The tents, collected in the fields on wild cherry trees, were handled in the same manner as the webs of webworms. Sprayed wild cherry foliage was placed in the jars daily and counts were made daily. Owing to the prevalence of the "wilt," or polyhedral disease, it was necessary to test these larvæ while in the earliest instars.

Potato-beetle larvæ.—Collected on potato plants, these larvæ were placed in cheesecloth cages, 9 inches square by 12 inches high. They were so well mixed before being placed in the cages that each cage contained about the same number in the various instars. Sprayed potato-plant foliage was given to them daily. Parasitism was common only in the last instar.

Grasshoppers.—The fourth, fifth, and sixth (adults) instars caught in the fields were tested in the cheesecloth cages. Having been unable to use the foregoing spray mixtures, bran mash, mixed with some of the same powdered arsenicals, served as food. Using Paris green (sample 64, containing 55.09 per cent As_2O_3) as a standard, and the regular formula [8] as a basis, a modified formula was derived, whereby a pint of poisoned bran mash containing each arsenical to

---

[8] Bran, 25 pounds; Paris green, 1 pound; lemons or oranges, 6; molasses, 2 quarts; and water, from 2 to 4 gallons.

be tested was prepared. A temporary preservative was added to the mash. The poisoned mash was so prepared that each pint had an arsenic content of 1.08 per cent. The grasshoppers were fed daily. Parasitism was common, causing a high daily mortality among the controls. The temporary preservative in the control food seems to have increased the mortality about 4 per cent.

Honeybees.—To obtain bees of practically the same age for insecticidal purposes, the brood chamber of a hive was moved 30 feet from the old stand. On the following day all the old bees had returned to the old stand, leaving only young workers (nurse bees and wax generators), the brood, and the queen in the brood chamber. Fifty of these young workers were placed in each of many screen-wire experimental cases and were fed the spray mixtures, diluted twenty times, in the following manner: One cubic centimeter of a diluted mixture was thoroughly mixed with 4 cubic centimeters of honey in a small feeder which was so covered with wire that the bees could not waste the food. The 50 bees were given 0.038 milligram of arsenic or arsenious oxid. If all consumed equal quantities, each one ate 0.0005 milligram of metallic arsenic when the arsenic oxid form was used, or 0.00057 milligram when the arsenious oxid form was employed. After the bees had eaten the poisoned honey they were given queen cage candy. The number found dead was recorded daily. Great care was taken to see that the bees always had plenty of food.

STATEMENT OF RESULTS.

Amount of food consumed.—Not having had time to calculate accurately the amount of food consumed during all of these tests, an effort was made to estimate it, but this was found possible only with the food eaten by the webworms and tent caterpillars. The amount consumed of the foliage placed daily in each jar of larvæ was estimated in tenths and fractional parts of tenths, if necessary. On the twentieth day the experiments were ended and the total amount of food eaten during this period was used in calculating the amount consumed per larva, counting one-hundredth of each daily feeding as a unit.

Criteria of toxicity.—In order to judge the value of these methods, so that the results obtained by using them can be properly interpreted, the following uncontrollable factors should be mentioned: (a) The insects always varied more or less in age and size. (b) The immature insects molted irregularly, causing an irregularity in feeding, as insects do not eat during the molting period, which may last from one to three days. (c) Disease and parasitism were often discovered several days after the experiments had been started. (d) The temperature often varied, causing the caterpillars, which are chiefly night "feeders," to eat less on cool nights than on warm nights. (e) Some insects die soon after eating a dose of poison, while others lie "sick" for several days before dying, which causes a great variation in their mortality record. (f) The sensitiveness of insects to poisons varies. (g) In applying the spray mixtures it was impossible to spray two bunches of foliage in such a manner that equal amounts of arsenicals adhered to all the leaves. Moreover, the metallic arsenic in the arsenites and arsenates varied slightly. No two arsenicals adhere equally well to leaves, and all of them have a tendency to collect in drops, causing an unequal distribution of the poison. Nevertheless, this spraying was done more thoroughly than is possible in practical spraying. (h) It was often difficult to separate the dead insects from those apparently dead. This was accomplished in a fairly satisfactory manner by placing these insects almost against the globe of an electric light. If they exhibited no signs of life after being subjected for five minutes to the heat from this light they were considered dead. (i) In these experiments it was impossible to feed definite amounts of the arsenicals to individual insects. In a very limited way it would be possible to feed insects singly, but it is almost impossible to make them eat definite amounts of poisons. It would be possible to feed definite amounts of arsenicals to individual bees. If they remain isolated singly in cages, however, they live for only a few hours, although when 50 or more are confined in one case they freely feed one another and usually live for 9 or 10 days.

Because of these uncontrollable factors, a large number of insects were used for each individual experiment and the experiments were repeated several times, if possible. The results thus obtained are only comparative and are based on the average time required to kill the insects tested rather than on the absolute single lethal doses required to kill them. It was assumed that the insects ate equal amounts of the poisons, although this may never have been true. In the light of these probable errors it is easy to explain the delayed deaths of many of the insects poisoned and the great variation in their daily mortality.

PRELIMINARY TESTS.

During the summers of 1917 and 1918, many preliminary tests were performed on silkworms, tent caterpillars, and fall webworms. While no conclusive data were obtained, the following indications may be given.

The 14 commercial acid lead arsenates (samples 1, 2, 3, 4, 13, 14, 29, 38, 39, 40, 44, 47, 48, and 49) used showed no important differences in insecticidal properties. All proved efficient. The two basic lead arsenates (samples 21 and 28) did not kill as quickly as did the acid lead arsenates. Only two of the five commercial calcium arsenates (samples 5, 6, 7, 24, and 34) tested proved efficient. The insoluble calcium meta-arsenate (sample 45) prepared in the laboratory had no effect, while the laboratory sample of water-soluble monocalcium arsenate (No. 46) killed quickly. The arsenious oxid samples (Nos. 9, 19, 27, and 37), arsenic oxids (samples 10 and 16), sodium arsenates (samples 25, 31, and 41), potassium arsenate (sample 26), and zinc arsenites (samples 23, 30, and 33) were usually efficient. One of these with a high percentage of water-soluble arsenic, however, was not necessarily more toxic than another with a lower percentage of water-soluble arsenic. The bases—lead oxid, (samples 12 and 20), calcium oxid (sample 11), and zinc oxid (sample 22)—had little effect when used alone. From the insecticidal viewpoint, there seems to be no advantage in combining calcium arsenate and lead arsenate (sample 8). When lime was added to the laboratory sample of calcium arsenate (No. 42) the toxicity seemed to be decreased.

RELATIVE TOXICITY OF COMMERCIAL LEAD AND CALCIUM ARSENATES.

Since the preliminary experiments indicated that the commercial acid lead arsenates do not differ greatly in toxicity, sample 39, one of those first used, was selected as a standard by which to judge the relative toxicity of other spray materials, because its arsenic oxid content (32.93 per cent) approaches most nearly the theoretical content (33.11 per cent).

In order to obtain comparable percentages of toxicity for the three arsenates tested against five species of insects, it was first necessary to place all the daily percentages of mortalities on the same basis. This was accomplished by subtracting the daily mortalities of the control insects fed nonpoisoned food from the daily mortalities of the insects fed sprayed food. Since the daily mortalities on any given day vary too much to serve as a fair percentage of toxicity, the average of the mortalities on the third, sixth, and tenth days have been taken. The records given in Table 13 under the twentieth day show whether or not the insecticides used were efficient. To test the effect of starvation on the insects, other controls without food were used also.

The results reported in Tables 13 to 21 are comparable only when the same combination of data and the same number of sets of insects have been used. Data on the number of sets tested and the variation and average number of insects used for each individual spray material, other than those given in the tables, therefore, are stated. For Table 13 these data are as follows: Silkworms, 1 set (variation 48–52, average 50); webworms (*H. cunea*), 2 sets (619–1224: 864); tent caterpillars, 4 sets (711–1126: 897); potato-beetle larvæ, 3 sets (132–157: 145); and grasshoppers, 3 sets (368–482: 420).

TABLE 13.—*Relative toxicity of commercial lead and calcium arsenates on 5 species of insects, after deducting mortality of control with food, 1919 and 1920.*

Sample No.	Arsenates and controls.	3 days.						6 days.					
		Silkworms.	Webworms (*H. cunea*).	Tent caterpillars.	Potato-beetle larvæ.	Grasshoppers.	Average.	Silkworms.	Webworms (*H. cunea*).	Tent caterpillars.	Potato-beetle larvæ.	Grasshoppers.	Average.
39	Acid lead arsenate....	96.0	39.1	53.1	61.5	37.6	57.5	100.0	91.7	86.5	72.3	31.1	76.3
28	Basic lead arsenate...	61.3	8.5	53.6	47.0	33.0	40.7	81.6	45.0	88.5	66.2	31.6	62.6
5	Calcium arsenate.....	96.0	12.5	54.3	67.5	63.6	58.8	100.0	69.1	89.6	66.9	32.6	71.6
7	.....do..............	14.3	3.6	49.7	45.6	48.0	32.2	28.6	15.6	85.2	47.0	32.6	41.8
56	.....do..............	59.6	4.3	51.8	54.8	62.4	46.6	94.3	33.7	87.6	54.9	32.6	60.6
57	.....do..............	64.0	1.1	43.9	60.5	61.6	46.2	86.0	27.8	82.9	73.3	32.6	60.5
58	.....do..............	12.5	2.7	45.1	50.6	42.6	30.7	18.7	18.7	85.6	70.4	32.6	45.2
59	.....do..............	72.5	3.8	60.3	57.8	61.0	51.1	96.1	42.1	81.4	60.8	32.6	62.6
	Control without food..	12.2	.0	.4	20.1	......		61.2	28.6	15.3	43.7	......	
	Control with food.....	.0	.0	1.9	14.6	35.5	10.4	.0	.7	5.5	20.7	67.4	18.9

TABLE 13·—*Relative toxicity of commercial lead and calcium arsenates on 5 species of insects, after deducting mortality of control with food, 1919 and 1920*—Continued.

Sample No.	Arsenates and controls.	Percentage of insects dead within—										Average toxicity.	Units of food eaten per insect (estimated), based on webworms (H. cunea) and tent caterpillars.
		10 days.						20 days.					
		Silkworms.	Webworms (H. cunea).	Tent caterpillars.	Potato-beetle larvæ.	Grasshoppers.	Average for 4 species.	Silkworms.	Webworms (H. cunea).	Tent caterpillars.	Potato-beetle larvæ.		
39	Acid lead arsenate....		84.5	87.3	52.5	All.	81.1		All.	All.	All.	71.6	2.9
28	Basic lead arsenate...	96.0	74.8	87.5	47.0	All.	76.3	100.0	All.	All.	All.	59.9	10.9
5	Calcium arsenate.....		84.0	87.7	53.7	All.	81.3		All.	All.	All.	70.6	9.1
7	....do..............	30.3	24.4	87.7	40.6	All.	45.8	44.9	20.7	All.	All.	39.9	66.0
56	....do..............	98.1	52.4	86.8	43.8	All.	70.3	100.0	49.8	All.	All.	59.2	30.8
57	....do..............	98.0	50.3	84.7	51.5	All.	71.1	100.0	45.7	All.	All.	59.3	29.9
58	....do..............	22.9	22.2	87.7	53.2	All.	46.5	29.2	20.5	All.	All.	40.8	69.1
59	....do..............	100.0	69.4	86.6	52.3	All.	77.1		51.9	All.	All.	63.6	18.5
	Control without food..	71.5	83.3	79.3	37.4	......	......	100.0	All.	All.	34.0	......	......
	Control with food.....	.0	14.4	12.3	42.5	78.3	17.3	0.0	41.8	50.5	57.1	15.5	100.0

Table 13 shows the following: The average percentages of toxicity of the acid lead arsenate (sample 39) and of one sample of calcium arsenate (sample 5) on five species of insects are practically the same; the percentage of toxicity for another calcium arsenate spray (sample 59) is a little lower; those for two other calcium arsenates (samples 56 and 57) and for basic lead arsenate (sample 28) are practically the same; while those for the remaining calcium arsenates (samples 7 and 58) are very low. Samples 7 and 58 were not efficient against all five species of insects tested. The basic lead arsenate acted much more slowly on the silkworms and webworms than did the lead arsenate, but, as a rule, only slightly more slowly on the tent caterpillars, potato-beetle larvæ, and grasshoppers. The quantity of food consumed is inversely proportional to the toxicity, being least for samples 39 and 5 and most for samples 58 and 7. The results in this table also show that starvation had little or no effect on the insects tested, but that the insects really died from the effects of the arsenates.

EFFECT ON TOXICITY OF ADDING LIME TO ARSENICALS.

According to the preliminary experiments conducted in 1917 and 1918, the laboratory sample of calcium arsenate (sample 42) and the same compound plus 0.3 gram of lime (sample 42A) killed 69 per cent and 68 per cent, respectively, of the webworms counted on the twelfth day. When the quantity of lime was doubled (sample 42B) the mortality was 50 per cent, and when it was quadrupled (sample 42C), 40 per cent. In 1919 many other experiments, in which a larger amount of lime was added to every 418 cubic centimeters of another laboratory sample of calcium arsenate, were performed, using silkworms, 1 set (variation 49–53, average 51); webworms (*H. cunea*), 2 sets (538–818: 622); tent caterpillars, 4 sets (785–1021: 943); webworms (*H. textor*), 1 set (181–325: 266); potato-beetle larvæ, 3 sets (290–361: 339); and potato-beetle adults, 1 set (37–41: 39). Deducting the mortalities of the controls and basing the average percentages of toxicity on the mortalities of the third, sixth, tenth, and twentieth days, the results for all these insects are: Sample 69, 45; sample 69A (sample 69 plus 0.5 gram lime), 32.7; sample 69B (sample 69 plus 1 gram lime), 29.1; sample 69C (sample 69 plus 2 grams lime), 26.5.

TABLE 14.—*Effect on toxicity of adding lime to arsenicals on 4 species of insects, 1919 and 1920.*

Sample No.	Arsenicals and control.	Percentage of insects dead within—									
		3 days.					6 days.				
		Silkworms.	Webworms (H. cunea).	Tent caterpillars.	Honeybees.	Average.	Silkworms.	Webworms (H. cunea).	Tent caterpillars.	Honeybees.	Average.
39	Commercial acid lead arsenate.	91.0	11.0	18.1	21.0	35.3	100.0	72.8	82.2	58.0	78.3
39C	Sample 39 plus lime (2 grams)..	69.0	6.3	18.0	14.0	26.8	93.0	38.3	81.1	40.0	63.1
69	Laboratory calcium arsenate...	32.7	5.4	42.3	12.0	23.1	53.8	39.7	91.6	44.0	57.3
69C	Sample 69 plus lime (2 grams)..	9.4	1.8	33.3	7.0	12.9	15.1	14.4	91.2	23.0	35.9
64	Commercial Paris green........	100.0	30.7	65.7	15.0	52.8	.....	85.2	99.0	62.0	86.6
64C	Sample 64 plus lime (2 grams)..	57.0	1.8	23.4	8.0	22.5	79.0	44.2	86.0	56.0	66.3
39	Commercial acid lead arsenate.	......	20.3	......	......	......	......	79.0	......	......	......
39L	Sample 39 (leaves sprayed with sample 11 lime)..............	......	20.5	......	......	......	......	78.7	......	......	......
57	Commercial calcium arsenate..	......	7.5	......	......	......	......	30.4	......	......	......
57L	Sample 57 (leaves sprayed with sample 11 lime)..............	......	2.3	......	......	......	......	12.2	......	......	......
	Control with food..............	.0	.0	.6	.0	......	.0	.0	8.8	12.0	......

Sample No.	Arsenicals and control.	Percentage of insects dead within 10 days.				Toxicity for—				Average toxicity.
		Silkworms.	Webworms (H. cunea).	Tent caterpillars.	Average.	Silkworms.	Webworms (H. cunea).	Tent caterpillars.	Honeybees.[1]	
39	Commercial acid lead arsenate.....	......	99.3	100.0	99.8	97.0	61.0	66.8	39.5	66.1
39C	Sample 39 plus lime (2 grams).	100.0	82.9	100.0	94.3	87.3	42.5	66.4	27.0	55.8
69	Laboratory calcium arsenate......	59.6	66.0	98.8	74.8	48.7	37.0	77.6	28.0	47.8
69C	Sample 69 plus lime (2 grams)......	22.6	30.2	100.0	50.9	15.7	15.5	74.8	15.0	30.2
64	Commercial Paris green...........	......	100.0	100.0	100.0	100.0	72.0	88.2	38.5	74.7
64C	Sample 64 plus lime (2 grams).	100.0	99.4	100.0	99.8	78.7	48.5	69.8	32.0	57.2
39	Commercial acid lead arsenate......	......	93.6	......	......	64.3	......	......	......	......
39L	Sample 39 (leaves sprayed with sample 11 lime)...............	......	95.1	......	......	64.7	......	......	......	......
57	Commercial calcium arsenate......	......	66.0	......	......	34.6	......	......	......	......
57L	Sample 57 (leaves sprayed with sample 11 lime)...............	......	36.4	......	......	17.0	......	......	......	......
	Control with food.................	.0	2.6	23.1	......	......	......	......	......	......

[1] Based on mortalities for third and sixth days only, because these controls, confined in small cases, lived for only 8.4 days on an average.

In 1920 these experiments were repeated on a larger scale. The following data are not given in Table 14: Silkworms, 2 sets (each of 50); webworms (*H. cunea*), 1 set (variation 136–194: 145); tent caterpillars, 3 sets (198–385: 280); and honeybees, 2 sets (each of 50). The percentages given for samples 69 and 69C are taken from the 1919 results, and should be compared only roughly with the other percentages given in Table 14. Reference to this table shows that the addition of lime to the three arsenicals employed reduced the toxicity in practically all cases.

There are two possible explanations for the reduction in toxicity due to the addition of lime. The excess lime may unite with the soluble arsenic and prevent it from functioning as a poison. This explanation is supported by practically all the results recorded, providing the excess lime did not decrease the percentage of arsenic in the food or on the leaves eaten. It did not reduce the percentage of arsenic in the poisoned honey, yet the lime in every case caused a decrease in toxicity to honeybees. In the case of the leaf-eating insects, the lime added theoretically reduced the percentage of arsenic on the leaves, because 2 grams of lime were mixed with every gram or less of the arsenical. Consequently, the dried spray material on the leaves would be greatly adulterated and the percentage of arsenic in it would be lowered. To determine the extent of the decrease in the arsenic, many leaves were sprayed with samples 39, 39C, 69, 69C, 64, and 64C. After repeating these experiments three times and analyzing the 18 samples of leaves sprayed, it was found that the addition of lime had reduced the arsenic on the leaves 26.3 per cent, while the excess lime on other leaves similarly sprayed had reduced the average toxicity of the same three arsenicals only 21.1 per cent.

In order to prevent the decrease of arsenic on the leaves, at the same time retaining an excess of lime on them, the following experiments were performed. Many leaves were sprayed, some with acid lead arsenate (sample 39) and others with calcium arsenate (sample 57). When dry, half of each lot was again sprayed with lime (sample 11) (2 grams of calcium oxid in 418 cubic centimeters of water). When all the leaves were dry, half of them were prepared as samples to be analyzed for arsenic and the other half were fed to fall webworms. These experiments were repeated twice, using 8,888 webworms in all. The results in Table 14 show that the lime (sample 39L) did not affect the toxicity of the acid lead arsenate (sample 39), but it (sample 57L) reduced the toxicity of the calcium arsenate (sample 57) 50 per cent. Analyses of the leaves sprayed with samples 39 and 39L showed that the lime reduced the arsenic 18 per cent, while in those sprayed with samples 57 and 57L the arsenic was reduced 29.4 per cent.

EFFECT ON TOXICITY OF ADDING BORDEAUX MIXTURE AND LIME-SULPHUR TO ARSENICALS.

Sanders and Brittain (41) reported that Bordeaux mixture and Wilson (51) reported that lime-sulphur, when added to arsenical spray mixtures, decrease the killing power of the arsenicals. Many experiments were performed by the writers in 1919 to determine whether or not these statements were true. The following insects were used: Webworms (H. cunea), 1 set (variation 102–476, average 241); tent caterpillars, 4 sets (742–1187: 919); and potato-beetle larvæ, 2 sets (130–264:153). After deducting the mortalities of the controls, the average percentages of toxicity of the three species of insects used are as follows: Sample 68 (laboratory sample of acid lead arsenate), 47.1; sample 50 (sample 68 plus lime sulphur), 40.1; sample 69 (laboratory sample of calcium arsenate), 55.6; sample 53 (sample 69 plus Bordeaux mixture), 42.8; sample 51 (sample 69 plus lime-sulphur), 41.8; sample 23 (commercial zinc arsenite), 51.4; and sample 54 (sample 23 plus Bordeaux mixture), 46. From these figures it seems that both Bordeaux mixture and lime-sulphur decreased the toxicities of the arsenicals used. Since silkworms and honeybees refuse to eat food containing lime-sulphur, the experiments in which they were used are not reported. All the other larvæ enumerated ate only about 25 per cent as much food as did the controls, while those that fed on foliage sprayed only with Bordeaux mixture and lime-sulphur ate 83 per cent and 54 per cent, respectively. Neither Bordeaux mixture nor lime-sulphur used alone had much insecticidal value against the insects tested.

In 1920 these experiments were repeated. Different arsenicals were tested, but the Bordeaux mixture (4–3.67–50) and lime-sulphur (1–30) were of the same strengths. The Bordeaux mixture and arsenicals were so mixed that each dry spray material consisted of practically 22 per cent of arsenious or arsenic oxid, and when the necessary amount of water was added, each had an arsenic or arsenious oxid content of 0.076 per cent. Table 15 gives the analytical results on these spray materials before water was added.

TABLE 15.—*Composition of Bordeaux mixture alone and in combination with arsenicals.*

Sample No.	Material analyzed.	Mois-ture.	Arsenious (As$_2$O$_3$) or arsenic (As$_2$O$_5$) oxid.		Base.	Carbon dioxid (CO$_2$).
			Total.	Water-soluble.		
		P. ct.	*P. ct.*	*P. ct.*	*Per cent.*	*P. ct.*
61	Laboratory sample of Bordeaux mixture (4–3.67–50).	0.68	....	....	15.90 (CuO) 54.49 (CaO)	3.52
91	Sample 61 plus acid lead arsenate (39)........	.24	22.06	0.12	5.60 (CuO) 18.16 (CaO) 42.52 (PbO)	1.17
92	Sample 61 plus calcium arsenate (57).........	.57	22.30	.26	9.09 (CuO) 53.10 (CaO)	5.29
55	Sample 61 plus sodium arsenate (25)..........	15.64	22.16	16.81	6.63 (CuO) 22.70 (CaO)	....
54	Sample 61 plus zinc arsenite (23).............	.37	23.05	.23	7.07 (CuO) 24.22 (CaO) 31.38 (ZnO)	1.95
30	Commercial Bordeaux and zinc arsenite mixture.	.46	24.33	.38	30.55 (ZnO) 8.92 (CaO)	.56

Table 16 shows the average percentages of toxicity against webworms and tent caterpillars of lead arsenate and of calcium arsenate alone, with Bordeaux mixture, and with lime-sulphur, and of sodium arsenate and zinc arsenite alone and with Bordeaux mixture.

TABLE 16.—*Effect on toxicity of adding Bordeaux mixture and lime-sulphur to arsenicals on four species of insects, 1920.*

Sample No.	Arsenicals and control.	Percentage of insects dead within—									
		3 days.					6 days.				
		Silkworms.	Webworms (H. cunea).	Tent caterpillars.	Honeybees.	Average.	Silkworms.	Webworms (H. cunea).	Tent caterpillars.	Honeybees.	Average.
39	Commercial acid lead arsenate....	91.0	11.0	18.1	21.0	35.3	100.0	72.8	82.2	58.0	78.3
91	Sample 39 plus Bordeaux mixture (61)............	78.0	7.4	11.3	12.0	27.2	99.0	40.0	88.1	46.0	68.3
93	Sample 39 plus lime-sulphur (60)..	......	6.5	34.0	......	20.2	......	60.7	88.9	......	74.8
57	Commercial calcium arsenate.....	56.0	8.4	14.4	12.0	22.7	85.0	27.1	72.8	44.0	57.2
92	Sample 57 plus Bordeaux mixture (61)..	52.0	3.3	10.1	12.0	19.3	83.0	11.7	72.2	20.0	46.7
94	Sample 57 plus lime-sulphur (60)..	......	4.2	37.4	......	20.8	......	21.0	93.5	......	57.2
25	Laboratory sodium arsenate......	99.0	28.8	36.6	33.0	49.3	100.0	72.2	91.4	62.0	81.4
55	Sample 25 plus Bordeaux mixture (61)........	77.0	3.7	33.8	20.0	33.6	99.0	43.5	94.2	53.0	72.4
23	Commercial zinc arsenite.........	96.0	12.5	68.9	25.0	50.6	100.0	37.5	96.9	44.0	69.6
54	Sample 23 plus Bordeaux mixture (61)..	83.0	9.1	68.1	18.0	44.5	95.0	30.0	98.4	54.0	69.4
	Control with food.................	.0	.0	.6	.0	......	.0	.0	8.8	12.0	......

Sample No.	Arsenicals and control.	Percentage of insects dead within—				Toxicity for—				Average toxicity for—	
		10 days.									
		Silkworms.	Webworms (H. cunea).	Tent caterpillars.	Average.	Silkworms.	Webworms (H. cunea).	Tent caterpillars.	Honeybees.[1]	All 4 species tested.	Webworms and tent caterpillars.
39	Commercial acid lead arsenate...	......	99.3	100.0	99.8	97.0	61.0	66.8	39.5	66.1	63.9
91	Sample 39 plus Bordeaux mixture (61).............	100.0	87.0	100.0	95.7	92.3	44.8	66.5	29.0	58.2	55.6
93	Sample 39 plus lime-sulphur (60)..	......	88.5	99.6	94.0	......	51.9	74.2	......	63.0	63.0
57	Commercial calcium arsenate....	97.0	65.4	100.0	87.5	79.3	33.6	62.4	28.0	50.8	48.0
92	Sample 57 plus Bordeaux mixture (61).............	97.0	47.5	100.0	81.5	77.3	20.8	60.8	16.0	43.7	40.8
94	Sample 57 plus lime-sulphur (60)..	......	76.0	100.0	88.0	......	33.7	76.9	......	55.3	55.3
25	Laboratory sodium arsenate.....	......	96.6	100.0	98.9	99.7	65.9	76.0	47.5	72.3	71.0
55	Sample 25 plus Bordeaux mixture (61).............	100.0	91.3	100.0	97.1	92.0	46.2	76.0	36.5	62.7	61.1
23	Commercial zinc arsenite.........	92.0	60.9	100.0	87.0	98.7	37.0	88.6	34.5	64.7	62.8
54	Sample 23 plus Bordeaux mixture (61).............	100.0	70.9	100.0	90.3	92.7	36.7	88.8	36.0	63.5	62.7
	Control with food.................	......	.0	2.6	23.1	......	......	......	......	......	......

[1] Based on mortalities for third and sixth days only.

GENERAL AVERAGE TOXICITY.

Four arsenicals without Bordeaux mixture and lime-sulphur $\begin{cases} 63.5 \text{ (all four species)} \\ 61.4 \text{ (webworms and tent caterpillars)}. \end{cases}$

Four arsenicals with Bordeaux mixture $\begin{cases} 57.0 \text{ (all four species)}. \\ 55.1 \text{ (webworms and tent caterpillars)}. \end{cases}$

Two arsenicals without lime-sulphur, 56.0 (webworms and tent caterpillars).
Two arsenicals with lime-sulphur, 59.1 (webworms and tent caterpillars).

The addition of Bordeaux mixture to the four arsenicals employed reduced the percentages of toxicity against silkworms, webworms, and honeybees, but reduced the toxicity against the tent caterpillars little, if any. The addition of lime-sulphur (sample 93) to the lead arsenate (sample 39) reduced the toxicity against webworms, but seemed to increase it against tent caterpillars. The addition of lime-sulphur (sample 94) to the calcium arsenate (sample 57) neither decreased nor increased the toxicity against webworms, but appeared to increase it against tent caterpillars. In the 1919 results, Bordeaux mixture and lime-sulphur reduced the rates of toxicity in all cases.

The following data are not given in Table 16: Silkworms, 2 sets (each of 50); webworms (*H. cunea*), 1 set (variation 107–332, average 141); tent caterpillars, 3 sets (118–557: 301); and honeybees, 2 sets (each of 50).

To determine the percentage of arsenic borne by leaves sprayed with the foregoing spray mixtures, many apple and mulberry leaves were sprayed at four different periods. The parts of arsenic per million parts of the leaves were as follows: Sample 39, 1,200; sample 91, 800; sample 93, 800; sample 57, 1,000; sample 92, 800; sample 94, 900; sample 23, 1,650; sample 54, 1,300; sample 25, 1,100; and sample 55, 1,100. The general average of those containing neither Bordeaux mixture nor lime-sulphur (samples 39, 57, 23, and 25) is 1,238 parts of arsenic, while those containing these two fungicides (samples 91, 93, 92, 94, 54, and 55) have a general average of 950 parts of arsenic. According to these figures, the fungicides reduced the arsenic content 23.3 per cent, whereas they reduced the general average toxicity only 11.5 per cent.

RELATIVE TOXICITY OF ARSENATES AND ARSENITES.

Toxicologists report that arsenites are more toxic than arsenates. Furthermore, on the basis of equal percentage of arsenious oxid and arsenic oxid, 16.2 per cent more metallic arsenic is present in the arsenites than in the arsenates. To secure additional data on this subject, a high-grade acid lead arsenate, a calcium arsenate, a sodium arsenate, a zinc arsenite, and a Paris green were selected in 1919 for comparison. The following insects were used: Silkworms, 1 set (variation 49–54, average 51); webworms (*H. cunea*), 2 sets (818–1725, average 1173); webworms (*H. textor*), 1 set (189–310, average 251); potato-beetle larvæ, 3 sets (282–404, average 345); and grasshoppers, 2 sets (181–302, average 242). After deducting the mortalities of the controls, the average percentages of toxicity were as follows: Acid lead arsenate (sample 39) 66, calcium arsenate (sample 5) 63.9, and sodium arsenate plus Bordeaux mixture (sample 55) 61.7, an average of 63.9 for the arsenates on five species of insects; zinc arsenite (sample 23) 57.6, and Paris green (sample 64) 65.5, an average of 61.6 for the arsenites. Thus the Paris green tested is equal to the arsenates in toxicity, and, as shown by the average, these two arsenites are not quite as toxic to insects as are the three arsenates employed, although the comparison is not fair in all respects. The smallest number of units eaten were sprayed with Paris green.

TABLE 17.—*Relative toxicity of arsenates and arsenites on 4 species of insects, 1920.*

Sample No.	Arsenicals and control.	Percentage of insects dead within—									
		3 days.					6 days.				
		Silkworms.	Webworms (*H. cunea*).	Tent caterpillars.	Honeybees.	Average.	Silkworms.	Webworms (*H. cunea*).	Tent caterpillars.	Honeybees.	Average.
39	Commercial acid lead arsenate...	91.0	11.0	18.1	21.0	35.3	100.0	72.8	82.2	58.0	78.3
25	Laboratory sodium arsenate.....	99.0	28.8	36.6	33.0	49.3	100.0	72.2	91.4	62.0	81.4
	Average for arsenates............	95.0	19.9	27.3	27.0	42.3	100.0	72.5	86.8	60.0	79.9
23	Commercial zinc arsenite........	96.0	12.5	68.9	25.0	50.6	100.0	37.5	96.9	44.0	69.6
64	Commercial Paris green..........	100.0	30.7	65.7	15.0	52.8	......	85.2	99.0	62.0	86.6
88	.....do......	100.0	38.9	59.3	25.0	55.8	......	86.7	97.5	55.0	84.8
89	.....do......	98.0	18.5	53.9	22.0	48.1	100.0	72.3	97.6	57.0	81.7
	Average for arsenites.............	98.5	22.7	61.9	21.8	51.8	100.0	70.4	97.7	54.5	80.7
90	Commercial London purple......	98.0	24.1	34.7	11.0	42.0	100.0	57.1	92.0	33.0	70.5
	Control with food................	0.0	0.0	0.6	0.0	......	0.0	0.0	8.8	12.0	......

Sample No.	Arsenicals and control.	Percentage of insects dead within—				Toxicity for—				Average toxicity
		10 days.								
		Silkworms.	Webworms (*H. cunea*).	Tent caterpillars.	Average.	Silkworms.	Webworms (*H. cunea*).	Tent caterpillars.	Honeybees.[1]	
39	Commercial acid lead arsenate......	......	99.3	100.0	99.8	97.0	61.0	66.8	39.5	66.1
25	Laboratory sodium arsenate........	......	96.6	100.0	98.9	99.7	65.9	76.0	47.5	72.3
	Average for arsenates..............	100.0	98.0	100.0	99.3	98.3	63.5	71.4	43.5	69.2
23	Commercial zinc arsenite............	......	60.9	100.0	87.0	98.7	37.0	88.6	34.5	64.7
64	Commercial Paris green.............	......	100.0	100.0	100.0	100.0	72.0	88.2	38.5	74.7
88	.....do......	......	100.0	100.0	100.0	100.0	75.2	85.6	40.0	75.2
89	.....do......	......	96.6	100.0	98.9	99.3	62.5	83.8	39.5	71.2
	Average for arsenites.............	100.0	89.4	100.0	96.5	99.5	60.8	86.5	38.1	71.5
90	Commercial London purple........	......	94.7	100.0	98.2	99.3	58.6	75.6	22.0	63.9
	Control with food..................	0.0	2.6	23.1	......	......	......	......	......	......

[1] Based on mortalities for third and sixth days only.

In 1920 experiments similar to the preceding ones were performed, using one lead arsenate, one sodium arsenate, one zinc arsenite, three Paris greens, and one London purple (an arsenate and an arsenite combined). The following data, which are not given in Table 17, were obtained: Silkworms, 2 sets (each of 50); webworms (*H. cunea*), 1 set (variation 90–136, average 120); tent caterpillars, 3 sets (207–507, average 288); and honeybees, 2 sets (each of 50). Table 17 shows that the average percentage of toxicity of the arsenates was 69.2, while that of the four arsenites was 71.5. The toxicity of the arsenites should be 16.2 per cent more than that of the arsenates, providing the toxicity is due to the arsenic, irrespective of its form of combination. According to the preceding figures, the toxicity of the four arsenites is only 3.3 per cent more than that of the two arsenates. Comparing the toxicity of the four arsenites with that of the lead arsenate, however, it is 7.8 per cent more, and comparing the toxicity of the three Paris greens with that of the lead arsenate, it is 11.5 per cent more. London purple (sample 90) has an average percentage of toxicity of 63.9, being practically the same as that of zinc arsenite. While this sample killed all of the webworms tested within 20 days, only about 90 per cent of those fed zinc arsenite died during the same period of time.

RELATIVE TOXICITY OF NEW ARSENATES.

In making a comparison of the relative toxicity of new arsenates, three commercial products and three pure laboratory products were used. The commercial acid lead arsenate (sample 39) was taken as a standard by which to judge the relative toxicity of the other products. The two other commercial products (sample 70, acid lead arsenate made by a new process, and sample 62, magnesium arsenate) and the laboratory sample of barium arsenate (sample 71) are practically new, while the laboratory samples of arsenates of aluminum (sample 73) and of copper and barium (sample 74) are totally new, as far as known.

In 1919 the following insects were tested: Silkworms, 1 set of 50; webworms (*H. cunea*), 1 set (variation 124–195, average 152); webworms (*H. textor*), 1 set (189–514, average 314); potato-beetle larvæ, 2 sets (150–355, average 260); and grasshoppers, 2 sets (181–305, average 265). After deducting the mortalities of the controls, the following figures were obtained. When silkworms, webworms (*H. cunea*), and potato-beetle larvæ were tested, the average percentages of toxicity were: Sample 39 (acid lead), 58.2; sample 70 (acid lead, new process), 57.3; and sample 62 (magnesium), 59.8. When silkworms, webworms (both species), potato-beetle larvæ, and grasshoppers were tested, the percentages were: Sample 39, 58.8; and sample 62, 54.2. When webworms (both species), potato-beetle larvæ, and grasshoppers were tested, the percentages were: Sample 39, 55; sample 71 (barium), 43.6; and sample 74 (copper and barium), 48.9. When webworms (both species) and potato-beetle larvæ were tested, the percentages were: Sample 39, 57.2; and sample 73 (aluminum), 34.6.

In 1920 these experiments were repeated, with the results shown in Table 18, as well as the following: Silkworms, 2 sets (each of 50); webworms (*H. cunea*), 2 sets (variation 647–897, average 776); webworms (*H. textor*), 1 set (189–514, average 314); honeybees, 2 sets (each of 50); and tent caterpillars, 3 sets (240–556, average 337).

TABLE 18.—*Relative toxicity of new arsenates on 5 species of insects, 1920.*

Sample No.	Arsenates and control.	Percentage of insects dead within—											
		3 days.						6 days.					
		Silkworms.	Webworms (H. cunea).	Webworms (H. textor).	Honeybees.	Tent caterpillars.	Average.	Silkworms.	Webworms (H. cunea).	Webworms (H. textor).	Honeybees.	Tent caterpillars.	Average.
39	Commercial acid lead arsenate	91.0	29.9	47.6	21.0	18.1	41.5	100.0	95.3	84.2	58.0	82.2	83.9
71	Laboratory barium arsenate	22.0	3.2	10.9	11.0	14.0	12.2	68.0	68.2	37.3	18.0	75.1	53.3
74	Laboratory copper barium arsenate	61.0	10.0	11.7	9.0	18.1	22.0	98.0	67.5	57.0	28.0	83.2	66.7
62	Commercial magnesium arsenate	91.0	13.8	5.2	4.0	......	......	100.0	85.2	46.5	31.0	......	......
70	Commercial acid lead arsenate (new process)	91.0	32.9	......	......	......	......	100.0	88.2	......	......	......	......
73	Laboratory aluminum arsenate	......	4.7	7.5	......	......	......	......	80.8	33.6	......	......	......
	Control with food	0.0	0.0	0.5	0.0	0.6	......	0.0	0.8	8.5	12.0	8.8	......

Sample No.	Arsenates and control.	Percentage of insects dead within—					Toxicity for—					
		10 days.										
		Silkworms.	Webworms (H. cunea).	Webworms (H. textor).	Tent caterpillars.	Average.	Silkworms.	Webworms (H. cunea).	Webworms (H. textor).	Honeybees.[1]	Tent caterpillars.	Average toxicity.
39	Commercial acid lead arsenate	......	100.0	100.0	100.0	100.0	97.0	75.1	77.3	39.5	66.8	71.1
71	Laboratory barium arsenate	92.0	88.2	72.1	99.0	87.8	60.7	53.2	40.1	14.5	62.7	46.2
74	Laboratory copper barium arsenate	100.0	95.2	82.7	100.0	94.5	86.3	57.6	50.5	18.5	67.1	56.0
62	Commercial magnesium arsenate	......	100.0	83.8	......	......	97.0	66.3	45.2	17.5	......	......
70	Commercial acid lead arsenate (new process)	......	99.2	......	......	......	97.0	73.4	......	......	......	......
73	Laboratory aluminum arsenate	......	98.3	80.9	......	......	......	61.3	40.7	......	......	......
	Control with food	0.0	24.7	16.9	23.1	......	......	......	......	......	......	......

[1] Based on mortalities for third and sixth days only.

COMPARATIVE AVERAGE TOXICITY.

Sample 39, 72.2; sample 62, 56.5.
Sample 39, 86.0; sample 70, 85.2.
Sample 39, 76.2; sample 73, 51.0.

RELATIVE TOXICITY OF PURE ARSENIC OXIDS AND OF BASES.

In order to judge as accurately as possible the relative toxicity of various bases when combined with the oxids of arsenic, the materials used are grouped in Table 19. In each mixture of the bases, 0.48 gram of the base was used in 100 cubic centimeters of water. At this rate from three to five times as much base was used as is present in the arsenical mixtures.

The following data are not given in Table 19: Silkworms, 1 set (variation 47–54, average 50); webworms (*H. cunea*), 1 set (161–761, average 280); tent caterpillars, 4 sets (565–1030, average 805); and potato-beetle larvæ, 2 sets (105–279, average 152).

TABLE 19.—*Relative toxicity of pure arsenic oxids and of bases on 4 species of insects after deducting mortality of control with food, 1919.*

		Percentage of insects dead within—									
		3 days.					6 days.				
Sample No.	Material and controls.	Silkworms.	Webworms (*H. cunea*).	Tent caterpillars.	Potato-beetle larvæ.	Average.	Silkworms.	Webworms (*H. cunea*).	Tent caterpillars.	Potato-beetle larvæ.	Average.
9	Arsenious oxid	40.0	21.6	4.6	19.2	21.4	58.0	67.3	50.5	23.1	49.7
10	Arsenic oxid	100.0	23.1	68.1	65.1	64.1	......	77.6	85.2	65.0	82.0
11	Calcium oxid	.0	.0	.0	.1	.0	.0	.0	.0	.7	.2
5	Calcium arsenate	96.0	12.5	54.3	64.8	56.9	100.0	69.2	89.6	63.4	80.6
12	Lead oxid	12.8	.0	.0	30.5	10.8	31.9	.0	1.5	46.3	19.9
39	Acid lead arsenate	96.0	39.1	53.1	50.4	59.6	100.0	91.8	86.5	51.2	82.4
22	Zinc oxid	.0	.0	.0	4.3	1.1	.0	.0	.0	12.0	3.0
23	Zinc arsenite	85.7	4.8	73.8	59.8	56.0	98.0	32.7	90.0	58.9	69.9
63	Magnesium oxid	.0	.0		5.1	......	.0	.0		5.5	......
62	Magnesium arsenate	96.0	7.2		73.8	......	100.0	51.6		70.3	......
65	Copper oxid	.0	.0		.0	......	.0	.0		.0	......
64	Paris green	100.0	18.7		65.7	......	......	67.0		64.9	......
74	Copper barium arsenate	......	10.0		63.1	......	......	66.9		68.9	......
72	Barium oxid	......	.0		.0	......	......	.0		4.1	......
71	Barium arsenate	......	4.3		57.9	......	......	43.7		63.4	......
	Control without food	12.2	.0	.4	......	......	61.2	28.7	15.3	......	......
	Control with food	.0	.0	1.9	14.6	4.1	.0	.6	5.5	20.7	6.7
	Control with food, omitting tent caterpillars										

TABLE 19.—*Relative toxicity of pure arsenic oxid and of bases on 4 species of insects after deducting mortality of control with food, 1919*—Continued.

Sample No.	Material and controls.	Percentage of insects dead within—											Units of food eaten per insect (estimated).[2]
		10 days.					20 days.						
		Silkworms.	Webworms (*H. cunea*).	Tent caterpillars.	Potato-beetle larvæ.	Average.	Silkworms.	Webworms (*H. cunea*).	Tent caterpillars.	Potato-beetle larvæ.	Total percentage dead (control mortalities not deducted).[1]	Average toxicity.	
9	Arsenious oxid	70.0	95.6	78.9	23.9	67.1	86.0	All.	All.	35.1	94.6	46.1	9.6
10	Arsenic oxid		94.2	87.6	51.7	83.4		All.	All.	All.	100.0	76.5	3.5
11	Calcium oxid	.0	.0	1.1	.0	.3	.0	.0	0.0	1.7	26.9	0.2	143.4
5	Calcium arsenate		92.7	87.7	51.8	83.0		All.	All.	All.	100.0	73.5	7.4
12	Lead oxid	46.8	.0	4.8	45.7	24.3	100.0	4.1	0.0	All.	65.3	18.3	148.6
39	Acid lead arsenate		93.7	87.3	45.5	81.6		All.	All.	All.	100.0	74.5	2.8
22	Zinc oxid	2.0	.0	.0	13.3	3.8	6.0	.0	0.0	24.1	35.0	2.6	119.8
23	Zinc arsenite	100.0	66.7	86.9	45.6	74.8		70.2	All.	All.	97.8	66.9	22.0
63	Magnesium oxid	.0	1.3		1.7		.0	2.2		8.6	29.6		105.5
62	Magnesium arsenate		84.7		55.5			74.8		All.	97.9		14.2
65	Copper oxid	2.0	.0		.0		2.0	2.5		0.0	27.0		106.9
64	Paris green		93.7		47.9			All.		All.	100.0		3.9
74	Copper barium arsenate		91.1		54.1			All.		All.	100.0		10.8
72	Barium oxid		6.4		5.1			7.7		8.7	47.2		70.3
71	Barium arsenate		66.9		52.1			66.3		All.	93.7		28.0
	Control without food..	71.5	93.6	79.3			100.0	All.	All.		100.0		
	Control with food.....	.0	4.1	12.3	42.5	14.7	.0	21.0	50.5	57.1	32.2	8.5	100.0
	Control with food, omitting tent caterpillars..............										26.0		

[1] First 8 and next to the last figures to be compared; next 8 and last figures to be compared.
[2] Based on webworms (*H. cunea*) and tent caterpillars.

Comparing the mortality of the insects fed on the various bases with that of the control insects (Table 19), it appears that calcium oxid is beneficial to insects (sample 11, 26.9 per cent, and control, 32.2 per cent), that zinc oxid (sample 22, 35 per cent, and control, 32.2 per cent), magnesium oxid and copper oxid (samples 63 and 65, 29.6 per cent and 27 per cent, and control, 26 per cent) are slightly injurious, that barium oxid (sample 72, 47.2 per cent, and control, 26 per cent) is moderately injurious, and that lead oxid (sample 12, 65.3 per cent, and control, 32.2 per cent) is the most effective of all the bases used.

Since the arsenious oxid (sample 9) used in the 1919 experiments had a low toxicity, a commercial white arsenic (As_2O_3) was used in the experiments conducted in 1920. Sample 9 contained only 17.77 per cent of water-soluble arsenious oxid, while sample 27 contained 38 per cent. To obtain its average toxicity on four species of insects in comparison with the toxicities of pure arsenic oxid (sample 10) and acid lead arsenate (sample 39), the following insects were used: Silkworms, 2 sets (each of 50); webworms (*H. cunea*), 1 set (variation 100–136, average 120); tent caterpillars, 3 sets (221–446, average 292); and honeybees, 2 sets (each of 50). The average percentages of toxicity are as follows: Sample 27 (arsenious oxid), 62.4; sample 10 (arsenic oxid), 74.3; and sample 39 (acid lead arsenate), 71.2.

RELATION OF WATER-SOLUBLE ARSENIC TO TOXICITY OF ARSENICALS.

No perceptible differences in mortality which could be attributed to the usually small differences in water-soluble arsenic oxid were observed in the 14 commercial acid lead arsenates used in the preliminary tests. Three of these arsenates which have high percentages of water-soluble arsenic oxid, however, killed no more insects than the others.

TABLE 20.—*Relation of water-soluble arsenic to toxicity of arsenicals, 1919.*

| Sample No. | Arsenicals and control. | Insects tested. | | Water-soluble arsenic, based on total arsenic in sample. | Toxicity after deducting mortality of control. | Food eaten per insect (estimated), based on webworms and tent caterpillars. |
		Number.	Species.[1]			
				Per cent.	*Per cent.*	*Units.*
18	Laboratory basic lead arsenate.............	1,184	sftl......	1.15	21.5	68.6
28	Commercial basic lead arsenate.............	1,939	...do.....	1.73	60.9	10.9
68	Laboratory acid lead arsenate.............	1,361	...do.....	.57	59.6	17.6
9	Pure arsenious oxid........................	1,529	...do.....	17.77	46.1	9.6
10	Pure arsenic oxid..........................	1,516	...do.....	100.00	76.5	3.5
23	Commercial zinc arsenite..................	1,441	...do.....	1.25	66.9	22.0
70	Commercial acid lead arsenate (new process).	422	·sfl.......	.69	66.9	2.8
39	Commercial acid lead arsenate.............	2,263	sftlg.....	.61	68.9	2.9
5	Commercial calcium arsenate..............	2,645	...do.....	.41	70.0	9.1
7	.....do	2,492	...do.....	.88	39.9	66.0
56	.....do	2,373	...do.....	1.31	59.2	30.8
57	.....do	2,393	...do.....	.20	60.1	29.9
58	.....do	2,114	...do.....	.52	43.1	68.1
59	.....do	2,657	...do.....	5.20	65.9	18.5
69	Laboratory calcium arsenate..............	2,298	...do.....	.88	52.5	55.0
45	Laboratory calcium meta-arsenate.........	1,232	ft........	.04	3.6	99.9
46	Laboratory monocalcium arsenate.........	1,758	...do.....	89.26	81.2	2.0
55	Laboratory sodium arsenate plus Bordeaux mixture.........................	2,674	sflgy.....		61.7	5.0
64	Commercial Paris green....................	2,059	...do.....	3.52	65.5	3.2
62	Commercial magnesium arsenate...........	1,651	flgy.....	4.64	50.2	18.3
71	Laboratory barium arsenate...............	1,706	...do.....	.68	43.6	22.2
74	Laboratory copper barium arsenate........	1,814	...do.....	6.27	48.9	15.6
73	Laboratory aluminum arsenate.............	1,482	fly.......	1.91	39.3	16.1
—	Control with food.........................	....	....	....	....	100.0

[1] s, silkworms; f, webworms (*H. cunea*); t, tent caterpillars; l, potato-beetle larvæ; g, grasshoppers; and y, webworms (*H. tertor*).

Table 20 shows that those arsenicals which are readily water soluble (samples 10 and 46) have extremely high percentages of toxicity, but that some of those which are almost insoluble in water (samples 5, 23, and 39) have percentages of toxicity nearly as high. The toxicity of the insoluble arsenicals does not appear to be based upon the water-soluble arsenic present, but upon the stability of the compound and how readily it can be broken down in the bodies of insects.

During all of these experiments no special study of the burning effects of the many arsenicals sprayed on foliage was made. The percentage of water-soluble arsenic is generally taken as a criterion for judging the burning effect on foliage. The following spray mixtures badly burned wild-cherry foliage: Sodium and potassium arsenates, sodium arsenate plus Bordeaux mixture, all the samples of arsenious and arsenic oxids used. calcium arsenates (samples 5,

34, 46, and 59), lead and calcium arsenates plus lime-sulphur (samples 50 and 51), and Paris green. The following slightly burned wild-cherry foliage: Zinc arsenite (samples 23 and 33), zinc arsenite plus Bordeaux mixture (sample 30), calcium arsenate (sample 32), and barium arsenate (sample 71). Zinc arsenite (sample 23) and Paris green slightly burned mulberry foliage.

RELATION OF ARSENIC RENDERED SOLUBLE BY INSECTS TO TOXICITY OF ARSENICALS.

Kirkland and Smith (*22*), in 1897, found that the alimentary tracts of the gypsy moth larvæ were alkaline to litmus. Analyses of the dialysate from washed and macerated alimentary tracts showed the presence of phosphorus and potash in proportions sufficient to form alkaline potassium phosphate, which is suggested as the cause of the alkaline reaction. Because of the report of these investigators, determinations of the hydrogen-ion concentration (pH value) were made on the water extracts of the bodies of the insects fed various arsenicals and also of the bodies of control insects. The results thus obtained showed a comparatively uniform acidity for all the insects tested. It is possible, however, that lactic or other acids are formed in the dead tissues of the insects. The buffer effect normally available may possibly have masked any slight changes in the reaction caused by the arsenicals fed. It is obvious that the pH data as here obtained, or ash determinations on dialysates of intestinal tracts as made by Kirkland and Smith, are inadequate to show the reactions (pH) of the living tissue of the intestinal tracts of insects.

The following methods were employed to determine the total arsenic and water-soluble arsenic in insects and also the hydrogen-ion concentration of the water extracts from the insects. The weights and number of the washed larvæ were recorded, after which the insects, parts of insects, or feces (dried in an oven at 105° C.) were macerated in a mortar containing about 20 cubic centimeters of distilled water. The macerated larvæ were then transferred to flasks and diluted to 500 cubic centimeters with distilled water. The solutions were shaken every 5 minutes for an hour, at the end of which they were filtered and aliquots were taken for the determination of the hydrogen-ion concentration and for the water-soluble arsenic. The rest of the solution, with the residue, was used for the total arsenic determination. The hydrogen-ion concentration was determined by the indicator method outlined by Clark and Lubs (*8*). The solutions used for determining the soluble arsenic and those with the residues for determining the total arsenic were placed in large porcelain casseroles, and nitric and sulphuric acids were added. They were then warmed on the steam bath and finally heated on the hot plate until the organic material was completely destroyed. Since the acids used, particularly the nitric acid, were not totally free from arsenic, a record of the quantities of acids used was kept. The solutions were then freed from nitric acid by adding water and by applying heat. Next enough water was added to make a volume of 100 cubic centimeters, and finally the arsenic was determined by the Gutzeit method, revised by Smith (*47*).

As preliminary tests, the following experiments were performed in 1919. Both sides of several mulberry leaves were heavily sprayed with acid lead arsenate (sample 39). After having been dried by an electric fan, the leaves were fed to 50 large hungry silkworms. When the silkworms had ceased eating, they were removed to clean cages where the feces, contaminated as little as possible, were collected and subsequently analyzed. The next morning a sample of 34 dead and dying silkworms was thoroughly washed for five minutes in running tap water, then, one worm at a time, in six different washes, the first four consisting of hydrochloric acid (2 per cent) and distilled water and the last two of distilled water alone. A pencil brush was used for scrubbing them. Analysis of the sixth wash showed the presence of no arsenic. These experiments were repeated five times. To determine how much of the arsenic had passed through the intestinal walls, the alimentary canals of three sets were removed by careful dissections.

The results of the analyses of these samples were as follows: 84 entire silkworms yielded 2.66 milligrams of arsenic oxid, being 54 per cent water-soluble; 72 silkworms with alimentary canals removed yielded 0.89 milligram of arsenic oxid, being 36.7 per cent water-soluble; the alimentary canals of these 72 silkworms yielded 1.03 milligrams of arsenic oxid, being 55.9 per cent water-soluble; and the 2.18 grams of dried feces from these 72 silkworms yielded 0.45 milligram of arsenic oxid. According to the figures obtained from these 72 silkworms, 37.6 per cent of the total arsenic eaten had passed through the walls of the alimentary canals, 43.4 per cent of it was retained inside these canals, and 19 per cent of it was voided with the feces. Reaction (pH) of water extract from the larvæ was neutral (7); from the alimentary canals, slightly alkaline (7.1); from the larvæ with the alimentary canals removed, slightly acid (6.2); and from the feces, acid.

The foregoing experiments were repeated on a larger scale by feeding 13 arsenicals sprayed on leaves to caterpillars of the catalpa-sphinx moth (*Ceratomia catalpæ* Bdv.). The results obtained indicate the following: (*a*) As a general rule, the higher the percentages of water-soluble arsenic in the larvæ and feces, the higher the rates of toxicity of those arsenicals; (*b*) the percentage of water-soluble arsenic in the arsenical ingested usually has little to do with the rate of toxicity; (*c*) the amount of arsenic found per caterpillar is fairly constant for all the arsenicals used; (*d*) the higher the ratio of total arsenic (per 100 grams of larval material or feces) found in the larvæ to that found in the feces, the higher the rate of toxicity; (*e*) the reaction (pH) of water extracts from the larvæ fed various arsenicals seems to bear no relation to the rate of toxicity.

In 1920 the preceding experiments were repeated on a much larger scale, using the following insects: Honeybees, 2 sets (each of 100); silkworms, 3 sets (each of about 25); *Ceratomia*, 2 sets (each of about 25). The procedure followed was the same as that in the preliminary tests, but, in order to determine the percentage of arsenic actually made soluble by the juices of the insects, the percentage under "control results" in Table 21 was subtracted from the percentage of arsenic found soluble in the bodies of insects. Since the solubility of a minute quantity of arsenic in 500 cubic centimeters of water proved to be greater than that of a larger quantity, an amount of arsenic approximating the average amount found in a sample of the insects analyzed was employed as a control.

TABLE 21.—*Relation of arsenic rendered soluble by insects to toxicity of arsenicals, 1919 and 1920.* . .

Sample No.	Arsenicals.	Total number of insects analyzed.		Percentage of arsenic.								
				Soluble in water on using minute amounts of arsenicals (control results).	Soluble in bodies of—				Made soluble by juices of—			
		Sets.	Individuals.		Honeybees.	Silkworms.	Ceratomia.	Average.	Honeybees.	Silkworms.	Ceratomia.	Average.
39	Commercial acid lead arsenate	8	310	17.3	44.5	46.0	83.5	58.0	27.2	28.7	66.2	40.7
28	Commercial basic lead arsenate	8	353	7.2	28.8	37.7	63.5	43.3	21.6	30.5	56.3	36.1
57	Commercial calcium arsenate	8	405	35.7	78.6	60.6	84.7	74.6	42.9	24.9	49.0	38.9
27	Commercial white arsenic	7	320	5.2	64.8	33.9	20.0	39.6	59.6	28.7	14.8	34.4
71	Laboratory barium arsenate	8	360	30.5	69.4	30.3	64.0	54.6	38.9	.0	33.5	24.1
45	Laboratory calcium meta-arsenate	6	336	2.4	41.8	39.1	22.6	34.5	39.4	36.7	20.2	32.1
64	Commercial Paris green	9	423	15.9	98.3	44.3	71.0	71.2	82.4	28.4	55.1	55.3
64C	Sample 64 plus lime (2 grams)	7	321	11.0	91.8	37.4	61.2	63.5	80.8	26.4	50.2	52.5
62	Commercial magnesium arsenate	9	546	37.9	80.3	59.9	98.7	79.6	42.4	22.0	60.8	41.7
90	Commercial London purple	6	293	33.2	84.3	48.4	95.1	75.9	51.1	15.2	61.9	42.7
23	Commercial zinc arsenite	6	292	6.0	58.4	63.8	73.9	65.4	52.4	57.8	67.9	59.4
74	Laboratory copper barium arsenate	10	570	6.2	74.6	59.2	58.8	64.2	68.4	53.0	52.6	58.0
10	Pure arsenic oxid	7	331	100.0	88.4	70.9	89.6	83.0	......	......	......	.....
25	Laboratory sodium arsenate	9	515	100.0	73.4	54.4	89.7	72.5	......	......	......	.....

Sample No.	Arsenicals.	Toxicity based on honeybees and silkworms.	Water-soluble arsenic, based on total arsenic in sample.	Average amount of arsenic per insect analyzed.				Average reaction (pH) of water extract from insect material.
				Honeybees.	Silkworms.	Ceratomia	Average.	
			Per ct.	*Mg.*	*Mg.*	*Mg.*	*Mg.*	
39	Commercial acid lead arsenate	78.5	0.61	0.0223	0.1212	0.0126	0.0520	6.0
28	Commercial basic lead arsenate	61.7	1.73	.0142	.0803	.0158	.0368	6.0
57	Commercial calcium arsenate	65.5	.20	.0099	.1245	.0189	.0511	6.0
27	Commercial white arsenic	51.0	38.00	.0091	.0914	.0285	.0430	6.0
71	Laboratory barium arsenate	69.5	.68	.0105	.0694	.0138	.0312	5.8
45	Laboratory calcium meta-arsenate	17.5	.04	.0120	.0676	.0110	.0302	5.9
64	Commercial Paris green	79.5	3.52	.0087	.1203	.0143	.0478	5.9
64C	Sample 64 plus lime (2 grams)	66.7	3.52	.0075	.1157	.0276	.0503	5.8
62	Commercial magnesium arsenate	71.0	4.64	.0120	.1460	.0173	.0584	6.0
90	Commercial London purple	73.7	5.30	.0068	.1315	.0305	.0563	5.8
23	Commercial zinc arsenite	77.5	1.25	.0132	.1430	.0220	.0594	6.0
74	Laboratory copper barium arsenate	66.0	6.27	.0058	.0875	.0177	.0303	6.0
10	Pure arsenic oxid	78.5	100.00	.0165	.1130	.0600	.0632	5.9
25	Laboratory sodium arsenate	82.4	100.00	.0180	.0968	.0169	.0439	5.9

The following deductions are made from the results shown in Table 21:

(a) Samples 45, 27, 23, 74, and 28 are very stable in water (slightly soluble as compared with control results); samples 64C, 64, and 39 are moderately stable in water; samples 71, 90, 57, and 62 are unstable in water; and samples 10 and 25 are totally water soluble.

(b) Sample 45 is least soluble and sample 10 is most soluble in the bodies of insects. Samples 10 and 25 were totally water soluble before they were eaten, but after being eaten only about three-fourths of the arsenic was obtained as soluble arsenic.

(c) While no general deductions can be made as to the average percentages of arsenic found soluble in the bodies of insects, when the figures under "control results" are subtracted from these averages, as a general rule, the higher the percentages of arsenic made soluble by the juices of the insects, the higher are the rates of toxicity. Using lead arsenate (sample 39) as a standard, the last statement is strongly supported by the results obtained with the first seven arsenicals (samples 39, 28, 57, 27, 71, 45, and 64), but it is not so strongly supported by the following five samples (64C, 62, 90, 23, and 74).

(d) The percentages of water-soluble arsenic in the original samples of arsenicals bear no relation to the toxicity of those arsenicals, except in the case of those which are totally water soluble.

(e) As a general rule, the larger the average amount of arsenic in the insects analyzed, the higher is the rate of toxicity of that arsenical. Using average weights of the undried insects fed on all 14 of the arsenicals and average amounts of arsenic per insect, a bee weighing 98 milligrams contained 0.0119 milligram of arsenic, a silkworm weighing 1,370 milligrams contained 0.1063 milligram, and a *Ceratomia* weighing 1,620 milligrams contained 0.0219 milligram of arsenic. Thus, although a silkworm is 14 times as large and a *Ceratomia* is 16 times as large as a bee, the silkworm contained 9 times as much arsenic as did the bee and 5 times as much as did the *Ceratomia*. This difference in amount of arsenic probably may be explained by the fact that for bees and silkworms the spray mixtures were used five times the usual strength, while for the *Ceratomia* the usual strength (1 pound to 50 gallons of water) was sufficient to kill the insects within 24 hours.

(f) None of the water extracts of the bodies of the insects fed on the various arsenicals showed an alkaline reaction, and the highest acid reaction was 5.8 (pH value). As an average pH value for the 14 arsenicals, the bees gave a value of 6; the silkworms, 5.7; and the *Ceratomia*, 6.1; and as an average pH value for any arsenical against all three insects, the only figures obtained are 5.8, 5.9, and 6. Again it is shown that the pH value has nothing to do with the percentage of arsenic rendered soluble by the insect juices.

Experiments like those performed on the three foregoing species of insects were also performed on another large but easily killed caterpillar (*Datana integerrima* G. & R.). As the number of these caterpillars was limited, only samples 39, 57, and 64 were used against this species, so that the results obtained could not be easily incorporated in Table 21. They are, however, similar in all respects to those already discussed.

MINIMUM DOSAGE OF LEAD ARSENATE REQUIRED TO KILL SILKWORMS.

By means of a needle-pointed pipette, an acid lead arsenate (sample 39) was dropped upon fresh mulberry leaves. Upon evaporation of the water from these drops, the portions of leaves bearing the white spots were fed to large hungry silkworms in the last instar.

One drop would occasionally kill a large worm but more often two drops were fatal. In almost every case three drops proved fatal within 24 hours. Therefore, for these larvæ three drops may be regarded as a minimum fatal dosage of acid lead arsenate. An analysis of 100 drops (4 sets) from the same pipette gave 0.0091 milligram of metallic arsenic as an average per drop, making 0.0273 milligram of arsenic a minimum fatal dosage for fully grown silkworms.

An analysis of 59 of the dead silkworms, each of which had eaten three drops of the arsenical, gave 0.0027 milligram of arsenic per larva, indicating that 90 per cent of the arsenic eaten had been voided in the feces before the larvæ died. Silkworms which had received a maximum dosage of the same arsenical voided in the feces only 19 per cent of the arsenic eaten, and *Ceratomia*, which had received an average dosage of the same poison, voided 64 per cent of the arsenic with the feces.

QUANTITY OF ARSENIC EATEN BY INSECTS IN FEEDING TESTS.

During the feeding tests many samples of dead larvæ were prepared for analyses, but only those of webworms (*H. textor*) and those of potato-beetle larvæ were finally analyzed. The webworm is one of the most difficult to kill by arsenic, while the potato-beetle larva is one of the most easily killed. Some of the webworms were washed as described on page 44, but most of them were not washed. Also several samples of feces (more or less contaminated) were analyzed. The percentage of toxicity, as shown in Table 22, is the average of the mortalities recorded on the third, sixth, and tenth days for the one species concerned.

TABLE 22.—*Arsenic consumed by insects in feeding tests, 1919.*

Species of insects and sample No.	Arsenicals and controls.	Condition of larvæ before being analyzed.	Number of larvæ analyzed.	Arsenic per larva.	Arsenic (parts per million) in—		Toxicity after deducting mortality of control.
					Larvæ.	Feces.	
Webworms (*H. textor*):				*Milligrams.*			
39	Commercial acid lead arsenate.	Washed and dried.	163	0.0017	359	527	....
39	....do.....	Dried..........	400	.0025	385	1,114	68.6
5	Commercial calcium arsenate.	Washed and dried.	200	.0014	303	746	....
5	....do.....	Dried..........	400	.0024	481	1,125	59.1
28	Commercial basic lead arsenate.	.....do..........	200	.0040	691	330	48.9
69	Laboratory calcium arsenate.	.....do..........	180	.0033	436	851	15.1
69B	Sample 69 plus 1 gram lime per 418 cc.	.....do..........	130	.0040	674	355	6.3
71	Laboratory barium arsenate.	.....do..........	160	.0027	399	365	31.5
62	Commercial magnesium arsenate.	.....do..........	200	.0050	747	539	36.5
55	Laboratory sodium arsenate plus Bordeaux mixture.	.....do..........	200	.0016	303	818	59.3
23	Commercial zinc arsenite.	.....do..........	200	.0055	917	903	63.6
64	Commercial Paris green.	.....do..........	200	.0050	911	946	62.6
73	Laboratory aluminum arsenate.	.....do..........	200	.0028	383	840	32.0
74	Laboratory copper barium arsenate.	.....do..........	200	.0053	613	306	41.8
	Control feces............					15	....

TABLE 22.—*Arsenic consumed by insects in feeding tests, 1919*—Continued.

Species of insects and sample No.	Arsenicals and controls.	Condition of larvæ before being analyzed.	Number of larvæ analyzed.	Arsenic per larva.	Arsenic (parts per million) in—		Toxicity after d ducting mortality of control
					Larvæ.	Feces.	
Potato-beetle larvæ:				*Milligrams.*			
39............	Commercial acid lead arsenate.	......do............	150	0.0017	141	......	62.1
28............	Commercial basic lead arsenate.	......do............	125	.0020	168	......	53.4
68............	Laboratory acid lead arsenate.	......do............	100	.0038	327	......	57.9
5............	Commercial calcium arsenate.	......do............	150	.0026	205	......	62.7
69............	Laboratory calcium arsenate.	......do............	110	.0043	311	......	61.8
69B............	Sample 69 plus 1 gram lime per 418 cc.	......do............	80	.0042	330	......	61.9
71............	Laboratory barium arsenate.	......do............	110	.0049	350	......	50.9
62............	Commercial magnesium arsenate.	......do............	130	.0029	223	......	57.1
55............	Laboratory sodium arsenate plus Bordeaux mixture.	......do............	100	.0028	257	......	51.8
23............	Commercial zinc arsenite.	......do............	100	.0018	172	......	54.7
64............	Commercial Paris green..	......do............	120	.0024	206	......	59.5
74............	Laboratory copper barium arsenate.	......do............	130	.0051	460	......	54.7

The following facts are evident from Table 22: About 40 per cent of the arsenic (samples 39 and 5) found in the samples of webworms was probably carried on the integuments of the larvæ. As a general rule, the higher the average toxicity, the smaller is the quantity of arsenic found in the larvæ. The ratio of arsenic found in the webworms to that found in their feces is about 3 to 5 for those arsenicals giving high toxicities, while for those arsenicals giving low toxicities the ratio is about 1 to 1.

PHYSIOLOGICAL EFFECTS OF ARSENIC ON INSECTS.

Symptoms of arsenic poisoning in the various insects used in the preceding experiments can not be fully described, because these insects were usually too sluggish to permit observation of the later symptoms, other than an occasional contortion of the body, the voiding of soft, watery feces, spewing at the mouth, and finally the complete loss of control of the legs.

Since honeybees are extremely active and are easily studied in observation cases, they were fed arsenic acid (sample 10) in honey at the rate of 0.00076 milligram of arsenic oxid or 0.0005 milligram of metallic arsenic per bee, providing all consumed equal quantities of the poisoned food. The poisoned bees lived for 5.4 days on an average, while the controls lived for 8.4 days on an average. On the second day after being poisoned many of these bees became more or less inactive, a few died, and subsequently but few of them were seen eating. By the third day they were dying rapidly, their abdomens were swollen, and they could not fly, although they could walk in a staggering manner, dragging their abdomens on the table. The only difference between the behavior of the bees subjected to nicotine poisoning (*29*, p. 91) and that of bees subjected to arsenic poisoning is that (*a*) nicotine acts more quickly, (*b*) its symptoms are more pronounced, and (*c*) in arsenic poisoning the abdomen is always more or less swollen, while in nicotine poisoning the abdomen is only rarely swollen. From the symptoms observed, it may be concluded that the bees fed arsenic might have died of motor paralysis, although the paralysis may be only a secondary cause.

Blythe (*4*, p. 567) says that flies, within a few minutes after eating arsenic borne on common arsenical fly paper, fall, apparently from paralysis of the wings, and soon die. Spiders and all insects into which the poison has been introduced exhibit a similar sudden death.

According to the textbooks on pharmacology by Cushny (*14*) and Sollmann (*49*), arsenic is termed, among other things, "a capillary poison." These authors state that arsenic is toxic to all animals having a central nervous system and also to most higher plants, but not to all the lower organisms. In mammals arsenic is cumulative, being stored in various organs, and it is excreted very slowly by the usual channels—urine, feces, sweat, milk, epidermis, and hair. With oral administration, the main part leaves by the feces, probably having never been dissolved.

TRACING ARSENIC IN TISSUES OF INSECTS.

All attempts to trace arsenic fed alone to fall webworms (*H. cunea*) by histological methods failed. The light-colored precipitate formed by the union of arsenic and silver nitrate was either washed out of the tissues or was obscured because the tissues were stained dark by the silver nitrate.

In an endeavor to trace arsenic in both the soluble and insoluble forms by stains and lampblack the following experiments were performed, using the method for tracing nicotine outlined by McIndoo (*29*, p. 106–109).

Four sets of fall webworms were fed leaves sprayed with an acid lead arsenate (sample 39), mixed with stains or lampblack as follows: First set ate arsenate mixed with indigo-carmine; second set ate arsenate mixed with carminic-acid; third set ate arsenate mixed with No. 100 carmine powder; and fourth set ate arsenate mixed with No. 100 lampblack powder. A day later those fed carmine were voiding reddish feces, and two days after being fed all of those nearly dead were fixed in absolute alcohol. The indigo-carmine and carminic-acid were soluble in water, but they were partially precipitated by absolute alcohol; the carmine was only slightly soluble in water, but totally insoluble in absolute alcohol; and the lampblack was soluble in neither water nor absolute alcohol.

Webworms fed indigo-carmine showed no stain. Those fed carmine-acid and carmine revealed pinkish intestines, those colored with the carmine being almost red. The intestinal contents of these larvæ were pink, but no carmine-acid could be observed outside the intestinal wall. In the larvæ fed carmine the stain was widely distributed. The nuclei in the cells of the intestine were strongly stained, while all the tissues outside the intestinal wall contained more or less of the stain. In the larvæ fed lampblack much of the powder could be observed inside the intestine, but very little (perhaps none in reality) outside the intestinal wall.

GENERAL PROPERTIES OF ARSENICALS.

Used alone, arsenious oxid burns the most resistant foliage, because of its high percentage of water-soluble arsenious oxid. To overcome this difficulty, Sanders and Kelsall (43) mixed a very finely divided arsenious oxid with Bordeaux mixture, to serve as a substitute for sodium arsenate and Bordeaux mixture, to control the potato beetle and late blight in Nova Scotia. Cooley (13) suggested the use of white arsenic with Bordeaux mixture for dusting potato vines and has successfully used white arsenic as a substitute for the expensive Paris green in bran mash to control grasshoppers in Montana. He considers crude arsenious oxid to be superior to the refined product, as the particles are finer. Most authors think that arsenious oxid possesses high insecticidal properties. The results of the investigation here reported, however, indicate that the toxicity of arsenious oxid varies greatly, depending on the degree of fineness of the crystals which influences the percentage of water-soluble arsenious oxid present. In no case did the toxicity equal that of an equivalent amount of arsenic oxid present in acid lead arsenate.

Acid lead arsenate, a satisfactory insecticide material, is to be recommended in general when an uncombined arsenical is to be used, as it possesses excellent adhesive and insecticidal properties, and burns foliage little if at all. Acid lead arsenate is compatible with Bordeaux mixture and with nicotine sulphate solutions. Lime-sulphur and acid lead arsenate are incompatible from a chemical standpoint, some soluble arsenic being formed. However, it is well recognized that acid or basic lead arsenates are used with lime-sulphur without serious foliage injury in most cases. A powdered acid lead arsenate contains about 32 per cent of arsenic oxid and about 64 per cent of lead oxid, while powdered basic lead arsenate contains about 23 per cent of arsenic oxid and about 73 per cent of lead oxid. Also, basic lead arsenate is more stable and less toxic than acid lead arsenate.

Paris green, a valuable insecticide on account of its high arsenic content, is said to dust well in spite of its high apparent density, but not to adhere well to foliage. It has no advantages over acid lead arsenate, but has several disadvantages, the burning of foliage being the principal one. The expensive copper sulphate and acetic acid used in its manufacture do not increase its power as a poison.

The amount of soluble arsenic in an arsenical is reduced by mixing it with Bordeaux mixture, and an unsafe arsenical may in certain cases be made safe by mixing it with Bordeaux.

Soaps contain alkalies which decompose arsenicals. The more soap used, the greater the decomposition. When calcium arsenate was mixed with sodium fish-oil soap, a smaller amount of soluble arsenic was formed than when acid lead arsenate was used in the mixture. Both of these mixtures are incompatible.

When acid lead arsenate or calcium arsenate is used in a kerosene-soap emulsion, soluble arsenic is rapidly formed. In the acid lead arsenate combination, six times as much arsenic is formed as in the calcium arsenate combination. Acid lead arsenate, therefore, should not be used in preparing kerosene-emulsion sprays, as the mixture is chemically incompatible. Gray (*16*) reports that basic lead arsenate is not affected by the alkali of soap.

When acid lead arsenate was mixed with solutions of nicotine sulphate, no chemical incompatibility was found. When calcium arsenate was used with nicotine sulphate, however, the latter was decomposed and free nicotine was formed. The SO_4 of the nicotine sulphate combined with free lime (CaO), if present, or with lime of the calcium arsenate, and large amounts of soluble arsenic were formed in certain mixtures. Free nicotine is present in all of these mixtures. The free nicotine is not dangerous but the soluble arsenic is. These mixtures are chemically incompatible. The findings in connection with the chemical compatibilities and incompatibilities of the various arsenicals, fungicides, and other materials tested are summarized in Table 23. Gray (*16*) in 1914 published a summary of data on the compatibilities of various spray materials which he had collected.

TABLE 23.—*Chemical compatibility of arsenicals combined with other spray materials.*

Arsenicals used.	Other spray materials used.				
	Lime sulphur.	Bordeaux mixture.	Kerosene emulsion.	Sodium fish-oil soap.	Nicotine-sulphate solution.
Acid lead arsenate....	Incompatible...	Compatible .	Incompatible...	Incompatible...	Compatible.
Calcium arsenate.....	Compatible....	....do......	.....do......	.....do.........	Incompatible.
Paris green..........		....do......			
Sodium arsenate......		....do......			

Sanders and Brittain (*41*) tested the comparative insecticidal properties of the arsenates of calcium, barium, and lead, alone and in combination with Bordeaux mixture, lime-sulphur, barium tetrasulphid, and sodium sulphid ("soluble sulphur"), on one species of insects. The results obtained showed that the presence of a fungicide had a marked influence on the efficiency of the arsenical investigated. The four arsenicals were 13 per cent more efficient when used with sodium sulphid than when used alone. The toxicity of the arsenicals was reduced when they were mixed with any of the other fungicides. The explanation given by these authors for the increased toxicity resulting from the use of sodium sulphid with an arsenical is that the sodium increases the palatability of the sprayed leaves, which causes the insects to eat ravenously for a few days. The insects thus take a large amount of arsenic into their systems in a short time and death rapidly ensues.

Mixing sodium sulphid with acid lead arsenate produces some lead sulphid and sodium arsenate. The sodium arsenate is soluble and therefore may be more active than the original acid lead arsenate. The results in Table 21 indicate that the soluble arsenicals are more toxic per unit of arsenic than are the insoluble ones, the greater toxicity being due to the water-soluble arsenic present in the compound or to the arsenic which is quickly rendered soluble inside the insects. Data obtained during this investigation suggest that the amount of arsenic present per unit of sprayed leaf is larger when a soluble arsenical is used in combination with a fungicide than when an insoluble arsenical is used. Accordingly it may be possible to explain chemically the increased activity or efficiency when sodium sulphid is used with arsenicals.

Evidence seems to show that it is not always true that an insecticide containing a high percentage of arsenic is more toxic than one containing less arsenic, for the reason that toxicity depends not alone upon the amount of arsenic present, but also upon its form of combination. The insecticidal rôle played by the base itself is small and sometimes nonexistent.

When lime or Bordeaux mixture was combined with the arsenicals the toxicity of the arsenicals was reduced. The fact that the addition of lime or Bordeaux mixture to the arsenicals reduced the toxicity of these insecticides to insects may be explained in two ways: (a) Leaves sprayed with the arsenicals combined with lime or Bordeaux usually contained less arsenic than those similarly sprayed with the arsenicals alone; (b) the toxicity was greater in the tests with honeybees fed honey containing the arsenicals alone than in tests in which bees ate honey containing the arsenicals with lime or Bordeaux mixture. These results support the theory that the calcium present prevents or counteracts the formation of soluble or more toxic arsenic compounds.

Based on the reported results, it would appear that if all seven species of insects used had been tested under similar conditions, their susceptibility to an acid lead arsenate would probably be in the following order, beginning with the insect most susceptible: Honeybees, silkworms, grasshoppers, potato-beetle larvæ, tent caterpillars, webworms (*H. textor*), and webworms (*H. cunea*).

The arsenious oxid ("white arsenic") samples were crystalline; the other commercial arsenicals generally lacked crystal outline and were probably for the most part amorphous. The calcium arsenates used contained some small "octahedral" crystals, but were largely composed of apparently amorphous material. The arsenious oxid samples gave variable results in the toxicity studies and wide variations were found in the results when calcium arsenates were used. On the other hand, the amorphous acid lead arsenates and the amorphous Paris green samples gave uniform toxicity data. The data show a relation between the uniformity of the products and uniformity of toxicity. Where the products were not uniform variations in toxicity were found.

Commercial arsenicals used for spraying or dusting purposes are usually judged chemically on the basis of the total arsenious or arsenic oxid contents and on the percentages of the total amount of these oxids which go into solution under certain conditions. The percentage of base present is also determined. Soluble arsenic oxids or arsenic rendered soluble after the application of arsenicals will burn foliage, the extent of the injury depending mainly on the amount of soluble oxid present or formed in the spray or solution applied. The results here reported indicate that it is the soluble arsenic or the arsenic rendered soluble by the insects that causes death. The rapidity with which arsenicals are made soluble in the bodies of insects seems to be the most important factor in connection with their toxicity. What happens to the soluble arsenic inside the insects is not known, except that part of it passes through the intestinal walls into the blood and is distributed to all parts of the body. A small portion of it reaches the nervous system, where it apparently kills by paralysis. The way arsenic affects the various tissues is not known, although Sollmann (49) reports that it is now generally believed that the arsenicals hinder protoplasmic oxidation in an unknown way. A successful insecticide must be sufficiently stable to be applied to foliage without injury and sufficiently unstable to be broken down in appreciable amounts in the bodies of the insects ingesting it.

SUMMARY.

Arsenious oxid, commercially known as white arsenic, or simply as arsenic, is the basis for the manufacture of all arsenicals. Samples of commercial arsenious oxid vary in purity, fineness, apparent density, and in the rate of solution in water (soluble arsenic), which accounts for the diverse chemical and insecticidal results reported in the literature. Arsenites are prepared by combining arsenious oxid with a base. Arsenates are produced by first oxidizing arsenious oxid to arsenic oxid (arsenic acid) and then combining the material with a base. Except for their water content of approximately 50 per cent, the paste arsenicals have the same general composition as the powdered arsenicals.

The usual lead arsenate on the market, acid lead arsenate $(PbHAsO_4)$, is well standardized and stable. Basic lead arsenate $(Pb_4PbOH(AsO_4)_3)$, also well standardized and stable, is being manufactured at present only to a limited extent. Chiefly because of its low arsenic and high lead contents, basic lead arsenate is more stable and therefore less likely to burn foliage than acid lead arsenate. It possesses weaker insecticidal properties and is somewhat more stable in mixtures than acid lead arsenate.

Commercial calcium arsenate (arsenate of lime), the manufacture of which is rapidly becoming standardized, contains more lime than is required to produce the tribasic form.

Paris green, an old and well standardized arsenical, is less stable and contains more "soluble arsenic" than commercial arsenates of lead or lime.

Laboratory samples of aluminum arsenate, barium arsenate, and a copper barium arsenate mixture, in the powdered form, were tested. The last named gave excellent insecticidal results.

The following combinations of insecticides and fungicides were found to be chemically compatible: Lime-sulphur and calcium arsenate; nicotine sulphate and lead arsenate; and Bordeaux mixture with calcium arsenate, acid lead arsenate, zinc arsenite, or Paris green. The following combinations were found to be chemically incompatible: Soap solution with either calcium arsenate or acid lead arsenate; kerosene emulsion with either calcium arsenate or acid lead arsenate; and lime-sulphur with acid lead arsenate.[9] Combined with nicotine sulphate, calcium arsenate always produces free nicotine, and unless a decided excess of free lime is present soluble arsenic is produced.

The combination of sodium arsenate with Bordeaux mixture as used in the experiments here reported gave no soluble arsenic.

---

[9] According to the Bureau of Entomology, this combination in large amounts is used successfully in the field.

Of all the arsenicals tested, acid lead arsenate and zinc arsenite were the most adhesive and Paris green the least adhesive on potato foliage. The use of lime with arsenicals applied to potato foliage did not increase their adhesiveness.

The suspension properties of the powdered arsenicals are of value in differentiating "light" from "heavy" powders, as determined by their apparent densities.

The physical properties of the commercial powdered arsenicals could not be satisfactorily determined by sieving, as they are generally amorphous and pack in the sieve on shaking. Arsenious oxid samples sometimes contain or consist of relatively coarse crystals, so that sieving may provide valuable data.

Microscopic examination gave little information concerning the desirable physical properties of the amorphous or seemingly amorphous powdered arsenicals. Differences in size of crystals present in the arsenious oxid samples were detected under the microscope.

The toxicity findings are based on the use of equivalent quantities of arsenious and arsenic oxids. Higher percentages of toxicity were found for acid lead arsenate than for basic lead arsenate. The different samples of calcium arsenate tested varied widely in toxicity. When lime or Bordeaux mixture was added to arsenicals, the toxicities were reduced. The average toxicity of the three samples of Paris green and that of one zinc arsenite tested was slightly more than that of an acid lead arsenate and a sodium arsenate. Of the four samples of arsenites, the Paris green samples gave the highest values, zinc arsenite being much less toxic. Based on equivalent metallic arsenic percentages, the Paris green samples gave values no higher than that of the acid lead arsenate tested. Several new arsenates tested did not show as high toxicities as did acid lead arsenate. Of the various bases tested, lead oxid showed some insecticidal value, while the oxids of zinc, magnesium, and copper showed little and lime no value. Arsenic acid, acid lead arsenate, and one sample of calcium arsenate gave high and practically equal toxicities. Arsenious oxid (white arsenic) gave lower and variable results. The percentages of water-soluble arsenic in the original arsenicals had little or no influence on the toxicity, except in the case of those arsenicals which were entirely or largely water soluble. These had high percentages of toxicity.

The determination of reaction in terms of the pH value of water extracts from the bodies of various insects fed all of the different arsenicals, and also from the bodies of control insects, showed uniformly a slight acidity. These results indicate that the arsenic compounds fed did not affect the pH values as determined on dead insects.

The minimum dosage of metallic arsenic required to kill a honeybee is approximately 0.0005 milligram, while 0.0273 milligram (or 54 times as much) is required to kill a full-grown silkworm. Honeybees, confined in cases, void none of the arsenic eaten, whereas silkworms void 90 per cent of the amount ingested. Thus, in reality about 6 times, rather than 54 times, as much arsenic is fatal to a silkworm as is required to kill a honeybee under the somewhat unnatural living conditions.

The conclusions that may be drawn from this investigation are that a chemical analysis of an arsenical does not give sufficient data to judge satisfactorily its insecticidal properties, and a toxicity study alone does not show that an arsenical is suitable for general insecticidal purposes, but both a chemical analysis and a thorough toxicity study are required in order to judge whether or not an arsenical is a satisfactory insecticide.

LITERATURE CITED.

(1) Association, of Official Agricultural Chemists.
　　Official and tentative methods of analysis as compiled by the committee on revision of methods, revised to November 1, 1919, 417 p., 18 figs. Washington, D. C.

(2) Avery, S., and Beans, H. T.
　　Soluble arsenious oxide in Paris green. In J. Am. Chem. Soc. (1901), 23: 111–117.

(3) Bedford, Duke of, and Pickering, S. U.
　　Lead arsenate. In 8th Rept., Woburn Exp. Fruit Farm (1908), p. 15–17.

(4) Blythe, A. W.
　　Poisons: Their effects and detection, 5th ed., p. 745. London (1920).

(5) Bradley, C. E.
　　Soluble arsenic in mixtures of lead arsenate and lime sulfur solution. In J. Ind. Eng. Chem. (1909), 1: 606–607.

(6) —— and Tartar, H. V.
　　Further studies of the reactions of lime sulfur solution and alkali waters on lead arsenates. In J. Ind. Eng. Chem. (1910), 2: 328–329.

(7) Brittain, W. H., and Good, C. A.
　　The apple maggot in Nova Scotia. Nova Scotia Dept. Agr. Bul. 9 (1917), 70 p.

(8) Clark, W. M., and Lubs, H. A.
　　The calorimetric determination of hydrogen-ion concentration and its applications in bacteriology. In J. Bact. (1917), 2: 1–34.

(9) Coad, B. R.
　　Recent experimental work on poisoning cotton boll weevils. U. S. Dept. Agr. Bul. 731 (1918), 15 p.

(10) —— and Cassidy, T. P.
　　Cotton boll weevil control by the use of poison. U. S. Dept. Agr. Bul. 875 (1920), 31 p.

(11) ——
　　Some rules for poisoning the cotton-boll weevil. U. S. Dept. Agr. Circ. 162 (1921), 4 p.

(12) Cook, F. C.
　　Pickering sprays. U. S. Dept. Agr., Bul. 866 (1920), 47 p.

(13) Cooley, R. A.
　　Latest developments in arsenical insecticides. In Better Fruit (1920), 15: 9.

(14) Cushny, A. R.
　　A textbook of pharmacology and therapeutics, 6 ed., 708 p., 70 figs. Philadelphia–New York (1915).

(15) Fields, W. S., and Elliott, J. A.
　　Making Bordeaux mixture and some other spraying problems. Ark. Agr. Exp. Sta. Bul. 172 (1920), p. 33.

(16) Gray, G. P.
　　The compatibility of insecticides and fungicides. Monthly Bul. Cal. Com. Hort. (1914), 3: 265–275.

(17) Haywood, J. K.
　　Paris green spraying experiments. U. S. Dept. Agr., Bur. Chem. Bul. 82 (1904), 32 p.

(18) —— and Smith, C. M.
　　A method for preparing a commercial grade of calcium arsenate. U. S. Dept. Agr. Bul. 750 (1918), 10 p.

(19) Howard, N. F.
　　Insecticide tests with Diabrotica vittata. In J. Econ. Entomol. (1918), 11: 75–79.

(20) KIRKLAND, A. H.
    A new insecticide (barium arsenate). U. S. Dept. Agr., Div. Entomol.
        Bul. 6 (1896), p. 27–28.
(21) ——— and BURGESS, A. F.
    Experiments with insecticides. In 45th Ann. Rept., Mass. Agr. Exp. Sta.
        for 1897, p. 370–389.
(22) ——— and SMITH, F. J.
    Digestion in the larvæ of the gypsy moth. In 45th Ann. Rept. Mass. State
        Bd. Agr. (1898), p. 394–401.
(23) LOVETT, A. L.
    The calcium arsenates. In J. Econ. Entomol. (1918), 11: 57–62.
(24) ———
    Insecticide investigations. Oreg. Agr. Exp. Sta. Bul. 169 (1920), 55 pp.
(25) ——— and ROBINSON, R. H.
    Toxic values and killing efficiency of the arsenates. In J. Agr. Research
        (1917), 10: 199–207.
(26) MCDONNELL, C. C., and GRAHAM, J. J. T.
    The decomposition of dilead arsenate by water. In J. Am. Chem. Soc.
        (1917), 29: 1912–1918.
(27) ——— and SMITH, C. M.
    The arsenates of lead. In J. Am. Chem. Soc. (1916), 38: 2027–2038.
(28) ———
    The arsenates of lead. In J. Am. Chem. Soc. (1917), 39: 937–943.
(29) MCINDOO, N. E.
    Effects of nicotine as an insecticide. In J. Agr. Research (1916), 7: 89–122.
(30) PATTEN, A. J., and O'MEARA, P.
    The probable cause of injury reported from the use of calcium and magnesium
        arsenates. Mich. Agr. Exp. Sta. Quart. Bul. (1919), 2: 83–84.
(31) PICKERING, S. U.
    Note on the arsenates of lead and calcium. In J. Chem. Soc. (1907), 91:
        307–314.
(32) QUAINTANCE, A. L., and SIEGLER, E. H.
    Information for fruit growers about insecticides, spraying apparatus, and
        important insect pests. U. S. Dept. Agr., Farmers' Bul. 908 (1918), p. 11, 73.
(33) RICKER, D. A.
    Experiments with poison baits against grasshoppers. In J. Econ. Entomol.
        (1919), 12: 194–200.
(34) ROBINSON, R. H.
    The calcium arsenates. Oreg. Agr. Exp. Sta. Bul. 131 (1918), p. 15.
(35) ———
    The beneficial action of lime in lime sulphur and lead arsenate combination
        spray. In J. Econ. Entomol. (1919), 12: 429–433.
(36) ——— and TARTAR, H. V.
    The arsenates of lead. Oreg. Agr. Exp. Sta. Bul. 128 (1915), p. 32.
(37) ———
    The valuation of commercial arsenate of lead. In J. Ind. Eng. Chem. (1915),
        7: 499–502.
(38) RUTH, W. E.
    Chemical studies of the lime sulphur lead arsenate spray mixture. Iowa
        Agr. Exp. Sta., Research Bul. 12 (1913), p. 409–419.
(39) SAFRO, V. J.
    The nicotine sulfate-Bordeaux combination. In J. Econ. Entomol. (1915),
        8: 199–203.
(40) SANDERS, G. E.
    Arsenate of lead vs. arsenate of lime. In Proc. Entomol. Soc. Nova Scotia
        for 1916, no. 2, p. 40–45.
(41) ——— and BRITTAIN, W. H.
    The toxic value of some poisons alone and in combination with fungicides,
        on a few species of biting insects. In Proc. Entomol. Soc. Nova Scotia for
        1916, no. 2, p. 55–64.
(42) ——— and KELSALL, A.
    Some miscellaneous observations on the origin and present use of some in-
        secticides and fungicides. In Proc. Entomol. Soc. Nova Scotia for 1918,
        no. 4, p. 69–73.
(43) ———
    The use of white arsenic as an insecticide in Bordeaux mixture. In Proc.
        Entomol. Soc. Nova Scotia for 1919, no. 5, p. 21–33; Agr. Gaz. Canada,
        (1920), 7: 10–12.

(44) SCHOENE, W. J.
    Zinc arsenite as an insecticide. N. Y. Agr. Exp. Sta. Tech. Bul. 28 (1913),
    p. 15.
(45) SCOTT, E. W., and SIEGLER, E. H.
    Miscellaneous insecticide investigations. U. S. Dept. Agr. Bul. 278 (1915),
    p. 47.
(46) SCOTT, W. M.
    Arsenate of lime or calcium arsenate. In J. Econ. Entomol. (1915), 8: 194–
    199.
(47) SMITH, C. R.
    The determination of arsenic. U. S. Dept. Agr., Bur. Chem. Circ. 102 (1912),
    12 p.
(48) SMITH, J. B.
    Arsenate of lime. In Rept. Entomol. Dept., N. J. Agr. Exp. Sta. for 1907,
    p. 476.
(49) SOLLMANN, TORALD.
    A manual of pharmacology. 1 ed., 901 pp. Philadelphia–London (1917).
(50) TARTAR, H. V., and WILSON, H. F.
    The toxic values of the arsenates of lead. In J. Econ. Entomol. (1915),
    8: 481–486.
(51) WILSON, H. F.
    Combination sprays and recent insecticide investigations. In Proc. Entomol.
    Soc. British Columbia, no. 3, n. s. (1913), p. 9–16.
(52) ⸺
    Insecticide investigations of 1914, and Bien. Crop Pest and Hort. Report for
    1913 and 1914, Oregon Agr. Expt. Sta., p. 137.
(53) ⸺
    Common insecticides: Their practical value. Wis. Agr. Exp. Sta., Bul.
    305 (1919), p. 15.

ORGANIZATION OF THE UNITED STATES DEPARTMENT OF AGRICULTURE.

Secretary of Agriculture...................... HENRY C. WALLACE.
Assistant Secretary .... C. W. PUGSLEY.
Director of Scientific Work.................... E. D. BALL.
Director of Regulatory Work ....
Weather Bureau.............................. CHARLES F. MARVIN, Chief.
Bureau of Agricultural Economics............ HENRY C. TAYLOR, Chief.
Bureau of Animal Industry .... JOHN R. MOHLER, Chief.
Bureau of Plant Industry .... WILLIAM A. TAYLOR, Chief.
Forest Service............................... W. B. GREELEY, Chief.
Bureau of Chemistry.......................... WALTER G. CAMPBELL, Acting Chief.
Bureau of Soils .... MILTON WHITNEY, Chief.
Bureau of Entomology......................... L. O. HOWARD, Chief.
Bureau of Biological Survey................... E. W. NELSON, Chief.
Bureau of Public Roads....................... THOMAS H. MACDONALD, Chief.
Fixed Nitrogen Research Laboratory .... F. G. COTTRELL, Director.
Division of Accounts and Disbursements........ A. ZAPPONE, Chief.
Division of Publications...................... EDWIN C. POWELL, Acting Chief.
Library...................................... CLARIBEL R. BARNETT, Librarian.
States Relations Service .... A. C. TRUE, Director.
Federal Horticultural Board................... C. L. MARLATT, Chairman.
Insecticide and Fungicide Board.............. J. K. HAYWOOD, Chairman.
Packers and Stockyards Administration.........⎫CHESTER MORRILL, Assistant to the
Grain Future Trading Act Administration .....⎭ Secretary.
Office of the Solicitor......................... R. W. WILLIAMS, Solicitor.

This bulletin is a contribution from

Bureau of Chemistry........................... WALTER G. CAMPBELL, Acting Chief.
Miscellaneous Division.................... J. K. HAYWOOD, in Charge.
Bureau of Entomology......................... L. O. HOWARD, Chief.
Fruit Insect Investigation................. A. L. QUAINTANCE, Entomologist in Charge.

58

UNITED STATES DEPARTMENT OF AGRICULTURE

In Cooperation with the
Clemson Agricultural College

DEPARTMENT BULLETIN No. 1148

| Washington, D. C. | ▼ | February 1, 1923 |

COMPARATIVE SPINNING TESTS OF SUPERIOR VARIETIES OF COTTON (GROWN UNDER WEEVIL CONDITIONS IN THE SOUTHEASTERN STATES; CROP OF 1921)

By WILLIAM R. MEADOWS, *Cotton Technologist*, and WILLIAM G. BLAIR, *Specialist in Cotton Testing, Bureau of Agricultural Economics.*

PURPOSE OF TESTS.

The spinning tests herein described were conducted to determine the relative spinning value of cotton commercially thought to be of superior character with that of a number of pure strains of superior varieties of cotton. All were grown under boll-weevil conditions in the southeastern cotton States during the season of 1921.[1]

IMPORTANCE OF PURE VARIETIES.[2]

Pure stocks of cotton seed produce larger and better crops because all of the plants in the field are alike, while in mixed stocks many of the plants are degenerate and unproductive and the lint is mixed and therefore of mediocre value. The use of pure seed means larger crops and better fiber.

The fiber from pure stocks is better not only because of its greater length or strength, but also because the fibers are more uniform, which is the first essential of high quality in cotton fiber.

Good cultural conditions simply give pure seed an opportunity for the expression of the full possibilities of the variety.

By superior varieties we do not necessarily mean long staples. There are superior short staple varieties as well as superior long staple varieties. Superiority consists of uniformity—uniformity of plants, uniformity of fruiting habit and of fruit: all of which results in uniformity in the length and in the character of the cotton, the most valuable spinning qualities to be had.

Pure seed is the first essential to a superior fiber.

---

[1] These spinning tests were conducted under the general supervision of William R. Meadows, cotton technologist, and under the direct supervision of William G. Blair, specialist in cotton testing, who was assisted by H. B. Richardson, C. E. Folk, and E. S. Cummings, assistants in cotton testing. The tests were made in the textile department of the Clemson Agricultural College, Clemson College, S. C.

[2] From a paper read by G. S. Meloy, investigator in cotton marketing, at the conference of the cotton division, New Orleans, La., June 23, 24, 25, 1920.

VARIETIES OF COTTON TESTED.

The following varieties were tested: Acala, Lone Star, Mexican Big Boll, Rowden, and typical North Georgia. All of the cotton was obtained from men of reputation for their plant-breeding work, with the exception of the typical North Georgia cotton, which was bought from a prominent cotton merchant as typical "North Georgia" cotton. This type of cotton always commands a premium over other cotton of the same grade and length of staple.

ORIGIN OF THE COTTON.

The Acala cotton consisted of 7 bales grown near St. Clair, Lowndes County, Ala.; the Lone Star consisted of 4 bales grown near Fayetteville, N. C.; the Mexican Big Boll consisted of 4 bales grown near McFarland, N. C.; the Rowden consisted of 4 bales grown near Monroe, N. C.; and the typical North Georgia cotton consisted of 4 bales bought from a merchant in Athens, Ga. The exact origin or history of the typical North Georgia cotton is unknown, except that it came from that region known commercially as typical "North Georgia" territory.

CLASSIFICATION OF THE COTTON.

Samples of cotton from the different bales were classed by a committee of the board of examiners. This committee is authorized to class cotton at the future exchanges under the provisions of the United States cotton futures act. The results of this classification are shown in Table 1.

TABLE 1.—Classification of the cotton of the different varieties.

Variety.	Grade.	Length of staple.	Variety.	Grade.	Length of staple.
		Inches.	Mexican Big Boll.....	Strict Middling...	Inches.
Acala.................	Middling.........	1		Good Middling....	1
	Middling..........	1 1/16		Good Middling....	1 full.
	Middling..........	1 1/16		Good Middling....	1 1/16
	Middling..........	1 1/16	Rowden..............	Good Middling....	1 full.
	Middling..........	1 1/16 full.		Good Middling....	1 1/8
	Middling..........	1 1/16 full.		Good Middling....	1 1/8
	Strict Middling...	1 1/16 full.		Good Middling....	1 1/8
Lone Star...........	Middling..........	1 1/16	Typical North Georgia	Good Middling....	1 full.
	Middling..........	1 1/16		Strict Middling...	1 1/8
	Strict Middling...	1 1/16		Strict Middling...	1 1/16
	Good Middling....	1 1/16		Strict Middling...	1 1/16

MECHANICAL CONDITIONS.

The five different varieties of cotton were run under identical mechanical conditions, which conformed to common mill practices for the grade and length of staple used.

PERCENTAGES OF WASTE.

Accurate weighings were made of the net amount of cotton fed to and delivered by each cleaning machine and of the net amount of waste discarded by each. From these weighings the percentage of visible, invisible, and total waste were determined. The percentages of waste for each variety are shown in Table 2.

TABLE 2.—*Percentages of waste from the different varieties of cotton.*

	Acala.	Lone Star.	Mexican Big Boll.	Rowden.	Typical North Georgia.
Grade..	Mid.	S. M.	G. M.	G. M.	S. M.
Length of staple (inches).......................	1⅛	1⅛	1 full....	1⅛	1¼
Picker waste: a	Per cent.	Per cent.	Per cent.	Per cent.	Per cent.
Opener-breaker motes and fly..................	1.31	1.26	.86	.86	.74
Finisher motes and fly........................	1.44	1.11	.91	.80	.85
Total visible............................	2.75	2.37	1.77	1.66	1.59
Invisible...............................	.68	.54	1.03	1.21	1.03
Total visible and invisible..............	3.43	2.91	2.80	2.87	2.62
Card waste: b					
Flat strips...........................	2.70	2.58	2.51	2.32	2.30
Cylinder and doffer strips............	1.02	.98	1.00	.73	.86
Motes and fly........................	1.96	1.65	1.47	1.32	1.60
Sweepings............................	.05	.11	.10	.07	.07
Total visible...........................	5.73	5.32	5.08	4.44	4.83
Invisible...............................	.83	.12	.29	.83	.47
Total visible and invisible..............	6.56	5.44	5.37	5.27	5.30
Pickers and cards: a					
Total visible...........................	8.28	7.54	6.71	5.97	6.29
Total invisible.........................	1.48	.65	1.31	2.02	1.49
Total visible and invisible..............	9.76	8.19	8.02	7.99	7.78

a Based on net weight fed to bale-breaker.   b Based on net weight fed to cards.

Table 2 shows that the percentages of total visible waste discarded by the different varieties of cotton, closely followed the grade when comparing the pure strains of cotton.

MOISTURE CONDITIONS.

The different varieties were run under as nearly identical moisture conditions as possible. Outside weather conditions caused higher relative humidities in the picker and card rooms than were desired. A relative humidity of 50 per cent was desired in the picker room. 60 per cent in the card room, and 70 per cent in the spinning room. Actual conditions which prevailed while the cotton was being machined are shown in Table 3. These averages were obtained from readings of self-recording hygrometers equipped with electric fans.

TABLE 3.—*Average temperatures and relative humidities during tests.*

Process.	Acala.		Lone Star.		Mexican Big Boll.		Rowden.		Typical North Georgia.	
	Temp.	Rel. hum.	Temp.	Rel. hum.	Temp.	Rel. hum.	Temp.	Rel. hum.	Temp.	Rel. hum.
	°F.	Per cent.	°F.	Per cent.	°F.	Per cent.	°F.	Per cent.	°F.	Per cent.
When opened.......	77	78	76	67	85	67	83	70	80	71
Finisher picker......	79	71	77	73	84	65	79	69	82	69
Cards..............	77	61	81	65	83	62	84	64	84	62
Drawing frames.....	77	60	82	62	83	62	84	65	84	62
Roving frames......	78	66	83	64	80	61	83	62	83	64
Spinning frame......	84	71	85	71	86	70	86	70	86	70

Samples for moisture tests were obtained at different periods during the day from the different manufacturing processes. The averages of these moisture tests are shown in Table 4.

TABLE 4.—*Percentages of moisture regain in cotton at the different manufacturing processes.*

Sample.	Acala.	Lone Star.	Mexican Big Boll.	Rowden.	Typical North Georgia.
	Per cent.	*Per cent.*	*Per cent.*	*Per cent*	*Per cent.*
From bale	7.78	7.81	8.47	8.78	9.20
Finisher picker lap	7.52	7.64	7.87	6.92	8.78
Lap from back of card	7.01	7.36	7.42	7.10	8.21
Card sliver	6.74	6.90	7.10	6.84	7.71
Finisher drawing sliver	6.66	7.12	7.27	6.38	7.61
Fine frame roving	6.96	6.97	6.62	6.62	7.25
Fine frame roving from creel of spinning frame	7.47	7.25	7.31	7.27	7.40
Yarn from spinning frame	7.84	7.64	7.38	7.48	7.53

The difference between the percentage of moisture in the bale and in the card sliver corresponds closely with the total percentage of invisible waste obtained from the pickers and cards.

Whenever cotton in process is subjected to a given relative humidity and temperature for two hours or more, the cotton assumes the moisture regain of that relative humidity and temperature.

The variation in moisture regain of the varieties is due to the different hygroscopic properties and the moisture in the bale of each variety.

Therefore, the differences in the moisture content (see Table 4) of the finisher picker lap and the lap from the back of the card, and the fine frame roving and the fine frame roving from the creel of the spinning frame are accounted for by the fact that the relative humidity of the picker room averaged 70 per cent, the card room 60 per cent, and the spinning room 70 per cent.

BREAKING STRENGTH OF YARNS.

The cotton of each variety was spun into 28's, 36's, and 44's yarn with twists equal to 4.25, 4.50, and 4.75 times the square root of the number spun. The average breaking strengths are shown in Table 5. These averages have been corrected for slight variations in the sizings of the yarn.

TABLE 5.—*Breaking strength in pounds per skein of 120 yards of yarn spun from the different varieties of cotton.*

No. of yarn.	New Draper Standard.	Twist multiplier.	Acala.	Lone Star.	Mexican Big Boll.	Rowden.	Typical North Georgia.
	Pounds.		*Pounds.*	*Pounds.*	*Pounds.*	*Pounds.*	*Pounds.*
28's	69	4.25	71.4	62.6	68.1	64.4	57.2
		4.50	71.2	62.9	67.2	62.9	56.2
		4.75	68.8	61.3	66.3	63.1	55.9
		Average.	70.5	62.3	67.2	63.5	56.4
36's	54	4.25	50.6	45.6	48.6	44.6	40.5
		4.50	50.4	43.7	46.8	44.0	39.9
		4.75	48.7	43.8	46.4	42.6	39.8
		Average.	49.9	44.4	47.3	43.7	40.1
44's	44	4.25	38.7	33.7	36.3	34.9	25.2
		4.50	38.7	33.9	33.7	33.8	25.9
		4.75	37.2	32.8	33.3	33.1	25.6
		Average.	38.2	33.5	34.4	33.9	25.6

The different varieties arranged in the order of their strength values, after allowing for the difference in the length of staple of the cotton, are as follows (strongest at top of list):

1. {Acala............}equal.
   {Mexican Big Boll..}
2. {Lone Star.........}equal.
   {Rowden...........}
3. Typical North Georgia.

IRREGULARITY OF YARNS.

The irregularity of the yarn was determined by calculating the average deviation of the sizings and breaking strengths per skein of 120 yards.

Table 6 gives the percentages of average deviation in the sizings per skein of 120 yards.

TABLE 6.—*Irregularity or average deviation in the sizings of the yarn.*

No. of yarn.	Acala.	Lone Star.	Mexican Big Boll.	Rowden.	Typical North Georgia.
	Per cent.	Per cent.	Per cent.	Per cent.	Per cent.
28's..	2.02	2.02	2.11	2.01	1.94
36's..	2.06	2.06	2.18	1.79	2.10
44's..	2.40	1.87	2.16	2.17	1.81

Table 6 shows that the yarns made from the different varieties of cotton were practically equal in evenness.

Table 7 gives the percentages of average deviation in the breaking strength per skein of 120 yards.

TABLE 7.—*Irregularity or average deviation in the breaking strengths of the yarn.*

No. of yarn.	Acala.	Lone Star.	Mexican Big Boll.	Rowden.	Typical North Georgia.
	Per cent.	Per cent.	Per cent.	Per cent.	Per cent.
28's	4.54	3.72	4.72	4.72	3.74
36's	4.51	3.86	5.09	3.98	3.86
44's	4.58	5.30	5.27	5.70	6.29

The different varieties arranged in order of evenness of strength are as follows:

1. Lone Star.
2. {Acala.................}equal.
   {Typical North Georgia..}
3. Rowden.
4. Mexican Big Boll.

MANUFACTURING PROPERTIES.

No difficulty was encountered in running any of the varieties, all showed excellent spinning qualities.

SUMMARY.

The cottons tested were from the crop of 1921, and consisted of the fiber of the following varieties: Acala, Lone Star, Mexican Big Boll, Rowden, and of typical cotton of the kind commercially known as "North Georgia." The Acala cotton was grown in Alabama, the Lone Star, Mexican Big Boll and Rowden were grown at different points in North Carolina, and the typical North Georgia cotton was grown in "North Georgia."

All of the cottons were tested under identical mechanical conditions.

The grades, lengths of staple, percentages of visible waste, strengths of the yarns, and percentages of average deviation or irregularity of the sizings and strengths as shown in Table 8, indicate that for hard twisted or warp yarns the varieties tested if placed in order of their merit and attractiveness from a spinner's viewpoint would fall in the following rank:

1. { Acala..............
     { Mexican Big Boll.. } equal.

2. { Lone Star...........
     { Rowden............ } equal.

3. Typical North Georgia.

TABLE 8.—*Grades, lengths of staple, percentages of visible waste, strengths of the yarn, and percentages of average deviation of the sizings and strengths of the yarn.*

	Acala.	Lone Star.	Mexican Big Boll.	Rowden.	Typical North Georgia.
Grade..	Mid.	S. M.	G. M.	G. M.	S. M.
Length of staple (inches).............................	1 1/4	1 3/16	1 full.	1 1/16	1 1/16
Percentage of visible waste.........................	8.28	7.54	6.71	5.97	6.29
Strength of yarn in pounds per skein of 120 yards:					
28's...	70.5	62.3	67.2	63.5	56.4
36's...	49.9	44.4	47.3	43.7	40.1
44's...	38.2	33.5	34.4	33.9	25.6
Percentage of average deviation or irregularity of sizing of the yarn:					
28's...	2.02	2.02	2.11	2.01	1.94
36's...	2.06	2.06	2.18	1.79	2.10
44's...	2.40	1.87	2.16	2.17	1.81
Percentage of average deviation or irregularity of strength of the yarn:					
28's...	4.54	3.72	4.72	4.72	3.74
36's...	4.51	3.86	5.09	3.98	3.86
44's...	4.58	5.30	5.27	5.70	6.29

These tests show clearly the desirability, from a spinning standpoint, of fiber produced by ure re strains of superior varieties of cotton over that produced fpom beordmercial seed even when grown in districts in which the reputation for character in cotton is excellent.

ORGANIZATION OF THE UNITED STATES DEPARTMENT OF AGRI-CULTURE.

Secretary of Agriculture........................... HENRY C. WALLACE.
Assistant Secretary............................. C. W. PUGSLEY.
Director of Scientific Work....................... E. D. BALL.
Director of Regulatory Work....................
Weather Bureau................................ CHARLES F. MARVIN, Chief.
Bureau of Agricultural Economics............... HENRY C. TAYLOR, Chief.
Bureau of Animal Industry..................... JOHN R. MOHLER, Chief.
Bureau of Plant Industry....................... WILLIAM A. TAYLOR, Chief.
Forest Service................................. W. B. GREELEY, Chief.
Bureau of Chemistry............................ WALTER G. CAMPBELL, Acting Chief.
Bureau of Soils................................ MILTON WHITNEY, Chief.
Bureau of Entomology........................... L. O. HOWARD, Chief.
Bureau of Biological Survey...................... E. W. NELSON, Chief.
Bureau of Public Roads......................... THOMAS H. MACDONALD, Chief.
Fixed Nitrogen Research Laboratory.............. F. G. COTTRELL, Director.
Division of Accounts and Disbursements........... A. ZAPPONE, Chief.
Division of Publications......................... JOHN L. COBBS, JR., Chief.
Library.. CLARIBEL R. BARNETT, Librarian.
States Relations Service......................... A. C. TRUE. Director.
Federal Horticultural Board...................... C. L. MARLATT, Chairman.
Insecticide and Fungicide Board.................. J. K. HAYWOOD, Chairman.
Packers and Stockyards Administration............} CHESTER MORRILL, Assistant to the
Grain Future Trading Act Administration.........} Secretary.
Office of the Solicitor........................... R. W. WILLIAMS, Solicitor.

This bulletin is a contribution from

Bureau of Agricultural Economics................. HENRY C. TAYLOR, Chief.
Division of Cotton Marketing................ WILLIAM R. MEADOWS, Cotton Technologist, in charge.

UNITED STATES DEPARTMENT OF AGRICULTURE

DEPARTMENT BULLETIN No. 1149

Washington, D. C.   ▼   May 9, 1923

ABSORPTION AND RETENTION OF HYDROCYANIC ACID BY FUMIGATED FOOD PRODUCTS.

By E. L. GRIFFIN, *Assistant Chemist*, and I. E. NEIFERT, *Junior Chemist, Insecticide and Fungicide Laboratory, Miscellaneous Division, Bureau of Chemistry;* N. PERRINE, *Assistant in Plant Fumigation, Federal Horticultural Board,* and A. B. DUCKETT,[1] *Scientific Assistant, Stored-Product Insect Investigations, Bureau of Entomology.*[2]

CONTENTS.

INTRODUCTION.

Hydrocyanic acid, in the gaseous form, is used extensively in the United States as a fumigant for the destruction of insects and rodents, particularly the brown rat (*Mus norvegicus*). Probably the earliest recorded use of this gas for killing insects[3] was that by J. T. Bell (*4*),[4] who in 1877 employed it to rid an insect cabinet of insect pests. Credit is given to, Dr. D. W. Coquillet for being the first to suggest the use of hydrocyanic acid gas for destroying insects on plants. In 1886, while employed as an agent of the United States Department of Agriculture, he began experiments with it which later showed its value for the destruction of scale insects infesting citrus trees (*14, 24*).

Since 1886 the use of hydrocyanic acid gas as a fumigant has been extended greatly, until it now includes the fumigation of dwellings, barracks, etc. (*12*), for the destruction of certain insects which are ordinarily classed as vermin, such as roaches, water bugs, and bedbugs, and the fumigation of warehouses and mills (*7, 8*) against certain insects that destroy food products. More recently this gas

---

[1] Deceased.
[2] H. L. Sanford assisted in the fumigation work and J. J. T. Graham assisted in making the analyses of the stored grains. As the plants and plant products coming in at the various ports of entry from foreign countries frequently are infested with insects new to the United States, E. R. Sasscer, entomologist in charge of the Plant Quarantine Service of the Federal Horticultural Board, outlined the fumigation procedure upon which the investigations herein reported were based, with the idea of determining whether or not various fruits, vegetables, and stored products fumigated with hydrocyanic acid gas in concentrations lethal to insects would be poisonous to consumers.
[3] Reference is made to the use of hydrocyanic acid gas generated rapidly by the action of sulphuric acid on potassium cyanide or sodium cyanide, and not to the use of potassium cyanide for killing insects in collectors' bottles, which probably is much the older practice.
[4] The numbers (italics) in parentheses throughout this bulletin refer to the bibliography on page 16.

29302—23—Bull. 1149——1

has been employed at ports of entry (9, 17) to prevent the introduction from foreign countries of many injurious insect pests that have not yet gained a foothold here. Among the most important of these pests are the pink boll worm and the citrus black fly. Fumigation with hydrocyanic acid gas is also a means for the prevention of epidemics of yellow fever (5) and bubonic plague (6, 13, 19). Ships coming from ports where these diseases exist are fumigated on arrival in order to kill mosquitoes and rats which carry the causative organisms.

Food products fumigated to destroy the insects with which they are infested come into contact with hydrocyanic acid. This is true in the fumigation of imported fruits and vegetables at ports of entry and in the fumigation of flour and grains in mills and warehouses. In destroying insects and rats in dwellings and ships, foodstuffs may not be removed during exposure to the gas. In any case there is the possibility of exposure to the fumigant of products intended for food.

Since hydrocyanic acid is extremely poisonous to man, it is important to know how much of it is absorbed and retained by foods. Very little work on this subject seems to have been done, although apparently the opinion that there is no danger in the fumigation of dry foods[5] is fairly general.

REVIEW OF LITERATURE.

Guthrie (10) was unable to find a trace of residual gas in oranges that had been fumigated with hydrocyanic acid gas, in the proportions recommended for actual practice, for three hours and then allowed to remain in the open air for a half hour. He states that "similar experiments were made on samples of apples and lemons * * * with the same result."

Townsend (22) reports that seeds, whether dry or moist, are capable of absorbing hydrocyanic acid, even when its concentration in the atmosphere is very low. He fed fumigated seeds (corn and wheat) to mice and concludes from his experiments that "dry grains and other seeds treated for several days with hydrocyanic acid gas of any strength will not be injured for food. * * * Damp grains and other seeds treated with hydrocyanic acid gas of any strength, even for short periods of time, should not be used for food until several hours after removing from the gas."

Schmidt (21) fumigated peaches, plums, pears, lemons, and apples with hydrocyanic acid gas, apparently in rather high concentration. He placed his material in a chamber of 9.4 liters capacity and, in the course of a half hour, carried over into it by means of a stream of air the acid freed from 20 grams of potassium cyanide. He gives no values for the rate at which the air entered. If the stream of air was just strong enough to get all the hydrocyanic acid over into the chamber, without carrying any out, the atmosphere surrounding the fruit would contain about 78 per cent of the fumigant. This is equivalent to treatment with the gas from 213 ounces of potassium cyanide or 160 ounces of sodium cyanide per hundred cubic feet, which would be from 50 to 150 times as concentrated as that used

---

[5] H. D. Young reports that the workmen engaged in citrus fruit fumigation in California often hang their lunches in the trees which they expect to finish about lunch time. Immediately after fumigation the lunches are removed and eaten with no ill effects.

in practice. Schmidt probably did not get as high a concentration as this, but it must have been very high. This idea is strengthened by the fact that he reports marked physical effects on his fruits. Some of his results are shown in Table 1.

TABLE 1.—*Hydrocyanic acid on fumigated fruits (Schmidt).*

Fruit.	Length of time fumigated.	Hydrocyanic acid present.	
		After ½ hour.	After 48 hours.
	Hours.	*Per cent.*	*Per cent.*
Peaches	2	0.33	0.05
Do	½	.06	.02
Plums	½	.04	.006
Do	20	.03	1 .008
Pears	½	.02	.005
Do	20	.02	2 .008
Apples	½	.01	.002
Do	24	.16	.08
Lemons	½	.003	....
Do	20	.07	3 .016

1 24 hours.   2 5 days.   3 14 days.

Schmidt found that peaches which had been fumigated for 18 hours gave off enough hydrocyanic acid to kill mice which were put in a jar with the fruit. He concludes that all fruits take up gaseous hydrocyanic acid and that certain fruits, for example peaches, take up the gas from even a very dilute atmosphere of it, so that it is possible that eating such fruit may cause some injury to health.

Quaintance (*18*) believes that very little, if any, gas is taken up by apples during fumigation with hydrocyanic acid. He and his associates have eaten freely of fumigated fruit, sometimes within 30 minutes of its removal from the fumigation box. These apples, of course, were first wiped.

Roberts (*19*) states that hydrocyanic acid fumigation does not injure any ordinary article of cargo.

Howard and Po enoe (*12*), in describing the method of fumigation against household insects, say "Liquids or moist foods, as milk, meat, or other larder supplies that are not dry and might absorb the gas, should be removed from the house." The inference is that other foods will not absorb enough of the fumigant to be dangerous. Their statement is apparently not based upon experimental evidence.

Bail and Cancik (*3*) say that fluids and moist foods should not be left in rooms which are being fumigated. They state that Heymons (*11*) found that fumigated flour was unchanged and nonpoisonous and that they found the same to be true for bran. After fumigating a food warehouse it is recommended that the food shall be used only after airing and that grain be shoveled over several times.

Bail (*2*) reports that Herr Hofrat v. Zeyneck found that after fumigation with 1 per cent by volume of hydrocyanic acid gas (time not stated) raw meat (minced) contained 186 parts of hydrocyanic acid per million, even after airing for 10 hours, moist vegetables contained 90 parts per million after airing for 2 days, fine flour contained 45 parts per million after 10 hours, and bran contained 30 parts per million. He recommends that all foods, whether wet or dry, be removed before fumigation.

Investigators in the United States Public Health Service (*1*) fumigated bread and milk with hydrocyanic acid and then fed them to white mice. They found that "when exposed to the cyanide gas in the concentration usually advised for fumigating tight compartments" they "did not absorb or adsorb sufficient cyanide to cause symptoms, when fed to white mice." With double the amount of hydrocyanic acid, "prolonged" exposure, and no aeration after fumigation, death of the mice resulted, but "after one or two hours exposure of the food to the air no symptoms were produced." They summarize, "The conclusion from these experiments is that the possibility of food poisoning occurring from food materials exposed to cyanide gas is extremely remote."

Lubsen, Saltet, and Wolff (*15*) state that hydrocyanic acid can be used for the destruction of insects in flour and other foodstuffs, since it does not affect foods, except milk and other liquids.

Marchadier, Goujon, and de Laroche (*16*) advise against the use of hydrocyanic acid fumigation for flour. They recognize its value for clothes and things of that type, but think that flour may hold enough of the gas to cause injury to health. They found a hydrocyanic acid content of 82 parts per million in one flour and say that the foods prepared from it (cakes, sauces, etc.) still had the taste of cherry laurel, even after cooking. They do not describe the treatment which the flour had received.

PURPOSE OF PRESENT INVESTIGATION.

There are no analytical data on the quantity of hydrocyanic acid absorbed under the usual conditions of fumigation, except those of Guthrie and of Bail, who give some results on five products, but none which indicate the rate of loss of hydrocyanic acid on aeration. Schmidt worked with excessive concentrations of the fumigant.

Experimental work was therefore undertaken in the United States Department of Agriculture to find how much hydrocyanic acid is absorbed under ordinary conditions of fumigation on a large number of fruits, vegetables, and seeds, and at what rate it is given off when the products are exposed to the air.

EXPERIMENTAL WORK.

FRUITS AND VEGETABLES.

Fruits and vegetables were bought in season in the open market and in a condition as nearly perfect as possible. They were divided into three lots.

One lot was analyzed without being fumigated, to guard against reporting as absorbed hydrocyanic acid any which might be present in the fruit naturally.

The second lot was fumigated at normal atmospheric pressure (NAP) by the "pot" method. The fumigant in this method was prepared by adding sodium cyanide to diluted sulphuric acid in the proportion of 1:1½:2. That is, for every avoirdupois ounce of sodium cyanide 1½ fluid ounces of sulphuric acid and 2 ounces of water are used.

The third lot was fumigated by a modification of the vacuum method described by Sasscer and Hawkins (*20*). The fumigant in this method was prepared from sodium cyanide, sulphuric acid, and water in the proportion of $2\frac{1}{2}$:1:1. That is, for every $2\frac{1}{2}$ fluid ounces of cyanide solution,[e] 1 fluid ounce of acid and 1 fluid ounce of water are used. The procedure is as follows: The material to be fumigated is placed in the fumigation chamber, in this case a horizontal iron retort with a capacity of 100 cubic feet, and the door is closed and clamped. The air is exhausted until the gauge registers 26 inches. At this stage the gas is generated by introducing into the generator the chemicals in the following order: Water, acid, cyanide in solution. The valve separating the generator from the fumigation chamber is opened, and the cyanide solution is allowed to flow slowly into the diluted acid in the generator. When all the cyanide solution has entered, the outside valve of the generator is opened, and the air is allowed to wash all of the gas over into the fumigation chamber. After washing for 5 minutes the vacuum in the fumigatorium is completely broken. The material is exposed to the gas for a period of time equal to 1 hour from the time the cyanide solution started to flow into the generator. To remove the gas-air mixture at the end of the exposure period, the fumigation chamber should be pumped to a vacuum of 25 inches. The valves of the chamber are then opened and the vacuum is broken. The chamber is opened and the material to be analyzed is removed.

Commercial 96–98 per cent sodium cyanide, usually at the rate of 4 ounces per hundred cubic feet of fumigated space, was used in this work, and the gas formed from it when treated with commercial 93 per cent sulphuric acid was allowed to remain in contact with the product for the time indicated. Even this dosage is higher than that now used in practice, usually $1\frac{1}{2}$ to 2 ounces of sodium cyanide per hundred cubic feet.

The temperature and humidity were accurately determined and recorded in each case.

Part of the material was analyzed immediately after fumigation, and part of it was stored in the refrigerator for 24 hours before being analyzed. Material which is usually pared before consumption was pared and separate analyses were made on the rind and flesh.

Hydrocyanic acid was determined, after distillation with tartaric acid, by the method of Viehoever and Johns (23). The results of these experiments are shown in Table 2.

TABLE 2.—*Hydrocyanic acid in fruits and vegetables after fumigation.*[1]

Product.	Sodium cyanide.		Temperature.	Relative humidity.	Period after fumigation.	Hydrocyanic acid in—		
	NAP	Vac.				Whole fruit.	Rind.	Flesh.
	Oz. per 100 cu. ft.	Oz. per 100 cu. ft.	°F.		Days.	Parts per million.	Parts per million.	Parts per million.
Apples:								
Ripe		4	64	43	1	[2]3		
Do		4	64	43	2	5		
Do		2	75	51	0	42		
Do		2	75	51	0.	36		
Do	4		72	33	0		7	6
Do	4		72	33	1		6	2
Do		4	74	23	0		97	42
Do		4	74	23	1		16	5

[1] All samples were exposed to the fumes for 1 hour, with the exception of the first pineapple sample, which was exposed for 70 minutes.
[2] Sample cut and allowed to stand overnight before analysis.

[e] This is made by dissolving sodium cyanide in water at the rate of 200 pounds to 50 gallons.

TABLE 2.—*Hydrocyanic acid in fruits and vegetables after fumigation*—Continued.

Product.	Sodium cyanide.		Temperature.	Relative humidity.	Period after fumigation.	Hydrocyanic acid in—		
	NAP	Vac.				Whole fruit.	Rind.	Flesh.
	Oz. per 100 cu. ft.	Oz. per 100 cu. ft.	°F.		Days.	Parts per million.	Parts per million.	Parts per million.
Avocadoes:								
Underripe		4	73	48	0		1,090	220
Do		4	73	48	1		250	78
Do	4		73	48	0		270	150
Do	4		73	48	1		170	93
Overripe		4	75.5	72	0		77	60
Do		4	75.5	72	1		95	41
Do	4		75.5	72	0		73	11
Do	4		75.5	72	1		75	41
Bananas:								
Ripe		4	64	43	2	20		
Do		2	75	51	0	80		
Do		2	75	51	0	95		
Do		4	73.5	40	0		440	110
Do		4	73.5	40	1		97	33
Do	4		73.5	40	0		210	61
Do	4		73.5	40	1		110	43
Beans, string (green):								
Fresh		4	77.5	43	0	1,100		
Do		4	77.5	43	1	280		
Do	4		77.5	43	0	480		
Do	4		77.5	43	1	440		
Beets:								
Good		4	64	42	0	130		
Do		4	64	42	0	160		
Do		4	67	53	0	49		
Do		4	67	53	1	57		
Do	4		67	53	0	54		
Do	4		67	53	1	49		
Cabbage:								
Good		4	64	42	0	220		
Do		4	64	42	0	240		
Do		4	67	39	0	190		
Do		4	67	39	1	54		
Do	4		67	39	0	160		
Do	4		67	39	1	39		
Carrots:								
Good		4	65	44	1	100		
Do		4	65	44	1	52		
Do		4	60	20	0		170	56
Do		4	60	20	1		120	44
Do	4		60	20	0		200	70
Do	4		60	20	1		150	80
Celery:								
Damp		4	65	44	0	300		
Do		4	65	44	0	310		
Do		2	75	51	0	190		
Fairly dry		4	67	39	0	120		
Do		4	67	39	1	75		
Do	4		67	39	0	74		
Do	4		67	39	1	70		
Corn, green, sweet:								
Fresh		4	82	65	0	230		
Do		4	82	65	1	150		
Do	4		82	65	0	430		
Do	4		82	65	1	380		
Cucumbers:								
Good		4	64	42	0	110		
Do		4	64	42	0	150		
Do		4	75.5	72	0		250	89
Do		4	75.5	72	1		58	17
Do	4		75.5	72	0		110	98
Do	4		75.5	72	1		120	45
Dasheen, small corms:								
Good		4	65	44	1	12		
Do		4	65	44	1	6		
Dasheen, large corms:								
Good		4	65	44	1	12		
Do		4	65	44	1	8		
Dasheen, tubers:								
Good		4	63	19	0		15	Trace.
Do		4	63	19	1		15	None.
Do	4		63	19	0		13	None.
Do	4		63	19	1		13	None.

TABLE 2.—*Hydrocyanic acid in fruits and vegetables after fumigation*—Continued.

Product.	Sodium cyanide. NAP	Sodium cyanide. Vac.	Temperature.	Relative humidity.	Period after fumigation.	Hydrocyanic acid in— Whole fruit.	Kind	Flesh.
	Oz. per 100 cu. ft.	Oz. per 100 cu. ft.	°F.		Days.	Parts per million.	Parts per million.	Parts per million.
Eggplant:								
Ripe		4	78	71	0	....	50	54
Do		4	78	71	1	....	44	61
Do	4		78	71	0	....	37	43
Do	4		78	71	1	....	42	42
Grapes (Worden variety):								
Ripe		4	82	65	0	430	....	....
Do		4	82	65	1	230	....	....
Do	4		82	65	0	420	....	....
Do	4		82	65	1	130	....	....
Grapefruit:								
Ripe		4	64	53	2	2	....	....
Do		2	75	51	0	20	....	....
Do		2	75	51	0	7	....	....
Do		4	73.5	40	0	....	62	2
Do		4	73.5	40	1	....	50	12
Do	4		73.5	40	0	....	62	2
Do	4		73.5	40	1	....	35	7
Lemons:								
Ripe		4	64	53	2	41	....	....
Do		2	75	51	0	120	....	....
Do		2	75	51	0	88	....	....
Overripe		4	73	55	0	....	230	21
Do		4	73	55	0	....	220	22
Do		4	73	55	1	....	160	14
Do		4	73	55	1	....	120	9
Ripe	4		74.5	58	0	....	290	11
Do	4		74.5	58	0	....	350	10
Do	4		74.5	58	1	....	110	17
Do	4		74.5	58	1	....	120	11
Lettuce:								
Damp		4	65	44	0	390	....	....
Do		4	65	44	0	270	....	....
Fairly dry		4	67	39	0	270	....	....
Do		4	67	39	1	49	....	....
Do	4		67	39	0	200	....	....
Do	4		67	39	1	41	....	....
Mameyes (*Lucuma mammosa*):								
Green		4	78	71	0	....	48	Trace.
Do		4	78	71	1	....	23	5
Green (soft)	4		78	71	0	....	54	4
Do	4		78	71	1	....	11	None.
Mammee apple (*Mammea americana*):								
Ripe	4		77.5	43	0	....	150	20
Mango (*Mangifera indica*):								
Green (soft)		4	78	71	0	....	140	76
Do		4	78	71	1	....	64	16
Green (firm)	4		78	71	0	....	140	32
Do	4		78	71	1	....	80	17
Muskmelon:								
Ripe		4	79	66	0	....	68	22
Do		4	79	66	1	....	54	28
Do	4		79	66	0	....	63	5
Do	4		79	66	1	....	70	21
Onions:								
Good		4	64	42	0	29	....	....
Do		4	64	42	0	20	....	....
Prime		4	78	71	0	Trace.	....	....
Do		4	78	71	1	None.	....	....
Do	4		78	71	0	Trace.	....	....
Do	4		78	71	1	None.	....	....
Oranges (Cuban) (Florida):[3]								
Good	1				5	....	None.	None.
Prime	1				5	....	None.	None.
Ripe		4	64	43	2	39	....	....
Do		2	75	51	0	29	....	....
Do		2	75	51	0	12	....	....
Nearly ripe		4	73	55	0	....	240	11
Do		4	73	55	0	....	240	7
Do		4	73	55	1	....	110	11
Do		4	73	55	1	....	100	11
Ripe	4		74.5	58	0	....	110	3
Do	4		74.5	58	0	....	100	3
Do	4		74.5	58	1	....	94	4
Do	4		74.5	58	1	....	87	4

[3] Fumigated at Key West, Fla.

TABLE 2.—*Hydrocyanic acid in fruits and vegetables after fumigation*—Continued.

Product.	Sodium cyanide.		Temperature.	Relative humidity.	Period after fumigation.	Hydrocyanic acid in—		
	NAP	Vac.				Whole fruit.	Rind.	Flesh.
	Oz. per 100 cu. ft.	Oz. per 100 cu. ft.	°F.		Days.	Parts per million.	Parts per million.	Parts per million.
Parsnips:								
Good		4	60	20	0		280	88
Do		4	60	20	1		280	71
Do	4		60	20	0		230	85
Do	4		60	20	1		80	50
Peaches:								
Ripe		4	73.5	51	0		130	65
Do		4	73.5	51	1		52	32
Do	4		73.5	51	0		92	3
Do	4		73.5	51	1		130	12
Pears:								
Ripe		4	73.5	51	0		72	22
Do		4	73.5	51	1		18	11
Do	4		73.5	51	0		92	14
Do	4		73.5	51	1		16	3
Peas (green):								
Fresh		4	77.5	43	0		[4] 530	1,100
Do		4	77.5	43	1		[4] 130	520
Do	4		77.5	43	0		[4] 420	1,400
Do	4		77.5	43	1		[4] 230	200
Peppers (green):								
Fresh		4	82	65	0	370		
Do		4	82	65	1	220		
Do	4		82	65	0	320		
Do	4		82	65	1	120		
Pineapple (Red Spanish):								
Ripe		4	71	49	0	88		
Do		4	71	49	0	120		
Green		4	71	40	0		180	88
Ripe	2		71	49	0	60		
Do	4		71	49	0	59		
Do	4		71	40	0		100	14
Green	4		71	40	0		100	6
Do	1.5		70	70	1		23	6
Do	1.5		70	70	2		6	None.
Pineapples (Cuban): [3]								
Ripe (bulk)	1.08				7	None.		
Green (bulk)	1.6				6	[5]None.		
Do	1.27		84		4	[5]None.		
Ripe (bulk)	1.31		84		4	[6]None.		
Green (crated)	1.46		84		4	[7]None.		
Do	1.46		84		4	[8]None.		
Green (bulk)	1.37		86		3	[6]None.		
Do	1.02		90		3	[6]None.		
Plantains:								
Green		4	78	71	0		490	130
Do		4	78	71	1		130	56
Do	4		78	71	0		170	160
Do	4		78	71	1		140	59
Potatoes (sweet):								
Good		4	65	44	1	49		
Do		4	65	44	1	83		
Do	4		72	33	0		39	10
Do	4		72	33	1		21	2
Do		4	68	34	0		69	31
Do		4	68	34	1		82	21
Potatoes (white):								
Good		4	65	44	1	11		
Do		4	65	44	1	19		
Do	4		72	33	0		20	6
Do	4		72	33	·1		8	2
Do		4	68	34	0		30	3
Do		4	68	34	1		8	1
Salsify:								
Good		4	64	42	0	200		
Do		4	64	42	0	190		
Fresh		4	63	19	0	110		
Do		4	63	19	1	49		
Do	4		63	19	0	110		
Do	4		63	19	1	54		

[3] Fumigated at Key West, Fla.
[4] Pod.
[5] 8 feet from generator.
[6] 6 feet from generator.
[7] 4 feet from generator.
[8] 14 feet from generator.

Before fumigation

After fumigation.

EFFECT OF HYDROCYANIC ACID ON FUMIGATED PRODUCTS.

Table 2·—*Hydrocyanic acid in fruits and vegetables after fumigation*—Continued.

Product.	Sodium cyanide.		Temperature.	Relative humidity.	Period after fumigation.	Hydrocyanic acid in—		
	NAP	Vac.				Whole fruit.	Rind.	Flesh.
	Oz. per 100 cu. ft.	Oz. per 100 cu. ft.	°F.		Days.	Parts per million.	Parts per million.	Parts per million.
Sapodilla:								
Ripe		4	76.5	70	0		550	120
Do		4	76.5	70	1		110	34
Do	4		76.5	70	0		450	110
Do	4		76.5	70	1		50	15
Squash:								
Ripe		4	73.5	40	0	130		51
Do		4	73.5	40	1	110		15
Do	4		73.5	40	0	94		36
Do	4		73.5	40	1	55		2 9
Strawberries:								
Ripe but firm		4	75.5	89	0	53		
Do		4	75.5	89	0	53		
Do		4	75.5	89	1	54		
Do		4	75.5	89	1	51		
Do	4		75.5	89	0	34		
Do	4		75.5	89	0	25		
Do	4		75.5	89	1	55		
Do	4		75.5	89	1	30		
Tangerines:								
Ripe		4	64	43	1	[2] 4		
Do		4	64	43	2	51		
Do		4	74	23	0		400	59
Do		4	74	23	1		85	23
Do	4		74	23	0		430	54
Do	4		74	23	1		98	16
Tomatoes:								
Ripe		4	64	42	0	120		
Do		4	64	42	0	89		
Do		4	67	53	0		74	17
Do		4	67	53	1		28	23
Do	4		67	53	0		56	12
Do	4		67	53	1		14	9
Green	1¼		47		0	7		
Do	1¼		47		1	2		
Do	1¼		47		3	2		
Do	1¼		70		0	[9] 2		
Do	1¼		70		1	[9] 2		
Do	1¼		70		3	[9] 2		
Turnips:								
Good		4	65	44	1	120		
Do		4	65	44	1	110		
Do	4		72	33	0		120	53
Do	4		72	33	1		45	31
Do		4	68	34	0		340	120
Do		4	68	34	1		99	43
Watermelon:								
Fresh	4		79	66	0	5		None.
Do	4		79	66	1	4		None.

[2] Sample cut and allowed to stand overnight before analysis.   [9] Sample stored at 70° F.

All the fumigated fruits and vegetables absorbed some hydrocyanic acid, but the quantities absorbed differed widely for different products. In general, the hard-skinned products, such as apples, oranges, lemons, watermelons, and grapefruit, had comparatively little of the gas in the flesh or edible parts. On the other hand, fruits and vegetables of a succulent nature or containing much chlorophyll absorbed larger quantities. Of course, in many cases these products are cooked before eating, so that most of the hydrocyanic acid, if not all, would have been driven off before they were eaten.

The physical effects on the products treated at the rate of 4 ounces of sodium cyanide per 100 cubic feet are noted in Table 3.

TABLE 3.—*Physical effects of hydrocyanic acid gas on fruits and vegetables.*

Product.	Effect of hydrocyanic acid.	Product.	Effect of hydrocyanic acid.
Apples.............	None.	Muskmelon.......	Decided softening.
Avocadoes........	Deterioration very much has-	Onions...........	None.
	tened.	Oranges..........	Do.
Bananas..........	Slight yellowing of the pulp;	Parsnips..........	.Do.
	some darkening of the epi-	Peas.............	Do.
	carp.	Peaches..........	Do.
Beans (green,	None.	Pears.............	Darkening of the epicarp.
string).		Peppers (green)...	None.
Beets.............	Do.	Pineapples........	Do.
Cabbage..........	Some wilting and yellowing.[1]	Plantains.........	Decided softening of the pulp
Carrots..........	None.		and browning of the epicarp.
Celery............	Severe wilting.[1]	Potatoes (sweet)..	None.
Corn(green, sweet)	None.	Potatoes (white)..	Do.
Cucumbers........	Do.	Salsify...........	Do.
Dasheen..........	Do.	Sapodilla.........	Do.
Eggplant..........	Do.	Squash...........	Do.
Grapes...........	Decided softening.	Strawberries......	Decided softening and severe
Grapefruit.......	None.		wilting.[1]
Lemons...........	Do.	Tangerines.......	None.
Lettuce..........	Immediate and severe wilting.[1]	Tomatoes........	Do.
Mameyea..........	Softening.	Turnips..........	Do.
Mammee apples...	None.	Watermelons......	Do.
Mango...........	Darkening of the epicarp.		

[1] Deterioration was so serious that the product was not marketable.

Some of the fumigated products show a tendency to speedy decay, probably because of a reduction of their natural resistance to putrefactive organisms (Pl. I). This is particularly noticeable in the case of the avocado. Refrigeration does not seem to prevent the disintegration to any great extent.

No very direct relation seems to exist between the quantity of hydrocyanic acid absorbed and the damage to the tissues. Green peas and string beans both absorbed large quantities and yet showed no deterioration. On the other hand, mameyea, pears, and muskmelons contained comparatively small quantities but deteriorated greatly.

Although Schmidt (*21*) reports severe deterioration of peaches due to fumigation, the lower concentration of gas in the experiments here reported gave no such effects.

SEEDS AND FLOUR.

Experiments with seeds and flour were undertaken to determine the following points: (*a*) The quantity of hydrocyanic acid absorbed during fumigation; (*b*) the rate at which it is dissipated on storage; (*c*) the effect of evacuating the chamber several times after fumigation on the quantity of hydrocyanic acid retained by the product; (*d*) the relation of the concentration of the fumigant to the quantity absorbed.

Navy beans, white field corn, cowpeas, wheat, and flour were tested. Sacks containing about 15 pounds of each were fumigated with the dosage indicated, by a modification of the method of Sasscer and Hawkins (*20*).

In the first series of experiments the products were put into the fumigation chamber, and air was pumped out until the vacuum gauge registered 26 inches. The hydrocyanic acid gas was then introduced, allowing 5 minutes for generation and 5 minutes for washing the gas from the generator to the fumigation chamber, after which the air was permitted to enter until normal atmospheric pressure had been attained. After the·products had been exposed to the fumigant in this manner for an additional 50 minutes outside air was drawn over them for 10 minutes to remove the hydrocyanic acid. They were then taken from the chamber for analysis.

The treatment of the second series was conducted in the same manner as that of the first, except that at the completion of the 50-minute exposure the chamber was again evacuated until the gauge read 25 inches, air was introduced until atmospheric pressure was reached and, after a further 2-minute aeration, the products were withdrawn for analysis.

The treatment of the third and fourth series was the same as that of the second, except that the evacuation at the end was repeated once and twice, respectively, with intermediate aerations of 2 minutes in each case.

Determinations of hydrocyanic acid were made, after distillation with tartaric acid, by the method of Viehoever and Johns (23), on the day of fumigation (except in the first series) and at intervals thereafter. A delay with the first series made it impossible to conduct the analyses on the same day. The products were stored in a large, well-ventilated room during the intervals, at a temperature of about 70° F. The results of the examinations are recorded in Tables 4, 5, 6, 7, and 8.

TABLE 4.—*Hydrocyanic acid (parts per million) in fumigated navy beans.*

Sodium cyanide.	Number of times chamber was evacuated.	Hydrocyanic acid after—							
		0 day.	1 day.	4 days.	7 days.	14 days.	30 days.	60 days.	90 days.
Oz. per 100 cu. ft.									
1........	0	....	3.3	3.3	1.7	0.8	None.	....	....
1........	1	....	8.3	3.3	2.5	.8	None.	....	....
1........	2	....	8.3	4.2	2.5	.8	0.8	0.4	0.4
1........	3	....	....	3.3	1.7	.8	.8	.6	Trace.
2........	0	20	4.2	2.5	1.7	1.2	1.2	1.2	1.2
2........	1	16	8.3	6.6	2.5	1.7	1.2	1.2	.4
2........	2	16	6.6	3.3	2.5	1.7	1.2	1.2	.4
2........	3	12	3.3	3.3	3.3	2.5	.4	.4	.4
4........	0	58	13	5.0	4.2	3.3	3.3	2.1	1.2
4........	1	42	17	5.0	3.3	2.5	2.1	2.1	1.7
4........	2	25	17	5.0	4.2	3.3	2.5	2.1	1.7
4........	3	42	20	4.2	3.3	2.5	1.7	1.7	1.7
6........	0	25	6.6	5.0	4.2	3.3	2.5	2.1	1.7
6........	1	42	27	10	6.6	5.0	3.3	2.9	2.5
6........	2	42	30	13	8.3	6.6	3.3	2.5	1.7
6........	3	58	20	12	10	6.6	3.3	2.5	1.7

TABLE 5.—*Hydrocyanic acid (parts per million) in fumigated field corn.*

Sodium cyanide.	Number of times chamber was evacuated.	Hydrocyanic acid after—							
		0 day.	1 day.	4 days.	7 days.	14 days.	30 days.	60 days.	90 days.
Oz. per 100 cu. ft.									
1........	0	....	7.5	2.5	1.2	None.	....	....	....
1........	1	....	4.2	2.1	.8	None.	....	....	....
1........	2	....	1.2	1.2	.8	None.	....	....	....
1........	3	....	....	.8	.8	None.	....	....	....
2........	0	62	5.8	1.7	1.7	1.2	1.2	0.8	0.8
2........	1	25	8.3	3.3	1.7	1.2	1.2	1.2	.4
2........	2	12	5.0	2.5	1.7	1.7	1.7	1.2	.8
2........	3	8	5.0	2.5	1.7	1.7	1.2	1.2	.4
4........	0	42	6.6	3.3	3.3	2.5	1.7	1.2	1.2
4........	1	25	10	3.8	3.3	2.9	2.9	2.1	1.7
4........	2	25	8.3	4.2	3.3	2.1	1.7	1.7	1.7
4........	3	17	6.6	3.3	2.5	2.5	2.1	2.1	1.7
6........	0	33	5.0	4.2	3.3	3.3	2.1	2.1	1.7
6........	1	33	10	6.6	5.8	5.8	5.8	5.0	4.2
6........	2	33	6.6	5.0	5.0	5.0	3.3	3.3	3.3
6........	3	33	12	6.6	6.6	5.8	4.2	3.7	3.3

TABLE 6.—*Hydrocyanic acid (parts per million) in fumigated cowpeas.*

Sodium cyanide.	Number of times chamber was evacuated.	Hydrocyanic acid after—							
		0 day.	1 day.	4 days.	7 days.	14 days.	30 days.	60 days.	90 days.
Oz. per 100 cu. ft.									
1........	0	....	6.2	4.2	3.3	2.5	1.7	1.2	1.2
1........	1	....	16	5.0	4.2	2.5	2.1	1.7	1.7
1........	2	....	4.2	4.2	4.2	2.5	1.7	.8	.8
1........	3	....	....	4.2	4.2	1.7	1.2	.8	1.2
2........	0	56	16	3.3	2.5	2.1	1.7	1.7	1.7
2........	1	33	16	5.0	3.3	2.5	2.1	2.1	1.7
2........	2	21	17	5.0	4.2	2.5	2.1	1.7	1.7
2........	3	16	11	4.2	3.3	3.3	2.1	2.1	1.7
4........	0	83	33	17	6.6	5.8	5.8	3.3	2.1
4........	1	50	33	13	5.0	5.0	5.0	4.2	3.3
4........	2	42	33	8.3	5.0	4.2	4.2	4.2	3.3
4........	3	42	23	6.6	5.8	5.8	5.0	3.3	3.3
6........	0	33	17	8.3	8.3	6.6	4.2	4.2	3.3
6........	1	83	27	8.3	8.3	7.5	7.5	6.6	5.0
6........	2	130	27	17	13	5.0	5.0	5.0	4.2
6........	3	100	40	13	12	10	6.6	6.6	5.0

No hydrocyanic acid was found in unfumigated samples of any of the products, showing that none of it was naturally present in them.

All of the seeds absorbed hydrocyanic acid on fumigation. The results obtained on the day of fumigation have little comparative significance, since much of the gas was loosely held and variations of three or four hours in the times of standing were unavoidable. They show, however, that the quantity then present is fairly large. Most of it disappears during the first few days. In fact, in most cases the hydrocyanic acid content, on the fourth day, was not more than 5 parts per million. After this time there was an extremely slow dis-

TABLE 7.—*Hydrocyanic acid (parts per million) in fumigated flour.*

Sodium cyanide.	Number of times chamber was evacuated.	Hydrocyanic acid after—			
		0 day.	1 day.	4 days.	7 days.
Oz. per 100 cu. ft.					
1.........	0	....	None.	....	....
1.........	1	....	None.	....	....
1.........	2	....	None.	....	....
1.........	3	....	....	None.	....
2.........	0	50	2.5	None.	....
2.........	1	83	3.3	0.8	None.
2.........	2	83	8.3	None.	....
2.........	3	83	3.3	None.	....
4.........	0	33	None.	....	....
4.........	1	150	3.3	None.	....
4.........	2	50	4.2	None.	....
4.........	3	120	6.6	None.	....
6.........	0	100	3.3	.8	None.
6.........	1	170	6.6	.8	None.
6.........	2	200	8.3	.8	None.
6.........	3	170	3.3	None.	....

TABLE 8.—*Hydrocyanic acid (parts per million) in fumigated wheat.*

Sodium cyanide.	Number of times chamber was evacuated.	Hydrocyanic acid after—							
		0 day.	1 day.	4 days.	7 days.	14 days.	30 days.	60 days.	90 days.
Oz. per 100 cu. ft.									
1........	0	....	5.0	3.3	2.5	1.7	1.2	1.2	1.2
1........	1	....	4.2	3.3	2.5	1.7	1.7	1.7	1.7
1........	2	....	4.2	3.3	2.5	1.7	1.7	1.2	1.7
1........	3	....		2.5	2.5	1.7	1.7	1.7	1.7
2........	0	17	8.3	3.7	3.3	2.5	2.1	2.1	2.1
2........	1	21	6.6	5.0	4.2	3.3	3.3	2.1	1.7
2........	2	13	5.0	3.3	2.5	2.5	2.5	2.1	1.7
2........	3	13	3.3	3.3	3.3	3.3	2.9	2.9	2.1
4........	0	17	6.6	6.6	5.0	4.2	4.2	4.2	3.3
4........	1	25	6.6	5.8	4.2	4.2	3.3	2.9	2.9
4........	2	17	6.6	5.0	4.2	4.2	4.2	4.2	3.3
4........	3	17	8.3	6.6	4.2	4.2	4.2	3.3	2.9
6........	0	17	5.0	3.3	3.3	3.3	2.5	2.9	2.5
6........	1	25	6.6	5.8	5.8	5.8	5.0	5.0	4.2
6........	2	33	6.6	6.6	5.0	5.0	4.2	4.2	3.3
6........	3	25	6.6	6.6	5.8	5.8	4.2	4.2	3.3

sipation, a very small quantity of the fumigant being present at the end of the 3-month experimental period in all but a few cases.

The flour differed from the seeds in that, while it at first took up a large quantity of hydrocyanic acid, the union seems to have been extremely weak and by the end of four days, or, at most, a week, no traces of it could be found.

Evacuating the fumigation chamber once, twice, or three times to get rid of the fumigant did not have much effect. In fact, a sample from the series in which the chamber had been evacuated two or three times frequently had a higher gas content than the corresponding sample in the series in which the chamber had not been evacuated.

The quantity of sodium cyanide used had a marked effect on the hydrocyanic acid absorbed by the product. This effect was noticeable after storage for 3 months.

MISCELLANEOUS PRODUCTS.

In the work of the Department of Agriculture it has at times seemed desirable to fumigate certain other material with hydrocyanic acid. These products have been analyzed, with a view of determining their safety for use after fumigation. The results are shown in Table 9.

TABLE 9.—*Residual hydrocyanic acid in miscellaneous products after fumigation.*

Product.	Period after fumigation.	Sodium cyanide.	Exposure.	Pressure.	Hydrocyanic acid.
	Days. (1)	Oz. per 100 cu. ft.	Hours.		Parts per million.
Beans, Brazilian	(1)	1	1¾	Vac.²	Less than 4.
Beans, Dwarf	2	1	1¾	Vac.	5
Cotton seed, Columbia:					
Whole seed	4	3	¾	Vac.	58
Hulls	4	3	¾	Vac.	110
Meats	4	3	¾	Vac.	None.
Whole seed	4	6	¾	Vac.	83
Hulls	4	6	¾	Vac.	140
Meats	4	6	¾	Vac.	None.
Cotton seed, Sea Island:					
Whole seed	4	3	¾	Vac.	75
Hulls	4	3	¾	Vac.	150
Meats	4	3	¾	Vac.	None.
Cotton seed, Trice:					
Whole seed	4	3	¾	Vac.	66
Hulls	4	3	¾	Vac.	140
Meats	4	3	¾	Vac.	None.
Whole seed	4	6	¾	Vac.	83
Hulls	4	6	¾	Vac.	150
Meats	4	6	¾	Vac.	None.
Cottonseed cake:					
Do	1	2	1	NAP³	8
Do	3	2	1	NAP	6
Do	7	2	1	NAP	5
Cowpeas, Groit	2	1	1¾	Vac.	66
Chestnuts:					
Whole	0	(4)	(4)	(4)	140
Shells	0	(4)	(4)	(4)	180
Meats	0	(4)	(4)	(4)	130
Honey:					
Capped	0	4	1	NAP	Trace.
Uncapped	0	4	1	NAP	9
Capped	1	4	1	NAP	None.
Uncapped	1	4	1	NAP	2

¹ Several.
² Vacuum fumigation by the method of Sasscer and Hawkins.
³ Fumigation at normal atmospheric pressure.
⁴ Unknown.

The hulls of the cotton seed and the shells of the chestnut absorb a large quantity of hydrocyanic acid. Unfumigated cottonseed hulls showed the presence of no hydrocyanic acid. Checks on the chestnuts were not available, but it does not seem possible that they would naturally contain such a large quantity. Hard rinds on fruits and vegetables tended to prevent absorption of the gas. No explanation is offered for this difference in behavior.

The absorption of hydrocyanic acid by uncapped honey was unexpectedly low. This was also surprising, in view of the fact that moist foods have a tendency to absorb the acid fairly rapidly.

SUMMARY.

Hydrocyanic acid gas, widely used as a fumigant against certain insects and rats, often comes in contact with materials intended for food. The quantity of hydrocyanic acid absorbed and retained by various fumigated foodstuffs has been determined.

All of the products examined absorbed the fumigant to some extent. Hard rinds of vegetables or skins of fruits had a tendency to decrease the absorption. Chlorophyll-bearing vegetables, or those of a succulent nature, in general, took up large quantities of hydrocyanic acid.

Some of the fruits and vegetables suffered physical injury (wilting, softening, or discoloration) because of fumigation to such an extent that they were unmarketable.

In the case of the seeds most of the hydrocyanic acid was rapidly dissipated, so that by the fourth day the content usually was not more than 5 parts per million. After this there was a slow dissipation, a very small quantity of the fumigant being present at the end of three months. The flour examined absorbed a large quantity of hydrocyanic acid but gave it off so rapidly that by the end of four days, or, at the most, a week, no traces of it could be detected.

Evacuating the chamber after fumigation was not effective in removing absorbed hydrocyanic acid.

The concentration of hydrocyanic acid gas used had, in general, a marked effect on the quantity absorbed by the product. This was noticeable even at the end of three months.

The quantities of hydrocyanic acid absorbed by various other products were determined also.

No conclusions as to the safety of fumigated foods for consumption are drawn in this bulletin. Chemical observations alone are included. Determinations of the quantities of hydrocyanic acid injurious to human health lie in the domain of the pharmacologist.

BIBLIOGRAPHY.

(1) ANONYMOUS.
    Adsorption of cyanide gas by foodstuffs. *In* U. S. Public Health Ser., Public Health Repts. (1920), **35**:1597.
(2) BAIL, OSKAR.
    Ungeziefervertilgung mittels Blausäuregas. *In* Gesundh. Ing. (1919), **42**:33–51.
(3) ———— and CANCIK, J.
    Ungezieferbekämpfung mit Blausäuredämpfen. *In* Centr. Bakt. Parasitenk. I Abt. Orig. (1918); **81**:109–124.
(4) BELL, J. T.
    How to destroy cabinet pests. *In* Can. Entomol. (1877), **9**:139–40.
(5) CORLETTE, C. E.
    Insecticidal fumigation in ships, with special reference to the use of hydrocyanic acid and to the prevention of ship-borne yellow fever. *In* Med. J. Australia (1916), **2**:384–7; 405–9.
(6) CREEL, R. H., FAGET, F. M., and WRIGHTSON, W. D.
    Hydrocyanic acid gas. Its practical use as a routine fumigant. *In* U. S. Public Health Ser., Public Health Repts. (1915), **30**:3537–50.
(7) DEAN, G. A.
    Insect control in flour mills. *In* Am. Miller (1922), **50**:752–3.
(8) ———— and SWANSON, C. O.
    Effect of common mill fumigants on the baking qualities of wheat flour. *In* Kans. Agr. Expt. Sta. Bull. 178 (1911), 155–207.

(9) FLORIDA STATE PLANT BOARD.
    Third Biennial Report. *In* Fla. State Plant Board, Quart. Bull. (1921),
    5:47–8; 99–101.
(10) GUTHRIE, F. B.
    Fumigation of fruit with hydrocyanic acid. *In* Agri. Gaz. N. S. Wales (1898),
    9:1191–2.
(11) HEYMONS.
    —— *In* Der Müller (1917), vol. 39, no. 21 (quoted by Bail and Cancik,
    loc. cit.).
(12) HOWARD, L. O., and POPENOE, C. H.
    Hydrocyanic-acid gas against household insects. U. S. Dept. Agr., Farmers'
    Bull. 699 (1916), 8 pp.
(13) LISTON, W. G.
    The use of hydrocyanic acid gas for fumigation. *In* Indian J. Med. Research
    (1920), 7:778–802.
(14) LODEMAN, E. G.
    The spraying of plants, p. 148. The MacMillan Co. (1916).
(15) LUBSEN, C., SALTET, R. H., and WOLFF, L. K.
    Over het gebruik van blauwzuur als insectendooden middel. *In* Nederl.
    Tijdsch. Geneeskunde (1920), 1:881–7, *through* J. Am. Med. Assoc. (1920),
    74:1614.
(16) MARCHADIER, GOUJON, and DE LAROCHE.
    L'acide cyanhydrique agent désinfectant des farines. *In* J. pharm. chim.
    (1921), ser. 7, 23:417–20.
(17) MONTGOMERY, J. H.
    Fumigation at Florida ports. *In* Fla. State Plant Board Quart. Bull. (1920),
    4:117.
(18) QUAINTANCE, A. L.
    Fumigation of apples for the San Jose scale. U. S. Dept. Agr., Bur. Ent.
    Bull. 84 (1909), 39 pp.
(19) ROBERTS, NORMAN.
    Cyanide fumigation of ships. *In* U. S. Public Health Ser., Public Health
    Repts. (1914), 29:3321–5.
(20) SASSCER, E. R., and HAWKINS, L. A.
    A method of fumigating seeds. U. S. Dept. Agr. Bull. 186 (1915), 6 pp.
(21) SCHMIDT, H.
    Ueber die Einwirkung gasförmiger Blausäure auf frische Früchte. *In* Arb.
    Kais. Gesundh. (1901–2), 18:490–517.
(22) TOWNSEND, C. O.
    The effect of hydrocyanic-acid gas upon grains and other seeds. *In* Md. Agr.
    Expt. Sta. Bull. 75 (1901), 183–198.
(23) VIEHOEVER, A., and JOHNS, C. O.
    On the determination of small quantities of hydrocyanic acid. *In* J. Am.
    Chem. Soc. (1915), 37:601–7.
(24) WOGLUM, R. S.
    Hydrocyanic-acid gas fumigation in California. U. S. Dept. Agr., Bur. Ent.
    Bull. 90 (1911), p. 1.

UNITED STATES DEPARTMENT OF AGRICULTURE

DEPARTMENT BULLETIN No. 1150

Washington, D. C.	▼	August 8, 1923

ACCOUNTING RECORDS AND BUSINESS METHODS FOR LIVE-STOCK SHIPPING ASSOCIATIONS.[1]

By FRANK ROBOTKA, *Assistant, Iowa Agricultural Experiment Station, and Collaborator, Bureau of Agricultural Economics.*

CONTENTS.

The cooperative marketing of live stock has experienced a more phenomenal growth than perhaps any other form of cooperative endeavor. Using Iowa as an illustration, the oldest association in the State was organized in 1904. Of all the associations in existence in the State in 1920, about 3 per cent were organized before 1910, only 8 per cent before 1915, and less than 25 per cent before 1918. About 75 per cent of the associations in existence in December, 1920, were organized during the years 1919 and 1920.[2]

Even though the history of the movement in other States differs in some respects from that in Iowa, by far the greatest development for the country as a whole has taken place within the past five years.

This rapid growth has brought to the front a number of problems, most of which may be traced directly or indirectly to small volume of business, inexperienced management and in some localities to competition among the associations. As a result there is a wide difference in the cost of shipping between the most efficient and the least efficient associations. The choice of markets is also important,

[1] Manuscript for this publication was prepared in collaboration with the Iowa State College of Agriculture and Mechanic Arts and is also published as Accounting Records for Live Stock Shipping Associations, by Frank Robotka. Iowa Agr. Exp. Sta. Bul. No. 209.

[2] Cooperative Live-Stock Shipping in Iowa in 1920, by E. C. Nourse and C. W. Hammans, Iowa Agr. Exp. Sta. Bul. No. 200.

especially in the Middle West, where in some cases associations are accessible to several markets.

The solution of many of these problems depends upon the management having a thorough knowledge of the relative advantages of different methods of handling live stock and operating the association, the relative costs of shipping to different markets, the relative merits of different methods of selling and weighing live stock, and the extent to which these factors influence the rate of shrinkage or loss due to dead and crippled animals.

The question of what business policy shall be pursued in connection with these and other problems can be answered intelligently only when the details regarding the different shipments are summarized and the results analyzed. Reliable figures which can be used for this purpose too frequently have not been preserved by shipping associations. In fact, bookkeeping has been neglected more among shipping associations than in most other types of farmers' organizations. Perhaps the chief reason for this situation is that it is a relatively simple matter to organize a shipping association. A group of farmers may meet in the morning, elect a board of directors and a set of officers, hire a manager and begin business the same day. The details of management and record keeping are usually left to be worked out as the necessity arises.

Another explanation for the frequent neglect of record keeping is to be found in the fact that each sale—that is, each shipment—is often treated as if it were a completed fiscal period. The entire proceeds are either paid out or reserved at the time of settlement and the shipment is considered a closed incident. Other causes are the small average annual income received by the managers, the lack of standardization of business practices, and the frequent changes of managers and directors. The fact that many associations also handle feed and other farm supplies, often on credit, has done much to complicate the situation.

The adoption of a simple but adequate system of records by the associations generally would be a long step in the direction of raising the standards of efficiency of operation, of building up the volume of business and of inspiring loyalty on the part of the members and confidence on the part of the community generally. Furthermore, it would lay the foundation for successful cooperation among the associations. The association which fails to meet any one of these essential conditions is not likely to be in a position to render the kind of service which the community has a right to expect of it.

The system of records and accounts recommended in this bulletin is based on the methods used by shipping associations in different parts of the country which experience has demonstrated are sound and practical. Its operation in a number of States has already demonstrated its adaptability under a wide range of conditions and methods of operation.[3]

---

[3] Some of the forms as presented are revisions of forms found in actual use, and others, particularly the shipment summary record and the cash journal, are original with the author. Final revisions were made at a series of conferences on shipping association business practices and accounting held in Chicago during the summer of 1921 under the auspices of the Illinois Agricultural Association, at which conferences the underlying principles involved and the forms themselves, substantially as here presented, were approved. In addition to the author, the following men took an active part in the discussions of the accounting records: S. W. Doty and F. G. Ketner, of Ohio, Ralph Loomis and T. D. Morse, of Missouri, and F. M. Simpson, of Illinois

The system is specifically designed to meet the needs of associations which make the shipping of live stock their main or only business. This includes associations which, in addition to shipping live stock, occasionally buy feed and other farm supplies which are unloaded directly from the car and paid for on delivery. Farmers' elevators or produce and supply associations which have a warehouse and carry a stock of supplies and which also ship live stock need only to add to their general ledger the special accounts necessary to handle the live-stock business. Such cash books and journals as may be in use also receive the entries for the live-stock transactions. However, all of the detail records and the shipment summary record herein recommended for shipping associations may be used with equal advantage by these other types of associations. Neither the cash journal nor the classification of accounts proposed in this system is designed or recommended for a mercantile or general produce business.

The purpose of each form and the method of using it is explained on the following pages.

WHAT FORMS ARE NEEDED?

A system of records, to be adequate, must provide for the keeping of two principal classes of records: The detail records or working papers, and the permanent records.

The detail records are needed to give evidence of the business transacted and to furnish the authority and data needed in making entries in the permanent records. As they contain the original calculations and figures they should be preserved carefully and filed conveniently for ready reference and verification in cases of dispute. Unless they are available when an audit is being made it is practically impossible to prove the accuracy of the books. The detail records which are included as part of the system and which experience has shown are necessary are:

> Form No. 1. Scale ticket.
> Form No. 2. Manifest.
> Form No. 3. Prorating sheet.
> Form No. 4. Member's statement and check voucher.
> Form No. 5. Shipment record envelope.

The permanent records are provided for the purpose of preserving the information contained in the detail records and classifying it so as to make it useful to the management, first, in determining the business standing and explaining changes made in it during a fiscal period; and, second, in deciding what changes should be made in the choice of markets, methods of handling the live stock, and in the business methods generally. The forms provided are:

> Form No. 6. Shipment summary record.
> Form No. 7. Cash journal.

To illustrate the use of each of these forms an imaginary shipment, No. 111, will be followed through the records.

SCALE TICKET.

A memorandum should be made on the scale ticket (Form No. 1) showing how the animals were marked and the number and weight of each kind and grade of live stock delivered by each shipper. The.

shipment number, date, and the name and address of the shipper should also be recorded. The home weight should be obtained separately for each grade of animals. Notations regarding the condition of the animals should be made on the ticket whenever there is reason to suspect that the animals have been fed excessively, or when there is a question as to whether certain ones may be subject to dock-

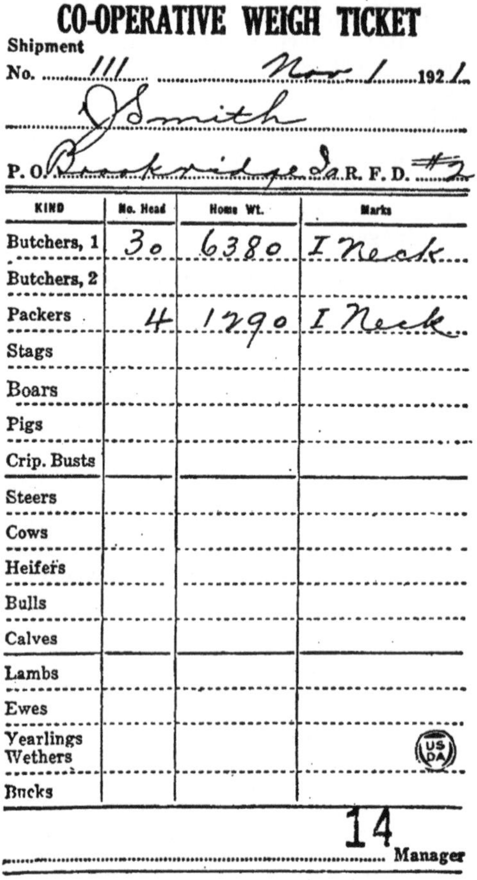

CO-OPERATIVE WEIGH TICKET

Shipment
No. ....*III*........ ....*Nov 1*...192*1*.

....

P. O. *Brookridge Ia*.R. F. D. ...*#2*...

KIND	No. Head	Home Wt.	Marks
Butchers, 1	*3o*	*6380*	*I neck*
Butchers, 2			
Packers	*4*	*1790*	*I Neck*
Stags			
Boars			
Pigs			
Crip. Busts			
Steers			
Cows			
Heifers			
Bulls			
Calves			
Lambs			
Ewes			
Yearlings Wethers			
Bucks			

14
.... Manager

FIG. 1.—Scale ticket (Form No. 1).

age or be sold subject to inspection. The original copy of the ticket should be given to the shipper and the carbon copy retained in the office.

MANIFEST.

A summary of the scale tickets for all the live stock included in the shipment should then be made on the manifest (Form No. 2) as shown in Figure 2. This form is also issued in duplicate, one copy being sent to the commission firm and the other retained in the office.

MANIFEST
OF LIVE STOCK SHIPPED BY

Shipping Assn. Form No. 2

Brookbridge Coop. Shpg Assn, Brookbridge — Shipment No. 111

Consigned to Cooperative Commission Co. Chicago — Date Shipped Nov. 1, 1921

Mail Account Sales to Jno. Clark, Mgr. Brookbridge, Ia. — Railroad C. & N.W.

Send Money to Same — Car Nos. I.C. 14980

Handling Instructions Weigh Packers separately; sell according to best judgment — Loaded 8:00 ~~A.M.~~ P.M.

HOME EXPENSES

Manager's Commission $____

Insurance Fund - - - - $____

Operating Expense - - $____

$____

Do not prorate $____

$____

Total $____

OWNERS	HOGS								MARKS	CATTLE						SHEEP				
	Butchers 1	Butchers 2	Packers	Stags	Boars	Pigs	Crips. Busts	Home Weight		Steers	Cows	Heifers	Bulls	Calves	Home Weight	Lambs	Ewes	Yrlgs. Wthrs.	Bucks	Home Weight
J. Smith	30							6380	I Neck											
"			4					1790	I "											
Bill Adams		75						7800	I Back											
			2					615	I "											
	30	75	6					16085												

FIG. 2.—Manifest (Form No. 2).

Full instructions should be given regarding the disposition of the returns, prorating, and the method of handling the live stock. If the commission firm is to prorate the home expenses also, the rates or amounts of the different items should be recorded in the blanks provided for this purpose in the upper right-hand corner of the form. Much confusion in prorating can be avoided by filling out the manifest carefully and completely.,

This completes the record work involved in receiving the live stock and loading it into the car. The results of the sale are necessary before the next step can be taken, which consists of prorating the returns.

PRORATING SHEET.

It is assumed that for shipment No. 111 the manager is to do the prorating. The manifest and the account sales received from the commission firm furnish all the information needed in connection with the distribution of the returns. It is assumed that the account sales shown on this page was received as a result of the sale of the live stock included in shipment No. 111. Figure 3 represents the prorating sheet (Form No. 3) as it appears after the returns have been prorated. The steps followed in arriving at the figures given on the prorating sheet are presented on pages 38, 39, 40.

[Account Sales for shipment No. 111.]

COOPERATIVE COMMISSION CO., UNION STOCK YARDS, CHICAGO, Nov. 2, 1921.

Sold for the Account of the Brookridge Cooperative Shipping Association, Brookridge, Iowa.

Buyer.	Head.	Kind.	Weight.	Mark.	Dockage.		Price.	Amount.
					Sows.	Stags.		
Armour...............	30	Hogs....	6,315	I. R. S....			10.00	$631.50
Swift...............	25	...do.....	7,720	I Back..			9.80	.756.56
Armour...............	6	Packers.	1,870	{4 I. R. S.} {2 I Back.}			9.00	168.30
			15,905					·1,556.36

I. C. 14980, 17,000 pounds @ 40¢................	$68.00	Freight.........................	$73.04
Switching-...............	3.00	Yardage 61, @ 12¢..............'....	7.32
War tax...................	2.04	Insurance.....:.............	.07
Total...................	73.04	Feed—5 bu. corn...'.............	5.00
		Inspection......................	.20
		Commission......................	18.00	103.63
		Net proceeds..............:.........	1,452.73

NOTE.—It will be noted that the weights shown here vary from those used in making up the prorate sheet (fig. 3). For explanation see note on page 39.

MEMBER'S STATEMENT.

When the calculations on the prorating sheet have been verified, statements and checks may be issued to the shippers. Form No. 4 is designed to be used for this purpose. The member's statement shows the details of the settlement with each shipper as calculated on the prorating sheet. The vouchers are issued in duplicate and are numbered consecutively. The statement bears the same number as the attached check, which number is inserted in the " check number " column on the prorating sheet as the checks are issued. The original copy is given to the shipper and the carbon copy is retained in the office. (See Fig. 4.)

In those cases where the association uses an ordinary check form separate from the member's statement, the member's statement without the attached check may be used. This statement (Fig. 5) is made in duplicate and bears the same number as the check issued in pay-

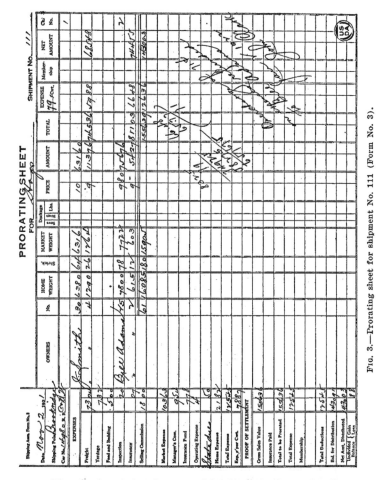

FIG. 3.—Prorating sheet for shipment No. 111 (Form No. 3).

ment. The check number is entered in the "check number" column on the prorating sheet. The original copy together with the check is given to the shipper and the carbon copy is retained in the office.

SHIPMENT RECORD ENVELOPE.

The purposes of the shipment record envelope are: (1) To provide a convenient means of filing for ready reference all the papers concerning each shipment; (2) to facilitate the classification of the debits and credits arising as a result of each settlement.

After the statements and checks have been issued, the blanks on the envelope should be filled out as indicated in Figure 6. The amount to be inserted opposite "Proceeds for live stock: Sold at market" will be the net proceeds as shown on the account sales. All of the other items will be obtained from the prorating sheet.

Shipping Association Form No. 4

MEMBER'S STATEMENT

Nº 94

Shipment No. *111* *Brookridge Cooperative Shipping Assn*

Brookridge Iowa, *Nov 2* 1921

Account of *J. Smith*   P.O. *Blank, Iowa* R.F.D. *2*

No.	Kind	Shrinkage Gain	Market Weight	Dock	Price	Amount		TOTAL	
3 0	*Good butchers*	64	6316		10	631	60		
4	*Pkrs*	76	1764		9	113	76		
								745	36

REMARKS:

(US DA)

	EXPENSES		
Species	Rate	Amount	
Hogs	0 79	59	88
Cattle			
Calves			
Sheep			
		59	88

Attached find Check for Balance due $685.48

Please ask about anything not understood.   Complete statement of each shipment is on file.
(Tear Off Before Depositing)

Brookridge Cooperative Shipping Assn.

Nº 94

Brookridge Iowa, *Nov 2* 1921

Pay to the order of *J. Smith* — $685.48/100

Six Hundred Eighty Five and 48/100 DOLLARS

J. Clark
Manager

FIG. 4.—Member's statement (Form No. 4).

It will be noted that the "home statement" on the shipment record envelope is also a proof of settlement, but it differs from that on the prorating sheet in that it is a statement of the disposition of the *net* amount of money remitted by the commission firm after deducting the expenses, rather than of the *gross* market value as on the prorating sheet.

Each shipment should be assigned a serial number, which should be entered in the upper right-hand corner of the envelope.

All papers pertaining to the shipment should be filed in the envelope, including the carbon copies of the scale tickets, a carbon copy of the manifest, a copy of the bill of lading, the account sales, the prorating sheet, carbon copies of the members' statements, and any other correspondence or papers pertaining to the shipment.

After settlement has been made summaries for the shipment should be recorded in the shipment summary record and the cash journal, as illustrated on the following pages.

SHIPMENT SUMMARY RECORD.

The shipment summary record is provided for the purpose of bringing together the useful information of a statistical nature regarding each shipment of live stock.

Shipping Association Form No. 4 - A

MEMBER'S STATEMENT

N? 95

Shipment No..............

.... 192........

Account of .... P.O................... ...................................R.F.D...........

No.	Kind	Shrinkage Gain	Market Weight	Dock	Price	Amount		TOTAL	

REMARKS:

	EXPENSES			
	Species	Rate	Amount	
	Hogs			
	Cattle			
	Calves			
	Sheep			

Attached find Check, No. .... for Balance due $............................
Please ask about anything not understood.   Complete statement of each shipment is on file.

FIG. 5.—Member's statement (Form No. 4–A).

The column headings and the sample entries on the form in Figure 7 indicate what facts are to be recorded on this form and the method of recording them. A summary of each shipment should be entered immediately after settlement has been made.

The figures for shipments No. 111 and No. 112 were taken directly from the manifests and the account sales illustrated in connection with the discussion of these shipments. (See page 41 for discussion of shipment No. 112.) The summaries consist of the *actual* weights, shrinkage, gross and net sales values, expenses, and home net value, rather than the prorated figures. The amount to be entered in the "home net" column is not the amount actually paid shippers, but it is the net value of the stock after all expenses have been deducted. The amount actually paid shippers is the home net value plus insurance paid for losses and plus or minus the small amount arising from dropping or adding fractions. The undivided balance and the insurance paid are the only items taken directly from the prorating sheet.

Separate summaries for hogs, cattle, calves, and sheep should be made on separate sheets of the shipment summary records. The summaries for the live stock shipped in mixed cars may be entered on the same sheets with those for the live stock in straight car shipments. Each summary should be totaled monthly and the totals to date brought down immediately below the monthly totals.

THE CASH JOURNAL.

The cash journal (Form No. 7) serves two very important purposes: (1) It provides a history showing day by day all cash receipts

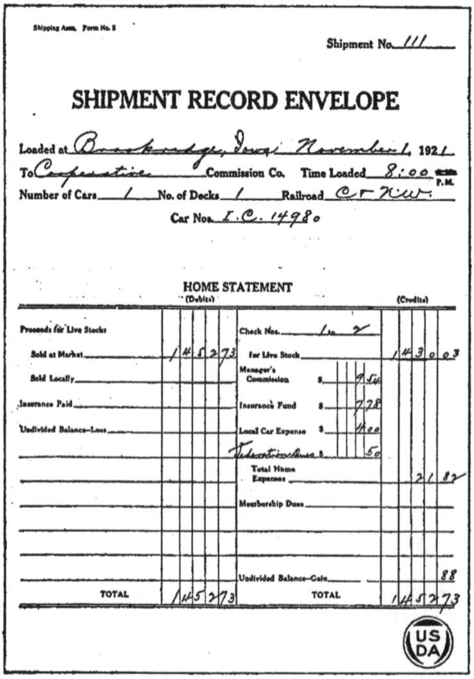

Shipping Assn. Form No. 5

Shipment No. 111

SHIPMENT RECORD ENVELOPE

Loaded at ________ November 1, 1921

To ________ Commission Co. Time Loaded 8:00 P.M.

Number of Cars 1 No. of Decks 1 Railroad ________

Car Nos. I.C. 14980

HOME STATEMENT

(Debits)			(Credits)
Proceeds for Live Stock:		Check Nos.	
Sold at Market	1452 73	for Live Stock	1430 03
Sold Locally		Manager's Commission $ 9 54	
Insurance Paid		Insurance Fund $ 7 78	
Undivided Balance—Loss		Local Car Expense $ 4 00	
		________ $ 50	
		Total Home Expenses	21 82
		Membership Dues	
		Undivided Balance—Gain	88
TOTAL	1452 73	TOTAL	1452 73

FIG. 6.—Shipment record envelope (Form No. 5).

and disbursements and other business transacted; (2) it classifies and summarizes the results of these transactions according to the accounts affected, thus making it a simple matter to determine the condition of any particular account or of the business as a whole.

The form (see Fig. 8) provides for recording the date and explanation of each transaction, and the number of the check issued, if any. The remainder of the form is divided into 11 pairs of columns. One pair of columns (a debit and a credit column) is to be used for each account.

MEMORANDA			
AMOUNT CLAIMED	COLLECTION FEE	NET AMOUNT COLLECTED	DATE RECEIVED
107 20	2 00 50	789 96	
25 75	3 00	22 75	Dec 5
19 44			
13 25			
180 29			
30 40			
69 13			
76 33			

SHIPMENT SUMMARY RECORD

(RIGHT-HAND PAGE)

DATE 1921	COMMISSION COMPANY	SHIP-MENT No.	No. DECKS		No. HEAD	No. SHIPPED	MARKET WEIGHT	SHRINKAGE		DOCKAGE		GROSS PROCEEDS	FREIGHT AND MARKET EXPENSES					MARKET NET
			TOTAL Decks	USED				TOTAL LBS.	LBS. CWT.	LBS.	SHRINK. DOCK.		FREIGHT	COMM.	FEED	INS. WARE.	COM. INSUR.	

FIG. 7.—Shipment summary record (Form No. 6).

CASH

[LEFT-HAND PAGE]

DATE 1921	EXPLANATIONS	CK. NO.	BANK		LIVE STOCK		MGR'S COMMISSION		INSURANCE FUND	
			DEPOSITS	CHECKS	SETTLEMENTS	NET PROCEEDS	PAYMENTS	DEDUCTIONS	PAYMENTS	DEDUCTIONS

FIG. 8.—Cash Journal

OPERATING THE CASH JOURNAL.

The operation of the cash journal is best illustrated by examples. Figure 9 shows how the following receipts of cash should be recorded. The numbers in parentheses correspond to the number of the illustrative transactions on pages 48 to 50.

(3) November 2. Received check for $1,452.73 from Cooperative Commission Co., representing proceeds of shipment No. 111.

(17) December 1. Received $40 in cash, representing membership fees paid by 40 new members.

(21) December 6. Borrowed $100 at the State Bank and gave a 90-day note bearing 7 per cent interest.

In transaction (3) live stock was exchanged for cash; in transaction (17) the privileges of membership were exchanged for cash; in transaction (21) an obligation to pay $100 in 90 days was exchanged for cash. In each case, the bank account is debited with the amount of cash received and deposited, and in each case that account which produced or parted with the value exchanged for the cash is credited.[4]

Entries for the following cash disbursements are shown in figure 10.

(2) November 1. Paid the Jones Feed Store for 8 bushels of corn for shipment No. 111; check No. 101 for $4.

(5) November 2. Paid Eureka Printing Co. for cash journal binder, $5 and stationery $5; check No. 103 for $10.

(8) November 4. Paid note at State Bank for $200 with interest $16; check No. 105 for $216.

(18) December 2. Paid John Clark, manager, commission on shipment No. 112; check No. 111, for $10.11.

In recording the disbursements the procedure is similar to that involved in recording the receipts, except that in this case the bank account is *credited* and the accounts representing the value received in exchange are *debited*. In transaction (2) the local car expense account is debited with the value (corn) received for the $4 cash expended. In transaction (5) personal property and office supplies were received; the cash journal binder, being a permanent piece of equipment, is debited to the yard and office equipment account, but the stationery, which will be used up in a relatively short time, is debited to general expense. In transaction (8) an obligation to pay was received (canceled) to the extent of $200, hence the debit to the indebtedness account. Interest expense was incurred to the extent of $16, which is debited to general expense under loss and gain. In transaction (18) expense was incurred for manager's services, hence the debit to the manager's commission account.

It should be noted that each transaction is entered on a separate line and that at least two accounts are affected. It will also be noted that the debits and credits arising from each transaction are equal.

Every transaction is an exchange of equivalent values, something of value is received and something of equal value is exchanged for it. According to a simple rule, an account is debited when value of the particular kind it represents is received, and it is credited when the same kind of value is parted with.

[4] As membership fees are usually used for general expenses, they are recorded in the loss and gain account as income. For exceptions, see discussion of "Loss and gain" account on page 20.

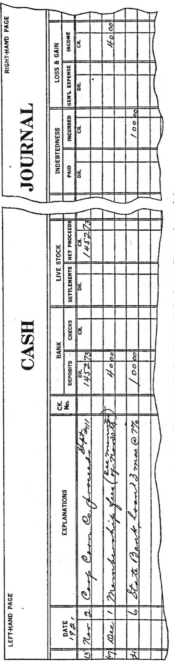

FIG. 9.—Cash Journal, showing method of recording cash receipts.

LEFT-HAND PAGE

CASH

	DATE 1921	EXPLANATIONS	CK. No.	BANK: DEPOSITS DR.	BANK: CHECKS CR.	LIVE STOCK: SETTLEMENTS DR.	LIVE STOCK: NET PROCEEDS CR.	MGR'S COMMISSION: PAYMENTS DR.	MGR'S COMMISSION: DEDUCTIONS CR.	INSURANCE FUND: PAYMENTS DR.	INSURANCE FUND: DEDUCTIONS CR.
2	Nov 1	Jones Feed Store, 8 bu Corn. Shpt. #111	101		4 00						
15	2	Eureka Ptg Co. Acct. Book $5.00 Sta. $5.00	103		10 00						
18	4	State Bank, paid note $200.- Int. $16.00	105		216 00						
18	Dec 2	John Clark, Mgr. Corn Shpt. #112	111		10 11			10 11			

RIGHT-HAND PAGE

JOURNAL

LOCAL CAR EXPENSE: PAYMENTS DR.	LOCAL CAR EXPENSE: DEDUCTIONS CR.	FEDERATION DUES: PAID OUT DR.	FEDERATION DUES: COLLECTED CR.	UNDIVIDED BALANCE: LOSSES DR.	UNDIVIDED BALANCE: GAINS CR.	EQUIPMENT: PURCHASES DR.	EQUIPMENT: INVENTORY DECREASES CR.	INDEBTEDNESS: PAID DR.	INDEBTEDNESS: INCURRED CR.	LOSS & GAIN: GEN'L EXPENSE DR.	LOSS & GAIN: INCOME CR.	NET WORTH: DECREASES DR.	NET WORTH: INCREASES CR.
4 00													
						5 00				5 00			
								200 00		16 00			

FIG. 10.—Cash journal, showing method of recording cash disbursements.

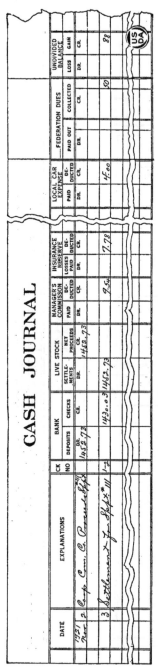

Fig. 11.—Cash Journal, showing entry for settlement with shippers.

When settlement is made for a shipment of live stock several ac.
counts are affected. The debit and credits arising from shipment
No. 111 are as follows (see Fig. 6):

DEBITS.		CREDITS.	
Account.	Amount.	Account.	Amount.
Live stock	$4,452.73	Bank	$1,430.03
		Manager's commission	9.54
		Insurance fund	7.78
		Local car expense	4.00
		Dues-State federation	.50
		Undivided balance-gain	.88
	1,452.73		1,452.73

The entry to be made in the cash journal would appear as shown
in Figure 11. For the sake of clearness, the entry for the receipt of
the proceeds is also recorded. The two entries, however, represent
two separate and distinct transactions.

· The Live-stock account is debited, indicating that the gross amount
due shippers from the sale of live stock·has been distributed. The
manager's commission account, the insurance fund account, the local
car expense account, and the federation dues account are each *credited*
with the amount deducted for each specific purpose. The amount
paid by checks is credited to the bank account. As complete distribution was not made, the undivided balance account is credited
with the 88 cents not distributed.

TRANSACTIONS WHICH DO NOT INVOLVE THE CASH ACCOUNT.

In the illustrations given above, cash was either received or dis-
bursed in each transaction. Although this is the case in the large
majority of transactions, it is occasionally necessary to record transactions in which cash is neither received nor paid out. For illustrations see transactions (25) to (28) on page 50 and entries for these
transactions dated December 31 in Figure 8.

ILLUSTRATIVE TRANSACTIONS.

In order to illustrate further the operation of the cash journal,
the business of an imaginary shipping association for the months
of November and December, 1921, together with a summary of the
previous 10 months' business is recorded on the cash journal pages
illustrated in Figure 8. (A list of these transactions is given on
pages 47 to 51.) It will be noted that the first entry records the
accumulated debits and credits in the accounts resulting from the
business transacted previous to November 1, 1921.[5] This entry is
then followed by the entries for the business transacted during November.

---

[5] As the management is responsible for the condition of the business as revealed by
the books, the manager or secretary should insist that the statement upon which the
opening entry is based be approved by the board of directors. If the books of a previous
secretary or manager are taken over they should first be approved by the board of
directors. The books should be examined by an auditing committee at intervals of
from one to three months, and a thorough audit by a skilled accountant should be
made each year, or each time a change in management is made. Strict adherence to
this rule would not only be a protection to the management and to the membership but
it would tend to keep those responsible for the affairs of the association in intimate
contact with the business.

At the end of the month, the totals of all the columns are brought down on the same line and are carried forward to the end of the year. However, in preparing the statement of resources and liabilities at the end of each month, the balances in the different accounts should be determined and only these used. (See statement of resources and liabilities for November 31, 1921, on p. 49.)

INFORMATION NEEDED TO DETERMINE THE BUSINESS STANDING.

· The records of many associations go no further than the prorating sheet, and information as to their business standing or the condition of their different accounts is not available. It is necessary, if proper accounting is to be done, that the results of the individual shipments be accumulated until the final reckoning at the end of the fiscal period, or oftener. As the estimates for insurance and overhead expenses are often intentionally made high or low, this final reckoning will reveal the excess or deficiency of such estimates and bring to light other items which may have been overlooked. Proper disposition can then be made of the excess reserved, or provision made for taking care of the deficiency.

. Furthermore, every association transacts some business which has reference to no particular shipment. Equipment is bought, claims are collected, money is borrowed or a note paid, office supplies are purchased, the premium on the manager's bond is paid, or farm supplies are shipped in. These transactions affect the standing of the business just as much as those which relate directly to specific shipments.

All of the business transacted, whether it affects cash or property, debts, reserves, expenses, net worth, or what not, should therefore be brought together and classified according to the accounts affected. Only when this is done will the association be able at all times to answer the question, "How do we stand?" with any degree of assurance that it is answered correctly.

The business standing of an individual or a business concern is revealed by the statement of resources and liabilities. In the case of a farmer purchasing a farm for $50,000 and paying $30,000 in cash and giving mortgage notes for $20,000, the statement of resources and liabilities would appear as follows:

Resources.		Liabilities.	
Farm	$50,000	Notes payable	$20,000
		Net worth	
		Owner's investment	30'000
	50,000		50,000

This statement shows, first, that the farm business, as a unit in itself distinct from the owner, is in the possession of property valued at $50,000. In the second place, the statement shows the kinds and the amounts of the different equities in the business. Note holders have a prior claim of $20,000 against the undivided property of the farm business. The remaining $30,000 represents the owner's equity.

If the owner had invested $40,000 instead of $30,000, the other items (value of farm and the indebtedness) remaining the same, the owner's claim against the business would be worth only 75 cents on the dollar, as there would be only $30,000 left after paying the note holders, who have a prior claim. The farm business in this case might be thrown into bankruptcy by the creditors. On the other hand, if the property was valued at $60,000, the other items remaining the same, there would be $40,000 left after paying off the note holders. In this case, each dollar of the owner's investment would be worth 133⅓ cents, and the financial condition of the farm would be considered very favorable.

A similar procedure is followed in determining whether or not any other kind of business concern is worth 100 cents on the dollar. An illustrative statement representing the affairs of an imaginary shipping association is presented below.

STATEMENT OF RESOURCES AND LIABILITIES OF THE BROOKRIDGE COOPERATIVE SHIPPING ASSOCIATION, NOVEMBER 1, 1921.

Resources.

Cash	$576. 02	
Yard and office equipment	1, 000. 00	
		$1, 576. 02

Liabilities.

Notes payable	$300. 00	
Federation dues	55. 00	
Insurance fund	799. 51	
Undivided balance	3. 51	
		1, 158. 02

Net worth.

Capital stock	400. 00		
Surplus (undivided profits)	18. 00		
		418. 00	1, 576. 02

It will be noted that the resources consist of cash and equipment amounting to $1,576.02; the liabilities amount to $1,158.02, consisting of outstanding notes, dues owed to a State association, the reserve for insurance and the undivided balance. The resources exceed the liabilities by $418, which amount represents the net worth of the association. As only $400 was put into the business originally, the difference of $18 represents surplus profits left in the business.

It will also be noted from this statement that the investment in the business came from stockholders, rather than from an individual owner, as in the case of the farm business. An association which is not incorporated is regarded as a partnership, in which case all of the members would be joint owners.

Each of the subdivisions in the statement shown above represents a separate account in the cash journal; in fact, it is from the accounts in this book that the information for such statements is obtained.

The accounts which a particular association needs depend upon the character of the business, if any, which it combines with live-stock shipping. Ordinarily all shipping associations need the following accounts:

1. Bank.
2. Live stock.
3. Manager's commission.
4. Insurance fund.
5. Local car expense.
6. Undivided balance.
7. Loss and gain.
8. Net worth.

Other accounts which are frequently needed are:

9. Federation dues (State or district federation).
10. Yard and office equipment.
11. Indebtedness (or notes payable).
12. Merchandise.

33703°—23——3

Each of these accounts is described and illustrated fully on the following pages.

DESCRIPTION OF THE ACCOUNTS.

THE BANK ACCOUNT.

It is good practice to handle all funds through the bank. All receipts of cash from whatever source will accordingly be entered in the "deposits" (debit) column and as checks are issued the amounts will be entered in the "checks" (credit) column. A debit balance indicates the amount of available funds in the bank and is an asset. A credit balance indicates an overdraft and is a liability.

Debit:

(1) With the available balance of cash in the bank as shown by the balance sheet at the time of opening the books.

(2) With all checks, drafts, and currency received from live stock and other sources, as well as proceeds of notes given for loans, as these items are deposited.

Credit:

(1) With an overdraft, if any, at time of opening the books.

(2) With the amounts of all checks drawn. The checks issued to shippers will be entered in total for each shipment.

All cash should be recorded in one bank account in the cash journal, even though the cash is divided into different funds at the bank or is carried in more than one bank. Where it is desired to divide the business between two banks it is preferable to change banks once or twice a year rather than to carry funds in both banks at the same time.

LIVE STOCK.

Debit:

(1) With net proceeds prorated at the time of the settlement for each shipment.

(2) With the purchase price of live stock purchased outright.

Credit:

(1) With the net proceeds received from commission firms for live stock shipped.

(2) With the amounts received for live stock sold locally.

A credit balance in this acount usually represent proceeds which have not yet been prorated to shippers and is a liability. However, if live stock is bought outright the account will show a gain if the credits exceed the debits, and a loss if the debits exceed the credits. At the end of the fiscal year any such gain or loss will be closed to the loss and gain account.

MANAGER'S COMMISSION.

Debit:

(1) With amounts of salary or commission as payments are made.

(2) With amounts paid manager in reimbursement of amounts advanced by him for association expenses.

Credit:

(1) With commission earned at the time settlement is made for shipment of live stock.

(2) With amounts advanced by manager for association expenses at the time the advances were made.

Where the manager is paid on the commission basis, the account will balance if he has been paid in full. A credit balance represents the amount of unpaid commission due the manager. If the manager is paid on a salary basis, the debit balance will represent the amount of expense due to manager's salary, which will be closed to the loss and gain account at the end of the year.

INSURANCE FUND.

Debit:

(1) With payments to shippers for losses.

(2) With payments of attorney's fees for collecting claims when such fees are paid by an association check.

Credit:

(1) With amount deducted from the proceeds of each shipment as the insurance charge.

(2) With amounts received in settlement of railroad claims.

The insurance fund account will usually show an excess of credits over debits, in which case the balance indicates that more has been reserved than actually paid because of losses.

Such a credit balance is a liability from the point of view of the association, as it represents deductions from returns due members in excess of the needs for insurance purposes. In a sense, this excess is held in trust for the members and in case of dissolution would be prorated back to them.

As the financial strength of an association depends to a considerable extent upon its ability to meet ordinary losses promptly without borrowing, it is important that a conservative credit balance be maintained in the insurance fund account. After a balance of several hundred to a thousand dollars (depending on the volume of business and other conditions) has been accumulated, the charge for insurance should be reduced to a point which will maintain the desired balance in the fund. The practice of some associations of drawing on the insurance fund for overhead and miscellaneous expenses is not to be commended, as the protection to members is likely to be impaired by an undue drain on this account. Where the membership fees are not adequate, special provision should be made for meeting overhead expenses. This may be done either by making a separate deduction from the proceeds of shipments for this purpose or, when a lump deduction is made for all purposes in general, by dividing the total deduction into two parts, one to be specifically reserved for insurance purposes and the other for overhead expenses. In order to avoid the possibility of using the insurance funds for purchases of equipment or otherwise rendering it unavailable for the payment of losses, some associations set aside the cash reserved for insurance in a separate deposit account in the bank, or even invest part of it in securities of a readily salable sort.

LOCAL CAR EXPENSE.

Debit:	Credit:
(1) With amounts paid for feed, bedding, partitions and other materials used in preparing cars for shipment.	(1) With deductions from proceeds from sales of live stock to cover any expense incurred in preparing cars for shipment, including local feed, bedding, partitions, rope, nails, etc.

The local car expense account will balance provided the deductions from returns exactly equal the expenses incurred in preparing cars for shipment. It happens sometimes, however, that supplies, such as feed, bedding, or lumber for partitions, are bought in quantities and charged against the shipments for which they are used. In such cases, the " payments " (debits) at a given time will exceed the " deductions " (credits) and the balance will represent the value of unused supplies on hand.

UNDIVIDED BALANCE.

Debit:	Credit:
(1) With losses on shipments when more is distributed than the actual balance available for distribution.	(1) With gains on shipments when less is distributed than the actual balance available for distribution.

Much time is often wasted in attempting to distribute returns to the cent. In calculating the shrinkage and expenses it is much more practicable to use rates figured to the nearest whole number or convenient fraction. Furthermore, when carloads of mixed grades are sold for a flat sum, it is necessary to "price the car up and down" according to grades when making returns to members. In all of the above cases the amount prorated may differ slightly from the actual returns. The difference is to be carried in the undivided balance account. Some of the older associations have adopted a flat rate of expense based on past experience which is applied on all shipments of a given species of livestock over a considerable period. In such cases gains, or losses occurring on individual shipments will also be entered in this account. At the end of the year the net balance should be closed to loss and gain or otherwise disposed of as decided by the board of directors.

LOSS AND GAIN.

Debit:	Credit:
(1) With general expense, such as postage, stationery, telephone, premium on manager's bond, interest paid, taxes and similar items.	(1) With deductions from proceeds from shipments of live stock to cover overhead expenses.
(2) With losses suffered in handling supplies or buying live stock.	(2) With membership fees.[6]
(3) With the balance in the undivided balance account at the end of the year when the overpayments exceed the underpayments.	(3) With extra charges made for handling stock for nonmembers.
(4) With the net gain at the end of the fiscal year when it is distributed in accordance with board action.	(4) With profits resulting from handling supplies or buying live stock.
	(5) With the balance in the undivided balance account at the end of the year when the underpayments exceed the overpayments.
	(6) With net loss at the end of the fiscal year when it is transferred to the net worth account.

The expenses of the ordinary shipping association fall into two classes, namely: Expenses incurred in preparing cars for shipment, which are not borne by the association but charged to the shippers and deducted from their returns; and, expenses which are not chargeable against any particular carload, that is, the overhead expenses, such as telephone, stationery and printing, advertising, interest on borrowed money, premium on manager's bond, and similar items. All such overhead expenses and any other items not charged to shippers and deducted from returns should be entered under " general expense " in the loss and gain account. The income from which such expenses are met will be entered under "income" in this account. This income will usually consist of membership dues,[7] in some cases supplemented by a special charge against shipments for this purpose. At the end of the fiscal year, after the necessary adjustments have been made, the loss and gain account will show either a net gain or a net loss, which should then be carried to the net worth account, or otherwise distributed as decided by the board of directors.

[6] See note on page 11.
[7] If the law under which the association is incorporated regards membership fees as capital contributions the same as capital stock, the amounts so collected should be credited to the net worth account as they represent the members' equity in the business. The same procedure should be followed even though the association is not incorporated, when more than a nominal fee is collected for the purpose of purchasing and installing scales, equipping yards or for other similar purposes.

NET WORTH.

Debit:	Credit:
(1) With the excess of liabilities over assets at the time of opening the books.	(1) With the par value of shares of stock outstanding at the time of opening the books.
(2) With the par value of shares of stock retired, or memberships redeemed where such memberships are redeemable.	(2) With the excess of assets over liabilities at the time of opening the books.
(3) With the net loss transferred from the loss and gain account at the end of the fiscal year.	(3) With the par value of additional shares of stock sold.
	(4) With the membership fees paid in, in case of associations incorporated under laws which hold memberships redeemable.
	(5) With net profits transferred from the loss and gain account at the end of the year.

It seldom occurs that the total resources of a concern exactly equal the total liabilities. If the resources at the time of opening the books exceed the liabilities, a free surplus exists. This balance represents the proprietors' (members' or stockholders') equity or interest in the business and will be entered on the credit side of the net worth account. Sales of shares of capital stock, if any, will also be entered in this column. However, if the liabilities or debts exceed the resources, the balance will represent the amount by which the association is unable to meet its obligations 100 cents on the dollar. The balance in this case will be entered in the debit column. At the end of the fiscal year the stockholders' or members' equity will be increased or decreased by the amount of the net gain or net loss shown by the loss and gain account.

In addition to the above, the following accounts are frequently needed.

FEDERATION DUES.

Debit:	Credit:
(1) With payments of current dues to State or district federation on account of membership in such federations.	(1) With deductions from proceeds of the sale of live stock for federation dues.

Associations which are members of a State or district federation of shipping associations, whose membership fees are collected out of the proceeds of shipments, will need a federation dues account. Any excess of the total collected over the amount paid out will represent the amount due the federation at any given time.

YARD AND OFFICE EQUIPMENT.

Debit:	Credit:
(1) With the value of equipment at the time of opening the books.	(1) With cost value of property sold or otherwise disposed of.
(2) With the purchase price of additional equipment bought.	(2) With estimated depreciation at the end of the fiscal year.
(3) With the freight and installation costs of equipment.	

Space is provided for two additional accounts. Associations which have invested money in yard and office equipment should use one pair of these columns for keeping track of such property.

INDEBTEDNESS.

Debit:	Credit:
(1) With payments made in settlement of outstanding obligations.	(1) With the amount of outstanding obligations at the time of opening the books.
	(2) With subsequent obligations incurred because of money borrowed or supplies purchased on account.

Where indebtedness is incurred an account should be opened with indebtedness or accounts payable, which will be credited with any obligation incurred and debited when it is paid.

MERCHANDISE.

Debit:	Credit:
(1) With the invoice price of supplies bought.	(1) With amounts received for supplies whether collected in advance or on delivery of supplies.
(2) With freight and other direct handling charges, such as extra labor, etc.	

If supplies of any kind are handled, an account should be opened with merchandise, which will be debited with the purchase price, freight, and any other direct costs incidental to the handling of such merchandise. The account will be credited with sales. When all of the merchandise has been sold the account will show either a gain or a loss, which should be transferred to the profit and loss account or prorated back to members at the end of the year.

If a larger number of accounts is needed than space is provided for in the cash journal, a short sheet providing space for six to eight accounts may be inserted between the left-hand and the right-hand pages of the journal. However, where the number of accounts needed is relatively large, a ledger should be used and the form of the cash journal modified accordingly.

ADVANCES TO SHIPPERS.

Some associations regularly make advances to shippers, if requested, at the time of the delivery of live stock. Where this is done, one of the blank pairs of columns in the cash journal should be headed " advances." All advance checks should be recorded in the cash journal as all other checks are recorded, and the amounts charged to the advances account. Deductions for advances will then be made on the prorating sheet, the amount being entered, with an appropriate notation, in the membership column. The advances deducted in making settlement will appear as one of the deductions on the credit side of the home statement on the shipment record envelope. The advances account will be credited when the entry for the settlement is made in the cash journal. As advances do not affect the value of live stock or the expenses of shipping, no record of the advances need be made in the shipment summary record.

SALES SUBJECT TO INSPECTION.

Separate returns are usually rendered to cover animals sold subject to inspection, even though the terminal weight of such animals has been included in determining the expense rate on the remainder of the shipment. A separate prorating sheet should be filled out when the returns for such animals are received, and a separate entry made in the cash journal simialr to that made for regular settlements. All the papers concerned in such sales should be pinned together and filed in the envelope with the other papers for the shipment.

When animals sold subject to inspection are condemned it sometimes happens that their tankage value does not cover the expenses. In such cases, the shipper owes the association the difference. As no debit will consequently appear in the live-stock account, when the cash journal entry is made the advances account should be debited for the amount due from the shipper when, such amounts are collected either in cash or by deduction from a subsequent shipment, the advances account will be credited.

THE NEED OF PERMANENT RECORDS.

Even when ordinary care is taken to file and preserve the papers containing information regarding the business transacted, it seems to be the general experience that sooner or later many or all of the papers are mislaid or destroyed. Unless the data they contain have been recorded in permanent book form, the association is unable to show what business has been done in the past or to verify the details of transactions.

RECORDS AS A PROTECTION TO MANAGERS, DIRECTORS, AND OTHERS.

Embarrassing situations traceable to this lack of records develop frequently. In a recent instance a question arose as to whether or not the funds of the association had been properly accounted for. Neither the secretary nor the manager had preserved a permanent record of the shipments made or other business done. As a result the association was unable to prove that the funds had not been properly accounted for, and the manager was unable to prove that he was free from blame. The fact that it was the practice to "check out" each shipment completely did not save the situation. Many an honest manager or officer has found himself in an exceedingly embarrassing position because of his failure to keep the few books needed to enable him to prove conclusively that his record is clear. Fidelity insurance companies usually require that proper records be kept as a condition to bonding officials responsible for the funds of an association.

In view of the responsibility which rests upon the manager and the board of directors in such matters, they should, for their mutual protection, insist that a complete, permanent record be made of all business transacted, that this record be kept in the same manner from year to year, irrespective of changes in the management. Furthermore, all accounts of sales and other details supporting records and working sheets should be preserved so as to make possible a verification of the entries made in the shipment summary record and the cash journal. Only when kept in this way will the records adequately serve as a protection to the manager, the directors, and the members, and be a reliable guide in determining business policies.

RECORDS AS A GUIDE TO MANAGEMENT.

Mismanagement is one of the most frequent causes of failures in business generally. The remedy for a large number of the cases of mismanagement is to substitute facts for guesswork in the determination of business policies. The judicious use of the figures covering the business from the time the association is organized eliminates much of the guesswork. For this purpose summaries are needed showing the values, numbers, weights, shrinkage, itemized expenses, losses, and other information resulting from the sale of live stock. These data are also needed in calculating averages which throw light on the relative economy of different methods of handling stock, the relative advantages or disadvantages of shipping to different markets, and in directing the attention of the management to variations in the rates of expenses, losses and shrinkage, with a view to ascertaining the causes of such variations and reducing these costs to a minimum. Each manager believes he is doing the best that can be done, until he learns that others have obtained better results than he. If all managers kept the essential figures in a uniform manner it would be a s.m pl er matter to compare notes and ascertain "how it was done."[1]

The relatively small amount of time required to keep these records will be found to have been well spent when information is desired regarding the results of operations. The time required in the preparation of the annual report can be reduced to the few moments needed in copying the desired totals from the records.

The value of these figures for publicity purposes is frequently overlooked. Many associations obtain valuable publicity by submitting their monthly and annual reports to the local papers to the county agents, to federations of cooperative live-stock shippers and by mailing mimeographed copies to the members.

MONTHLY AND ANNUAL REPORTS.

Illustrations of the different schedules which a satisfactory report should include will be found on the following pages. These schedules consist of the following:

A. Financial statements.
    1. Statement of resources and liabilities.
    2. Statement of income and expenses.
B. Statement of results of shipping.
    1. Volume and value of live stock handled.
    2. Analysis of expenses and deductions.
    3. Analysis of shrinkage.
    4. Analysis of losses.
C. Report of money handled.
    1. Cash receipts and disbursements.
    2. Bank reconciliation.
    3. Analysis of undivided balance account.
    4. Analysis of insurance fund account.

ANNUAL REPORT OF THE BROOKRIDGE COOPERATIVE SHIPPING ASSOCIATION FOR THE FISCAL YEAR ENDING DECEMBER 31, 1921.

A. FINANCIAL STATEMENTS.

A 1.—*Statement of resources and liabilities.*

Resources.			Liabilities.	
Cash in bank		$19.62	Notes payable	$200.00
Prepared expenses (feed)		17.50	Insurance fund	500.00
Equipment	$1,255			
Less depreciation	50			700.00
		1,205.00	*Net worth.*	
		1,242.12	Capital stock paid in	395.00
			Surplus beginning of year	$000.00
			Net profits this year	147.12
			Total surplus	147.12
				1,242.12

A 2.—*Statement of income and expenses.*

Net proceeds received for live stock		$192,478.56
Railroad claims collected, gross		1,016.21
Total		193,494.77
Net amount paid shippers for undamaged stock	$188,230.46	
Losses paid	1,287.90	
Total paid shippers	189,518.36	
Add increase carried forward in insurance fund held for benefit of shippers	500.00	
Total accruing to shippers		190,018.36
Balance available for expenses		3,476.41
Add cash membership fees received		40.00
Total gross income		3,516.41

Expenses.

Manager's commission		$2,339.40
Local car expenses		646.89
Attorney's fees		203.50
State federation dues		62.50
Total		3,252.29
Premium on manager's bond	$37.50	
Interest	16.00	
Depreciation	50.00	
Printing and stationery	9.00	
Telephone	2.50	
Miscellaneous	2.00	117.00
Total for all expenses		3,369.29
Net profit carried to surplus		147.12

B. STATEMENT OF RESULTS OF SHIPPING.

B 1.—*Volume and value of live stock handled.*

Kind of live stock.	Number of carloads.		Number of head.	
	This year.	Last year.	This year.	Last year.
Hogs	120	92	8,815	6,610
Cattle	3	7	123	288
Mixed	2	5		
Total	125	104		

	Hogs.	Cattle.
Gross sales value	$201,973.21	$4,792.21
Added out of insurance fund	1,287.90	
Total	203,261.11	4,792.21
Total expenses and deductions	17,833.13	701.83
Paid shippers [8]	185,427.98	4,090.38

[8] Home net value less gain in undivided balance plus insurance paid.

B 2.—*Analysis of expenses and deductions.*

	Hogs.		Cattle.
Freight, switching, war tax	$9,429.16		$390.16
Feed	971.73		28.50
Yardage	1,055.88		39.68
Selling commission	2,239.57		99.03
Inspection and insurance	32.80		.35
Total freight and terminal expenses	13,729.14		557.72
Manager's commission	2,248.95		90.45
Deducted for insurance	1,133.89		38.12
Local car expense	634.01		12.88
State federation dues	60.61		1.89
Membership fees deducted	20.00		
Undivided balance:			
Gains	$17.35	1.47	
Losses	10.82	6.53	.70	.77
Total home deductions	4,103.99		144.11
Total all expenses and deductions	17,833.13		701.83

B 3.—*Analysis of shrinkage.*

	Hogs.	Cattle.
Home weight _____pounds	2,290,951	95,880
Market weight _____do	2,271,439	93,620
Shrinkage _____do	19,512	2,260
Shrinkage, per 100 pounds _____do	0.852	2.4
Average value of shrinkage, per 100 pounds, market weight, cents	[1]7.034	[1]10.6

B 4.—*Analysis of losses.*

Number of dead	106
Number of cripples	142
Total damaged	248
Losses paid	$1,287.90
Claims collected, gross	$1,016.21
Less collection fees	203.50
Net amount of claims collected	812.71
Net losses	475.19
Net losses, per 100 pounds market weight, cents	2.09
Net losses of sales value, per cent	0.235

C. REPORT OF MONEYS HANDLED.

C 1.—*Cash receipts and disbursements.*

Receipts.

Cash balance Jan. 1, 1921		
Received for live stock:		
Hogs	$188,244.07	
Cattle	4,234.49	
Total		$192,478.56
Capital stock sold		400.00
Membership fees, cash		40.00
Borrowed at bank		400.00
Claims collected		1,016.21
Total receipts		$194,334.77

[1] For method of calculation, see footnote on p. 39.

Disbursements.

Net value of live stock:
Hogs		$184,166.61
Cattle		4,091.15
Total		188,257.76

Less:
Membership fees	$20.00	
Undivided balance	7.30	27.30

Paid shippers for undamaged live stock	188,230.46
Losses paid	1,287.90

Total paid shippers	$189,518.36
Scales and scale house	1,000.00
Adding machine	250.00
Account book	5.00
Manager's commission	2,339.40
Feed, bedding, etc.	664.39
Attorney's fees, collecting claims	203.50
State federation dues	62.50
Paid for certificate of capital stock	5.00
Paid note at State bank	200.00
Premium on manager's bond	37.50
Printing and stationery	9.00
Interest	16.00
Telephone	2.50
Miscellaneous expenses	2.00

Total disbursements	$194,315.15
Balance	19.62

C 2.—*Bank reconciliation.*

Balance as per bank statement		$102.12

Less outstanding checks as follows:
No. 107	$20.00	
No. 115	62.50	82.50
Balance on our books		19.62

C 3.—*Analysis of undivided balance.*

Balance Jan. 1, 1921		$000.00
Gains on shipments, 1921	$18.71	
Losses on shipments, 1921	11.41	
Excess on gains over losses	7.30	
Transferred to loss and gain	7.30	
Carried forward		000.00

C 4.—*Analysis of insurance fund account.*

Balance Jan. 1, 1921		$000.00

Deducted during 1921:
Hogs	$1,133.89	
Cattle	38.12	
Total deducted	1,172.01	
Add claims collected	1,016.21	
Total credits	2,188.22	

Losses paid:
Hogs _____ $1, 287. 90
Cattle _____ 000. 00

Total losses paid_____ 1, 287. 90
Attorney's fees _____ 203. 50

Total debits_____ $1, 491. 40
Credit balance _____ 696. 82
Deduct amount transferred to loss and gain_____ 196. 82

Net increase carried forward_____ $500. 00

Total carried forward_____ 500. 00

ANALYZING THE BUSINESS.

If the information contained in the records and reports is to be utilized to the fullest extent in determining business policies, it must be analyzed and reduced to terms which will serve as measures of efficiency. The most successful association is the one which, first, receives the highest price obtainable for each class' and grade of live stock, and, second, pays the shipper the largest proportion of each dollar of gross sales, considering the services performed.

The analysis presented in Table 1 is based on the actual results obtained by three Iowa shipping associations in shipping hogs in 1921. It will be noted that even these associations, selected at random from the same territory, show wide differences in expenses, shrinkage, and losses. The extent to which these differences are justified must be determined by the management of each association in the light of its local conditions and other factors. It is not the purpose here to attempt to explain these differences, but rather to emphasize the fact that only by keeping adequate records and analyzing the results will the leaks in the marketing of live stock be revealed and their causes eliminated.

TABLE 1.—*Comparison of the results obtained by three Iowa associations in shipping, 1921.*

	Association A.	Association B.	Association C.
Numbers of straight carloads shipped.....................	120	140	144
Markets to which shipped................................	X	X & Y	X & Z
	Cents per 100 lbs.[1]	Cents per 100 lbs.[1]	Cents per 100 lbs.[1]
Freight, switching, war tax..............................	41. 5	34. 0	38. 5
Feed..	4. 3	2. 6	3. 1
Yardage...	4. 6	2. 7	3. 8
Selling commission......................................	9. 9	7. 4	8. 8
Insurance, inspection...................................	0. 1	0. 1	0. 1
Total freight and terminal expenses..................	60. 4	46. 8	54. 3
Manager's commission...................................	9. 9	6. 8	5. 7
Local car expense.......................................	2. 8	1. 9	2. 3
Insurance charge..	5. 0	6. 0	5. 0
Federation dues...	0. 3	0. 3	0. 3
Undivided balance and membership fees..................	0. 1	0. 2	0. 0
Total home expenses and deductions..................	18. 1	15. 2	13. 3
Total all expenses and deductions...................	78. 5	62. 0	67. 6
Less undivided balance, insurance fund balance, and membership fees....................................	3. 0	2. 9	0. 3
Net shipping expenses..............................	75. 5	59. 1	67. 3

[1] Based on market weight.

TABLE 1.—*Comparison of the results obtained by three Iowa shipping associations in shipping, 1921*—Continued.

	Association A.	Association B.	Association C.
	Cents per 100 lbs.	*Cents per 100 lbs.*	*Cents per 100 lbs.*
Cost of shrinkage [2]	7.03	9.75	12.25
Total of net expense and cost of shrinkage	82.53	68.85	79.55
General expenses, not included in above	0.5	0.70	0.30
Insurance fund charge	5.0	6.0	5.0
Losses paid	5.7	5.7	2.0
Claims collected, net	3.6	2.1	0.0
Net losses	2.1	3.6	2.0
Per cent of gross sales value paid shippers	91.8	94.2	93.0
Average price paid shippers per 100 pounds, dollars	8.16	8.48	9.10

[2] Calculated as follows, i. e., for hogs:

Paid shippers for hogs (Statement B 1)	$185,427.98
Add excess of insurance fund charge over losses paid, including net amount of claims collected	658.70
Add undivided balance—gain	6.53
Total	186,093.21
Deduct proportionate share of general expenses not deducted in determining amount paid shippers above	112.32
Net value of hogs	185,980.89

$185,980.89÷2,271,439 (market weight)=8.188¢=net value of hogs per lb.; 19,512 pounds of shrinkage, at 8.188¢=$1,597.64=Total cost of shrinkage; $1,597.64÷2,271,439 (market weight)=7.034¢=Cost of shrinkage per 100 lbs.

WHO SHOULD KEEP THE BOOKS?

The question frequently arises as to whether the manager or one of the officers should keep the records. Although local conditions will to a considerable extent decide this question in each case, it will ordinarily be found more convenient and satisfactory if the books are kept at the place of business or some other place where they are accessible to the members and the management. Inasmuch as practically all the business contacts with members and others are made by the manager, he is most frequently called upon to answer questions regarding the business, and, therefore, has occasion most frequently to refer to the books. Furthermore, the manager of the association is in a position of leadership, and the directors and members look to him to take the initiative in determining the business policies. Unless he has the figures regarding the business conveniently available for constant reference and analysis, he is in very much the same position as the pilot without a compass

It is not, of course, always possible in practice to make ideal arrangements regarding the clerical work. In fact, the manager who understands the handling and marketing of live stock and who is also qualified or adapted to do clerical work is the exception rather than the rule. The disbursement of the funds and the bookkeeping is therefore frequently done by some other officer of the association, usually the secretary, or the local bank. In some cases, the manager attends to the prorating and issues the checks for live stock and the secretary-treasurer issues the checks for the home expenses. The chief disadvantage of the latter plan is that all of the records are seldom, if ever, available at one place or at one time.

The prime considerations to be kept in mind are: (1) Safeguarding the funds which can be accomplished by bonding those responsible for the funds, by monthly audits by an auditing committee, and annual audits by a qualified, disinterested accountant; (2) having all of the records accessible at one place, preferably at the place of business, or at the bank; (3) having the records kept up to date and according to approved methods. If neither the manager nor the secretary is qualified to do the clerical work some one who is qualified can usually be induced to assume this responsibility. Economy in the matter of keeping the records is usually dearly bought.

Whether the manager or the secretary keeps the books, or whether the work is delegated to hired help, it is highly desirable that both the manager and one or more members of the board of directors possess a sufficient knowledge of accounting so that they can intelligently judge the results obtained and the method of obtaining them, and can supervise the work when delegated to hired help.

MARKETING METHODS.

The foregoing discussion of forms, accounts, and procedure is based on certain conclusions reached after an extensive study of cooperative live stock marketing methods. In view of the many different methods used in handling the business at home as well as at the markets, this discussion of records and accounts would be incomplete unless supplemented by an analysis of the business practices. Moreover, only by free and thorough discussions of the different methods used will real progress be made in standardizing the practices and in eliminating those methods which are unsound and uneconomical.

TERMINAL MARKET METHODS.

The chief objective of the cooperative live stock shipping movement is to obtain for the shipper the actual market value of his particular kind and quality of live stock, less the actual cost of marketing it. The extent to which this ideal will be realized depends upon the prevailing methods of selling and weighing the live stock at the central markets and handling it at home, and upon the methods used in prorating. A clear understanding of the methods of handling the live stock at the terminal markets is necessary if real progress is to be made in realizing this ideal.

The prevailing method of handling hogs seems to be to sell and weigh by grades and to prorate the shrinkage either on the entire load or separately on the bulk of the load and on the throwouts and packers. On some markets a considerable number of hogs are sold as straight carloads, the salesman pricing the animals in each individual lot on their merits and prorating the shrinkage either on the entire load or separately on the bulk of the load and on the throwouts. Less frequently loads are sold according to marks, unless it happens that given lots fall into specific grades which are sold to different buyers. In such cases the shrinkage is ascertainable separately for each lot and may be charged to the individual owners as it actually occurs.

Much the same methods are used in handling calves and sheep, except that selling and weighing by grades prevail to a greater extent than in the case of hogs. The grading frequently consists merely of culling out the off grades and selling the bulk of the load as a separate lot.

Cattle are generally sold and weighed by ownership, each owner being charged with the actual shrinkage on his animals. However, when the cattle in a load run fairly uniform as to grade and quality, they may be sold as one lot. Even in such cases individual weights are usually obtained.

The same methods do not predominate to the same degree on all the markets. The practice of selling and weighing by grades prevails to a greater extent on some markets than on others, depending partly on custom, the adequacy of the handling facilities, the practices of packer, order and other buyers, the volume of cooperative shipments, and partly on the custom and attitude of the salesmen of commission firms. Whether or not a market is receiving shipments from territory in which cooperative shipping is of recent origin also has its influence. It may be said, however, that on all markets the commission firms which solicit cooperative shipments (and most of them now do so) attempt in so far as it is possible to carry out the instructions of the managers with respect to selling, weighing, and prorating.

Naturally the manager of a shipping association is vitally concerned in having the live stock handled in such a way as to net the shipper the largest possible return. In order that the manager may attain this end what shall be his instructions to the commission firm regarding methods of weighing and selling? The following discussion of the relative merits of the different methods should aid him in deciding this question in the light of the conditions under which he is operating.

The question seems to resolve itself into three main problems: (1) Selling the live stock so as to obtain the largest gross amount possible; (2) weighing so as to reduce the shrinkage to the minimum; (3) selling and weighing in such a way as to make possible a fair division of the total returns and the shrinkage among the different shippers.

SELLING METHODS.

Selling each owner's live stock separately is usually impracticable, except in the case of cattle. More time and labor is required to handle a load under this method and it is more difficult to find buyers who are willing to take the time and trouble to make their purchases piecemeal. More sorting is required, resulting in more shrinkage, and the number of drafts on the scales is increased. The net return is more likely than not to be disappointing to the shippers.

The chief advantage claimed by many shippers for this method is that it materially reduces the shrinkage, but it is doubtful if this is the case. The chief objection is that when the animals are not of uniform grade and quality, the pricing of the load according to grades is based on the salesman's opinion rather than on actual sales which, unless arrived at conscientiously, may result in an unfair distribution of the returns among the shippers. This objection can, however, be overcome to a considerable extent, if not entirely, by home grading by a competent manager.

The main disadvantages of selling by ownership might be avoided by selling the carload as a unit for a flat sum. Some salesmen maintain that more can usually be obtained for a straight carload than for a load which is divided into several lots according to ownership.

It is reasonable that buyers prefer to buy in larger units than the individual lots of live stock in a typical cooperative shipment. It is even claimed that it is often possible to " work off ", inferior animals to better advantage by this method than by grading the load; in other words, to "make the good hogs sell the poor ones." The extent to which careful buyers can be imposed upon to this extent is a question.

Selling according to quality or grade predominates on many of the important markets and is without doubt the most desirable method, especially where the animals in the load represent a considerable range in quality and where the spread in the market price for the different grades is wide. Each shipper's animals then actually sell on their merits, as nearly as this ideal can practically be approached. Excessive shrinkage is avoided, and buyers, not being compelled to take undesirable animals in order to get the desirable ones, are inclined to bid more nearly what each grade is actually worth. More than this, no manager can hope to obtain for his shippers. Where a shipping association has a sufficient volume of business, this sorting can be done at the shipping point and only animals of one grade loaded in a car.

WEIGHING.

The methods used in weighing the animals are of at least as much concern to the manager of a shipping association as the methods of selling. He is concerned not only in keeping the shrinkage down to the minimum, but also in dividing the total shrinkage on a fair basis among the different shippers.

As each group of animals sold at a given price must be weighed separately, it follows that the method of sale determines to a large extent the method of weighing. The weighing problem resolves itself into the question of the merits of dividing shrinkage according to ownership or of prorating it uniformly on some fair basis.

Weighing by marks.—The advantage claimed for the method of weighing by marks is that the actual shrinkage incurred on each lot can be definitely ascertained and charged to the individual shipper. This is always desirable in the case of cattle, as the shrinkage differs widely on account of the wide differences in the quality and condition of the animals and on account of different methods of feeding and handling the cattle. These differences are of less significance in the case of calves. Wide differences often occur in the shrinkage of different lots of hogs and sheep. Hogs or sheep coming from green pastures will shrink more than those coming from the feed lot. Animals driven or hauled different distances to the shipping point often show considerable differences in shrinkage. One of the problems of the manager is to single out the shipper who feeds heavily before delivering his live stock. Weighing by ownership is the most effective method of doing this. Managers frequently request separate weights only on lots which they suspect have been filled before delivery.

The chief disadvantage of weighing by marks is that excessive shrinkage usually results. Extra shrinkage resulting from weighing according to marks has been reported as high as several hundred pounds in some cases. Naturally this difference will vary with the number of lots in the load. This difference in shrinkage is due to loss of fill, respiration, and to the fact that yard scales usually register weights in 10-pound intervals. Another objection which is made to this method of weighing is that more facilities and labor are required at the yards, which eventually must be reflected in higher yardage and commission rates. The premium often paid by order buyers, who are usually eager to get their cars loaded promptly for shipment east, is sometimes lost to cooperative shippers because of the delay occasioned by weighing by marks. Altogether, this method of weighing does not make for economy in live-stock marketing.

Weighing by grades.—The disadvantages of weighing by marks may be avoided by weighing by grades. When separate weights are requested on lots which the manager suspects have been filled and when shippers have learned how to handle live stock properly before delivering it at the shipping point, weighing by grades will make possible as nearly correct a distribution of shrinkage as it seems practicable to make.

GRADING AND PRORATING AT HOME.

On most markets, an extra charge of $2 to $6 per carload is made when extra work on account of individual ownership is required. Some of the local packing plants and reload stations, particularly in the Middle West, refuse to handle shipments when such extra work is involved, thus practically closing such markets to cooperative association. This raises the question of the practicability of grading and prorating at home. There is a marked tendency among the older associations to perform this service at home. In some cases, where a local market is the only advantageous outlet for a shipping association, this work has been done by the manager from the beginning.

Successful grading at the shipping point requires that the manager be familiar with market grades and keep closely in touch with market conditions. It also requires that there be a fair volume of business. The manager could, of course, remove the basis for the extra charge and such objections as might be made to handling cooperative shipments because of the extra service required, by crediting each shipper with the weight of each grade of live stock delivered and distributing the returns on the basis of his grading. This he could do whether the shipment consisted of one car or several. However, a further advantage, and perhaps a more important one, is to be gained when the volume of business is such that the live stock may be sorted and shipped to market as straight carloads of uniform grades. Not only is the work involved in handling reduced to the minimum, but the stock is placed before the buyers to the best advantage.

In practice, only two things are necessary for the successful working of such a system, viz, a capable and impartial manager, and members who are true cooperators. This last requirement means that (1) the shippers shall ship regularly through the association, so that any slight error in sorting would average out over a series of shipments; (2) that they shall have the cooperative point of view, so that they will be ready to accept that method of doing business which results in greatest economy and best results for all; and (3) all shippers must be so loyal to the organization and their fellow members that they will give their stock proper treatment prior to shipment, rather than stuffing, salting, or using other devices for securing a fraudulent home weight or an excessive fill at the market.[9]

The question of prorating at home presents somewhat the same problems as grading. No doubt commission firms in most cases are better equipped than the shipping associations to do this work. On the other hand, inasmuch as the alert manager insists on checking the work anyway, he can with but little extra effort make the original calculations. Too frequently, because of the dependence upon the commission firm to do this work, the local management is unaware of the methods used or the problems involved. A critical knowledge of these methods and problems is essential to progress in realizing the ideal of the shipping association, namely, to obtain for each shipper what his live stock is actually worth less the cost of marketing it.

Conditions are gradually becoming more favorable for grading and prorating at home. Managers and officers are acquiring experience, and the development of the local association in many States seems to be in the direction of consolidating the business under fewer and better qualified managers. The work of prorating would be greatly facilitated by the adoption of a uniform system of records and the use of labor-saving devices, such as calculating machnes, computation tables, and suitable printed working forms and permanent records.

PROBLEMS INVOLVED IN PRORATING.

Much of the success of a shipping association depends upon whether the shrinkage and expenses are charged and the returns distributed fairly among the different shippers. Prorating, or the calculation of the returns due the individual shippers, is therefore one of the most important operations to be performed in the management of a shipping association.

Prorating involves the following problems: (1) Distributing shrinkage; (2) distributing the gross amount among the different grades of live stock when a carload of mixed grades is sold for a lump sum; (3) dividing the expense among the different kinds of stock in a mixed car; (4) prorating when a shipment consists of more than one car; (5) distributing the total expenses among the individual shippers according to the live stock shipped by each.

Distributing shrinkage.—The usual practice in distributing shrinkage is to charge cattle with their indivdual shrinkage, which of course, necessitates obtaining individual weights at home as well as at the market. In the case of hogs, calves, and sheep, however, the usual practice is to prorate the total shrinkage on some uniform basis, preferably so much per 100 pounds.

Shrinkage is sometimes prorated on the head basis, which method is equitable only when the animals included are of approximately uniform size and weight. When the shrinkage differs for different grades of animals, as, for instance, between good butcher hogs and packers, the rate for each grade showing a marked difference should be calculated separately. As already noted in the foregoing, any lots of animals which may unduly influence the average shrinkage

---

[9] Cooperative Live Stock Shipping in Iowa in 1920, by E. G. Nourse and C. W. Hammans, Iowa Agr. Exp. Sta. Bul. No. 200.

should be weighed separately at the market and the owners charged with the actual shrinkage.

Distributing flat sum among different grades in carload.—Where a carload of hogs of mixed grades is sold for a flat sum, the commission firm usually indicates on the account sales the market value of the different animals in the shipment. Where hogs, calves, or sheep are graded locally the proceeds are distributed on the basis of the market quotations prevailing on the day of sale for the different grades.

Dividing the expenses when mixed loads are shipped.—The question of mixed loads is of more importance in some localities than in others. However, nearly all associations ship some mixed loads. Much difference of opinion prevails as to the method to be used in dividing the different items of expense between the species. It is urged by some, for instance, that the extra freight should be charged to the hogs, and by others, to the cattle, calves or sheep. Still others urge that the total expenses should be divided equally among the different kinds of stock on the weight basis.

The problem of dividing the expenses centers mainly about the item of freight. Obviously, it is not fair to members shipping 16,000 pounds of hogs in a load to charge them with the freight burden due to the inclusion of 1,000 or 2,000 pounds of cattle. It would be still more unfair to charge the cattle with the extra burden. Even if the freight were divided equally on the weight basis, it would pay the hog shippers much better to ship their 16,000 pounds in a carload by themselves. The weight basis of division seems to be the only practicable basis. When distribution on this basis puts an undue burden on either group of shippers, the only solution is not to load in such unfavorable proportions. By educational work and progressive leadership on the part of the management the community may be made to see the penalty paid for shipping in unfavorable proportions. It should be clear not only to the management of a shipping association but to the membership as well, that an association shipping under excessive freight burdens due to improper mixing is laboring under a considerable handicap, especially when competing with agencies which may take special care to avoid such burdens.

The division of the other items of expense involves no special difficulties. The yardage charge is divided according to the rate per head actually applying on each species. The cost of corn is charged to the hogs and the cost of hay to the cattle. Inspection applies to hogs only. Fire insurance, because of the smallness of the amount, may be arbitrarily charged to the bulk of the load. The selling commission is a per-head charge and should be divided on that basis. For instance in shipment No. 112, on page 41, the rate applying on hogs was assumed to be 30 cents, or $15.60 for the 52 head; and on cattle, 90 cents per head or $4.50 for the 5 head. The total commission at these rates would be $20.10. If, however, $18 is assumed to be the maximum commission applying on a single car, the proportion chargeable to hogs would be as $15.60 is to $20.10, or 77.6 per cent, and the proportion chargeable to cattle would be as $4.50 is to $20.10, or 22.4 per cent.

The manager's commission and the insurance fund charge for shipment No. 112 would be divided as follows: Manager's commission, 6 cents per 100 pounds for hogs and 4 cents per 100 pounds for cattle; insurance one-half of 1 per cent of the gross sales value of each kind of stock. (See p. 41.) The local car expenses usually consist chiefly of feed and bedding. Each species should be charged with the feed it receives, and the bedding may be divided on the basis of the space occupied by each species in the car or on the weight basis. Ropes and special crates for vicious animals should be charged to the owners of the animals requiring their use.

Prorating when shipment consists of more than one car.—When several cars of the same kind of live stock are shipped the same day, should the returns, shrinkage, and expenses be averaged, or should each car be prorated as a separate unit? If 25 farmers deliver 200 head of hogs for shipment, the fact that three cars may be required to transport the hogs is and should be of no concern to them. Each patron is entitled to the same price for the same grade of live stock and should be assessed at the same rate of expense as every other patron whose stock was included in the shipment.

In actual practice, however, the solution is not always so simple. When only one grade of hogs is loaded into each of several cars included in a shipment to one market, the expenses can be averaged for the entire shipment, the shrinkage in the case of the hogs can be calculated separately for the good butcher hogs and the packers, and also for the "throwouts" when their shrink is abnormal. In the case of calves and sheep, the rates of shrinkage should be calculated separately for the bulk of the load and the culls or "throwouts," whenever the rates show a marked difference.

As each car in the above case is assumed to contain but one grade of live stock, each grade can be priced to the shippers in accordance with the actual sales. If two or more cars of the same grade sold for different prices the proceeds should be averaged.

Where the shipment consists of several cars of mixed grades it is clear that all shippers should receive the same price of the same grade of stock, even though the animals were distributed among the several cars and might actually have sold for different prices.

An entirely different situation is presented when part of the shipment goes to one market and another part to another market. In this case the shrinkage and expenses should be calculated separately for the cars going to each market. A question arises, however, as to the distribution of the net proceeds. If the manager has misjudged the relative merits of the different markets, he finds himself in an embarrassing position when attempting to explain to a shipper why his stock brought less than that of a neighbor, whose stock happended to be included in a car shipped to another market which turned out to be the highest one that day. If the stock is graded and each grade shipped to the most advantageous market, it might still happen that the lower grade would bring the same or a higher price than the higher grade, and the manager would have the same difficulty in attempting to explain the inconsistency.

In spite of these difficulties, the manager is presumed to have used his best judgment and to have patronized the market offering the best average results for each class and grade of livestock. Each shipment to a different market should therefore be treated as a separate unit. If dissatisfaction results frequently, it means that the manager misjudges frequently. A thorough knowledge of the different markets, the relative costs of shipping, to them, and other factors concerned are essential on the part of the management if the greatest possible success is to be achieved. Some managers shift the responsibility for the choice of markets to the shippers themselves or to the shipper who owns the bulk of the load.

Distributing the total expenses among the shippers.—Little uniformity exists in the methods used in distributing the expenses among the shippers. This is true whether the prorating is done at home or by the sales agency. In the case of some of the older associations, particularly in the Northwest and in some of the Corn-Belt States, all of the expenses are added together and charged to the shipper at so much per 100 pounds. In other cases the attempt of the cooperator to obtain the actual market value of his stock less the actual expenses of marketing, seems to have been interpreted as meaning that the member's statement must show in dollars and cents how much he has contributed toward each of the six to a dozen different items of expense, calculated on two or three different bases. Between these two methods there exists a wide range of variations.

Under the method of prorating illustrated in the following pages all expenses are added together, irrespective of the basis on which charge was made against the shipment as a whole, and divided among the shippers equally on the weight basis. The advantages of this method are:

(1) The work involved in prorating is reduced to the minimum, as only one calculation is necessary in determining the amount of expenses to be charged each shipper, compared with the large number of calculations involved in the detailed method of prorating. The extra work involved in prorating is reflected in the extra charge of $2 to $6 per car made by commission firms for handling cooperative shipments.

(2) The distribution of expenses among the shippers is as fair on the average as is practically possible. Inasmuch as each 100 pounds of livestock in a shipment receives practically the same service, it seems logical to distribute the expenses on the weight basis.[10] Efficiency in marketing calls for handling the shipment in such a manner as will yield the highest possible net price per 100 pounds for the entire shipment, rather than striving for individual accounting of each shipper's stock at any cost.

(3) The single-rate method of prorating conveys to the shipper in an emphatic manner the factors which determine the financial results of the shipment, i. e., the weight and shrinkage, the selling price, the total expenses in dollars and cents, and the rate per 100 pounds. It is believed the educational benefits of cooperative shipping can be realized more fully by presenting the detailed information regarding expenses, etc., in the form of comparatively monthly summaries than by presenting them on the individual member's statement. Variations in expenses, losses, and shrinkage can be explained more satisfactorily when based on more extensive data than a single shipment affords

---

[10] It is sometimes urged that it is only fair that the expenses should be passed on to the shipper on the same basis as they were actually incurred. Carried out to its logical conclusion, this would necessitate the determination of the amount of feed actually consumed by each lot of live stock separately. It would mean weighing by ownership to determine actual shrinkage by lots. It might even mean that shippers should assume the risk of losses individually.

and the danger of overemphasizing the importance of minor details or drawing conclusions from an extreme instance is reduced.

Whether the expenses are reduced to one rate per 100 pounds or split up into several rates and applied on different bases, present practice seems to favor having each shipment bear its own expenses. There is some tendency, however, particularly among the older associations, to favor a fixed rate of expense applying over a period of time. The chief argument in favor of this method is that it spreads the risk of variations in expenses over a larger number of cars. The variations in the expenses of different shipments are likely to be greater in the case of small associations than large ones because of the greater difficulty in getting enough live stock to make a full load without excessively delaying shipments. Differences as high as 20 cents per 100 pounds are not uncommon. Certainly it is no fault of the shipper when his live stock happens to be included in a shipment which, because of short weight or for other reasons, incurs relatively high expenses. It seems entirely logical to spread this risk over a number of cars, just as the risk of loss due to dead or crippled animals is spread.

Another argument in favor of this method is that the shipper knows beforehand just what it will cost to ship. Furthermore the work involved in prorating is reduced to the minimum.

If the fixed rate is to be applied fairly, however, it must take into consideration differences in the costs of shipping the different species of live stock both in straight and mixed loads, seasonal differences in costs, and differences in the costs of shipping to the different accessible markets. Many associations apply, even on carlot shipments owned by a single shipper, rates which reflect the difference in the amount of service required in handling them.

FILLING OUT THE PRORATING SHEET.

The steps followed in calculating the returns for shipment No. 111, the prorating sheet for which appears in Figure 3 on page 7, are as follows:

1. Insert shipment number, date, shipping point, car number and railway in the spaces provided therefor.

2. Fill in the blanks under "expenses." The freight and terminal expenses will be obtained from the account sales received from the commission company and in this case amount to $103.63. Assume the home expenses to be as follows:

Manager's commission (6 cents per 100 pounds on market weight, of 15,905 pounds)	$9.54
Insurance fund (one-half of 1 per cent of gross market value of $1,556.36)	7.78
Local car expense (8 bushels corn at 50 cents)	4.00
Dues (State association)	.50
Total	21.82

3. Calculate the rate of expense per 100 pounds by dividing the total expense, $125.45, by the market weight, 15,905 pounds (market weight includes dockage, if any), which gives a result of 78.87 cents per 100 pounds.

To avoid the awkward fraction in figuring the expenses, a rate of 79 cents per 100 pounds is used in calculating each shipper's expenses in this illustration.

4. List each owner's delivery of live stock according to the price ranges on the account sales (or if graded at home, according to the home grades) and insert the home weights.

5. Calculate the rates of shrinkage as follows:

Kind.	Home weight.	Market weight.	Shrinkage.		
			Lbs.	Rate.[1]	Rates used in prorating.
				Per cent.	Per cent.
Butcher hogs	14,180	14,035	145	1.02	1.00
Packer hogs	1,905	1,870	35	1.84	2.00
Total	16,085	15,905	180	1.119	....

[1] The rates of shrinkage are obtained by dividing the shrinkage in pounds by the home weight. In actual practice, shrinkage is frequently computed by using even percentage figures, rather than the actual figures. This practice has been followed in the illustrations in this bulletin (1 per cent instead of 1.02 per cent and 2 per cent instead of 1.84 per cent and, as will usually be the case, has resulted in weights being used on the prorate sheet (Fig. 3) which vary slightly from those on the accounts sales (page 7).

6. Calculate each shipper's shrinkage by multiplying the home weight by the rate determined above for each kind of live stock, and prove the shrinkage calculations by comparing the total shrinkage deducted plus the market weight with the total home weight. Where the shrinkage rate used in prorating has been rounded up or down, the total pounds of shrinkage and the total market weight as shown on the prorating sheet may be a few pounds more or less than the actual shrinkage and market weight.

7. Calculate the gross amount due each shipper, using the prices given on the account sales. In the case of dead or crippled animals, the calculations on the prorating sheet are carried through at the prices such animals would have brought undamaged. Any difference in the prorated market weight and the actual weight due to averaging the shrinkage will also result in a slight discrepancy between the calculated gross sales value and the gross sales value shown on the account sales. The gross sales value obtained on the prorating sheet will also be greater than that shown in the account sales when damaged animals are calculated at the price they would have brought undamaged.

8. Calculate the amount of expenses to be deducted from each shipper's returns by multiplying the market weight by the rate obtained under (3) page 7. Here again the total prorated expenses may differ slightly from the actual expenses on account of rounding the expense rate up or down to facilitate calculation.

9. Ascertain the net amount due each shipper and prove the deduction of expenses by comparing the sum of the expenses and net amount with the gross amount.

10. By carrying out the calculations indicated under "proof of settlement" in the lower left-hand corner of the prorating sheet, the total difference between the prorated results and the actual results of the shipment will be determined. The gross sales value will be found on the account sales. To this will be added insurance payments, if any, to obtain the total to be prorated. The total deductions will consist of the total expenses listed on the left-hand margin of the prorating sheet, plus membership fees, if any. Subtracting the total deductions from the total to be prorated will give the balance for

distribution, that is, the amount which could actually have been distributed had shrinkage been calculated exactly to the pound and ex-

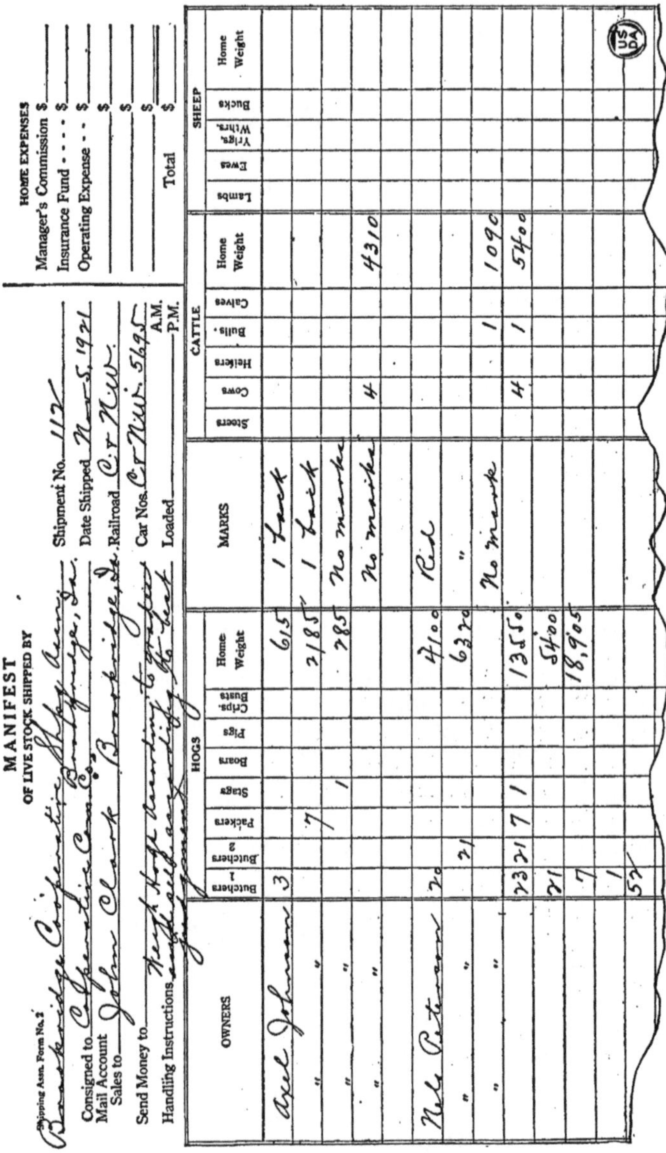

Shipping Assn. Form No. 2

MANIFEST
OF LIVE STOCK SHIPPED BY Brookridge Coöperative Shipping Assn., Ia.

Consigned to Coöperative Com. Co.
Mail Account Sales to John Clark, Brookridge, Ia.
Send Money to
Handling Instructions

Shipment No. 112
Date Shipped Nov. 5, 1921
Railroad C. & N. W.
Car Nos. C. & N. W. 5695
Loaded ___ A.M. P.M.

HOME EXPENSES
Manager's Commission $
Insurance Fund $
Operating Expense $
Total $

OWNERS	Hogs: Butchers 1	Hogs: Butchers 2	Hogs: Packers	Hogs: Stags	Hogs: Boars	Hogs: Pigs	Hogs: Crpls. Busts	Hogs: Home Weight	MARKS	Cattle: Steers	Cattle: Cows	Cattle: Heifers	Cattle: Bulls	Cattle: Calves	Cattle: Home Weight	Sheep: Lambs	Sheep: Ewes	Sheep: Yrlgs. Wthrs.	Sheep: Bucks	Sheep: Home Weight
Axel Johnson	3							615	1 Jack											
" "			7					2185	1 tail											
" "				1				285	No marks											
" "									No marks		4				4310					
Nels Peterson	20							4100	Red											
" "		21						6320	"											
" "									No mark				1		1090					
	23	21	7	1				13550			4		1		5400					
	21							5400												
	7							18,905												
	1																			
	52																			

FIG. 12.—Manifest for shipment No. 112.

penses to the penny. In the illustration it is found that $1,430.03 was actually distributed, whereas $1,430.91 was available for distribution, hence the undistributed balance-gain of 88 cents.

PRORATING MIXED SHIPMENTS.

The prorating of carloads containing more than one kind of live stock is discussed under prorating on page 36. However, in order to illustrate more fully the procedure involved, and assumed carload referred to as shipment No. 112 containing 13,505 pounds of hogs and 5,400 pounds of cattle is carried through the records in the following pages. Other complications such as reimbursement for dead and crippled animals, dockage, and membership deductions, are also introduced into this shipment.

For the purpose of this illustration, it is assumed that the scale tickets show that live stock was delivered as shown in the manifest illustrated in figure 12.

It is assumed that the account sales shown on this page represents the results of the sale of this shipment.

[Account sales for shipment No. 112.]

Cooperative Commission Co., Union Stock Yards, Chicago, November 6, 1922.

Sold for the account of the Brookridge Cooperative Shipping Association, Brookridge, Iowa.

Buyer.	Head.	Kind.	Weight.	Dockage.			Marks.	Price.	Amount.
				Sows.	Stags.	Lbs.			
Swift......	22	Hogs....	4,465				2–1; 20 No. mk....	$10.00	$446.50
Hinkle.....	1	Dead....	200				I 1($10).............	1.00	2.00
Armour....	20	Hogs....	5,940				No mark..........	9.50	564.30
Hinkle......	1	Crip.....	310				1($9.50)...........	7.00	21.70
Swift.......	7	Packers.	2,140	1		40	1.................	8.00	168.00
Cudahy.....	1	Stag....	280		1	70		7.00	14.70
Brennan....	3	Cows....	3,300					6.00	198.00
Do.....	1	Cow.....	930					7.00	65.10
Do.....	1	Bull....	1,050					5.00	52.50
									1,532.80

C. & N W, 5694, 22,000 pounds, @ 40 cents....$88.00	Freight....................$93.64	
Switching................. 3.00	Yardage 52, @ 12 cents; 5, @ 30 cents 7.74	
War tax................. 2.64	Insurance................. .07	
——	Hay, 100 pounds................. .75	
93.64	Corn, 5 bushels................. 6.25	
	Inspection................. .20	
	Commission................. 18.00	
	——	126.65
	Net proceeds................. 1,406.15	

1 Undamaged value per 100 pounds.

In prorating the returns for this shipment, the shrinkage is first ascertained separately for the butcher and the packer hogs as follows:

Kind.	No.	Home weight.	Market weight.	Shrinkage.	
				Lbs.	Per cent.
Butchers.................	44	11,035	10,915	120	1 1.1087
Packers.................	7	2,185	2,140	45	1 2.06

1 The shrinkage in pounds, divided by the home weight gives the rate of shrinkage in pounds per 100 pounds or as a percentage of the home weight.

The rate of 1.1 per cent was actually used in calculating the shrinkage of the butcher hogs, but in the case of the packers 2 per cent was used instead of 2.06 per cent. The stag and the cattle were charged with their actual shrinkage.

The expenses are next divided item by item between the hogs and the cattle. The freight and terminal expenses appear on the account sales and the home expenses are assumed to be as follows:

Manager's commission:
 Hogs, 13.335 pounds, terminal weight, at 6 cents 100 pounds_ $8.00
 Cattle, 5,280 pounds at 4 cents_____ 2.11
                    ———— $10.11
Insurance fund one-half of 1 per cent of gross sales value_____ 7.66
Local car expense_____ 3.50
State federation dues___ _____ .50

  Total_____ 21.77
 Also deduct membership fees $2 (Johnson $1, Peterson $1).

The division of the expenses is shown in the following table. The total expenses are shown in the first column, the amount chargeable to hogs in the second column and to cattle in the third column. The total expense for each species is then determined and the rate per 100 pounds calculated on the basis of the terminal weights.[12]

Expenses.

Expenses.	Total.	Hogs.	Cattle.
Freight, switching, and war tax..	$93.64	$67.42	$26.22
Yardage...	7.74	6.24	1.50
Feed..	7.00	6.25	.75
Insurance inspection..	.27	.20	.07
Selling commission..	18.00	13.97	4.03
Total market expense...	126.65	94.08	32.57
Manager's commission..	10.11	8.00	2.11
Insurance fund..	7.66	6.08	1.58
Operating expenses $3.50, dues $0.50......................................	4.00	2.88	1.12
Total home expenses...	21.77	16.96	4.81
Total expenses..	148.42	111.04	37.38
Rate per 100 pounds...cents..	....	83.28	70.8

To facilitate the calculation of the expenses to be charged each shipper, the rate for hogs was rounded down to 83 cents and for cattle up to 71 cents.

All data needed in prorating are now before us. A separate prorating sheet is used for each kind of live stock, and after the expenses have been transferred to the prorating sheets the calculations are carried out as explained in prorating shipment No. 111.

Referring to the accompanying prorating sheets for shipment No. 112, (See Figs. 13 and 14) it should be noted that in calculating the returns for the hogs, nothing appears on the prorating sheet to indicate that one hog was dead and another crippled. As these hogs were received in good condition they are to be paid for at the price they would have brought undamaged and the difference is to be charged to the insurance fund account. These animals are therefore included with the undamaged animals in carrying out the calculations. The amount of $25.75 appearing opposite "insurance paid" under proof of settlement includes $18, the difference between the $2 which the dead hog actually brought and the $20 it would

---
[12] See discussion of method on p. —._

have brought undamaged at $10 per 100 pounds, according to notations made on the account sales by the commission firm. Similarly the loss on the crippled hog amounts to $7.75, making a total of $25.75 for both hogs.

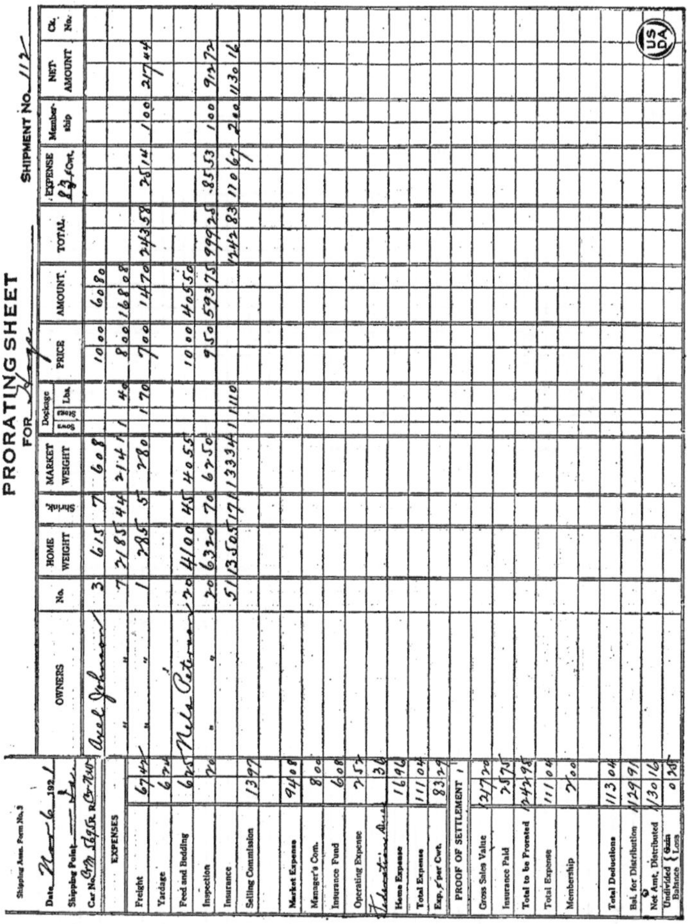
PRORATING SHEET

Shipping Assn. Form No. 3

FOR Hogs SHIPMENT No. 112

Date Nov 6 1921

Shipping Point — Ia.

Car No. C.M. 5695 R.R. C-N.W.

EXPENSES	
Freight	67 42
Yardage	6 74
Feed and Bedding	6 25
Inspection	20
Insurance	
Selling Commission	13 97
Market Expense	94 08
Manager's Com.	8 00
Insurance Fund	6 08
Operating Expense	2 52
Federation Dues	36
Home Expense	16 96
Total Expense	111 04
Exp. ¢ per Cwt.	83 29
PROOF OF SETTLEMENT	
Gross Sales Value	1217 20
Insurance Paid	25 75
Total to be Prorated	1242 95
Total Expense	111 04
Membership	2 00
Total Deductions	113 04
Bal. for Distribution	1129 91
Net Amt. Distributed	1130 16
Undivided Balance { Gain / Loss	0 25

OWNERS	No.	HOME WEIGHT	Shrink.	MARKET WEIGHT	Dockage Sows	Dockage Stags	Dockage Lbs.	PRICE	AMOUNT	TOTAL	EXPENSE 83 ¢ Cwt.	Membership	NET AMOUNT	Ck. No.
Axel Johnson	3	615	7	608				10 00	60 80					
" "	7	2185	44	2141	1		40	8 00	168 08					
" "	1	285	5	280		1	70	7 00	14 70	243 58	25 14	1 00	217 44	
Nels Peterson	20	4100	45	4055				10 00	405 50					
" "	20	6320	70	6250				9 50	593 75	999 25	85 53	1 00	912 72	
	51	13505	171	13334	1	1	110			1242 83	110 67	2 00	1130 16	

FIG. 13.—Prorating sheet for hogs, shipment No. 112.

The items of 25 cents, undivided balance-loss on the prorating sheet for hogs, and the 11 cents, undivided balance-gain on the prorating sheet for cattle, may be analyzed as follows:

		Losses.	Gains.
Hogs:			
Actual expense	$111.04		
Expenses prorated	110.67		
Loss		$0.37	
Actual shrinkage on packer hogs	45 lbs.		
Shringage prorated	44 lbs.		
Loss	1 lb. @ 8¢	.08	

Hogs—Continued.   Losses. Gains.
   Actual shrinkage on butcher hogs_____ 120 lbs.
   Shrinkage prorated_____ 122 lbs.

      Gain _____ 2 lbs.@10. $0. 20
      Total_____ $0. 45   . 20
  · Undivided balance-loss_____   . 20
                                                                   . 25

Cattle:
   Actual expenses _____ $37. 38
   Expenses prorated_____   37. 49

          Undivided balance-gain_____   . 11

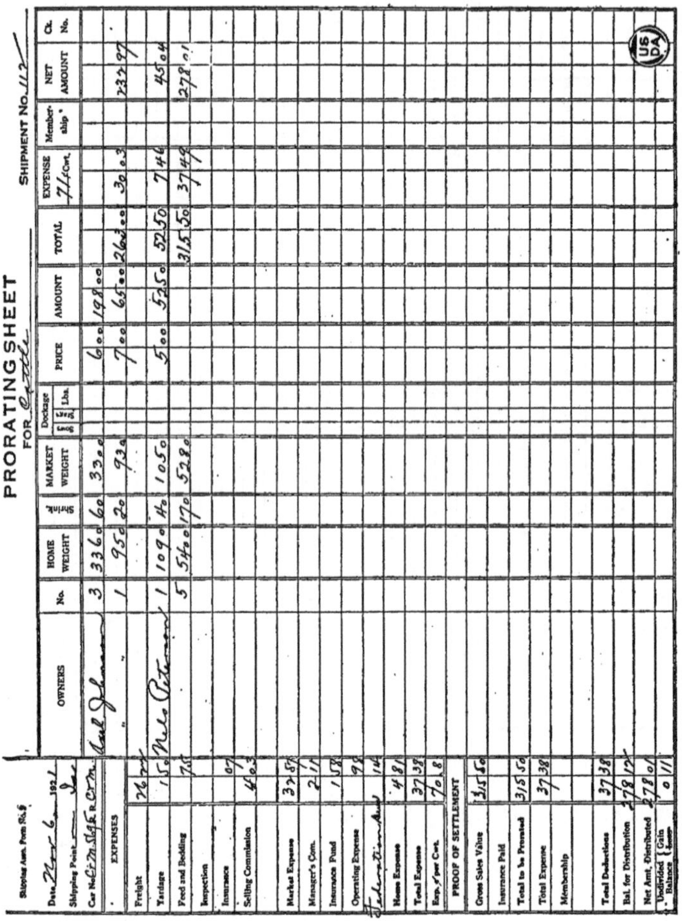

Fig. 14.—Prorating sheet for cattle, shipment No. 112.

    A member's statement showing the results of the sale of the live stock delivered by Axel Johnson in shipment No. 112 is shown in Figure 15.

The data to appear on the shipment record envelope for shipment No. 112 are shown in Figure 16.

It will be noted that when the undivided balances on both prorating sheets are combined for this shipment, there was a net overpayment of 14 cents, which is obtained by subtracting the underpayment of 11 cents on the cattle sheet from the overpayment of 25 cents on the hog sheet.

Shipping Association Form No. 4

MEMBER'S STATEMENT

Nº 97

Shipment No. 112

Brookbridge Iowa, Nov 6 1922

Account of Axel Johnson P.O. Brookbridge, Ia. R.F.D.

No.	Kind	Shrinkage Gain	Market Weight	Dock	Price		Amount		TOTAL	
3	Good Hogs	7	608		10	00	60	80		
37	Packers	44	2141	40	8	00	168	08		
1	Stag	5	280	.70	7	00	14	70	243	58
3	Cows	80	3300		6	00	198	00		
1	Cow		930		7	00	65	00	263	00

REMARKS:

EXPENSES					
Species	Rate		Amount		506 58
Hogs	83		25	14	
Cattle	71		30	03	
Calves					
Sheep					
Membership			1	00	56 17

Attached find Check for Balance due $ 450.41

Please ask about anything not understood. Complete statement of each shipment is on file.

(Tear Off Before Depositing)

Brookbridge Cooperative Livestock Shipping Association

Nº 97

Brookbridge Iowa, Nov 6 192 2

Pay to the order of Axel Johnson $450.41

Four Hundred Fifty and 41/100 DOLLARS

To State Bank, Iowa. John Clark Manager

FIG. 15.—Member's statement showing the results of sale of stock included by Axel Johnson in shipment No. 112.

By referring to the illustrative entries in the shipment summary record for shipment No. 112 it will be noted that the data are summarized separately for hogs and cattle. Reference is made to transaction (14), on page 49, for the cash journal entry to be made for the settlement for this shipment.

SHORT WEIGHT AND MIXED CARLOADS.

The following tables [13] are presented to illustrate the effect on the freight cost per 100 pounds of shipping carloads containing less than

[13] Tables prepared by C. W. Crickman, assistant in agricultural economics, Iowa State College.

the minimum weight and of shipping mixed carloads containing hogs and cattle. The figures apply to a standard 36-foot single-deck car and the rates used were 36 cents per 100 pounds for hogs and 34 cents for cattle. Similar tables may be readily constructed for other kinds of live stock, for cars of different capacity, for different minimum weights, and based on different rates.

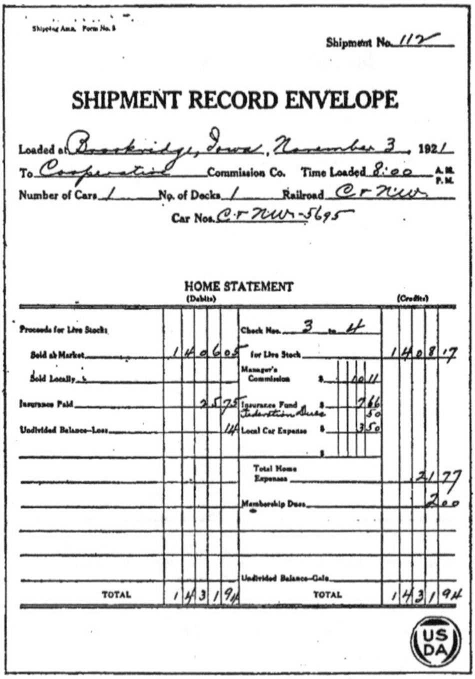

Shipping Assn. Form No. 5

Shipment No. 112

SHIPMENT RECORD ENVELOPE

Loaded at Brookridge, Iowa, November 3, 1921

To Cooperative Commission Co. Time Loaded 8:00 A.M.

Number of Cars 1 No. of Decks 1 Railroad C&NW

Car Nos. C&NW-5695

HOME STATEMENT

(Debits)		(Credits)	
Proceeds for Live Stock:		Check Nos. 3 to 4	
Sold at Market	1406 05	for Live Stock	1408 17
Sold Locally		Manager's Commission $ 10 11	
Insurance Paid	25 75	Insurance Fund $ 7 66 Federation Dues 50	
Undivided Balance—Loss	14	Local Car Expense $ 3 50	
		Total Home Expenses	21 77
		Membership Dues	2 00
		Undivided Balance—Gain	
TOTAL	1431 94	TOTAL	1431 94

FIG. 16.—Shipment record envelope for shipment No. 112.

TABLE 2.—*Freight cost on short-weight cars.*

Hogs.		Cattle.	
Weight.	Cost per 100 pounds of live stock shipped.	Weight.	Cost per 100 pounds of live stock shipped.
Pounds.	*Cents.*	*Pounds.*	*Cents.*
17,000	36.0	22,000	34.0
16,000	38.2	21,000	35.6
15,000	40.8	20,000	37.4
14,000	43.7	19,000	39.4
13,000	47.1	18,000	41.6
12,000	51.0	17,000	44.0
11,000	55.6	16,000	46.7
10,000	61.2	15,000	49.9

By referring to Table 2 it will be seen that the cost of freight rises rapidly as the weight of live stock loaded falls below the minimum weight. The matter of getting the proper weight into the car is often a difficult problem for the manager to solve. Even though the member is under contract and delivers the exact number of head of live stock listed, his estimates of the weight are often wide of the mark. The result is a constant swinging from short-weight to overloaded cars. The properly loaded car is, of course, not necessarily the one which contains at least the minimum weight. In fact, experience seems to show that, particularly in the case of hogs, the saving in freight cost resulting from loading to the minimum weight or over it is frequently more than counterbalanced by excessively heavy shrinkage and losses due to dead and crippled animals.

The alternative of shipping a short-weight partly-filled carload of hogs, cattle, or sheep is of course to ship a mixed load.[11] When the manager has a choice, his problem is to decide which is the more economical alternative. Many communities, however, produce live stock in such quantities and in such proportions that the mixed carload is the rule rather than the exception. In this case the manager's problem is to select such proportions of two or more different kinds of live stock as will reduce the freight burden to the minimum.

From observations made, it would seem that this problem is not generally understood, and that relatively little attention is given to an effort to obtain just the right mixture which can be shipped at the lowest costs. It is probable that careful study of the proper load will reflect as large savings to the shippers as can be made in any other way.

ILLUSTRATIVE TRANSACTIONS.

NOTE.—See Figure 8 for cash journal entries for the following transactions.

For the purpose of this illustration, it is assumed that totals have accumulated in the different accounts as indicated below, as a result of the business transacted up to November 1, 1921. This business is assumed to consist of livestock handled as summarized on the first line in the shipment summary record (see p. 9). Eighty shares of capital stock at $5 per share have been sold; $300 have been borrowed at the bank, and $1,000 have been invested in scales and other equipment. The manager has been paid in full and the deductions for local car expenses just equal the amount which has been disbursed for this purpose. The totals which have accumulated are shown in the following trial balance.

Trial balance November 1, 1921.

	Debits.	Credits.
Bank	$172,655.49	$172,079.47
Live stock	170,965.03	170,965.03
Manager's commission	2,070.09	2,070.09
Insurance fund (including railway claims)	1,226.00	2,025.51
Local car expense	578.60	578.60
Federation dues		55.00
Undivided balance	8.96	12.47

[11] The freight on a mixed load of live stock is calculated at the highest rate based on the highest minimum represented by the live stock in the car.

	Debits.	Credits.
Equipment _____	$1,000.00	_____
Indebtedness_____	_____	$300.00
Loss and gain _____	_____	18.00
Net worth _____	_____	400.00
Total_____	348,504.17	348,504.17

The condition of the business affairs is revealed by the following statement of resources and liabilities constructed from the balances in each of the foregoing accounts:

Statement of Resources and Liabilities of the Brookridge Cooperative Shipping Association November 1, 1921.

Resources.		Liabilities.	
Cash _____	$576.02	Notes payable _____	$300.00
Equipment _____	1,000.00	Insurance fund _____	799.51
		Federation dues_____	55.00
Total _____	1,576.02	Undivided balance_____	3.51
		Net worth.	
		Capital stock paid in_____	400.00
		Loss and gain _____	18.00
		Total _____	1,576.02

November 1.

(1) The board of directors has approved both the trial balance and the statement of resources and liabilities constructed from it. The cash journal will, therefore, be opened by entering in each account therein the accumulated debits and credits given in the foregoing trial balance.

(2) Paid Jones Feed Store for feed for shipment No. 111; check No. 101, for $4.

November 2.

(3) Received from Cooperative Commission Co. proceeds of shipment No. 111, $1,452.73.

(4) Paid Bell Telephone Co. November telephone bill, check No. 102, $2.50.

(5) Paid Eureka Printing Co. for cash journal binder $5 and stationery $5, check No. 103, $10. (The permanent binder should be debited to the yard and office equipment account and the stationery to general expense.)

November 3.

(6) Settlement for shipment No. 111 as per home statement on the shipment record envelope for this shipment.

Accounts debited.		Accounts credited.	
Live stock _____	$1,452.73	Bank (checks 1–2)_____	$1,430.03
		Manager's commission _____	9.54
Total_____	1,452.73	Insurance fund _____	7.78
		Local car expense_____	4.00
		Federation dues_____	.50
		Undivided balance–gain_____	.88
		Total_____	1,452.73

(7) Paid Jno. Clark, manager, commission for shipment No. 111, check No. 104, $9.54.

November 4.

(8) Paid Blank State Bank $200 note with interest $16, check No. 105, $216.

November 5.

(9) Paid Smith Hardware Store for rope for shipment No. 112, check No. 106, $1.

(10) Paid Farmer's Elevator Co. 40 bushels of corn, check No. 107, $20.

November 6.

(11) Received from Cooperative Commission Co., proceeds from shipment No. 112, $1,406.05.

November 7.

(12) Paid Tribune Printing Co. for advertising circulars, check No. 108, $4.
(13) Paid National Surety Co. for premium on manager's bond; check No. 109, $37.50.
(14) Settlement for shipment No. 112. (See shipment record envelope on p. 10 for this shipment).

Accounts debited.		Accounts credited.	
Live stock	$1, 406. 05	Bank (checks 3–4)	$1,408. 17
Insurance fund (losses paid)	25. 75	Manager's commission	10. 11
Undivided balance loss	. 14	Insurance fund	7. 66
		Local car expense	3. 50
Total	1, 431. 94	Federation dues	. 50
		Loss and gain (membership fees)	2. 00
		Total	1, 431. 94

November 25.

(15) Paid United States Office Equipment Co. for Burroughs adding machine No. 36980, check No. 110, $250.
(16) In order that the cash journal may show the results of all shipments made during November, as recorded in the shipment summary record, shipments No. 113 to No. 122 will, for the purpose of this illustration, be entered in summary form. It will be assumed that the manager's commission and the local car expenses have been paid in full for these shipments. The debits and credits arising from these transactions are as follows:

	Debits.	Credits.
Bank	$18, 654. 75	$18, 760. 33
Livestock	18, 654. 75	18, 654. 75
Manager's commission	249. 66	249. 66
Insurance fund	236. 65	121. 52
Local car expense	60. 79	60. 79
Federation dues		6. 50
Undivided balance	2. 31	5. 36
	37, 858. 91	37, 858. 91

Total all columns at the end of the month, entering all of the amounts on the same line. See Figure 8 on page 10*b*. If the debits and credits arising from each transaction have been correctly entered, the sum of the debit totals at the end of the month should equal the sum of the credit totals.

A statement of resources and liabilities based on the balances in the different accounts at the end of November appears as follows:

Statement of resources and liabilities, November 31, 1921.

Resources.		Liabilities.	
Yard and office equipment	$1, 255. 00	Bank overdraft	$63. 52
Prepaid expense (feed)	17. 50	Notes payable	100. 00
		Due Jno. Clark, manager	10. 11
		Insurance fund	674. 07
		Federation dues	62. 50
		Undivided balance	7. 30
		Net worth.	
		Capital stock paid in_ $400. 00	
		Less loss and gain___ 45. 00	
			355. 00
Total	1, 272. 50	Total	1, 272. 50

December 1.

(17) Received in cash $40 from 40 new members, as per the minutes of the November 31 meeting of the Board of Directors.

December 2.

(18) Paid John Clark, manager, commission on shipment No. 112, check No. 111, $10.11.

December 5.

(19) Received from C. & NW. Ry. $25.75 in settlement of claim of November 7.

December 6.

(20) Paid Stephen Stone, attorney's fees for collecting claim of November 7, check No. 112, $3.

(21) Borrowed at the State Bank on 3 months note at 7 per cent $100 to cover overdraft.

December 9.

(22) Paid Sinclair Oil Co., for 10 gallons gasoline, check No. 113, $2.

December 15.

(23) Bought of J. Andrews, retiring member, capital stock certificates No. 24, check No. 114, $5.

(24) Paid State federation dues for 1921, 50 cents on 125 cars, check ,No. 115, $62.50.

Fiscal year adjustments.

(25) The Board of Directors voted to charge off depreciation on the equip-- ment estimated at $50 for the year. (This amount will be credited to the yard and office equipment account and debited to the loss and gain account.)

(26) The credits in the insurance fund account at this point exceed the debits by $696.82. The Board of Directors, it is assumed, decided to carry forward only $500 in this account. Hence the excess of $196.82 will be transferred to loss and gain by debiting the former account and crediting the latter.

(27) The Board of Directors also decided to close the credit balance of $7.30 in the undivided balance account to loss and gain. Debit undivided balance account and credit loss and gain.

Had the credit balances in the two above instances been in excess of the needs of the business, the directors might have voted to refund the excess to the shippers as a patronage dividend. Preferably such refunds should be first credited to indebtedness when the refund is decided upon by the directors, and, subsequently when, paid, debited to indebtedness.

Distribution of net income.

The loss and gain account at this point shows a credit balance of $147.12 which represents the excess of all deductions and income over all expenses incurred. As profits can be distributed legally only by action of the Board of Directors, it is assumed the board has voted to carry the balance of $147.12 to surplus.

(28) In accordance with the above action of the Board of Directors debit loss and gain account with the balance of $147.12 and credit same to net worth.

All columns should again be totaled as was done at the end of November. As this marks the end of the fiscal year, the smaller side of each account should be deducted from the larger and only the balance carried forward to the new fiscal year.

Annual report.

Suggestions for the preparation of the annual report will be found on pages 24 to 28, where statements based on the illustrative figures in the accompanying cash journal and shipment summary record will be found.

January 2, 1922·

(29) Bill Adams came to the office and stated that he had been overcharged in the settlement made for shipment No. 111. A recalculation of his expenses, which appear on the prorating sheet in Figure 4 shows the overcharge to be 71 cents. This amount is paid Mr. Adams by check No. 116. Debit undivided balance account.

ORGANIZATION OF THE
UNITED STATES DEPARTMENT OF AGRICULTURE.

Secretary of Agriculture_____ HENRY C. WALLACE.
Assistant Secretary_____ C. W. PUGSLEY.
Director of Scientific Work_____ E. D. BALL.
Director of Regulatory Work_____
Weather Bureau_____ CHARLES F. MARVIN, Chief.
Bureau of Agricultural Economics_____ HENRY C. TAYLOR, Chief.
Bureau of Animal Industry_____ JOHN R. MOHLER, Chief.
Bureau of Plant Industry_____ WILLIAM A. TAYLOR, Chief.
Forest Service_____ W. B. GREELEY, Chief.
Bureau of Chemistry_____ WALTER G. CAMPBELL, Acting Chief.
Bureau of Soils_____ MILTON WHITNEY, Chief.
Bureau of Entomology_____ L. O. HOWARD, Chief.
Bureau of Biological Survey_____ E. W. NELSON, Chief.
Bureau of Public Roads_____ THOMAS H. MACDONALD, Chief.
Fixed Nitrogen Research Laboratory_____ F. G. COTTRELL, Director.
Division of Accounts and Disbursements__ A. ZAPPONE, Chief.
Division of Publications_____ EDWIN C. POWELL, Acting Chief.
Library_____ CLARIBEL R. BARNETT, Librarian.
States Relations Service_____ A. C. TRUE, Director.
Federal Horticultural Board_____ C. L. MARLATT, Chairman.
Insecticide and Fungicide Board_____ J. K. HAYWOOD, Chairman.
Packers and Stockyards Administration_____⎫ CHESTER MORRILL, Assistant to the.
Grain Future Trading Act Administration___⎭ Secretary.
Office of the Solicitor_____ R. W. WILLIAMS, Solicitor.

This bulletin is a contribution from

Bureau of Agricultural Economics_____ HENRY C. TAYLOR, Chief.
Division of Costs of Marketing_____ A. V. SWARTHOUT, in charge.
324

UNITED STATES DEPARTMENT OF AGRICULTURE

DEPARTMENT BULLETIN No. 1126

Washington, D. C. ▼ April 23, 1923

THE EFFECT OF BORAX ON THE GROWTH AND YIELD OF CROPS

By

J. J. SKINNER and B. E. BROWN, Biochemists, and
F. R. REID, Assistant Biochemist
Office of Soil-Fertility Investigations, Bureau of Plant Industry

CONTENTS

WASHINGTON
GOVERNMENT PRINTING OFFICE
1923

UNITED STATES DEPARTMENT OF AGRICULTURE
BULLETIN No. 1128

Washington, D. C.   PROFESSIONAL PAPER   February 20, 1923

DECAYS AND DISCOLORATIONS IN AIRPLANE WOODS

By

J. S. BOYCE, Pathologist
Office of Investigations in Forest Pathology
Bureau of Plant Industry

CONTENTS

WASHINGTON
GOVERNMENT PRINTING OFFICE
1923

UNITED STATES DEPARTMENT OF AGRICULTURE
BULLETIN No. 1132

Washington, D. C.   PROFESSIONAL PAPER   March 21, 1923

THE RESULTS OF PHYSICAL TESTS
OF ROAD-BUILDING ROCK
FROM 1916 TO 1921,
INCLUSIVE

CONTENTS

WASHINGTON
GOVERNMENT PRINTING OFFICE
1923

UNITED STATES DEPARTMENT OF AGRICULTURE

DEPARTMENT BULLETIN No. 1134

| Washington, D. C. | PROFESSIONAL PAPER | April 26, 1923 |

SELF-FERTILIZATION AND CROSS-FERTILIZATION IN PIMA COTTON

By

THOMAS H. KEARNEY, Physiologist in Charge of Alkali and Drought Resistant
Plant Investigations, Bureau of Plant Industry

CONTENTS

WASHINGTON
GOVERNMENT PRINTING OFFICE
1923

UNITED STATES DEPARTMENT OF AGRICULTURE

DEPARTMENT BULLETIN No. 1136

Washington, D. C. ▼ May 12, 1923

KILN DRYING HANDBOOK

By

ROLF THELEN, In Charge, Section of Timber Physics, Forest Products Laboratory, Forest Service

CONTENTS

WASHINGTON
GOVERNMENT PRINTING OFFICE
1923

ORGANIZATION OF THE UNITED STATES DEPARTMENT OF AGRICULTURE.

UNITED STATES DEPARTMENT OF AGRICULTURE

DEPARTMENT BULLETIN No. 1138

| Washington, D. C. | PROFESSIONAL PAPER | February, 1923 |

VITAMIN B IN THE EDIBLE TISSUES OF THE OX, SHEEP, AND HOG

I. Vitamin B in the Voluntary Muscle
II. Vitamin B in the Edible Viscera

By

RALPH HOAGLAND, Senior Biochemist, Biochemic Division, Bureau of Animal Industry

CONTENTS

WASHINGTON
GOVERNMENT PRINTING OFFICE
1923

UNITED STATES DEPARTMENT OF AGRICULTURE

DEPARTMENT BULLETIN No. 1141

EVAPORATION OF FRUITS

By

JOSEPH S. CALDWELL,

Plant Physiologist, Office of Horticultural and Pomological Investigations
Bureau of Plant Industry

CONTENTS

WASHINGTON
GOVERNMENT PRINTING OFFICE
1923

UNITED STATES DEPARTMENT OF AGRICULTURE

DEPARTMENT BULLETIN No. 1147

Washington, D. C. ▼ June 9, 1923

CHEMICAL, PHYSICAL, AND INSECTICIDAL PROPERTIES OF ARSENICALS

By

F. C. COOK, Physiological Chemist, Insecticide and Fungicide Laboratory
Miscellaneous Division, Bureau of Chemistry

and

N. E. McINDOO, Insect Physiologist, Fruit Insect Investigations
Bureau of Entomology

CONTENTS

WASHINGTON
GOVERNMENT PRINTING OFFICE
1923

Lightning Source UK Ltd.
Milton Keynes UK
UKHW010617030119
334852UK00010B/958/P